HISTORY

OF THE

CONFEDERATE STATES NAVY

FROM ITS ORGANIZATION

TO THE SURRENDER OF ITS LAST VESSEL.

ITS STUPENDOUS STRUGGLE WITH THE GREAT NAVY OF THE
UNITED STATES ; THE ENGAGEMENTS FOUGHT IN THE RIVERS
AND HARBORS OF THE SOUTH, AND UPON THE HIGH SEAS;
BLOCKADE - RUNNING, FIRST USE OF IRON-CLADS
AND TORPEDOES, AND PRIVATEER HISTORY.

BY

J. THOMAS SCHARF, A. M., LL.D.

AN OFFICER OF THE LATE CONFEDERATE STATES NAVY,

*Author of "Chronicles of Baltimore," "History of Maryland," "History of Baltimore," "History
of St. Louis," "History of Western Maryland," "History of Philadelphia," "History of
Westchester County, N. Y.," etc. Also, Member of Historical Societies of Virginia,
Georgia, South Carolina, Maryland, Pennsylvania, New York, Wisconsin, Minnesota, Philosophical Society of Ohio, etc., etc.*

PROFUSELY ILLUSTRATED.

THE FAIRFAX PRESS

J. THOMAS SCHARF.

PREFACE.

IT is no exaggeration of the services rendered in the late war by the navy of the United States, to say that without its aid the armies of the Union would not have been successful; that if the United States had been as destitute of a navy and of naval resources as the Southern Confederacy was, that the Union would have been dissolved; that without Farragut and Foote, Grant and Sherman would occupy in history the same plane with McDowell and Banks, Burnside and Hooker; that when the navy was not co-operating McDowell was hurled back on Washington; McClellan was driven from Richmond to seek protection under the guns of the navy on James River; that Pope was bounced from Cedar Mountain and, ricochetting at Manassas, rested like a spent ball under the defences of the capital; that in the West the "tin-clad" navy conveyed the army to Fort Henry, and was its effective left wing at Donelson; that the Mississippi River from Cairo to its mouth was firmly held by the Confederates until Foote from the North and Farragut from the South broke its barriers and opened its navigation; that Vicksburg and Port Hudson successfully defied and defeated the land forces, and surrendered as much to the navy as to the army; that Sherman would never have undertaken the "march to the sea" if the navy had not provided protection on the seaboard; that Grant, in the Wilderness, diverted by Lee from his direct march on Richmond, sought the friendly help of the navy in his campaign to capture the Confederate capital; that the blockade from the Chesapeake Bay to the mouth of the Rio Grande shut the Confederacy out from the world, deprived it of supplies, weakened its military and naval strength, and compelled exhaustion, by requiring the consumption of everything grown or raised in the country; that there was not an act in either army that surpassed in magnificent courage the bold defiance by Lieut. Morris, of the U. S. Navy, of death alike from shot and drowning, on the deck of the sinking *Cumberland*, rather than surrender the ship.

And it was in the school of that navy that Buchanan, Tatnall, Ingraham, Mitchell, Semmes, Wood, Hollins, Tucker, Jones, Maffitt, Maury, Wilkinson, Davidson, Pegram, Brown, Bulloch, Brooke, and their associates, learned examples of heroic seamanship which enabled them to write the story of the Confederate Navy in high relief across the page of history.

That story it is the province of this book to tell, but the difficulties and embarrassments which have surrounded the subject can be known only to the author. Of official records there are very few of any kind in existence, and not a complete set for any department, or of the operations at any port, or of any vessel, except that preserved by Admiral Semmes of the *Alabama*. To meet that difficulty the author was compelled to rely mainly on the aid and assistance of Confederate naval officers. But while willing and anxious to aid in every way, these officers possessed but very few records and were unwilling to rely merely on their memory. However, in reply to letters sent out by the author, much reliable information was obtained and valuable suggestions made, which when followed up led to the solving of many difficulties and the clearing away of much doubt and uncertainty. The "Official Records," now being published by the United States Government, have in the published volumes but very little that refers to naval affairs. Thus, the author has been compelled to rely upon his own unequaled collection of naval material, which he has been fifteen years in collecting, on contemporary accounts of operations, collected and preserved in newspapers, private letters, and individual papers, which compared with Federal authorities and such official Confederate records as escaped destruction, were again in many chapters referred to those officers now living who participated in the scenes and actions described for their supervision and correction.

The author's object was the truth, the whole truth as far as practicable, and nothing but the truth, in all he wrote. Many worthy and deserving officers, who fully and faithfully performed their arduous duties, have not received mention in the book, solely because the author had not the record which would enable him to relate the service rendered; while there is abundant authority to establish the truth of all that is told in the book, much valuable service has been lost to history by the destruction of records.

It is to be hoped that the book will serve to excite surviving officers, and the representatives of those deceased, to search for and recover lost manuscripts, so that future editions may add to this labor of love, the record of services omitted in this.

Notwithstanding the difficulties which beset the author, many facts have been brought to light, doubtful statements settled, errors corrected, and character rescued from misrepresentation and falsehood. Histories of the U. S. Navy written during the war, or immediately after its close, have undertaken to give accounts and details of Confederate action and motive, without the facts, and without knowledge of the circumstances of the Confederate side of the question, or of the particular action described. Errors, not necessarily intentional, but unavoidable, have thus been introduced into history, which the author of this work has endeavored to correct and explain. While vindicating the political views of Confederate officers, no criticism has been found necessary of those whose convictions of duty impelled them to take the "other side."

If, therefore, in this effort to relate the deeds of daring, the instances and examples where ingenuity, enterprise and device rose above the embarrassments of restricted and limited resources, we have exhibited a partiality or seemed to detract from the glory of the parent navy, it must be attributed to sympathy with a common suffering, rather than a purpose to lesson that renown in which every American must now participate. Time has deprived prejudice of its rancor, politics of its bitterness, and, without changing convictions of duty, has united both sections of the Union under the government instituted by our fathers, and under its influence each party to the war can now read with profit the deeds of those who

> " Gashed with honorable scars,
>   Low in glory's lap they lie,
> Though they fell they fell like stars,
>   Streaming splendor through the sky."

That navy at all times carries in pride, and we hope will always bear in triumph, that flag which now belongs alike to North and South. If we tell how the stars and bars wrested victory from the stars and stripes, we shall only exhibit the heroism of Americans, and make plain a glory that belongs to all the citizens of the Great Republic.

The author heartily acknowledges the intelligent aid and generous encouragement which he has received from his publishers ; and he also acknowledges his indebtedness to the publishers of Admiral Porter's " Naval History of the Civil War," for the loan of maps and illustrations.

Baltimore, May 1st, 1887.

INTRODUCTION

The author, himself an officer of the late Confederate States Navy, describes the great struggle with the Navy of the United States at the time of the War Between the States, the engagements fought in the rivers and harbors of the South and upon the high seas, blockade-running, the first use of iron-clads and torpedoes, and the history of privateers.

The volume, long out of print, was written a score of years after the end of the civil conflict and in large part is based on research and interviews with Confederate naval officers, supplemented by Scharf's own first-hand observations. His general thesis is a simple one: that unless the Union had had the aid and assistance of the United States Navy, they would not have won a war in which their ground forces were hopelessly outclassed. The examples given in support of this are numerous: that when the United States Navy was not cooperating, General McDowell was hurled back on Washington; that McClellan was driven from Richmond to seek protection from the Navy on the James River; that Pope was bounced from Cedar Mountain; and that Sherman would never have undertaken the "march to the sea" if the Navy had not been providing protection on the seaboard.

Yet he feels impelled to emphasize the heroism and selflessness of those very members of the Confederate Navy who, underprovided and underarmed, still kept the stars and bars flying until, in many cases, they went down with their ships. And he defends the concept of states' rights which is still an issue in our times and argues the loyalty of those men who chose to cast their lot with the Southern Confederacy instead of with the Union which those same states had helped create.

The book is controversial; the detailed and dramatic accounts of the principal naval conflicts of the war years, which have the sustained interest and suspense of superior fiction, are colored by the author's emotional involvement in the very events he is relating. But if the history reads like fiction, it is nonetheless authentic history; if each chapter reads like an exciting adventure story, it nevertheless offers valuable information as to what really happened over a century ago by one who was there.

LIST OF ILLUSTRATIONS.

CONTENTS.

CHAPTER I.

INTRODUCTION.

WHILE it does not enter within the scope of this work to discuss the political subjects which, after long years of debate, culminated in the late war between the States, yet we are confronted at the very threshold of our undertaking with the moral question : Whether there was either violation of oath, or ingratitude to the United States, in resigning commissions in that service, and accepting commissions under their States, by those officers who had been educated in the military and naval schools at West Point and Annapolis?

That question involves in its solution the theories upon which the Constitution of the United States was framed. For, if it was ordained and established by *one people*, then the relation of citizenship to the United States was wholly outside of all relation to the States, and the allegiance of those officers was due directly and entirely to the United States. If, on the contrary, the Constitution was ordained and established by the States, in their sovereign and independent character, then allegiance was due primarily to the States, and became due to the United States only through the action of the States. If, therefore, the States, by their sovereign act, transferred the allegiance of their citizens to the United States, that allegiance could only be by the act of the State, and remain due only so long as the State continued a party to the Constitution of the United States.

Whether the theory of a national, or of a compact, government be the true theory of the Constitution, now and hereafter, it is not necessary to discuss. The compact theory of the United States Constitution, announced in 1800 to all the States, and denied by none, continued to be held by the people of the Southern States down to the year 1861. From that theory was derived the axiom of political faith, that the State, and not the citizen, was the contracting party to the Constitution, and that the power, right and duty of continuing with or withdrawing from the Union remained with the State. Hence

all Southern men held that the sovereign act of the State was
obligatory on her citizens, and of such efficacy that disobedience by her citizen to the ordinance of secession would have
been *treason* to the State.   In the political relations of States
there are questions which the State only can determine ; of
these that of allegiance is the first and of most importance.   At
the formation of the Constitution of 1789, the States transmitted the allegiance of their citizens to the United States.
The act of the State, by which the citizen was bound to obey
the authority of the United States, did not divest the citizen of
his duty to obey the State, but made allegiance to the United
States to be the citizen's duty because the State was one of
the United States.   That act of the State did not create a
double allegiance—one to the State, and another to the United
States—but transferred, while the State was a party to the
United States Constitution, the *single* allegiance of her citizen
to the United States through and by virtue of the act of the
State.

Under any theory of *double* allegiance it would have been
impossible for the citizen to have escaped committing the
crime of treason.   For, if the State should be driven by
oppression to withdraw from the Constitution of the United
States, her citizen, under this *double* allegiance, would have
been bound to the United States.   Hence, if the citizens should
obey their own State, they would be pursued and hunted
down as traitors to the Federal government; and, if forsaking
the State to which their allegiance was originally exclusively
due, they should adhere to the Federal government, they
would be traitors to their own State and enemies to their fire-
sides.   Such a scheme of government would be a monstrous
engine of cruelty and oppression, which no man can believe
the fathers of the Constitution erected to crush and grind
their posterity between the upper and the nether millstones
of the two governments, and then pronounce it to be a scheme
"to secure the blessings of liberty to themselves and their
posterity."

With the officers of the army and navy there was no
party politics — but they held a *faith* or conviction upon the
relation of their States to the Federal Union, disconnected
from all party association, which did not permit them to discuss whether their States were acting wisely or prudently —
but only that their States had acted, and that they were bound
by the sovereign act of their States.   It was their sense of
duty — their view of citizenship, their conviction of allegiance
to the State—that impelled them to resign their commissions in
the service of the United States and cast their fortunes with
their States.

By ordinance of the Virginia Convention, it was "ordained
that all officers, civil and military, and the people generally of
this State, be and they are hereby released from any and all

oaths which they may have taken to support the Constitution of the late confederacy, known as The United States of America, and that the said oaths and the said Constitution are inoperative and void, and of no effect."

Thus a political oath, taken by virtue of a command from the State, was absolved and released by a like sovereign act of the State.

As to the resignation of those officers, Admiral Semmes very justly remarks :

"It must be admitted, indeed, that there was some little nerve required on the part of an officer of the regular army or navy to elect to go with his State. His profession was his only fortune ; he depended upon it for the means of subsisting himself and family. If he remained where he was, a competency for life, and promotions, and honors, probably, awaited him ; if he went with the South, a dark, uncertain future was before him ; he could not possibly better his condition, and, if the South failed, he would have thrown away the labor of a life-time. The struggle was hard in other respects. All professions are clannish. Men mutually cling together who have been bred in a common pursuit, and this remark is peculiarly applicable to the army and the navy. West Point and Annapolis were powerful bonds to knit together the hearts of young men. Friendships were there formed which it was difficult to sever, especially when strengthened by years of after-association in common toils, common pleasures, and common dangers. Naval officers, in particular, who had been rocked together in the same storm, and had escaped perhaps from the same shipwreck, found it very difficult to draw their swords against each other. The flag, too, had a charm which it was difficult to resist. It had long been the emblem of the principle that all just governments are founded on the consent of the governed, vindicated against our British ancestors in the War of the Revolution; and it was difficult to realize the fact that it no longer represented that principle, but had become the emblem of its opposite : that of coercing unwilling States to remain under a government which they deemed unjust and oppressive."

Of the same tenor is the testimony borne by Capt. Bulloch and Parker, and by the sentiments of affection in every Southern officer who resigned from the United States Navy. It required no sacrifice and entailed no inconvenience to remain loyal to the Union ; but to resign from that service involved every consideration which might deter a man not actuated by exalted principles.

There could not, therefore, be any violation of an oath which had been taken by command of the State, after the State absolved and released her citizen from its obligation and commanded his services in her own defence.

As to ingratitude, in resigning after education in the military and naval schools—the same reasons apply with equal force. Those schools had been established and maintained by the States, in their associated capacity as "The United States of America," for the defence only of the States, for outside of the States there was nothing to defend. The citizens of the States were appointed cadets from the States, maintained by the taxes of citizens of the States, and were appointed to the army and navy which was designed only to protect and defend the States. It is hardly necessary to say that it never was within the contemplation of the States, when the schools at West Point and Annapolis were established, to conjecture or suppose that the graduates would ever be called upon to fight against the States — even for the union of the States. But in 1861 events had presented to the States that most un-expected result — the soldiers and sailors, educated by the Federal government in its character of agent of the States, were called upon by that agent to fight against its principal — by the servant to make war on the master; by the creature to destroy the creator. In that anomalous condition of the relations of the States to the Federal Union, the *élèves* of West Point and Annapolis returned to their States without the least ingratitude to the United States, which had lost sight of its origin and assumed a mastery where only a service or agency was designed.[1]

Such was the firm and honest sense of duty entertained not only by these officers, but taught and inculcated in the political literature of the Southern States, and incorporated in the great principles of government and parties from the election of Mr. Jefferson in 1800 to the close of Mr. Buchanan's in 1860. The resolutions of Virginia and Kentucky, in 1798, was the *magna charta* of political principles not only for the Southern States, but New England, in 1815, drew from them her justifica-tion of opposition to the war with Great Britain. That those resolutions had been assailed and the inference of the right of secession controverted by eminent statesmen and jurists at the North is not denied, but they retained throughout the South their great cardinal features of political faith. In obey-ing convictions directly resulting from the teachings of Mr. Jefferson and Mr. Madison, ratified and confirmed by the re-peated elections of both of the authors of those resolutions, the officers discharged a duty as binding upon their consciences as was their faith in the Supreme Being.

[1] At the beginning of the war a great deal was said about the way the body of the officers who commanded the army and navy was con-stituted with reference to the North and the South, and much speculation was rife as to the course these gentlemen would pursue in case of conflict between the two sections. Mr. Seward, in the political campaign of 1860, de-nounced both services as mere slave-catching and slave-keeping institutions, and declared for the abolition of both when he was speaking in the West, where the Navy was particularly unpopular.

The impression, in 1860, seemed prevalent that the majority of the officers in both branches of the service came from the South, and had Southern prejudices, but the army and navy registers give the following tables, from which it will be seen that there was a majority in favor of the North in both services—a majority of 112 in the army, and of 253 in the navy:

ARMY.	South.	North.
Generals	2	2
Colonels	14	18
Lieutenant-Colonels	11	18
Majors	51	59
Captains	151	189
Lieutenants	238	293
Total	467	579

NAVY.	South.	North.
Captains	34	45
Commanders	62	52
Lieutenants	135	190
Surgeons	25	44
Assistant Surgeons	44	35
Paymasters	30	34
Chaplains	7	16
Masters	15	29
Midshipmen	14	37
Acting Midshipmen	60	178
Boatswains	14	27
Gunners	20	26
Total	460	713

CHAPTER II.

WANT OF PREPARATION FOR WAR.

IN the same line of reckless aspersion as that against the resigned officers was the charge made against the Southern States of having, while in the Union, prepared resources of arms and collected munitions of war to effect its dissolution.

In support of that assertion, the Potter Committee of the Federal Congress reflected with severity upon the transfer of certain arms to the Southern States during the year 1860, prior to the election of Mr. Lincoln, and when secession was being discussed in the same language which had been used on that subject for thirty years before. But the subsequent secession of the Southern States gave point and application to the charge that Secretary Floyd had prepared the South for war by arming the States with United States arms. The raid of John Brown into Virginia had put into actual war the continued threat of the avowed Abolitionists, who regarded the Constitution as a "compact with the devil and a league with hell" —and who swore to

> "Tear down that flaunting lie !
> Half-mast the starry flag !
> Insult no sunny sky
> With hate's polluted rag."

For defence against those attacks of invasion the peaceful policy of Virginia had rendered her wholly unprepared. Northern cupidity availed itself of that excitement and vociferously cried to Congress for the manufacture of more arms. Pittsburgh manufacturers lobbied a bill through Congress for the manufacture of cannon to arm the unfinished Southern forts.

The appropriation for casting these cannon was passed by Congress, without the knowledge or solicitation of Secretary Floyd, under the industrious lobbying of Pittsburgh iron-founders. The guns were cast in obedience to law, and the early shipment of them in advance of the full completion of the forts, though not in advance of the readiness of the forts to receive their armament, was due more to the fact that the Pittsburgh iron-founders were bound by their contract to deliver them before receiving their pay than to the special eagerness of the Secretary to get them off. The Secretary simply obeyed a mandate of Congress, and the Pittsburgh contractors simply obeyed the influences of cupidity. But those guns never reached the Southern forts, their shipment was stopped in Pittsburgh by Secretary Holt. Much was also said about one hundred thousand muskets having been ordered to be sold to one Belknap at two and one-half dollars each, as being a part of the same scheme to arm the South. But that order was made under a standing law and in pursuance of numerous reports of competent boards of ordnance officers, declaring the Government would do well to get rid of them at two dollars. Those muskets never came to the South ; for, though offered to and urged upon the Southern States, they would not take them. Virginia had previously taken a few thousand, Mississippi as many more, and Alabama a still greater number. Probably South Carolina and Georgia took also a few thousand; but when a hundred thousand more could have been had for a song they paid no attention to the subject. The offer to the States was at two dollars ; the offer to Belknap was not till afterwards, and at two and one-half dollars. Belknap's scheme was to sell the muskets in Europe, and not to the South, as the committee's report insinuated.

For years prior to 1860 it had been the policy of the Federal war department to allow all the rifles and muskets manufactured at the Federal armories to be deposited in Northern arsenals. That at Watervliet, near Troy, N. Y., contained probably one-half of all the arms of improved patterns owned by the Federal government.

The attack of John Brown upon Virginia, and the numerous efforts of Northern emissaries to excite Southern slaves to insurrection, suggested the importance of distributing their quota of these fine guns among the Southern States. Accordingly, orders were issued in 1860, by Secretary Floyd, to transfer the Southern quota of the arms from the Northern arsenals.

On May 30th, 1860, prior to the nomination even of Mr. Lincoln, an order was made for the transfer of the quota of arms to the Southern arsenals. Under which order the transfer was as follows :

	Percus'n Muskets.	Altered Muskets.	Percus'n Rifles.
Charleston (S. C.) Arsenal,	9,280	5,720	2,000
North Carolina Arsenal,	15,408	9,520	2,000
Augusta (Ga.) Arsenal,	12,380	7,620	2,000
Mt. Vernon, Ala.,	9,280	5,720	2,000
Baton Rouge, La.,	18,820	11,420	2,000

The number of arms transferred to these arsenals under this order being 114,868.

That transfer of arms was made prior to the nominations of political parties in 1860, long anterior to the presidential election and entirely without the least expectation of secession or war. The safety of persons and property at the South, the preservation of order and social life in the slave-holding States, had been put in jeopardy by Northern incendiaries, and that transfer of arms was justified by what had already taken place at Harper's Ferry under John Brown, and by the sympathy shown to and martyrdom conferred upon that insurrectionist and incendiary. The portion borne by the Southern States in the expenditures of the Federal government entitled them to the custody of a fair quota of this sort of public property. They were taken under undisputed legal right; and more than the portion taken belonged to the Southern States by right of property fairly paid for. That transfer of arms was the act of the Federal government, and not the preparation for war by any State.

But the charge of previous preparation for war was believed by many at the North, and has been since the war repeatedly asserted by writers who ought to have known better. If those who made the assertion had shown that preparation for war had been even commenced, that materials of war had been collected, that any steps had been taken to make successful an attempt to dissolve the Union, there might be some probability in the assertion. But the fact is now apparent and within the reach of all, that, until the organization of the Confederate States, there was not a ship owned by any State, nor the least effort made to procure one; that there was not a piece of ordnance of any kind; not a yard in which a yawl-boat could be built; not a machine shop capable, without material alterations, of constructing the simplest piece of naval machinery; not a rope-yard, not a percussion-cap machine; only one powder mill, no supply of nitre, or sulphur, or lead—not the least preparation of any kind.

Why was it that there were no preparations? The answer must be found in the conviction of all men, that none could be needed—because secession was a peaceful remedy—and war would not follow separation from a Union which owed its existence to a peaceable secession from an older Union. Hence there was no preparation for war—until President Lincoln's Proclamation, calling on all the States for 75,000 men to recapture the forts, etc., held by the seceded States, made war not only imminent but actual. It was that proclamation which brought the two sections of the Union face to face in war, as independent and hostile Republics, but without the least preparation on the part of either. The United States was in better condition and situation for war than the Confederate States, but not without less preparation. That government had the small army as a nucleus for a larger, and all the ships of the navy—for no Southern officer who resigned brought a ship with him to the

Confederacy. They did not presume to take upon themselves the duty of dividing the navy among the States, notwithstanding it was the common property of all the States. In the excitement of the times, it would have been pardonable conduct to have brought their ships to the defence of the States; but their delicate sense of honor, and a sailor's duty to the government whose commission he bore, required that he should divest himself of every selfish motive before he returned his commission to the Federal government. In the light of such honorable conduct, the petty malice with which Secretary Welles was actuated, when he endeavored to stigmatize these officers with having "*deserted the service*," reacts with more effect against the character of the Secretary than against the conduct of these officers.

The forts, arsenals, etc., situated in and attached to the soil of the States, had all been conveyed to the United States, with the reservation of the State's right of re-entry and occupation, when the forts, etc., ceased to be used for the defence of the State. The property was held *in trust* for all the States, as a means of defending all, through the avenues of commerce in the particular State. Hence, when the State, in which the fort, arsenal and dock-yard was situated, withdrew from the Union, the purposes of the trust ended, and she resumed her right and jurisdiction over the fort. The money expended in improving the fort was, of course, to have been returned to the United States in the settlement of accounts between the seceded States and the United States;[1] and that was one of the objects of the diplomatic mission of Messrs. Forsyth and Crawford to the government at Washington, in March, 1861.

Every act of the seceded States had been peaceful, and there was no occasion for war until the authorities at Washington put in practice their new scheme or theory invented by President Lincoln: that he would re-occupy and hold the forts in the seceded States. The little garrison at Sumter could not have effected the result of the issue between the Confederate States and the United States, whether it yielded under the pressure of a want of supplies, or was delivered to South Carolina under the constitutional view that it belonged to that State. But Major Anderson and his little command offered an excellent opportunity for the application of the new theory to re-occupy and hold the forts, etc.—and, better, it could be so managed as to make the Confederates States *fire the first gun.*[2]

---

[1] The Provisional Constitution of the Confederate States provided that:
"The government hereby instituted shall take immediate steps for the settlement of all matters between the States forming it and their other late confederates of the United States, in relation to the public property and public debt at the time of their withdrawal from them: these States hereby declaring it to be their wish and earnest desire to adjust everything pertaining to the common property, common liabilities, and common obligations of that Union, upon the principles of right, justice, equity and good faith."—Stat. at Large, Prov. Gov't, C. S A., pp. 27, 28.

[2] The New York *Herald* of April 5, 1861, said: "We have no doubt Mr. Lincoln wants the Cabinet at Montgomery to take the initiative by capturing the two forts in its waters, for it would give him the opportunity of throwing upon the Southern Confederacy the responsibility of commencing hostilities. But the country and posterity will hold him just as responsible as if he struck the first blow."

It is no part of our purpose to trace the course of that devious and disgraceful diplomacy which, in Washington City, during March and April, 1861, was running both above and below the surface—the Secretary of State promising peace and the evacuation of Sumter, and the Secretaries of War and Navy preparing military and naval expeditions to force the firing of the first gun upon the Confederates. Secretary Welles, in the *Galaxy* for November, 1870, told the story of the double and triple negotiations by which the war was inaugurated, and a few extracts will fully sustain us in saying that war, and not peace, was the object of the Washington authorities. Mr. Welles says:

" Mr. Seward from the commencement doubted not only the practicability of reinforcing Sumter, but the expediency of any attempt to provision the garrison, therein differing from every one of his colleagues, though in perfect accord with General Scott. The subject in all its aspects was less novel to him than the rest of us, and from some cause his conclusions were wholly unlike the others. If not indifferent, he had none of the zeal which inspired his colleagues, but seemed to consider it an unimportant or settled question. The insurgents had possession of Fort Moultrie, Castle Pinckney, and, in fact, all the defences of Charleston; what benefit, he asked, could we derive from retaining this isolated fortress, if it were possible to do so ?"

Mr. Welles was one of those colleagues whose "zeal," not born of wisdom, circumvented the patriotic and pacific purposes of Mr. Seward. Indeed, the *Galaxy* article on " Fort Sumter," when read between the lines, is a covert and insidious impeachment of Mr. Seward's loyalty to the Republican purpose of forcing war upon the South, hence Mr. Welles further says :

"The Secretary of State was the only member of the Cabinet who did not cordially concur in these conclusions (to reinforce and provision Fort Sumter), and he could not successfully controvert them. He did not, however, give his earnest approval, but, in acquiescing, reiterated what he had previously urged: that the attempt, if made, would prove a failure; that the failure would strengthen the secessionists and weaken the government; that in the attitude of parties it would be received as the commencement of hostilities, would foreclose all measures of reconciliation, and place the Administration in a wrong and false position."

Mr. Welles, writing in the spirit of a partisan rather than in that of a statesman, admits that the " political necessities " demanded the attempt to reinforce Sumter. The subsequent events demonstrated the wisdom of Seward; and Mr. Welles, in attempting to impeach the party fidelity of Mr. Seward, demonstrates the efforts of the latter to keep faith with his plighted word to the Governor of South Carolina, that the situation at Sumter should not be changed. The *Galaxy* article, notwithstanding it uncovers much that was hidden and unknown of the doings about Sumter, also discloses that the opening of the war by the South was the object for which all but Seward, and, perhaps, Mr. Lincoln, were playing in their desperate game prior to the assault upon Fort Sumter.

The object of Mr. Lincoln and his party was accomplished: *the first gun was fired by the Confederates.* In the excitement which followed, men did not remember that between nations the aggressor is not he who first uses force, but he who first makes force necessary. The scheme, or rather the trick, succeeded, by which the North was to be aroused and angered into war. The "blood-letting" policy avowed by Mr. Z. Chandler[1] had been successfully shifted to the South, and yet had been the means of arousing the North. The "Peace Convention" had "*ended in thin smoke,*" as Mr. Chandler desired, by having delegates of the "stiff-backed" sort sent to Washington to defeat every effort at peace and reunion.

The recital of the facts, as they existed at the South in 1861, establishes beyond controversy that no preparation for war had been made by any Southern State prior to secession—that not one of the States desired war—that there ought not to have been war—and that there would not have been war, except to "save the Republican party from rupture." The facts of the times[2] and the acts of men cannot be covered up from the search and exposure of the historian, who, when he comes to write the causes of the terrible war of 1861–5, must discover and expose those who, to secure themselves in the possession of political place, deliberately played with the excited passions and feelings of the hour, to involve the country in war, and dissolved the Union, so that its reconquest would perpetuate their party ascendancy, or that the loss of the Southern States would deprive their political opponents of the great bulk of their strength, and thus secure for themselves the possession of power in either the reconstructed Union or in the dismembered and divided Northern part.

The State of South Carolina adopted her Ordinance of Secession on Dec. 20th, 1860. Major Anderson complicated the difficulties of a peaceful arrangement by evacuating Fort Moultrie and occupying Fort Sumter on Dec. 25th; but his act was not without material aid to South Carolina, for he left behind him all the guns of Fort Moultrie. This was the first supply of munition of war obtained by South Carolina. It is no part of the purpose of this work to discuss whether Major Anderson did wrong in abandoning Fort Moultrie—*the fact* gives the information of how South Carolina was able to girdle Sumter with her batteries and compel its surrender. After Major Anderson occupied Sumter, the South Carolina authorities occupied both Fort Moultrie and Castle Pinckney, Fort Johnson, and the United States arsenal in Charleston.

In pursuance of her purpose and in preparation for the defence of her soil, the Governor of South Carolina, on the 30th December, 1860, informed Commander T. T. Hunter, United States Lighthouse Inspector at Charleston, that he could depart the State, but prohibited him from removing any property of

---

[1] Letter to Gov. Austin Blair, Feb. 11, 1861. [2] Z. Chandler, Feb. 11, 1861.

the United States from the buoy-shed. On the 1st of January, the Governor forbade the removal of vessels belonging to the lighthouse establishment from Charleston, but the Inspector (Commander Hunter) was allowed to leave by land. On the 8th, the removal of the light-vessel at Rattlesnake Shoals, off the harbor of Charleston, was reported to the Lighthouse Board, and the board was informed that the three tenders in the harbor of Charleston had been seized by the authorities of South Carolina.

The information of the removal of buoys and a light-ship at Rattlesnake Shoals, on Morris Island, and at the entrance of Charleston Harbor, was made public, January 26, 1861, by Raphael Semmes, then the Secretary to the U. S. Lighthouse Board.

The U. S. revenue cutter *Wm. Aiken* was lying at Charleston and was a first-class boat of ninety tons; she was ready for service and was armed with one forty-two pounder pivot gun, and her crew, on a war footing, numbered thirty men. She was seized by the State authorities, and with the steam cutter *Gray*, purchased by the authorities, were the first ships in the navy of South Carolina.

Mississippi passed her Ordinance of Secession on January 9; 1861, and made provisions for a State army, and appointed Hon. Jefferson Davis her Major General to command her army, and authorized such measures as were practicable to obtain the arms necessary for it. The State had few serviceable weapons, and no establishment for their manufacture or repair. Her authorities seized the fort on Ship Island, and the U. S. Hospital on the Mississippi River.

Florida seceded on January 10, 1861, and on the 12th the navy-yard, Forts Barrancas, McRea, and Marion, and the arsenal at St. Augustine, were seized. It is said that the Chatahoochee arsenal contained 500,000 rounds of musket cartridges, 300,000 rifle cartridges, and 50,000 pounds of gunpowder. The coast survey schooner *F. W. Dana* was also taken possession of.

Alabama seceded on January 11, 1861, and took possession of Fort Morgan, containing about 5,000 shot and shell, also Mt. Vernon arsenal, containing 20,000 stand of arms, 1,500 barrels of powder (150,000 pounds), some pieces of cannon and a large amount of munitions of war. The revenue cutter *Lewis Cass*, and the tender *Alert*, belonging to the lighthouse establishment, were seized at Mobile by order of the commanding officer of the State troops at Fort Morgan. On the 21st, T. Sanford, Collector of the Customs at Mobile, notified Commander Handy that he, " in the name of the sovereign State of Alabama, takes possession of the several lighthouses within the State, and all appurtenances pertaining to the same." Mr. Sanford had resigned his commission as U. S. Collector on the 12th of the same month.

On the 1st of February, Commander Handy transmitted to Washington a copy of a letter addressed to R. T. Chapman, late of the U. S. navy, by T. Sandford, Collector, appointing him Lighthouse Inspector in place of Commander Handy, to whom the appointment was tendered by the authorities of Alabama, but who refused to accept it.

Georgia seceded on Jan. 18, 1861, and seized Forts Pulaski and Jackson, and the arsenal at Augusta, containing two twelve-pounders, two cannons, 22,000 muskets and rifles, and large stores of powder, balls, grape, etc., and U. S. steamer *Ida*.

On the 6th of February, the keeper of the St. Simon's light, near Darien, Ga., reported that his light had been obscured by a party of persons claiming authority from the State; but the light was not extinguished.

On the 8th, Capt. W. H. Whiting, of the United States Engineers, reported that possession had been taken of his office, furniture, etc., in Savannah, by the authorities of the State.

Louisiana seceded on Jan. 26, 1861, and seized Forts Jackson and St. Philip, on the Mississippi, and Fort Pike, on Lake Ponchartrain, and the arsenal at Baton Rouge. The latter contained 50,000 small arms, 4 howitzers, 20 pieces of heavy ordnance, 2 batteries, 300 barrels of powder. At Bellville iron-works the armament of the revenue cutter *Lewis Cass* was stored, and that was also obtained by the State.

On Jan. 14, 1861, the United States barracks below New Orleans, which was being used as a hospital, was taken possession of by the Louisiana authorities. But this seizure, though, in one sense, of a military character, was rather an embarrassment than an aid to war, since all it contained was 216 invalids and convalescent patients. The removal of the sick patients was requested by Capt. C. M. Bradford, which request being reported by Collector F. H. Hatch to Secretary of the Treasury, John A. Dix, the latter telegraphed Jan. 27, 1861, to "remonstrate with the Governor against the inhumanity of turning the sick out of the hospital," and that telegraph was followed by a letter, which, with many variations on the duty of humanity, protested against the request of Capt. Bradford. All of which was needless, as the Governor had before their receipt ordered the sick to be left unmolested, and Collector Hatch was informed that his protest was unnecessary, as "the authorities would never have exercised the least inhumanity towards these patients ; for, if the barracks had been required for the use of the troops Louisiana has been compelled to raise for her protection and defence, her charity hospital— justly the glory and pride of her munificence, into whose portals the afflicted of all nations can enter without money and without price—would have amply provided for their wants. In closing this communication, I am constrained to observe, in reply to the remark in your letter of the 28th, that you 'fear no public property is likely to be respected'; that, in compliance with the ordinance of the Convention of the people of Louisiana, the State took possession of the public property, in trust, to prevent any abuse of the same by the Federal government, which, it was believed, would pervert that which the Constitution intended for defence to the purposes of destruction. This property she will be ready to render a just and true account of at the proper time."

The Treasurer of the branch mint at New Orleans was *ex-officio* Assistant Treasurer of the United States. It appears from the report of Secretary of the Treasury, John A. Dix, that, on the 21st January, 1861, there were in the hands of the Treasurer of the branch mint at New Orleans, the following sums :

As Treasurer of the Mint, ...	$389,267 46
As Assistant Treasurer to the credit of the Treasurer of the United States, ...	265,445 14
As Assistant Treasurer to the credit of disbursing officers, ...	225,374 80
Total, ...	$880,087 40

On January 21, 1861, Secretary Dix drew a draft for $350,000 on the Assistant Treasurer at New Orleans in favor of Adams' Express Company, which was not paid on presentation because there were not sufficient funds in hand to pay the draft, and the Assistant Treasurer declined paying any part until he could pay the whole. This reply Mr. Dix regarded as evasive and designed to create delay, in order that the action of the Louisiana Convention might prevent the transfer of any part of the property of the United States beyond the power of the Convention. Whether so intended or not, the delay had that effect, for the State authorities seized the mint and its contents on January 31.

The Custom House at New Orleans and its contents were seized by the State authorities on the 31st of January, 1861, and Collector Hatch retained the position under the State. Under the revenue system of the United States, goods in bond were permitted to pass the port of entry, and the customs' duty could be paid at the interior Custom House. To continue that system would have deprived Louisiana, then a sovereign State, of her right to collect revenue from imports at her chief port of entry. Hence the collector at New Orleans refused to pass goods in bond, for transportation to port of delivery in States of the United States, without the duty being paid at New Orleans. This would have subjected importers in St. Louis, Louisville, and other river ports to the hardships of paying double duty —first to Louisiana, and second to the United States. This was practically a fatal blow at the free navigation of the Mississippi River, as well as a means of supplying revenue to Louisiana. Such action on the part of the State rose above its relations to the ports above New Orleans, and took the importance of an international question. The free navigation of the

Mississippi River was recognized as a natural right, and, when Lousiana ratified the Confederate Constitution, that right of free navigation was accorded by Act of Congress, February 25, 1861—which declared and established the free Navigation of the Mississippi River "to the citizens of any State upon its borders, or upon the borders of any of its navigable tributaries, of all ships, boats, or vessels, without any duty or hindrance, except light-money, pilotage, and like charges."[1]

The U. S. revenue cutter, which was lying at New Orleans for repairs, was seized by the State authorities. The U. S. revenue cutter *Robert McClelland*, under command of Capt. J. G. Brushwood of the revenue service, was ordered from the lower Mississippi to New Orleans by Collector Hatch and seized by the State authorities. To prevent that seizure, Secretary Dix, on January 19, 1861, ordered W. Hemphill Jones to proceed to New Orleans and take possession of the *McClelland*. Capt. Brushwood refused to recognize Mr. Jones' authority, which refusal being communicated to Secretary Dix, he ordered, by telegraph, Lieut. Caldwell to arrest Capt. Brushwood, assume command of the cutter, if Brushwood interfered to treat him as a mutineer, and "if any one attempted to haul down the American flag, shoot him on the spot!" This spirited order came too late—the State authorities already had possession of the cutter.

Texas seceded on February 1, 1861, and seized Forts Chadbourne and Belknap, and General Twiggs surrendered government stores valued at $1,300,000, consisting of $55,000 in specie, 35,000 stand of arms, 26 pieces of mounted artillery, 44 pieces dismounted, with ammunition, horses, wagons, forage, etc., etc. In Galveston Bay, the revenue cutter *Dodge* was seized, and Fort Brown surrendered.

Arkansas seceded May 6, and the arsenal at Little Rock, containing 9,000 small arms, 40 cannon, and some ammunition, was taken possession of.

The following is a list of the seizures of vessels made by the States as they seceded from the Union, and which formed the nucleus of the Confederate States navy:

Name of Vessel.	Number of Guns.	Styles of Guns.	Crew.
McClellan	5	4 side guns and 1 pivot	35
Lewis Cass	1	68-pounder	45
Aiken	1	42-pounder	45
Washington	1	42-pounder	45
Dodge	1	Pivot	—

And, in addition to the above, the following:

Name.	Class.	Guns.	How obtained.
James Gray	Propeller	1	Purchased at Charleston.
Bonita	Brig	1	Captured Slaver.
Nina	Steam gunboat	1	——
Everglade	Steamer	—	——
Fulton	U. S. War Steamer	3	Seized at Pensacola.

[1] Stat. at Large, Prov. Gov't, C. S. A., pp. 36–38.

The gun on the *James Gray* was a forty-two-pounder columbiad, and those on the *Fulton* thirty-two-pounders.

RECAPITULATION.

Vessels 10
Number of Guns 15

The weight of metal these fifteen guns carried was comparatively light, only one being a sixty-eight-pounder, three forty-two-pounders, and the rest of still less calibre.

The *Fulton* had been wrecked off Pensacola, and was of very little account, but was repaired and rebuilt by the Confederate government. [1]

The seceded States met, by delegates, at Montgomery, on the 4th of February, 1861, and adopted the Provisional Constitution of the Confederate States of America. On that day the Confederacy had neither army or navy, and the States which composed it had only such munitions of war as every State in the United States had at all times—namely, their volunteer soldiery —badly armed, poorly drilled, and in very limited numbers. The evidence of preparation nowhere existed, but the peaceful condition of public affairs plainly told that no purpose of dissolution had been long maintained, but that it was the sudden appearance of a long-dreaded danger that had driven them to the last alternative in a federative union—Secession ; and that the States expected it to be peaceful, but that Mr. Lincoln and his advisers had outwitted and overreached all the precautions of peace taken at the South, and, by deftly and cunningly drawing the fire of the Charleston batteries, had inaugurated war. The latent spirit of devotion to the Union, which the echoes of the guns at Charleston aroused into such

[1] At the breaking out of the war the United States owned ten navy-yards, viz. : — Kittery, Me.; Portsmouth, N. H.; Charlestown, Mass.; Brooklyn, N. Y.; Philadelphia, Pa ; Washington, D. C.; Norfolk, Va.; Pensacola, Fla.; Mare Island, Cal.; Sackett's Harbor, N. Y.

The following list shows the number and rate of vessels built at each of these yards before 1861:

Yard.	Ships of the Line.	Frigates.	Sloops.	Brigs.	Screw St'rs.	Side-wheel St'rs.	Total.
Portsmouth....	—	—	—	—	—	—	—
Charlestown...	2	1	4	1	4	—	12
Brooklyn ..	1	1	4	1	4	1	12
Philadelphia...	2	2	3	—	4	2	13
Washington....	1	3	2	—	1	1	8
Norfolk..	2	1	4	1	4	1	13
Pensacola.. ...—	—	—	—	—	2	—	2
Mare Island....—	—	—	—	—	—	1	1
Sackett's Harbor.........	1	—	—	—	—	—	1
Kittery........	1	2	3	—	2	1	9

STORE-SHIPS, RECEIVING-SHIPS, ETC.

Purchased vessels......................... 9

BUILT AT OTHER PLACES.

Erie, Pa., steamer Michigan, then on the Lakes.

Pittsburgh, Pa., Allegheny. ...Receiving-ship at Baltimore.
Charlestown, Mass., Independence ....Pacific receiving-ship.
Boston, Mass., Princeton..... Philadelphia receiving-ship.
Charlestown, Mass.. Warren...Panama receiving-ship.
Charlestown,Mass., Falmouth, Aspinwall receiving-ship.

By the secession of Virginia and Florida the Federal government lost the Norfolk and Pensacola navy-yards ; but, owing to the rigid blockade, they were of little service to the Confederacy. The Norfolk navy-yard was one of the oldest and perhaps the most valuable in the United States. From its stocks were launched two ships-of-the-line, one frigate, four sloops-of-war, one brig. four screw steamers and one side-wheel steamer, besides doing a vast amount of refitting and rebuilding of vessels. The Pensacola yard had only turned out two vessels—the *Pensacola*, a second-class screw steamer of 2,158 tons. Her hull was built there, but she was completed at the Washington navy-yard. The other vessel built at Pensacola was the *Seminole*, a third-class screw steamer of 801 tons. It will thus be seen that the Northern navy-yards had always built the largest number of vessels.

terrible force and proportion, stopped not to consider the trick
by which the war had been begun.   It only saw the flag of the
Union in the smoke of battle, and, whether right or wrong,
rushed to its defence.   But neither that expression of loyalty
to the Union, nor the extraordinary efforts in its defence, nor
the triumphs of its army and navy, will be able to cover up
and conceal from the reprehension of history the shameful
subterfuge of provisioning Sumter as a start to war; but history will separate the glory of the people's defence from the
shame of the politician's trick.

Jefferson Davis

HON. STEPHEN RUSSELL MALLORY,

SECRETARY OF THE NAVY OF THE CONFEDERATE STATES.

CAPTAIN FRENCH FORREST.

CONFEDERATE STATES NAVY.

CHAPTER III.

ORGANIZATION OF THE NAVY.

DELEGATES from the seceded States met at Montgomery, Alabama, in February, 1861, and on March 11th unanimously adopted the "Constitution for the Provisional Government of the Confederate States of America." This Constitution, and the one afterwards adopted as the permanent Constitution of the Confederate States, empowered Congress "to provide and maintain a navy," and made the President the Commander-in-Chief of the Army and Navy.

The first statute enacted by the Confederate Congress continued in force all the laws of the United States not inconsistent with the Constitution of the Confederate States, until altered or repealed by Congress. By that legislation, law and order were maintained in the midst of a total change of foreign and domestic relations, the public business continued without interruption, and private intercourse experienced no shock. All officers connected with the customs revenue were continued in office, and the existing postal arrangements were left undisturbed. Thus the people in the Confederate States passed into their new relations without the least interruption of their business affairs.

Before either of the Cabinet departments were constituted by law, Congress, on February 14th, passed a resolution authorizing "the Committee on Naval Affairs to procure the attendance at Montgomery of all such persons versed in naval affairs as they may deem advisable to consult with." C. M. Conrad, the Chairman of the Committee, immediately upon the passage of the resolution, addressed telegrams to a number of United States navy officers whose sympathies were with the South, requesting them to repair to Montgomery at their earliest convenience. Among those who received a telegram from the chairman of the committee was Commander Raphael Semmes, who was still at his post, in Washington, performing his duties at the Lighthouse Board. Commander Semmes immediately tendered his resignation, which was accepted on the 15th, and on the 18th he arrived at Montgomery, where a number of navy officers had preceded him. On the following day he attended a joint session of the military and naval committees, which discussed the military and naval resources of the country, and devised such means of defence as was within their reach to enable the Confederacy to meet the most pressing exigencies of the situation. But few naval officers of any rank had as yet withdrawn from the old service: Rousseau, Tatnall, Hollins, Ingraham and Randolph were all the captains, and Farrand, Brent, Semmes and Hartstene were all the commanders. Of those who were present before the committees, besides Semmes, was Rousseau, Ingraham, and Randolph, of the old navy. As the result of the deliberations of the committee, Congress, on the 20th, passed an act to "provide munitions of war," by purchase and manufacture. Jefferson Davis having been inaugurated President on the 18th of February, on the 21st dispatched Commander Semmes to the United States, and at the same time sent Caleb Huse to Europe to purchase arms and munitions of war.[1]

On the same day, "the act to establish the Navy Department" was passed, providing for a Secretary of the Navy, a chief clerk, and such other clerks as may be authorized by law.[2]

The Secretary of the Navy, under the President, was to have charge of all matters and things connected with the navy. Bureaus of ordnance and hydrography, of orders and details, of medicine and surgery, of provisions and clothing, were also provided; and the Secretary of the Navy was required to prepare and publish regulations for the general government of the navy, and all laws of the United States relating to the navy and its officers, and not inconsistent with this act, were enacted as laws for the government of the Confederate navy.

[1] The letter of instruction to Com. Semmes was written by Mr. Davis, who then was without Cabinet officers or even a private secretary, and is full, precise, and much in detail, exhibiting a minute acquaintance with bureau duties, with the resources of the North, and with the men there who would furnish the supplies needed. Com. Semmes found "the people everywhere not only willing but anxious to contract" with him, and he purchased large quantities of percussion-caps in the city of New York, and sent them by express without any disguise to Montgomery. He made contracts for batteries of light artillery, powder and other munitions, and succeeded in getting large quantities of the powder shipped, and it was agreed between the contractors and Com. Semmes that when the telegraph was used certain sign or agreed words should be substituted for those of military import—to avoid suspicion. He made a contract for the removal to the South of a complete set of machinery for rifling cannon, and with the requisite workmen to put it in operation. "Some of these men," says Com. Semmes, "who would thus have sold body and soul to me for a sufficient consideration, occupied high social position and were men of wealth." In social intercourse, at their private residences, Com. Semmes found them ready to help on the cause of the Confederate States with their "aid and comfort," and in a much more efficient manner than was charged against Secretary of War, Floyd, who merely sent to the Southern States the proper quota of their arms.

While in New York, on that mission, Com. Semmes received from Secretary Mallory, who had been appointed to the Navy Department, a letter of date March 13th, directing him to select and purchase two steamers of strength and light draft. But Com. Semmes could find none. The month of March was closing, and as the new Federal Administration became fixed in their positions the hopes of peace departed and the clouds of war began to thicken; yet, curiously enough, the New York and Savannah steamers continued to run, "carrying the Federal flag at the peak and the Confederate flag at the fore," in one of which steamers, on the last day of March, Com. Semmes embarked, and arrived in Montgomery on the 4th of April, 1861.

[2] The act of March 8th established the clerical force of the Navy Department to consist of a chief clerk, a corresponding clerk, and three other clerks, and a messenger.

The act of March 16th authorized the President to appoint four captains, four commanders, thirty lieutenants, five surgeons, five assistant surgeons, six paymasters, and two chief engineers, and to employ as many masters, midshipmen, engineers, naval constructors, boatswains, gunners, carpenters, sailmakers, and other warrant and petty officers and seamen, as he may deem necessary, not to exceed in the aggregate three thousand. The act also made provision for a marine corps, to consist of one major, one quartermaster, one paymaster, one adjutant, one sergeant-major, one quartermaster-sergeant, and six companies, each company to consist of one captain, one first and one second lieutenant, four sergeants, four corporals, one hundred men and ten musicians, with pay and allowance the same as in the infantry.

Under the law passed February 21st, the President immediately called to the Navy Department, as Secretary of the Navy, Hon. Stephen Russell Mallory, of Florida.[1]

Secretary Mallory immediately organized his department by assigning Capt. Franklin Buchanan to the Bureau of Orders and Detail; Commander George Minor to that of

[1] Mr. Mallory was born in the Island of Trinidad, near the coast of Venezuela, in the year 1813. He was the second son of Charles Mallory, and Ellen his wife, who at the time of his birth were living in or near the town of Port of Spain, in Trinidad. Charles Mallory, his father, was from the town of Reading, Conn., a civil engineer by profession, and for some years before the birth of Stephen had been engaged as a civil engineer on some public work at Port of Spain.

Ellen Russell, the mother of Stephen Russell Mallory, was born at Carrick-on-Suir, County Waterford, Ireland. When about thirteen years of age she was adopted by two bachelor uncles, her mother's brothers, who were planters in Trinidad, and taken by them to their home in that island, where she met Charles Mallory, and was married to him when she was not more than sixteen years of age. Charles and Ellen Mallory had but two children—John, who was born about 1811, and Stephen. John died when he was about fourteen years old, at Key West.

When Stephen was about a year old his parents left Trinidad and came to the United States. Charles Mallory's health was feeble, and after trying the climate of Havana for a short time, he removed to Key West about 1820, when the island was inhabited by only a few fishermen. He died of consumption at Key West about two years afterwards, leaving his widow and the two boys. Before settling at Key West, or going to Havana, Mr. and Mrs. Mallory visited Mobile, Ala., and while there concluded to place the youngest boy, Stephen, at a school on the eastern shore of Mobile Bay, at a place that was known as "the village." Stephen, who could not have been more than six or seven years old, remained there for six months or a year, and then went over to Key West, where his parents were then living. He remained at Key West until he was about fourteen years of age, when his mother, who was then a widow and had lost the oldest boy John, sent him to the Moravian School for boys at Nazareth, Pa. He was at that school about three years, and returned to Key West when about sixteen or seventeen. This was all the schooling he ever had.

When about nineteen years of age he received the appointment of Inspector of Customs at Key West, which he held for several years, and was subsequently appointed Collector of Customs at Key West. While Inspector of Customs he studied law with Judge William Marvin, at that time Judge of the United States District Court at Key West, and was admitted to the Bar about 1839. During the Indian war in Florida he volunteered and served for those years in active operations against the Seminoles.

In 1838 he married Angela Moreno, daughter of Francisco Moreno of Pensacola, Fla.; she is still (1886) alive. After leaving the office of Collector of Customs at Key West, and having attained a high reputation as a skillful practitioner of the law, in 1850 he was selected as a delegate to the great commercial convention which met at Nashville; but, though heartily favoring its purpose, was compelled by other engagements to decline the honor. In 1851 he was elected by the Florida Legislature to the United States Senate for six years, his opponent being Hon. David L. Yulee. Mr. Mallory was at Key West at the time, and did not even know that he was a candidate for the office. Mr. Yulee contested his election before the United States Senate, having as his attorney the late Edwin M. Stanton, afterwards the Federal Secretary of War; but failed to make good his contest. The Senate unanimously awarded the position to Mr. Mallory, and he took his seat in December following. At the expiration of his term as Senator, Mr. Mallory was again elected by the Florida Legislature to succeed himself in 1857, and continued to represent Florida in the Senate until the secession of his State in 1861, when he resigned his seat and at once took an open and active part with the States of the South. He returned to his home at Pensacola, to which place he had removed from Key West in 1858. During most of his service in the Senate he was Chairman of the Committee on Naval Affairs, a position his familiarity with marine matters qualified him to fill. He was also a member of the Committee on Claims. As a speaker he never gained a high reputation in

Ordnance and Hydrography; James A. Semple, paymaster, to that of Provisions and Clothing, and W. A. W. Spotswood, surgeon, to that of Medicine and Surgery. Capt. Raphael Semmes was, upon his return to Montgomery, appointed to the Lighthouse Board, which had been made a bureau of the Treasury Department. Edward M. Tidball was appointed Chief Clerk of the Navy Department, March 13, 1861.

The appointment of Mr. Mallory has been criticised with great severity, but no single good reason has been shown as to his incompetency or unfitness; his loyalty to the Confederacy was by innuendo impeached, but the malice which invented the aspersion was too apparent to give it probability. He could not command success, but he deserved it by faithful and diligent labor, and by intelligent and discreet effort.

When a Senator of the United States, he had been Chairman of the Naval Committee, where the information derived from his previous employment at Key West soon enabled him to obtain a thorough knowledge of the organization, equipment and general disciplinary rules of the U. S. navy. He found himself at the head of a naval department on the eve of a great war, without a ship or any of the essentials of a navy; he had not only to organize and administer, but to build the

the Senate. He was not a showy orator, but occasionally delivered speeches showing careful preparation and a clear knowledge of the subject treated. His vote was always for the South on every question, and he could be counted upon to support any measure his more able leaders proposed. In 1858 Mr. Buchanan tendered him the appointment of Minister to Spain, which he declined. On the secession of Florida he was appointed Chief Justice of the Admiralty Court of the State, but declined the high honor.

During the time he was at his home he took an active part in all matters relating to the defence of his State, and on January 28, 1861, sent the following warning letter to the United States authorities through the "Hon. John Slidell, or Hon. R. M. T. Hunter, or Governor Bigler": "We hear the *Brooklyn* is coming with reinforcements for Fort Pickens. No attack on its garrison is contemplated, but, on the contrary, we desire te keep the peace, and if the present status be preserved we will guarantee that no attack will be made upon it; but if reinforcements be attempted, resistance and a bloody conflict seem inevitable. Should the Goverment thus attempt to augment its force—when no possible call for it exists, when we are preserving a peaceful policy—an assault may be made on the fort at a moment's warning. All preparation are made. Our whole force—1,700 strong—will regard it as a hostile act. Impress this upon the President, and urge that the inevitable consequence of reinforcements under present circumstances is instant war, as peace will be preserved if no reinforcements be attempted. If the President wants an assurance of all I say from Colonel Chase, commanding the forces, I will transmit it at once. *I am determined to stave off war if possible.*"—*Official Records, Series* 1, *Vol. II., p.* 354. But that not being possible, he accepted the portfolio of Secretary of the Confederate Navy of President Davis and held it continuously through the war. He was a gentleman of excellent sense, unpretending manners, and probably conducted

his department as successfully as was possible with the limited naval resources of the South.

Mr. Mallory left Richmond in company with Mr. Davis on the abandonment of that city by the Confederate Government, and accompanied the President to Washington, Ga., where they separated, Mr. Mallory going to La Grange, Ga., where his family was then living. He was in La Grange about a week, when he and Hon. Benjamin Hill, who was also there, were arrested, taken to Atlanta, and thence carried to Fort Lafayette in New York Harbor. He was arrested on May 20, 1865, and his devoted wife in a letter written at the time thus describes the event:

"Night before last, at half-past twelve o'clock, we were aroused from sleep by a heavy knock at the door, and a threat of breaking it open followed before any one had time to answer. When a light was procured the servant opened the door, and some twenty armed men entered to arrest my husband; at the same time another party went to Senator Hill's house, at which Mr. Mallory was staying, and there arrested him. Mr. Mallory was hurried off like a malefactor, without being given even enough time to put on proper clothing. They would not listen to the tears and entreaties of his wife and children to let him remain wlth them only until daylight. I sent Buddie to Atlanta as soon as it was daylight with clothing and money."

Mr. Mallory was confined in Fort Lafayette ten months, being released on parole in March, 1866. He returned to Pensacola in July, 1866, still under parole, and resumed the practice of law, and successfully continued it until his death, November 9, 1873.

Mr. Mallory was a hard student all his life, and though his three years at Nazareth were about all the real schooling he ever had, he, nevertheless, at the age of thirty-five, was able to speak French and Spanish correctly and fluently. His mother lived to see him in the United States Senate, she dying at Key West about the year 1855.

ships and boats, provide as best he could their ordnance, and create a naval force in a country which in a few days was shut out from the world by an almost impenetrable blockade, and which possessed within its limits resources only in the rude, crude and unmanufactured state. The timber for his ships stood in the forest, and when cut and laid was green and soft ; the iron required was in the mines, and there were neither furnaces nor workshops; the hemp required for the ropes had to be sown, grown, reaped, and then there were no rope-walks. The Southern States had never produced a sufficiency of iron for the use of their people in time of peace, and now that war was greatly to multiply the uses of that indispensable metal, the price rose from $25 to $1,300 per ton; and yet neither money nor industry could supply the demand which the navy, the army, the fast-wearing rails and engines of the railroads, and all the other necessities a great war required.

With not a rolling-mill capable of turning out a $2\frac{1}{2}$-inch iron plate, nor a workshop able to complete a marine engine, and with a pressing need to build, equip and maintain ships-of-war, the embarrassments and difficulties which Mr. Mallory encountered may be estimated. When the Confederate government was formed in February, 1861, Virginia had not seceded, and the Tredegar Iron Works and Belona Foundry, at Richmond, were not accessible to the use of the Confederate States navy, and the Pensacola navy-yard with its dock-yard was not a yard of construction, but merely for shelter and repair.

From the 21st of February to the 15th of April there was not time enough, with all the appliances of a first-class manufacturing people, to organize a navy and build and equip its ships; and yet that was what the Confederate Navy Department had before it. When the navy-yard at Norfolk fell into the hands of Virginia, it was burnt and damaged, yet was of inestimable service to the Confederate navy, after being transferred to the Confederate States. The administration of Mr. Mallory is not to be judged and condemned by its failure, but it will excite surprise and win admiration for what was accomplished with the means and resources at his command. The efforts made and the results accomplished will be best understood and appreciated in connection with the operations of attack and defence; but we shall, for the benefit of a clearer understanding of the merits and demerits of the Navy Department, briefly review the administrative acts in connection with the organization of *personnel* and material in advance of those movements of offensive and defensive action.

At the time of the organization of the Confederate government, its treasury was not only absolutely empty, but the legislation and agency for collecting the necessary means of support had to be adopted and applied. Under even the most favorable circumstances, time and experience would be necessary before the supply of money could be collected and on hand to meet expenses which had already begun. But this difficulty was aggravated and increased beyond calculation in the face of an impending conflict with the United States. In this emergency, early in March, 1861, the Convention of the State of Louisiana, by ordinance, transferred to the Confederate States the "Bullion Fund," then in the hands of A. J. Guirot, State Depositary, and which was seized in the U. S. Mint, amounting to $389,267.46, and the further sum of $147,519.66, the amount collected from customs between the 31st January and March 1, 1861.

The total expenditures of the Confederate government from February, 1861 to August, 1862, a period of eighteen months, were $347,272,958.58; the receipts were $302,482,096.60. Of the expenditures the navy used $14,605,777.86.[1]

The resignations of naval officers from the U. S. navy followed the secession of the State of which they were citizens. South Carolina being the first State that severed her connection with the United States, the first resignation came from her officers, and as each of the other States withdrew from the Union, their officers, following the sense of duty of their allegiance, resigned their commissions, until by June 3, 1861, about one-fifth of the officers of the United States navy had resigned. A publication of that date gave a list of all the resignations, with the entire number of officers in the service, as follows:

	Whole Number.	Southerners Resigned.	Southerners Remaining.
Captains	93	16	22
Commanders . . .	127	34	30
Lieutenants	351	76	75
Surgeons	69	11	20
Passed Assistant Surgeons .	43	10	11
Assistant Surgeons . .	36	7	11
Paymasters . . .	64	10	17
Chaplains . . .	24	1	5
Profs. Mathematics . .	12	1	6
Masters . . .	45	6	10

[1] The aggregate appropriations for each department of the Confederate government early in March, 1861, was:

Legislative......................	$55,740
Executive........................	33,050
Department of State..............	44,200
Treasury Department	70,800
War Department..................	59,000
Navy Department.................	17,300
Post Office Department.	44,900
Judiciary........................	63,200
Mint and independent treasury.....	80,000
Foreign intercourse..............	100,000
Lighthouses.....................	150,000
Expenses of collecting revenue....	545,000
Executive mansion................	5,000
Miscellaneous....................	200,000
Total.....................	**$1,468,190**

The Act of March 15 appropriated
1. For pay of officers of the navy.... $131,750
2. For pay of marine corps.......... 175,512
3. For provisions and clothing...... 133,860
4. For pay of warrant and petty officers, etc...... 168,000
5. For expenditure for coal........ 235,000
6. Probable cost of 10 gunboats...... 1,100,000
7. For completing and equipping steamer *Fulton*, at Pensacola. .. 25,000
8. For pay of officers, etc , at Pensacola navy-yard 54,363
9. For compensation of ex-clerk in Navy Department.... 6,000

Total...... .... $2,028,685

	Whole Number.	Southerners Resigned.	Southerners Remaining.
Midshipmen	55	5	15
Acting Midshipmen . .	267	106	22
Gunners	47	2	9
Carpenters . . .	45	1	19
Sailmakers	40	3	11
Marine Corps.			
Captains	13	3	3
First Lieutenants . .	20	6	4
Second Lieutenants . .	20	5	7
Chief Engineers . . .	28	4	4
First Assistants . . .	43	6	17
Second Assistants . .	29	1	9
Third Assistants . .	92	7	23
	1,563	321	350

Commander Henry J. Hartstene, in command of the gunboat *Pawnee*, apprehending that he might be ordered to Charleston, asked to be relieved, and then resigned. Lieut. Thomas P. Pelot and Lieut. J. R. Hamilton resigned immediately after ascertaining that South Carolina had seceded. Lieut. Haralton addressed the "Southern officers of the U. S. navy" a warm appeal, under date of Jan. 14, 1861, to resign and accept commissions from their States. His earnest appeal to the officers, "to bring with you every ship and man you can, that we may use them against the oppressors of our liberties," received no response, and not a United States vessel was delivered up by a Southern officer.

After the secession of the States those officers were scattered throughout the States, some in shore batteries, others devising means of defence, procuring ordnance supplies, and in one way and another doing all in their power to aid in the defence of their States. These officers were transferred by their States to the Confederate States for appointment in the navy, and to the same rank they held in the navy of the United States. Thus, at its very beginning, the new government found itself embarrassed with a wealth of officers, while it was poor beyond description in every other essential of a navy.

To provide for the officers who had resigned from the U. S. navy, the Confederate navy, as provided for by the act of February 21, 1861, was increased by the Amendatory Act of April 21, 1862, and made to consist of

"Four admirals, 10 captains, 31 commanders, 100 first lieutenants, 25 second lieutenants, 20 masters, in line of promotion; 12 paymasters, 40 assistant paymasters, 22 surgeons, 15 past assistant surgeons, 30 assistant surgeons, 1 engineer-in-chief, and 12 engineers.

"That all the admirals, 4 of the captains, 5 of the commanders, 22 of the first lieutenants and 5 of the second lieutenants shall be appointed solely for gallant or meritorious conduct during the war. The appointments shall be made from the grade immediately below the one to be filled and without reference to the rank of the officer in such grade, and the service for which the appointment shall be conferred shall be specified in the commission: Provided, that all officers below the grade of second-lieutenant may be promoted more than one grade for the same service.

"That the warrant officers shall be as follows : 20 passed midshipmen, 106 acting midshipmen, 50 first assistant engineers, 150 second assistant engineers, 150 third assistant engineers, 10 boatswains, 20 gunners, 6 sail-makers, and 20 carpenters.

"That the annual pay of the additional grades created by this act shall be as follows :—Admiral, $6,000; second lieutenant, for service afloat, $1,200; when on leave or other duty, $1,000; master in the line of promo-tion, $1,000 for service afloat; when on leave or other duty, $900; past mid-shipman, $900 for service afloat; when on leave or other duty, $800.

"That the annual pay of assistant paymasters shall hereafter be, when on service afloat, $1,200; on other duty, $1,100."

By the latter act the following was established as the pay table of the officers of the navy :

Grades.	Pay per annum.
Admiral	$6,000
Captains—	
When commanding squadrons	5,000
All others at duty on sea	4,200
On other duty	3,600
On leave or waiting orders	3,000
Commanders—	
On duty at sea first five years after date of commission	2,825
On duty at sea second five years after date of commission	3,150
On other duty first five years after date of commission	2,662
On other duty second five years after date of commission	2,825
All other commanders	2,250
Lieutenants Commanding—at sea	2,550
First Lieutenants—	
On duty at sea.	1,500
After seven years' sea service in the navy	1,700
After nine years' sea service in the navy	1,900
After eleven years' sea service in the navy	2,100
After thirteen years' sea service in the navy	2,250
On other duty	1,500
After seven years' sea service in the navy	1,600
After nine years' sea service in the navy	1,700
After eleven years' sea service in the navy	1,800
After thirteen years' sea service in the navy	1,875
On leave or waiting orders	1,200
After seven years' sea service in the navy	1 266
After nine years' service in the navy	1,333
After eleven years' sea service in the navy	1,400
After thirteen years' sea service in the navy	1,450
Second Lieutenants—	
Duty afloat	1,200
When on leave or other duty	1,000
Fleet Surgeons	3,300
Surgeons—on duty at sea—	
For first five years after date of commission as surgeon	2,200
For second five years after date of commission as surgeon	2,400
For third five years after date of commission as surgeon	2,600
For fourth five years after date of commission as surgeon	2,800
For twenty years and upwards after date of commission	3,000
On other duty—	
For first five years after date of commission as surgeon	2,000
For second five years after date of commission as surgeon	2,200
For third five years after date of commission as surgeon	2,400
For fourth five years after date of commission as surgeon	2,600
For twenty years and upwards after date of commission	2,800

The loss and destruction of naval records render it impossible to follow the changes and details that took place in the Confederate Navy Department. In the earlier days of the war many assignments were made hurriedly and for immediate necessity which the imperfect records do not explain or consecutively follow, and officers are found discharging duties at stations for which no orders are now obtainable.

The difficulty is further increased by the simultaneousness of the preparations for war in every part of the country, and at every port, in every river, and along the whole coast. The States, after secession, ordered the officers who resigned from the U. S. navy to different places within their limits, and they remained at those posts after the formation of the Confederate government until ordered elsewhere. Thus, South Carolina, before the formation of the Confederate government, preparing for the capture of Fort Sumter, had assigned Capt. Hartstene to the command of her naval forces in Charleston harbor, where, on the 8th of January, the first gun in the war was fired at the *Star of the West* on her ill-advised attempt to reinforce Sumter.

General Beauregard, after the formation of the Confederate government, assumed command of the Confederate forces beleaguering Fort Sumter, and in erecting the batteries which surrounded the fort was aided by Confederate naval officers. In his report of April 27, 1861, he mentions " the naval department, especially Capt. Hartstene, as perfectly indefatigable in guarding the entrance into the harbor "; and the same officer as having had charge of the arrangements with the United States fleet off the harbor for the transportation of Major Anderson's command to some port of the United States; Captains Hamilton, Hallonquist, and Lieut. Valentine for the rapidity and accuracy of their mortar practice; and Surgeon A. M. Lynah, C. S. navy, for intelligent professional arrangements in anticipation of the casualties of battle.

Hon. G. V. Fox, afterwards Assistant Secretary of the U. S. Navy Department, while in New York arranging for the expedition, which, under his direction, was designed to relieve Sumter, encountered the agents of the State of South Carolina negotiating to purchase two tugs; and writing to Mr. Blair, under date of March 1, 1861, Mr. Fox mentions " Hartstene, now a captain in the Confederate States navy, who thinks he has prevented an attack upon Sumter so far, but says it will soon be done and will be a very sanguinary affair. Paul Hamilton commands the floating battery now launched. They have four tugs, which do not amount to much compared to one of these powerful New York ones." When Mr. Fox visited Charleston, March 21, he was carried down to Fort Sumter under the escort of Capt. Hartstene, who commanded the little fleet of three steamboats which kept watch and ward over the outer harbor of Charleston, lighting the entrance with floating lightwood fires, and directing the motion of the Drummond lights whenever the alarm of "the boats are coming" might be signalled.

The States which provided the *personnel* of the navy, also, under the resolution of the Confederate Congress of March 15, 1861, in reference to property captured from the United States, turned over the ships seized by them at the time of their secession. This bare nucleus of a navy, Congress, on March 15, 1861, authorized the President to increase by construction or purchase of ten steam gunboats for coast defences, whereof five were to be of a tonnage not exceeding seven hundred and fifty tons, and five of one thousand tons. In consequence of the resolution of the same date, the States turned over to the Confederate government the forts, arsenals, navy-yards, dock-yards and other property formerly belonging to the United States. This transfer placed at the disposal of the Navy Department the navy-yard at Pensacola, Florida, which having been a yard mainly for shelter and repairs, was but indifferently adapted to building purposes, and, lying in an exposed position, was of no immediate aid to the Navy Department.

The efforts of the Confederate Navy Department in organizing the naval stations were directed in March, 1861, to New Orleans, whither a commission, composed of Commander L. Rousseau, Commander E. Farrand and Lieut. Robert T. Chapman, was sent on the 17th of that month to purchase or contract for constructing the new gunboats authorized by Congress. Under their administration at New Orleans, the *Sumter*, the first Confederate cruiser, was dispatched to sea from that city on April 18, 1861.

Commander L. Rousseau, thus appointed to the command of the New Orleans naval station, was chiefly engaged in the examination of river craft for conversion into gunboats, and collecting such material as the city and adjacent country afforded suitable to naval purposes. He continued in command until July 31st, when he was relieved by Capt. George N. Hollins.

Capt. Duncan N. Ingraham, C. S. navy, in charge of naval affairs in the waters of Alabama, was ordered, May 20, 1861, to ascertain the practicability of obtaining wrought-iron plates of from two to three inches in thickness; and whether, if such plates could be furnished according to a given form, dimension and weight, what would be the price per pound, together with the best means of forwarding them to New Orleans. Capt. Ingraham reported that neither the Tennessee Iron Works nor the Messrs. Hillman & Co., on the Cumberland River, in Kentucky, would undertake work for the Confederate States in the then condition of the country in which their works were located, and that Messrs. Wood & Co. were not prepared to roll heavy work under any circumstances. He also ascertained that the mills at Atlanta, Georgia, could not roll such iron as was needed, as it would involve an entire change in their mill, which they declined to make at that time; but afterwards, in November, 1861, the Atlanta mills were changed and became a mill for rolling iron plates for vessels-of-war.

On November 16, 1861, Capt. Ingraham was assigned to duty in Charleston harbor, and ordered to superintend the preparation and armament of the batteries for its defence, assign to duty the naval officers at his disposal as ordnance officers at the batteries, and to execute all orders relating to the naval operations in the harbor which he might receive from Flag-officer Tatnall.

Capt. Victor M. Randolph, late of the United States navy, was appointed by the State of Florida to the command of the navy-yard at Pensacola, and assisted Colonel Wm. H. Chase, then in command of the State forces around Pensacola, in the reduction of that navy-yard; Commander Ebenezer Farrand and Lieut. Francis B. Renshaw were also officers of the United States navy, and on duty at the Pensacola navy-yard. Capt. Farrand continued to command the navy-yard until its evacuation and destruction by order of Gen. Braxton Bragg, March 11, 1862. The Navy Department entered into contracts with Ollinger & Bruce, November 4, 1861, and with F. G. Howard, October 29, 1861, for the construction of two gunboats at the head of Pensacola Bay, thirty-five miles from Fort Pickens; which, under the supervision of Commander Farrand, were well and strongly built, and their destruction was condemned by Commander Farrand as unnecessary. He considered that they could have been removed up Escambia River, out of reach of the enemy's gunboats, and there completed, where they would have rendered important service in any attack by the enemy on Pensacola. It was the action of the commander, General Samuel Jones, under positive orders of General Bragg, and not the Navy Department, or its executive officer, Commander Farrand, that thus destroyed two valuable gunboats. It is not true, as Admiral Porter says, that "Pensacola was evacuated by the Confederates . . . on a scare, they thinking that Farragut's fleet was on its way to take it" —but the evacuation was rendered necessary, in General Bragg's opinion, because "our fate may depend on two weeks in the valley of the Mississippi." The letter from which we extract that remark was written March 1, 1862, and ordered the troops from Pensacola to the valley of the Mississippi after all the guns and other military and naval stores had been removed. Among the troops defending Pensacola was Capt. Thom's company of marines, which were transferred to Virginia November 29th, at which date General Bragg renewed a request made "as early as last spring, and frequently since, for some young naval officers, but without success," notwithstanding he had "two steam gunboats commanded by landsmen."

Commander Tatnall resigned his commission in the United States navy on February 21, 1861, and was appointed senior flag-officer in the navy at Georgia, February 28th, and commissioned a captain in the Confederate Navy in March, 1861. The Navy Department immediately assigned Capt. Tatnall to the command of the naval defence of the waters of Georgia and South Carolina, with directions to improvise as best he could a squadron, to be composed of such light steamers and river craft as he might be able to secure. Contracts for the building of four gunboats at Savannah, Ga., and of two at Saffold, in that State, were made by the Navy Department during the first year of the war.

The Proclamation of President Lincoln, April 15, 1861, calling upon Virginia and the other States for 75,000 troops to enable the United States authorities to repossess and hold the forts, etc., seized by the seceded States, had no uncertain signification in Virginia. There it was understood and accepted as the declaration of war on the part of the United States. Virginia could be no neutral in that war and had no desire to occupy any such position. It was apparent that her territory would become the Flanders of the war, and that between her northern and southern boundaries would be fought those great battles upon the results of which would depend the fate and fortune of the Confederate States.

Among the first acts of the State Convention after the adoption of the Ordinance of Secession, on April 17, 1861, was Ordinance No. 9, passed on the same day, by which the Governor of the State, after being authorized and required to call for volunteers, was also directed to "immediately invite all efficient and worthy Virginians and residents of Virginia in the army and navy of the United States to retire therefrom, and to enter the service of Virginia, assigning them to such rank as will not reverse the relative rank held by them in the United States service, and will at least be equivalent thereto."

By the same Ordinance the Governor was ordered to "repel invasion and see that in all things the commonwealth take no detriment," and to that end an appropriation of $100,000 was made.

An invitation was also extended by the Convention to all Virginia officers in the Revenue service and Coast Survey of the United States to enter the service of the State, and the Governor was authorized to make proper provision for them.

A commander-in-chief of the military and naval forces of the State, with the rank of Major General, was authorized by Ordinance of April 19, 1861, who should, when appointed, take rank over all other military and naval officers of the State without regard to date of commission.

The oath to support the Constitution of the United States, which had been taken by citizens of Virginia while the State

was a member of that confederacy, was declared inoperative
and void, and of no effect, and the statutory provisions of the
State which heretofore gave efficacy to that oath were repealed.

Having thus disrobed herself of the constitution and
union of the United States, Virginia prepared as best she
could to meet the responsibilities of her acts. A provisional
army was created, and on April 27th an Ordinance establishing the navy of Virginia was passed, to consist of 2,000 seamen and marines, with their proper officers. The officers
were to be those of the U. S. navy who had or who might
thereafter avail themselves of the invitation extended by
Ordinance No. 9, of April 17th. The Governor was directed
to prescribe the pay, rations, and allowances, which were to
be the same in all respects as those then in the U. S. navy;
Virginians on the retired list of the U. S. navy were to be
provided for by the Governor, and to perform such duties as
they were able to discharge; the rules for the government of
the U. S. navy were directed to be revised by a Board of
officers to be ordered by the Governor, and made applicable to
the navy of Virginia; the term of enlistment for seamen was
fixed at three years, and for marines at five years; a medical
department was directed to be organized by the Governor, to
which none but surgeons and assistant surgeons late of the
U. S. navy were to be appointed.

An Auditing Board for all claims and expenditures for the
army and navy was appointed, consisting of George W.
Munford, John R. Tucker, and Jonathan M. Bennett.

On the 22d of April, 1861, Robert E. Lee, late a colonel in
the U. S. cavalry, was appointed by Governor Letcher and
confirmed by the convention to be Commander-in-chief of the
army and navy of Virginia, and immediately entered upon
the duties of his position.

Two days after that appointment, on April 24th, a convention between Virginia and the Confederate States of America
was entered into, which provided that : Until the union between the State and the Confederacy was fully completed the
whole military and naval operations, offensive and defensive,
of the State, in the impending conflict with the United States,
shall be under the chief control and direction of the President
of the Confederate States, and that, after the completion of
said union, the State would turn over to the Confederate
States all the public property, naval stores and munitions of
war then in her possession, acquired from the United States,
and that whatever expenditures of money the State might incur would be met and provided for by the Confederate States.
The Constitution of the Confederate States was ratified and
ordained, and proclaimed binding on the people of Virginia
by Ordnance No. 56, adopted June 19, 1861.

In the interval between April 17th and June 19th the
States seized the Gosport navy-yard, Harper's Ferry, two

steamers at Richmond, and began to fortify the Potomac, Rappahannock, York and James Rivers with batteries, under the command and direction of her naval officers.

Commodore French Forrest, having resigned his commission in the U. S. navy, was appointed in the Virginia navy, and assigned to duty as flag-officer at the Norfolk navy-yard immediately upon its evacuation by the United States authorities; at the same time Capt. Arthur Sinclair, also of the old navy, was appointed to the same rank in the navy of Virginia, and assigned to the command of Fort Norfolk; Robert B. Pegram and Catesby Ap R. Jones were appointed on April 18, 1861, captains in the Virginia navy, and James H. Rochelle, a lieutenant. These officers were immediately ordered to Norfolk, under the following order addressed to Capt. Pegram : "You will immediately proceed to Norfolk and there assume command of the naval station, with authority to organize naval defences, enroll and enlist seamen and marines, and temporarily to appoint war officers, and do and perform whatever may be necessary to preserve and protect the property of the Commonwealth and the citizens of Virginia." This order was of date April 18th, but was superseded in a few days by that assigning Flag-officer Forrest to the command of the naval station at Norfolk.

Lieut. John M. Brooke, of the C. S. navy, was assigned to duty, as aide-de-camp, at the headquarters of Major Gen. Robert E. Lee, then commanding the army of Virginia, and Commander M. F. Maury was attached to the Advisory Council of the State of Virginia; Wm. L. Maury and Wm. Taylor Smith, lieutenants in the Virginia navy, were assigned to duty under Gen. Philip St. George Cocke, commanding on the line of the Potomac, and were engaged in erecting batteries of that river; Capt. William C. Whittle, of the navy, was assigned to duty at Gloucester Point. Capt. Thos. J. Page while in the Virginia navy was aide-de-camp to Governor Letcher. Capt. Wm. F. Lynch was assigned to duty on the Potomac River. Commander A. B. Fairfax was ordnance officer at the Norfolk navy-yard, and Lieut. H. H. Lewis was on duty on the Rappahannock. Capt. J. Wilkinson was assigned to the duty of constructing Fort Powhatan on the James River.

The naval school established by Secretary Mallory at Richmond, under the superintendence of Lieut. Wm. H. Parker, proved of great benefit to the service. The exigencies of defence required not only trained officers, but men capable of training others. The naval academy educated and trained a large number of the younger officers of the service, some of whom subsequently acquired great distinction.

The number of experienced seamen in the Southern States prior to the war was very limited, and these were entirely absorbed by the Conscript Law of February 17, 1864, placing in the military service all white men residents of the Confederate States between the ages of seventeen and fifty; notwithstanding the law of May 1, 1863, provided for the transfer of all seamen and ordinary seamen from the army to the navy, in practice this law was almost entirely disregarded—the only favorable response that was made to numerous calls made on the army for seamen, under this law, was to an order from the War Department of March 22, 1864, which directed the transfer to the navy of 1,200 men, under which 960 men were transferred from all the armies on the east of the Mississippi River. The law of October 2, 1862, gave the right of election to all persons enrolled, or about to be enrolled, at any time before being assigned to any company, who should prefer the navy or marine corps, to be enlisted in that service, but this availed very little to the navy; and notwithstanding naval officers were sent to the different conscript camps to facilitate recruiting for the navy, a favorable result was not attained; hence, recruiting for the navy was barely sufficient to supply the deficiencies occasioned by deaths, discharges and desertions. In 1864 the whole number of enlisted men in the navy was 3,674.

The United States naval register of 1861 shows a navy of 90 vessels, of which number 21 are designated as unserviceable, 27 available but not in commission, and 42 in commission; there were distributed to the home squadron 12 vessels of 187 guns; Mediterranean, 3 vessels, 37 guns; coast of Brazil, 2 vessels, 53 guns; East Indies, 3 vessels, 42 guns; while those in the Pacific aggregated the 42 vessels in commission, which mounted 555 guns, and with over 7,000 men. With the vessels not then in commission, but which were immediately put in commission, Admiral Porter enumerates as the "old navy," 76 vessels, mounting 1,783 guns. Mr. Welles, the United States Secretary of the Navy, took immediate steps for the purchase of 136 vessels, which were altered and commissioned, and mounted with 518 guns ; and also began the construction in different yards, both of the government and of private parties, 52 vessels to carry 256 guns, which, by December of 1861, composed a navy of 264 vessels, carrying 2,557 guns, manned by 22,000 seamen, and of an aggregate tonnage of 218,016 tons.

Prof. Soley enumerates five distinct measures which were immediately adopted by the Administration at Washington to increase the naval force:

First. To buy everything afloat that could be made of service—a measure which was impossible for Mr. Mallory to imitate, because in the Confederacy there was nothing afloat to buy, and no money with which to purchase.

Second. The United States immediately began, and pushed with unexampled energy, the construction of eight sloops-of-war. This was another measure impossible to Mr. Mallory, who had neither ship-yards nor ship-carpenters, neither the means of building nor the power to buy.

Third. To contract with private parties for the construction of heavily armed iron-plated screw gunboats; these "ninety-day gunboats" were for service at sea. Nine of these gunboats passed the forts below New Orleans with Admiral Farragut.

Fourth. For service in narrow waters, twelve paddle-wheel steamers —" double - ender"— and twenty-seven of a larger class; some of which were of iron, were contracted for and built with the greatest dispatch.

Fifth. The iron-clads.

In addition to these five types of vessels, there was also an "immense river fleet, composed of river steamboat rams, iron-clads, tin-clads, and mortar boats"; and lastly, under the sting of the *Alabama*, the *Florida*, and other "commerce-destroyers." the Federal government undertook the construction of a class of war-vessels,—"large wooden steamers, with fine lines, excessively long and sharp and narrow, of light draft for their size, in which every quality was sacrificed to speed"—their main purpose was to destroy the "commerce-destroyers," as well as, under other circumstances, "to do a little commerce-destroying themselves." The Appendix to Prof. Soley's "Blockade and Cruisers" shows 126 wooden vessels constructed between 1861 and 1865, mounting 1,307 guns, and 74 iron-clads, mounting 213 guns—a total of 200 vessels, mounting 1,520 guns.

Against that naval force, Prof. Soley says:

" The Confederate States had at its disposal a small number of trained officers, . . . some of these, like Buchanan, Semmes, Brown, Maffitt, and Brooke, were men of extraordinary professional qualities; but, except its officers, the Confederate government had nothing in the shape of a navy. It had not a single ship-of-war. It had no abundant fleet of merchant-vessels in its ports from which to draw reserves. It had no seamen, for its people were not given to seafaring pursuits. Its only ship-yards were Norfolk and Pensacola. Norfolk, with its immense supplies of ordnance and equipment, was, indeed, valuable ; but though the 300 Dahl-gren guns captured in the yard were a permanent acquisition, the yard itself was lost when the war was one-fourth over. The South was without any large force of skilled mechanics; and such as it had were early summoned to the army. There were only three rolling mills in the country, two of which were in Tennessee ; and the third, at Alabama, was unfitted for heavy work. There were hardly any machine shops that were prepared to supply the best kind of workmanship, and in the beginning the only foundry capable of casting heavy guns was the Tredegar Iron Works, which, under the direction of Commander Brooke, was employed to its fullest capacity. Worst of all, there was no raw materials, except the timber that was standing in the forests. Under these circumstances, no general plan of naval policy on a large scale could be carried out, and the conflict on the Southern side became a species of partisan, desultory warfare."

Without assenting to the conclusion of Prof. Soley, it must be admitted that his picture of Confederate naval prospects at the beginning of the war is not overdrawn or too highly colored. Not dismayed by the unpromising prospects before him, Secretary Mallory obtained the passage of the secret acts of Congress of May 10, 1861, which authorized the dispatch of Naval Agent James D. Bulloch to England, where he arrived on June 4, 1861. But, anticipating legislation on March 13th, an officer was sent to New York to examine and ascertain whether vessels could be purchased there suitable for war purposes; and, if he could, to procure them. On the 19th of March, an engineer officer was dispatched to New York, Philadelphia and Baltimore in search of suitable vessels for naval purposes, and his report was that but one vessel of the character desired could be found in any Northern city, and that was the steamer *Caroline*, of Philadelphia. There negotiations were rendered abortive by the outbreak in Baltimore on the passage of Massachusetts troops through that city, and the agents returned to Montgomery. The agents in Canada reported, 5th of June, that the U. S. government had secured every available steamer in Canadian waters.

The subject of iron-clad ships was brought by the Navy Department to the attention of the naval committee by letter of May 8, 1861, in which Mr. Mallory, after reviewing the history of iron-clad ships in England and France, continued:

"I regard the possession of an iron-armored ship as a matter of the first necessity. Such a vessel at this time could traverse the entire coast of the United States, prevent all blockades, and encounter, with a fair prospect of success, their entire navy.

"If to cope with them upon the sea, we follow their example and build wooden ships, we shall have to construct several at one time, for one or two ships will fall an easy prey to her comparatively numerous steam frigates. But inequality of numbers may be compensated by invulnerability, and thus not only does economy but naval success dictate the wisdom and expediency of fighting iron against wood without regard to first cost. . . . Should the committee deem it expedient to begin at once the construction of such a ship, not a moment should be lost. An agent of the department will leave for England in a day or two charged with the duty of purchasing vessels, and by him the first step in the measure may be taken."

The recommendation of that letter was embodied in a law, and the *Merrimac* was expected to be the kind of vessel therein suggested. The report of the Secretary of the Navy, July 18, 1861, says:

"The frigate *Merrimac* has been raised and docked at an expense of $6,000, and the necessary repairs to hull and machinery to place her in her former condition is estimated by experts at $450,000. The vessel would then be in the river, and by the blockade of the enemy's fleets and batteries rendered comparatively useless. It has, therefore, been determined to shield her completely with three-inch iron, placed at such angles as to render her ball-proof, to complete her at the earliest moment, to arm her with the heaviest ordnance, and to send her at once against the enemy's fleet. It is believed that thus prepared she will be able to contend successfully against the heaviest of the enemy's ships, and to drive them from Hampton Roads and the ports of Virginia. The cost of this work is estimated by the constructor and engineer in charge at $172,523, and, as time is of the first consequence in this enterprise, I have not hesitated to commence the work, and to ask Congress for the necessary appropriation."

Lieut. James H. North was sent abroad in May to procure iron-clad ships, if possible; but finding it impracticable to purchase in Europe, the department commenced the construction of such vessels in the waters of the South. It was recognized by Secretary Mallory in his report of November 20, 1861, that "iron-clad steamships capable of resisting the crushing weight of projectiles from heavy ordnance must at an early day constitute the principal part of the fighting vessels of all naval powers"; and to secure iron for covering, construction and ordnance of naval vessels, the department, as soon as Virginia entered the Confederacy, contracted with Joseph R. Anderson & Co. and the Messrs. Deane for a supply of all classes of iron, including ordnance and projectile, as far as those shops could supply.

At various dates from June 28th, 1861, to Dec. 1st, 1862, Secretary Mallory entered into thirty-two contracts, for the construction of forty gunboats, floating batteries and vessels-of-war, with parties in various cities, from Norfolk to New Orleans and Memphis. In addition to these, the department had vessels under construction superintended by its own officers. This did not include the vessels under contract and construction in foreign countries.

These contracts were with John Hughes & Co., Myers & Co., Ritch & Farrow, David S. Johnston, Frederick G. Howard, Ollinger & Bruce, H. F. Willink, Jr., Gilbert Elliott, William A. Graves, N. Nash, Krenson & Hawkes, F. M. Jones, Wm. O. Safford, Lindsey & Silverton, Henry D. Bassett, Porter & Watson, I. E. Montgomery and A. Anderson, Howard & Ellis, Thomas Moore and John Smoker, for the immediate construction of forty-two gunboats and floating batteries. Many of these vessels were constructed and delivered, and performed valuable service in the Confederate navy.

The building of these gunboats was hindered by a variety of causes, and in many instances their completion prevented by the enemy capturing the localities where the boats were being built. Such failures could not have been prevented by the Navy Department, and the wonder is, not that greater success did not attend Secretary Mallory's efforts, but that so much was done with such limited means, and in spite of the active and unremitting advances of a powerful enemy.

The preparation in 1861 of an iron-clad fleet of gunboats at St. Louis by the U. S. government attracted the attention of the Navy Department at Richmond, and immediate steps were taken to have reliable mechanics sent to St. Louis and employed on those boats who would obtain accurate information of their strength and fighting character and the progress made toward their completion. These reports, with an accurate plan and description of the *Benton,* were made to Mr. Mallory. In consequence of which, it was deemed of more immediate importance to defend New Orleans against an attack from above rather than from the Gulf.

To this end the Act of Congress of August 30th was passed, authorizing and directing the "preparation immediately of floating defences best adapted to defend the Mississippi River against a descent of iron-plated steam gunboats." Under this act contracts were made, August 24, 1861, at Memphis, for the construction of the *Tennessee* and the *Arkansas*, both to be completed by December 24, 1861. The enemy's fleet, building at St. Louis, threatened the Cumberland and Tennessee Rivers, and the country through which these rivers flowed equally with that along the banks of the Mississippi. The Legislature of Tennessee, apprehending an invasion along the line of one or perhaps both of those rivers, called the attention of Congress, by joint resolution of date June 24, 1861, to their unprotected condition; and efforts to purchase and adapt to defensive purposes the river steamboats *Helman*, *Jas. Johnson*, *J. Woods*, and *B. M. Runyon*, lying at Nashville, were immediately undertaken, and were in such progress that, on November 8, Gen. C. F. Smith, U. S. army, commanding at Paducah, called the attention of the authorities at Washington to the fact that, " some eight miles above Fort Henry, the enemy has been for many weeks endeavoring to convert river steamers into iron-clad gunboats. This fort is an obstacle to our gunboats proceeding to look after such work." The construction of the gunboat *Eastport*, on the Tennessee River, was commenced, but not being completed when the forts fell was destroyed by the orders of Gen. A. S. Johnston.

Near the end of the first year of the war, on March 4th, 1862, Mr. Mallory, in response to a resolution of the House of Representatives, urged that the immediate procurement of "fifty light-draft and powerful steam-propellers, plated with five-inch hard iron, armed and equipped for service in our own waters, four iron or steel-clad single deck, ten-gun frigates of about two thousand tons, and ten clipper propellers with superior marine engines, both classes of ships designed for deep-sea cruising, three thousand tons of first-class boiler plate iron, and one thousand tons of rod, bolt and bar iron"; and under the head of munitions of war the Secretary enumerated as necessary for immediate use, " two thousand pieces of heavy ordnance, ranging in calibre from six to eleven inches, and in weight from six thousand to fourteen thousand pounds, two thousand tons of cannon powder, one thousand tons of musket powder for filling projectiles and pyrotechny, four thousand navy rifles, and four thousand navy revolvers, and four thousand navy cutlasses, with their equipment and ammunition." There were required, he further urged, "three thousand instructed seamen, four thousand ordinary seamen and landsmen, and two thousand first-rate mechanics," and he requested that five millions of dollars be immediately placed in Europe.

A joint select committee of the two Houses of Congress was raised on the 27th of August, 1862, to investigate the administration of the Navy Department. New Orleans had fallen, and the great gunboats *Louisiana* and *Mississippi*, of which so much was expected and had been promised, had been burned, without delivering any seriously damaging blow at the enemy. Norfolk had been captured, and with her fall the great navy-yard at Gosport had returned to the control of the United States, and the pride of the Confederate navy, the *Virginia*, while riding triumphant in Hampton Roads, had been destroyed by the match in Confederate hands. Disappointment and disaster made men unjust in their review of causes, and a scapegoat was attempted to be made of the Secretary of the Navy. His department was charged with incompetent management, with wastefulness of means, with partiality and favoritism, and with the responsibility for the loss of New Orleans and Norfolk—for the unnecessary destruction of the *Mississippi* and the *Virginia*.

In their report the committee state that they inquired into everything relating to the materials and the operations of the navy of the Confederate States; the means and resources for building a navy; the efforts to purchase or build vessels and to obtain ordnance stores; the naval defences of the Mississippi River, and especially of New Orleans, of the Cumberland, Tennessee and James Rivers, and of the city of Norfolk.

Before the war but seven steam war-vessels had been built in the States forming the Confederacy, and the engines of only two of these had been contracted for in these States. All the labor or materials requisite to complete and equip a war-vessel could not be commanded at any one point of the Confederacy.

In justification of the Secretary of the Navy, the committee state that he had invited contracts for building gunboats wherever they could be soonest and best built and most advantageously employed, and that his contracts were judicious and seemed to have been properly enforced. In relation to the destruction of the *Mississippi* at New Orleans, the committee say, the contractors—Messrs. Tift—undertook her construction without pecuniary reward, and prosecuted the work on her with industry and dispatch, and that neither they nor the Secretary were censurable for the incompleteness of that vessel when the enemy reached New Orleans, or for her destruction.

With reference to what the department had accomplished since its organization, the committee state that it erected a powder mill which supplies all the powder required by our navy; two engine-boiler and machine shops, and five ordnance workshops. It has established eighteen yards for building war-vessels, and a rope-walk, making all cordage, from a rope yarn to a nine-inch cable, and capable of turning out 8,000 yds. per month.

Of vessels not iron-clad the Department has purchased and otherwise acquired and converted to war-vessels. 44
Has built and completed as war-vessels 12
Has partially constructed and destroyed, to save from the enemy . . . 10
And has now under construction. 9
Of iron-clad vessels it has completed and has now in commission . . . 12
Has completed and destroyed, or lost by capture 4
Has in progress of construction, and in various stages of forwardness . 23

It had also one iron-clad floating battery, presented to the Confederate States by the ladies of Georgia, and one iron-clad ram, partially completed and turned over to the Confederacy by the State of Alabama.

In spite of all embarrassments and difficulties, the navy had afloat in November, 1861, the *Sumter*, the *Dixie*, the *Jeff. Davis*, the *Gordon*, the *Merrimac*, the *Petrel*, the *Everglade*, the *Savannah* (captured), the *Webb*, the *McClelland*, the *McRae*, the *Yorktown*, the *Patrick Henry*, the *Resolute*, the *Sallie*, the *Bonita*, the *James Grey*, the *Calhoun*, the *Ivy*, the *Dodge*, the *Lady Davis*, the *Lewis Cass*, the *Washington*, the *Nina*, the *Jackson*, the *Tuscarora*, the *Pickens*, the *Bradford*, the *Nelms*, the *Coffee*, the *Nashville*, the *Manassas*, the *George Page*, the *Judith* (destroyed), and several other vessels. The *personnel* of the navy then consisted of—Captains, 9; Commanders, 25; Lieutenants, 24; Midshipmen, 6; Surgeons, 7; Paymasters, 8; Chief Engineer, 1; First Assistant Engineer, 1; Navy Agents, 2; Colonel of Marines, 1; Lieut. Colonel of Marines, 1; Major of Marines, 1; Captains of Marines, 2; Second Lieutenants of Marines, 3.—Total, 87.

Notwithstanding the military reverses of 1861 and 1862, by which so many important points were taken possession of by the enemy, the Navy Department, in May of 1863, had twenty-three gunboats in progress of construction, twenty of which were of iron and three of wood. The report of Naval Constructor John L. Porter, of November 1, 1862, shows that an iron-clad steamer had just been launched at Richmond, and that at the same place an iron-clad ram was then on the stocks, and four torpedo-boats under construction. At Halifax, N. C., a gunboat of light draft for use in the waters of the Sound would be ready in two months; at Edward's Ferry, on the Roanoke River, a wooden gunboat of light draft, for operations on that river, was approaching completion, and at the same place an iron-clad gunboat for Albemarle Sound was awaiting her machinery. At Wilmington, N. C., there was being built an iron-clad steamer, of such draft of water as would enable her to go out and in at all stages of the tide; the machinery of this steamer was being completed at Columbus, Ga., under the supervision of Chief Engineer J. H. Warner,

C S. navy.   At Pedee River Bridge, a wooden gunboat had just been completed with two propellers, the engines of which were built at the naval works at Richmond, and that there was also on the stocks at the same place a small side-wheel steamer for transportation purposes on the Pedee River, as well as a torpedo-boat.   At Charleston, an iron-clad steamer was nearly completed, with citadel armor-plated, with iron six inches thick, and mounting six guns; also two first-class steamers, for which there was no iron available at that time. At Savannah, an iron-clad was ready for launching, whose engines were also built by Chief Engineer Warner at Columbus, and another iron-clad was also ready for her armament. At Columbus, Ga., a double propeller iron-clad steamer awaited the rising of the river for launching, an.: the steamer *Chattahoochee* had just been thoroughly overhauled and repaired.   At Mobile, a large iron-clad side-wheel steamer, built by Montgomery & Anderson, and two light-draft, double propeller, iron-clad steamers, by Porter & Watson, on the Tombigbee River, awaited iron for plating.

"It will be seen," says Mr. Porter, "that everything has been done to get up an iron-clad fleet of vessels which could possibly be done under the circumstances; but in consequence of the loss of our iron and coal regions, with the rolling mill at Atlanta, our supply of iron has been very limited.   The mills at Richmond are capable of rolling any quantity, but the material is not on hand; and the amount now necessary to complete vessels already built would be equal to four thousand two hundred and thirty tons, as follows :

		Tons.
At Richmond, for two vessels.		575
" Wilmington, for one vessel.		150
" Charleston, for two vessels.		800
" Savannah, for two "		750
" Columbus, for one vessel		280
" Mobile, for three vessels		1,250
On Tombigbee, for three vessels.		425
	Total	4,230 "

Before the war there was no powder stored in any Southern States, except such small quantities of sporting powder as was usual in a country whose people were engaged in field sports.   But of powder for military and naval purposes, that captured at the Norfolk navy-yard, and some obtained in the arsenals in the Southern States, amounting in all to about 60,000 pounds, was the only supply on hand.

"I earnestly beg," Governor F. W. Pickens, of South Carolina, wrote, on September 1, 1861, "if possible, that you will order me, if you have it at Norfolk, 40,000 pounds of cannon powder.   I loaned the Governor of North Carolina 25,000 pounds, and also the Governor of Florida, for Fernandina and Saint Augustine, 5,000 pounds, besides what I sent to Memphis, Tenn.   If I could be sure of getting 40,000 pounds as a reserve for Charleston, I would immediately order a full supply of cannon powder for about 100 guns I have now on our coast below Charleston. As it is, I fear to drain Charleston entirely. I bought for the State, last December and January, about 300,000 pounds from Hazard's Mills in Connecticut, but I have distributed all of it but about 40,000 pounds." About the same time, General John B. Grayson wrote: "As sure as the sun rises, unless cannon powder, etc., be sent to Florida in the next thirty days, she will fall into the hands of the North. Nothing human can prevent it. There are not 4,000 pounds of powder at every post combined." At Fort Pulaski, in September, 1861, the powder in the magazine was " about 45,000 pounds"—on which the navy held an order for 1,800 pounds. The Governor of Florida was writing also : " No powder or fuses—we need guns of larger calibre and ammunition—Florida wants arms. She has never received a musket from the Confederate States." The same demand for powder and arms came up to Richmond from every centre of military operations.

The stock of percussion-caps amounted to less than half a million, if that amount was available, and there was not a machine for making them in all the Southern States. Major Gorgas, in his monograph, says :

" We began in April, 1861, without an arsenal, laboratory or powder mill of any capacity, and with no foundry or rolling-mill except at Richmond, and before the close of 1863, within a little over two years, we supplied them. During the harassments of war, while holding our own in the field defiantly and successfully against a powerful enemy; crippled by a depreciated currency; throttled with a blockade that deprived us of nearly all the means of getting material or workmen; obliged to send almost every able-bodied man to the field ; unable to use slave-labor, with which we were abundantly supplied, except in the most unskilled departments of production ; hampered by want of transportation even of the commonest supplies of food; with no stock on hand even of articles such as steel, copper, leather, iron, which we must have to build up our establishments—against all these obstacles, in spite of all these deficiencies, we persevered at home, as determinedly as did our troops on the field against a more tangible opposition ; and in that short period created, almost literally out of the ground, foundries and rolling mills at Selma, Richmond, Atlanta and Macon, smelting works at Petersburg, chemical works at Charlotte, North Carolina; a powder-mill far superior to any in the United States, and unsurpassed by any across the ocean, and a chain of arsenals, armories and laboratories, equal in their capacity and improvements to the best of those in the United States, stretching link by link from Virginia to Alabama."

The work of preparing for the manufacture of ordnance, ordnance stores and naval supplies was greatly advanced by the Bureau of Ordnance and Hydrography under Commander George Minor, C. S. navy, Lieut. Robert D. Minor, C. S. navy, and Commander John M. Brooke, whose banded guns, manufactured under his supervision at the Tredegar Works in Richmond, proved so remarkably efficient throughout all the conflicts of the war. The Ordnance Bureau at Richmond sent to New Orleans from May, 1861, to May, 1862, 220 heavy guns.

The Bureau of Ordnance and Hydrography later in the war was transferred to Commander John M. Brooke, and in its various departments and different stations became the most valuable branch of the navy. The ordnance works at Richmond, Va., under Lieut. R. D. Minor and R. B. Wright, supplied nearly all the equipments of the vessels in James River and at Wilmington, as well as the carriages for the heavy navy guns in batteries on shore. The employés enrolled in a naval battalion were frequently called from their work to the field, thus interrupting and delaying work far more valuable than any field service it was possible for them to render. At Charlotte, N. C., the naval ordnance works, under the superintendence of Chief Engineer H. A. Ramsay, became one of the most important and valuable aids to the naval service. It was the only establishment where heavy forging could be done; and there the shaftings for steamers and the wrought-iron projectiles were forged and finished; gun-carriages, blocks, and ordnance equipments of nearly every description, including the productions of an ordnance laboratory, were manufactured in great quantities and with great regularity, because its operations were less liable to interruption by calls upon its workmen for service in the fields. At Selma, Commander Catesby Ap. R. Jones superintended the various branches of the foundry employed chiefly in the manufacture of guns specially adapted for service against iron-clads. Forty-seven of these guns were supplied from these works to the defences of Mobile, and twelve were in batteries at Charleston and Wilmington. The naval powder mills at Columbia, under the superintendence of P. B. Gareschi, became in time capable of fully supplying the demands of the navy, and the powder there manufactured was of an excellent quality.

Lieut. D. P. McCorkle, in charge of the ordnance works at Atlanta, finding his plant threatened by the movements of the enemy, transferred the whole machinery and stores to Augusta, and set to work in temporary buildings to manufacture shot, shells, gun-carriages for Charleston, Savannah and Mobile.

The great and pressing demands for ordnance and ordnance stores for the defences of the country, at every point, rendered it impossible for the Navy Department at Richmond to comply promptly with requisitions made upon the Bureau of Ordnance from every assailed point in the Confederacy. To meet the urgent demands of the navy at New Orleans, a laboratory was established on a large scale in that city for the preparation of fuses, primers, fireworks, etc., and to authorize the casting of heavy cannon, the construction of gun-carriages, and the manufacture of projectiles and ordnance equipments of all kinds. The laboratory was first under the direction of Lieut. Beverley Kennon, C. S. navy, and afterwards under Lieut. John R. Eggleston, and then of Acting Master W. A. Robins. General Lovel had already set up a powder mill and was manufacturing an excellent powder, which he supplied to both the army and navy as far as it was possible, but the constant and ever-recurring urgent demands upon his mills were greatly beyond their possible supply. By December 5, two powder mills were in running order and turning out two tons of powder per day, and contracts for two hundred tons of saltpetre, promised to relieve the pressing needs of the defences of the city from the danger of a short supply. But the explosion of one of the mills on December 28, just as the ships of the enemy were assembling at Ship Island, caused great anxiety. Contracts for powder at 83 cts. per pound were ordered and entered into; and on Jan. 13, 1862, the supply at New Orleans was reported at 116,750 pounds. On Jan. 22, 1862, the price of powder under contracts had risen to $1.14 per pound, with an advance of two-thirds of the price before its manufacture began.

In addition to this want of ordnance stores, the navy was further embarrassed in its supply of coal—the incursions of the army at some points contiguous to the coal supply was to a great extent the cause of this; so that, in the last year of the war, the mines at Richmond, in North Carolina and in Alabama, were the only sources of supply, but deficiencies of transportation increased the difficulty of obtaining coal from those mines for distant points on the seaboard.

The navy erected at Petersburg rope-walks, which proved adequate to all the demands of the navy and supplied also the army, the coal mines, the railroads and the canal companies. Cotton, manufactured with tar, was found to be a valuable substitute for hemp cordage.

Thus, the Confederate States, which, in 1861, were totally destitute of every appliance, of all machinery, of all tools and mechanics, for the manufacture of naval ordnance of any kind, while fighting a multitudinous enemy over a vast territory, and surrounded by the navy of the enemy which closed every port, was able to erect at Richmond, Atlanta, Augusta, Selma, New Orleans, Charlotte, Columbia, Petersburg, Columbus, those extensive works which, before the war closed, supplied her navy and batteries with all the ordnance they required. These various works developed into usefulness as the war progressed, notwithstanding its exacting demands upon the country for every man capable of bearing arms. Their efficiency was frequently retarded by the calls to arms which took the workmen from the shop to the field, and at all times the comparatively small number of mechanics available for work at these stations was a matter of serious embarrassment.

If the United States surprised the nations of the world by the development of its war power during that war, a careful examination of what was accomplished in the Confederate States will be found to have greatly exceeded the results in the United States when the conditions and circumstances of the two parties to the war are considered and contrasted. If, while fighting each other and each party destroying everything that could not be removed, these grand results were respectively accomplished—what limit shall be set to the capabilities of such a people united and excited by the same determination in their defence of their common country ?

COMMANDER JOHN M. BROOKE,
CONFEDERATE STATES NAVY.

CAPTAIN JAMES D. BULLOCH,

CONFEDERATE STATES NAVY AGENT IN ENGLAND.

CHAPTER IV

PRIVATEERS, OR LETTERS OF MARQUE.

A S we have seen, the surrender of Fort Sumter on the 13th of April, 1861, was the initial act of the war between the States. On the 15th the President of the United States issued a proclamation, calling out troops to the number of 75,000. President Davis, on the 17th, published a counter - proclamation, inviting applications for letters of marque and reprisal to be granted under the seal of the Confederate States, against ships and property of the United States and their citizens. [1]

Doubting the constitutional power of the executive to grant letters of marque to private armed ships, President Davis, with characteristic regard for law, determined not to commission privateers until duly authorized by Congress. That body assembled in special session on April 29, in obedience

[1] After appropriately recognizing the condition of public affairs, and inviting energetic preparation for immediate hostilities, he said:

"Now, therefore, I, Jefferson Davis, President of the Confederate States of America, do issue this, my proclamation, inviting all those who may desire, by service in private armed vessels on the high seas, to aid this government in resisting so wanton and wicked an aggression, to make application for commissions or letters of marque and reprisal, to be issued under the seal of these Confederate States; and I do further notify all persons applying for letters of marque to make a statement in writing, giving the name and suitable description of the character, tonnage, and force of the vessel, name of the place of residence of each owner concerned therein and the intended number of crew, and to sign each statement, and deliver the same to the Secretary of State or Collector of the Port of Entry of these Confederate States, to be by him transmitted to the Secretary of State, and do further notify all applicants aforesaid, before any commission or letter of marque is issued to any vessel, or the owner or the owners thereof, and the commander for the time being, they will be required to give bond to the Confederate States, with at least two responsible sureties not interested in such vessel, in the penal sum of $5,000; or if such vessel be provided with more than 150 men, then in the penal sum of $10,000, with the condition that the owners, officers, and crew who shall be employed on board such commissioned vessel, shall observe the laws of these Confederate States, and the instructions given them for the regulation of their conduct, and shall satisfy all damages done contrary to the tenor thereof by such vessel during her commission, and deliver up the same when revoked by the President of the Confederate States. And I do further specially enjoin on all persons holding offices, civil and military, under the authority of the Confederate States, that they be vigilant and zealous in the discharge of the duties incident thereto; and I do, moreover, exhort the good people of these Confederate States, as they love their country—as they prize the blessings of free government—as they feel the wrongs of the past, and these now threatened in an aggravated form by those whose enmity is more implacable because unprovoked—they exert themselves in preserving order, in promoting concord, in maintaining the authority and efficacy of the laws, and in supporting, invigorating all the measures which may be adopted for a common defence, and by which, under the blessings of Divine Providence, we may hope for a speedy, just, and honorable peace.'

to a proclamation of the President, in which he advised legislation for the employment of privateers. On the 6th of May Congress passed an act, entitled, "An act recognizing the existence of war between the United States and the Confederate States, and concerning letters of marque, prizes, and prize goods." The first section of this act was as follows :

"The Congress of the Confederate States of America do enact that the President of the Confederate States is hereby authorized to use the whole land and naval force of the Confederate States to meet the war thus commenced, and to issue to private vessels commissions or letters of marque and general reprisal, in such form as he shall think proper, under the seal of the Confederate States, against the vessels, goods, and effects of the United States, and of the citizens or inhabitants of the States and territories thereof ; provided, however, that property of the enemy (unless it be contraband of war) laden on board a neutral vessel, shall not be subject to seizure under this act ; and provided further, that vessels of the citizens or inhabitants of the United States now in the ports of the Confederate States, except such as have been since the 5th of April last, or may hereafter be, in the service of the Government of the United States, shall be allowed thirty days after the publication of this act to leave said ports and reach their destination ; and such vessels and their cargoes, excepting articles contraband of war, shall not be subject to capture under this act during said period, unless they shall have previously reached the destination for which they were bound on leaving said ports."

The act then proceeded to lay down in detail regulations as to the conditions on which letters of marque should be granted to private vessels, and the conduct and behavior of the officers and crews of such vessels, and the disposal of such prizes made by them, similar to the regulations which have been ordinarily prescribed and enforced with respect to privateers in the United States, and by the maritime powers of Europe.

The fourth and seventh sections were as follows :

"That, before any commission or letters of marque and reprisal shall be issued as aforesaid, the owner or owners of the ship or vessel for which the same shall be requested, and the commander thereof for the time being, shall give bond to the Confederate States, with at least two responsible sureties not interested in such vessel, in the penal sum of $5,000, or, if such vessel be provided with more than 150 men, then in the penal sum of $10,000, with condition that the owners, officers, and crew who shall be employed on board such commissioned vessel shall and will observe the laws of the Confederate States, and the instructions which shall be given them according to law for the regulation of their conduct, and will satisfy all damages and injuries which shall be done or committed contrary to the tenor thereof by such vessel during her commission, and to deliver up the same when revoked by the President of the Confederate States.

" That before breaking bulk of any vessel which shall be captured as aforesaid, or disposal or conversion thereof, or of any articles which shall be found on board the same, such captured vessel, goods, or effects, shall be brought into some port of the Confederate States, or of a nation or State in amity with the Confederate States, and shall be proceeded against before a competent tribunal ; and after condemnation and forfeiture thereof, shall belong to the owners, officers, and crew of the vessel capturing the same, and be distributed as before provided ; and in the case of all captured vessels, goods, and effects which shall be brought within the jurisdiction of the Confederate States, the district courts of the

Confederate States shall have exclusive original cognizance thereof, as the civil causes of admiralty and maritime jurisdiction ; and the said courts, or the courts being courts of the Confederate States into which such cases shall be removed, in which they shall be finally decided, shall and may decree restitution in whole or part, when the capture shall have been made without just cause. And, if made without probable cause, may order and decree damages and costs to the party injured, for which the owners and commanders of the vessels making such captures, and also the vessels, shall be liable."

A further act, entitled, "An act regulating the sale of prizes and the distribution thereof," was likewise passed by the Congress of the Confederate States on the 14th of May, 1861.

Meanwhile, on the 19th of April, the President of the United States issued a further proclamation, in which, after referring to the proposed issue of letters of marque, declared that he had deemed it advisable to set on foot a blockade of the ports within the States of South Carolina, Georgia, Alabama, Florida, Mississippi, Louisiana and Texas, in pursuance of the laws of the United States and the law of nations in such cases provided. By another proclamation, dated the 27th of April, the blockade was so extended as to include the Southern ports as far north as Virginia.

The blockade declared by the foregoing proclamations was actually instituted, as to the ports within the State of Virginia, on the 30th of April;[1] and was extended to the principal ports on the sea-board of the Confederate States before the end of May. The Federal cruisers soon began to make prizes of neutral ships for alleged breach of blockade, and they were condemned with very short shrift by the United States prize-courts.

On the 3rd of May, 1861, the proclamation of the blockade was published in the London newspapers; on the 10th of May copies of the proclamation of blockade, and of the counter-proclamation of President Davis, were received by Lord Russell from the British Minister at Washington, and finally the blockade was officially communicated to Lord Russell by the United States Minister on the 11th of May.

On the 6th of May, Lord Russell stated in the House of Commons, that. after consultation with the law officers, the government had come to the conclusion that the Southern Confederacy must be treated as belligerents; and, on the 14th, Her Majesty's Proclamation of Neutrality was issued, which

---

[1] The following is an official copy of the notice of blockade served on Captain Russell of the steamer *Louisiana*, of the Chesapeake Bay line of steamers, running between Baltimore and Norfolk :

" UNITED STATES FLAG-SHIP *Cumberland*,
" OFF FORTRESS MONROE,
" VIRGINIA, April 30, 1861.

" *To all whom it may concern :*

"I hereby call attention to the proclamation of his Excellency Abraham Lincoln President of the United States, under date of April 27, 1861, for an efficient blockade of the ports of Virginia and North Carolina, and warn all persons interested that I have a sufficient naval force here for the purpose of carrying out that proclamation.

" All vessels passing the capes of Virginia, coming from a distance and ignorant of the proclamation, will be warned off, and those passing Fortress Monroe will be required to anchor under the guns of the fort and subject themselves to an examination.

" G. J. PRENDERGRAST,
" Flag-Officer, Commanding Home Squadron."

acknowledged the existence of a civil war, and thereby recognized the Confederate States as belligerents. The example of Great Britain was soon followed by the chief maritime powers in the following order: France, June 10th; Netherlands, June 16th; Spain, June 17th; Brazil, August 1st. The remaining powers issued "notifications" at various dates, prohibiting the entry of privateers or prizes into their ports, and defining the conditions under which the public vessels of both parties should be permitted to enter and receive supplies, and drawing no distinction between them as belligerents.[1]

Mr. Seward could not bring himself to a dignified acquiescence in the common verdict of the great maritime powers of Europe. He indulged in repeated and petulant complaints, and urged with vehement earnestness that all the world should be subservient to his will, and should re-fashion the code of public law to suit his policy.[2] He wished to practice all the rights which a state of war confers upon a belligerent, but begged to be excused from performing the duties which attach in equal degree to that condition.

Notwithstanding the English government considered the privateers of the Confederate States as the lawfully commis-

---

[1] The Secret Service of the Confederate States in Europe, by James D. Bulloch, Naval representative of the Confederate States in Europe during the Civil War.—Vol. II., p. 294. Commander Bulloch's account of the purchasing, building, and equipment of the Confederate cruisers abroad is straightforward, sincere, and adorned by the graces of style. It is probably the ablest book from the Southern side yet written.

[2] He affirmed that the so-called government at Richmond merely represented "a discontented faction." Writing to Mr. Dayton on the 30th of May, 1861, he says : "The United States cannot for a moment allow the French government to rest under the delusive belief that they will be content to have the Confederate States recognized as a belligerent power by States with which this nation is at amity. No concert of action among foreign States so recognizing the insurgents can reconcile the United States to such a proceeding, whatever may be the consequences of resistance."—Geneva Arbitration. United States Appendix, Vol. I., p. 192, quoted by Sir A. Cockburn, p. 82; Bulloch, Vol. II., p. 294.

The views of the British government were expressed in a dispatch to Lord Lyons, her Majesty's Minister at Washington, dated June 21, 1861. Lord Russell, in the dispatch referred to, mentions that Mr. Adams had complained of the Queen's proclamation of neutrality as having been hasty and premature, and then adds : "I said (to Mr. Adams), in the first place, that our position was of necessity neutral; that we could not take part either for the North against the South, or for the South against the North. To this he willingly assented, and said that the United States expected no assistance from us to enable their government to finish the war. I rejoined that if such was the case, as I supposed, it would not have been right either towards our admirals and naval commanders, nor towards our merchants and mercantile marine, to leave them without positive and public orders ; that the exercise of belligerent rights of search and capture by a band of ad-

venturers clustered in some small island in the Greek Archipelago or in the Atlantic would subject them to the penalty of piracy; but we could not treat 5,000,000 of men, who had declared their independence, like a band of marauders or filibusters. If we had done so, we should have done more than the United States themselves. Their troops had taken prisoners many of the adherents of the Confederacy; but I could not perceive from the newspapers that in any case they had brought these prisoners to trial for high treason, or shot them as rebels."

The policy of the British government was more fully explained and justified in a letter from Lord Russell to Mr. Adams, dated May 4, 1865. He says: "What was the first act of the President of the United States ? He proclaimed on the 19th of April, 1861, the blockade of the ports of seven States of the Union. But he could lawfully interrupt the trade of neutrals to the Southern States upon one ground only, namely, that the Southern States were carrying on war against the government of the United States ; in other words, that they were belligerents. Her Majesty's government, on hearing of these events, had only two courses to pursue, namely, that of acknowledging the blockade and proclaiming the neutrality of her Majesty, or that of refusing to acknowledge the blockade, and insisting upon the rights of her Majesty's subjects to trade with the ports of the South. Her Majesty's government pursued the former course as at once the most just and the most friendly to the United States. * * * So much as to the step which you say your government can never regard ' as otherwise than precipitate,' of acknowledging the Southern States as belligerents. It was, on the contrary, your own government which, in assuming the belligerent right of blockade, recognized the Southern States as belligerents. Had they not been belligerents, the armed ships of the United States would have had no right to stop a single British ship upon the high seas."—United States Documents, Vol. I., pp. 214, 215, quoted by Sir A. Cockburn, pp. 80, 82, 83.

sioned vessels of a belligerent nation, and did not take Mr. Lincoln's view of the "artificial crisis" in America, yet it did not suffer the privateers of the Confederacy to refit and sell their prizes in the English ports.

On the 1st June, 1861, Her Britannic Majesty's government issued orders by which the armed ships of both belligerents, whether public ships-of-war or privateers, were interdicted from carrying prizes made by them into the ports, harbors, roadsteads, or waters of the United Kingdom, or of any of Her Majesty's colonies or possessions abroad.

The government of the Confederate States remonstrated warmly against these orders, as practically unequal in their operation, and unduly disadvantageous to the belligerent whose ports were blockaded. The Secretary of State of the United States expressed his satisfaction with them, as likely to "prove a death-blow to Southern privateering." These orders were strictly enforced throughout the whole period of the war, and no armed vessel was suffered to bring prizes into any British port. The foreign powers admitted the legality of the blockade, and as a necessary and legitimate consequence they acknowledged the Confederate States as belligerents, and threw open their ports to both parties on the same conditions and under precisely similar restrictions. "What Mr. Seward wanted," truthfully says Commander Bulloch, "was that Europe should permit the United States to remain in the enjoyment of every privilege guaranteed by treaties of peace, free and unrestricted access to the ports, the right to buy arms and transport them unmolested across the sea, to engage men and forward them to the battle-fields in Virginia without question, and, at the same time, that the whole world should tolerate a total suppression of trade with eleven great provinces, and suffer the United States to seize ships on the high seas, and hale them before prize-courts, unless they were protected by the certificate of an American Consul."[1]

The European Powers having acknowledged the existence of a *de facto* government at Montgomery, and afterward at

---

[1] The Supreme Court of the United States, through Justice Grier, gave the following judgment of a prize case brought before it: "To legitimatize the capture of a neutral vessel or property on the high seas, a war must exist *de facto*, and the neutral must have a knowledge or notice of the intention of one of the parties belligerent to use this mode of coercion against a port, city, or territory, in possession of the other. * * * The proclamation of the blockade is itself official and conclusive evidence to the court that a state of war existed which demanded and authorized a recourse to such a measure under the circumstances peculiar to the case. The correspondence of Lord Lyons with the Secretary of State admits the fact and concludes the question."

The European powers, acting upon this decision, acknowledged the Confederate States as belligerents. They saw eighteen or more great States, acknowledging a central government at Washington, engaged in war with eleven other great States, adhering to a common authority at Richmond. This was the actual condition of affairs. All the special pleading of the politicians at Washington, all the *finesse* of diplomatic reasoning, could not alter the facts. Foreign powers perceived the actual state of affairs, and the proclamations of neutrality, and the regulations specifying the conditions upon which their ports might be used, were framed in accordance with the fact that there was a state of war between two separate powers, and although one could glory in the full-fledged title of "a government *de jure*," and the other was shackled with the more restrictive appellation of "a government *de facto*," yet in regard to belligerent rights and duties they were placed on precisely the same footing by the common consent and common action of the whole civilized world.—*Bulloch*, Vol. I., p. 303.

Richmond, by eleven great States, with a population of more than six millions of people, that acknowledgment carried with it the concession of all belligerent rights. Privateering being one of these rights, the right of the Confederate government to issue letters marque to private vessels to enable them to capture those of the enemy, was as well established by the code of international law as any other vested in a belligerent for its protection and defence.' All governments have resorted to privateering whenever they found it available against a maritime foe. The United States always regarded the right as unquestionable, and never surrendered it, though Great Britain, France, Austria, Prussia, Russia, Sardinia, and Turkey agreed among themselves to do so in 1856 by the treaty of Paris. [1]

When the circular invitation of the Powers was sent to the United States government in 1856, Secretary of State Wm. L. Marcy, in his letter, dated July 28th, to the foreign Plenipotentiaries, proposed to amend the rules by the addition of a new article, excepting private property at sea from capture. No action was taken on the proposal, and the negotiations were suspended until Mr. Lincoln's accession to office. [2]

[1] The following is the language of the terms of the treaty :

"1. Privateering is and remains abolished.

2. The neutral flag covers enemy's goods with the exception of contraband of war.

3. Neutral goods, with the exception of contraband of war, are not liable to capture under the enemy's flag.

4. Blockades in order to be binding must be effective—that is to say, maintained by a force sufficient really to prevent access to the coast of the enemy.

The governments of the undersigned Plenipotentiaries engage to bring the present declaration to the knowledge of the States which have not taken part in the Congress of Paris, and to invite them to accede to it.

Convinced that the maxims which they now proclaim cannot but be received with gratitude by the whole world, the undersigned Plenipotentiaries doubt not that the efforts of their governments to obtain the general adoption thereof will be crowned with full success.

The present declaration is not and shall not be binding except between those powers who have acceded or shall accede to it.

Done at Paris, the 16th of April, 1856."

[2] In his letter to the foreign powers Mr. Marcy strongly defended privateering. He said, among other things, that:

" In regard to the right to employ privateers, which is declared to be abolished by the first principle put forth in the 'Declaration,' there was, if possible, less uncertainty. The right to resort to privateers is as clear as the right to use public armed ships, and as incontestable as any other right appertaining to belligerents. The policy of that law has been occasionally questioned—not, however, by the best authorities ; but the law itself has been universally admitted, and most nations have not hesitated to avail themselves of it ; it is as well sustained by practice and public opinion as any other to be found in the maritime code.

"There is scarcely any rule of international law which particular nations in their treaties have not occasionally suspended or modified in regard to its application to themselves. Two treaties only can be found in which the contracting parties have agreed to abstain from the employment of privateers in case of war between them. The first was a treaty between the King of Sweden and the States General of the United Provinces, in 1675. Shortly after it was concluded, the parties were involved in war, and the stipulation concerning privateers was entirely disregarded by both. The second was the treaty of 1785, between the United States and the King of Prussia. When this treaty was renewed in 1799, the clause stipulating not to resort to privateering was omitted. For the last half-century there has been no arrangement, by treaty or otherwise, to abolish the right until the recent proceedings of the Plenipotentiaries at Paris. * * *

" In a work of much repute, published in France almost simultaneously with the proceedings of the Congress at Paris, it is declared that ' The issuing of letters of marque, therefore, is a constantly customary belligerent act. Privateers are bona fide war vessels, manned by volunteers, to whom, by way of reward, the Sovereign resigns such prizes as they make, in the same manner as he sometimes assigns to the land forces a portion of the war contributions levied on the conquered enemy." — Pistoye et Duverdy, des Prises Maritimes. * * *

" No nation which has a due sense of self-respect will allow any other, belligerent or neutral, to determine the character of the force which it may deem proper to use in prosecuting hostilities; nor will it act wisely if it voluntarily surrenders the right to resort to any means, sanctioned by international law, which under any circumstances may be advantageously used for defence or aggression. * * * The importance of privateers to the community of nations, excepting only those of great naval strength, is not only vindicated by history, but sustained by high authority. The following passage in the

About a week after President Davis' proclamation was issued, announcing his purpose of issuing letters of marque, Mr. Seward instructed the Minister of the United States at London to re-open negotiations, and offered to accede unconditionally to the Paris Declaration. This proposal seemed to point too strongly to an effort to treat President Davis, Lee and Stonewall Jackson as common brawlers or "rebels," and the "piratical rovers" as unworthy of shelter or assistance, and fit only to be pursued and destroyed as a common enemy and a common pest, which the British government refused.[1] As the United States were thus debarred from any present advantage to be derived from the adoption of the rule, the whole question was dropped, and both belligerents were kept under the same restrictions.[2]

The right, therefore, of President Davis to issue " letters of marque " was not questioned by any of the European

treatise on maritime prizes, to which I have before referred, deserves particular attention :

"Privateers are especially useful to those powers whose navy is inferior to that of their enemies. Belligerents, with powerful and extensive naval armaments, may cruise upon the seas with their national navies; but should those States, whose naval forces are of less power and extent, be left to their own resources, they could not hold out in a maritime war; whilst by the equipment of privateers they may succeed in inflicting upon the enemy an injury equivalent to that which they themselves sustain. Hence, governments have frequently been known, by every possible appliance, to favor privateering armaments. It has even occurred that sovereigns, not merely satisfied with issuing letters of marque, have also taken, as it were, an interest in the armament. Thus did Louis XIV. frequently lend out his ships, and sometimes reserve for himself a share in the prizes." * * *

"History throws much light upon this subject. France, at an early period, was without a navy, and in her wars with Great Britain and Spain, both then naval powers, she resorted with signal good effect to privateering, not only for protection, but successful aggression. She obtained many privateers from Holland, and by this force gained decided advantages on the ocean over her enemy. Whilst in that condition, France could hardly have been expected to originate or concur in a proposition to abolish privateering. The condition of many of the smaller States of the world is now, in relation to naval powers, not much unlike that of France in the middle of the sixteenth century. At a later period during the reign of Louis XIV., several expeditions were fitted out by him, composed wholly of privateers, which were most effectually employed in prosecuting hostilities with naval powers. * * *

"The ocean is the common property of all nations, and instead of yielding to a measure which will be likely to secure to a few—possibly to one—an ascendancy over it each should pertinaciously retain all means it possesses to defend the common heritage."

[1] Sir Admiral Cockburn said : "Men refused to see in the leaders of the South the 'rebels' and the 'pirates' held up by the United States to public reprobation."

" Whatever the cause in which they are exhibited, devotion and courage will ever find respect, and they did so in this instance. Men could not see in the united people of these vast provinces, thus risking all in the cause of nationality and independence, the common case of rebels disturbing peace and order on account of imaginary grievances, or actuated by the desire to overthrow a government in order to rise upon its ruins. They gave credit to the statesmen and warriors of the South—their cause may be right or wrong—for the higher motives which ennoble political action, and all the opprobrious terms which might be heaped upon the cause in which he fell could not persuade the world that the earth beneath which Stonewall Jackson rests does not cover the remains of a patriot and a hero."—*Geneva Arbitrat'n,* p. 72, 114.

[2] The President of the United States was himself at one time an avowed secessionist or revolutionist. In a speech delivered in the House of Representatives on the 12th of January, 1848, Mr. Lincoln, then an honorable member from Illinois, used this language:

"Any people anywhere being inclined and having the power have a right to rise up and shake off the existing government and form a new one that suits them better. This is a most valuable, sacred right—a right which, we believe, is to liberate the world. Nor is this right confined to cases in which the whole people of an existing government may choose to exercise it. Any portion of such people that can may revolutionize and make their own of so much of the territory as they inhabit. More than this: a majority of any portion of such people may revolutionize, putting down a minority intermingled with or near about them, who may oppose their movements. It is a quality of revolutions not to go by old lines or old laws, but to break up both and make new ones."—*Appendix, Congressional Globe,* 1st Session, 30th Congress, p. 94. See also on this subject, opinion of Alexander Hamilton, Bancroft's *History of the United States,* pp. 213 and 232; also to language of John Adams in same work. Also *Rawle on the Constitution,* p. 292. Appendix to the Virginia edition of *Blackstone's Commentaries* by St. George Tucker in 1802, pp. 73, 74; Dwight's *History of Connecticut,* pp. 435, 436, 437; 8th *Mass. Reports,* 546; Scharf's *History of Maryland,* Vol. III., pp. 338 to 346, etc.

powers, and he was justified in his course by the acts of the *de facto* government of the revolted colonies in 1776, and by the more formally recognized government at Washington, in 1812–15, and 1861–5.

In July, 1861, the U. S. House of Representatives passed a resolution authorizing the Secretary of the Treasury to employ a sufficient force to protect the commerce of the United States from the Confederate privateers. The object of this act was to send out privateers to capture those of the Confederacy that were annoying U. S. commerce.

In October following, Secretary Welles wrote the following letter in relation to granting letters of marque:

"NAVY DEPARTMENT, WASHINGTON, Oct. 1, 1861.

"In relation to the communication of R. B. Forbes, Esq.—a copy of which was sent by you to this department on the 16th ultimo, inquiring whether letters of marque cannot be furnished for the propeller *Pembroke*, which is about to be dispatched to China—I have the honor to state that it appears to me that there are objections to, and no authority for, granting letters of marque in the present contest. I am not aware that Congress, which has the exclusive power of granting letters of marque and reprisal, has authorized such letters to be issued against the insurgents; and were there such authorization, I am not prepared to advise its exercise, because it would, in my view, be a recognition of the assumption of the insurgents that they are a distinct and independent nationality. Under the act of August 5, 1861, 'supplementary to an act entitled an act to protect the commerce of the United States and to punish the crime of piracy,' the President is authorized to instruct the commanders of 'armed vessels sailing under the authority of any letters of marque and reprisal granted by the Congress of the United States, or the commanders of any other suitable vessels, to subdue, seize, take, and, if on the high seas, to send into any port of the United States any vessel or boat, built, purchased, fitted out or held,' etc. This allusion to letters of marque does not authorize such letters to be issued, nor do I find any other act containing such authorization. But the same act, in the second section, as above quoted, gives the President power to authorize the 'commanders of any suitable vessels to subdue, seize,' etc. Under this clause, letters permissive, under proper restrictions and guards against abuse, might be granted to the propeller *Pembroke*, so as to meet the views expressed by Mr. Forbes. This would seem to be lawful and perhaps not liable to the objections of granting letters of marque against our own citizens, and that, too, without law or authority from the only constituted power that can grant it. I have the honor to transmit herewith a copy of a letter from Messrs. J. M. Forbes & Co., and others, addressed to this department, on the same subject."   GIDEON WELLES."

With the view of destroying Confederate privateers, the United States Congress, in March, 1863, passed a bill authorizing the President to issue letters of marque.

"By this measure," the New York *Herald*, of March, 8th, 1863, said, "Mr. Lincoln will have power to cause the ocean to swarm with our 'militia of the seas.' * * * The American republic is not guided by the policy of European powers. It is not bound by the declaration of the Congress of Paris, for the simple reason that it did not agree to it. At the time, Mr. Marcy, on the part of the United States, offered to agree to the proposition to abolish privateering if the European Powers would agree to abolish all captures on the sea of private property, except contraband of war—thus extending to the ocean the rule that prevails in modern times exempting private property from capture on the land. England and France objected, particularly England, by whose influence the offer was rejected. Again, since our civil war began, Mr. Seward proposed to England and France to adopt the proposition in the declaration of Paris, to abolish privateering, provided they would agree to treat it as piracy all over the world, like the African slave trade. But, though no nation could be aggrieved by the establishment of this rule, and although all the minor powers of Europe had agreed to the proposition of the Paris Conference—even those in the interior, who had not a single ship on the sea—yet the Western Powers refused the overture of the American government, on the ground that it was then too late."

The *Royal Gazette* of England, on July 21, 1863, commenting upon the act passed by the U. S. Congress, authorizing the issuing of letters of marque, said:

" The U. S. Congress, in its last session, authorized the President, if he deemed it proper, to issue letters of marque. His having not done so, in view of the destruction of property by the *Alabama* and the *Florida*, is severely censured by a writer in one of the late New York papers. This writer suggests that a reward of $500,000 be given to any letter of marque that should capture and bring into any of the ports of the United States any Confederate privateer, or $250,000 for the sinking or otherwise destroying of such a privateer. The writer concludes by observing that the 'almighty dollar might then be the means of bringing privateering to an end.'

"We can hardly understand why such a measure should be adopted. When patriotism is not sufficient to induce men to serve their country, is it probable that the dollar will? Will the dollar inspire courage to a man when the sight of his lowered flag fails to do so ? And, besides, are there not enough U. S. ships-of-war skimming the seas after the *Alabama* and the *Florida*, the only two known Confederate privateers, and are these Federal vessels not commanded by admirals and officers that the Union boasts of ? The issuing by the Washington government of letters of marque would be, indeed, an acknowledgment of the inefficiency of their navy compared to the two or three comparatively small vessels-of-war owned by the Confederacy, and of the incapacity of the men at the head of their fleet."

If the precedents established by the United States were just and lawful acts of war, then similar acts done by authority of the *de facto* government of the Confederate States in 1861-5 were not " criminal" and " nefarious."

The license or " letters of marque," issued by a belligerent government to a private armed ship, to capture the ships and goods of the enemy at sea, had its origin in the Middle Ages, when princes issued to their subjects licenses to cross the march or frontier of a neighboring power in order to make reprisals for an injury. It was extended to the high seas in the fourteenth century. But the practice was not general till the end of the sixteenth century. The first instance in which the aid of privateers was deemed important in war was in the struggle between Spain and her revolted provinces of the Netherlands. The Prince of Orange, the leader of the revolt, issued letters of marque against Spain in 1570, and his privateers became terrible. Ever since that time the use of

privateers has been legalized in Europe, unless where parties
agree by treaty to abolish it as against each other. The
French were the first, on a large scale, to send out those
scourges of the sea. The British imitated their example, and
their illustrious naval commander, Drake, was a privateersman. At the close of the French war with England, by the
peace of Amiens, the latter nation had 30,000 French sailors
in prison. In our Revolutionary war with England, the
American privateer played a very important part.

On May 20, 1775, articles of confederation and perpetual
union were entered into by the delegates of the several colonies of New Hampshire, Massachusetts, etc. A resolution was
at the same time passed, that after the expiration of six
months (from July 20, 1775) all the ports of the said colonies
were declared to be thenceforth open to the ships of every State
in Europe that would admit and protect the commerce of the
colonies. [1]

Although by the above articles the colonists usurped the
rights of sovereignty with regard to peace and war, the entering into alliances, the appointment of civil and military
officers, etc., still their connection with Great Britain was
maintained, and no *de facto* independent government was
established.

On June 12, 1775, General Gage issued a proclamation, by
which a pardon was offered in the King's name to all those
who should forthwith lay down their arms, threatening the
treatment of *rebels* and traitors to all those who did not accept
the proffered pardon. This proclamation was looked upon as
the preliminary to immediate action, and on the 17th June
hostilities commenced between the colonists and royal troops
in the neighborhood of Charlestown. In July, 1775, the confederacy assumed the appellation of the *Thirteen United Colonies*,
and General Washington was appointed to the command of
the army of the confederation. Hostilities were carried, not
only in the colonies, but Canada was also invaded by the
colonial forces.

The first act of the Congress for the formation of a navy
was promulgated on October 13, 1775, when two vessels were
ordered to be armed, and on the 30th of the same month two
more armed vessels were ordered to be fitted for sea. On
November 25, 1775, resolutions were passed, directing seizures
and capture under commissions obtained from the Congress,
together with the condemnation of British vessels *employed
in a hostile manner* against the colonies; the mode of trial
and of condemnation was pointed out, and the shares of the
prizes were apportioned. On November 28, 1775, Congress
adopted rules for the regulation of the navy of the *United
Colonies*. On the 13th December, a report was sanctioned for

---

[1] The trade of the British colonists in America at this period was carried on solely by British
and colonial shipping.

fitting out a naval armament, to consist in the whole of thirteen ships. On the 22d December, officers were appointed to command the armed vessels. On January 6, 1776, a regulation was adopted relative to the division of prizes and prize-money taken by armed vessels. On March 23, 1786, resolutions were adopted authorizing the fitting out of *private armed vessels* to cruise against the enemies of the *United Colonies.* On April 2d, 1776, the form of a commission for private armed vessels was agreed upon, and on the 3d April instructions to the commanders of private armed vessels were considered and adopted. *They authorized the capture of all ships and other vessels belonging to the inhabitants of Great Britain* on the high seas, or between high-water and low-water marks, except vessels bringing persons who intended to reside and settle in the United Colonies.

The whole of these laws were promulgated previously to the final Declaration of Independence issued on July 4, 1776. In the meantime, the different powers of Europe, notwithstanding the declarations of neutrality in the conflict between Great Britain and her colonies, more particularly France, Spain, and Holland, almost openly expressed their sympathy with the cause of the colonists, and aided them with arms and money, and allowed the fitting out of ships, the repairs and armaments, of privateers in their ports, even previous to the receipt of the Declaration of Independence of the colonies, passed on July 4, 1776 ; the letter from the American Committee of Secret Correspondence to Mr. Silas Deane, their agent in Paris, inclosing the *Declaration of Independency,* with instructions to make it known to the powers of Europe, not being received until November 7, 1776.

The exploits of Paul Jones by land and sea, making raids upon the British coasts, and sometimes capturing English ships-of-war, are more like romance than reality. The deeds of Captain Reed, of the *General Armstrong,* are well known. The letters of marque issued by the Continental Congress were held to be valid two years before the new government was recognized by any foreign power; and during the first year the American privateers captured 530 British vessels and their cargoes, valued at $5,000,000. During the Revolutionary war this country had 1,500 privateers on the ocean, having 15,000 guns.

In 1781, according to the Salem (Massachusetts) *Gazette,* privateering was the principal business of the town. In Mr. Niles' volume, containing "principles and acts of the Revolution," will be found, at p. 376, a "list of privateers fitted out and chiefly owned in Salem and Beverly, from March 1 to November 1, 1781," embracing 26 ships, with 476 guns and 2,645 men ; 16 brigs, with 206 guns and 870 men ; 8 schooners, with 50 guns and 235 men ; 2 sloops, with 14 guns and 70 men ; and 7 shallops, with 120 men.

Massachusetts has taken the lead in several operations in this country. She and some of the other New England States took the leading part in the slave trade; she also took the lead in the early part of this century in secession, or nullification. [1] Before the Declaration of Independence, and of course long before the formation of the present Constitution, as early, indeed, as the 10th of November, 1775, the State of Massachusetts passed a law to authorize the fitting-out of privateers and to establish a court for the trial and condemnation of prizes. [2] That law preceded by fifteen days the action of the old Continental Congress upon the same subject; for it was on the 25th of November, 1775, that the Congress passed a law authorizing privateering. Massachusetts was two weeks ahead of Congress, and she passed a law to institute and encourage privateering. Massachusetts did not stand alone in this act, her lead was followed by other States; by Pennsylvania, Maryland and other commonwealths. The Continental Congress encouraged the practice.

The records of the Council of Maryland show that up to April 1, 1777, licenses to privateers were issued by the Council of Safety, and that these vessels were so active that their prizes captured and sent into the Chesapeake realized over $1,000,000. From April 1, 1777, to March 14, 1783, a period of six years, the privateers which sailed out of the Chesapeake, furnished with letters of marque and reprisal, numbered 248, carrying in all 1,810 guns and 640 swivels. We find in the list of owners of these vessels and their commanders some of the very best people in the State, and the ancestors of a number of those who were distinguished on the Union side during the late war between the States. We need only refer to the names of John Rodgers, David Porter, Alexander Murray, Joshua Barney, Robert Morris (the great financier of Philadelphia, the friend of Washington and Franklin), Robert Purviance, Alexander McKim, James Calhoun, the first Mayor of Baltimore, and William Patterson, the father of Madame Bonaparte.

In 1793, when the war broke out between France and Great Britain, Baltimore sent to sea some forty or fifty privateers

---

[1] On the 1st of August, 1812, Governor Strong, of Massachusetts, addressed a letter to the three judges of Massachusetts, in which, amongst other things, he propounded to the judges this question : " Whether it was for the President of the United States, or for the States themselves, respectively, to determine the Constitutional exigency upon which the militia of the States were liable to be ordered out into the service of the Federal government?" The reply of the judges was, " That that right was vested solely in the commanders-in-chief of the militia of the several States." This question, it is true, was never formally adjudicated by the judges, but this was their answer to the question; and it was as much as to say (so far as the Governor, and the judges at least could say so) that if the President enforced, or attempted to enforce, this right that was claimed for him, the State of Massachusetts would resist it: and she did resist it, for, in point of fact, she never furnished her quota, or even a solitary militiaman, we believe, under the requisition which was made upon her by the President. What was this but secession, or revolution, or practical nullification in the most ultra shape ? We all know how persistently the conscription and impressment scheme of President Monroe, for raising an army in 1815, was resisted and opposed by five of the New England States; how it first led to a legislative protest and resolutions on the part of Connecticut, strongly tinctured with secession and nullification; and how it afterwards led to that celebrated conclave called the Hartford Convention, which met on the 15th of December, 1815, and whose members were nothing more or less than a set of nullifiers or secessionists under the cloak of federalism.

[2] Hildreth's *History of the United States*, Vol. III., p. 101.

under the French flag to cruise against British commerce. A great number of these vessels were afloat within three months, not only equipped, armed and fitted out in port, but they were owned, officered and manned by citizens of Baltimore. These vessels were in the French and Spanish service even after the British cruisers blockaded every French and Spanish port from Antwerp to Genoa, and they made captures while the war continued. The records of the Supreme Court of the United States abound with admiralty appeals in cases of this kind during the French war, the British owners trying to recover their vessels captured by American privateers sailing under the French flag.

In the war of 1812 the number of British ships captured by American privateers was immense. In less than five months after the declaration of war Baltimore sent to sea forty-two armed vessels, carrying 330 guns, and manned by 3,000 men. The *Rossie*, in forty-five days, took prizes valued at $1,289,000. The next cruise of this vessel, from July to November, yielded $1,500,000. The *Rolla* in a brief cruise took seven vessels, 150 men and $2,500,000. The *Amelia*, in eighty-five days, took $1,000,000. The *Harpy*, in twenty days, took $500,000. The damage done by these vessels to British commerce is hard to exaggerate. In three years the American privateers captured over 2,000 vessels, of which nearly one-third were taken by the Baltimore letters of marque.

The whole number of privateers and private-armed ships that were commissioned as cruising vessels, and all others actively engaged in commerce during our war with Great Britain in the years 1812, 1813, and 1814, were 250 sail. They belonged to the different ports in the United States as follows: From Baltimore, 58 ; from New York, 55; from Salem, 40; from Boston, 32; from Philadelphia, 14 ; from Portsmouth, N. H., 11 ; from Charleston, 10 ; from Marblehead, 4 ; from Bristol, R. I., 4; from Portland, 3; from Newburyport, 2; from Norfolk, 2; from Newbern, N. C., 2; from New Orleans, 2; from New London, 1 ; from Newport, R. I., 1 ; from Providence, R. I., 1; from Barnstable, Mass., 1; from Fair Haven, Mass., 1; from Gloucester, Mass., 1 ; from Washington City, 1 ; from Wilmington, N. C., 1; from other places belonging to Eastern ports, 3. Total, 250.

When the South American war of independence occurred, the United States furnished a great many privateers to nearly all the new States. The commodore of the Columbian navy was a Baltimorean, and the same city fitted out privateersmen for Venezuela, Chili, Buenos Ayres, Peru, and several other States, which preyed both upon Spanish and Portuguese commerce. The Portuguese Minister, in 1816, complained to President Monroe that twenty-six of these vessels had been fitted out and armed in Baltimore alone, and in 1819 they were reported to have captured fifty Portuguese vessels.

The British, in the Revolutionary war, spoke of the Chesapeake Bay as "a nest of pirates," and the Spanish Minister at Washington in 1817, Don Luis de Onis, wrote to Mr. Monroe that "it is notorious that * * * whole squadrons of pirates have been fitted out" from Baltimore and New Orleans. He complained that the privateer *Swift*, which, sailing under the flag of Buenos Ayres, had just captured the Spanish polacca *Pastora*, "is now in Baltimore River, and her captain, James Barnes, who has so scandalously violated the law of nations, the neutrality of this government and the existing treaty, has had the effrontery to make a regular entry of his vessel at the Custom House of Baltimore, declaring his cargo to consist of bales and packages, containing silks, laces, and other valuable articles—all, as you may suppose, plundered from the Spaniards."[1]

In 1861, when the Southern Confederacy recognized privateering as a legitimate instrument of warfare, the North called it piracy, as the British did in the war of 1776 and 1812. But President Davis, having the example of his revolutionary ancestors before him for fitting up and sending forth armed vessels to prey upon the commerce of the enemies of his country, soon availed himself of the opportunity. Simultaneous with the issuing of the proclamation of Mr. Lincoln, blockading the Southern ports, the Collectors of the various ports were directed by the U. S. Secretary of the Treasury to refuse clearances to any vessels bound for ports in the States which had seceded or which might afterwards secede. Accordingly, the lines of steamers, from New York and Baltimore to Charleston and Savannah and New Orleans, discontinued their trips, and those steamers which remained in New York were immediately chartered by the Federal government to carry troops. The *Nashville*, being at Charleston, was seized by the authorities there; the *Star of the West*, at Indianola, with provisions on board for the troops in Texas, was also seized by the armed steamer *Matagorde*, at New Orleans. The *Yorktown* and *Jamestown* steamers were seized by Governor Letcher, at Richmond. Besides these steamships, a half-dozen revenue cutters and a number of schooners were seized in the South and converted into war-vessels. These seizures created considerable commotion in mercantile circles North, where the most of them were owned. In the meanwhile, the authorities at the North seized all the vessels and other property, belonging to the citizens of the South, in their respective ports.

In retaliation for the seizure of Southern property by the United States, the citizens of Mobile seized the brig *Belle of the Bay*, lying in that port, loaded with rice from Boston. Another party seized the schooners *Daniel Townsend*, the *Stag*

---

[1] This reads like some of the letters of U. S. Minister Adams to Lord Russell in regard to the cruises of the *Alabama* and other Confederate men-of-war.

and *Anna Smith*, loaded with assorted cargoes. The State Artillery Continentals chartered the steamer *Gunnison*, and captured the *R. L. Gamble*, and anchored her under the guns of Fort Morgan; but she was afterwards released. The Montgomery (Alabama) *Mail* of the 29th of May, said : "We learn that there are now quite a number of privateers in the service of the Confederate government cruising off the Gulf and Atlantic coast, all well armed and manned—dispatches having been received in the city showing that hundreds of others are fitting out at various points for the same purpose."[1]

Shortly after the secession of South Carolina, the State appropriated $150,000 to establish a sea-coast police under the direction of Governor F. W. Pickens, with authority to purchase three screw-propellers. The Governor established a State navy similar to that of the United States. He enlisted thirty-two men for each of his boats, with a captain and first lieutenant, besides ordinary crews, firemen and engineers. He intended to station one of his boats in Charleston, another at Beaufort, and the third at Georgetown. He found it exceedingly difficult to procure boats suitable for the service and had to content himself with fitting out small schooners. They kept up communication between the points named, and gave protection, as far as they were able, from invasion by lawless bands in small crafts and skippers that infested the coast.

On the 13th of March, South Carolina put afloat her first vessel-of-war since the Revolution in 1776; ·Gov. Pickens purchased her at Richmond, Va., and altered her for service; armed with twenty-four pounders she was regularly equipped. The Governor directed her to be named *Lady Davis*, in compliment to the lady of the first President of the Confederate States. Her officers were Lieut. Thomas B. Huger, commanding, with Lieuts. William G. Dozier and John Grimball.

The *Lady Davis* made several captures of Federal vessels off Charleston, and, on May 1, she fired on a schooner that escaped from the port, belonging to Freetown, Mass., and wounded one of the crew.[2]

---

[1] A correspondent of the New York *Herald*, writing from Montgomery on May 7, 1861, says:

"But it may be asked, who will take these letters of marque? Where is the government of Montgomery to find ships? The answer is to be found *in the fact that already numerous applications have been received from the ship-owners of New England, from the whalers of New Bedford, and from others in the Northern States for these very letters of marque*, accompanied by the highest securities and guarantees! This statement I make on the very highest authority. I leave it to you to deal with the facts."

[2] The following is a copy of clearance of vessels from the port of Charleston, S. C., with the alterations in the seals, etc.:

DISTRICT OF THE PORT OF CHARLESTON, }
STATE OF SOUTH CAROLINA. }

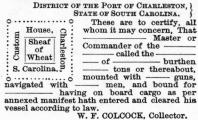

These are to certify, all whom it may concern, That ———— Master or Commander of the ———— called the ———— of ———— burthen ———— tons or thereabout, mounted with ———— guns, navigated with ———— men, and bound for ———— having on board cargo as per annexed manifest hath entered and cleared his vessel according to law.

W. F. COLCOCK, Collector.

The privateer *Savannah* was the first captured, and the first that received a commission from the Confederate States— her letters of marque being indorsed No. 1, and was as follows:

JEFFERSON DAVIS,

PRESIDENT OF THE CONFEDERATE STATES OF AMERICA.

To all who shall see these presents, greeting :—Know ye, that by virtue of the power vested in me by law, I have commissioned, and do hereby commission, have authorized, and do hereby authorize, the schooner or vessel called the *Savannah* (more particularly described in the schedule hereunto annexed), whereof T. Harrison Baker is commander, to act as a private armed vessel in the service of the Confederate States, on the high seas against the United States of America, their ships, vessels, goods and effects, and those of her citizens, during the pendency of the war now existing between the said Confederate States and the said United States.

This commission to continue in force until revoked by the President of the Confederate States for the time being. Schedule of description of the vessel—name, schooner *Savannah ;* tonnage, 53 $\frac{41}{95}$ tons ; armament, one large pivot gun and small arms; number of crew, thirty.

Given under my hand and the seal of the Confederate States, at Montgomery, this 18th day of May, A.D. 1861.

JEFFERSON DAVIS.

By the President—R. TOOMBS, Secretary of State.

The *Savannah* was a fast-sailing schooner of about fifty-four tons, having been formerly pilot boat No. 7 in Charleston harbor. She carried one eighteen-pound gun amidships upon a swivel, and was provided with a crew of thirty-two men, including officers, as well as a necessary supply of arms, ammunition, etc. In May she was fitted out in Charleston as a privateer; on Sunday, June 3, she went to sea under the command of Capt. Thomas Harrison Baker. The instructions to the commanders of all letters of marque or privateers were as follows :

1. The tenor of your commission, under the Act of Congress, entitled, "An act recognizing the existence of war between the United States and the Confederate States, and concerning letters of marque, prizes and prize goods," a copy of which is hereto annexed, will be kept constantly in your view. The high seas referred to in your commission you will understand generally to refer to the low-water mark; but with the exception of the space within one league, or three miles, from the shore of countries at peace with the United States and the Confederate States. You nevertheless execute your commission within the distance of the shore of the nation at war with the United States, and even on the waters within the jurisdiction of such nation, if permitted to do so.

2. You are to pay the strictest regard to the rights of the neutral vessels; you are to give them as little molestation or interruption as will consist with the right of ascertaining their neutral character, and of detaining and bringing them in for regular adjudication in the proper cases.

You are particularly to avoid even the appearance of using force or seduction, with a view to deprive such vessels of the crews or the passengers, other than persons in the military service of the enemy.

3. Towards enemy's vessels and their crews you are to proceed, in exercising the rights of war, with all the justice and humanity which characterize this government and its citizens.

4. The master, and one or more of the principal persons, belonging to the captured vessels, are to be sent, as soon after the capture as may be,

to the judge or judges of the proper courts in the Confederate States, to be examined upon oath, touching the interest or property of the captured vessel and her lading; and, at the same time, are to be delivered to the judge or judges all papers, charter parties, bills of lading, letters and other documents and writings found on board, and the said papers to be proved by the affidavit of the commander of the captured vessel, or some other person present at the capture, to be produced as received, without fraud, addition, subtraction or embezzlement.

5. Property, even of the enemy, is exempt from seizure on neutral vessels, unless it be contraband of war.

If goods contraband of war are found on any neutral vessel, and the commander thereof shall offer to deliver them up, the offer shall be accepted and the vessel left at liberty to pursue its voyage, unless the quantity of contraband goods shall be greater than can be conveniently received on board your vessel, in which case the neutral vessel may be carried into port for the delivery of the contraband goods.

The following articles are declared by this government contraband of war, as well as all others that are so declared by the laws of nations, viz.:

All arms and implements serving for the purpose of war by land or sea, such as cannons, mortars, guns, muskets, rifles, pistols, petards, bombs, grenades, balls, shot, shell, pikes, swords, bayonets, javelins, lances, horse furniture, bolsters, belts, and generally all other implements of war.

Also, timber for ship-building, pitch, tar, rosin, copper in sheets, sails, hemp, cordage, and generally whatever may serve directly to the equipment of vessels, wrought iron and planks only excepted.

Neutral vessels, conveying enemy's dispatches or military persons in the service of the enemy, forfeit their neutral character, and are liable to capture and condemnation. But this rule does not apply to neutral vessels bearing dispatches from the public ministers or ambassadors of the enemy residing in neutral countries.

By the command of the President of the Confederate States,

ROBERT TOOMBS, Secretary of State.

FORM OF BOND.

Know all men by these presents : That we (Note 1.) ——, are bound to the Confederate States of America, in the full sum of (Note 2.) —— thousand dollars, to the payment whereof, well and truly to be made, we bind ourselves, our heirs, executors and administrators, jointly and severally, by these presents.

The condition of this obligation is such, that whereas, application has been made to the said Confederate States of America, for the grant of a commission of letter of marque and general reprisals, authorizing to —— (Note 3.) or vessel called the ——, to act as a private armed vessel in the service of the Confederate States on the high seas, against the United States of America, its ships and vessels, and those of its citizens, during the pendency of the war now existing between the said Confederate States and the said United States.

Now, if the owners, officers and crews, who shall be employed on board of said vessel when commissioned, shall observe the laws of the Confederate States and the instructions which shall be given them according to law for the regulation of their conduct, and shall satisfy all damages and injuries which shall be done or committed contrary to the tenor thereof by such vessel during her commission, and shall deliver up said commission when revoked by the President of the Confederate States, then this obligation shall be void, but otherwise shall remain in full force and effect.

Signed, sealed and delivered in the presence of ——, on this —— day of ——

A. B. }
C. D. } witnesses.

NOTE 1.—This blank must be filled with the name of the commander for the time being, and the owners and at least two responsible sureties interested in the vessel,

NOTE 2.—This blank must be filled with a " five " if the vessel be provided with only one hundred and fifty men, or a less number; if with more than that number, the blank must be filled with a "ten."

NOTE 3.—This blank must be filled with the character of the vessel, " ship," " brig," "schooner," " steamer," etc.

On the 4th of May, Capt. Baker fell in with the brig *Joseph*, of Rockland, Maine, from Cardenas, Cuba, with a cargo of sugar consigned to Welch & Co., of Philadelphia. The *Joseph* fell an easy prize, and was sent into Georgetown, S. C., where she was condemned and sold. The *Savannah*, having accompanied the *Joseph* almost into port, put to sea again in search for other prizes. Soon after the two vessels parted company, the U. S. brig *Perry*, man-of-war, hove in sight, a little north of the Hole in the Wall; but as her guns were run back, her port-holes closed, and the vessel otherwise purposely disguised, she was mistaken for a merchantman, and the *Savannah*, flushed with success, made all sail for the supposed prize. The privateer had got within a mile of the brig before Capt. Baker discovered his blunder, when he put about. The *Perry* at once gave chase, crowding all sail, and fired several shots, four of which were returned by the eighteen-pounder of the *Savannah*. Two of the shots from the *Perry* went through the foresail of the privateer; the shots of the *Savannah* did not take effect. Capt. Baker, seeing no possible chance to escape, surrendered his vessel. The officers and crew were taken on board the *Perry*, and were subsequently transferred to the *Minnesota*, lying off Charleston. The *Minnesota* put a prize crew of seven upon the *Savannah*, Midshipman McCook commanding, and they brought her to New York, where she arrived on June 15th, 1861. The U. S. steamer *Harriet Lane*, on June 25th, brought the officers and the remainder of the crew of the *Savannah* to New York.

The capture of the *Savannah*, and the placing of her crew in irons on board of the frigate *Minnesota*, excited considerable discussion. A great deal of debate also arose in relation to the disposition that should be made of them. The war press of New York claimed that, if they were to be considered privateers, they should have been hung at the yard-arm, and they demanded, at all hazards, the execution of the death penalty. Though the Confederate government was recognized by the courts as belligerent, and a state of war was held to exist,[1] the government of the United States attempted to

[1] In the case of the prize bark *Hiawatha*, the point presented by the counsel for her owners, in conjunction with the counsel for other vessels seized under similar circumstances, were that the court had no jurisdiction; that the public disturbances which then existed did not constitute a state of war under the law of nations : that no lawful blockade had been established or maintained, or violated under the law of nations; that no State, or combination of States, could be treated as enemies of the United States government ; that the President

put those engaged in hostilities at sea upon a different footing, and to bring them to trial for piracy. The proclamation of Mr. Lincoln, on April 19, gave expression to this principle. In it he said: "And I hereby proclaim and declare that if any person under the pretended authority of the said States, or under any other pretence, shall molest a vessel of the United States, or the person or cargo on board of her, such person will be held amenable to the laws of the United States for the prevention and punishment of piracy."

A privateer, as the name imports, is a private armed ship, fitted out at the owner's expense, but commissioned by a belligerent government to capture the ships and goods of the enemy at sea, or the ships of neutrals when conveying to the enemy goods contraband of war. A privateer differs from a pirate in this, that the one has a commission and the other has none. A privateer is entitled to the same rights of war as the public vessels of the belligerent. A pirate ship has no rights, and her crew are liable to be captured and put to death by all nations, as robbers and murderers on the high seas. The policy of neutrals recognizing privateers as legitimate belligerent ships is founded on the interests of humanity and the common desire to prevent piracy. If privateers were not recognized by neutral nations they would become pirates, and, instead of making prisoners of the crews of prize vessels, they would massacre them, appropriate the cargoes and sink the ships. But, being recognized, they are under the surveillance of the government commissioning them as well as the governments of neutral nations, and they are responsible for their acts to both. The government, moreover, which issues letters of marque is liable to neutral nations for the misdeeds of its privateers. To a government with a small navy, or no navy, and with slender resources, privateers are a great advantage, because they not only cost the government nothing, being owned and equipped by private individuals, but, on the contrary, they are a source of revenue, for they are obliged to pay a percentage on the value of their captures, in consideration of their license.

The fact that the war was a civil one afforded no reason for a distinction between combatants at sea and combatants on land. As naval warfare is no more criminal than land warfare, those captured in the one occupation are as much entitled to be treated as prisoners-of-war as those captured in

had no power to establish a blockade, or declare a state of war, without the authority of Congress.

The exception as to the jurisdiction of the court was overruled by Judge Betts of New York. A state of war, the judge maintained, did exist, and, under the law of nations, the rights of a war waged by a government, to subdue an insurrection or revolt of its own citizens or subjects, are the same in regard to neutral powers as if hostilities were carried on between independent nations, and apply equally in captures of property for municipal offences, or as prizes of war. It is sufficient to establish the legality of the blockade, to show that the ports blockaded are under the power and use of the enemies of the United States. So far as their own acts can make them so, the insurgents who hold these ports are as alien and foreign to the United States government as if they had declared themselves citizens and subjects of various South American States; they thus make themselves avowed enemies of the United States and are waging a war for the dismemberment of the nation and destruction of the government.

the other.[1] The rights and privileges of privateering had been maintained and asserted by the United States, and the separate and distinct existence of the Confederate States as a political power had up to the time of the capture of the *Savannah* been also practically recognized in many ways by the U. S. government. From the outset of the controversy, the Southern States had been scrupulously exact, or rather superstitiously exact, in recognizing the courtesies and civilities of warfare. Gen. Robert Anderson, who began the war as a subordinate, against pledges and promises, was treated for weeks with more attention and courtesies than were bestowed on many Confederate officers. When taken prisoner, he and his command were released with unusual honor. Gen. Harney was taken prisoner at Harper's Ferry and released with honor. Lieut. Col. Morris, U. S. army, was twice or thrice arrested on good grounds, and yet was discharged. Many prisoners were taken in Texas and at other places and honorably released.

It is not necessary to multiply instances to prove that the South, because she was compelled to defend her rights by war, deserved an honorable war, modified by all the limitations and amenities of modern war among Christian and civilized nations. The outrages, therefore, perpetrated upon the Southern privateersmen stirred the gall of every earnest man in the Confederate States. In the deficiency of a navy proper, these gallant men, commissioned by the Confederate government as their militia of the sea, went forth to punish their enemy to the extent of their ability. It was the only naval resource of the South, and accorded with the laws and customs of nations. It was a right which the United Colonies in 1776, and the United States in 1812, freely exercised against their mother

---

[1] Judge Daly, of New York, who from the first outbreak of the war had been distinguished for his zeal in the Union cause, in January, 1862, addressed a letter to Senator Harris in opposition to the enforcement of the alleged laws against Southern privateers. He said:

" What is the difference between the Southern soldier who takes up arms against the government of the United States upon the land and the Southern privateersman who does the same upon the water? Practically there is none; and if one should be held and exchanged as a prisoner-of-war, the other is equally entitled to the privilege. The court before which the crew of the *Jefferson Davis* were convicted as pirates held that they could not be regarded as privateers, upon the ground that they were not acting under the authority of an independent State with the recognized rights of sovereignty. This objection applies equally to the man-of-warsmen in the Southern fleets, and to every soldier in the Southern army, none of whom are acting under the authority of a recognized government. The Constitution defines treason to be the levying of war against the United States, and the giving of aid and comfort to its enemies. All of them are engaged in doing this ; and although the Southern privateersmen may fall specifically under the provisions of the act defining piracy, the guilt of the one is precisely the same as that of the other. The question then arises — as there is in point of fact no difference between them — is every seamen or soldier that shall be taken in arms against the government to be hung as a traitor or a pirate ? * * *

" It is natural that we should have hesitated to consider the Southern States in the light of belligerents before the rebellion had expanded to its present proportions; but now we cannot, if we would, shut our eyes to the fact that war, and war upon a more extensive scale than usually takes place between contending nations, actually exists. It is now, and it will continue to be, carried on upon both sides by a resort to all the means and appliances known to modern warfare, and, unless we are to fall back into the barbarism of the Middle Ages, we must observe in its conduct those humane usages in the treatment and exchange of prisoners which modern civilization has shown to be equally the dictate of humanity and of policy. * * *

" The existing embarrassment is easily overcome; further prosecutions can be stopped, and in respect to the privateersmen who have been convicted, the President, acting upon the suggestion of the court that tried them, can, by the exercise of the pardoning power, relieve them from their position as criminals and place them in that of prisoners-of-war."

country, and in 1856 peremptorily refused to waive by treaty stipulation. Yet, in 1861, because it bore disagreeably upon their commerce, the practice was denounced by the United States, and the captured Confederate privateersmen were subjected to the ignominious treatment of common felons. Paraded in chains through the streets of northern cities, for the gaze of the hostile rabble, they were put in the wretched dungeons of " the Tombs," surrounded by filth and vermin. Here for long months they were kept, that confinement and anxiety might prey upon their health, and that wounded self-respect might fret their hearts in the torture of humiliation. They were then dragged forth before the public gaze of their infuriated enemies to be tried for their lives as the worst of criminals—enemies to the whole human race. These were the men the Confederacy sent forth to fight their battles under the flag of their government, and this was the treatment they met with as prisoners at the hands of a government which claimed that it was conducting the war according to the laws and usages of civilized nations.

On the 17th of July, Thomas H. Baker, John Harleston, Charles Sidney Passailaigue, Henry C. Howard, Joseph C. de Carmo, Handy Ornan, Patrick Daly, Wm. C. Clark, Albert Ferris, Richard Palmer, John Murphy, Alexander C. Coyle, and Martin Galvin, the thirteen remaining crew of the *Savannah*, were arraigned in the U. S. Circuit Court, in New York, to plead to their indictment. They were handcuffed in pairs, and attended by ten U. S. deputy marshals. The indictment against them was a very long and elaborate document, to which they pleaded "not guilty." The counsel for the prosecution were E. Delafield Smith, U. S. District Attorney, William M. Evarts, Samuel Blatchford, and Ethan Allen ; for the prisoners, Daniel Lord, James T. Brady, Algernon S. Sullivan, Joseph E. Dukes, Maurice Mayer, Isaac Davega, S. L. M. Barlow, G. R. J. Bondin, and Jeremiah Larocque.

After the reading of the indictment the prisoners were remanded to the Tombs, followed by a large crowd of excited people, where they remained in confinement until the day set for their trial. On the 23d of October, the trial began in the U. S. Circuit Court, before Judges Nelson and Shipman, and terminated on the 31st in the disagreement of the jury. After a consultation of twenty hours, the jury could not agree upon a verdict, four members out of the twelve being in favor of an acquittal ; the remaining considering the prisoners guilty on some of the counts only. The trial deserved and attracted a great share of public attention during its progress, as it involved principles of international law and of national polity of the most delicate character. The management of the case was highly creditable to the counsel on each side, and it was heard before two of the ablest Federal judges in the country, and a highly intelligent jury of New York City.

The facts in the case were few and simple, and were admitted by the defence. "The only question for the Court and jury to decide," said the New York *Herald*, in commenting on the case, "was whether the act amounted to piracy, either under international law or under the United States statute. Arguments were made to show that it was not piracy under the law of nations, because a pirate is designated as the enemy of the human race, whereas the privateer only wars on the commerce of a particular nation. Under the United States statute, however, the prisoners appeared to be amenable, if the law were to be strictly and technically construed. But the opinions and precedents of all jurists who wrote, and of all courts that decided, and all governments that treated of the offence, were remarkably unanimous on the point, that in a state of foreign war, or domestic revolution, those who warred upon the ocean were entitled to the same humanities as those who warred upon the land. There could be no good reason, it was urged, why our government should treat as prisoners-of-war, or should discharge, on taking the oath of allegiance, the rebels taken on land with arms in their hands fighting against the republic, while they should treat as pirates or felons those who warred against the United States on the high sea. And the precedent of Great Britain in that respect was cited to show that when the American colonies revolted against her, and when the ocean swarmed with

---

[1] The 9th Section of the Act of Congress of 1790, under which the prisoners were tried, is as follows:

"That if any citizen shall commit any piracy or robbery aforesaid, or any act of hostility against the United States, or any citizen thereof, upon the high seas, under color of any commission from any foreign prince or State, or on pretence of authority from any person, such offender shall, notwithstanding the pretence of any such authority, be deemed, adjudged and taken to be a pirate, felon and robber, and on being thereof convicted, shall suffer death."

It may be well to observe that this act was taken from the British statute of 11 and 12 Will. 3, c. 7; the 8th section of which provided as follows:

"That if any of his Majesty's natural born subjects or denizens of this kingdom shall commit any piracy or robbery or any act of hostilities against others, his Majesty's subjects, upon the sea, under color of any commission from any foreign prince or State or pretence of authority from any person whatsoever, such offender and offenders and every of them, shall be deemed, adjudged and taken to be pirates, felons and robbers."

This statute was in force during the American Revolution, just as much as the Act of Congress of 1790 was in force during the Southern Revolution; and there was no more reason then for applying the act of 1790 against citizens of the Confederate States than there was for applying the statute of 11 and 12 Will. 3, c. 7, against citizens of the United States from 1775 to 1783.

In 1775 Gen. Gage, of the British army, regarded prisoners as persons "whose lives by the law of the land are destined to the cord."— *Sparks' Collection of the Writings of Washington*, Vol. III., p. 500. In his reply, Gen. Washington, on the 11th of August, 1775, said that he "resolved to adopt the same mode of treatment towards the British prisoners then in his possession which was practiced by Gen. Gage."— *Ibid*, p. 500, 501. Congress was of a like opinion with the American general. After the King's proclamation of the 23d of August, 1775, Congress declared and published "that whatever punishment shall be inflicted upon any persons in the power of our enemies, for favoring, aiding or abetting the cause of American liberty, shall be retaliated in the same kind and the same degree upon those in our power who have favored, aided or abetted, or shall favor, aid or abet, the system of ministerial oppression."— *Ibid.* p. 204. And when Col. Allen was taken prisoner near Montreal and thrown into irons, Gen. Washington, following the order of Congress, wrote on the 18th of December, 1775, to Gen. Howe, that "whatever treatment Col. Allen receives, whatever fate he undergoes, such exactly shall be the treatment and fate of Brigadier Prescott, now in our hands." This, it will be seen, was before the Declaration of Independence. After that Declaration, a general exchange of prisoners was proposed and acceded to, to wit: of officers for officers of equal rank, soldier for soldier and sailor for sailor.—Vol. IV., pp. 23, 512, also pp. 105, 108, etc.

American privateers, she never treated those who fell into her
hands in any other manner than as prisoners-of-war. These
arguments and precedents had their weight with the jury, and
helped to save the accused from the verdict of guilty."

Meanwhile, pending the trial of the officers and crew of
the *Savannah*, the Confederate government threw out the
menace of retaliation, which, after the first battle of Manassas, it was in a position to carry out. It decided, if one drop
of Southern blood was shed by Northern courts for defending
the Confederate States on the seas, it was to be paid for, with
interest, in Charleston. Self-protection and the enforcement
of the laws of nations and of humanity alike required, in this
instance at least, full and ample retaliation.

As soon as President Davis received intelligence that the
crew of the *Savannah* had been placed in irons and were to be
tried for piracy, he sent Col. Richard Taylor, of his staff, as a
special messenger to Mr. Lincoln, with a communication,
under date of July 6th, 1861, in which he said:

"Having learned that the schooner *Savannah*, a private armed vessel
in the service, and sailing under a commission issued by authority of the
Confederate States of America, had been captured by one of the vessels
forming the blockading squadron off Charleston harbor, I directed a
proposition to be made to the officer commanding the squadron, for an
exchange of the officers and crew of the *Savannah* for prisoners-of-war
held by this government, 'according to number and rank.' To this proposition, made on the 19th ultimo, Capt. Mercer, the officer in command of
the blockading squadron, made answer on the same day that 'the prisoners
(referred to) are not on board of any of the vessels under my command.'

"It now appears, by statements made, without contradiction, in newspapers published in New York, that the prisoners above mentioned were
conveyed to that city, and have been treated not as prisoners-of-war, but
as criminals; that they have been put in irons, confined in jail, brought
before the courts of justice on charges of piracy and treason; and it is even
rumored that they have been actually convicted of the offenses charged,
for no other reason than that they bore arms in defence of the rights of
this government, and under the authority of its commission.

"I could not, without grave discourtesy, have made the newspaper
statements above referred to the subject of this communication, if the
threat of treating as pirates the citizens of this Confederacy, armed for its
service on the high seas, had not been contained in your proclamation of
the 19th of April last; that proclamation, however, seems to afford a sufficient justification for considering these published statements as not devoid of probability.

"It is the desire of this government to so conduct the war now existing as to mitigate its horrors as far as may be possible; and, with this
intent, the treatment of the prisoners captured by its forces have been
marked by the greatest humanity and leniency consistent with public obligation. Some have been permitted to return home on parole, others to
remain at large, under similar conditions, within this Confederacy, and all
have been furnished with rations for their subsistence, such as are allowed
to our own troops. It is only since the news has been received of the treatment of the prisoners taken on the *Savannah*, that I have been compelled
to withdraw these indulgences, and to hold the prisoners taken by us in
strict confinement..

"A just regard to humanity and to the honor of this government
now requires me to state explicitly, that, painful as will be the necessity,

this government will deal out to the prisoners held by it the same treatment and the same fate as shall be experienced by those captured on the *Savannah;* and if driven to the terrible necessity of retaliation, by your execution of any of the officers or crew of the *Savannah,* that retaliation will be extended so far as shall be requisite to secure the abandonment of a practice unknown to the warfare of civilized man, and so barbarous as to disgrace the nation which shall be guilty of inaugurating it.

"With this view, and because it may not have reached you, I now renew the proposition made to the commander of the blockading squadron, to exchange for the prisoners taken on the *Savannah* an equal number of those held by us, according to rank."

Col. Taylor was permitted to go to Washington, but was refused an audience with Mr. Lincoln, and was obliged to content himself with a verbal reply from Gen. Scott that the communication had been delivered to him, and that he would reply in writing as soon as possible.

No answer ever came, however, and the Confederate authorities were compelled to select by lot, from among the Federal prisoner in their hands, a number to whom they proposed to mete out the same fate which might await the crew of the *Savannah.* [1] But fortunately Mr. Lincoln was induced, from some cause, to *recede* from his position—albeit he never deigned an answer of any sort to Mr. Davis' letter—and the horrors of retaliation were thus averted. Perhaps the Federal government was influenced in this matter by what occurred in the British House of Lords, on the 16th of May, soon after Mr. Lincoln's proclamation, declaring the Confederate privateers *pirates,* reached that country. On this subject the Earl of Derby said:

"He apprehended that if *one thing was clearer than another, it was that privateering was not piracy,* and that no law could make that piracy, as regarded the subjects of one nation, which was not piracy by the law of nations. Consequently the United States *must not be allowed to entertain this doctrine,* and to call upon Her Majesty's government *not to interfere.* He knew it was said that the United States treated the Confederate States of the South as mere rebels, and that as rebels these expeditions were liable to all the penalties of high treason. That was not the doctrine of this country, because we have declared that they are entitled to all the rights of belligerents, *The Northern States could not claim the rights of belligerents for themselves, and, on the other hand, deal with other parties not as belligerents, but as rebels.*"

[1] The following correspondence discloses the names of the prisoners the Confederates had selected to await the fate of the *Savannah* privateersmen, etc.:

"C. S. A. WAR DEPARTMENT,
"RICHMOND, Nov. 9, 1861.

"SIR—You are hereby instructed to choose by lot from among the prisoners-of-war of highest rank one who is to be confined in a cell appropriated to convicted felons, and who is to be treated in all respects as if such convict, and to be held for execution in the same manner as may be adopted by the enemy for the execution of the prisoner-of-war Smith, recently condemned to death in Philadelphia. You will also select thirteen other prisoners-of-war, the highest in rank of those captured by our forces, to be confined in the cells reserved for prisoners accused of infamous crimes, and will treat them as such so long as the enemy shall continue so to treat the like number of prisoners-of-war captured by them at sea, and now held for trial in New York as pirates. As these measures are intended to repress the infamous attempt now made by the enemy to commit judicial murder on prisoners-of-war, you will execute them strictly, as the mode best calculated to prevent the commission of so heinous a crime.

"Your obedient servant,
"J. P. BENJAMIN,
"Acting Secretary of War.
"To Brig. Gen. JOHN WINDER, Richmond, Va."

"HEADQUARTERS DEPARTMENT OF HENRICO,
"RICHMOND, Va. Nov. 11, 1861.

"Hon. J. P. BENJAMIN, Secretary of War:
"SIR—In obedience to instructions contained in your letter of the 9th inst., one prisoner-of-

Lord Brougham said that "it was clear that privateering was not piracy by the law of nations."

Lord Kingsdown took the same view. "What was to be the operation of the Presidential proclamation upon this subject was a matter for the consideration of the United States." But he expressed the opinion that the enforcement of the doctrine of that proclamation "would be an act of barbarity which would produce an outcry throughout the civilized world."

Up to this time there had been no formal *cartel* for the exchange of prisoners, and the policy of the Washington government seemed to be that they would not treat with "rebels" in any way which would acknowledge them as "belligerents." But many prisoners, on both sides, were released on parole, and a proposition made in the Confederate Congress to return the Federal prisoners taken at First Manassas, without any formality whatever, would doubtless have prevailed but for the difficulty in reference to the crew of the *Savannah*.

The pressure upon the Federal government by friends of the prisoners became so great that they were finally induced to enter into a *cartel* for the exchange of prisoners on the very basis that the Confederates had offered in the beginning. The Confederate Gen. Howell Cobb and the Federal Gen. Wool entered into this arrangement on the 14th of February, 1862—the only unadjusted point being that Gen. Wool was unwilling that each party should agree to pay the expenses of transporting their prisoners to the frontier, and this he promised to refer to his government.

At a second interview, the 1st March, Gen. Wool informed Gen. Cobb that his government would not consent to pay these expenses, and thereupon Gen. Cobb promptly receded from his demand, and agreed to the terms proposed by the other side. But Gen. Wool, who had said at the beginning of the negotiation, "I am alone *clothed with full power* for the purpose of arranging for the exchange of prisoners," was now

war of the highest rank in our possession was chosen by lot, to be held for execution in the same manner as may be adopted by the enemy for the execution of Smith, recently condemned to death in Philadelphia. The names of the six colonels were placed in a can. The first name drawn was that of Col. Corcoran, Sixty-ninth Regiment, N. Y. S. M., who is the hostage chosen to answer for Smith. In choosing the thirteen from the highest rank to be held to answer for a like number of prisoners-of-war captured by the enemy at sea, there being only ten field officers, it was necessary to draw by lot three captains. The first names drawn were Capts. J. B. Ricketts, H. McQuade and J. W. Rockwood. The list of thirteen will therefore stand: Cols. Lee, Cogswell, Wilcox, Woodruff and Wood; Lieut. Cols. Bowman and Neff; Majors Potter, Revere and Vodges; Capts. Ricketts, McQuade and Rockwood.

"Respectfully, your obedient servant,
"JOHN H. WINDER,
"Brigadier General'

"HEADQUARTERS DEPARTMENT OF HENRICO,
"RICHMOND, Va., Nov. 12, 1861.
"Hon. J. P. BENJAMIN,
"Secretary of War, Richmond, Va.:
"SIR—In obedience to your instructions, all the wounded officers have been exempted as hostages to await the result of the trial of prisoners captured by the enemy at sea. I have therefore made selections by lot of Capts. H. Bowman and T. Keffer to replace Capts. Ricketts and McQuade, wounded.

"The list of thirteen will now stand: Cols. Lee, Cogswell, Wilcox, Woodruff and Wood; Lieut. Cols. Bowman and Neff; Majors Potter, Revere and Vogdes; Capts. Rockwood, Bowman and Keffer.

"Respectfully, your obedient servant,
"JOHN H. WINDER,
"Brigadier General."

The prisoners were sent to Charleston, S. C., where they were put in jail in close confinement, to abide the issue of the trials of the privateersmen at the North.

under the necessity of stating that " his government had changed his instructions." And thus the negotiations were abruptly broken off, and the matter left where it was before. The vacillating conduct of the Federal government was of easy explanation, and in perfect accord with their double dealing throughout the war. After these negotiations had begun, the capture of Forts Henry and Donelson had given the United States a considerable preponderance in the number of prisoners held by them, and they at once reverted to their original purpose of not treating with " rebels" on equal terms.

But Jackson's Valley campaign, the Seven Days' Battles around Richmond, and other Confederate successes again reversed the "balance of power," and brought the Federal government to terms, to which the Confederate authorities were *always* willing. Accordingly negotiations were again entered into by Gen. D. H. Hill on the part of the Confederacy, and Gen. John A. Dix on the part of the United States, and the result was, on July 22d, 1862, the adoption of a *cartel* of exchange.

The rigid observance of this *cartel* would have prevented all the horrors of prison life North and South, and have averted the great mortality in Southern prisons, and the greater mortality in Northern prisons, if it had been faithfully carried out by the Federal authorities.

In the meantime, on the 2d of February, 1862, Hon. Alfred Ely, member of Congress from New York, captured at the first battle of Manassas, had an interview with Mr. Lincoln and Secretary Seward, when it was determined to place the privateersmen in confinement at New York and Philadelphia upon the same footing as other prisoners-of-war. On the 3d, the following prisoners confined in the Tombs were transferred to Fort Lafayette in obedience to orders received from Washington, and were subsequently exchanged :

FROM THE *Savannah.*—T. Hamilton Baker, John Harleston, Henry Howard, Handy Ornan, Wm. Clark, Alex. C. Coyle, C. S. Passailaigue, Joseph Cuig De Carmo, Patrick Daly, John Murphy, Martin Galvin. FROM THE *Dixie.*—George Gladden, Charles Forrester, J. P. M. Catro, John Journell, John H Marshall. FROM THE *Sumter.*—Henry Spence, John Davis, A. D. Hodgier, John O'Brien, Wm. May, Peter Thompson, John Donnelly, James Milner, Eugenie Ruhl. FROM THE CONFEDERATE MAN-OF-WAR *Florida.*—John Williams, Patrick McCarthy, James Reilly, Archibald Wilson.

The brig *Jefferson Davis*, formerly the slaver *Echo*, built in Baltimore in 1854, and condemned in Charleston, was fitted up in the latter city as a privateer, and on the 28th of June, 1861, started out upon a privateering expedition. The *Davis* was 230 tons register and rated 1½. She was full-rigged and carried four waist guns, two eighteen-pounders, and two twelve-pounders, and one long eighteen-pounder of old English make amidships. Her officers were Capt. Louis M. Coxetter, Lieuts. Postell and Stewart, Surgeon Babcock, Capt. of Marines, Mr. Sanfrau, four prize-masters, and a crew of 70 men.

Soon after leaving Charleston, the *Jefferson Davis* reaped a rich harvest in capturing Federal vessels, with an estimated value of $225,000. On the 6th of July, the brig *John Welsh*, bound from Trinidad to Falmouth, Eng., with a cargo of sugar, was captured off Hatteras. Capt. J. C. Fifield, of the *John Welsh*, says:

"After the work of transferring the stores had been completed, Capt. Coxsetter mustered all hands aft and said to them : 'Boys, if you molest the crew of that brig or their things to the value of a rope-yarn, I will punish you to the utmost of my power. Do you understand ? Now go forward.' Turning to his officers, he said : 'Gentlemen, I desire that you do everything in your power to make the stay of these gentlemen as agreeable as possible.' He then invited me to dine with him in his cabin, while my mate was taken into the officers' mess."

A prize crew in charge of Prize-master Stephens was then put in charge of the captured vessel, and she was ordered to put in the nearest Southern port. On the same day the schooner *Enchantress*, from Boston, bound to St. Jago, was captured off Montauk. She was placed in charge of Wm. Smith, formerly a Savannah pilot, as prize-master, and ordered South. On Sunday, the 7th of July, about 150 miles from Sandy Hook, the *Jefferson Davis* captured the schooner *S. J. Waring*, of Brookhaven, L. I., with a valuable cargo, bound to Montevideo. Montague Amiel, a Charleston pilot, was put in charge as prize-master, with a man named Stevens as mate, and Malcolm Siding as second mate, and two men. The *Davis* left William Tillman, a colored cook, two seamen, and Bryce Mackinnon, a passenger, on board. Late in the afternoon the schooner was headed South. The remaining crew and the passenger were in hopes of a recapture by some U. S. vessel, and made themselves agreeable and sociable to the privateersmen, and in consequence they suspected nothing until the night of the 16th of July, when fifty miles to the southward of Charleston.

Seeing no prospect of their hopes being realized, and the prize-captain and first mate being asleep in their berths, and the second mate at the wheel, the others dozing or asleep, the preconcerted plan was carried into effect by the steward, William Tillman (colored), killing the three with a hatchet, and throwing the bodies overboard. One of the remaining men was tied up that night, and both were released in the morning on promise to help work the vessel, and were treated accordingly.

After retaking the vessel, the charge of her devolved on the steward. Neither he nor the others understood navigation, but having once got hold of the land he brought her safely up to the pilot ground, when Charles E. Warner, of the pilot-boat *Jane,* took charge, and brought the schooner up to the battery in New York Harbor.[1]

On July 9th, the *Jefferson Davis* captured the ship *Mary Goodell,* Capt. McGilvery, from New York for Buenos Ayres. As she drew eighteen feet of water, and was useless to the privateer, she was allowed to go, five of her crew joining the *Davis.* All the prisoners captured by the privateer were put aboard of the *Mary Goodell,* and she sailed for Portland, Me. On the same day, the brig *Mary E. Thompson,* of Scarsport, bound to Montevideo, loaded with lumber, was made a prize of. After venturing to within 100 miles southeast of Nantucket shoals, and reaping a rich harvest, the *Jefferson Davis* steered her course for the South American coast, where she captured several valuable cargoes. The havoc made by the *Jefferson Davis* among the merchant ships of the enemy, within sight of the Atlantic shores, created the greatest excitement in all the Northern ports. Immediately upon the receipt of the news of her seizures, the government at Washington ordered a fleet of revenue-cutters and gunboats to be dispatched in quest of the daring privateer. The command of the fleet from New York was confided to Capt. Howard, and the cutters *Jackson, Crawford* and *Varina* went promptly to sea in tow of the steamer *Mercury.* The *Henrietta* and the gunboat *Iroquois* started in pursuit on the 13th of July. From Boston the revenue-cutters *Morris* and *Caleb Cushing* sailed on the same mission on the 12th, and the frigate *Vincennes* sailed on the following day with orders to cruise off Nantucket for a week in search of the *Jefferson Davis.*

The privateer arrived at St. John's, P. R., on July 26th. Before entering the port, a boat and ten men were sent in for provisions, but not being allowed to land, the brig was allowed to go in. The captain-general informed the commander of the

---

[1] Shortly before the hour of midnight on the 16th of July, Capt. Montague Amiel was asleep in his cabin, together with Stevens, the mate, in the berth next to him. The second mate, Malcolm Siding, was also asleep on the poop deck, and the other two seamen composing the privateer prize crew were lounging leisurely at the forehead part of the ship.

Tillman stole up from between decks, with hatchet in hand, and first went down into the captain's cabin, who was sound asleep in bed. He then raised his axe and gave him a vigorous blow on his skull, from which he seemed to be launched into eternity. for he moved not an inch. The negro next proceeded to deal with the mate, who was also reclining near his captain fast asleep, and dealt with him in the same summary and terrible manner. After leaving both these dead men below, Tillman came on the poop deck and struck the second mate a fearful blow over the temple. The unfortunate man was just rising from his reclining position with little expectation that he was about being launched into eternity. He then went below once more, took hold of the captain's body and flung him overboard, doing the same with that of the mate and second mate. The coast being now clear, he

called out to the two remaining of the crew aft, telling them that they must obey him as captain of the vessel, or he would throw them overboard also. The men yielded up without a murmur, when he had them at once ironed, but subsequently released them on their consenting to assist in bringing the vessel to a Northern port. Tillman afterwards related that the time consumed in killing the men and throwing them overboard and getting the vessel under his command only consumed seven and a half minutes.

Mr. Mackinnon, the passenger on board of the *Waring,* afterwards gave the following account of the steward's bloody work:

"I was awakened from a light sleep by a peculiar sound in the captain's room, which I knew instinctively could only have been produced by an axe cleaving Amiel's skull. No sooner did the '*thush*' strike upon my ear than I leaped out of bed, and leaning against the door-casing in the partition, saw the steward dart through the twilight—for he had extinguished the light— noiselessly as a rat, across the cabin towards the second mate's room. I also saw, at the same glance, Capt. Amiel rise from his berth and attempt to follow him, but the blood blinded him, and he fell to the floor, with a horrid gurgling

Jefferson Davis that he must leave within twenty-four hours, and immediately dispatched the steam - corvette *Herman Cortez*, mounting six guns, outside the harbor to watch her movements. After procuring a supply of water and provisions, the privateer sailed on the 29th.

On the 5th of August, after chasing several vessels without success, the *Davis* captured the schooner *Windward* from Turk's Island, with a cargo of salt. On the following day the privateer made prize of the brig *Santa Clara*, of Eastport, loaded with sugar from Porto Rico, bound to New York. It had been the intention of Capt. Coxetter, of the *Davis*, to burn or sink the *Windward*, but, having so many prisoners, he put them on board that vessel and set them free. On July 21st the *Davis* had captured the bark *Alvarado*, bound from the Cape for Boston, with a valuable cargo of wool, hides, etc. She was sent into the Confederacy. The bark *California* was also captured by the *Jefferson Davis*, but not having sufficient men to put a prize crew on board was allowed to proceed.

Capt. Coxetter, finding that his provisions and water were short, and that his crew had been reduced to one-half of his original number, made sail for the Florida coast, intending to run into a Confederate harbor. When about 800 miles east of Cape Florida, says the Richmond *Enquirer*, she came in contact with the ship *John Crawford*, Capt. Edge, from Philadelphia, bound to Key West, with arms and coal for the U. S. forces. She was found to draw twenty-two feet of water, and could not possibly be brought in. The officers and crew, numbering in all twenty-two persons, were taken on board the privateer, the vessel fired, and holes bored in her sides and bottom. This was about four o'clock in the morning, and about good daylight the ship was wrapped in flames,

sound in his throat. All this was but the work of a second. The cleaving of the skull, like the flash from a gun preceding the report, was followed by a weak, faint cry, like that of a sick child, and the gurgling in the throat. I knew then that his wound was mortal. Stooping side-ways, the steward entered the second mate's cabin, and once more swung his axe, but not so effectively.

"The mate started up with a '—— —— you; don't strike me again,' and clutched at the steward's breast, but eluding the wounded man, he ran on deck to where the man lay near the wheel-house, and keeping his axe behind him, demanded ' what all this noise was about?' The mate who had been aroused by the outcries of the captain and mate, had raised himself up on his elbow, and stared at the steward in a half-stupid, half-fascinated way, not seeing the pistol which Stedding, the man at the helm, had pointed at him for use in case of necessity. As he turned his face toward the steward, the latter drove his weapon home into the base of his skull. Stedding and the steward then tumbled him overboard. He rose on the wave, with a hoarse cry, when about two lengths astern, the water having raised him; but he must have soon gone down to his long account.

" Then the steward came down to the cabin, where I still stood while Stedding stood, pistol in hand, to guard the deck. The captain cried faintly twice to me by name, ' Help me—help me,' but he was past help. Another swishing blow of the axe. and he did not repeat the cry. Then the steward returned to the second mate's cabin, where, seated on a pile of starch boxes, his legs drawn up, and his head between his knees, was the half-stupefied man. Again and again the axe fell, and again and again the cry, ' Don't do that,' fell on my ear, each time fainter than the last. Stedding now came down, and the steward and he took the corpse of the captain by the feet, and dragging it up the companion-way, tossed it overboard. Meantime I had got some irons out, hoping to intercede to save bloodshed. Stedding and the steward once more came down, and each taking the second mate by the shoulder led him out from the place where he had crouched on the starch boxes. He seemed to walk, with their assistance, as they went up the companion-way, but his head lay a pulpy mass upon his shoulder, and a moment after a loud splash alongside told the fate of another of the privateers."

going down shortly afterwards. It was found impossible to secure any of the arms, as they were stowed under the coal.

On August 16th, the *Jefferson Davis* was off St. Augustine, Florida, but the wind blowing half a gale, she could not venture in. On the following day, while trying to cross the bar, the privateer stuck. A small boat was sent ashore with Dr. Babcock and Lieut. Baya, and the prisoners were landed. The officers and crew of the privateer then went ashore, and were greeted with the most enthusisastic demonstrations by the inhabitants. About half-past nine two lightboats went off to the brig along with Capt. Coxetter and other officers. The starboard guns were thrown overboard to lighten the vessel, in order to clear her decks of water and save as much as possible of the supplies on board the brig.

Every effort was made to save everything on board, but it was supposed that the guns thrown overboard stove her in and caused her to bilge. The lightboats, however, were filled with a large amount of provisions and baggage, and finally succeeded in saving all the small arms on board.

The ladies threw open their houses, and they were received with cheers upon cheers. Cheers were given for the *Jefferson Davis*, for the Southern Confederacy, and the utmost hilarity and rejoicing for the safe arrival of the privateersmen was manifested. While there they were sumptuously provided for, and furnished with every comfort that could possibly be devised.

During the voyage of the *Jefferson Davis*, a conspiracy existed among the prisoners and a portion of the crew to kill the captain and officers, and take the vessel into New York. After the return of the privateer to the Confederacy, the conspiracy was disclosed by one of the crew, and upon their arrival in Charleston the suspected ones were arrested, and tried before Judge Magrath on October 11th. Only one of the men proved to be guilty of the charge.

Wm. Smith, one of the crew of the *Jefferson Davis*, was convicted in the U. S. Circuit Court, at Philadelphia, on Oct. 25th, upon an indictment of piracy. Thos. Quigley, David Mullins, and Edward Rockford, of the crew of the same privateer, were also convicted in the same court, Oct. 29th, upon the same charge. When the U. S. government, after the trial of the *Savannah* privateersmen, decided to place the crews of the privateers upon the same footing with other prisoners taken from the Confederates, on Feb. 5th, 1862, the four men belonging to the *Jefferson Davis* and the thirty-four of the *Petrel*, who were confined in the jail at Philadelphia, were sent to Fort Lafayette.[1]

---

[1] The following were the names of the privateersmen : William Smith, Thomas Quigley, Daniel Mullins, Edward Rockford, Wm. Perry, Richard M. Harvey, Chas. Campbell, August Peyrupet, Robert Barrett, Henry Mills, Edward Flynn, Austin C. Williams, Henry Aulinaus, Daniel Courtney, John M. Morgan, George Hankins, Asa Delahey, John Cunningham, Robert R. Jeffries, William H. Hurlehunt, Geo. S. Harrison, John Mack, Hugh Managoort, William Ryan, George Moaden, John Cronin, Michael Delton, Henry A. Rumn, John Mullins, C. H. Marriott, G. H. Roberts, T. A. Brookbanks, Richard Lewis, Edward Murphy, John H. Edwards, Thomas Wood, John G. S. Luckett.

Capt. Coxetter, of the *Jefferson Davis*, after the wreck of his vessel, went into the blockade-running service, and commanded the steamers *Autonica* (*Herald*), and the *Beauregard* (*Havelock*). In his last trip in the *Beauregard* to Charleston, S. C., in 1863, he was fired at fifteen times by the Federal blockaders. He was very successsul in the service, but owing to bad health was compelled to retire.

The steamer *Gordon* was owned by the Florida Steamship Company, and, before the war, ran on the line between Charleston and Fernandina. She was about 500 tons burden, carried two guns, and was commanded by Capt. Lockwood. She succeeded in running the blockade at Charleston, and made several valuable prizes. Her name was changed to the *Theodora*, and she frequently ran the blockade.

About the middle of July, 1861, the privateer steamer *Gordon*, from Charleston, captured and carried into Hatteras Inlet the brig *Wm. McGilvery*, from Cardenas bound to Bangor, Me., with a cargo of molasses; also the schooner *Protector*, from Cuba to Philadelphia, with a cargo of fruit. The privateer steamer *Mariner* at the same time captured a schooner loaded with fruit. The schooner *Frank Lucas*, of Philadelphia, about May 1st, reported that off the eastern shore of Virginia she was chased by three sailing-vessels ; and the Norfolk correspondent of the Richmond *Examiner*, on Aug. 1st, said: " Another privateer left our waters yesterday afternoon, the *Smith*, carrying two guns of heavy calibre." On the 15th of August, the schooner *Priscilla*, bound to Baltimore from Newbern, N. C., arrived at her destination, bringing the captains and crews of several vessels which were captured off Cape Hatteras and taken into the port of Newbern. The steamer *Coffee*, or *Winslow*, as she was afterwards called, was a small steamer and carried two guns. It is said that she was lost or abandoned in the neighborhood of Hatteras after making several captures. The schooner *Priscilla*, loaded with salt, was captured by the Confederate privateer steamer *Winslow*, Capt. Carsen. The Confederates took out the salt, and, because the schooner was owned in Baltimore, she was released, Baltimore vessels being exempted from capture. The *Priscilla* brought to Baltimore the captain and crew of the brig *Itasco*, of Warrenton, Me., loaded with sugar, captured off Hatteras, on August 4th, by the steamer *Winslow ;* also Capt. Carlisle and the crew of the brig *William McGilvery*, of New York, and the crew of the steamer *Sea Witch*, of New York, captured by the steamer *Gordon*, and the officers and crew of the schooner *Henry Nutt*, of Philadelphia. The following captured vessels were at this time in the harbor of Newbern: schooner *Transit*, of New London, captured on the 23d of June; *Wm. S. Robbins* and *J. W. Hewes*. The gunboat *Ninon* chased the *Winslow* off Cape Hatteras, but could not overtake her. The Baltimore brig *R. R. Kirkland* was boarded to the southward of the

Gulf Stream in July, by two privateer schooners, and thirty miles south of Hatteras by a privateer steamer, but was released because she belonged to and was bound for the neutral port of Baltimore. The privateers reported to Capt. Knight that they had captured a bark belonging to New Bedford, from Philadelphia, loaded with coal; also a schooner. On July 25th, the schooner *John Elliott*, from Boston for St. Domingo, reported that she had been chased by three privateers on three successive days. The British schooner *Favorite*, from Picton, on the 20th of July, when about sixty miles east of Halifax, was chased by a privateer schooner of about 100 tons.

The privateer schooner *Dixie*, of about 150 tons burden, after a very successful cruise, passed through the "efficient blockade," and with guns booming and colors flying, on August 27th, startled from their gravity the quiet people of the "nest of rebellion" and anchored under the guns of Castle Pinckney. The *Dixie* was commanded by Thomas J. Moore, with Lieuts. George D. Walker, John W. Marshall, and L. D. Benton; Gunner, Charles Ware; Boatswain, George O. Gladden, and a crew of twenty-four men. Capt. Moore, upon his return to Charleston, gave the following interesting account of his cruise :

"The *Dixie* weighed anchor in Charleston harbor on July 19th. On the following day, aided by a stiff breeze, she succeeded in getting out safely to sea. The privateer pursued a southeasterly course without any incident of special moment until Tuesday, the 23d ult. At an early hour on that day Capt. Moore made a sail upon the lee-quarter, and tacking ship soon overhauled her. A gun fired across the bow of the stranger speedily brought her to. The captain was ordered to come on board the *Dixie*, and his papers showed his vessel to be the bark *Glen*, of Portland, Maine, bound to Fort Jefferson, Tortugas, with a cargo of coal. Without further ceremony, the Yankee skipper was informed of the business of his captors, and made prisoner. A prize crew was put aboard the *Glen*, who did not take her to Fort Jefferson, and the *Dixie* went on her way rejoicing. On Thursday, the 25th, the schooner *Mary Alice*, of New York, from the West Indies, with a cargo of sugar, bound for New York, hove in sight. A messenger from Long Tom explained the meaning of the Stars and Bars, and the *Mary Alice* was soon a prize.[1] On the 27th, two sails were for a short time in sight, but a heavy squall came up, accompanied by a waterspout, which passed close ahead of the privateer; and, when this subsided, the vessels had disappeared. On Monday, the 29th, two sails were again descried, but the *Dixie* was unable to come up with them. On the 30th, the hermaphrodite brig *Robert R. Kirkland*, of Baltimore, loaded with salt, consigned to a firm in that city, was spoken. She was, of course, permitted to pass. The captain of the brig, however, was induced to take on board the cook of the *Glen*, the prisoners on board the *Dixie* having become more numerous than was desirable. On the evening of the 31st, no less than nine sail were visible. About sundown the *Dixie* gave chase to one of these vessels, which, from information obtained from one of the prisoners, was believed to be the bark *Albertina*, armed with two rifled-cannon. Two of the guns of the privateer were loaded with grape and canister, and when the stranger was sufficiently near, a shot was fired across her bow, which had the desired effect of bringing her to. She proved to be the bark *Rowena*, of Philadelphia, from Laguayra, with

---

[1] This vessel was afterwards recaptured by the blockaders.

coffee for Philadelphia. The *Rowena*, as well as her coffee, was of course duly "bagged." But inasmuch as her crew numbered thirteen, besides four passengers, Capt. Moore deemed it prudent to go aboard of her himself as prize-master, taking with him several of the prisoners, and leaving on board the *Dixie* a crew of four men, under command of Lieut. L. D. Benton, with the remainder of the prisoners.

"The privateer being now in latitude 30 deg. 38 min., longitude 76 deg. 25 min., and with the bark *Rowena* in her wake, was headed west. On August 2d, she made a strange steamer, but managed to elude her. On Sunday, August 4th, before daylight, a vessel's light was discovered to the eastward, but the *Dixie* kept shy of her. Shortly after daybreak, a steamer was plainly seen in the same direction. For a while she gave chase to the *Dixie*, but Lieut. Benton finding himself off a well-known and convenient harbor of our coast, now a port of entry, decided to run in without delay. The steamer, finding her chase ineffectual, hauled off to the southward."

On the 25th of August, the schooner *Agricola*, from Ellsworth, Me., was overhauled twenty miles northeast from Cape Ann by the privateer schooner *Freely*, of Charleston, S. C. The *Freely*, not wishing anything the *Agricola* had on board, allowed her to resume her voyage. The privateer *Sallie*, formerly the fore-and-aft schooner *Virginia*, about 140 tons, and mounting one long gun amidships, with a crew of forty men, commanded by Captain Libby, ran the blockade from Charleston on the 10th of October. On the 13th, when off Charleston, she captured the brig *Granada*, with a cargo of 400 hogsheads of sugar, melado and molasses, and a quantity of cedar consigned to New York. A privateer brig sailed from St. John's, P. R., on the 6th of September, after having obtained a supply of water and provisions. The schooner *Herbert Marston*, with a cargo of sugar consigned to New York, and valued at $30,000, on the 3d of July, was captured by a North Carolina privateer steamer twenty-five miles southeast of Hatteras, and towed into Hatteras Inlet, where she was anchored under a battery. The brig *B. F. Martin*, with a cargo of machinery, was captured on the 23d of July, 1861, off Hatteras, and the crew taken prisoners by the privateer *York*, commanded by Capt. Jeffrey. The *York* was a large pilot-boat built in Baltimore, and armed with one rifled cannon. In running down the coast to get to Hatteras Inlet, the *Martin* was intercepted by the U. S. ship *Savannah*, which gave chase. The brig at once sheered into shore and eluded capture in the shallow water. While there, the U. S. steamer *Union* came along and shelled the *Martin*, setting her on fire and destroying her cargo, valued at $25,000. The brig *Hannah Butty*, from Savannah, Ga., to some Northern port, was captured on June 25th, laden with molasses, by the steamer *Coffee*. She was brought into Hatteras Inlet together with the schooner *Gordon*, bound for Philadelphia, laden with fruit. At this time the two principal ports of North Carolina, Wilmington and Beaufort, were not under very rigid blockade, and an active trade was carried on from them in naval stores, and the importation of provisions and military supplies. The trade was with Nassau and other British ports.

The revenue cutter *Aiken*, which had been seized in Charleston by the authorities of South Carolina before the firing on Fort Sumter, was fitted out as a privateer, and called the *Petrel*, and placed under the command of Capt. Wm. Perry. On July 27th the privateer schooner sailed out of Charleston, and stood for the U. S. frigate *St. Lawrence*, which she mistook for a merchantman, as all her ports were closed. When the *Petrel* got within range she fired three shots without doing any damage. The *St. Lawrence* returned with shot and shell a terrific fire, one shell exploding in the hull of the *Petrel*, and sinking her instantly. The boats of the frigate were lowered, and picked up thirty-six out of forty of the privateer's crew, who were taken aboard, and their feet and hands heavily manacled. The remaining four were drowned. The prisoners were afterward removed to the U. S. gunboat *Flag*, and brought to Philadelphia. They arrived in that city on the 6th of August, and were lodged in Moyamensing prison. On August 9th they were escorted from prison in two omnibuses, handcuffed, and had a preliminary hearing before U. S. Commissioner Hazlett. On the way out to the coaches, a dense mob hooted the prisoners and threatened to hang them. In the Circuit Court of Philadelphia, on November 4th, while the Assistant District Attorney was urging the trial of the crew of the *Petrel*, Judge Grier said he could not consent to have the regular business of the court interrupted. " It seems like a farce to try them at this time, when the country played civil war. The dictates of humanity would counsel the government to treat captives on the sea the same as those taken on land, and he could not understand the policy of hanging the first and holding the latter as prisoners or releasing them. Let the rebellion be crushed—and God grant that it may be speedily—and these men might be tried for treason or piracy, and he would assist, no matter how much he might be called Jeffreys or Scroggs."

The privateer schooner *Beauregard* was fitted out by a stock company in Charleston, and, on October 14th, President Davis commissioned her to act as a private armed vessel in the service of the Confederate States on the high seas. She was commanded by Capt. Gilbert Hays; John B. Davis, First Lieutenant; Joseph H. Stuart, Second Lieutenant; Archibald Lilly, Purser, and twenty-three seamen. Several of the officers and men had served on the privateer *Jefferson Davis*. The *Beauregard* was 101 tons burden and carried a rifled pivot gun, throwing a twenty-four pound projectile.

The *Beauregard* sailed from Charleston on the 7th of November, and, when about 100 miles east-northeast of Abaco, she was captured early on the morning of the 12th by the U. S. bark *W. G. Anderson*. The privateer saw no vessel before her capture, and did not fire a gun after leaving port. No resistance was made by the *Beauregard*, the superiority of the armament of the *Anderson*—six thirty-two-pounders and one rifled-cannon, and a crew of 110 men—being so great that it would have been madness to measure their strength. While the *Anderson* was approaching the *Beauregard*, however, her crew were engaged in throwing over shell, shot, muskets, etc., and before the capture most of the ammunition was destroyed, the sails and rigging cut to pieces, and pivot gun spiked. The crew, 27 in number, were at once placed in irons and transferred to the *Anderson*. A prize-crew was placed in charge of the *Beauregard*, and she was brought into Key West. After an examination on board, the officers and crew were taken to the shore and placed in the county jail. [1]

The Convention of Georgia having placed that State outside of the Union, at the same time adopted a resolution calling upon her citizens—officers of the U. S. army and navy—to resign, and give their services to Georgia. In response to this call, Capt. Josiah Tatnall, Commander James D. Bulloch, Lieuts. Julian Myers, Wm. A. Wayne, C. M. Morris, John Kell, A. E. Armstrong, C. J. Graves, Wilburn B. Hall, George A. Borchert, R. F. Armstrong, and many other officers of distinction in the "old navy," resigned their commissions and tendered their services to their State.

Among the first to accept service under Georgia was Lieut. Wilburn B. Hall, who had just arrived in New York in command of a captured slaver, which had been seized off the coast of Africa by the U. S. frigate *Constellation*, with 700 slaves aboard. Immediately upon his arrival in the United States, Lieut. Hall resigned his commission and reported at Milledgeville for orders. Governor Brown, like his associates of the other sea-coast States, was at that time engaged in establishing a sea-coast police, to guard against attempts of Northern slave-dealers to carry off slaves from the coasts and sell them in Cuba; thus transferring their slave trade from the African coast to that of the Southern States adjacent or near to Cuban waters. [2] To guard against these depredations, a sea-coast police was necessary. Accordingly, upon his arrival at the capital of Georgia, Lieut. Hall had a conference with Adjut. Gen. H. C. Wayne, who directed him, on behalf of the State, to return to New York and purchase a rapid steamer for coast service. The Governor and Adjutant General said they had no apprehension of war, and that the State only wanted a rapid steamer capable of mounting two howitzers to overhaul vessels engaged in illicit trade, and to give protection to the citizens of Georgia residing along the

[1] All the privateersmen belonging to the various vessels were exchanged in June, 1862, at City Point, on the James River.

[2] It is a fact not generally known that no vessel with slaves was ever captured by the United States on the coast of Africa, owned by Southern men—all of them, with but one exception, having been fitted out at the North. The exception was the *Wanderer*.

coast. It was their belief, that, though the situation between the two sections looked serious, "the whole matter would be accommodated, and that *war ships would not be needed.*" To accomplish his mission, Lieut. Hall had $15,000 placed to his credit, and started for New York, where he purchased the steamer *Huntress.* The vessel had run as a mail-boat between Boston and Portland, and was very fast, making, in smooth water, twenty knots with ease. She was about 500 tons, 230 feet in length, very narrow beam, low in the water, immense side-wheels, and painted black. Her engines were very fine, and her accommodations ample, but she was old. For the purpose she was intended, however, the *Huntress* was a great bargain.

Notwithstanding that Lieut. Hall was dogged day and night by government spies, with the aid of Engineer George W. Tennent, afterwards of the C. S. navy, he equipped his vessel, secured his crew, and about the middle of March got safely to sea in a great storm, at midnight, running between the U. S. steamers *Vanderbilt* and *Harriet Lane,* who were guarding the port of New York. Being forced to make some harbor from the equinoctial storm which was raging along the coast, Lieut. Hall sought refuge in Hampton Roads, and anchored close under the guns of Fortress Monroe. Having put himself in communication with friends on shore, Lieut. Hall soon learned that his vessel was suspected, and that her seizure was certain to take place on the following morning. He therefore resumed his voyage in the face of a fierce gale in the night. After being storm-driven for more than eight days and terribly battered, starboard wheel-house knocked to pieces, coal and stores almost entirely consumed, the *Huntress* arrived in a deplorable condition at Charleston. She entered the harbor flying the Confederate flag, and a flag bearing the coat-of-arms of the State of Georgia—being, it is believed, the first vessel to raise the Southern flag on the high seas. As the *Huntress* passed in between Fort Moultrie, flying the Confederate flag, and Fort Sumter, flying the U. S. flag, with Anderson in a state of siege, she was saluted by Moultrie. Lieut. Hall supplied his vessel with coal, and sailed for Savannah, where he reported to Capt. Tatnall. Having been accepted, and war having begun, the *Huntress* was turned over to the C. S. navy, and placed under the command of Lieut. C. M. Morris, Lieut. Hall being ordered to command the C. S. steamer *Savannah.* The *Huntress* served on the Georgia coast until the battle of Port Royal, in which she took an active part, when she escaped to Charleston. After the negro pilot Smalls stole the steamer *Planter* out from Charleston, the *Huntress* took her place as a dispatch-boat in the harbor. Being very fast, the Confederate government changed her name to the C. S. steamer *Tropic,* and made her a blockade-runner. After successfully eluding and passing through the blockade ships of the enemy off Charleston, the *Huntress*, with a cargo of cotton belonging to the Confederate government, was burned at sea by accident.

The *Everglade*, or *Savannah*, to which Lieut. Hall was ordered from the *Huntress*, was a small side-wheel steamer, purchased by the State of Georgia for $34,000. She was changed into a gunboat, for the purpose of cruising as a coast-guard at the mouth of the Savannah River. Her officers, as first appointed, were as follows : Commander, J. McIntosh Kell; Midshipmen, R. F. Armstrong, S. N. Hooper, J. A. Merriweather; Chief Engineer, Joshua Smith; Assistant Engineer, Norval Meeker; Clerk, William J. Bennett. The *Everglade* had her name changed to the *Savannah*. At the attack on Port Royal by the Union forces she figured as the flag-ship of Commodore Tatnall.

The steamer *Nina*, mounting one gun, was used along the coast of South Carolina as a gunboat. The brig *Bonita*, built in New York in 1853, was 276 tons burden, and a fast sailer. She was formerly engaged in the slave trade, but was captured on the coast of Africa, taken to Charleston, and afterwards to Savannah, where she was seized by order of Gov. Brown and converted into a privateer. The *Lewis Cass* was a clipper-built topsail schooner, of 100 tons burden, and was in the U. S. revenue service when she was seized at Savannah. She was converted into a privateer, armed with one long sixty-eight-pounder taken from the Pensacola navy-yard. Her crew numbered forty men and officers.

The privateer schooner *Judith* was of 250 tons, and carried four broadside guns and one pivot gun amidships. She was destroyed at the Pensacola navy-yard by the Union forces, who boarded her, spiked her guns, and then fired her.

On the 4th of May, the Georgia privateer schooner *Five Brothers*, Capt. Wm. Barquedo, with a crew of eighteen men, in Cumberland Sound, seized the brig *Elisha Doane*, of Boston, loaded with lumber. The *Doane* was detained by a prize-crew for eight days, and then released by order of Gov. Brown.

Soon after the secession of Louisiana, Capt. Lawrence Rosseau, a true son of that State, who had entered the U. S. navy on the 16th of January, 1809, and who had been in its service for many years, resigned his commission and accepted rank under his native State. Gov. Moore appointed him commander of the Louisiana navy, with headquarters at New Orleans. When the delegates at Montgomery formed a Provisional Government, Captain Rosseau was one of the first to report for duty under the new Confederacy. In February, Capts. Rosseau, Ingraham and Randolph, with other naval officers, were before the Naval Committee at the Confederate capital, and assisted in devising means for the establishment of a navy. Soon after the organization of the Navy Department,

Capt. Rosseau was ordered to New Orleans, where he aided in sending out a number of privateers to cruise against the commerce of the enemy, and had the high honor of equipping and sending to sea the first Confederate man-of-war—the *Sumter*. Early in March, 1861, he was ordered to purchase for the Confederate Government the steamship *Habana*, afterwards named the *Sumter*, in honor of the victory over Fort Sumter, and fit her out as a cruiser. On the 26th of the same month he entered the naval service of the Confederate States.

Immediately upon the receipt of the news in New Orleans that President Davis had invited privateers to prey upon the enemy's commerce, several stock companies were organized and several hundred thousand dollars were subscribed in a few hours for the purpose of fitting out vessels. About the 14th of May, the privateer steamer *Calhoun*, of 1,058 tons burden, under the command of Capt. J. Wilson, with a crew of 100 men and several pieces of cannon, hastened out of New Orleans to the Balize on her cruise in the Gulf. She soon captured the bark *Ocean Eagle*, from Portland, Me., with a cargo of 3,147 casks of lime, valued at $24,000. Having put a prize-crew on board, and towing the vessel into the Mississippi, the *Calhoun* resumed her voyage. The *Calhoun* also captured the ship *Milan*, with 1,500 bags of salt, valued at $20,000, and the schooner *Ella*, from Tampico, with a cargo of fruit, valued at $5,000.

The *Calhoun* was afterwards engaged in blockade-running, and while on her way from Havana to New Orleans with a large and valuable cargo of military stores, valued at $300,000, was chased by a Federal cruiser and abandoned. Capt. Wilson, who commanded the *Calhoun*, was formerly the captain of the brig *Minnie Schiffer*, the vessel that rescued the passengers of the ill-fated steamer *Connaught*.

The steamer *Wm. H. Webb*, immediately upon the breaking out of the war, was converted into a gunboat and privateer. She steamed out of New Orleans in May, and on the 24th captured, about ninety miles from the Passes, three Massachusetts whalers, the brig *Panama*, and schooners *John Adams* and *Mermaid*. The prizes reached New Orleans on the 27th, and had on board 215 barrels of whale and sperm oil.

The privateer steamer *V. H. Ivey*, of about 200 tons, armed with two thirty-two pound rifled guns, in May steamed out of New Orleans and captured the ship *Marathon*, from Marseilles, in ballast, valued at $35,000; ship *Albino*, from Boston, with a cargo of ice, valued at $25,000.

The privateer steamer *Music* captured during the same time a splendid new ship—the *Marshall*, from Havre, in ballast, valued at $50,000, and the ship *John H. Jarvis*, from Liverpool, in ballast, valued at $20,000. The schooner *Vigilante*, with a cargo of provisions, was captured on July 21st, in Jourdan River, by Lieuts. J. V. Toulone and J. Colly, with a detachment of the Shieldsboro' Rifles. All of these vessels were condemned and sold in New Orleans by C. B. Beverly, the Confederate States Marshal.[1]

On April 18th, 1863, Congress passed "an act to establish a volunteer navy" According to the provisions of this act, any person or persons who produced to President Davis satisfactory evidence as to character, competency and means, were to be, under certain regulations, commissioned by the Confederate government, as regular officers of the volunteer navy, to procure and fit out vessels of over 100 tons burden for cruising against the enemy. Such officers were to be "worthy to command," and such vessels were to be "fit for the service," and they were to be "received into the volunteer navy," "to serve during the war," and " subject to all the laws, rules and regulations of the regular navy, except as otherwise provided for." The grades of rank were fixed in the act from commander down, and pay was provided, which, however, was small, the compensation being prizes (ninety per cent. of which went to the captors, and ten per cent. to the wounded and widows and orphans of those slain), and a bonus of twenty-five per cent. for every armed vessel, or military and naval transport of the enemy, burnt, sunk or destroyed, and twenty-five dollars for every prisoner captured and brought in from such vessels.

The passage of this act, it was thought, would add considerably to the navy of the Confederacy, that was doing so much on the high seas for the South. Immediately after the passage of the Act of Congress, "the Virginia Volunteer Navy Company" was organized, and over a million and a half dollars was subscribed for stock. The subscribers were men of capital and influence, who saw in the measure a means of most seriously damaging the enemy, as well as handsomely rewarding those who embarked in it.

The company was chartered by the Legislature of Virginia on October 13th, 1863, with the following incorporators:

---

[1] The New York *Herald* of June 2d, 1861, says: " On the 26th of last month there were under seizure, or as prizes in the port of New Orleans, the following vessels :

SHIPS.

Name.	Master.	Hail From
Abællino	Smith	Boston.
Ariel	Delano	Bath, Me.
American Union.	Lincoln	Bath, Me.
C. A. Farwell	Farwell	Rockland.
Express	Frost	Portsmouth, N.H.
Enoch Train (probably)	Burwell	Boston.
J. H. Jarvis..	Rich	Boston.
Marathon	Tyler	New York.
Marshall	Sprague	Providence.
Milian	Eustis	Bath, Me.
Robert Harding.	Ingraham	Portland.
State of Maine..	Humphrey..	Portland.
Toulon	Upshur	New York.
Wilbur Fisk (probably)	Pousland	Boston.

BARKS.

Name.	Master.	Hail From
Chester	Bearse	Boston.
Ocean Eagle	Luce	Thomaston.

SCHOONERS.

E. S. Janes	Townsend..	——
Henry Travers	Wyatt	Baltimore.
Ella	Howes	Philadelphia.

" Of the above vessels some doubt attaches to the seizure of the *Enoch Train* and *Wilbur Fisk*, but the probabilities are that they have been confiscated. The seizures made by the Confederates up to the last accounts may be thus enumerated :

Off the different ports	12
In port	30
Steamers captured on the Mississippi	15
Total	57

Samuel J. Harrison, Baker and Baskerville, Dunlap, Moncure
& Co., Joseph R. Anderson & Co., J. L. Apperson, R. H.
Maury & Co., W. F. Watson, J. P. George, John Robin Mc-
Daniel, R. M. Crenshaw, Thomas Branch, D. B. Dugger,
Thomas R. Price & Co., Matthew Bridges, William B. Jones
& Co., William B. Isaacs, Bolling W. Haxall, and such other
persons as were then or afterward associated with them. The
capital of the company was not to be less than $1,000,000, nor
more than $10,000,000. The officers were Samuel J. Harrison,
President; Robert Archer, J. L. Apperson, Thomas W. Mc-
Cance and J. R. McDaniel, Directors.

Owing to the unfavorable turn of affairs in the South and
the blockade of Southern ports, the company did not embark
in privateering.

"The Old Dominion Trading Company" of the city of
Richmond, which was chartered by the Legislature of Virginia
on October 3d, 1863, with a capital of not less than $100,000,
and not to exceed $2,000,000, in shares of $500 each, did a considerable business in blockade-running. The incorporators
were: A. Morris, P. C. Williams, Wm. G. Payne, D. O. Hufford
and E. D. Keeling.

The privateers of the Confederacy carried on their destruction of U. S. commerce for many months with considerable immunity. There was no limit to their boldness or scope
to their operations. By August 1, 1861, three privateer steamers were reported in latitude 7 deg. 47 min. North, longitude
22 deg. 48 min. West. The British mail-steamer *Tyne*, on
August 17th, reported seeing a privateer steamer between Rio
Janeiro and Pernambuco. A letter from the Island of St.
Thomas, dated Aug. 5th, said that several privateers had been
seen in the neighborhood, and two of them, well armed and
equipped, refitted and provisioned at St. John's, in the island
of Porto Rico. The Liverpool underwriters, as early as June,
had permitted the pith of President Davis' rules for privateers to be posted in their rooms, and an American ship—the
first—on May 23d, hoisted the Confederate flag in the Prince's
dock. The operations of the privateers upon commerce put
up insurance premiums so high upon all freights taken in
American vessels as to cause many U. S. merchants to turn
their vessels over to English owners, who sailed them under
the English flag.

Notwithstanding all the naval preparations made by the
U. S. government from the beginning of the war to August,
1861, only two small privateers had been captured or destroyed,
the *Savannah* and the *Petrel;* only two of their prizes had
been retaken by government vessels, and two by the crews.
The little privateers, on the other hand, had captured within
the same length of time nearly sixty Federal vessels. How
many had been captured of which we have no account, it is
impossible to say. Several privateers, whose names are now

CAPTAIN CHARLES M. MORRIS, C. S. N.,

COMMANDER OF THE "FLORIDA."

COMMANDER MATTHEW F. MAURY,

CONFEDERATE STATES NAVY.

unknown, and of which we have no record, were undoubtedly afloat along the coast or in mid-ocean, or near the shores of countries where the American foreign trade was chiefly carried on.   Many prizes, no doubt, were burnt or sunk, as in the case of some of those taken in the early part of the war by the *Sumter;* and it is doubtful if we shall ever hear of them. " We are satisfied," says the New York *Herald* of Aug. 10th, 1861, " that already $20,000,000 worth of property has been lost in various ways through the operations of these highwaymen of the seas, increasing daily in numbers, and becoming more and more daring from impunity.   The worst effect, is not the loss of the vessels and their cargoes, but the destruction of our trade.   Our commerce with the West Indies was immense before the pirates commenced their depredations. Now no Northern vessel will get a charter or can be insured for any reasonable premium.   English bottoms are taking all our trade.   When the *Great Eastern* was here, she could have been filled with cargo, if her draft of water were not so great. Thus our shipping interest is literally ruined."

CHAPTER V.

VIRGINIA WATERS.

THE secession of Virginia from the Union, following immediately after the assault upon Sumter, dispelled all hope at Washington that Virginia would not ally herself with the Confederate States. It was accepted, and possibly intended, as a virtual declaration that, in any collision between the Federal and Confederate forces, Virginia would arraign herself on the side of the latter. It was regarded at Washington as a hostile act, and the waters of the State as having been opened to invasion whenever the government should deem it proper to send a force to occupy the rivers, bays and harbors of the State. In the same light it was accepted at Richmond, and Gen. Lee, in reporting to Governor Letcher, June 15th, 1861, the state of military and naval preparations to that date, says:

"Arrangements were first made for the establishment of batteries to prevent the ascent of our rivers by hostile vessels. As soon as an examination was made for the selection of sites, their construction was begun, and their armament and defence committed to the Virginia navy."

Among the very first of those arrangements, Gen. Lee dispatched Capt. Wm. F. Lynch of the State navy to examine the defensible points on the Potomac, and to take measures for the establishment of batteries to prevent the vessels of the enemy from navigating that river. In the discharge of that duty, sites for batteries along that river were immediately selected, and arrangements made for their speedy erection. But the entire command of the river being in the possession of the U. S. government, a larger force was required for the protection of the batteries than could be spared at that early day from the field of active operations.

Alexandria, Va., the practical head of navigation so far as Virginia was concerned, was occupied immediately by a small force of State troops under Lieut. Col. A. S Taylor, but their exposed position was soon found to be untenable, and the city was evacuated on May 5th, 1861, Col. Taylor's force falling back eight miles to Springfield, on the Orange & Alexandria Railroad. That force consisted of only two companies of raw recruits, numbering 150 privates, armed with flint muskets of 1818, without cartridges; the Mt. Vernon Guard, 86 privates, armed with new muskets, 52 men without accoutrements, and 15 without arms, and all with very little ammunition. [1] Such a force was useless for defence, and only provocative of attack. The retention of the command and navigation of the Potomac was even more indispensable to the Federal authorities for the maintenance of their capital than to the Confederates for defence, and, therefore, the *Pawnee*, Commander S. C. Rowan, carrying a battery of fifteen guns, was put in commission as soon as Virginia seceded, and under the protection of her guns the first Zouave regiment of New York Volunteers, under Col. Ellsworth, occupied Alexandria on May 24th. The removal of the flag from the staff on the Marshall House was avenged by Mr. Jackson, the owner, who sacrificed his life in taking that of Col. Ellsworth. Among all the acts of personal bravery during the war, not one exceeds in heroism that total indifference to personal safety which inspired the noble Jackson to brave in his single person a whole regiment of the enemy. The uselessness of the act may detract from its wisdom, but cannot lessen its heroism. The authorities at Washington had on April 23d the U. S. steamers *Anacostia* and *Pocahontas*, the latter a vessel of some 1,800 tons, at the navy-yard, to keep the navigation of the Potomac open.

On April 24th, Major Thos. H. Williamson of the Engineers, and Lieut. H. H. Lewis of the Virginia navy, by order of Gen. Ruggles, examined together the ground at Aquia Creek, and selected Split Rock Bluff as the best point for a battery, as the channel there could be commanded from that point by guns of sufficient calibre. Cream Point, on the other side of the creek, was not defensible with the small force then under Gen. Ruggles, and hence was not fortified. [2] The Aquia Creek landing and the protection of the steamer *George Page*, which had been seized, were regarded as of secondary importance, except in the moral influence upon the neighborhood. The position at Aquia was difficult to defend, since it was easily turned by way of Potomac Creek, and exposed to disaster from an attack in the rear. But it would serve the purpose of drawing the attention of the enemy from Freestone and Mathias Points, which would control the navigation of the river, and which, when occupied, would render the battery at Aquia Creek of little importance. [3] To this end, Capt. Wm. F. Lynch, Commander Robert D. Thorburn and Lieuts. H. H. Lewis and John Wilkinson, of the State navy, erected at Aquia a battery of thirteen guns, about May 14th, to protect the terminus of the

[1] *Official Records*, Series 1, Vol. II, p. 27.—Report of Col. Taylor.

[2] Report of Major Williamson and Lieut. Lewis,

April 24th, 1861, *Off. Rec.*, Series 1, Vol. II., p. 779.

[3] Report of Gen. Ruggles, May 6th, *Off. Rec.*, Vol. II, p. 810.

railroad to Richmond. While serving to protect the railroad, that battery was also a threat to close the navigation of the Potomac, and was so considered at Washington. U. S. naval authorities immediately organized the Potomac flotilla, consisting of the *Freeborn*, carrying three guns, the *Anacostia*, of two guns, and the *Resolute*, of two guns; the whole commanded by Commander James H. Ward. The Aquia Creek battery was commanded by Capt. Wm. F. Lynch and other officers of the Virginia but afterwards of the Confederate navy.

On April 29th, Lieuts. Wm. L. Maury and Wm. Taylor Smith, of the State navy, having ascertained reliably the number of Federal troops in Washington City to be very largely in excess of that holding the Confederate lines on the Potomac, advised Gen. Ruggles against erecting a battery above Aquia Creek, and that the two eight-inch guns, ammunition, etc., then in Alexandria, be removed to some point of greater security; which was immediately done, and not too soon, as the enemy occupied Alexandria on May 24th. Capt. Lynch, on May 6th, diverted the guns, first intended for Mathias Point, to Aquia Creek, to protect the approaches to Fredericksburg from the Potomac, and the guns were placed in position by Commander Thorburn, and the necessary preparation of defence actively undertaken and completed within forty-eight hours. The difficulty of enrolling men for any naval service, even in shore batteries, by naval officers, was experienced at that early day, and for that reason Gen. Ruggles was compelled to man the batteries with companies of volunteers, as well as to detail infantry to work in erecting the batteries for the heavy guns.

On May 31st and June 1st, 1861, the first battle of the war between the navy of the United States and batteries of the Confederate States was fought. On the first day, the U. S. steamers opened their fire on the battery, and fired fourteen shot and shell, slightly wounding one man in the hand, but doing no other damage, and not by any means justifying the remark of Admiral Porter that, "the batteries were silenced altogether in two hours, and the secessionists driven to their earthworks on hills overlooking the landing." Nothing of that kind occurred. On June 1st, about 10 A. M., the U. S. Potomac flotilla renewed their attack upon the battery, and after throwing 397 shot and shell retired, having hurt no one in the battery and doing no injury to the works. [1]

The report of Capt. W. F. Lynch, then of the Virginia navy, dated June 2d, 1861, to Capt. Samuel Barron, Virginia navy, in charge of Naval Detail and Equipment, shows that·

"On Friday, at 10:30 P. M., two out of three steamers abreast of the battery opened fire upon us, and continued the cannonade for three hours, when they withdrew. The largest steamer very much resembled the *Crusader*. As they kept at long shot, mostly beyond our range, I economized ammunition, and only fired fifty-six times. One of the steamers had a rifled

[1] *Official Records*, Report of Gen. Ruggles, 1st Series, Vol. II., pp. 55 and 57.

gun, the shell from which penetrated through the sand bank, and one of them exploded in and completely demolished the room occupied by the officers and myself. Upon our part no one was injured; but lookers-on from the hills and opposite shores state that the enemy was repeatedly struck.

"Yesterday, the steamers which had laid off during the night were reinforced by the *Pawnee*, and at 11:30 A. M. they commenced a brisk cannonade, which continued with little interruption until about 4:30 P.M., during which the *Pawnee* fired 392 shot and shell, and the other steamer 207, the greater portion of the latter being rifled shells.

"Our sand banks not being *en barbette*, we could only fire as the enemy came within range through the embrasures. This, added to the long distance at which he kept, and the necessity of occasionally repairing damages to the breastwork, combined with my desire to save ammunition, constrained me to withhold fire, except when something like a fair shot presented. The houses in the rear were very much knocked about, and the railroad track torn up in three or four places; but, thanks to a kind Providence, who seems to smile benignly on our cause, no one with us was injured.

"As the enemy had on Friday made the buildings at the extremity of the wharf his line of sight upon the battery, I had all the furniture, etc., together with the weather-boarding, conveyed to the rear of the battery, and in the course of the forenoon set fire to and blew up the platform and outer end of the bridge.

"I have spoken of Commander Thorburn's zeal in the first engagement, and cannot too highiy applaud the spirit and alacrity, tempered by deference to orders, of Commander Cooke and Lieut. Trobel. With the exception of Gunner's Mate Cunningham and Master's Mate Larmour, whose services were of inestimable value, our guns' crews consisted of only volunteer militia, who stood their ground bravely.

"We had yesterday, in addition to our guns, a small rifled one from Capt. Walker's battery, under the immediate command of Lieut. Robertson, of Tennessee, which rendered efficient service.

"In connection with the transportation of the Columbiads to the summit of a lofty hill, I cannot speak in too highly commendable terms of the zeal and untiring energy of Lieut. Chas. C. Simms."

The result, or rather want of result, of the cannonade of the earth battery at Aquia Creek by the Federal gunboats, attracted the immediate attention of Gen. Lee, and on June 10th he wrote to Gen. Holmes, commander at Fredericksburg:

"It is probable, that realizing the inutility of cannonading the batteries at Aquia Creek with smooth-bore guns, the naval force of the United States will hereafter employ rifled cannon of large calibre at long range. It is therefore advisable that the batteries should be rendered as secure as possible by the application of some such means as were so successfully employed at Charleston. Railroad iron, laid at an angle of about forty-five degrees with the horizon, on the exterior slope, the upper ends projecting above the exterior crest, would probably answer the purpose."

In that first battle, the accurate firing of the battery under Capt. Lynch, C. S. navy, was attested by the damage done to the flotilla—the *Freeborn* being obliged to return to Washington for repairs. The U. S. Potomac flotilla had been increased by the *Pawnee*, Commander Rowan, and, though a number of the shots from the battery struck the hulls of the

vessels, there was no irreparable damage. [1] The Federal newspaper accounts of this "opening of the ball" were extravagant
in expression, and far beyond the facts of the fight; "the observer, through a telescope," who "saw a number of the bodies
of them carried away in wagons," was himself carried away
in imagination. One finger was the total loss sustained in
the battery. Nor was the official report of Commander Ward,
May 31st, 1862, more accurate in his conjectures of damage
inflicted by the battery of his flotilla, while his commendation of the working of the gun-carriage of his own invention
was not wholly without a business look. The report of Commander Ward, of June 1st, is not without its testimony in behalf
of Capt. Lynch and the other Confederate naval officers who
commanded the Aquia Creek batteries. He reported that:

"Several shots came on board of us, causing the vessel to leak badly,
and, besides other injuries, clipping the port wheel, the wrought-iron
shaft being gouged by a shot which would have shattered it if of cast
iron. * * * I proceeded to Washington to repair damages and refill
my exhausted magazine. The *Pawnee* remains meantime below to supply
my place in the blockade. Capt. Rowan of that ship joined me last night,
replenishing my exhausted stores, and most gallantly opened fire this
morning, having followed my lead in shore towards the batteries. His
ship received numerous wounds, both below and aloft, inflicted by the
enemy's shot. On account of her size, she being more easily hit, she appeared to be their favorite mark, and was herself often a sheet of flame,
owing to the rapidity of her repeated charges."

Major Thomas H. Williamson, Chief Engineer of the State
of Virginia, as early as May 4th recommended the establishment of a battery at Mathias Point, on the Potomac, where a
bluff-headland, twenty feet above the water, commanded the
channel at a distance of about three-quarters of a mile,
for more than a mile of sailing. Capt. Lynch, C. S. navy,
was also consulted, and, upon the recommendation of these
officers, a battery of ten heavy guns was constructed. But,
before the battery was commenced, a small party of the enemy,
on June 24th, landed at Mathias Point, and burned the house
of Dr. Howe; and two days after, on June 26th, Commander
Ward, of the U. S. Potomac flotilla, dispatched Lieut. Chaplin
with a party from the *Resolute*, protected by the *Reliance*, and
provided with implements for holding the Point and erecting
a battery. About 1 P. M. the Confederate pickets reported that
the enemy had landed, and that, under the heavy fire of shell
and shot from the enemy's steamers, they had been compelled
to retire. A vigorous attack was immediately made by the
Confederate troops under Col. R. M. Mayo, and the enemy
were driven to their boats and vessels, having sustained very
heavy loss. Capt. Ward, commander of the Potomac flotilla,
was killed and many wounded. Col. Mayo reported the "absolute necessity" for a battery of heavy artillery at the Point,

1 *Porter's Hist.*, p. 41.

and the battery was erected, which, in conjunction with that erected soon afterwards at Evansport, completed the blockade of the Potomac.

In August the Confederate authorities determined to erect the batteries at Evansport, near the mouth of Quantico Creek, which had been recommended by Capt. Lynch on June 4th. Brig. Gen. French, with a portion of the command of Gen. Holmes, was ordered to erect the batteries under the direction of Commander Frederick Chatard of the C. S. navy, assisted by Commander H. J. Hartstene and Lieut. Charles W. Read, all of the navy. The place selected for their erection was admirably suited for offence and defence. The construction of the batteries was an exceedingly difficult undertaking, and had to be carried on with the greatest secrecy and caution, for the river was most rigidly patroled by the Federal gunboats night and day, while larger vessels and transports were passing up and down at all hours. It seemed almost impossible under such circumstances that four powerful batteries, mounting in all about twenty heavy guns, could be constructed without interruption at the very river's edge ; yet it was accomplished. A stinted growth of pines skirting the edge of the Potomac Bluff formed the screen behind which the work was performed. Two of the batteries were nearly completed and fully manned when discovered on the morning of October 15th, 1861. Their armament consisted of nine-inch Dahlgrens, forty-two-pounder navy guns, two rifled thirty-two-pounders, and an Armstrong gun, which carried a ball of 135 pounds' weight. It was received from England by way of Bermuda, and brought in by the blockaders. The Potomac there being but a mile and a half wide, with a channel close to the Virginia shore, was completely commanded by the guns of the Confederate batteries. Before the batteries were established the bosom of the broad river was whitened with the sails of transport fleets, and its waves were plowed by rapid war steamers continually passing between Washington and the sea. After the establishment of the batteries nothing was to be seen but the dark and swelling river, and occasionally a small schooner stealing furtively along the Maryland shore. On these insignificant crafts our gunners did not care to waste their ammunition. Sometimes, in the darkness of night, a steamer managed to slip past; but for all practical purposes the river was closed against the enemy.

The first shot that notified Capt. Chatard that his batteries were discovered came from the sloop-of-war *Pocahontas* as she was passing down the river. The garrisons had been in the fortifications but a few days, and the troops in Battery No. 2, at Freestone Point, preparatory to unmasking their position, had been ordered to cut the small pines in front of them on one side, so that each one of them afterward could be easily leveled by a single blow of an axe. A storm of wind coming on at night blew some of the pines down, so that when the *Pocahontas* came by early in the morning the battery and the men at work were discovered through the openings. She promptly notified the Confederates of the discovery by a shell which struck the battery square in the centre of the rampart, pushing its way clean through to the woodwork inside, but injured no one. The *Pocahontas* fired but the single shot and passed on. About a mile astern, and following in her wake, the *Seminole* was steaming majestically down the river. Orders were instantly given in the battery to prepare for action. All concealment was now thrown off. A party of men with axes soon leveled the thin green pines in front, and the details, hurriedly told off, sprang with alacrity to the guns, which were quickly loaded with shot and shell. Promptly they opened on her, shot after shot followed in quick succession, and the *Seminole*, without hastening her speed, gallantly replied to every shot, and poured her broadsides into the batteries in quick succession.

A letter from the U. S. steam-sloop *Seminole*, published in the Philadelphia *Bulletin*, and dated Oct. 16th, shows the accuracy of firing attained by the batteries under the instruction and drill of the Confederate naval officers. The *Seminole* was going from Washington to Old Point, and passing Evansport batteries encountered their fire:

"They sent us at least thirty rifled balls and shells, all splendidly aimed, their guns being evidently well manned. Some of their shot and shell went over us, about eight or nine feet clear of the deck, and only a few feet above my head. These fell or burst from twenty to forty rods beyond on our port side. Some burst just outside, before reaching us, and some just over our heads. Fragments of shell flew about the deck, and splinters in thousands.

"*We were struck eleven times.* One ball cut away the main stays, scattering bits of iron chain down on the deck. One shot cut through and shivered the mizzen mast. Several banged clear through the ship, in at one side and out at the other. One rifled ball came through in that way, struck and carried away the brass hand-rail guard around the engine hatch, and went out through the opposite side of the ship. This ball went within five feet of me, and sent a piece of brass, bent double like a boomerang, whizzing over my head. How the balls do hiss, and the shells sing aloud—a perfectly distinct, fascinating, locust-like song ; but growing louder and faster as they come nearer, plunging, hissing and bursting through the air ! * * *

"The fight was a severe one, and without knowing what the other side suffered, I do know that the *Seminole* suffered severely."

Early on the morning following the firing on the *Seminole*, the *Pawnee*, in passing the batteries, received seven shots. One of them, a thirty-two-pounder, struck amidships, about eighteen inches above the water-line. A second took effect on the starboard quarter, passing through the dingy, and made its appearance in the ward-room, but was prevented from entering by striking on the plank shear. A third struck the bluff of the starboard bow, while a fourth struck the vessel in the waist, passing from one side through to the other, cutting a hammock in two in its course. The splinters flew around in all directions, but she was not seriously damaged, and nobody was hit.

It was supposed that the Confederates were making arrangements for some offensive demonstration from the vicinity of Aquia Creek for crossing into Maryland, and shortly after the batteries were unmasked a division of troops was detached from the Army of the Potomac and sent to southern Maryland, and General Hooker given the command. The line stretched along the river from Port Tobacco, opposite Aquia Creek, to within about twenty miles of Washington. The troops were encamped well back from the river, but the bank was closely picketed by batteries and sentries day and night.

Before the arrival of Hooker's troops, a small steamer—the *George Page*—which the Confederates had captured during the early part of their occupation, and which had been armed and newly christened the C. S. steamer *City of Richmond*, ran out of Aquia Creek late in October during a storm, under the darkness and fog, and came up the river anchored inside of Quantico Creek. On October 24th she came out in the Potomac and crossed over to the Maryland side and shelled the camp of Gen. Sickles' Excelsior brigade. necessitating the changing of their position to a more distant location and out of the reach of the *Page's* guns. The *Page* gave great annoyance to the enemy and kept up the apprehension of a Confederate landing in Maryland. Capt. Parks, of the U. S. tug *Murray*, reported in Washington, October 23d, that the steamer was seen crossing to Maryland at Budd's Ferry between Evansport and Shipping Point, that she was protected by the Confederate batteries "which have recently thrown balls from their rifled guns across the river (which was a mile and a half wide), and to a distance of two miles into Maryland." At the time the *George Page* was playing about the river, under the protection of the Confederate batteries, a Northern correspondent said :

" The United States squadron off Indian Head consists of the following vessels: *Yankee* (flagship), Commander Craven; *Pocahontas*. Commander Wyman; *Seminole*, Commander Gillis ; *Penguin*, Commander ———; *Union*, Lieut. Com. Harrell; *Valley City*, Lieut. Commanding Chaplin ; *Jacob Bell*, Lieut. Commanding McCrea ; *Island Bell*, Master Commanding Harris; *Rescue*, ———, commanding; *Herbert*, ———; *Murray*, Midshipman Commanding McGlensey ; *Reliance*, Master Commanding Hannum ; *Resolute*, Master Commanding Foster, and *Satellite*. Thus our squadron consists of various descriptions of vessels, from the smart and powerful sloop-of-war *Pocahontas* to those tiny twin sisters, *Resolute* and *Reliance*, each mounting one brass twenty-four, and are probably the smallest men-of-war in the world. Beside these there are six large launches, each armed with either a twenty-four howitzer, or a rifled cannon of the same calibre. In naming the foregoing vessels, I have by no means exhausted the catalogue. There are a number of gunboats further down the river guarding the entrance to Aquia Creek, and keeping a sharp look-out on Mathias Point and other suspicious places. Among these is the *Freeborn*, which, under the command of the late gallant Commander Ward, was of so much service in keeping the navigation of the river clear during the earlier period of the present struggle."

And the New York *Herald*, October 25th, taunted the Navy Department at Washington with insufficiency because,

"In the interval, on the Lower Potomac River, between the principal batteries of the rebels, the rebel steamer *George Page*, poking her nose out of Aquia Creek, has suddenly made her appearance, and has been complimenting the Sickles brigade on the Maryland shore with a few specimen shells. Next we shall probably hear of another mosquito fleet, and of the capture of some of our river transports, unless we put an end, and that very soon, to this rebel blockade of the Potomac. Rome, we know, was not built in a day; but these rebel batteries, built in a night, ought not to require more than one day's work to silence them. But let us wait with patience, for good news, we think, is close at hand."

On November 14th, Gen. Hooker, in reporting the burning of a schooner off Mattawoman Creek by a party of rebels from Cockpit Point, says that "it was executed with an air of true heroism"; and later, November 27th, the newspapers said:

"Last night, the *Harriet Lane*, and the other vessels of the flotilla off Indian Head, had their cables ready for slipping at a moment's notice, had the rebel steamer *George Page* made her appearance out of Quantico Creek, but as she did not quit her retreat she gained another lease of existence. *Apropos* of the *Page*, Dr. Russell's remarks in the London *Times* about her and her supposed achievements and capabilities are pure invention. She has never landed any troops in Maryland; only one attempt was made to do so, on the day she came out of Aquia Creek, but the sight of a single Union soldier caused her to turn back and run into Quantico Creek, whence she never dared to stir till Friday night, when she attempted to capture the store-ship *Wyandunk*, but the opportune appearance of the *Hale*, with her formidable batteries, once more drove her back like a rat to its hole. The rebels are capricious in their attentions to passing vessels. Sometimes they will let several pass without a shot, but open fire on the last. It would appear from this, that when they open on an unarmed vessel it is merely for target practice. Last night and to-day several schooners passed unmolested. Perhaps they are short of ammunition."

On the morning of January 2d, 1862, an experiment was tried by the enemy to reduce the Confederate battery at Cockpit Point. The correspondent of the New York *Herald*, on board the U. S. steamer *Stepping Stones*, said:

"At ten o'clock the *Anacostia* approached the battery, and took up a position somewhat above and opposite the Mattawoman Creek. She threw in a number of shells, several of which were seen to explode in the rebel battery. The *Yankee* then got underway and stood for the battery, ranging herself right opposite. She commenced by firing two shells from her bow gun, a sixty-four-pounder, and afterwards continued to pour in her fire on the enemy from her after guns, consisting of a thirty-two-pounder and twenty-four brass howitzer, and a twelve-pounder brass rifled cannon. The enemy replied to the *Yankee*, for the *Anacostia* was so placed that the batteries could not hit her, throwing four shots, the second of which struck the *Yankee*, entering the forecastle on the port side, her head being up the river, and knocking away a knee entirely; passing to the starboard side, the shot smashed another knee and dropped on the floor, its force being spent. The shot was from a rifled gun, and weighs eighty pounds."

Of these almost daily occurrences no official reports from either side are to be obtained, and all information must be gathered from the contemporaneous accounts in the newspapers of the day, which, notwithstanding the tone of exaggeration and the bitterness of feeling, then quite natural, are yet reasonably accurate and to be relied on for information of many gallant actions which illustrate American character, and which would have been lost to history but for the zealous and indefatigable newspaper correspondent. Their letters, particularly those in the Federal papers, often contain the only accounts that have survived those events, which, unimportant to the general conduct of the war, were nevertheless of great value in training the soldier and the sailor.

The efficiency of the Potomac batteries, though not enough to close the river, was, under the management of Capt. Frederick Chatard of the C. S. navy, such as to compel the U. S. steamer *Pensacola* to creep by at night under cover of darkness, and signalled by lights from the *Resolute*, *Freeborn, Yankee, Reliance*, the *Wyandunk* and the *Stepping Stones*.[1] The *George Page*, from her lair on Quantico Creek, gave great annoyance to the navigation of the river, compelling the convoy of the *Reliance* or the *Wyandunk* to every little schooner or oyster-boat. From May, 1861, to March, 1862, the N. Y. *Tribune*, of March 1st, said:

"There has been no safe communication by water between this city and the capital of the nation during all this time—a period of six months. This is one of the most humiliating of all the national digraces to which we have been compelled to submit. It has been most damaging to us in the eyes of the world. No one circumstance has been used more to our disadvantage with foreign nations than this. And it has helped the Confederates just in proportion as it has injured us. It has been their haughty boast that they had maintained steady and effectual sway over the great channel of commerce between this city and Washington, through which the immense supplies of our grand army of the Potomac would naturally have passed. Our own government has been subjected to very heavy expense, and great inconvenience, in consequence of this blockade. The inhabitants of Washington have at times suffered from a scarcity of both food and fuel from the same cause. If occasionally some vessel has got past the enemy's guns, it has been under the cover of darkness, or at a considerable risk, in the same way that our blockade of the Southern coast is often run by the Confederates.

"Has all this damage and disgrace been a matter of necessity to us? or could it by a different policy, by energy and capacity, have been avoided? Let facts answer: In the month of July last Mr. Marshall O. Roberts, of this city, offered to keep the Potomac River open, and free from all obstruction by the enemy's guns, for the period of twelve months, at his own expense; if he succeeded, the government to pay him whatever

[1] N. Y. *Herald*, Jan. 12th, 1862.

they thought proper; if he did not, he would charge nothing. He was in Washington at that time, with one of his ships, fully prepared to carry his offer into immediate execution. The proposition was made to a leading member of the Cabinet, who at once reported it to President Lincoln, and subsequently informed Mr. Roberts that it was accepted with great satisfaction and pleasure—as any man in his senses would suppose it must have been. But it seems that the matter was subsequently referred to the Secretary of the Navy, and he rejected the proffered service. The malicious may say he did so because he could not see any way for his brother-in-law, Mr. George D. Morgan, to make anything out of it in the shape of fat commissions or otherwise. We are sure that such conclusions as this would do Mr. Welles great injustice. His errors are all of judgment, not of intention. But, whatever the reason, the Potomac has remained blockaded, to the infinite injury and disgrace of our government."

The Chicago *Times* describes the effect of this blockade of the *Potomac* as most seriously felt:

"Washington is now beginning to feel some of the evils of the beleaguered city. With its principal avenue closed by hostile batteries, and in the hands of its enemies, it is dependent on the single-track rail road from Baltimore here for every article of daily consumption. This would be no inconvenience at all in ordinary times, when the National Capital is only a mere village of 20,000 inhabitants. But now, when its ordinary population is augmented by an army of 200,000 men and 40,000 horses, it is a very different matter. The railroad is taxed beyond its utmost capacity. Yet, in spite of all, the supplies that arrive are not equal to the demand. In regard to provender for the horses, it has become so scarce that the whole country for many miles around has been scoured for forage with very indifferent success."

And the Cincinnati *Commercial* said:

"The severe inconveniences suffered from the blockade of the Potomac affect already nearly every person in the community, and unless relief can be had in some way, it must soon ripen into actual distress. Fuel and wood are the chief necessaries of life in the winter season. The supply of both is wholly exotic as regards Washington."

It was not only the inconvenience which these batteries gave, but they were of so much military importance that Mr. Lincoln, in General Orders No. 3, March 8th, 1862, ordered: "That no more than two army corps (about fifty thousand troops), of the said Army of the Potomac, shall be moved *en route* for a new base of operations until the navigation of the Potomac from Washington to the Chesapeake Bay shall be freed from enemy's batteries and other obstructions."

The Annual Report of Secretary Welles, December 1st, 1862, says: "The active operations of the Potomac flotilla ceased in a great measure after the erection of the extensive rebel batteries on the Virginia shore in the autumn of 1861. For several months the commerce on this important avenue to the national capital was almost entirely suspended, though at no time was the passage of our armed vessels prevented "— and he ought to have added—except by stealing by under cover of darkness, directed by signal lights from other vessels and points on the Maryland shore, and when they could not be seen or heard from the Confederate batteries.

In consequence of the blockade of the Potomac by the Confederate batteries, an immense quantity of freight was carried over the Washington branch of the Baltimore and Ohio railroad, running from Baltimore to the capitol. It was estimated that more than sixty vessels, including many large steamships, arrived at Locust Point, Baltimore, daily, and their cargoes were immediately forwarded to Washington. For some days the daily average of cars over this road numbered over four hundred, and to supply the increasing demand for transportation, in October, 1861, a wagon-train of nearly one hundred wagons was established between Baltimore and Washington. This immense amount of business which the exigencies of the war created, rendered it necessary that the Washington branch of the Baltimore and Ohio should be carefully guarded, and a sentinel was placed at every quarter of a mile of the road.

Among the fortifications erected at Harper's Ferry by Gen. Joseph E. Johnston were the naval batteries under Lieut. Charles M. Fauntleroy, of the navy, which were placed on the northern and southern salients of the village at Harper's Ferry, and were designed to envelop with their fire the whole town of Bolivar, and the approaches by the immediate banks of the Potomac and Shenandoah Rivers. On May 23d, 1861, these batteries mounted but two thirty-two-pounders each on plain platforms, and the guns on ships' carriages. The number of guns intended was six to each battery, and they would have been very formidable in resisting an attack upon the town.[1]

During Gen. Lee's command of the Virginia military and naval forces, prior to their being turned over to the Confederate States, Commander H. H. Lewis, of the navy, advised him " that the points lowest down the Rappahannock River, where batteries would be effective in preventing the passage of vessels, are at Lowery's and Accoheek Points, about seven miles below Tappahannock. The channel does not exceed three-quarters of a mile from these points, and a small redoubt with five or six guns on each point would close the passage to any vessels that are likely to attempt it."[2] In consequence of this recommendation, Fort Lowery was erected with four thirty-two-pounders and an eight-inch columbiad, and on May 4th Gen. Lee directed Gen. Daniel Ruggles, commanding at Fredericksburg, to assign a portion of the troops under his command for the protection of that battery. The point was selected because there the river was narrowest and the channel the most difficult, and could be best defended by the guns that were then available; at the same time, examinations of Gray's Point and Cherry Point were made for batteries, and Col.

---

[1] *Off. Rec.*, Vol. II., p. 869.   [2] *Off. Rec.*, Vol. II., p. 811.

Talcott was ordered to complete the battery at Gray's Point with the utmost dispatch and secrecy.

These batteries in the early days of the war held the Rappahannock River above them from the operations of raiding gunboats of the enemy, and enabled the formation of those naval expeditions into the waters of the Chesapeake which were so fruitful in dash and enterprise under Col. John Taylor Wood, aide to the President, and also of the C. S. navy.

During the first year of the war, the Washington authorities were under the impression that gunboats were being constructed at Fredericksburg. These impressions were created by reports from negroes, who also reported that the *St. Nicholas*, which Col. Thomas had captured, and the *Virginia*, had been armed. These boats were never armed, but were used only as transports between Fredericksburg and Fort Lowery. Capt. S. V. Spencer, of the Potomac flotilla, suggested to Secretary Stanton, March 17th, 1862, that a "few hundred troops might land at Taylor's, opposite Maryland Point, and march over to a place called Hop's Yard Wharf (a distance of seven miles), where the steamer *Neales* stops to land passengers, and surprise her, taking her past the batteries under her own colors"; but the Secretary did not commend the expedition.

The movement of land forces in the early part of March, 1862, caused the retirement of the defensive line of Gen. Holmes to the Rappahannock River, and Fort Lowery was made the depot of provisions and supply for the right of Gen. Holmes' army, and Col. Maloney was ordered to concentrate his forces for the protection of that fort. Naval matters, on both the Potomac and Rappahannock Rivers, were, with the exception of Confederate States naval expeditions, brought to an end in March, 1862, by the retrograde movements of the armies from the line of the Potomac to that of the Rappahannock River. This movement caused the removal of all guns and supplies and troops from the batteries of the Lower Potomac to Fredericksburg; and the occupation of the peninsula between those rivers by the U. S. troops under Gen. Hooker. In that retrograde movement the steamer *George Page* was burned by the Confederates in Quantico Creek, March, 1862, having for nearly one year baffled every effort of the U. S. Potomac flotilla to destroy and capture her. Close beside the burning *Page* lay the remains of the *Fairfax*, another capture in the Potomac, which was snatched from the tow of the *Resolute* in October, and whose valuable cargo of hay, cement and furniture was very acceptable—and near by lay the hulk of a schooner—all evidences that the Potomac flotilla had been met on many occasions by the enterprise and dash of the Confederate navy, and which its superior advantages had not been able to circumvent or overcome. The batteries built by the Confederate naval officers. Capt. Lynch, Lieuts. Lewis, Read and Thorburn, were described by those officers of the U. S. army who entered them after evacuation, "as perfect gems of engineering skill," but which ceased to be any longer of use or value, through the movements of the army which protected and defended their rear. They yielded to the force of military, not naval, events.

On April 20th, 1861, the form and position for a water battery on Gloucester Point, on York River, was selected, which would cover all the channel-way with its line of fire, and to mount thirty-one guns; the faces bearing on the channel were arranged for five and nine guns, respectively; the fifteen intermediate guns were to be arranged on the arc of a circle, of about 120 degrees. The lines of fire would cross the channel so near, that that part of the battery was to be armed with eight-inch howitzers, while the faces were to be provided with eight-inch columbiads. All the high ground in rear of the battery was intended to be covered with a large field-work for the protection of the battery. On the Yorktown site a very good position for a six-gun battery was selected near the river bluff. J. J. Clarke was left by Col. Andrew Talcott in charge of the work.

Col. Wm. B. Taliafero was appointed colonel of Virginia volunteers, and on May 3d was assigned to the command of the troops he could collect at Gloucester Point, where Capt. W. C. Whittle, of the Virginia navy, was then constructing the battery. On the 7th, the day Gen. Taliafero assumed command at Gloucester Point, Col. Dimick, in command of Fortress Monroe, was informed "by Flag-officer Pendergrast that a three-gun battery had been discovered by him at Gloucester Point, and that the steamer *Yankee* exchanged several shots with it; but as there was one eight-inch gun in the battery, and those of the steamer were of much shorter range, her commander hauled off."[1] The facts are, that the guns in battery were six-pounder guns, and complaint being made of a waste of ammunition in firing at the *Yankee* so far off, Capt. Whittle disclaimed all authority for the firing, and Gen. Taliafero on the 8th of May urged Gen. Lee to order to that point some effective sea-coast guns. At that date there were six nine-inch guns at the river, and the next day three thirty-two-pounders arrived at West Point, but the *Yankee* was driven off by six-pounder guns.[2] Gen. Lee, on May 11, urged that it was very important that the Gloucester Point battery be pushed forward as fast as possible, and that all labor necessary for its speedy completion be devoted to it. On the same day, Gen. Taliafero wrote to Gen. Lee that the defences had greatly improved, two heavy nine-inch guns being in position on the water battery, and two more of the same kind of guns ready to be placed in battery; that two companies of infantry and one of artillery had been mustered into service, and that with the company of

---

[1] *Off. Doc.*, Vol. II., p. 27.　　　[2] *Off. Rec.*, Vol. II., p. 821.

cavalry he had the means to prevent a landing from boats. May 14th the water battery was armed with three nine-inch guns, and were being instructed in the working of the guns by Commander T. J. Page, of the Virginia navy. Major George W. Randolph, of the Richmond Howitzer Battalion, on June 18th, wrote to Gen. Lee, that "there are in Yorktown, besides the field pieces of my battalion, four columbiads on the water battery, two brass twelve-pounders, one twelve-pounder navy howitzer and two iron six-pounders," and, after calling attention to the extended lines of defence and the necessity for more large guns, added, "that Capt. Ingraham, the Chief of the Naval Bureau of Ordnance, can supply us with eight thirty-two-pounders of twenty-seven hundred-weight, and four forty-two-pounder carronades with navy carriages. * * * Capt. Ingraham can also furnish us four boats, capable of transporting 400 or 500 men, which will be very useful in preserving the communications between Yorktown and Gloucester Point. Two of the guns are at Gloucester Point, and two at West Point; but Capt. Whittle authorizes me to say that they are not ready for them at either place, and that he should prefer seeing them mounted at Yorktown." There had been sent to Gloucester Point eight nine-inch guns; two thirty-two-pounders of fifty-seven hundred-weight; three thirty-two-pounders of thirty-three hundred-weight; one thirty-two pounder of twenty-seven hundred-weight, which constituted its battery on June 25th. The defences were incomplete and liable to be taken by parties landing below the batteries on the Gloucester side, and carrying or turning them; to prevent which, Gen. Magruder, on July 9th, called on Capt. Whittle, at West Point, to send down the two thirty-two-pounders at that point and for a regiment of infantry, to enable Col. Crump to hold the Point against any ordinary force that could be brought in boats to assail it. The ease with which the enemy could land a large force below Gloucester Point, and take the land and water defences in their rear, kept Gen. Lee "anxious for the safety of that position"; for, if the Point was once in the possession of the enemy, the navigation of York River to West Point would be open, as Gloucester Point commanded Yorktown; and his letters to Gen. Magruder, in the month of July, show how urgently he pressed the commanding officer on the peninsula to complete the earthworks for the defence of Gloucester Point.

In reference to the relative rank of navy and army officers, Gen. Lee addressed the following order to the officers at Gloucester Point, for the regulation of all mixed commands:

"As there are no sailors in the service, it is impossible to serve river batteries by them, and artillery companies must perform this duty. Naval officers, from their experience and familiarity with the peculiar duties connected with naval batteries, their management, construction, etc., are eminently fitted for the command of such batteries, and are most appropriately placed in command of them. In a war such as this, unan-inimity and hearty co-operation should be the rule. Petty jealousies about slight shades of relative command, and bickering about trivial matters, are entirely out of place and highly improper, and, when carried so far as to interfere with the effectiveness of a command, become both criminal and contemptible. Within the ordinary limits of a letter it is impossible to provide for every contingency that may arise in a command which is not centred in a single individual. It is therefore hoped that mutual concessions will be made, and that the good of the service will be the only aim of all."

With that circular an order was transmitted to Col. Peyton, at Yorktown, that the naval officer assigned to naval batteries would command all troops when in the battery, either for drill, instruction or fighting, but that in camp the officer of the particular command would have charge of the troops, but must make no order that would impede the naval officer in the proper discharge of his duties.

Commander James L. Henderson, of the navy, in command of the naval batteries at Gloucester Point, was retained by Gen. Magruder several weeks after the order detaching him, while awaiting the arrival of Lieut. Chas. M. Fauntleroy, and the repeated letters of Gen. Magruder for Lieut. Fauntleroy's services show the high appreciation in which that officer was held.

Complaint was made by Gen. Magruder that the gun-carriages of the naval batteries, having been made of green pine, had given indications of breaking down; that their manner of construction prevented their being elevated sufficiently to explode a fifteen-second fuse; that carriages of good pattern promised by the Navy Department had never been sent; and that the depth of water at the mouth of York River being ample for the largest ships, the defences were liable to assault, while the guns in battery on their present carriages could not reach the ships. Capt. George Minor, Chief of the Naval Ordnance Bureau, immediately had other and proper carriages made and replaced the defective ones.

The subject of building gunboats on the upper waters of York River was brought to the attention of the Virginia State authorities as early as May 11th, prior to that State joining the Confederacy, by Capt. Wm. C. Whittle, then commanding defences in York River. In a letter of that date to Capt. S. Barron, then in the Virginia Office of Detail and Equipment, Capt. Whittle urged that "an energetic naval constructor" be at once directed to commence, on the Pamunkey River, the construction of one or more steam-propeller boats, to carry each two eleven-inch shell guns, and to be manned by eighty to one hundred men; that much timber suitable to such boats was already cut, and an inexhaustible supply was standing everywhere in the surrounding forests. And, again, September 24th, Capt. Whittle renewed the request, and sent Gabriel F. Miller, a constructor from Matthews County, to Capt. F. Buchanan, then in charge of the C. S. Office of Orders and Detail, as a man every way reliable and fully competent, and ready to undertake at once the construction, at West Point, of a steam-propeller gunboat—that the timber could be had on the Pamunkey River hard by. Capt. Whittle urged that such vessels, so valuable then, would be the true foundation for a navy composed of vessels of 800 or 1,000 tons, and manned by 100 men each, such as the river trade in Virginia waters could supply. The suggestions were unheeded by both the State and Confederate authorities. It was the opinion of Capt. Whittle that a fleet of these small gunboats, secure behind the batteries at Yorktown and Gloucester Point, sallying forth when occasion offered, and intercepting every unarmed boat and vessel that approached Fortress Monroe, would have compelled the enemy to convoy all supplies to the fort, or have starved the fort into surrender. That convoy service would have weakened the blockading squadrons, as well as the expeditions to Southern waters, and those boats, in conjunction with the army, would have made an important diversion, probably fruitful in many important captures.

As late as January 23d, 1862, General Magruder wrote to the War Department that the work at Gloucester Point was not half finished; that the works at Yorktown, though trebled in strength in the last two months, were still unfinished, both as regards the protection of the men against the enemy's shells, guns and mortars at sea, as well as his attacks by land.

The victory of the *Virginia* in Hampton Roads, on March 9th, created such consternation in all military and naval circles that intelligence of every kind was eagerly caught at by the Federal officers. The "contraband" was a prolific source of information. One of these was received on board the *Wachusett*, April 13th, of whom Mr. I. S. Missroon says : "He is *not* intelligent"; but, notwithstanding, he communicated that Gen. Magruder had asked for and expected the *Merrimac* (*Virginia*) to come to the York River; that "the battery at Gloucester Point is commanded by Jeff Page, late of the U. S. navy, a good officer; Richard Page, also formerly of the navy, in command of the upper works at Gloucester; that they are very sanguine of sinking vessels, and have practiced their firing, which is very accurate; says Page (Jeff) can kill a dog a mile. He knows the roads and creeks. I will send his p. m. If you want him, telegraph. Would it not be well to communicate to Flag-officer Magruder's expectation of the *Merrimac* coming here ? It can do no harm."[1]

The naval batteries at Gloucester Point and Yorktown, though incomplete and imperfect, had served their purpose fully, holding the enemy's fleet in check, barring their way up that river to the rear of the Confederate army on the peninsula, and were abandoned, not to the U. S. navy, but to the exigencies of the C. S. army, which, retiring beyond the Chickahominy River, rendered the batteries useless.

[1] *Off. Rec.*, Vol. XI., Part III., p. 99.

CAPTAIN FREDERICK CHATARD,

CONFEDERATE STATES NAVY.

COMMANDER JOHN TAYLOR WOOD,
CONFEDERATE STATES NAVY.

CHAPTER VI.

CAPTURES IN VIRGINIA WATERS.

ABOUT the middle of June, 1861, Lieut. H. H. Lewis, of the C. S. navy, while visiting the Potomac River at Aquia Creek with Gen. Holmes, observed the steamer *St. Nicholas*, of Baltimore, approach without challenge or inquiry the U. S. steamer *Pawnee*, range alongside without question from the *Pawnee*, and put provisions and other articles on board. There was neither stoppage or delay of the *St. Nicholas* before reaching the side of the *Pawnee*. Interested at this unusual proceeding in actual war, Lieut. Lewis called Gen. Holmes' attention to the matter, and finding from repeated observation that the same unchallenged intercourse took place, Lieut. Lewis formed a plan upon that fact for the capture of the *Pawnee*, by first seizing the *St. Nicholas* lower down the river, putting upon her a force of naval officers and a detachment of infantry, and steaming, as was usual, alongside of the *Pawnee*, board and overpower her crew. Appealing to Gen. Holmes for a detail of 300 men from a Tennessee regiment which had many Western steamboat-men in its ranks, Lieut. Lewis met with a refusal by Gen. Holmes, who regarded the risk too great for him to assume the responsibility. He was referred to the Secretary of War, and on his way to Richmond met Capt. M. F. Maury, of the navy, at Fredericksburg, to whom he explained the plan of capture. Capt. Maury, approving heartily of the plan, returned with Lieut. Lewis to Richmond, and laid the plan before Mr. Mallory, who entered warmly into the enterprise, and talked it over with the Secretary of War, L. P. Walker. That officer, under date of June 25th, wrote to Gen. Holmes: "You are authorized to co-operate with Lieut. Lewis, C. S. navy, with any part of the force under your command, as you may deem advisable, in the operations which he has explained to this department, and with which you are acquainted." To this letter Gen. Holmes suggested that he be *ordered* to make the detail, and Mr. Mallory wrote to the Secretary of War: "Gen. Holmes suggests that instead of obtaining volunteers from him, you order the Tennessee regiment to the duty required in our joint machinations against the 'peace and dignity' of Abraham and the *Pawnee*, and that a line from you to Col. Bate would 'enthuse' them, etc. Capt. Maury calls on you, at my request, to attend to this. Our commander, Lewis of the navy, will command the party afloat, and will succeed." Secretary Walker immediately wrote to Gen. Holmes, June 27th : "If you deem the suggestions of Commander Lewis feasible, you are authorized to detail 500 troops for the purpose of co-operating with him. In doing this it will be proper to select from the lifferent regiments under your command. If, however, you do not concur with Commander Lewis in the feasibility of the undertaking, it will be proper for you to send a detachment of troops to Cone River to support him in the event he should find it necessary to run in at that point." To this letter Gen. Holmes replied to Secretary Walker, June 27th : "In answer to yours relative to co-operating with Commander Lewis, Confederate navy, I have respectfully to say that I did not feel justified in ordering volunteer troops on an expedition so fraught with ruinous consequences if it failed, and the success of which required that so many contingencies should be effectually accomplished. I referred the matter to the colonels of regiments, and they declined to volunteer their men."[1]

Foiled in an enterprise which he considered both feasible and gallant, Lieut. Lewis proceeded to duty on the lower Rappahannock, where in a few days after he was surprised by a visit from Capt. George N. Hollins, of the C. S. navy, and Col. Thomas, who informed him that they were on their way to Baltimore to seize the *St. Nicholas*, run her into Cone River, and turn her over to his command. Returning immediately to Fredericksburg, Lieut. Lewis found there several naval officers and a part of the first Tennessee regiment under Col. Bate, and embarking on the steamer *Virginia*, they landed at Monasteon on the Rappahannock, and marched that evening across to Cone River, where, at three o'clock the next morning, the *St. Nicholas* arrived.

Such was the inception of the earliest and not the least bold and daring exploit of individual coolness, pluck and dash of the war—the capture of the steamer *St. Nicholas* on the Potomac River, on the morning of Saturday, June 29th, 1861. Events had already shaped themselves into a state of actual war. Maryland, though still in the Union, was, in the sentiment of a very large portion of her people, in thorough accord with the people of the seceded States. A similarity of institutions and a long association of trade, business, and social intimacy united and bound her people and her interests with those of the people of the South. In the counties of that State

1 *Off. Rec.*, Vol. II., p. 949, 958.

in the peninsula between the bay and the Potomac, were the homes of the bulk of her slave-holding people, and every feeling of interest and of sympathy were warmest and strongest for the people of the Confederate States.

In St. Mary's County resided the Hon. Richard Thomas, one of Maryland's most honored citizens, who for many years had enjoyed the confidence and regard of her people, and who had presided for several sessions over the Maryland Senate. A large slave-holder, and thoroughly Southern in every principle of politics and every personal sympathy, his children had been educated and instructed in those principles of government which had obtained complete ascendancy over all the slave-holding States. Among his sons was Richard Thomas, whose sympathies were thoroughly enlisted with the South. Bold, brave, intelligent, and ardently desiring to signalize his advent in the South with an exploit which would serve to illustrate the spirit and purpose with which the sons of Maryland espoused the Southern cause, Richard Thomas planned and executed the capture of the steamer *St. Nicholas* with all that indifference as to the odds that might be against success which existed all over the South at the beginning of the war. Fully aware that the success of his attempt would add very much to the strength of the Confederacy on the waters of the Chesapeake Bay, he was not indifferent to the fact that, if unsuccessful, the very recklessness of the effort would illustrate that spirit of individual heroism so necessary in every contest between unequal forces.

That the expedition was not one of inconsiderate rashness is shown by the precautions taken to hold the steamer after capture. Col. Thomas visited Richmond, where he made known to Gov. Letcher his plans and purposes, and arranged to have a detachment of troops on the Virginia shore, together with naval officers, to take charge of the steamer. To that end, a detachment from Col. Bate's (1st) Tennessee regiment, then near Fredericksburg, was ordered to take position on the Potomac in the neighborhood of Cone River, and to be in position on the morning of June 29th, the day the *St. Nicholas* was regularly due at the ports on the Maryland shore. In company with the infantry, Lieuts. H. H. Lewis, Robert D. Minor, C. C. Simms, of the C. S. navy, Lieut. Thorburn of the Virginia navy, and fifteen sailors from the steamer *Yorktown*, were also dispatched from Richmond to lend assistance. The infantry and the naval force were promptly in place, having marched across the peninsula of the northern neck, and arrived almost simultaneously with the captured steamer.

These preliminary precautions taken and arranged, Col. Thomas repaired to Baltimore and gathered together the very few men in whom he could confide. These were necessarily very few in number, though very determined in purpose and fully resolved to succeed; no contemporaneous account states

8

the exact number of "passengers" that started in the boat. On Friday evening, June 28th, the *St. Nicholas*, a side-wheel steamboat of about 1,200 tons, regularly plying between Baltimore and Georgetown, D.C., touching at regular points on the Potomac, received on board a very quiet, demure, rather *passé* lady, with a French accent and rather masculine features; but reserved in deportment, and rather uneasy as to the time the boat would reach Washington. In all other respects the "French lady's" behavior attracted no attention. The "passengers," booked for different stopping-places, dispersed themselves about the boat, holding but little conversation among themselves and none whatever with the French lady. The officers of the boat observed nothing peculiar in the conduct of any of the passengers, and certainly nothing in that of the "lady." The boat proceeded on her course, with no occurrence worthy of note, until the landing at Point Lookout was made, when two more "passengers" came aboard, one of these an "elderly-looking" man. With nothing to attract attention, that "elderly-looking" passenger took his position on deck in rear of the ladies' cabin, giving apparently more attention to the weather, the water, or the skies, than to the boat or her passengers.

Upon casting-off from the wharf at Point Lookout, the *St. Nicholas* headed up stream for Washington, and when a mile or so from the wharf there might be seen climbing over the deck rail, immediately above the window of the cabin to which the "French lady" had retired, an active and determined man, clad in Zouave uniform and fully armed with sword and revolvers. The "French lady" had doffed her wig, her curls, her petticoats, and donned the uniform of the Zouave and was ready for action. Exchanging a few hurried words with the "elderly passenger," he, too, was suddenly changed into Capt. George N. Hollins, formerly of the U. S. navy, but having resigned his commission in that service now about to assume the command of the *St. Nicholas* in the service of the Confederate States. The few hurried words exchanged, both officers repaired below decks, where further transformations were immediately made among twenty-five "passengers," who now appeared as Zouaves, armed and determined to have and to hold the steamer. Surprised and astounded, the officers and crew of the boat found that resistance would be unavailing, and quietly yielded possession of the boat. The real passengers on the boat, though greatly alarmed by the unexpected turn which had been given to affairs aboard, were quieted with the assurances of safety and respect. The St. Mary's (Md.) *Beacon*, of July 6th, 1861, says:

"Throughout the whole night not a single act of rudeness was perpetrated, all the passengers being treated with the greatest civility. The ladies were told by the commander that they were in the hands of Southern gentlemen, and would be treated as his own sisters. Whatever opinions may be entertained of the capture itself, no one who was present on that eventful night can say aught but in praise of the gentlemanly deportment of all concerned."

A passenger on board the *St. Nicholas,* who witnessed Col. Thomas' appearance on deck, and his conversation with Capt. Hollins, "suspected nothing of the truth, supposing that a government boat was boarding her for the purpose of inquiry." So quiet was the execution of this well-considered and arranged plan of capture that every man knew his duty, the moment for his appearance, and the exact part he was to take.

Such was the account given of this exploit in the Union papers of that day; but Col. Alexander, one of Col. Thomas' men, and who was subsequently captured and confined in Fort McHenry with Thomas, gives a somewhat different version. He says:

"The detail that accomplished the capture of the *St. Nicholas* got on in small groups at different landings as ordinary passengers. When I got aboard, the first person I saw in the cabin was Col. Thomas, who was of small stature, dressed as a lady, carrying on an animated conversation with a Federal officer. He spoke French fluently and was passing himself off as a French lady. It was from this circumstance that the nickname was afterward given him. It was amusing to note how admirably he performed his part, tossing a fan about and putting on all the airs of an animated French woman, much to the enjoyment of the Federal officer with whom he was conversing. Our whole force was by this time aboard, known to each other by private signals. Thomas, when he saw that everything was ready for the *émeute,* excused himself from his companion and retired to his state-room. We all knew that the time had now arrived for action, and we gathered together awaiting the reappearance of Thomas. It was but a few moments when, with a shout, he sprang from his state-room in the dress of a Zouave, armed with cutlass and pistol. The balance of us made a rush to the state-room, where our arms were concealed, and likewise secured pistols and cutlasses. In a few moments we overpowered the passengers and crew, secured them below the hatches, and the boat was ours. We then proceeded immediately to the rendezvous where we expected to take aboard our infantry reinforcements, but owing to the long delay before they arrived word of our movements got abroad, and the enemy were placed on their guard. Had our infantry regiment been at the appointed place in time, the *Pawnee* certainly, and perhaps the entire Potomac fleet, would have been captured."

Immediately after the capture of the steamer, all lights upon her were extinguished, and her head was turned to the Virginia shore, where she arrived at 3:30 in the morning, and stopped at the wharf at Cone River, where she was boarded by the officers of the C. S. navy, and the Tennessee infantry appeared for her protection. Embarking a portion of the infantry, the *St. Nicholas,* now under command of Capt. Hollins, headed up the Potomac in search of the U. S. steamer *Pawnee,* the capture of which was contemplated by surprise and boarding; but, not finding the *Pawnee,* the steamer rounded and stood down the river for the bay. Between Smith's Point and the mouth of the Rappahannock River, Capt. Hollins met the schooner *Margaret*, from Alexandria (Va.) to New York, whose mate, Mr. E. Case, gave to the N. Y. *Times* the following account:

"On Saturday, the 29th day of June, we passed Smith's Point, at the mouth of the Potomac; we saw the steamer *St. Nicholas* come out of a river on the Virginia shore, called Cone River. She passed us, and paid no attention to us, we thinking all the while it was rather strange for her to be sailing down the bay, as it was out of her course. Her object, we soon found out, was to seize the brig *Monticello* and the schooner *Mary Pierce*, which were bound up the bay as we were going out.

"In a few minutes the *St. Nicholas* headed up the bay again; she came up and passed us, then turned again and bore down on us. Capt. Hollins hailed us, and asked what schooner it was. We told him the schooner *Margaret*. He then inquired what it was loaded with, and we told him. He then sung out that we were a prize to the Southern Confederacy. The *St. Nicholas* was then run close alongside; then about twenty-five armed men jumped on board, and drove all hands on board the steamer. When I got on deck, and before they drove me into the hold, I looked around me, and who should I see but the traitor, Capt. Thomas Skinner, formerly master of the steamer *Jamestown!*

"They then took the schooner in tow, and took us up the Rappahannock River as far as the depth of the water would permit. That night they came again alongside, and coaled the *St. Nicholas* from our cargo. Next morning we started for Fredericksburg, and took the *Mary Pierce* in tow, and towed her within fifteen miles of the town. At dark, on the 30th, we came alongside of the dock; they kept us on board all night. The next morning early we were marched out, closely guarded by soldiers, and were placed on board the cars for Richmond, not having eaten anything worth speaking of for twenty-four hours."

The vessels then captured by Capt. Hollins with the *St. Nicholas* were:

Brig *Monticello*, from Brazil, bound to Baltimore, with 3,500 bags of coffee. [1]

Schooner *Mary Pierce*, from Boston, bound to Washington City, with 260 tons of ice.

Schooner *Margaret*, from Alexandria, bound to Staten Island, with 270 tons of coal.

Lieutenant Simms, C. S. navy, was put in charge of the *Monticello;* Lieut. Robert D. Minor, C. S. navy, in charge of the *Mary Pierce;* and Lieut. Thorburn, of the Virginia navy, in charge of the *Margaret*.

The people in the Confederacy needed coffee, ice and coal, their government needed the steamer and the vessels, and it is not surprising that the bold officers and brave men who brought in supplies so much needed should have been loudly praised and profusely complimented. On the *Monticello* were found a number of bags containing the mails and dispatches from the United States squadron in Brazil, from which the movements of the ships in that squadron were learned by the Confederate government. The ice captured was sold in Fredericksburg for $8,000. Col. Thomas repaired to Richmond,

[1] The *Monticello*, after being taken up the Rappahannock River, was released by her captors after the coffee had been taken out, and permitted to return to Baltimore, where she was owned.

where every attention and compliment awaited and were lavishly bestowed upon him. The State of Virginia, by Governor Letcher, on July 1st, commissioned him, under the name of Richard Thomas Zarvona, a colonel in the volunteer forces of the State. During his visit, his friends insisted on seeing him in his costume of the "French lady," as he appeared on the steamer *St. Nicholas.* To gratify them, he left the room, promising to return promptly, provided the company was not enlarged, as the joke was to be strictly private. Unfortunately, the circle was shortly after disturbed by the entrance of a strange lady, for whom, however, room was made, and to whom a seat was tendered with customary Virginia gallantry. The rest of the company broke up into knots, leaving the stranger to herself, and discussing in whispers the propriety of keeping the colonel out until a favorable opportunity presented itself. Suddenly their embarrassment was relieved by the action of the lady, who, lifting her skirts to a modest height, displayed a soldier's uniform and end of a cutlass. The effect may be imagined !

The capture of the *St. Nicholas* illustrates the difficulty which the United States authorities encountered at the beginning of the war in preventing communication across the Potomac between the sympathizing Marylanders and their compatriots in Virginia. Chas. Worthington, the Baltimore agent of the steamer *St. Nicholas,* writing to the Secretary of the Navy, July 1st, after describing how the steamer had been spirited away, gives at length the precautions he had taken with Capt. Ward to prevent any such occurrence : "The arrangement," says Mr. Worthington, "we made was mutually satisfactory, and he promised to meet her (the steamer) every Saturday morning at the mouth of the Potomac, and give her a pass to proceed on her trip. But, alas ! he is no more "— Col. Thomas had timed his enterprise so well that he slipped through the unguarded door of the mouth of the Potomac, and accomplished effectually his daring exploit.

At the session of the Confederate States District Court in Richmond, February 3d, 1862, in the admiralty case of George N. Hollins *et al.* against the steamer *St. Nicholas,* her cargo, tackle and apparel, the marshal reported that he had placed the amount of the sale of the vessel, etc. ($18,924.73), in bank to the credit of the case.

The *St. Nicholas* was burned at Fredericksburg in 1862, when that city was evacuated, along with many other vessels. [1]

[1] The following is the list of vessels destroyed at that place by the Confederate military authorities previous to the evacuation of the town: Steamer *Virginia,* steamer *St. Nicholas,* schooner *May,* owned by McConkey, Parr & Co., Baltimore, Md ; *A. Henry Armstrong,* valued at $45,000; schooner *Ada,* owned by Samuel G. Miles, of Baltimore, valued at $3,500; schooner *Northern Light,* valued at $2,000; *Reindeer,* owned by Capt. W. C. Moore, Middlesex County, Va., valued at $1,500; *Decapolis,* valued at $700 ; *Mary Pierce,* owned by R W. Adams and L. B. Eddens, Fredericksburg, Va., valued at $5,600; *Helen,* Capt. Solomon Phillips, Essex Company, valued at $2,000; *W. J. Valiant,* valued at $1,500; *Anglo-Saxon,* owned by Segars & Perkins, Middlesex Company, valued at $1,500; *Dazzling Orb,* Fredericksburg, Va , valued at $600; *Putala,* owned by A. Williams and B. Walker, Lancaster County, Va , valued at $1,500; *James Henry,*

Col. Zarvona, prompted by his success, if not spirited by the praise and flattery it elicited, determined to return to Baltimore, and possibly with the purpose of accomplishing another daring feat. In spite of all persuasion, and against the advice of friends—indeed, against the application of force on the part of some of his admirers—he set out in a schooner in July for Maryland, and landed at Fair Haven, in the Bay.

On July 4th, certain parties were seen inspecting the steamer *Columbia*, of the same line as the *St. Nicholas*, while lying at Fardy's ship-yard, near Federal Hill, Baltimore. They went aboard and inquired of Capt. Harper what was her speed, how much coal was on board, and whether she could be chartered. The steamer *Logan*, of the Baltimore and Fredericksburg line, and the steamer *Virginia*, were already in the possession of the Confederates; the steamer *William Selden*, of the Baltimore Steam Packet Company, was being used by the Confederates in Norfolk harbor. These captures had made the Union authorities more vigilant and suspicious. It was also reported to the authorities in Baltimore that several parties had left the city on the Monday night preceding, in omnibuses, and it was presumed that their purpose was to co-operate with Col. Zarvona, whose arrival at Fair Haven, in Anne Arundel County, had also been reported. To effect the capture of the "French lady" and her whole party, an expedition was arranged by Provost Marshal Kenly, and placed under command of Lieut. Thomas H. Carmichael and John Horner, of Baltimore. The steamer *Chester*, according to one contemporaneous authority, and a sloop, according to another, was equipped at Fort McHenry with an armament of two twenty-four-pounders, an artillery company, an infantry company, and a *posse* of police officers. Proceeding to Fair Haven, the officers arrested Neale Green, a noted barber, doing business on Pratt Street, Baltimore, on the charge of having been engaged in the assault on the 6th Massachusetts regiment on the 19th of April; and with Green in charge the officers returned to Baltimore on September 19th, 1861, on board the steamer *Mary Washington*, while the *Chester* proceeded down the bay in search of the schooner which brought Col. Zarvona to Fair Haven. The Baltimore *American*, of July 9th, has the following account of the capture of Col. Zarvona:

"Shortly after leaving, the lieutenant entered into conversation with a number of passengers, and ascertained that Capt. Kirwan, with the engineer and another officer of the steamer *St. Nicholas*, as well as others

owned by Capts. Mullin and Dickinson, Richmond County, Va., valued at $400; *J. Wagner*, Lancaster County, Va., valued at $225; *Active*, Capt. Henry Taylor, Richmond County, Va., valued at $2,200; *Sea Breeze*, owned by Miles, of Baltimore, Crabb & Sanger, Richmond, Va., valued at $2,000; *Mary Miller*, owned by G. Burgess, of Northumberland County, Va., and Miller, of Middlesex County, Va., valued at $4,000; *Nannie Shrevel*, owned by E. Mann, valued at $2,500; *Lucy Renn*, owned by a citizen of Gloucester County, Va., valued at $600; *Hiawatha*, owned by Mr. Garland Richardson, valued at $2,000; sloop *Amethyst*, owned by Capt. Charles Gutheridge, Fredericksburg, valued at $900; including the value of the *Virginia* and *St. Nicholas*.

In connection with the burning of bridges and vessels, from $15,000 to $20,000 worth of cotton was also burned.

who had been taken prisoners when the steamer was seized by Thomas, the 'French lady,' and his party, had been released by them and was returning to this city on the *Mary Washington*. The officers also ascertained that among the passengers on board were seven or eight of the captors, with Capt. Thomas himself, who, doubtless exhilarated by the success attending their first achievement, were disposed to make another venture, probably on the steamer *Columbia* or some other steamer plying on the Maryland rivers.

" As soon as satisfactory information on this point was obtained and each one of the party recognized beyond doubt, Lieut. Carmichael directed Capt. Mason L. Weems, the commander of the *Mary Washington*, to proceed, on reaching this harbor, to land the passengers at Fort McHenry. The direction was given while the steamer was at Annapolis. Shortly after, while Lieut. Carmichael and Mr. Horner were in the ladies' cabin, they were approached by Thomas, who desired to know by what authority the order had been given for the steamer to touch at Fort McHenry. The lieutenant informed him that it was through authority vested in him by Col. Kenly, Provost Marshal of Baltimore. On hearing this, Thomas drew his pistol, and calling his men around him, threatened to seize and throw Carmichael and Horner overboard. The latter drew their revolvers and defied the other party to proceed to execute their threats. The utmost confusion prevailed in the cabin for a short time, the female passengers running out screaming, but the other male passengers stood up with Carmichael and Horner, and compelled Thomas and his companions to remain quiet. Matters thus stood on the boat until the steamer approached the fort wharf, when the lieutenant went up and informed Gen. Banks of his important capture.

" The General instantly ordered out a company of infantry, who marched to the steamboat and secured all the accused excepting Thomas, for whom search was made for an hour and a half. He was then found concealed in the drawer of a bureau in the ladies' cabin, in the aft part of the boat. At first it was apprehended that Thomas would make a desperate resistance, but he disclaimed any such design, alleging that he was too weak to resist. He and the other prisoners were then marched to the fort and placed in confinement."

The arrest created a "tremendous excitement" in Baltimore, where Col. Thomas was well known, and had many friends among the best families in the city. On his person was found his commission as colonel in the volunteer forces of Virginia;[1] but that did not protect him from treatment such as a pirate would have received. His imprisonment, upon becoming known at Richmond, was firmly protested against, and measures of retaliation adopted, which arrested all proceedings against him on the charge of piracy, but did not

---

[1] The following are copies of papers found on Col. Thomas at the time of his arrest at Fort McHenry:

" *The Commonwealth of Virginia to Richard Thomas Zarvona, greeting* :

Know you, that from special trust and confidence reposed in your fidelity, courage and good conduct, our Governor, in pursuance of the authority vested in him by an Ordinance of the Convention of the State of Virginia. doth commission you a colonel in the Active Volunteer forces of the State, to rank as such from the first day of July, eighteen hundred and sixty-one.

{ L. S. } In testimony whereof, I have hereunto signed my name, as Governor, and caused the seal of the Commonwealth to

be affixed, this second day of July, eighteen hundred and sixty-one.

JOHN LETCHER.

CITY OF RICHMOND, VIRGINIA, *To Wit* :
This day appeared before me, Joseph Mayo, Mayor of the City of Richmond, Richard Thomas Zarvona, and qualified to the within commission by taking the oath prescribed by law.

Given under my hand this 2d day of July, A.D. 1861.

JOSEPH MAYO, Mayor.

EXECUTIVE DEPARTMENT. }
RICHMOND, July 3, 1861. }
Permit Col. R. T. Zarvona, of the Potomac Zouaves, to pass at will, *free*, over the roads and

secure the treatment due to him as a prisoner-of-war. He was confined in Fort McHenry for several months, during which he made several ineffectual efforts to escape, and was, early in 1862, transferred to Fort Lafayette. During his imprisonment reports were circulated that his health had been impaired, and that his mental condition indicated cruelty in the treatment he had received. These reports caused the U. S. Senate to direct the Committee on Military Affairs of the Senate to inquire into and report as to the truths of those reports. Senator Wilson reported, February 16th, 1863, that:

"Richard Thomas Zarvona was committed to this fort on December 3d, 1861, and was allowed the same privileges as the other prisoners until the 3d March, 1862, on which date he was placed in close confinement by order of the Secretary of War, dated 28th day of February, 1862. After that date he was not allowed to leave his room except to go to the water-closet—which is situated on the sea wall—in charge of a member of the guard, of which privilege he took advantage on the night of the 31st of April, 1862, and attempted to escape by jumping overboard and swimming to the Long Island shore. Since that time he has not been out of his room except to see his mother, who visited him in October last by permission of the Secretary of War.

"The room in which he is confined, is one of those intended for quarters, 25 feet long and fifteen feet wide, with nine windows, one of which is closed, because it opens upon the court where the other prisoners exercise. The room is the same which Senator Wall, with some others, occupied while confined here. He is permitted to supply himself, through the commanding officer of the post, with anything he may wish in the way of food (in addition to the regular ration which is issued to him) and clothing. He is not permitted the use of papers or books, as he has taken advantage of these privileges to communicate to parties outside.

"As regards Thomas' health, Acting Assistant Surgeon W. H. Studley, of the fort, under date of February 2d, says: 'I have this day examined Col. Richard Thomas Zarvona, Confederate States army, and found that his health is generally good, according to his own admission. That it is better than when he entered the fort. In reference to his mental condition, I find him sound and rational, but somewhat eccentric in some of his ideas, and yet not more so than in thousands who may be said to be born with a certain turn of character. Therefore, in my opinion, I should deem his peculiarities perfectly consistent with sanity of mind.'

"The report of Assistant Adjt. Gen. D. D. Townsend, to the Secretary of War, dated February 10th, says: Col. Richard Thomas, *alias* Richard Thomas Zarvona, was captured on board the steamer *Mary Washington*, near Annapolis, February 7th, 1861, and confined at Fort McHenry, Baltimore, Maryland. He was recognized on the steamer as a man who headed a party which captured the steamer *St. Nicholas*, plying between Baltimore and the Potomac, and was indicted by the Grand Jury of Maryland District for the offence and for treason. When

rivers of this Commonwealth upon his own certificate, and upon like certificate pass his men and baggage.

All officers, civil and military, will respect him, and give him such facilities as he may require, in their power to afford.

By order,

S. BASSETT NEUCH,
Aide-de-Camp to Governor of Virginia.
Approved: JOHN LETCHER."
He also had with him a letter of credit on a Baltimore house for the sum of $1,000, declaring that the check of Col. Zarvona to that

amount would be duly honored by Messrs. R. H. Maury & Co., of Richmond.

July 14, 1861, Asst. Adj. Gen. Robert Williams at Fort McHenry, reported by direction of Major Gen. Banks, "that the schooner *Georgiana*, owned by Thomas and his party, and with which a portion of them had been lying in wait for the capture of other steamers from Baltimore, has been taken possession of, and is now at the dock of this port, having been run aground and deserted by her crew. No capture of rebels was made on board of her."—*Official Records*, Series 1, Vol. II., p. 749.

search was made for him on the *Mary Washington*, he was found dressed in female apparel, and concealed in a bureau in one of the state-rooms. Gen. Dix, in his report of February 20th, 1862, thinks he should be treated as a 'pirate and a spy.' There are four witnesses against him as to the first crime, who were at Fort McHenry the last of September. The evidence of the second charge consists in his being taken in disguise as a female, with a commission of Colonel 'in the active volunteer forces' of Virginia upon his person at the time. In consequence of the report made in his case, he has not been placed in the list of prisoners-of-war, but is held confined at Fort Lafayette."

There was no truth in the statement that Col. Zarvona was "dressed in female apparel."

Such feats of resolution and daring inspire a whole people with admiration, and create that spirit of enthusiasm which takes no reckoning of the odds against success. Col. Zarvona may have been eccentric, every man that acts outside of the dull line of other men is set down as eccentric; but the coolness and resolution with which he faced danger, and the indomitable energy with which he executed his enterprise, show that he was well fitted to lead in a desperate undertaking. Some idea of the resources of this young man may be formed from the novel means by which he tried to effect escape. With a number of tin cans securely corked and tied around his waist, he threw himself into the water and swam boldly from Fort Lafayette toward the Long Island shore; but being discovered by the sentinel, a boat was sent after him and he was recaptured and brought back to the fort. He continued to languish in the gloomy cell at Fort Lafayette for two years— an object of admiration and pity to every man and woman in the South. His imprisonment was reported to be rigorous in the extreme, and his confinement close and severe. His repeated efforts to escape may have rendered these measures necessary—but their report caused retaliation to be instituted in Richmond, by the confinement at hard labor in the Penitentiary of two Federal officers, and the announcement of the purpose to mete out to them whatever might befall Col. Zarvona. In response to a resolution, adopted by the Virginia House of Delegates on the 23d of January, 1863, in relation to the efforts made by Governor Letcher to obtain the release of Col. Zarvona, the Governor said that "at the time of his capture, Col. Zarvona was acting under orders from me, and was employed on secret service for the accomplishment of an object regarded as one of the first importance to the interests of the State and the Confederacy." In response to this communication, the Legislature, on March 28th, 1863, adopted a resolution authorizing and directing the Governor to transfer the prisoners captured by the State Line to the Confederate government, except those held as hostages for Col. Zarvona and others. These acts of retaliation procured the release of Col. Zarvona, and he was exchanged and returned to Richmond in April, 1863. That one so conspicuous in the earliest period of the war for coolness and courage should have played no further part, is remarkable, but not the less a fact.[1]

On Wednesday night, Aug. 19th, 1863, Lieut. John Taylor Wood, C. S. navy, left Richmond in command of a party numbering sixty men; the inception, organization and destination of the expedition were so well concealed that the first intimation received in Richmond of the expedition was the information of its complete success.[2]

The United States Chesapeake flotilla, commanded by Capt. Craven, was chiefly engaged in arresting intercourse between the United States and the Confederate States along the waters of that bay. To that end armed steamers were kept cruising off the mouths of rivers and creeks, and at the mouth of the Rappahannock the steamers *Satellite* and *Reliance* were doing duty in August, 1863. These steamers carried, on the former, one thirty-two-pounder smooth-bore gun and one twelve-pounder howitzer; and the latter mounted one thirty-pounder Parrott and one twenty-four-pounder howitzer, each with a crew of forty men. As they lay off Stingray Point, at the mouth of the Rappahannock, they offered a temptation which to the courage, dash and enterprise of Lieut. Wood was too inviting to be resisted.

The point of departure, the lower end of Middlesex County, Va., was reached, and embarking in four small boats Lieut. Wood's command pulled steadily and swiftly for the two vessels.

The challenge of the watches on board had scarcely died away on the midnight air before the boarders were clambering up the sides of the two vessels, cutting their way through the hammock netting, which had been triced up in anticipation of attack, driving the crews below and mastering the prizes. Three minutes finished the work. The assault was so quickly made that the crews had no opportunity to use their heavy guns, and the fighting was entirely hand-to-hand, in which Lieut. Hoge, Midshipman H. S. Cooke, and three men were wounded, and Capt. Waters of the *Reliance*, with eight others, were severely wounded and two killed. This affair, so brilliant in conception and execution, was described in the Washington City *Evening Star* by N. H. Stavey, Paymaster's Clerk of the *Satellite*, who was wounded in the fight. He said:

---

[1] Col. Thomas had originally intended to raise a regiment of Maryland Zouaves, and the first company was organized in Richmond on July 4th, 1861, by the election of the following officers ; William Walters, Baltimore, Captain; G. W. Alexander, First Lieutenant; John W. Torsch, Second Lieutenant; F. M. Parsons, Jr., Third Lieutenant; Chas. Simms, Orderly Sergeant; Charles Hemling, Second Sergeant; F. Duffin, Third Sergeant; J. L. Quinn, Fourth Sergeant; John D. Mitchell, First Corporal; William Uncle, Second Corporal; John H. Russick, Third Corporal; William A. Ryan, Fourth Corporal. The company was ordered to Tappahannock on the Rappahannock River, to re-cruit and drill, and wait for the release of its colonel from imprisonment; but, owing to the great length of time he was confined, the scheme of organizing a regiment of Zouaves was abandoned, and the company of Maryland Zouaves was soon after consolidated with other Confederate commands and performed gallant service throughout the war.

[2] Lieut. Wood with a boat's crew of thirteen men, on the night of October 7th, 1862, boarded, captured and burned the steamer *Francis Elmore*, which was lying at anchor off Lower Cedar Point in the Potomac River. The captain and crew were sent prisoners to Richmond.

"The attacking party numbered sixty-eight men, mostly sailors belonging to the *New Merrimac*, at Richmond, with some of Wheat's battalion, and approached in four boats, each containing about seventeen men, the two boats which approached the *Satellite* being in command of Col. Wood, an aide and relative to Jeff. Davis, and the two who boarded the *Reliance*, in charge of Lieut. Hoge, of the *Merrimac*. Both of these officers, we believe, formerly were attached to our navy.

"At the time of the attack (twelve o'clock Saturday night) it was dark and a heavy sea was running. The assailants were not discovered on the *Satellite* until nearly to the boat, when the officer ran below to call the executive officer, and by the time he returned the vessel was boarded and the crew were in a fight with the rebels, which lasted some ten or fifteen minutes, during which Thomas Damon, a fireman, and —— Lawson, who originally came from the rebel army, were killed, and Ensign R. Sommers received two cutlass wounds on the left arm, and was shot through the neck; N. H. Stavey, Paymaster's Steward, shot in the arm; Wm. Bingham, Master-at-Arms, Samuel Chin (colored), and two others, slightly. The fight on board the *Satellite* is represented to have been desperate, and several of the rebels were wounded; but the crews were obliged to give way. It is said that the Captain of the *Satellite* (Robinson) behaved in a very cowardly manner when he came on deck in his underclothes. Finding the crew in a desperate hand-to-hand encounter with the rebels, he cried out, "For God's sake, don't shoot. I surrender."

"The party which boarded the *Reliance*, Acting Ensign Walters, also was resisted, the officers and men fighting desperately, but were obliged to succumb to this attack; Lieut. Hoge was either killed or wounded, and Ensign Walters was shot through the stomach, the ball coming out at the hip. After Mr. Walters was wounded he crawled into his pilot-house and blew his whistle for help, not being aware that the *Satellite* had been already taken. Mr. McCauly, the engineer of the *Reliance*, when he found his boat in possession of the rebels, put his engines out of gear, rendering them useless.

"After they captured both boats the rebels proceeded with them to Urbana, where the officers and crews were put on shore, and they put out with the steamers again for the mouth of the river, where they lay all day Sunday; but on Sunday night they went to the Eastern Shore and captured three schooners, one a large coaler, from Philadelphia, which they took up to Urbana; and after burning one of them, went, as they said, to Port Royal, where they would remove the machinery and destroy the boats."

Immediately upon securing the two steamers, the boats in which Lieut. Wood had made the attack were made fast astern, everything was hauled taut on board, ropes coiled up, and guns prepared for a fight. Lieut. Wood was on board the *Satellite*, and Lieut. Francis L. Hoge being wounded, Lieut. Wm. E. Hudgins, the second officer in command, was put in charge of the *Reliance*. He was ordered to follow close after the *Satellite*, which was to be taken up the river by Pilot Moore. The engineers, Messrs. Bowman and Tennent, soon got up steam, and reported the vessels ready to move.

Lieut. Hoge was the first to reach the deck of the *Reliance*, and fighting his way forward with great gallantry, was struck in the neck by a pistol ball, and fell upon the deck. Midshipman Cooke, though hit by two balls, continued to direct the fight until the enemy surrendered. Lieut. Hudgins took command of the *Reliance*, and just as the first gray streak of day appeared in the East the *Satellite* moved out, followed closely by Lieut. Hudgins. The run up occupied some three hours, and a little after sunrise we dropped the anchors off Urbana. The first thing was to get the wounded and prisoners ashore. Midshipman Matt. P. Goodwyn had charge of this, and in a short time all were landed and delivered into the hands of the cavalry of Col. T. L. Rosser, who had co-operated with the expedition, and was ready to take charge of the prisoners to Richmond.

When captured, the Federal steamers had but a few hours supply of coal, and the *Currituck*, their companion-steamer, had gone for coal for the little squadron. Lieut. Wood, however, determined to make the supply on hand serve his purpose, and expecting resistance from the *Currituck*, Col. Rosser detailed Capt. Clay's company of sharp-shooters to assist on the *Satellite*. Capt. Fendall Gregory and Lieut. Nunn, of Rosser's regiment, also volunteered.

Owing to the difficulty of making and keeping up steam on the *Reliance*, Lieut. Hudgins was unable to accompany Lieut. Wood in his cruise over the waters of the Chesapeake Bay, and the *Satellite*, on Sunday night, went out alone, and reached the mouth of the river at eleven o'clock. The sea was quite high, with a strong southeasterly wind, and every prospect of an approaching storm. Having so little coal, it was impossible to go far; but Lieut. Wood started boldly up the bay to see what there was afloat. The waves were every moment getting higher and the *Satellite* creaked and groaned in every seam, and ran heavily against the sea, as if trying to commit suicide at the chagrin of capture. Although much indisposed, Pilot Moore managed her admirably, and kept her well against the storm. After cruising awhile up the bay, her course was turned towards the eastern shore. Some few sails were seen looming up through the dark, but they were small and hardly worth the time when larger game was expected. At one o'clock the sea was very high, and about all the *Satellite* could stand. It would have availed little then to have made out a sail, for the sea was too rough for boarding, and small boats would probably have swamped in such weather. At two o'clock the *Satellite* turned back, and a little before day made Stingray Point. Fearing the *Currituck* might have returned during the night and dropped into the anchorage, Lieut. Wood sent up a signal light; but it was not answered, and the *Satellite* ran safely inside.

In the gray of Monday morning the steamer ran some five miles up the river, and came to anchor near Gray's Point. Being out all night, as well as the two nights previous, everybody was much exhausted, and, as soon as the anchor dropped over the side, nearly all dropped to sleep upon the deck. Having suffered severely from sea-sickness during the night, the cavalry men were a forlorn-looking set, and it was pitiful to see their pale, uneasy faces.

Nothing of importance occurred during the day. The sea still ran high, and the wind increased in strength. About night three sails made their appearance in the bay, all beating down upon the starboard tack directly towards the *Satellite*. Lieut. Wood made out towards them, and for an hour or two chased the larger of the two down towards Gwin's Island and the mouth of the Piankatank. About nine o'clock she was overhauled, and proved to be the schooner *Golden Rod*, laden with coals from Baltimore, and bound for Maine. The other two sail (schooners both) had anchored just inside the point, and these were picked up upon the return. They were the *Two Brothers* and the *Coquette*, anchor-sweepers, from Philadelphia. Both had a number of very fine anchors and cables on board. Taking the three in tow, the *Satellite* ran up to Urbana again, and let go anchors. As the *Reliance* had but a few bushels of coal left, she was sent up to Port Royal that morning, but after the capture of the *Golden Rod* she was ordered to return.

Running the *Satellite* alongside the schooner, Lieut. Wood took on board coal to last a day or two, and prepared to run down the river. The schooners were made ready for burning, and instructions left with Lieut. Hudgins to take charge of them and apply the match should the enemy appear before the return of the *Satellite*.

Remaining but a few hours of Tuesday at Urbana, for the purpose of ministering to the wounded in the fight, Lieut. Wood again ran down the river and laid under lee of the land, some two miles from the bay, waiting patiently for "something to turn up." The sea seemed to be higher than before, and the white foam caps flashed in the light, and the heavy breakers dashed upon the beach with their continuous, saddening roar. It was too much for the *Satellite*—the elements were against her. From a picket it was ascertained that the *Currituck* had arrived off the Piankatank, communicated with the shore, and afterwards steamed rapidly in the direction of Fortress Monroe. It was evident, then, she was aware of the nature of Lieut. Wood's exploit, and had gone for aid. Sure enough, later in the evening, the black smoke-stacks of three large gunboats became visible in the distance.

Had the weather been favorable, Lieut. Wood intended to have run out before the steamers came up; but the pilots decided the sea was too rough for the engines. This being the case, Lieut. Wood had the choice of an unequal fight or a retreat up the river. The odds were too great for the former, and the *Satellite* headed for Urbana.

Lieut. Hudgins had returned with the *Reliance* and was coaling alongside the captured schooner, and the *Satellite* was quickly moored close to the *Reliance*. The storm continuing with great violence put an end to all movements by either side, and when Wednesday morning broke clear and cold the

river was very rough.   However, a pilot was obtained from
the shore and preparations were made to run up to Port Royal,
where the steamers and the prizes could be dismantled.   The
larger schooner drew eleven feet of water, and this the pilot
thought too much to be gotten up without difficulty; so at daylight she was fired.   Taking the other two prizes in tow the
Satellite started on, pilot Moore bringing up the *Reliance* close
behind.   After a few miles he brought her alongside the *Satellite*, and the two then worked together, making quite good
time against the strong ebb-tide and the high headwind.

The Confederate flag was flying from the *Satellite*, and
from some old bunting on board the officers of the *Reliance*
improvised a small flag of the new pattern—the white ground
with battle-flag union.   The advance caused considerable excitement on the route: the people did not know what to make
of it.   Some stared in mute astonishment, others thought it a
trick of the Yankees, others again greeted the little fleet with
enthusiastic cheers.

Upon arrival at Port Royal, where was stationed some
Confederate artillery, the approaching fleet was hailed and
warned not to approach the shore.   But a boat dispatched
from the vessels explained their true character and changed a
hostile aspect into pleasant and welcoming shouts.

Early on Thursday, Lieut. Wood reported to the officer in
command at Port Royal, where a detachment of Confederate
cavalry and artillery had been protecting a foraging train.
The Federal troops were at King George C. H., some fifteen
miles distance, and from which an attack might be expected
as soon as the news of the arrival of the captured steamers
was made known.   After two days' hard work, there was
nothing left upon the *Satellite* and the *Reliance*, and their
guns were on shore and in battery to resist any approach of
the enemy.

This bold and unexampled expedition was particularly annoying to the administration of the Federal Navy Department.
It had occurred in the very track of their communication between Washington and McClellan's base of operations.   It
was liable to repetition, and the captured vessels offered the
means of greater expedition among the many vessels sailing
on the Chesapeake Bay.   The *Currituck*, as anticipated by
Lieut. Wood, did report his exploit to the gunboat *Meigs*, and
an expedition for their recapture started, but returned empty-
handed.

In the meantime Lieut. Wood had arrived at Port Royal
and was securing the fruits of his enterprise.   Four wagons
were set to work transporting the cargo and other captured
material to Milford Station, on the R. F. and P. R. R.   Lieut.
Wood went to Richmond to procure more transportation,
leaving Lieut. Hudgins in command.   To Washington the
report was carried "by Capt. Bates, of Gen. Sickles' staff,

that information had been received at the headquarters of the
Third Army Corps that Gen. Kilpatrick succeeded in sinking
the recently captured gunboats *Reliance* and *Satellite*, on the
Rappahannock, twelve miles below Fredericksburg."

Nothing of the kind occurred; the Federal cavalry did attack and did attempt to destroy the vessels, but was driven off
by Col. Hardwick with an Alabama regiment that happened
to be in Port Royal protecting a foraging train.   Everything
valuable was taken from the captured steamers, and on Friday they were burned by Lieut. Wood.   Gen. Kilpatrick's
attack was on Tuesday evening and Wednesday morning preceding.   It accomplished nothing whatever toward the destruction of the *Satellite* and *Reliance*, which were burned on
Friday, by the order of Lieut. Wood, because they could not be
of any further service to the Confederacy.   The expedition
was a most brilliant success, illustrating the dash and enterprise of the C. S. navy, and a mortifying blow upon the
U. S. Chesapeake flotilla, as well as securing valuable material
for the navy and the army of the Confederacy.   In its moral
effect it aroused enthusiasm and kept alive the spirit of resistance, teaching the lesson that amid reverses there was still
the chance of victory and the hope of success.

The capture of these two steamers was investigated by a
U. S. Naval Court of Inquiry, which reported that it was the
result of a complete surprise, and by order of Secretary Welles
the officers commanding the steamers were dismissed the
service.

CHAPTER VII.

HAMPTON ROADS.

THE magnificent estuary of Hampton Roads, lying behind the guns of Fortress Monroe and the Rip Raps, receives the waters of the James River, which flow immediately past Richmond; while on the Elizabeth River, its other principal tributary, the greatest naval station and ship and ordnance yard of the United States is located. The central position of this great harbor, almost equally distant from the north and from the south portion of the Atlantic sea-board, made its possession and control of the greatest importance to both sections of the Union. And while the storm of war was gathering, and yet had not taken positive shape, both parties —at least Virginia and the United States—kept the possession of this harbor constantly in view. The report that the guns of Fortress Monroe had been turned " landward" produced very great excitement in the Virginia Convention, even after resolutions looking to secession had been overwhelmingly defeated; and, if the report had not been contradicted, would have precipitated action quite as decided as did Mr. Lincoln's proclamation calling for 75,000 troops. While this anxiety about the possession of the Roads was very great, neither Virginia nor the United States seemed disposed to disturb the uncertain calm of public affairs by open efforts to secure the possession of the harbor; but both seemed to tacitly submit to the *status quo* in the hope that events might yet be so shaped as to avoid collision. But while President Lincoln and Mr. Seward were endeavoring to prevent a collision in Charleston, and to preserve their pledged word with South Carolina that the situation should not be changed, it was a part of the secret purpose of the war wing of the Republican party, headed by Secretaries Welles and Stanton, not only to precipitate a collision in Charleston Harbor but to provoke a like assault at Norfolk.

To that end, before Sumter was assaulted, and while the Virginia Convention was anxiously holding the State to her moorings in the Union, against the efforts of the secession

minority, Mr. Welles addressed his order of April 10th to Capt.
C. S. McCauley, commandant of the navy-yard at Norfolk,
to prepare the steamer *Merrimac* for sea, and to dispatch her
to Philadelphia. The right of the government to control the
movements of its war-ships is undeniable, but the *prudence*
of changing the situation of affairs at Norfolk, just after the
State Convention had refused to secede, can only be commended as a sequence to Mr. Welles' purpose to force Virginia
into hostile action, as he was about to compel South Carolina
to assault Sumter. The expedition of Capt. Fox to Charleston Harbor, and the letters of the Secretary to Capt. McCauley, of the 10th, 11th, and 12th of April, are not only contemporaneous, but they are important parts in the scheme to
preserve the unity of the Republican party by involving the
country in civil war. Hoping and believing that the bad
faith involved in dispatching the Fox expedition to Charleston would light the fires of strife, Mr. Welles determined to
force Virginia to declare her position, and no better device
could have been selected than that of changing the peaceful
situation of affairs at Norfolk. In furtherance of that scheme
he dispatched, on the 14th of April, Engineer Isherwood to
Norfolk with orders to take charge of the *Merrimac*, repair her
machinery, and remove her to Philadelphia. The condition
of her machinery was such that she could have been removed
on the 18th, but Capt. McCauley, anxious not to assume the
responsibility of provoking the State of Virginia into secession, refused on the 16th to permit the frigate to be removed.
Secretary Welles, knowing that the Fox expedition had resulted in collision, wrote to Capt. McCauley on the 16th April
that "no time should be lost in getting her (the *Merrimac's*)
armament on board," and in placing that vessel and the others
capable of being removed, with the public property, ordnance,
stores, etc., "beyond the reach of seizing"; and confident that
he had fired the train of civil war, he concluded his letter of
the 16th with instructions that "the vessels and stores under
your charge you will defend at any hazard, repelling by force,
if necessary, any and all attempts to seize them, whether by
mob violence, organized effort, or any assumed authority."
The *Cumberland* frigate had been ordered to Vera Cruz before Mr. Welles' scheme for provoking assault by South Carolina had been worked through the Cabinet of Mr. Lincoln;
but, after the fall of Sumter, the *Cumberland's* departure
was rendered "inexpedient" by "a state of things" which
Mr. Welles had brought about; so, on the 16th April, he
ordered Capt. Pendergrast, of the *Cumberland*, *not* to depart
for the Gulf, because "events of recent occurence, and the
threatening attitude of affairs in some parts of our country,
call for the exercise of great vigilance and energy at Norfolk."
    Affairs at Norfolk were not managed by Secretary Welles
with the same success which had crowned his expedition under

Capt. Fox to Sumter, where, to use the language of the Secretary's panygerist, Chaplain Boynton, it was "very important that the rebels should strike the first blow in the conflict."[1]

A timidity, both moral and physical, existed among the Federal officers at the Norfolk navy-yard, which prevented any fixity of purpose or any resolution of action. Whether to fly from the yard with the ships, or stay and defend both yard and ships, was a very difficult question to decide, and, whichever way determined, involved the most serious consequences. Those officers found themselves on the very verge of war, not with a foreign nation, but with their fellow-citizens — their friends and relatives—with States in the Union under one political theory, and out of the Union under another. The moral embarrassments that surrounded them involved no suspicion of their loyalty, and their gallantry before and after prevents any question of their courage on that occasion.

Governor Letcher, of Virginia, on the 18th of April, after the passage of the Ordinance of Secession, ordered Major Gen. William B. Taliaferro, of the State Militia, to "forthwith take command of the State troops which are now or may be assembled at the city of Norfolk," to which city he was ordered to depart instantly; and on the same day, Robert B. Pegram and Catesby Ap R. Jones were appointed captains in the navy, and Capt. Pegram was ordered "to proceed to Norfolk and there assume command of the naval station, with authority to organize naval defences, enroll and enlist seamen and marines, and temporarily to appoint warrant officers, and to do and perform whatever may be necessary to preserve and protect the property of the commonwealth and of the citizens of Virginia," and he was further directed to co-operate with the land forces under Gen. Taliaferro.

Under these orders, Gen. Taliaferro, with Capt. Henry Heth and Major Nat. Tyler of his staff, and Capts. Pegram and Jones, repaired to Norfolk, arriving on the night of the 18th. The situation of affairs, both Federal and State, at Norfolk, on the morning of the 19th of April, was that the Federal authorities had there "the U. S. frigate *Cumberland*, twenty-four guns, fully manned, ready for sea, and under orders for Vera Cruz; the brig *Dolphin*, four guns, fully manned, and ready for sea; the sloop *Germantown*, twenty-two guns, fully

[1] Of Chaplain Boynton's History of the Navy during the Rebellion, Admiral Porter says: "He received his information from that (the Navy Department) source, and naturally followed it as that to be put in his history, whereas a historian should leave nothing undone to obtain a true statement of affairs. Mr. Boynton, while writing his history, held an appointment under the Navy Department, which he could only hold as long as his writings were acceptable to its chief; * * * Where articles were prepared for his book, he could not very well reject or revise them without severing his relations with a party who had given him an easy office, in order that he might have time to devote himself solely to writing his Naval History. Many officers of the navy say it is only a history of the Naval Department." It is not surprising that a book written under such inspiration should have been not only unjust and partial in United States naval matters. but foul-mouthed with epithets toward Confederate affairs. Its reliability is clouded with suspicion of its motives, and its statements poisoned with the malice of its patron.

manned, ready for sea; the sloop *Plymouth*, twenty-two guns, ready for sea; the marines of the navy-yard, and the guards of the frigate *Raritan*, sixty guns, in ordinary; the frigate *Columbia*, fifty guns, in ordinary; the frigate *United States*, fifty guns, in ordinary; the steam-frigate *Merrimac*, forty guns, under repairs; the ship of the line *Delaware*, seventy-four guns, in ordinary; the ship of the line *Columbus*, seventy-four guns, in ordinary, and the ship of the line *Pennsylvania*, 120 guns, "receiving-ship"—all lying at the yard or in the stream. The yard was walled around with a high brick inclosure, and protected by the Elizabeth River, and there were over 800 marines and sailors with officers.

On the side of Virginia the situation was: that of Gen. Taliaferro with his staff ; Capt. Heth and Major Tyler, two volunteer companies—the Blues of Norfolk and the Grays of Portsmouth—and Capts. Pegram and Jones of the navy. These were the only troops in Norfolk, until after the evacuation of the navy-yard and the departure of the Federal ships.

Whatever information may have been received by Capt. McCauley on "Friday, the 19th of April," about Virginia state troops arriving at Portsmouth and Norfolk in numbers from Richmond, Petersburg, and the neighborhood, had its only foundation in the *ruse de guerre* practiced by Wm. Mahone, President of the Norfolk and Petersburg Railroad, by running empty cars up the railroad a few miles, where they received some citizens from the neighborhood, and then returning to the city, with every man yelling with all his might, and thereby creating the desired impression of large reinforcements pouring into the city.

It was not until Saturday night, the 20th, that the first reinforcements arrived from Petersburg, numbering about 400 men; on Sunday the Richmond *Grays*, and on Monday three companies from Georgia arrived, and after that troops continued to arrive until the post was fully garrisoned. At the evacuation of the yard, the State force was only the two volunteer companies in Norfolk and Portsmouth—the aggregate of which was outnumbered by the command on board any one of the U. S. ships in the navy. The batteries spoken of by Commander McCauley as being thrown up opposite the navy-yard, and which he said "were distinctly seen from the masthead of the *Cumberland*, though screened from sight below by the intervening trees"—*had no existence then*, nor at any other time. Gen. Taliaferro, having no means at his command with which to oppose the passage of the ships from the navy-yard, relied largely upon the demoralization existing in the yard, for the effect of his promise "that to save the effusion of blood, he would permit the *Cumberland* to leave the port unmolested, if the destruction of property should be discontinued." The reply of Com. Paulding "that any act of violation on *their* part would devolve upon them the consequences"—

was received by Gen. Taliaferro as a Parthian arrow shot by a flying foe; and having literally no force of any kind that could *molest* ships-of-war, he was forced to see the flying squadron escape. The obstructions placed in the channel of Elizabeth River were *not* so placed as to prevent the men-of-war from escaping—for it was not desirable to shut up in Elizabeth River so formidable a force of armed ships as then floated on her waters. Those obstructions were a part of the intimidation mode of assault which Mr. Mahone carried out on land, and the old hulks in the water—designed only to threaten the closing of the river—and the capture of the ships by the large land force that was represented as arriving on the noisy but empty cars. At the same time, an opening was left, which Lieut. Murray found—a golden bridge for a flying foe—through which ships which could not be captured might escape.

Capt. McCauley's report shows that on the 20th he was informed by Col. Heth, Gen. Taliaferro's aide-de-camp, that there were no batteries being constructed, and Lieut. Selfridge, of the *Cumberland*, confirmed the statement. The State had seceded but three days before, and Gen. Taliaferro had been in Norfolk but two days, so that under ordinary circumstances the Federal officers would have realized the impossibility of there being any formidable force threatening the yard. These officers were demoralized by the political situation, and did not understand how to make war on a State, and were not prompt to commence hostilities on Virginia cities, as long as the administration at Washington had not declared war. Even the naval critic will find extenuation and apology for these gallant and brave men, who found themselves confronted with the appalling horror of being the first to commence civil war.

The Norfolk navy-yard, which fell into the hands of Virginia on the 20th April, was three-quarters of a mile long and a quarter mile wide. It was by far the most extensive and valuable one in the United States. It had a granite dry dock like that at Charlestown, Mass. The yard was covered with machine shops, houses for officers, and store-houses of various kinds. It was provided with two ship-houses complete, and one unfinished ; marine barracks, sail loft, riggers' loft, gunners' loft, shops for carpenters and machinists, and a large amount of tools and machinery, besides great quantities of materials, provisions, and ammunition of every description. There were 1,198 guns of all kinds captured with the yard, of which fifty-two were nine-inch Dahlgren guns. Lying at the yard was the *Merrimac*, worth $1,200,000 ; the *Plymouth* and *Germantown*, twenty-two guns each ; and the *Dolphin*, four guns—all efficient vessels. The old *Pennsylvania* was in commission as a receiving-ship; and the *Delaware*, eighty-four; *Columbus*, eighty guns ; and the *Columbia* and *Raritan*, fifty guns each, were lying in ordinary at the yard, and the ship-of-the-line *New York* was on the stocks. The *Cumberland*, Commodore Pendergrast, lay in a position that commanded completely the cities of Norfolk and Portsmouth. The total property was estimated by the U. S. Navy Department at $9,760,181.

Immediately upon the withdrawal of the U. S. ships, the citizens broke into the yard and began the work of saving property. The magnificent dry-dock was found mined and containing twenty barrels of powder, the train to which had failed, from some cause unknown, to ignite the mine, and the dry dock was saved. The ships that were scuttled and fired were saved from total destruction by sinking, the ship-houses and much other valuable property were destroyed, but a vast amount of property of inestimable value to the Confederate States was saved. On Monday morning, Lieut. C. F. M. Spottswood raised the flag of Virginia over the yard, and the State assumed authority over all the property.

The report of William H. Peters, made to the Governor of Virginia, of an inventory of property captured at the fall of the Norfolk navy-yard, makes the following statement:

"It is difficult to estimate the value of property destroyed on the night of April 20th, 1861, when the Federal forces, having previously fired the navy-yard, evacuated it. The extensive row of buildings on the north front of the yard, containing large quantities of manufactured articles and valuable material—such as pivot gun-carriages, several full suites of sails for frigates and sloops of-war, a very large number of hammocks and bags, and immense quantities of canvas, cordage, etc., etc., were, with their contents, entirely destroyed. Ship-houses A and B, which were very large wooden structures, the former containing the line-of-battle ship *New York*, on the stocks, were also totally destroyed. So, also, were the buildings used as barracks; the latter, however, were of but little value."

The report gives the following account of the attempt to destroy the dry dock:

"The dry dock did not escape attention. Twenty-six barrels of powder (a quantity sufficient to have destroyed the dock and every building at the south end of the yard) were found disturbed in the culvert on its north side, and across the head of the dock. These barrels were connected by a train, continuing on to the inner steps at the bottom of the dock, where it is supposed slow matches were placed for ignition at a prearranged moment. The plan, however, was happily discovered in time to frustrate it. Lieut. C. F. M. Spottswood, of the navy, to whom the discovery was reported early on the morning of the 21st, promptly directed the opening of the gates, when the dock was flooded, and thus saved from destruction."

The number of guns in the yard is not stated, but the following general remarks are made:

"Many heavy cannon were spiked, and for the time rendered useless; but they have since been restored. Some had their trunnions broken off. The small arms (of which there were in the yard 1,329 carbines, 274 rifled muskets, 950 naval pistols, and 337 Colt's revolvers) were in part carried off in the frigate *Cumberland*, and the remainder broken and thrown overboard.

" I had purposed offering some remarks upon the vast importance to Virginia, and to the entire South, of the timely acquisition of this extensive naval depot, with its immense supplies of munitions of war, and to notice briefly the damaging effects of its loss to the government at Washington; but I deem it unnecessary, since the presence at almost every exposed point on the whole southern coast, and at the numerous inland intrenched camps in the several States, of heavy pieces of ordnance, with their equipments and fixed ammunition, all supplied from this establishment, fully attests the one, while the unwillingness of the enemy to attempt demonstrations at any point, from which he is obviously deterred by the knowledge of its well-fortified condition, abundantly proves the other—especially when it is considered that both he and we are wholly indebted for our means of resistance to his loss and our acquisition of the Gosport navy-yard."

To the report there are appended elaborate tabular estimates of the value of the property seized. The worth of the land is given as follows:

Navy-yard, proper, containing eighty-six acres . .	$246,000 00
St. Helena, containing thirty-eight acres . . .	12,000 00
Naval hospital, containing 100 acres	20,000 00
Fort Norfolk, containing six acres	10,000 00
Total	$288,000 00

The estimates of the improvements are:

Improvements at navy-yard	2,944,800 00
Improvements at St. Helena	8,300 00
Improvements at naval hospital	622,800 00
Improvements at naval magazine	136,580 68
Improvements at other points	226,000 00
Total	$3,938,480 68

The worth of the vessels partially destroyed is thus estimated:

Merrimac, steam-frigate	$225,000 00
Plymouth, first-class sloop	40,000 00
Germantown, first-class sloop	25,000 00
Pennsylvania, line-of-battle ship	6,000 00
Delaware, line-of-battle ship	10,000 00
Columbus, line-of-battle ship	10,000 00
Columbia, frigate	5,000 00
Dolphin, brig	1,000 00
Powder boat	800 00
Water tank	100 00
United States	10,000 00
Total	$332,900 00

The value of the steam-engines and other apparatus is estimated at $250,676. The following is a recapitulation:

Value of territory	$288,000 00
Value of buildings and other improvements . .	3,938,480 68
Value of vessels	332,900 00
Value of engines, machinery, etc.	250,676 00
Total	$4,810,056 68

Gen. Taliaferro's appearance at Norfolk, as commanding officer of the Virginia forces, made it apparent to the people of that city, as well as to the officers of the navy-yard, that the Convention had passed the Ordinance of Secession. From that moment the intensest excitement prevailed, for upon the prudence of the Virginia troops the safety of both Norfolk and Portsmouth depended. The Federal naval force in Elizabeth River was known to be too formidable for attack, and yet any imprudent or threatening preparations might invite severe and destructive retaliation. The demoralization existing in the navy-yard was well known in both cities, and was felt to be rather a danger than an aid towards the capture of the yard. The excitement which prevailed was by no means any indication of a sentiment of opposition to the secession of the State, and the statement made in the report of the Select Committee of the U. S. Senate,[1] * * * "that at least a majority of the citizens of both Norfolk and Portsmouth were on the side of the Union, and would have been warmly and openly so had the government shown a strong hand and a timely determination to defend itself," has no foundation whatever in truth and fact. That "an election for Mayor was held in Portsmouth a few days previous to the surrender, at which the Union candidate was elected by an overwhelming majority," no more proves the disloyalty of the people of that city to Virginia than the fact that the Virginia Convention, but a few days before the fall of Sumter, refused by an overwhelming majority to pass the Ordinance of Secession, established the loyalty of the State to the Union. Both the election in Portsmouth, and the defeat of secession in the Convention, preceded the fall of Sumter and the proclamation of Mr. Lincoln, which revolutionized public sentiment throughout the State. Neither is it true, as stated by that committee, that "a voluntary military association, considerable in numbers and influence, was formed in Norfolk for the exclusive purpose of assisting in the defence of the yard against the insurgents." From the 17th to the 20th—three days—was too short a period for the formation of a voluntary military organization, and there were no "insurgents" or other persons threatening the yard. The crowd that on the wharf *jeered* at the *Pawnee* as she passed up on the evening of the 20th, the committee of the Senate represents as *cheering* the steamer for her "deliverance of them from the perils and dishonor of a war against that Union which they loved." *Many of* that same crowd had, the night before, labored with great zeal and industry in bringing the kegs of powder from the U. S. magazine to the lighters which carried it to Richmond; and if their loyalty to the Union had been as intense as the committee represents, it would have conveyed information to the navy-yard of what was taking place.

[1] Report Com., No. 27—27th Congress, 2d Sess.

The averment of the Senate Committee in their report that "the officers of the yard were traitors in disguise, and continued nominally in the service of the government only that they might the more effectually compass their treasonable designs," has foundation only in the violence of the partisan passions of the committee. The officers alluded to were Capt. John R. Tucker, Commander Robert G. Robb, Lieut. C. F. M. Spottswood, and others, who, as long as the State (Virginia) remained in the Union, desired to preserve the peaceful attitude of public affairs at Norfolk, and to that end, in perfect honesty of purpose, and with fidelity to their oaths as United States officers, persuaded Capt. McCauley to do no act which would further complicate the situation at Norfolk. Not one of those officers would have surrendered the yard to any mob, or failed to defend it against unauthorized demand; but when the State of Virginia seceded from the Union, and asserted her right to the yard, a very different question was presented. If the government at Washington would not declare war against a State, was it reasonable to expect officers of the navy to be quick to commence hostilities ? Capt. McCauley was instructed by Secretary Welles, on April 10th, that "it is desirable that no steps should be taken to give needless alarm, but it may be best to order most of the shipping to sea or other stations"; and that as regarded the steamer *Merrimac*, "in case of danger from unlawful attempts to take possession of her, that she should be placed beyond their reach." Such carefully worded orders left to that officer the responsibility of determining what would be "unlawful attempts." The naval officers had witnessed arsenals, forts, and army surrendered to the demands of States throughout the South without even demur or objection by either the executive or legislative authority of the United States; they had seen the flag of the Union fired upon, and the *Star of the West* driven from Charleston Harbor on the 8th of January, and neither President Buchanan nor President Lincoln accepted the act as one of war, but both had submitted and continued negotiations looking toward a peaceful determination of affairs. They had seen eight States secede from the Union and organize a separate and independent government without war, or even a preparation for hostilities by the United States. It was not within the duty of naval officers to interpret the proclamation of President Lincoln of April 15th, in regard to "combinations too powerful to be suppressed by the ordinary course of judicial proceedings," and calling on the States for 75,000 troops to "disperse" the "*persons* composing the combinations," as a declaration of war against the States. And when on the 16th of April, the next day after the publication of that proclamation, Secretary Welles again wrote to Capt. McCauley, without even mentioning that call for troops, or intimating any purpose of the government to resist the demands of States, he alluded to "mob violence, organized effort, or any assumed authority," he still avoided the use of language which would prescribe the officers' duty in the case of the State demanding possession of the navy-yard. The carefully worded orders of Secretary Welles might well have caused all the naval officers at Norfolk, whatever may have been their political opinions on the right of secession, to hesitate long before taking upon themselves the responsibility of hostilities which the government of Washington avoided, and to prefer destroying United States *property* to assuming the duty of either refusing the demand of the State of Virginia or of commencing hostilities.

It was the unauthorized act of some of the people of Norfolk which placed the first imperfect obstructions in the channel; and, subsequently to the evacuation, the old ship *United States* was taken from the navy-yard by a tug and sunk at the mouth of the river. [1]

The burning of the navy-yard at Norfolk is almost a matter of inheritance; our forefathers, in the Revolution, burned the first navy-yard, to prevent it from falling into the hands of the British, the United States authorities again burned it, in 1861, to deprive the State of Virginia of its use, and the following year, for the third time, the yard was committed to the flames by the Confederate army.

The connection of the State of Virginia with the navy-yard begun after its evacuation by the Federal officers, by assigning to its command Flag-officer French Forrest, who assumed command, about April 25th, over all naval property of every kind; and at the same time Gen. Walter Gwynn superseded Gen. Taliaferro in command of the land forces. Gen. Gwynn was directed by Gen. Lee in exercising the command, to advise with, and as far as practicable to act, in relation to naval matters, in consonance with the views of the senior naval officer present ; and it was further suggested to him that the interests of the State might be best served by employing naval officers in the construction and service of water batteries. The naval officers had laid out at Penner's Point a battery to mount twelve guns ; and on Soller's Point had marked out lines for three batteries of six guns each ; and they had prepared the grounds in front of the naval hospital for mounting fourteen guns on two faces, half of which, on April 27th, were ready for service, with navy furnaces for heating shot. This work was begun immediately after the evacuation, amid the greatest confusion and excitement caused by the movements of the *Pawnee* up and down Elizabeth River, as though meditating a visit back to Norfolk. Three guns and carriages were hastily

[1] It may be mentioned here, that Major Nat Tyler, in command of the party trying to sink the old ship, broke and destroyed two whole boxes of axes and did not succeed in cutting through her sides, and that her final sinking was due to the suggestions of an old sailor, to bore through from the inside.

moved from the navy-yard, and mounted in rear of the ground required to be broken for the battery ; 150 bales of cotton were sent over by Major Tyler to make a temporary cover for the men between the guns, should the *Pawnee* or *Cumberland* venture back toward Norfolk. No such attempt was made, and the cotton was afterwards piled away to prevent its damage. At Fort Norfolk, Col. Talcott mounted guns to bear on the channel of Elizabeth River, and constructed a battery of five guns between the fort and the wharf. By moonlight, on Sunday night, Col. Talcott and one assistant examined the ground on Craney Island, and Monday morning labor commenced to arrive from the plantations, until 120 working-men, with carts, constructed a battery for twenty guns—which covered all the channel-way from N. 58 W. to E. By the 27th April, batteries to mount sixty-one guns were under construction, and were soon after completed. Of these, fourteen were at the naval hospital, twelve at Penner's Point, and twenty on Craney Island ; at the same time, residents near Bushy Bluff began, and soon completed, a battery for four guns ; at Soller's Point a battery was afterwards erected. Capt. Dimmock, State Colonel of Ordnance, suggested to Gen. Lee the necessity for a laboratory to work upon all ammunition for the heavy pieces for stationary batteries, and that Norfolk was the most suitable place for the same, and that Capt. Minor, of the navy, approved of this suggestion ; but Norfolk was not considered a safe place at that time for such a work, and, on May 30th, Lieut. John M. Brooke, of the navy, acting Aide-de-camp to Gen. Lee, instructed Gen. Gwynn to remove from Norfolk all "materials," etc., such as powder, shot, cannon, pikes, and shells, as are not required for the defence of that city. The pikes were to do service with cavalry in the stead of sabres, of which there was a very great deficiency.

Notwithstanding the seizure of the navy-yard at Norfolk, commercial and hostile intercourse continued between Norfolk and Baltimore until April 30th, when Capt. Pendergrast, flag-officer commanding home squadron, announced that he had a sufficient naval force off Fortress Monroe for the purpose of carrying out President Lincoln's Proclamation of Blockade. From that date all communication, other than such as was surreptitiously carried on, ceased between Virginia and the United States. The *Wm. Selden*, of the Baltimore Steam Packet Company, carrying the mails between Norfolk and Baltimore, having been allowed to pass in, notwithstanding an official announcement of effective blockade, was seized at Norfolk by the Confederate authorities. On May 1st, the blockade of the James River commenced.

Commander Archibald B. Fairfax was put in charge of the ordnance department of the navy-yard, and he immediately begun that important work of banding and rifling the thirty-two-pounders of fifty-seven and sixty-three hundred-weight.[1]

These banded guns were regarded by Capt. W. H. Parker as the "most important improvement made in our ordnance during the war," and when placed on the small steamer *Harmony* enabled her to place herself out of the "range of the guns of the U. S. frigates in Hampton Roads, and yet succeeded in hitting her several times." It was Capt. Fairfax that fitted out the Confederate vessels in Norfolk.

Brig. Gen. Benjamin Huger, of the volunteer forces of Virginia, was assigned to the command of the troops in and around Norfolk, and relieved Gen. Gwynn on May 24th; and on the 27th reported to Gen. Lee that the enemy from Fortress Monroe had landed from seven steamers many troops at Newport News, and that other steamers with troops had arrived at Fortress Monroe. The movements were considered as threatening the Nansemond River, which extends far back into the country on the south side of the James to the town of Suffolk, where it is crossed by the Norfolk and Petersburg railroad. The effect of that, or any other movement by which Suffolk would be held, would have severed all communication between Norfolk and Richmond, isolated the former city, and regained the navy-yard for the United States. To guard against such a movement, Gen. Lee diverted Georgia and North Carolina troops from their march to Virginia to Norfolk, and ordered Lieut. John M. Brooke, of the navy, to Petersburg, and thence to Zuni, for the protection of the bridges and to observe the movements of the enemy—if any should be made to the south side of the James. The battery erected at Jamestown by Gen. Magruder was placed under the protection of the steamer, under the command of Capt. James Barron, on May 28th. The position of the Federal detachment at Newport News, while threatening to the State authorities, was itself exposed and liable to assault. To that end, Col. Francis J. Thomas, commanding at Suffolk, Virginia, two Maryland companies—a regiment from North Carolina and two companies of cavalry—asked permission, May 31st, of Gen. Lee, to cross the James River and strike a blow and then retire : that he could bring a tug and a steamboat into Nansemond River, which could transport his command across. He was ordered by Gen. Lee to get the boats ready, but not to make the attack at once, unless completely prepared for success. The reinforcement of the detachment at Newport News postponed Col. Thomas' intended assault, and induced Gen. Lee, June 18th, to order Lieut. R. R. Carter,

[1] Of these banded guns, Admiral Louis Goldsborough, U. S. N., wrote to Mr. Secretary Welles : "His (the Confederate's) gun is the thirty-two pounder of fifty-seven and sixty-three hundred-weight, beautifully fortified at the breech-end by a long and massive wrought-iron cylindrical ring, and so rifled in the bore as to admit of the use of round shot and grape, as well as shells, by the simple interposition of a junk wad between the charge of powder and the shot or stand of grape. His ordnance arrangements throughout exhibit great skill and ingenuity."

commanding the Confederate[1] steam-tender *Teaser*, to unite with the batteries at Jamestown Island in defence of James River, and to be employed in obtaining intelligence of the movements of hostile vessels and the landing of troops on either side of the river.

On May 30th, Flag-officer Forrest announced to Gen. Lee that "we have the *Merrimac* up, and just hauling her into the dry dock." By the 27th of June, the sloop-of-war *Germantown* was gotten afloat, and her fine battery of ten large guns were recovered from the bottom of the river uninjured, though a little rusty. The spars and rigging of the *Germantown* were burned off, but the hull was found uninjured materially; the *Plymouth* was being rapidly repaired, she was the least injured of any of the vessels. The hull of the *Merrimac* was found not to be materially injured, and the machinery was thought at that early review of the ship not to require any very great repairs. On July the 25th, while there was no work being done on the *Merrimac*, all the machine shops were engaged, under Commodore Forrest, in repairing damages done by the fire, and getting ready for work on the vessels. The northern wall of the yard had been lined with many pieces of heavy ordnance, and the defences of Norfolk were nearly completed.

While the military and naval authorities at Norfolk were putting the Elizabeth River in a state of defence to protect Norfolk, Portsmouth, and the navy-yard from assault by the U. S. forces, then assembling at Fortress Monroe, the James River, which opened a practicable route to Richmond, was also being prepared to prevent any ascent to the capital of the State, and afterwards of the Confederate States. Gen. Lee, on April 29th, ordered Col. Talcott to proceed up James River to the vicinity of Burwell's Bay, and select the most suitable point for the erection of a battery to prevent the ascent of the river by the enemy, and, after laying-off the works, to leave their completion to Lieut. C. Ap R. Jones of the Virginia navy, and then to proceed to the mouth of the Appomattox or to old Fort Powhatan, and select sites for defensive fortification to be constructed under the supervision of Commander J. W. Cooke.

The battery at Fort Powhatan was constructed, and placed under the command of Capt. Harrison F. Cocke, who had resigned his commission in the U. S. navy; and Lieuts. John Wilkinson and C. S. and George Noland, C. S. navy, were attached to the battery, which was supported by several companies of Virginia volunteers. It was situated a short distance below City Point, and mounted six or eight forty-two-pound guns on ships' carriages, which had been transported from the Norfolk navy-yard. When the position was considered no

---

[1] The proclamation of Gen. Letcher of June 8th transferred to the authorities of the Confederate States the command of all the officers, seamen and marines of the Provisional Navy of Virginia.

longer tenable, the guns were removed, and Lieut. Wilkinson was ordered to the command of a battery at Aquia Creek.

Col. J. B. Magruder, of the Provisional Army of Virginia, was placed in command of the troops and military operations on the peninsula on May 21st, with directions to take measures for the safety of the batteries at Jamestown and Yorktown. Gen. Lee, on June 15th, wrote to Governor Letcher, that for the defence of James River two batteries and two steamers have been provided, mounting altogether forty guns, ranging in calibre from thiry-two-pounders to eight and nine-inch Columbiads ; that arrangements were also in progress for mounting sixty guns of different weight in the defences around Richmond, and a naval battery of six to twelve-pounder howitzers was in progress of organization. The two steamers mentioned by Gen. Lee were the *Yorktown,* late the *Patrick Henry,* of the New York and Old Dominion Steamship Line, and the *Jamestown,* of the same line, afterwards called the *Thomas Jefferson.*

The naval defences of James River were placed under the charge of Capt. George N. Hollins, C. S. navy, on July 10th, 1861, who was advised by Gen. Lee to push forward the armaments as fast as possible, and to continue the examination of the river from Day's Point to Mulberry Point, with a view of ascertaining the best methods of commanding its navigation. The batteries at Mulberry Point and on the point opposite, as well as interrupting, the navigation of Swash Channel, was called to the attention of Capt. Hollins. Under the advice of Lieut. Jones, of the navy, the defences at James-town Island were strengthened by the erection of a battery on the Point to command the entrance into the creek, and armed with two thirty - two - pounder (fifty - seven hundred-weight) guns.

The *Patrick Henry,* though not at all fitted for fighting, had to be taken as the best that the State could do when she seceded. By taking off her cabins, strengthening her decks, Lieut. William Llewellyn Powell,[1] her executive officer, was able to make " her answer pretty well." Lieut. Powell is believed to have been the first officer to fully comprehend the necessity for shielding the ships with iron, and, urging this improvement upon the Secretary of the Navy, he obtained permission to make the experiment on the *Patrick Henry.* One-inch iron plates were put abreast her boilers, extending a foot, perhaps two, below the water-line, and ran a few feet forward and abaft her engines and boilers. One inch, though not much protection, was all the merchant-ship could bear; and iron shields, in the form of a V, on the spar-deck forward and abaft her engines, which, when fighting head or stern on, afforded good protection from raking shots, as well as afforded

---

[1] He resigned from the navy and died a brigadier-general at Fort Morgan before its fall.

some protection to the walking-beam of that side-wheel steamer.

The *Jamestown*, the sister-ship of the *Yorktown*, became the *Thomas Jefferson*, but was always known by the name of the *Jamestown*. The *Jamestown*, the *Patrick Henry* and the *Teaser*, a river tug mounting one gun, composed the C. S. James River squadron, which was under the command of Capt. John R. Tucker. However much may have been hoped for from this little fleet, its possibilities of usefulness were limited more by the discretion and dash of the commander than by the fighting power of the ships. The iron shield of the *Patrick Henry* was a protection, but the vulnerability of the ship was but little helped by the thin shield of iron over her engines and boilers. Capt. Tucker, however, was not the man to accept the excuse of the weakness of his fleet for not seeking the enemy. So, on the 13th of September, he steamed down to Newport News to feel the enemy and put a limit to gunboat excursions up James River. Off the point lay the U. S. steamer *Savannah*, the U. S. sloop *Cumberland*, the U. S. steamer *Louisiana*, and on the land the heavy batteries of the enemy as well as a battery of light artillery on the banks of the stream. Capt. Tucker had, on the 7th of the month, taken position, at Gen. Magruder's request, off Mulberry Island Point, where Harden's Point battery on the south closed the river to the enemy. Of this naval skirmish there is no report by Capt. Tucker, but the New York *Herald* correspondent gives the following "facts":

"On the afternoon of Friday, the 13th inst., the *Yorktown* came down James River, and, choosing her distance, opened fire upon the fleet, the shots striking near the *Savannah*, which ship returned her fire from her large guns—the shot, however, falling a long way short. She also threw shells from her lower-deck guns, which burst in the air not more than one-third of the distance to the steamer. The *Cumberland* sloop-of-war fired two or three times, but, finding the shot fell short, ceased firing. The Sawyer gun in our battery on shore was fired too, but the shot struck from a quarter to half a mile ahead of the steamer. In the meantime, the U. S. steamer *Louisiana* got under way and advanced three-quarters of a mile towards the *Yorktown* and opened an effective fire upon her, which was continued for more than an hour, the *Yorktown* directing all her fire at the *Louisana*, none of the shot, however, striking her, although several came very near.

"The *Yorktown* was finally forced to retire by a cross-fire from the *Louisiana* and Lieut. Cooke's battery of light artillery, which had gone up the bank of the river until the steamer was in range."

The gunboats from Newport News and Fortress Monroe, together with armed tugs, had become annoying in the James River, and Capt. Tucker, learning that they were in the habit of ascending the river at night and withdrawing in the morning, was induced to take the first favorable opportunity to surprise and attack them. The morning of the 2d of December, being dark and suitable for the enterprise, he left his anchorage, off Mulberry Island, at 4 A. M., and proceeded cautiously down the river, all lights carefully concealed. At early daylight he discovered four steamers anchored in line, near the side of the frigates, but in supporting distance of them and the battery at Newport News. He rounded-to at a supposed distance of a mile, and commenced the attack with his port battery and pivot guns, which was returned by the steamers and the battery on shore from rifled and other guns. Many of the rifled shells came near and over the *Patrick Henry*, and one struck her, going through the pilot-house and exploding in the starboard hammock nettings, producing slight injury, and wounding one of the pilots and a seaman very slightly by the splinters. The engagement lasted two hours, when he returned to his anchorage, the enemy evincing no disposition to advance either during the engagement or afterwards. He expended twenty-eight shells and thirteen solid shot, some of which must have struck, but with what injury to the enemy he was unable to say. At the request of Gen. Magruder, the *Patrick Henry* and *Jamestown* remained between Mulberry Point and Harden's Bluff batteries.

By Act of Congress of December 24th, conferring army rank upon such officers of the navy as were commanding batteries on shore, Commander R. F. Pinkney, commanding Fort Norfolk, Commander Charles F. McIntosh, commanding Fort Nelson, and Commander W. L. Maury, commanding Sewell's, were appointed lieutenant colonels; and Lieuts. George W. Harrison, commanding Penner's Point battery, R. R. Carter, commanding Pig Point battery, were appointed majors, and B. P. Loyall, assigned to Roanoke Island, was appointed captain. [1]

The three batteries at Cedar Point, Barrel Point and Pagan Creek, were in charge of Commander R. L. Page until he was relieved and sent to Gloucester Point. Gen. Huger says the batteries at Dog's Point and Harden's Bluff were also under the command of naval officers.

The months of January and February, 1862, witnessed no naval movements or engagements in the waters of Hampton Roads and James River, but the time was used to strengthen the defences on shore and to complete the work on the *Merrimac* or *Virginia*. The correspondence of Union officers show very accurate information of the kind of change being made in the *Merrimac*, as well as the progress towards her completion. Gen. McClellan advised Gen. Wool, on February 21st, that "the iron-clad steam monitor and a large frigate will be at Hampton Roads within the time you specify"; to which Gen. Wool replied, that "five days" was "the time

---

[1] Brevet Capt. J. S. Taylor, formerly a lieutenant in the U. S. navy, but who had not been appointed in the C. S. navy, but to a second lieutenancy in the army, was commanding Lambert's Point battery. Gen. Huger recommended him for promotion "as a most valuable artillery officer." Another naval officer holding commission in the army, was Brevet Capt. Jas. E. Milligan, signal officer—he was in the revenue service, resigned, and took service under the State of Virginia.

stated when the *Merrimac, Yorktown* and *Jamestown* would attack Newport News." The information received of the *Virginia* by the U. S. Navy Department was such that Secretary Welles wrote to Capt. John Marston, March 7th, to " send the *St. Lawrence, Congress* and *Cumberland* immediately into the Potomac River ; use steam to tow them up. I will also try and send a couple of steamers from Baltimore to assist. Let there be no delay." The order came too late. The *Virginia* had done her work upon the *Congress* and *Cumberland* so effectually that their sailing days were over forever.

CHAPTER VIII.

THE FIRST IRON-CLAD.

THE honor of having planned a vessel so novel in form, and so effective in battle, was early the subject of discussion in the Confederacy ; and ever since has remained unsettled and disputed. In the March, 1884, number of the *Century*, Lieut. John Taylor Wood, of the late C. S. navy, awards the honor to "Lieut. (George) John M. Brooke, an accomplished officer of the old navy," who he says proposed to Secretary Mallory to make and rebuild this ship (the *Merrimac*) as an iron-clad. His plans were approved, and orders were given to carry them out."

Commander John M. Brooke testified before the Investigating Committee of the Confederate Congress that:

"The Secretary and myself had conversed upon the subject of protecting ships with iron-cladding very frequently, and at last I proposed to him a plan. That was early in June, 1861, just after the Secretary came here from Montgomery. He approved of the plan, and I asked him to send to Norfolk for some practical ship-builder to draw out a plan in detail. He sent for one, and one of the employees of the yard, whose opinion then I did not favor, except that I heard he was a regular constructor there, was sent up. He said he knew nothing of drafting, and although he approved of the general plan, he could not make the drawing. This was what I wanted done chiefly. He was here a few days, and complained of being made sick by the water, and was therefore permitted to return to Norfolk. I then determined to go on with the drawing myself, but asked the Secretary to send for the naval constructor at Norfolk, and naval engineer, so that they might be consulted in relation to the vessel. They came up, and this constructor brought with him a model. I should have said that the name of the constructor was J. L. Porter. This model is now one of the models in the Secretary's room. It consisted of a shield and hull, the extremities of the hull terminating with a shield, forming a sort of box or scow upon which the shield was supported. The Secretary directed the constructor, Chief Engineer Williamson, and myself to meet him at my office here. We met there and this model was examined by us all, and the form of the shield was approved. It was considered a good shield, and, for ordinary purposes, a good boat for harbor defence. The Secretary then called the attention of Mr. Porter and Mr. Williamson to the drawing, giving a general idea of the vessel I proposed. The difference between the model and my drawing consisted in the one I proposed,

10

having the ends prolonged and shaped like those of any fast vessel, and, in order to protect them from the enemy, were to be submerged two feet under water, so that nothing was to be seen afloat but the shield itself. The object of having these parts of the vessel submerged was to gain speed and to have buoyancy without exposing the hull, and to avoid increasing the draft of water. Mr. Porter and Mr. Williamson, after looking at the drawing, approved of it, and the Secretary directed us to get up a vessel on that plan. Mr. Porter's shield and the one I proposed were almost identical. Mr. Porter, being a draftsman, immediately drew a plan of such a vessel of comparatively light draft. I think she was to draw something over eight feet of water. Mr. Williamson and myself went to look for engines. We went to the Tredegar Works and inquired there, but there were no suitable engines to be had. Mr. Porter completed the draft and it is now in my office. Mr. Williamson subsequently stated that the engines of the *Merrimac* could be repaired and made valuable, but that they could not be used well in any other vessel unless she had equal draft of water, or nearly equal. Mr. Williamson proposed to put the shield on the *Merrimac*. Mr. Porter and myself thought the draft too great, but were nevertheless of the opinion that it was the best thing that could be done, with our means; and Mr. Porter was ordered by the Secretary to Norfolk to make the plan of the vessel in accordance with the plan which we had approved, and which I mentioned before as having been submitted to the Secretary. Mr. P. did so. He sent up drawings which were after same general description as those he made before in accordance with my suggestion. Mr. Porter was directed to perform all the duties of constructor in connection with alteration of the ship. Mr. Williamson was directed to attend to the engines, and I was directed to attend to having iron prepared at Richmond for her, and the work was then prosecuted with all the energy possible, in my opinion. It was a difficult matter to get iron from Richmond to Norfolk, there being over 700 tons of iron sent down in the course of her construction. After the vessel was launched, Mr. Porter stated to me that he had accidentally omitted in her calculations some weights which were on board the ship, in consequence of which she did not draw as much water when launched as he anticipated."

Secretary Mallory, in a report to the Confederate Congress, of date March 29th, 1862, says: that on the 10th day of June, 1861, Lieut. John M. Brooke, C. S. N., was directed to aid the department in designing an iron-clad war-vessel, and framing the necessary specifications:

"He entered upon this duty at once, and a few days thereafter submitted to the department, as the results of his investigations, rough drawings of a casemated vessel, with submerged ends and inclined iron-plated sides. The ends of the vessel and the eaves of the casemate, according to his plan, were to be submerged two feet; and a light bulwark or false bow was designed to divide the water and prevent it from banking up on the forward part of the shield with the vessel in motion, and also to serve as a tank to regulate the ship's draft. His design was approved by the department, and a practical mechanic was brought from Norfolk to aid in preparing the drawings and specifications.

"This mechanic aided in the statement of details of timber, etc., but was unable to make the drawings; and the department then ordered Chief Engineer Williamson and Constructor Porter from the navy-yard at Norfolk to Richmond, about the 23d of June, for consultation on the same subject generally, and to aid in the work.

"Constructor Porter brought and submitted the model of a flat-bottomed, light-draft propeller, casemated battery, with inclined iron-covered sides and ends, which is deposited in the department. Mr. Porter and Lieut. Brooke have adopted for their casemate a thickness of wood and iron, and an angle of inclination nearly identical.

"Mr. Williamson and Mr. Porter approved of the plan of having submerged ends to obtain the requisite flotation and invulnerability, and the department adopted the design, and a clean drawing was prepared by Mr. Porter of Lieut. Brooke's plan, which that officer then filed with the department.

"The steam-frigate *Merrimac* had been burned and sunk, and her engine greatly damaged by the enemy, and the department directed Mr. Williamson, Lieut. Brooke and Mr. Porter to consider and report upon the best mode of making her useful. The result of their investigations was their recommendation of the submerged ends, and the inclined casemates for this vessel, which was adopted by the department."

The following is the report upon the *Merrimac:*

"In obedience to your orders, we have carefully examined and considered the various plans and propositions for constructing a shot-proof steam battery, and respectfully report that, in our opinion, the steam-frigate *Merrimac*, which is in such condition from the effects of fire as to be useless for any other purpose, without incurring very heavy expense in rebuilding, etc., can be made an efficient vessel of that character, mounting * * * heavy guns; and from the further consideration that we cannot procure a suitable engine and boilers for any other vessel without building them, which would occupy too much time. It would appear that this is our only chance to get a suitable vessel in a short time. The bottom of the hull, boilers, and heavy and costly parts of the engine, being but little injured, reduce the cost of construction to about one-third of the amount which would be required to construct such a vessel anew.

"We cannot, without further examination, make an accurate estimate of the cost of the proposed work, but think it will be about * * * the most of which will be for labor, the materials being nearly all in the navy-yard, except the iron plating to cover the shield.

"The plan to be adopted in the arrangement of the shield for glancing shot, mounting guns, arranging the hull, etc., and plating, to be in accordance with the plan submitted for the approval of the department.

"We are, with much respect,
"Your obedient servants,
"WILLIAM P. WILLIAMSON,
"Chief Engineer Confederate States Navy;
"JOHN M. BROOKE,
"Lieutenant Confederate States Navy;
"JOHN L. PORTER,
"Naval Constructor."

"Immediately upon the adoption of the plan, Mr. Porter was directed to proceed with the constructor's duties. Mr. Williamson was charged with the engineer's department, and to Mr. Brooke were assigned the duties of attending to and preparing the iron and forwarding it from the Tredegar Works, the experiments necessary to test the plates and to determine their thickness, and devising heavy rifled ordnance for the ship, with the details pertaining to ordnance.

"These gentlemen labored zealously and effectively in their several departments. Mr. Porter cut the ship down, submerged her ends, performed all the duties of constructor, and originated all the interior arrangements by which space has been economized, and he has exhibited energy, ability and ingenuity. Mr. Williamson thoroughly overhauled her engines, supplied deficiencies, and repaired defects, and improved greatly the motive-power of the vessel.

"Mr. Brooke attended daily to the iron, constructed targets, ascertained by actual tests the resistance offered by inclined planes of iron to heavy ordnance, and determined interesting and important facts in connection therewith, and which were of great importance in the construction of the ship ; devised and prepared the models and drawings of the ship's heavy ordnance, being guns of a class never before made, and of extraordinary power and strength.

" It is deemed inexpedient to state the angle of inclination, the character of the plates upon the ship, the manner of preparing them, or the number, calibre and weight of the guns; and many novel and interesting features of her construction, which were experimentally determined, are necessarily omitted.

" The novel plan of submerging the ends of the ship and the eaves of the casement, however, is the peculiar and distinctive feature of the *Virginia*. It was never before adopted. The resistance of iron plates to heavy ordnance, whether presented in vertical planes or at low angles of inclination, had been investigated in England before the *Virginia* was commenced, and Major Barnard, U. S. A., had referred to the subject in his ' Sea-coast Defences.'

" We were without accurate data, however, and were compelled to determine the inclination of the plates and their thickness and form by actual experiment.

" The department has freely consulted the three excellent officers referred to throughout the labors on the *Virginia*, and they have all exhibited signal ability, energy and zeal."

To that report, and to articles in the Richmond *Enquirer*, claiming for Lieut. Brooke the honor of the plan of the *Virginia*, Naval Constructor John L. Porter, of the C. S. navy, immediately replied, through the *Enquirer*, that the "greatest injustice " had been done to Engineer Williamson and himself by both the report of Secretary Mallory and the article of the *Enquirer*. Constructor Porter admits that Lieut. Brooke had "made an attempt to get up a floating battery at the Navy Department," and that the master ship-carpenter had been sent for to come up and assist him, but asserts that after trying for a week he failed to produce anything, and the master returned to his duties at the yard. He adds, that Secretary Mallory then sent for him to come to Richmond, at which time he carried up the model of an iron-clad floating battery, with the shield of the present *Virginia* on it, and before he ever saw Lieut. Brooke; and that model was then at the Navy Department. Constructor Porter says that the Secretary then ordered the Board, whose report is embodied in Secretary Mallory's report to Congress. As the report of that Board specifically mentions having "carefully examined and considered the various plans and propositions for constructing a shot-proof steam battery," it would appear that other plans and propositions, as well as that of Constructor Porter's, had been examined and considered. To this suggestion Constructor Porter replied:

" If it is intended to convey the idea that we (the Board) were to examine any plan of Lieut. Brooke, I never so understood it; neither did we act in accordance with any such idea, as our report will show. The report next refers to my model, which I carried up with me, the shield and plan of which is carried out on the *Virginia ;* but the report seems to have lost sight of the fact that the eaves and ends of my model were submerged two feet, precisely like the present *Virginia*. The ship was cut down on a straight line, fore and aft, to suit this arrangement, and the shield was extended over her just as far as the space inside to work the guns would admit of. Where the shield stopped, a strong deck was put in to finish out the ends, and plated over with iron, and a rough breakwater built on it to throw off the water forward. The report next states, that Mr. Porter approved of the plan of submerged ends, and made a clean drawing of Lieut. Brooke's plan, which that officer then filed with the department. How could I disapprove of my own model, which had submerged ends two feet? And the only drawing I ever made of the *Virginia* was made in my office at this navy-yard, and which I presented to the department on the 11th day of July just sixteen days after this Board had adjourned, having been ordered to Richmond on other business. This drawing and plan I considered my own and not Lieut. Brooke's. So soon as I presented this plan, the Secretary wrote the following order, when everything was fresh in his mind concerning the whole matter:

"NAVY DEPARTMENT,
"RICHMOND, July 11th, 1862.

"*Flag-officer F. Forrest:*

"SIR: You will proceed with all practicable dispatch to make the changes in the form of the *Merrimac*, and to build, equip, and fit her in all respects according to the design and plans of the constructor and engineers, Messrs. Porter and Williamson.

[Signed] "S. R. MALLORY,
"Secretary of the C. S. Navy."

"What, I would ask, could be more explicit than this letter, or what words could have established my claims any stronger if I had dictated them. The concluding part of this report says: 'The novel plan of submerging the ends of the ship and the eaves of the casement, however, is the peculiar and distinctive feature of the *Virginia*.' This may all be true; but it is just what my model calls for; and if Lieut. Brooke presented rough drawings to the department carrying out the same views it may be called a singular coincidence. And here I would remark, that my model was not calculated to have much speed, but was intended for harbor defence only, and was of light draft, the eaves extending over the entire length of the model, and submerged all around two feet, sides and ends, and the line on which I cut the ship down was just in accordance with this; but if Lieut. Brooke's ideas, which were submitted to the Secretary in his *rough drawings*, had have been carried out, to cut her ends down low enough to build tanks on to regulate the draft of the vessel, she would have been cut much lower than my plan required, for all the water which now covers her ends would not alter her draft over three inches, if confined in tanks. All the calculations of the weights and displacements, and the line to cut the ship down, was determined by myself, as well as her whole arrangements. That Lieut. Brooke may have been of great assistance to the department in trying the necessary experiments to determine the thickness of the iron, getting up her battery, and attending to the shipment of the iron, etc, I do not doubt, but to claim for him the credit of designing the ship is a matter of too much interest to me to give up. Engineer Williamson discharged his duties with great success; the engine performed beyond his most sanguine expectations, and these, with the improvement of the propeller, has increased her speed three miles per hour.

"The Confederacy is under many obligations to Secretary Mallory for having approved the report of this Board in making the *Merrimac* a bomb-proof ship. Her performance has changed the whole system of naval defences so far as wooden ships are concerned. Europe, as well as America, will have to begin anew; and that nation which can produce iron-clad ships with greatest rapidity will be the mistress of the seas.

"In this communication I disclaim any disrespect to the Secretary of the Navy whatever ; he has not only been my friend in this government, but was a true and serviceable one under the U. S. government, and has rendered me many acts of kindness, for which I have always esteemed him; but the present unpleasant controversy involves a matter of so much importance to me that I shall be excused for defending my claim not only as the *constructor* but the originator of the plan of the *Virginia*.

"JOHN L. PORTER,
"Confederate States Navy Constructor."

After the ship had been in progress of construction, Secretary Mallory wrote to Flag-officer Forrest, at the navy-yard, urging the "utmost dispatch" in the construction of the ship, and adds:

"Chief Engineer Williamson and Constructor Porter, severally in charge of the two branches of this great work, and for which *they will be held specially responsible*, will receive, therefore, every possible facility at the expense and delay of every other work on hand if necessary."

Mr. Porter continues:

"Of the great and skillful calculations of the displacement and weights of timber and iron involved in the planning and construction of this great piece of naval architecture, and of her present weights, with everything on board, no other man than myself has, or ever had, any knowledge. If he has, let him show it; for while public opinion said she would never float, no one, save myself, knew to the contrary, or what she was capable of bearing. After the *Merrimac* was in progress for some time, Lieut. Brooke was constantly proposing alterations in her to the Secretary of the Navy, and as constantly and firmly opposed by myself, which the Secretary knows.

"To Engineer Williamson, who had the exclusive control of the machinery, great credit is due for having so improved the propeller and engines as to improve the speed of the ship three knots per hour.

"I never thought for a moment that, after the many difficulties I had to encounter in making these new and intricate arrangements for the working of this novel kind of ship, that any one would attempt to rob me of my just merits ; for, if there was any other man than myself who had any responsibility about her success or failure, I never knew it, only so far as the working of the machinery was concerned, for which Engineer Williamson was alone responsible."

These extracts are from letters published in the *Enquirer* on March the 8th, and March the 29th, 1862. In the Charleston (S. C.) *Mercury*, of April the 8th, 1862, a private letter from Constructor Porter says :

"I received but little encouragement from any one while the *Virginia* was progressing. Hundreds—I may say thousands—asserted she would never float. Some said she would turn bottom-side up ; others said the crew would suffocate ; and the most wise said the concussion and report from the guns would deafen the men. Some said she would not steer; and public opinion generally about here said she would never come out of the dock. You have no idea what I have suffered in mind since I commenced her; but I knew what I was about, and persevered. Some of her inboard arrangements are of the most intricate character, and have caused me many sleepless nights in making them; but all have turned out right, and thanks are due to a kind Providence, whose blessings on my efforts I have many times invoked.

"I must say I was astonished at the success of the *Virginia*. She destroyed the *Cumberland* in fifteen minutes, and in thirty more the *Congress* was captured. The *Minnesota* would have shared the same fate, but she got aground, and the *Virginia* could not get at her."

President Davis, in his "Rise and Fall of the Confederate Government," awards the honor to Lieut. Brooke; Capt. Wm. H. Parker, says that "it was claimed by Commander John M. Brooke and by Naval Constructor John L. Porter," and that Lieut. Wm. L. Powell was the first to appreciate the use of iron in naval warfare and to advise its adoption, and that, "in the case of the *Merrimac*, the originality consisted in the designs and not the use of iron."

Weighing carefully all the evidence, it appears at this time that there was some similarity of plan between that offered by Lieut. Brooke and the model exhibited by Constructor Porter; but that the model, rather than the "rough drawings," received the approval of the Board and adoption by the department. That to Constructor Porter is due the honor of the plan—the only really original thought or idea about the ship;—that to Engineer Williamson is due the credit of repairing and adapting the engines of the *Merrimac* to the propulsion of the new *Virginia*, and that to Lieut. Brooke belongs the honor of providing the iron sheathing and the remarkable battery by which her destructive work was accomplished.

That division of the honor does not by any means relieve from responsibility for errors which arose from the divided authority between the Naval Constructor at Norfolk and the Bureau of Construction at Richmond. In consequence of this, the calculations in the displacement of the ship proved erroneous, and Mr. Porter found himself 200 tons short, by reason of calculating for a different suit of armor from that which was finally ordered for the ship, after the experiments made by the Ordnance Board on Jamestown Island. This increased her already great draft of water, and eventually impaired her usefulness in action in Hampton Roads. And yet so great was her buoyancy that it required a very large amount of pig-iron as ballast to bring her down to the proper depth, which would submerge her ends beneath the water. Without a complete submergence of her hull, the *Virginia* would have been utterly worthless in action.

Her appearance in the water "was that of the roof of a house. Saw off the top of a house at the eaves (supposing it to have ordinary gable-ended shelving-sides roof), pass a plane parallel to the first through the roof some feet beneath the ridge, incline the gable-ends, put it in the water, and you have the *Merrimac* as she appeared. When she was not in action her people stood on the top of this roof, which was, in fact, her spar-deck."

The *Merrimac* frigate, out of which the *Virginia* was constructed, was built at Charlestown in 1855, and was pierced for
forty guns, her last service in the U. S. navy had been with the
Pacific squadron; she had been the sister-ship of the *Minnesota* and the *Roanoke*, and was lying in Elizabeth River, opposite the navy-yard, on the eventful night of April 20th, 1861,
when the navy yard was burned, and the vessels scuttled and
sunk. On April 25th, her battery was removed and dispatched
to batteries, on Sewell's Point and other places, for the
defence of Norfolk. On May 30th, the *Merrimac* was raised
and pulled into the dry dock.

The work of her transformation into the *Virginia* began
immediately by cutting her down to the old berth-deck, to
within three and a half feet of her light water-line. Both ends
for seventy feet were covered over, and when the ship was in
fighting trim were just awash. On the mid-ship section, for a
length of 170 feet, was erected, at an angle of forty-five
degrees, a roof of pitch-pine and oak, twenty-four inches
thick, extending from the water-line to a highth over the
gun-deck of seven feet. Both ends of this shielded roof
were rounded so that the pivot guns could be used as bow and
stern chasers or quartering. Over the gun-deck was a light
grating, making a promenade about twenty feet wide, and
nearly 170 long.

The iron plating which covered the wood-backing was
rolled at the Tredegar Iron Works at Richmond, and was
two inches thick. The underlayer being placed horizontal,
and the upper laid up and down—the two being four inches
thick—were bolted through the woodwork, and clinched inside.
The *Virginia*, thus armored, was further provided with a cast-
iron prow, which projected four feet, but imperfectly secured,
as the test of battle proved. Another defect was the unprotected condition of her rudder and propeller. The pilot-house
was forward of the smoke-stack, and covered with the same
thickness of iron as her sides. The same motive-power of the
Merrimac propelled the *Virginia*, but it was so radically defective that both engine and boilers had been condemned in
the last cruise of the *Merrimac;* and when to those defects are
added the injury sustained from the fire which burned and
the water in which she was sunk, it was not possible for the
limited resources at the command of the Confederate Bureau
of Construction to do more than repair. Every effort was
made to hasten the completion of the ship. Flag-officer Forrest, on January 11th, 1862, expressed his high appreciation of
the voluntary offer of the "blacksmiths, finishers and strikers
to perform extra work gratuitously in order to expedite the
completion of the *Merrimac*."[1] But notwithstanding every

[1] The agreement of the blacksmiths, and
strikers, and finishers, was as follows: " We, the
undersigned blacksmiths, finishers and strikers,
agree to do any work *that will expedite the completion of the Merrimac,* free of charge, and continue
on until eight o'clock every night; or any other

exertion to finish the ship and to have her ready for action before McClellan's advance from Washington to the peninsula, the unavoidable delay in preparing and transporting the plating from Richmond to the Norfolk navy-yard prevented an earlier completion of the ship. The Tredegar Works at Richmond were the only shops within the Confederate lines where plates of the kind required could be rolled, and their limited resources were taxed in the preparation of every kind of war material. It was impossible for the very few experienced workmen who could be collected together, no matter how ready and willing, to do more than was accomplished, both at the Tredegar Works and at the navy-yard, to expedite the transformation of the *Merrimac* into the *Virginia*. In many instances the very tools required by the workmen had to be improvised and made; not only was the ship to be radically changed, but the Tredegar Works had also to be converted from an ordinary iron workshop, for the manufacture of the engines of locomotion in peaceful times, to those of destruction and defence in the midst of a terrible and exacting war. There were no patterns to follow in constructing this experimental iron-clad; the theory, drawings and calculations of the constructor had to be verified as they proceeded, and errors, if any, corrected as the work progressed.

And it is not the least remarkable fact in the history of the experiment, that the *Virginia* and the *Monitor* should have been so very much alike in their general outline and form. The submerged hull and machinery and the protection of the battery were the same in both vessels, the difference being only in the round turret of the *Monitor* and roof-shaped casemate of the *Virginia*.

The armament of the *Virginia* consisted of two seven-inch rifled guns, heavily reinforced around the breech with three-inch steel bands shrunk on; these were the first heavy guns so made, and were the work of Lieut. Brooke, and they were the bow and stern guns of the battery; there were also two six-inch guns of the same make, and six nine-inch smooth-bore broadside — ten guns in all. There was no Armstrong gun, as so often asserted, on the ship. Her entire battery was the work of Lieut. Brooke.

work that will advance the interests of the Southern Confederacy.

BLACKSMITHS AND STRIKERS.

James A. Farmer, M. S.; Chas. Snead, 1st Foreman; Wm. T. Butt, 2d Foreman; Pat. Parks, Jno. West, Jno. Cain, Jas. Watfield, H. Tatem, Wilson Guy, Miles Foreman, Hugh Minter, Jno. Green, Thos. Bloxom, Jas. Mitchell, Joseph Rickets, Thos. Franklin, Jas. Patterson, Wm. Gray, Jno. Moody, Hillory Hopkins, E. Woodward, H. Reynolds, Southey Rew, Julius Morien, Jos. Askew, Anthony Butt, Thos. Bourke, Wm. Hosler, David Wilkins, Jas. Wilbern, Wm. Reynolds, Walter Wilkins, Thos. Kerby, Samuel Davenport, Jas. Larkin, Lewis Ewer, Jno. Davis, Jas. Watson, Sr., James Flemming, Samuel Hodges, Alex. Davis, Thomas Guy, Smith Guy, Michael Conner, Wm. Perry, Patrick Shanasy, Lawson Etheredge, Joshua Daily, Jas. Morand, Miles Foreman, Jos. West, Thos. Powell, Wm. Shephard, Jno. Curran, Opie Jordan, Wiley Howard.

FINISHERS.

Jno. B Rooke, Elias Bridges, Anderson Gwinn, John Stoakes, E. H. Brown, Harvey Barnes, Lemuel Leary, William Jones, John Rhea, William Leary, John Wilder Frederick Bowen, Charles Sturdivant, Jesse Kay, William Shipp, William Pebworth, Lawrence Herbert, T. I. Rooke, Calder Sherwood, George Collier, Henry Hopkins, George Bear, Walter Thornton, Edward Walker, Thomas Dunn."

Such was the *Virginia;* her defects were many and of a most serious character. She was absolutely dependent for her movement on her defective machinery; for this once out of order, she became helpless, while hurtful to her assailant only when her assailant came within the range of her battery. Her great draft of water rendered her action dependent on the tides, and menaced her helplessness should she move out of the narrow channel where the water was deep enough for her. Her ram was useless against a vessel drawing less water, which, by retiring into

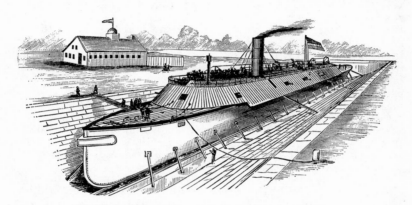

THE VIRGINIA (MERRIMAC) IN DRY-DOCK, AFTER BEING ARMORED.

shoal water, reduced the action to a duel of heavy guns, where the stoutness of iron sides would carry off the palm of victory. The officers assigned to the *Virginia*, February, 1862, were:

Flag-officer, Capt. Franklin Buchanan;[1] Lieutenant, Catesby Ap R. Jones; Executive and Ordnance Officers, Charles C. Simms, R. D. Minor (flag), Hunter Davidson, John Taylor Wood, J. R. Eggleston and Walter Butt; Midshipmen, R. C. Foute, H. H. Marmaduke, H. B. Littlepage, W. J. Craig, J. C. Long and L. M. Rootes; Paymaster, James Semple;

[1] Franklin Buchanan was born in Baltimore, Md., on the 11th of September, 1800. He was a grandson of Governor McKean, of Pennsylvania, and a brother of Paymaster Buchanan, who was in the U. S. ship *Congress* when she was destroyed in the fight with the *Virginia*. When a youth, Franklin Buchanan resided in Pennsylvania, from which State he was appointed a midshipman. He entered the U. S. navy on the 28th of January, 1815; became a lieutenant January 13th, 1825; master commander, September 8th, 1841; first superintendent of the Annapolis Naval Academy, 1845-7; captain, September 14th, 1855. On the 19th of April, 1861, when the Sixth Massachusetts regiment was attacked on its passage through Baltimore, Capt. Buchanan was in charge of the navy-yard at Washington. He immediately resigned his commission, but finding that Maryland did not secede, petitioned to recall his resignation, but was refused. On the 5th of September, 1861, he entered the service of the C. S. navy, and was assigned to duty as Chief of Orders and Details. He was ordered to the command of the *Virginia* on February 24th, 1862, and after she had been cut loose from her moorings and was on her way down the harbor, Capt. Buchanan called "all hands to muster," and delivered the following spirited address to the crew: "Men, the eyes of your country are upon you. You are fighting for your rights—your liberties—your wives and children. You must not be content with only doing your duty, but do *more than your duty !* Those ships "(pointing to the Union fleet) "must be taken, and you shall not complain that I do not take you close enough. Go to your guns !" How well the officers and gallant crew of that "monster of the deep" performed their whole duty, the following pages will tell. When Capt. Buchanan was severely wounded and taken below, a feeling of deep sadness pervaded the entire crew, but they soon rallied when Lieut. George Minor,

Surgeon, Dinwiddin Phillips; Assistant Surgeon, Algernon S. Garnett; Captain of Marines, Reuben Thorn; Engineers: H. A. Ramsay, Acting Chief; Assistants, John W. Tynan, Loudon Campbell, Benj. Herring, C. A. Jack and R. Wright; Boatswain, Charles H. Hasker; Gunner, C. B. Oliver; Carpenter, Hugh Lindsey; Clerk, Arthur Sinclair, Jr.; Volunteer Aide, Lieut. Douglas Forrest, C. S. army; Capt. Kevil, commanding detachment of Norfolk United Artillery; Signal Corps, Sergeant Tabb.

Flag-officer Buchanan was ordered February 24th, 1862, to the command of the naval defences of the James River, and to hoist his flag on the *Virginia*, or any other vessel of the squadron, which was to consist of the *Virginia*, the *Patrick Henry*, the *Jamestown*, the *Teaser*, the *Raleigh*, and the *Beaufort*. Secretary Mallory in his order added :

" The *Virginia* is a novelty in naval construction, is untried, and her powers unknown ; and hence the department will not give specific orders as to her attack upon the enemy. Her powers as a ram are regarded as very formidable, and it is hoped you will be able to test them. Like the bayonet charge of infantry, this mode of attack, while the most destructive, will commend itself to you in the present scarcity of ammunition. It is one also that may be rendered destructive at night against the enemy at anchor. Even without guns the ship would, it is believed, be formidable as a ram.

" Could you pass Old Point and make a dashing cruise in the Potomac as far as Washington, its effect upon the public mind would be important to our cause.

" The condition of our country, and the painful reverses we have just suffered, demand our utmost exertions ; and convinced as I am that the opportunity and the means for striking a decisive blow for our navy are now, for the first time, presented, I congratulate you upon it, and know that your judgment and gallantry will meet all just expectations.

"Action, prompt and successful just now, would be of serious importance to our cause."

Of officers there were an ample supply, and they were among the best and bravest, the most skillful and experienced, which the navy of the United States had turned out. But the crew that was to work and fight this new kind of man-of-war, where were they to come from ? There had been no

---

himself wounded and sent below, appeared on deck and delivered to them the following message from the flag-officer: "Tell Mr. Jones to fight the ship to the last. Tell the men that I am not mortally wounded, and hope to be with them very soon." The cheers that greeted the delivery of this message, it is said, resounded far above the cannon's roar, and every man was again quickly at his post, dealing death and destruction with their heavy guns. Congress was in session when the engagement took place, and shortly thereafter passed a bill creating the grade of admiral in the navy, to which position Buchanan was nominated by the President and confirmed by the Senate on August 21st, 1862. He commanded the Confederate fleet in Mobile Bay in August, 1864, on board of the iron-clad *Tennessee*, where he was wounded and defeated by Admiral Farragut and taken prisoner. After the war he was president of the Maryland Agricultural College. He died in May, 1874, at "The Rest," his splendid residence in Talbot

County, Maryland. He was the organizer and founder of the Naval Academy at Annapolis; he co-operated in landing the troops at Vera Cruz, under Gen. Scott, and was one of the leading spirits of the navy there at the capture of San Juan d'Ulloa; was among the first to step foot on the soil of Japan in the expedition of Commodore Perry, which opened the ports of that erst forbidden land to the world at large, but with especial kindness to our own country— and later was honored by a grateful President with the position of commandant of the navy-yard at Washington, overlooking the entire affairs of the naval establishment of the country; and still later he was called by the warm impulses of his Maryland brethren to be the President of the Maryland Agricultural College — in all of which positions he not only acquitted himself with credit and honor, but left a legacy of discipline and order and gentlemanly bearing that leaves its impress to the present hour.

merchant marine at the South to supply experienced sailors, and but few of the sailors of the U. S. navy were in Southern ports when the rupture of the Union occurred. To meet that pressing exigency, Lieut. Wood visited Gen. Magruder's army at Yorktown, and from a New Orleans regiment selected eighty sailors out of 200 volunteers who had seen service in the ships that visited New Orleans; these with a few seamen from Norfolk who had escaped from the Confederate flotilla in Pamlico Sound at the fall of Roanoke Island, and with other volunteers from the army, a crew of 300 men was formed, which proved to be "as gallant and trusty a body of men as any one could wish to command, not only in battle, but in reverse and retreat."

ADMIRAL FRANKLIN BUCHANAN,
CONFEDERATE STATES NAVY.

LIEUTENANT COMMANDER WILLIAM HARWAR PARKER,

CONFEDERATE STATES NAVY.

CHAPTER IX.

THE NAVAL BATTLE IN HAMPTON ROADS.

THE first Confederate iron-clad, so unlike in every respect to any other afloat, the officers and men strangers to each other and new to every part of the ship, was immediately launched from the dock into battle, and from what was supposed to be an experimental trial of sailing and floating capacity into the fiercest fight of modern times. Discharging workmen as the *Virginia* moved out into the channel, Flag-officer Buchanan turned her prow into waters swarming with enemies, and covered with the line-of-battle ships that had never lowered their flag to an enemy. Immediately her defects became apparent; not more than five knots an hour could be got out of her, and she obeyed her rudder so reluctantly that from thirty to forty minutes were required to turn her. Her draft of twenty-two feet confined her to a narrow channel, and deprived her of every advantage attainable by manœuvring. But, in that unmanageable water-logged vessel, Capt. Buchanan, on the 8th of March, 1862, steamed slowly down Elizabeth River, accompanied by the steam-tugs *Beaufort*, Lieut. Commanding W. H. Parker, and the *Raleigh*, Lieut. Commanding J. W. Alexander, to make her "trial trip" a trial of battle. The movement was hailed with huzzas from citizens and soldiers, from wharves and batteries; but silently, and without response, the gallant ship and her escorts, followed by Commander Forrest and staff, plowed their way toward the enemy. Down the deep channel of the Elizabeth River, passing Confederate batteries at Craney Island and on the right bank, the *Virginia* and her escort reached Hampton Roads at Sewell's Point. At Fortress Monroe lay the *Minnesota*, 40 guns ; the *Roanoke*, 40 guns, and the *St. Lawrence*, 50 guns ; together with the gunboat *Dragon*, the gunboat *Mystic*, the gunboat *Whitehall*,[1] the gunboat *Oregon*, which was destroyed by a shell ; the gunboat *Zouave*, which was seriously damaged and

---

[1] The *Whitehall* had three killed, and was burned by a shell from a Confederate gunboat.

forced to retire from action, and the *Cambridge.* At Newport News, riding at anchor, was the *Cumberland,* 30 guns, and the *Congress,* 50 guns. In addition to this formidable battery of guns afloat must be added the batteries at Newport News and the guns on the land side of Fortress Monroe, and the *great gun* in position at the Rip-raps. Notwithstanding the information which leaked through the lines as to the progress that was making upon the *Virginia* at the navy-yard, her appearance, if not unexpected, was at least unprepared for. The *Congress* and the *Cumberland* lay at anchor off Newport News, with boats hanging to lower booms, washed clothes flying in the wind from the rigging, and no indication whatever of preparation or readiness for battle, until the *Virginia* was within three-quarters of a mile, when every man was astir, boats were dropped astern, booms got alongside, and the ships were cleared for action.

Into that circle of great guns from line-of-battle ships, shore batteries, and gunboats, whose concentrated fire could be directed to almost any position in the Road, Captain Buchanan led his little fleet, comprised of the *Virginia,* 10 guns; the *Beaufort,* 1 gun; and the *Raleigh,* 1 gun; when in action to be reinforced by the *Patrick Henry,* 12 guns, Commander John R. Tucker; the *Jamestown,* Lieut. Commanding J. N. Barney, 2 guns; the gunboat *Teaser,* Lieut. Commanding W. A. Webb, 1 gun. Total, 27 guns, against an armament of over 300 guns, of which 100 could be brought into action at every moment, and on every point.

At Sewell's Point, Capt. Buchanan turned the *Virginia,* with the gunboat escort, towards Newport News, to engage the "frigates *Cumberland* and *Congress,* gunboats and shore batteries."[1] Reserving fire until within less than a mile, Lieut. Charles C. Simms, with the forward pivot gun of the *Virginia,* opened the engagement with the *Cumberland,* and the action became general almost immediately. To reach her selected foe the *Virginia* had to pass the *Congress,* to which she gave a broadside, and received an equally liberal compliment. From the *Cumberland,* the *Congress,* the gunboats and shore batteries, there was now poured upon the *Virginia* and her little escort the concentrated fire of 100 heavy guns at short range. Standing on, the *Virginia* brought her *ramming* powers into action, and struck the *Cumberland* under the starboard forechannels, delivering the fire of her bow pivot gun at the very moment of crushing through the sides of the *Cumberland.* The destruction was very great, "killing ten men at gun No. 1, among whom was Master's Mate John Harrington, and cutting off both arms and legs of Quarter Gunner Wood. As the *Merrimac* rounded-to and came up, she again raked the *Cumberland* with heavy fire. At this fire sixteen men at gun

---

[1] Report of Flag-officer Franklin Buchanan; date, March 27th, 1862.

No. 10 were killed or wounded, and all were subsequently carried down in the sinking ship.[1]

The blow, hardly perceptible on the *Virginia*, had been received by the *Cumberland* nearly at right angles. Heading up stream, to turn the gallant but very slow-moving ship, enabled Lieut. Wood to bring the after pivot gun into action, which was turned upon the *Congress* just as she slipped her anchor, loosed her bow topsail, and run up her jib, to effect escape.

The effort was unavailing; the *Congress* grounded, and the *Virginia*, at a distance of 200 yards, riddled her sides. Notwithstanding that the hole in the side of the *Cumberland* was " big enough to drive a horse and cart through," Lieut. Morris continued as gallant a fight as the records of any navy offer; slowly sinking, deck after deck was submerged, the forward magazine drowned, the after magazine was used to fight the ten-inch gun; but in thirty-five minutes the ship canted to port, and her gallant officers and men delivered their parting fire and immediately leaped into the water, and the *Cumberland* sank with the " American flag flying at the peak."[2]

Before the waters of Hampton Roads had closed over the *Cumberland*, the dark smoke of the Jamestown squadron was seen, as the ships and boats hurried under press of steam to the scene of battle. Dashing past the Federal shore batteries, Capt. John R. Tucker led the van in the *Patrick Henry*, closely followed by the *Jamestown*, Lieut. Commanding Barney, and the little *Teaser*, Lieut. Webb, puffing with all the energy of a short-winded tug. Making a gallant run past the batteries, they " were exposed to a heavy fire. Their escape was miraculous, as they were under a galling fire of solid shot, shell, grape and canister, a number of which passed through the vessels without doing any serious injury, except to the *Patrick Henry*, through whose boiler a shot passed, scalding to death four persons and wounding others. Lieut. Commanding Barney promptly obeyed a signal to tow her out of the action. As soon as damages were repaired, the *Patrick Henry* returned to her station and continued to perform good service during the remainder of that day and the following."

The part taken by the little James River squadron is not the least remarkable part of that great fight. It was lost sight

---

[1] Moore's *Rebellion Record*, Vol. IV., p. 273.

[2] OFFICERS OF THE " CUMBERLAND."

The following is a list of the officers on board the *Cumberland* during the fight :—First Lieut. George Morris, commanding; Second Lieut. F. O. Selfridge; Sailing Master, Mr. Stivison; Chaplain, Rev. Mr. Leinhardt. drowned; Boatswain, Edward Bell; Gunner, Eugene Mack; Carpenter, William L. Leighton; Sailmaker. David Bruce; Master's Mate, John Harrington, killed; Master's Mate, —— Wyman; Master's Mate, —— O'Neil; Paymaster's Clerk, Hugh Knott; Acting Master, —— Randall; Acting Master, —— Kennison; Master Smith, Victor M. Smith; Marine Officer, Charles M. Hayward.

The *Cumberland* was commanded by Capt Radcliffe, who was detailed to attend a Court of Inquiry on board the flag-ship *Roanoke*. When the fight commenced he mounted a horse and rode rapidly to Newport News, but only reached there in time to find his vessel sinking.

Commandant William Smith had previously commanded the *Cumberland*, but was detached and ordered to the command of the *Sabine*, of the Gulf blockading fleet. While waiting transportation he remained on board the *Cumberland*. and as a volunteer gave valuable assistance. Lieut. Morris, who, by the absence of Capt. Radcliffe, was in command, by the general testimony of his brother officers did his duty in the most gallant manner.

of in the battle of the iron-clad giants, but in the days of oak walls would have been recorded with honorable mention among the acts of bravery and seamanship which illustrate a navy. Capt. Pendergrast, of the *Congress*, reported that: "In the meantime the *Patrick Henry* and *Thomas Jefferson*, rebel steamers, approached us from up the James River, firing with precision, and doing us great damage. Our two stern guns were our only means of defence. These were soon disabled, one being dismounted, and the other having its muzzle knocked away. The men were knocked away from them with great rapidity, and slaughtered by the terrible fire of the enemy."

Capt. Wm. Watson, of the gunboat *Dragon*, reports that:

"Arriving at the *Minnesota*, took position and opened fire on the *Yorktown* and *Jamestown*. Kept it up until dark, when we received orders to cease firing, and lay by the ship until morning. At 2 A. M. tried to tow the *Minnesota* off the bottom, and succeeded only to ground in another and more exposed place. Made fast for the night. Second day, at 8 A. M., we were ordered to take up position as best we could, and opened fire on the *Yorktown* and *Jamestown* with good effect ; could plainly see our shells bursting on the enemy. At 12 M. received orders to go alongside of the *Minnesota*, and be ready to assist in towing her off. Made fast on the port side, being in direct line of the *Merrimac's* batteries. At the same moment received two shots from her, one taking effect in the boiler, blowing up the vessel, together with the captain and three men; seriously wounding Charles J. Freese ; badly scalding Ben. S. Hungerford, and breaking the legs of — McDonald, which will have to be amputated. Received orders to get on board the *Minnesota*. Vessel on fire. Shortly after received orders to get bags and hammocks on board of the *Whitehall*."

Capt. Balsir, of the gunboat *Whitehall*, reported that, "although her heavy batteries had no effect on the iron monster *Virginia*, still the rebel steamers *Yorktown* and *Jamestown* will remember the accurate gunnery of the *Whitehall* for some time to come." Capt. Van Brunt, of the *Minnesota*, reported that, "at 4 P. M., the *Merrimac, Virginia, Jamestown* and *Patrick Henry* bore down on my vessel. Very fortunately, the iron battery drew too much water to come within a mile of us. She took a position on my starboard bow, but did not fire with accuracy, and only one shot passed through the ship's bow. The other two steamers took their position on my port bow and stern and their fire did most damage in killing and wounding men, inasmuch as they fired with rifled guns; but with the heavy gun that I could bring to bear upon them, I drove them off, one of them apparently in a crippled state."

Mrs. Susan Archer Weiss, an eye-witness, describes "the saucy *Teaser*" as follows: "By this time the *Jamestown* and *Patrick Henry* had joined the *Merrimac*, taking a position which concealed her from our view. We were told afterward by Federal officers that the little *Teaser* (commanded by Capt. Webb) pushed her way in between the *Patrick Henry* and *Jamestown*, and advancing close to the shore fired her one gun

in face of the battery of sixty guns.   Probably her insignifi-
cance saved her, for now every shot seemed concentrated upon
the *Merrimac*, and the air and the very ground where we
stood seemed trembling with the roar of shot and shells.   So
dense was the smoke that we could discern nothing except
that the Confederate vessels were constantly shifting their
position in front of the fleet, which was now lying close in
shore."

While the battle between the *Virginia* and the Federal
ships at Newport News was in progress, the small fry of Capt.
Buchanan's squadron—the *Roanoke* and the *Raleigh*—gallantly attacked the *Congress*, "killing and wounding many of
her crew."   Witnessing the easy destruction of the *Cumberland*, Lieut. Pendergrast, upon whom the command of the
Congress devolved on the death of Lieut. Joseph B. Smith, set
her fore and top sails, and, with the assistance of the gunboat
Zouave, drew the vessel ashore, where it was impossible, on
account of her draft, for the *Virginia* to ram her to pieces.
The movement was necessary, for Capt. Buchanan says:

"Having sunk the *Cumberland*, I turned our attention to the *Congress*.   We were some time in getting our proper position, in consequence
of the shoalness of the water, and the great difficulty of managing the
ship when in or near the mud.   To succeed in my object, I was obliged to
run the ship a short distance above the batteries on James River in order
to wind her.   During all the time her keel was in the mud, of course she
moved but slowly.   Thus we were subjected twice to the heavy guns of
all the batteries in passing up and down the river, but it could not be
avoided.   We silenced several of the batteries, and did much injury on
shore.   A large transport steamer alongside the wharf was blown up, one
schooner sunk, and another captured and sent to Norfolk.   The loss of
life on shore we have no means of ascertaining."

But there was no escape for the *Congress* even in shoal
water, for "at half-past two the *Merrimac* took a position
astern of us at a distance of 150 yards, and raked us fore and
aft with shells, while one of the smaller steamers kept up a fire
on our starboard quarter."[1]

The movement of the *Virginia* to get into position for attacking the *Congress* was mistaken for retreat, and was loudly
cheered by the gunners and crew of the frigate; but their mistake was corrected, when, in a few moments, from her raking
position the *Virginia* opened on the *Congress*, carrying carnage, havoc and dismay through the ship, and causing a white
flag to be displayed at the gaff, half-mast and main.

The report of Lieut. Pendergrast says:

"Seeing that our men were being killed without the prospect of any
relief from the *Minnesota*, which vessel had run ashore in attempting to
get up to us from Hampton Roads, not being able to get a single gun to
bear upon the enemy, and the ship being on fire in several places, upon
consultation with Commander Wm. Smith we deemed it proper to haul

[1] Report of Lieut. Pendergrast.
11

down our colors without any further loss of life on our part. We were soon boarded by an officer of the *Merrimac*, who said he would take charge of the ship. He left shortly afterwards, and a small tug came alongside, whose captain demanded that we should surrender and get out of the ship, as he intended to burn her immediately. A sharp fire with muskets and artillery was maintained from our troops ashore upon the tug, having the effect of driving her off.

"The *Merrimac* again opened fire on us, although we had a peak to show that we were out of action.

"After having fired several shells into us, she left us and engaged the *Minnesota* and the shore batteries; after which, Lieutenant Pendergrast states, the wounded were taken ashore in small boats, the ship having been on fire from the beginning of the action from hot shot fired by the *Merrimac*."

Upon this point there is a difference of report as well as of opinion. Capt. Buchanan says that, on seeing the white flag,

"Our fire immediately ceased, and a signal was made for the *Beaufort* to come within hail. I then ordered Lieut. Commanding Parker to take possession of the *Congress*, secure the officers as prisoners, allow the crew to land, and burn the ship. He ran alongside, received her flag and surrender from Commander Wm. Smith and Lieut. Pendergrast, with the side-arms of those officers. They delivered themselves as prisoners-of-war on board the *Beaufort*, and afterwards were permitted, at their own request, to return to the *Congress*, to assist in removing the wounded to the *Beaufort*. They never returned, and I submit to the decision of the department whether they are not our prisoners. While the *Beaufort* and *Raleigh* were alongside the *Congress*, and the surrender of that vessel had been received from the commander, she having two white flags flying, hoisted by her own people, a heavy fire was opened upon them from the shore and from the *Congress*, killing some valuable officers and men. Under this fire the steamers left the *Congress;* but, as I was not informed that any injury had been sustained by those vessels at that time, Lieut. Commanding Parker having failed to report to me, I took it for granted that my order to him to burn her had been executed, and waited some minutes to see the smoke ascending from her hatches. During this delay we were still subjected to the heavy fire from the batteries, which was always promptly returned."

It is probably true, as suggested by Admiral Porter,[1] that the garrison at Newport News did not comprehend the state of affairs on the *Congress* when it opened fire on that ship, and the *Beaufort* and the *Raleigh*, which were engaged in removing the Federal wounded from the burning *Congress*. But Admiral Porter errs in saying that, "although the white flag was still flying, the *Merrimac* (*Virginia*) opened fire on the *Congress*. This certainly would have been inhuman, since the crew of the *Congress* were not responsible for the acts of the troops on shore." Capt. Buchanan's report gives full explanation :

"The steam-frigates *Minnesota* and *Roanoke*, and the sailing frigate *St. Lawrence*, had previously been reported as coming from Old Point; but, as I was determined that the *Congress* should not again fall into the hands of the enemy, I remarked to that gallant young officer, Flag Lieut. Minor, 'That ship must be burned.' He promptly volunteered to take a boat and

---

[1] *The Naval Hist. of the Civil War,* p. 125.

burn her, and the *Teaser*, Lieut. Commanding Webb, was ordered to cover the boat. Lieut. Minor had scarcely reached within fifty yards of the *Congress* when a deadly fire was opened upon him, wounding him severely and several of his men. On witnessing this vile treachery, I instantly recalled the boat and ordered the *Congress* to be destroyed by hot shot and incendiary shell. About this period I was disabled, and transferred the command of the ship to that gallant, intelligent officer, Lieut. Catesby Jones, with orders to fight her as long as the men could stand to their guns."

In the effort to remove the wounded from the *Congress*, Lieut. Taylor and Midshipman Hutter of the *Raleigh* had been killed, notwithstanding the white flag floated from the masts of the *Congress*. This fire from the shore batteries killed and wounded a number of Federal men on the *Congress*, and became so hot and destructive as to compel the *Beaufort* and the *Raleigh* to retire with only thirty wounded prisoners, and to leave the rest to share the fate of the burning ship, in which over 150 perished. The inhumanity which Admiral Porter imagined to exist in the conduct of Capt. Buchanan, finds its actual existence in the rash and absurd folly of the shore batteries attempting defence of the *Congress* at a time when she was on fire, had surrendered, and her wounded were being removed. It was this unnecessary slaughter of friend as well as foe that Capt. Buchanan regarded as " vile treachery," to be punished by burning the ship, which, having surrendered, was yet being defended by shore batteries.

Very great indignation was felt and expressed by the Confederates that their kindness to the captured officers of the *Congress* should have been availed of by them to escape, after surrendering their swords and themselves as prisoners-of-war. Lieut. Wood, having been ordered by Commander Buchanan to go alongside the *Congress* to " take the officers and wounded men prisoners, to permit the others to escape, and then to burn the ship," promptly placed the *Beaufort* alongside the burning frigate, and sent an officer to direct the commander of the *Congress* to come to him. In a few minutes, Lieut. Austin Pendergrast came down the side of the *Congress*, accompanied by Capt. William Smith, who was acting as a volunteer. " These two officers," Lieut. Wood says, "landed on the hurricane deck of the *Beaufort* where I was, and surrendered the ship. As they were without side-arms, I thought it proper to request them to return to their ship and get them. This they did, though Pendergrast delivered to me a ship's cutlass instead of the regulation sword. I now told Pendergrast my orders, and asked him to get his officers and wounded men on board as quickly as possible, as I wanted to burn the ship. He said there were sixty wounded men on board the frigate, and begged me not to burn the vessel. I told him my orders were peremptory. While we were engaged in this conversation, the wounded men were being lowered into the *Beaufort*, and just then the *Raleigh* came

alongside.   Lieut. Taylor came on board and said that Capt.
Alexander had sent him to me for orders.   I directed him to
take the *Raleigh* to the starboard side of the *Congress* and
assist in getting off the wounded men.   I had scarcely given
him the order when a tremendous fire was opened on us from
the shore by a regiment of soldiers—Medical Director Shippen
says it was the Twentieth Indiana.   At the first discharge
every man on the deck of the *Beaufort*, save Capt. Smith and
Lieut. Pendergrast, was either killed or wounded.   Four
bullets passed through my clothing, one of which carried off
my cap cover and eye-glass, and another slightly wounded me
on the knee.   Lieut. Pendergrast now begged me to hoist the
white flag, saying that all his wounded men would be killed.
I called his attention to the fact that they were firing on the
white flag, which was flying at his mainmast-head, directly
over our heads.   I said I would not hoist it on the *Beaufort;*
in fact, I did not feel authorized to do so without consulting
Commander Buchanan.   I said,' Tell your men to stop firing.'
He replied,' They are a lot of volunteers, and I have no control
over them.'   This was evident.   The lieutenant then *requested*
permission to go on board the *Congress* with Capt. Smith, and
assist in getting the wounded down.   This I assented to.
Capt. Smith and Lieut. Pendergrast did not return, but escaped
to shore; and, after surrendering themselves prisoners-of-war,
took advantage of the permission given for the humane purpose of saving their wounded, and violated their implied
parole and escaped."

It must be said that the *Congress*, not having hauled her
colors down, as is usual in naval warfare, the right to continue
fire until the colors are struck is not altered by flying the
white flag.   That does not of itself constitute a surrender—it
implies a parley, during which firing ceases temporarily, to ascertain the object of the white flag.   Under these circumstances
were Capt. Smith and Lieut. Pendergrast prisoners-of-war,
and were they justified in escaping, or if they escaped from
the burning ship to save their lives, were they not in military
honor and custom bound to have returned to their captors?
Their position was not the same as that of Capt. Semmes at the
sinking of the *Alabama*.   Smith and Pendergrast had been in
the *actual possession* of their captor, and on board his ship, and
had surrendered their swords in token of their capture.   Capt.
Semmes never was within the power of Capt. Winslow of the
Kearsarge.   From the deck of the *Beaufort*, Smith and Pendergrast were *permitted* to go to the *Congress* for a specific purpose of helping to save their own wounded men.   Capt.
Semmes leaped into the ocean, preferring the risk of drowning
to capture by Capt. Winslow.   The officers of the *Congress* had
come on board the ship of their captor, and surrendered their
swords, and the opportunity to escape, which they embraced,
was extended to them in the office of humanity, but was taken

advantage of by them to the discredit of the honor of American sailors.

In the fight between the *Virginia* and the *Congress* and the *Cumberland*, the former received no material injury except the loss of ram in the side of the *Cumberland*, and the breaking off the muzzle of two of the broadside guns. Her armor was not the least damaged, as the balls that struck glanced off, "having no more effect than peas from a pop-gun," though she was the focus upon which the fire of more than 100 heavy guns was concentrated for over three hours. But everything outside was swept away by the fire to which she was exposed. One anchor, the smokestack, and steampipes, stanchions, railings, boat-davits, and flag-staff were all shot away, and finally a boarding pike bore her colors in triumph out of the fight. Her loss was two killed and eight wounded, among the latter Capt. Buchanan, so seriously as to be compelled to transfer the command to Lieut. Jones, and, with Lieut. Minor, to be carried the next day to the naval hospital at Norfolk. The loss in the Confederate fleet aggregated in killed and wounded twenty-one.

The *Minnesota*, the *Roanoke*, and the *St. Lawrence*, upon seeing the approach of the Confederate fleet from Norfolk, were not slow to get underway. Each of these ships grounded before coming within short range—the *Minnesota* so firmly as not to be got afloat for four tides; the *Roanoke* grounded also, but was soon gotten off with the assistance of tugs, which towed her round; and the *St. Law*rence in tow of the *Cambridge*, passed the *Roanoke*, but she also grounded, but was gotten off; "after which," Capt. Purviance reported, "a powerful broadside from the spar and gun decks of the *St. Lawrence*, then distant about half a mile, thrown into the *Merrimac*, induced her to withdraw, whether from necessity or discretion, is not known." The parting broadside of the *St. Lawrence* was merely coincident with the withdrawal of the *Virginia*. Capt. Buchanan says :

"The ships from Old Point opened their fire upon us. The *Minnesota* grounded in the north channel, where, unfortunately, the shoalness of the channel prevented our approach. We continued, however, to fire upon her until the pilots declared that it was no longer safe to remain in that position, and we accordingly returned to the south channel (the middle ground being necessarily between the *Virginia* and *Minnesota* (the *St. Lawrence* and the *Roanoke* having retreated under the guns of Old Point), and again had an opportunity of opening upon the *Minnesota*, receiving her heavy fire in return; and shortly afterwards upon the *St. Lawrence*, from which vessel we also received several broadsides."

The *St. Lawrence* carried off a token from the *Virginia*— "one of her projectiles of formidable dimensions." Capt. Purviance says:

"An eighty-pound shell penetrated the starboard quarter about four inches above the water-line, passed through the pantry of the ward-room, and into the state-room of the assistant surgeon on the port side, completely demolishing the bulkhead, and then struck a strong iron bar which secured the bull's-eye of the port. It returned into the ward-room expended. It fortunately did not explode, and no person was injured. The damage done by this shot proved the power of the projectiles which she employed, and readily explained the quick destruction of our wooden and antiquated frigates. Our position at this time was one of some anxiety."

The *St. Lawrence* was gotten off by the gunboat *Young America.* The ship's carpenter of the *Minnesota* reported the damage done to that frigate as follows :

"Port side received one shell on after-quarter at the water-line, which cut through the planking; one shell between main and mizzen rigging, below air-port-line, which passed through chief engineer's state-room, crossing and tearing up the deck over the cock-pit, and striking the clamp and knee in carpenter's state-room, where it exploded, carrying away the beam clamp and knee, and completely demolishing the bulkheads, setting fire to the same and ripping up the deck. One shell passed through hammock netting abaft of main rigging, striking the spar deck on starboard side, cutting through four planks, then ricochetting, carrying away trunk and axle of gun-carriage, and wounding water-ways. Two shells passed through No. 8 port, carrying away planking, timbers and deck clamps, and splintering several beams and castings. One shell passed through forward part of No. 6 port, carrying away planking timber and upper sill. One shell under fore-rigging, which cut away sheet cable, penetrating planking timber and splintering deck clamps. One shell on starboard side carried away hammock nettings and gangway boards. There are several wounds on port side received from fragments of exploding shell. One shell passed through the mainmast fourteen feet above deck, cutting away one-third of the mast and bursting some of the iron bands. One shell struck the spar deck in starboard gangway, cutting it up. One passed from port to starboard gangway, forward of mainmast, where it exploded, wounding two boats."

Darkness had closed over the water, and put an end to further fighting for that day. The Confederate fleet steamed proudly and triumphantly back to its anchorage, having sent a thrill of joyful enthusiasm throughout the length and breadth of the Confederate States, dismay and disgrace all over the United States, and revolutionized naval construction throughout the world. From that anchorage, and by the blaze of the burning *Congress,* the crews of the Confederate vessels saw waving from the masts of the sunken *Cumberland* the flag of the United States, and heard the booming of the guns of the burning *Congress,* until her magazine, exploding, scattered over the waters of the Roads the fragments of the frigate ; the stranded *Minnesota* lying riddled, the *Roanoke, St. Lawrence, Mystic,* and other gunboats, huddled under the guns of Fortress Monroe, and no flag but the *Stars and Bars* waving in defiance over all the waters of the Hampton Roads.

CHAPTER X.

THE VIRGINIA (MERRIMAC) AND MONITOR.

AT daybreak on Sunday, March 9th, 1862, the positions of the various vessels in Hampton Roads were as follows: Off Sewell's Point lay the Confederate fleet: the *Virginia*, the *Patrick Henry*, the *Jamestown*, the gunboats *Raleigh* and *Teaser*. Off Newport News the masts of the *Cumberland* rose above the waters of Hampton Roads, and the floating *debris* of the *Congress* told the story of the battle of the 8th. In the north channel, hard and fast aground, lay the *Minnesota*, with her sides well riddled, while, close beside, the queer-looking *Monitor* guarded the stranded frigate. Towards Fortress Monroe, the *Roanoke*, the *St. Lawrence*, and the many gunboats of the Federal fleet kept at a respectful distance from the dreaded *Virginia*. The central figure in the picture was unquestionably the *Monitor*, of whose construction and reputed prowess full particulars had been received by the Confederate authorities. Whatever her merits might prove, the fact that she was iron-clad was sufficient, after the previous day's experience, to make her visit inopportune and undesired to the victors of the night before. Beside the towering frigate, the little *Monitor* presented the appearance of a pigmy beside a giant. A "tin can upon a shingle," or a "cheese box on a plank," were the familiar similes that greeted her appearance. But though small and insignificant in appearance, she was known to be the product of American inventive genius, of American energy, industry and enterprise. The officers who were to engage her in battle were too familiar with the resources, the energy, and the skill of Northern enterprise to doubt her prowess or to expect an easy victory. But whatever she might prove herself to be, she was there, watching and guarding the prize of yesterday's victory, and must be fought, let the result be what it would. Lieut. Jones, commanding the *Virginia*, was not the man to decline any contest after yesterday's triumph—still less to retire before testing the endurance and capabilities of that last product of Yankee invention.

Without waiting longer than necessary for an early breakfast —about eight and a quarter o'clock, the *Virginia* led the way to the second trial of strength and endurance, followed by the *Patrick Henry*, the *Jamestown*, the *Raleigh* and the *Teaser*, and steamed straight for the *Minnesota*. The battle was to be fought below the "middle ground"—in the deeper channel of the lower Roads, nearer to Fortress Monroe and the Rip-raps, and immediately off the Confederate Battery at Sewell's Point. Moving very slowly, the *Virginia* made straight as the channel would permit for the *Minnesota* and the *Monitor*, and opened fire from her bow pivot gun, and, closing the distance, delivered her starboard broadside at shorter range. The *Monitor* promptly accepted the challenge and stood boldly for the *Virginia*, passing her and delivering the fire of her eleven-inch gun directly upon the armored side of the *Virginia*. Both vessels turned and approached each other—the *Monitor* firing with the greatest deliberation at intervals of seven or eight minutes, and the *Virginia* oftener from her greater number of guns. It was soon apparent to both commanding officers that each had found a foeman worthy of his ship, and that the test was to be the strength of their country's *iron* rather than of the seamanship or courage of her sailors. The poetry of a naval battle was not there; it was simply a game of enormous iron bolts hurled upon thick iron plates from iron guns of heretofore unknown dimensions. The contest was not between ships, but between metal monsters with impenetrable sides.

The *Virginia* was working badly, the *Monitor* beautifully. The damage to the smokestack of the *Virginia* in the fight of the day before impeded the making of steam, and Chief Engineer Ramsay reported great difficulty in obtaining the necessary draft for his boilers. In addition to this, the great draft of the *Virginia* caused her to touch bottom and drag in the mud. Her twenty-three feet of draft confined her to a narrow channel, while the *Monitor's* twelve-feet draft enabled her to take any position she desired. The *Monitor* was the better boat—more obedient to her helm, more easily turned, and equally invulnerable, but not without apparent embarrassments. Her pilot-house, immediately in front of her turret, impeded the fire of her guns; and her commander, shut off in the pilot-house from her executive officer in the turret, had to pass his order through speaking-tubes, which were broken early in the action, and afterward by two *landsmen*, who were so unfamiliar with the technical communications that they were often misunderstood. Nevertheless, the *Monitor* was the superior ship in all the essentials necessary in action. It was not long before the experience of battle showed to Lieut. Jones the impossibility of perforating the turret, and he directed his fire upon the pilot-house with better results, and soon a shell from the *Virginia* "struck the forward side of the pilot-house, directly in the sight-hole or slit,

THE BATTLE OF THE IRON-CLADS. MARCH 9TH, 1862

COMMANDER CATESBY AP R. JONES,

CONFEDERATE STATES NAVY.

and exploded, cracking the second iron-log, and partly lifting the top, left an opening. Worden was standing immediately behind this spot, and received in his face the force of the blow, which partly stunned him, filling his eyes with powder and utterly blinded him,"[1] and the command devolved on Lieut. S. D. Greene.

Two hours of hard blows from the *Virginia* had made no impression on the *Monitor*, and the same amount of pounding had done no greater injury to the *Virginia*; and the battle continued at close quarters for some time, at less than fifty yards, without apparent damage to either side.[2] Under these circumstances, Lieut. Jones determined to try the same engine of destruction that the day before had broken through the wooden walls of the *Cumberland*; and, if not able to break in the sides of the *Monitor*, to run her down, or to fasten on to her and board her. Owing to the defective stearing-gear of the *Virginia*, this required nearly an hour of manœuvring for position, which was mistaken by observers for retreat, or evidence of damage inflicted; and when at last the opportunity offered, there was not room enough for the ship to get that headway which might have crushed the *Monitor* with the weight, if not by the blow, of the *Virginia*; so, when the ships came together, the agile, swift-turning *Monitor* eluded the blow, which amounted to nothing more than a small indentation. The ram of the *Virginia* had been broken off in the *Cumberland*, but it is very doubtful if under any headway that the *Virginia* could have acquired in that narrow channel of the Roads, any prow would have done material damage to the *Monitor*. Neither was it found practicable to board the *Monitor*, as was intended by Lieut. Jones, as she dropped astern before the boarders could get on board.

During this duel, from nine to eleven o'clock, between the iron-clads, the *Yorktown* and *Jamestown* participated, and received the fire of the *Monitor* and *Minnesota*. The latter vessel had received from the steamer *Rancocas* 100 solid shot, which she used against the *Virginia*, but with no perceptible injury to her iron sides. The *Virginia* used shells exclusively, the only solid shot that she carried being of large windage for use as hot shot; but as the solid shot from the *Monitor* and *Minnesota* did not injure the four-inch iron sides of the *Virginia*, it is not probable that solid shot from the guns of the *Virginia* would have done any more injury upon the nine-inch iron bulwarks of the *Monitor*. In the close contact of less than forty yards, the rapid firing of both ships enveloped them in dense clouds of smoke, almost totally concealing the contestants, from which they would emerge in their evolutions to receive the cheers of their respective friends, with their flags flying, to indicate that no victory had been won by either side.

[1] Commander S. D. Greene, in *Century*, March, 1885: p. 761. [2] Greene and Wood, in the *Century*, March, 1885.

As the ships steamed round each other for position, the *Virginia* would turn her guns upon the stranded *Minnesota* and endeavor to destroy her.   One of these shots took effect in the steamer *Dragon*, lying alongside the frigate, and exploded her boiler.

In the ineffectual effort of the *Virginia* to ram the *Monitor*, the latter delivered two shots from her eleven-inch guns directly and squarely upon the armored sides of the former, the effect of which was to knock down all the crews of the after-guns, and the concussion producing bleeding from nose and ears; the impact of these solid shots forced in the wooden backing of the shield two or three inches, and if such shots had been repeated at the same spot might have broken through and penetrated into the ship.

The battle raged almost continuously for four hours, and about 12 M. terminated without material damage to either ship, and certainly without decisive victory for either flag.   So far as damage done can indicate success, the *Virginia* could claim the palm of victory.   She had sunk the *Cumberland*, burned the *Congress*, riddled the *Minnesota*, destroyed the *Dragon*, burned the *Whitehall*, injured the *Roanoke* and *St. Lawrence*, [1] and left her mark upon the *Monitor*.   More than thirty prisoners had been captured, and over 250 of her enemies killed and wounded.   Not a vessel of the Confederate squadron had been disabled, or even seriously injured.   The *Patrick Henry* was compelled to haul out of the fight of the first day for a few hours to repair damage, but was at her post during all of the second day's fight; the clean sweep made of everything outside of the *Virginia*, and the loss of flag-staff and of one mast in the fleet, was the total damage done the Confederate ships.

Whether the *Monitor* or the *Virginia* first withdrew from action is yet unsettled.   Lieut. Jones says : "At length the *Monitor* withdrew over the middle ground where we could not follow, but always maintaining a position to protect the *Minnesota*," [2] which was the objective of Lieut. Jones' fight on the 9th.   "To run our ship ashore on a falling tide would have been ruin.   We waited her return for an hour; and at 2 P. M.

[1] Chief Engineer Allan C. Stiners of the *Monitor* reported, March 9th, 1862 : "We were struck twenty-two times, pilot-house twice, turret nine times, side armor eight times, deck three times.   The only vulnerable point was the pilot-house.   One of your great logs (nine by twelve inches thick) is broken in two.   The shot struck just outside of where the captain had his eye, and it has disabled him by destroying his left eye, and temporarily blinding the other.   The log is not quite in two, but is broken and pressed inwards one and a half inches. [The ' log ' alluded to is made of wrought iron of the best material.]   She tried to run us down and sink us, as she did the *Cumberland* yesterday, but she got the worst of it.   Her bow passed over our deck, and our sharp upper edge side cut through the light iron shoe upon her stern, and

well into her oak.   She will not try that again.   She gave us a tremendous thump, but did not injure us in the least.   We are just able to find the point of contact.

" The turret is a splendid structure.   I don't think much of the shield, but the pendulums are fine things, though I cannot tell you how they would stand the shot, as they were not hit.

"You were very correct in your estimate of the effect of shot upon the man on the inside of the turret when it was struck near him.   Three men were knocked down, of whom I was one ; the other two had to be carried below; but I was not disabled at all, and the others recovered before the battle was over."

[2] *Century*, March, 1885, p. 744.

steamed to Sewell's Point, and thence to the dock-yard at Norfolk, our crew thoroughly worn out from the two fights." Although there is no doubt that the *Monitor* first retired—for Capt. Van Brunt, commanding the *Minnesota*, so states in his official report—"the battle was a drawn one, so far as the two vessels engaged were concerned. But in its general results the advantage was with the *Monitor*." On the other hand, Commander Greene,[1] after explaining the reasons for the *Monitor* retiring temporarily from action, immediately after the wounding of Capt. Worden, says: "During this time the *Merrimac*, which was leaking badly, had started in the direction of the Elizabeth River, and on taking my station in the pilot-house and turning the vessel's head in the direction of the *Merrimac*, I saw that she was already in retreat. A few shots were fired at the retiring vessel and she continued on to Norfolk. I returned with the *Monitor* to the side of the *Minnesota*."

A more disinterested observer of the fight than Lieut. Green, and yet one quite as likely to be as observant of all that transpired between the two iron-clads, was Commander Van Brunt, of the *Minnesota*. The destruction of that frigate was the prime object of Lieut. Jones, and the *Monitor* was the only barrier that interposed between the destroyer of the *Cumberland* and the *Congress*, and the stranded frigate. The voluntary testimony of a witness whose opportunity of observation was the best, whose interests were antagonistic to the *Virginia*, and whose motives were anything than partial to his enemy, ought to receive greater weight than that of Lieut. Green shut up in the pilot-house, excited by the contest, and personally and professionally interested in the result of the fight. The official report of Commander Van Brunt on this point is as follows:

"By the time she had fired her third shell the little *Monitor* had come down upon her, placing herself between us, and compelled her to change her position; in doing which she grounded, and again I poured into her all the guns which could be brought to bear upon her. As soon as she got off she stood down the bay, the little battery chasing her with all speed, when suddenly the *Merrimac* turned around and ran full speed into her antagonist. For a moment I was anxious, but instantly I saw a shot plunge into the iron roof of the *Merrimac*, which surely must have damaged her, for some time after the rebels concentrated their whole battery upon the tower and pilot-house of the *Monitor*, and soon after the *latter* stood down for Fortress Monroe, and we thought it probable she had exhausted her supply of ammunition or sustained some injury. Soon after the *Merrimac* and the two other steamers headed for my ship, and I then felt to the fullest extent my condition. I was hard and immovably aground, and they could take position under my stern and rake me. I had expended most of my solid shot, my ship was badly crippled, and my officers and men were worn out with fatigue; but even in this extreme dilemma I determined never to give up the ship to the rebels, and after consulting my officers, I ordered every preparation to be made to destroy

[1] *Century*, March, 1885, p. 760.

the ship after all hope was gone to save her. On ascending the poop deck I observed that the enemy's vessels had changed their course and were heading for Craney Island."

We have italicized the word "latter" to call attention to the statement of Commander Van Brunt, that it was the *Monitor* which "stood down for Fortress Monroe"—her house of refuge, and her place of safety. Upon seeing the *Monitor* standing down for Fortress Monroe, he realized that the

THE "MERRIMAC" IN PROFILE.

destruction of his own ship was now possible, and he prepared himself to destroy her, when to his surprise he observed the *Virginia* to have changed her course for Craney Island.

Commander Foxhall Parker, in a paper read before the Naval Institute on "The *Monitor* and the *Merrimac*," perpetuates errors in regard to the fight, which repeated publications have exposed, and which he ought to have avoided. After describing the wounding of Capt. Worden, and Lieut. Green's assuming command, and bringing the *Monitor* back into action, Commander Parker continues : "as the *Monitor* turned, however, so did the *Merrimac*, and, to the surprise of all not on board of her, she steamed at full speed for Norfolk, * * * wholly

THE "MONITOR" IN PROFILE.

leaving the battle-field, and seeking shelter under the rebel batteries, thus by all the laws of war acknowledging herself vanquished." It is only necessary, in refutation of that statement, to refer to the above extract from the report of Commander Van Brunt, "whose officers and crews, Commander Parker says, were anxious spectators, as we may well conceive, of this novel combat, upon whose issue the fate of their own ship depended." The statement of an officer as deeply interested in the result of the conflict as Capt. Van Brunt was, and an eye-witness of the scene, will outweigh with history the fancy sketch of one who wrote to please the popular prejudice rather than to relate the facts as they actually occurred.

Capt. W. H. Parker, of the C. S. N., who commanded the *Beaufort* in both battles, wrote under date, College Station,

Prince George County, Md., February 9th, 1875, to Commander Catesby ap R. Jones, that:

"The *Beaufort* and *Raleigh* were canal boats running on the Albemarle Canal and Sound. Armament — one rifled thirty-two-pounder (banded). The *Beaufort* had also one twenty-four-pounder carronade. Crew and officers about thirty-five men. I perfectly understand that your narrative was intended to give an account of the proceedings of the *Virginia* only. It is truthful and correct, and such is the universal opinion. All I wanted was to show that I was not in command of a mere *Tug* boat on that eventful day. If I had seen your *MS.* before you published it, I don't know that I could have suggested anything you have not said. I think your account is just what it should be, and reflects credit upon you. In my opinion it will kill Worden's claim without any further testimony. *Foxhall* [a brother of W. H. Parker] *tells me he wrote his narrative from Worden's notes and at his request.* No doubt Worden put it out as a 'feeler.' When Foxhall (last month) showed me Worden's printed petition (for prize money) I said, 'Well! Fox - I thought well of Worden and am sorry he has put his name to a lie !' I think Fox regrets having written his article. I had a letter from Selfridge (a lieutenant on the *Cumberland*) on the subject. He wanted to know if the *Cumberland* was not entitled to as much credit (if any) as the *Monitor*. I answered him 'just about as much.' Major John Lee, of Washington, has written also. I referred him to your account, and told him Worden's assertions were hardly worthy a serious denial. Dr. Pinkney swears Worden shall not get the million he asks for, and indeed he has brought a hornet's nest about his ears. If I had any hope that honor and truth would ever again be valued in this country I should say Worden would live to regret his action.

"Very truly yours,

"WM. H. PARKER."

Prof. Soley says: "Seeing the *Monitor* draw off, Van Brunt, under the supposition that his protector was disabled and had left him, prepared for the worst, and made ready to destroy his ship. But, at this point, the *Merrimac* withdrew to Norfolk. As she moved off, Green fired at her twice, or at most three times. He then returned to the *Minnesota*, and remained by her until she got afloat. To have followed the *Merrimac* under the batteries of Sewell's Point would have been running a greater risk than the circumstances would warrant, considering the important interests in Hampton Roads, of which the *Monitor* afforded the sole protection." But if the *Virginia* had been defeated by the *Monitor*, and was in retreat to Norfolk, was it not the imperative duty of the commander of the *Monitor* to have followed the *Virginia* and destroyed her, or disabled her further, and would not that destruction have been the best and most complete protection to all the "important interests" at Hampton Roads ?[1]

---

[1] In a letter to the New York *Graphic*, in 1879, Commodore John Marston, U. S. N., claims the credit of saving the country by disobeying orders. At the time of the arrival of the *Monitor* in Hampton Roads, the Commodore was in command at that point, and says he had an imperative order to send the *Monitor* to Washington. The *Virginia* having already come down, *sunk* the *Cumberland* and burned the *Congress*, the Commodore resolved to disregard the order, at the risk of his commission, and send the *Monitor* up to Newport News to look out for the *Virginia*. Capt. Worden cheerfully acquiesced, and the result is known. "Where," asks the Commodore, "would the United States at this moment have been if I had not disobeyed my orders? There was nothing to prevent the *Merrimac* going to Philadelphia, New York, or Boston, and the fall of either of those cities would have been the signal for Europe, but especially for England, to acknowledge the independence of the South."

In a report made on this battle by Lieut. (afterward Admiral) Worden, he says :

"The *Merrimac* having been thus checked in her career of destruction, and driven back crippled and discomfited, the question arises, should she have been followed in her retreat to Norfolk? That such a course would commend itself very temptingly to the gallantry of an officer and be difficult to resist, is undeniable ; yet I am convinced that under the condition of affairs then existing at Hampton Roads, and the great interests at stake there, all of which were entirely dependent upon the *Monitor*, good judgment and sound discretion forbade it. It must be remembered that the pilot-house of the *Monitor* was situated well forward in her bows, and that it was considerably damaged. In following in the wake of the enemy it would have been necessary, in order to fire clear of the pilot-house, to have made broad 'yaws' to starboard or port, involving, in the excitement of such a chase, the very serious danger of grounding in the narrow portions of the channel and near some of the enemy's batteries, whence it would have been very difficult to extricate her; possibly involving her loss. Such a danger her commanding officer would not, in my judgment, have been justified in encountering, for her loss would have left the vital interests in all the waters of the Chesapeake at the mercy of future attacks of the *Merrimac*. Had there been another iron-clad in reserve at that point to guard those interests, the question would have presented a different aspect, which would not only have justified him in following, but perhaps made it his imperative duty to do so.

"The fact that the battle with the *Merrimac* was not more decided and prompt was due to the want of knowledge of the endurance of the eleven-inch Dahlgren guns with which the *Monitor* was armed, and which had not been fully tested. Just before leaving New York, I received a peremptory order from the Bureau of Ordnance to use only the prescribed service charge, viz., fifteen pounds, and I did not feel justified in violating those instructions at the risk of bursting one of the guns, which, placed as they were in turret, would almost entirely have disabled the vessel. Had I been able to have used thirty-pound charges, which experience has since shown the guns capable of enduring, there is little doubt in my mind that the contest would have been shorter and the result more decided. Further, the crew had been but a few days on board, the weather bad, the mechanics at work on her up to the moment of sailing, and sufficient opportunity had not been afforded to practice them properly at the guns, the mode of manipulating which was entirely novel."

Are these reasons satisfactory, if the *Virginia* was believed to have been defeated, crippled and discomfited? Were the channels too narrow for the *Monitor*, drawing only twelve feet ? And what was the fleet then floating the flag of the United States in Hampton Roads and guarding those interests ? There were in Hampton Roads, besides the *Monitor*, 2 guns, the *Roanoke*, 40 guns; the *Minnesota*, 48 guns; the *St. Lawrence*, 50 guns; *Brandywine*, 50 guns; *Cambridge*, 5 guns; *Mount Vernon*, 3 guns; *Mystic*, 4 guns; *Mount Washington*, 4 guns; *Braziliera*, 6 guns; *S. R. Spaulding*, 3 guns; *Young America*, 2 guns; *Delaware*, 2 guns, and *Charles Phelps*, 1 gun. —Total, 220 guns. Surely, a fleet strong enough to protect the interests in Hampton Roads from a "crippled and discomfited" vessel of 10 guns, which they said retreated to dry dock ! The *Congress*, 50 guns; *Cumberland*, 24 guns; *Whitehall*, 2 guns; *Dragon* and *Zouave*, each 1 gun, had been destroyed; but, with the exception of the *Minnesota*, all the above were afloat and quite able to protect the Roads from the James River squadron.

But if the *Monitor* was the victor on the memorable 9th of March, and the *Virginia* was "crippled and discomfited" and forced to fly to Norfolk, what necessity was there for the following order?

"NAVY DEPARTMENT, March 10th, 1862.

"It is directed by the President that the *Monitor be not too much exposed*, and that in no event shall any attempt be made to proceed with her unattended to Norfolk. If vessels can be procured and loaded with stone and sunk in the channel, it is important that it should be done.

"The *San Jacinto* and *Dakota* have sailed from Boston to Hampton Roads, and the *Sabine*, in tow of *Baltic* and a tug from New York. Gunboats will be ordered forthwith. Would it not be well to detain the *Minnesota* until other vessels arrive?

"CAPTAIN G. V. FOX,　　　　　　　　　　"GIDEON WELLES.

"*Assistant Secretary of the Navy, Fortress Monroe.*"

These preparations for a stone blockade against the *Virginia* look like precautionary measures against another such victory over the *Virginia*.

There are other official records, cotemporaneous with the fight, which show that the Federal authorities did not believe the *Virginia* defeated or disabled. Assistant Secretary Fox wrote to Secretary Welles, March 8th, 1862, 9 P.M., that "nearly all here are of the opinion that the *Merrimac* is disabled. I was the nearest person to her, outside of the *Monitor*, and I am of opinion she is not seriously injured." Assistant Secretary of War, P. H. Watson, on March 9th, wrote to Henry B. Fenwick, of New York, that:

"The *Merrimac*, an armor-clad vessel belonging to the rebels, issued from Norfolk yesterday, and captured several of the United States blockading vessels, and threatens to sweep our whole flotilla from Chesapeake Bay. Under these circumstances, it is of the last importance to capture or destroy the *Merrimac*, and the whole wealth and power of the United States will be at command for that purpose. As this movement was anticipated, and the subject of discussion between you and myself last December, you have, no doubt, thought of various modes by which it could be met and overcome most promptly. The Secretary of War desires you quietly to call a meeting of from three to nine persons, at your discretion, of the best judgment in naval engineering and warfare, to meet immediately at your father's house, or some other convenient and suitable place, and to sit as a committee to devise the best plan of speedily accomplishing the capture or destruction of the *Merrimac*. I would suggest the name of Abram S. Hewitt as a member of the committee. You will bear in mind that every hour's delay to destroy the *Merrimac* may result in incalculable damage to the United States, and that the plan or plans for her destruction should be submitted at the earliest hour practicable for the approval of this department, to the end that their execution may not be unnecessarily delayed a moment. To enable you to communicate hourly with this department, the Telegraphic Company is directed to transmit all messages from you at the expense of the government. Acknowledge this dispatch the moment you receive it. Spare no pains or expense to get the committee together immediately. Act with the utmost energy. You and each member of the committee will consider this whole matter confidential."

Evidently the War Department at Washington did not believe the fiction that the *Virginia* had been defeated, discomfited and disabled. On the same day, Gen. McClellan telegraphed to the commanding officers at Fort Delaware, Fort Mifflin, Fort Trumbull, New York Harbor, Newport, R. I., Boston and Portland, Me., that "the rebel iron-clad steamer *Merrimac* has destroyed two of our frigates near Fort Monroe, and finally retired last night to Craney Island. She may succeed in passing the batteries and go to sea. It is necessary that you place your fort in the best possible condition for defence, and do your best to stop her should she endeavor to run by. Anything that can be effected in the way of temporary batteries should be done at once." From Baltimore, Gen. Dix telegraphed Col. Warren, commanding Fort Federal Hill: "She (the *Merrimac*) may pass Fort Monroe and come here. You will make the same arrangements which would be necessary if we were in the presence of an enemy." Secretary Stanton telegraphed the Governors of New York and Massachusetts, that "the opinion of the naval commanders here is that the *Merrimac* will not venture to sea, but they advise that immediate preparations be made to guard against the danger to our ports, by large timber rafts protected by batteries. They regard timber rafts, guarded by batteries, as the best protection for temporary purposes." Com. Dahlgren, at Washington, telegraphed Gen. Hooker, "the *Merrimac* got out of harbor, and had pretty much used up our ships at Hampton Roads. It is impossible to say what she may attempt; but, as a proper precaution, it is proposed to be ready to block the channel of this river in the event of an attempt to enter it. By direction of the President, it has been agreed on by Gen. McClellan, Gen. Meigs, and myself, the Secretary of War present, to fill some canal-boats and other crafts, and tow them down near the place where it would be advisable to sink them. I wish you would, therefore, send up some steamers to tow them down. You have, no doubt, received my dispatch to send some fast vessel to observe the mouth of the Potomac. Let this duty be well looked to." Com. Dahlgren urged upon the President the necessity of blocking the Potomac, and to Gen. McClellan wrote: "I am making arrangements to place an eleven-inch gun and some ten-inch mortars on Giesborough Point, and that the steamer *Sophia* will leave G Street wharf in ten minutes, having in tow eight canal-boats loaded with sufficient stone to sink them; another steamer with eight more will leave in the course of the night." These are but a portion of the official records which show the fright and consternation produced by the *Virginia*, which, it was alleged, had been defeated, discomfited and disabled. "The performances of the *Merrimac*," says Gen. McClellan, "placed a new aspect upon everything, and may probably change my whole plan of campaign just on the eve of execution." On March

9th, Assistant Secretary Fox wrote to Secretary Welles, "the performance of the *Monitor* to-day against the *Merrimac* shows a slight superiority in favor of the *Monitor*. She is an ugly customer, and it is too good luck to believe we are yet clear of her." The steamer *Commodore* was directed to be held for a messenger to recall Gen. Burnside from the North Carolina Sound, and Secretary Welles ordered the *Oneida*, and "any vessels you have," to be sent to Hampton Roads. "Send the *Wachusett* to Hampton Roads; have the work on the other gunboats carried on day and night with all force possible to put on them, and when ready send them to Hampton Roads." "If *Chocura* and *Penobscot* have not sailed, send them to Hampton Roads as soon as steam can be gotten up; also the *Marblehead*, or any other gunboat ready." To Commodore Hiram Paulding, commandant at the New York Navy Yard, he telegraphed March 17th: "Send what gunboats you have at the yard to Hampton Roads at once." To Capt. Wm. L. Hudson, commandant at the Boston Navy Yard, he telegraphed at the same time: "Send what gunboats you have at the yard to Hampton Roads at once." And as Secretary Welles was in despair crying for gunboats to be sent to Hampton Roads, Dahlgren and Meigs were running canal boats loaded with stone down the Potomac.

"The possibility of the *Merrimac* appearing again paralyzes the movements of this army by whatever route is adopted," was the opinion of Gen. Barnard expressed to Assistant Secretary Fox; and if the *Virginia* had been turned towards Fortress Monroe, Meigs and Dahlgren would have filled the Potomac brimful of stone; while McClellan and Wool relied on filling the channel between Craney Island and Sewell's Point as the surest means of sealing up the terrible *Virginia ;* and "to take the battery at Sewell's Point, it would require the *Monitor*. Neither of us (Wool and Goldsborough) think it would do to use the *Monitor* for that service, lest she should become crippled. She is our only hope against the *Merrimac*." It was actually proposed by Secretary Stanton to let the destruction of the *Merrimac out by contract*, and to that end John Tucker, Assistant Secretary of War, wrote to Com. Vanderbilt. New York, March 15th, 1862: "The Secretary of War directs me to ask you for what sum you will contract to destroy the *Merrimac*, or prevent her from coming out from Norfolk—you to sink or destroy her if she gets out—answer by telegraph, as there is no time to be lost." To which Mr. Vanderbilt replied that he could "make no satisfactory reply to the inquiry made of him, but will be in Washington on Monday next to confer with the department."[1]

In the meantime, Com. Vanderbilt presented the steamer *Vanderbilt* to the government, and on March 20th, Secretary

[1] *Off. Rec.*, Series 1, Vol. IX. p. 15-31.

12

Stanton wrote to him at New York: "The President desires to turn to the utmost account your patriotic and generous gift to the government of the great steamship *Vanderbilt*, and to use and employ that ship for *protection and defence against the rebel iron-clad ship Merrimac.*"[1] Two days afterward, on the 22d, Secretary Stanton wrote to Major Gen. John E. Wool, commanding at Fortress Monroe: "The steamship *Vanderbilt* sailed from New York last night for Fortress Monroe. She has been given to the War Department and accepted by the President, and is designed to serve and be employed under the instructions of this Department for the convoy and protection of government transports at Fortress Monroe and *especially for the destruction of the Merrimac.*"[2] Secretary Stanton, on the 27th, gave Cornelius Vanderbilt a letter of introduction to Gen. Wool and he proceeded to Fortress Monroe to "aid in the destruction of the *Merrimac.*" He also placed at his disposal, beside his own steamer (the *Vanderbilt*), which had arrived at Fortress Monroe, the steamer *Matamora.*[3] Assistant Secretary of War P. H. Watson, writing from Cherrystone, Va., on March 28th, 1862, to Hon. E. M. Stanton, Secretary of War, said: "Yesterday afternoon I visited the *Vanderbilt*, and found her preparations are far advanced and that she is at any moment ready for action. Her steam is kept constantly up. There are seven steamers here, all ready to act as rams, with more or less efficiency, but by their combined operations abundantly able to destroy the *Merrimac*. In my judgment it is impossible for the *Merrimac* to come down to Fortress Monroe without being sunk by the rams. She can run up James River; she can attack Newport News, and do what she pleases above Fortress Monroe, as the channel above is too narrow and crooked to admit of the steam rams being worked against her with effect; but while remaining up there out of our reach she can do us no harm. Commodore Goldsborough is fully awake to the importance of destroying the *Merrimac*, and has a clear comprehension of the manner in which that can best be done with the means at his command. I think he will do his duty both skillfully and bravely, and I have no doubt with success. Mr. Vanderbilt fully approves Commodore Goldsborough's plan of battle, and desires the steamer *Vanderbilt* to remain under Goldsborough's command.[4] I have directed her so to remain until otherwise ordered by you. The large guns are not made available as they ought to be. The fifteen-inch gun is not yet ready to be used with any efficiency, although it is mounted upon a carriage. It is important to have the great gun made available immediately for *defence against the Merrimac.*"[5] On April 7th, 1862, Gen. McClellan

[1] *Official Records*, Series 1, Vol. XI. Part III. p. 26. The italics are ours.

[2] *Ibid*, p. 29.

[3] *Ibid*, p. 43.

[4] Gen. Wool had turned the *Vanderbilt* over to Flag-officer Goldsborough on March 24th, which met with the disapproval of Secretary Stanton on the 27th.—*Off. Rec.* Ser. 1, Vol. XI. Part III. p. 43.

[5] *Ibid*, p. 46.

in despair, wrote to Gen. Wool: "I wish the *Merrimac* would come out, so that we could get our gunboats up the James River;" and Commodore Goldsborough, in reply, said: "I dare not leave the *Merrimac* and consorts unguarded. Were she out of the way everything I have here should be at work in your behalf; but as things stand you must not count upon my sending any more vessels to aid your operations than those I mentioned to you."[1] Gen. Wool on April 11th, in a letter to Secretary Stanton, said: "The *Merrimac, Jamestown, Yorktown,* and several gunboats and tugs appeared between Newport News and Sewell's Point. The only damage done us is the capture of three small vessels, one empty, one loaded with hay, and the other loaded, it is said, with coal. * * No effort was made to prevent the capture."[2] At 5 P. M., in the same afternoon, Gen. Wool telegraphed to the Secretary: "*Merrimac* came down toward the *Monitor* and *Stevens*. The latter fired four or five rounds and the *Merrimac* one round, when she, with her consorts, returned to Craney Island."[3]

Flag-officer Goldsborough, in a letter to Mr. Lincoln, on May 9th, said: "On the *Merrimac's* appearance outside of the wrecks [at Sewell's Point], the *Monitor* had orders to fall back into fair channel way, and only to engage her seriously in such a position that this ship [the *Minnesota*], together with the merchant vessels intended for the purpose, could run her down. If an opportunity presented itself, the other vessels were not to hesitate to run her down, and the *Baltimore*, an unarmed steamer of light draught, high speed, and with a curved bow, was kept in the direction of the *Monitor* expressly to throw herself across the *Merrimac*, either forward or aft of her plated house. But the *Merrimac* did not engage the *Monitor*, nor did she place herself where she could have been assailed by our ram vessels to any advantage, or where there was any prospect whatever of getting at her."[4]

It was probably fortunate that the ships fitted up for the purpose of running the *Virginia* down did not make a serious attempt. Their own destruction, instead of that of the *Virginia*, would most likely have been the consequence.

---

[1] *Off. Rec.* Ser. 1, Vol. XI. Part III. pp. 77, 80.

[2] *Ibid*, pp. 88, 89.

[3] *Ibid* p. 89. J. S. Missroon, of the *Wachusett*, writing to Gen. McClellan, on April 14th, 1862, said he had received intelligence from a " contraband " who was "*not* intelligent," and who came on board from Gloucester, in a canoe, "that the battery at Gloucester Point is commanded by Jeff Page, late of the U. S. navy, a good officer; Richard Page, also formerly of navy, in command of one of the upper works at Gloucester; that they are very sanguine of sinking vessels, and have practiced their firing, which is very accurate; says Page (Jeff) can kill a dog at a mile." *Ibid*, p. 99. This same officer, on April 23d, writing to Commodore Goldsborough about the batteries in the neighborhood of Yorktown, which were nearly all com-

manded by C. S. naval officers, said: "Their cannon are managed and served with surprising accuracy, exceeding anything I have heretofore known, and there is every indication of a most determined resistance." *Ibid*, p. 123. Speaking of the gallant and efficient services rendered by some of the naval officers under his command, Major Gen. J. B. Magruder, in his official report of operations on the Peninsula, under date of May 3d, 1862, says: " That accomplished officer, Capt. Thomas Jefferson Page of the navy, successfully applied the resources of his genius and ripe experience to the defence of Gloucester Point. My thanks are due to Capt. Chatard of the navy, for valuable services as inspector of batteries, and to Lieut. Col. Noland, late of the navy, the efficient Commander of the batteries at Mulberry Island Point."

[4] *Ibid*, p. 155.

In further corroboration and explanation of the stone blockade of the Potomac, and of the extraordinary proposition of the U. S. Secretary of War to *contract with Vanderbilt* for the destruction of the *Virginia*, ex-Secretary Welles wrote to the Philadelphia *Times*, of December 3d, 1877, as follows:

"On the evening of that memorable Sunday I received from Dahlgren, who was in command of the navy-yard, a message, stating that he, and all the force he could command, were employed in loading and preparing the boats which had been sent to the yard. He supposed by my order and with my approval, although he had received no word from me. I replied that I had purchased no boats, given no orders, and that if I rightly apprehended the object and intention of the work in which he was engaged, I did not approve it. When I called on the President the next morning Stanton was already there, stating some grievance, and, as I entered, he turned to me and inquired my reason for countermanding his orders. He proceeded to state that he had directed the purchase of all the boats that could be procured in Washington, Georgetown and Alexandria, which were being laden with stone and earth, under the direction of Col. Meigs and Dahlgren, with a view of sinking them at Kettle Bottom Shoals, some fifty miles or more below, in order to prevent the ascension of the *Merrimac*. That while the officers whom he had detailed, he supposed with my approval, were actively engaged, they had been suddenly stopped by an order from me to Dahlgren. He was still complaining when Dahlgren, and I believe Meigs also, came in, and I then learned that great preparations had been made to procure a fleet of boats, which were to be sunk at Kettle Bottom to protect Washington. I objected, and said I would rather expend money to remove obstacles than to impede navigation; that the navy had labored through the fall and winter to keep open this avenue to the ocean; that the army had not driven the rebels from the Virginia shore, nor assisted us in this work, though they had been greatly benefitted by our efforts in the transportation of their supplies, forage, etc.; that to our shame there was but a single railroad track to the capital, though we had here an army of more than 100,000 to feed, and that I should not consent to take any of the naval appropriation to cut off water communication, unless so ordered by the President ; but should protest against obstructing the channel of the river. Our conversation was very earnest, and the President attentively listened, but with an evident inclination to guard in every way against the *Merrimac*, but yet unwilling to interrupt ocean communication, so essential to Washington. Giving the interview a pleasant turn, he said it was evident that Mars not only wanted exclusive control of military operations (Stanton had manifested much dissatisfaction with McClellan as General-in-chief), but that he wanted a navy, and had begun to improvise one. Having already got his fleet, the President thought he might as well be permitted to finish his work, but he must not destroy communication on the Potomac or cripple Neptune. The boats purchased might be loaded and sent down the river, but not sunk in the channel until it was known the *Merrimac* had entered the river or was on its way hither. Whatever expense was incurred must be defrayed by the War Department. With this understanding Dahlgren was authorized to supervise and assist Stanton's squadron.

"In addition to his fleet of canal boats, scowboats and other craft, Cornelius Vanderbilt, who owned several large steamers, a man of well-known energy and enterprise, was invited by Stanton to Washington for consultation and advice. He was informed that the egress of the *Merrimac* must be prevented, and the vessel destroyed whenever she appeared ; that the War Department did not rely upon the *Monitor*, but proposed to stop and destroy her independent of the navy, and that he had more confidence in the capability, suggestions and prowess of individuals like

Vanderbilt, who depended on their own resources, than on naval officers, who were circumscribed by their education and trained to a particular service. He concluded by asking the great steamboat chief if he could in any way destroy or overcome the *Merrimac.*

"Gratified with the summons, and complimented by the confidence expressed in his superior ability by the Secretary of War, Vanderbilt responded that he could destroy the *Merrimac,* and was ready to do so, but he wanted the *Monitor* out of the way, and must be permitted to do the work subject to no control of naval officers or any interference from them or from naval vessels. If they would all get out of the way he would run down the *Merrimac* with his big ship '*Vanderbilt.*' The employment of this great ship corresponded with Stanton's ideas of power and force. He was delighted, and went with Vanderbilt to the President, who assented to the scheme, but was unwilling to dispense with the *Monitor,* which had done so well, and suggested that an encounter of the large wooden steamer with the armored ship might result in the destruction of the *Vanderbilt* instead of the *Merrimac.* In that event a good sale would be made of the *Vanderbilt,* and the government might be compelled to pay largely for the experiment without being benefitted. Vanderbilt replied that he would take the risk; that he was anxious to assist the government; that he had already offered his vessel to the Secretary of the Navy on his own terms, and would have given her to him, but the Secretary wouldn't take her; he would make a present of her to the President, requiring, however, that the engineers and employees on board should be retained at present wages. Pleased with the suggestion that the *Merrimac* might be run down, and thus a double security provided against her, not only the *Vanderbilt,* but the *Baltic,* and one or two other large merchant steamers, were chartered and stationed in Hampton Roads."

Mr. Welles is a competent witness *in favor* of the *Virginia's* victory, though it must be confessed that he ceases to be entirely reliable when he comes to relate subsequent events. Continuing his narrative, he says:

"These immense vessels, lofty and grand, were anchored near Fortress Monroe, where they remained for two months, at no small expense, awaiting the appearance of the *Merrimac,* but no opportunity occurred to run her down; that vessel, in her conflict with the *Monitor,* sustained serious injury, and her officers, dreading more the novel craft which she had encountered on the 9th of March than the large wooden steamers, never again descended Elizabeth River to the Roads."

Indisputable evidence exists to contradict the statement of Mr. Welles that the *Virginia* "never again descended Elizabeth River to the Roads," in the established facts that she captured prizes from under the guns of the *Monitor, Vanderbilt,* and the forts, that she drove off the fleet from Sewell's Point, and repeatedly offered battle in the Roads. The Honorable Secretary seems, in 1877, to have forgotten a letter he wrote of date November 7th, 1874, to G. V. Fox, in relation to this same fight. That letter was as follows :

"HARTFORD, Nov. 7th, 1874.
"MY DEAR SIR: Your favor of the 2d inst., in the Catesby Jones narrative, I duly received and read with interest. You ask me whether you had better give it to the press. I see no objection, if his name goes with it. Of course, his statement is tinged with his feelings and views, for which allowance will be made. But he is a man of character, and presents the case as he understands it. I am always glad to read the

statements of reliable men among the secessionists, and they are often quite as truthful as representations and histories on our side.

"Truly yours,   GIDEON WELLES.

"G. V. Fox, Boston."

In 1876, ex-Assistant Secretary of the Navy G. V. Fox prepared an account of the *Monitor* for an encyclopædia in which he gave a short and fair description of the fight in Hampton Roads. The proof sheets Mr. Fox sent to Commander Catesby Jones, who immediately wrote to Mr. Fox the following letter:

"NEW YORK, June 20th, 1876.

"MY DEAR FOX: Your *Monitor* article has been forwarded to me from Selma. Thanks for it. It is by far the fairest Northern account of the fight that I have seen. There are, however, some errors which I will mention, knowing how desirous you are that it shall be a true history.

"You say the *Merrimac* 'was armed with an approved broadside battery of rifled guns.'

"Each broadside consisted of *three* smooth-bore guns and but one rifle gun.

"Of the first day's fight, you say : 'By five o'clock the battle was over.'

"It continued at least one and a half hours later. We fought until it was so dark that we could not see to point the guns with accuracy. We did not leave the vicinity of the *Congress* until after the pilots had several times urged me to seek an anchorage, and, in fact, did not leave until they would not be responsible if we did not.

"Of the second day's fight you say : 'Once whilst the vessels were thus separated, the *Merrimac* fired three shells at the *Minnesota*.' Do you refer to the time when the *Monitor* ran into shoal water to hoist up shot as stated by Worden ? And again you say: 'When near noon the *Monitor* hauled off.' * * * This movement laid open the *Minnesota* to another attack from the *Merrimac*, but her commander did not, as previously, avail himself of it.' You also say that 'the *Merrimac* fired forty-six shells at the *Monitor* and four at the *Minnesota*.'

"The unavoidable inference being, that we only fired at the *Minnesota* when the *Monitor* had hauled off, but this is very erroneous. We frequently fired at the *Minnesota* whilst we were fighting the *Monitor*, and we actually fired more shell at the wooden vessel on the second day than we did at the iron-clad. I had intended to have incorporated in my narrative the exact expenditure of powder and shell, but lost it, and as the gunner's memory was entirely at fault, I did not allude to the matter at all.

"On the first day you say 'It was full sea there at 1.56 P. M., and whilst the *Cumberland* was' riding ' to the last of the flood the *Merrimac* ran into her.'

"When we ran into the *Cumberland*, she had canted with her head toward the Newport News side, so that on approaching her, we did not have to change our course in order to give her a fair blow.

"On the second day you say we passed the bar ' at meridian three hours before high water.' Are you not mistaken as to the time of high water ? I think you must be. If not, the pilots misled me. We only determined to leave when we did, because they said if we did not, we could not leave until the next day. The tide was running flood when the fight commenced. I wanted to fight the *Minnesota* with our starboard battery, two of the guns on the port side being disabled, but owing to the flood-tide we had to keep the vessel's head down stream, and fire at the *Minnesota* with the port battery. We certainly would not have returned to Norfolk had I have supposed it wanted three hours of high water. My impression too is that it was ebb tide when we arrived at the Navy Yard which would not have been the case if you are right. The pilots were very cautious, and would not consent to move the vessel except under the most favorable conditions of tide, etc.

"As all Confederate accounts called our vessel the 'Virginia,' it would have been well to have mentioned it, or, at the next centennial the two names may be believed to refer to different vessels.

"You incorrectly state that we lightened one inch for twenty-four tons consumption, it should be for fifteen tons; but the prow and anchor being lost from the bows caused her to come up much more forward than aft.

"You say we were 'under repairs' more than a month. It did not require that length of time to repair her. We were endeavoring to complete her, but could not. She never was completed.

"My name is incorrect.

"I have written hurriedly amid interruptions, but believe I have no more to say. Address, etc.

"CATESBY AP R. JONES.

"G. V. Fox, Boston."

To this criticism ex-Secretary Fox replied as follows:

"BOSTON, Aug. 2d, 1876.

"MY DEAR COMMANDER : I received both of your letters. When your first arrived I had packed up my things for the Beach and could not reply, by authority, to your criticisms. I am not keeping house and when I leave the hotel I give up my rooms and stow away my things. However I will do the best I can, taking up your remarks seriatim.

"'Approved battery of rifle guns.' I gave the battery at first as you sent it, and should have left out 'rifle guns' or put in rifle *and smooth bore.* 'By five o'clock the battle was over,' I have not been able to obtain uniformity upon this point, and will seek more light. The number of shot fired by the *Merrimac* I feel sure you gave me, but cannot get your letters before fall. See Van Brunt's report, and the different officers' reports of the *Minnesota.* If you can give me any more authentic proof upon this subject, should like it. The high tides are from the Coast Survey office, taken actually on that day at Old Point, and computed for N. News and Norfolk, therefore you must have rammed the *Cumberland* before 1.56 P. M., immediately after which the *Congress* surrendered. I gave three hours to finishing her. I never wrote your name as it is printed. I will put it *M.* and *Virginia.* The histories all use *Merrimac.* I could not get a proof until it was printed, and now the first edition is out, but it will be followed immediately by another which I shall be happy to correct where I can see any way to do so. My account differs from all Northern accounts as well as the Count de Paris', but it accords with the views I stated to Mr. Lincoln and Gen. McClellan after I had witnessed the contest.

"The exact truth about all these matters is what I am seeking for, the source is immaterial. Where there is a conflict I must use the best judgment I possess to endeavor to reconcile them. The log-books I found not to be of much use. Give me all your criticisms at your leisure and I will investigate each one carefully.

"Yours truly,

"G. V. Fox."

"BOSTON, Aug. 3d, 1876.

"DEAR COMMANDER : Capt. Selfridge, who was a lieutenant on board the *Cumberland,* writes me that the *Merrimac* struck the *Cumberland* three times, the last one being the mortal blow. Is that so ?

"I wrote you yesterday.

"Yours truly,

"G. V. Fox."

Later in 1876, on December 23d, Mr. Fox again wrote to Commander Jones as follows :

"BOSTON, Dec. 23d, 1876.

"DEAR COMMANDER: I have yours of the 19th inst. When I was in New York the other day, I called at the Cyclopædia office, and they told me that any corrections I wish to make could be inserted whenever they printed another edition, which happened every year almost. They confined me to the same space, because they print say 500 copies to an edition, then sell those and are ready to use the same plates for another 500. They insert corrections by cutting out a space of metal and inserting another. I have all your letters and other correspondence tied up in a bundle, and whatever fact you send me I will look into it and correct it unless the weight of evidence on the other side throws it into a doubt.

"With regard to the displacement and rise per ton, I got the figures from old John Lenthal. I enclose the article. You can go over it very carefully at your leisure and send me the facts as they seemed to you.

"If we divest ourselves of passion, and meet the political difficulty with the calmness and good judgment I witnessed at Columbia, S. C., where the provocation to fling discretion to the winds is greater than any State has hitherto been subjected to, then we shall pull through. If we lived in a hereditary form of government, and were subjected to the wrongs which now threaten us, an appeal to arms would be the proper course, but the multiplicity of our elections enable us to overthrow a government after a while, no matter how much cheating goes on. The South are setting our people a great example, and winning esteem from the North in spite of prejudice.

"Whichever party makes a blunder by forcing matters in the next three months will disappear from history. The experiment of an appeal to force, to remedy political troubles, has not resulted satisfactorily to any section or to our common country. A happy Christmas to you and Mrs. J.

"Sincerely,

"G. V. Fox."

It will be seen from the above letter that the Encyclopædia article on the *Monitor* was subject to repeated emendations and alterations. When it appeared first in 1874, its publication drew from Mr. J. Ericsson the following letters of protest:

"NEW YORK, Nov. 24th, 1874.

"MY DEAR SIR: I am quite at a loss to understand why you have opened a fresh discussion about the *Monitor* and *Merrimac* fight, so happily disposed of by several patriotic writers, to the satisfaction of the country—I may say to the satisfaction of the whole world. No one knows better than yourself the shortcomings of that fight, ended at the moment when the crew had become well trained and the machinery got in good working order. Why? Because you had a miserable executive officer who, instead of jumping into the pilot-house when Worden was blinded, ran away with his impregnable vessel. The displacement of the top plate of the pilot-house, which I had designed principally to keep out spray in bad weather, was really an advantage by allowing fresh air to enter the cramped iron-walled cabin—certainly that displacement offered no excuse for discontinuing the fight, the revolving turret and the good steering qualities of the *Monitor* rendering it unnecessary to fire over the pilot-house.

"Regarding the rebel statement before me, I can only say that if published it will forever tarnish the lustre of your naval administration, and amaze our people who have been told that the *Merrimac* was a terrible ship, which but for the *Monitor* would have destroyed the Union fleet, and burnt the Atlantic cities.

"In fact, that the *Monitor* had saved the country. Need I say that Jones' statement will be published in the professional journals of all civilized countries, and call forth sneers and condemnation from a legion of *Monitor* opponents.

"Poor Count Platen, and Alderspanes, the criticism and blame that will be heaped upon them by the present king's party will be insupportable. How the changes will be rung on the statement of the *Merrimac's* commanding officer that the *Cumberland* could have sunk his vessel (admitted to be 'unseaworthy,' the hull being covered by only one-inch plating), yet the *Monitor* was unable to inflict any damage, not a man on board the *Merrimac* wounded or killed. But the *unarmed Cumberland* destroyed two guns, killing and wounding several of the *Merrimac's* crew.

"Again, the *Monitor*, when challenged to come out, 'hugged the shore under the guns of the fort.' Counter statements, even if believed, would never be published. But I have said enough. Should the rebel statement be published its effect will be more damaging than probably any incident of my life.

"Please find your several documents enclosed,

"Yours truly,

"J. ERICSSON.

"P. S.—The original written under strong emotion, being nearly unintelligible, I forward the copy.

"Yours,

"J. ERICSSON."

"The rebel statement before" Mr. Ericsson. was the account of the fight between the *Monitor* and the *Virginia*, written by Commander Catesby ap R. Jones, and published in the *Southern Historical Society Papers*, p. 65 to 75, No. 2-3, Vol. XI., which is as follows:

"When on April 21st, 1861, the Virginians took possession of the abandoned navy-yard at Norfolk, they found that the *Merrimac* had been burnt and sunk. She was raised; and on June 23d following, the Hon. S. R. Mallory, Confederate Secretary of the Navy, ordered that she should be converted into an iron-clad, on the plan proposed by Lieut. John M. Brooke, C. S. N.

"The hull was 275 feet long. About 160 feet of the central portion was covered by a roof of wood and iron, inclining about thirty-six degrees. The wood was two feet thick; it consisted of oak plank four inches by twelve inches, laid up and down next the iron, and two courses of pine; one longitudinal of eight inches thickness, the other twelve inches thick.

"The intervening space on top was closed by permanent gratings of two inch square iron two and one-half inches apart, leaving openings for four hatches, one near each end, and one forward and one abaft the smoke-stack. The roof did not project beyond the hull. There was no knuckle as in the *Atlanta, Tennessee* and our other iron clads of later and improved construction. The ends of the shield were rounded.

"The armor was four inches thick. It was fastened to its wooden backing by one and three-eighths inch bolts, countersunk and secured by iron nuts and washers. The plates were eight inches wide. Those first made were one inch thick, which was as thick as we could then punch cold iron. We succeeded soon in punching two inches, and the remaining plates, more than two-thirds, were two inches thick. They were rolled and punched at the Tredegar Works, Richmond. The outside course was up and down, the next longitudinal. Joints were broken where there were more than two courses.

"The hull, extending two feet below the roof, was plated with one-inch iron; it was intended that it should have had three inches.

"The prow was of cast-iron, wedge-shape, and weighed 1,500 pounds. It was about two feet under water, and projected two feet from the stem; it was not well fastened.

"The rudder and propeller were unprotected.

"The battery consisted of ten guns, four single-banded Brooke rifles, and six nine-inch Dahlgren shell guns. Two of the rifles, bow and stern pivots, were seven-inch, of 14,500 pounds; the other two were six four-inch (thirty-two pounds calibre), of 9,000 pounds, one on each broadside. The nine-inch gun on each side nearest the furnaces was fitted for firing hot shot. A few nine-inch shot, with extra windage, were cast for hot shot. No other solid shot were on board during the fight.

"The engines were the same the vessel had whilst in the United States navy. They were radically defective, and had been condemned by the United States government. Some changes had been made, notwithstanding which, the engineers reported that they were unreliable. They performed very well during the fight, but afterwards failed several times, once whilst under fire.

"There were many vexatious delays attending the fitting and equipment of the ship. Most of them arose from the want of skilled labor, and lack of proper tools and appliances. Transporting the iron from Richmond also caused much delay; the railroads were taxed to supply the army.

"The crew, 320 in number, were obtained with great difficulty. With few exceptions they were volunteers from the army; most of them were landsmen. Their deficiencies were, as much as possible, overcome by the zeal and intelligence of the officers; a list of them is appended. In the fight one of the nine-inch guns was manned by a detachment of the Norfolk United Artillery.

"The vessel was by the Confederates called *Virginia*. She was put in commission during the last week of February, but continued crowded with mechanics until the eve of the fight. She was badly ventilated, very uncomfortable, and very unhealthy. There was an average of fifty or sixty at the hospital, in addition to the sick list on board.

"The Flag-officer, Franklin Buchanan, was detained in Richmond in charge of an important bureau, from which he was only relieved a few days before the fight. There was no captain; the ship was commissioned and equipped by the executive and ordnance officer, who had reported for duty in November. He had by special order selected her battery, and was also made responsible for its efficiency.

"A trial was determined upon, although the vessel was in an incomplete condition. The lower part of the shield forward was only immersed a few inches, instead of two feet as was intended; and there was but one inch of iron on the hull. The port-shutters, etc., were unfinished.

"The *Virginia* was unseaworthy, her engines were unreliable, and her draft, over twenty-two feet, prevented her from going to Washington. Her field of operation was therefore restricted to the bay and its immediate vicinity; there was no regular concerted movement with the army.[1]

"The frigates *Congress* and *Cumberland* temptingly invited an attack. It was fixed for Thursday night, March 6th, 1862; the pilots, of whom there were five, having been previously consulted. The sides were slushed, supposing that it would increase the tendency of the projectiles to glance. All preparations were made, including lights at obstructions. After dark the pilots declared that they could not pilot the ship during the night. They had a high sense of their responsibility. In justice to

[1] There was, however, an informal understanding between Gen. Magruder, who commanded the Confederate forces on the Peninsula, and the executive officer, to the effect that Gen. Magruder should be kept advised by us, in order that his command might be concentrated near Hampton when our attack should be made. The movement was prevented in consequence of a large portion of the command having been detached just before the fight.

them it should be stated that it was not easy to pilot a vessel of our great draft under favorable circumstances, and that the difficulties were much increased by the absence of lights, buoys, etc., to which they had been accustomed.

"The attack was postponed to Saturday, March 8th. The weather was favorable. We left the navy-yard at 11 A. M., against the last half of the flood tide, steamed down the river past our batteries, through the obstructions, across Hampton Roads, to the mouth of James River, where, off Newport News, lay at anchor the frigates *Cumberland* and *Congress*, protected by strong batteries and gunboats. The action commenced about 3 P. M. by our firing the bow-gun[1] at the *Cumberland*, less than a mile distant. A powerful fire was immediately concentrated upon us from all the batteries afloat and ashore. The frigates *Minnesota, Roanoke* and *St. Lawrence* with other vessels, were seen coming from Old Point. We fired at the *Congress* on passing, but continued to head directly for the *Cumberland*, which vessel we had determined to run into, and in less than fifteen minutes from the firing of the first gun we rammed her just forward of the starboard foe chains. There were heavy spars about her bows, probably to ward off torpedoes, through which we had to break before reaching the side of the ship. The noise of the crashing timbers was distinctly heard above the din of battle. There was no sign of the hole above water. It must have been large, as the ship soon commenced to career. The shock to us on striking was slight. We immediately backed the engines. The blow was not repeated. We here lost the prow, and had the stem slightly twisted. The *Cumberland*[2] fought her guns gallantly as long as they were above water. She went down bravely, with her colors flying. One of her shells struck the sill of the bow-port and exploded; the fragments killed two and wounded a number. Our aft nine-inch gun was loaded and ready for firing, when its muzzle was struck by a shell, which broke it off and fired the gun. Another gun also had its muzzle shot off; it was broken so short that at each subsequent discharge its port was set on fire. The damage to the armor was slight. Their fire appeared to have been aimed at our ports. Had it been concentrated on the water-line we would have been seriously hurt, if not sunk. Owing to the ebb-tide and our great draft we could not close with the *Congress* without first going up stream, which was a tedious operation, besides subjecting us twice to the full fire of the batteries, some of which we silenced.

"We were accompanied from the yard by the gunboats *Beaufort*, Lieut. Commander W. H. Parker, and *Raleigh*, Lieut. Commander J. W. Alexander. As soon as the firing was heard up James River, the *Patrick Henry*, Commander John R. Tucker, *Jamestown*, Lieut. Commander J. N. Barney, and the gunboat *Teaser*, Lieut. Commander W. A. Webb, under command of Capt. John R. Tucker, stood down the river, joining us about four o'clock. All these vessels were gallantly fought and handled, and rendered valuable and effective service.

"The prisoners from the *Congress* stated that when on board that ship it was seen that we were standing up the river, that three cheers were given under impression that we had quit the fight. They were soon undeceived. When they saw us heading down stream, fearing the fate of the *Cumberland*, they slipped their cables, made sail, and ran ashore bows on. We took a position off her quarter, about two cables' length distant, and opened a deliberate fire. Very few of her guns bore on us, and they were soon disabled. The other batteries continued to play on us, as did the *Minnesota*, then aground about one and one-half miles off. The *St. Lawrence* also opened on us shortly after. There was great havoc on board the *Congress*. She was several times on fire. Her gallant

---

[1] It killed and wounded ten men at the after pivot gun of the *Cumberland*. The second shot fired from the same gun killed and wounded twelve men at her forward pivot gun.

[2] She was a sailing frigate of 1,726 tons, mounting two ten-inch pivots and twenty-two nine-inch guns. Her crew numbered 376; her loss in killed and wounded was 121.

commander, Lieut. Joseph B. Smith,[1] was struck in the breast by the fragment of a shell and instantly killed. The carnage was frightful. Nothing remained but to strike their colors, which they did. They hoisted the white flag, half-masted, at the main and at the spanker gaff. The *Beaufort* and *Raleigh* were ordered to burn her. They went alongside and secured several of her officers and some twenty of her men as prisoners. The officers urgently asked permission to assist their wounded out of the ship. It was granted. They did not return. A sharp fire of musketry from the shore killed some of the prisoners and forced the tugs to leave. A boat was sent from the *Virginia* to burn her, covered by the *Teaser.* A fire was opened on them from the shore, and also from the *Congress*, with both of her white flags flying, wounding Lieut. Minor and others. We replied to this outrage upon the usages of civilized warfare by reopening on the *Congress* with hot shot and incendiary shell. Her crew escaped by boats, as did that of the *Cumberland.* Canister and grape would have prevented it; but in neither case was any attempt made to stop them, though it has been otherwise stated, possibly from our firing on the shore or at the *Congress.*

"We remained near the *Congress* to prevent her recapture. Had she been retaken, it might have been said that the Flag-officer permitted it, knowing that his brother[2] was an officer of that vessel.

"A distant and unsatisfactory fire was at times had at the *Minnesota.* The gunboats also engaged her. We fired canister and grape occasionally in reply to musketry from the shore, which had become annoying.

"About this time the Flag-officer was badly wounded by a rifle-ball, and had to be carried below. His bold daring and intrepid conduct won the admiration of all on board. The Executive and Ordnance officer, Lieut. Catesby Ap R. Jones, succeeded to the command.

"The action continued until dusk, when we were forced to seek an anchorage. The *Congress* was riddled and on fire. A transport steamer was blown up. A schooner was sunk and another captured. We had to leave without making a serious attack on the *Minnesota*, though we fired at her as we passed on the other side of the Middle Ground, and also at the *St. Lawrence.*[3] The latter frigate fired at us by broadsides, not a bad plan for small calibres against iron-clads, if concentrated. It was too dark to aim well. We anchored off our batteries at Sewell's Point. The squadron followed.

"The *Congress*[4] continued to burn; 'she illuminated the heavens, and varied the scene by the firing of her own guns and the flight of her balls through the air,' until shortly after midnight, 'when her magazine exploded, and a column of burning matter appeared high in the air, to be followed by the stillness of death.' [Extract from report of General Mansfield, U. S. A.] One of the pilots chanced, about 11 P. M., to be looking in the direction of the *Congress*, when there passed a strange looking craft, brought out in bold relief by the brilliant light of the burning ship, which he at once proclaimed to be the *Ericsson.* We were therefore not surprised in the morning to see the *Monitor* at anchor near the *Minnesota.* The latter ship was still aground. Some delay occurred from sending our wounded out of the ship; we had but one serviceable boat left. Admiral Buchanan was landed at Sewell's Point.

"At 8 A.M. we got under way, as did the *Patrick Henry, Jamestown,* and *Teaser.* We stood towards the *Minnesota* and opened fire on her. The pilots were to have placed us half-a-mile from her, but we were not at

---

[1] His sword was sent by flag of truce to his father, Admiral Joseph Smith.

[2] One of the sad attendants of civil war, divided families, was here illustrated. The Flag-officer's brother was paymaster of the *Congress.* The first and second lieutenants had each a brother in the United States Army. The father of the fourth lieutenant was also in the U. S. army. The father of one of the midshipmen was in the U. S. navy.

[3] A sailing frigate of fifty guns and 1,726 tons.

[4] A sailing frigate of 1,867 tons, mounting fifty guns. She had a crew of 434, of whom there were 120 killed and missing.

any time nearer than a mile. The *Monitor*[1] commenced firing when about a third of a mile distant. We soon approached, and were often within a ship's length; once while passing we fired a broadside at her only a few yards distant. She and her turret appeared to be under perfect control. Her light draft enabled her to move about us at pleasure. She once took position for a short time where we could not bring a gun to bear on her. Another of her movements caused us great anxiety; she made for our rudder and propeller, both of which could have been easily disabled. We could only see her guns when they were discharged; immediately afterward the turret revolved rapidly, and the guns were not again seen until they were again fired. We wondered how proper aim could be taken in the very short time the guns were in sight. The *Virginia*, however, was a large target, and generally so near that the *Monitor's* shot did not often miss. It did not appear to us that our shell had any effect upon the *Monitor*. We had no solid shot; musketry was fired at the look-out holes. In spite of all the care of our pilots we ran ashore, where we remained over fifteen minutes. The *Patrick Henry* and *Jamestown*, with great risk to themselves, started to our assistance. The *Monitor* and *Minnesota* were in full play on us. A small rifle-gun on board the *Minnesota*, or on the steamer alongside of her, was fired with remarkable precision.

" When we saw that our fire made no impression on the *Monitor*, we determined to run into her if possible. We found it a very difficult feat to do. Our great length and draft, in a comparatively narrow channel, with but little water to spare, made us sluggish in our movements, and hard to steer and turn. When the opportunity presented all steam was put on; there was not, however, sufficient time to gather full headway before striking. The blow was given with the broad wooden stem, the iron prow having been lost the day before. The *Monitor* received the blow in such a manner as to weaken its effect, and the damage was to her trifling. Shortly after an alarming leak in the bows was reported. It, however, did not long continue.

" Whilst contending with the *Monitor*, we received the fire of the *Minnesota*,[2] which we never failed to return whenever our guns could be brought to bear. We set her on fire and did her serious injury, though much less than we then supposed. Generally the distance was too great for effective firing. We blew up a steamer alongside of her.

" The fight had continued over three hours. To us the *Monitor* appeared unharmed. We were therefore surprised to see her run off into shoal water where our great draft would not permit us to follow, and where our shell could not reach her. The loss of our prow and anchor, and consumption of coal, water, etc., had lightened us so that the lower part of the forward end of the shield was awash.

" We for some time awaited the return of the *Monitor* to the Roads. After consultation it was decided that we should proceed to the navy-yard, in order that the vessel should be brought down in the water and completed. The pilots said if we did not then leave, that we could not pass the bar until noon of the next day. We therefore at 12 M. quit the Roads and stood for Norfolk. Had there been any sign of the *Monitor's* willingness to renew the contest, we would have remained to fight her. We left her in the shoal water to which she had withdrawn and which she did not leave until after we had crossed the bar on our way to Norfolk.

" The official report says: ' Our loss is two killed and nineteen wounded. The stem is twisted and the ship leaks; we have lost the prow, starboard anchor, and all the boats; the armor is somewhat damaged, the steam-pipe and smoke-stack both riddled, the muzzles of the

[1] She was 173 feet long and forty-one feet wide. She had a revolving circular iron turret eight inches thick, nine feet high and twenty feet inside diameter, in which were two eleven-inch guns. Her draft was ten feet, less than half that of the *Virginia*.

[2] She was a screw steam frigate of 3,200 tons, mounting forty-three guns of eight, nine and ten-inch calibre. She fired 145 ten-inch, 349 nine-inch, and thirty-four eight-inch shot and shell, and 5,567 pounds of powder. Her draft was about the same as the *Virginia*.

two guns shot away; the colors were hoisted to the smoke-stack, and several times cut down from it.' None were killed or wounded in the fight with the *Monitor*. The only damage she did was to the armor. She fired forty-one shots. We were enabled to receive most of them obliquely. The effect of a shot striking obliquely on the shield was to break all the iron, and sometimes to displace several feet of the outside course; the wooden backing would not be broken through. When a shot struck directly at right angles, the wood would also be broken through, but not displaced. Generally the shot were much scattered; in three instances two or more struck near the same place, in each case causing more of the iron to be displaced, and the wood to bulge inside. A few struck near the water-line. The shield was never pierced; though it was evident that two shots striking in the same place would have made a large hole through everything.

"The ship was docked; a prow of steel and wrought iron put on, and a course of two-inch iron on the hull below the roof extending in length 180 feet. Want of time and material prevented its completion. The damage to the armor was repaired; wrought iron port-shutters were fitted, etc. The rifle guns were supplied with bolts of wrought and chilled iron. The ship was brought a foot deeper in the water, making her draft 23 feet.

"Commodore Josiah Tatnall relieved Admiral Buchanan in command. On the 11th of April he took the *Virginia* down to Hampton Roads, expecting to have a desperate encounter with the *Monitor*. Greatly to our surprise, the *Monitor* refused to fight us. She closely hugged the shore under the guns of the fort, with her steam up. Hoping to provoke her to come out, the *Jamestown*[1] was sent in, and captured several prizes, but the *Monitor* would not budge. It was proposed to take the vessel to York River, but it was decided in Richmond that she should remain near Norfolk for its protection.

"Commodore Tatnall commanded the *Virginia* forty-five days, of which time there were only thirteen days that she was not in dock or in the hands of the navy-yard. Yet he succeeded in impressing the enemy that we were ready for active service. It was evident that the enemy very much overrated[2] our power and efficiency. The South also had the same exaggerated idea of the vessel.

"On the 8th of May a squadron, including the *Monitor*, bombarded our batteries at Sewell's Point. We immediately left the yard for the Roads. As we drew near, the *Monitor* and her consorts ceased bombarding, and retreated under the guns of the forts, keeping beyond the range of our guns. Men-of-war from below the forts, and vessels expressly fitted for running us down, joined the other vessels between the forts. It looked as if the fleet was about to make a fierce onslaught upon us. But we were again to be disappointed. The *Monitor* and the other vessels did not venture to meet us, although we advanced until projectiles from the Rip-raps fell more than half a mile beyond us. Our object, however, was accomplished; we had put an end to the bombardment, and we returned to our buoy.

"Norfolk was evacuated on the 10th of May. In order that the ship might be carried up the James River, we commenced to lighten her, but ceased on the pilots saying they could not take her up. Her shield was then out of water; we were not in fighting condition. We therefore ran her ashore in the bight of Craney Island, landed the crew, and set the vessel on fire. The magazine exploded about half-past four on the morning of the 11th of May, 1862. The crew arrived at Drury's Bluff the next day, and assisted in defeating the *Monitor*, *Galena* and other vessels on the 15th of May.

"Commodore Tatnall was tried by court-martial for destroying the *Virginia*, and was 'honorably acquitted' of all the charges. The court

---

[1] French and English men-of-war were present. The latter cheered our gunboat as she passed with the prizes.

[2] Some of the Northern papers estimated her to be equivalent to an army corps.

stated the facts, and their motives for acquitting him. Some of them are as follows : 'That after the evacuation of Norfolk, Westover on James River became the most suitable position for her to occupy ; that while in the act of lightening her for the purpose of taking her up to that point, the pilots for the first time declared their inability to take her up. That when lightened she was made vulnerable to the attacks of the enemy. The only alternative, in the opinion of the court, was to abandon and burn the ship then and there, which, in the judgment of the court, was deliberately and wisely done.' "

List of officers of the C. S. iron-clad *Virginia*, March 8th, 1862 :

Flag-officer, Franklin Buchanan ; Lieutenants, Catesby Ap R. Jones (Executive and Ordnance officer , Charles C. Sims, R. D. Minor (flag), Hunter Davidson, J. Taylor Wood, J. R. Eggleston, and Walter Butt; Midshipmen, Foute, Marmaduke, Littlepage, Craig, Long, and Roots; Paymaster, James Semple; Surgeon, Dinwiddie Phillips; Assistant Surgeon, Algernon S. Garnett; Captain of Marines, Reuben Thom; Engineers, H. A. Ramsey, Acting-Chief; Assistants, Tynan, Campbell, Herring, Jack and White; Boatswain, Hasker; Gunner, Oliver; Carpenter, Lindsey; Clerk, Arthur Sinclair, Jr.; Volunteer Aide, Lieutenant Douglass Forrest, C. S. A.; Captain Kevil, commanding detachment of Norfolk United Artillery; Signal Corps, Sergant Tabb.

The following letter from Commander Jones to the Hon. A. H. Stephens was intended to set history right from the errors into which even Vice-President Stephens has fallen:

"SELMA, ALABAMA, Dec. 21st, 1875.

"DEAR SIR: A few days since my attention was called to that portion of your history of the United States that relates to the contest between the *Virginia* and *Monitor*. You will excuse the Commander of the *Virginia* for saying that you have done her scant justice. Your history states that 'the *Monitor* attacked the *Virginia* and so damaged her that she was compelled to retire to her moorings.' This conveys an erroneous impression. The *Virginia* did not return to Norfolk until after the *Monitor* had put an end to the fight by running off into shoal water beyond the reach of our guns.

"I would refer you to a detailed account of the fight giving some facts not previously made known. It was written by me, at the request of the Southern Historical Society, and published in the December (1874) number of the *Southern Magazine* of Baltimore. It has been endorsed by all of our officers that I have seen or heard from who participated in the fight or witnessed it.

"In regard to the *Monitor's* running into shoal water, it is admitted by Admiral Worden, in his official report and in an article published last year by Commander Parker, U. S. navy, which was written at the request of Worden and after consulting with him. I enclose a copy of a letter from Ericsson, the inventor and builder of the *Monitor*, with the understanding that it is not to be published, as the writer never supposed that I would see it. It was sent to me by G. V. Fox, Assistant Secretary of the U. S. navy during the war, to whom it was addressed. It fully sustains my narrative.

"If you have not seen my article, I can send it to you with Parker's and other Northern versions of the fight.

"Your prominence in the Confederacy and your able vindication of it since the war has endeared you to the whole South. And no one from our section is as well known or as highly esteemed in the North as yourself. Full credit will be given to your history. It is even more taught in the schools here. I must therefore ask that you make a change in your account of the fight between the *Virginia* and *Monitor*.

"The above has been written to you as a historian, I would now, in connection with the same fight, write you as a member of Congress.

" Parker's article mentioned above was very generally published and commented upon by the Northern press. I have understood it was written to pave the way for a preposterous claim made by Admiral W. for prize-money. Strange to say, he succeeded at the last session in obtaining favorable reports from the Naval Committees of the Senate and House. Each of them introduced a bill to give as prize-money a sum equal in amount to the value of the *Virginia*, not less than a $1,000,000.

" Further action in Congress was prevented, I am told, by the opportune publication of my narrative.

"The law of prize is that a vessel capturing one of equal or superior force is entitled to the value of the captured vessel. And when the vessel is sunk, as in the case of the *Kearsage* and *Alabama*, it is customary for Congress to grant a sum to be divided as prize-money. I have not seen Worden's petition, and am at loss to know upon what ground he asks for prize-money. He certainly did not capture or sink the *Virginia*. The fight continued for over three hours, and though he commanded the better vessel, he was the first to quit the fight. In my testimony before Commander Tatnall's court-martial, I said that the *Monitor* ought to have sunk the *Virginia* in fifteen minutes. In my narrative I refrain from expressing any opinion as to lack of skill on the part of the *Monitor*, but it may be inferred from the facts I give. I would call your attention to an article in the November ('74) number of the *Southern Magazine* of Baltimore, in reply to Commander Parker, by Col. Morris, who witnessed the fight. He dwells upon the only material point of difference in the official reports. I have written in regard to Worden's claim for prize-money as it is probable that he would again petition Congress.

" I was pleased to hear that your health had improved, and hoping that it may now be quite restored,
"I am with respect and esteem,
"Yours truly,
"CATESBY AP R. JONES.
"Hon. ALEX. H. STEPHENS,
"*Crawfordsville, Ga.*"

During the winter of 1864–5, Capt. Wm. F. Lynch, C. S. navy, was detailed by the Navy Department to write a report on the battles and combats fought or participated in by the Confederate States navy. Commodore Lynch wrote to Flag-officer Tucker, then commanding the C. S. naval forces at Charleston, for information in relation to the battle of Hampton Roads, and the subsequent repulse of the U. S. squadron at Drury's Bluff; Flag-officer John R. Tucker having, as Commander Tucker of C. S. S. *Patrick Henry*, been present at both of these engagements. Commander James H. Rochelle was at the same time executive officer of the *Patrick Henry*. When Flag-officer Tucker received Capt. Lynch's letter, Lieut. Rochelle was in command of the Confederate iron-clad *Palmetto State*, at Charleston, and Flag-officer Tucker requested him to give his recollection of the principal events connected with the *Patrick Henry*. In compliance with this request Lieut. Com. Rochelle prepared and sent to Flag-officer Tucker the following able and interesting letter:

"Confederate Steamship 'Palmetto State,' }
"Charleston, S. C., January 30th, 1865. }

" *Flag-officer* John R. Tucker,
"*Commanding Afloat at Charleston, S. C.*

"Dear Sir : I am glad to learn from you that Commodore Lynch has been directed by the department to prepare a narrative of the memorable and gallant deeds of the Confederate navy ; judging from the former works of the Commodore, I think we may congratulate ourselves that the navy has fallen into good hands, and feel confidence that the proposed book will not only be a valuable contribution to the history of this giant war, but also a pleasant addition to the literature of the day. Hitherto there has been no effort made to popularize the navy, our officers, trained in an illustrious and exclusive service, have looked with a feeling akin to contempt on both the praise and blame of the periodical press; hence the only records of the navy are to be found in dry and terse official dispatches, exceedingly uninteresting to unprofessional readers, and unintelligible to the great mass of the people. Let us hope that the forthcoming work will be popular with the people, remove many of the prejudices against our service, and assist the present generation to the just conclusion that the Confederate navy has done well its part, notwithstanding the almost complete lack in the Confederate States of all the necessary constituents of naval strength. Among the naval events that Commodore Lynch will be called upon to relate, the career of the Confederate steamship *Patrick Henry* will, perhaps, claim a prominent place, and if you think there is anything in this letter which will aid the Commodore to a fuller understanding of the services of that vessel, you are quite at liberty to send it to him.

"The *Patrick Henry*, a side-wheel steamer of beautiful model and of about fourteen hundred tons burthen, was called the *Yorktown* before the war, and was one of a line of steamers running between Richmond and New York. She was considered a fast boat, and deserved the reputation. When the Commonwealth of Virginia seceded from the Union this vessel was, fortunately, in James River. She was seized by the State, and the Governor and Council determined to fit her out as a man-of-war. She was taken up to the wharf at Rocketts, Richmond, and the command conferred upon Commander John Randolph Tucker, late an officer of the U. S. navy, who had resigned his commission in that service in consequence of the secession of Virginia, his native State. Naval Constructor Joseph Pearce, with a number of mechanics from the Norfolk navy-yard, commenced the necessary alterations, and in a short time the passenger steamer *Yorktown* was converted into the very creditable man-of-war steamer *Patrick Henry*, of 10 guns and 150 officers and men.[1] The vessel being properly equipped, so far as the limited resources at hand could be used, proceeded down James River and took a position off Mulberry Island, on which point rested the right of the Army of the Peninsula under Magruder. It was dull work laying at anchor off Mulberry Island; the officer and crew very rarely went on shore, the steamer being kept always with banked fires, and prepared to repel an attack which might have been made at any moment, the Federal batteries at Newport News and the guard vessels stationed there, the *Congress, Cumberland*, and several gunboats being plainly in sight. After a while the monotony became so irksome that Commander Tucker took the *Patrick Henry* down the river to within long range of the Federal squadron and opened on them with his two heavy guns with the hope of inducing a single gunboat to ascend the river and engage vessel to vessel. The challenge was not accepted, and the enemy having moved a field battery of rifled guns up the bank of the river, and taken a secure position from which they

---

[1] At the battle of Hampton Roads the officers of the *Patrick Henry* were, as well as can be remembered at the present (1887) time, Commander John Randolph Tucker, commanding; Lieut. James Henry Rochelle, Executive officer; Lieut. Wm. Sharp, Lieut. Francis Lyell Hoge; Surgeon, John T Mason; Paymaster, Thomas R. Ware; Passed Assistant Surgeon, Frederick Garretson; Acting Master, Lewis Parish; Lieut. of Marines, R. H. Henderson; Midshipmen, John Tyler Walker, A. M. Mason, M. P. Goodwyn.

opened an annoying fire, the vessel was steamed slowly back to her station off Mulberry Island. The Northern papers stated that in this little affair, which took place on September 13th, 1861, the fire of the *Patrick Henry* did considerable damage to the frigate *Congress*. About this time intelligence was received that one or two of the Federal gunboats came up the river every night on picket duty and anchored about a mile and-a-half above their squadron at Newport News. Here was a chance; so on the night of the 1st of December, 1861, the *Patrick Henry* again went down the river, keeping a sharp look-out for the expected picket boat. Not a sign of a vessel was seen, and when day broke there were the Federal squadron and batteries looming up against the dawn with all the gunboats quietly at anchor near the larger vessels. As the *Patrick Henry* could not have returned unseen, Commander Tucker opened fire. The Federals were evidently taken by surprise, and it was some minutes before they replied to the fire. They soon got to their guns, however, and the sun as it rose was greeted with a roar of artillery that shook the windows in Norfolk and roused the people of that then gay city from their slumbers at a most inconvenient hour.

"The Federal fire was well directed, and one officer and several men were wounded on board the *Patrick Henry*. One gunboat in particular, commanded by Lieut. H. K. Davenport, was noted for the precision with which she used her rifled guns. The old sailing-master of the *Patrick Henry*, a seaman of sixty winters and many gales, was much pleased with the manner in which Davenport used his guns. He said to some one standing near him, 'look at that black, ugly little craft yonder, well, whenever you see a puff of smoke go up from her, look out, for, as sure as you are born, there will be a blue pigeon about.' The skirmish having continued for an hour or more, and nothing to be gained by prolonging it, the *Patrick Henry* returned to her usual anchorage.

"In February, 1862, the ladies of Charles City, a county bordering on James river, desired to present to the *Patrick Henry* a flag which they had made for her, as an evidence of their confidence in the vessel, and their appreciation of the services she had done them by keeping marauding expeditions from ascending the river to pillage, plunder, and perhaps destroy the famous old country seats that are to be found on its banks. But the flag was destined never to be presented, such stirring times were at hand that the few hours necessary for the ceremony could not be spared. The iron-clad *Virginia* was about to make an attack upon the Federal batteries and vessels at Newport News, and the *Patrick Henry* was ordered to participate in the battle.

"The day before the attack was to be made, the *Patrick Henry* was moved down to Day's Neck, and an anchorage taken, from which any vessel coming out from Norfolk could be seen.

"The 8th of March, 1862, was a bright, placid, beautiful day, more like a May than a March day. All eyes on board the *Patrick Henry* were watching for the *Virginia*. About one o'clock in the afternoon she came steaming out from behind Craney Island, attended by her satellites—the gunboats *Beaufort* and *Raleigh*. Grand, and strong, and confident, a Hercules of the waters, she moved straight upon the enemy.

"It was not necessary to 'call all hands up anchor' on board the *Patrick Henry*, the anchor was 'raised with a run,' and under a full head of steam the vessel sped on her way to aid her powerful friend.[1]

The *Patrick Henry* was rigged as a brigantine; square yards to the foremast and fore-and-aft sails alone for the mainmast. At Norfolk, when she was about to be employed in running by the batteries of Newport News at night, it was thought best to take both of her masts out, in order to make her less liable to be discovered by the enemy. Signal poles, carrying no sails, were established in their place. When she became the schoolship of the Naval Academy in 1863, her square-rigged foremast was replaced, so that the midshipmen could be exercised in reefing and furling and such other exercises as were practicable on board a vessel in harbor. A bowsprit was also put in and rooms or cabins were erected on the hurricane-deck, as appears in the engraving in the chapter on the Naval Academy to be found elsewhere.

"The Confederate vessels in James River formed 'in line ahead' as they approached the batteries at Newport News. The *Patrick Henry*, 10, Commander Tucker, leading; next came the *Jamestown*, 2, Lieut. Com. Barney; and next the *Teaser*, 2, Lieut. Com. Webb. The *Virginia* reached the scene of action first; amidst the iron hail which fell harmlessly on her armor, she ran into and sank the *Cumberland;* a hearty cheer from the James River vessels greeted her success. But there was no time to give up to exultation, the long line of the Newport News batteries were close at hand, and in order to reach the naval combat it was necessary to pass them. The guns of the *Patrick Henry*[1] were elevated for a range of 800 yards, that being the distance at which the pilots expected to pass the batteries.

"And now the hush which preceded the shock of battle settled alike on Federal and Confederate. Through the embrasures of the Federal batteries glimpses could be caught of the men at their guns, but not a sound came from them. As the *Patrick Henry* ranged up abreast of the first battery she delivered her fire, and the flash from her guns had scarcely vanished when the Federal works were wrapped in smoke, and their projectiles came hissing through the air. The first shots from the *Patrick Henry* went over the batteries, her guns having been elevated for a range of 800 yards, consequently she was passing the batteries at less than that distance, and to this circumstance is to be attributed her not having been sunk or disabled by them. The enemy supposed she would pass as far from them as the channel would allow, and had elevated their guns for that range; the vessel passing closer than they thought she would, their shot for the most part passed over her. She was struck, however, several times during the passage; one shot passed through the crew of No. 3 gun, wounding two men and killing one, a volunteer from the army, who had come on board to serve only for the fight. His last words as he fell were, 'Never mind me, boys.'

"Having passed the batteries with less damage than was expected, the *Patrick Henry* became engaged in the thick of the fight; whilst the forward guns were engaging one enemy, the after-guns were firing at another. The situation of the Confederate wooden vessels at this time seemed desperate. The Newport News batteries were on one side; on the other, the frigates *Minnesota, St. Lawrence and Roanoke* were coming up from Old Point Comfort, and in front of the beach was lined with field batteries and sharpshooters. Fortunately for the Confederate wooden vessels, the *Minnesota, St. Lawrence* and *Roanoke* grounded, and the smaller vessels which accompanied them, warned by the fate of the *Cumberland*, returned to Old Point. The *Minnesota*, though aground, was near enough to take part in the action, and opened a heavy fire on the Confederate squadron.

"About this time Flag-officer Buchanan hailed the *Patrick Henry*, and directed Commander Tucker to burn the *Congress*, which vessel had run ashore, hauled down her ensign, and hoisted a white flag. The gunboats *Raleigh, Beaufort* and *Teaser* had attempted to burn her, but had been driven off by a heavy artillery and infantry fire from the Federal troops on the beach. The pilots of the *Patrick Henry* declared that that vessel could not get alongside the *Congress* in consequence of an intervening shoal. This determined Commander Tucker[2] to approach the

---

[1] When the *Patrick Henry* was first put in commission, her battery consisted of ten medium 32-pounders in broadside, one 10-inch shell gun pivoted forward, and one 8-inch solid shot gun pivoted aft. The 8-inch solid shot gun was the most effective gun on board, and did good service both at the battle of Hampton Roads and the repulse of the Federal squadron at Drury's Bluff. The captain of this gun was an excellent seaman gunner, named Smith. He was promoted to boatswain, and served under Commander Rochelle on board of the *Palmetto State* at Charleston, S. C.

[2] The name of my dear and deeply-lamented friend, Admiral John Randolph Tucker, has been necessarily so frequently mentioned in this letter as commander of the *Patrick Henry*, that it will not be out of place to say a few words as to his career.

During the course of his honorable and eventful life Admiral Tucker served in three navies, rendering gallant, faithful and important services to each of them, but probably the most brilliant, if not the most important, of all his services was rendered whilst he commanded the *Patrick Henry*. Born in Alexandria, Va., in the

Congress as near as the shoal would permit, and then to send his boats and burn her; the boats were prepared for the service, and the boats' crews and officers to command them held ready, whilst the vessel was steaming into the *Congress.* This movement of the *Patrick Henry* placed her in the most imminent peril; she was brought under the continuous and concentrated fire of three points; on her port-quarter were the batteries of Newport News, on her port-bow were the field-batteries and sharpshooters on the beach, and on her starboard-bow the *Minnesota.* It soon became evident that no wooden vessel could long float under such a fire; several shots struck the hull; a piece was shot out of the walking beam; as the sponge of the after-pivot gun was being inserted in the piece, the handle was cut in two by a shot. * * * Half in prayer and half in despair at being unable to perform his duty, the sponger exclaimed, 'Oh, Lord ! how is the gun to be sponged ?' and he was much relieved when the quarter-gunner of his division handed him a spare sponge. This state of things could not last long; a rifled shot from the field batteries penetrated the steam-chest, the engine-room and fire-room were filled with steam, five or six of the firemen were scalded to death, the engineers were driven up on deck, and the engines stopped working. The vessel was enveloped in a cloud of escaped steam, and the enemy, seeing that some disaster to the engines or boilers had occurred, increased his fire. At this moment, no one knew what had happened, the general impression being that the boiler had exploded; and it is an unmistakable evidence of the courage and discipline of the crew that the fire from the *Patrick Henry* did not slacken, but went on as regularly as before the damage. As the vessel was drifting towards the enemy the jib was hoisted to pay her head around, and the *Jamestown,* Lieut. Commanding Barney, gallantly and promptly came to her assistance, and towed her from her perilous position. The engineers soon got one boiler to work—the other was so badly damaged that they were unable to repair it at the time—and with the steam of one boiler alone, the *Patrick Henry* returned to the conflict. Night, however, soon closed in, and as in the darkness it was impossible to distinguish friend from foe, hostilities ceased, the victory of this day being without dispute with the Confederates.

"During the battle the shores of the Confederate side of the 'Roads ' were lined with spectators from Norfolk and the adjacent camps, who seemed greatly to enjoy the 'historical piece' that was enacted before them.

year 1812, he entered the navy of the United States as a midshipman in 1826, and made his first cruise in the frigate *Brandywine.* In 1837 he was promoted to the rank of lieutenant, and in 1855 to that of commander. During the Mexican war he commanded the bomb-brig *Stromboli.* In 1861, when commanded so to do by the Virginia Convention, he resigned his commission in the U. S. navy and entered the Confederate service, with the rank of commander. He commanded the C S. steamer *Patrick Henry* at the naval conflict in Hampton Roads; and at Drury's Bluff, having landed his crew and mounted the principal guns of his vessel on the bluff, he materially aided in repulsing the Federal squadron. Soon after the battle of Drury's Bluff he was promoted to the rank of captain, and ordered to Charleston, where he commanded the Confederate naval forces as flag-officer of the station. When Charleston was evacuated he returned to Drury's Bluff, which station he commanded until Richmond was evacuated, when he reported with his command to Gen. Lee. His services in the civil war ended at Sailor's Creek, where, after a most gallant resistance, he surrendered to Gen. Keifer; who some years after the close of the war returned him his sword.

During the war between the Republics of Peru and Chili and Spain, Admiral Tucker commanded, with the commission of rear-admiral, the combined fleets of the two republics. His last service was the exploration and survey of the upper Amazon and its tributaries, being President of the Peruvian Hydrographic Commission of the Amazon.

He died of disease of the heart, at his residence in Petersburg, Virginia, on the 12th of June, 1883, and was buried by the side of his wife, in the cemetery at Norfolk.

It would require a volume to do anything like justice to the character and career of this most noble and gallant man. His firmness on all occasions of duty was of proof, though no one was more gentle in the ordinary intercourse of private life. None served with him without feeling that he was a man fitted for high destinies, for he was of a nature, an experience, and a professional skill, well calculated to command respect and inspire confidence. In the course of my life I have had many opportunities of hearing character discussed among sea officers; few escape criticism of some sort or other for their professional acts, and fewer still as men, yet I do not remember a single instance in which I have ever heard a whisper of complaint against the professional or private conduct of John Randolph Tucker. J. H. R., 1886.

"The night after the battle the Confederate squadron anchored under Sewell's Point, at the mouth of the harbor of Norfolk. There was little time for sleep that night, for the conflict was to be renewed the next morning, and it was necessary to make many repairs and preparations. Soon after midnight a column of fire ascended in the darkness, followed by a terrific explosion. The Federal frigate *Congress*, which had been on fire all the evening, had blown up, the fire having reached her magazine.

"At the first peep of dawn, on the 9th of March, the Confederate squadron was under way, it having been determined to destroy the *Minnesota*, that frigate being still aground near Newport News. As the daylight increased the *Minnesota* was discovered in her old position, but the *Minnesota* was not the only thing to attract attention; close alongside of her there lay such a craft as the eyes of a seaman does not delight in; an immense shingle floating on the water, with a gigantic cheese-box rising from its centre; no sails, no wheels, no smoke-stack, no guns, at least, none that could be seen. What could it be? On board the *Patrick Henry* many were the surmises as to the strange craft; some thought it a water tank sent to supply the *Minnesota* with water; others that it was a floating magazine replenishing her exhausted stock of ammunition, but few were of the opinion that it was the *Monitor*, which the Northern papers had been boasting about for a long time.

"All doubts about the stranger were soon dispelled; as the *Virginia* steamed down upon the *Minnesota* the cheese-box and shingle steamed out to meet her. It was, indeed, the *Monitor*, and then and there commenced the first combat that had ever taken place between iron-clads. [1]

"The *Patrick Henry* and the other Confederate wooden vessels took little part in the events of the day, except to fire one shot at the *Monitor*, at very long range, as she passed and repassed at one time during her manœuvering with the *Virginia*. At one time the *Virginia* did not seem to move, and apprehensions were entertained that she had got aground or that some part of her machinery was damaged. Signal flags were run up on board of her, but the flags did not blow out clear, and it was some minutes before the signal officer of the *Patrick Henry* could make out the numbers. At length he reported the signal to be, as well as he was able to read it, 'disabled my propeller is.' [2]

"No wooden vessel could have floated twenty minutes under the fire that the *Virginia* was then undergoing from the *Monitor* and the *Minnesota*, but if her propeller was disabled it was necessary to attempt to tow her back to the cover of the Confederate batteries. So the *Patrick Henry* and *Jamestown* started to make the attempt, but they had gone only a short distance when the *Virginia* was seen to move and her propeller to turn, showing that she required no assistance. That evening all the Confederate vessels went into the harbor of Norfolk.

"Flag-officer Tatnall having relieved Flag-officer Buchanan, who had been seriously wounded in the first day's fight in Hampton Roads, and all the vessels having been refitted, on the 13th of April the squadron again sailed out to meet the enemy. In case the *Virginia* should not be able to capture or destroy the *Monitor*, the gunboats *Beaufort* and *Raleigh* and two small steamers were assigned the duty of carrying the *Monitor* by boarding. [3] The squadron steamed about in Hampton Roads for two

---

[1] The combat between the *Virginia* and the *Monitor* was an indecisive action so far as those two vessels were concerned; at least such was my opinion after witnessing the fight from the distance of about a mile. Both vessels were skillfully and gallantly fought, and neither could claim a victory over the other. If the *Monitor* had been silenced, the *Minnesota* would have been destroyed, and probably much other damage done to the Federal forces. If the *Virginia* had been defeated, the city of Norfolk would have been at the mercy of the *Monitor*. J. H. R., 1886.

[2] Some years after the conclusion of the war I showed a copy of this letter to my friend, Capt. Catesby ap Roger Jones, who was in command of the *Virginia* during the fight with the *Monitor*. Capt. Jones informed me that the signal officer of the *Patrick Henry* did not read the *Virginia's* signal correctly; I forget what Capt. Jones said the signal was, but it did not indicate that the *Virginia* was in distress, or that she desired assistance. J. H. R., 1886.

[3] One of these small steamers was the tender of the Norfolk navy-yard. She was manned for

days in succession, and the *Jamestown* captured two of the Federal transports, but the *Monitor* did not leave her anchorage at Fortress Monroe.[1]

*   *   *   *   *

" I am, sir, very respectfully, your obedient servant,
" J. H. ROCHELLE,
" *Lieut. Com. Confederate Iron-clad ' Palmetto State.' "*

" When the Federal squadron entered James River, the *Patrick Henry* ran up to Drewry's Bluff, and her officers and crew aided materially in getting that position ready for defence.   The Confederate steamship *Jamestown* was sunk to complete the obstructions of the river, her guns having been previously landed and placed in battery on the Bluff.   One solid shot eight-inch gun and two rifled 32-pounders were landed from the *Patrick Henry*, mounted in pits dug in the brow of the Bluff, and manned by the officers and crew of the vessel.

" On the 15th of May, 1862, the Federal squadron, consisting of the *Galena, Monitor, Naugatuck, Port Royal,* and *Aroostook,* made the well-known attack on the Confederate batteries at Drewry's Bluff, which was the only defensible position between the squadron and Richmond.   The *Galena* and the *Monitor* were the only vessels which engaged the batteries at effective range.   The *Galena* was managed with great skill and daring. She steamed to about 800 yards of the batteries, and opened with much precision a most damaging fire.   After a hot action of about four hours duration, the Federal squadron was beaten off, and steamed away down the river.   The guns on the Bluff were worked by the officers and crews of the *Patrick Henry, Jamestown, Virginia,* and a battalion of artillery.   The most effective gun on the Bluff was the *Patrick Henry's* eight-inch solid shot gun ; the working of this gun was personally directed by Capt. John R. Tucker, and the execution done by it was manifest.

" After the action at Drewry's Bluff, the *Patrick Henry's* officers and crew were permanently attached to the naval batteries at that place.   The vessel herself became the schoolship of the Confederate States naval school, and was destroyed when Richmond was evacuated by the Confederates, to prevent her falling into the hands of the enemy."—J.H.R., 1886."

A writer in *The United Service* Magazine for November, 1880, says :

" The first grand naval triumph of the South was the victory achieved by the iron-clad *Virginia,* in the memorable battle of Hampton Roads, on the 8th of March, 1861.   An event interesting not only for the immediate issues involved, but as introducing a new element in naval warfare, and inaugurating a revolution in the means and methods of future encounters."

Then, after a graphic and correct account of the battles of the 8th and 9th, in which the palm of victory is awarded to the *Virginia,* the writer concludes :

" The *Virginia* came out of the conflict a historical ship.   In all future narratives of naval war she will loom up conspicuously as having determined a new line of development in naval forces, leading to a complete revolution in the naval systems of the whole world, as well as those of

the occasion by officers and men of the *Patrick Henry,* under the command of the executive officer of that vessel, and was christened by the men *Patrick Henry Junior.* J. H. R., 1886.

[1] The conclusion of this letter has been lost. It went on to relate the services of the *Patrick Henry* up to the date of the letter. These services may be briefly recounted: When the Con-

federate authorities determined upon the evacuation of Norfolk. the *Patrick Henry* was employed to remove what public property could be saved from the navy-yard to Richmond.   The hulls of several uncompleted vessels were towed past the Federal batteries at Newport News. The running past the batteries was always done in the middle of the night, moonless nights being chosen; so far as we ever knew, we were not once discovered by the enemy.

coast and harbor defences. The triumph of that vessel was a brilliant one, but short-lived."

" J. H. C.," in the Oct. number of *The United Service*, says:

"The victory (on the 8th) of the *Virginia* had been most brilliant. She had almost unaided destroyed two large ships of war, with a loss of several hundred men, and driven off the rest of the fleet. Her own loss was scarcely enough to set off her triumph. She had shown a wondering world that wooden vessels could not stand for an instant against the iron-clads, and now the world looked on, curious to see her prowess against a foeman of her own class."

And after describing the battle of the 9th as one of which " both sides claimed the victory, and, indeed, its honors seem to be evenly divided," relates the scheme of destroying the *Virginia* by running her down with immense wooden steamers—adds:

"Another occasion was sought on the 8th of May, when a portion of the Union fleet, including the *Monitor*, bombarded the battery at Sewell's Point. This brought the *Virginia* upon the scene, but no good opportunity occurred to run her down. In fact, the scheme was impracticable; and it was probably fortunate that the ships fitted up for the purpose did not make a serious attempt. Their own destruction instead of that of the iron-clad would most likely have been the consequence."

These official records, and private documents and statements, ought to dispose of all claim to a victory over the *Virginia*, as they reveal a state of consternation and dismay in Washington not surpassed even by that caused by the first battle of Bull Run.

At the second session of the Forty-third Congress, the fiction of a victory of the *Monitor* over the *Virginia*, on the 9th of March, 1862, was made the subject of an application by the officers and crew of the U. S. steamer *Monitor*, who participated in the action in Hampton Roads, for the payment to them by the United States of the actual value of the *Virginia* and her armament "at the date of said action, not exceeding $200,000, to be distributed in lieu of the bounty provided by Section 4,635 of the Revised Statutes of the United States, and in proportion fixed by law in cases where the capturing or destroying vessel was acting independently of the commanding officer of a fleet, squadron, or division, and for the appropriation of $200,000." The memorial or application was referred, in the House of Representatives, to the Committee on Naval Affairs, but no action was taken on it until January 9, 1882, when it was again presented to the House of Representatives with like reference. A report was submitted by the Committee, recommending the passage of the bill, but it failed to become a law. At the second session of the Forty-seventh Congress, the memorial was again made the subject of two bills, Senate Bill No. 369, and House Bill No. 3,840, for an appropriation of $200,000 for distribution among the officers and crew of the *Monitor*, not as prize-money for the capture or destruction of the *Virginia*, for the facts were too baldly patent to warrant any such claim, but because the *Monitor* had been "in the action with the rebel iron-clad *Merrimac*" on that day. But the "statement of the reasons for making such a grant of *prize*-money," claimed that reward "for damage to the Confederate iron-clad *Merrimac*, March 9th, 1862, and her subsequent destruction." The facts were, however, too patent and potent, and both bills failed to pass. The subject was renewed at the first session of the Forty-eighth Congress, and in the House of Representatives it was again referred to the Committee on Naval Affairs.

Mr. Ballentine, from the Committee on Naval Affairs, to whom the House Bill No. 244, had been referred, in 1884, submitted a very interesting and strong adverse report. It said:

"The memoralists claim that the *Monitor* so disabled the *Merrimac* as to make her destruction necessary, and, further, that she prevented the *Merrimac* from going below Old Point, thus saving Baltimore and Washington from capture, and even New York City from menace. The testimony which has been set out at length does not, in the opinion of the Committee, sustain either of these opinions, but quite the contrary. It is only necessary to refer to the full description of the *Merrimac* to show that, without greatly lightening her, which could not have been done without impairing her power to fight, and exposing her to the projectiles which would have been hurled against her, had she ventured outside of Cape Henry, she would have inevitably foundered.

"On the other point, all of the evidence leads as clearly to the opinion that the *Monitor*, after her engagement with the *Merrimac* on the 9th of March, declined again to engage her, though offered the opportunity, and that so great doubt existed with the U. S. naval and military authorities as to the power of the *Monitor* to successfully meet the *Merrimac*, *that orders were given to her commander* by the President *not to bring on an engagement.*[1]

"It also appears that the *Merrimac* so far from being seriously injured, was enabled after the engagement to protect the approaches to Norfolk and Richmond until after the evacuation of Norfolk. If, then, it be proven that the destruction of the *Merrimac* was not the result of injuries inflicted by the *Monitor*, which we assume to be true, what claim have the memorialists for compensation? It is not pretended that they are entitled to compensation in the nature of prize-money. The act of June 30, 1864, sec. 10 (Vol. 13, page 309), provides for the payment of *bounty money* to the officers and crew of the U. S. naval vessels, who *sink* or otherwise *destroy* vessels of the enemy in engagements, or which it may be necessary (for the captors) to destroy in consequence of injuries received in action; but the case presented does not, in our opinion, come within the meaning of the statute. * * Officers of the navy are entitled to prize-money when they capture or destroy property, provided it is in a line where the law of capture applies, but not otherwise. On the destruction of a vessel, the price of that vessel may be awarded as prize money

[1] In support of its statement, the Committee quote many of the extracts heretofore given by us, and the following letter addressed to the Secretary of the Navy by Adjt. Gen. L. Thomas, under date of March 13th, 1862: "I am directed by the Secretary of War to say that he places at your disposal any transports or coal vessels at Fortress Monroe, for the purpose of closing the channel of the Elizabeth River to prevent the *Merrimac* from again coming out." They also submitted a letter from Secretary Welles to the Secretary of War, under date of March 13th, in which he said: "I have the honor to suggest that the Department can easily obstruct the channel of Norfolk, so as to prevent the exit of the *Merrimac*, provided the army will carry Sewell's Point batteries in which duty the navy will give great assistance." They also mention the fact that in a council of war, held at Fairfax Court House, March 13th, 1862, present Gens. Keyes, Heintzleman, McDowell and Sumner, at which it was decided that Gen. McClellan's plan to attack Richmond by York River should be adopted, provided, first, "that the enemy's vessel *Merrimac* can be neutralized."

CAPTAIN J. R. TUCKER,

CONFEDERATE STATES NAVY.

CAPTAIN JOSIAH TATNALL
CONFEDERATE STATES NAVY.

under the rule, but where the enemy's vessel is not destroyed, no such rule obtains, and never has obtained, in this or any other civilized country. It is claimed that this money should be awarded the petitioners on the ground that the *Monitor* saved from destruction Washington, Baltimore and other large cities of the North, and also saved from destruction the vessels which were in the harbor. The question presented by the memorialists is not one of the saving of New York or Washington, or of the vessels which were in Hampton Roads for the presumed purpose of making battle and protecting the U. S. forts and property; but the question is, was there any *destruction* of the *Merrimac* by the *Monitor*, or *such a destruction* as to bring this application within the purview and meaning of the law ? If the answer to this be in the affirmative, it is singular that the officers and crew of the *Monitor* have not long since received their money. * * * We assume that the proof shows that the only serious damage sustained by the *Merrimac* was inflicted by the *Cumberland*, and that the *Merrimac* went back to Norfolk when her adversaries were out of her reach; and they being in shoal water, and she, on account of the great depth of water which she drew, unable to attack them, went into dock for repairs, and again came out and offered battle, which was refused; and that eventually on the evacuation of Norfolk by the Confederate forces, she was destroyed by her officers and crew, to *prevent her falling into the hands of the Union forces*, and that, therefore, her destruction was *not* the result of her engagement with the *Monitor*, and that if the proof shows this state of facts to exist that the claim of the petitioners in this memorial ought not to be allowed."[1]

From the testimony submitted by the Committee, they add, "we feel assured that neither Gen. Magruder, nor any of his superiors had the slightest apprehension of any damage to be feared from the *Monitor*. So far from this, their dispatches show that they felt full confidence that the *Virginia* (or *Merrimac*) was master of the situation in the waters from Norfolk to Hampton Roads. * * The testimony shows clearly, that the only serious injury received by the *Merrimac* was from the *Cumberland;* and this official testimony is fully sustained by affidavits made by Capt. Catesby Jones, White, and Littlepage, and the statement of the latter was made here in Washington, when the question was up, and when all the surroundings seemed to favor the claim of the petitioners."[3]

[1] In support of these points the committee submitted considerable testimony, among which was an extract from the official report of Brig. Gen. Joseph K. F. Mansfield of the engagement, made to Gen. John E. Wool, bearing date March 12, 1862, in which he says: "Our ships were perfectly harmless against the *Merrimac*, as their broadsides produced no material effect on her."

[2] "On March 10, P. H. Watson, Assistant Secretary of War. telegraphed to Henry B. Renwick, New York City, and advises that three large and swift steamers be fitted up to run down and destroy the *Merrimac*." If the vessel had been destroyed the day before, there was no necessity for this.

[3] The statement of Midshipman H. B. Littlepage, referred to, who was a midshipman on board of the *Virginia* during the engagement in Hampton Roads, and up to the time of her destruction, was as follows:

"*To the Editor of The Post* (Washington, D. C.).

"From the article which appeared in the columns of *The Post* this morning, I learn that the officers and men of the *Monitor* have memorialized Congress for prize-money for the disabling of the *Merrimac* by that vessel. As there is not an officer or man who was on the *Monitor* on that memorable occasion who does not know that the *Monitor* did not disable the *Merrimac*. I cannot conceive upon what grounds the claim for prize-money is made. It reminds me of the old sailor. who whenever he heard others speaking of fine horses, would always tell of the remarkable traits of his own horse. He told it so often that he actually believed he had a horse, and when the ship went into Vera Cruz he bought a fine Mexican saddle for it. The statement that the *Merrimac* was disabled and driven from Hampton Roads into Norfolk is entirely incorrect and absurd. It only convinces me that I. R. G., like many others who have written upon this subject. was not there. The *Monitor* was neither the direct nor the remote

In conclusion the Committee add: "From the above mentioned facts, we think it clearly appears (1) that the *Monitor*, after her engagement with the *Merrimac*, on the 9th of March, never again dared encounter her, though offered frequent opportunities; (2) that so much doubt existed in the minds of the Federal authorities as to her power to meet the *Merrimac*, that orders were given her commander, not to fight her voluntarily; that the *Merrimac*, so far from being seriously injured in her engagement, efficiently protected the approaches to Norfolk and Richmond until Norfolk was evacuated; that the *Merrimac* could not have gotten to Washington, or Baltimore, in her normal condition; that she could not have gone to sea at all; that although she could have run by the Federal fleet and Old Point (barring torpedoes in the channel), and threatened McClellan's base at Yorktown, in exceptionally good weather, yet would have had to leave the James River open. * * Holding to these views, we respectfully report adversely to the passage of the bill."

While the subject was being discussed in Congress, Lieut. Commander William H. Parker, C. S. N., who commanded the *Beaufort* in the Hampton Roads engagements, sent to the *Norfolk Landmark* the following interesting statement of the question:

"NORFOLK, VA., Dec. 11, 1882.

"*To the Editor of the 'Landmark':*

"The claim of the crew of the U. S. steamer *Monitor* for prize-money for the destruction of the Confederate vessel *Virginia* (*Merrimac*), has naturally called forth many letters from those engaged in the naval operations in Hampton Roads from March 8, 1862, to May 6, 1862.

cause of the destruction of the *Merrimac*. If prize-money is to be awarded, let it be given to the gallant officers and crew of the *Cumberland*, which went down with her colors flying after doing nearly all the damage sustained by the *Merrimac* on the 8th and 9th of March, 1862. The broadside fired by the *Cumberland* just as the *Merrimac* rammed her, cut one of the *Merrimac's* guns off at the trunnions, the muzzle of another, tore up the carriage of her bow pivot gun, swept away her anchors, boats and howitzers, riddled her smoke-stack and steam-pipe, and killed and wounded nineteen men.

"The next day in the fight with the *Monitor* the *Merrimac* did not have a man killed or wounded, nor a gun disabled. The only damage sustained by her worth mentioning was by ramming the *Monitor* with her wooden stem, her cast-iron bow having been wrenched off the day before in the *Cumberland*. This probably saved the *Monitor* from a similar fate. 'Tis true the *Monitor* struck us some powerful blows with her eleven-inch guns when only a few feet from us, but not one of her shots penetrated our armor. If instead of scattering her shot over our shield she had concentrated them upon some particular spot, a breach might have been made. When the *Merrimac* left Hampton Roads for Norfolk, the *Monitor* had passed over the bar and hauled off into shoal water, where we could not reach her—the *Merrimac's* draft being over twenty-two feet, and hers only about ten. As there was nothing more to fight, the tide being

favorable, the *Merrimac* returned to Norfolk, where she was docked. She was then thoroughly overhauled and equipped for fighting an iron-clad. A prow of steel and wrought iron was put on. Bolts of wrought-iron and chilled-iron were supplied for the rifle guns, and other preparations made especially for the *Monitor*. They were such as to make all on the *Merrimac* feel confident that we would either make a prize of or destroy the *Monitor* when we met again. On the 11th of April, all being ready for the expected fray, the *Merrimac* again went to Hampton Roads. The *Monitor* was laying at our moorings, at the mouth of the Elizabeth River, publishing to the world that she was blockading the *Merrimac*. Greatly to our surprise she refused to fight us, and as we approached, she gracefully retired, and closely hugged the shore under the guns of Fortress Monroe. As if to provoke her to combat, the *Jamestown* was sent in. and she captured several prizes, in which the *Monitor* seemed to acquiesce, as she offered no resistance. French and English men-of-war were present; the latter cheered and dipped their flags as the *Jamestown* passed with the prizes.

"On the 6th of May, when the *Merrimac* had returned to Norfolk for supplies, a squadron consisting of the *Monitor*, *Naugatuck* and *Galena* (iron-clads , and five large men-of-war, commenced to bombard our batteries at Sewell's Point. The *Merrimac* immediately left Norfolk for the scene of conflict. As she approached the squadron at full speed the *Vanderbilt*, one

"I commanded the *Beaufort* in the battles of the 8th and 9th of March, and in the operations under Commodore Tatnall, to which I shall allude. In fact, I may say I commanded a consort of the *Merrimac* from the time she was put in commission until she was blown up. I, therefore, profess to be familiar with her history.

"The battle of March 8th I propose describing at some future day, in order to show more particularly what part the wooden vessels took in that memorable engagement. The battle of March 9th * * * that between the *Monitor* and *Merrimac*—has been fully described by Capt. Catesby Jones, her commander, and by other of her officers. I do not propose here to repeat it; but there are some points in relation to the operations subsequent to that engagement which have either been unnoticed, or but lightly touched upon. These points are in my judgment so important, and bear so immediately upon the claim of the *Monitor* for prize-money, that I venture to submit the following:

"I. After the battle of the 9th of March, the *Merrimac* went into dock to replace the prow, or ram, which had been lost in sinking the *Cumberland*, to exchange some of her guns, and to make some small repairs to her armor and machinery On the 11th of April, Commodore Tatnall, who had succeeded Commodore Buchanan in the command, went down with his entire squadron, consisting of the *Merrimac*, *Patrick Henry*, *Jamestown*, *Teaser*, *Beaufort* and *Raleigh*, to offer battle to the Federal fleet then lying in Hampton Roads or below Old Point. Three merchant vessels were run on shore by their masters between Newport News and Old Point, and were partially abandoned. The *Jamestown* and *Raleigh* towed them off almost under the guns of Old Point and the Federal fleet. Their flags were hauled down and hoisted Union down under the Confederate flag as a defiance to induce the fleet to attempt to retake them. The fleet, under Flag-officer Goldsborough, consisted of a large number of wooden vessels, some of them very heavy frigates, the *Monitor*, the *Naugatuck* (a small iron-clad), and even the *Vanderbilt*, a powerful steamer specially prepared 'to run down and sink the *Merrimac*.'

"An English and a French man-of-war were present in the Roads and went up to Newport News, evidently to witness the serious engagement, which we, at least, expected. Their crews repeatedly waved their hats and handkerchiefs to our vessels as we passed and repassed them during the day.

"The *Merrimac*, with her consorts, held possession of the roads, and defied the enemy to battle during the entire day, and for several days after * * the Federal fleet lying in the same position below Old Point. Towards sunset of the first day the *Merrimac* fired a single gun at the enemy ; it was immediately replied to by the *Naugatuck*, lying, I think, inside Hampton Bar.

"I do not know what Commodore Tatnall thought about attacking the Federal fleet as it stood, nor do I know what his instructions were, but I *do* know that our officers generally believed that torpedoes had

of the fastest steamers then afloat, which we understood had been fitted with a prow especially for ramming us, joined the other ships. We regarded the attack as an invitation to come out, and we expected a most desperate encounter. Much to the disappointment of our Commodore, and greatly to the relief of many others besides myself, as soon as the *Merrimac* came within range, they seemed to conclude that Sewell's Point was not worth fighting about, and all hurried below the guns of Fortress Monroe and the Rip-raps. The *Merrimac* pursued at full speed until she came well under the fire of the latter fort, when she retired to her moorings at the mouth of the river. After the evacuation of Norfolk the *Merrimac* was taken above Craney Island and blown up on the 11th of May. The *Monitor* was then up the James River, having gone up the day before, and was probably more than fifty miles away. She had refused the

gage of battle offered her by the *Merrimac* daily since the 11th of April.

"Wherefore doth she claim prize-money?

"In stating the above facts, I do not wish to detract one iota from the just deserts of the brave officers and men of the *Monitor*. They did their whole duty, but not more gallantly than their less fortunate comrades on the *Cumberland*, *Congress*, *Minnesota*, and other ships in the Roads, and are therefore no more entitled to prize-money. Those on the *Merrimac* by no means regarded the *Monitor* as a lion in her path. Having served on the *Merrimac* from the time work was first begun upon her until the night of her destruction, in justice to all concerned, and that honor may be done to whom honor is due, I simply desire the facts to be known.

"H. B. LITTLEPAGE.

"WASHINGTON, Feb. 21."

been placed in the channel between Old Point and the Rip-raps; indeed, we supposed that to be the reason why Flag-officer Goldsborough declined to fight us in the Roads; moreover, fighting the entire fleet, *Monitor*, *Naugatuck*, *Vanderbilt*, and all in the Roads, was one thing, and fighting the same under the guns of Old Point and the Rip-raps, was another.

"II. The *Merrimac* remained for some days in this position, offering battle, and protecting the approaches to Norfolk and Richmond, and then went up to the navy-yard to water. I think it was on the 8th day of May that Flag-officer Goldsborough took advantage of her absence to bombard Sewell's Point with a number of his vessels—the *Monitor*, *Galena*, aud *Naugatuck* included—all three iron-clads. When the fact was known in Norfolk, the *Merrimac* cast off from her moorings and steamed down to take a hand in the fight. *As soon as her smoke was seen* the entire fleet fled, and again took refuge below the guns of Old Point, where the *Merrimac* declined to pursue, for reasons satisfactory to her gallant commander.

"III. From this time, until the 10th of May, the *Merrimac* maintained the same attitude. On that day she was blown up by her commander in consequence of the evacuation of Norfolk by the Confederates. Then, *and not till* then, Commodore John Rodgers was sent up the James River with the *Galena*, *Monitor* and *Naugatuck*, all iron-clads, to attack Drewry's Bluff or Fort Darling, and make an attempt on Richmond.

"IV. The above facts go to show what Flag-officer Goldsborough thought of the *Merrimac*, and in citing them, I wish it to be understood that I intend to cast no imputations upon him and his gallant officers. I have been told by some of them that he had positive orders from his government *not to attack the Merrimac;* and I believe it to be the case. * * *

"V. The memorial claims that the *Monitor* not only whipped the *Merrimac* on the 9th of March, but that she ever after prevented her from going below Old Point; and thus saved Baltimore, Washington, and even New York!!! The answer to this is, that the *Merrimac* could not have gone to Baltimore or Washington without lightening her so much that she would no longer have been an iron-clad : that is, she would have risen in the water so as to expose her unarmored sides. As to her going outside of Cape Henry it was impossible ; she would have foundered. She could not have lived in Hampton Roads in a moderate gale.

"I served in the *Palmetto State* at Charleston, a similarly constructed vessel, but better sea-boat, and infinitely more buoyant, and have seen the time when we had to leave the outer harbor and take refuge in the inner in only a moderate blow !

"VI. From the above-mentioned facts I think it clearly appears (1.) that the *Monitor*, after her engagement with the *Merrimac* on the 9th of March, never again dared encounter her, though offered frequent opportunities ; (2.) that so much doubt existed in the minds of the Federal authorities as to her power to meet the *Merrimac*, that orders were given her commander not to fight her voluntarily; (3.) that the *Monitor* never ventured above Old Point from the 9th of March until after the destruction of the *Merrimac* by her own crew, save on the occasion above referred to; (4.) that the *Merrimac*, so far from being seriously injured in her engagement, efficiently protected the approaches to Norfolk and Richmond until Norfolk was evacuated; (5.) that the *Merrimac* could not have gotten to Washington or Baltimore in her normal condition; (6.) that she could not have gone to sea at all ; (7.) that, although she could have run by the Federal fleet at Old Point (barring torpedoes in the channel) and threatened McClellan's base at Yorktown, in exceptionally good weather, yet would have had to leave the James River open.

"VII. For the truth of the very important facts mentioned in sections I., II. and III., I am willing to abide by the log-book of the *Monitor*, the dispatches of Flag-officer Goldsborough, or the testimony of Commander Dana Greene, U. S. navy, who was the gallant and efficient executive officer of the *Monitor* from the day she left New York until she foundered off Cape Hatteras.

"VIII. In conclusion I would like to say, and I do so most cheerfully, that the *Monitor* made her appearance in Hampton Roads at a critical time—the night of the 8th of March, 1862—and although an untried vessel, of a new and peculiar construction, did on the next day what the whole Federal fleet present declined to do—she fought the *Merrimac*.

" If the claim for a reward was put upon this ground alone, no one would be more gratified to see it granted her gallant crew than myself; but to claim prize-money on the ground that the *Monitor* defeated and permanently disabled the *Merrimac*, thus saving Washington and New York, etc., is in view of the facts cited, in my humble opinion, preposterous.   " Very respectfully, etc.,   "WM. H. PARKER."[1]

The history of the fight between the *Monitor* and the *Virginia* established the fact beyond controversy that the *Virginia* sustained no more damage from the *Monitor* than the latter received from the former, and that all the damage received by the *Virginia* was on the 8th of March, in her action with the *Cumberland, Congress, Minnesota*, and other wooden vessels, and that her *" subsequent destruction "* was the work of her own officers and crew, in consequence of military operations on land, and distant many miles from the waters of Hampton Roads. McClellan turned the flank of the *Virginia* away up on the peninsula, and exposed her base at Yorktown to capture, and she was no longer able to supply her necessities, repair her engines, and keep herself afloat. The *Monitor* and the other men-of-war in Hampton Roads had neither part nor lot in the destruction of the *Virginia*.

Prof. Soley, in his effort to reason out a victory for the *Monitor,* says:

" But assuming for the moment that the *Merrimac* was left in possession of the field, why did she not continue her operations ? The retreat of the *Monitor* would have left matters in precisely the situation in which the *Merrimac* supposed them to be when she came out in the morning. It is to be presumed that her object was to destroy the *Minnesota*. The *Monitor* had prevented her for four hours from doing this; now, however, if the *Monitor* had retreated, why did she not attack the frigate ?

" Instead of continuing the fight, the *Merrimac* steamed to Norfolk. Jones gives as his reason for returning that he believed the *Monitor* to be entirely disabled. What ground he had for forming such a belief does not appear. It has also been suggested that his pilots led him to suppose that delay would prevent him from crossing the bar. But what need had he to cross ? The bar was a mile above Sewell's Point; he had anchored safely the night before under the battery, and after destroying the *Minnesota*, supposing that the *Monitor* had disappeared—he could do the same again, and go up to Norfolk at his leisure. If, however, his injuries were so great that he was compelled to lose no time in returning to Norfolk, it would seem that, instead of his having defeated the *Monitor*, the *Monitor* had defeated him. In truth, the claim that the *Merrimac* was victorious is singularly bold, in view of the fact, that half an hour after the last shot was fired the *Minnesota* was lying aground in the very spot she had occupied in the morning, the *Monitor* was lying alongside her, neither of them materially injured, and the supposed victor was standing as fast as possible to Elizabeth River, in order to cross the bar before ebb-tide."

It is one thing to win a victory, and another thing to reap the entire fruits of that victory, and many a victory has

---

[1] The *Merrimac* was christened the *Virginia* by the Confederate authorities; but I have pre-ferred in this article to give her the name she was best known by.—W. H. P.

been complete of which the full fruitage was lost. That the
first battle of Bull Run was a complete victory is generally
admitted, but the fruits were lost by unavoidable and unfore-
seen circumstances. The fruits of Lee's victory over Burnside at Fredericksburg were barred against him by the Rappahannock River, and so the "middle ground" of Hampton
Roads, impassable to the *Virginia*, prevented her from completing her victory by destroying the *Minnesota*. The Confederate army was damaged very greatly both at Manassas
and at Fredericksburg, but no writer has claimed for McDowell
and Burnside victories in those battles because their armies
were not *totally* destroyed. It was not the bar a mile above
Sewell's Point that the pilots advised Jones about, but the
"middle ground" which interposed between the *Minnesota*
and the *Virginia*. They were unwilling to be responsible for
the ship if she attempted to cross that "middle ground," or
hazard further fighting in her position, on an ebb-tide. Lieut.
Wood says: "At length the *Monitor* withdrew over the middle ground, where we could not follow, but always maintaining a position to protect the *Minnesota*. To have run our
ship ashore on a falling tide would have been ruin. We waited
her return for an hour, and at about 2 P. M. steamed to
Sewell's Point." These are the badges of defeat upon which
the Confederates claim that the *Virginia* compelled the *Monitor* to withdraw from the fight. And when to these is added
the fact, now brought out by Lieut. Greene, that the Navy Department, by *positive orders*, forbid the *Monitor* to engage the
Virginia unless in defence, the conclusion is irresistible that
in the first great battle of the iron-clads the Confederate ship
and navy won the laurels of victory. In this claim we detract
nothing from the valor, seamanship and gallantry with which
Worden handled and fought the *Merrimac*. Until blinded by
the casualty of battle, he fought his ship with a gallantry only
equalled by Lieut. Jones; and, when the command devolved
on Greene, it was no want of courage that caused him to withdraw from the "middle ground," but the prudence of a
thoughtful sailor that would take account of damage, and
ascertain the true condition of his ship, the command of which
had so suddenly descended to him.

The affidavit of a deserter, one James Byers, who stole the
steam-tug *J. B. White*, and fled from Norfolk to Newport
News, has been repeatedly used by Federal writers and in
public documents published by Congress, to establish the
claim of very great injury done the *Virginia* by the *Monitor*.
That affidavit, quoted by the Committee of the Senate when
considering the bill for prize money to the officers and crew
of the *Monitor*, recites:

"The *Merrimac* came back into the river badly disabled, and almost
in a sinking condition. Tugs had to be used to get her into the dry dock
at the navy-yard, the crew pumping and bailing water with all their

might to keep her afloat. I saw her in the dock at Norfolk next day, was on board of her, and made a personal examination of the ship. The effect of the *Monitor's* guns upon the *Merrimac* was terrible.   Her plated sides were broken in, the iron plating rent and broken, the massive timbers of her sides crushed; and the officers themselves stated that she could not have withstood the effect of the *Monitor's* guns any longer, and that they barely escaped in time from her."

The sworn statement of a deserter, made to ingratiate himself with his new-found friends, will not receive credence from impartial history, but the following letter from Lieut. Green of the *Monitor*, coming from an honorable source, is entitled to every respect:

"UNITED STATES STEAMER MONITOR, ⎰
"HAMPTON ROADS, March 12th, 1862. ⎰

"On Sunday last we met the *Merrimac* at 9.15 A. M., and, after a hard fight of four hours, drove her back to Norfolk.   Our noble and gallant captain was wounded near the close of the fight, and I was called to take command of the vessel.   Up to that time I had fired every gun myself, and have the satisfaction of knowing that I put five shots of 170 pounds straight through this infernal machine, and wounded her captain.

"Lieut. T. O. Selfridge (Lieut. Jaffers has since taken command) is at present in command, and as soon as the *Merrimac* makes her appearance we are going to lay this battery alongside of her and stay there until one or the other sinks.

"Our vessel is a complete success, and we are not materially damaged. We received twenty-one shots."

It was simply impossible for Lieut. Green, shut up in the turret of the *Monitor*, with no look-out, except the port-holes when open for firing, to have seen the effect of his shots, and when he says he "put five shots of 170 pounds straight through this infernal machine and wounded her captain," he drew largely upon his imagination, for he really did neither. Nor is there any truth in the remark made on page 12 of the "Statement" accompanying Senate Bill 369, Forty-seventh Congress, first session, that : "Finally, however, a shot from the *Monitor*, whose guns had been depressed for that purpose, struck the *Merrimac* on her only vulnerable part, the junction of the casemate with the side of the ship, causing a leak, which induced her officers to abandon the contest."   No such shot struck the *Virginia*, and consequently there was no leaking from the effect of the shot, and no abandonment of the contest from that cause.

The *Virginia* was leaking, not from injury inflicted by the *Monitor*, but from that received in the battle of the 8th, when she rammed the *Cumberland* to the bottom, for in doing that splendid feat she twisted off her ram, which caused her to leak ; and Boatswain Hasker, of the *Virginia*, explains that leak was further opened when the *Virginia* rammed the *Monitor*, "which leak," he adds, "was stopped partially by shoving a bale of oakum against the stem apron"; and again, "in consequence of our stem being twisted, we were leaking badly, and only had time to steam to Norfolk, and get in the dry dock by high-water."

Whatever process of reasoning Federal writers may adopt to satisfy themselves that the *Monitor* defeated the *Virginia*, to make good their claim they must go further and explain why the *Monitor*, if the victor in the first fight, never again came out of shoal water to engage the *Virginia;* but that her gallant and brave crew of officers and men submitted to the deep humiliation of seeing three Federal transports captured in Hampton Roads, and dragged around the arena with the flags *Union down*, in the presence of the French and English cruisers, as will presently appear.

Capt. Buchanan and Lieut. Jones both bore testimony to the skill and bravery of all the officers under their command in the actions of both days:

"To that brave and intelligent officer, Lieut. Catesby Jones, the executive and ordnance officer of the *Virginia*," says Capt. Buchanan in his official report, "I am greatly indebted for the success achieved. His constant attendance to his duties in the equipment of the ship; his intelligence in the instruction of ordnance to the crew, as proved by the accuracy and effect of their fire—some of the guns having been personally directed by him—his tact and management in the government of raw recruits, his general knowledge of the executive duties of a man-of war, together with his high-toned bearing, were all eminently conspicuous, and had their fruits in the admirable efficiency of the *Virginia*. If conduct such as his —and I do not know that I have used adequate language in describing it —entitles an officer to promotion, I see in the case of Lieut. Jones one in all respects worthy of it.   As flag officer, I am entitled to some one to perform the duties of flag-captain, and I should be proud to have Lieut. Jones ordered to the *Virginia* as lieutenant commandant, if it be not the intention of the department to bestow upon him a higher rank.

"Lieut. Simms fully sustained his well-earned reputation. He fired the first gun, and when the command devolved upon Lieut. Jones, in consequence of my disability, he was ordered to perform the duties of executive officer. Lieut. Jones has expressed to me his satisfaction in having had the services of so experienced, energetic, and zealous an officer.

"Lieut. Davidson fought his guns with great precision. The muzzle of one of them was soon shot away ; he continued, however, to fire it, though the wood-work around the port became ignited at each discharge. His buoyant and cheerful bearing and voice were contagious and inspiring.

"Lieut. Wood handled his pivot gun admirably, and the executive officer testifies to his valuable suggestions during the action. His zeal and industry in drilling the crew contributed materially to our success.

"Lieut. Eggleston served his hot shot and shell with judgment and effect; and his bearing was deliberate, and exerted a happy influence on his division.

"Lieut. Butt fought his gun with activity, and during the action was gay and smiling.

"The Marine Corps was well represented by Capt. Thom, whose tranquil mien gave evidence that the hottest fire was no novelty to him. One of his guns was served effectively and creditably by a detachment of the United Artillery of Norfolk, under the the command of Capt. Kevill. The muzzle of their gun was struck by a shell from the enemy, which broke off a piece of the gun, but they continued to fire as if it was uninjured.

"While the *Virginia* was thus engaged in getting her position for attacking the *Congress*, the prisoners state it was believed on board that ship that we had hauled off; the men left their guns and gave three cheers. They were soon sadly undeceived, for a few minutes after we opened upon her again, she having run on shore in shoal water. The carnage, havoc and dismay caused by our fire compelled them to haul down their colors, and to hoist a white flag at their gaff and half-mast, and another at the main. The crew instantly took to their boats and landed.

"Midshipmen Foute, Marmaduke, Littlepage, Craig and Long rendered valuable services. Their conduct would have been creditable to older heads, and gave great promise of future usefulness. Midshipman Marmaduke, though receiving several painful wounds early in the action, manfully fought his gun until the close. He is now at the hospital.

"Paymaster Semple volunteered for any service, and was assigned to the command of the powder division, an important and complicated duty, which could not have been better performed.

"Surgeon Phillips and Assistant Surgeon Garnett were prompt and attentive in the discharge of their duties ; their kind and considerate care of the wounded, and the skill and ability displayed in the treatment, won for them the esteem and gratitude of all who came under their charge, and justly entitled them to the confidence of officers and crew. I beg leave to call the attention of the department to the case of Dr. Garnett. He stands deservedly high in his profession, is at the head of the list of assistant surgeons, and there being a vacancy, in consequence of the recent death of Surgeon Blacknall, I should be much gratified if Dr. Garnett could be promoted to it.

"The engines and machinery, upon which so much depended, performed much better than was expected. This is due to the intelligence, experience and coolness of Acting Chief Engineer Ramsay. His efforts were ably seconded by his assistants, Tynan, Campbell, Herring, and Jack White. As Mr. Ramsay is only acting chief engineer, I respectfully recommend his promotion to the rank of chief ; and would also ask that Second Assistant Engineer Campbell may be promoted to first assistant—he having performed the duties of that grade during the engagement.

"The forward officers, Boatswain Hasker, Gunner Oliver and Carpenter Lindsey, discharged well all the duties required of them. The boatswain had charge of a gun and fought it well. The gunner was indefatigable in his efforts ; his experience and exertions as a gunner have contributed very materially to the efficiency of the battery.

"Acting Master Parrish was assisted in piloting the ship by Pilots Wright, Williams, Clark and Cunningham. They were necessarily much exposed.

"It is now due that I should mention my personal staff. To that gallant young officer, Flag Lieut. Minor, I am much indebted for his promptness in the execution of signals, for renewing the flag-staffs when shot away—being thereby greatly exposed—for his watchfulness in keeping the Confederate flag up ; his alacrity in conveying my orders to the different divisions, and for his general cool and gallant bearing.

"My aide, Acting Midshipman Rootes, of the navy, Lieut. Forrest, of the army, who served as a volunteer aide, and my clerk, Mr. Arthur St. Clair, Jr., are entitled to my thanks for the activity with which my orders were conveyed to the different parts of the ship. During the hottest of the fight, they were always at their posts giving evidence of their coolness. Having referred to the good conduct of the officers in the flag-ship immediately under my notice, I come now to a no less pleasing task when I attempt to mark my approbation of the bearing of those serving in the other vessels of the squadron.

"Commander John R. Tucker, of the *Patrick Henry*, and Lieut. Commanding J. N. Barney, of the *Jamestown*, and W. A. Webb, of the *Teaser*, deserve great praise for their gallant conduct throughout the engagement. Their judgment in selecting their positions for attacking the enemy was

14

good: their constant fire was destructive, and contributed much to the success of the day. The 'general order,' under which the squadron went into action, required that, in the absence of all signals, each commanding officer was to exercise his own judgment and discretion in doing all the damage he could to the enemy, and to sink before surrendering. From the bearing of those officers, on the 8th, I am fully satisfied that that order would have been carried out.

"Commander Tucker speaks highly of all under him, and desires particularly to notice that Lieut. Col. Cadwallader St. George Noland, commanding the post at Mulberry Island, on hearing of the deficiency in the complement of the *Patrick Henry*, promptly offered the services of ten of his men as volunteers for the occasion, one of whom, Geo. E. Webb, of the 'Greenville Guards,' Commander Tucker regrets to say, was killed.

"Lieut. Commanding Barney reports ' every officer and man on board of the ship performed his whole duty, evincing a courage and fearlessness worthy of the cause for which we are fighting.'

"Lieut. Commanding Webb specially notices the coolness displayed by Acting Master Face and Third Assistant Engineer Quinn, when facing the heavy fire of artillery and musketry from the shore, whilst the *Teaser* was standing in to cover the boat in which, as previously stated, Lieut. Minor had gone to burn the *Congress*. Several of his men were badly wounded.

"The *Raleigh*, early in the action, had her gun-carriage disabled, which compelled her to withdraw. As soon as he had repaired damages as well as he could, Lieut. Commanding Alexander resumed his position in the line. He sustained himself gallantly during the remainder of the day and speaks highly of all under his command. That evening he was ordered to Norfolk for repairs.

"The *Beaufort*, Lieut. Commanding Parker, was in close contact with the enemy frequently during the day, and all on board behaved gallantly.

"Lieut. Commanding Parker expresses his warmest thanks to his officers and men for their coolness. Acting Midshipman Foreman, who accompanied him as volunteer aide, Midshipmen Mallory and Newton, Captain's Clerk Bain and Mr. Gray, pilot, are all specially mentioned by him."[1]

Capt. Buchanan was immediately promoted to be Admiral of the C. S. navy, and in consequence of his wound was temporarily relieved from the command, and Commander Josiah Tatnall, on March 25th, 1862, was ordered to assume command of the naval defences of the waters of Virginia, and to hoist his flag on board the *Virginia*, with the same vessels composing the fleet.

As soon as the news of the battles in Hampton Roads reached Savannah, Capt. Tatnall wrote, March 12th, 1862, to Capt. Buchanan:

"MY DEAR BUCHANAN: The reports from Norfolk have kept us in a state of hopeful but painful anxiety in regard to your unexampled combat off Newport News, until the accounts of last evening reported the result, and the return of the ships to Norfolk. I congratulate you, my dear friend, with all my heart and soul, on the glory you have gained for the Confederacy and yourself. The whole affair is unexampled, and will carry

[1] On the 16th of April, 1862, the Confederate Congress passed the following "*Resolution of thanks to the officers and crews of the ' Patrick Henry,' ' Jamestown,' ' Teaser,' and other vessels, for gallant conduct* :

"*Resolved by the Congress of the Confederate States of America*, That the thanks of Congress are due and are hereby tendered to the officers and crews of the *Patrick Henry, Jamestown, Teaser*, and other vessels engaged, for their gallant conduct and bearing in the naval combat and brilliant victory on the waters of James River. on the 8th and 9th of March, 1862."

your name to every corner of the Christian world, and be on the tongue of every man that deals in salt water. That which I admire most in the whole affair is the bold confidence with which you undertook an untried thing. To have faltered, or to have doubted, might have been fatal; but you proved yourself (as the old navy always esteemed you) a man not of doubt or faltering when you had undertaken an adventure. If your wound be severe, I shall regret it; but if it be not so, your friends will not find fault, as it crowns your worth.

"I hope Congress will make you Admiral, and put you at the head of the navy. You have my vote for it, from my very heart, and I am sure all your seniors will cry 'Amen.' You don't know how much you have aided in removing the gloom which recent military events had cast over us. Do let some friend at your bedside write me one line to tell me the nature of your wound. God bless you, my dear Buchanan."

Evidently, neither Buchanan nor Tatnall knew that the *Virginia* had been defeated, as alleged, and had retreated to Norfolk.

Commander Tatnall assumed command on the 29th of March, and on April 1st received from Secretary Mallory the information and suggestion contained in the following letter:

"The inclosed note, sent to me by a friend from Baltimore, will inform you of some interesting points about the *Monitor*. This vessel has achieved a high reputation by her recent combat with the *Virginia*; and the enemy, no less than our own people, look forward to a renewal of it as a matter of course, and with very deep interest. I confess to a very deep interest in your success over her, for I am fully convinced that the result of such a victory may save millions of money, and perhaps thousands of lives; and hence I cannot avoid communicating to you matters relating to the *Monitor* which perhaps may have but little influence in determining the mode of assailing her.

"The *Scientific American*, in a recent number, publishes a neat woodcut of the vessel and gives some *data* of her construction. She has, I perceive, two four-sided ventilators, about three feet diameter, and three feet high, which, it is alleged, slide down even with the deck when in action. But little preparation to resist boarders exists, it would seem; and a wet sail thrown over her pilot-house would effectually close the steersman's eyes. Her grated turret, her smokestack, ventilators, and air-holes invite attack with inflammables and combustibles; and it would seem that twenty men thus provided, once upon her deck, as her turret is but nine feet high, might drive every man out of her.

"You will leave with your ship and fleet to attack the enemy when in your judgment it may seem best, and I need not add that I have every confidence that you will accomplish all that any man with such means can.

"Please telegraph me when you will probably leave; and to avoid the leaky telegraph, you can say 'Captain Smith will leave here on —— at—— o'clock.' Good, fearless pilots are all-important, and I suggest that before you sail you confront them with the chart. Their refusal to place the *Virginia* closer than one mile to the *Minnesota*, notwithstanding Buchanan's earnest appeals, induces me to say this."

The Confederate Secretary of the Navy could not have regarded the *Virginia* as defeated by the *Monitor* when urging another attack as soon as possible. "Do not hesitate," wrote Secretary Mallory on April 4th, "or wait for orders, but strike, when, how and where your judgment may dictate. Take her (the *Virginia*) out of the dock when you deem best, and this point is left entirely to your decision."

From the 11th of March to the 4th of April the *Virginia* was in the dry dock undergoing repairs, and, indeed, trying to get completed, as originally designed.   While in the dock her hull was partially covered with two-inch iron plates, four feet below her shield, for a distance of 180 feet; a new and heavier ram was more strongly secured at her bow; the damage done to her armor was repaired and wrought-iron shutters were in part fitted to her ports, and rifled guns, supplied with steel-pointed shot, were provided for her bow and stern guns. These changes, and another 100 tons of pig iron in her fan-tails, increased her draft, and, while improving her powers of attack and defence, yet retarded her speed to about four knots an hour.

Flag-officer Tatnall, on April 4th, sent the following dis-patch to Secretary Mallory: "The *Virginia* is at this moment going out of the dock, and I shall drop down into the Roads to-morrow and act against the enemy according to circumstances," and he expressed his regret that he could not fit the remainder of the iron covers for the ports, or render, for want of time, four of the six originally fitted available in action, and he added: "The ability to close our ports while loading would be (particularly in close action with the *Monitor*) of great advan-tage; for, if it be found that both vessels are impenetrable to shot, the contest will be narrowed to the dismounting of guns, and while ours will be exposed the whole time, hers will be exposed but about one-sixth of the time."   Capt. Buchanan advised Tatnall most earnestly not to engage the *Monitor* without port covers, because, he said, that two of her guns had been disabled, and all the wounds incurred had been by shots through the ports.   In that opinion Lieut. Jones also coincided; and it became even more necessary should an attempt be made to pass Fortress Monroe; in that event, open ports would ex-pose the battery to the danger of being dismounted by the shots from the heavy guns in the fort and on the Rip-raps. In addition to these serious drawbacks, Engineer Ramsay, on April 5th, called attention to the utter unreliability of the en-gines of the *Virginia*.   Mr. Ramsay had been in the *Merrimac* during her last cruise, was familiar with the bad working of her engines, and now urged upon Flag-officer Tatnall, that, as the engines never having been reliable, they were now not to be depended upon, adding: "At the time I was ordered to the vessel I was informed that it was not the intention to take the ship where a delay, occasioned by a derangement in the machinery, would endanger her safety"; and he further said: "The engines of this ship are not disconnected, and one can-not be worked alone.   As long as the vacuum of the forward engine holds good, the engines might be run by working the after-engine high pressure; but as the vacuum of either engine is at all times precarious, and, if the vacuum of the forward engine should fail, the engines would stop.   Using one engine high pressure would also require a great deal of steam, which the boilers cannot generate for any length of time."

These embarrassing difficulties delayed the departure until April 11th. The day previous, Tatnall informed the department at Richmond, that it was his purpose to attack the enemy's transports lying above the forts near Hampton Roads, and not only to throw down the gage of battle, but add to it the insult of actual injury, and thus compel the *Monitor* to accept battle on the old ground. It was Tatnall's conviction that the *Monitor*, then lying off Hampton Creek, would certainly come to the protection of the transports; and with this impression he wrote to Secretary Mallory: "I shall not notice her (the *Monitor*) until she closes with me, but direct my fire on the transports. There must be, however, a combat with the *Monitor*."

From first assuming command, Flag-officer Tatnall was aware that his ship was not equal to public expectation, and that it was hardly probable that he would find in Hampton Roads the opportunity that his gallant friend Buchanan had so gloriously embraced. To run the gauntlet between Fortress Monroe and the Rip-raps was to open the way to Norfolk for the *Monitor*, as well as to hazard the safety of the *Virginia* with her open ports, and yet he wrote that he saw "no chance for me but to pass the fort and strike elsewhere, and that if the *Virginia* was needed at Yorktown, where McClellan's army was intrenched and his transports around him, the *Virginia* would "at once attempt" the passage of the fort.

With these high purposes, the *Virginia* and the gunboats steamed down to the Roads on the morning of April 11th. The Fortress Monroe correspondent of the New York *Herald* witnessed the movement, and sent the following account:

"The alarm gun was fired at twenty minutes past seven o'clock, and, as soon as the appearance of the *Merrimac* was generally known, the docks, beach, ramparts of the fortress, and other points commanding a view, were crowded with spectators.

"The *Merrimac*, after showing herself beyond Sewell's Point, appeared to be heading this way. She did not long continue on this course, however, but turned towards the James River, followed by six other gunboats, which had come round the point in her company. Of the latter, the *Jamestown* and the *Patrick Henry* were recognized. Among the others were supposed to be the *Raleigh* and *Teaser*.

"Arriving at a point about halfway between Sewell's Point and Newport News Point, and near the place where the French war-vessels *Gassendi* and *Catinet*, and the English steamer *Rinaldo*, had placed themselves early in the morning, the whole fleet came to a stop, while the *Jamestown*, followed at some distance by the *Patrick Henry* and a small tug, continued on her course.

"The intention of the *Jamestown* was not at first perceived. As she came around, leaving Newport News on her left, it was seen that her object was to capture two brigs and a schooner which were anchored near the shore, about two miles from the point.[1] This was done without the

---

[1] The following were the vessels alluded to: Brig *Marcus*, of Stockton, N. J.; brig *Saboah*, of Providence, and schooner *Catharine T. Dix*, of Accomac. The two brigs were loaded with

slightest difficulty, and the assistance of the small tug being rendered, the three prizes were taken off under the rebel flag.

"The whole affair was concluded in less than half an hour, and the *Jamestown*, having rejoined the fleet, was ordered to tow the prizes to Craney Island. Taking one brig in tow astern, and the others alongside, she moved slowly away.

"Slightly alarmed at this bold dash, quite a number of schooners in the upper harbor availed themselves of a favorable wind and sailed.

"Up to this time (2 P. M.) the rebel fleet have remained in the position in which they first placed themselves, and nothing more has been done The tide is now out, and probably no new movement will be made for some hours. If the *Merrimac* should then see fit to pay us a visit she will be appropriately welcomed."

The N. Y. *Herald* of April 15th, commenting upon the affair of the 11th, says:

"The public are very justly indignant at the conduct of our navy in Hampton Roads on Friday last. The Confederate fleet, headed by the *Merrimac*, came down to Craney Island, and one of the Confederate gunboats very coolly captured three Union vessels. The *Monitor*, the Stevens battery, the *Octarora*, and the other Union vessels-of-war, took no apparent notice of this proceeding. Not one of the vessels there even moved towards the *Merrimac*. From all appearance, the Confederate fleet might have captured every vessel in the Roads without resistance, so long as the *Merrimac* kept her position off Craney Island.

"Among the spectators of this national disgrace were representatives of the French and English navies. They must have formed a very high opinion of our navy from this sample. Excelling the Confederate fleet in the number and efficiency of our vessels, we yet waited for an attack, and submitted even to the capture of the unarmed vessels we were there to defend rather than make the first assault. Was it want of force that caused this remarkable inaction? Look at our ships in Hampton Roads, and, from the *Minnesota* to the *Monitor*, we challenge the world to show us finer war-vessels. Was it cowardice, then? Look at our brave sailors, and remember what they have done for the Union, and their cowardice seems impossible. No; it was red tape which anchored our gallant ships, and kept them from attacking the enemy; it was red tape which tied the hands of our brave sailors, and restrained them from victory. The wretched imbecility of the management of the Navy Department has paralyzed the best sailors and the best navy of the world."

Again the N. Y. *Herald*, of April 13th, says that, "at four o'clock in the afternoon (of the 11th), the *Merrimac* fired three shots in the direction of Hampton Creek, as a challenge to our fleet to come out and fight. The *Monitor*, meantime, continued at her usual anchorage, and as for the *Vanderbilt*, and the rest who were to run the *Merrimac* down, we have no account of their presence. Where were they? It is no wonder that 'the bold impudence of the manœuvres of the rebel fleet, contrasted with the apparent apathy of our fleet, excited surprise and indignation' among the spectators."

hay—one of them having stalls for the accommodation of horses. The schooner was not loaded.

The crews of these vessels were made prisoners, with the exception of a portion of the crew of one of the brigs, who escaped to Camp Hamilton by means of their small boats. The vessels were brought up and anchored in the river between Craney Island and Norfolk, and the prisoners taken off by the steamer *Raleigh* and carried to the navy-yard about two o'clock and placed in safe keeping.

The prisoners numbered thirteen in all—eleven white men and two negroes. The latter, as also three of the white men, were from the eastern shore of Virginia.

The "*sauve qui peut*" was given by the signal-gun of the *Minnesota* when the *Virginia* made her appearance, and the race for safety is thus described by the *Herald's* Fortress Monroe correspondent:

"The large fleet of Union schooner transports which was anchored in the Roads, on seeing the rebel fleet, slipped their moorings, and, favored by wind and tide, were soon out of harm's way. Many of those in Hampton Cove, restricted by the narrow and serpentine channels, not being able to get out of the way by themselves, were assisted by the steam-tugs, of which there are a number here. The little *Monitor*, which has been anxiously awaiting the reappearance of the *Merrimac*, on seeing the latter approach, got ready for action by clearing her decks, lowering her smoke and steam pipes, slipping her anchor, and in less than ten minutes was ready for action. The orders from Flag-officer Goldsborough were, however, to act strictly on the defensive, and to give battle only when the rebel craft should approach a given point."

Another correspondent adds, that "the events of this morning are much commented upon, and have caused a considerable feeling of irritation and some humiliation," that "the capture was affected almost under the bows of the French and English cruisers, and we may be sure that our national prestige was not increased in their eyes by what they saw." Lieut. Greene, in his article in the *Century* of March, 1885, does not mention this bold defiance by the *Virginia*, but says: "For the next two months we lay at Hampton Roads. Twice the *Merrimac* came out of the Elizabeth River, *but did not attack.*" It was Tatnall's expectation that the *Monitor* would come into water deep enough *to be* attacked, and, while he would not have declined a duel at long range, he expected the same gallantry from Lieut. Selfridge that had been shown by Capt. Worden, who had *advanced* to the attack the moment the *Minnesota* was threatened. But the *Monitor* now witnessed, without an effort to prevent, the capture and carrying off of three transports, if not from under its guns, certainly from within the range of its artillery. As Lieut. Barney of the *Jamestown* towed his captures,[1] with the U. S. flags hoisted Union down to taunt their protectors, and induce them to come up and endeavor to retake them, and dragged them under the stern of the English corvette *Rinaldo*, Capt. Hewitt, he was enthusiastically cheered.

It was not for the capture of transports that Tatnall steamed to Hampton Roads; that capture was made to provoke the *Monitor* into deep water, where his new mode of attack by boarding could be attempted. To that end Tatnall had determined to surround the *Monitor* with the Confederate fleet—and with their crews divided each into three parties to have boarded the *Monitor*. Numbers one in each vessel were charged with covering the ventilators after having thrown into them ignited combustibles that would suffocate; numbers

---

[1] Parker's *Recollections of a Naval Officer*, p. 274.

two of each party were to wedge the turret; while numbers three were to cover the pilot-house and blind the steersman. Accurate and secret information had been acquired in regard to the *Monitor*, and while Tatnall was prepared to sacrifice largely of his command he felt confident of capturing the *Monitor* if once he could grapple her. And while Lieut. Greene has said that the *Monitor's* commander was prepared for such an attempt, and that it would have failed, a demonstration of its failure in actual conflict was, perhaps, prevented by the *Monitor* declining battle. It is due to Lieut. Greene to quote his reason for not accepting the challenge : " We, on our side, had received positive orders not to attack in the comparatively shoal waters above Hampton Roads, where the Union fleet could not manœuvre." The reason of the order might have applied to the *Virginia* with her draft of *twenty-three* feet, but did not apply to the *Monitor* with a draft of twelve feet. Moreover, before the *Virginia* had been felt, the *Monitor* accepted battle in the same " comparatively shoal waters," why then was it ordered to decline fight in the same waters ? The reason for the restraining order is to be found in the stubborn fact, that, notwithstanding all the clamor of victory for the *Monitor*, the *Virginia* was believed at Washington to have received no material injury, and while her defective machinery was not known, the authorities at the Federal capital did not repose confidence in the ability of the *Monitor* to prevent the advent of the Confederate ram at Washington. Secretary Welles related what took place at a Cabinet meeting called after the fight in Hampton Roads, at which he reports Mr. Stanton as saying:

" ' The *Merrimac* will change the whole character of the war; she will destroy, *seriatim*, every naval vessel; she will lay all cities on the sea-board under contribution. I shall immediately recall Burnside ; Port Royal must be abandoned. I will notify the governors and municipal authorities in the North to take instant measures to protect their harbors.' He had no doubt, he said, that the *Merrimac* was at this moment on her way to Washington; and looking out of the window, which commanded a view of the Potomac for many miles, 'not unlikely we shall have a shell or cannon ball from one of her guns in the White House before we leave this room.' Mr. Seward, usually buoyant and self-reliant, overwhelmed with the intelligence, listened in responsive sympathy to Stanton, and was greatly depressed, as, indeed, were all the members."

Evidently the Cabinet of Mr. Lincoln did not believe the *Virginia* had been defeated by the *Monitor*, and they therefore positively ordered the *Monitor* to remain in shoal waters, and to avoid another fight. It was owing to the apprehensions of the Cabinet at Washington, and not the prudence of Lieut. Jeffers, that " the capture of these vessels almost within gunshot of the *Monitor* did not effect her movements," as Tatnall reported on April 12th, when he " moored the *Virginia* to the buoy off Sewell's Point in sight of the enemy's ships."

Notwithstanding Tatnall knew that the *Monitor* in Hampton Roads was the superior ship, and possessed great advantages over the *Virginia*, he boldly invited another trial, and was greatly disappointed when the invitation was declined. On the 21st of April he advised the Navy Department, that "the enemy's vessels of light draft can go from Fortress Monroe to Newport News, a distance of but six miles, with impunity." At that writing he had sent into James River, by the enemy's batteries at Newport News, the *Patrick Henry*, the *Jamestown*, *Raleigh*, *Beaufort* and *Teaser*, and was alone in Hampton Roads. The chart of the Roads shows that nine to ten feet of water can be carried near the land, and inside Hampton Bar, from Fortress Monroe to Newport News, and by that route the enemy's gunboats and light-draft vessels could pass into James River, and that consequently the navigation of James River by the light-draft vessels of the enemy could not be prevented by the *Virginia* unless that vessel was permanently placed at the mouth of James River. In such a position Norfolk was open to the *Monitor;* for, if Tatnall was ready when ordered to run between Fortress Monroe and the Rip-raps with the *Virginia,* he felt that the batteries at Craney Island and Sewell's Point could not protect Norfolk from the *Monitor.*

As it was, the *Virginia* was mistress of Hampton Roads, for he said, "the enemy's great fleet of war-vessels and transports, with a few exceptions of small transports, is not in Hampton Roads, but in Chesapeake Bay, below the forts, so that to reach them I must pass the forts." Why the *Virginia* did not pass the forts into the Chesapeake Bay is explained in the same dispatch, because that movement involved the abandonment of Norfolk, and the risk of losing the ship by attempting the passage without the means of closing her ports, and also because, "I have the best authority (a French officer of rank) that obstructions of some kind have been placed in the channel, probably in the centre, and from thence to the Rip-raps, so as to compel me, if made aware of them, to pass close to the guns of Fortress Monroe." Thus, the *Monitor* was not only ordered to stay in shoal water and to avoid a fight, but the *Virginia* was barred out of the Chesapeake Bay by obstructions between Fortress Monroe and the Rip-raps.

On the 8th and 9th of March the C. S. fleet had successfully encountered, defied and beaten a force equal to 2,890 men and 230 guns as follows:

	Men.	Guns.
Congress (burnt)	480	50
Cumberland (sunk)	360	22
Minnesota (riddled)	550	40
Roanoke (scared off)	550	40
St. Lawrence (peppered)	480	50
Gunboats (two or three disabled)	120	6
Forts (silenced)	200	20
Ericsson	150	2
Total	2,890	230

From the 11th of March to the 11th of April, the *morale* of her victory kept the enemy close under the guns of Fortress Monroe, even while the *Virginia* lie in the dock at the navy-yard undergoing repairs. From the 11th of April to the 11th of May, she steamed over the waters of Hampton Roads, capturing transports, defying the enemy, and not one of them dare dispute the supremacy she had conquered.

Upon these facts Admiral Porter[1] attempts to throw doubt. The following account of the affair of the 8th of May is copied in his History:

"On the 8th of May, the *Merrimac* again appeared, and found the *Monitor, Galena* and *Naugatuck*, and a number of heavy ships, shelling the works at Sewell's Point; but on the appearance of the iron-clad they all returned below Fortress Monroe. Tatnall stood direct for the *Monitor*, which retreated with the other vessels, the *Merrimac* and consorts following close down to the Rip-raps, where shot passed over the ship and a mile beyond. Tatnall remained for some hours in the Roads, until finally, in disgust, he gave an order to Lieut. Jones to fire a gun to windward and take the ship back to her buoy."

This, Admiral Porter says, is a "Confederate" account, which he finds does not agree with the following extract from Admiral Goldsborough's report:

"By direction of the President, our vessels shelled Sewell's Point, yesterday, mainly with a view to see the practicability of landing a body of troops thereabouts. The *Merrimac* came out, but was even more cautious than ever. The *Monitor* was kept *well in advance*, and so that the *Merrimac* could have engaged her without difficulty had she been so disposed; but she declined to do so, and soon returned and anchored at Sewell's Point."

Admiral Porter admits that the capture of the transports "was a humiliation and should not have been suffered, but prevented at all hazards." According to either of the above accounts of the affair of the 8th, an opportunity to wipe out that "humiliation" was offered by the *Virginia* and declined by the *Monitor;* and when Admiral Goldsborough's report is read with the remark of Lieut. Greene, that the officer commanding the *Monitor*, "that he had received positive orders not to attack;" the "Confederate account" has more of the appearance of truth than that from Admiral Goldsborough. Lieut. Commander Wm. Harwar Parker, an officer in the Confederate fleet, sustains the "Confederate account."[2]

"On the 8th of May," he says, "only two days before we evacuated Norfolk, while the *Merrimac* was at the navy-yard, Flag-officer Goldsborough took advantage of her absence to come above Old Point with the *Monitor* and a number of other vessels, and bombard Sewell's Point. When the news was telegraphed to Norfolk the *Merrimac* cast off her fasts and steamed down the harbor. As soon as her smoke was seen, the entire Federal fleet fled below Old Point again, and was

[1] *Naval History of the Civil War*, p. 132.   [2] *Recollections of a Naval Officer*, p. 276.

pursued by the *Merrimac* until under the guns of Fortress Monroe. There is no doubt about the fact of this." If Admiral Porter really sought for something "on record" to substantiate the "Confederate account," he overlooked the "Recollections of a Naval Officer," by Lieut. W. H. Parker, where will be found, on page 277, a refutation of the very extract from Admiral Goldsborough. Lieut. Wood confirms this statement in every particular given above of the defiance, on the 8th of May, by the *Virginia*, and the retreat of the U. S. squadron.

The New York *Herald's* Fortress Monroe correspondent, under date of May 8th, describes the movement against Sewell's Point, by the *Naugatuck* (the Stevens' Battery), the *Monitor*, the *Dacotah*, the frigate *San Jacinto*, gunboat *Seminole*, and the *Minnesota*, and the cannonade from 12 to 3 P. M., when

"A dense smoke was seen in the direction of Norfolk, and in a few minutes the rebel battery *Merrimac* hove in sight. The flag-officer thereupon signalized our vessels to withdraw, which command was obeyed, and our vessels, in returning, gave the rebel works parting salutes with their iron hail. The *Monitor*, with the others, took up the retrograde movement, the evident intention being, no doubt, to coax the *Merrimac* into deep water, where a fair fight might be had. The *Merrimac* came steaming down the Elizabeth River very rapidly, the black smoke coming out of her pipe, showing they were using tar or some other combustible material in their boiler furnaces to accelerate her speed. At ten minutes past three the flag-ship *Minnesota*, and by twenty minutes past three the *Merrimac*, had attained a position at a point about two miles west of Sewell's Point, covering the rebel works there. Our wooden vessels had then reached a point within two miles of the fort. The *Monitor* remained at a point about a mile astern of her consorts, and within a mile of her adversary. The *Merrimac* suddenly stopped, it being apparent that she was merely acting on the defensive. She turned around and got her bow headed for Norfolk, and, subsequently, backed down half a mile ; the *Monitor* all this time remained stationary, and, although the vessels were within easy range, not a shot was exchanged at her, the apparent design of the commanders of the opposing vessels being not to fire, except at close quarters. At forty-five minutes past three, the *Merrimac* started in the direction of Norfolk, closely followed by the *Monitor*, the *San Jacinto*, and the other vessels of the fleet, who appeared determined to have another dash at the rebel works. Shortly after four o'clock, the *Merrimac* stopped off the north end of Craney Island ; our vessels also stopped, the antagonists eyeing each other with the deepest interest. By this time the *Arago*, *Vanderbilt* and *Illinois*, which were to take a part in any subsequent action should the rebel craft give them a chance, came steaming up the Roads until they reached a point between the Rip-raps and the fortress ; here they were signalized by the flag-officer to return, as the *Merrimac* was not likely to leave her cover under Craney Island. The flag-ship *Minnesota* also wore around and returned to her anchorage. The result of the engagement so far was practically *nil*, as the rebel batteries replied with more celerity when our vessels retired than they did at the first of the engagement. All our vessels came out of the fight unscathed, and not a man on our side was hurt. At 5:30 P. M., the *Monitor* and all the vessels returned to their anchorage."

Is there not abundant "record" evidence in all these published accounts to establish the fact that the *Monitor* retired before the *Virginia* on the 8th of May, 1862? Finally, Flag-officer Tatnall's official letter of May 14th confirms the truth of the "Confederate account" in every particular, as follows:

"We found six of the enemy's vessels, including the iron-clad steamers *Monitor* and *Naugatuck*, shelling the battery (Sewell's Point). We passed the battery and stood directly for the enemy for the purpose of engaging him, and I thought an action certain, particularly as the *Minnesota* and *Vanderbilt*, which were anchored below Fortress Monroe, got underway and stood up to that point, apparently with the intention of joining their squadron in the Roads. Before, however, we got within gunshot the enemy ceased firing and retired with all speed under the protection of the guns of the fortress, followed by the *Virginia*, until the shells from the Rip-raps passed over her."

And Lieut. Parker (W. H.) says: "A little after sunset, as she (the *Virginia*) was slowly turning in the channel for the last time that day, she fired a single shot in the direction of Fortress Monroe. It was promptly replied to by the *Naugatuck*. I have reason to recollect this shot from the *Naugatuck*, for it was the first from the long-range guns I had seen. I was talking to Hunter Davidson, who was near me on the vessel, when we heard the whistling of this shot, which dropped in the water between us. Much surprised, I sent for my chart and found the distance to be 3½ miles. Long-range guns were then just coming into use, and caused Bill Arp afterwards to exclaim: 'Blamed if they wasn't shooting at me before I knew they were in the country.'" Flag-officer Goldsborough, in a dispatch dated 9th May, gives the following reason for the *Monitor* retiring on the day before, when the *Virginia* offered battle. He says:

"The *Monitor* had orders to fall back into fair channel-way, and only to engage her seriously, in such a position, that this ship, together with the merchant vessels intended for the purpose, could run her down, if an opportunity presented itself. The other vessels were not to hesitate to run her down, and the *Baltimore*, an unarmed steamer of light draft, high speed, and with a curved bow, was kept in the direction of the *Monitor* expressly to throw herself across the *Merrimac*, either forward or aft of her plated house; but the *Merrimac* did not engage the *Monitor*, nor did she place herself where she could have been assailed by our ram vessels to any advantage, or where there was any prospect whatever of getting at her."

In other words, the *Virginia*, though offering battle to the *Monitor*, did not offer the other vessels, namely, the *Naugatuck*, *Minnesota*, *Vanderbilt*, and three others, together with the *Baltimore*, "with a curved bow," the opportunity to run her down. The *Monitor*, dry-nursed by a whole fleet of Federal ships, so as not to be "*too much exposed*," as President Lincoln directed, and falling back into a fair channel-way to escape the *Virginia*, is *argued* to have won a victory by the Senate Committee in the following extract:

"Thus it conclusively appears that the *Monitor* remained constantly ready to confront her powerful antagonist had the latter been disposed for the conflict. But her injuries were too severe, and the chastisement she had received at the hands of the little iron raft too fresh in the minds of her masters, to induce a repetition of the encounter of the 9th of March; and, notwithstanding the fact that the gallant and skillful Worden was then on a bed of pain, far from the battle-ground, helpless and disabled from the honorable wounds received by him in the engagement, and no longer directed her movements, it appears that the *Merrimac* took good care to keep out of the range of the *Monitor's* guns by whomsoever they might have been directed."

The forty-five days of glorious, gallant defiance of the whole Federal fleet at Fortress Monroe by Flag-officer Tatnall in the *Virginia* were drawing to a close. Thirteen of those days the *Virginia* had passed in the dry dock, but on every one of the other thirty-two days she had carried her colors in open defiance of the largest and best-appointed fleet that ever bore the flag of the United States. The punishment she inflicted cannot be concealed, but the defiance she offered has been misrepresented and misstated, and the terror she excited is a matter of history. But her days were drawing to a close. Confederate military exigency on land, not the Federal naval supremacy in Hampton Roads, was the cause of her destruction. Without Norfolk in which to coal and repair, the *Virginia* could not maintain herself a week in the Roads; with Norfolk open to her, she had successfully defied and defeated all the naval power of the Federal Union. But when the military authorities, whether wisely or unwisely, abandoned and evacuated Norfolk, there was nothing else for Tatnall to do but to destroy the *Virginia*, and prevent her falling into the hands of the Federal forces.

Whatever criticism may be passed upon the haste, as well as the necessity, for evacuating Norfolk, none whatever can be made upon Flag-officer Tatnall's action in regard to the *Virginia*.

The destruction of the *Virginia* on the 11th of May, 1862, was the most distressing occurrence of the war up to that time. [1] The people, ignorant of her defects, but having witnessed her prowess, and gone wild over her triumphs, believed her capable, not only of whipping any enemy, but of steaming in any waters. Restless under seeing the ship in Hampton Roads, they urged through the press, " on to Yorktown," "on to Washington," "on to New York." When, therefore, the news flashed over the country that the gallant vessel, which had done so much, and of which so much more was expected, had been destroyed, the public indignation knew no bounds, the wildest clamor broke forth, and the manifestations of public dissatisfaction were so great and outspoken, that Flag-officer Tatnall asked, in the following letter to Secretary Mallory, that a Court of Inquiry might investigate the *cause* of the destruction of the *Virginia*:

" RICHMOND, May 14th, 1862.
"SIR—In detailing to you the circumstances which caused the destruction of the C. S. steamer *Virginia*, and her movements a few days

---

[1] On May 11th Gen. McClellan telegraphed to Secretary Stanton: "I congratulate you from the bottom of my heart upon the destruction of the *Merrimac*."

previous to that event, I begin with your telegraphic despatches to me of the 4th and 5th insts., directing me to take such a position in the James River as would entirely prevent the enemy's ascending it.

"Gen. Huger, commanding at Norfolk, on learning that I had received this order, called on me and declared that its execution would oblige him to abandon immediately his forts on Craney Island and Sewell's Point, and their guns, to the enemy. I informed him that, as the order was imperative, I must execute it, but suggested that he should telegraph you and state the consequences. He did so, and on the 5th inst. you telegraphed me to endeavor to afford protection to Norfolk as well as the James River, which replaced me in my original position. I then arranged with the General that he should notify me when his preparations for the evacuation of Norfolk were sufficiently advanced to enable him to act independently.

"On the 7th inst., Commodore Hollins reached Norfolk with orders from you to consult with me and such officers as I might select in regard to the best disposition to be made of the *Virginia* under the present aspect of things.

"We had arranged the conference for the next day, the 8th ; but on that day, before the hour appointed, the enemy attacked the Sewell's Point battery, and I left immediately with the *Virginia* to defend it.

"We found six of the enemy's vessels, including the iron-clad steamers *Monitor* and *Naugatuck*, shelling the battery. We passed the battery, and stood directly for the enemy for the purpose of engaging him, and I thought an action certain, particularly as the *Minnesota* and *Vanderbilt*, which were anchored below Fortress Monroe, got underway, and stood up to that point, apparently with the intention of joining their squadron in the Roads. Before, however, we got within gunshot, the enemy ceased firing, and retired with all speed, under the protection of the guns of the fortress, followed by the *Virginia*, until the shells from the Rip-raps passed over her.

"The *Virginia* was then placed at her moorings near Sewell's Point, and I returned to Norfolk to hold the conference referred to.

"It was held on the 9th, and the officers present were Col. Anderson and Capt. ——, of the army, selected by Gen. Huger, who was too unwell to attend himself, and of the navy, myself, Commodore Hollins, and Capts. Sterrett and Lee, Commander Richard L. Jones, and Lieuts. Ap. Catesby Jones and J. Pembroke Jones.

"The opinion was unanimous that the *Virginia* was then employed to the best advantage, and that she should continue for the present to protect Norfolk, and thus afford time to remove the public property.

"On the next day, at 10 A. M., we observed from the *Virginia* that the flag was not flying on the Sewell's Point battery, and that it appeared to have been abandoned. I dispatched Lieutenant J. P. Jones, the Flag Lieutenant, to Craney Island, where the Confederate flag was still flying, and he there learned that a large force of the enemy had landed on the Bay shore, and were rapidly marching on Norfolk, that the Sewell's Point battery was abandoned, and our troops were retreating. I then dispatched the same officer to Norfolk, to confer with Gen. Huger and Capt. Lee. He found the navy-yard in flames, and that all the officers had left by railroad. On reaching Norfolk, he found that Gen. Huger and all the officers of the army had also left ; that the enemy were within half a mile of the city, and that the mayor was treating for its surrender.

"On returning to the ship, he found that Craney Island and all the other batteries on the river had been abandoned.

"It was now seven o'clock in the evening, and this unexpected confirmation rendered prompt measures necessary for the safety of the *Virginia*.

"The pilots had assured me that they could take the ship, with a draft of eighteen feet, to within forty miles of Richmond.

"This, the chief pilot, Mr. Parrish, and his chief assistant, Mr. Wright, had asserted again and again ; and on the afternoon of the 7th, in my cabin, in the presence of Commodore Hollins and Capt. Sterrett, in reply to a question of mine, they both emphatically declared their ability to do so.

"Confiding in these assurances, and, after consulting with the first and flag lieutenants, and learning that officers generally thought it the most judicious course, I determined to lighten the ship at once, and run up the river for the protection of Richmond.

"All hands having been called on deck, I stated to them the condition of things, and my hope that by getting up the river before the enemy could be made aware of our designs, we might capture his vessels which had ascended it, and render efficient aid in the defence of Richmond ; but that to effect this would require all their energy in lightening the ship. They replied with three cheers, and went to work at once. The pilots were on deck and heard this address to the crew.

"Being quite unwell I had retired to bed. Between one and two o'clock in the morning the first lieutenant reported to me that, after the crew had worked for five or six hours and lifted the ship so as to render her unfit for action, the pilots had declared their inability to carry eighteen feet above the Jamestown Flats, up to which point the shore, on each side, was occupied by the enemy.

"On demanding from the chief pilot, Mr. Parrish, an explanation of this palpable deception, he replied, that eighteen feet could be carried after the prevalence of easterly winds, and that the winds for the last two days had been westerly.

"I had no time to lose. The ship was not in a condition for battle, even with an enemy of equal force, and their force was overwhelming. I therefore determined, with the concurrence of the first and flag lieutenants, to save the crew for future service by landing them at Craney Island, the only road for retreat open to us, and to destroy the ship to prevent her falling into the hands of the enemy. I may add that, although not formally consulted, the course was approved by every commissioned officer in the ship. There was no dissenting opinion. The ship was accordingly put on shore as near the mainland, in the vicinity of Craney Island, as possible, and the crew landed. She was then fired, and after burning fiercely fore and aft for upwards of an hour blew up a little before five on the morning of the 11th.

"We marched for Suffolk, twenty-two miles, and reached it in the evening, and from thence came by railroad to this city.

"It will be asked what motives the pilots could have had to deceive me. The only imaginable one is that they wished to avoid going into battle.

"Had the ship not been lifted, so as to render her unfit for action, a desperate contest must have ensued with a force against us too great to justify much hope of success, and, as battle is not their occupation, they adopted this deceitful course to avoid it. I cannot imagine another motive, for I had seen no reason to mistrust their good faith to the Confederacy.

"My acknowledgments are due to the First Lieut. Ap. Catesby Jones, for his untiring exertions, and for the aid he rendered me in all things. The details, firing for the ship and landing the crew, were left to him, and everything was conducted in the most perfect order.

"To the other officers of the ship, generally, I am thankful for the great zeal they displayed throughout.

"The *Virginia* no longer exists, but 300 brave and skillful officers and seamen are saved to the Confederacy.

"I presume that a Court of Inquiry will be ordered to examine into all the circumstances I have narrated, and I earnestly solicit it. Public opinion will never be put right without it. I am, sir, with great respect, your obedient servant,
"JOSIAH TATNALL,
"Flag-officer Commanding.

"Hon. S. R. MALLORY, Secretary of the Navy."

The request for a Court of Inquiry was promptly complied with, and the members detailed, and, strangely enough, was composed of three officers who had been applicants for the command of the *Virginia*, and to whom Tatnall had been preferred by the department. The officers of the Court of Inquiry were Flag-officers Forrest, Ingraham and Capt. Lynch. The special matter before them was, " to investigate and inquire into the destruction of the steamer *Virginia*, express an opinion as to the necessity of destroying her, and state particularly whether any and what disposition could have been made of that vessel."

The Court of Inquiry found, in its opinion, that, first, the destruction of the *Virginia* was unnecessary ; second, that the *Virginia* could, with a little more lessening of draft, have been taken up James River to Hog Island, and there she would have prevented the larger vessels of the enemy and the transports from ascending ; and there, the court was of opinion, she could have been supplied, and then could have been taken into consideration the expediency or practicability of striking a last blow at the enemy or destroying her. The conclusions of the Court of Inquiry, while not in terms condemnatory of Flag-officer Tatnall, were so to all intents and purposes, and excited marked astonishment throughout all military and naval circles, as well as among the intelligent portion of the people. Nevertheless, a portion of the press continued to assail the gallant Tatnall with epithet and innuendo, until some of the officers of the *Virginia* entered their protest with the Navy Department against the approval of the finding of the Court of Inquiry, alleging that, after being lightened sufficiently to ascend James River, the *Virginia* "was comparatively helpless against iron-clad vessels, and would have fallen an easy prey to the enemy," and, without discussing the points made by the Court of Inquiry, unqualifiedly indorsed the action of Flag-officer Tatnall. The whole question arising out of the situation and condition of the *Virginia* was clearly and forcibly presented in the Richmond (Va) *Enquirer* by an officer of the *Virginia*, and, as far as one so deeply interested could be relied on, fully exonerated Flag-officer Tatnall.

"JUNE 23d, 1862.

"To the Editors of the Enquirer:

" GENTLEMEN—Much has been said and written about the destruction of the *Virginia*, and the late Court of Inquiry has expressed the opinion 'that it was unnecessary at the time and place it occurred;' that the vessel might have been 'taken to Hog Island in James River, and there prevented the passage of the enemy's gunboats and transports up the river.' In all that I have seen and heard against the matter, there has not occurred one idea worthy the consideration of an intelligent naval officer; and although the times are troubled with weighty matters, requiring the public to look to the future and not to the past, I propose to investigate the subject before us *now*, that it may not fester in the minds of those ignorant of naval matters, and become an incurable national sore. There are but three conceivable things that could apparently have been done with the *Virginia*, viz.: to take her a certain distance up James River, to remain in Hampton Roads, or to pass Old Point. Before discussing them, let me say that the *Virginia* drew twenty-two feet six inches water, was 312 feet long, her sides, inclined at a horizontal angle of about thirty-five degrees, extended *below the surface of the water*, and her gun-deck ports only five feet above it. First, in order to have taken the vessel to Hog Island, she had to be lightened to twenty feet. This draft would have brought her inclined armor above the water, and left about two-fifths of her perpendicular sides aft covered only by one inch of iron for two feet in depth, exposing her magazine to every well-depressed shot at close quarters, and her after 'stern post,' which, if broken, would have destroyed her propeller and rudder.

"The best position of Hog Island, which the *Virginia* could have taken, is thirty-five miles above Newport News, and the shoalest water occurs about four miles above Newport News, where the river is nearly six miles wide. Had the vessel got aground here, which is highly probable, as her helm had no command of her when her keel was near the bottom, she would, at low tide, have been an easy prey to any of the enemy's vessels. Being very sharp under water, with a deep keel, she would have keeled over, exposing her naked sides, and rendering her battery useless. But suppose she got to Hog Island safely, where the narrowest part of the river is about two miles wide. The *Galena* (iron-clad), the *Aroostook*, and *Port Royal*, all armed with heavy eleven-inch guns, had gone up the river two days before the evacuation of Norfolk. The *Monitor* and *Naugatuck* (iron-clad) could have passed a half-mile from the *Virginia* in perfect safety; and these vessels are exactly those, and no others, that made the attack at Drury's Bluff. They could have remained in the river, received their ammunition and provisions from Gen. McClellan, and their water anywhere. What 'gunboats,' then, would the *Virginia* have 'prevented from going up James River'?

"Gen. McClellan has been supplied by way of the York River. There was no reason why any transports should go up James River; and to this day, six weeks having elapsed, we have no reliable information that one of the enemy's transports has come up the river! Then what 'transports' would the *Virginia* have 'prevented from going up James River'? If she could not have done either of these things, as, in the opinion of the Court of Inquiry she should have done, what use was she at Hog Island? It must be seen that a vessel of the importance of the *Virginia* would have been surrounded by the enemy's pickets, night and day; therefore she could never have obtained water or supplies of any kind. To have attempted her destruction at Hog Island would have been, as at any other place but the one where she was destroyed, to give her to the enemy, because she had about 340 souls on board, and but two small boats, each capable of holding about twenty people; and is it to be supposed that the enemy were so foolish as to permit more than one landing to be made without exacting a pledge that the vessel should not be destroyed? Oh, no! The *Virginia* had no means of making rafts while she could fight her guns. Hence the Court of Inquiry expected 300 men to stand on her decks, see the match touched to the magazine, and be blown into eternity, or jump overboard and be washed into it, as only one out of about forty could swim, the crew having been transferred from the army, with very few seamen among them.

"Secondly. To remain in Hampton Roads would have been to do nothing, but finally surrender the vessel to the enemy. She could have inconvenienced them by stopping their water communication with Norfolk, but Suffolk and 'Ocean View' beach would have been sufficient landings for them. There was nothing in the Roads to fight, unless they played Don Quixote and charged Old Point with about as much effect as he did the windmills, occasionally feeling a slight reaction from the Lincoln gun 480-lb. shot. Now, if she could not blockade James River at Hog Island, she could not do it at the mouth, where it is five miles wide. But we have

15

seen that the *Virginia* had inclined sides, with her gun-deck ports only five feet above the water, hence, whenever the wind blew fresh it raised a sea that washed into the ship and would soon have sunk her ; for a vessel of that build, with her greatest bearings below the surface of the water, will go down very rapidly. Now this might have occurred any night when too dark to see where to go. On one occasion the ship had to return to Norfolk when off Craney Island because there was too much sea in the Roads.

"Thirdly. The *Virginia* could only have passed Old Point and gone to York River, or any of the Chesapeake's tributaries, in the smoothest weather. If she got to York River she could have done nothing still; for, many hours before her arrival there, the enemy's vessels would have known it from Old Point, and gone into the numerous bends and creeks where the *Virginia* could never have reached them. She could not have laid in the narrow channel between Gloucester Point and Yorktown and block-aded the river, for, if not sunk by the sea in a few days, she would have been by the enemy's heavy, long, big rifle bolts from the heights above, without being able to elevate her guns and return the fire. As to going up Chesapeake Bay, or following the enemy's vessels, that would have been madness. The ship was not seaworthy. What vessel would have stopped and fought her under favorable circumstances ? Will the Court of Inquiry tell us where that 'final blow' could have been 'struck at the enemy'?

"Now, Messrs. Editors, the *Examiner* of this morning, speaking of the Court of Inquiry, gives vent to some very unkind remarks regarding the officers of the *Virginia*. It should have recollected that the opinion of a Court of Inquiry is not a final decision; but that, when the exigencies of the service will permit it, a court-martial has to take up the case.

"The latter court may be composed of thirteen members, the former of three, and until the 'finding' of the court-martial is promulgated, would it not be proper for those interested to take an intelligent view of the facts in the matter, and not be blindly pricked into a position from which they will be ashamed, perhaps, to recede ?

"There was no panic, precipitation, or even haste in the destruction of the *Virginia;* no step was ever taken with more deliberation and cool-ness. How nonsensical to suppose that the officers who had served their country a life-time, and the brave crew who had stood by the old ship since her first conception, through all the fatiguing delays to her comple-tion, when many doubted her success, and who fought the battle of New-port News, and thrice since had seen the enemy's vessels fly before them, should have been panic-stricken by hearing that the enemy had sur-rounded them *on shore!* What harm could have been done the ship from *the shore ?* None, except to prevent landing. No, it is hardly sensible to suppose that the officers were afraid of the *enemy*, but they were afraid of his getting the ship, or to the certainty of having to destroy their own lives to prevent it, which the country hardly expected of them under the circumstances.

"I think it is clearly shown by the foregoing facts, that, had any other disposal been made of the ship, she would finally have fallen into the enemy's hands without having done our cause any service before-hand. Her great draft of water, extreme length, unwieldiness, and unsea-worthiness, rendered her the most difficult of vessels to manage. She was of no service but in *deep, smooth water*. Deep water is constantly rough; if not, it must be too narrow for the *Virginia* to have worked in. She was intended only for the defence of Norfolk harbor ; but, after fighting the battle of Newport News, the public mind magnified her to a power which it was supposed could lay the Northern ports under contribu-tion. The officers were not called upon to disabuse them of this highly flattering idea, until now, in their own defence. But, because they have to do it as a defence, an intelligent reader will not believe they were fairly arraigned for trial. I have been writing this article under the supposition that the officers were responsible for the destruction of the vessel, because the Court of Inquiry has committed an act of supererogation in thus charging them. But the *Virginia* had a flag-officer in command, and a braver, truer man never trod under his country's flag. His feeble health has not, in the slightest degree, impaired his judgment, and every step he took in command of that ship proved the fact. He it was whom the Court of Inquiry had to deal with. They had only to state whether the act was necessary or not, and the facts leading to it, and the commander was responsible. Who ever thinks of investigating a defeat or a retreat, and charging the officers with their opinions or advice asked by the general commanding? A man in any responsible position is expected to inform himself before taking any step, but no one asks or cares where he got his information. He is put there to judge. You might as well hold the lawyers responsible for the 'decision of a jury,' a court, or judges. They deliver the verdict, and it is executed. The captain gives the order, and the ship is destroyed.

"Now, I deny that there is one single word in all the evidence before the Court of Inquiry to show that the officers were panic-stricken, or that they were actuated by any other sense than a clear, deliberate understanding of the awful necessity of the occasion. They were perfectly aware how high the ship was held in the public estimation, and of the outburst of indignation that would meet her unexpected destruction, because the public may be very good judges of military matters; but it requires a life-time to become a seaman and a judge of nautical affairs. Never was a commander forced by his own country into a more painful position; but, with a high moral courage worthy of the man, he coolly and calmly gave the order to destroy his ship. It took nearly four hours to accomplish it, proving there was no panic or precipitancy. The small arms and sufficient ammunition were all saved; the men were formed in military order, and marched to Suffolk, twenty-two miles, after ten hours of the most arduous labor, and made a narrow escape from capture by the enemy, who, it was expected, would cut them off as they passed near Portsmouth.

"For myself I am not only satisfied that the destruction of the *Virginia was necessary,* 'at the time and place it occurred,' but I assert that her destruction at the time saved the city of Richmond. Moral effect is a much more active agent in our affairs than the people are yet accustomed to recognize, and it is now generally conceded that the victory of Manassas has done us more harm than good. The Southern people are high-spirited and determined when aroused, but they are fond of ease and pleasure, and will seek them whenever to be found. Hence, after victory come demoralization and a 'laying back' upon our laurels, whilst the wary foe, nerved to madness, prepares for revenge. The people had trusted that the existence of the *Virginia* insured our blockade of James River; and although the gallant and energetic officers of the *Patrick Henry* and *Jamestown* were working hard at Drury's Bluff, yet the means at their command were insufficient to render the position impassable by the time the enemy's gunboats could have come up. Suddenly it bursts upon the public ear, 'The *Virginia* is destroyed!' Then came 'hot haste,' and munitions of war and things that could assist the barricade were hurried night and day to the Bluff. The officers and crew of the *Virginia* having pushed through to Richmond; traveling unceasingly, worn out, and broken down, were sent immediately down; and ankle deep in mud, exposed to unceasing rain for three days, without provisions or a change of clothing, they assisted, day and night, in mounting heavy guns and placing obstructions to the enemy's passage of the river. The last gun was not quite ready for action when the burst of the enemy's shell over their heads told that the strife was at hand. It did come, and how gallantly the little navy maintained its reputation on that day the good citizens of Richmond may be willing to acknowledge; and perhaps they may sometimes think that some of these men were not 'panic-stricken' when they destroyed the *Virginia*.

"In conclusion, Messrs. Editors, I say that the destruction of the *Virginia* required the exercise of a moral courage which will outlive the late Court of Inquiry and the inconsiderate editorials of the press. I am proud to have been one of her crew from beginning to end, but the proudest moments, in connection with her, were those in which I saw the flames burst from her hatches, and felt that the enemy's tread would never pollute her decks.   RAY."

As soon as the finding of the Court of Inquiry was made known, Flag-officer Tatnall demanded a court-martial, which was immediately ordered, and convened on the 5th of July, 1862, and was composed of the following officers:

Captains: Lawrence Rousseau, Franklin Buchanan, Sidney S. Lee and George N. Hollins; Commanders: Robert G. Robb, Murray Mason, Eben Farrand, A. B. Fairfax, M. F. Maury and George Minor; Lieutenants: W. L. Maury and Robert B. Pegram; Judge Advocate: Robert Ould.

The defence of Flag-officer Tatnall, read before the court, is the true and circumstantial history of the cause and manner of the destruction of the *Virginia*.

"*Mr. President and Gentlemen:*

"After serving fifty years with unblemished reputation, you may well imagine the concern I feel at being arraigned before you on charges affecting my judgment and conduct in the face of the enemy.

"It is known to the court that this trial grew out of the finding of a Court of Inquiry convened to inquire into the facts attending the destruction of the steamer *Virginia* whilst under my command in Hampton Roads 'on the 11th of May last,' with instructions to report their opinion as to the necessity of destroying her, and particularly ' whether any and what other disposition could have been made of the vessel;' and that the Court of Inquiry, upon the evidence of much the same witnesses that you have heard, reported that she ought not to have been destroyed at the time and place she was. That I, having been instructed (Norfolk being evacuated) to prevent the enemy from ascending the James River, the ship, with very little more, if any, lightening of draft, with her iron sheathing still extending three feet under water, could have been taken up to Hog Island, in James River (where the channel is narrow); could there have prevented the larger transports and vessels of the enemy from ascending; and that such disposition should have been made of her; and if it should be ascertained that her provisions could not be replenished when those on board were exhausted, then the proper time would have arrived to take into consideration the expediency or practicability of striking a last blow at the enemy, or destroying her.

"The substance of the finding of the Court of Inquiry, so far, may probably be embraced in the first charge and specification of ' culpably ' destroying the ship in Hampton Roads, ' when, with the draft to which she had been, or might have been reduced, she could have been carried up James River to a place of usefulness, free from immediate danger.'

"But there is a further part of the finding of the Court of Inquiry (and the most injurious of all to myself), which is not, as it seems, clearly, although such is avowed by the Judge Advocate to have been his intentions, embraced in the charge before the court. I have applied to the Secretary of the Navy to have it made the subject of specific charge, but was informed by that officer that he had referred the matter to the Judge Advocate, who expresses the opinion that it is substantially so embraced. In that point of view I may refer to it. It is as follows : 'In conclusion, the court are of the opinion that the evacuation of Norfolk, the destruction of the navy-yard and other public property, added to the hasty retreat of the military under Gen. Huger, leaving the batteries unmanned and unprotected. no doubt conspired to produce in the minds of the officers of the *Virginia* the necessity of her destruction at the time, as, in their opinion, the only means left of preventing her from falling into the hands of the enemy; *and seems to have precluded the consideration of the possibility of getting her up James River to the point or points indicated.* The innuendo here is not to be misunderstood. It implied that the destruction of the ship was the effect of panic on the part of those engaged in it.

"Nothing could be more blighting to the honor and reputation of an officer than this imputation, if sustained ; and in this connection I desire to remind the court of the healing scope and efficacy of the judgment they have the power to pronounce, if the proof in the case shall appear to entitle me to it. The court may not only pronounce a dry verdict of acquittal, but it may do more. 'Trial before courts-martial (says De-hart, p. 180) must often involve the investigation of divers particulars, under various and distinct charges. Circumstances which are embodied in the charges, and upon which constructive guilt is charged, are necessarily dependent upon *motive*, by which the degree of criminality is determined.

"'It consequently rests with the court to ascertain this particular degree, and declare it by their finding, and the verdict may be *special*, as it is not necessary that it be *general*, as to the guilt or innocence of the prisoner.' And again (p. 182), 'Courts-martial have at times stated the motives of acquittal, *and given an opinion of the conduct of the accused at length.*'

"Now I respectfully and confidently invoke—nay, claim—of this enlightened body of military men the fullest inquiry into and report of my motives and conduct in regard to the destruction of the *Virginia ;* and am fully prepared to stand or fall by its award.

"It will be perceived that the first charge of 'culpable' destruction of the *Virginia* is by no means narrowed by the first specification of culpably, and without sufficient reason for so doing, destroying, by fire, the steamer *Virginia.*

"It is as broad and undefined as the charge itself, involving all the circumstances in which I was placed, as respects every possible use to which the ship could have been devoted at any time previous to her destruction. This would seem to invite an allusion to the events which preceded the contemplated evacuation of Norfolk; after which, it will be seen I was left no alternative but to attempt to defend James River.

"When, on the 25th of March last, I was ordered to the defence of the waters of Virginia, and to hoist my flag on the steamer *Virginia*, I could scarcely be supposed insensible to the peril of reputation to which I became exposed from the extraordinary and extravagant expectations in the public mind, founded on ignorance of the character of the ship, and the recent brilliant success of Commodore Buchanan under the circumstances which could not again be looked for. The frigates of the enemy were incautiously at anchor in Hampton Roads, and the opportunity was seized by that gallant officer with a judgment and promptness which insured the glorious result which, while it could not exalt him too highly in public estimation, unfortunately produced a false estimate of the ship, dangerous to the reputation of his successor. From the day of his success to the evacuation of Norfolk, I do not think that a single vessel of the enemy has anchored in Hampton Roads, excepting a few gun-boats and small transports lying either under the guns of the forts or on flats unapproachable by the *Virginia.*

"Yet, for the very brief space of time when the ship was out of dock, or not in the hands of the yard, but under my command (thirteen days out of forty-five), the court will, I may be permitted to say, perceive in the evidence no signs of indisposition on my part to make her as annoying and destructive as possible to the enemy.

" Aware that Hampton Roads furnished me no field for important operations, I early turned my thoughts to passing the forts and striking unexpectedly at some distant point, say New York, or Port Royal and Savannah, and in a letter of the 10th of April to the Secretary I conveyed my views as follows :

" ' I have been aware from the first that my command is dangerous to my reputation, from the expectation of the public, founded on the success of Commodore Buchanan, and I have looked to a different field from his to satisfy them.

" ' I shall never find in Hampton Roads the opportunity my gallant friend found.

" ' There is no chance for me but to pass the forts and strike elsewhere, and I shall be gratified by your authority to do so as soon as the ship shall be in a suitable condition.'

" It will be perceived that this letter was written under the influence of expectations of improvement in the condition of the ship, created by the letters received by me from the Secretary of the Navy, informing me of her weak points, and the changes in her armor which were then in progress. How much these expectations were disappointed is made manifest from the evidence. Even the designed improvements were not fully effected, and at no time did the *Virginia* attain the power and capacity of a sea-going vessel, or exceed the measure of usefulness originally designed for her—that of harbor defence.

" When, in compliance with the Secretary's order, I consulted Commodore Buchanan on the character and power of the ship, he expressed the distinct opinion then, as he has testified here, that she was unseaworthy, and he informed me then that she was not sufficiently buoyant, and that in a common sea she would founder.

" Her construction was such that the moment the sea struck her the water would rush into her ports.

" Mr. Porter, the naval constructor of the ship, has testified that he informed me he had reported to the Secretary of the Navy that the ship could not go to sea with safety. And such were the radical defects of her engines, as greatly to retard and interfere with her operations even in the smooth waters of Elizabeth City and Hampton Roads.

" The official report of Acting Chief Engineer Ramsay, of the 5th of May (made part of your record), is in this point so important as to challenge special attention.

" Moreover, it is in evidence that on five trips made from Norfolk to Hampton, a distance of but ten miles, the engines failed twice, obliging me, on one occasion, to return to Norfolk to repair them; and on another, making it necessary to work one of her engines at high pressure, ' just managing (to use the words of the chief engineer in his report of the 5th of May to Lieut. Catesby Jones) to reach her anchorage at Norfolk.' Under these untoward circumstances, I was mortified beyond measure by frequent suggestions, not only from unofficial but high official sources, of important services to be performed by the *Virginia*, founded on the most exaggerated ideas of her qualities, among them the feasibility of passing the forts and going into York River to assist the military operations at the peninsula.

" It was while these conceptions formed the subject of anxious reflections with me that the chief engineer volunteered his report to me of the 5th of May, in which he enters particularly and at length into the subject of the ship's capacity. He says, as to her engines, ' that from present and past experience he is of opinion that they cannot be relied on; that in the two years' cruise of the *Merrimac* they were continually breaking down when least expected, and the ship had to be sailed under canvas the greater part of the cruise; that the engines gave out the day before, as he had already reported, after running only a few hours, and, as he could not insure their working any length of time, he deemed it his duty to report, etc.; that at the time he was ordered to the vessel, *he was informed that it was not the intention to take the ship where a delay, occasioned by a derangement in the machinery, would endanger her safety, and that she would always be accessible to the navy-yard for repairs*, which was the reason why he had deferred this report, etc. He adds: 'Each time that we have gone down, I have had to make repairs, which could not have been done aboard ship very well, or, if done at all, would have required a great deal of time.'

"The pilots, too—my only source of information as to the feasibility of carrying the ship past the forts into York River—report in writing substantially (their report is of record) that they could not, with any probability of success, take the ship there by night, and that it would require a clear day; that they must see the land, and that if it should come on to blow, or the weather be thick, there was no harbor in which they could place her. They say: 'If the lights, light-boats and buoys, which were found necessary for the navigation of the channel, still existed, there would be no trouble in reaching York River, except so far as the enemy may have obstructed the way, for there is plenty of water. If the weather were smooth and clear, and the lead and compass could be relied on, we could still take the *Virginia* to Yorktown. But the lights, light-boats and buoys having been removed, the compasses of the ship being almost useless from local attraction, and the lead equally so by the fire of the enemy, we have serious doubts as to our ability to carry the draft of twenty-three feet with any reasonable prospect of success.'

"And the 'extensive flats,' say they, 'inside of York River, on both sides, offer a safe retreat to a large fleet from the fire of a vessel of this draft; and all vessels in Poquosin River, or at anchor off Shipping Point, are not to be approached by the *Virginia* nearer than four miles.'

"That the enemy had obstructed the way was plain to view, from the unusual manner in which they used the channel between the forts; that they had done so most effectually may be safely inferred from the resources of material and skill at their command, and their known industry in their use. To have attempted to pass this obstructed channel in open day, in full fire of both forts, and all their men-of-war, some twenty in number, including the *Monitor* and other iron vessels and steamers fitted for the express purpose of running her down (see the testimony of Lieut. Catesby Jones), would indeed have merited the epithet of folly, which, in the opinion of that gallant officer, the effort would have deserved.

"Thus it will be seen that I was in command of a ship that could not go to sea, nor even into Chesapeake Bay, without great hazard (and that without reference to the enemy), and that with a great draft of water, in narrow channels, she was in a great degree trammeled by pilots not reliable, as is clearly shown by the record and the Secretary's letters to me of the 1st and 8th of April, on file, thus depriving me of the privilege of manœuvring her freely, and by my own judgment.

"I had nothing left me but to be patient, to attempt what I thought was in the compass of the ship's power, and to carry out the orders of the Secretary of the Navy.

"During the short time she was not in dock, or in the hands of the navy-yard (some thirteen days), it is proved that she went down to the Roads and offered fight to the *Monitor*.

"She covered the gunboats at that time while they made prizes. She showed herself several times at Sewell's Point, giving the enemy the impression she was ready for any service. On one occasion she drove the enemy off from bombarding Sewell's Point. She also kept the Roads clear of the enemy's men-of-war.

"From a letter from the Secretary of the Navy, of the 9th of April, inclosing one from Gen. Lee of the same date, suggesting operations in the direction of Yorktown, I extract the following paragraph:

"'I regard the *Virginia* as of the first importance to the safety of Norfolk, and hence, though the suggestion of Gen. Lee of a dash at the enemy on York River holds out temptation to go at him at once, it should not be made if Norfolk is to be thereby exposed to capture.'

" From another letter from the Secretary, of the 12th of April, the following is also extracted:

" ' No immediate necessity for your leaving the Roads exists, and concurring with you in the opinion you express, that were the *Virginia* to pass the forts Norfolk would be in danger of immediate capture, you will not subject it to this hazard without the sanction of this department.'

" This sanction was never given. I will only add, in this connection, as evidence of my willingness to undertake, under these adverse circumstances and embarrassments, any hazardous enterprise which the government might deem of public service, an extract from my reply to the Secretary's letter of the 8th of April :

" ' If the presence of the *Virginia* at Yorktown be deemed at Richmond of such paramount importance as to call for the passage of the forts at all hazards, I shall, on hearing from you by telegraph to that effect, attempt it at all hazards.'

" And again, in a letter of the 30th of April, I wrote :

" ' I am prepared to run any hazard with her (the ship), under the advice and direction of the department, but, in view of your instructions to me, am not prepared to abandon Norfolk and Hampton Roads for a distant field of action, and for an object of very doubtful attainment.'

" The foregoing imperfect recital covers the events of my campaign occurring before the evacuation of Norfolk. I rely on it to vindicate the propriety of my motives and conduct previous to that event. As the specification that ' the ship,' at the draft to which she was or might have been reduced, could have been carried up James River to a place of usefulness, free from immediate danger, is designed, as the Judge Advocate avows, to conform with the part of the finding of the Court of Inquiry, already stated, that she should have been carried to Hog Island, in James River, and in her lightened condition employed there as a war vessel, it would seem that a comparison of the prudence and wisdom of that course with the course actually pursued, will exhaust this part of the subject, and leave the court under no difficulty of decision between the two.

" Now, that the *Virginia* could have been fought as a war vessel anywhere after being lightened to twenty-six feet six inches, by which her knuckle was exposed, rests upon no opinion, military or unmilitary, that has ever been expressed, except that of the Court of Inquiry. On the contrary, the testimony is unanimous the other way, including that of Mr. Porter, the naval constructor, and that her iron sheathing when so lightened, though it did extend three feet six inches below the water (it is omitted from the finding that a considerable portion of it was only one inch thick, its original thickness, the additional covering, with two additional inches, not extending the whole way), would not have protected her.

" Then, as to the eligibility of Hog Island as a place of retreat, it is unanimously condemned by every military opinion which has been expressed upon it ; and it is not a little remarkable that in the proceedings of the Court of Inquiry no military opinion is asked at all on this point.

" It rests on the opinion of Pilots Parrish and Wright alone. *They* told the court the ship could have been lightened at Hog Island with the same facility as where she was lightened, and that she could have protected the river, because the enemy would have to pass in close reach of her guns ; that is, we were bound to lighten her some to get her up to Hog Island.

" She could protect the river as well at Hog Island, as the enemy's vessels would have to pass her in 400 yards, within range of her guns, and that was so clearly demonstrative of the superior eligibility of Hog Island as the place of resort, that the court thinks nothing could have blinded our eyes to it but the evacuation of Norfolk, the destruction of the navy-yard and other public property, added to the hasty retreat of the military under Gen. Huger, leaving the batteries unmanned and un-protected, no doubt conspiring to produce in the minds of the officers of the *Virginia* the necessity of her destruction at the time, as in their opinion the only means left of preventing her from falling into the hands of the enemy, and seeming to have precluded the consideration of the possibility of getting up James River to the point or points indicated. Comment here is surely unnecessary. Nor can it be necessary to dwell on the alternative presented by the Court of Inquiry, of destroying the ship at Hog Island, or, in her then exposed condition, '*making a last dash at the enemy*,' consisting of twenty sail, including the *Minnesota*, the *Monitor*, and three other iron-clad steamers, the ram *Vanderbilt* and others ; or should we, after passing through them, have gone down to Cape Henry, rounded the Horse Shoe—the lighter vessels of the enemy, drawing sixteen feet, the while passing the swash channel and reaching Yorktown hours before us—and come to Yorktown only to find the enemy's vessels placed in safety above us, and then, with boats lost and provisions consumed, have hoisted a flag of distress, or a flag of truce, and sur-rendered at discretion ? A glance at the evidence will show that the idea of carrying the ship to Hog Island, and keeping her there for defence, if ever conceived, could only have been dismissed as vain and futile.

"Lieut. Catesby Jones says :

"'I think it ought not to have been done, because the enemy was in possession of the batteries above Hog Island.

"'The *Galena* and other gunboats were also up the river. There had been batteries of our own opposite Hog Island, which commanded the anchorage which the *Virginia* would have to have taken, and if there were no guns there the enemy could easily have placed them there.

"'The ship, with her inclined armor above the water, which at that place we could have had no means of bringing below the water, was not in a condition to contend against such batteries and the gunboats.

"'She would necessarily have to have been at anchor, and could not change her position.

"'We did not have much water on board, and, as the water at Hog Island was not fresh, we could not have stayed there long.

"'The proper place in James River to which the steamer should be taken up was a matter of discussion between Commodore Tatnall and myself, and he was of opinion she could be taken up to Westover, which was above the enemy's batteries, in communication with Richmond, and where there was a good position for batteries on shore to assist us in pro-tecting the river.'

"Again he says, speaking of the feasibility of sinking her to her original draft at Hog Island :

"'She could not, by any means in our power, have been sunk to her depth of twenty-three feet, and she be preserved as a steamer of war. I think there was water enough to sink her to twenty three feet at Hog Island; but of this I am not certain. If we had put water in her it would have put out the fires, and drowned the magazine and shell-room, and any idea of aid from the shore in sinking her was forbidden; for, to say nothing of the hostile occupation of both shores, we had only two small boats to the ship, carrying fifteen men each in smooth water.' Surely this is sufficient.

"It only remains to consider briefly the course actually adopted ; whether it was prudent or culpable, either in its conception or in its at-tempted execution, under the circumstances.

"The plan of taking the ship up to a narrow part of James River, and there assuming a defensive point, was by no means a sudden thought with me, dictated by the hasty and unexpected evacuation of Norfolk.

"After the determination to retreat from Yorktown, and, as a conse-quence of that measure to evacuate Norfolk, whereby both banks of the James would necessarily fall into the hands of the enemy, it had occurred to me as the best means of defending the river to which I had been specially ordered, and had been communicated to the gallant officers near me, who shared my confidence and counsel.

"The attempt was precipitated, it is true, by the unexpected advance of the enemy on Norfolk.

"The last orders I received from the Secretary of the Navy in regard to the *Virginia* were by telegraph on the 5th and 6th of May, four days before the abandonment of Norfolk.

"The effect of both was to direct me to protect Norfolk as well as James River, and if possible to prevent the enemy from ascending it. As to this, it may be here remarked, as I had signified to the Secretary my inability, with the five vessels under my command, to prevent this, I wrote him on the 21st of April that his gunboats could go from the forts to Newport News, a distance of six miles, with perfect impunity; and that, to prevent misconstruction, I wished it understood that I could not prevent it, or their army from crossing, except so far as the force of steamers I had placed in the river could do so

"On the 9th of May, the day before evacuation, a conference of officers of the army and navy was held, by the suggestion of the Secretary of the Navy (in which Commodore Hollins, a member of the court, participated), in which it was decided that the *Virginia* should remain at Sewell's Point, to cover Norfolk, until after the evacuation. Commodore Hollins has testified to what has occurred in that conference.

"He says that it was expected, in the last resort, the ship would be taken up James River to a point of safety for herself, and to protect Richmond; and when asked where he was to have gone to find such a place, he answered, 'I do not know anything further than what the pilots said—up to Harrison's bar'; and when asked, if I had not been able to take her up there what disposition I was expected to make of her, he replied, that he did not take that into consideration at the time, as he thought it was a thing which could be done, from what the pilots said; and it is in proof that on the 9th, the day before the unexpected evacuation on the 10th, I consulted with Capt. Lee, the commandant at the navy-yard, as to the best mode of taking her up without a loss of ballast, and with a view to having the use of her ballast after we got up.

"We arranged that I would take the two empty water tanks, two large floats, and two launches, and not thinking that the enemy would be in Norfolk the next day, I prepared to return to the navy-yard for all these things. My plan was to place the ship in a narrow part of the river, in fresh water, above the batteries of the enemy on either shore (both being in their hands), in easy communication with Richmond, whence her supplies might be drawn, and with the shore, where batteries of our own might protect and co-operate with her, and material might be obtained to sink her to the required draft, and there to defend the river. What might have been the effect if the plan had succeeded (particularly in the present attitude of the opposing armies) must be left to conjecture; at all events, it was the best course that suggested itself in trying and difficult circumstances, and I have not yet been taught by any criticism that it has encountered that a better could be devised.

"The plan, however, in its execution, necessarily depended on two conditions—the one, that the ship could be lightened to eighteen feet draft; the other, that with that draft she could be carried as high up as the plan required.

"It is said the first of these conditions was impossible, and that I did not take the requisite means to inform myself that it was so.

"I have to reply, that the Secretary of the Navy, in his letter of March 25th, assigning me to the ship and advising me whom to consult about her, says:

"'Your Flag-officer, Lieut. Jones, is said to have fought the ship gallantly, and *he is thoroughly informed about her.*'

"Constructor Porter bears the same testimony to Lieut. Jones' thorough information about her, and that officer was not only then of opinion, but swears to his belief now, that she could be lightened to eighteen feet; and this was one main source of information on which I relied.

"To the constructor, Mr. Porter, I applied through Paymaster Semple for information on the subject, who swears positively that he obtained the constructor's written report, that the ship could be lightened to even seventeen feet, and would have stability to that draft in James River. Now, whether Mr. Semple misunderstood Mr. Porter or not, there can be no doubt of the nature of the reply communicated to me through a reliable source, upon which, in the nature of things, having no knowledge of my own, I was obliged to rely. Nor will the positive and reliable testimony thus given be much shaken by Mr. Porter's flippant answer to the question why he did not give full information—'That I never spent a thought on the subject—I was busy—I supposed the officers all knew what they were about, and I gave all the information that was asked of me.'

"It will be recollected he was apprised of the meditated disposition of the ship, and had been asked for written official information on the subject.

"Then, could the ship be carried to Harrison's Bar with eighteen feet, and did I resort to the proper source of information on the point whether she could be or not ?

"I had been early warned against the pilots, yet with no charts accessible, and none of the officers having any knowledge of the sounding of the river, on what else could I rely?

"As early as the 8th of April the Secretary writes to me:

"'You are very much in the hands of your pilots. I am convinced they might have placed the ship nearer to the *Minnesota* in the late engagement than they did, and that they erred from a high sense of their responsibility only.'

"But there is ground for the belief that a much darker stain is attached to their conduct.

"It is significant that the statements of a number of witnesses, embarked in a common business, on an important inquiry, should be found altogether so wholly destitute of the traces of sincerity and truth ; and when it appears that an object was to be obtained by such means, it is hard to resist the conclusion of complicity and combination to attain it. That object would seem to have been the destruction of the ship rather than to go with her beyond the forts or up James River, in the presence of the enemy's fleet.

"For without proceeding with the dissection of so much tergiversation and falsehood, '*experimentum in corpore vile*,' it is proved as irrefragably as anything can be established by human testimony, that when the destination of the ship seemed to be past the forts and up York River, they were pressing in their representations to all the officers who have testified, that they could carry the ship up to Harrison's Bar with eighteen feet of water; and when that project seemed to be abandoned, and the prospect was that the ship, when lightened to that draft, would be carried up James River, perhaps into the presence of the enemy, they permitted, nay, encouraged, the lightening to proceed in their presence, until she became helpless, and then surprised her officers with the declaration that they were unable to carry her up at the draft of eighteen feet, to which it was proposed to reduce her, in the then present state of winds and tides, a qualification which they had never before expressed.

"And they now here falsely declare that, by the general understanding of the officers, the ceasing to lighten the ship was owing to the discovery that she could not be reduced to eighteen feet, when it is established beyond doubt or cavil that no such impression prevailed among them, and that it was owing simply and solely to their own sudden and unexpected announcement that she could not ascend the river with that draft.

"They are convicted, too, by several unimpeachable witnesses, of the declaration (in the teeth of their disclaimer here, after it was known that the attempt would be made to ascend the river, the enemy's fleet having gone up), that nothing remained to do but to abandon the ship and destroy her; one of them expressing to one witness his opinion of the hardship that they—the pilots—with dependent families, should be exposed to the dangers probably to be encountered in the ship.

"He must be a savage judge, indeed, who would visit me with a penalty for the fraudulent impositions practiced on me by these men.

"The attempt to ascend the river (frustrated by the treachery to which I have alluded, and resulting in the ship's destruction), was undoubtedly hastened beyond expectation.

"On the 9th it was supposed that the evacuation and removal of the public property would occupy a week or more, during which I was to cover the evacuation, and, so far as might be, prevent the enemy's ascent.

"On the 10th, information of our design having been traitorously conveyed to the enemy, he was in full march in force on Norfolk. The city, navy-yard, and batteries were abandoned, and the naval and military force had retired.

"Nothing remained but still, under increased embarrassments, to prosecute my original design. It was defeated by no fault of mine, but it is shown beyond dispute that from the officers who commanded and superintended the lightening of the ship, to the crew who went to the work with a cheer—in the work itself, in the destruction of the ship, in the landing and retreat of the crew, all was order, deliberation and energy. And any assumption to the contrary is not only unsupported, but is in the teeth of everything that has been proved in any stage of this cause.

"There is a charge of 'improvident conduct' in lightening the steamer at the bight of Craney Island, instead of taking her up James River, and there lightening her when the necessity for doing so arose, and to the extent of that necessity.

"It is easily disposed of. The ascent, to be successful, required that the lightening of the ship should have been done, not in, but out of, the presence of the enemy—a result which could more probably be attained by lightening her at once, where she was, instead of being probably compelled in the ascent to carry out the design in his sight. Other reasons might be given, but this seems sufficient.

"Again, some question has been made as to the place where the ship was abandoned and destroyed. The best information I could get recommended that as the easiest place of retreat. It is in proof, by the Secretary of War, that the danger was, when both shores became open to the enemy, that he would pass his forces over to the south side and intercept retreat by the southern bank.

"In that view time was precious,—the landing should be effected at once. The result was, that the retreat of the crew was successful, and in thirty-six hours' time they had reached Drewry's Bluff, ready to co-operate, as they did, in the gallant defence made at that place.

"Thus perished the *Virginia!* and with her many high-flown hopes of naval supremacy and success. That denunciation, loud and deep, should follow in the wake of such an event might be expected from the excited mass who on occasions of vast public exigency make their wishes the measure of their expectations, and recognize in public men no criterion of merit but perfect success. But he who worthily aspires to a part in great and serious affairs must be unawed by the clamor, looking to the right-judging few for a present support, and patiently waiting for the calmer time when reflection shall assume a general sway, and by the judgment of all, full justice, though tardy, will be done to his character, motives and conduct.   "Respectfully submitted,   "J. TATNALL."[1]

[1] The testimony of two of the lieutenants of the *Virginia*—J. T. Wood and Charles King—was not taken by the court-martial, owing to their unavoidable absence. They had testified, however, before the Court of Inquiry that they approved of the effort to take the ship up the James River, and that her destruction was the best disposition that could have been made of her.

The testimony and witnesses before the court-martial and Court of Inquiry were the same, excepting that the Secretary of War and Surgeon Phillips did not testify before the Court of Inquiry.—*Flag-officer Tatnall.*

The testimony of the witnesses and the statements of parties being all before the court, it was cleared for deliberation. After mature consideration the court unanimously found as follows:

"That the first specification of the first charge is not proved.
"That the second specification of the first charge is not proved.
"And that the accused is not guilty of the first charge.
"That the first specification of the second charge is not proved.
"That the second specification of the second charge is not proved.
"And that the accused is not guilty of the second charge.
"That the specification of the third charge is not proved.
"And that the accused is not guilty of the third charge.

"The court do further find that the accused had, while in command of the *Virginia*, and previous to the evacuation of Norfolk, thrown down the gage of battle to the enemy's fleet in Hampton Roads, and that the enemy had declined to take it up; that the day before Norfolk was evacuated, a consultation, at the instance of the Secretary of the Navy, was held by a joint commission of the navy and army officers as to the best disposition to be made of the ship; that the accused was in favor of passing Fortress Monroe and taking the ship into York River, or of running before Savannah with her; that in this he was overruled by the council, who advised that he should remain on this side of Fortress Monroe for the protection of Norfolk and Richmond; and that, in accordance with this advice, he proceeded to regulate her movements; that after the evacuation of Norfolk, Westover, on James River, became the most suitable position for her to occupy; that, while in the act of lightening her for the purpose of taking her up to that point, the pilots, for the first time, declared their inability to take her up, even though her draft should be reduced to its minimum of eighteen feet; that by the evacuation of Norfolk and the abandonment of our forts below Westover, both banks of the James River, below that point, were virtually given up to the enemy; that the ship being thus cut off from Norfolk and Richmond, was deprived of all outward sources of supply, save those of the most precarious and uncertain character; that her store of provisions would not last for more than three weeks; that, when lightened, she was made vulnerable to the attacks of the enemy; and that, after having been lightened, there was no available means of bringing her down to her proper draft and fighting trim; and that she had but two small boats, each capable of landing not more than fifteen or eighteen men at a time, even in smooth water.

"Such being the facts and circumstances under the influence of which the *Virginia* found herself after the evacuation of Norfolk, it was, in the opinion of the court, only necessary for the enemy to continue to refuse battle, as he had done since it was first offered by Capt. Tatnall early in April, and thenceforward to keep a strict watch about the *Virginia*, in order, when her provisions were exhausted, to make her his prize, and her crew his prisoners.

"Being thus situated, the only alternative, in the opinion of the court, was to abandon and burn the ship then and there; which, in the judgment of the court, was deliberately and wisely done by order of the accused.

"Wherefore, the court do award to the said Capt. Josiah Tatnall an honorable acquittal.

"L. Rosseau, Captain.
"Geo. N. Hollins, Captain.
"M. Mason, Commander.
"A. B. Fairfax, Commander.
"George Minor, Commander.
"R. B. Pegram, Lieutenant.

"Franklin Buchanan, Captain.
"Robert G. Robb, Commander.
"Eben Farrand, Commander.
"M. F. Maury, Commander.
"Wm. L. Maury, Lieutenant.
"Robert Ould, Judge Advocate."

Such was the end of the *Virginia*, a vessel constructed out of the burned and scuttled remains of the *Merrimac*, planned and fashioned crudely because of the limited resources of the Confederacy, armed with the banded guns, the work of Lieut. J. M. Brooke, manned with a crew of soldiers collected from regiments and a few sailors that remained in Norfolk after the evacuation, but commanded by the ablest, and bravest, and most skillful officers of the C. S. navy. She was a prodigy and a nondescript in naval construction. In her short career she not only inflicted immense loss on her enemy, defied the best production of unrestricted American genius, but revolutionized naval construction throughout the world. From her performance was given the first glimpses of the new system of naval warfare that was opening upon all navies; and she taught the nations that the end of wooden fighting-ships had come. The shots that sounded on her four-inch armament were heard and heeded in Europe, and England, France, and continental powers learned that no weapon of offence or defence was left to them, so efficient as a large armor-clad and very swift ram. Even in her weakness from over-draft and inefficient motive power, the *Virginia* carried the lesson, "that armor-plated floating batteries are the cheapest and most effectual protection to coasts and harbors," and in her short but glorious career she prefigured that of the Confederacy itself—brilliant in courage and endurance, but wanting greatly in those weightier matters which constitute a great and powerful nation.

The military movements of the armies on the peninsula, by which Gen. Joseph E. Johnston retired from the Yorktown lines to the west side of the Chickahominy, caused the order for the evacuation of Norfolk. The military necessity it is not our purpose to discuss; it put an end to all naval operations in Hampton Roads, and the little Confederate fleet, withdrawing up James River, took station behind the fortifications at Drewry's and Chapin's Bluffs. Norfolk was evacuated by the Confederates, the navy-yard and ships were burned, and Gen. Wool marched into the empty fortifications.

The loss of the navy-yard was a very great diminution of Confederate naval resources, while the destruction of the *Virginia* was equal almost to the loss of an army of many thousand men. Indeed, the official records show that she was far more feared at Washington than Gen. Lee's army, and that the terror excited by her exploits reached to every Atlantic city.

CHAPTER XI.

MISSISSIPPI RIVER FROM CAIRO TO VICKSBURG.

THE Mississippi River and its tributaries—that "inland sea," to which the Supreme Court of the United States extended maritime jurisdiction, because of its "two thousands of miles of public navigable waters, including lakes and rivers, in which there is no tide"—was too important to the great Northwest for its outlet to the ocean to be controlled by any power foreign to the United States.

The erection of batteries near Vicksburg by the State of Mississippi, in December and January, 1861, caused great excitement throughout the Northwest. "There was a good deal of fierce talk on both sides," said the N. Y. *Herald* of January 28th, 1861:

" And some Western governors drew ensanguined pictures of possible difficulties to take place among the canebrakes and woodyards of the Mississippi. It appears, however, that these batteries were temporary affairs, built to prevent the reinforcement of the forts at points below Vicksburg, more especially those at New Orleans. The Louisiana Convention made haste to declare that the navigation of the river should be free to all 'friendly States and powers.' The governor of Mississippi recommends that the 'most prompt and efficient measures be adopted to make known to the people of the Northwestern States that peaceful commerce on the Mississippi River will neither be interrupted nor annoyed by the people of Mississippi.' We agree with the governor in the statement that 'this will preserve peace between the South and the Northwest, if it can be preserved.' * * * We regard the course of Louisiana and Mississippi upon the matter of the river navigation as being not only very important in a commercial point of view, but likewise a very cheering sign that our political affairs are not in such a bad way as to be altogether hopeless. Let Chicago rejoice and Wall Street be comforted. Trade, 'the calm health of nations,' will still flow unrestricted from the Falls of St. Anthony to the Delta of the Mississippi."

Notwithstanding these assurances of free navigation by Louisiana and Mississippi, as well as by the first acts of the Confederate Congress: "That the peaceful navigation of the Mississippi River is hereby declared free to the citizens of any State upon its borders, or upon the borders of its navigable tributaries,"[1] the great northwestern section of the United States was unwilling to accept, as a concession from a foreign power, a right so essential and indispensable to the prosperity and progress of its peoples. If there had been no sentiment of union to rouse the spirit of war for its preservation, this right of freely navigating without let or hindrance, without permission or question, the Mississippi, from its source to the Gulf, would have involved the two republics in war before the lapse of a single decade.

The Louisville *Journal* of Jan. 24th, 1861, had the following indignant protest against the blockade of the Mississippi River:

"It appears that the respectable Kentucky secessionist who informed us that the cannon placed at Vicksburg by the order of the governor were withdrawn from the Mississippi shore on Tuesday of last week was mistaken. The battery still frowns from the bank, compelling all descending boats to come up to, undergo a formal search, and pay wharfage, although they have no business in the port. And now, as we learn from telegraphic dispatches, a battery of sixteen thirty-two pounders has been planted upon the Memphis bluff to bring boats to there as they are brought to at Vicksburg. This really seems almost incredible. It is hard to bring ourselves to believe that the people of Memphis, always deemed so loyal, can tolerate any such a high-handed proceeding, such a wrong and insult to all the States that use the Mississippi River for purposes of navigation. Much as we dislike violence in all its forms, we should suppose that the Memphis population, in spite of the Minute Men, or any other organization, secret or open, would rise up in their wrath and tumble the obstructing battery into the river. We wonder whether batteries are to be planted at all the ports of all the States on the Lower Mississippi for overhauling all descending boats, examining their cargoes with an eye to seizure or confiscation, and enforcing the payment of wharfage. If so, how long before the river cities will either break up the navigation to which they owe their existence and on which they depend for its continuance, or else bring upon themselves and their States the armed hosts of the States that shall feel themselves aggrieved?

"The Louisiana State Convention is very careful to stipulate for the free navigation of the Mississippi. Yesterday the following resolution was reported to the Convention, to be added to the ordinance of secession:

"'We, the people of Louisiana, recognize the right of free navigation of the Mississippi River and tributaries by all friendly States bordering thereon; we also recognize the right of the ingress and egress of the mouths of the Mississippi by all friendly States and Powers, and hereby declare our willingness to enter into stipulations to guarantee the exercise of those rights.'"

As if to force the Southern States, against their wish and purpose, to prevent the free navigation of the Mississippi River, the U. S. Surveyor of the Customs at Louisville, Ky., May 8th, was instructed to prevent the shipment of arms, ammunition and provisions to the seceded States, including Tennessee, North Carolina and Arkansas, and to intercept such shipments passing by or going through Louisville.

The administration at Washington thus took the first steps to interrupt the free navigation of the Mississippi. It was

---

[1] Approved, Feb. 26th, 1861.

by successive steps against the interests and the purposes of the Southern States that from one act to another, by one provocation and another, the two sections did exactly what was against their material interest, because of their fears of injury by the authorities of each section. But commercial intercourse was not wholly interrupted by the Proclamation of Mr. Lincoln, of April 19th.

The Cairo correspondence of the Cincinnati *Commercial*, of May 25th, says:

"Somewhat singular is the manner in which matters are being conducted at the different ports in relation to articles destined South. A few days since, the Surveyor of the Port at St. Louis permitted the steamer *Falls City* to clear with some 10,000 or 15,000 barrels of lime for New Orleans. Upon her arrival here, as you are aware, she was stopped, and the lime taken off. Yesterday a flatboat loaded with the same article arrived from Louisville. She underwent an examination by the authorities at Evansville, and was allowed to pass. This lime was also stopped here. The orders upon this subject must be general and consistent. This peculiar execution of them should be remedied, so that the great inconvenience and consequent dissatisfaction might be avoided, and the object of the blockade more easily and speedily accomplished. Considerable anxiety is manifested here in relation to the steamer *Prince of Wales*. It is thought that she has been seized at Memphis, as an article in yesterday's *Avalanche*, in speaking of the seizure of the *Sovereign*, and the expected arrival of the *Prince*, sounded somewhat of rapaciousness.

"The steamship *Catawba* was seized at New Orleans, April 25th, 1861, by a number of citizens under Capt. Shirens, on their own responsibility; she was released afterwards by orders from Governor Moore, who had received instructions from the Confederate government prohibiting and disapproving of any obstruction to commerce in Southern ports. The Collector of New Orleans was notified to the same effect. Orders were also sent to the Collector at Galveston, to raise the embargo at that port—general government alone having such power. The *Catawba* sailed for New York, full of freight and passengers. She was owned principally in New Orleans and Mobile. She was only seized on the ground of expediency and not out of retaliation.

"Governor Moore, in reply to a dispatch relative to the seizure of boats and Southern property in the Ohio River, was instructed by the government at Montgomery to wait till the reports were confirmed, and then only to retaliate by seizing property belonging to citizens of Ohio."

When war became inevitable by the assault on Sumter, Attorney General Bates, on April 17th, wrote to James B. Eads to hold himself in readiness to aid the U. S. government with his information and experience of the Mississippi as to the best manner of recapturing and holding the navigation of all Western waters. On the 29th of April, Mr. Eads [1] submitted a plan of operations with a description of the kinds of gunboats suitable for operations on Western rivers. The plan, approved by Commodore Paulding, was intrusted to Capt. John Rodgers to be put in execution. After further consultation with Mr. Eads, the *Conestoga, Taylor* and *Lexington*, powerful freight and passenger Ohio River steamboats, were altered at Cincinnati and converted into gunboats. While

[1] *Life of Admiral Foote*, p. 164.

16

these boats were not iron-plated they were protected by oak bulwarks from musket balls. [1]

Mr. Eads became the successful bidder for the seven gun-boats, advertised for construction by the U. S. quartermaster in July. These gunboats were each of 600 tons, and drew six feet water, and carried thirteen guns each. They were built very strong, and plated with two-and-a-half-inch iron, and could steam nine miles per hour. Their form and dimensions gave very great steadiness, and the accuracy of the fire of their guns was almost equal to those on land batteries. These seven boats were the *DeKalb, Carondelet, Cincinnati, Louisville, Mound City, Cairo*, and *Pittsburg*. The *Benton* was added later; she became the flag-ship of Admiral Foote, who, in September, 1861, assumed command in Mississippi waters. This was a powerful squadron, aggregating a tonnage of 5,000, heavily armored, fully equipped, and mounting 157 large guns, without which all the armies of the great West would not have been able to have regained and held the navigation of the Mississippi River.

The efforts of Secretary Mallory to organize a fleet on the Mississippi River were necessarily confined to adapting river craft to war purposes. While the immense resources of the United States were able in 100 days to put afloat, armed and equipped, the fleet of gunboats on the Mississippi River, the Confederate Navy Department was confined to altering steam-boats; and even that work was hindered and delayed by want of skilled workmen, scarcity of material at ports, and embarrassments from defection and deficient transportation.

New Orleans and Memphis were the only points on the Mississippi River in the least adapted to ship-building or repairing. At the latter city, the *Tennessee* and *Arkansas* were put under contract for completion by December 24th, 1861.

The secession of Tennessee and her adoption of the Confederate Constitution enabled the Confederate authorities to

---

[1] The first active service of the *Lexington* was to seize the *W. B. Terry*, at Paducah, Ky., Aug. 25th, 1861; and that act, called for by no conduct, hostile or injurious, to the United States, or any citizens thereof, provoked to capture by Kentuckians of the steamer *Samuel Orre*, belonging to Evansville, Ind., and worth, with her cargo, $25,000. Thus, one uncalled for outrage led to others, and on the 28th of July, Col. A. A. Hunt, Capt. G. B. Massey and Lieut. W. H. Branham, left the city of Mobile for the purpose of capturing the packet *Cheney*. On their arrival at Columbus, Ky., they found her running under the orders and signals of Gen. Prentiss. There being some doubt as to where she belonged, Col. Hunt sent Capt. Massey to Cairo, with instructions to remain there until he could ascertain her proper ownership. On the return of Capt. Massey, it was rendered certain that she belonged to the enemy. Col. Hunt, having been informed that the packet carried United States troops secreted upon her, made known the object of his expedition to a few reliable friends in Columbus, and received the aid of T. W. Doughty, S. W. Rennich and W. Gray.

On the arrival of the *Cheney* at Columbus, on Thursday, the 1st of August, as she landed she was boarded, the captain, clerk and other officers arrested—the short space of twenty minutes being allowed them to get ashore. Col. Hunt then took command of the boat, bringing her down the Mississippi River to the headquarters of Gen. G. J. Pillow, to whom he reported the prize. Gen. Pillow then ordered Col. Hunt, with the packet, to Memphis to report to Maj. Gen. Polk.

As she left for Columbus a shout arose from a large assemblage on the levee. At Hickman she was presented with a Confederate flag, and three hearty cheers for the success of the adventurers were given. As she progressed down the river, salutes were fired, and other demonstrations of joy were manifested. At Randolph, Capt. Tom Demmons, of the Woodruff guard, was detailed with a detachment of his men to guard her to Memphis.

She arrived at the wharf with a large U. S. flag flying beneath a handsome Southern banner. .

The *Cheney* was worth probably $25,000, and was a capital prize.

occupy and fortify Memphis, Randolph, Fort Pillow, and Island No. 10. The neutral position of Kentucky compelled the Confederates to construct their defences of the Cumberland and Tennessee Rivers within the borders of Tennessee, but as near as possible to the Kentucky line. Fort Donelson on the west side of the Cumberland, and Fort Henry on the east side of the Tennessee, prolonged the defensive line of the Confederates from Island No. 10 to the eastward. The fortified points closed the Mississippi, the Cumberland and the Tennessee Rivers.

About the 1st of September the United States land forces occupied the point of land immediately opposite the town of Columbus, Ky., and indicated most unmistakably a purpose to possess and fortify the town itself. The demonstration of such a purpose was promptly met by Gen. Polk, who, notwithstanding the neutrality of Kentucky, felt bound to defend his lines, and that Columbus offered the best position to that end. " The necessity justifies the action," was President Davis' telegram of September 4th, and the " profound gratification " of the citizens of Columbus expressed to Gen. Polk was but the partial expression of the sentiment of the great majority of the people of Kentucky.

Almost simultaneously with the occupation of Columbus, Ky., by the Confederates, Paducah was seized by the U. S. forces. This occupation of Columbus, Ky., and the extension of the advance lines of military defence to Bowling Green, Ky., constituted a position which could not be turned, but which when once broken would have to be abandoned throughout its whole length. Columbus on the Mississippi River, defended by its batteries, was also protected by the Confederate fleet of Flag-officer Hollins, consisting of the *McRae* (flag-ship), the *General Polk*, the *Ivy*, the *Jackson*, the *floating battery* (the Pelican dry dock of New Orleans), to which, in January and February, the *Pontchartrain*, the *Maurepas*, and the *Livingston* were added.

The destruction of records, and the deaths of officers, render it a difficult matter to ascertain with exact accuracy what Confederate vessels composed Hollins' fleet. Capt. Mitchell,[1] enumerated the *Polk*, the *Ivy*, the *McRae*, the *Jackson*, the *floating battery* of New Orleans, the *Calhoun*, and says that in January and February the *Pontchartrain*, the *Maurepas* and *Livingston* were added. Commodore Hollins, the better authority, because commanding the fleet, before the same Committee,[2] enumerated the *McRae*, the *Livingston*, the *Maurepas, Polk*, and the *Ivy;* and in reply to the question, "Did you not have the *Manassas* at one time ?" replied, "She came part of the way up, but she was sent back again, having ran aground and injured herself." Lieut. C. W. Read, executive

---

[1] Testimony before Investigating Committee of Congress, p. 38.

[2] Testimony before Investigating Committee of Congress, p. 47.

officer of the *McRae*,[1] enumerates at Columbus the *Manassas* (1 gun), *McRae* (8), *Polk* (5), *Jackson* (2), and *Calhoun* (2), and says that the *Pontchartrain* and *Ivy*, *Maurepas* and *Livingston* were added.

These were converted river boats, and the very great difference between a gunboat and a steamboat with a gun on it must be borne in mind when reading of Confederate crafts on interior waters in the early days of the war. The desultory operations of the enemy's flotilla, making reconnoissances, and hunting out masked batteries on river-banks, offered no opportunity for important actions on either side, and while Lieut. S. L. Phelps, U. S. N., commanding the U. S. steamer *Conestoga*, reported that, on Sept. 10th, 1861, while reconnoitering Lucas' Bend with the *Conestoga* and the *Lexington*—

"Two steamers of the enemy came up from Columbus, one of them the gunboat *Yankee*, opened fire upon us, but I found our guns could not reach them where they lay below the batteries. At about ten o'clock I again dropped down with this vessel, determined to try a shot at the rebel gunboat. The first shot must have struck her on the ricochet, as it touched the water close alongside, and she at once started down stream."

This observation of a picket-boat is not even reported in Confederate accounts.[2]

By the commencement of the year 1862, the Federal flotilla had been increased by the following iron-plated gunboats, built and fitted for war purposes: The *Benton* (flagsteamer), the *Carondelet*, the *Essex*, the *Louisville*, the *Mound City*, the *Cincinnati*, the *Cairo*, the *Pittsburg*, and the *St. Louis*—carrying each ten heavy guns,[3] all under command of Flag-officer Andrew H. Foote. This fleet of twelve vessels—nine of which were iron-plated—was opposed to the Confederate fleet of Flag-officer Hollins—of old steamboats, which, on Feb. 28th, numbered five boats, which could bring but twenty guns to bear upon an enemy;[4] these boats were shielded with iron to protect the machinery only, and which "looked very much like a cow-catcher," but offered no protection to the hull of the boats.

Flag-officer Hollins had been in command of the naval station at New Orleans from August 1st, 1861, having then superseded Captain Rosseau—and was relieved of the command of the naval station by Commander Wm. C. Whittle, in February, 1862, when he proceeded up the river with the fleet

[1] *Reminiscences of the Confederate States Navy*—S. Hist. Soc.: Paper, Vol.—, No. —, p, 336.

[2] Admiral Walke, *Naval Scenes*, p. 30, gives to it a very great importance, and makes the Confederate steamer to have "on board their 'President' Jeff. Davis, and Gen. Jeff. Thompson, Gen. Polk, and others of like renown." As President Davis was in Richmond, Va., on that day, and was not at Columbus at any time during its occupancy by the Confederates, there was no occasion for "the cool and crafty Jeff. Thompson" to devise a "plan of escape" by means of pretended dispatches for U. S. headquarters. Neither was the ram *Manassas* at that or any other time at Columbus—the whole story was a *canard* put upon the credulous admiral, for which he is now responsible, without the least authority to establish its truth.

[3] Porter's *History of the Navy* and Walker's *Naval Scenes*.

[4] Testimony of Capt. Hollins before Investigating Committee, p. 54.

above enumerated, which by changes of one kind and another was reduced to the *McRae*, the *Polk*, the *Livingston*, the *Maurepas* and the *Ivy*. In his examination before the Investigating Committee Capt. Hollins was asked: "Were all these boats iron-plated?" His reply was: "Only in their bow—they looked very much like a cow-catcher. This was intended, not to guard the men at all, but as a protection to the machinery." * * * "You stated that you had four boats with nine guns and one with but two, making thirty-eight altogether. I understood you to say, you could bring forty guns to bear upon the enemy?" "I stated I could bring twenty guns to bear upon the enemy going down."

The fall of Forts Henry and Donelson broke the Confederate line near the centre, and permitting the ascent of the Cumberland and Tennessee Rivers to the interior of the State of Tennessee and up to the boundary of Alabama, compelled the evacuation of Columbus, and a re-alignment from Island No. 10, which became the advance Confederate post on the Mississippi River. This island is situated at the turn of a long bend in the river fifty-five miles below Cairo, and is, by its situation, a very defensible position, which was made so strong and formidable by land defences as to deter the enemy for weeks from attempting to run its blockade. Being inaccessible to assault by land forces, its batteries, for many miles along the shores, held the river and completely sealed the navigation. The swift current of the Mississippi and the sharp turn of the river at the bend rendered the movements of the enemy's iron-clads very difficult and hazardous. Any injury to their motive-power or steering apparatus would render the injured boat an easy capture, since the current would swiftly carry it under the Confederate batteries, whose seventy guns, scattered in separate batteries along the river-banks and on the island, would soon have destroyed even the iron-clads. The gallant conduct of Commander H. Walker, of the U. S. steamer *Carondelet*, running the blockade of Island No. 10 on the night of April 4th, and which was followed by Commander Thompson in the *Pittsburg* on the night of April 6th, enabled Gen. Pope to transport his army across the river to the Tennessee bank, and this movement, taking the batteries in rear, compelled the evacuation of Island No. 10.[1]

[1] The floating battery, at Island No. 10, was under the command of Lieut. S. W. Averett, formerly of the U. S. navy. This battery was the Pelican dry dock of Algiers, opposite New Orleans, and was without motive power of any kind. It floated, that was all, and, when hauled by some other boat, could be moved as desired; at other times it drifted, unless anchored or tied up. The pumping engine in her hold enabled her to be lowered or raised in the water, and a slanting cover of timbers, surmounted by a coating of sheet-iron, erected over her, protected her pumping engine from shot and shell. Her deck was flush, without bulwarks, except a single sill around it, corresponding to the port sill on a ship, in its appearance and uses. All the guns on its starboard, or in-shore side, for both ends went down, had been transferred to shore batteries, while six were left on board of her on her port side, which faced the river and the enemy's flotilla. While, above the island, on the left of the Confederate works, the battery was the most exposed, of all the defences, to the enemy's fire during the long bombardment. She could be reached by the enemy's fire across the low bank of sand, which caused the bend in the river above the island, and was thus exposed to mortar shells and shot from rifled cannon, whose range was superior to that of any of the guns on the battery.

Lieut. Read says that "one day we received information that the tin-clad U. S. steamer *Carondelet* was ferrying the men of Gen. Pope's army over to a point above Tiptonville, and the general commanding at No. 10 urged Capt. Hollins to attack the gunboat with his fleet; for, if the enemy got possession of Tiptonville and the road by which supplies were sent to No. 10, the evacuation or capture of that place was certain. Capt. Hollins declined to comply with the request of the general, saying, that as the *Carondelet* was iron-clad, and his fleet were all wooden boats, he did not think he could successfully combat her. Lieuts. Dunnington, Fry and Carter, of the gunboats *Ponchartrain, Maurepas* and *Polk*, begged Commodore Hollins to allow them to attack the enemy's gunboat, but the old commodore was firm in his decision to remain inactive. The three gunboats mounted together seventeen guns, eight and nine-inch smooth-bores and six and seven-inch rifles."

The incident narrated by Lieut. Read is disingenuously stated, in that it omits to mention that the *Pittsburg*, an iron-clad steamer, followed the *Carondelet* below Island No. 10, and was within easy call at Tiptonville; that the two *iron-clads* carried eighteen heavy guns, in casemate, and were protected throughout their hull and armament with iron, while their powers as rams were greatly superior to that of any of Hollins' fleet. With that explanation, the inactivity of Capt. Hollins to sacrifice the only Confederate vessels on the upper Mississippi will not appear so strange to the reader as it does to Lieut. Read.

The fall of Island No. 10 opened the Mississippi to the enemy down to Fort Pillow, where, on April 14th, Flag-officer

even when fired with the highest charges, either at extreme elevation or on ricochet. During the last ten days of the bombardment, the battery was the target of nearly every shot. A long, flat boat, used as quarters for the Pelican Guards, moored between the battery and the bank, was sunk; one of the battery's guns was wrecked by a rifle shot, and her sides perforated by mortar shells and rifle shots, until she leaked so badly that she careened to the port side until the water washed over her deck, and almost touched the muzzles of her guns. In that trying predicament, her gallant commander kept his post, sometimes on the top of her roof or over the pumps, and always endeavoring to so use his guns as to reach the enemy—while hurrying forward repairs, and endeavoring, by all means known to a skillful officer, to maintain the battery at the post assigned to her. Compelled, by her disabled condition, to drop down the river out of range, the battery was pumped out, and, besides other damage, there was found two vertical holes, about three feet in length, below her water line, caused by mortar shells. All damages being repaired during that day and night, the battery was reported early the next day ready to take any position to which Gen. Machall would assign her, and have her towed to any station he might select. She was taken to the south end of the island, where she remained, and, protected by her batteries, and by

her men armed with small arms, the defences of the south end and mainland, until every gun had been abandoned. She was then scuttled, but, drifting on a bar, was captured by the enemy.

It has been intimated that the floating battery was abandoned without giving notice to the officers on the island, but the most reliable evidence exists of the error of the statement, and that Lieut. Averett did not leave the floating battery until advised by Lieut. Williamson, of the First Alabama Regiment, that he had sent information to the officers on the island.

Lieut. Col. Joseph Barbiere, in his interesting work on "Scraps from the prison table at Camp Chase and Johnson's Island," says:

"We have omitted the floating battery in our mention of the guns. This impromptu affair was commanded by Capt. Averitt, formerly of the U. S. navy, an officer of nerve and intelligence. He had four guns. This, with the battery of the Southern Guards, and the five brass pieces of the Point Coupe Artillery, two small mortars, more ornamental than otherwise, make a grand total of fifty-three guns, the great portion of which were of light metal. The enemy report the capture of 120. We surrendered not exceeding 2,600 men; the enemy report 7,000. They publish the capture of seven generals; we had one, and two acting brigadiers. If there is any glory in such a capture, the bombastic Pope is welcome to it."

Foote says: " Five rebel gunboats rounded the point below us, when the gunboats, the *Benton* in advance, immediately got underway and proceeded in pursuit; and when within long range opened upon the rebels, followed by the *Carondelet, Cincinnati*, and other boats.   After an exchange of some twenty shots, the rebel boats rapidly steamed down the river, and kept beyond our range until they reached the batteries of Fort Pillow, a distance of more than thirty miles." Such skirmishes as the above find no record in Confederate reports—Capt. Hollins, before the Committee of the Confederate Congress, merely remarking that " at New Madrid we were engaged off and on for nearly seventeen days—night and day."[1] On the day that the above skirmish is reported to have taken place, Capt. Hollins received from Capt. Whittle, at New Orleans, a dispatch that the enemy was in force at the mouth of the river, and begged him to come down, as his services were needed there.

On receipt of that telegram, Capt. Hollins proceeded immediately to New Orleans, having first advised the Navy Department of his call, and the urgency that demanded his presence there, as he was the officer commanding the defences afloat of the Mississippi River.   Lieut. Read, in his " Reminiscences," again overdraws the facts of this correspondence when he says:

" Commodore Hollins telegraphed to the Secretary of the Navy for permission to go with all the vessels of his fleet to the assistance of the forts below New Orleans.   The Secretary replied to Commodore Hollins to remain where he was, and to ' harass the enemy as much as possible.'   The Commodore answered, that as all the enemy's gunboats on the upper Mississippi were iron-clad, while those on the lower river were wood, like our own, he was of opinion that he could be of more service with his fleet below New Orleans than at Fort Pillow.   Without waiting to hear further from the department, the Commodore started down the river on the *Ivy.*"

Mr. Mallory's reply to Capt. Hollins' dispatch was that : " Your dispatch received yesterday proposed to abandon opposition to the enemy's descent of the river by your fleet, and to carry your fleet to the mouth of the river.   This proposition is totally inadmissible ; every effort that nautical skill, invention and courage can put forth must be made to oppose the enemy's descent of the river, and at every hazard. You inform me that you have gone to New Orleans at the urgent request of Capt. Whittle.   You will, therefore, send these orders to the senior in command of your squadron, by telegraph.   The *Louisiana* must join your squadron at the earliest practicable moment."   That telegram was dated April 11th, and was sent to Hollins in New Orleans, and

<hr>

[1] Page 48.

received by him there, and he received no other orders. The command of the fleet at Fort Pillow devolved on Commander Pinkney. Between the judgment of Capt. Hollins and that of Secretary Mallory, as to the nature of the defence of New Orleans, the reader cannot fail, by the light of facts now existing, to see that Hollins' idea of strengthening the fleet below New Orleans was correct, while that of Secretary Mallory would, as late as April 10th, have further depleted that defence by sending the *Louisiana* up the river to resist the fleet of Capt. Davis rather than down to the forts to meet that of Admiral Farragut. Mr. Mallory's opinion that New Orleans' danger was from above and not from below, was fixed until the very sound of the enemy's guns above the forts caused him to realize his great error.

The command of Hollins' little fleet devolved on Commander Pinkney at Fort Pillow. The *McRae*, in obedience to Capt. Hollins' order, proceeded to New Orleans—the *Ivy* had carried the commodore ; and when Fort Pillow was evacuated the fleet was scattered, the *Maurepas* and *Pontchartrain* going up White River,[1] where, under the gallant lieutenants, Joseph Fry and Dunnington, they rendered efficient service— the *Livingston* and *Polk* to the Yazoo River, where they were most ingloriously but effectually burned.

Capt. Hollins entertained a firm conviction that his little fleet, united with that at the forts and aided by the forts and all the appliances there, could have driven Admiral Farragut out of the river. That opinion he expressed before the Court of Inquiry to the effect that:

"I had often passed the Yankee batteries, and knew they could pass ours, and I was anxious that my squadron, which was up the river, should be ordered down to resist Farragut, *feeling satisfied that I could have cut him off*. I should have fought him to the greatest advantage. Farragut's ships would have been exposed—bow foremost—to my broadsides, and the sides of his vessels to the fire of the forts ; had he exposed the stern of his vessels to the fire of the forts, they would have been sunk in a short time."

That opinion is characterized by a writer in the *United Service Magazine* as "braggardism," but Farragut seems to have held the same opinion as to the advantage of coming down stream as against fighting up, and against the current. In a letter of June 3d, to Secretary Welles, he points out the very advantages which Hollins claimed for his proposition, saying:

"Few gunboats, although they have heavy batteries, are nearly all so damaged that they are certainly not in a condition to contend with iron-clad rams coming down upon them with the current, as are those of the upper Mississippi, which are built for the purpose, are iron-clad, and are designed to contend with the enemy's gunboats coming up against the current."

[1] Lieut. C. W. Read.

It was the advantage of fighting with the current, and against vessels struggling against the current, that induced Capt. Hollins to add:

"Had my squadron been at the mouth of the river, I could have kept the enemy from crossing the bar ; their heavier ships had to be lightened very greatly; their armament, etc., taken out before they could be got over: I could then have whipped their smaller craft with my squadron, and have prevented their larger ones getting over, if it had not been in my power to have destroyed them."

Upon his arrival at New Orleans, the brave old fighting sailor received a telegram from Secretary Mallory, calling him to Richmond to sit on a court-martial, and thus one of the best and bravest of the Confederate naval officers was removed from the scene of war to be a member of a court to try Commodore Tatnall for destroying the *Virginia*.

The scattering and destroying of the C. S. fleet at Fort Pillow left the defence of the river to the Montgomery flotilla.

While this *River Defence* expedition was no part of the C. S. navy, but was under the command of the general of the army in the Mississippi Department, and control of the War Department, yet its history is necessary to a full understanding of Mississippi River defences.

On January 15th, 1862, in obedience to a telegram from Secretary of War Benjamin, Gen. Lovell seized fourteen steamers at New Orleans; they were the *Mexico, Texas, Orizaba, Charles Morgan, Florida, Arizona, William Heines, Atlantic, Austin, Magorda, Matagorda, William H. Webb, Anglo-Saxon,* and *Anglo-Norman*. In announcing this seizure, Gen. Lovell called the attention of the Richmond authorities to

"Capt. Higgins, who lately resigned (from the navy), with a view of fitting out some of these vessels for war purposes under State authority. This seizure puts an end to his business. He is an officer of the old navy, of experience, skill, and high reputation as a bold and efficient officer. His services would be of great value in assisting to fit out a fleet here, and in fighting it afterwards."

This broad hint to the authorities was of no avail, because Mr. Benjamin, in his reply, informed Gen. Lovell of the passage by the Confederate Congress of laws Nos. 344 and 350,[1] and that these vessels were

"'Not to be a part of the navy, for the acts intended a service on the rivers, and will be composed of the steamboat-men of the Western waters.' The expedition was to be 'subject to the general command of the military chief of the department where it may be ordered to operate, but the boats will be commanded by steamboat captains and manned by steamboat crews, who will be armed with such weapons as the captains may choose, and the boats will be fitted out as the respective captains may desire. The intention and design are to strengthen the vessels with iron

[1] Approved January 9th, 1862, for floating defences for the Western waters, by which $1,000,000 was appropriated, to be expended at the discretion of the President by the Secretary of War or Secretary of the Navy, as he shall direct, and authorizing the President to appoint officers of the regular navy to the command.

casing at the bows, and to use them at high speed to run down, or run over and sink, if possible, the gunboats and mortar rafts prepared by the enemy for attack at our river defences. These gunboats and mortar rafts have been so far protected by iron plates and by their peculiar construction as to offer, in the judgment of the President and of Congress, but small chances of our being able to arrest their descent of the river by shot or shell, while, at the same time, their weight, their unwieldy construction and their slow movement, together with the fact that they show very little surface above the water-line, render them peculiarly liable to the mode of attack devised by the enterprising captains who have undertaken to effect their destruction by running them down, if provided with swift and heavy steamers, so strengthened and protected at the bows as to allow them to rush on the descending boats without being sunk at the first fire.

"Capts. Montgomery and Townsend have been selected by the President as two of those who are to command these boats. Twelve other captains will be found by them and recommended to the President for appointment. Each captain will ship his own crew, fit up his own boat, and get ready within the shortest possible delay. It is not proposed to rely on cannon, which these men are not skilled in using, nor on fire-arms. The men will be armed with cutlasses. On each boat, however, there will be one heavy gun, to be used in case the stern of any of the gunboats should be exposed to fire, for they are entirely unprotected behind; and, if attempting to escape by flight, would be very vulnerable by shot from a pursuing vessel.

"I give you these details as furnishing a mere outline of the general plan to be worked out by the brave and energetic men who have undertaken it. Prompt and vigorous preparation is indispensable."

The above fourteen vessels were appraised by a Board consisting of Messrs. Bogart, Stephenson, Frost, Grinnel, Milliken and Naval Constructor Porter at $900,000, but the sale was made for $563,000. Gen. Lovell urged that the captains in charge of this expedition should recommend to the President some competent person to have general control of the fleet in fitting it out, and making general rules for its control and management; and added, prophetically, that "fourteen Mississippi captains and pilots would never agree about anything after they once get under way."

The River Defence expedition was not fully organized before Gen. Lovell called the attention of the War Department to "considerable dissatisfaction" which had been expressed at some of the captains appointed by Montgomery and Townsend. The list of captains as appointed by Montgomery and Townsend was: Capts. John A. Stephenson, Isaac Hooper, Burdett Paris, John H. Burke, James Beverly Smith, James C. Delancy, Joseph Davis McCoy, William H. H. Leonard, James Henry Hart, George Willholland Phillips, William W. Lamb, and Joseph A. Sturtevant.

The fleet was fitted out at an enormous expense in consequence of the rise in price of every article to over 300 per cent.; the fitting out, provisioning, and coaling the fourteen ships costing to April 15th over $800,000—which, in addition to the $563,000 which were paid for the steamers and other expenses, made the total outlay over the $1,500,000 appropriated.

To the high prices paid for every article must be added the increase of cost arising from the fact noted by Gen. Lovell that "the river pilots (Montgomery and Townsend), who are at the head of the fleet, are men of limited ideas—no system and no administrative capacity whatever." The fleet never impressed Gen. Lovell with any conviction of usefulness—who advised the Secretary that he feared "that their powers of execution will prove much less than have been anticipated, in that unless some competent person of education, system, and brains is put over each division of the fleet, it will, in my judgment, prove an utter failure. No code of laws or penalties has been established, and it is difficult to decide how deserters from the fleet are to be tried and punished. There is little or no discipline or subordination, too much 'steamboat,' and too little of the 'man-of-war,' to be very effective," and he expressed the opinion that for this fleet to compensate for the outlay some good head ought to be placed in charge of it. That was never done, and this expensive fleet totally failed to render any appreciable service whatever to the public defence.

The evacuation of Columbus, Ky., before the fleet was completed, rendered its primary object—the destruction of the enemy's fleet at Cairo—impossible, and the breaking by the flood of the raft at the forts below New Orleans rendered it impossible for Gen. Lovell to put guns on the boats of the fleet, and compelled him to keep six of the steamers at New Orleans.

This anomalous, inefficient, useless and expensive expedition was planned and gotten up by the pilots, Montgomery and Townsend, and urged upon Congress by the whole Mississippi delegation and by Gen. Polk.

When the time for action came, "the River Defence fleet proved a failure, for the very reasons set forth in my (Gen. Lovell) letter to the department of April 15th—unable to govern themselves, and unwilling to be governed by others, their almost total want of system, vigilance, and discipline rendered them nearly useless and helpless when finally dashed upon suddenly on a dark night."

It will be seen, when the fight at the forts comes to be considered, that Gen. Duncan could get no intelligent obedience to his orders from Capt. Stephenson, and that the *fire* boats in charge of Capt. Stephenson were so handled that, instead of burning the enemy's boats, they set fire to the forts' wharves, lighting up the defences of the forts and obscuring the position of the enemy, so that Gen. Duncan took the fire boats out of the control of Capt. Stephenson and turned them over to Lieut. Renshaw, C. S. N.; and Com. Mitchell of the navy bears emphatic testimony to Stephenson's positive refusal during the fight at the forts to receive orders himself or allow any of the River Defence vessels to obey any order from a naval officer, asserting that all the officers and crews of the River Defence fleet "had entered the service with the distinct understanding or condition that they were not to be placed under the orders of naval officers"; and Com. Mitchell further testified before the Court of Inquiry that he was "not aware that the River Defence fleet did any service in resisting the enemy; if they did, it did not come under my (his) observation, nor has it in any way been brought to my notice; that four of the vessels were destroyed by the enemy or set on fire and abandoned by their own crew; that the *Resolute* was run ashore and abandoned by her officers and crew, and was burned by order of Com. Mitchell, and that the *Defiance* was discovered abandoned, having escaped without any material damage."[1] The responsibility for this senseless and abortive River Defence fleet rests neither with the Confederate Navy Department, nor with any naval officer.

It was from this River Defence expedition that Flag-officer Davis, U. S. N., won the laurels of the "first naval engagement of the war, pure and simple, where the squadrons of both sides were pitted against each other."[2] The engagement alluded to was the first battle of Fort Pillow, on May 10th, 1862. The Confederate boats engaged were the *General Bragg*, commanded by Capt. W. H. H. Leonard; the *General Stirling Price*, First Officer J. E. Hawthorne; the *Sumter*, Capt. W. W. Lamb; the *General Van Dorn*, Capt. Isaac D. Falkerson; the *General Jeff. Thompson*, Capt. J. H. Burke; the *Colonel Lovell*, Capt. J. C. Delancy; the *General Beauregard*, Capt. J. H. Hunt.[3]

The "log" of the *Price*, from New Orleans to Memphis, written by L. F. Delisdemier, the purser of that vessel, gives the following particulars of her cruise up the Mississippi, and the first naval engagement of the war:

"*Tuesday, March 25th,* 1862.—Left New Orleans at 9 P. M., with the following officers : J. H. Townsend, captain; T. E. Henthorn, first officer; L. F. Delisdemier, purser ; George L. Richardson, second officer ; William Branden, chief engineer ; J. H. Frobees, assistant engineer.

"*March 28th.*—Laid up last night, on account of fog ; left Red River at 10 A. M. ; passed the *General Bragg* to-day.

"*Saturday, 29th.* Arrived at Vicksburg at 4 P.M., and found the *Bragg* had stopped here; left at 5:30 P.M.; found no iron there. Weather pleasant.

"*Monday, 31st.*—Arrived at Eunice at 8 P. M. Informed the railroad agent that we wanted some iron. He said he had none. Our captain then told him he would have to tear up his track, and set the men at it, and soon had some three miles torn up and ready to carry on board.

"*Thursday, April 3d.*—Left Eunice yesterday afternoon, after getting on board all the iron that we wanted to finish the *Price* and *Van Dorn.* Arrived at Memphis at 3 P.M.; found the *Bragg* had arrived yesterday afternoon. At 4 P.M. the *Van Dorn* came up. Capt. Townsend, being senior captain, set all available men at work to finish the boats as soon as possible.

"*Friday, April 11th.*—Weather rainy. Received order to leave Fort Pillow. Got two pilots to-day, viz.: W. W. Hayden and Oscar Postall. Left Memphis at 6:30 P. M.

"*Saturday, April 12th.* – Arrived at the fort, and reported to the General at 6 :30 A. M., and then dropped down to coal. Orders were sent

[1] *Off. Record,* Vol. VI.

[2] Porter, p. 166.

[3] It will be observed from the names of these vessels that the C. S. navy was permanently excluded from all connection with this expedition.

down for us to escort the transport *Lockland* up the river on a foraging expedition. We started at 5 P. M.; left orders for the *Van Dorn* to follow us. Those of Hollins' fleet went up ahead of us; passed them at 11 P. M. at anchor near Island No. 25. As soon as we rounded the bend saw a United States transport and gave her chase. She either heard us or saw our smoke, and started up the river. We chased her about eight miles, when she met the Federal fleet at the mouth of the Obion River.

"*Sunday, 13th*, 1 A. M.—Sent a note to Capt. Huger, flag-officer on the *McRea*, notifying him of the presence of the enemy. At 5 A. M. received his answer that he would be along after daylight; 8:30, the look-outs report the fleet coming up; dropped out into the stream and formed in line of battle, and stood up to meet the enemy; and when within three miles of us, the U. S. gunboat *Benton* opened on us; her shot fell short. The C. S. gunboat *Maurepas* replied to her from a nine-inch Dahlgren, also falling short. The Federals now showed their whole fleet, consisting of eleven gunboats and eight mortars. So Capt. Huger, knowing it to be folly to contend with them, left us alone with them. We then rounded to, and waited until the enemy came within two miles, and let them have the contents of our stern guns, and then we went after the balance of the fleet. The Yankees followed us, and kept up a running fire, but without any damage. We arrived at the fort at 11:30, and reported the fleet coming down. The guns were immediately manned, and all waited for the appearance of the fleet. At half-past two they made their appearance, but only exchanged a few shots, rounded to, and went up the river about six miles.

"*Monday, the* 14th.—This morning, the Federals opened fire on the fort, and every fifteen minutes they gave three shells. The bombardment was kept up till 9 P. M. A scouting party from our boat and the *Van Dorn*, under command of First officer T. E. Henthorn, went out this morning on the Arkansas shore, and went within six hundred yards of the Federal fleet, and report them forming in line of battle and dropping down stream, stern foremost. 10 P. M.—No demonstration made by fleet as yet.

"*April* 15th, *Tuesday*.—First-officer T. E. Henthorn, with a party of thirteen men and officers from the River Defence fleet, have gone out again this morning. The bombardment was renewed at an early hour this morning, and has been kept up at regular intervals of ten minutes. They have three mortar boats in position, at the distance of three and a half miles, and lay around a point opposite the forts. 10 P. M.—The firing ceased at 8 P. M. The scouting party have just returned; report three men captured at Mr. Lamies', by Federal mounted infantry; were chased by a party, but made their escape.

"*Wednesday,* 16th *April.*—Went down to Mr. Lamies', and moved him and family on board of steamer transport *Charm*, and sent them below, under convoy of the *Bragg*. A party of fifty 'Feds.' came down last night, to capture one of our boats, but not finding us, they returned at daylight. This morning a party of U. S. soldiers appearing in sight, gave them a few rounds of grape. Scouts report fifteen men killed and wounded; burnt ninety bales unginned cotton, and thirty bales of cotton.

"*April* 17th.—Went down and moved Mr. Morgan to a place of safety.

"*Thursday, May* 8th.—The bombardment has been kept up day by day, but no damage done; loss: two killed. This morning the *Sumter*, *Bragg*, and *Van Dorn* were ordered to go up and cut out the mortar floats. Arrived at the field where they had been posted, but found they had been moved up the fleet. The *Sumter* remained there until 9 A. M.; the Federals firing a few shot at her, but did not come down, and commenced a furious bombardment, throwing over two hundred and fifty shells, but most of them fell short.

"*Saturday, May* 10th.—Agreeably to the decision of the council of war, held yesterday, the fleet left their moorings at 7 A. M., and the several positions in line of battle, as follows: The *Bragg, Sumter, Sterling*

Price, Van Dorn, Jeff. Thompson, General Lovell, Beauregard, and *Little Rebel.* On rounding the point, the Federal fleet was plainly visible in 'Bulletin Bar,' with the exception of the *Cincinnati,* who had come down as a protection to the mortar, but made (as soon as we appeared) for the balance of the fleet. According to orders, the *Bragg* immediately gave her chase, and soon overtook her, striking her a violent blow on the larboard bow, dismounting one of her forward guns and slewing her round. The *Cincinnati* fired a broadside into the *Bragg,* one shot going through her, killing a cook. The *Price* next in turn started for her, and at the same time delivering an effective fire at the mortar, silencing it. The *Cincinnati* kept a running fire as the *Price* kept away from her, soon overtaking her, and struck her aft a little starboard of midships, carrying away her rudder and stern-post, disabling her; the *Sumter* came soon after, and also struck her, and she then lifted on the bar and sunk. The *Van Dorn* in the meantime had come up. Those of the Federal fleet came down to the assistance of the *Cincinnati,* and surrounded the *Van Dorn,* who made a sudden dash at the *Mount City,* striking her amidships, driving in her hull about six feet, causing her to leak badly; but as the Federal gunboats are all built in water-tight compartments, it was some time before she sank; she was able to make the bank. The U. S. gunboat *Pittsburg* was disabled, by getting between the fires of the two fleets. The firing between both fleets was rapid and heavy, and our boats were struck several times, doing some damage to the cabins, but only one was damaged in the hull, and that was the *General Price,* who received a shell (128 pounds) between wind and water, cutting off the supply pipes and causing her to leak. As the 'Feds.' had drawn off into shoal water, where we could not reach them, Commodore J. E. Montgomery signaled the fleet to retire, which was done in good order, all dropping down stream, below the guns of the fort. The total loss was two killed; but several firemen were wounded with splinters, and one man had his arm broken. The only damage was to the upper works of the *Van Dorn* and *Price,* with the exception of damage done the *Price* as reported. As soon as we arrived at Fulton, commenced to repair damages.

"*Sunday,* 11*th.*—All damages on our boats repaired, and all ready for another engagement with the enemy. At 4 P. M. scouts came in from Osceola, report the loss of the enemy to be three boats sunk, and several killed and wounded. The enemy are hard at work raising their boats. The *Little Rebel* went up on a reconnoissance to-day. On her appearance, the Yankees took their mortar floats and started up the river.

"*Tuesday, June* 3*d.*—The bombardment has been kept up, but no damage done to the fort. Second officer John C. Rawson, and a party of seven men, went after ice and were captured. At 3:30 P. M. two gunboats and three rams came down to cut out the *Jeff. Thompson,* but the fort opened on them, and they retired. The C. S. fleet then went up to the fort, and were actively employed in taking on shot and shell, and commissary stores, as the fort is to be evacuated.

"*Wednesday, June* 4*th,* 1862.—The fort being completely demolished, the fleet started down the river. At Randolph, the *Van Dorn* got aground, and had to send men in the woods to cut spars and spar her off.

"*June* 5*th.*—Arrived at Memphis at 1 P. M. 9 P. M. all were aroused by the report of a cannon, and a rush was made to find out the cause, and found the *General Lovell* out in the stream dropping down. All then dropped out in the stream, in line of battle, but the "Feds." not making their appearance, returned to our anchorage. The tug *Gordon Grant,* was sent up as a picket boat, but grounded, and had to be burnt.

The official accounts of the fight, which will be found in the notes, show that the victory, if any, belonged to the River Defence service of the Confederate States; that so far as injury inflicted either to vessels or crew can measure the result, the

U. S. flotilla suffered the loss of the *Cincinnati* and the *Mound City*, and that the losses were greater in Capt. Davis' fleet than in that of Capt. Montgomery.[1] The contemporaneous accounts in the newspapers are now seen to have been so full of errors, if not of misrepresentations, that they are utterly unreliable, while the official report of Gen. W. K. Strong from Cairo to Major Gen. Halleck was hardly more veracious than Falstaff's fight with the men in buckram. Admiral Porter is

[1] Report of Capt. J. E. Montgomery, *Off. Rec.*, Vol. X., p. 888.

FLAG-BOAT LITTLE REBEL,
FORT PILLOW, Tenn., May 11th, 1862.

SIR: I have the honor to report an engagement with the Federal gunboats at Plum Point, four miles above Fort Pillow, May 10th.

Having previously arranged with my officers the order of attack, our boats left their moorings at 6 A. M., and proceeding up the river, passed round a sharp point, which brought us in full view of the enemy's fleet, numbering eight gunboats, and twelve mortar boats.

The Federal gunboat *Carondelet* [should be the *Cincinnati*] was lying nearest us, guarding a mortar boat that was shelling the Fort. The *General Bragg*,Capt. Leonard, dashed at her; she firing her heavy guns and retreating towards a bar where the depth of water would not be sufficient for our boats to follow. The *Bragg* continued boldly on under fire of nearly the whole fleet, and struck her a violent blow that stopped her further flight, then rounded down the river under a broadside fire, and drifted until her tiller-rope,that had got out of order, could be readjusted. A few moments after the *Bragg* struck her blow, the *General Sterling Price*, Flag-officer J. E. Hawthorne, ran into the same boat, a little aft of her starboard midship, carrying away her rudder, stern-post, and a large piece of her stern. This threw the *Carondelet's* [*Cincinnati*] stern to the *Sumter*, Capt. W. W. Lamb, who struck her, running at the utmost speed of his boat.

The *General Van Dorn*, Capt. Isaac D. Fulkerson, running according to orders, in rear of the *Price* and *Sumter*, directed his attention to the *Mound City*, at the time pouring broadsides into the *Price* and *Sumter*. As the *Van Dorn* proceeded, by skillful shots from her thirty-two pounder, W. G. Kendall, gunner, silenced a mortar boat that was filling the air with its terrible missiles. The *Van Dorn*, still holding on the *Mound City's* midship, in the act of striking, the *Mound City* sheered, and the *Van Dorn* struck her a glancing blow, making a hole four feet deep in her starboard forward quarter, evidenced by splinters left on the iron bow of the *Van Dorn*. At this juncture the *Van Dorn* was above four of the enemy's boats.

As our remaining boats, the *Jefferson Thompson*, Capt. J. H. Burke, the *Colonel Lovell*, Capt. J. C. Delancy, and the *General Beauregard*, Capt. J. H. Hart, were entering boldly into the contest in their prescribed order, I perceived from the flag-boat that the enemy's boats were taking position where the water was too shallow for our boats to follow them, and as our cannon were far inferior to theirs, both in number and size, I signalled our boats to fall back, which was accomplished with a coolness that deserves the highest commendation.

I am happy to inform you, while exposed to close quarters to a most terrific fire for thirty minutes, our boats, although struck repeatedly, sustained no serious injury.

Our casualties were two killed and one wounded—arm broken.

Gen. M. Jeff. Thompson was on board the *General Bragg*, his officers and men were divided among the boats. They were all at their posts ready to do good service should an occasion offer.

To my officers and men I am highly indebted for their courage and promptness in executing all orders.

On the 11th instant I went, on the *Little Rebel*, in full view of the enemy's fleet. Saw the *Carondelet* [the *Cincinnati*] sunk near the shore, and the *Mound City* sunk on the bar.

* * *   J. E. MONTGOMERY,
Senior Captain,
Commanding River Defence Service.

To Gen. G. T. BEAUREGARD.

On the same day, Gen. M. Jeff. Thompson reported to Gen. Beauregard, confirming in every particular Capt. Montgomery's account of the battle.

The First Report of Capt. Davis, commanding the U. S. flotilla, was as follows:

UNITED STATES FLAGSHIP BENTON,
ABOVE FORT PILLOW, MISSISSIPPI RIVER,
May 10th, via Cairo, May 11th.

Hon. Gideon Welles, Secretary of the Navy:

The naval engagement for which the rebels have been preparing took place this morning. The rebel fleet, consisting of eight iron-clad gunboats, four of which were fitted with rams, came up handsomely. The action lasted one hour. *Two of the rebel gunboats were blown up and one sunk*, when the enemy retired precipitately under the guns of the fort. Only six vessels of my squadron were engaged. The *Cincinnati* sustained some injury from the rams, but will be in fighting condition to-morrow. Capt. Stembel distinguished himself. He is seriously wounded. The *Benton* is uninjured. Mortar boat No. 16, in charge of Second Master Gregory, behaved with great spirit.

The rebel squadron is supposed to be commanded by Commodore Hollins.

C. H. DAVIS, *Captain,*
Commanding Western Flotilla,
Mississippi River pro tem.

The second report was :

UNITED STATES FLAG STEAMER BENTON,
OFF FORT PILLOW, May 11th.

Hon. Gideon Welles, Secretary of the Navy :

SIR—I have the honor to inform the department that yesterday morning, a little after seven o'clock, the rebel squadron, consisting of eight iron-clad steamers—four of them, I believe, fitted as rams—came around the point at the bend above Fort Pillow, and steamed gallantly up the river, fully prepared for a regular engagement.

The vessels of this squadron were lying at the time tied up to the bank of the river—three on the eastern and four on the western side—and (as they were transferred to me by Flag-officer

but little more correct in his account:[1] "although the Confederate vessels made great holes in the *Mound City* and the *Cincinnati*, and were considerably damaged themselves [*they sustained no injury whatever*], they all succeeded in escaping. The *Cincinnati*, after proceeding some distance up the river, sunk near the Tennessee side. The *Cairo* assisted the *Mound City* to the first island above the scene of action, where she also sunk"; and he adds that the "small list of casualties for such a desperate brush would seem to indicate rather indifferent gunnery practice on the part of the Federals, who, with their heavy ordnance, ought to have swept the enemy from the face of the water, as his vessels were of wood and lightly built. The attack on the Federal vessels was, however, by a new method; for this was the first time ramming had been practiced on this river during the war, and the *Cincinnati* and *Mound City* had been put *hors de combat* almost at the beginning of the action. The Confederate commander-in-chief was not accustomed to command vessels *en masse*, and does not seem to have understood the necessity of concert of action." Each Confederate vessel seems to have been fighting on her "own hook." And yet he asserts that "Flag-officer Davis had the satisfaction of winning the first naval squadron fight." A little more of that kind of satisfaction would have left Commodore Davis without a vessel. That this "victory" of May 11th was not entirely satisfactory to Commodore Davis appears from a dispatch to Secretary Stanton from Col. Chas. Ellet, Jr., commanding the U. S. ram flotilla at Fort Pillow, on June 4th, in which it is stated that,

"While the strength of the rebel batteries seems to be greatly overrated, their fleet of rams and gunboats is much larger than mine. It consists of eight [?] gunboats, which usually lie just below the fort, and four [?] others at Randolph, a few miles further down. Commodore Davis will not join me in a movement against them, nor contribute a gunboat to my expedition, nor allow any of his men to volunteer, so as to stimulate the

Foote) ready for action. Most of the vessels were prompt in obeying the signal to follow the motions of the commander-in-chief.

The leading vessels of the rebel squadron made directly for mortar boat No. 16, which was for a moment unprotected. Acting Master Gregory and his crew behaved with great spirit during the action; he fired his mortar eleven times at the enemy, reducing the charge and diminishing the elevation.

Commander Stembel, in the gunboat *Cincinnati*, which was the leading vessel in the line on that side of the river, followed immediately by Commander Kilty, in the *Mound City*, hastened to the support of the mortar boats, and were repeatedly struck by the enemy's rams, at the same time that they disabled the enemy and drove him away.

The two leading vessels of the enemy's line were successively encountered by this ship. The boilers, or steam chest, of one of them was exploded by our shot, and both of them were disabled. They, as well as the first vessel encountered by the *Cincinnati*, drifted down the river.

Commander Walke informs me that he fired a fifty-pound rifle shot through the boilers of the third of the enemy's gunboats, of the Western line, and rendered her for the time being helpless.

The action lasted during the better part of an hour, and took place at the closest quarters. The enemy finally retreated, with haste, below the guns of Fort Pillow.

I have to call the especial attention of the department to the gallantry and good conduct exhibited by Commander Stembel and Kilty, and Lieut. Commanding S. L. Phelps.

I regret to say, that Commander Stembel, Fourth Master Reynolds, and one of the seamen of the *Cincinnati*, and one of the *Mound City*, were severely wounded. The other accidents of the day were slight.

I have the honor to be your most obedient servant,

C. H. DAVIS,
Captain Commanding Mississippi Flotilla pro tem."

[1] *History of the Navy*, p. 166.

pride and emulation of my own. I shall therefore first weed out some bad material and then go without him."

Premising that, instead of twelve gunboats, Capt. Montgomery's fleet consisted of only *seven;* six of which carried two guns, and one carried four, making a total of sixteen guns; the reluctance of Commodore Davis to risk his flotilla was an inheritance handed down to him by Flag-officer Foote, who on March 12th wrote to Secretary Welles : " I shall be very cautious, as I appreciate the vast responsibility of keeping our flotilla from falling into the rebels' hands, as it would turn the tide against us"; and again on the 20th: "Were we to attempt to attack these heavy batteries with the gunboats, or attempt to run the blockade and fail, as I have already stated in a former communication, the rivers above us—Mississippi, Ohio and Cumberland—would be greatly exposed, not only frustrating the grand object of the expedition, but exposing our towns and cities bordering on those rivers." These considerations, like those that operated to keep the *Monitor* out of reach of the *Virginia* in Hampton Roads after the first fight, were conclusive with Commodore Davis, after his experience with the rams on May 10th, to take no risks in such expedition as that proposed by Col. Ellet, Jr.

Brig. Gen. Villepigue, in obedience to orders from Gen. Beauregard, evacuated Fort Pillow on June 4th, and that opened the river to Memphis; below which the River Defence expedition of Capt. Montgomery had retired to obtain coal.

On the morning of the 6th of June, the Federal fleet of gunboats, Commodore Davis, at Memphis, commanding, consisted of the flag-ship *Benton,* Lieut. Commanding S. L. Phelps; the *Louisville,* Commander B. M. Dove; the *Carondelet,* Commander Henry Walke; the *Cairo,* Lieut. Commanding N. C. Bryant; and the *St. Louis,* Lieut. Commanding Wilson McGunnegle, and the ram fleet of Col. Ellet, Jr., of the *Queen of the West,* the *Monarch,* the *Lancaster,* and the *Switzerland,* iron-shod, and especially constructed, as to draft and power, for operation by ramming. This ram fleet, like that of Montgomery, was independent of the navy, and not under command or obedient to the orders of naval officers. The combined fleets of the enemy numbered in all nine vessels, while that of Montgomery numbered eight vessels; but the inequality in number of guns was as eighty-four to fourteen, and, in the character and adaptability to fighting, the odds were also greatly in favor of the Federal fleet. To that disparity must also be added the *morale* and experience of educated naval and army officers, and the *esprit de corps* of both United States services as against the total want of both in Montgomery and the other Mississippi pilots who had been improvised into officers afloat, without any of the essential characteristics, except that of personal courage.

17

As the battle of Memphis was a fight more particularly between the ram fleets, its particulars are best derived from the commanders of those fleets. The movements of the United States ram fleet, given by Col. Ellet, Jr., were, that:

"Approaching Memphis, the gunboats were in advance. I had received no notice that a fight was expected, but was informed, on landing within eight miles of Memphis, that the enemy's gunboats had retreated down the river. My first information of the presence of the enemy was a shot which passed over my boat. I had four of my most powerful rams in the advance in any emergency. The others were towing the barges. On advancing to the attack I expected of course to be followed by the *Monarch*, the *Lancaster*, and the *Switzerland*. The *Monarch* came in gallantly. Some of the officers of the *Lancaster*, which now held the next place in the line, became excited and confused, but the engineers behaved well. The pilot erred in signals and ran the boat ashore and disabled her rudder. The captain of the *Switzerland* construed the general signal order to keep half a mile in the rear of the *Lancaster* to mean that he was to keep half a mile behind her in the engagement, and therefore failed to participate. Hence the whole brunt of the fight fell upon the *Queen* and the *Monarch*. Had either the *Queen* or the *Switzerland* followed as the *Monarch* did, the rebel gunboat *Van Dorn* would not have escaped, and my flag - ship would not have been disabled. Three of the rebel rams and gunboats which were struck by my two rams sank outright and were lost. The *Gen. Price* was but slightly injured, and I propose to add her to my fleet."

At daylight of the morning of June 6th, Montgomery moved up the river to engage the enemy—in ignorance of the presence of the combined fleets—while the gunboats were firing at long range. The United States ram fleet accepted the challenge, and, advancing ahead of the Federal gunboats, steamed rapidly to the front, and gallantly engaged the *Gen. Lovell*, which the *Queen of the West* struck with a crushing blow amidship, breaking through her timbers, and almost instantly filling her with water; she drifted and sunk on the Tennessee shore. The *Queen*, recovering from her shock with the *Lovell*, was rammed by the *Beauregard*, and so much injured that she, too, floated to the Arkansas shore. Boats from the shore were instantly pushed out to rescue the drowning crew, but received a heavy and well-directed fire from the sharp-shooters on the rams, by which many were killed and wounded. Flag-officer Davis, in his report, says, that while the rams were engaged, "the firing from our gunboats was continuous and well-directed. The *Gen. Beauregard* and the *Little Rebel* were struck in the boilers and blown up." The gunboats were too far off for accurate observation. The *Beauregard*, rushing at the United States ram *Monarch*, missed her object and ran into the *Price*, tearing off her wheel-house and disabling her so that she floated out of the fight and sunk on the Arkansas shore. The *Lovell* and the *Price*, thus destroyed, reduced Montgomery's fleet to five. The *Little Rebel* next came in for her *coup de grace*, by a heavy shell from the gunboats striking her near the water-line, and, exploding among her machinery, gave her pilot time only to turn her head to the shore, where the current drifted her, and she sank. Capt. Montgomery and Capt. Fowler escaping ashore, saved themselves and part of the crew in the swamps on the Arkansas side. The *Bragg* and the *Sumter* and the *Jeff. Thompson* continued the hopeless fight—backing down stream, followed by rams and gunboats. The *Van Dorn*, having a most valuable cargo of powder and other munitions of war, and seeing the hopelessness of the contest, steamed rapidly to Vicksburg, where she arrived in safety. The *Bragg* and the *Sumter*, though run ashore, were captured before they could be destroyed, and the *Jeff. Thompson* was blown up by her officers. Thus, six of the River Defence fleet were destroyed in its second battle with the enemy. No list of Confederate casualties is now obtainable. Capt. Cable, of the *Lovell*, perished, and Col. Ellet, of the United States ram fleet, died in a few days of wounds received in the battle.

Capt. J. Henry Hart, who commanded the steamer *Beauregard*, gives the following interesting account of the fight at Memphis:

"Our gunboat flotilla arrived at Memphis on the evening of the 5th of June, 1862, to await the arrival of the Federal fleet, which came down about nine o'clock of the same evening, and laid on 'Paddy's Hen and Chickens,' in sight of Memphis. On being informed of this, our commodore sent up a small tug, in charge of Capt. Bennett, as a picket. By some mismanagement she got aground on the foot of the island, and she could not be got off with her own power; consequently the torch was applied, and she was left to her fate in flames. Nothing more of importance happened during the night, but the general understanding with all the fleet was, that we would not make a stand.

"After daylight, on the morning of the 6th, we could see by the movements of the enemy that they were making preparations to come down, for the heavens were one solid cloud of black smoke. In the meantime we were not idle in making preparations to back out in the stream, which we did, one after another, until our whole fleet, eight in number, were drawn in line of battle. It was here we received the first intelligence that we were going to make a stand. The enemy was now in full view, coming down in line of battle. The following boats were sent up to draw the Federal gunboats off of the bar: *General M. Jeff. Thompson, Sumter, General Beauregard*, and *Colonel Lovell*, from the fact that they had sixty-four pound guns mounted on their bows. The fire was opened by the *Thompson*, but not until she had fired three rounds did the enemy make any reply. The fire on the Federal side was opened by the flagship *Benton*. The fight now became general. Brisk firing, from both sides was the order of the day. It was while the battle was raging with intense fury, between our rams and the Federal gunboats, that their rams made their appearance; first came the *Queen of the West*, which made a bee-line for the *Colonel Lovell*, which tried to back out of the way, but in so doing got in such a position as to show her opponent a broadside, when she ran into her and sunk her immediately, in water to her hurricane deck, in the channel of the river. Life-boats were immediately dispatched from the *Little Rebel*, to assist her crew in getting ashore. Before the *Queen of the West* could regain her position, the Confederate ram *Sumter* struck her in midships, sending her ashore, during the balance of the engagement. Next came the *Switzerland*, bearing down on the *Sumter*. The *Beauregard* next in turn singled out the *Switzerland* for her antagonist. The Federal ram, seeing her intention, drew off from the *Sumter*, and headed down on the *Beauregard;* they struck head on, but glanced, placing the *Switzerland hors de combat*, knocking down her bridge-tree, when she had to go ashore, where she threw out her sharpshooters as pickets.   Next came the Federal ram *Monarch*, in chase of the *Jeff. Thompson*, she at the same time rounding to, head up stream, followed by the *Monarch;* here the *General Price* was put under a heavy head of steam, to overtake the *Monarch*, which she did, striking her a heavy blow in the starboard quarter, driving in her hull, and rounding her to, after which she stopped to back around and give her another blow; but, unfortunately, the *Beauregard* had made a dash at the *Monarch*, and missed her object, and striking the *Price* on the port-side, completely disabling her.   During this, with only one wheel left, she managed to get ashore, but too late for the crew to make their escape; disabled as she was, the enemy kept up a constant fire into her; for humanity's sake the "stars and bars" were hauled down.   It was about this time the *Beauregard* got headed up again to meet another of her adversaries, when a shell was shot into her hull and burst, damaging her boilers and hull; killed one engineer, and wounding three others, and scalding three firemen.   She was unfit for duty, floated down the river about one-fourth of a mile, and sunk in twenty feet water, face to the enemy, and colors flying.   It was about this time the *Little Rebel* made a dash at one of the rams; but before she could reach her received a shot in her boilers, when she kept her course into the shore, where all but three made their escape.   In the meantime, the *Sumter* had been run ashore, and crew all escaped; also the *Thompson* was run ashore, and burned to the water's edge.   The *General Bragg* stood off and looked at the fight, likewise the *General Earl Van Dorn;* neither offering any assistance.   The *Bragg*, in attempting to round to, to make good her retreat, was run into by one of the Federal rams, which drove in her side.   The crew of the *Bragg* nearly all made their escape in yawls and life-boats.   The *Van Dorn*, handling much better than the *Bragg*, was fortunate in making good her escape.   Thus ended one of the hottest naval engagements ever fought in the Mississippi.

"The following is a list of the principal officers, as far as we can ascertain:

"*Earl Van Dorn*—Captain, Isaac Fulkerson; Purser, Charles Reynolds; First Officer, John W. Jordan; Second Officer, John Mardis; Chief Engineer, William Hurst; First Assistant Engineer, John Swift, William Camon and William Molloy.

" *General Sterling Price*—Captain, Thomas E. Henthorn; Purser, L. F. Delisdeimer; First Officer, N. J. Henthorn; Second Officer, George L. Richardson; Chief Engineer, William Brauden; First Assistant Engineers, William Orin, W. W. Hayden and Oscar Postall.

" *General Beauregard* — Captain, J. Henry Hart; Purser, J. C. Haynes; First Officer, R. D. Court; Second Officer, John Rawson; Chief Engineer, Joseph Swift; First Assistant, Edward Connolly; Pilot, J. Pope Altram.

" *General Bragg*—Captain, W. H. H. Leonard; Purser, William Riply; First and Second Officers, names unknown; Chief Engineer, John Porter; First Assistant Engineer, Henry Sisson; Pilot, James Russel.

"*Sumter*—Captain, Wallace W. Lamb; Purser, John Wilbanks; First Officer, Lemuel Murray; Second Officer, name unknown; Chief Engineer, Robert T. Patterson; First Assistant Engineer, John Ramsey; Pilots, Thad Siederburg and Moses Gray.

"*Little Rebel*—Captain, J. White Fowler; Purser, Charles Smedly; First Officer, James Wall; Second Officer, name unknown; Chief Engineer, Gus Mann; First Assistant Engineer, William Reeder; Pilots, Newton Pue and John Bernard.

" *General M. Jeff. Thompson*—Captain, John Burk; Purser, James Bissell; First Officer, Louis Camfield; Second Officer, Henry Moore; Chief Engineer, Thomas Mitchell; Pilots, Barney Arnold and Daniel Thomas.

" *General Lovell*—Captain, James C. Dellaney; Purser, Hardy; First Officer, Thomas Johnson; Pilot, William Cable.

"Commodore of the fleet, J. E. Montgomery.

"The Federal fleet consisted of sixteen mortar-boats, six rams, and eight gunboats, besides any number of tugs and transports."

Col. Ellet's dispatch to Secretary of War Stanton is as follows:

"OPPOSITE MEMPHIS, June 6th, *via* Cairo, June 8th.

" *To Hon. E. M. Stanton, Secretary of War:*

"The rebel gunboats made a stand early this morning opposite Memphis, and opened a vigorous fire upon our gunboats, which was returned with equal spirit. I ordered the *Queen*, my flag-ship, to pass between the gunboats and move down ahead of them upon the two rams of the enemy, which first boldly stood their ground.

"Lieut. Col. Ellet, in the *Monarch*, of which Capt. Dryden is First Master, followed gallantly. The rebel rams endeavored to back down stream, and then to turn and run, but the movement was fatal to them. The *Queen* struck one of them fairly, and for a few minutes was fast to the wreck. After separating, the rebel steamer sunk. My steamer, the *Queen*, was then herself struck by another rebel steamer and disabled, but, though damaged, can be repaired. A pistol-shot wound in the leg deprived me of the power to witness the remainder of the fight.

"The *Monarch* also passed ahead of our gunboats, and went most gallantly into action. She first struck the rebel boat that struck my flag-ship and sunk the rebel. She was then struck by one of the rebel rams, but not injured. She then pushed on and struck the *Beauregard* and burst open her side. Simultaneously, the *Beauregard* was struck in the boiler by a shot from one of our gunboats.

"The *Monarch* then pushed at the gunboat *Little Rebel*, the rebel flag-ship, and having but little headway pushed her before her, the rebel commodore and crew escaping. The *Monarch* then finding the *Beauregard* sinking, took her in tow until she sank in shoal water. Then, in compliance with the request of Commander Davis, Lieut. Col. Ellet dispatched the *Monarch* and the *Switzerland* in pursuit of the one remaining gunboat and some transports which had escaped the gunboats.

"Two of my rams have gone below.

"I cannot too much praise the conduct of the pilots and engineers and military guard of the *Monarch* and *Queen*, the brave conduct of Capt. Dryden, or the heroic bearing of Lieut. Col. Ellet. I will name all parties to you in a special report. I am myself the only person in my fleet who was disabled.

[Signed]   CHARLES ELLET,
" Col. Commanding Ram Fleet."

This dispatch was also sent to the Federal War Department:

"OPPOSITE MEMPHIS, June 6th, *via* Cairo, 8th.

"*Hon. Edwin M. Stanton, Secretary of War:*

"It is proper and due to the brave men on the *Queen* and the *Monarch* to say to you briefly that two of the rebel steamers were sunk outright and immediately by the shock of my two rams, one with a large amount of cotton, etc., on board was disabled by accidental collision with the *Queen*, and secured by her crew, after I was personally disabled.

"Another, which was also hit by a shot from the gunboats, was sunk by the *Monarch*, and towed to shoal water by that boat. Still another, also injured by the fire of our gunboats, was pushed in to the shore and secured by the *Monarch*. Of the gunboats I can only say that they bore themselves, as our navy always does, bravely and well.

[Signed]   CHAS. ELLET, JR.,
" Col. Commanding Ram Fleet."

This battle between the ram fleets on the Mississippi very nearly destroyed the River Defence expedition, and demonstrated the folly which conceived and executed a plan of defence expensive and inefficient, and which, intrusted to men incapable of commanding because unwilling to obey, was certain to meet with an early and ruinous defeat.

Neither the Navy Department nor any naval officer was at any time identified with this fleet, and, as whatever it accomplished belongs to those commanding it, so the responsibility for its failure, destruction and expense rest on the C. S. War Department.

The city of Memphis, being without defences of any kind, was surrendered to the Federal authorities, and the Mississippi from Cairo to Vicksburg was open to navigation by Federal gunboats; but its banks, infested with guerrilla bands, still rendered its use too hazardous for trade and business.[1]

---

[1] On the morning of the 6th of June, Brig. Gen. M. Jeff. Thompson and Capt. Montgomery were given by Gen. Beauregard joint command of the River Defence. It proved a very short and a very inefficient defence—for at 12:30 A. M. on the 6th, after receiving Gen. Beauregard's dispatch, Gen. Thompson reports, June 7th, that he "immediately wrote a note to the Commodore (Montgomery), asking what I should do to co-operate with him. He requested two companies of artillery to be sent aboard at daybreak (all of my men were at the depot awaiting transportation to Grenada). I at once ordered the companies to hold themselves in readiness. At the dawn of day I was awakened with the information that the enemy were actually in sight of Memphis. I hurried on board to consult with Montgomery. He instructed me to hurry my men to Fort Pickering Landing, and sent a tug to bring them up to the gunboats, which were advancing to attack the enemy. I hastened my men to the place indicated, but before we reached it our boats had been either destroyed or driven below Fort Pickering, and I marched back to the depot to come to this place (Grenada) to await orders.

"I saw a large portion of the engagement from the river bank, and am so sorry to say that in my opinion many of our men were handled badly, as the plan of battle was very faulty. The enemy's rams (Col. Ellet's fleet) did most of the execution, and were handled more adroitly than ours; I think, however, entirely owing to the fact that the guns and sharp-shooters of the enemy were constantly employed, while we were almost without either. The *Colonel Lovell* was so injured that she sank in the middle of the river; her captain, Jas. Delancy, and a number of others, swam ashore. The *Beauregard* and *Price* were running at the *Monarch* (Yankee) from opposite sides, when the *Monarch* passed from between them, and the *Beauregard* ran into the *Price*, knocking off her wheel-house, and entirely disabling her. Both were run to the Arkansas shore and abandoned. The *Little Rebel*, commodore's flag-boat, was run ashore and abandoned after she had been completely riddled, and I am satisfied the commodore was killed. The battle continued down the river, out of sight of Memphis, and it is reported that only two of our boats, the *Bragg* and *Van Dorn*, escaped."

CAPTAIN GEORGE N. HOLLINS,
CONFEDERATE STATES NAVY.

COMMANDER CHARLES F. McINTOSH, C. S. N.

CHAPTER XII.

BUILDING A NAVY AT NEW ORLEANS.

AMONG the earliest acts of the C. S. Navy Department, March 17th, 1861, for the increase of the navy, was the appointment of a commission, consisting of Commander L. Rousseau, Commander E. Farrand, and Lieut. Robert T. Chapman, to purchase and contract for building the ten gunboats authorized by Acts of Congress, March 15th and August 19th, 1861, which were to be ship-rigged propellers of 1,000 tons burden, capable of carrying at least one ten-inch and four eight-inch guns. These vessels were to be of light draft and great speed. The commission entered upon its duties early in April, 1861, at New Orleans, and at Algiers opposite, where there were several ship-yards which had been formerly largely engaged in building and repairing river craft of all descriptions; but no war vessel had ever been built at New Orleans.

The commission did not find at New Orleans one vessel suitable for war purposes, but upon instructions from the Secretary it examined and purchased the *Habanna* and the *Marquis de la Habanna*, the former becoming the *Sumter* and the latter the *McRae*. Instructions for building vessels were given to Commander Rousseau, at New Orleans, on March 27th, and upon his report, after examination on April 22d, the steam-propeller *Florida* was purchased and fitted up for service on the lakes. An ineffectual effort was made to purchase a steamer offered for sale by Hollingsworth & Co., of Wilmington, Del., but the vessel failed to reach New Orleans. The *Star of the West*, captured in Texas, was used as a receiving-ship, as she was not adapted to war purposes. Commander Rousseau, after a thorough examination of all the facilities at New Orleans for rolling iron plates, ascertained and reported that it was not possible to roll plates from 2½ to 5 inches in thickness in any shop in New Orleans. His examination of the steamer *Miramon* was not favorable; but on the 9th of May he purchased the steamer *Yankee*, which was afterwards called the *Jackson*, and fitted her out, and with the *McRae* sent them up the river to Columbus, Ky. In Federal accounts of up-river operations this vessel is always styled the *Yankee*.

On the 21st of May, 1861, Congress enacted a law, amending the tenth section of the act, recognizing a state of war with the United States; so that, in addition to the bounty therein mentioned, the government of the Confederate States would pay to the cruisers of any private armed vessel commissioned under said act twenty per cent. on the value of such vessel belonging to the enemy as may be destroyed by such private armed vessel. Under that act, the ram *Manassas* was built at New Orleans by private subscription; but after Commodore Hollins' successful clearing of the enemy's fleet from the mouth of the Mississippi River, on the 12th of October, 1861, the *Manassas* was purchased by the C. S. government.

THE "MANASSAS."

The *Manassas* was constructed out of the *Enoch Train*, built in Boston, in 1855, by J. O. Curtis. Her correct dimensions were: Length on deck, 128 feet; breadth of beam, 26 feet; depth of hold, 12 feet 6 inches; depth of hold to spar deck, 12 feet 6 inches; draft of water, when loaded, 11 feet; 387 tons burden. Her frame, when built, was of white oak, and cross-fastened with iron and tree-nails. Her engine was of the inclined description, with two cylinders 36 inches in diameter, and a stroke of piston of 2 feet 8 inches. She was a propeller. Her machinery was constructed by Harrison Loring, of Boston; Capt. John A. Stephenson, a commission merchant of New Orleans, undertook the conversion of the *Enoch Train*. She was built up with massive beams, seventeen inches in thickness, making a solid bow of twenty feet, and fastening them in the most substantial manner. Over this impenetrable mass was a complete covering of iron plates, riveted together, and fitted in such a way as to render her bomb-proof. Her only entrance was through a trap-door in her back, and her port cover sprang back as the gun was withdrawn. Her shape above water was nearly that of half a sharply pointed egg - shell, so that a shot would glance from her no matter where it struck. Her back was formed of twelve-inch oak, covered with one-and-a-half-inch bar-iron. She had two chimneys so arranged as to slide down in time of action. The pilot-house was in the stern of the boat. She was worked by a powerful propeller, but could not stem a strong current. She carried only one gun, a sixty-eight-pounder, in her bow. To prevent boarding, the engine was provided with pumps for ejecting steam and scalding water from the boiler over the whole surface. Such was the craft which in the earliest days of the war the enterprising people of New Orleans, without aid from city, State or Confederacy, contrived, and which proved not only, as Capt. Hollins said, the "most troublesome vessel of them all" at the fight at the passage of the forts, but which cleared the river in October, 1861, of the blockading fleet.

In the interval between March 17th, 1861, and February 1st, 1862, the utmost efforts of the Navy Department were made to put afloat a naval force competent to meet that being prepared at St. Louis by the United States. To that end, river boats were purchased and converted, not into gunboats, but into steamboats with guns on them. They were side-wheel steamboats of light draft, and though substantially built for commercial uses, were too frail to withstand the effect of heavy ordnance. They had no rails and no breast-works, but were pierced for eight or nine guns. Their armament was old navy smooth-bore forty-two-pounders, with a rifle thirty-two-pounder to each boat.

The movements of the enemy's fleet down the river compelled Commodore Hollins, in December, 1861, to take his improvised fleet of steamboats up the river. This was composed of the *General Polk*, the *Ivy*, the *Livingston*, the *Maurepas*, the *McRae* and the *Manassas*, which last was, as we have stated, sheathed with one and one-half inches of iron. In January and February, 1862, the *Bienville, Ponchartrain* and *Carondelet* were completed, all of which were also converted river boats. The *Livingston*, built by Hughes & Co., under contract with the Secretary of the Navy, had more of the pretensions of a gunboat than any of the others; she was completed on the keel of a ferry or tow-boat, laid before hostilities began, and was more substantially constructed than her consorts.

The floating batteries *New Orleans* and *Memphis*, the gunboats *Mobile* and the *Leger*, in Berwick's Bay, the *St. Mary's* and the *Calhoun*, with twenty-six fire-boats, were all prepared, and, as far as they were capable of being adapted to war purposes, were completed in less than nine months at New Orleans alone.

The character and strength of the enemy's fleet on the upper and lower Mississippi having been fully reported to the Confederate Navy Department, a more effective means of defending the river from these threatened attacks was submitted to and approved by Capts. Ingraham and Collins, Lieut. Brooke, and Naval Constructor Pierce, and for that purpose $800,000 was appropriated by the Act of Congress of July 30th, 1861.

The construction of the *Louisiana* by E. C. Murray was begun in New Orleans on October 15th, 1861. The blockade of the river having begun prior to that date, the timber had to be procured from Lake Ponchartrain and from the forests along the New Orleans and Jackson Railroad. There was used in her construction 1,700,000 feet. The engines of the steamer *Ingomar*

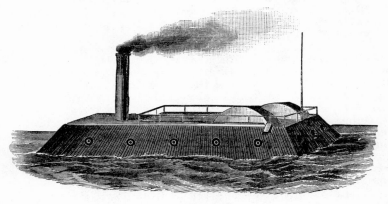

THE "LOUISIANA."

were bought and transferred to the *Louisiana*, but it required two months for their removal by Leeds & Co. The contractor used 500 tons of railroad iron in the vessel. Delays of construction were frequent, in consequence of strikes among the hands for higher wages, from having to wait for iron, and from alteration in the port-holes. Mr. Murray, the contractor, had been a practical ship-builder for twenty years, and had built over 120 boats—steamers and sailing-vessels; but with all possible diligence on his part, it was not within his power to complete the boat earlier than thirty days before the fall of New Orleans. It was a practical impossibility to have completed the boat earlier than she was launched, while other vessels were building at New Orleans, and the blockade of the river prevented the receipt of timber and iron from abroad. The gunboat *Livingston* was under construction at that time in the yard of John Hughes & Co., but was not iron-shielded. The *Bienville* and *Carondelet*—the former built by Hughes & Co., and the latter by Naval Constructor Sidney D. Porter—were also being at this time built in New Orleans yards. The *Livingston* was completed February 1st, 1862, the *Bienville* April 5th, 1862, and the *Carondelet* March 16th, 1862, the first in seven months, the second in six months; and in November, 1861, Mr. Mallory had at New Orleans, under construction, a fleet consisting of the floating battery *New Orleans*, 20 guns, the floating battery *Memphis*, 18 guns; the gunboat (incomplete) to carry 6 guns; the gunboat *Grotesque*, afterwards the *Maurepas*, 6 guns; the *Lizzie Simmons*, afterwards the *Ponchartrain*, 6 guns; the *Bienville* and *Carondelet* (incomplete) each to carry 6 guns; the *Pickens* and the *Morgan*, each 3 guns, and the two iron-clads, the *Louisiana* and the *Mississippi*, each, when complete, to mount 16 guns. When the Federal fleet reached New Orleans, Capt. Porter, U. S. N., wrote to Senator Grimes, of Iowa, that of the naval vessels constructed at New Orleans, "the best one I saw floating by me was a dry dock turned into a floating battery, mounting 16 guns, and the entire engine, which was to propel it, hermetically sealed by a thick iron turret against shot. She was sunk, but floated down to Southwest Pass, and is now aground on the bar and can be easily raised."

The failure to complete at New Orleans the iron-clad steamer *Mississippi* was a matter of much discussion and of crimination against the Navy Department. Of that vessel, Commodore Hollins stated before the joint committee that "she was the greatest vessel in the world. I don't suppose there was ever such a vessel built." Of the same tenor was the testimony of Capt. Sinclair, C. S. N.: "She was entirely a new conception, and a remarkably fine vessel, and very formidable, in my opinion. I am satisfied that she could have, as I stated before, kept that river clear against the blockade. That vessel, as I have said, was entirely a new conception. She was a ship that was most creditable to the country, as far as my judgment goes." Capt. Porter, U. S. N., in his letter of May 6th, 1861, to Senator Grimes, bore testimony to the strength of the *Mississippi*, by saying:

"In New Orleans our naval officers found the most splendid specimen of a floating battery the world has ever seen (a sea-going affair, and had she been finished and succeeded in getting to sea, the whole American navy would have been destroyed. She was 6,000 tons, 270 feet long, 60 feet beam; had four engines, three propellers, four inches (and in some places more) of iron, and would steam eleven knots an hour. She cost Mr. Mallory & Co. $2,000,000."

The projectors of the *Mississippi* were the Messrs. Nelson and Asa F. Tift. These gentlemen were brothers, the former a citizen of Georgia, and the latter a citizen of Florida, who had been a member of the Convention of that State which passed the Ordinance of Secession, which Mr.

Tift signed, and for this his property in that State, at Key West, had been seized by the authorities of the United States, and Mr. Tift removed to Georgia, to the estate of his brother. These unimportant facts are stated because super-servicable Confederates, like the Hon. Henry S. Foote, of Mississippi, who abandoned the Confederacy in the hour of its supreme trial, and made his individual peace with Mr. Lincoln, endeavored by insinuation and innuendo to impeach the loyalty of the Messrs. Tift to the Confederate cause.

At the breaking out of the war, Mr. N. Tift considered that the weakest point of the Confederacy, as well as the strongest point of the United States, was on the water, where the greatest deficiency of the Confederacy existed, and where the supreme necessity existed for maintaining, at least, the ability to hold communication with foreign nations, and there the enemy possessed the means and the skill of inflicting the most serious injury to our means of defence both on water and land. To contribute all that was in his power towards the public defence, he set his mind to considering the best means of attack and defence which the Confederates could make, in their then situation of almost utter destitution of mechanics skilled in naval architecture, as well as of the means of building the ships. To supply necessities, and overcome obstacles, Mr. Tift saw that it was necessary to work the abundant pine timber into vessels by the ordinary house-carpenter. And that, if war-vessels made of green pine timber could be shielded with iron, the Confederate States would have taken a very important step in equalizing the conditions of war with the United States. To that end he applied his mind, and perfected the model of the *Mississippi.* Having submitted his design to the judgment of his brother, they both went to Richmond, where the model, which had been examined and approved in Savannah by Commander Tatnall, and in Charleston by prominent naval officers, was submitted to the examination of Mr. Mallory. The Messrs. Tift asked no compensation for their model, did not seek fortune by contracting to build the ship, but tendered their services to the government *without compensation* to superintend the building of the vessel.

The model of the *Mississippi* was the adaptation of straight timber to her construction, in a new and simple form, upon which the ordinary house-carpenter could work, and by which strength and efficiency could be obtained, rather than the old lines of curved frames, crooks and knees, peculiar to the old style of naval architecture. The model avoided the necessity of employing skilled ship-carpenters and joiners, of which there were very few in any of the ports of the Confederate States. All surfaces of the *Mississippi* were flat, or in straight lines, except the four corners which connected the two ends of the ship with her sides. There was to be no frame;

but the work was solid for the required thickness, which was three feet, and to be covered with three-inch iron plates. The model first submitted to the Navy Department was during construction lengthened in the middle division 20 feet, by which two sets of 8 boilers, each 42 inches in diameter, and 30 feet long, gave the necessary steam to work 3 engines 36 inches in diameter, 2 feet stroke shelf valves, with 3 propellers 11 feet in diameter, on wrought-iron shafts.

The *Mississippi* was 260 feet long, 58 feet extreme breadth, 15 feet depth of hold, about the same size as the U. S. steamers *Colorado* and *Roanoke*. The Algerine *News Boy*, of December 30th, gives the following items:

"The bottom of this gunboat is twenty-two inches thick, in solid planks, solidly bolted and calked, and its walls two feet solid in thickness, with numerous thick keelsons to brace it.

"The hold will be fourteen feet in depth, and on its summit will be placed the battery, composed of several heavy rifled and shell guns, all under casemates.

"Above this is a cupola, which will contain various conveniences, and be surmounted with another battery, and a shooting-gallery for sharp-shooters.

"The vessel is to be strengthened by iron bolts through and through, and be plated over with three-inch iron. She will be drawn by three propellers, worked by powerful engines. Another such a gunboat will immediately follow this one. Near by is another just begun, still larger, which will combine the breadth of the floating battery with some of the advantages of a self-propelled boat."

Much difficulty was experienced in procuring a first-class designer, and after trying several who failed to satisfy the projectors of the ship, E. M. Ivens and Chief Engineer Warner completed the designs, and Acting Naval Constructor Pierce was appointed superintendent; and on September, 25th, 1861, the preparation of the ship-yard was commenced on the east side of the river, immediately above the corporate limits of the city, and within the corporate lines of Jefferson City, on the property of Mr. Millandon, who tendered its use without charge. There Constructor Pierce commenced his preparations for building on the 28th of September. In thirty days he made the body, and put the floors in the ship; in two months the sides had risen three feet high; in 110 days the wood-work was completed. This extraordinary dispatch was owing to the peculiar plan of construction.

Before the Investigating Committee of the Confederate Congress, E. C. Murray, a practical ship-builder of twenty years and the contractor for building the *Louisiana*, testified that:

"I think the vessel was built in less time than any vessel of her tonnage and character, and requiring the same amount of work and materials, on this continent. That vessel required no less than 10,000,-000 feet of lumber, and, I suppose, about 1,000 tons of iron, including the false works, blockways, etc. I do not think that amount of materials were ever put together on this continent within the time occupied in her construction. I knew many of our naval vessels requiring much less material than were employed in the *Mississippi*, that took about six or twelve months in their construction. She was built with rapidity, and had at all times as many men at work upon her as could work to advantage. She had, in fact, many times more men at work upon her than could conveniently work. They worked on nights and Sundays upon her, as I did upon the *Louisiana*, at least for a large portion of the time."

Contracts for every part of the steam machinery were made immediately with the Messrs. Jackson & Co., of the Patterson Iron Works, at New Orleans, to be completed in ninety days. There was not a foundry and hammer in the Confederacy capable of making the wrought-iron shafts for the vessel. Three of these shafts were required; that for the middle to be fifty feet long, and those on the sides each forty feet long, and all nine inches in diameter. The middle shaft was fitted up at the Tredegar Works in Richmond and did not reach New Orleans until April 9th, at which time one of the side-shafts was at Leeds & Co.'s, and the third shaft was just forged and would not be ready for nine or ten days. New Orleans fell on April 24th; Capt. Whittle was informed that the *Mississippi* would be ready for her guns on April 23d, and ready for service on the 1st of May; the plating was going on as fast as possible, but it would require from twelve to fourteen days to completely shield the ship with iron.

It was not the purpose of the projectors to launch the ship until the shafts and propellers had been put in, but Capt. Mitchell and Capt. Sinclair having given their opinion that the enemy might pass the forts at any moment, the *Mississippi* was launched on the 19th of April with her iron on below the surface of the gun-decks, and the remaining iron was being rapidly put on; the furnace work was completed and all the machinery on board; the wood-work was entirely done, and two weeks of more time would have seen the *Mississippi* fully completed, equipped and commissioned.

When the Federal fleet passed the forts, the *Mississippi* in her unfinished state could neither fight nor run away, and Commander Sinclair, who was in charge of her, made every effort to obtain boats to tow the vessel up the river. To that end he employed the *St. Charles* and the *Peytona*, which, after an unaccountable delay of nearly twelve hours, was unable to move the ship up stream on account of the current, there being a freshet at the time which made the current even stronger than usual. After the whole night spent in fruitlessly trying to move the ship up stream, and finding that they were losing ground and floating down towards the approaching enemy, the *Mississippi* was committed to the flames and burned to the water's edge, and sunk in the river.

Commander Arthur Sinclair testified before the Court of Inquiry, that

"The *Mississippi* might doubtless have been launched and towed up the river many days previous to the enemy's passing the forts, and there finally completed; but her completion would have been greatly retarded, as all the workshops, material, workmen—in fact, the whole naval establishment—would have had to be transferred from New Orleans to the place of transfer, and there was no place of safety above, that I know of, short of Fort Pillow, and all above on the river was then menaced by the enemy. Her completion was a momentous affair, and, therefore, the work was prosecuted up to the last moment with all the energy in our power. I received no orders from the commander of the station, Commander Whittle, under whose orders I was, or from the Navy Department, to remove her until the morning of April 24th, the day upon which the enemy passed the forts. On that day Commander Whittle sent for and informed me that the enemy had passed the batteries, and were coming up, at the same time directing me to take the ship up the river, if possible, to some place of safety, but not to let her fall into the hands of the enemy. I immediately sent orders to the steamers engaged by the Messrs. Tift to proceed at once up to the ship-yard for the purpose of taking the ship in tow. The officers sent by me upon this duty returned, and informed me that the steamers referred to had been detained by order of Gen. Lovell. I called myself upon Col. Lovell, the general being out of his office upon business, and obtained from him the release of two of the three which were engaged for this purpose, the *Peytona* and the *St. Charles*. Although directed to proceed at once, they did not reach the ship-yard until late in the evening. The captains of these boats showed every disposition—in fact, determination—to thwart me in my wishes, and, to accomplish my ends, I had, with my own officers, to lash and secure them alongside, and furnished one of them, the steamer *St. Charles*, with an engineer, as the captain said he had only one. I finally succeeded in getting off, but found, after many hours of hard tugging against a powerful current, that I could not succeed. Assistance was promised me by Col. Baggs (or Biggs) of the Safety Committee, but none was received. Still unwilling to give up the ship, I went myself back to the city in the *Peytona*, and urged the aid of the steamers, but in vain. Every variety of excuse was offered by their captains, and no disposition manifested to help me; in fact, a fixed determination not to move in the matter. While thus negotiating, the enemy hove in sight, and I at once started back for the ship, four miles above, intending to fire her; but the officer in charge, Lieut. Waddell, anticipated me, and applied the torch. After remaining in the stream until the ship was nearly consumed, I held a council of war with my officers, and it was determined to return to the city and offer our services to Gen. Lovell. I was on my way back when I met Lieut. McCorkle, of the navy, who informed me that the enemy were off Canal Street, and that Gen. Lovell had marched his troops out. I then proceeded up the river with my officers to Vicksburg. I will also state that the assistance of several steamers, which passed up the river, while engaged in towing the *Mississippi*, was asked and refused. I also engaged the services of navy workmen to accompany me up in the ship to try and finish her, and put on board, while awaiting the arrival of the steamers, much of the material for her completion. Some was afterwards put aboard the steamer *St. Charles* before firing the ship, and taken up to Vicksburg and saved

"The *Mississippi* was launched on Saturday, April 19th, and burned the Friday following. In this connection, I would state that on my arrival at New Orleans there was a great desire upon the part of many persons expressed that the ship should be launched. The Tifts objected, and I agreed with them that to launch her in her then condition would cause much delay in shipping her propellers, and involve the expense of building the box or dry dock for that purpose, of which I have already spoken; but, finding the attack about to be commenced, I recommended her being launched to her builders, the Tifts, in which Commander Mitchell joined me: the suggestion was heeded, but not until many days after, for reasons which they assigned; * * * if the *Mississippi* had been completed, and with her armament and men on board, she alone could have held the river against the entire Federal fleet coming up from below; and she would have been the most formidable ship that I ever knew or heard of—very creditable to her projectors, builders and country."

Admiral Porter remarks in his Naval History, that if New Orleans had " been left three months longer to perfect its defences and finish its work of offence, our wooden fleet would have been driven North, and the entire Southern coast would have been sealed against us. The blockade would have been raised, and the independence of the South recognized by the powers of Europe "; that "truly the Queen City of the South was doing her share of building rams to annihilate our navy and commerce, but where were our rams that should have been built by the North, which boasted of its great skill and resources ? These should have been ready to sally out within three months after the war began, to drive the *Louisiana, Manassas, Mississippi, Tennessee, Arkansas, Albemarle* and others back to their holes, or crush them like so many eggshells." The *Mississippi* was raised by the Federal authorities, and sent to Brooklyn navy-yard.

Admiral Farragut's experience of the Confederate gunboats constructed out of frail river craft was sufficient for him to say that " the rebel gunboats cannot stand before ours; but what they dignify by the name of iron-clad rams is an article entirely different, and, had they succeeded in getting any one of those on the Mississippi finished before our arrival, it would have proved a most formidable adversary "; and that

" We have destroyed, or made the enemy destroy, three of the most formidable rams in the country. Arthur Sinclair declared that the *Mississippi* (ram) which he was to command was far superior to the *Merrimac.* But we were too quick for them. Her machinery was not in working order, and when I sent after her they set her on fire, and she floated past us, formidable even in her expiring flames. Mitchell commanded the other as flag-officer. Poor Charlie McIntosh was her captain, and is now going on shore in a dreadful condition. It is not thought he will live, but he has a good constitution, and that will do a great deal for him.

" Their fleet has suffered very much in this affair, both in reputation and in vessels. We destroyed them all, some fourteen or fifteen, and many lives were lost."

While this work of building ships and converting old steamboats into vessels - of - war was going on, there were naval expeditions undertaken from New Orleans, which served to keep alive the spirit of naval enterprise and to teach those lessons which can only be learned in time of war.

While the *McRae* was being fitted out, her officers were impatient to be about some duty other than that which held them down in New Orleans. Capt. Higgins, formerly of the U. S. navy, but at that time acting as aid to Gen. Twiggs, undertook to capture the launches of the enemy prowling and marauding in the Mississippi Sound; and obtaining volunteers from Lieut. Thomas B. Huger, of the *McRae,* started with two lake steamers, armed with one thirty-two pounder, one eight-inch gun, and two howitzers. The steamer *Oregon*, commanded by Capt. A. L. Myers, and the steamer *Swaim*, by Lieut. A. F. Warley, C. S. N., proceeding to Bay St. Louis, and filling bags with sand, they left the bay at nine o'clock on July 6th for the cruising-ground of the enemy, the *Swaim* taking the mainland or side passage, and the *Oregon* the outside, and proceeded to Ship Island Pass.

Finding no enemy in sight, the *Oregon* proceeded to sea from Ship Island, and soon saw two vessels and gave chase. They proved to be two Confederate fishing-smacks. The *Oregon* then returned to Ship Island, and Capt. Higgins, who was in command of the expedition, deemed it advisable to take possession of Ship Island. Accordingly he signalled the *Swaim* to come to and go alongside of the island. The *Oregon* then came alongside the *Swaim*, and both proceeded to disembark the men and munitions of war, provisions, etc. After the disembarkation the guns on the boats were put in battery, and protected by sand-bags.

The *Swaim* was left at the island while the *Oregon* proceeded to New Orleans, *via* Pass Christian, for the purpose of sending a dispatch to Gen. Twiggs to send forward reinforcements of ammunition and men. There she was ordered to take on board guns, gun-carriages, and munitions to reinforce Ship Island—Major Twiggs, and Capt. Higgins and Major Smith, using every possible effort to get everything in readiness. The steamer *Grey Cloud* was also taken into requisition, and was loaded and got underway, also well armed. The *Oregon* followed the same night with provisions, and proceeded directly to Ship Island.

On Tuesday morning, when within eight miles of the fort on Ship Island, Capt. Myers saw a large U. S. steamer and a tender lying off about two miles outside the island. At this moment the troops at the sand batteries opened fire on the steamer, which was immediately returned, and the battle commenced in good earnest. The *Grey Cloud* coming up slowly, the *Oregon* took off her ammunition and proceeded at once to the scene of action, Major Smith directing the *Grey Cloud* to follow at a safe distance.

Having arrived at the island, Capt. Myers proceeded at once in his yawl, with Major Smith, with a load of shell and powder, being received with cheers by Capt. Thom, of the C. S. marines, and the sailors and soldiers, who at once carried the supplies to the batteries. The enemy had fired some thirty odd rounds of shell and round shot, which sank in the sand, and were used by our sailors in returning fire. The explosion of the enemy's shells did no other damage than slightly to injure one man in the leg.

The steamers immediately commenced landing their guns and provisions, during which time the enemy again opened

18

fire, the shot falling short, but being returned with great effect. It is supposed that the attacking steamer, the *Massachusetts*, was hulled three times, and a shell was seen to explode over her decks, which, it was supposed, did some damage, as she immediately hauled off and put for the Chandeleur Islands, a distance of twelve miles.

After taking possession of the island, Capt. Higgins detailed the following officers, with the marines and sailors, to hold and defend it: Lieut. Warley, commanding; Lieut. R. T. Thom, of the marines; Surgeon Lynah and the midshipmen. After the enemy had retired, the steamer *Swain* arrived with Lieut. Col. H. W. Allen, of the Fourth Regiment, from Mississippi City, with three companies, who set to work fortifying the island.

The proclamation of blockade, issued by Mr. Lincoln on the 19th of April, 1861, was put in force for the Mississippi River in June following, when the *Powhatan*, Lieut. D. D. Porter, took station off the Southwest Pass; and the *Brooklyn*, Commander Charles Poor, off Pass à l'Outre. But the escape of the *Sumter* from the latter pass soon called the attention of the U. S. naval authorities to the necessity of a closer watch over the many exits from New Orleans, and suggested the holding of the "head of the passes" by a naval force. This point, where the vast volume of the waters of the Mississippi divides into three great outlets to the ocean, is distant sixteen miles by the Southwest Pass, and fourteen miles by Pass à l'Outre, from the bar. The river at the "head of the passes" broadens into a bay two miles wide, and from the telegraph station to the point of firm land, between Southwest and South Passes, the distance is also two miles—so that there is wide and deep water at the head—ample to float a fleet, and for naval manœuvres. To hold the "head of the passes" the Federal authorities attempted to erect a battery on the point of firm ground at the junction of the Southwest and South Passes, but the movements of Captain Hollins, about to be related, broke up the battery before it was more than marked out. In that deep and broad water, the Federal squadron, consisting of the screw-steamer *Richmond*, twenty-two nine-inch guns, Capt. John Pope; the *Vincennes*, sloop-of-war, ten guns, Commander Robert Handy; the sloop *Preble*, eleven guns, Commander Henry French, and the screw-steamer *Water Witch*, four guns, Lieut. Francis Winslow, arrived on the 12th of October, 1861. The squadron mounted forty-seven guns, and, properly handled and commanded, could have successfully met and destroyed the little Confederate fleet which Capt. George N. Hollins had improvised. The ships of Hollins' fleet were the *McRae*, whose defective machinery had prevented her from following the *Sumter* to sea, and changed her destination from a cruiser to a River Defence craft, was at that time commanded by Lieut. Com.

Joseph Fry, who after the war commanded the *Virginius*, and met so sad a death in Cuba. The *Ivy*, the *Tuscarora*, the *Calhoun*, the *Jackson*, and the ram *Manassas*, under Lieut. Warley, and the unarmed tow-boat *Watson*, under Lieut. Averett—the whole under command of Capt. Hollins.

In the early morn of the 13th of October, the U. S. S. *Richmond* lay at anchor taking in coal from a schooner alongside. The night was intensely dark, and it was almost impossible to see twenty yards ahead. The *Manassas* put on a heavy head of steam and dashed on in the direction where it was thought the enemy were lying. Suddenly a large ship was discovered only a length ahead, and, before Lieut. Warley could fire the signal-rocket into her they went together with an awful crash! An appalling shriek was heard on board of the *Richmond*, or the schooner, as the ram crushed into the *Richmond*, and broke loose the schooner, the latter having acted as a cushion, and breaking somewhat the force·of the ram's blow. Immediately, the *Richmond* fired a rocket, beat to quarter, and poured a shower of iron hail on the dark waters and into the still darker air. Though the force of the *Manassas*' blow broke in the side of the *Richmond*, it was not without injury to her own machinery. This was most inopportune and perilous; and the *Richmond*, soon observing that something was wrong, began playing upon her with all the power of her guns. Lieut. Warley found that only one engine would work, and with that he began working his way out of reach towards shore; but the shot fell thick and fast around, and upon the "old turtle," and her fate seemed hanging on a hair, when the brave little *Tuscarora* and the *Watson*[1] came up with five barges on fire, and soon cut them adrift on the stream. A ram and a fire-raft were too much for Capt. Pope's nerves, and signalling "danger" with a red light, he ordered the *Preble* and the *Vincennes* to proceed down the Southwest Pass, which they did, not standing on the order of their going. His official report says:

"At this time three large fire-rafts, stretching across the river, were rapidly nearing us, while several larger steamers and a bark-rigged propeller were seen astern of them. The squadron proceeded down the river in the following order: First, the *Preble;* second, the *Vincennes;* third, the *Richmond;* fourth, the *Water Witch;* with the prize schooner *Frolic* in tow. When abreast of the pilot settlement, the pilot informed me that he did not consider it safe to venture to turn this ship in the river, but that he believed he could pass over the bar. I accordingly attempted to pass over the bar with the squadron, but in the passage the *Vincennes*

---

[1] "The *Watson* did not run aground as has been stated, did not suffer any mishap, made no blunder, had no confusion, and made so little noise as she steamed to her position 'to turn loose her fire-boats on the enemy's ships,' that the Confederate fleet above her in the river supposed she had been disabled and was drifting helplessly between the flames of her own fire-boats—one on either side—and under the shot and shells of the enemy's ships into their midst. The expedition was a complete success so far as opening the way to the sea from New Orleans was its object, but the officers of the *McRae* were greatly disappointed, when it was discovered that her machinery was so defective as, in the judgment of Flag-officer Hollins, to render the steamer unfit for sea service.—*Extract from private letter of Lieut. Averett.*

and *Richmond* grounded, while the *Preble* went over clear. This occurred about eight o'clock, and the enemy, who were now down the river with the fire steamers, commenced firing at us, while we returned the fire from our port battery and rifled gun on the poop—our shot, however, falling short of the enemy, while their shell burst on all sides of us, and several passed directly over the ship."

Capt. Hollins did not know what had been the result of the firing, neither did the rest of the officers. It was too dark to make observations, and he did not wish to risk signals. So daylight was waited for impatiently. It came at last, and presented the following picture: The enemy, some miles down, heeling it for the open sea by way of the Southwest Pass. The *Manassas* close in shore, among the willows, concealed as well as possible; the *Tuscarora* aground on the bank, and the *Watson* not far off. The *Tuscarora* was soon pulled off by the rest, and the fleet commenced a pursuit of the retreating enemy. They soon came within range, and a heavy cannonade began. The *Richmond* drew up on the outside, and the other vessels of the enemy soon got aground, but near by, but were in a great measure protected by the *Richmond's* guns.

The fight ended not with the return of light, for Pope says:

"At half-past nine Commander Handy, of the *Vincennes*, mistaking my signal to the ships outside the bar to get underway for a signal to him to abandon his ship, came on board the *Richmond* with all his officers and a large number of the crew, the remainder having gone on board the *Water Witch*. Capt. Handy before leaving his ship had placed a lighted slow match at the magazine. Having waited a reasonable time for an explosion, I directed Commander Handy to return to his ship with his crew, to start his water, and, if necessary, at his own request, to throw overboard his small guns for the purpose of lightening his ship, and to carry out his kedge with a cable to heave-off by. At 10 A. M. the enemy ceased firing and withdrew up the river. During the engagement a shell entered our quarter port, and one of the boats was stove by another shell."

Cotemporaneous, but not official, accounts report Handy as appearing on the deck of the *Richmond* with the large flag of the United States wrapped in folds around his person, [1] and reporting that he had put a slow match to the magazine of the *Vincennes*. The *Manassas* drew off from the collision with the *Richmond* without trouble, though she undoubtedly twisted her prow badly when swayed to one side by the current, for it was found broken and bent to one side. The balls which struck her bounded off without effecting any damage, except in one case, when a ball hit on the bluff of the bow and made an ugly, though not serious, dent in the iron.

In the actual fight, the other Confederate vessels took no part—their presence, however, and the fire-rafts added to the enemy's demoralization, and they shared in the artillery duel

[1] Porter's *Naval History* and Soley's *Blockade*.

at long range. The Confederates took great credit for this gallant dash at the enemy; but it may well be asked, why, after having done so much, they did not do more? A demoralized and retreating enemy, aground, and scrambling to get over the bar, offered the opportunity of winning the fruits of victory by following up the blow. All day Friday the ships lay fast aground, and offered a fair opportunity to the victorious Confederates, but they had steamed back to New Orleans. A letter from on board the *Richmond* says: "On Saturday we were glad to see the *McClellan* coming in from sea with two rifled Parrott guns for us. She made fast to us, and before midnight we had the steamer *South Carolina* at anchor near us. On Sunday the two steamers succeeding in towing our ship and the *Vincennes* off the bar, and here we are, all afloat, and ready for any emergency."

No Confederate report, except newspaper accounts, of this very gallant little affair is extant, if any was ever made. But it is to be taken for granted that good and sufficient reasons moved so gallant a sailor as Capt. Hollins to abandon the scene of action at the time he did. There were many half-won victories by the Confederates in the war, both on land and water, of which history can give no explanation—and this one is not an exception. Heavy censure and unsparing ridicule were visited upon the officers of the Federal fleet—greater than they deserved—for they were new to the situation, and fresh from that national fear of "masked batteries"—rams and fire ships—all of which passed off as the experience of war in reality increased. Unlimited praise was extended to Hollins and his officers, without either the authorities or the public stopping to inquire why he left the stranded fleet without at least trying to destroy them. The war was young in the Fall of 1861—all its honors had been won by the Confederates; and when the *Bull Run* of the "Passes" was reported, "cowardice and pusillanimity" were charged upon Captains Pope and Handy, while Hollins, like Beauregard, was never required to say why he did not follow the retreating foe. If historians of the U. S. navy blush as they record the flight of their ships at the "Passes," those of the Confederate navy must express an almost equal dissatisfaction at the lack of results that the victory brought. The blockade was not raised, as Capt. Hollins claimed, for the Federal fleet remained off the mouths of the "Passes"—and soon after returned and held the head of the "Passes" until Farragut and his fleet recaptured the control of the river.

CHAPTER XIII.

MISSISSIPPI RIVER FROM THE GULF TO VICKSBURG.

THE movement by the Federal Administration at Washington, to open the Mississippi River, begun by Com. Foote at Cairo, in the summer of 1861, was continued from the Gulf by Admiral Farragut, in the spring of 1862. During the winter and early spring the largest and best appointed fleet that ever flew the U. S. flag was organized, and placed under the command of the boldest, ablest and most enterprising officer in that service. In order to hold what Farragut might capture, an army of 15,000 men, under Gen. Butler, was dispatched in the wake of the admiral's squadron. The combined fleet of men-of-war, mortar-schooners and transports arrived on the 16th of April, below Forts Jackson and St. Philip, which guarded the river approach to New Orleans. The Federal fleet,[1] consisting of 46 vessels, carrying 348 guns and 21 mortars, anchored below; and on the

[1] Vessels composing Farragut's fleet:

Flag-ship *Hartford*, twenty-five guns, Capt. Richard Wainwright; executive officer, Lieut. J. S. Thornton.

Steam-sloop *Brooklyn*, twenty-four guns, Capt. Thomas T. Craven; executive officer, Lieut. R. B. Lowry.

Steam-sloop *Richmond*, twenty-six guns, Capt. James Alden.

Steam-sloop *Mississippi*, twelve guns, Capt. M. Smith; executive officer, Lieut. Dewey.

Steam-sloop *Verona*, ten guns, Capt. Chas. S. Boggs.

Steam-sloop *Pensacola*, twenty-four guns, Capt. Henry W. Morris; executive officer, Lieut. Francis Roe.

Steam-sloop *Oneida*, nine guns, Commander S. Phillips Lee; executive officer, Lieut. Sicord.

Steam-sloop *Iroquois*, nine guns, Commander John De Camp; executive officer, David B. Harmony.

Gunboat *Westfield*, six guns, Capt. William B. Renshaw.

Gunboat *Katahdin*, six guns, Lieut. Commanding George Preble.

Gunboat *Pinola*, five guns, Lieut. Commanding Crosby.

Gunboat *Clifton*, five guns.

Gunboat *Cayuga*, five guns, Lieut. Commanding Harrison.

Gunboat *Itaska*, five guns, Lieut. Commanding C. H. B. Caldwell.

Gunboat *Kennebec*, five guns, Lieut. Commanding John Russell.

Gunboat *Kanawha*, five guns, Lieut. Commanding John Febiger.

Gunboat *Sciota*, six guns, Lieut. Commanding Edward Donaldson.

Gunboat *Miami*, six guns, Lieut. Commanding A. D. Harroll.

Gunboat *Owasco*, five guns, Lieut. Commanding John Guest.

Gunboat *Winona*, four guns, Lieut. Commanding Edward T. Nichols; executive officer, John G. Walker.

Gunboat *Wissahickon*, five guns, Lieut. Commanding Albert N. Smith.

Gunboat *Kineo*, five guns, Lieut. Commanding George H. Ransom.

Schooner *Kittatinny*, nine guns, Acting Volunteer Lieut. Lamson.

Gunboat *Harriet Lane*, six guns, Lieut. Commanding J. M. Wainwright, with Commander David D. Porter, who had twenty-one schooners, composing "Porter's mortar fleet," each carrying a heavy mortar, and two thirty-two guns.

morning of April 18th, commenced the bombardment of the forts.[1]

At that time the defences of New Orleans consisted of Forts Jackson and St. Philip, under Gen. Johnson K. Duncan, the former fort mounting seventy-five guns, and the latter fifty-three guns, both together manned by about 700 men. The naval defence consisted of the C. S. steamer *Louisiana*, 16 guns, Capt. Charles F. McIntosh; the ram *Manassas*, one thirty-two-pounder, Lieut. A. F. Warley; the *McRae*, 7 guns, Lieut. Thomas B. Huger; the *Jackson*, 2 guns, Lieut. F. B. Renshaw; launch No. 6, Acting Master Fairbanks; launch No. 3, one howitzer, Acting Master Telford, the fleet under command of Commodore John K. Mitchell. Co-operating with the fleet of Commodore Mitchell were two Louisiana State gunboats: the *Governor Moore*, two thirty-two-pounder rifled guns, Commander Beverley Kennon, C. S. N., and the *Gen. Quitman*, Capt. Grant; in addition was the remnant of the River Defence fleet of converted tow boats : the *Warrior*, Capt. Stephenson; the *Stonewall Jackson*, Capt. Phillips; the *Resolute*, Capt. Hooper; the *Defiance*, Capt. McCoy, and the *R. J. Breckenridge*, all under command of Capt. John A. Stephenson, and mounting from one to two guns each.[2] There were also the following unarmed steamers, acting as tenders and for towing purposes: the *Phoenix*, to the *Manassas*; the *W. Burton*, Capt. Hammond, and the *Landis*, Capt. Davis, to the *Louisiana;* also the *Mosher*, Capt. Sherman; the *Belle Algerine*, the *Star*, Capt. La Place, and the *Music*, Capt. McClellan.

To a complete understanding of the effort of the Confederate navy in defence of the city of New Orleans, a full

[1] Commander Beverley Kennon, in the *Century Magazine* for July, 1886, says :

" The *Navy Register* of January, 1863, gives Flag-officer Farragut's seventeen vessels 193 guns, and Commander Porter's seven vessels, sixty-five guns. The frigate *Colorado*, being unable to cross the bar, transferred April 11th her twenty-four-pounder howitzer to the *Sciota* ; on the 6th of April, four nine-inch guns to the *Oneida* and *Iroquois*; and, on April 9th, *three* officers, 142 men, and her spar-deck battery of twenty eight-inch guns, for distribution in the fleet. Add thirty-eight thirty-two pounders, and nineteen thirteen-inch mortars on board the 'bombers,' and twenty-nine twelve-pounder howitzers, one to each of twenty-four vessels, the five larger ones having two, both in their tops, and we find they had in all three hundred and sixty-nine guns of recent construction, fully equipped with latest improvements, and commanded and handled by trained men. Excepting one sailing ship and the mortar vessels, all of the guns were mounted on board steamers, the larger ones protecting their boilers and engines by tricing up abreast them on their outer sides their heavy chain cables, sixty links of one of them weighing more than *all the iron on the bows and elsewhere on all the Confederate State and River Defence Fleet*, numbering nine vessels, and all built of wood. In the above list of guns, about twenty-six were eleven-inch pivots; about 140 were nine-inch; about fifty-four were eight-inch ; about sixty were thirty-

two-pounders; about forty were rifled twenty to eighty-pounders, nineteen were thirteen-inch mortars, thirty were howitzers. To meet them the Confederates had 128 guns of assorted sizes in the two-forts, and forty-one on board their vessels. Of this number thirty-two only were of recent manufacture and fully equipped. The remainder were out of date by several years, and were commanded and manned, as a rule, by inexperienced though brave men; 122 were old-time thirty-two pounders. There were also three seven-inch and thirteen six-inch rifles, four brass field-pieces, eleven mortars (eight ten and one thirteen-inch), four eight-inch, four nine-inch, and eight ten-inch guns; total, 169. If I have erred, it is in not giving all the guns on the United States ships, as the *Register* always gives the least number mounted. Howitzers are never included any more than pistols, but when mounted in a vessel's tops to be fired at men on an exposed deck, as was the case with the Federal ships in this action, they become formidable weapons."

[2] It is necessary to mention the presence of the River Defence boats, but by reference to a former page where this expedition is described at length, it will be seen that their presence was more of an "embarrassment than an aid " in the action at the forts. Admiral Porter in his Naval History says: " Little assistance came to the fleet from the employment of these boats, on account of the insubordination of their division commander.''

account of the fighting condition of the vessels composing the fleet of Commodore Mitchell is necessary. This is the more required because northern writers have endeavored to exalt the performances of the U. S. navy by magnifying the fighting capacity of Confederate vessels. To that end Admiral Porter, in a letter to Senator Grimes, of Iowa, of May 6th, 1862, from Ship Island, set the key-note by saying of the *Louisiana*:

"That vessel was 4,000 tons, 270 feet long, and had sixteen heavy rifle guns, all made in Secessia. She intended to take position that night when she would have driven off all our fleet, for as a proof of her invulnerability one of our heaviest ships laid within ten feet of her and delivered her whole broadside, making no more impression on her than if she was firing peas. The *Louisiana's* shot, on the contrary, went through and through the above-mentioned sloop-of-war, as if she was glass.

"The iron ram *Manassas* hit three vessels before her commander ran her ashore and abandoned her. She has been a troublesome customer all through."

The real condition of the *Louisiana*, as given by Lieut. William C. Whittle, Jr., is that

"The *Louisiana* was in an entirely incomplete condition when she was sent down from New Orleans, and Commodore William C. Whittle, the naval commander at New Orleans, only sent her down in that condition in obedience to positive orders from Richmond to do so, and against his remonstrance and better judgment. Her guns were not mounted and the machinery of her two propellers was not put together. The machinery of her miserably conceived wheels, working in a ' well ' in her midship section, one immediately forward of the other, was in working order, but when she cast off her fasts at New Orleans on, I think, April 20th, 1862, the wheels were started, but with them she went helplessly down the stream, and tow-boats had to be called to take her to her destination. That point was where she was afterwards destroyed, on the left bank of the river, just above Fort St. Philip, where she was tied up to the river bank, with her bow down stream. Machinists and mechanics were taken down in her and worked night and day to complete the work on the machinery, and to prepare the ship for service.

"Our gallant and efficient commander, the lamented Charles F. McIntosh, aided by active, zealous and competent officers, bent all their energies to put the ship in a fighting condition, and by the time the Federal fleet came up to run by the batteries, on April 24th, all the guns, except I think two, were mounted. At that time the work on the machinery of the propellers was far from completion and the vessel was, in that regard, as helpless as when she went there.

"The port-holes for the guns were so miserably constructed as simply to admit of the guns being run out, and were so small as not to admit of training laterally or in elevation."

Commodore Mitchell testified before the Court of Inquiry as to the number of vessels, their armament and condition, that :

"The principal vessel of my command, the steamer *Louisiana*, iron-clad, mounting sixteen guns, was without sufficient motive power even to stem the current of the Mississippi without the aid of her two tenders, the *Landis* and *W. Burton*. Her two propellers were not ready

LIEUTENANT THOMAS B. HUGER,

CONFEDERATE STATES NAVY.

COMMANDER JOHN K. MITCHELL,
CONFEDERATE STATES NAVY.

for use, and were designed more to assist in steering than in the expectation of adding to her speed, and her rudder had little, if any, power to control her movements. Most of her guns had to be dismantled, after arriving at Fort St. Philip, and shifted to pivots where they could be worked, and one of them was not in position in the action of April 24th, being dismounted. The crew of the *Louisiana*, aided by the men from the *McRae*, were employed constantly night and day, in arranging the battery for action. The decks were thus, from this cause and the presence of numerous mechanics employed in completing machinery for the propellers, the ironing of the decks, and calking wheel-houses, much incumbered, and being very cramped at best for room, prevented the proper exercise of the men at their guns. This condition of her motive power and battery rendered her not only unfit for offensive operations against the enemy, but also for defence, as, being immovable, her guns all around could only command about 40 degrees of the horizon, leaving 320 degrees of a circle on which she could have been approached by an enemy without being able to bring a gun to bear upon him. Her guns, from the small size of her ports, could not be elevated more than 4 to 5 degrees, which with our best guns would not have given a range probably of more than 2,000 yards. The means for purchasing her anchors were inadequate, and it was utterly impossible to weigh them, when once they were let go, either from the bow or stern, and, indeed, her steering apparatus prevented her being anchored by the stern in the middle of the river, a position, under all the circumstances, I should have preferred to being tied to the river bank, by which more guns might have been used against the enemy, and the vessel might have been warped or sprung, so as to bring some of her guns to bear upon any given point. The quarters for the crew of the *Louisiana* were wholly insufficient, and for her officers there were none at all, except on the shield deck or roof, under a tented awning. Most of the officers and crew had to live on board two tenders, which were also required as tugs, without which the vessel could not be moved at all. The shield of the *Louisiana* was effective, for none of the enemy's projectiles passed through it; but as it only extended to the water line, a shot between wind and water must have penetrated the perpendicular pine sides. In addition to the *Louisiana*, the following vessels of the C. S. navy were under my command at the forts, viz.: The steamer *McRae*, Lieut. Com. Thomas B. Huger, with six light thirty-two pounder smooth-bore broadside guns, and one nine-inch shell gun pivoted amidships—total, seven; the steamer *Jackson*, Lieut. Com. F. B. Renshaw, two pivoted smoothbore thirty-two pounders, one forward and one aft; the iron-plated ram *Manassas*, Lieut. Com. A. F. Warley, one thirty-two pounder in bow; launch No. 3, Acting Master Telford, and one howitzer, twenty men; launch No. 6, Acting Master Fairbanks, one howitzer and twenty men. Also, the following converted sea steamers into Louisiana State gunboats, with pine and cotton barricades to protect the machinery and boilers, viz.: The *Governor Moore*, Commander Beverley Kennon, two thirty-two-pounder rifled guns; the *General Quitman*, Capt. Grant, two thirty-two-pounder guns. All the above steamers, being converted vessels, were too slightly built for war purposes. The following unarmed steamers belonged to my command, viz.: The *Phœnix*, Capt. ——, tender to the *Manassas;* the *W. Burton*, Capt. Hammond, tender to the *Louisiana*, and the *Landis*, Capt. Davis, tender to the *Louisiana*. The following-named steamers, chartered by the army, were placed under my orders, viz.: The *Mosher*, Capt. Sherman, a very small tug; the *Belle Algerine*, Capt. ——, a small tug; the *Star*, Capt. La Place, used as a telegraph station, and the *Music*, Capt. McClellan, tender to the forts. The two former were in bad condition, and were undergoing such repairs as could be made below previous to the 24th. On arriving below I delivered to Capt. Stephenson written orders from Major Gen. M. Lovell, requiring him to place all the River Defence gunboats under my orders, which consisted of the following converted tow boats, viz.: 1st, the *Warrior*, under the immediate command of Capt. Stephenson ; 2d, the *Stonewall Jackson*, Capt. Philips; 3d, the *Resolute*, Capt. Hooper; 4th, the *Defiance*, Capt. McCoy, and 5th, the *General Lovell*, —— ——. The *R. J. Breckenridge* —— ——, joined the evening before the action. All of the above vessels mounted from one to two pivot thirty-two pounders each, some of them rifled. Their boilers and machinery were all more or less protected by thick double pine barricades, filled in with compressed cotton, which, though not regarded as proof against heavy solid shot, shell, and incendiary projectiles, would have been a protection against grape and canister, and ought to have inspired those on board with sufficient confidence to use their boats boldly as rams, for which they were in a good measure prepared with flat bar iron casing around their bows. In thus using them their own safety would be best consulted, as well as the best way of damaging the vessels of the enemy."

In the "Naval History of the Civil War," Admiral Porter says : "The machinery (of the *Louisiana*) consisting of twin screw engines, and central paddles, was unfinished, and her inactivity at the time of the fight was due to that fact." With that knowledge of the cause of the *Louisiana's* "inactivity," Admiral Porter, in the *Century* for April, 1885, attempts to cast an imputation upon Commodore Mitchell by saying:

"Fortunately for us, Commodore Mitchell was not equal to the occasion, and the *Louisiana* remained tied up to the bank, where she could not obstruct the river or throw the Union fleet into confusion while passing the forts."

On the 22d of April. Gen. Duncan wrote to Commodore Mitchell :

" It is of vital importance that the present fire of the enemy should be withdrawn from us, which you alone can do. This can be done in the manner suggested this morning under the cover of our guns, while your work on the boat can be carried on in safety and security. Our position is a critical one, dependent entirely on the powers of endurance of our casemates, many of which have been completely shattered, and are crumbling away by repeated shocks ; and, therefore, I respectfully but earnestly again urge my suggestion of this morning on your notice. Our magazines are also in danger."

Upon the receipt of that request Commodore Mitchell held a consultation with his officers, and it was unanimously and wisely determined that it would be unwise to comply with Gen. Duncan's request, as Lieut. Whittle said :

"For the reason that it would place her under the fire of the whole Federal fleet commanded by Admiral Farragut without its being in her power to reach them by a single shot, in consequence of her ports not admitting of an elevation of more than five degrees, and, in addition, to the terrific fire of Admiral Porter's mortar fleet, '2,800 shells in twenty-four hours,' any one of which falling upon her unprotected upper deck would have gone through her bottom and sunk her : under which combined fires it would be impossible for any work to be done on our machinery, which we so hoped to complete in time for service when the Federals should come up."

Fair and just criticism of the conduct of officers on either side of the late war, is proper, and useful to the avoidance of errors and mistakes on future occasions, but the misrepresentation and unprofessional innuendoes of Admiral Porter are unworthy alike of an officer and of a historian.

It is not probable that Admiral Farragut would have steamed on to New Orleans and left the *Louisiana*[1] in his rear, if he had not been aware that she was unable to move from her position at the bank of the river, or if he had formed the opinion of her fighting power which Admiral Porter expressed.

In aid of the forts and the fleets defending the passage of the river there was a formidable obstruction placed between Forts Jackson and St. Philip, consisting of heavy logs between forty and sixty feet in length, lashed together by large chains across the river under the logs, and fastened on both sides of the river by planting very heavy anchors. There were also about thirty anchors let into the bottom of the river. So powerfully had this raft been built and fastened on both shores, and so thoroughly had it been anchored, that it was believed by those who constructed it that nothing save the giving way of the bottom of the Mississippi itself could break it. It was impossible for vessels to pass the forts while the raft was across the river. It held three months, but was swept away finally by the high water, the rapid current and the drift. A steamer and men were constantly employed to attend to the raft, and to keep away the drift, etc., which, however, it was found impossible to do. This raft cost not less than $55,000 or $60,000, and had it not been for the unprecedented high water, it is supposed that it would have answered the purpose for which it was intended.

---

[1] Wm. C. Whittle, Jr., who was third lieutenant on the *Louisiana* during the contest against Farragut's fleet in the Mississippi, sent to the *Century* the following statement concerning her armament:

"The hull of the *Louisiana* was almost entirely submerged. Upon this were built her heavy upper works, intended to contain her battery, machinery, etc. This extended to within about twenty-five feet of her stem and stern, leaving a little deck forward and aft, nearly even with the water, and surrounded by a slight bulwark. The structure on the hull had its ends and sides inclined inward and upward from the hull, at an angle of about forty-five degrees, and covered with T railroad iron, the lower layer being firmly bolted to the woodwork, and the upper layer driven into it from the end so as to form a nearly solid plate and a somewhat smooth surface. This plating resisted the projectiles of Farragut's fleet (none of which perforated our side), although one of his largest ships lay across and touching our stem and in that position fired her heavy guns. Above this structure was an open deck which was surrounded by a sheet-iron bulwark about four feet high, which was intended as a protection against sharp-shooters and small arms, but was entirely inefficient, as the death of our gallant commander, McIntosh, and those who fell around him, goes to prove.

"The plan for propelling the *Louisiana* was novel and abortive. She had two propellers aft, which we never had an opportunity of testing.

The novel conception, which proved entirely inefficient, was that right in the centre section of the vessel there was a large well, in which worked the two wheels, one immediately forward of the other. I suppose they were so placed to be protected from the enemy's fire.

"The machinery of these two wheels was in order when my father, Commodore W. C. Whittle, the naval commanding officer at New Orleans, against his better judgment, was compelled to send the vessel down to the forts. The vessel left New Orleans on the 20th of April, I think. The work on the propellers was incomplete, the machinists and mechanics being still on board, and most of the guns were not mounted. The centre wheels were started, but were entirely inefficient, and, as we were drifting helplessly down the stream, tow-boats had to be called to take us down to the point, about half a mile above Fort St. Philip, on the left side of the river, where we tied up to the bank with our bow down stream. Thus, as Farragut's fleet came up and passed, we could only use our bow-guns and the starboard broadside.

"Moreover, the port-holes for our guns were entirely faulty, not allowing room to train the guns either laterally or in elevation. I had practical experience of this fact, for I had immediate charge of the bow division when a vessel of Admiral Farragut's fleet got across our stem, and I could only fire through and through her at point blank instead of depressing my guns and sinking her."

After the raft was carried away another obstruction was placed across the river, as soon as possible, by anchoring small vessels, and running chains from one to the other, after their masts were removed. The men worked night and day to accomplish this. The obstruction thus made remained in position until within two or three days of the fight, when it too was carried away in a storm by fire vessels breaking adrift above it and coming down against it, which they did with great violence, the current being very rapid and the wind blowing very hard. Vessels were immediately set to work to put this obstruction in position again, but the enemy would not allow them to do it, firing upon them whenever they attempted it. The obstructions between the forts cost not less than $100,000.

The mending of the obstruction was a work of difficulty, the breaking of it one of scarcely any labor; so that whether Capt. Bell, when dispatched by Admiral Farragut, found his work anticipated by the current, or was aided by defective patching of the obstructions, is not material. A way was open when the enemy's fleet moved up, on the morning of the 24th of April, 1862. The first division of the enemy's fleet, consisting of eight gunboats, under command of Capt. Bailey, moved through the obstruction, having Fort St. Philip for its objective. The *Cayuga*, flag-ship of Bailey's division, in fifteen minutes had run by both forts, and was above and beyond the range of the guns of Fort St. Philip. Capt. Bailey says he "encountered" the Montgomery flotilla, consisting of eighteen gunboats, including the ram *Manassas* and the iron battery *Louisiana*. As the "Montgomery flotilla" never numbered but twelve vessels, and six had been destroyed a month before at Memphis, there were but six of that flotilla at the forts; so, instead of eighteen, Capt. Bailey encountered but six, for that was all that were left of that flotilla. If that was a "moment of anxiety to Capt. Bailey it could not have been produced by the 'Montgomery flotilla,' for they immediately left the scene of the fight, not standing on the order of their going." Commander Beverley Kennon says:

"Suddenly two, then one Confederate ram darted through the smoke from the right to the left bank of the river, passing close to all of us. They missed the channel for New Orleans, grounded on and around the point above, and close to Fort St. Philip; one was fired and deserted, and blew up soon after, as we passed her; the others, the ram *Defiance* and ram *Resolute*, were disabled and deserted."

At the report of the first gun on that morning, Lieut. Warley, on the *Manassas*, and Commander Beverley Kennon on the *Governor Moore*, started for the approaching fleet of the enemy. The little tug-boat, the *Belle Algerine*, was fouled and disabled, but cleared by the *Governor Moore*, which pressed forward and, hampered for room to gather headway for ramming, was compelled to make haste slowly, by moving under the east bank to the bend above, and then to turn down stream. From the bend, Commander Kennon witnessed the

burning of the telegraph steamer *Star*, and the companion ship
of the *Governor Moore*, the *Quitman*, which had been set on
fire at their berths on the right bank by the enemy's fleet.

Once clear of the entanglement with the *Louisiana*, *McRae*
and the *Manassas*, and out of the cross-fire of the forts, the
Governor Moore encountered the *Oneida* and the *Cayuga*, on
her port beam. To the hail, "What ship is that?" Com.
Kennon replied, "the U. S. steamer *Mississippi*," which was
also a side-wheel steamer; but he could not deceive the commander of the *Oneida*, whose reply was with a starboard
broadside at a few feet distance, while the *Cayuga* was not less
prompt with another broadside at a distance of thirty yards.
The *Pensacola* or the *Brooklyn*, the haze of the early morning

THE C. S. STEAMER "GOVERNOR MOORE."

and the smoke of battle preventing the exact distinguishing of vessels, poured in a charge of shrapnel from howitzers in her tops, which killed and wounded twelve men at
the guns. The *Pinola*, five guns, close on the port-quarter
of the *Governor Moore*, delivered a fire which killed five men.
This combined attack cut the *Moore* up very badly, but just
then, seeing a large two-masted steamer rushing up stream,
and recollecting that Gen. Lovell was on board the *Doub-
loon*, and but a short distance ahead, Com. Kennon moved
to engage the steamer, which proved to be the *Varuna*,
which he could see, while a dark background of woods partially covered the *Moore* from observation. The chase for
a fight continued for several miles up the river; the *Varuna*
evidently mistaking the *Moore* for a Federal vessel until
Com. Kennon, at broad daylight, revealed his true character
by discharging a gun at the *Varuna*, which promptly accepted battle. At close quarters the two vessels continued

to pour their shots into each other until, a fair opportunity offering, Com. Kennon rammed the *Varuna* twice near the starboard gangway — receiving her broadside at the very instant of striking and sinking his enemy, which, as she lay on the bank, was also rammed by the *Stonewall Jackson*. The *Moore*, having finished the *Varuna*, turned down stream to meet the approaching ships of the enemy. The *Oneida* had lost time by imperfect information and mistaken signals, and was not aware that the *Varuna* was ahead up stream, until Commander Lee came upon the stranded *Varuna*, and her triumphant foes. As the *Moore* came round to head down stream, the *Oneida* fired a shower of heavy projectiles which crashed through the *Moore*, and swept her decks already nearly without a working or a fighting force. The *Oneida's* shots quickly disabled the *Moore*, and she was beached just above the sunken *Varuna*. Such is the account given by Kennon of the fight between the *Varuna* and the *Moore*, but on the other hand, Capt. Boggs, of the *Varuna*, says: "While still engaged with her [the *Moore* and not the *Morgan*, as Capt. Boggs calls Com. Kennon's ship,] another rebel steamer, iron-clad, [1] with a prow under water, struck us in the port gangway, doing considerable damage. She backed off for another blow, and struck again in the same place, crashing in the side; but by going ahead fast, the concussion drew our port around, and I was able, with the port guns, to give her, while close alongside, five eight-inch shells abaft her armor. This settled her, and drove her ashore in flames." That could not have been the *Stonewall Jackson*, for that vessel escaped and was destroyed thirteen miles above the forts, and out of gunshot of the enemy; and as no other Confederate vessel was present, it is probable that Com. Kennon's account of the disabling and sinking the *Varuna* is the correct one. Capt. H. W. Morris, of the *Pensacola*, in his report claims the credit of having fired the shots that disabled the *Moore*. "The ram (the *Moore*) after having struck the *Varuna* gunboat, and forced her to run on shore to prevent sinking, advanced to attack this ship, coming down on us right ahead. She was perceived by Lieut. F. A. Roe, just in time to avoid her by sheering the ship, and she passed close on our starboard side, receiving, as she went, a broadside from us." It is proper to say that in the report of the officers commanding the *Cayuga*, the *Oneida*, the *Pinola*, and the *Brooklyn*, each claims to have been engaged with the *Governor Moore*. If all are correct, she sustained more of the battle than all other Confederate vessels.

As soon as the enemy's approach was known the *McRae* stood over towards the opposite side of the river, and was soon engaged by the gunboat *Iroquois*, to which the *McRae* gave first one and then the other broadside. Just at that moment the *McRae* discovered a short distance astern two ships—one

---

[1] There was no *iron-clad* about the *Moore* or the *Stonewall Jackson*.

on each quarter — coming rapidly up. Calling all hands to quarters to repel boarders, which were expected from the approaching steamer, Lieut. Commander Huger was much surprised to see the enemy pass without firing a gun, having mistaken the *McRae* for one of his own gunboats—but as the *McRae* stood across the river, the enemy discovered his error and opened with their starboard guns. Lieut. Read says:

"One of their shells striking us forward, and exploding in the sail-room, set the ship on fire. The engine and deck pumps were immediately started, but owing to the combustible nature of the articles in the sail-room, the fire burned fiercely. The sail-room was separated from the shell lockers by a third bulkhead. The commander directed the ship to be run close into the bank, and ordered me to inform him when the fire should reach the shell locker bulkhead. I repaired to the scene of fire, and succeeded in smothering and extinguishing it. Two large ships and three gunboats were now engaging us, at a distance of about 300 yards. We backed off the bank with the intention of dropping down near the forts, when the *Manassas* came to our relief. She steered for the enemy's vessels, and as soon as they discovered her, they started up the river.

"Just as we were backing off the bank, Lieut. Commanding T. B. Huger fell severely wounded.[1] I now directed the course of the vessel across and up the river, firing the starboard guns as rapidly as possible, and, I think, with much accuracy. We soon reached a position which furnished a view of the river around the first bend above the forts, where I discovered eleven of the enemy, and not deeming it prudent to engage a force so vastly superior to my own, I determined to retire under the guns of the forts. Having dropped a short distance, and getting into an eddy, I thought it best to turn and steam down; as the ship was turning, the tiller ropes parted. The ship was instantly stopped, and the engines reversed, but too late to avoid striking the bank. I endeavored to back her off the shore, but could not succeed. One of the river fleet, called the *Resolute*, had been run ashore early in the morning, just above where we were now lying, and had a white flag flying. I sent Lieut. Arnold, with ten men on board of her, with orders to haul down the white flag, and fight her guns as long as possible.

"At 6:30 the enemy stood up the river—and as soon as our guns would no longer bear we ceased firing. At 7 a tow-boat came up from the forts, and hauled us off.

"The *McRae* received three shots through her hull—all near the water-line. Most of the enemy's shell passed over us; every stay was carried away, and three-fourths of the shrouds. One shell passed through the smoke-stack—also, a number of grape.

"The sides of the ship received a large number of grape and canister which did not pass through. The enemy's firing upon the whole was very bad."

The centre division of the Federal fleet, composed of the *Hartford*, *Brooklyn* and *Richmond*, under Admiral Farragut, followed the leading division through the obstructions, and,

[1] Lieut. Thomas B. Huger, who died in New Orleans on the 25th of April, 1862, from wounds received in the engagement with the U. S. fleet on the day before, was a son of Dr. Benj. Huger, of Charleston, South Carolina. He belonged to a family which has always borne honorable connection with the history of the United States. He was appointed in the navy as midshipman on the 5th of March, 1835, and made his first cruise in the ship-of-the-line *North Carolina*.

The Navy Register of 1861 gave Lieut. Huger sixteen years and three months of sea service, three years shore duty, and six years and six months unemployed. At the time he resigned from the U. S. navy, he was First Lieutenant of the steam sloop *Iroquois*, on the Mediterranean Station, and was among the first to tender his resignation. He was a brave and chivalric officer, and his death was lamented by his associates in the C. S. navy.

passing the forts, was met by the Confederate tug *Mosher*, whose brave captain, Sherman, pushed a burning raft alongside the *Hartford*, under the very muzzles of her guns. The flames quickly leaped up the sides and rigging, and the mizzen shrouds were instantly afire. The disciplined crew responded to the call for firemen, and the flames were soon extinguished. This attack showed what might have been done if the material wasted in rafts abandoned singly to the current had been expended in organized attack of several rafts at a time, controlled by steam-power and launched at propitious moments. This incident Admiral Farragut mentioned on the same day in a letter to Capt. Porter, saying: "The ram (it was a tug-boat) pushed a fire-raft on me, and, in trying to avoid it, I ran the ship on shore. He again pushed the raft on me, and set the ship on fire all along one side. I thought it was all up with us, but we put it out and got off again, proceeding up the river, fighting our way." Porter says: "The fire was a sharp one; and, at times, rushing through the ports, would drive the men back from the guns. Seeing this, Farragut called out: 'Don't flinch from that fire, boys; there's a hotter fire than that for those who don't do their duty! Give that rascally little tug a shot, and don't let her get off with a whole coat.'"

Commander Albert Kautz, who was at this time lieutenant on the *Hartford*, in a letter to the editor of the *Century*, thus describes this memorable scene:

"No sooner had Farragut given the order ' Hard-a-port,' than the current gave the ship a broad shear, and her bows went hard up on a mud-bank. As the fire-raft came against the port side of the ship, it became enveloped in flames. We were so near to the shore that from the bowsprit we could reach the tops of the bushes, and such a short distance above Fort St. Philip that we could distinctly hear the gunners in the case-mates give their orders; and as they saw Farragut's flag at the mizzen, by the bright light, they fired with frightful rapidity. Fortunately, they did not make sufficient allowance for our close proximity, and the iron hail passed over our bulwarks, doing but little damage. On the deck of the ship it was as bright as noonday, but out over the majestic river, where the smoke of many guns was intensified by that of the pine-knots of the fire-rafts, it was dark as the blackest midnight. For a moment it looked as though the flag-ship was indeed doomed, but the firemen were called away, and, with the energy of despair, rushed aft to the quarter-deck. The flames, like so many forked tongues of hissing serpents, were piercing the air in a frightful manner, that struck terror to all hearts. As I crossed from the starboard to the port side of the deck, I passed close to Farragut, who, as he looked forward and took in the situation, clasped his hands high in air, and exclaimed, ' My God, is it to end in this way !' Fortunately, it was not to end as it at that instant seemed, for just then Master's Mate Allen, with the hose in his hand, jumped into the mizzen rigging, and the sheet of flame succumbed to a sheet of water. It was but the dry paint on the ship's side that made the threatening flame, and it went down before the fierce attack of the firemen as rapidly as it had sprung up. As the flames died away, the engines were backed 'hard,' and, as if providentially, the ram *Manassas* struck the ship a blow under the counter, which shoved her stern in against the bank, causing her bow to slip off. The ship was again free; and a loud, spontaneous cheer rent the air as the crew rushed to their guns with renewed energy."

The disagreement briefly stated in these extracts, was a material matter in the responsibility which rested on the officers of the Confederate army and navy, to whom was entrusted the defence of New Orleans. To a complete understanding of the situation and to ascertain the reasons of the disagreement between the commanding officers in the forts and afloat, the accompanying diagram will illustrate the positions taken by Commander Mitchell as well as that indicated and desired by Gen. Duncan.

In his testimony before the Confederate Court of Inquiry upon the fall of New Orleans, Gen. Duncan says, that on April 22, "everything afloat, including the tow-boats and the entire control of the fire barges, was turned over to Capt. John K. Mitchell, C. S. navy," that :

"In an interview with Capt. Mitchell, on the morning of this date, I learned that the motive power of the *Louisiana* was not likely to be completed within any reasonable time, and that in consequence it was not within the range of probabilities that she could be regarded as an aggressive steamer, or that she could be brought into the pending action in that character. As an iron-clad invulnerable floating battery, with sixteen guns of the heaviest calibre, however, she was then as complete as she would ever be.

"Fort Jackson had already undergone and was still subjected to a terrible fire of thirteen-inch mortar-shells, which it was necessary to relieve at once to prevent the disabling of all the best guns at the fort; and, although Fort St. Philip partially opened out the point of woods concealing the enemy and gallantly attempted to dislodge him or draw his fire, he nevertheless doggedly persisted in his one main object of battering Fort Jackson. Under these circumstances I considered that the *Louisiana* could only be regarded as a battery, and that her best possible position would be below the raft, close in on the Fort St. Philip shore, where her fire could dislodge the mortar-boats from behind the point of woods and give sufficient respite to Fort Jackson to repair *in extenso*. This position (X on the accompanying diagram) would give us three direct cross-fires upon the enemy's approaches and at the same time ensure the *Louisiana* from a direct assault, as she would be immediately under the guns of both forts. Accordingly, I earnestly and strongly urged these views upon Capt. Mitchell in a letter of this date (copy lost), but without avail, as will be seen by his reply, attached as document D.[1]

---

[1] [Inclosure D.]

CONFEDERATE STATES STEAMER "LOUISIANA,"}
OFF FORT JACKSON, LA., April 22, 1862. }

GENERAL: I have the honor to acknowledge the receipt of yours of this date, asking me to place the *Louisiana* in position below the raft this evening, if possible. This vessel was hurried away from New Orleans before the steam power and batteries were ready for service, without a crew, and in many other respects very incomplete, and this condition of things is but partially remedied now. She is not yet prepared to offer battle to the enemy, but should he attempt to pass the forts, we will do all we can to prevent it, and it was for this purpose only that she was placed in position where necessity might force her into action, inadequately prepared as she is at this moment.

We have now at work on board about fifty mechanics, as well as her own crew and those from other vessels, doing work essential to the preparation of the vessel for battle. Under these circumstances it would, in my estimation, be hazarding too much to place her under the fire of the enemy. Every effort is being made to prepare her for the relief of Fort Jackson, the condition of which is fully felt by me, and the very moment I can venture to face our enemy with any reasonable chance of success, be assured, general, I will do it, and trust that the result will show you that I am now pursuing the right course.

I am, very respectfully, your obedient servant,
JNO. K. MITCHELL,
Commanding C. S. Naval Forces; lower Mississippi.

GENERAL JOHNSON K. DUNCAN,
Commanding Coast Defences, Fort Jackson, La.

P. S.—The *Jackson*, with Launch No. 3, will go up to the quarantine this afternoon to watch the enemy, as suggested in your note this morning. Respectfully, etc.,
J. K. M.

"Being so deeply impressed myself with the importance of this position for the *Lousiana* and of the necessity of prompt action in order to
ensure the success of the impending struggle, I again urged this subject

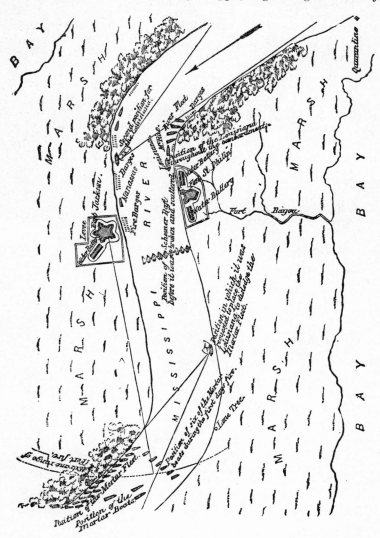

DIAGRAM OF BOMBARDMENT OF FORTS JACKSON AND ST. PHILIP, APRIL 16TH–19TH, 1862.

upon Capt. Mitchell, during the latter part of the same day, as absolutely
indispensable and imperative to the safety of New Orleans and to the
control of the lower Mississippi. My efforts were ineffectual to get him

to move the boat from her original position above the forts. His reply is attached, as document E, in which he is sustained by all the naval officers present having the command of vessels.

"I also addressed him two other notes through the day—one in regard to sending the fire barges against the enemy, and the other relative to keeping a vigilant lookout from all his vessels, and asking for co-operation should the enemy attempt to pass during the night.

"Bombardment continued throughout the day and night, being at times very heavy. During the day our fire was principally confined to shelling the point of woods from both forts, and apparently with good results, as the mortar fire was slackened toward evening. The casemates were very much cut up by the enemy's fire, which was increased at night.

"There was little or no success in sending down fire barges as usual, owing in part to the condition of the tow-boats *Mosher, Music* and *Belle Algerine*, in charge of the same, explained by attached document G. This does not excuse the neglect, however, as there were six boats of the river fleet available for this service, independent of those alluded to, and fire barges were plentiful.

"*April 23.*—The day broke warm, clear and cloudless. No immediate relief being looked for from our fleet, the entire command was turned out to repair damages under a very heavy fire of the enemy.

"The bombardment continued without intermission throughout the day, but slackened off about 12 m., at which hour there was every indication of an exhaustion on the part of the mortar flotilla; hence it became evident that the tactics of the enemy would necessarily be changed into an attack with broalsides by his larger vessels. In consequence, these views were laid before Capt. Mitchell, and he was again urged to place the *Louisiana* at the point before mentioned, below the raft and near the Fort St. Philip bank of the river, to meet the emergency. (See attached document H.) Capt. Mitchell's reply is attached, in documents E, I, J, and K, wherein he positively declines again to assume the only position which offered us every possible chance of success, and Capts. [Chas. F.] McIntosh, [Thomas B.] Huger, and Warley sustain Capt. Mitchell in his views of the case.

"Just before sundown, under a very heavy mortar fire, the enemy sent up a small boat, and a series of white flags were planted on the Fort St. Philip bank of the river, commencing about 350 yards above the lone tree upon that shore. (See diagram.)

"This confirmed my previous views of an early and different attack from the usual mortar bombardment, especially as I presumed that these flags indicated the positions to be taken up by the several vessels in their new line of operations.

"As nothing was to be expected from the *Louisiana* after the correspondence during the day, I could only inform Capt. Mitchell of this new movement of the enemy (see attached document L), and particularly impress upon him the necessity of keeping the river well lit up with fire barges, to act as an impediment to the enemy and assist the accuracy of our fire in a night attack.

"Lieut. [Geo. S.] Shryock, C. S. N. (Capt. Mitchell's aide), came on shore about 9 P. M. to inform me that the *Louisiana* would be ready for service by the next evening—the evening of the 24th. I informed him that time was everything to us, and that to-morrow would in all probability prove too late. Lieut. Col. Higgins warmly seconded my opinion, and warned Lieut. Shryock that the final battle was imminent within a few hours.

"In regard to lighting the river, Lieut. Shryock stated that fire barges would be regularly sent down throughout the night every two hours, and as none had been sent up to that hour (9:30 P. M.), he left, informing me that this matter would be attended to as soon as he arrived on board. To my utter surprise, not one single fire barge was sent down the river, notwithstanding, at any hour of this night. It was impossible for us to send them down, as everything afloat had been turned over to Capt. Mitchell by order of the major general commanding, and the fire barges and the boats to tow them into the stream were exclusively under his control. In consequence of this criminal neglect, the river remained in complete darkness throughout the entire night. The bombardment continued all night and grew furious toward morning."

The reply of Commander Mitchell, which is referred to by Gen. Duncan as inclosure E, is accompanied, as he states, by the concurring views of his subordinate officers as to the impracticability of placing the *Louisiana* at point X, in the diagram; but he added, that through the labors of the mechanics then at work on the *Louisiana* he hoped " that by to-morrow night the motive power of the *Louisiana* will be ready, and that in the meantime her battery will be in place and other preparations will be completed so as to enable her to act against the enemy. When ready you will be immediately advised."

Though the darkness and smoke of battle prevented Gen. Duncan from observing how the *Louisiana* was fought, he was able, notwithstanding the obscuring media, to observe the *Defiance*, the *Manassas*, the *McRae*, the *Resolute*, the *Warrior*, and the enemy's fleet. The disappointment and chagrin of defeat, it is probable, may have made Gen. Duncan dissatisfied with the reasons of Commander Mitchell and his officers for not complying with the request to take position in the *Louisiana* below the forts, but in the light of all the facts and circumstances now available, the refusal of Commander Mitchell will be sustained by military and naval critics. That " to-morrow " came heralded by the passage of the forts by the enemy's fleet, and thus the opportunity was lost, cannot be charged upon the conduct of Com. Mitchell, but must be credited to the enterprise and dash of Farragut, who waited not for the completion of the Confederate defences, but took advantage of their incompleteness and steamed past the forts and the fleet. The incompleteness of the *Louisiana*, and the unfinished condition of the *Mississippi*, were due to circumstances, perhaps, beyond control of the Confederate Navy Department, but there were defects of organization—in this, that there were two separate and distinct organizations afloat—one under the Secretary of War and the other under the Secretary of the Navy, entirely independent of each other; and, though cordially co-operating, yet doing so under different and sometimes conflicting orders.

During the proceedings of the Court of Inquiry the Judge Advocate raised the point that the court had no jurisdiction to inquire into and pronounce upon the official conduct of the naval officers in command at or near the forts, and after hearing argument upon the point, the court directed that " the order convening the court did not restrict its investigation to the conduct of Major Gen. Mansfield Lovell and the troops of his command except as to the mere evacuation of the city.

In relation to the capture of the city the words of the order preclude the idea of such restriction, and they do not imply it in respect to the defence. "It is required of the court, too, in these matters, to examine into the attending facts and circumstances, without limit as to persons or arm of the service"—so the witnesses were permitted to enter into naval as well as army matters. In the Report of Facts the Court found that: "Between Gen. Lovell and the naval officers on duty in Department No. 1 there existed good feeling and a desire to co-operate for the public defence." Gen. Lovell often supplied the navy with guns and ammunition. During the bombardment it was designed by Gens. Lovell and Duncan that the *Louisiana* should be placed in a position from which they thought she could enfilade and drive off the mortar-fleet of the enemy, but this request was not complied with—Com. J. K. Mitchell, commanding the defences afloat, alleging in reply, that the *Louisiana* was without motive power, and in the position indicated her guns could not be given sufficient elevation to reach the enemy, while she would be in full range of his mortar-fleet, and that her top-deck was flat and vulnerable. These statements are proven to be true. He also added, as his opinion, sustained by a council of naval officers, that "the desired movement would result in the destruction of the vessel by the enemy," and upon that finding of facts, the opinion of the court was that "the non-completion of the iron-clad gunboats *Louisiana* and *Mississippi* made it impossible for the navy to co-operate efficiently with Gen. Lovell."

The following is the finding and opinion of the Naval Court of Inquiry into the official conduct of Commander Mitchell:

"C. S. NAVY DEPARTMENT, RICHMOND, Dec. 5, 1863.
" Finding and opinion of a Naval Court of Inquiry, convened in the city of Richmond, Va., January 5, 1863, by virtue of the following precepts ·

"C. S. NAVY DEPARTMENT,   ⎫
"OFFICE OF ORDERS AND DETAIL,   ⎬
"RICHMOND, December 24, 1862.   ⎭

"SIR : By order of the Secretary of the Navy you are hereby appointed president of a court of inquiry to be convened in this city on the 5th of January next.

"Capt. S. S. Lee and Commander Robt. G. Robb have been ordered to report to you and with you will compose the court.

"Mr. George Lee Brent will report to you as recorder. You will inquire into the whole official conduct of Commander John K. Mitchell, C. S. N., while in command of the steamer *Louisiana* and in charge of the vessels of the Confederate navy at and below New Orleans and report the same to this department, with your opinion whether the said officer did or did not do all in his power to sustain the honor of the flag and prevent the enemy from ascending the Mississippi River, and if he did not to what extent did he fail so to do.

"Respectfully, your obedient servant,
"F. FORREST, *Chief of Bureau.*

"*Flag-officer Samuel Barron,* C. S. N., *commanding, etc., James River, Va.*"

FINDING OF THE COURT.

"That Commander Mitchell assumed command of the *Louisiana* at New Orleans on the 20th of April, 1862, and from that time until the destruction of the vessel only a period of eight days was embraced.

"That the whole force under his command consisted of the *Louisiana*, the *McRae*, the *Manassas*, the *Jackson* and one launch.

"That on the day he took command Capt. Mitchell descended the River Mississippi in the *Louisiana* and took up a position on the left bank of the river, about half a mile above Fort St. Philip.

"That on leaving New Orleans the machinery of the *Louisiana* was incomplete, her motive power imperfect and her battery improperly mounted. That she could not on a fair trial stem the current of the Mississippi with her own motive power aided by two steam tugs.

"That every exertion was made by Commander Mitchell, the officers and mechanics, to get the *Louisiana* in a proper state of efficiency for defence of the passage of the river, and that the defects in mounting the battery had been remedied and the battery served with efficiency, with the exception of two guns out of place. It appears that a request, or order, was sent by Gen. Duncan, commanding Fort Jackson, to Commander Mitchell to change the position of the *Louisiana* to a point lower down the stream, which, by a council of officers, was unanimously deemed impracticable, and to a certain extent impossible on account of the great depth of water, and that such change of position would endanger the safety of the *Louisiana*. That in the position Gen. Duncan desired the *Louisiana* to assume she would have been in range of the mortar boats of the enemy and perfectly helpless, inasmuch as she could not give her guns more than five degrees elevation, not enough to reach the enemy. That the best disposition possible was made of the vessels under the command of Commodore Mitchell to resist the passage of the enemy.

"That on the 24th of April the enemy appeared and his passage was hotly contested by the *Louisiana*, the *McRae* and the *Manassas*. That the *Jackson* was previously sent up the river to guard certain passes and the launch down the river to signal the approach of the enemy, and that they took no part in the fight. That every possible resistance was offered by the vessels mentioned to the passage of the enemy up the river.

"That at no time was the *Louisiana* able to leave her moorings and pursue the enemy, from want of sufficient motive power. That the interval between the passage of the enemy and the destruction of the *Louisiana* (four days) was employed in completing the machinery, to render her more able to cope with the enemy, and that it was Commander Mitchell's intention to make an attack when the *Louisiana* was capable of doing so.

"That Commander Mitchell, when he heard that Gen. Duncan, in command of Fort Jackson, had accepted the terms of surrender offered the day before by Capt. Porter, U. S. N., remonstrated with Gen. Duncan against such a course, but was told it was too late, as a flag of truce boat had already been sent ; that the enemy appeared in overwhelming force, and that at the time it was determined in council to destroy the *Louisiana* the position of affairs was as follows : There were from ten to fourteen large vessels of Flag-officer Farragut's fleet above the *Louisiana* and the mortar fleet and gunboats of Capt. Porter were below. Two vessels of the enemy, with white flags flying, were coming up the river in sight to accept the surrender of Forts Jackson and St. Philip, which had white flags in answer to them. That the *Louisiana* could not move from where she was moored to the bank, nor could she fire on the boats with flags of truce flying, and in a short time the forts would be in the hands of the enemy and the *Louisiana* between them. It was then unanimously determined in a council of the officers to destroy the *Louisiana*, as it was the only course left to prevent her from falling into the hands of the enemy. This destruction was accordingly effected under the direction and supervision of Commander Mitchell, in an orderly and deliberate manner, and every precaution was taken to insure the safety of his men.

OPINION.

" And the court is of the opinion, from all the evidence adduced, that Commander Mitchell did all in his power to sustain the honor of the flag and to prevent the enemy from ascending the Mississippi River, and that his conduct and bearing throughout the period of his service while in command of the vessels of the navy for the defence of the Mississippi River, under the trying and embarrassing circumstances under which he was placed, was all that could be expected by the country and the naval service of a capable and gallant officer.

" S. BARRON, *Flag-officer,*
" *President of the Court.*

" GEO. LEE BRENT, *Recorder.*"

"NAVY DEPARTMENT, March 17th. 1863.

" Proceedings and finding approved. Office of Orders and Detail will dissolve the court.

" S. R. MALLORY, *Secretary of the Navy.*"

" C. S. NAVY DEPARTMENT,
" OFFICE OF ORDERS AND DETAIL,
" RICHMOND, March 18th, 1863.

" *Flag-officer S. Barron, Commanding, etc.*

" SIR—The Naval Court of Inquiry on Commander Mitchell, of which you are the presiding officer, is hereby dissolved. The court convened in this city on the 5th of January, and has been continued thus long in session awaiting the attendance of Gen. Mansfield Lovell and Lieut. Col. Edward Higgins, who were summoned to appear before it as witnesses by orders from the War Department. Learning that one of these gentlemen, Lieut. Col. Higgins, cannot be spared from his present command, and that Gen. Lovell has made no answer to the summons from the War Department, although they have been more than two months since summoned again and again, there is no course left but to dissolve the court, which is done accordingly, and you will so inform the members and the Judge Advocate. You will be pleased to have this letter, or a certified copy, spread upon the records of the court.

" Respectfully your obedient servant,

" F. FORREST, *Chief of Bureau.*

" The foregoing is ordered to be published for the information of all whom it may concern.

" S. R. MALLORY, *Secretary of the Navy.*"

The tug escaped from the *Hartford,* though afterwards she was destroyed. The *Brooklyn* followed the *Hartford* through the obstructions, but as soon as she appeared above the forts was engaged by the *Manassas,* Lieut. Com. A. F. Warley, who made directly for the *Brooklyn's* starboard side, which he struck twice but the *Brooklyn's* chain protection turned the blows, which glanced from her side, and in the darkness the *Manassas* passed astern of the *Brooklyn* and turned up the river, where, near quarantine, the *Mississippi* turned and attempted to run the *Manassas* down, but by a quick turn of the helm, the ram escaped the blow, but ran ashore, where her injection pipes were cut by her crew and she drifted afterwards away from the bank and sank below the forts. The *Manassas* proved herself to be the most troublesome ship in the Confederate fleet. At different times in that dark morning she rammed the *Brooklyn,* the *Hartford,* and the *Mississippi.*

A writer in the *Army and Navy Journal*, controverting the right of the crew of the *Mississippi* to bounty money for her destruction, says:

"It is certainly true that the *Mississippi* destroyed the *Manassas* by pouring a broadside into her, which punched several holes in her armor, and set her on fire, so that her small crew were glad to run her on shore and abandon her. I believe she afterwards drifted off, and, passing the forts, occasioned something of a panic among the mortar schooners, who took her for a live, and not a defenceless monster. The *Mississippi*, however, was ordered to the duty of destroying her. She turned down stream to meet her coming up, in consequence of an order from the *Hartford*, and, going down, pressed the *Kineo*, Lieut. Com. Ransom, to assist her. The meeting was witnessed by all, or nearly all, the fleet, and was watched as one of the pretty things of that fight, being performed in broad daylight. Why, then, should the *Mississippi* be singled out to receive bounty for the destruction of that rebel ram?"

Who should have the money? is an unimportant question to any but the recipient, but the facts upon which any money

THE RAM "MANASSAS" AS SHE APPEARED AFTER BEING SET ON FIRE BY HER COMMANDER.

was awarded ought to have been first settled. Capt. Smith, of the *Mississippi*, asserts having fired a broadside into the *Manassas*, but did that broadside, which laid the foundation of the claim for bounty, destroy the *Manassas?* That it did not is established by Lieut. Read, who says that "at 8:30 we anchored near the *Louisiana*, while we were aground the ram *Manassas* was discovered floating helplessly down the river. I sent a boat to her and ascertained that she was *uninjured*, but had her injection pipes cut, and that it would be impossible to save her."

The whole Federal fleet, except the *Itasca*, *Kennebec*, *Winona* and the mortar boats as they passed the forts, was met by the *Louisiana* lashed to the shore, and able to use but a part of her battery, yet receiving uninjured the broadside of nearly every Federal vessel.

Admiral Farragut, convinced that the *Louisiana* tied to the bank, however formidable she might be to an attacking party, was harmless herself to assault, left her, and sailed with his whole fleet that was above the forts, to New Orleans. Around the *Louisiana* lay the *McRae* and the *Resolute*, with the tender *Landis*.

William C. Whittle, Jr., third lieutenant of the *Louisiana*, says:

" The *Louisiana* had used her guns against all of the Federal fleet as they passed, and every man had fought bravely and well, and chafed under their powerlessness from causes and defects beyond their efforts to correct to do more. There she lay, with her little flag bravely flying, after having resisted every projectile from Admiral Farragut's fleet.

" The guns used during the action on board the *Louisiana* were those of the bow division, pointing down the river, and those of the starboard broadside division, pointing across the river, the former consisting of two nine-inch smooth-bore shell guns, and one seven-inch rifle, and the latter, I think, one 32 pound rifle and two eight-inch smooth-bores.

" Of the bow division I had immediate command. I was the third lieutenant. During the conflict, one of the largest of Admiral Farragut's fleet, as if her steering gear was disarranged, was caught in the eddy current and came right athwart our hawse, her starboard side nearly if not actually touching our stem, with only the length of our short forward deck outside of her armor between her side and our armor. In that position we received her fire without any shot perforating, and the three guns of my division were fired as fast as they could be loaded and discharged. But here the abortively constructed port-holes prevented our depressing our guns to sink her.

" It was at this time that our brave commander, Charles F. McIntosh, received his death wounds. [1] When this vessel was placed in this position, as if anticipating that she intended to try to board us, and chafing under the forced inactivity of our vessel, he called away his men to repel the attack and gallantly led them to the upper deck, when he was shot down, as were numbers of his brave followers. A braver man or set of men never gave up their lives to any cause."

Statements and counterstatements, all differing and disagreeing in language and purport have been made as to the destruction of the *Louisiana*, and questions of honor raised as to Commodore Mitchell's destroying the vessels while flags of truce were flying over the forts and over the enemy's vessels. As there existed no power of command on the part of Gen. Duncan over the C. S. fleet which Commodore Mitchell commanded, each officer was free to follow his own dictates of duty. That Commodore Mitchell, in destroying the *Louisiana*, took caution that no injury should fall to the enemy's fleet while under the flag of truce, is abundantly shown by the sequel as well as proven by the statement of Lieut. Wm. C. Whittle, Jr., who says:

" I think it was on April 27th that Commodore Mitchell was informed by Gen. Duncan that he had received a demand from Admiral Porter to surrender and offering terms of capitulation, and that he had peremptorily refused. Our work was still going on, night and day, on our machinery. The next morning we were to test the efficiency of it. At daylight a note from Gen. Duncan came off to say that during the night a portion of his garrison had mutinied or deserted and that, not knowing the extent of the disaffection, he had determined to accept the terms offered by Porter.

[1] Commander McIntosh died on the 28th of April, 1862.

" Commodore Mitchell was, of course, astonished and, jumping into a boat, went ashore and asked if the note was genuine. The reply was that it was. He learned that a portion of the garrison of Fort Jackson, from New Orleans, becoming uneasy about their families, had deserted. He remonstrated and urged that the garrison of St. Philip was true, as was the crew of the *Louisiana*, but he was told that it was too late, as a messenger had been dispatched.

" Commodore Mitchell returned to the *Louisiana*. Admiral Porter's fleet, led by the flagship, *Harriet Lane*, was then seen coming up under a flag of truce, in reply to a flag of truce on Fort Jackson. A consultation was called by Commodore Mitchell. The decision was, that with an enemy above, an enemy below soon to be in possession of our forts, with limited supplies, no reliable motive power, to destroy the vessel.

" An orderly but rapid transfer to the unarmed tender *Landis* was made, and the magazines and charges in our guns were drowned as far as practicable. Commodore Mitchell, Lieuts. Wilkinson, Ward and I were the last to leave the *Louisiana*, after firing her effectually. Commodore Mitchell then called me to him and told me to go in a boat indicated to Admiral Porter's flagship, then anchored off Fort Jackson, distant about a mile, and say to him, with his compliments, that he had fired the *Louisiana* and drowned, as far as he could, the magazines and charges in the guns, but that she was secured to the bank with rope fasts, which might burn, and as he was indisposed to do him any damage while under a flag of truce, in answer to a similar flag from the forts, he notified him in case his burning ship should drift down among his fleet.

" I started down in the boat, two men pulling. When I got about one-third of the distance I felt the boat tremble and, looking around, saw that the *Louisiana* had blown up at or near the spot where I left her. I went on, however, and going alongside of the *Harriet Lane* was received by my old Naval Academy schoolmate, Edward Lee, who was on deck. I asked for Admiral Porter and was told that he was below. A messenger was sent down to him. The reply came back that he was arranging the terms of capitulation of the forts. In a short time he came up. I delivered the message of Commodore Mitchell.

" He said, ' Where is the *Louisiana* ?' A strange question from one who had been ' fairly shaken from his seat ' and whose flagship had been ' thrown on her side.' I replied that she had been blown up."

Admiral Porter, in his " Naval History," takes no account whatever of Lieut. Whittle having arrived on board the *Harriet Lane*, and advised the officer on deck of the purpose of Commodore Mitchell to burn the *Louisiana*, but leaves the reader to suppose that no intimation of the purpose to destroy the *Louisiana* had been given, and continues—that he remarked—" this is sharp practice, but if you can stand the explosion when it comes, we can. We will go on and finish the capitulation." But unfortunately for this pretended indifference to danger, the facts upset the probability of the remark having been made. The *Louisiana had blown up before the officer reported below of her being on fire.* The explosion took place while Lieut. Whittle was rowing to the *Harriet Lane*, and before he had informed his old schoolmate Edward Lee, on the deck of the *Harriet Lane*, of Commander Mitchell's message. The shock which Porter, in the *Century* for April, 1885, says " fairly shook us all from our seats, and threw the *Harriet Lane* over on her side"—ought to have rendered his question to Lieut. Whittle—" where is the *Louisiana* ?" totally unnecessary.

In a letter to Admiral Farragut, Commander Mitchell says: "Lieut. Whittle was sent in a boat, with a flag of truce, to inform Commander Porter that in firing the *Louisiana*, her magazine had not been effectually drowned, and that, though efforts were made to drown the charges in the guns, they may not have succeeded. This information was given in consideration of the negotiations then pending under flag of truce between him and Fort Jackson; but while the message was on its way the explosion took place—a fact that does not affect the honorable purposes intended by it."

Commodore Mitchell was no part of Gen. Duncan's command, nor did the latter pretend to any power to include the navy in the terms of his capitulation, but expressly disclaimed all connection with or power over the navy. It was within the province of Commodore Mitchell to continue the fight, to surrender, or to destroy his ships and effect escape if possible. His consideration for the flag of truce between the enemy and the forts will commend his conduct, while his purpose to prevent the enemy from obtaining possession of his ship will be endorsed and sustained by every principle and precedent of naval warfare. The subsequent harsh treatment of Commodore Mitchell and the officers of the *Louisiana* resulted from the report which Porter made, but as soon as the authorities at Washington ascertained from Commodore Mitchell the truth and facts of the destruction, they were released from confinement and treated as prisoners of war.

Of the thirteen Confederate ships, the *Governor Moore*, disabled and aground, was burned by her commander, Beverley Kennon; the C. S. S. *Jackson* escaped to New Orleans; the *Manassas* disabled, was destroyed by Lieut. Commander Warley; the *Stonewall Jackson*, of the Montgomery flotilla, escaped up the river and was destroyed by her officers, thirteen miles above the forts; the *Quitman* and the *Star* were abandoned at the very opening of the fight and burned; the *Warrior* was abandoned and burned on the Fort St. Philip side of the river; to the north of her, on the other side of the river, the *Breckenridge* (or *Defiance*) perished in the same ignoble manner—having taken no part in the fight except escaping from it.

The *Louisiana*, the *McRae*, the *Resolute*, of the Montgomery flotilla (which was abandoned by her crew, and taken possession of by Lieut Arnold and the men from the *McRae*, and brought back into the fight), with the *Burton* and the *Landis*, unarmed tenders, survived the fight, and for two days maintained their positions above the forts. Nor did Capt. Porter, who had with him the gunboats *Itasca*, the *Winona*, the *Kennebec*, the *Harriet Lane*, the *Westfield*, the *Miami*, and the mortar fleet. attempt their capture or even offer them battle.

The fall of New Orleans, and the recovery of the control and navigation of the Mississippi River, was due to the enterprise, sagacity and courage of Admiral Farragut and his officers, aided by the concurrence of many circumstances, which it was the duty and ought to have been the business of the Confederate authorities, army and navy, to have prevented and guarded against. Mr. Mallory wasted money in trying to be economical, and delayed important matters while he was hurrying them with all his energies. The mistaken conviction that the danger to New Orleans was from up the river, rather than from the Gulf, was not only firmly held, but was persisted in after it was known that Farragut was in the Gulf, with the largest and best appointed fleet that the United States had ever organized. As late as the middle of April, and even when Farragut was working his fleet over the bar at the mouth of the Mississippi, Mr. Mallory retained the idea that the real danger which threatened New Orleans was from the seven "tin-clad" gunboats of Flag-officer Davis, then up the river at Fort Pillow; and even after Commodore Whittle at New Orleans had recalled Hollins from up the river to the defence of New Orleans against the fleet of Farragut—Mr. Mallory still believing that the real attack was to be from Davis rather than by Farragut, would have sent the *Louisiana* up the river to meet Davis rather than down to the forts to engage Farragut. Reliance for the safety of New Orleans was placed upon Forts Jackson and St. Philip, notwithstanding the advice and opinion of the ablest naval officers in the Confederate service, given to the Naval Committee at Montgomery, that steam vessels could run by the forts. In that opinion Semmes, Rousseau, Bulloch, Hollins, Whittle and others, not only concurred but urged that the safety of the city could only be assured by defences afloat acting in co-operation with the batteries of the forts. Yet every vessel that could carry a gun was sent up the river, and the forts were left unaided for months to defend the approach to New Orleans. The presence of the *Louisiana*, at the time Farragut appeared before the forts, was due to the assumed authority of Com. Mitchell, and in spite of the order of the Navy Department of April 10th to send her as soon as completed to Fort Pillow. The *McRae* and the *Jackson* were at the fight, because Capt. Hollins had ordered them down the river when he went to aid in the defence of the city, in response to Commodore Whittle's telegram,[1] and these were in New Orleans,

---

[1] Capt. William Conway Whittle was born in Norfolk, Va., in 1805, and was appointed a midshipman in the U. S. navy May 10th, 1820. He served in various positions and in every grade in the "old navy" from midshipman to commander inclusive, and on a large number of vessels, among which were the *Ontario, Fairfield, Columbia, Brandywine* and *Ohio.* He was in Florida during the Seminole disturbances, and in the Mexican war he was wounded at the battle of the Tuspan, and afterwards commanded the dispatch steamer *Col. Harney.* In 1853 he commanded the U. S. sloop *Decatur* on the banks of Newfoundland, and in 1854 and 1855 the U. S. sloop *Dale* on the coast of Africa. He resigned from the U. S. navy in 1861 upon the secession of Virginia, and was in the Virginia navy. On June 11th, 1861, he was transferred to the C. S. navy. He commanded the naval defences on York River, Va., and the Confederate flotilla on the upper Mississippi, and the Naval Station at New Orleans. He honorably served the Confederacy in various places and during the whole war. On October 23d, 1862, he was promoted to Captain, to rank from February 8th, 1862. He died in Virginia in 1878.

against the judgment of Mr. Mallory. These facts are not re-called with any purpose of sustaining the charge of inefficiency which was preferred against the Confederate Secretary of the Navy, but to show how a mistaken view of the enemy's purpose led to the weakening of the defences of the city, and that that error was in spite of the advice and opinion of naval officers.

The divided command at New Orleans, by which the army and navy were responsible to no common authority, contributed to that want of concert which hindered and embarrassed the fighting capacity of both arms when the hour came which needed all the efforts of each. The confidence reposed in the rams of Montgomery's flotilla, and in the capacity and courage of their captains — men without education, without naval training, with no *esprit de corps*—was repaid by almost instant flight after the exhibition and display of acts of insubordination criminal and contemptible. There is nothing about the naval defence of New Orleans to which a Confederate can look back without a feeling of disappointment, except the magnificent courage and seamanship displayed by Kennon in the *Moore*, by Huger and Read in the *McRae*, by Warley in the *Manassas*, and by Mitchell and his officers in the immovable *Louisiana*.

Having destroyed every vessel of the Confederate navy below New Orleans, Admiral Farragut found himself before the city, with his victorious ships, but even then the unconquerable spirit of her people could not be made, even by threats which Farragut would never have executed, to haul down the flag of Louisiana from the staffs of the public buildings. However much Farragut may have disappointed the people of the South, by remaining in the navy of the United States, there were about the old sailor those instincts and ideas of a Southern man which must have often returned to him and cost him much mental suffering. No man can shake off in a moment all the associations and convictions of a lifetime, and turn at the prompting of self-interest against the people among whom he was born, had been bred, honored, promoted, and whom he loved and respected. Loyalty to the Union will not explain such a revolution in a Southern man; and neither will the honors and applause which follow success completely eradicate the quiet rebukes which conscience gives, nor completely hide the blush that follows, when old friends turn away and refuse to recognize the apostate. "It is a strange thought," he wrote to his wife, "that I am here [in New Orleans] among my relatives, and yet no one has dared to say 'I am happy to see you.'"

His Southern birth was not forgotten at the North, and notwithstanding his victories, his triumphs, and his apostasy to the South had cut him off from the friends of his youth and manhood, and separated him from the associates of his early naval training, Secretary Welles says:[1]

"That the last days of this brave, truthful, amiable, and exemplary man, for whom his countrymen had, and always will retain, a deep and abiding affection and regard, should have been subjected to petty annoyances from a few who were envious of his fame, or incapable of doing him justice. Although honored and loved by his countrymen, and at the head of the navy, he does not appear to have had the confidence of those who administered its affairs for the last eighteen months of his life, or to have been consulted in matters which personally and officially interested and legitimately belonged to him as naval chief."

It is the old story—they loved the treason, and they rewarded with honors and prize-money the exploits of the apostate son of the South, but they never took him wholly and singly to their hearts. Secretary Welles continues:

"In various ways ignoble and ungenerous minds hastened to mortify the great and unassuming naval chief. In derogation of his real rank and position as chief and head of the navy, he was made port admiral or usher, to wait upon and receive naval officers at New York, an employment which self-respect and regard for the navy compelled him to decline. Among other indignities was that of ordering the uniform and the flag of admiral, which he had adopted when the Government created and conferred upon him the office, to be changed and substituting therefor a different uniform and another flag, wholly unlike the coat he wore, and unlike the symbol of rank which was identified with him, and which from the time the office was created had floated above him. Farragut would neither change his coat nor permit the tawdry substitute for the admiral's flag to wave over him. On his special personal application, which he felt humiliated to make, the Secretary of the Navy permitted him to be spared these indignities during his life, but it was with the knowledge that the flag which he had earned —the emblem he had chosen and prescribed as the symbol of highest naval rank—was to be buried with him. It would be painful to dwell on the many annoyances to which this brave and noble officer was subjected during the last few months of his existence."

[1] *Galaxy*, December, 1871.

CAPTAIN WILLIAM C. WHITTLE, C. S. N.

COMMANDER ISAAC N. BROWN, C. S. N.

CHAPTER XIV.

THE RAMS "ARKANSAS," "QUEEN OF THE WEST," "INDIANOLA," AND "WEBB."

THE immense preparations for building gunboats at St. Louis and other Western cities, by the United States, as heretofore explained, greatly alarmed the Legislature of the State of Tennessee, which, by joint resolutions of June 24th, 1861, called the attention of the Confederate Government to the exposed and undefended condition of all Western waters, and asked for an immediate appropriation of $250,000, for their defence. These resolutions were laid before Congress by a special message from President Davis on July 31st, and the Act of August 24th, making additional appropriations for the navy, included a clause, "for the construction, equipment and armament of two iron-clad gunboats for the defence of the Mississippi River, and the city of Memphis, $160,000."[1] On the day of the approval of that act, Secretary Mallory entered into a contract with John T. Shirley, of the city of Memphis, "to construct and deliver to the Secretary of the Navy of the Confederate States, on or before the 24th day of December, 1861, two vessels of the character and description provided in the plans and specifications" of the Department. Heavy penalties were imposed for delay beyond, and like amounts to be paid for each day previous to, the 24th of December, were embraced in the contract.

The two *vessels* were the rams *Arkansas* and *Tennessee*. The constructor of the *Arkansas* was Prime Emmerson, of Memphis, Tenn. It was necessary for the contractor to begin his work by building two saw-mills, such as would saw long pine timber, which was brought from a distance of 104 miles by railroad; and in addition, the oak timber had to be prepared in five other saw-mills, which were located from ten to twenty miles away.

[1] It is said that this sum was found totally inadequate, and in order to raise funds, which were supplied tardily by the government, Capt. Shirley was compelled to sell his homestead.

The iron was purchased partly in Memphis and more largely in Arkansas, on the other side of the Mississippi River, and was altogether railroad iron. The bolts and spikes had to be rolled on the Cumberland River, and the first lot of these was seized by Confederate officers at Nashville, and taken and put into an iron boat under construction at that city. This required to have the spikes and bolts again rolled, and with increased difficulty. The complement of iron was picked up at one place and another in fifty and one hundred pound lots, wherever it could be found. Very little success attended efforts to procure ship-carpenters in New Orleans, St. Louis, Mobile, and Nashville. Details of these carpenters from the army were refused notwithstanding the efforts of the Secretary of the Navy. The contract was for the completion of the vessels in four months from August 24, 1861, but over seven months passed before their completion. The successful passage of Columbus and Island No. 10, by the enemy, opened the way down to Memphis, and the passage of the Federal fleet of the forts below New Orleans, it was then thought opened the way up to Memphis, and hence the destruction of the *Tennessee*, and the removal of the *Arkansas* to Greenwood, on the Yazoo River, became a necessity. In the removal a barge laden with 400 bars of drilled railroad iron was sunk in the Yazoo, which compelled a delay of several weeks before the barge was raised. Every bar of iron required six holes to be drilled through, and the steam machinery at Memphis for that purpose had to be taken down and transported, and set up before the new iron could be drilled. The *Arkansas* was removed to the Yazoo in April, 1862, before the actual fall of Memphis. These boats were commenced in October, and their construction carried on together; the *Tennessee's* frame having been completed and the planking on her; and the *Arkansas* had her wood-work entirely completed, and her hull covered with iron nearly to the main deck. The iron for the *Tennessee* was on the Arkansas side of the river, when, on the evening before the enemy arrived at Memphis, the boat was burned. The failure to complete the *Tennessee* was due to causes and circumstances beyond the control of either the Secretary of the Navy or the contractor—to the unprepared condition of the country for the speedy completion of such ships. Those natural and unavoidable impediments to speedy work were increased by the refusal of Gen. Polk to detail the carpenters in his army to work upon the rams. The Secretary wrote to him on December 24th, 1861, that:

"The completion of the iron-clad gunboat at Memphis, by Mr. Shirley, is regarded as highly important to the defences of the Mississippi.

"One of them at Columbus would have enabled you to complete the annihilation of the enemy.

"Had I not supposed that every facility for obtaining carpenters from the army near Memphis would have been extended to the enterprise,

I would not have felt authorized to have commenced their construction then, as it was evident that ruinous delays must ensue, if deprived of the opportunity to obtain mechanics in this way.

"These vessels will be armed with very heavy guns, and will be iron-clad, and with such aid as mechanics under your command can afford, they may be completed, I am assured, in sixty days.

"Now I ask, therefore, that you will extend to this department the necessary aid."

The refusal of Gen. Polk is the more extraordinary and unaccountable because he had particularly and emphatically endorsed and recommended Mr. Shirley to the Navy Department, as the contractor for these boats, and Gen. Polk ought to have known, without Secretary Mallory's statement, that "unless mechanics could be obtained from the forces under your command, the completion of the vessels will be a matter of uncertainty." That failure by Gen. Polk to comply with the request of the Secretary caused the latter, on January 15th, to bring the matter to the attention of the President, who was then informed officially that:

"The two iron-clad ships being built at Memphis, and which would be worth many regiments in defending the river, progress very slowly from the difficulty of procuring workmen; Gen. Polk, in command there, having declined to permit the contractor to have any from his forces.

"I have the honor to ask, therefore, that such measures may be adopted as will secure to this department the services of such ship-wrights, carpenters and joiners in the army as may be willing to work for it in the construction of vessels."

On the 10th of April, 1862, Capt. Hollins, then in command of the Upper Mississippi, telegraphed the Navy Department that three iron-clad gunboats of the enemy had passed Island No. 10, and was advised by the Secretary of the Navy to "act according to your best judgment—do not let the enemy get the boats at Memphis;" and on the same day, Commander McBlair, in command of the *Arkansas*, was advised by the Secretary of the passage of Island No. 10 by the enemy's fleet, and to "get your boat to New Orleans, and complete her as soon as possible, if she is in danger at Memphis." But on April 25th, Commander McBlair advised the Department by telegraph that in consequence of the passage of the forts below New Orleans by the enemy's fleet, that he would take the *Arkansas* up the Yazoo River, carrying the material for completing the gunboat, and also carrying the engines of the boat on the stocks, and that arrangements would be made to destroy the *Tennessee*. Accordingly, on the approach of the enemy's gunboats to Memphis the *Tennessee*, being on the stocks, was burned, and the *Arkansas* towed down to the mouth of the Yazoo and up that river to Yazoo City. Below the city, batteries were speedily erected and armed, and a raft was built across the river to protect the ram while being finished from the gunboats of the enemy.

On the 26th of May, 1862, Lieut. Isaac N. Brown,[1] C. S. N., received orders "to assume command of the *Arkansas* and finish the vessel without regard to expenditure of men or money." On the 28th this efficient officer took command at Greenwood. He found the *Arkansas surrounded* by refugee merchant steamers and four miles from dry land. Nothing could be done at that place toward rendering the vessel effective. The barge which had brought down some of the railroad iron intended for armor was sunk in the Yazoo River, the guns and machinery lying on deck, and but one blacksmith's forge and five carpenters were at work. The timber from which the gun-carriages were subsequently made was still growing in the woods. The outlook was certainly anything but encouraging. In two days time the barge was raised from the bed of the river with the railroad iron, and the *Arkansas* taken 160 miles nearer the enemy to Yazoo City. Fourteen forges and 200 carpenters were immediately employed, and divided into day and night parties, were set to work upon the ram. Iron armor was brought by wagons from the railroad, twenty-five

[1] Isaac N. Brown, son of Rev. Samuel Brown, of the Presbyterian Church, was born in Livingston County, Ky,, and appointed an officer in the U. S. navy from Mississippi on the 15th of May, 1834. He served five years on the West India station and Gulf of Mexico, and performed efficient service in the Seminole war on the Florida coast in open boats, and also in the interior. In 1840 he stood his examination at the naval school, then in Philadelphia, and passed No. 1. He served in the Mexican War, first in the Gulf, and was present at the capture of Vera Cruz. He was then transferred to the Pacific coast, where he performed arduous service during the remainder of the war. His service afloat took him three times around Capes Horn and Good Hope, including a voyage to Australia, and going twice around the globe. For a time he served on the Coast Survey, and also at the U. S. Naval Observatory, then under the charge of Commander M. F. Maury. He served one cruise as Executive officer of the U. S. frigate *Susquehannah* in the Mediterranean, and assisted in the first attempt to lay the Atlantic cable. He was the Executive officer of the U. S. frigate *Niagara* when that vessel returned to their homes the first Japanese Embassy to the United States. On the return of the *Niagara* to Boston in 1861, Lieut. Brown finding two governments where the year previous he had left but one, promptly resigned his commission after having given twenty-seven years of his life to the naval service of the United States. He entered the service of the C. S. navy on June 6, 1861, with the rank of lieutenant, and was assigned for duty at the headquarters of the Army of the West, to aid in the defences of the Mississippi River. When Randolph, Fort Pillow and Columbus were armed with heavy guns, Lieut. Brown was sent to Nashville with instructions to purchase and change into gunboats certain river steamers for the defence of the Cumberland River. This work was entered into with his accustomed vigor, but was interrupted by the withdrawal of the Confederate forces from the Cumberland as a line of defence. He was then ordered to New Orleans to contract for and superintend the construction of four iron-clad gunboats. He was pushing this work at the ship yards at Algiers, opposite New Orleans, when that unfortunate city fell into the hands of the enemy. Lieut. Brown proceeded to Vicksburg where he received on May 26th, 1862, a telegraphic order from the Navy Department to assume command of the gunboat *Arkansas.* For his gallant service on board of the *Arkansas* he was promoted to the rank of Commander on August 25th, 1862. After her destruction, during his absence on account of sickness, he resumed command of her surviving officers and men, and was engaged on shore duty in the batteries at Port Hudson. In a short time most of the officers were detached for service on the seaboard, leaving Lieut. Brown with a small command with which he defended the defences on the Yazoo River. While engaged in this duty he destroyed the Federal iron-clads *DeKalb* and *Cairo* by torpedoes in the Yazoo. He was then assigned by Lieut. Gen. Pemberton to the command of a body of troops, and in conjunction with an improvised cotton-clad squadron of river steamers, materially aided in the repulse of an expedition composed of 10,000 men, with several iron-clads, under the command of Gen. Ross, which made an attack on Fort Pemberton. In this engagement a small detachment of the crew of the *Arkansas* with a sixty-four-pounder gun rendered the most effective service. After the fall of Vicksburg Commander Brown was ordered to the command of the C. S. iron-clad *Charleston,* at Charleston, S. C., where he performed good service in the defence of that heroic city. After the fall of Charleston he was appointed to the command of all the naval defences west of the Mississippi, including the coast of Louisiana and Texas. Before reaching his destination, however, he received intelligence of the cessation of hostilities. Returning on parole to his plantation in Mississippi, without a dollar, he overcame the difficulties of his situation, and surrounded by his interesting family cultivated it for the following twenty years. Half of this time he was disfranchised, but on the restoration of his citizenship he declined to take any part in civil or political affairs. Commander Brown is now [1887] a resident of Corsicana, Texas, though still retaining his property in Mississippi.

miles distant, drilling machines started, gun-carriages contracted for, and the work energetically and intelligently pushed.[1]

While working thus assiduously on the ram, Lieut. Brown ordered Lieut. Read to go down to Liverpool Landing, and take measures to protect the *Polk* and the *Livingston*, of the Hollins fleet, which had taken refuge up the Yazoo, from the enemy's gunboats. Lieut. Read's instructions were to protect the two gunboats with cotton, turn their heads down the stream, keep steam up, and be prepared to fight and ram any gunboat of the enemy that might present itself on the river. But Commander Pinkney, then awaiting the arrival of Capt. William F. Lynch, who was to take command of all the naval forces in Western waters, determined to await the arrival of Capt. Lynch, and would not for that reason assent to the programme of operations designed by Lieut. Brown. There remained nothing then to do but to push forward the completion of the ram. Upon his arrival, Capt. Lynch inspected the ram, and dispatched to Secretary Mallory that "the *Arkansas* is very inferior to the *Merrimac* in every particular. The iron with which she is covered is worn and indifferent, taken from a railroad track, and is poorly secured to the vessel; boiler iron on stern and counter; her smoke-stack is sheet iron."[2] Nevertheless, Lieut. Brown completed the ram, and armed her with ten guns: two eight-inch Columbiads in the two forward or bow ports; two nine-inch Dahlgren shell guns, two six-inch rifled, and two thirty-two pounders, smooth bores in broadside, and two six-inch rifles astern. Her engines were new, having been built at Memphis, and on the trial trip had worked well; she had two propellers and separate engines.

[1] Lieut. George W. Gift, a gallant officer of the *Arkansas*, says: "The ship was in a very incomplete condition. The iron of her armor extended only a foot, or a little more, above the water line, and there was not a sufficiency of iron on hand to finish the entire ship. Of guns we had enough, but were short four carriages. In the matter of ammunition and outfit for the battery we were also very deficient. It was fearfully discouraging, but Brown was undismayed. He summoned the planters from the neighborhood and asked for laborers and their overseers. Numbers of forges were sent in, and the work commenced. The hoisting engine of the steamboat *Capital* was made to drive a number of steam drills, whilst some dozen of hands were doing similar work by hand. A temporary blacksmith shop was erected on the river bank, and the ringing of the hammer was incessant. Stevens went to Canton and got the four gun-carriages. I have often been greatly amused when thinking of this latter achievement. He made no drawing before his departure, not knowing that he could find a party who would undertake the job. Being agreeably disappointed in this latter respect, he wrote back for the dimensions of the guns. With two squares I made the measurements of the guns (all different patterns) and sent on the data. In a week or a little more, Stevens appeared with four ox teams and the carriages. However, it would take more space than is necessary to recite all that was done and how it was done. It is sufficient to say that within five weeks from the day we arrived at Yazoo City, we had a man-of-war (such as she was) from almost nothing—the credit for all of which belongs to Isaac Newton Brown, the commander of the vessel."—*Southern Hist. Society Papers*, Vol. XII., No. 5, May 1884.

Brig. Gen. M. L. Smith, who first assumed command of Vicksburg and its defences, on the 12th of May, 1862, in obedience to orders from Major Gen. Lovell, in his official report, dated August, 1862, says: "As bearing immediately upon the defence of this place, measures had also been taken to push the *Arkansas* to completion, It was reported the contractor had virtually suspended work; that mechanics and workmen were leaving; that supplies were wanting; finally, that a very considerable quantity of iron prepared for covering her had been sunk in the Yazoo River. Steps were taken to promptly furnish mechanics and supplies, and bell-boat being obtained and sent up to the spot, the prepared iron was soon recovered. It was considered fortunate that soon after this Capt. Brown was assigned to the duty of completing the boat, as after his assignment this important work gave me no further concern."

[2] Lieut. C. W. Read in *So. Hist. Papers*, Vol. I., No. 5, May 1876.

Her boilers were in the hold below the water line, and her speed was about six knots in still water, or four miles an hour when turned against the current of the river ; she drew fourteen feet of water, and her full complement of officers and men was about 200. The crew of the *Arkansas* was formed of various detachments of men from lately burned gunboats, and of sixty Missouri volunteers from Col. Jeff. Thompson's command, who had never before been on board a gunboat, or seen a heavy gun. They were under the command of Capts. Harris and McDonald. It required all the zeal and ability of these officers to get the crew trained at their guns during the two days they were on board before the conflict with the enemy's fleet.

The naval officers formerly belonged to the old navy, and were young, ardent and skilled. The officers of the *Arkansas* were :

Executive Officer, First Lieutenant Henry K. Stevens; Lieutenants, John Grimball, A. D. Wharton, Charles W. Read, Alphonso Barbot, George W. Gift; Surgeon, H. W. M. Washington; Assistant Surgeon, Charles M. Morfit; Assistant Paymaster, Richard Taylor; First Assistant Engineer, George W. City; Second Assistant Engineer, E. Covert; Third Assistant Engineers, William H. Jackson, E. H. Brown, James T. Doland, John S. Dupuy, James S. Gettis; Acting Masters, Samuel Milliken, J. L. Phillips; Midshipmen, Richard H. Bacot, Dabney M. Scales, Clarence W. Tyler; Master's Mate, J. A. Wilson; Gunner, T. B. Travers; Pilots, J. H. Shacklett, William Gilmore, James Brady and John Hodges.

The model of the *Arkansas* was a combination of the flat bottomed boats of the West and the keel built steamers designed for navigation in deep waters. Her bow was made sharp, and her stem tapered, so as to permit the waters to close readily behind her. In the centre of her hull she was very broad and of great capacity, and for nearly eighty feet along the middle was almost flat bottomed. Her engines were low-pressure, and her two propellers acted independently. It is said she also had a steam hose apparatus by which she could repel boarders—a novelty first introduced in naval warfare. The iron mail of the *Arkansas* was of ordinary railway iron running horizontally, of a single thickness. The quarter and stern had a thin coating of boiler iron. The wheel was within the shield, but the top of the pilot-house, two feet above the shield deck, and through which the pilot looked while steering, was in an unfinished state, having bar-iron over it. The top of the shield was flat and covered with inch bar-iron. The constructor's design was to have made the shield of the " gun box," as Commander Brown called his vessel, solid fore and aft, with side batteries only, and with an iron beak for ramming. This plan was somewhat changed by Commander Brown, so far as to admit of two guns forward and two aft,

1 It is said the militia went into the engagement with the skin of their hands and fingers peeled off, caused by constant exercise at the tackles of the great guns.

with three on each broadside. This gave her a battery of ten guns, four of them mounted on railroad iron *chassis*, and the six broadside guns on carriages constructed at Canton. Notwithstanding the use of every available means, the *Arkansas* could not be made available for service before it became necessary, on account of the rapidly receding waters in the Yazoo, to move the ram down the river, across Satartia bar, below which there was deep water. This was on the 13th of July, six weeks after beginning work on the mere hull at Greenwood. Lieut. C. W. Read was sent with one of the pilots to sound the bar at Satartia. They found plenty of water for the *Arkansas,* but the pilot reported that if the river continued to fall as it had been doing for several days, in five more days there would not be enough for the ram to get down. The man who placed the obstructions in the river said they could not be moved inside of a week. Lieut. Brown instructed Lieuts. Grimball, Gift and Read to examine the obstructions, and report if it was practicable to remove them, so as to allow the *Arkansas* to pass through, and if so, in what time the work could be done. The officers visited the rafts, and after a careful examination reported that they could be removed in less than half an hour.

As soon as Lieut. Commander Brown received this information, he decided to consult with Major Gen. Earl Van Dorn, commanding the defences of Vicksburg, and who had received authority from President Davis to use the *Arkansas* as part of his force. Lieut. C. W. Read was dispatched to Vicksburg to explain the position of the *Arkansas,* and to ask for instructions. He was also directed to reconnoitre the position of the enemy's fleets above Vicksburg. Lieut. Read set out on his mission, riding all night—some fifty miles—and arrived at the general's headquarters about eight o'clock on the following morning and delivered his message. Gen. Van Dorn wrote a letter to Lieut. Brown in which he said that thirty-seven vessels of the enemy were in sight from Vicksburg, and "plenty more up the river,' but believed the *Arkansas* could run past them. He therefore commanded Lieut. Brown to take his vessel through the raft at Haines Bluff, and after sinking the Confederate steamer *Star of the West* in the opening of the obstructions, to go out of the Yazoo and attack the upper fleet of the enemy, to the cover of the Vicksburg batteries.

The Yazoo empties into an old channel of the Mississippi, twelve miles above the city of Vicksburg, and this old channel runs into the main river, three miles below the mouth of the Yazoo. In order to reach the landing and get under cover of the Confederate batteries on shore, it was necessary for Commander Brown to pass his vessel by no less than forty of the most formidable sloops, gunboats, rams and transports then in the service of the U. S. navy.

The distance from Satartia bar to where the combined fleets of Davis, Farragut, and Ellet were waiting the attack of the *Arkansas*, was less than sixty miles of open river; but as it was difficult to see why such an immense force should not meet the assailant half-way, it was not without anxiety that in the first twenty miles of the descent of the Yazoo the discovery was made that (owing to the defects in the engine and in the construction of the after-magazine) the steam had dampened the powder, so as to render it unfit for use. Fortunately the day was clear and the July sun very hot. The *Arkansas* was moored to the bank and, though looking for the enemy's approach at any moment, the powder was landed and spread in the sun to dry. This occupied the greater part of the 14th, and it was midnight before the ram reached Haines Bluff, a few miles from the main river. Here the anchor was let go until early dawn of the 15th of July, a memorable day, on which Gen. Van Dorn truly says, Lieut. Brown "immortalized his single vessel, himself, and the heroes under his command, by an achievement the most brilliant ever recorded in naval annals."

On the night of the 14th, two deserters from the *Arkansas* came on board the U. S. gunboat *Essex*, and stated that the *Arkansas* meditated an attack on the Federal fleet either that night or the following morning. Flag-officers Farragut and Davis, who had joined their fleets on June 28th, above Vicksburg, did not believe the Confederates had sufficient resources to build a formidable vessel in such an out-of-the-way place, but moved by the persistency of the two deserters, they finally decided on the following day to send an exploring expedition up the Yazoo " to procure correct information concerning the obstructions and defences of the river, and ascertain if possible the whereabouts of the ram *Arkansas*."

Soon after daylight on the morning of the 15th, Lieut. Commander Brown ordered the anchors of the *Arkansas* to be raised, and substituting an inferior vessel in place of the *Star of the West* in the obstructions, proceeded down the Yazoo. It was the intention to have made the attack on the Federal fleet at daylight, but on starting from the temporary anchorage the ram ran aground and lost valuable time. At sunrise three of the enemy's vessels were seen rapidly ascending Old River. They were in a line abreast, the iron-clad *Carondelet* of thirteen guns in the centre, the iron-clad ram *Queen of the West* on the starboard, and the gunboat *Tyler* on the port side. At this moment the commander of the *Arkansas* called the officers around him on the shield, and addressed them in these words : "Gentlemen, in seeking the combat as we now do, we must win or perish. Should I fall, whoever succeeds to the command will do so with the resolution to go through the enemy's fleet, or go to the bottom. Should they carry us by boarding, the *Arkansas* must be blown up, on no account must

she fall into the hands of the enemy. Go to your guns!"
Lieut. Gift says :

"Many of the men had stripped off their shirts and were bare to the
waists, with handkerchiefs bound round their heads, and some of the
officers had removed their coats and stood in their undershirts. The
decks had been thoroughly sanded to prevent slipping after the blood
should become plentiful. Tourniquets were served out to division officers
by the surgeons, with directions for use. The division tubs were filled
with water to drink ; fire buckets were in place ; cutlasses and pistols
strapped on ; rifles loaded and bayonets fixed ; spare breechings for the
guns, and other implements made ready. The magazines and shell-rooms
forward and aft were open, and the men inspected in their places. Before
getting under way, coffee (or an apology therefor) had been served to the
crew, and daylight found us a grim, determined set of fellows, grouped
about our guns, anxiously waiting to get sight of the enemy.

"Shortly after sunrise, the smoke from several steamers was discovered by Capt. Brown, who with the First Lieut. Henry K. Stevens,[1]
stood on a platform entirely exposed to the enemy's fire. This was the
signal for fresh girding up, last inspections and final arrangements for
battle. Lieut. John Grimball and myself divided the honor of commanding the eight-inch Columbiads. He fought the starboard and I the port
gun. Midshipman Dabney M. Scales was his lieutenant, and a youngster
named John Wilson, of Baltimore, was mine. Lieut. A. D. Wharton, of
Nashville, came next on the starboard broadside, with Midshipman R. H.
Bacot for his assistant. Lieut. Charles W. Read, of Mississippi, had the
two stern chasers, both rifles, to himself, and the remaining two guns on
the port side were under command of Lieut. Alphonso Barbot. Each
lieutenant had two guns. Grimball and myself had each a bow-chaser
and a broadside gun. The two Masters, John L. Phillips and Samuel
Milliken, were in charge of the two powder divisions. Stevens busied
himself passing about the ship, cool and smiling, giving advice here and
encouragement there. Our commander, Lieut. Isaac Newton Brown,
passed around the ship, and after making one of his sharp, pithy speeches,
returned to his post with glass in hand to get the first sight of the approaching enemy."

Just then the *Carondelet*, for which the *Arkansas* had
been steadily standing, fired her bow guns, at short range,
wore round and accompanied by her consorts made for the
fleet six or eight miles below. The bow guns of the *Arkansas* were now well served in the chase, whose superior speed,
so evident at the beginning of this running fight, soon slackened under the effect of the *Arkansas'* raking fire. In the
meanwhile the latter experienced much annoyance from the
guns and small arms of the other vessels of the Federal
squadron, and from their attempts to gain positions for ramming and raking astern; but whenever the *Arkansas*, leaving the *Carondelet*, steered for them, as alternately and frequently she had to do, they would return to their positions in
the line abreast with the *Carondelet*. In half an hour this
latter vessel, superior in guns and armor to the *Arkansas*,
was silenced and ran in among the willows, where her pursuer, owing to her great depth of water, not caring to follow,
left her, she no longer having the power or apparent disposition

[1] Afterwards killed on board steamer *Cotton*, in Bayou Teche, La.

to offer further resistance, and if not actually surrendering, showing no colors, nor having a man or officer in sight.[1] The consort vessels, too, gave up the fight, abandoning their chief, made their way, at a speed far surpassing that of the *Arkansas*, for the shelter of their main fleet.

In justice to Commander Henry Walke, of the *Carondelet*, we insert his official report of the action. He says:

"We had reached six miles up, when we discovered a formidable looking ram gunboat, since proved to be the celebrated *Arkansas*. The *Queen of the West*, *Tyler* and *Carondelet* at once proceeded down the river to avoid being inevitably sunk, firing upon her with our stern, and occasionally with our side guns. The enemy vigorously returned the fire from her heavy bow guns as she pursued, and had greatly the advantage of us from being thoroughly protected by iron. We had continued the fight about one hour when the *Arkansas* came up, with the evident intention of running us down. I avoided the blow, and as we passed exchanged broadsides at very close quarters. I endeavored to board her, but she passed us too quickly, and I could only fire our bow guns fairly at her stern. Not a shot entered her, however, the shot easily glancing off her invulnerable stern.

"At this moment our wheel ropes were cut off for a third time, and we had to run the boat into shore. As she swung round, we gave the rebel vigorous discharges from our bow and starboard guns. * * * We had now received severe damages in our hull and machinery, more than twenty shots having entered the boat. In the engineer's department, three escape pipes, the steam guage and two water pipes were cut away. In the carpenter's department, nineteen beams were cut away, thirty timbers damaged, and three boats rendered useless. Our deck pumps were cut away also. We had some thirty killed, wounded and missing.

"When the escape pipes were cut away many of the hands jumped into the water."

The following extract from the "log" of the gunboat *Tyler*, gives a partial account of her engagement with the *Arkansas :*

"At 4 A. M. got under way, ran alongside of the *Lancaster* and sent a boat on board of her, which returned with a pilot. At five stood on up the river, followed by the ram *Queen of the West*, the *Carondelet* being ahead. Arrived at the mouth of the Yazoo River at forty-five minutes past five; stood on up. At 7 A. M. discovered a steamer standing down the river, at the distance of a mile, which proved to be the rebel ram *Arkansas*, and immediately opened fire on her with our bow guns, which was returned. The *Carondelet* about a mile and a half astern, and the *Queen of the West* about a quarter of a mile.

[1] As the *Arkansas* passed the *Carondelet* lying helpless and discomfited on the river bank, she fired a broadside while almost touching her. Commander Brown says: "No return fire came from the *Carondelet*, save the working of her engines, no sound or sight of anything to indicate that a live man remained; nor any flag or signal flying to tell which side she belonged to." Lieut. Brown was all this time on the shield of the *Arkansas*, in full view, from his boots to the crown of his cap — within easy pistol range — and not a shot was fired at him. He even walked to the after part of the shield, as his vessel swung off from the *Carondelet* into deep water, as the *Arkansas* was a vessel of more than twice her draft, and when near to her addressed a short speech to Commander Henry Walke of the *Carondelet*, which he could have plainly heard had he been on deck. Notwithstanding the contrary statements of Commander Walke, the truth was that the *Carondelet* had been rendered by the fire of the *Arkansas* a helpless wreck. Indeed he ran away before being shot at.

Lieut. Read says: "We had decreased our distance from the *Carondelet* rapidly, and were only 100 yards astern, our shot still raking him, when he ceased firing and sheered into the bank; our engines were stopped, and ranging up alongside with the muzzles of our guns touching him, we poured in a broadside of solid shot, when his colors came down.

"We commenced backing down the river, keeping up a fire with the guns that could be brought to bear. Finding that she was gaining on us rapidly, we rounded down stream and stood for the *Carondelet*, which vessel was standing down stream, and took a position on her port bow, about one hundred yards distant, keeping up a continuous fire on the ram from our stern gun, and an occasional fire from our broadside battery, the *Carondelet* having already opened on the ram with her stern guns.

"About half-past seven the rebel ram closed with and struck the *Carondelet*, and forced her against the left bank of the river, receiving a discharge from her stern guns. Standing past her, she received the fire of her broadside guns, and stood directly for us, at that time distant about two hundred yards.

"We then stood down the river at all speed, and managed to keep the ram from two hundred to three hundred yards distant from us, keeping up a rapid fire from our stern gun and an occasional discharge from our broadside batteries as we could bring them to bear, receiving the fire of her two bow guns, and occasional discharges from her broadside batteries.

"At half-past eight came within sight of the fleet; forty-five minutes past eight rounded to under the stern of the *Essex*, delivering a broadside at the rebel ram as she was standing down past the fleet.

"At this time the ram was receiving the fire of most all the vessels of our flotilla."

The *Tyler* was a great deal cut up in the engagement, fourteen shot having struck her, eleven of which penetrated the vessel. During the last half hour of the engagement the after part of the gunboat was full of steam, caused by the escape pipe being cut. She had on board during the engagement a detachment of the Fourth Wisconsin regiment, detailed as sharpshooters. Her commander reported a loss of eight killed and sixteen wounded.

The *Tyler* succeeded in reaching the Federal fleet nearly half an hour in advance of the *Arkansas*, thus giving sufficient time to prepare for the reception of the unwelcome visitor. None of the vessels had much steam up, though all had fires in their furnaces. Instantly the utmost efforts were made to get the gunboats ready to manoeuvre in case the *Arkansas* should really make an attack.

In this minor conflict with Commander Walke and his consorts several casualties occurred among the officers and crew of the *Arkansas*. Chief Pilot John Hodges, a man of much worth, was mortally wounded at the wheel, and the wheel partly shot away, and the Yazoo River pilot, J. H. Shacklett, disabled and carried below. Lieut. Commander Brown, at his station on the upper or shield deck, received a severe contusion on the top of his head, and soon after was struck by a Minie ball which grazed his left temple, causing him to fall insensible through the hatchway to the gun-deck within the shield. While being carried to the cockpit he regained consciousness, sent his bearers to their guns, and resumed his place on the shield. He escaped further wounds save slight ones in the shoulder and right hand. Lieut. George W. Gift, a brave son of Tennessee, received a wound in the arm from a splinter. One of the crew, whose curiosity overcame his discretion, putting his head out of the port, while his gun was run in for loading, had it cut cleanly off by a cannon ball. Several others were slightly wounded.

The now alarming fact was reported by the executive officer to the commander, that the temperature of the fire-room had risen to 130 degrees, and that the firemen had to be relieved every ten minutes, the steam which at the beginning of the chase was at 120 pounds, had gone down more than one half. Under this state of things, leaving out the original calculation of slow speed, under full pressure, the use of the *Arkansas*, as a ram, became hopeless, and the alternative of a fight through the Federal fleet, with guns alone, had to be accepted.

Lieut. Gift, in his interesting "story of the *Arkansas*," says that :

"It is quite probable that they [*Carondelet*, *Queen of the West*, and *A. O. Tyler*] imagined we would take to our heels when we saw the odds which were against us. They were mistaken. Owing to the fact that our bow-ports were quite small, we could train our guns laterally very little; and as our head was looking to the right of the enemy's line, we were compelled to allow them to begin the action, which was quite agreeable, as we had levelled all our guns with a spirit-level the day before, marked the trunnions, and agreed that we would not fire until we were sure of hitting an enemy direct, without elevation. The gunnery of the enemy was excellent, and his rifle-bolts soon began to ring on our iron front, digging into and warping up the bars, but not penetrating. Twice he struck near my port, and still we could not "see" him. The first blood was drawn from my division. An Irishman, with more curiosity than prudence, stuck his head out the broadside port, and was killed by a heavy rifle-bolt which had missed the ship. Stevens was with me at the time; and fearing that the sight of the mangled corpse and blood might demoralize the gun's crew, sprang forward to throw the body out of the port, and called upon the man nearest him to assist. "Oh ! I can't do it, sir!" the poor fellow replied, "it's my brother." The body was thrown overboard. This incident of the brother was related to me by Stevens afterwards, for by that time I had enough to do ahead. As soon as we could point straight for the enemy, with safety from grounding, the pilot steered direct for the *Tyler*, and I got the first shot, with an eight-inch shell, with five-second fuse. It struck him fair and square, killing a pilot in its flight and bursting in the engine-room. She reported seventeen killed and fourteen wounded, and I think this shell did the better part of the day's work on her. Unfortunately, the gun recoiled off its *chassis*, and I was out of the action for five or ten minutes. However, Grimball made up for it. He had the best gun captain—Robert McCalla—in the ship, and a superb crew, and his gun seemed to be continually going out and recoiling in again. The broadside guns thus far were not engaged ; but they were not to remain entirely idle. The 'mustang,' summoning courage, shot up as though he would poke us gently in our starboard ribs. Capt. Brown divined his intent, and gave notice in time. The starboard battery was trained sharp forward, and as the *Queen* ranged up, Scales gave her the first shell, followed quick by Warton and Bacot. This settled the account on that side. The Lieut. *Col.* had business down the river, and straightway went to attend to it—that is to say, to quote Gwin [Lieut. Commander of the *Tyler*], he 'fled ingloriously.' This left us with the *Tyler*, now getting pretty sick, and the *Carondelet*, to deal with.

"It was, I think, somewhere about this stage of the fight that a bolt entered the pilot-house and mortally wounded John Hodges, Mississippi pilot, and disabled Mr. Shacklett, Yazoo River pilot, and broke the forward rim of the wheel. James Brady, the remaining Mississippi pilot, took charge, however, and by his admirable judgment and coolness kept the vessel in deep water until she got into the Mississippi, where he knew what he was about. The fight had been an advance on our part; we had never slowed the engines, but stood forward as though we held such small fry in contempt. Gwin handled and fought the *Tyler* with skill as long as there was any hope; but he finally took to his heels, badly crippled, and went after the 'mustang.' What Walke did in the *Carondelet*, in the first part of the engagement, I am not competent to say, as I was mounting my gun, but I think he was 'hacked' quite early, and did but little. At any rate, when I came on the scene again (not more than ten minutes had elapsed from the first gun), and ran out my gun, the *Carondelet* was right ahead of us, distant about one hundred yards, and paddling down stream for dear life. Her armor had been pierced four times by Grimball, and we were running after her to use our ram, having the advantage of speed. Opposite to me a man was standing outside on the port-sill loading the stern chaser. He was so near that I could readily have recognized him had he been an acquaintance. I pointed the Columbiad for that port and pulled the lock-string. I have seen nothing of the man or gun since. We were now using fifteen pound charges of powder and solid shot, which latter were hastily made in Canton, and had *very* little windage; so that I think we bored the fellow through and through from end to end. It was an exceedingly good thing we had. If his stern guns were not dismounted, the crews had deserted them, for they were not used after my gun came into action the second time. I think I had hit four times, and our beak was nearly up to him, when Brady discovered that he was taking to shoal water with the hope of our grounding—we drew four [eight] feet more water than she. Therefore, we sheered off, and passed so close that it would have been easy to have jumped on board. Stevens passed rapidly along the port broadside, and saw the guns depressed to their utmost, and bid us wait for a good chance and fire down through his bottom. As we lapped up alongside, and almost touching, we poured in our broadside, which went crashing and plunging through his timbers and bottom. Although his four broadside guns—one more than we had—were run out and ready, *he did not fire them*. We were running near the left or Vicksburg side of the river (we are now in what is called Old River), and, as soon as passed, we headed for the middle of the stream, which gave Read his first opportunity—and right well did he use it. His rifles 'spoke' to the purpose, for the enemy *hauled down his colors*. In an instant, Capt. Brown announced the fact from the deck, and ordered the firing to cease; but the ship still swinging, gave Wharton and the others a chance at her with the starboard guns before it was known that he had surrendered. White flags now appeared at her ports, and the news of our victory was known all over the ship in a moment.

"Talk about yelling and cheering; you should have heard it at the moment on the deck of the *Arkansas* to have appreciated it. In fifteen minutes, without being checked in our progress, we had thrashed three of the enemy's vessels—one carrying arms as good as ours, and two more guns than we, and one of the others was a famous ram, whilst the third, though of but little account, gave moral support to the others. It was glorious. For it was the first and *only* square, fair, *equal* stand-up and knock-down fight between the two navies in which the Confederates came out first best. From the beginning our ship was handled with more pluck, decision, and judgment than theirs (the *Tyler* excepted); our guns were better fought and better served. Not an officer or man doubted the result from the beginning. We went in to win, and we *won*. We now had no time to stop to secure our prize, as the enemy would be apprised of our coming and swarm in the river like bees if we did not hurry. These fellows we had beaten were but skirmishers of a main army. Consequently we pushed down the river."

On nearing the fleet, a line of men-of-war, seemingly interminable, on the east side of the river, inside of that line a moving mass of rams and iron-clads, on the west side an occasional gunboat, and directly ahead, as if by bulk alone to bar the way, a large ram and a double hull iron-clad flying the flag of an admiral. The grand river was level with its banks, and, as witnesses to the scene about to open and of the prelude just described in Old River, lay the Union camp of many thousand men of all arms, while numerous bomb vessels and an immense fleet of transport steamers lay securely on the west bank near the great host of auxiliaries to the naval investment of Vicksburg. It was not time for the commander of the *Arkansas* to count the hostile ships amidst which he was taking his brave comrades. There were in the Federal squadron at least six iron-clads, each singly superior in armor, guns and speed to the *Arkansas;* seven rams and ten sea-going ships of war among which were some of superior force, the whole commanded by Rear Admirals Farragut and Davis, to say nothing of the river defence fleet under Col. Ellet. 3,000 men, 300 heavy guns, and a vast squadron of iron-clads, gunboats, frigates, etc., against a solitary Confederate vessel of ten guns and 200 men.

The commander of the *Arkansas* had called his little vessel a "box of guns," but as she slowly moved into the Federal line of fire between the hours of seven and eight o'clock on the morning of Tuesday, July 15th, 1862, she became a citadel of flame. Passing grandly along within half a cable's length of Farragut's line, the *Arkansas* received and returned the fire of the entire fleet, and as the enemy closed in astern, from their double inshore line, the Confederate guns at the same moment were fired ahead, astern, port and starboard, dealing death at every point of the compass. The rapid succession of broadsides, commingled with bursting shells, and the sharp hissings of grape, shrapnell and Minie balls, all these, though the noise of the cannonade was heard forty miles from the scene of action, seemed slight to the officers and crew of the *Arkansas* compared with the horrible din and constant concussion of the missiles crushing against and through the side of their vessel. The bright, clear morning was for a time so obscured by smoke, that the red flash from the cannon's mouth produced the illusion of a nocturnal combat. Slowly the combat drifted along the dreadful line, for now the breechings of the *Arkansas'* boilers had been shot away and steam fell to twenty pounds. The temperature in the shield around the guns rose to 120 degrees, and the exhausted firemen coming from below found little relief, save in the nearer excitement of the battle.

The first vessel encountered by the *Arkansas* was gunboat No. 6 of Farragut's fleet, carrying one heavy eleven-inch Dahlgren and two small twelve-pounders at the bow. This boat received several shots from the *Arkansas*, and replied vigorously with her big gun. Without stopping her engines, the *Arkansas* ran past No. 6, and next encountered the *Louisville*, which gave her the full benefit of her broadside and bow guns. The *Arkansas* had by this time reached a position where her shot were effective in every direction, and she used all her guns at the same moment, firing at transports and gunboats indiscriminately. None of the boats were able to give the *Arkansas* more than one or two broadsides before she was out of reach. Most of the balls were thrown at short range, but many of the solid projectiles glanced off, while the shells were shivered into a thousand fragments by the force of the concussion alone. The *Benton, Louisville* and *Cincinnati* moved as speedily as they could turn in the river, and followed closely upon the heels of the *Arkansas*.

As the Confederate ram passed the *Hartford, Iroquois, Richmond, Sumter, Louisville, Oneida, Cincinnati, Sciota, Wissahickon, Winona* and *Essex*, she received a heavy broadside from each. Two of the enemy's eleven-inch solid shot, however, crushed through the sides of the *Arkansas*, doing fearful execution among her men. The iron on her port side, though pierced but twice, had been so often struck with heavy projectiles that it was very much loosened. A few more heavy shots would have caused nearly all of it to have fallen from the sides of the vessel. In many instances solid shot seemed to flatten against her armor, while shells were scattered into thousands of fragments. A shot from one of the boats, at short range, is said to have struck at right angles upon her side and rebounded, falling into the water close to the vessel from which it was discharged. It is also said by those who saw the engagement, that a flash of fire denoted the spot where every ball struck, so terrible was the concussion and so strong the resistance.

The *Arkansas* during her progress down the river put holes in the *Hartford*, the *Iroquois, Richmond* and *Benton*, and half of the gunboats. Her iron prow was prominent to view ; but she did not attempt to use it upon any of the boats after the first attack. The U. S. ram *Lancaster* at one time started for the *Arkansas*, intending to run her down; but before proceeding far she received three shots from the bow guns of Grimball and Gift, one of which severed her steam pipe, by which a number of her crew were scalded, three of them fatally. A daring ram attacking astern, was blown off by the rifle guns of Read and Scales. The iron-clad *Benton*, the flag-ship of Rear-Admiral Davis, guarding the gorge through which led the way to Vicksburg, moved out of the way of the gallant *Arkansas*, and received for her courtesy, through her stern ports, from their very muzzles, the contents of the *Arkansas'* starboard guns. The Federal line was now forced, and the *Arkansas* emerged from the volcano of flame and smoke, from an hour's horizontal iron hail of every description, from thirty-two to two hundred-pounders, hurled by a fleet of about forty formidable

war vessels,—shattered, bleeding, triumphant! The brave
men from below, almost suffocated, hurried up on the shield-
deck and formed a group of hero faces around their commander; just then a heavy rifle shell passed close over their
heads,—it was the last shot noticed, and in another half hour
they were welcomed by the patriotic shouts of the army at
Vicksburg—and the siege of that city was virtually raised!

The enemy continued the pursuit until a shot from one of
the Confederate batteries on shore, thrown into their foremost
vessel, announced that the *Arkansas* was no longer alone in
the unequal contest. The enemy then hauled off their vessels
and returned to their anchorage up the river.

We cannot close this interesting story of the *Arkansas*,
without adding the graphic account of her passage through
the Federal fleet, written by Lieut. G. W. Gift, who was one of
her officers and an eye-witness to what he describes :

"We left the *Carondelet* sinking and pursued the *Tyler* and *Queen of
the West*. Both were swifter vessels than the *Arkansas*, and in our efforts
to overtake them we worked off steam too rapidly and the result was
when we entered the Mississippi River they had gained sufficiently on us
to notify the fleets of Farragut and Davis of our approach, and that before we had come in sight around the point. The result was instant and
rapid preparations by the squadrons for our reception. Steam was hurried up on all the river vessels, and they weighed or slipped anchor, and
took up such positions as would enable them to hit us and at the same
time keep away from our powerful beak, if possible. On coming in sight
of them the scene was one of intense interest. A dozen or more vessels
were steaming about in an uneasy, uncertain way, somewhat after the
manner of a brood of chickens on the approach of a hawk. Tugs, transports and hospital vessels were smoking up or trying to hide. The heavy
sloops-of-war and gunboats of Farragut's squadron were anchored in the
middle of the stream with fires out, but with batteries manned and ready
for battle. On the banks batteries of field artillery were run up and sev
eral thousands of soldiers prepared to shoot Minie balls into our ports
The 'mustang' rams—the same that beat our 'mustang,' Montgomery,
in front of Memphis a short time before—were under way also, but they
did not come to the front too close, with a chap carrying guns and men
who knew how to handle them. I think I do not over-estimate the force
of the enemy when I say he had twenty pennants flying ; and we were
about to attack him in an unfinished and untried vessel, with engines
totally and entirely unreliable. As we stood down to them there was a
decided and painful pause. We were in range, but preferred to save our
strength and ammunition for a close grapple. One of my best men was
a tall, athletic young Irishman who had greatly distinguished himself
for zeal and courage half an hour before. Putting his eye to the gun he
peeped out ahead and saw the immense force assembled to oppose us. In
an instant he was overcome, and exclaimed : 'Holy mother, have mercy
on us ; we'll never get through there!' I had been watching the changing panorama ahead with many doubts and misgivings. A half dozen I
would not have minded, but two dozen were rather more than we had
bargained for. But we had ventured too far to think of backing out ;
through we must go. The first vessel which stood out to engage us was
' No. 6' (*Kineo*), against which we had a particular grudge, inspired by
Read, who desired us all to handle roughly any seagoing vessel we should
see with ' No. 6' on her smoke-stack, as that vessel was engaging the
McRae, above Forts Jackson and St. Philip when Lieut. Com. Huger was
killed. Read, who was first lieutenant under Capt. Huger, and devotedly

attached to him, saw the ' No. 6' by the flashes of the guns, and had ever since treasured the hope of getting alongside the fellow some day. This ' No. 6' came out like a game-cock, steamed to the front to take the fire of a great monster from which ' mustangs' and river iron-clads were hiding and fleeing. I sent my powder boy to Read with a message to come forward, as his friend was in sight. He came leisurely and carelessly, swinging a primer lanyard, and I think I have never looked at a person displaying such remarkable coolness and self-possession. On observing the number ahead his eye was as bright and his smile as genuine as if he had been about to join a company of friends instead of enemies. We were now getting close aboard ' No. 6,' and he sheered with his port helm and unmuzzled his eleven-inch pivot gun charged with grape. It was hastily pointed, and the charge fell too low to enter our ports, for which it was intended. This broke the terrible quiet which hung over us like a spell. Every man's nerves were strung up again, and we were ready for the second battle. With a sharp touch of the starboard helm Brady showed me ' No. 6,' straight ahead, and I gave him a shell through and through, and as we passed he got the port broadside. He did not follow us up. These two shots opened the engagement. Soon we were a target for a hundred or more guns, which poured in an unceasing and terrible fire. Generals Breckenridge, Van Dorn and others viewed the engagement from the top of the court-house in Vicksburg, and were appalled at the apparent rashness of attempting the passage. The fire of the enemy was almost unceasing, nor were we idle by any means. As we have said before, every gun was fully manned, and wherever we looked, in every direction, we saw gunboats. It was only necessary to load the guns and fire and we hit. The rams were taking up a position to come out and strike us as we passed. One of them, the *Lancaster*, was slowly moving across our path, and I heard Brady ask Capt. Brown if he should cut the boat in two. The captain returned an affirmative answer, and the game pilot steadied our ship for the ram. I had in a five-second shell, which I wished to get rid of before we got to the iron-clads, and so set it in motion. It struck his mud-drum, emptying the hot steam and water into the small, barricaded engine-room, where the crew and a company of sharp-shooters were seeking protection, about a hundred of whom were killed. The poor fellows came pouring up the scuttles, tearing off their shirts and leaping overboard as soon as they reached the air. But that gave us no rest. The shot struck upon our sides as fast as sledge-hammer blows. Capt. Brown was twice knocked off the platform, stunned, his marine glass was broken in his hand, and he received a wound on his temple ; but recovering himself, he gallantly—no, heroically—resumed his place, and continued to direct the movements of his ship from a position entirely exposed to the fire of not only great guns, but thousands of sharp-shooters, who were pattering the balls all around and about him. The man of steel never flinched, but carried us straight and clear through. I know that this great battle, and the great commander, have been ignored by the *sect* which ruled the navy, but when the history of our *corps* is written, Brown will rank first. Some one called out that the colors had been shot away. It reached the ear of Midshipman Dabney M. Scales, and in an instant the glorious fellow scrambled up the ladder which was being swept by a hurricane of shot and shell, deliberately bent on the colors again, knotted the halyards and hoisted them up, and when they were again knocked away would have replaced them had not he been forbidden by the captain. Midshipman Clarence Tyler, aide to the captain, was wounded at his post alongside the captain. We were passing one of the large sloops-of-war when a heavy shot struck the side abreast of my bow-gun, the concussion knocking over a man who was engaged in taking a shot from the rack. He rubbed his hip, which had been hurt, and said they would ' hardly strike twice in a place.' He was mistaken, poor fellow, for immediately a shell entered the breach made by the shot, and bedding itself in the cotton-bale lining on the inside of the bulwark proper, exploded with terrible effect. I found myself standing in a dense, suffocating smoke, with my cap gone and hair and beard singed. The smoke soon cleared away, and I found but one man (Quartermaster Curtis) left. Sixteen were killed and wounded by that shell, and the ship set on fire. Stevens, ever cool and thoughtful, ran to the engine-room hatch, seized the hose and dragged it to the aperture. In a few moments the fire was extinguished, without an alarm having been created.

"The Columbiad was fired but once after its crew was disabled. By the aid of an army captain (whose name, I am sorry to say, I have forgotten, belonging to a Missouri battery, Curtis and myself succeeded in getting a shot down the gun, with which we struck the *Benton*. The ill-luck which befell the crew of the bow gun was soon to be followed by a similar misfortune to the crew of my broadside gun. An eleven-inch shot broke through immediately above the port, bringing with it a shower of iron and wooden splinters, which struck down every man at the gun. My Master's Mate, Mr. Wilson, was painfully wounded in the nose, and I had my left arm smashed. Curtis was the only sound man in the division when we mustered the crew at quarters, at Vicksburg. Nor did the mischief of the last shot end with my poor gun's crew. It passed across the deck, through the smoke-stack, and killed eight and wounded seven men at Scales' gun. Fortunately, he was untouched himself, and afterward did excellent service at Grimball's Columbiad. Stationed on the ladder leading to the berth-deck was a quartermaster named Eaton. He was assigned the duty of passing shells from the forward shell-room, and also had a kind of superintendence over the boys who came for powder. Eaton was a character. He had thick, rough, red hair, an immense muscular frame, and a will and courage rarely encountered. Nothing daunted him, and the hotter the fight, the fiercer grew Eaton. From his one eye he glared furiously on all who seemed inclined to shirk, and his voice grew louder and more distinct as the shot rattled and crashed upon our mail.

"At one instant you would hear him pass the word down the hatch: 'Nine-inch shell, five-second fuse. Here you are, my lad, with your rifle shell; take it and go back, quick. What's the matter that you can't get that gun out?' and, like a cat, he would spring from his place, and throw his weight on the side tackle, and the gun was sure to go out. 'What are you doing here, wounded? Where are you hurt? Go back to your gun, or I'll murder you on the spot. Here's your nine-inch shell. Mind, shipmate (to a wounded man), the ladder is bloody; don't slip; let me help you.'

"I have thrown in this slight sketch to show that our men were beginning to straggle, so badly were we cut up. But still the ship was not disabled; seven guns were yet hammering away, and the engines were intact. But steam was down to a terribly low ebb. The party who fitted up the boilers had neglected to line the fire front with non-conducting materials; the consequence was that when a heavy fire of coal was put in the whole mass of iron about the boilers became red-hot, and nearly roasted the firemen, who had also got a tub of ice-water of which they drank freely. The result was that we had to hoist them all out of the fire-room during the action, and Grimball headed a party to supply their place. But I will not detain the reader. We got through, hammered and battered though. Our smoke-stack resembled an immense nutmeg-grater, so often had it been struck, and the sides of the ship were spotted as if it had been peppered. A shot had broken our cast-iron ram. Another had demolished a hawse-pipe. Our boats were shot away and dragging. But all this was to be expected, and could be repaired. Not so on the inside. A great heap of mangled and ghastly slain lay on the gun-deck, with rivulets of blood running away from them. There was a poor fellow torn asunder, another mashed flat, whilst in the "slaughter-house" brains, hair and blood were all about. Down below fifty or sixty wounded were groaning and complaining, or courageously bearing their ills without a murmur.

"All the army stood on the hills to see us round the point. The flag had been set up on a temporary pole, and we went out to return the cheers the soldiers gave us as we passed. The generals came on board to embrace our captain, bloody, yet game."

As soon as the *Arkansas* came in view of the lower fleet of the enemy a great commotion was noticed. Vessels were running hither and thither as if expecting an immediate attack. Presently flames burst out from one of the mortar-boats lying hard aground, and in thirty minutes she had burned to the water's edge. At the same time, several regiments of infantry, camped on shore, piled up their commissary stores, set them on fire, and fled to the transports, which immediately went down stream, the remainder of the fleet following until nearly out of sight, when seeing that the *Arkansas* was not pursuing, came to a halt and returned to its former anchorage.

The New York *Herald*, in its account of the engagement, makes the following table of the total loss of the Federal fleet and the number of shots received by each vessel:

	Killed.	Wounded.	Shots Received.
Carondelet	5	20	20
Tyler	8	16	14
Lancaster	18	10	1
Benton	1	3	6
Sumter	0	0	12
Champion	0	0	3
Dickey	0	0	3
Great Western	0	0	1
Farragut's Fleet	10	20	13
Total	42	69	73

It was ten minutes to nine o'clock in the morning, when the *Arkansas* moored to the wharf at Vicksburg. Her smoke-stack was riddled, and she was otherwise considerably damaged. The scene which followed the landing of the *Arkansas* was of the most thrilling character. Crowds in the city rushed to the wharf frantic with joy. As Commander Brown presented himself to view, the warm, fresh blood still trickling down his furrowed cheeks from his wounded head, the enthusiasm became irrepressible. All felt that the gratitude of the country, and the admiration of the navy, were due to Commander Brown and his brave officers and crew for their most brilliant achievement.

Immediately upon his arrival at Vicksburg, Lieut. Brown sent the following official dispatch to the Navy Department at Richmond:

" VICKSBURG, MISS., July 15, 1862.
"*To Hon. S. R. Mallory:*

"We engaged to-day from 6 to 8 A.M. with the enemy's fleet above Vicksburg, consisting of four or more iron-clad vessels, two heavy sloops-of-war, four gunboats, and seven or eight rams. We drove one iron-clad vessel ashore, with colors down and disabled, blew up a ram, burned one vessel,

21

and damaged several others. Our smoke-stack was so shot to pieces that we lost steam, and could not use our vessel as a ram. We were otherwise cut up, as we engaged at close quarters. Loss, ten killed, fifteen wounded, and others with slight wounds.

"[Signed]   ISAAC N. BROWN,
Lieut.-Commanding."

In recognition of Lieut. Brown's successful feat of gallantry, ranking among the most brilliant of the war, the following tribute was paid him by the Confederate Government:

" CONFEDERATE STATES OF AMERICA, NAVY DEPARTMENT, } " RICHMOND, August 4th, 1862. }

"Commander Isaac N. Brown, C.S.N., commanding steam sloop Arkansas, Vicksburg, Miss.:

" SIR:—Your official report of the engagement of the 15th ultimo, between the screw sloop *Arkansas*, under your command, and the enemy's fleet before Vicksburg, together with the details of the loss sustained by your ship, have been this day received.

" Upon the receipt of your telegraphic dispatch, announcing this achievement, the following response was made :

" RICHMOND, July 18, 1862.

"Lieut.-Commanding Isaac N. Brown, C.S.N., commanding the Arkansas, Vicksburg, Miss.:

" Your telegram announcing the action between the sloop-of-war *Arkansas* under your command, and the enemy's fleet before Vicksburg, has been received, and I am requested by the President to express, in behalf of the country, whose cause you have nobly sustained, his thanks to yourself, your officers and crew.

" For gallant and meritorious conduct you are promoted, and made a commander for the war.

" S. R. MALLORY, *Secretary of the Navy.*

" A grateful country, while deploring the loss of the gallant dead who fell upon this memorable occasion, will place their names upon the roll of her heroes, and cherish them with respect and affection.

" You will please furnish the department with a perfect list of your officers and crew, in order that their names may become known to the country and the service which they have so signally served.

" I am, respectfully, your obedient servant,

" S. R. MALLORY, *Secretary of the Navy.*"

The War Department also received, at the same time, the subjoined dispatch from Gen. Earl Van Dorn:

" VICKSBURG, July 15.

" The sloop-of-war *Arkansas*, under cover of our batteries, ran gloriously through twelve or thirteen of the enemy's rams, gunboats and sloops-of-war.

" Our loss is ten men killed, and fifteen wounded. Capt. Brown, her commander and hero, was slightly wounded in the head.

" Smoke-stack of the *Arkansas* is riddled, otherwise she is not materially damaged, and can soon be repaired.

" Two of the enemy's boats struck their colors, and ran ashore to keep from sinking.

" Many killed and wounded—glorious achievement for the navy, her heroic commander, officers, and men.

" One mortar boat disabled and aground, is now burning up. All the enemy's transports and all the vessels-of-war of lower fleet, except a sloop-of-war, have gotten up steam and are off to escape from the *Arkansas*.

" EARL VAN DORN, *Major General Commanding.*"

In General Orders No. 51, under date of July 22d, Adjutant and Inspector General S. Cooper, by order of the Secretary of War, paid the following compliment to the officers and crew of the *Arkansas* :

"Lieutenant Brown and the officers and crew of the Confederate steamer *Arkansas*, by their heroic attack upon the Federal fleet before Vicksburg, equalled the highest recorded examples of courage and skill. They prove that the navy, when it regains its proper element, will be one of the chief bulwarks of national defence, and that it is entitled to a high place in the confidence and affection of the country."

Congress also passed the following joint resolution of thanks to Lieut. I. N. Brown, and all under his command :

"*Resolved*, by the Congress of the Confederate States of America, That the thanks of Congress are hereby cordially tendered to Lieut. Isaac N. Brown, and all under his command, for their signal exhibition of skill and gallantry on the fourteenth day of July last, on the Mississippi River, near Vicksburg, in the brilliant and successful engagement of the sloop-of-war *Arkansas* with the enemy's fleet.
"Approved Oct. 2, 1862."

It was "with deep mortification" that Admiral Farragut announced to the Federal Naval Department the successful achievement of the *Arkansas;* and Lieut.-Col. Ellet commanding the steam-ram fleet, in a letter to Flag-officer Davis, of the gunboat flotilla, said: "The continued existence of the rebel gunboat *Arkansas* so near us is exercising a very pernicious influence upon the confidence of our crews, and even upon the commanders of our boats." The Federal naval officers feared that the *Arkansas* would run down to New Orleans and capture that city. Immediately after she sought, shelter under cover of the upper batteries at Vicksburg, all the commanders of the Federal fleet were called aboard of Commodore Farragut's flag-ship, the steam sloop-of-war *Hartford*, for consultation. A plan was immediately formed to get the entire upper fleet between the *Arkansas* and New Orleans, and in passing, if possible, sink or capture the ram. An eye-witness gives the following graphic description of Farragut's fleet attempting to destroy the Confederate ram.

"The fleet of Commodore Davis accordingly took up a station at about dark, and opened on the batteries to draw their fire. They succeeded admirably, and at an unexpected moment the fleet of large vessels struck into the channel and descended the river. As each boat arrived opposite the *Arkansas* she slackened and poured her broadside into her. She answered as well as she could in such a storm of missiles, and put one or two balls into our vessels, but her main occupation was to be still and take it. Upwards of a hundred guns, some of them throwing ten-inch shots, poured their deadly charges into her. Seven-inch steel-pointed shot were fired into her. The firing was tremendous. The *Sumter* also ran into her and tried to knock a hole in her hull, but seemingly might as well have run into a rock. The batteries of course joined the engagement, and poured shot into our vessels as well as they could in the darkness.

"The roar of guns was like an earthquake, and nothing more terrific ever was conceived than this grand artillery duel by night. It lasted an hour, and then our vessels passed below and took up their old anchorage.

"In the morning messengers were despatched to see what damage the *Arkansas* had sustained. By going up the opposite bank of the river, she could be plainly seen. Two battles, such as no boat in the world ever went through before, had failed to demolish her."

As the Federal ships and gunboats moved slowly down stream, all the while throwing shot and shell by broadside at the Confederate batteries, into Vicksburg, and at the *Arkansas*, the ram returned the salutations most heartily. Amidst the terrific booming of cannon and the bursting of shells, could be heard the rattle of musketry from a brigade of infantry, which poured volleys into the enemy's rigging and exposed places. For near an hour and a half the roar was deafening and incessant, and to add to the sublimity of the picture, two houses in the city, soon after dark, caught on fire from the shells, and lighted up everything far and wide.

During the furious bombardment, the *Arkansas* changed her position a few hundred feet, having gotten under way to fight to greater advantage, but found it impossible to generate sufficient steam, owing to her smoke-stack being riddled. A well-directed 225-pound wrought-iron bolt struck near the water line of the *Arkansas*, passed through the port side into the dispensary, on the berth-deck, opposite the engine-room, mashed up all the drugs, etc., carried in an ugly lot of iron fragments and splinters, passed over the engine-room, disabling the engine, grazed the steam chimney, and lodged in the opposite side of the ship, between the wood-work and the iron plates. Several of the firemen and Charles Gilmore, one of the pilots, were killed, and James Brady, who had stood at the wheel while in Old River and in passing through the combined fleets above Vicksburg, was wounded and knocked overboard, and an engineer and several others were wounded. Lieut. Stevens stopped the leak, while the bow guns and port broadsides never ceased to pour into each passing vessel a constant fire of shot and shell. The enemy's fleet passed so close to the *Arkansas* that her shots could be distinctly heard crashing through the sides of their ships, and the groans of their wounded were also heard. With the exception of the destructive shot described, the *Arkansas* was not materially injured, but brought five of her guns to bear on the passing vessels.

Lieut. Gift, describing the passage of Farragut's fleet before Vicksburg and the attempt of the enemy to destroy the *Arkansas*, says:

" Our arrival at Vicksburg was hailed with delight by all the army. The officers came on board to see the marks of the struggle, whilst squads of eager privates collected on the bank to get a near view of the wonderful craft which had just stood so much hammering. This attracted a daring band of sharp-shooters to the other bank, and we were forced to open with our heavy guns to disperse them, which was easily accomplished by half a dozen discharges. The enemy below showed decided signs of demoralization. A mortar boat which had been allowed to get aground was hastily set on fire and blown up. A sea-going vessel (commanded by Craven), left to guard the transports, sprung her broadside athwart the stream to be ready for an attack. Everything got up steam, and Porter's flag-boat opened with a hundred-pounder Parrott gun in a spiteful, angry fashion, throwing her shot over and beyond us. If we had a smoke-stack, proper boiler fronts, good engines, a new crew, and many other things, how we would have made a smash of those fellows! But as our smoke-stack was so riddled, the draft was destroyed, and as our engines were troublesome, faulty affairs, and our crew were nearly all killed, wounded, or used up, we had to bide where we were, and see the chance slip away from us. Read cast many longing glances down the river, and I think would have been perfectly willing to undertake the task, broken down as we were. But there is a limit to human endurance; we could do no more, and we rested. During the day the telegraph informed Capt. Brown that he had been promoted to the rank of commander, and we were thanked from Richmond for our brilliant achievement. Our dead were removed on shore for burial, and our wounded were taken to an army hospital. As soon as we arrived at Vicksburg the detachment of soldiers left us to rejoin their command, which reduced our force to a very low ebb. As well as we could, we put the ship to rights, and the day wore away. As soon as dark began to set in, it was evident that the enemy meant mischief.

"Everything was under way, and soon the guns from the upper battery opened quick and sharp, to be replied to by the broadsides of the heavy ships coming down, the *Richmond* (Alden) leading. Our plucky men were again at their quarters, and steam was ready should we be compelled to cast off and take our chances in the stream against both fleets. About that time things looked pretty blue. It is true that we were under the batteries at Vicksburg, but practically we had as well have been a hundred miles from there. The guns were perched on the high hills; they were not provided with sights, and if ever they hit anything it was an accident or the work of one of Brooke's rifles.[1]

"This we well knew, and stripped this time for what we supposed would be a death struggle. The sea-going fleet of Farragut was to pass down, drag out, and literally mob us; whilst the iron-clad squadron of Davis was to keep the batteries engaged. Down they came, steaming slowly and steadily, and seemed to be on the look-out for us. But they had miscalculated their time. The darkness which partially shrouded them from the view of the army gunners, completely shut us out from their sight, inasmuch as our sides were the color of rust and we lay under a red bank; consequently, the first notice they had of our whereabouts came from our guns as they crossed our line of fire, and then it was too late to attempt to check up and undertake to grapple with us. They came by singly, each to get punished, as our men were again feeling in excellent spirits. The *Hartford* stood close in to the bank, and as we spit out our broadside at her, she thundered back with an immense salvo. Our bad luck had not left us. An eleven-inch shot pierced our side a few inches above the water-line, and passed through the engine-room, killing two men outright (cutting them both in two) and wounding six or eight others. The medicines of the ship were dashed into the engine-room, and the *debris* from the bulkheads and splinters from the side enveloped the machinery. The shot bedded itself so far in the opposite side that its position could be told by the bulging protuberance outside. On account of my disabled arm, I had turned over my division to Scales, and remained with Capt. Brown on the platform. To be a spectator of such a scene was intensely interesting and exciting. The great ships with their towering spars came sweeping by, pouring out broadside after broadside, whilst the batteries from the hills, the mortars from above and below, and the iron-clads, kept the air alive with hurtling missiles and the darkness lighted up by burning fuses and bursting shells. On our gun-deck every

---

[1] Not then in position at Vicksburg.

man and officer worked as though the fate of the nation hung on his individual efforts. Scales was very near, and I could hear his clear voice
continually. He coaxed and bullied alternately, and, finally, when he
saw his object in line, his voice rose as clear as a bell, and his 'ready! fire!'
rang out like a bugle note. The last vessel which passed us was that
commanded by Nichols ('Bricktop'), and she got one of our shots in her
out-board delivery. He pivoted his eleven-inch gun to starboard, heeled
his vessel to keep the leak above water, and drifted past the batteries
without further damage.

"We had more dead and wounded, another hole through our armor
and heaps of splinters and rubbish. Three separate battles had been
fought, and we retired to anything but easy repose. One of our messmates
in the ward-room (a pilot) had asserted at supper that he would not again
pass through the ordeal of the morning for the whole world. His mangled
body, collected in pieces was now on the gun-deck; another had been sent
away to the hospital with a mortal hurt. The steerage mess was short
four or five members, whilst on the berth-deck many poor fellows would
never again range themselves about the mess-cloth.   *   *   *   *
The enemy now had a fleet above and below us, and though foiled and
angry, he made no immediate active effort to do us more harm, other than
to shell us incessantly by day, and once by night, with mortar shells. Half
a dozen or more thirteen-inch mortars kept missiles continually in the air,
directed at us. We were twice struck by fragments, otherwise the business was very harmless."

On the morning after the passage of the Federal fleet below Vicksburg, the enemy finding that the *Arkansas* was still
at her moorings, comparatively uninjured and with steam up,
opened on her all their mortar boats above and below the town,
throwing their huge thirteen-inch shells thick and fast around
her. As the mortar-shells fell with terrible force almost perpendicularly, and as the *Arkansas* was unprotected on upper
decks, boilers amidship, a magazine and shell-room at each
end, it was very evident that if she was struck by one of these
heavy shells, it would cause her destruction. Her moorings
were changed frequently to impair the enemy's range; but day
and night from the 16th to the 22d of July, the officers and
crew were exposed to the falling bombs. Quite a number exploded a few feet above decks, and sent their fragments into
the decks, and several burst so near under the water, as to
shake the vessel with earthquake force. [1]

[1] "When the *Arkansas* started down the Yazoo
her crew were seamen with the exception of
about fifty soldiers—volunteers from a Missouri regiment. The seamen had been on the
Yazoo swamps some time, and in consequence
were troubled with chills and fever. Many had
been killed, a large number wounded, and a
greater portion of the remainder sent to the
hospital on the arrival at Vicksburg. The day
after we reached the city the Missouri volunteers, who had agreed to serve only for the trip,
went on shore and joined their command; so
we were now very short-handed. Capt. Brown
asked Gen. Van Dorn to fill up our complement
from the army, which he readily assented to do,
provided the men would volunteer, and make
application for transfer through proper channels. At first quite a number volunteered, but
when they got on board and saw the shot-holes
through the vessel's sides, and heard sailors' reports of the terrible effect of shell and splinters,

and were made aware of the danger of the
mortar-shell that fell continually around the
ship, those volunteers found many pretexts
to go back to their commands; many took
the 'shell fever,' and went to the hospital.
As a general thing, soldiers are not much
use on board ship, particularly volunteers,
who are not accustomed to the discipline
and routine of a man-of-war. A scene that
occurred on board the *Arkansas* one day at
Vicksburg is illustrative. We were engaged
hauling the ship into a position near one of our
batteries; but having but few sailors to haul on
the wharf, we were progressing slowly, when
Lieut. Stevens, the executive officer, came on
deck, and perceiving a crowd of volunteers sitting on deck playing cards, he said rather
sharply: 'Come, volunteers, that won't do; get
up from there and give us a pull.' One of the
players looked up at Lieut. Stevens and replied:
'Oh! hell! we aint no deck hands;' and eyeing

Notwithstanding the immense hammering the *Arkansas* received from the combined fleets of the enemy, in a few days she was ready to assume the offensive. Upon one occasion, while under the command of Capt. William F. Lynch, who had relieved Commander Brown for a few hours, to enable him to go ashore and take a dinner and a sound sleep, of which he was in great need and which he had not had for more than a week, the *Arkansas* left her moorings in front of Vicksburg, and proceeded up the river beyond the range of the batteries with the intention of destroying the enemy's mortar boats. Her appearance created the greatest excitement in the enemy's fleet, and though the mortar boats were under the protection of the Eads iron-clads, each of them superior in arms and armament to the *Arkansas*, the boats were taken in tow and run up the river at a speed far surpassing that of the Confederate ram. As the *Arkansas* had but a limited supply of coal, and there was 1,000 miles of open river ahead, the pursuit was abandoned, and she returned to the city. On the next day Commander Brown resumed his command, and in attempting to ascend the river to drive off the Federal mortar fleet, the starboard engine became disabled, and it was with difficulty he could return to his moorings in front of the city.

On the 21st of July, Flag-officers Farragut, Davis, and W. D. Porter held a council of war on board the *Benton*, at which Commander Porter volunteered the service of the *Essex* to make an effort to destroy the *Arkansas*, and the following programme was agreed on:

"That on the morning of the 22d, precisely at four o'clock, the whole available fleet under command of Flag-officer Davis was to get under way, and when within range to bombard the upper batteries at Vicksburg; the lower fleet under Flag-officer Farragut was to do the same, and attack the lower batteries; the *Essex* was to push on, strike the rebel ram, deliver her fire, and then fall behind the lower fleet."

In accordance with this plan Commodore Porter got under way, passed the *Benton*, and proceeded down the river.

the man sitting opposite to him, was heard to say: 'I go you two better!'

"Both of our surgeons being sick, Capt. Brown telegraphed out into the interior of Mississippi for medical volunteers. In a day or two a long, slim doctor came in from Clinton; and as he was well recommended, Capt. Brown gave him an acting appointment as surgeon, and directed him to report to Lieut. Stevens for duty. It was early in the morning when he arrived; the enemy had not commenced their daily pastime of shelling us; the ship's decks had been cleanly washed down, the awnings spread, and everything was neat and orderly. The doctor took breakfast in the ward-room, and seemed delighted with the vessel generally. Before the regular call to morning inspection the officer of the powder division started around below to show the new medical officer his station during action, and the arrangement for disposing of the wounded, etc., etc. In going along the berth-deck, the officer remarked to the doctor that in a battle there was plenty to do, as the wounded came down in a steady stream. The 'medico' looked a little incredulous; but a few minutes afterwards, when he perceived the road through which an eleven-inch shell had come, his face lengthened perceptibly; and after awhile, when the big shell began to fall around the vessel, he became rather nervous. He would stand on the companion-ladder and watch the smoke rise from the mortar-vessels, and would wait until he heard the whizzing of the shell through the air, when he would make a dive for his state-room. As soon as the shell fell he would go up and watch out for another. Occasionally when a shell would explode close to us, or fall with a heavy splash alongside, he would be heard to groan: 'Oh! Louisa and the babes!'" — *Reminiscences of the C. S. Navy, by C. W. Read, Southern Historical Society Papers.* Vol. I. No. 5. May 1876.

A more opportune moment to destroy the *Arkansas* could not have been chosen, as many of her officers and all but twenty-eight of her crew were ashore in the hospitals, and she laid helpless at anchor with a disabled engine.

At daylight on the 22d of July, the iron-clad fleet above Vicksburg dropped down and commenced firing rapidly at the Confederate upper batteries. Farragut's fleet engaged the lower batteries, and the mortar-vessels opened upon the city and forts. The cannonading was tremendous, and fairly shook the earth. In about half an hour after the firing had begun, the large and formidable iron-clad ram, the *Essex*, emerged from the smoke above and made directly for the *Arkansas*. Commander Brown received the attack at anchor, with a crew sufficient to work two guns, but with the aid of his officers he was able to man all the guns which could be brought to bear. When the muzzles of the guns of both vessels were nearly touching each other, the broadside of the *Arkansas* was exchanged for the bow guns of the *Essex*. As the latter struck the *Arkansas* one of her ten-inch solid shots struck the armor of the *Arkansas* a foot forward of the larboard forward port, cutting off the ends of the railroad iron and driving the pieces forward diagonally across from forward to aft, split upon the breech of the starboard after gun, killing eight men and wounding six, half of the crew. The *Essex* swung alongside of the *Arkansas*, when the latter gave her a port broadside with guns depressed, which apparently disabled the *Essex*, for she ceased firing and drifted down the river.[1]

Commander Porter, in his official report, says that as he passed the *Benton*:

"Flag-officer Davis hailed me and 'wished me success.' I now pushed on, according to my understanding of the programme, and precisely at half-past four A. M. the enemy's upper batteries opened upon me, but I heard no response at this time from our fleets. I arrived at the ram, delivered my fire and struck her; the blow glanced, and I went high on the river bank with the bows of the ship, where I lay ten minutes under three batteries of heavy guns. I backed off and loaded up. The enemy had drawn up three regiments of sharp-shooters and several batteries of field pieces, ranging from six-pounders to twenty-four pounders. I found it impossible under these circumstances to board the rebel boat, though such was my original intention. After I delivered my fire at but five feet from the ram we distinctly heard the groans of her wounded and saw her crew jumping overboard. At this time I began to look for aid from the fleets, but without result. I ordered the pilots to get the *Essex's* head up stream, with the intention of holding on until the lower fleet came up, and then make another attack on the ram. At this time I was under the guns of three batteries, one of which was not over one hundred feet off. A heavy ten-inch shot from the nearest battery struck my forward casemate about five feet from the deck, but fortunately did not penetrate. A rifle seven and a half-inch shot from the same battery

---

[1] In the engagement the two vessels were so close to each other that several of the officers and crew of the *Arkansas* had their faces blackened and severely hurt by the powder which flashed through the ports of the *Arkansas* from the guns of the *Essex*.

struck the casemate about nine feet from the deck. It penetrated the iron, but did not get through, though so severe was the blow that it started a four-inch plank two inches and eighteen feet long on the inside. A conical shell struck the casemate on the port side as we were rounding to, penetrated the three-quarter-inch iron and came half way through the wooden side. It exploded through, killing one man and slightly wounding three. A small piece grazed my head, and another piece tore the legs of the First Master's pantaloons.

"I had now been under fire for upwards of an hour, and thirty minutes of the time from eighty-feet to one hundred yards of some of the enemy's heaviest batteries. I still looked for the arrival of the lower fleet, but saw nothing of it. I held on for a short time longer, but the enemy began to fire with such rapidity and we were so close that the flashes of his guns through my gun-holes drove my men from the guns. At last, through the smoke, I saw the lower fleet nearly three miles off, and still at anchor. Seeing no hope of relief or assistance, I now concluded to run the gauntlet of the enemy's lower forts and seek an anchorage below the fleet. I therefore reluctantly gave the order to 'put her head down stream;' but I was determined to be in no hurry. They had now plenty of time to prepare, and so rapid was their fire that for half an hour the hull of this ship was completely enveloped in the heavy jets of water thrown over her by the enemy's shot, shell and rifle balls. The department may have some idea of the amount and number of shot, shell, plugs and rifle missiles thrown at this vessel when they are now informed we were two hours and a-half under fire of seventy heavy guns in battery, twenty field-pieces and three heavy guns on board the ram. During that time this vessel was heavily struck forty-two times, and only penetrated twice."

Soon after the *Essex* had encountered the *Arkansas*, the ram *Queen of the West*, under the command of Lieut.-Col. Alfred E. Ellet, commander of the steam-ram fleet, attempted to run her down. The ram passed the batteries under a terrific fire, and ran into the *Arkansas*, which made both vessels tremble from stem to stern. The *Arkansas* seemed to shrink and yield before the tremendous blow, and for a moment it was thought her side would give way; but she re-acted and the ram flew back from her, and, in moving toward her again, ran into the river bank. The *Queen of the West* reversed her engines and ran on again so forcibly as to strain her own works badly. By this time the *Queen* had been struck twenty or twenty-five times. Her smoke-stack was perforated with balls; one of her steam-pipes had been shot away; in various places large holes had been put through her sides and bow. As she was seriously injured in her hull, and leaking, and liable to be captured by the Confederates, Col. Ellet determined if possible to effect his escape. As he passed the *Arkansas*, the ram gave him a parting broadside which nearly ended the career of the *Queen*. The *Queen* moved up the river, and the Confederate batteries increased their fire. Heavy shot and shell fell before, behind, and around her, and every few seconds one would go tearing through her deck or cabin. As she passed one of the upper batteries, a thirty-four pound shot struck her in the rear, went through every one of her larboard state-rooms, in which no person happened to be at the time, into the captain's office, penetrating the iron safe, and passing out, shattered the wooden carriage of one of the mounted brass pieces on the boiler deck, dismounting the gun, and hitting it, left a deep indentation in the metal.

The *Queen* ran by the batteries through a terrible fire and made her appearance above the bend in the river riddled with shot. A correspondent of the New York *Tribune* said:

"The *Queen* presents a most dismantled and forlorn appearance, and is as nearly shot to pieces, for any vessel that will float, as can well be imagined. The many who have visited her since her terrible experience are with difficulty persuaded that not one of her crew was killed or dangerously wounded. She has the semblance of a complete wreck, and it will be necessary to send her North at once for repairs, though some think her injury too great for remedy—that she is not worth the mending.

"Shells exploded in her cabin, shivering her furniture, crockery, and state-rooms to pieces. The wardrobe of the crew was converted into rags, and hardly a whole garment or a pair of boots or shoes can be found on the boat. She is dented and damaged, and blackened and splintered, and singed and shattered, as if she had passed through a score of the fiercest battles, and presents as good an example of the amount of injury that may be done to a boat without absolutely destroying her as it would be convenient to present, or easy to discover in twelve months' service on the flotilla."

Lieut. Gift, in his account of the engagement of the *Arkansas* with the *Essex* and the *Queen of the West*, says:

"Our crew was fearfully used up on the 15th. Daily we sent more men to the hospital, suffering with malarious diseases, until we had not in a week more than thirty seamen, ordinary seamen and landsmen, and I think but four or five firemen. Many of the younger officers had also succumbed; those of us who were left were used up also. We slept below, with our clothes on, in an atmosphere so heated by the steam of the engines as to keep one in a constant perspiration. No more men were to be had. It was disheartening enough to see a ship which but a week before was the pride of the country now almost deserted. On the morning of the 22d of July, a week after our arrival, as we awakened early in the morning by the drum calling us to quarters, great commotion was observed in the fleet above. Everything seemed under way again, and it was evident that we were soon to have another brush. On our decks were not men enough to man two guns, and not firemen enough to keep steam up if we were forced into the stream! Rather a doleful outlook! We were moored to the bank, head up the river, as a matter of course. The fires under the boilers were hastened, and every possible preparation made for resistance. In a few minutes we observed the iron-clad steamer *Essex* ('Bill Porter' commanding) steaming around the point and steering for us. The upper battery opened, but she did not reply. Grimball unloosed his Columbiad, but she did not stop. I followed, hitting her fair, but still she persevered in sullen silence. Her plan was to run into and shove us aground, when her consort, the *Queen of the West*, was to follow and butt a hole in us; and thus the dreaded ram was to be made way with. On she came like a mad bull, nothing daunted or overawed. As soon as Capt. Brown got a fair view of her, followed at a distance by the *Queen*, he divined her intent, and seeing that she was as square across the bow as a flat boat or scow, and we were as sharp as a wedge, he determined at once to foil her tactics. Slacking off the hawser which held our head to the bank, he went ahead on the starboard screw, and thus our sharp prow was turned directly to her to hit against. This disconcerted the enemy and destroyed his plan. A collision would surely cut him down and leave us uninjured. All this time we had not been idle spectators. The two Columbiads had been ringing on his front and piercing him every shot; to which he did not reply until he found that the shoving game was out of the question; then, and when not more than fifty yards distant, he triced up his three bow port shutters and poured out his fire. A nine-inch shot struck our armor a few inches forward of the unlucky forward port, and crawling along the side entered. Seven men were killed outright and six wounded. Splinters flew in all directions. In an instant the enemy was alongside, and his momentum was so great that he ran aground a short distance astern of us. As he passed we poured out our port broadside, and as soon as the stern rifles could be cleared of the splinters and broken stanchions and wood-work, which had been driven the whole length of the gun box, we went ahead on our port screw and turned our stern guns on him, every man—we had but seventeen left—and officer went to them. As he passed he did not fire; nor did he whilst we were riddling him close aboard. His only effort was to get away from us. He backed hard on his engines and finally got off; but getting a shot in his machinery just as he got afloat, he was compelled to float down stream and join the lower fleet, which he accomplished without damage from batteries on the hills. He fired only the three shots mentioned. But *our* troubles were not over. We had scarcely shook this fellow off before we were called to the other end of the ship—we ran from one gun to another to get ready for a second attack. The *Queen* was now close to us, evidently determined to ram us. The guns had been fired and were now empty and inboard. *Somehow* we got them loaded and run out, and by the time she commenced to round to, I am not sure, but I think we struck her with the Columbiads as she came down, but at all events the broadside was ready. Capt. Brown adopted the plan of turning his head to her also, and thus received her blow glancing. She came into us going at an enormous speed, probably fifteen miles an hour, and I felt pretty sure that our hour had come. I had hoped to blow her up with the thirty-two pounder as she passed, but the gun being an old one, with an enlarged vent, the primer drew out without igniting the charge. One of the men—we had no regular gun's crews then, every man was expected to do ten men's duty—replaced it and struck it with a compressor lever; but too late, his boilers were passed, and the shot went through his cylinder timbers without disabling him. His blow, though glancing, was a heavy one. His prow, or beak, made a hole through our side and caused the ship to careen, and roll heavily; but we all knew in an instant that no serious damage had been done, and we redoubled our efforts to cripple him so that he could not again attempt the experiment. As did the *Essex*, so he ran into the bank astern of us, and got the contents of the stern battery; but being more nimble than she, was sooner off into deep water. Returning up stream he got our broadside guns again, and we saw that he had no disposition to engage us further. As he passed the line of fire of the bow guns he got it again, and I distinctly recollect the handsomest shot I ever made was the last at her. He was nearly a mile away, and I bowled at him with the gun lying level. It *ricochetted* four or five times before it dropped into his stern. But it dropped there. As I have said before, the *Essex* was drifting down stream unmanageable, and now would have been our time to have ended her in sight of both squadrons, but we had but seventeen men and they well-nigh exhausted. Beating off these two vessels, under the circumstances, was the best achievement of the *Arkansas*. That we were under the batteries of Vicksburg did not amount to anything. I do not believe that either vessel was injured by an army gun that day. We were left to our fate, and if we had been lost it would have been no unusual or unexpected thing. The *Essex* used in one of her guns that day projectiles that were probably never used before, to wit: Marbles that boys used for playing. We picked up a hundred unbroken ones on our forecastle. There were 'white-allies,' 'chinas,' and some glass marbles. I wish the naval reader to understand that the *Essex* did not return the fire as she lay alongside us, did not attempt to board, although he had a picked crew for that purpose, and fired but three guns in the fight, and thereafter kept her ports closed. Brown, no longer able to play the lion, assumed the *role* of the fox with consummate skill."

Notwithstanding the terrific engagements the *Arkansas* had passed through, in her combats with the two Federal fleets on the Mississippi River, she was comparatively uninjured, and on the following day, after her contest with the *Essex* and *Queen of the West*, she was seen steaming up and down the river in front of the batteries at Vicksburg in contempt of all the efforts that had been made to destroy her.

The Federals held Baton Rouge, the capital of Louisiana, forty miles below the mouth of Red River, with a land force of about 5,000 men, in connection with two powerful fleets. It was a matter of great necessity for the Confederates that the navigation of Red River should be opened as high as Vicksburg. Supplies, much needed, existed there, hard to be obtained from any other quarter, and strong military reasons demanded that the Confederates should hold the Mississippi at two points, to facilitate communication and co-operation between the military district of Mississippi and the trans-Mississippi department. The capture of Baton Rouge, and the forces of the Federals at that point, would open the Mississippi, secure the navigation of Red River, then in a state of blockade, and also render easier the recapture of New Orleans. To this end Major Gen. Earl Van Dorn gave orders to Gen. Breckenridge to move upon Baton Rouge. To ensure success he also ordered the *Arkansas* to co-operate with the land forces by a simultaneous attack from the river. In his official report, he says: "All damages sustained by the *Arkansas* from the fleets of the enemy had been repaired, and when she left the wharf at Vicksburg for Baton Rouge, she was deemed to be as formidable, in attack or defence, as when she defied a fleet of forty vessels-of-war, many of them iron-clads."

With such effective means, Gen. Van Dorn deemed the taking of Baton Rouge and the destruction or capture of the enemy on the land and water the reasonable result of the expedition. By epidemic disease, the land force under Major Gen. Breckenridge was reduced to less than twenty-five hundred effective men. The *Arkansas*, after passing Bayou Sara, within a short distance of Baton Rouge, in ample time for joint action at the appointed hour of attack, suddenly became unmanageable, from a failure in her machinery and engine, which all the efforts of her engineers could not repair. The gallant Breckenridge, advised by telegram every hour of her progress toward Baton Rouge, and counting on her co-operation, attacked the enemy with his whole effective force, drove the Federals from all their positions, and forced them to seek protection under the cover of their gunboats.

In his official report of operations at Vicksburg and Baton Rouge, dated September 9th, 1862, Major Gen. Earl Van Dorn says: "I think it due to the truth of history to correct the error, industriously spread by the official reports of the enemy, touching the destruction of the *Arkansas*. She was no trophy won by the *Essex*, nor did she receive injury at Baton Rouge from the hands of any of her adversaries. Lieut. Stevens, her gallant commander,[1] finding her unmanageable, moored her to the shore. On the cautious approach of the enemy, who kept at a respectful distance, he landed his crew, cut her from her moorings, fired her with his own hands, and turned her adrift down the river. With every gun shotted, our flag floating from her bow, and not a man on board, the *Arkansas* bore down upon the enemy, and gave him battle. Her guns were discharged as the flames reached them, and when her last shot was fired, the explosion of her magazine ended the brief but glorious career of the *Arkansas*. 'It was beautiful,' said Lieut. Stevens, while the tears stood in his eyes, 'to see her, when abandoned by commander and crew, and dedicated to sacrifice, fighting the battle on her own hook.' I trust that the official report of Commander Lynch will do justice to the courage, constancy and resolution of the officers and men, who were the last crew of the *Arkansas*."

From a statement of Lieut. Read, of the *Arkansas*, it appears the ram steamed leisurely down the river from Vicksburg to within fifteen miles of Baton Rouge, when her starboard engine broke down. Repairs were immediately begun, and at eight o'clock were partially completed, though she was not in a condition to encounter many of the Federal vessels on account of the injury received. On rounding the point near Baton Rouge, the starboard engine again broke down,

[1] Important repairs were yet necessary to the engines of the *Arkansas*, and to replacing and refastening her shattered armor. While these were under way, Commander Brown obtained a furlough from the Navy Department until the repairs were made and the *Arkansas* was ready for action. He proceeded to Grenada, Miss., about six hours ride by rail from Vicksburg, where his family had taken refuge. Immediately upon his arrival he was taken severely ill, and while unable, as he thought, to get out of bed, he received intelligence from Commander Stevens informing him that he had received instructions from Gen. Earl Van Dorn to co-operate with Gen. Breckenridge in the attack on Baton Rouge. Commander Brown sent positive orders to Lieut. Stevens not to move his vessel until he could join it, as the *Arkansas* was not ready for action. Commander Brown caused himself to be taken to the depot, and being unable to sit up, was put in the mail car and laid on the mail bags until he arrived at Jackson, Miss., 130 miles distant. At the latter place Commander Brown heard that the *Arkansas* had left Vicksburg four hours before, and was then on her way to Baton Rouge. It appears that Gen. Van Dorn was peremptory in his orders for the co-operation of the *Arkansas*, and Lieut. Stevens being undecided, had referred the matter for his decision to Capt. Wm. F. Lynch, the senior officer of the C. S. navy in the West, who was at Jackson, Miss. Ignorant or regardless of the condition of the *Arkansas*, Capt. Lynch ordered Lieut. Stevens to disobey the instructions of Commander Brown and comply with the request of Gen. Van Dorn. In this way the *Arkansas* was placed under the command of Lieut. Stevens, with orders to run 300 miles against time. When her engines broke down within sight of Baton Rouge, Lieut. Stevens, who was as humane as he was true and brave, finding that he could not bring a single gun to bear upon the approaching enemy, sent all his officers and crew ashore over the bow, and remained alone to set his ship on fire. This he did so effectually that he had to jump over the stern into the river, and save himself by swimming, and the *Arkansas*, whose decks had never been pressed by the foot of an enemy, with colors flying was blown into the air. After the destruction of the *Arkansas*, Commander Brown joined the camp of Gen. Breckenridge at Baton Rouge, and passed a night in his tent, who, seeing he was still an invalid, that great and good man insisted on his taking his narrow camp mattress, while he slept on the ground beside him.

and the ram drifted ashore in sight of the city on the Arkansas side. Repairs were immediately begun, and the ship got afloat at five o'clock the same evening. The engineer reported that the engines were unreliable. It was determined to make a trial trip up the river to ascertain the strength of the engines, and the *Arkansas* proceeded some five hundred yards when the engines again broke more seriously than ever. The crew were engaged all night in repairs. On the following morning at eight o'clock the lookouts reported the Federal fleet coming up the river. The ram was moored head down stream and cleared for action, and in this condition her officers and crew determined to fight her to the last. At this moment the engineer reported the engines ready for service, and that they would last half a day. The lines were cut, and the *Arkansas* started for the *Essex* with the intention of running her down. The ram proceeded about three hundred yards in the direction of the *Essex* when the starboard engine again suddenly stopped. The *Arkansas* was then steered for the river bank, her stern down, the *Essex* pouring a hot fire into her. In this condition the ram opened fire with her stern gun. The *Essex* continued to advance, and when within four hundred yards, the crew of the *Arkansas* were ordered ashore. and the vessel cut adrift and set on fire. After all hands were ashore the *Essex* fired upon the disabled vessel most furiously. In an hour after her abandonment, as she was drifting down upon the Essex, the fire communicated to her magazine, and all that remained of the noble *Arkansas* was blown up.

Lieut. Gift in continuation of his narrative of the "story of the *Arkansas*" says :[1]

"Capt. Brown was sick in Grenada, and telegraphed Stevens not to go down, as the machinery was not reliable. Application was made by Gen. Van Dorn to Commodore Lynch, who gave the order to proceed down the river as soon as possible. The vessel was hurriedly coaled and provisioned, and men and officers hastened to join her. Capt. Brown left his bed to regain his ship, but arrived too late. He subsequently followed down by rail and assumed command of the crew shortly after the destruction of the vessel. The reader must not construe any remark here to reflect on Stevens. Such is not my intention. He was a conscientious Christian gentleman, a zealous and efficient officer. In the performance of his duty he was thorough, consistent and patriotic. His courage was of the truest and highest type; in the face of the enemy he knew nothing but his duty, and always did it. Under this officer we left Vicksburg thirty hours before Gen. Breckinridge had arranged to make his attacks. The short time allowed to arrive at the rendezvous made it imperative that the vessel should be driven up to her best speed. This resulted in the frequent disarrangements of the machinery and consequent stoppages to key up and make repairs. Every delay required more speed thereafter in order to meet our appointment. Another matter operated against us. We had been compelled to leave behind, in the hospital, our chief engineer, George W. City, who was worn out and broken down by excessive watching and anxiety. His care and nursing had kept the machinery in

[1] Southern Historical Society Papers for January and February, March, April and May, 1884. Vol. XII. Nos. 1 and 2, 3, 4, 5.

order up to the time of leaving. We soon began to feel his loss. The engineer in charge, a volunteer from the army, had recently joined us, and though a young man [1] of pluck and gallantry, and possessed of great will and determination to make the engines work, yet he was unequal to the task. He had never had anything to do with a screw vessel or short-stroke engines, and, being zealous for the good repute of his department, drove the machinery beyond its powers of endurance.

"The reader may wonder why the machinery of a vessel of so much importance should have been entrusted to a strange and inexperienced person, and ask for an explanation. Were there not other engineers than Mr. City in the navy, and, if so, where were they? There were dozens of engineers of long experience and high standing at that time in the navy, most of whom were idle at Richmond and other stations. At or near the mouth of Red River, the engines had grown so contrary and required to be hammered so much that Stevens deemed it his duty to call a council of war to determine whether it was proper to proceed or return. The engineer was summoned, and gave it as his opinion that the machinery would hold out, and upon that statement we determined to go ahead. A few miles below Port Hudson, he demanded a stoppage to key up and make all things secure before going into action. We landed at the right bank of the river, and I was dispatched with Bacot to a house near by to get information. After a deal of trouble we gained admittance, and learned that the naval force of the enemy at Baton Rouge consisted of our particular enemy the *Essex*, and one or two small sea-going wooden gunboats. This was very satisfactory. We learned, also, that Breckenridge was to attack at daylight; that his movements had been known for several days on that side of the river; yet it will be borne in mind that the important secret could not be entrusted to high officers of the navy until a few hours before they were to co-operate in the movement. At daylight we heard our gallant troops commence the engagement. The rattle of the volleys of musketry, mixed with the deep notes of artillery, informed us that we were behind, and soon came the unmistakable boom of heavy navy guns, which plainly told us that we were wanted; that our ironsides should be receiving those missiles which were now mowing down our infantry. In feverish haste our lines were cast off and hauled aboard, and once more the good ship was driving toward the enemy. Like a war-horse she seemed to scent the battle from afar, and in point of speed outdid anything we had ever before witnessed. There was a fatal error. Had she been nursed then by our young and over-zealous engineer she would have again made her mark in the day's fight. We were in sight of Baton Rouge. The battle had ceased; our troops had driven the enemy to the edge of the water, captured his camps and his positions, and had in turn retired before the heavy broadsides of the *Essex*, which lay moored abreast of the arsenal. Our officers and crews went to quarters in high spirits, for once there was a chance to make the army and country appreciate us. Baton Rouge is situated on a "reach" or long, straight stretch of river, which extends three or four miles above the town. We were nearly to the turn and about to enter the "reach;" the crew had been mustered at quarters, divisions reported, and all the minute preparations made for battle which have before been detailed, when Stevens came on deck with Brady, the pilot, to take a final look and determine upon what plan to adopt in his attack on the *Essex*. It was my watch, and we three stood together. Brady proposed that we ram the *Essex*, and sink her where she lay, then back out and put ourselves below the transports and wooden gunboats as soon as possible to cut off their retreat. Stevens assented to the proposal and had just remarked that we had better go to our stations, for we were in a hundred yards of the turn, when the starboard engine stopped suddenly, and, before the man at the wheel could meet her with the helm, the ship ran hard and

[1] I have forgotten his name.

fast aground, jamming herself on to some old cypress stumps that were submerged. We were in full view from the position Gen. Breckenridge had taken up to await our attack. All day long he remained in line of battle prepared to move forward again, but in vain. On investigation it was found that the engine was so badly out of order that several hours must be consumed before we could again expect to move. There lay the enemy in plain view, and we as helpless as a sheer hulk. Hundreds of people had assembled to witness the fight. In fact, many ladies in carriages had come to see our triumph. They waved us on with smiles and prayers, but we couldn't go. But Stevens was not the man to give up. A quantity of railroad iron, which had been laid on deck loose, was thrown overboard, and in a few hours we were afloat. The engineers had pulled the engine to pieces and with files and chisels were as busy as bees, though they had been up constantly then for the greater parts of the two preceding nights. At dark it was reported to the commanding officer that the vessel could be moved. In the meantime some coal had been secured (our supply was getting short) and it was determined to run up stream a few hundred yards, and take it in during the night, and be ready for hot work in the morning. Therefore we started to move; but had not gone a hundred yards before the same engine broke down again; the crank pin (called a "wrist" by Western engineers) of the rock-shaft broke in two. Fortunately one of the engineers was a blacksmith, so the forge was set up and another pin forged. But this with our improvised facilities used up the whole night. Meantime the enemy became aware of our crippled condition, and at daylight moved up to the attack. The *Essex* led, and came up very slowly, at a rate not to exceed two miles an hour. She had opened on us before the last touch had been given to the pin, but it was finished and the parts thrown together. As the ship again started ahead Stevens remarked that we were brought to bay by a superior force, and that he should fight it out as long as we would swim. The battle for the supremacy of the river was upon us, and we must meet the grave responsibility as men and patriots. His plan was to go up the river a few hundred yards and then turn on and dispatch the *Essex*, then give his attention to the numerous force of wooden vessels which had been assembled since the morning before. The pleasant sensation of again being afloat and in possession of the power of locomotion, was hardly experienced before our last and final disaster came. The port engine this time gave way, broke down and would not move. The engineer was now in despair, he could do nothing, and so reported. The *Essex* was coming up astern and firing upon us. We had run ashore and were a hopeless, immovable mass. Read was returning the fire, but the two ships were scarcely near enough for the shots to tell. We were not struck by the *Essex*, nor do I think we struck her. An army force was reported by a mounted 'home guard,' to be coming up the river to cut off our retreat. Stevens did not call a council of war, but himself assumed the responsibility of burning the ship. I recollect the look of anguish he gave me, and the scalding tears which were running down his cheeks when he announced his determination. Read kept firing at the *Essex* until Stevens had set fire to the ward-room and cabin, then all jumped on shore, and in a few moments the flames burst up the hatches. Loaded shells had been placed at all the guns, which commenced exploding as soon as the fire reached the gun-deck. This was the last of the *Arkansas*."

The war has been over for more than twenty years, but the errors in the bulletins of the fight are uncorrected even in the histories written long after the excitement of the conflict has passed away. Farragut's reports, as highly colored as a newspaper correspondence, recur in Porter's history without even a note of explanation to make plain the real facts, and W. D. Porter's report that the *Essex* blew up the *Arkansas* finds a place in the records of the war to continue the delusion. Admiral Porter does indeed cast doubt on both reports, saying: "The *Arkansas* was soon set on fire and totally destroyed—whether from the shells of the *Essex* or by the Confederates to escape capture, is not known. The Confederates claim that one of her engines was disabled, and that she was destroyed by them; but be that as it may, her destruction was due to the presence of the *Essex* and her two consorts." And Admiral Farragut[1] says: "Although Bill Porter *did not* destroy her, he was the cause, and thought his shells did the work! for they would hardly have destroyed her unless he made the attack. I insist that Porter is entitled to the credit of it."

The destruction of the *Arkansas* resulted from her disabled condition, and from the impossibility of repairing her engines anywhere on the Mississippi River. Admiral Porter regards the statements of the Confederate officers destroying the *Arkansas* as a "very unlikely story," and that "it is not credible that a vessel, which had run the gauntlet of the two fleets under Farragut and Davis, at Vicksburg, inflicting great injury in return, would avoid a conflict with the *Essex* (a vessel of weaker hull and very much less speed), unless she had been first so crippled by the *Essex's* guns that her commander saw no hope of success." That is a conclusion which the facts do not warrant; and as illogical as to say that "while Admiral Farragut 'did not attach much importance to Confederate rams,' he had seen enough of the performances of the *Arkansas* to know that if properly managed she was the most formidable vessel on the Mississippi River, and that there would be no security against her while she floated." It is not true that "the events that took place on board the ram, except through vague reports, have never come to light." Lieut. Stevens' report, supplemented by the statements of Lieutenants Gift and Read, and the prisoners mentioned by Flag-officer Farragut in his report to the Secretary of the Navy, dated August 10, 1862,[2] fully shows all that took place on the ram, and that she was no trophy to the *Essex's* shells—for they broke harmless on her armored sides, and inflicted no injury on her hull, her armament, or her machinery. The inherent defects of a badly constructed engine, built under circumstances

[1] Life and Letters, p. 289.

[2] Flag-officer Farragut in his report to Secretary Welles, on August 10th, 1862, says:
"SIR: Since forwarding the reports of Lieuts. Fairfax, Ransom, and Roe, we have picked up a number of prisoners from the ram *Arkansas*, all of whom I have catechised very closely. They agree very well respecting her exit from the Yazoo, and her passing the fleets; they also agree as to the number of killed and wounded on each of these occasions, making in all eighteen killed and a large number of wounded. At Vicksburg they plated the deck with iron, and fortified her with cotton inside. She then came down in command of Lieut. H. K. Stevens, (Brown having been taken sick at Vicksburg,) with the intention of making a combined attack with Gen. Breckenridge upon Baton Rouge; but her port engine broke down. They repaired it in the course of the day, and went out to meet the *Essex* the next morning, when they saw her coming up; but the starboard engine gave way, and they ran her ashore, she being perfectly unmanageable.

"They say that when the gunboats were seen coming up, and the *Essex* commenced firing, the captain set the ram on fire and told the crew to run ashore. They also state that the gunboats *Webb* and *Music* were sent for to tow her up the river, but they did not arrive, and neither of them had been seen. This is the statement."

22

that could not be improved, disabled the *Arkansas* in the very presence of her enemy, and rendered her destruction necessary to prevent her becoming the trophy of battle. The letter of S. L. Phelps to Admiral Foote,[1] shows that "the *Arkansas* fairly caught the vessels napping, and, coming upon them so unexpectedly, was able to drive her furious, and, as it actually proved, destructive way through the fleet. The first attempt of Farragut to destroy her was unsuccessful, doubtless owing to the darkness; and the second attempt by Davis was not followed up by a general attack of the lower fleet owing, it would seem, to a misunderstanding." This second attempt Mr. Phelps pronounced "a fizzle;" and the epithet applies with equal force to the attempt to claim for the *Essex* the honor of destroying the *Arkansas*.[2]

The junction of the fleets of Admiral Farragut and Flag-officer Davis, above Vicksburg, had been attained without material loss, but not without some feelings of disappointment on the part of Farragut. In a letter of June 2d, 1862, he expresses his feelings at what the Navy Department had required of him. "The government appear to think we can do anything. They expect me to navigate the Mississippi, nine hundred miles, in the face of batteries, iron-clad rams, etc., and yet, with all the iron-clad vessels they have North, they could not get to Norfolk or Richmond. The iron-clads, with the exception of the *Monitor*, were all knocked to pieces. Yet I am expected to take New Orleans, and go up and release Foote from his perilous situation at Fort Pillow, when he is backed by the army and has iron-clad boats built for the river service, while *our* ships are to be periled by getting aground and remaining there till next year; or, what is more likely, be burned to prevent them falling into the enemy's hands. A beautiful prospect for the 'hero' of New Orleans."[3] Every vessel on the Mississippi, floating the Confederate flag below Vicksburg, had been swept out of existence, and all that remained above that city were scattered in rivers and bayous. Of the fleet formerly under Hollins, the *Polk* and the *Livingston* found a hiding-place up the Yazoo River, where they were burned by Commander Pinkney, and the *Van Dorn*, of the Montgomery flotilla, shared the same fate.[4]

---

[1] Life of Admiral Foote, p. 351.

[2] Lieut. Commander George M. Ransom, of the U. S. gunboat *Kineo*, in his report to Flag-officer Farragut, on August 6th, 1862, says: "I believe that she [the *Arkansas*] had suddenly become helpless by some failure of her engines; and seeing our approach, so formidable to her in her crippled condition, doubtless they set her on fire and abandoned her. About one o'clock her magazine exploded, and the ram *Arkansas* was *extinct*."

Flag-officer Farragut, in reporting this fact to Secretary Welles, on August 7th, said: "It is one of the happiest moments of my life that I am enabled to inform the department of the destruction of the ram *Arkansas*."

[3] Life of Farragut, p. 269.

[4] A Yazoo City correspondent of the Jackson *Mississippian*, July 12th, 1862, writes:

"Two of the enemy's gunboats, or rather hay-plated rams, made a reconnoitering trip up the Yazoo River as high as Liverpool yesterday, and returned immediately on seeing the fire produced by the burning of the gunboats *Livingston*, *Polk* and *Van Dorn*—the two former having been burnt by order of Commodore Pinkney, chief in command—the *Van Dorn* catching fire from the other burning vessels, thus destroying these three valuable boats.

"Capt. Isaac N. Brown had procured 400 bales of cotton and had it placed on the *Livingston* and *Polk*, with a view of making fire-ships of

In March, 1863, Acting Rear Admiral David D. Porter sent an expedition up the Yazoo Pass, under the command of Lieut. Commander Watson Smith. Soon after entering the Tallahatchie, Lieut. Smith was taken sick, and Lieut. Commander James P. Foster took command. The expedition was composed of the iron-clads *DeKalb* and *Chillicothe*, and the steamers *Rattler* and *Lioness*, with a large land force under Gen. Quimby. It proceeded as far as Fort Pemberton on the Tallahatchie River, which the gunboats engaged for several days, but were finally repulsed by Commander Isaac N. Brown, C. S. navy, and a small force of Confederates who were defending it. Lieut. Commander Foster, in his official report to Rear Admiral Porter, on April 13th, 1863, said:

"The first attack made on Fort Pemberton was on the 11th of March, on a reconnoisance, about 11 A. M., when five or six shots were exchanged, doing little or no damage. On the afternoon of the same day the *Chillicothe* again went down and opened fire on the fort. During the action the *Chillicothe* had four men killed and fifteen wounded; after having a whole gun's crew disabled the *Chillicothe* withdrew.

"On the 13th the *Chillicothe* and *Baron DeKalb* got under way at 11:30 A. M., and commenced the attack on Fort Pemberton, at 780 yards. The *Chillicothe* remained in action one hour and thirty-eight minutes. During this action she received forty-four shots; and after expending nearly all of her ammunition of five-inch and ten-inch shells, retired by order of the commanding officer. On the retiring of the *Chillicothe* the fort ceased firing, although the *DeKalb* remained, and kept firing slowly during the remainder of the day.

"On the 18th we retired, believing the fort too strong for the forces there engaged, and being short of ammunition.

"The day after leaving Fort Pemberton the *Chillicothe*, *DeKalb*, light-drafts, etc., arrived before the fort again; and at the suggestion of Gen. Quimby the *Chillicothe* took her old position before the fort, firing three shots for the purpose of drawing the enemy's fire; failing in this, she withdrew. We, along with those on shore, were under the impression that the enemy blew up a torpedo just forward the *Chillicothe's* bow.

"We remained twelve days waiting for the army to do something; and when General Quimby was ordered to withdraw his forces, we brought up the rear."

On the 15th of March, the enemy landed an eight-inch gun from the gunboat *Baron DeKalb*, with a supply of ammunition, and placed it in battery on shore, with a crew to work it.

them, connecting them by a chain, and with steam up to run head on and destroy any ascending boat. This design would have been carried out by Capt. Brown and his officers but for the untimely and unnecessary sacrifice by Commodore Pinkney. Not only were these valuable vessels thus needlessly destroyed, but also the clothing of the crew, provisions, small boats, small arms, chains and anchor from which the *Arkansas* expected to supply herself.

"All these vessels were moored to the shore and protected by batteries, only at the time needing men to man the guns to drive back the enemy's vessels; but the gallant commodore's whole thoughts seemed bent upon the destruction rather than the protection of the boats, and not a man was sent to the guns ashore.

"Before the boats were fired a squad of militiamen offered their services to remove the provisions from the boats, assuring Pinckney that all care should be taken of them; but he would not allow anything to be carried ashore, preferring that all should be destroyed.

"Capts. Brown and Carter just arrived at the scene of this wanton destruction as the boats were fired—too late to save them by their counsels if they had been heeded, for both these gentlemen condemned the act in unmeasured terms.

"It is not known what became of the commodore after his 'brilliant' performance, as Capt. Brown sought to have an interview with him, but could not do so. Nor is it known how much the gallant chief saved of his personal effects, for he certainly saved nothing for his country—but he did heroically manage to have taken ashore, without injury, a pair of pet chickens and a poodle dog."

On the 19th, they took the gun on board from the shore battery, and retired with severe loss in both killed and wounded. The *DeKalb* was considerably cut up, losing ten gun-deck beams, having the wheel-house and steerage badly knocked to pieces, and various other damages to the wooden parts of the vessel. The *Rattler* was considerably damaged, and lost several in killed and wounded.

The Federals reported that they caused the Confederates to sink the steamers *Star of the West, Magnolia,* and *Natchez.*

On the 15th of May, 1863, Rear Admiral Porter came up the Yazoo, with a formidable fleet of gunboats, to co-operate with Gens. Grant and Sherman, in their siege of Vicksburg. On the 18th, he put his fleet in communication with the Federal land force near Snyder's Bluff, and sent them provisions from below. In the meantime, the Confederates were evacuating Haines' Bluff, which Lieut. Commander Walker, of the *DeKalb,* found abandoned when he reached that point. The works at Haines' Bluff were designed by C. S. navy officers. and were very formidable. The fortifications and the rifle-pits extended about a mile and a quarter.

Having blown up the magazines, and destroyed the works generally, Acting Rear Admiral Porter started Commander Walker up the Yazoo River, with sufficient force to destroy all the Confederate property above the obstructions. In the meanwhile, Gen. Grant was closely investing Vicksburg, and had already in his possession the most commanding points.

As the Federal gunboats approached Yazoo City, the Confederate navy-yard, and all pertaining to it, was burned by Commander Isaac N. Brown, C. S. N., to prevent its falling into the enemy's possession. The Federal vessels arrived at Yazoo City, at 1 P. M. on the 21st of May, and were met by a committee of citizens, who informed Commander Walker that the place had been evacuated by the military and naval authorities, and asked protection. Lieut. Commander Walker, of the U. S. gunboat *Baron DeKalb,* in his report says:

"The vessels burned were the *Mobile,* a screw vessel, ready for her planking, the *Republic,* which was being fitted out for a ram, and a vessel on the stocks—a monster—310 feet long and 70 feet beam.

"The navy-yard contained five saw and planing-mills, an extensive machine shop, carpenter and blacksmith shops, and all the necessary fixtures for a large building and repairing yard, which with a very large quantity of lumber were burned. I also burned a large saw-mill above the town.

" Most of the public stores had been removed; such as I found in town were taken on board the vessels or destroyed."

After the return of the expedition under Lieut. Commander Walker to Yazoo City, Acting Rear Admiral Porter sent him up again, with instructions to capture transports, so as to break up all transportation on the river. In his report, dated

June 1st, 1863, Lieut. Commander Walker from the "Mouth of the Yazoo," said:

"I left this place on the morning of the 24th of May, with the *DeKalb*, *Forest Rose*, *Linden*, *Signal* and *Petrel*. I pushed up the Yazoo as speedily as possible for the purpose of capturing or destroying the enemy's transports in that river. The *Signal* knocked down her smoke-stacks and returned the same night. Leaving the *DeKalb*, with orders to come on as fast as possible, I pushed on with the *Forest Rose*, *Linden* and *Petrel*, to within fifteen miles of Fort Pemberton, when I found the steamers *John Walsh*, *R. J. Lockland*, *Golden Age* and *Scotland*, sunk on a bar, completely blockading it up.

"Failing in my efforts to make a passage through the blockade, I fired them, destroying all but such parts of the hulls as were under water. These steamers were fine boats, in good order, and if I had had the means could have been raised and saved. I remained at that point during the night, and next morning at daylight was attacked by a force of the enemy, but after a sharp fire of a few minutes they beat a hasty retreat. Our only loss was two men belonging to the *Petrel*, wounded. Returning down the Yazoo, I burned a large saw-mill twenty-five miles above Yazoo City. At Yazoo City I landed and brought away a large quantity of bar, round, and flat iron from the navy-yard. Arriving at the mouth of Big Sunflower, I proceeded up that river about 180 miles, until stopped by shoal water. At Indian Shoot I sent Volunteer Lieut. Brown, of the *Forest Rose*, with boats through to Rolling Fork. He found a quantity of corn belonging to the rebels, which he burned. At the mouth of Bayou Quirer, hearing of steamers, I sent Lieut. Brown, with the boats of the *Forest Rose* and *Linden*, up after them. After ascending ten miles he burned the *Dew Drop* and *Emma Bett*. The *Linden* burnt the *Argo* in a small bayou about seventy-five miles up Sunflower.

"I also found the *Cotton Plant* sunk in Lake George, with nothing out of water but the tops of her smoke-stacks.

"At Gawin's Landing, on the Sunflower, I found and brought away a cutter which was lost on the Deer Creek expedition. Returning, I arrived here last evening."

In July a naval and military expedition was sent to Yazoo City to capture the Confederates who had re-occupied that place. The army and navy made a combined attack on the works which the Confederates abandoned. While the Federal gunboat *Baron DeKalb* was moving slowly along she ran foul of a torpedo planted in the river by Commander Isaac N. Brown, C. S. N., which exploded and sunk her. Acting Rear Admiral Porter says: "Many of the crew were bruised by the concussion, which was severe, but no lives were lost. The officers and men lost everything. She went down in fifteen minutes."

At the retreat from Fort Pillow, the *Maurepas*, under Lieut. Commander Fry, and *Pontchartrain*, under Lieut. Commander John Dunnington, of Hollins' fleet, were sent up White River. The short service of the *Maurepas* is best told by the report of her commanding officer, Lieut. Fry:

"C. S. Gunboat 'Maurepas,' }
"Des Arc, Ark., June 6th, 1862. }

"General: I arrived at this place on the 22d ult., with a crew of less than ten men, exclusive of my firemen and coal passers. It was absolutely necessary, if I proposed doing anything besides frightening the enemy, that I should have the co-operation of a land force, which, despite all my efforts, I was unable to obtain. One or two companies of cavalry would have sufficed if I could get no more; but the first colonel I could hear from concluded I was under his command, and ordered me to stay where I was until further orders. This order, of course, I disregarded; as, according to my judgment, no man under the rank of a Brigadier-General can possibly form a correct judgment of the contingencies governing the movements of a gunboat.

"Having armed a few citizens, I proceeded with them to act as sharp-shooters up the river to Jacksonport. At Grand Glaze some 200 of the enemy's cavalry preceded us ten minutes. The turns of the White River resemble a bow-knot, and cavalry, and even infantry, by cutting across points could keep ahead of us; and in ambuscade, could have killed every man on board of us. We, however, never saw the enemy till we got near Jacksonport, which place had been evacuated in part in anticipation of our arrival with a large land force. The enemy (Ninth Illinois Cavalry) retreated in time across Black River. I fired about ten shots into the woods in the direction of their flight. * * * * * * *

"The gentlemen who volunteered their services to me rendered efficient assistance in rolling out and burning the cotton. My crew destroyed the sugar. The river had fallen so that we rubbed hard in getting up, and was falling so rapidly that I had not a moment to spare. I barely saved the boat as it was, and had to leave unburned about 900 bales. These were housed, and our party had determined to burn the house containing them, but on the representation of a person who came to me and said that it would burn the town, I prevented it. I learned subsequently that it might have been destroyed without risk to the city.

"The citizens, in their enthusiasm, got some of my men drunk, and my citizens in some instances left off work to plunder. One got the Provost-Marshal's trunk, containing his commission, uniform, and some papers. I have the original book containing the oath of allegiance exacted from the citizens as the price of their being at liberty and exempt from plunder(!)

"A man named Peoples rides a fine horse, goes heavily armed, and pilots Federal scouts on foraging expeditions. At his nod one is spared and another sacrificed. His house was close to the Federal camp. I stopped at his place, burnt the house, corn-crib, etc., considering it important as a retaliatory measure. I have taken prisoners several persons who have voluntarily taken the oath of allegiance, arrested suspicious persons, and caused the arrest of a traitor spy named Lewis Smith, who has served in our army, and was greatly trusted. I have the Federal vouchers for his pay in my possession. The visit of my boat will not be without its fruit. * * * * * * *

"Respectfully, your obedient servant,
"JOSEPH FRY."[1]

A Federal expedition was fitted out at Memphis, consisting of the *Mound City, St. Louis, Lexington, Conestoga*, and a number of transports, and was dispatched up White River to the relief of Gen. Curtis. Resistance to such an expedition by the *Maurepas* would have been futile, so her commander sunk her and two wooden boats across the channel at St. Charles, Ark., and placing the guns of the *Maurepas* in battery on the heights, brought the Federal expedition to a halt, and compelled an action, in which one of the shot from Fry's guns penetrated the steam-chest of the *Mound City*, and the escaping steam soon compelled her crew to take to the water. In

[1] Life of Capt. Joseph Fry, p. 163.

contemporaneous accounts of this engagement, a very improbable story gained considerable circulation that Lieut. Commander Fry had ordered his men to fire on the struggling men in the water. The improbability that a man of Fry's character could give such an order, is confirmed by its impossibility, on account of Fry being at least a quarter of a mile further down the river when the gun was fired which exploded the steam-chest of the *Mound City*. At the point below, Lieut. F. M. Roby had command of one Parrott gun, and Lieut. Commander Fry was with him. [1]

Lieut. Fry's account of the affair [2] is that "it had been reported to him that the Federals were sending small boats loaded with armed men from the gunboats below, with a view of cutting off his retreat from the rear. Under these circumstances, Lieut. Roby, with five or six riflemen, was stationed to open fire on these boats, in order to interfere with their design of cutting off his retreat. It was that justifiable and proper firing that was misrepresented as a shooting of drowning and struggling men while in the water. His report from on board the U. S. naval hospital ship *Red Rover*, to which he was carried when captured and wounded, was : "I sunk the *Maurepas* to close the channel on White River, to prevent the Federal gunboats (four in number) from ascending. I then landed

---

[1] The following is the official report of Flag-officer Davis :

UNITED STATES FLAG SHIP "BENTON,"}
MEMPHIS, June 19, 1862. }

SIR: The *Conestoga*, Lieut. Commanding G. W. Blodgett, arrived here to-day from White River. She brings information of the capture of two batteries at St. Charles, eighty miles from the mouth, the first of which mounted four Parrott guns and the second three forty-two-pounder rifled guns. Three guns, it is understood, were taken from the gunboat *Mariposa*, *i.e.*—*Maurepas*, which, after being dismantled, was sunk. There is now but one gunboat remaining in White River, the *Pontchartrain*, mounting three or five guns, and having her machinery protected by iron and cotton.

The enemy has attempted to block up the river by driving piles and by sinking boats, but no serious obstructions have yet been discovered.

The *Conestoga* will return to White River to-night with reinforcements, accompanied by an additional transport, laden with commissary stores.

The victory of St. Charles, which has probably given us the command of White River, and secured our communication with Gen. Curtis, will be unalloyed with regret but for the fatal accident to the steam drum and heater of the *Mound City*, mentioned in my telegraphic dispatch. Of the crew, consisting of one hundred and seventy-five officers and men, eighty-two have already died, forty-three were killed in the water or drowned, and twenty-five are severely wounded, and are now on board the hospital boat. Among the latter is Capt. Kilty. They promise to do well. Three officers and twenty-two men escaped uninjured.

After the explosion took place, the wounded men were shot by the enemy while in the water, and the boats of the *Conestoga*, *Lexington* and *St. Louis*, which went to the assistance of the

scalded and drowning men of the *Mound City*, were fired into, both with great guns and muskets, and were disabled, and one of them forced on shore to prevent sinking.

The forts were commanded by Lieut. Joseph Fry late of the U. S. N., who is now a prisoner and wounded.

The department and the country will contrast these barbarities of a savage enemy with the humane efforts made by our own people to rescue the wounded and disabled, under similar circumstances, in the engagement of the 6th inst Several poor fellows, who expired shortly after the engagement, expressed their willingness to die when they were told that the victory was ours.

I have the honor to be, very respectfully, your obedient servant,

C. H. DAVIS,
Flag-officer Commanding Western Flotilla.

To Hon. GIDEON WELLES,
Secretary of the Navy.

[2] A correspondent of the Baltimore *Gazette* contributed the following brief account of Capt. Joseph Fry, of the C. S. N., who afterwards commanded the *Virginius* :

" He was born in Florida, and served many years in the U. S. navy; from the latter he resigned to join the Confederacy, in which he held the rank of lieutenant. As such he served on the Mississippi, first under the command and on the flagship of Commodore Hollins at New Orleans. After the fall of that city he had command of a small gunboat which the Federal fleet drove into one of the smaller Western rivers—the White, I think—and finding it impossible to save her, he sunk his boat, landed his battery on a bluff, and opened a fire that disabled one of his pursuers, and drove the remainder off. The fleet, however, returned, and throwing a body of some 500 marines in his

my crew, and assisted by Capt. Dunnington, with two guns' crew from the *Pontchartrain*, and some forty or fifty riflemen, fought the gunboats, until a large land force in our rear compelled me to retire up the bank of the river. I lost six or eight of our men, and was the only officer captured or wounded that I know of."

The report of Lieut. John W. Dunnington, C. S. N., of the engagement at St. Charles, Arkansas, was as follows:

"Confederate States Gunboat 'Pontchartrain,' ⎰
"Little Rock, Ark., June 21st, 1862. ⎱

"General: As the senior officer in command of the naval forces, in the absence of Capt. Fry, C. S. N., I beg leave to submit the following report of the engagement between our forces and the enemy's gunboats at St. Charles, on the morning of the 17th instant:

"I reached St. Charles on Monday evening, 16th instant, about 6 P. M., with the men I carried with me to work the two rifled thirty-two-pounder cannon, which I had previously placed there in battery. I found our forces there under arms. The smoke of the enemy's gunboats was plainly seen from the bluff, and the pickets who had come in reported two gunboats, one tug, and two transports below, advancing. Owing to the unexpected approach of the enemy, Capt. Fry had not time to land his guns, but immediately placed his vessel across the river above my battery of rifled guns, and intended to resist their progress. Finding the enemy did not advance, after dark it was determined to sink the gunboat *Maurepas*, the transports *Eliza G.* and *Mary Patterson*, in a line across the river. The sinking of the transports was entrusted to Capt. Leary.

rear, while some four or five steamers opened on his front, made it hot for his two guns and sixty or seventy men. Fighting all around to the bitter end, Fry never did surrender, and the first knowledge he had of the battle's finish was when restored to consciousness in a Federal hospital, when he found himself severely wounded in the shoulder, and learned that his little band had been nearly all killed or wounded before the bluff was taken. After he was exchanged and was assigned to duty, his wound breaking out afresh, compelled him reluctantly to yield regular service, and, still suffering with his shoulder and a semi-paralyzed arm, he undertook the lighter duty of commanding a Confederate steamer, the *Eugenie*, in the blockade running. In this steamer, one of the few sailing regularly under the Confederate flag, Capt. Fry proved himself a skillful, daring commander, and was uniformly successful. On one occasion the *Eugenie*, loaded with gunpowder, grounded outside of Fort Fisher under the guns of the blockading squadron, and when, in view of the heavy cannonade which was opened upon her, he was commanded from the fort, from Wilmington, and finally from Richmond, to abandon his boat and save his crew from what was considered the inevitable explosion, Fry positively refused to do so; stood by his ship, lightened her, got a good tide, carried her safely in—a measure of cool gallantry not easily surpassed, as he was utterly defenceless, carrying no armament. He simply stood the chance of being blown up without the excitement of battle to sustain his nerve, while, on the other hand, the adjacent coast made escape easy.

"From this service Fry was withdrawn to superintend the construction of torpedoes, and for that purpose went to Scotland, where the closing of the ports rendered his efforts fruitless. After the war I heard of him in New Orleans, working on some patents for saving ships and curing timber, and very poor. Of his connection with the Cubans I know nothing, and can only suppose his poverty and natural love of adventure combined to bring about his murder. Personally, he was a tall, well-made, handsome man, with the most mesmeric eyes I have ever seen, having great power of control, both over himself and others. His mind was remarkably good and well cultivated. He was a deep reader and thinker, fond of speculating on abstruse subjects, and apt to be led by his genius to extreme views. In disposition he was sweet, but firm tempered; a true friend and a strong enemy, not given, perhaps, to a large circle, but very sociable and conversible with his intimates, and, withal, as modest as brave.

"As an old naval officer having personal experience of the laws of blockade, he both knew the legal limits of his liability if captured, and trusted the flag he bore from protection from all other penalties. Had the *Virginius* been a Cuban privateer, as alleged, as such she would have carried a battery, and Capt. Fry would never have surrendered without resistance. Had he borne a Cuban commission, three or four shots over his steamer, within reach almost of Jamaica's coast, would never have brought him to. The truth must be he commanded an American steamer, and believed that the flag under which he had so long served, which had conquered him, could and would insure him at least civilized treatment."

Capt. Fry and fifty-three of his comrades were cruelly murdered by the Cuban authorities on November 7th, 1873, and ninety-three more were under sentence of immediate execution, but were saved by the intercession of Sir Lambton Lorraine of the British man-of-war *Niobe*.

Capt. Fry, with his own crew, sank the *Maurepas*, remaining on deck till the gun-deck was submerged. The blockading of the river was necessarily so hastily done that no ballast or weight could be placed in the transports. About daybreak the last vessel was sunk, and the river blockaded temporarily. Supposing the enemy would make the attack at early daylight, one rifled Parrott gun and ammunition, in command of Midshipman [F. M.] Roby, was moved some 400 yards below the rifled battery and placed in position. The sailors who manned the different batteries were ordered to sleep within a few feet of their guns. Shortly after daylight two rifled Parrott eight-pounder guns, that had been sent to the rear for want of ammunition, were brought up and placed in position near the guns commanded by Midshipman Roby. These three guns were manned by the crew from the *Maurepas*, and Captain Fry in person superintended the fighting of them. One twelve-pounder howitzer from the *Maurepas*, manned also by the crew, was sent down the river to assist Capt. Williams in checking the enemy's advance by land.

" At 7 A. M. on the morning of the 17th, the pickets reported the enemy getting up steam. At 8:30 they had advanced up the river to our lines, and two gunboats commenced throwing shell, grape and canister among our troops on the right bank of the river. They advanced very slowly, attempting to find our heavy guns. When they arrived abreast of Capt. Fry's rifled guns, they opened on his battery very rapidly for three-quarters of an hour, endeavoring to silence his guns. Failing to do so, they slowly moved up the river until they came within point-blank range of one of the rifled thirty-two-pounders. The leading gunboat stopped to fight that gun; but, finding the gun still farther up was firing at her, she moved up the river to get its position, and, in doing so, placed herself between the two guns and in point-blank range. The other gunboat, in obedience to signal, I suppose, came abreast of the lower battery, and opened a brisk fire upon us. About this stage of the action, 10 A. M., Capt. Fry sent me word the enemy were landing a large force below. All the available men that could be found were immediately sent to Capt. Williams' assistance. At 10:30, a shot from the rifled thirty-two pounder farthest up the river penetrated the leading gunboat, and either passed through the boilers, steam-chest, or pipe, filling the entire vessel with steam, and causing all that were not killed or scalded with steam to jump into the river. The vessel was completely deserted, and drifted across the stream into the bank, near Capt. Fry's battery. He immediately hailed, and directed their flag hauled down. They failing to do so, although the order was given by some of their own officers in hearing of our own people, our own men were directed to shoot those in the water attempting to escape. The two rifled guns were immediately directed to fire upon the lower gunboat, which was still engaging us. She was struck several times, and soon ceased firing, slowly dropping down the river, I think, materially damaged, as she made no effort to assist the boat we had blown up, or save their friends in the river. Near 11:30, Capts. Fry and Williams came to my battery and told me the enemy had completely surrounded us; the battery of small rifled guns had been spiked, and our people were in retreat. I trained one of the rifled guns to take a last shot at the enemy, and, as we fired, their infantry appeared over the brow of the hill, about fifty yards distant, and opened on us with musketry. Capt. Fry then proposed to make a stand with the sailors, and attempted to hold the guns, but they were only armed with single-barreled pistols, which they had fired at the enemy in the water. Nothing was now left but to save all the men we could, and, as the enemy had us under a cross-fire the men were ordered to retreat, the officers bringing up the rear, until scattered in the woods. I had confined in single irons, at my battery, six prisoners, captured by Capt. Fry at Little Red River. Deeming it inexpedient to bring them away, and as Capt. Fry told me he had no positive proof against them, I left them for the enemy. The gallantry of Capts. Fry and Williams was so conspicuous as to cause general notice and remark. To my own officers and several of Capt. Fry's who served with me, I am particularly indebted.   Mr. William Smith (acting master), Mr. William Barclay (engineer), Midshipman Roby, who commanded one of the guns, Mr. W. L. Campbell, and Dr. Addison, of the *Maurepas*, acted with great gallantry, and displayed a coolness and courage unsurpassed by any one in the engagement.   To Col. Belknap, one of the citizens of St. Charles, we are all indebted for the untiring energy and zeal with which he assisted before and during the action.   He was always where he was needed, encouraging the men and assisting the officers.   I am unable to furnish a list of killed and wounded, but do not think the numbers exceed three up to the time of the retreat.   For the operations of the infantry, I respectfully refer you to Capt. Williams.   I herewith inclose a rough sketch of St. Charles and the surrounding country, including the position of our batteries and that of the enemy's gunboats.

"I am, sir, with great respect,

"J. W. DUNNINGTON,
"*Commanding Gunboat 'Pontchartrain.'*

"*Maj. General* HINDMAN,
"*Commanding Trans-Mississippi District.*"

Capt. A. M. Williams, C. S. Engineers, made the following report of the same engagement:

"HEADQUARTERS TRANS-MISSISSIPPI DISTRICT, }
LITTLE ROCK, ARK., June 21st, 1862. }

"SIR : I have to report that on the evening of the 16th information was brought me that the enemy's gunboats were advancing on Saint Charles, which was soon substantiated by advance of our pickets, posted down the river.   We immediately made preparations to receive them, the artillerymen keeping their positions at the guns during the night, and my command being thrown out to prevent a surprise.   We also, to prevent the enemy's gunboats passing our position, under orders from Major Gen. Hindman, scuttled the steamboats *Eliza G.* and *Mary Patterson.* Capt. Fry, of the C. S. navy, who was in command at Saint Charles, scuttled the gunboat *Maurepas*, thus forming an obstruction across the river that could not be moved until our batteries were silenced.   The enemy, however, made no demonstrations during the night.   On the morning of the 17th, about 8:30 o'clock, two gunboats, two transports and one tug appeared in sight and prepared to engage us.   The men under my command, consisting of detachments from Capts. Jones', Hearin's, Smith's and Johnson's companies, Col. Pleasants' regiment, numbering about thirty-five men, were, by order of Capt. Fry, deployed as sharpshooters, and posted along the river below the battery.   At 9 A. M we engaged the enemy's pickets and drove them in.   The firing disclosed our position to the gunboats, from which the enemy commenced a furious fire of grape and shell, before which my men fell back to a more secure position.   At this time the enemy opened fire upon our light battery of four guns, manned by the crew of the *Maurepas*, to which they replied gallantly.   At 10 A. M., the heavy battery under command of Capt. Dunnington, C. S. N., opened fire on them, and soon blew up one of their boats and silenced the other.   When the explosion took place, the boat's crew jumped into the water and into boats, to escape the scalding steam that was pouring out of every hole and crevice.   I immediately ordered all the sharp-shooters that remained on the field, about twenty in number, to the river bank to shoot them.   Numbers of them were killed in the water.   At this time, about 11 o'clock, I discovered the enemy landing below, and immediately ordered men to take possession of Col. Belknap's house, for the purpose of holding them in check.   When we reached the top of the hill near the house, the enemy poured into us a furious fire of musketry at a short distance.   I at once made a reconnoissance of their position in person, and ascertained that we were almost surrounded by a force of several hundred men. I informed Capt. Fry of our situation and was ordered by him to fall back to the battery, which I did with the few men who remained with me. When we reached the battery the enemy were on our front and right flank, and poured into us a galling cross-fire of musketry. Capt. Fry gave the orders to retreat, and immediately the men scattered and ran the gauntlet of a heavy cross-fire for nearly half a mile, the officers bringing up the rear. I cannot make an accurate report of our loss, not knowing who have made their escape. It is, however, very slight. The enemy's loss must have been very heavy. They admit a loss of 140 killed, drowned and scalded. All our stores and artillery fell into the hands of the enemy. I respectfully call your attention to the coolness and intrepid bearing exhibited by Capt. Fry, our commander, who, from disease, could not make his escape, and was, I understand, severely wounded and taken prisoner. Capt. Dunnington in this engagement has proved to the world that the Federal gunboats are not invulnerable. You are respectfully referred to his report for more minute information. I would also call your attention to the gallantry of a portion of my command, some twenty in number, whose names I cannot give, and particularly to the intrepid manner in which Privates [J. H.] Bruce and [G. W.] Everett, of Capt. Hearin's company, behaved themselves. I take great pleasure in acknowledging the services of Cols. Belknap and Finch, and Messrs. Herman and Margins. The thanks of the country are due them for assistance rendered in encouraging and cheering the men, and bringing them up. * * *

"I am, very respectfully, your obedient servant,
"A. M. WILLIAMS, *Captain of Engineers.*
" *Colonel* [R. C.] NEWTON, *Assistant Adjutant General.*"

Several days after this battle, the enemy having been re-inforced by an additional gunboat and six transports, and with a land force of about 4,000 men, made a demonstration against Devall's Bluff. Intrenchments were thrown up and three heavy guns from the *Ponchartrain*, manned by a portion of her crew, were put in position. Obstructions were also put in the channel to detain the enemy's vessels under fire. A regiment and battalion of Arkansas infantry just organized and armed, partly with shot-guns, sporting rifles, and partly with pikes and lances, were sent to the bluff, together with three batteries of artillery, and with the Texas regiment already there, were formed into a brigade, under Brig. Gen. Allison Nelson.

Evidently alarmed by the resistance met at St. Charles, Col. G. N. Fitch, the Federal commander, moved very slowly up stream, fired upon from both banks by Major Gen. T. C. Hindman's cavalry, dismounted, and by citizens. At Clarendon, twenty-five miles below Devall's Bluff, Col. Fitch landed a regiment of infantry and moved it forward on the west side to reconnoitre, escorted by the tug *Tiger*. After advancing five miles it was compelled to retire with a loss of fifty-five in killed and wounded.

On the 4th of January, 1863, Gen. McClernand determined to make an attack on Fort Hindman, or Arkansas Post (as the Federals called it), on the Arkansas River, and requested the co-operation of the navy. Acting Rear Admiral Porter detailed three iron-clads, the *Louisville, Baron De Kalb* and *Cincinnati*, with all the light draft gunboats in his Mississippi squadron. Among the latter were the *Rattler, Black Hawk, Romeo, Juliet, Marmora, Signal, Forest Rose, Glide* and the ram *Monarch,* Col. Charles Ellet. The Federal naval forces were under the command of Acting Rear Admiral David D. Porter in person, and the troops were commanded by Gens. McClernand and Sherman.

Fort Hindman, or Arkansas Post, as the Federals called it, was a regular bastioned work, one hundred yards exterior side, with a deep ditch some fifteen feet wide, and a parapet eighteen feet high. It mounted eleven guns of various sizes. The accompanying diagram gives an accurate plan of the work.

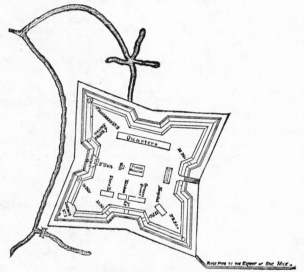

PLAN OF FORT HINDMAN, OR ARKANSAS POST.

The fort was commanded by John W. Dunnington, colonel commanding third brigade, and first lieutenant C. S. navy. In the defence of the place he displayed the most conspicuous gallantry, and before he surrendered, all his heavy guns were broken by the Federal shot, and were lying about in fragments on the ground. A large number of his killed and wounded were lying in the ditches, and many of his brave garrison who also belonged to the C. S. navy were sick in the hospital. After the capture of Fort Hindman, and the officers and crew of the C. S. gunboat *Ponchartrain,* the gunboat was sent to Little Rock, where she was afterwards destroyed to prevent her from falling into the hands of the enemy.

On the 9th of January, the Federal gunboats ascended the Arkansas River, as high as Fort Hindman, when the army landed within about four miles of the fort. The Confederates had thrown up heavy earthworks and extensive rifle-pits all along the levee, and the fort itself was built close to the river; the fort not being more than twenty yards from the bank. While the Federal army was making a detour to surround the fort, the iron-clads and gunboats moved up to the attack. At 5:30 P. M. the *Louisville, Baron DeKalb* and *Cincinnati* advanced to within 400 yards of the fort, which immediately opened upon them, making some good shots, and inflicting considerable damage. Owing to the terrific fire and superior guns of the enemy, in a short time the fort ceased firing, nearly all the guns being disabled. At dark the Federal vessels dropped down the river and tied up to the bank. Just before dark the light-draft iron-clad *Rattler* passed the fort and enfiladed it in the rear. In passing the fort, the cabin works of the *Rattler* were knocked to pieces and she was raked from stem to stern in the hull. The *Rattler* got past the fort, but becoming entangled in the obstructions placed in the river to impede the progress of the Federal gunboats, had to return.

During the night Lieut. Dunnington and his brave garrison worked with great zeal to repair damages, preparatory to the struggle which they anticipated would take place on the following day, when the land forces of the enemy would be in position to assault the fort. All the night of the 9th the heavy strokes of the hammers of the Confederates could be heard through the Federal fleet on the iron covering of their casemates; at daylight, the tired garrison, having remained up all night to repair their nearly demolished fort, were patiently waiting for the Federal gunboats to renew the attack. These were ordered to take position again not further than fifty yards from the fort, and begin to fire as soon as possible. The battle began, and soon became hot. In a short time all the guns in the works were dismounted and silenced. The *Black Warrior* having taken a regiment of infantry on board, was run to the bank alongside the fort to board it. At the same time a messenger was sent to Gen. Sherman informing him of the condition of the fort, and that if he would send a storming party from the land side, the navy would assault it from the water. At this time the fort was a complete ruin and surrounded on all sides by an overwhelming force. Lieut. Dunnington and his brave set of navy officers and men, however, had no thought of surrendering. Admiral Porter says: "While waiting for Sherman's troops the *Black Hawk* laid alongside the fort, her high upper works on a level with the embrasures, while three boat guns on wheels, on the upper deck, completely commanded the inside of the works, which presented a dreadful scene of killed and wounded. A large number of artillery horses had been killed in the fort, and the shells and shrapnel had made sad havoc with the dead and

dying men, mixed up with the killed and wounded animals.
It was a scene ever to be remembered. In the meantime,
while waiting for Sherman's assaulting party, all firing had
ceased on both sides and the victorious sailors were quietly
looking on at the dreadful havoc that had been made inside
the works, not anticipating that the enemy would make any
more resistance. Their colors had been shot away and had
not been hoisted again."

As the assaulting column of the soldiers of the enemy got
within twenty yards of Lieut. Dunnington and his garrison,
who were "concealed behind or underneath the buildings that
had been knocked down," they rose together and "poured in a
withering volley from about four hundred and fifty muskets,
and nearly every bullet told." The enemy staggered at this
unexpected volley and retreated. At that moment white flags
were hoisted by several men contrary to orders and the Confederates laid down their arms and surrendered. Lieut. Com.
Dunnington sent for Admiral Porter and surrendered to him
in person. Gen. Churchill, Confederate commander of all the
forces around the fort, surrendered to Gen. McClernand.

Rear Admiral H. Walke, U. S. N., in his "Naval Scenes and
Reminiscences of the Civil War in the United States," says:

"As a prisoner of war, a few days after the battle, on his way up to
Cairo [Lieut. J. W. Dunnington, C. S. N.,] said that he had no thought of
surrendering when he first heard that the white flag was raised on all their
flag-staffs by order of their commander-in-chief. He ordered it down from
his flag-staff, and hoisted the Confederate flag again and continued the
fight for some time after, even when he was told that their army had surrendered, and declared that he would not strike his colors. On being informed that all their works in the rear had surrendered to our army, and
that the consequences would be terrible to their troops if he persisted
in firing any longer, he surrendered to Admiral Porter."

The defence of Fort Hindman was one of the most gallant
events of the war. It was enfiladed from all sides by gunboats and rifled field-pieces, which not only destroyed the
houses and light work inside the fort, but also destroyed all
the guns and casemates. Admiral Porter says : "No fort
ever received a worse battering, and I know of no instance
on record where every gun in a fort was dismounted or destroyed." The list of killed and wounded in the Confederate
navy garrison was very large; the list of officers captured
was as follows :

"John W. Dunnington, colonel commanding third brigade, and first
lieutenant C. S. navy, commanding naval forces; Joseph Preble, acting-
master C. S. navy; Frank Ranger, acting master C. S. navy; F. M. Roby,
first lieutenant and brigade ordnance officer and midshipman C. S. navy;
N. M. Read, assistant surgeon C. S. navy: W. S. Campbell, major and
quartermaster third brigade and captain's clerk C. S. navy; Howell
Quigley, second assistant engineer C. S. navy; Samuel Suttioan, third
assistant engineer C. S. navy; Joseph Nutter, master's mate C. S. navy;
W. A. Lang, captain's steward C. S. navy; George Elliott, boatswain's
mate; John McDonald, boatswain's mate; W. C. Fisher, master-at-arms;

Charles Lettig, quartermaster; John B. Hassett, quartermaster; Michael Kemmett, quartermaster; John Shephard, quartermaster; P. J. Fitzpatrick, purser's steward; James Hussey, surgeon's steward; Richard Scott, gunner's mate; Charles Loewenberg, ship's cook; T. J. Jackson, wardroom cook; Charles Crowley, seaman; Charles Williams, seaman; Patrick Kelly, ordinary seaman; Pliney Cox, ordinary seaman; John Lee, ordinary seaman; Henry Peters, landsman; Edward Walsh, first-class fireman; George Dehman, first-class fireman; John Fuller, coalheaver; Aleck Martin, first-class boy; John Brown, first-class boy; Christopher Kain, second-class boy; Michael Knackley, second-class boy; Samuel H. Bink, captain, acting general; A. M. Williams, captain of engineers.

The enemy also lost heavily in killed and wounded. Lieut. Com. John G. Walker, of the U. S. gunboat *Baron DeKalb*, in his official report to Acting Rear Admiral Porter on January 12th says, that in the attack on the evening of the 10th his vessel was struck several times :

"In the attack on the 11th, one of the ten-inch guns was struck in the muzzle, and both gun and carriage destroyed; one thirty-two-pounder carriage struck and destroyed; one of the iron plates on forward casemate badly broken by shot; the wood-work about two of the ports badly torn by shot, and one lower deck beam cut off by a plunging shot through the deck. The other injuries, although considerable, can be repaired on board in a few days. I lost two men killed and fifteen wounded; two probably mortally, and several seriously.

"Before going into action, I covered the bow sides and pilot-house with slush, which, I think, was of much assistance in turning the shot, as the vessel was repeatedly struck by eight and nine-inch shot, at very short range, and the iron was in no case penetrated. The loss was from shot and shell entering the ports."

The *DeKalb, Louisville,* and *Cincinnati* each had several men killed and wounded.

Early in January, 1863, Rear Admiral Porter gave orders that the Federal ram *Queen of the West*, Capt. E. W. Sutherland, should pass the Confederate batteries at Vicksburg, destroy the steamboat *City of Vicksburg*, lying opposite the city, and then run past the lower Confederate batteries. The *Queen of the West* was one of the celebrated Union ram fleet organized and equipped at Pittsburgh, Pa., by Col. Charles Ellet. The fleet was at first established under the cognizance of the Federal Secretary of War, and was under the control of that department until about the beginning of 1863, when it was transferred to the Navy Department and placed under the control of Rear Admiral D. D. Porter. The fleet played an important part in the operations of the United States forces on the Mississippi River from and after the fall of Island No. 10.

The *Queen of the West* was a freight-boat, formerly in the St. Louis, Cincinnati and New Orleans trade, and before she was converted into a ram was considered a model of strength and speed. When Col. Ellet, the originator of the ram fleet, who died in consequence of wounds received in the naval conflict at Memphis, was organizing this branch of the Union service, the *Queen of the West* was one of the first boats selected. She was strengthened as to her hull by heavy oak timbers, and as to machinery by a bulwark of solid wood-work twenty-four inches thick, extending from stem to stern, and so inclosing the boilers and engines that they were considered safe from shot and shell from guns of no heavier calibre than six or twelve pounders. When she ran the batteries at Vicksburg she was further strengthened by two rows of cotton bales, extending entirely around her, from the guards to the upper deck. Her pilot-house was also similarly protected. To guard against the effect of plunging-shot, there was a layer of cotton bales upon the gun-deck. Her armament consisted of a bow gun, a large thirty-two-pounder rifled Parrott upon her main-deck, one twenty-pounder rifled Parrott, and three twelve-

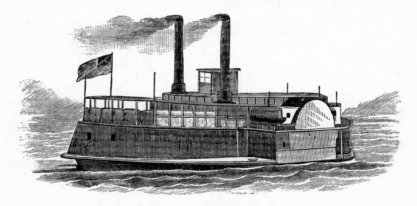

"QUEEN OF THE WEST," CAPTURED BY THE CONFEDERATES, FEBRUARY 4TH, 1863.

pounder brass howitzers upon her gun-deck. Besides her officers and crew, she usually carried a detail of sharp-shooters.

The *Queen of the West* was first brought into prominence in the naval engagement above Memphis on June 8th, 1862, in which she took a very active part. When the Confederate ram *Arkansas* made her first appearance in the Yazoo River, previous to her run into the Mississippi, one of her opponents was the ram *Queen of the West*. In the attempt to capture the *Arkansas* before Vicksburg on the 22d of July, 1862, the *Queen of the West* took a very important part. During the attack upon Vicksburg, in December following, she took an active part in the affair with the Confederate battery at Haines Bluff, near the mouth of the Yazoo.

In compliance with the instructions of Rear-Admiral Porter, on the morning of February 2d, 1863, the *Queen of the West* having made all arrangements deemed necessary to insure her safety, under the command of Col. Charles R. Ellet started to pass the Confederate batteries at Vicksburg, and sink the Confederate steamer lying before that city. Owing to the delay caused by re-arranging her steering apparatus, she did not reach the city until after sunrise, when the batteries opened a heavy fire upon her all along the shore. In passing the steamer *Vicksburg*, the *Queen of the West* attempted to destroy her by ramming, but ran obliquely into her, which only staved in a few of her deck planks near the guards and forced her high into the mud. Several incendiary projectiles were at the same time fired into the *Vicksburg* which set her on fire, but was soon extinguished. At this moment one of the Confederate shells set the cotton on fire near the starboard wheel of the *Queen of the West*, while the discharge of her own gun ignited that portion which was on the bow. The flames spread rapidly, and the dense smoke rolling into the engine room nearly suffocated the engineers. Col. Ellet, knowing that if he attempted to run again into the steamer *Vicksburg*, his ram would certainly be burned, ordered her to be headed down stream. Every man was then put to extinguishing the flames, which after much exertion they accomplished by throwing the burning cotton overboard.

The *Queen of the West* passed the batteries without suffering any material injury, although she was struck twelve times, and had one casemated gun dismounted and destroyed. Having reached the mouth of the proposed canal below Vicksburg, the *Queen* came to anchor, and Col. Ellet officially informed Admiral Porter of his passage of the batteries. The remainder of her crew having come on board she started on her adventurous cruise down the Mississippi River. Passing Warrenton, under a heavy fire from the batteries at that point, she proceeded to the mouth of Big Black River and Natchez, without creating any excitement whatever. About fifteen miles below the mouth of Red River the *Queen* captured the steamboat *A. W. Baker* which had discharged her cargo at Port Hudson, and was bound up Red River for another. Several Confederate officers were seized on board of the steamer. While engaged in plundering the steamboat another was announced coming down the river. Leaving a guard on the *A. W. Baker*, Col. Ellet captured the steamboat *Moro* loaded with military stores for the Confederate forces at Port Hudson. Proceeding up the Red River he captured the steamboat *Berwick Bay*, also loaded with military supplies. The coal of the *Queen of the West* running short, some of the captured stores were transferred to the ram and she steamed down the Red River and up the Mississippi with her prizes. Finding that the progress of the prizes was so slow, and knowing that he could not wait to bring them up, Col. Ellet concluded to burn them. Thus the *Berwick Bay*, the *Moro* and the *Baker* were destroyed.

The ram returned in safety to near the lower end of the canal, where she was supplied with coal, which had run the

23

batteries in a barge. The *De Soto*, a small steam ferry-boat, having been captured by Gen. Blair's brigade, was turned over to Col. Ellet as tender to the *Queen of the West*. She was surrounded with a bulwark of cotton bales and armed with a thirty-two pounder rifle upon her bow. The two steamers having received 20,000 bushels of coal, on February 10th, were lashed together and moved down the river on another expedition. On the same evening, the *Queen of the West*, with her tender, the *De Soto*, ran past the Confederate batteries at Warrenton without receiving a shot. She passed Natchez the following day, and anchored for the night at the mouth of Old River, forty-five miles below. On Thursday, the 12th, she cruised in the Atchafalaya, capturing and destroying a train of army wagons, seventy barrels of beef, and an artillery wagon containing baggage. Upon her return she was fired into from the right bank of the Atchafalaya by the citizens. On Friday morning the *Queen* again entered the Atchafalaya, and in retaliation burned every house, barn, sugar-mill, and negro quarters between the mouth of the river and Semmesport. At the latter place she captured a Confederate mail, and first learned of the occupation of Berwick Bay and lower Atchafalaya by Admiral Farragut. On Friday afternoon the boats entered Red River, and anchored for the night at the mouth of Black River. At ten on Saturday morning, the *Queen of the West* captured the Confederate steamer *Era No. 5*, laden with stores for the army at Little Rock. Col. Ellet had heard that a Confederate battery was in position eighty miles from the mouth of Red River, at Gordon's Landing, and as he approached it all his prisoners declared that he could easily capture it. Finley Anderson, a correspondent of the New York *Herald*, was on board of the *Queen of the West*, with Mr. Bodman of the Chicago *Tribune*, and Joseph McCullagh, "Mack" of the Cincinnati *Commercial*. Mr. Anderson says:

"Col. Ellet had pressed into his service the pilot of the captured *Era*, and placing him in the pilot house, forced him to assist at the wheel. She moved slowly up the river at 'slow bell,' but with a full head of steam in her boilers, and instead of taking the bend of the river outside the eddy, ran inside, and in an instant was hard aground and immovable as the hills.[1] It was at this very instant that the three rifled thirty-two

---

[1] A correspondent of the Memphis *Appeal* gave the following account of the capture of the *Queen of the West*, through the exploit of her gallant Confederate pilot, who was taken from the Confederate steamer *Era*, and ordered to the wheel of the *Queen of the West* under the bayonets of a guard of Federal soldiers:

"On the morning of the 12th instant, the *Era* No. 5, with Mr. George Wood as her pilot, steamed out from her mooring at Alexandria, loaded for Black River, which empties into the Red River, some forty miles above her mouth. On reaching Gordon's Landing, some seventy-five miles below Alexandria, where we have a military post, consisting of —— casemated guns and —— Parrott pieces, the *Era* was stopped and told that the night before (Wednesday) a

suspicious looking craft had made her appearance in the mouth of Red River, consequently she tied up for further developments. Other boats, as many as four, came down and were likewise stopped; they remained awhile and then returned up the river.

"Saturday morning, the 14th, at daylight, the *Era* steamed up and plowed her way down to her destination, supposing she could reach the mouth of Black River with safety, as nothing had then been heard of the *Queen of the West* coming up. Gliding down her watery path, she was bounding onward with full steam, when some ten miles above the mouth of Black River, her turning point, she was met at a bend in the river, fired into, one shot hitting her pilot house, and was captured by the *Queen of the West*, which

pounders in Fort Taylor opened fire. Each shot told with fearful accuracy. Solid shot crashed through her cabins as if they were made of paper. Shell exploded between her chimneys, upon her decks, over her pilot house—all about her, and she fixed and immovable. Every exertion was made to back her off, but all was of no avail. In her present position none of the *Queen's* guns were effective. The rebels had the range perfectly, and if firing at a target in broad daylight could not have done better execution. Presently word came from the engine room that the lever was shot away, then that the escape pipe was broken, and almost immediately after the terrible roar and tumult of rushing steam showed that her steam chest was penetrated.

"At this time no one thought of saving the boat. It needed all their exertions to save themselves. It was at first thought the boiler had exploded, but though the vessel shook and reeled as if from an earthquake shock, it was soon discovered the boilers were unhurt. Soon the rushing steam entered every part of the vessel, the main-deck, the hold, the cabin and pilot house My informant was in the pilot house, and with difficulty prevented suffocating by filling his mouth with a woollen rag lying hard by. With some difficulty he escaped to the cabin, and from thence to the hurricane roof, where many of the crew and the three journalists were gathered.

"All this time the crash of the shell and roar of the guns were fearfully distinct, the shot hissing and screaming in dangerous proximity to their heads. Some leaped overboard and were drowned. Others tumbled cotton bales into the river and attempted to float with the current. Mr. Anderson was last seen standing, undecided whether to risk escape on a cotton bale or risk capture by remaining. Bodman swung himself from the hurricane roof, and reached the *De Soto* in a skiff. McCullagh sought a cotton bale, and debated whether he should trust his precious body upon it. While thus engaged the bale floated beyond his reach, and immediately thereafter a shell alighted upon it, and exploding, blew it into a thousand fragments. 'Mac' seized another bale, and reached the *De Soto* in safety. Col. Ellet escaped in like manner.

"The enemy hearing no reply to his guns, and discovering from the rush of steam that some accident had occurred, slackened his fire and

was steaming upward on forbidden waters. The crew and passengers of the *Era* were taken prisoners, and all were guarded on board the *Era*, by a band of Abolition soldiers, save Mr. George Wood, the pilot, who was ordered aboard the *Queen of the West*, and, with heavy threats, directed to her pilot wheel to assist her pilot in directing her onward to the capture of our fort. On they glided, but not distrustful, and much elated at their success, till they came in reach of our battery at five P. M., when she commenced firing, still advancing. Our batteries challenged her by opening most furiously from their hidden recesses. Still she advanced, till, as I was told by one of our lieutenants, who was there, she came within a quarter of a mile of our battery and on the opposite shore in full range for our guns, when the gallant Wood, who directed her wheel, had her rounded, ran her aground, breaking her rudder and thus crippling her and turning her broadside to give our guns a fair chance. This gallant man, in the confusion, made good his escape, as it was a life and death case with him. Thus crippled and disabled by the hand that drove her on to her destiny, she lay like a wounded falcon, at the mercy of her adversaries.

"The night was dark and stormy, the heavens overhung with clouds, which now and then pealed forth their muttering thunder, and drenched the earth with rain Thus in the rainstorm this crippled *Queen* lay beaten by the tempest. Our batteries made some four or five shots in her guard around the upper deck, and

two holes through her chimney stacks, and one happy shot through her main body, which was providentially guided to the cutting of her steampipe, but no other damage was done her. Thus grounded and crippled, it was then contemplated to blow up her magazine, and thus destroy her by fire, but the surgeon protested against it, as fortunately her captain lay on board mortally wounded by a rifle shot received near Semmesport, so Col. Ellet consented to let her lay, for the sake of humanity to her dying commander. She was well barricaded with cotton bales. On seeing all hope of success gone, the commanding officer, Col. Ellet, made his escape, with nearly all his crew, by getting on cotton bales and floating down the river. She raised the white signal, as the storm abated, as it was seen by the light of a burning warehouse, but it was not answered till next morning. Thirteen of the crew remained in silence till daylight, then her white banner was still afloat, and then, and not till then, our Southern sons of thunder crossed the river and formally took possession of this proud and haughty triumph, as she lay a victim of a single hand, the gallant Wood.

"The results of the capture are one thirty-two-pound rifle Parrott gun, one twenty-four-pound rifle Parrott gun, three twelve-pound Porterfield brass pieces, and one thirteen-pound brass piece—damaged, a fine supply of ordnance stores, a good deal of quinine, three fine cases of surgical instruments, and provisions in abundance."

sent boats to reconnoitre. Three yawls, loaded with men, approached the vessel, to whom the crew remaining on board signified their surrender. Thus the *Queen of the West*, with all her guns and ammunition, fell a prize into the hands of our enemies.

"The *De Soto* was less than a mile below where the accident to the *Queen of the West* occurred, and came up as near the point as prudence justified. She picked up the floaters, and sent her yawl for the survivors, but before it reached the *Queen of the West* all who remained on board were in the enemy's hands and prisoners, herself narrowly escaping capture. The river banks began to be lined with soldiers, who demanded, in voices plainly discernible by those on board, the surrender of men swimming for their lives. Fearing a re-enactment of the White River tragedy, Col. Ellet thought proper to order the *De Soto* to move down the river. She was turned, and slowly floated down with the current, picking up poor unfortunates as she ran. The steamer had not proceeded more than three miles before she ran aground in a sharp turn of the river, and unshipped her rudder. For fifteen miles and for three hours she was unmanageable, and moved with the current, sometimes head on and at other times stern on. At eleven o'clock she reached the *Era*, and found the men and prisoners undisturbed. The coal barge had sunk, and Col. Ellet was forced to leave it.

"Just as they reached the *Era* the pilot caused the second rudder to be unshipped. She was now totally unmanageable, and there was no alternative left but to destroy her. A man was sent on board, who knocked out her water pipes and then laid a train to a keg of powder placed under the boilers, and setting a slow match on fire the *Era* had barely time to move a hundred rods or so before the *De Soto* exploded with a tremendous report. Her magnificent thirty-two pounder Parrott, the chief object of Col. Ellet's care, lies forty feet below the surface of the river.

"It was nearly twelve o'clock Saturday night before the *Era* was well under way again. Col. Ellet knew that the gunboat *Webb* was at Alexandria, sixty miles above Gordon's Landing, and he was certain she would attempt to pursue him. All hands were set to work to throw overboard the corn with which she was laden, and in the fog, thunder, lightning and rain she worried her way out of the Red River into the Mississippi. They cursed the fog then; they blessed it afterwards.

"Sunday morning the *Era* had reached the mouth of Old River. All day long, with no fuel but the corn with which she was laden, and a few cords of water-soaked cypress, which she found on the bank of the Mississippi, and with which she found it impossible to make steam enough to give her headway, the fleeing steamer attempted to get up the river. Forty miles in twenty-four hours is poor sailing under the most unfavorable circumstances; yet the *Era* made scarcely that. At Union Point she was run aground. This delayed her three hours. How this delay affected the fugitives may easily be imagined. They knew that the *Webb* was at Alexandria, sixty miles above Gordon's Landing, and they felt assured she would start in pursuit when she heard of their repulse at Fort Taylor. At the best, even if she laid over for the fog—a thing hardly likely under the circumstances—she could be but a short distance behind. Those on board, anticipating their capture, were discussing the probabilities of escape by skiffs and yawls to Port Hudson.

"The carpenter had managed to construct a spar from the forest near where the *Era* was aground, and after three hours' hard work the steamer was afloat again. Colonel Ellet's first duty afterwards was to place the pilot under arrest.

"They had just passed Ellis' Cliffs, when, through the fog, the lookout discovered the black chimney of some passing steamer. At that distance, and because the hull of the steamer was still enveloped in dense vapor, it was impossible to make her out. That she burned coal, as was evident from the black smoke pouring from her chimneys, was enough to

satisfy the crew of her character. ' It was the Federal steamer *Indianola*.'
No more fear of the *Webb*.

" The *Era* was laid alongside the *Indianola* and coaled. The crew
had eaten nothing for thirty-six hours, and were nearly famished. The
Indianola fed them. They were coatless and bootless, some of them, and
the *Indianola* clothed them. They had lost their arms and ammunition
in the *Queen*, and these were supplied by the *Indianola*."

Scarcely was the *Era* well settled in her new position beside
the *Indianola* when the Confederate ram *Webb* hove in sight,
having been dispatched by Gen. Richard Taylor to overtake
the escaped crew of the *Queen*. The *Indianola* cleared for
action and fired two shots, when the *Webb* with her consorts
returned up the Red River. The *Era*, having been protected
with cotton bales, seized on the plantation belonging to the
heirs of Dr. Jenkins, above Red River, proceeded up the
Mississippi, and finally anchored in good condition below
Vicksburg.

On Monday following her capture, the *Queen of the West*
was towed up to the forts on Red River, and finally to Alexandria, a distance of sixty miles, where by working night and day
she was soon repaired, and on February 19th, 1863, placed
in the Confederate service under the command of Capt. James
McCloskey.

After meeting the steamer *Era No. 5*, with those who
escaped from the *Queen of the West*, the *Indianola* proceeded
to the mouth of Red River in pursuit of the Confederate
ram *Webb*. Ascending the river some twenty or thirty miles,
Capt. Brown, the commander of the *Indianola*, ascertained
that the *Queen of the West* had been removed from the
bar where she was captured, and was repaired and ready for
action. The *Indianola* then hastened down the river to the
Mississippi, and reached Grand Gulf, where she was overtaken by the Confederate fleet under the command of Major
J. L. Brent.

Major Gen. Richard Taylor, commanding the Confederate
forces in the Western District of Louisiana, with headquarters
at Alexandria, on February 19th, 1863, ordered Major J. L.
Brent to take supreme command of an expedition which was
then fitting out on Red River for the capture of the U. S. iron-
clad *Indianola*. Major Brent's fleet consisted of the gunboats
Queen of the West, Capt. James McCloskey; the *Webb*, Capt.
Charles Pierce; the steamer *Dr. Batey*, and the tender *Grand
Era*. The steamer *Grand Duke* was also placed at his disposal if he deemed it advisable to use her. Major W. M.
Levy, commanding post at Fort De Russey, was at the
same time ordered to lend Major Brent all the assistance in
his power for fitting out the expedition in the shortest possible
time.

The movements of the expedition under the command
of Major Brent are fully narrated in his official report to

Major E. Surget, Gen. Taylor's A. A. General, which is as follows :

"MAJOR GENERAL R. TAYLOR'S GUNBOAT EXPEDITION,
"C. S. WEBB, THIRTY MILES BELOW VICKSBURG,
"OFF PRIZE IRON-CLAD INDIANOLA,
"February 25th, 1863.

"MAJ. E. SURGET, A. A. General:

"*Major*—My last dispatch to you, exclusive of the telegram sent you last night, was from Natchez. The Federal iron-clad *Indianola* had forty-eight hours start of us at Acklin's Landing; at Natchez she was less than twenty-five hours in advance. We left Natchez on the evening of the 23d inst., and I found that we could easily overhaul her on the morning of the 24th, but I determined not to do so, in order that I might bring the enemy to an engagement only at night, considering for many reasons that this time was most advantageous to us.

"We reached Grand Gulf before sunset, and there learned that the enemy was only about four hours in advance of us. As we were running more than two miles to his one, the time required to overtake him could be easily calculated, and I determined to overtake and bring him to action early in the night.

"We came up with the *Indianola* about 9:40 last night, just above New Carthage, near the foot of Palmyra Island, and I immediately signalled the *Webb* to prepare for action.

"Our order of approach was as follows: The *Queen of the West* about 500 yards in advance of the *Webb*, and the *Batey*, Lieut. Col. Brand commanding (whom I wrote you joined us with a force and steamer fitted out at Port Hudson), over two miles in the rear, and lashed to my tender the *Grand Era*.

"The moon was partially obscured by a veil of clouds, and gave and permitted just sufficient light for us to see where to strike with our rams, and just sufficient obscurity to render uncertain the aim of the formidable artillery of the enemy.

"We first discovered him when about 1,000 yards distant, hugging the western bank of the Mississippi, with his head quartering across and down the river.

"Not an indication of life appeared as we dashed on towards him, his lights obscured, and his machinery apparently without motion.

"We had also covered our lights, and only the fires of the *Era* could be seen, two miles back, where she was towing the *Batey*.

"The distance between him and the Queen had diminished to about 500 yards, when, for the first time, we could clearly distinguish the long black line of the two coal barges which protected his sides from forward of his bow to nearly abreast his wheels.

"The impatient desire of our men to open fire could be scarcely restrained, but I would not allow it, as the vast importance of traversing the distance to be passed over without drawing the fire of his powerful guns was too apparent. At last, when within about 100 yards, I authorized Capt. McCloskey to open fire, which he accordingly did with his two Parrott guns and one Cross twelve-pounder ; but at the second round the twenty-pounder Parrott was disabled by blowing out its vent-piece.

"Our intention was to dash our bow near the enemy's wheel-house, just in rear of the coal barge, but when about fifty yards distant he backed and interposed the barge between us and him. Our bow went crushing clear through the barge heavily loaded with coal, and was not arrested until struck with a violent shock, and scattered some of his timbers amidship, deeply indenting the iron plating of his hull.

"So tremendous had been the momentum of our attack, made under full pressure of steam, that for some minutes we could not disengage ourselves, but remained with our bows against the sides of the *Indianola*, held fast by the pressure of the coal and barge through which we had crushed. In this position, our sharp-shooters kept up fire, sweeping the deck of the enemy, who feebly answered.

"After a brief interval, one end of the coal barge sunk, and the other drifted down the current; and the *Queen*, finding herself free, immediately rounded up stream to add to her next charge the additional power obtainable from the descending current of the river. Just then the *Webb* came dashing by us, and plunged into the *Indianola* with great force, just in rear or on the turn of her bow.

"Some of the iron plating was loosened, but this blow of the *Webb* produced no serious external injury, though prisoners since report that it disabled the left-hand engine.

"As the *Webb* approached on this her first charge, the two eleven-inch Dahlgren guns, in the forward casemate of the enemy, opened on her at seventy-five yards distant, but fortunately she was untouched.

"The vigor of the *Webb's* onset forced the enemy around, and carrying her forward laid her across and in actual contact with these monitor guns, if run out in battery. Dashing safely around from this perilous position, the *Webb* swung across the bow and on to the starboard side of the enemy, getting between him and his remaining coal barge, breaking its fastenings and setting it adrift.

"The result of our first onset was to strip the *Indianola* of the two coal barges which protected her sides, and to injure her to some extent in her wheel, which was apparent from the subsequent want of rapidity and precision in her movements.

"As soon as the *Webb* swept away clear of the enemy, the *Queen* swung around, and again dashed upon him, who, this time with partial success, endeavored to break the force of the onset by presenting his bow to our blow. But his movements were too torpid, and not entirely successful, which tends to confirm the belief that his machinery was injured by the first blow.

"The *Queen* struck a little forward of midships, but, as she was turning, the force of the blow glanced along his side and passed his wheel-house.

"Just as the *Queen* swung clear of his stern, he opened upon us with two nine-inch guns in his after iron casemate at so near a range that the flames of the guns almost touched us—their heat being felt.

"One shot struck the *Queen* on her starboard shoulder, and knocked away ten or twelve bales of cotton, causing us to list over, and then a shell entered under our front port-hole, on the port side, struck the chase of a brass twelve-pounder gun and exploded, killing two men, wounding four, and disabling two pieces.

"This time the *Queen* swung around rapidly up stream, and in a very brief interval, dashed on the enemy for the third time, striking a little to the rear of his starboard wheel-house, crashing through and shattering his framework, and loosening some of his iron plates. By this time the *Webb* had run up stream, making a wide circuit, had turned and, for her second onset, came charging on with a full head of steam just as the *Queen* had rounded out after her third blow, and striking the enemy very nearly in the same place where the *Queen* had just before hit him.

"Through and through his timbers, crushing and dashing aside his iron plates, the sharp bow of the *Webb* penetrated as if it were going to pass entirely through the ship. As the *Webb* backed clear, the *Indianola*, with all the speed she could raise, declined further fight, and ran down the river towards the western bank, with the intention, as afterwards appeared, of getting a line out on shore, in order that the officers and crew might land and abandon their steamer. In fact, a line was got out on shore, but not fastened, and three of the crew effected their escape, but were captured to-day by the cavalry of Major Harrison.

"After the *Queen* had struck the enemy for the third time, she was for some time almost unmanageable—she had listed so much over on the port side that one of her wheels was raised nearly out of the water, and presented every appearance of sinking.

" Capt. McCloskey righted her a little by throwing over cotton from his upper deck.

" He was able to bring her around very slowly, but still this gallant commander succeeded wearing her with difficulty, and headed her for her fourth charge.

" Whilst the *Webb* had her bow knocked off to within fourteen inches of the water line, her splended machinery was unhurt, and she quickly and gallantly bore up for her third charge, when bearing down and approaching the enemy, Capt. Pierce reports that he was hailed from the enemy's deck, announcing his surrender, and begging to be towed ashore as he was sinking. Capt. Pierce further represents that he then placed a line on board and commenced towing the *Indianola*, when the line parted.

" As the *Queen of the West* was running off from her last charge, making a circuit to obtain room and space to add increased momentum to her onset, we encountered the steamer *Batey*, Lieut. Col. Brand commanding, who had cast from the tender *Grand Era*, and was hovering around to enter the fight when an opportunity offered.

" The *Batey* is a frail steamboat, with but little power, and incapable of being used as a ram. She was crowded with two hundred and fifty gallant volunteers from the forces at Port Hudson, who had embarked in the *Batey* with the resolution to fight the enemy by boarding him. We called out to them that the opportunity for boarding had arrived, as it was apparent the enemy was disabled and much demoralized.

" Lieut. Col. Brand with his command gallantly bore away, approached the enemy after the line from the *Webb* had parted, and gave, as I am informed by him, the command, ' prepare to board,' when he was greeted by a voice from the *Indianola*, announcing her surrender, and that she was in a sinking condition.

" Lieut. Col. Brand then boarded her upper deck, and received the sword of the Federal commander, Lieut. Brown. This result must have been very gratifying to Col. Brand, as it was obtained without the loss or injury of a single man of his command. Upon my reaching the deck of the *Indianola*, Lieut. Col. Brand most handsomely acknowledged that the capture was entirely due to the *Queen of the West* and to the *Webb*, and he has so officially reported. I have no doubt, if it had been necessary, that Col. Brand and his gallant command would have again demonstrated that nothing can resist the desperation of troops who regard not their own lives, but victory.

" Upon taking possession, I immediately appointed Lieut. Thomas H. Hardy prize-master. We found our prize a most formidable gunboat, mounting two eleven-inch guns aft, all protected by thick iron casemates utterly impenetrable to our artillery, even at the very shortest range. The motive power consisted of side-wheels and two propellers. She was filled with a valuable cargo, embracing supplies, stores, etc. The officers and crew, amounting to over one hundred, fell into our hands as prisoners. Nothing shows more clearly how well she was protected than the fact that our artillery, though frequently fired at the range of twenty and thirty yards, utterly failed to injure her. Lieut. Handy, of the *Webb*, fired an eighty-pound shell from his rifled and banded thirty-two-pound gun so close to the forward casemate of the enemy that it actually enveloped his port-holes in flames, and yet no injury was sustained by the casemate.

" Our sharp-shooters deliberately and coolly fired at every onset.

" Notwithstanding all these circumstances, the enemy lost but one man killed and none wounded. The *Webb* had one man wounded, and the *Queen* two killed and four wounded.

" The fire of the enemy was terrific, and delivered at short range mostly. His huge shot and shell were directed a little wide of the mark, except the two shot that struck the *Queen*, and one shot that passed through the bulwarks of the *Webb*. This was remarkable, as he frequently fired at such close range that the flames of his enormous guns almost enveloped our bows.

"The escape from destruction of the feeble crafts, that were five times precipitated upon the iron sides of this powerful war-steamer, mounting an armament of 9 and 11-inch guns, was providential.

"On taking possession, we found our prize rapidly making water which we could not arrest. Seeing that she would sink, I did not wish that this should take place on the western side of the river, where the Federal forces could easily have retaken her, and therefore made fast to her with two of my steamers, and towed her over the river to the eastern side, where she sunk in the water up to her gun-deck, just as we reached the shallow water, thus losing us the enormous value of her capture, as well as the valuable stores that were in her hold.

"I am much indebted for the success of this expedition to the skill and gallantry of my officers and men. Capt. James McCloskey, commanding the *Queen*, combined with the courage of the soldier the skill and aptitude that characterizes the sailor of our western waters. Lieut. Thomas H. Handy, of the Crescent Artillery, commanded the troops on the *Webb*. He exhibited skill and courage in handling his command, and in person assisted in manning the thirty-two-pound rifled gun. Lieut. Rice, of the Twenty-first Tennessee, was on the *Webb* with a detachment from his regiment, and bore himself well and gallantly. Lieut. Prather, also on the *Webb*, served his two field-pieces entirely unprotected with praiseworthy courage, and was well seconded by Mr. Charles Schuler, acting as chief of one of the guns.

"Capt. Charles Pierce, a civilian, commanded and controlled the movements of the *Webb*. It was he who selected the weak spots of the enemy, and with a steady hand and eye dashed the *Webb* against the *Indianola*.

"Not only did the officers act well, but I have nothing but commendations for the private soldiers.

"Capt. Caines' and Lieut. Rice's company, of the Twenty-first Tennessee, and the detachment of Lieut. Doolan, adjutant of Major Burnett's battalion of Texans, and a detachment from the Third Maryland Artillery, were in the expedition, and acted with courage and discipline when under fire.

"Capt. J. W. Mangum, Assistant Adjutant Gen. of Brigadier Gen. Moore, accompanied the expedition as a volunteer and acted as my adjutant. He comported himself gallantly under fire; and throughout the expedition rendered me valuable services.

"I herewith submit the report of Capt. McCloskey, commanding the *Queen*. He mentions favorably Capt. Caines and Lieut. Miller, of the Twenty-first Tennessee; Lieut. Doolan, adjutant of Major Burnett's battalion; Sergt. E. H. Langley, of the Third Maryland Artillery, acting as lieutenant in charge of the two Parrott guns; and the volunteers, Capt. J. H. White, slightly wounded, acting with efficiency as ordnance officer; Capt. Tank and Lieuts. Fisk and Stanmeyer, both wounded; and Lieut. R. R. Hyams, who, as quartermaster and commissary, exhibited much energy. As I was on board the *Queen* during the action, the conduct of the officers and men was under my own eye, and I cheerfully endorse the commendation of Capt. McCloskey. He also speaks highly of the intrepid promptness and skill of his pilots and engineers, and of the conduct of Assistant Surgeon Blanchard, who manifested much care and coolness, coming on the gun-deck in the midst of the action and personally supervising the removal of the wounded.

"Sergt. Magruder, of the signal corps, also deserves mention for having rendered very important services in the discharge of the responsible duties devolved upon him.

"Capt. Pierce, of the *Webb*, verbally reports to me that his pilots and engineers behaved themselves with coolness and bravery, and discharged their duties with promptness and energy.

"I have no doubt that this is correct, from the skillful manner in which his boat was handled.

"This report is dated from the *Webb*, as I have dispatched the *Queen*, Capt. McCloskey, to Warrenton, and, if possible, to Vicksburg.

"I am, major, yours respectfully,

"J. L. BRENT, *Major Commanding.*"

The *Indianola* lost in the engagement two killed and five wounded out of a crew numbering in all about 120 men. The *Indianola* was one of the most formidable iron-clads on the Mississippi River. She was 174 feet long, fifty feet beam, ten feet from the top of her deck to the bottom of her keel. Her sides of oak were thirty-two inches thick, covered with three-inch iron plates. Her decks were also covered with iron. Her casemates stood at an angle of twenty-six and one-half degrees and were covered with three-inch iron on heavy oak backing. Her coal bunkers were seven feet thick alongside of her boilers.

U. S. IRON-CLAD "INDIANOLA," CAPTURED BY THE CONFEDERATES, MAY 24TH, 1863.

The entire machinery being in the hold. She had seven engines, two for working the side-wheels, one on each quarter stern, two for her two propellers, between the wheels, two for her capstans, and one for supplying water and working the bilge and five pumps. She had also hose for throwing scalding water from the boilers that would reach from stem to stern. She had also five large fire-flued boilers. The pilot-house was also thoroughly iron-clad, and instant communication could be had with the gunners and engineers, enabling the pilot to place the vessel in just such position as might be required for effective action. Her forward casemates had two eleven-inch Dahlgren guns, and her after casemate two nine-inch guns. Her forward casemate was pierced for two guns in front, one on each side, and two aft, so that she could fire two guns forward, one on each side, and four angling sideways and astern. She was one of a number of gunboats built by Joseph Brown, on the Ohio River, in 1863, and cost about $100,000.

When captured, the *Indianola* was in a sinking condition. She was run on a sand-bar on the Mississippi side of the river, and the *Queen of the West* was dispatched to Vicksburg to bring down mechanics to repair and raise her. Before the Confederates succeeded in raising her, she was blown up to prevent her recapture by the Federals.

In April, Capt. Fuller, in command of the *Queen of the West*, determined to make an attack on the Federal gunboats then lying in the Teche. A company of infantry had been placed on board, and a regiment on the steamer *Minna Simma*, which accompanied her. The Federal fleet, composed of the gunboats *Estrella*, *Calhoun* and *Arizona*, under the command of Commodore Cook, encountered the *Queen of the West* at Grand Lake. At a quarter past five A. M., on April 14th, 1863, the fight commenced, the *Estrella* firing the first gun, the *Arizona* and *Calhoun* following. The *Queen* did not reply until she was within three-quarters of a mile, when she fired rapidly from one to another of the gunboats. The intention of the Union vessels was to surround the *Queen of the West*, open a tremendous cross fire upon her, and, if necessary, run her down. When within a half a mile of the *Arizona*, the *Queen* turned slowly to the left and steamed for her, with the evident intention of running her iron prow into her. At the same time the *Calhoun* started for the *Queen of the West*, for the same purpose, when the latter, as if uncertain what to do, stopped her engines and appeared to stand at bay, while the Federal shell and shot were flying around her from every quarter. Suddenly at this time a cloud of white smoke was seen to rise, as if from the deck of the ram, followed a moment after by a dense, black smoke and then a sheet of flame. It appears that one of the shells struck and burst in a box of ammunition, instantly setting her upper decks and rigging in a blaze.

As soon as the Federal fleet saw their powerful enemy on fire, her guns silent, and her crew running here and there in wild confusion—some throwing overboard cotton bales with which she was barricaded, while others jumped into the river —all feelings of enmity vanished. Commodore Cook immediately blew the signal-whistle to cease firing, and assist in rescuing the crew; and as the *Estrella*, *Calhoun* and *Arizona* steamed up to the doomed vessel to save and succor those on board of the *Queen of the West*, boats were lowered, drowning men rescued, and all on board of the burning ram were transferred to the decks of the gunboats. In the confusion, the *Minna Simma* steamed off as rapidly as possible. Ninety-five persons were taken out of the water and from on board the *Queen of the West*; but notwithstanding these humane exertions to rescue those on board, it is believed forty of them were drowned. As soon as the crew and officers and soldiers were rescued the ram was abandoned. She drifted about for some time, the flames each moment raging more fiercely until they reached her magazine, when she exploded with a noise which was heard for miles around.

The ram *Webb*, which aided very materially in capturing the *Indinnola*, was originally called the *William H. Webb*. Before the war she was used in New York as a tow boat, and as an ice breaker in winter, for which purpose she was specially constructed, being of great strength and fitted with powerful engines. She was purchased by some of the New Orleans merchants for the purpose of towing the heavily laden ships to and from the city. She was a low-pressure side-wheel steamer, about two hundred feet long, and noted for her power and speed. When the war broke out she was still in New Orleans, and was seized by the Confederate authorities and converted into a ram and gunboat, by placing heavy solid timbers in her bow, running about thirty feet aft and bolting them firmly and strongly together.

In the latter part of May, 1861, the *Webb* seized three vessels laden with oil and made prizes of them, but after the establishment of the Federal blockade her privateering operations ceased. Upon the evacuation of New Orleans by the Confederates, the *Webb* was sent up the Red River to Shreveport, La. Very little was heard of her again until she attacked, with her consort, the ram *Queen of the West*, the ironclad *Indianola*, in the Mississippi, and, after a desperate struggle, in which she rammed her several times, compelled her to surrender. On the passage of the Vicksburg batteries by the Federal fleet, the *Webb* retreated to the Red River, which she ascended far above Alexandria, where she remained until after the failure of the Banks' expedition up that river, when it is said Lieut. Commander Charles W. Read, of the C. S. navy, conceived the idea of converting her into a Confederate cruiser, to prey upon the commerce of the United States, and submitted the project to Secretary Mallory. The *Webb*, at this time, was lying at Shreveport, La., and the mouth of Red River below was strongly blockaded by a Federal fleet. Besides this blockade, the Mississippi was being constantly patroled by Federal gunboats and other armed craft. New Orleans was literally full of Federal troops, while Federal war vessels lined her levee and occupied and guarded the channel both above and below the city, and further down, Forts Jackson and Philip presented formidable obstacles to the success of such an enterprise as the brave and intrepid Read proposed to undertake. It is said that it was the design of Read, if he should reach the mouth of the Mississippi in safety, to surprise and capture the ship *Pampero*, guardship at the mouth of the river, and then go to Havana, sell the cargo, and sink and destroy whatever he could capture *en route* and then run the blockade into Galveston.

The plan was approved, it is said, by Secretary Mallory, and Commander Read made immediate preparations to carry his enterprise into effect. With Lieut. W. H. Wall as his executive officer, Master Samuel P. Blanc, Midshipman Scott,

Surgeon W. J. Addison and other navy officers, Commander Read left Richmond for the scene of his daring undertaking with sealed orders. Arriving at Shreveport, Commander Read reported to Lieut. Commander Robert R. Carter, commander of the naval defences at that point, and in compliance with orders from the Secretary of the Navy was placed in command of the *Webb*. Every assistance was rendered Commander Read to get his vessel ready for her hazardous expedition. A rough bulwark was built around her forecastle to protect her as much as possible from the sea, and several hundred bales of cotton were piled up around her machinery, to protect it from the guns of the enemy while running the blockade. For fuel, pine knots were substituted for coal. A month's rations and water were placed on board, and the vessel received a good white-washing to prevent her from being seen at night. Her armament consisted of one thirty-two pound rifled gun, mounted on the forecastle, and two twelve pound iron cannon on the quarter-deck. Engineers and pilots were secured, and the craft was manned by volunteers from Gen. E. Kirby Smith's command.

Information of the intended expedition of the *Webb* reached Admiral Lee of the Federal navy, and he dispatched a fleet of iron-clads and gunboats to the mouth of the Red River to prevent her escape. Among them were the monitor *Manhattan* and the iron-clads *Lafayette* and *Choctaw*.

Everything being prepared, the *Webb* left Shreveport, La., on the Red River, twenty-five miles below Alexandria, on Monday, April 16th, 1865. She stopped at Cotes' Landing, and took on board 250 cords of wood. Arriving at the mouth of Red River on the night of April 23d, 1865, with all lights screened, and her safety-valve tied down, she was allowed to drift with the current by the Federal gunboats. Scarcely had she run the gauntlet when a musket was fired at her from the *Manhattan*, quickly followed by a discharge of canister from a howitzer on her deck. The moment the *Webb* was discovered, the engines were started at full speed, and she rushed down the river at the rate of twenty miles an hour, leaving far astern the *Lafayette* and a gunboat which had started in pursuit. Her speed was slackened when the gunboats were out of sight, and she steamed along easily, so as to pass the forts below New Orleans in the night. Ten miles above the city, Commander Read sent a boat ashore and cut the telegraph wires to the city, but unfortunately for him not before a dispatch had been sent from Donaldsonville to New Orleans that she had passed the Federal fleet, giving the Federal authorities in the latter city three hours' notice in advance of her approach. On nearing New Orleans the Union ensign was hoisted at half-mast—on account of President Lincoln's death—and her crew, dressed in Federal army overcoats, sat around on the cotton, on deck, and on the guards, coolly

smoking and picking their teeth, as if they were only innocent soldiers. The fleet lying at New Orleans were prepared
for the approach of a ram, but looking for something of the
Merrimac style of iron-clads, and not for the innocent-appear-
ing army transport, laden with cotton, and thronged with soldiers, that steamed leisurely down the river. The ram had
nearly passed the Federal fleet when the pilot of the *Lackawanna*, an old steamboat man, at once recognized her as the
Webb, and so informed Capt. Emmons. Several shots were
fired at her by the *Lackawanna* and *Ossipee*, which laid above
Algiers, and could use their guns without endangering the
town. In an instant, the American flag was hauled down and
the Confederate colors run up. The *Webb* was hit several
times, but she dashed forward at the rate of twenty-five miles
an hour and ran by the *Portsmouth, Quaker City, Florida,
Ossipee*, and other vessels, whose batteries were manned, but
which could not be fired in consequence of the danger of killing innocent people who thronged the streets and levee of Algiers, watching for the ram. The excitement in New Orleans
was intense. The news soon spread, and in a few moments it
was reported that President Davis and Gen. E. Kirby Smith
were passengers, and that John Wilkes Booth was at the
helm; that gold and silver in untold quantities were on board,
together with all the valuable and official documents of the
Confederacy. The *Webb* passed the city on the afternoon
of April 24th, under a full head of steam, with astonished
crowds on the levee to witness the extraordinary sight.
Her pilot was ordered to "keep the channel and run through
anything that attempts to cross your track." Her torpedo
was triced up in front and every man was at his station.
Plugs were provided for plugging shot-holes that might be
made near the water-line, and, altogether, a ship never rode
the waters more gracefully and defiantly than this little vessel
as she dashed along through the muddy Mississippi, scattering
the white spray far out in her front and on her sides. As she
passed the French man-of-war she dipped her flag. When the
Webb approached the Federal ordnance ship *Fearnought*,
Commander Read ordered the torpedo lowered and the vessel
run into. In the eagerness and haste of lowering the torpedo the spar gave way, and the current carried it under the
starboard wheel. Seeing the danger, Commander Read very
coolly cried out, "Stop the engine and cut away the guy-
ropes." Prompt obedience of this order sent the torpedo to the
bottom of the river, and saved the *Webb* perhaps from being
blown up by its own torpedo. Commander Read afterwards expressed great satisfaction that he was unable to
blow up the *Fearnought*, as the vessel had over three
hundred barrels of powder on board, which would have
blown herself, as well as the *Webb*, out of the water.
The *Hollyhock*, the *Florida*, the *Quaker City*, and the *Ossipee*

were dispatched by the Federal commander in pursuit of the *Webb*, the *Hollyhock* far ahead. When the *Webb* had proceeded about twenty-three miles away from the city, and had slowed her engines to allow the *Hollyhock* to come up, the masts of the sloop-of-war *Richmond* were seen over a point of the river bank. Thinking that she had been placed there to trap him, Commander Read ordered the pilot to put the *Webb* at her, to blow her up with a torpedo, and then to hurry on. On the pilot informing him that a flat laid between them, and that the *Webb* must go around the curve in the channel and pass under the *Richmond's* broadside, he said he had tested her guns before, and would not try them again. He then ordered the *Webb* to be run ashore, and every man to look out for himself. This was at once done on the left bank of the river. The vessel was fired and Commander Read, and his officers and men, took to the swamp. When the *Florida* and *Hollyhock* arrived later, the *Webb* was in a mass of flames, and too far burned to save. Finding that they were surrounded by cavalry sent down from the city to effect their capture, the officers and crew returned to the wreck, where a gunboat was lying alongside, commanded by a naval officer, and desiring to fall into the hands of the U. S. navy rather than the army, the officer was called on shore, and received the officers and crew of the *Webb*, as prisoners of war. They were at once conveyed to New Orleans and placed on board the *Lackawanna*, and finally transferred to the *Florida*, which conveyed them to New York. They arrived in the latter city on May 6th, and on May 10th were consigned to Fort Warren, in Boston harbor. They remained in Fort Warren until the surrender of Gen. E. Kirby Smith, when they were allowed to return to their homes.

CHAPTER XV

NORTH CAROLINA WATERS.

THE most cursory examination of the map of the Southern States will show to the reader that the sounds of North Carolina were no less important to the defence of that State than Hampton Roads was to that of Virginia, and that if the blockade of the Southern coast was to be effective indeed, then these sounds, as coaling stations and harbor of refuge, were of prime importance to the United States. The long, low sandy islets that separated the waters of the ocean from those of the sounds, were indented with inlets, which often changing positions, and always treacherous, were yet, at one or two points always navigable for vessels that could ride with safety in the shoal waters of the sounds.

From Cape Charles to Cape Lookout that island chain extended but inclosed no inland water of importance until Albemarle Sound was reached; there Roanoke Island separated that sound from the larger and deeper water of Pamlico Sound, upon the eastern border of which Cape Hatteras jutted farthest out into the ocean, and Hatteras Inlet and Ocracoke Inlet offered the only safe and reliable entrances from the ocean. Oregon Inlet, near Roanoke Island, had been at all times unsafe for any but the smallest of crafts. The command of the broad waters of these sounds, with their navigable rivers extending far into the interior, would control more than one-third of the State and threaten the main line of railroad between Richmond and the sea-coast portion of the Confederate States. Roanoke Island, between Albemarle and Pamlico Sounds, was the commanding position in those waters. These sounds were connected with the waters of Hampton Roads by the Albemarle and Chesapeake Canal, capable of passing vessels of light draft from Norfolk to Elizabeth City. From Albemarle Sound, the Pasquotank River afforded navigation to Elizabeth city; the Perquimans River to Hertford; the Chowan River to Winton; the Roanoke River to Plymouth.

COMMANDER JOSEPH FRY, C. S. N.

COMMANDER JOHN NEWLAND MAFFITT,

CONFEDERATE STATES NAVY.

From Albemarle Sound, the Pamlico River extended to Washington, from whence the Tar River was navigable to Tarboro; the Neuse River opened wide and deep communication with Newberne, and further up to Kingston and Beaufort, and Morehead City, below Cape Lookout, were accessible also from Pamlico Sound. A large portion of the population of this large and fertile area was, if not actually hostile to the Confederate cause, so indifferent to its success, as to avail themselves of the first and every opportunity to evade the duty of defence and to secure the protection of the enemy for their persons and property.

The State of North Carolina, immediately after passing the Ordinance of Secession, began the work of defending the possession of these sounds. The steamer *Winslow*, a small side-wheel steamboat, was fitted out by the Governor of the State, and on the outside of Hatteras began to annoy and destroy the commerce of the United States. Under Thomas M. Crossan, formerly of the U. S. navy, the *Winslow* captured and brought into the sounds, for condemnation, many prizes, among them the brig *Hannah Butley*, with molasses; the bark *Lenwood*, with 6,000 bags of coffee; the schooner *Lydia French*, the brig *Gilvery*, with 315 tierces of molasses; three unknown brigs, the schooner *Gordon*, with fruit; the schooner *Priscilla*, with 600 bushels of salt; a brig and three schooners; the brig *Itasca*, with 500 hogsheads of molasses; the schooner *Henry Nut*, with mahogany and logwood, and the schooner *Sea Witch*, with fruit. The outcry that went up from commercial circles at the North may have had no little to do in influencing the naval authorities to block the outlet from which the little *Winslow* inflicted such damages.

After the State united herself to the Confederate States, her navy, consisting of the *Winslow*, the *Ellis*, the *Raleigh*, and the *Beaufort*, all ordinary steamboats, armed with one gun each, were turned over to the Confederate States.

The defence of the entrances to these sounds was undertaken by the erection of batteries at Hatteras and Ocracoke Inlet and at Beaufort; on the interior waters, Newberne, Roanoke Island, and the mouth of the Neuse River, were defended under the State by small batteries, which were not completed when the State adopted the Constitution of the Confederate States.

Major R. C. Gatlin[1] was appointed Commander of the "Southern Department Coast Defences," with headquarters at Wilmington, N. C.; promoted to Brigadier General in August, 1861, he was assigned to the command of the Department of North Carolina and the coast defences of the State.

---

[1] Gen. Gatlin was a major in the U. S. army, Fifth infantry, when the State seceded. He had been captured at Fort Smith by the forces of the State of Arkansas, April 23d, 1861, and released on parole, and resigning his commission accepted service under North Carolina, and was transferred by her Ordinance to the Confederate States Army.

24

The importance of seizing and retaining possession of the North Carolina Sounds was as apparent and urgent upon the United States as their defence was to the Confederate States. These safe and commodious anchorages not only afforded protection against the storms which so often prevail along the Atlantic coast, but they were depots from which the very central line of inland communication of the Confederates might be broken, and, moreover, they were the "back door" to Norfolk, by which the navy-yard might be regained.

To the Navy Department of the United States is due the credit for seeing the importance of these sounds, and taking early steps to regain their possession and control. The preparation and concentration of a naval expedition was commenced in the summer of 1861, and so far completed by the 25th of August that the infantry detail, numbering 860 men under Gen. B. F. Butler, was taken aboard, and on the 26th of August the expedition sailed. The expedition consisted of the steam frigate *Minnesota*, Capt. G. I. Van Brunt, the flagship of Commodore Stringham ; the steam frigate *Wabash*, Capt. Samuel Mercer ; the *Monticello*, Commander John P. Gillis ; the *Pawnee*, Commander S. C. Rowan ; and the revenue-cutter *Harriet Lane*, Capt. John Fanner. The steamer *Adelaide*, Commander Henry S. Stellwagen, with 500 infantry from the Twentieth New York regiment, Col. Weber ; and the *Peabody*, Lieut. R. R. Lowry, with 220 infantry of the Ninth New York regiment; 100 men of the Union coast-guard, Capt. Nixon ; and sixty men of the Second U. S. artillery, Lieut. Learned. As the means of landing through the surf, the transports towed two schooners with very large iron surf-boats. On the same afternoon the expedition anchored off Hatteras Inlet, and preparations were immediately made for landing the troops, as well as to attack the batteries from the war vessels. The frigate *Susquehanna* joined the expedition off Hatteras and took part in the bombardment.

The entrance to Hatteras Inlet is endangered by a bar which covers the whole front of the inlet, and is further impeded by a "bulkhead" on the sound side only, while the water is very seldom of greater depth than seven and a half feet. Of the forts defending the inlet, Fort Hatteras, the larger, mounting twenty-five guns, was separated from Fort Clark by a shallow bay about half a mile wide. The surf, though heavy and dangerous along the beach, was not such as to prevent the landing of troops, and a detachment was put on shore during the bombardment, at a point far beyond the reach of the guns of the fort and without resistance from the Confederates, whose garrison was unequal to defence, and only large enough to give importance to its capture.

Flag-officer Capt. Samuel Barron, [1] C. S. N., to whom had been assigned the duty of commanding the defences, did not arrive at Hatteras until the 28th of August, one day after the bombardment had been going on. Col. Martin's little force, the Seventh North Carolina Volunteers, exhausted and worn down with constant fighting, had been driven from Fort Clark to Fort Hatteras, when Major Andrews, commanding all the forces on land, awaited another regiment from Newberne. The land forces of the enemy took possession of Fort Clark and defended it with naval howitzers brought with them. At the urgent request of Major Andrews, Flag-officer Barron assumed command. He found Col. Martin utterly prostrated by the severe action and the duties of the day.

There were but two guns mounted on the side next to Fort Clark, both thirty-two pounders, and one gun on the corner next the bar, an eight-inch shell gun. During the night Major Andrews tore away a traverse on the back face of the work and brought another gun to bear in the same direction. The companies of the command, under Capts. Cobden, Lamb and Sutton, having been in action all the previous day, displaying great courage and devotion, were perfectly exhausted. He

[1] Admiral Samuel Barron was born in Virginia, and entered the U. S. navy as midshipman, on January 1, 1812. He was attached to the *Brandywine* when she conveyed Gen. Lafayette to France, in 1825; was promoted to be lieutenant March 3, 1827, commander July 15, 1847, and captain in 1855. At the beginning of the war he was appointed chief of the Bureau of Detail in the U. S. Navy Department. He entered the C. S. navy on the 10th of June 1861, with the rank of commander, and put in charge of the naval defences of North Carolina and Virginia, with the rank of flag-officer. He did not arrive at Fort Hatteras until after the fall and evacuation of Fort Clark. He was requested by Col. Martin, in command of the North Carolina troops, to take command of the land officers, and conduct the defence of Fort Hatteras, as it was armed with navy guns and the officers and men were not accustomed to the management of them. Commodore Barron then assumed the general direction of the defences. He was engaged all night in preparing to defend Fort Hatteras, by transferring the officers and men from the other forts to do it. During the fight the next day (the 29th of August) Commodore Barron did not have a single gun that could reach the enemy's ships, while their batteries were throwing shells into the fort every few seconds.

The following were the articles of capitulation agreed upon at the surrender of the forts, at the inlet of Hatteras, N. C.,—the first agreed upon after the war began:

"OFF HATTERAS INLET, }
"U. S. FLAG-SHIP 'MINNESOTA,' Aug. 29, 1861. }

"*Articles of capitulation between Flag-officers Stringham, commanding the 'Atlantic Blockading Squadron,' and Benjamin F. Butler, U. S. army, commanding on behalf of the United States Government, and Samuel Barron, commanding the naval force for the defence of North Carolina and Virginia, and Col. Martin, commanding the forces, and Major Andrews, commanding the same forces, at Fort Hatteras.*

"It is stipulated and agreed between the contracting parties that the forces under the command of the said Barron, Martin and Andrews, and all munitions of war, arms, men, and property under the command of said Barron, Martin, and Andrews, be unconditonally surrendered to the Government of the United States in terms of full capitulation.

"And it is stipulated and agreed by the contracting parties on the part of the United States Government that the officers and men shall receive the treatment due to prisoners of war.

"In witness whereof, we, the said Stringham and Butler, on behalf of the United States, and the said Barron, Martin and Andrews, representing the forces at Hatteras Inlet, hereunto interchangeably set our hands this twenty-ninth day of August, A. D. 1861, and of the independence of the United States the eighty-fifth year.

"S. H. STRINGHAM,
"*Flag-officer Atlantic Blockading Squadron.*

"BENJ. F. BUTLER,
"*Major-General U. S. Army, commanding.*

"S. BARRON,
"*Flag-officer Confederate States Navy, commanding Naval Defences South and North Carolina.*

"WM. F. MARTIN,
"*Colonel 7th Regiment Infantry North Carolina Volunteers.*

"W. S. G. ANDREWS,
"*Major, commanding Forts Hatteras and Clark.*"

After the surrender Commodore Barron was sent to Fort Warren, Boston Harbor, until exchanged in 1862. During the remainder of the war he was in England and France engaged in carrying out the plans of his government, in getting war vessels afloat. He secured for the Confederacy the cruisers *Stonewall* and *Georgia*. After the close of the war he returned to Virginia and now (1887) resides, a great invalid, at Loretto, Essex County, Virginia.

placed the batteries in charge of fresh troops, as follows:
Nos. 2 and 3 of the channel battery under the command of
Capt. Thomas Sparrow, assisted by his Lieuts., Shaw and
Thomas; Nos. 4 and 5 of the same battery were under command of Lieut. Col. George W. Johnston. assisted by First
Lieut. Mose and Second Lieut. George W. Daniels; No. 6, facing the bar, and No. 7, facing Fort Clark, were placed in
charge of Major Henry A. Gillion, assisted by Lieuts. Johnston and Grimes; No. 8, a gun mounted on naval carriage,
was commanded by Lieut. William H. Murdaugh, of the
C. S. N., assisted by Lieut. Wm. Sharp[1] and Midshipman J. M.
Stafford.   Capt. Thomas H. Sharp had command of No. 1,
but owing to the wrenches not fitting the eccentric axles, was
unable to bring it into action. He staid by his gun during
most of the engagement, but could not fire. Thus, the Confederates had but three guns they could bring to bear (if the
enemy took up his position of the previous day), viz.: Nos. 6,
7 and 8.

At 7:40 A. M. of the 29th the enemy opened fire from the
steam-frigate *Minnesota* (forty-three guns), *Wabash* (forty-
three guns), *Susquehanna* (fifteen guns), frigate *Cumberland*

[1] William Sharp entered the navy of the United
States September 9th, 1841, and resigned as a
lieutenant at the Norfolk navy-yard, where he
was stationed, on the day Virginia seceded. He
entered the service of the Confederate States
navy on June 10th, 1861, and was first placed
on duty in the Navy Department at Richmond, by and with Commodore Samuel Barron.
Later he was stationed at a fort on the Naval
Hospital Grounds, Norfolk, commanded by Capt.
Chas. F. McIntosh. where he was for some weeks
engaged in drilling several regiments in heavy
artillery. Later, Commodore Barron was ordered
to North Carolina in charge of the Water Defences
of that State, and he was sent as his aide with
headquarters at Newberne. On the morning after
the arrival of the U. S. squadron under Commander S. H. Stingham with Gen. B. F. Butler on
board, off Hatteras Inlet, he attended Commodore
Barron to the vicinity of that locality, witnessed
the first day's fight, and at 9 P.M. of the same day,
at the request of Col. W. F. Martin, commanding
Fort Hatteras, Commodore Barron relieved him,
and the navy officers entered it at once.
Early next day the Federal fleet returned from
their anchorage, and commenced the attack on
Fort Hatteras, as Fort Clark (to the northward)
had surrendered on the previous day, and rained
Minie balls over their heads throughout the
morning. The guns of Fort Hatteras were harmless to the fleet, while nearly every shot from
them told against the Confederates. During the
action Lieut. Sharp was wounded in the face and
fell, remaining insensible for some time. He
was taken up, supposedly dead, by Col. Charles
Heywood, U. S. Marine Corps, who entered the
fort with Gen. B. F. Butler when he landed, and
received the surrender. Lieut. Sharp was sent
off to the flag-ship *Minnesota*, which went to
New York immediately, and was landed as a
prisoner at Fort Columbus, Governor's Island,
commanded by Col. Loomis, U. S A. After a
stay of some months, he was sent to Fort Warren,
Boston Harbor, in November, 1861, commanded
by Gen. Justin Dimmick, U. S. A.

After some weeks, in charge of Lieut. W. F.
Spicer, U. S. N., and a marine guard, he was
taken to Boston, placed on the Old Colony R. R.
and taken to the U. S. receiving ship *North
Carolina*, Brooklyn navy-yard. On the same day
he was sent to the gunboat *Connecticut*, Capt.
Maxwell Woodhull, which steamed for Hampton Roads, he being sent as a prisoner to the
U. S. frigate *Congress*, Capt. Wm. Smith. On
November 2 ', 1861, he was exchanged for Lieut.
John L. Worden, U. S. N., and was landed in
Norfolk. In a few days afterwards, he was
ordered to the C. S. steamer *Patrick Henry* at
Richmond, and had charge of her forward division in the Hampton Roads battles of March
8th and 9th, 1862. Some weeks later he was assigned to the command of the Confederate gunboat *Beaufort*, relieving Lieut. W. H. Parker,
and was one of four sent to Hampton Roads
with the intention to attempt boarding the
Monitor. The *Monitor* did not come out and
nothing was accomplished. Soon after that he
towed the schooner *Kaigan's Point* at night past
the blockading squadron off Newport News,
and to Drewry's Bluff, loaded with iron for the
Tredegar Iron Works at Richmond.
After a while he was stationed at Charlotte,
N. C., thence accompanying Commodore Barron to Murfreesboro, Tenn., where their expectations of getting to Nashville to block up the
Cumberland were frustrated by the Federal army
being in possession. Returning to Richmond
he was one of a board of examiners to examine
Midshipmen, which sat in Mobile, Savannah,
Charleston and Richmond
Then he was sent to re-command the gunboat
Beaufort, remaining till the winter of 1863,
when he was sent to Winston, N. C., to relieve
Commander James W. Cook in supervising the
construction of the iron-clad steamer *Neuse*. He
remained on this duty till the spring of 1864,
when he was sent to Charleston, S. C., in charge
of the Naval Ordnance Department, and continued there until Sherman's advance through
Georgia. This was his last service.

(twenty-four guns), steamer *Pawnee* (ten guns), and *Harriet Lane* (five guns), and a rifled battery of three guns erected in the sand-hills three miles east of Fort Clark.

Bringing seventy-three guns of the most approved kind and heaviest metal to bear on the forts, the shells thrown being nine-inch, ten-inch, and eleven-inch Dahlgren, Paixhan, and Columbiad ; while, from the position taken, the guns of the forts were unable to reach them with the greatest elevation. The men of the channel battery were ordered to leave their guns and protect themselves as well as possible, the council of the commanding officers having decided that it was to be an action of endurance until reinforcements came up. After a few shots had been fired, and it was ascertained that the guns could not reach them, the Confederate firing ceased, and only answered the fire of the enemy occasionally, to show that the forts had not surrendered. The shower of shell in half an hour became literally tremendous, falling into and immediately around the works not less, on an average, than ten each minute, and, the sea being smooth, the firing was remarkably accurate.

One officer counted twenty-eight shells, and several others counted twenty, as falling in a minute. At a quarter to eleven o'clock a council of the officers was held, and it was determined to surrender. A white flag was raised, and the firing ceased at eleven o'clock. Thus for three hours and twenty minutes Fort Hatteras resisted a storm of shells perhaps more terrible than ever fell upon any other work. At the time the council determined to surrender, two of the fort's guns were dismounted, four men were reported killed, and between twenty-five and thirty badly wounded.[1] One shell

---

[1] Among the severely wounded was Lieut. William H. Murdaugh, who had his left arm shattered by a shell and was slightly wounded in the knee by a fragment of a shell. Lieut. Murdaugh, after the acceptance of his resignation in the old navy, reached Richmond in June, 1861. The duty to which he was first assigned was that of making surveys in James River, in connection with the establishment of batteries and the obstruction of channels. Lieut. Commander Robert R. Carter, of Virginia, was associated with him in this work. After this duty was faithfully discharged, Lieut. Murdaugh went with Commander Barron to the defences of North Carolina, where he was assigned to the command of a vessel, but before he could take charge, the affair at Fort Hatteras came off. in which he was severely wounded. While unfit for active service from his wound, he was on ordnance duty at the Norfolk navy-yard. He was with Capt. French Forrest in the tug *Harmony* in Hampton Roads during the two days' fight When it was determined to evacuate Norfolk, he was sent off to select a place for an ordnance depot to which the stores and tools from the Ordnance Department of the navy-yard could be removed. He selected Charlotte, N. C , as the place and rented machine shops and store houses for the purpose. Charlotte was an important workshop all during the war, and was never pressed by the foot of the enemy until resistance ceased on the part of the Confederates. From Charlotte, Lieut. Murdaugh was ordered to the command of the steamer *Beaufort*. on James River, and afterwards was sent abroad to purchase ordnance supplies. Commander Bulloch, in his admirable work on "The Secret Service of the Confederate States in Europe," says: "Among the officers sent to Europe for service in the iron-clad vessels it was hoped might be got to sea was Lieut. William H. Murdaugh. Besides having the special experience and general professional knowledge which fitted him for ordnance work, he possessed admirable tact and judgment, and also the reticence and faculty of self-control which are essential for the satisfactory performance of duties requiring secrecy. The special ordnance stores were nearly all overlooked and certified by him. The whole of the work was performed creditably, and the goods passed out of the manufacturer's hands, and went through the shipping-ports, without attracting notice or causing any embarrassing scrutiny. The execution of the foregoing special orders brought Lieut. Murdaugh into constant and confidential communication with me, and I was most desirous to appoint him to another and still more important service, but the war came to an abrupt end just before the maturity of the enterprise in which he was to have had a leading part."

had fallen into the room adjoining the magazine, and the
magazine was reported on fire.

Articles of capitulation of unconditional surrender were
demanded and the whole command became prisoners of war. [1]

An officer of the C. S. steamer *Ellis,* who witnessed the
bombardment and surrender of Fort Hatteras, in a letter to the
Washington (N. C.) *Dispatch,* gave the following account of
the affair:

" Proceeding up the Sound, we came up with the little despatch boat
M. C. Downing, just from Hatteras, bringing up the intelligence that the
patriotic little band of 100 men who were at Fort Clark, a little above
Fort Hatteras, after making a desperate resistance, firing their last shot,
had evacuated the fort, having previously rendered the guns useless by
spiking and dismounting them, and that the vandal horde of the North,
led on by a traitorous Methodist minister, had landed and taken possession of the fort, and now the 'Stars and Stripes' were floating over the
time-honored soil of the Old North State; that Fort Hatteras was still
gallantly fighting, but was in need of men and munitions of war. The
men we could easily supply, but the ammunition we had not. The little
steamer then passed ahead after ammunition, and we with beating and
anxious hearts eagerly waited the time when we should cheer our noble
companions by our presence. Just at this time we saw the steamer *Winslow* approaching with a plenty of ammunition, and the following officers
on board: Capt. Samuel Barron, Lieuts. Sharp and Murdaugh, and Surgeon Greenhow. She came to anchor about two and a-half or three miles
from the fort. This was indeed cheering, and our expectations knew no
bounds. All this time a severe and constant cannonade was being kept
up, the fleet firing continual broadsides of shell, while we replied at intervals with shot, our shell having been expended. The shot and shell dropped thick and fast upon the fort and island, but so far no one was hurt,
except two men killed and Lieut. Knight wounded, while retreating from
Fort Clark. In the face of the dreadful storm of iron, our captain, with
that firmness and tranquility which ever characterizes the true officer and
gentleman, ran the C. S. steamer *Ellis* near the fort, which now of course
became the prominent mark for the Yankees, as we were not only a gunboat, but our decks were crowded with men. Protected by our Heavenly
Father, though the balls whistled close and fast by us, we remained unhurt. One thing I can vouch for is, that there is not a man upon this little steamer but who has grown familiar with that peculiar whizzing
sound which always accompanies a ball in its flight through the air.
Several rifle cannon balls passed in close proximity to us, and though perhaps it was the first time that some of them had ever heard a cannon fired,

---

[1] Major W. S. G. Andrews, in his official report
to the Adjutant Gen. of North Carolina, says :
" I desire especially to speak of the conduct of
the officers and men at the naval gun, who fired
frequently to try the range. Lieut. Murdaugh
was badly wounded, Lieut. Sharp was knocked
down by a shot which passed through the parapet near his head and brought the blood from
his ear and cheek in considerable quantity, killing a man at his side, at the same time knocking
down and covering Col. J. A. Bradford with sod
and earth ; and Midshipman Stafford cheered
on the men, behaving in a most gallant manner.
After the fall of Lieut. Murdaugh his men bore
him to the commodore's boat and he escaped.

An officer of the steamer *Winslow* said: " Lieut.
Murdaugh, the friend and brother officer of
Capt. Barron, who was brought on board of the
Winslow during the engagement, with a severe
wound in the left arm, informed me that he

never saw a man possessed of more cool courage
than animated Capt. Barron in that hour of
peril ; and he says also, that the resolution to
surrender the fort was the result of calm and
serious deliberation, actuated by decided feelings of honor and patriotism. The gallant lieutenant, who also behaved most nobly in the engagement, will, when he recovers from the
effects of his wound, bear me out in the statement of facts, which I think ought in justice to
be made. I know, what every one who witnessed
the engagement must feel, and that is, that Capt.
Barron is as brave as he is honorable, and that
in his conduct at Hatteras he was actuated by a
strict sense of duty alone."

Another officer, writing from Hatteras, says :
" Capt. Barron, though forced to yield by overwhelming batteries, he, and those who fought
with him in that conflict of fire, are worthy of
their country's approbation and honor."

yet the crew and officers stood it with most perfect nonchalance, exhibiting throughout the whole action perfect confidence in their officers, and a reliance upon the Almighty hand. After safely landing the troops, we again returned to the *Winslow*, and taking a plentiful supply of ammunition, we went alongside the schooners and took all the troops on board, and safely landed everything at the fort. Our escape was truly miraculous. Nobly has the *Ellis* performed her duty in this terrible encounter, and it is due to her that her services should be acknowledged. Too much praise cannot be given to her commander and crew.

"The enemy, after an incessant fire of about six hours, having sounded all about, and planted buoys ready for the dreadful work of to-morrow, retired for the night, and no doubt employed themselves for the coming struggle. Nearly all night we were employed in making the fort impregnable, as we then thought. *Much of the disaster which occurred on Thursday may be attributed to the fact that we did not possess our-selves of Fort Clark by the bayonet that night;* but wiser and older heads than mine thought otherwise. Certain it is, in my opinion, it was one of the causes, second only to the shameful neglect of the authorities in not properly fortifying the coast, that caused our defeat. From these two causes we have the following result: the possession of Hatteras, the key of the Sound; the road open to invasion at any moment; Capt. Barron, Lieut. Sharp, and about 700 or 800 gallant men prisoners, taken by the Abolition Kangaroos, besides prolonging, in my opinion, the war for half a year.

"I must not here forget to mention a trivial circumstance, it may seem, but one which exhibits the brave man and patriot. On going to the fort about two o'clock at night, Lieut. Murdaugh might be seen standing, in the clear moonlight, upon the well-defended ramparts at Hatteras. He was calmly superintending the works about the guns, having one fixed so as better to bear on the enemy with which he himself intended to fight. No one who saw him could doubt but that he would do good service. The next morning, August 29th, a day ever memorable to those who witnessed or participated in this sublime but terrible contest, rose calm and beautiful. This was just what the Yankees wished. All the morning I was busily engaged in going to and fro on duty to Capt. Barron, who was very anxious for me to go on shore and help about the guns, as they had not many in the fort who knew much about gunnery; but as we had not the officers to spare, Capt. Muse would not consent for me to go. I will here mention a fact to show how close the Yankees were to the fort. While ashore, standing on the ramparts, in company with Capt. Barron, Lieut. Sharp and Lieut. Barron, all of us being in uniform, were of course a good mark, and the Yankees thought so too, for whiz went a ball in close proximity to the captain's head, while several struck in the parapet immediately under us. It will here be proper to state that Midshipman J. M. Stafford had been sent ashore, where, during the fight, he fully performed his duty and rendered valuable service, conducting himself with manly coolness surpassing his years.

"At 8:30 A. M., the frigate *Wabash* steamed up, and as she passed Fort Clark the Stars and Stripes were waved three times to her from the parapet of the fort, which she acknowledged by dipping her colors. She then rounded to, dropped anchor, and opened fire upon the fort. She was immediately joined by the *Susquehanna, Cumberland,* and *Minnesota,* in an incessant fire of shell which dropped thick and fast around and in the fort. The fort replied at intervals, and the *Susquehanna* was evidently damaged, as she withdrew from the range of the fort, and only fired two more shots during the engagement, her place being supplied by the *Roanoke.* Fort Clark now also opened on Fort Hatteras, together with several other land batteries which they had erected on shore, one of these, consisting of rifle cannon, seemed to pay particular attention to us; and as they gradually got our range, they came near hitting us several times, so that we changed our position, and the guns were then turned on the fort.

All eyes were now turned to that gallant little fort fighting against such desperate odds. One continual stream of shell fell upon it, but still it does not fire ! What can be the matter ? Look, there goes the fort again ! Again ! But alas ! all fall far short. The reason is now evident ; they cannot reach the vessels, while every shot almost from them tells upon the fort. Amid a perfect hail-storm of iron a boat leaves the fort. What can it want? My God, they are bringing the wounded to the steamer! What a terrible scene ! Never shall I forget it. They approach. Surely that blackened face, that body almost covered with blood cannot be the noble and chivalrous Lieut. Murdaugh. Alas ! it is. He has fallen, manfully battling against them by the side of his gun, with words of encouragement upon his lips. After firing three or four effective shots, which crippled the *Susquehanna*, and finding they were out of range of our guns, he remarked to his men, ' Well, boys, we will wait till they come up, when we will give it to them again.' But he had hardly uttered these words ere an eleven-inch shell exploded close by, sent two or three fragments of shell through his left arm, completely shattering it to pieces, causing great pain, exhaustion and loss of blood. He was supplied with lint by Mr. Tredwell, one of our officers, who had very thoughtfully provided some for his own use, should he be wounded, and who, during the whole action, behaved, as did all the officers, with the utmost coolness and firmness. He was taken on board the *Winslow*, and placed under the care of Surgeon Greenhow, of the C. S. navy, an intelligent and successful surgeon, where he was properly cared for.

"The bombardment of Fort Hatteras, by the flower of the Federal navy, was a scene which will ever be present to the minds of those who witnessed it. On that day many a fireside was made desolate ; many a mother and wife made to weep over the sad fate of those who were nearest to them, and whose bloody and mangled corpses, perhaps, now lay stark and still upon the blood-stained beach of Hatteras. But such scenes as these are the necessary attendants of war. But what is that appearing on the fort ? *A white flag !* Surely those who were that morning so buoyant and full of joy and hope at the prospect of beating the Yankees, cannot now be suing for peace ! Yet it is so. Such a continual stream of shell was more than the gallant little fort could stand ; the bomb-proof had given way, and every shell now played sad havoc among them ; so, laying aside their pride, they yielded to necessity, and to prevent any more sacrifice of life, had resigned themselves to months of imprisonment, perhaps, in the loathsome dens of the Tombs ! It was truly a humiliating sight.

"The fight lasted for a day and a half, out of which time there were fourteen hours of incessant firing, during which time they threw some 400 or 500 shot and shell. After finding the fort had surrendered, and that we could be of no possible use, we left for Ocracoke, to take on board the sad and weeping wives of the officers, now prisoners, and shall proceed to Washington, N. C."

Of this engagement Admiral Porter [1] remarks that " in days of wooden ships one gun mounted on shore was considered equal to five on shipboard ; but even this allowance made the squadron superior to the forts, without considering the heavier guns and better equipment of the frigates;" and to those advantages must be added the still more important fact that the squadron took position beyond the range of any gun on shore—and thus, without the possibility of injury, were able to " almost smother " the people in the forts. " This was our first naval victory—indeed, our first victory of any kind, [2]

[1] *Naval History*, p. 45.   [2] *Naval History*, p. 47.

and great was the rejoicing thereat throughout the United States."

Thus, on the 31st of August, the important position at Hatteras Inlet was captured, and that at Ocracoke Inlet abandoned by the Confederates, and safe entrance to the fleets of the enemy gained to the sounds and rivers of North Carolina. Notwithstanding the loss of Hatteras Fort and the ability of the enemy to cover the waters of the sound with their gunboats, they soon discovered that they must hold their conquest with a force ever present to defend it. Capt. Wm. F. Lynch[1] succeeded Flag-officer Barron, who had been taken prisoner in the command of the naval defences, and, ever alert and active, received information on October 1st that the enemy was sending reinforcements of men and supplies to Chicamacommico, a station about forty miles north of Hatteras Inlet, on the narrow strip of sand that divides the sound from the ocean. With the *Raleigh*, Lieut. Commander J. W. Alexander; *Junaluska*, Midshipman W. H. Vernon, commanding, assisted by Midshipman James M. Gardner, and the *Curlew*, Capt. Lynch proceeded to intercept any steamer that might be found cruising in the sound. Midshipman commanding Taylor was left in charge of the floating battery, and Midshipman Gregory on the *Cotton Plant*. At 5 P. M. the Federal steamer *Fanny*, loaded with ammunition and supplies for the Federal post at Loggerhead Inlet, was sighted. The armament of the *Fanny* was two rifled cannon, and she had just a few hours before received from the *Putnam* a rifled cannon and ammunition for the Twentieth Indiana Regiment.

Col. Claiborne Snead, of Augusta, Ga., describing the spirited affair, says:

" On the first day of October, 1861, the army of occupation of Roanoke Island consisted of the Third Georgia Regiment, under the command of Col. A. R. Wright and Col. Shaw's North Carolina Regiment. Here these Georgians, just one day after the fall of Fort Hatteras, solitary and unaided, planted the Confederate flag. The night previous, when only a detachment of four companies had arrived in Pamlico Sound, they

---

[1] Capt. Wm. F. Lynch, C. S. N., was born in Virginia in 1801, and entered the U. S. service as a midshipman, January 26th, 1819. He was promoted a lieutenant in May, 1828, and originated his famous expedition to the Dead Sea and River Jordan, which received the sanction of the government. He sailed from this country for Smyrna in the naval store-ship *Supply* in November, 1847. He visited Constantinople to obtain the requisite authority and protection from the Turkish government to pass through Palestine. He made this necessary overland journey on camels, and by the aid of Arabs and others. His party was landed in the Bay of Acre in March, 1848, and in the following April began the work of navigating the Jordan to the Dead Sea. A thorough exploration and sounding of the sea were made. Among other curious features of the labor was the establishment by a series of levels of the depression of the Dead Sea below the level of the Mediterranean, a former survey by Lieut.

Symonds, of the British navy, being fully corroborated as correct, and the depression established as 1,312 feet. On his return Lieut. Lynch published a narrative of his expedition, which has passed through several editions and attained a position among standard works.

On his return he was promoted a commander. He prepared to engage in an expedition into Africa, but the exploration was abandoned. In 1851 he published a volume entitled *Naval Life; or, Observations Afloat and on Shore.* In 1856 he was promoted captain, and this position he retained until his resignation on April 21st, 1861. Immediately after his resignation from the U. S. navy he entered the service of Virginia and was assigned to duty on the Potomac River and the coast defences of the State. He entered the C. S. navy on June 10th, 1861, with the rank of captain. After his gallant defence of the coast of North Carolina he was assigned to duty on the Mississippi River. He died at Baltimore, October 17th, 1865.

received the unwelcome tidings of the surrender of this fort to which they were proceeding as a reinforcement. Hence, they landed, and from that day till the period of which we now write, they were continuously at work, working by day, and frequently the moon shining on, or the darkness of night enveloped them still at work, building entrenchments and batteries on this and Croatan Island and other adjacent points, for the protection of the inland coast of North Carolina.

"The North Carolina regiment had but recently arrived, having been previously in garrison at Fort Oregon, on Oregon Inlet, the extreme northern point on Hatteras Island, the evacuation of which had been necessitated by the fall of Fort Hatteras on the extreme point south.

"Receiving information that a Federal steamer had been seen just south of Roanoke Island, Col. A. R. Wright, commanding as senior officer of the Confederate forces, determined at once to intercept and capture her, and if possible to learn the intentions of the enemy, who were evidently meditating some hostile movement upon his position. He was warmly seconded by Commodore Lynch, a man of iron nerve and justly celebrated for his exploration of the Dead Sea, who was then in command of what was commonly called "The Mosquito Fleet," composed of light draft miniature vessels, drawing from two to six feet of water. These vessels were thus peculiarly constructed with the view to avoid the danger of the shallows and frequent rough state of the waters of Albemarle and Pamlico Sounds. But the disaster at Hatteras, with the occupation of the inlet by the United States Navy, and the consequent opening of all the sounds and tributary rivers of northeastern North Carolina to the inroads of the enemy, caused a hasty transformation of these crafts into men-of-war, which, if not really formidable, were sufficient to command respect and frighten off the Federals till the final attack on Roanoke Island by Burnside with an overwhelming land and naval force.

"From this little fleet the steamers *Junaluska*, *Raleigh* and *Curlew* were selected for the projected expedition, but as neither of these boats had received any armament except the *Raleigh*, which had a couple of six-pounder smooth-bore boat howitzers, it became necessary to provide guns and crews for them. In Fort Bartow, an earth-work just completed near the "marshes," there was a long navy thirty-two pounder which had been recently rifled and reinforced with heavy steel rings in the navy-yard at Portsmouth. This gun had but a few days previously been mounted and placed in position *en barbette* in the fort. It was determined to remove it and place it temporarily on a pivot on the bow of the *Curlew*, which was a large side-wheel steamer, formerly used as a passenger boat on the Albemarle Sound. During the night this difficult task was accomplished. An old twelve-pounder smooth-bore gun, mounted on a field carriage, was placed in the stern of the *Curlew*, and these two guns composed her armament. On the *Junaluska*, a small propeller tug-boat, drawing three and a half feet, was placed a six-pounder field gun. Crews to work these guns were selected from three companies of the Third Georgia regiment. These men had been practiced for a few days with the guns in the fort, but neither of them had ever seen a cannon discharged, and were therefore perfectly green and inexperienced in the use of such guns. Few of them had ever been on shipboard, their whole naval experience being comprised in the fact that they had been transported from Norfolk to the Island a few days previous on a canal barge drawn by the little tug *Junaluska*."

"Having received their armament, guns, crews and a small force of infantry composed of the "Dawson Greys," the "Governor's Guards," and the "Athens Guards," all of the Third Georgia regiment, were distributed on board the three little vessels, armed with Enfield rifles. Weighing anchor they proceeded down the sound in the direction of Hatteras Inlet, moving slowly and cautiously in order to keep within the narrow channels and to avoid the dangerous shoals. In less than two hours the object of the cruise was plainly seen, when an advance upon her was ordered, the *Curlew* (Commodore Lynch's flag-ship, upon which was Col. Wright, commanding the expedition), leading; and when within range a brisk fire was opened which was promptly responded to, her guns being well worked and aimed with precision. Each vessel advanced rapidly with the intention of grappling and boarding the foe that exhibited so much spirit in her responsive fire; but after fifteen or twenty shots, one shell exploded on the deck of the *Fanny* (for that was the name of the U. S. steamer), when immediately her colors were struck, and a few moments thereafter up to her masthead went the Confederate ensign amid the shouts of the victors.

"She carried two rifled guns, a crew of forty-nine men, besides a large amount of army stores valued by some as high as $100,000. Among the latter were 1,000 new overcoats, which were turned over to the Third Georgia regiment, and contributed greatly to their comfort during the ensuing winter.

"The prisoners were sent to Norfolk, while the *Fanny* became a part of the Mosquito fleet; and subsequently, with her every now and then, Capt. Hunter, a vigilant, active and energetic C. S. naval officer, would run down the sound and send greetings with shell into Fort Hatteras.

" This victory was important in more respects than one. It was our first naval success in North Carolina and the first capture made by our arms of an armed war-vessel of the enemy, and dispelled the gloom of recent disasters. The property captured was considerable, much needed, and highly esteemed at that time. But more important than all was the information obtained as to the movements and intentions of the enemy. These stores were found to be intended for the Twentieth Indiana regiment at Chickacommico, twenty miles distant, on Hatteras Island, where a camp had been established with a view to make it a *point d'appui* from which to attack Roanoke Island."

The Federal account of the engagement, by Gen. Mansfield, is that "not a shot struck the *Fanny*, and some eight or nine shots were fired at the enemy, one of which took effect. Then the cable was slipped and the *Fanny* was run ashore some 2¾ miles still from the beach, and the crew abandoned her in a boat, and the officer in charge, Capt. Hart, hoisted a white flag, and surrendered before a gun was fired on either side." It is not for us to reconcile the discrepancies in a report which, while mentioning an "attack" in which "eight or nine shots were fired at the enemy" yet concludes with the statement that the vessel was "surrendered before a gun was fired on either side."[1] Capt. Lynch reports that "after an engagement of 35 minutes the *Fanny* surrendered, and we made prisoners of the entire force—47 men, 2 officers and 1 negro. The *Fanny* mounted two rifled guns and made a gallant resistance, but the superior weight of our guns gave us the advantage." Want of fuel compelled Capt. Lynch to return and set his sailors to work cutting and chopping wood.

While bestowing a full page to the most minute description of the destruction of some abandoned material in the fort at Ocracoke, Admiral Ammen dismisses the capture of the *Fanny* with a single line : "this speedily led to the capture of the *army* tug *Fanny* and a considerable quantity of army stores." The prize had very valuable stores on board; besides

[1] Brig. Gen. J. K. T. Mansfield's report in Vol. IV., p. 595, Official Records.

the powder, shell, and fixed ammunition for her rifled guns, there were 65,000 musket balls and buckshot cartridges, 7,000 Minie ball cartridges, and a large quantity of blankets, overcoats and shoes.   The loss of the *Fanny* eventually led to the Twentieth Indiana regiment being sent elsewhere.[1] The information obtained by Capt. Lynch in his expedition of the 1st led him to attempt a more important one on the 4th, with the whole of his little fleet, with a portion of Col. A. R. Wright's regiment on board.

Col. Claiborne Snead, in describing this expedition, says :

"Hatteras Island, whereon occurred the scene of which we write, is a narrow strip of land lying between the Atlantic Ocean and Pamlico Sound, about forty miles in length and from one-fourth to half a mile in breadth. It was a bald sand beach, interspersed here and there at a distance of a league or more with chaparral or small clusters of trees resembling the oasis of a desert, and is inhabited by a class of people who subsist by fishing and hunting, as well as from the cargoes of vessels stranded upon the stormy coast. They are commonly called "wreckers," and seem to do a lucrative business, from the numberless wrecks scattered along the beach. The warning rays of the light-house, the extreme point east, are not seen or cannot be heeded by vessels riding along this, the roughest point of the American coast. The misfortunes of the sea-farer bring to these people a day of joy, all the mysteries connected with which will never be revealed until old ocean unearths her account on the day of judgment. The islanders mingle but little with the world; apparently indifferent to this outside sphere, they constitute a world within themselves. During the late war their indifference or neutrality was evinced by raising white flags to the house-tops on the approach of either Confederates or Federals.

"By the capture of the U. S. steamer *Fanny*, on the first day of October, 1861, it was ascertained that the enemy had established a camp at Chicamacommico, about forty miles from Fort Hatteras, and near the southern extremity of Roanoke Island. The Twentieth Indiana regiment had there gone into camp, whither the *Fanny*, when captured, was proceeding with commissary and quartermaster's supplies. A large force was soon to follow: and, in fact, a majority of the prisoners captured on this vessel were Zouaves of Col. Hawkins' New York regiment, who were pioneers of the projected reinforcements. The situation of the Confederates was alarming. It was evident that the new position taken by the enemy was intended as a base of operations—the *point d'appui* from which to assail Roanoke Island and capture the small garrison thereon. The Third Georgia regiment and Col. Shaw's North Carolina regiment, with Commodore Lynch's "Mosquito fleet," comprised our entire defence, while reinforcements could not be obtained nearer than Norfolk by a long and difficult route through Albemarle Sound, Dismal Swamp Canal and the Elizabeth River. On the other hand, the Federal forces, daily accumulating at Fort Hatteras, had behind them, on an open sea, a powerful navy, efficient both in attack and in the transportation of troops.

"Col. A. R. Wright, senior officer, commanding, seeing that a crisis was near at hand, and fully appreciating the danger of being isolated and attacked at a disadvantage, determined at once to move forward and strike the first blow. He had the warm co-operation of Commodore Lynch, who in this, as in every other emergency, showed himself as zealous an officer as he was skillful and brave.

---

[1] The cargo of the *Fanny* was valued in the reports of her loss at "about $150,000 worth of property on board," and she was "one of the most useful gunboats." "A part of her cargo consisted of 250 of Sawyer's shells, 75,000 canister shot, 1,000 overcoats, 1,000 dress coats, 1,000 pairs of pantaloons, and 1,000 pairs of shoes.

"All preparations having been made which the limited means at hand would permit, at one o'clock on the morning of the 5th day of October, the third Georgia regiment, with Lieut. Col. Reid in command, and Colonel Shaw's North Carolina regiment, were embarked on the steamers *Curlew*, *Raleigh*, *Junaluska*, *Fanny*, *Empire*, and *Cotton Plant*. Passing through Croatan Sound into and down Pamlico Sound, the little fleet arrived off Chicamacommico, and about three miles therefrom, just after sunrise. All the vessels were of too deep a draft to get nearer this point of the island, except the *Cotton Plant*, which was enabled to advance a mile further on. Upon her, Colonel Wright, with three companies of the third Georgia and two six-pound boat howitzers, commanded by Lieut. J. R. Sturgis, with forty men, proceeded towards the shore, the officers and men wading in water up to their middles for three fourths of a mile, and opening a rapid fire upon the enemy, who stood in line of battle on the beach, twelve hundred strong according to their muster-rolls. Soon after the firing commenced they began a retreat, moving hastily and in great disorder towards Fort Hatteras.

"Orders were immediately sent to the North Carolinians to move down the sound on board the *Empire*, to a point opposite the light-house, twenty miles distant, and there intercept and cut off the enemy.

"The rest of the Third Georgia having been signalled to advance, effected a landing in the same way as the three preceding companies. Then commenced a chase which has been properly styled "Chicamacommico Races." The attacking party scarcely numbered seven hundred men, some of whom, with their own hands, drew the two howitzers through the deep sand, pursued the retreating foe flying pellmell for twenty-six miles, killing eight and capturing forty-two men. About six miles from the starting point, Col. Wright being in advance of his command, overtook a part of the rear guard, who fired on him, bringing down his horse, but with one hand seizing a small Yankee boy and holding him in front as a shield, and with pistol in the other, he advanced upon the party and captured Sergt. Major Hart, who fired the shot, together with four others of his regiment. Night alone closed the pursuit at Kinakeet, where the Confederates, exhausted from fatigue, went into camp.

"On the following morning, learning that Col. Shaw had not effected a landing at the point where he was expected to intercept the enemy, orders were given to countermarch back to Chicamacommico. And it is proper here to say that Col. Shaw failed to carry out his part of the programme not from indisposition or want of energy. His transport grounded on the shoals at a considerable distance from the shore. Persevering in his efforts to reach the land, he, with his men, commenced to wade, but were stopped by intervening deep sluices, and compelled to return.

"At about one o'clock, just after the Third Georgia regiment had emerged from the grove of Kinakeet upon a long, barren sand beach, the Confederate Light Guards, commanded by Lieut. C. Snead, being deployed in front as skirmishers on a line stretching from the ocean to the sound, in order to pick up any straggling Federals who might have been passed over in the preceding day's pursuit, the U. S. steamer *Monticello* hove in sight on the southeast, hugging the shore closely, which she could safely do in the waters of this particular locality. When within range she opened with round shot, following the fire up with shell, grapeshot and canister, moving in close proximity and at even pace with the Confederates, and keeping up a furious cannonade till the shades of evening closed the scene. Fortunately a rough sea, causing her to careen alternately from side to side, prevented precision in the aim of her guns; and every man who started in the pursuit from Chicamacommico returned in safety, except a member of the Governor Guards, who died from exhaustion."

The Confederates captured on the expedition Lieut. F. M. Peacock, U. S. N., Lieut. J. W. Hart, Twentieth Indiana regimet, besides forty-two privates belonging to the Ninth New York and Twentieth Indiana regiments. The U. S. naval report of this affair is one of the most remarkable made during the war. It is by Lieut. D. L. Braine, October 5th, 1861:

"At half-past 1 P. M. we discovered several sailing vessels over the woodland Kine Keet, and at the same time a regiment marching to the northward, carrying a rebel flag in their midst, with many stragglers in the rear; also two tugs inside, flying the same flag. As they came out of the woods of Kine Keet we ran close in shore and opened a deliberate fire upon them, at the distance of three-quarters of a mile. At our first shell, which fell apparently in their midst, they rolled up their flag and scattered, moving rapidly up the beach to the northward. We followed them, firing rapidly from three guns, driving them up to a clump of woods, in which they took refuge, and abreast of which their steamers lay. We now shelled the woods, and could see them embarking in small boats after their vessels, evidently in great confusion and suffering greatly from our fire. Their steamers now opened fire upon us, firing, however, but three shots, which fell short. Two boats filled with men were struck by our shells and destroyed. Three more steamers came down the sound and took position opposite the woods. We were shelling also two sloops. We continued firing deliberately upon them from half-past 1 P. M. until half-past 3 P. M. * * * Six steamers were now off the point, one of which I recognized as the *Fanny*. At twenty-five minutes to 5 P. M., we ceased firing, leaving the enemy scattered along the beach for upwards of four miles. I fired repeatedly at the enemy's steamers with our rifled cannon, a Parrott thirty-pounder, and struck the *Fanny*, I think once. I found the range of this piece much short of what I had anticipated, many of the shot turning end over end, and not exceeding much the range of the smooth-bore thirty-two pounder."

Of that affair Gen. J. K. F. Mansfield said, October 14th, 1861: "Under the circumstances Col. Brown probably did well. No guns were fired at him by the enemy, nor was he attacked"—because he fled before the Confederates could land. Continuing, Gen. Mansfield said:

"We lost some stragglers along the road. Not a man was killed, that I have heard of, except an old inhabitant shot by the rebels. *I do not understand the report of the navy in this matter*. The rebels had landed only about 500 out of about 2,000 supposed to be on board their fleet of nine steamers and vessels, besides flats, that approached the landing. I did not learn that a vessel of the rebels was taken or sunk or that a man was killed by the shells from the ships of war. I did hear that they carried off all the small fishing vessels belonging to the inhabitants." [1]

Admiral Ammen finds more importance in the highly colored report of Lieut. Braine than Gen. Mansfield did, and Admiral Porter in perpetuating the misstatements of Lieut. Braine, says: "Two of the boats loaded with men were struck by shells and sent to the bottom, several officers were killed, and the shore for a distance of four miles was strewn with killed and wounded"—and yet Gen. Mansfield, after investigating the conduct of the officers commanding the Indiana regiment,

[1] *Official Record*, Vol. IV., p. 626.

visiting the ground, and questioning the parties engaged in the retreat, wrote to Gen. Wool, "that I did not learn * * * that a man was killed by the shells from the vessels of war." And there was neither vessel or man injured by Lieut. Braine's shells.

In November, the French man-of-war *Prony*, Commander De Pontage, was wrecked on the beach below Hatteras, and Lieut. Commander J. W. Alexander, in the C. S. steamer *Winslow* (formerly the *Coffee*), was sent to her relief; but striking on a sunken vessel in the sound, the *Winslow* was sunk and burned. The officers and crew of the *Prony* were saved by the *Ellis* and the *Seabird* without the loss of a man, and the wreck of the *Prony* burned to prevent its falling into the possession of the enemy. Commander De Pontage and his officers were carried to Norfolk by Commander Lynch, where they were cordially and hospitably received by Flag-officer Forrest.

The capture by the U. S. forces of Hatteras Inlet and the sand-banks of the sound brought most forcibly to the attention of the Confederate authorities the defenceless condition of the sound waters and rivers of North Carolina, which Gen. Gatlin had been persistently urging with little avail since he was placed in command.

Upon hearing of the fall of Hatteras he wrote to the War Department for four regiments and a light battery for the eastern counties, and that now it was imperatively necessary to fortify every river running into the sounds. The loss of Hatteras exposed so many points to attack and invasion, some of them of great importance from their connection with the railroad and public works, that Gen. Gatlin again urged the importance of sending at least two regiments to Newberne and ten to Wilmington. Brig. Gen. Joseph R. Anderson was ordered to Wilmington, November 30th, the order assigning him to duty saying that one regiment of Georgia volunteers had been sent from Norfolk to Roanoke Island; that two regiments were at the mouth of Cape Fear River, five companies in Fort Macon, one regiment and two battalions at Newberne—that the whole force available in North Carolina at all points was equal to seven regiments, one battalion, and one light battery; that a large number of heavy guns had from time to time been sent to the State, and that an additional number could be furnished if needed. At that time Fort Macon had not one practical gunner, only forty reliable fuzes, no rifled cannon, no ordnance officer, and only raw troops without proper supplies. It was the hope of Col. Wright at Roanoke Island " to have seven guns mounted to-night (September 6th) on the Pah Pauh Battery, and will commence on Wein Point Battery as soon as they can get the engineers to look after the work." The British ship *Alliance*, learning from a British man-of-war that the blockading fleet would attack Fort Macon on September 7th, communicated the information to Col. Brydges, at which time there were no gunners who could manage the guns, and Gen. Clarke called on Secretary Mallory for officers who understand the use of naval guns. Capt. Lynch determined to go into the fort with the crew of the *Winslow*, and placed Lieut. W. H. Parker of the navy, who remained for two weeks instructing the soldiers in the working and handling of naval guns. Gen. Clarke recognized this assignment of a naval officer to Fort Macon as very satisfactory, and asked that Fort Caswell might be served also with naval officers. The Georgia regiment was landed on Roanoke Island by Lynch's little fleet, which proceeded to Oregon Inlet and removed the troops and guns. The *Winslow* and *Ellis*, when retreating from Hatteras, had removed the guns and troops from Ocracoke Inlet.

The work of fortifying Roanoke Island was pressed with vigor and energy, but under most embarrassing circumstances. The " front wheels and axles of the wagons" were taken for limbers for twelve and twenty-four pounders, and the latter were found so heavy that all the teams in the island could not move it to its battery. But, worse than all, the North Carolina troops were disorganized and demoralized, and Col. Wright could "hope nothing from them;" and Commander Thomas T. Hunter regarded " the maintenance of Roanoke Island possible only so long as it is defended by troops from another State, or from a more loyal part of North Carolina."

The Secretary of the Navy had sent from Norfolk to North Carolina, up to October 20th, 242 guns, including six rifled thirty-two-pounders, and he found himself unable to do any more, as the vessels of the navy needed guns. The condition of the sound defences at the middle of October is. shown by Gen. D. H. Hill as follows :

" Fort Macon has but four guns of long range, and these are badly supplied with ammunition, and are on very inferior carriages.

" Newberne has a tolerable battery, two eight-inch Columbiads and two thirty-two pounders. It is, however, badly supplied with powder. This is also the condition of Washington. Hyde, the richest county in the State, has ten landings and only one gun—an English nine-pounder of great age and venerable appearance.

"Roanoke Island is the key of one-third of North Carolina, and whose occupancy by the enemy would enable him to reach the great railroad from Richmond to New Orleans; four additional regiments are absolutely indispensable to the protection of this island. The batteries also need four rifled cannon of heavy calibre. I would most earnestly call the attention of the most Honorable Secretary of War to the importance of this island. Its fall would be fatal as that of Manassas. The enemy now has 8,000 men at Hatteras, and Roanoke Island will undoubtedly be attacked."

This was a very greatly exaggerated estimate of the number of troops at Hatteras, which on December 1st, 1861, numbered only 1,712 officers and men present.[1] But under the impression that the enemy was very strong at Hatteras, Gen. D. H. Hill issued. October 17th, a peremptory order against any expedition for offensive operations without his previous sanction and authority. This order prevented Capt. Lynch and Col. Wright from undertaking an expedition against Hatteras. They had a large number of flats or large fish boats, enough to transport 1,200 or 1,500 men. Capt. Lynch's fleet was ready and he was willing and anxious to make the attack, but the order of Gen. Hill was peremptory, and thus a naval and military expedition was stopped which might have released eastern North Carolina from capture. The enemy's preparation in October of the Port Royal expedition was at first suspected of having either Beaufort, N. C., or Roanoke Island as its objective; and its effect was to increase to a limited extent the efforts to defend eastern North Carolina. In observing the movements of the Federal vessels, Capt. Lynch, on October 30th, started up the sound and looked in on the abandoned forts at Beacon Island and Ocracoke, and finding no enemy at either place, continued on to Hatteras Inlet, and when near the position of the inner buoy the enemy opened fire upon the *Curlew*, Commander Thomas T. Hunter, C. S. N., from the fort and two or three of their steamers, without injury. On coming within easy range, Capt. Lynch sighted the rifled gun at the *Harriet Lane*,[1] and fired, the fort and two steamers continuing to fire as rapidly as possible. The *Curlew* fired six shells of twenty-five and twenty fuse, and as the course of the steamer was necessarily changed to keep in the narrow channel, the stern gun was fired at them five times, training it well forward. It is uncertain whether the enemy sustained any injury, although many of the crew and officers thought the fourth shell took effect amidship of a very long three-masted steamer lying near the *Harriet Lane*, and another burst between the two. A small steamer was seen employed towing a merchant vessel either out of danger or out of range of the fort. The enemy fired twenty-three shells, only one of which came near.

Having taunted and invited the enemy to accept battle, and finding them reluctant, Capt. Lynch withdrew and waited within half a mile of the buoy, hoping to draw the small steamer outside. When the fort returned the shot, the *Curlew* stood back, fired another shell, and then sailed back to Roanoke Island.

The long delay on the part of the U. S. authorities which ensued after the fall of the Hatteras forts, before the sounds of North Carolina were again visited by that navy, appears very strange, considering the importance of these inland seas to both parties to the war. Hatteras, without the complete control of the sounds, was a barren victory, for though the

[1] "This surveying steamer *Corwin* is the *Harriet Lane* mentioned in the report of the rebel Capt Hunter, of the naval battle at this place about the 1st inst., and one of the vessels he was supposed to have seriously damaged." —*N. Y. Herald, Hatteras letter, Nov. 16th.*

25

occupancy of the inlet might prevent the egress of privateers
and blockade-runners, yet its possession only was not so
severe a blow at the Confederate cause as the newspapers had
represented it to be.

The U. S. Navy Department again took the initiative, and
in January, 1862, organized a naval expedition for the purpose
of completely controlling the waters of the sounds. The annoyance to and destruction of commerce, it was found, continued as well after the fall of Hatteras as before, and public
sentiment in loud complaint urged the department to do
something with its immense navy to better protect the coastwise commerce than had resulted from the capture of Hatteras. Moreover, it was known that within the waters of
those sounds there were building some powerful iron-clads,
which, if permitted to be completed, would not only enable
the Confederates to retain supremacy in the sounds, but recapturing Hatteras, to issue to sea, and raise the blockade of
Beaufort and Wilmington. But while the navy might capture,
it could not hold the interior points, and it was therefore
necessary that a combined expedition of army and navy
should be dispatched to the sounds; and to this end Rear-
Admiral Louis M. Goldsborough, U. S. N., and Major Gen. A.
E. Burnside, were selected to command the navy and army
contingents. A fleet of seventeen vessels, mounting 48 guns,[1]
and an army of 17,000 on transports, sailed from Fortress Monroe, January 11th, 1862, and arrived off Hatteras on the 12th.
From that day till the 4th of February the expedition was engaged in getting over the bar and bulkhead at Hatteras, and
on the 8th appeared before Roanoke Island. Gen. H. A. Wise
was appointed to the command of the Confederate forces on
Roanoke Island on January 22d. With the military defence
of Roanoke Island this work has no proper connection, except
to express the opinion that greater want of preparation was
nowhere else shown in all the war; that a more inadequate
force was nowhere else intrusted with the defence of an important position; and to confirm the language of Gen. Gatlin,
that the authorities " failed to make timely efforts to maintain the ascendancy on the Pamlico Sound, and thus admitted
Burnside's fleet without a contest : we failed to put a proper
force on Roanoke Island, and thus lost the key to our interior

[1] The fleet was composed of the *Stars and Stripes*, Lieut. Com. Worden, four 8-inch 55 cwt. and one 20-pdr. Parrott gun; *Louisiana*, Lieut. Com. Murray, one 8-inch 6½ cwt., one 32-pdr. of 57 cwt., two 32-pdrs. of 3 cwt , one 12-pdr. rifled Dahlgren; *Hetzel*, Lieut Com. Davenport, one 9-inch, one 80-pdr. cwt.; *Underwriter*, Lieut. Com. Seffers, one 8-inch 63 cwt., one 80-pdr rifled, one 12-pdr. rifled, one 12-pdr. smooth-bore; *Delaware*, Lieut. Com. Quackenbush, one 9-inch, one 32-pdr. 57 cwt., one 12-pdr rifled; *Valley City*, Lieut. Com. Chaplin, four 32-pdr. 42 cwt., one 12-pdr. rifled; *Southfield*, Act. Vol. Lieut. Com. Behm, three 9-inch, one 100-pdr. rifled; *Hunchback*, A. V. Lieut. Com. Colhoun, three 9-inch and one 100-pdr. rifled; *Morse*, Acting Master Hayes, two 9-inch; *Whitehead*, Acting Master French, one 9-inch; *Seymour*, Acting Master Wells, one 30-pdr. rifled, one 12-pdr. rifled; *Shawsheen*, Acting Master Woodward, two 20-pdr. rifled ; *Lockwood*, Acting Master Graves, one 80-pdr. rifled, one 12-pdr. rifled, one 12-pdr. smooth-bore; *Ceres*, Acting Master McDiarmid, one 30-pdr. rifled, one 32-pdr. of 33 cwt ; *Putnam*, Acting Master Hotchkiss, one 20-pdr rifled; *Brinckner*, Acting Master Giddings; and *Granite*, Acting Master's Mate Boomer, one 32-pdr.

coast; and we failed to furnish Gen. Branch with a reasonable force, and thus lost the important town of Newberne."

On that day Capt. Lynch, from on board the *Seabird*, off Roanoke Island, informed Secretary Mallory of the enemy's readiness to advance from Hatteras with a fleet of twenty-four gunboats seven large steamers, and sixteen transports, and that :

"To meet these, I have two old side-wheel steamers, and six propellers — the former possessing some speed; the latter slow in their movements and one of them frequently disabling its shaft; but my greatest difficulty is in the want of men. So great has been the exposure of our crew that a number of them have necessarily been invalided; consequently the complements are very much reduced, some of them one-half. I have sent to Washington, Plymouth, Edenton and Elizabeth City for recruits without success, and an earnest appeal to Commodore Forrest brought me only four. To meet the enemy I have not more than a sufficient number of men to fight half the guns."

The military defence of the island and that by the navy are so connected that it is proper to explain in brief the provisions for defence on the island, and its adjacent waters. By a strange omission, and against suggestions amounting almost to orders, the defence of the island was made north of Ashby's Point, which was left dependent for defence upon two pieces of field artillery; and there was "no battery on Sandy Point," which Admiral Goldsborough regarded as an "omission to guard the point," which was the most favorable one on the island for the debarkation of troops, and where it was made unmolested and undisturbed. The forts upon the island were Fort Bartow, the most southern end of the defences on the west side—a sand fort well covered with turf, armed with six long thirty-two-pounders in *embrasure,* and three thirty-two-pounders *en barbette;* next Fort Blanchard on the same side of the island, about two and a half miles from Fort Bartow—a semi-circular sand fort, turfed, and mounting four thirty-two-pounders *en barbette;* twelve hundred yards from Fort Blanchard, on the same side of the island, stood Fort Huger, a turfed sand fort, with a low breastwork in rear, with a *banquette* for infantry, armed with eight thirty-two-pounders in *embrasure,* ten rifled thirty-two-pounders *en barbette,* and two small thirty-two pounders *en barbette* on the right. On the east side of the island, three miles from Fort Bartow at Midgett's Point, there was a battery of two thirty-two-pounders, guns *en barbette,* and in the centre of the island a mile from Fort Bartow, and one mile from Midgett's Point, there was a redoubt, or breastwork, across the road, about seventy or eighty yards long, with embrasures for three guns, with a swamp on the right and a marsh on the left, supposed to be impassable to infantry; and on other side of the sound, nearly opposite Fort Huger, there stood Fort Forrest, mounting seven twenty-two-pounders. A barrier of piles extended from the east side of Fulker's

Shoals toward the island, having for its object to compel
vessels passing on the west side to approach the shore bat-

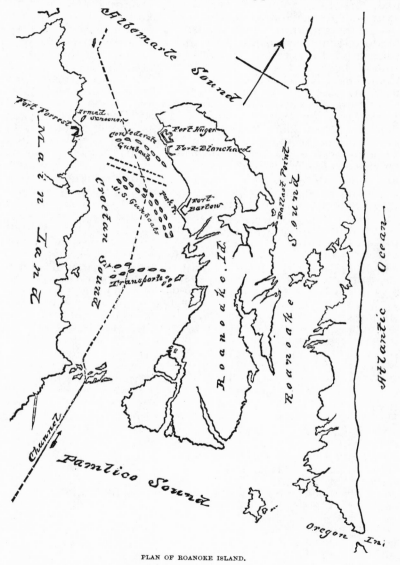

PLAN OF ROANOKE ISLAND.

teries, but up to the day of the battle a space of 1,700 yards
was open opposite Fort Bartow, since vessels had been sunk

and piles driven on the west side of Fulker's Shoals. These completed the land defences of the island, which, when manned, left 1,024 men, of whom 200 were on the sick list, available to resist Burnside's army of 17,000.

In the sound, between the island and the mainland, Commodore Lynch had his fleet of seven vessels—the *Seabird* (flagship), Lieut. Com. Patrick McCarrick, one 32-pounder smooth bore. and one 30-pounder Parrott ; the *Curlew*, Lieut. Com. Thos. T. Hunter, one 32-pounder; the *Ellis*, Lieut. Com. J. W. Cooke, one 32-pounder ; the *Appomatox*, Lieut. Com. C. C. Sims, one 32-pounder; the *Beaufort*, Lieut. Com. W. H. Parker, one 32-pounder ; *Raleigh*, Lieut. Com. J. W. Alexander, one 32-pounder; *Fanny*, Midshipman Commander Taylor, one 32-pounder ; *Forrest*, Lieut. Com. James L. Hoole, one 32-pounder; the *Black Warrior*, Lieut. Harris, two 32-pounders. Of these vessels, the *Seabird* was a wooden side-wheel steamer, and the *Curlew* an iron side-wheel steamer, the others were screw tugboats built for the canals; the *Black Warrior* was a large schooner. The armaments of the fleets were as 11 to 48, [1] and even with the land batteries that could be used in the battle, the disparity in numbers, as well as weight of metal, was still very largely in favor of the U. S. fleet. At 11 o'clock, the enemy's fleet, consisting of about thirty gunboats and schooners, advanced in two divisions, the rear division having the schooners and transports in tow. The advance and attacking division again sub-divided, one assailing Capt. Lynch's squadron, and the other firing upon the forts with nine-inch, ten-inch and eleven-inch shell, spherical case, a few round shot, and every variety of rifled projectiles. The fort replied with four guns (all that could be brought to bear), and after striking the foremost vessel several times, the enemy's fleet fell back so as to mask one of the guns of the fort, leaving but three to reply to the fire of the whole fleet. The bombardment continued in that manner throughout the day, and the enemy withdrew at dark. Com. Lynch's squadron retained its position most gallantly, notwithstanding the disparity of guns, and only retired after exhausting all its ammunition and the loss of the *Curlew* and the disabling of the *Forrest*, and wounding her gallant young commander, Lieut. Hoole. On the morning of February 7th, 1862, the enemy succeeded in landing a large infantry and artillery force at Hammond (a point north of Ashby's Landing, and out of reach of the few field-pieces at Ashby's, and defended by a swamp from the advance of the Confederate infantry, and protected by his gunboats), and effected a permanent lodgment on the island. Having landed a force amounting nearly to 15,000 infantry and artillery, the enemy was able to outflank the

---

[1] Capt. Parker says : "At daylight the next morning, the *Appomatox* was dispatched to Edenton, and as she did not return till sunset, and the *Warrior* did not take any part in the action, this reduced our force to seven vessels and eight guns."—*Recollections of a Naval Off.*, p. 229.

Confederate line, upon which there "were but 803 men [left] for infantry duty," and compelled the abandonment of the first line of defence; repeating the movement, the enemy compelled the abandonment of Fort Bartow, and also of Forts Blanchard and Huger.

Upon the evacuation of the forts, Capt. Lynch held a consultation with his officers on the propriety of retreating to Norfolk, through the Chesapeake and Albemarle Canal, or to Elizabeth City on the Pasquotank River. By going to Norfolk all the vessels might have been saved, but that would have been a total abandonment of the waters of North Carolina, to defend which Com. Lynch had been sent to the sounds. For that reason it was decided to retreat to Elizabeth City, the terminus of the Dismal Swamp Canal, by which it was hoped to obtain ammunition from Norfolk. Having communicated this determination to Col. Shaw, in command on Roanoke Island, through Lieut. Parker, the squadron got under way for Elizabeth City, the *Seabird* towing the *Forrest*. The night was pitchy dark, and as no vessel could show a light without discovering to the enemy the retreat, navigation without collision required all the skill and nerve of the officers. On the morning of February 8th, Com. Lynch had the satisfaction of finding his six steamers at Elizabeth, and immediately dispatched Capt. Hunter to Norfolk for ammunition. The next morning, having found a few rounds of ammunition, he steamed out of the river in the *Seabird*, taking the *Raleigh* with him, to reconnoitre and ascertain the purpose of the enemy.

The fleet of Commander Goldsborough, consisting of the *Louisiana*, the *Hetzel*, the *Underwriter*, the *Delaware* (flagship), the *Perry*, the *Valley City*, the *Morse*, the *Seymour*, the *Whitehead*, the *Lockwood*, the *Ceres*, the *Shawsheen*, *Brinckner*, and *Putnam*, after getting through the obstructions, followed close upon the retreating squadron of Commander Lynch; for as the enemy's flotilla passed into Albemarle Sound, the smoke of Commander Lynch's steamers was seen not far distant near the opposite shore, heading for Pasquotank River. Chase was immediately signaled by Commander Rowan, commanding the flotilla, and an effort made to cut off the steamers before they could reach the river. But Lieut. Parker was too quick and safely steamed in, and as night closed on the enemy, he discontinued the chase, and anchored at 8 P. M. within ten miles of Fort Cobb, on Cobb's Point.

Capt. Lynch's reconnoitering detachment found Commander Rowan's fleet, which immediately sent two steamers in pursuit—compelling Lynch to return to Elizabeth City, which place he reached about 5 P. M. About daylight on the 10th, Commander Rowan's flotilla weighed anchor and with the *Underwriter*, *Perry*, *Morse* and *Delaware*, the *Ceres*, *Louisiana*, *Hetzel*, *Valley City* and *Whitehead*, proceeded up the river, and discovered Lynch's six steamers behind the battery at Cobb's Point—which contained four thirty-two-pounders taken from the lost *Curlew*—the schooner *Black Warrior*, two thirty-two pounders, which was moored on the opposite side of the river.   The armament of the respective forces was eight guns to thirty-two—six vessels to fourteen.   The *Raleigh* had escaped to Norfolk, and the *Forrest* was drawn up on the ways at Elizabeth City. At 8:30 A. M., the enemy's flotilla was seen steaming swiftly up the river—and at that moment the Confederate infantry in the fort fled, and Lieut. Parker, of the *Beaufort*, was ordered with his crew to occupy the abandoned fort; and, quick to obey the order, he dispatched the *Beaufort* to Norfolk, under the pilot, and with his men repaired to the fort.   The enemy, while this change was taking place, had got into line and was received by the fire of the guns of the fort under Parker and his men from the *Beaufort*. Capt. Lynch was caught on shore, by his row-boat being cut to pieces by one of the enemy's first shots.   The flotilla under Commander Rowan reserved its fire until close to the fort and the vessels of Capt. Lynch, when without slacking its speed it passed the fort and fell upon the little fleet of Capt. Lynch—the *Perry* rammed and sunk the *Seabird*, the *Ellis* was speedily captured after a desperate defence, in which her gallant commander, James W. Cooke, was badly wounded— the schooner *Black Warrior* was set on fire and abandoned by her crew—the *Fanny* was run on shore and blown up by her officers.   The *Appomatox* was fought with great success by Lieut. Commander Simms until her gun was accidentally spiked, when she was drawn off, firing her howitzer from the stern, and made for the mouth of the canal, but being about two inches too wide she could not enter and was then set on fire by Lieut. Simms.   Parker from the fort witnessed the destruction of the fleet, but was powerless to prevent or even annoy the enemy while at their work of destruction, and seeing that he could do no further service, spiked the guns and withdrew his men, and with Capt. Lynch and the survivors retreated to Norfolk. Midshipman Wm. C. Jackson, in swimming from the *Ellis*, was wounded and taken on board the *Wetzel*, where he received every attention and kindness until he died the next day.   The *Forrest* was burned on the ways to prevent her falling into the hands of the enemy. [1]

1 The following officers and men of the C. S. navy were captured and paroled upon signing a paper worded as follows :
"OFF ROANOKE ISLAND, NORTH CAROLINA, ON BOARD U. S. VESSEL-OF-WAR, February 12th, 1862.
"Belonging to the Confederate States navy, and held as a prisoner of war by the authorities of the United States, I, understanding that this paper is intended to release me on parole, do hereby pledge my sacred honor that, until duly exchanged, I will neither take up arms against the United States, serve against them in any manner or way, nor divulge, to their prejudice, anything I may have heard or seen during my captivity."
Their names and rank are :
J. W.Cooke, lieut. commanding; J.W. B.Greenhow, surgeon; E. Holt Jones, assist. surgeon; P. McCarrick, master commanding; Jerry Bowden, colored boy; Stephen Beasly, seaman; Thomas T. Baum, ordinary seaman; Eames Williams, landsman; John Thornton, ordinary seaman; James Barnett, seaman; Iowa Gregory, ordinary seaman; Elias Williams, seaman; James A. Peters, midshipman; J. W. Wolmsley, third

Speaking of the engagement in Albemarle Sound, Commander John N. Maffitt, C. S. N., in his Reminiscences, says: " Commodore Lynch was appointed to the command of the naval forces in the waters of North Carolina. Early in February, 1862, he hoisted his flag on board the *Seabird*, a small passenger steamer. The six remaining vessels of his force were of the same flimsy character. Burnside entered the sound with sixty-seven vessels. Twenty-five were powerful, well-armed gunboats, mounting the heaviest naval ordnance; the remainder transported a large army with its equipment and all military requirements.

"Nothing daunted, the heroic Lynch, on the 7th of February. 1862, formed his line of battle abreast of the Confederate batteries established on Roanoke Island."

"The boldness and unflinching attitude of these diminutive rebel vessels in defying immense odds in power and number, elicited from many Federals flattering expressions of admiration for this exhibition of decided pluck by their nautical enemies—a chivalry of sentiment too rarely indulged in by either side during the war. To disparage the courage of an enemy is to detract from the honors of the victor.

"The unequal contest commenced at 10 A. M., and continued until 5 P. M., when Lynch was forced to retire, having expended all his ammunition, not a cartridge remaining in the fleet; in fact the *Ellis*, Capt. Cooke, had continued fighting for hours on borrowed powder. Several vessels were seriously damaged. The *Curlew* was struck by a 100-pound shot between wind and water; the commander ran her ashore and applied the torch. The casualties in the fleet were numerous. The commodore hastened to Elizabeth City and sent to Norfolk by express for ammunition. On its arrival he started back for Roanoke Island, but returned to Elizabeth City on receiving information of the surrender. Here the determined Lynch, with a few remaining vessels, decided to make a final stand for weal or woe.

"On the morning of the 10th, fourteen Federal gunboats, flushed with their recent success, dashed impetuously upon the Confederates, and in spite of a desperate resistance their immense preponderance of force swept everything before them. The commanders of the *Fanny*, *Accomac*, and *Seabird*, seeing that capture was inevitable, fired their steamers and escaped with their crews. The *Beaufort* and *Raleigh* passed through the canal and arrived in safety at Norfolk. The *Ellis*, commanded by James W. Cooke, resisted to the bitter end. Boarders swarmed on board of her, and were met, cutlass in hand, by the dauntless captain, who, though badly wounded by a musket ball and by a thrust from a bayonet, fought with the fierceness of a tiger, refusing to surrender or haul down his flag.

" Overpowered by numbers he was borne to the deck; and would have been slaughtered on the spot but for the generous interference of an old associate, who caused him to be safely conveyed to Commodore Rowan's flag-ship, where extreme kindness was extended.

"The regular officers of the navy had not expunged from their bearing the ancient chivalry of the profession ; brave prisoners received at

assistant engineer; George Livingston, captain's clerk; Jas. McCarrick, master's mate; John W. Young, seaman; J. W. Ballance, landsman, John W. Phillips, quartermaster; Thomas Johnston, gunner's mate; John A. Wilson, seaman; William Maro, second-class fireman; James T. Sullivan, ordinary seaman; J. J. Henderson, third assistant engineer; Junius Hanks, third

assistant engineer ; Reuben Willis, pilot ; Joseph F. Weaver, carpenter; Alfred Reid, officer's cook; Josiah W. Butt, quartermaster; Edwin T. R. Jones, carpenter's mate; John W. Horton, ship's cook, George W. Dowdy, seaman; Jas. L. Day, seaman; William R. Scraggs, second lieutenant, company D., artillery corps, Wise legion.

their hands that generous consideration taught by the examples of Decatur, Stewart, Bainbridge, and other grand old nautical fathers. If during the struggle there was a departure from the golden rule of honor, the perpetrator was anathematized by the navy proper, which, through all the labyrinths and horrors indigenous to civil war, humanely endeavored to ameliorate its harshness.

"The naval battles in Albemarle Sound and off Elizabeth City reflected much credit upon the personal courage of all the Confederate officers therein engaged. With mere abortions for gunboats, badly armed and sparse of ammunition, they confronted without hesitation the well-equipped and powerful vessels of the North.

"Even those who, to prevent capture, fired their steamers, fought their guns amid raging flames and banners flying, retreating at last with the stubbornness of the Old Guard, that 'were conquered, but not subdued.' This defeat, like those of Hatteras Inlet and Port Royal, being inconsiderately weighed in the scales of popular estimation, as a natural sequence the navy was pronounced 'short of weight.' Success is the vital spark that excites confidence and admiration. Without the smiles of good fortune all the ability man can possibly be endowed with is unappreciated."[1]

Thus Roanoke Island was lost. It was the key to all the rear defences of Norfolk: it unlocked two sounds (Albemarle and Currituck), eight rivers—North, West, Pasquotank, Perquimans, Little, Chowan, Roanoke and Alligator, four canals—the Albemarle and Chesapeake, the Dismal Swamp, the Northwest and the Norfolk, and two railroads—the Petersburg and Norfolk and the Seaboard and Roanoke. It guarded more than four-fifths of Norfolk's supplies of corn. pork and forage, and it cut the command of Gen. Huger off from all its most efficient transportation. Its possession by the enemy endangered the existence of Huger's army, threatened the navy-yard at Gosport, and to cut off Norfolk from Richmond, and both from railroad communication with the South Atlantic States. It lodged the enemy in a safe harbor from the storms of Hatteras, gave him a rendezvous and a large and rich range of supplies, and the command of the seaboard from Oregon Inlet to Cape Henry. It ought to have been defended by 20,000 men, instead of the single brigade of Gen. Wise and the little fleet of seven small vessels of Capt. Lynch. That the enemy did not appreciate the value of his capture, and the importance of the waters he had won, is as little to the credit of the military and naval authorities of the United States as the loss of the position was discreditable to the Confederate authorities.

From Elizabeth City Commander Rowan dispatched the *Louisiana*, the *Underwriter*, the *Perry*, and the *Lockwood* to Edenton, where a vessel was being built, which was destroyed. Upon the return of the expedition from Edenton, Commander Rowan dispatched a portion of his fleet to block the Chesapeake and Albemarle Canal, and while he was blocking it at one end, the Confederates were doing the same work further

[1] *Reminisc. ces of the Confederate Navy, United Service Magazine,* Oct. 1880.

up, and thus the back door of Norfolk was effectually closed
by the labors of its assailants and defenders.

The Confederate navy in the waters of the sounds of North
Carolina was in that first action, if not entirely destroyed,
dissipated and scattered; the enemy not encountering a single
armed vessel in any one of the expeditions up the rivers and
to the towns of that large section of that State.

The official report of Commodore Lynch of the participation of his fleet in the defence of Roanoke Island and Elizabeth
City, on the 7th of February, was as follows:

"FLAG-SHIP 'SEABIRD,' ⎫
"OFF ROANOKE ISLAND, February 7th, 1862. ⎭

"SIR: I have the honor to report that the enemy, at 10 A. M., to-day,
with twenty-two heavy steamers and one tug, made an attack upon this
squadron and the battery at Pork Point.

"As his numerical force was overwhelming, we commenced the action
at long range, but as our shell fell short, while his burst over and around
us (owing, I think, to the superior quality of his powder), we were eventually compelled to shorten the distance.

"The fight lasted continuously from 10 A. M. to 5:30 P. M., throughout
which the soldiers in the battery sustained their position with a gallantry
which won our warmest approbation. The fire was terrific, and at times
the battery would be enveloped in the sand and dust thrown up by shot
and shell.

"And yet their casualties was only one man killed and three wounded.
The earthwork, however, was very much cut up. I mention the battery
because, in all probability, communication will reach you before intelligence will be received from appropriate official source. The enemy approached in two divisions, the rear one having the schooner transports in
tow.

"The advance, which was the attacking division, again subdivided,
and one portion assailed us and the other the battery. Repeatedly, in the
course of the day, I feared that our little squadron of seven vessels would
be utterly demolished, but a gracious Providence preserved us.

"Master-Commanding Moall, of the Forrest, received a wound in the
head, which is pronounced serious, if not mortal. I yet trust that this
promising young officer, who so bravely fought his ship, will be spared to
the service. Midshipman Camm, of the Ellis, and ——— of the Curlew,
each lost an arm, which, with three others slightly wounded, constitute
the sum of our personal casualties.

' I am sorry to say that the Curlew, our largest steamer, was sunk,
and the Forrest, one of the propellers, disabled. We have received other
injuries from the shot and shell, but comparatively of light character,
and could, with the exception of the Forrest, be prepared to renew the
action to-morrow, if we only had ammunition. I have not a pound of
powder nor a loaded shell remaining, and few of the other vessels are better off. During the latter part of the engagement, when the ammunition
was nearly exhausted, I sent to the upper battery for a supply, but ten
charges were all that could be spared, and those were expended at dark,
as the enemy was withdrawing from the contest.

"In all probability the contest will be renewed to-morrow, for the
enemy having landed a force below the battery will doubtless endeavor
to divert its fire. I have decided, after receiving the guns from the wreck
of the Curlew, to proceed direct with the squadron to Elizabeth City, and
send express to Norfolk for ammunition. Should it arrive in time we will
return to aid in the defence; if not, will there make a final stand, and
blow up the vessels rather than they shall fall into the hands of the
enemy.

"There are reasons for retiring upon Norfolk, but it would be unseemly thus to desert this section of country. If I have erred in judgment, by a speedy notification the error will be corrected.

"Commander Hunter, Lieut. Commanders Cooke, Parker, and Alexander, and Masters Commanding McCarrick, Taylor, and Hoole, bravely sustained the credit of the service, and every officer and man performed his duty with alacrity. Lieut. Commanding Simms, although absent on detailed service, exhibited such an eagerness to participate in the conflict as to give full assurance that, if gratified, he would have upheld his high reputation.

"I am, very respectfully, your obedient,

"W. F. LYNCH, Flag-officer.

"The Hon. S. R. MALLORY, Secretary of the Navy."

But though defeated, and all the naval vessels destroyed, and the enemy controlling all the waters of the North Carolina Sounds—the hope yet remained of regaining control and re-establishing Confederate authority over the district watered by the rivers and sounds of eastern North Carolina. While new vessels were being constructed in the upper waters, the enemy was watched with eagerness for any unguarded point where an enterprising and bold assailant might make an effort to capture a gunboat to form the beginning of a force afloat. The long period of inactivity, with only patrol duty by gunboats in the sounds and rivers, produced a carelessness and want of watchfulness which offered the opportunity desired.

In January, 1864, the Confederate naval commanders at Richmond, Wilmington and Charleston, received orders from the Navy Department to select a boat's crew of fifteen able and trusty seamen, under the command of an experienced officer, from each of the gunboats then lying at the above-named ports, and report with their arms and boats to Commander John Taylor Wood, of the C. S. navy, and Colonel on the President's staff, at Wilmington, N. C. By the latter part of January everything was in readiness; the men were well armed, and accompanied by four boats and two large launches, they left Wilmington by the Kingston railway, under the command of Col. Wood. The utmost secrecy had been observed by those in command as to the object of the expedition and its destination.

The town of Newberne, a place of some note in North Carolina, lies on a point of land at the junction of the Trent and Neuse Rivers with Pamlico Sound. Roanoke Island was captured on the 14th of February, 1862, and following that event Newberne surrendered to the Federals. They at once threw up fortifications, which extended over an area of twenty miles, and in order to strengthen their position and provide against the chances either of surprise or capture, three or four of their gunboats were either anchored off the wharf at Newberne, or else kept cruising up and down the Neuse or Trent Rivers. The largest of these gunboats was the *Underwriter*, a large side-wheel steamer, which fired the first gun in the attack on Roanoke Island. and participated in most of the engagements fought along the North Carolina coast. The *Underwriter* had engines of 800 horse power, and carried four guns, one six-inch rifled Dahlgren, one eight-inch of the same pattern, one twelve-pound rifle, and one twelve-pound howitzer. Jacob Westervelt, of New York, Acting Master U. S. navy, was her commander.

The expedition under Col. Wood reached Kingston early on the morning of Sunday, January 31st; the boats being at once unloaded from the cars and dragged by the men to the river and launched in the Neuse. The distance between Kingston and Newberne by rail is about thirty miles, but the tortuous and circuitous course which the river takes, makes the journey by water at least twice that length. Bending silently to the muffled oars, the expedition moved down the river. Now, the Neuse broadened until the boats seemed to be on a lake; again, the tortuous stream narrowed until the party could almost touch the trees on either side. Not a sign of life was visible, save occasionally when a flock of wild ducks, startled at the approach of the boats, rose from the banks, and then poising themselves for a moment overhead, flew on swift wing to the shelter of the woodland or the morass. No other sound was heard to break the stillness save the constant, steady splash of the oars and the ceaseless surge of the river. Sometimes a fallen log impeded the progress, again a boat would run aground, but as hour after hour passed by, the boats still sped on, the crews cold and weary, but yet cheerful and uncomplaining. Night fell, dark shadows began to creep over the marshes and crowd the river; owls screeched among the branches overhead, through which the expedition occasionally caught glimpses of the sky. There was nothing to guide the boats on their course, but the crew still kept hopefully on, and by eleven o'clock the river seemed to become wider, and Col. Wood discovered that he had reached the open country above Newberne.

When in sight of the town, Col. Wood ran his boats into a small stream, and succeeded in getting them close to the shore. The party landed on what seemed to be a little island covered with tall grass and shrubs. Here the men found temporary shelter, and rations were served.

At midnight the men were called to quarters, and the object of the expedition was explained. Major Gen. G. E. Pickett, who was then commanding the Confederate forces operating against Newberne, was to open fire on the enemy's lines around the town, thus drawing his attention inland, while Col. Wood and his command, under cover of the diversion, were, if possible, to capture one or more of the gunboats and clear the river. Arms were inspected and ammunition distributed, and everything made ready to embark on what each of the party felt was a perilous enterprise. In order to distinguish the Confederates in the dark, each man was furnished with a white badge, to be worn around the left arm, and the pass-word "Sumter" was given.

The firing of Pickett's command was now heard on the right. In company with Hoke's brigade, a part of Corse's and Clingham's and some artillery, Gen. Pickett had made a reconnoissance within a mile and a half of Newberne. He met the enemy in force at Batchelor's Creek, killed and wounded about one hundred in all, captured thirteen officers and 280 men, fourteen negroes, two rifled pieces and caissons, 300 stands of small arms, besides camp and garrison equipage. His loss was thirty-five killed and wounded.

While the engagement at Batchelor's Creek was in progress, Acting Volunteer Lieut. G. W. Graves, of the U. S. steamer *Lockwood*, commanding the Federal vessels at Newberne, communicated with Acting Master Westervelt, commanding the *Underwriter*, and Acting Master Josselyn, commanding the *Hull*, ordering them to be in readiness for a move. Early on the morning of the 1st of February, Lieut. Graves ordered the *Underwriter* to get under way and take up position on the Neuse River, so as to command the plain outside of the Federal line of works, and the *Hull* to take a station above her. At 9 A. M. the *Underwriter* had reached the position assigned her, but the *Hull*, soon after getting under way, got aground, and could not be got off during the day. Soon after this, hearing from Gen. J. W. Palmer, in command of the Union forces, that the Confederates were planting a battery near Brice's Creek, Lieut. Graves, in the *Lockwood*, proceeded as far up the Trent River as he could get, and laid there for the night.

In the meantime, Col. Wood had again launched his boats in the Neuse, and arranged them in two divisions, the first commanded by himself, and the second by Lieut. B. P. Loyall. After forming parallel to each other, the two divisions pulled rapidly down stream. When they had rowed a short distance, Col. Wood called all the boats together, final instructions were given, and this being through with, he offered a fervent prayer for the success of his mission. It was a strange and ghostly sight, the men resting on their oars with heads uncovered, the commander also bareheaded, standing erect in the stern of his boat ; the black waters rippling beneath ; the dense overhanging clouds pouring down sheets of rain, and in the blackness beyond an unseen bell tolling as if from some phantom cathedral. The party listened—four peals were sounded and then they knew it was the bell of the *Underwriter*, or some other of the gunboats, ringing out for two o'clock. Guided by the sound, the boats pulled toward the steamer, pistols, muskets and cutlasses in readiness. The advance was necessarily slow and cautious. Suddenly, when about three hundred yards from the *Underwriter*, her hull loomed up out of the inky darkness. Through the stillness came the sharp ring of five bells for half-past two o'clock, and just as the echo died away, a quick, nervous voice from the deck hailed, "Boat ahoy !" No answer was given, but Col. Wood kept steadily on. "Boat ahoy ! Boat ahoy ! !" again shouted the watch. No answer. Then the rattle on board the steamer sprang summoning the men to quarters, and the Confederates could see the dim and shadowy outline of hurrying figures on deck. Nearer Col. Wood came, shouting, "Give way !" "Give way, boys, give way !" repeated Lieut. Loyall and the respective boat commanders, and give way they did with a will. The few minutes that followed were those of terrible suspense. To retreat was impossible, and if the enemy succeeded in opening fire on the boats with his heavy guns all was lost.

The instructions were that one of the Confederate divisions should board forward and the other astern, but, in the excitement, the largest number of the boats went forward, with Col. Wood amidships.

In the meantime, the *Underwriter*, anchored within thirty yards of two forts, slipped her cable and made efforts to get up sufficient steam from her banked fires, to move off, or run the Confederates down. This movement only hastened the boarding party, and the crews pulled rapidly alongside. Lieut. George W. Gift, believing that the *Underwriter* was moving, gave orders to Midshipman J. Thomas Scharf, who was in command of the boarders in the bow of his launch, to open fire on the steamer with the howitzer which was mounted in the bow, and endeavor to cripple her machinery. One shot was fired which struck in the pilot-house, and before the howitzer was reloaded the boats were alongside, and the crews scrambling on deck. The enemy had by this time gathered in the ways just aft of the wheel-house, and as the Confederates came up they poured into them volley after volley of musketry, each flash of which reddened the waters around, enabling the attacking party to note their position. In spite of the heavy fire, the boarders were cool and yet eager, now and then one or more were struck down, but the rest never faltered. When the boats struck the sides of the *Underwriter*, grapnels were thrown on board, and the Confederates were soon scrambling, with cutlass and pistol in hand, to the deck with a rush and a wild cheer, that rung across the waters, the firing from the enemy never ceasing for one moment. The brave Lieut. B. P. Loyall was the first to reach the deck, with Engineer Emmet F. Gill, and Col. Wood at his side. Following in their steps came Lieuts. Francis L. Hoge, Wm. A. Kerr, Philip Porcher, James M. Gardner, F. M. Roby, Henry Wilkinson, George W. Gift, Midshipmen Saunders, H. S. Cook, J. T. Scharf, and William S. Hogue, gallantly leading their men.

The firing at this time became so hot that it did not seem possible that more than half the Confederates would escape with their lives. Col. Wood, with the bullets whistling around him, issued his orders as coolly and unconcernedly as if the enemy had not even been in sight. All fought well. There was no halting, no cowardice; every man stood at his post and did his duty. The conduct of the officers was beyond all praise. Cool and collected in every movement, they executed their parts well. From Commander Wood down to the youngest midshipman, not one faltered. Conspicuous among all was the conduct of the marines, a company of them under Capt. Thomas S. Wilson being distributed through the boats. As the Confederates came up to the ship the marines rose and delivered their fire, taking accurate aim, reloading still under the heavy fire from the enemy. When on board they obeyed their orders promptly, and, forming on the hurricane deck, not even the explosion of the monster shell fired by the enemy from one of the shore batteries among them could break the ranks or turn a man from his post.

Once on the deck of the *Underwriter* the onslaught was furious. Cutlasses and pistols were the weapons of the Confederates, and each selected and made a rush for his man. The odds were against the attacking party, and some of them had to struggle with three opponents. But they never flinched in the life-and-death struggle, nor did the gallant enemy. The boarders forced the fighting. Blazing rifles had no terrors for them. They drove back the enemy inch by inch. Steadily, but surely, the boarders began to gain the deck, and crowded their opponents to the companion-ways or other places of concealment; while all the time fierce hand-to-hand fights were going on on other portions of the vessel. Now, one of the Confederates would sink exhausted—again, one of the enemy would fall on the slippery deck. Rifles were snatched from the hands of the dead and the dying, and used in the hands as bludgeons did deadly work. Down the companion-ways the attacked party were driven pell-mell into the ward-room and steerage, and even to the coal-bunkers, and after another sharp but decisive struggle the enemy surrendered. The *Underwriter* was captured, its commander slain,[1] and many of its officers and men killed and wounded, or drowned. The Confederate loss was over one-fourth of the number engaged —six killed and twenty-two wounded. E. F. Gill,[2] the Confederate engineer, lay in the gangway mortally wounded, and Midshipman Saunders,[3] a gallant boy, cut down in a hand-to-hand fight, breathed out his young life on deck.

The *Underwriter* was moored head and stern between Fort Anderson and Fort Stevenson, and scarcely a stone's

[1] Acting Master Joseph Westervelt, the commander of the *Underwriter*, was born in New York, and appointed from that State, Feb. 8th, 1862. His body was not recovered until Feb. 28th, 1864.

[2] Emmet F. Gill was born in Virginia, and appointed from that State a Third Assistant Engineer in the Provisional Navy of the Confederate States on February 19th, 1863. At the time of his death he was stationed on the iron-clad *Fredericksburg*, at Richmond, Va.

[3] Palmer Saunders was born in Virginia, and appointed from that State on August 14th, 1861, a midshipman in the C. S. navy. He was cut through the head several times with a cutlass, and afterwards shot in the stomach. He was a very promising young officer.

throw from the shore. The sound of the firing was heard at the batteries, and by the time the Confederates captured the boat, which took about ten minutes, the Federals on shore fired a shell into her, which struck the upper machinery and exploded on deck. All of the shore batteries then opened fire on the doomed vessel, either careless of or not realizing the fact that their own wounded must be on board; and the captors soon found that a rapid movement would have to be made. The prisoners were ordered into the boats, and the Confederates who were on board began to prepare for action. Lieut. Hoge opened the magazines and manned the guns. Steam, however, was down and the machinery disabled, and with a heavy fire from the batteries pouring upon them, it was seen that the Confederates could not take sufficient time to carry off their prize. It was, therefore, determined to set fire to the vessel. The Confederate wounded and those of the enemy were carefully removed to the boats alongside, the guns were loaded and pointed towards the town, fire was applied from the boilers, and in five minutes after the boarders left, the *Underwriter* was in one mass of flames from stem to stern, burning with her the dead bodies of those of the brave antagonists who had fallen during the action.

The Confederates retired under a heavy fire from the shore batteries, and also from a volley of musketry, which whistled along the water. They turned once more up the Neuse, and pulled away from the town. As they rounded a point of woods they took a last look at the burning steamer, now completely enveloped in flame, the lurid light flaming in the sky and flashing for miles across the water. Although hidden from view, they could see by sudden flashes in the sky, and by the dull, heavy booming sound which came to them upon the night air, that the shell-room was reached and that the explosion had begun. Turning into Swift Creek, about eight miles from Newberne, the party landed on the shore to care for the wounded and receive intelligence from Gen. Pickett. It was part of the Confederate plan, if the military had been successful in their attack on the enemy's works on the land side of Newberne, for the boats to land a large force of infantry on the water side of the forts and to attempt to carry them by assault. Owing to the failure of some of his command to co-operate in the demonstration, Gen. Pickett withdrew his troops from before Newberne, and the naval force, on the next morning, retired up the river.

During the attack on the *Underwriter*, which was defended with great gallantry, the other gunboats took the alarm and made up the Trent as fast as steam could carry them, and luckily for the Confederates they did not dare to take part in the fight. When the shell exploded on the deck of the *Underwriter*, it is said that Acting Master Westervelt, the commander, leaped overboard, and was killed hanging to a hawser. Edgar

G. Allen, the engineer of the *Underwriter*, who escaped, in his report to Lieut. Graves, under date of February 2d, 1864, says:

"I, together with eighteen or twenty of the crew, being put into the whale boat belonging to the *Underwriter*. * * * We then shoved off and were proceeding up the stream, the boat I was in being astern the rest, when I discovered that, in their hurry to get off, they had put only two men as guard in the boat. This fact I discovered by the one in the stern steering (by whom I was sitting) hailing the other boats, which were some fifty yards ahead of us, and asked them to take off some of us, as the boat was so overloaded it could make no headway, and also saying they wanted a stronger guard, as all but two were prisoners. One of the other boats was turning to come back, when I snatched the cutlass from the belt of the guard and told the men to pull for their lives. Some of the men, the other guard among them, jumped overboard and swam for the land. I headed the boat for the shore and landed at the foot of the line of breastworks, delivered my prisoner to the commanding officer, and procuring an ambulance, took one of our disabled men to the hospital."

The *Underwriter* lost in the engagement about nine killed, twenty wounded and nineteen prisoners. Twenty-three of her officers and men escaped.

In recognition of the distinguished gallantry displayed in the capture of the *Underwriter*, the Confederate Congress, on February 15th, 1864, unanimously passed the following:

"*Joint resolution of thanks to Commander John Taylor Wood and the officers and men under his command, for their daring and brilliant conduct.*

"*Resolved, by the Congress of the Confederate States of America, That* the thanks of the Congress of the Confederate States are due, and are hereby tendered, to Commander John Taylor Wood, Confederate States Navy, and to the officers and men under his command, for the daring and brilliantly executed plans which resulted in the capture of the U. S. transport schooner *Elmore*, on the Potomac River; of the ship *Alleghany*, and the U. S. gunboats *Satellite* and *Reliance;* and the U. S. transport schooners *Golden Rod*, *Coquette* and *Two Brothers*, on the Chesapeake; and more recently, in the capture from under the guns of the enemy's works of the U. S. gunboat *Underwriter*, on the Neuse River, near New-berne, North Carolina, with the officers and crews of the several vessels brought off as prisoners."

"This was rather a mortifying affair for the navy" (U.S.) says Admiral Porter, "however fearless on the part of the Confederates. This gallant expedition," he continues, "was led by Commander John Taylor Wood. * * It was to be expected that with so many clever officers who left the Federal navy and cast their fortunes with the Confederates, such gallant actions would often be attempted," and it is his opinion that "had the enemy attacked the forts the chances are that they would have been successful, as the garrison was unprepared for an attack from the river, their most vulnerable side."[1]

---

[1] Most of the officers associated with Col. Wood were promoted for their daring and desperate act in capturing the *Underwriter*. Lieut. Loyall received the following letter from Secretary of the Navy S. R. Mallory in recognition of his distinguished gallantry:

NAVY DEPARTMENT, C. S. A. }
RICHMOND, Feb. 10th, 1865. }
Commander BENJAMIN P. LOYALL, P. N. C. S.:
SIR: You are hereby informed that the President has appointed you, by and with the advice and consent of the Senate, a COMMANDER in the

26

The experience which old steamboats mounting a gun, and called by the sounding name of a gunboat, brought to the Confederate authorities, was of a kind to teach the lesson that, as the vessels which could regain the sounds must be built, it was wiser to build iron-clad steamers of light draft, and to carry one or two guns, than to attempt to strengthen any river craft and convert them into gunboats.

The Confederate Navy Department on January 13th, 1862, entered into a contract with Gilbert Elliott, agent for J. G. Martin, of Elizabeth City, N. C., to construct and deliver to the Navy Department, at Elizabeth City, the hulls of three gunboats, within four months after the 6th day of January, 1862. The capture of Roanoke Island, followed by the occupation of the Pasquotank River, frustrated that contract. Again, on April 16th, 1862, another contract was entered into with the same party for the construction of "one gunboat, to be iron-clad," wherein it was stipulated "that if the work is interrupted by the enemy, the party of the first part is to receive compensation for the work done upon the boat to the time of such interruption. The contract as published in the report of the Investigating Committee, does not indicate in what waters that iron-clad was to be built. On September 17th, 1862, another contract with Martin & Elliott, of Elizabeth City, was made for the construction at Tarboro', N. C., of the hull of one gunboat, to be iron-clad, and to be completed on or before the first day of March, 1863. On October 17th, 1862, a contract with Howard & Ellis, of Newberne, N. C., was entered into for the construction, at White Hall, N. C., of the hull of one gunboat, to be iron-clad, and completed on or before the first day of March, 1863.

Almost a year before the battle of Plymouth and the exploit of the *Albemarle*, Lieut. Commander C. W. Flusser, of the *Miami*, obtained all the particulars of the construction of "a rebel iron-clad battery nearly completed on the Roanoke River above Plymouth"—and on June 8th, 1863, advised Acting Rear Admiral S. P. Lee, with the following description:

"The battery is built of pine sills fourteen (14) inches square, and is to be plated with railroad iron. The steamer intended to tow her is one hundred and thirty-four (134) feet long, and twenty-four (24) feet beam, with two screws. The boat has six ports, two on each side, and one on either end. She carries a pivot gun forward, and another aft. Each gun works out of three ports. The battery carries two guns on each of two opposite faces, and one on each of the two remaining sides. The boat is built on the plan of the former *Merrimac*. The roof (slanting) of the

Provisional Navy of the Confederate States of America, "for *gallant and meritorious conduct as second in command and executive officer of the naval expedition which, on the night of the 1st of February, 1864, cut out from under the guns of the enemy at Newberne, N. C., the Federal gunboat Underwriter and destroyed her.*"

You are requested to signify your acceptance or non-acceptance of this appointment.

S. B. MALLORY, *Secretary of the Navy.*

When the Confederates landed in Swift Creek, they took their wounded ashore, where two of the crew died. They were buried in the afternoon, the funeral services being read by Lieut. Loyall. It was a very solemn scene. The boats crews were formed in a square around the graves, with the officers in the centre. After the funeral services, Lieut Loyall offered up a beautiful prayer, thanking God for their victory and safe return.

battery and all parts exposed are to be covered with five inches of pine, five inches of oak, and then plated with railroad iron. So say the workmen. *We* are driving piles in the river, and preparing to receive them. I do not doubt we shall whip them if they venture down."

At the same time Lieut. Flusser enclosed the following plan:

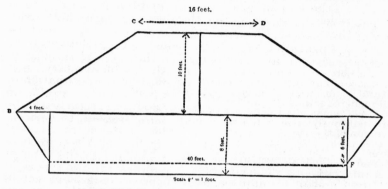

16 feet.

A. B. C. D. E, F is to be plated.
Perpendicular line between C D denotes the entrance to the vessel.

DIAGRAM OF THE RAM "ALBEMARLE."

On August 8th, 1863, Rear Admiral Lee wrote to Secretary Welles, that:

"The iron-clad on the Roanoke River at Edward's Ferry, forty miles above Rainbow Bluff, heretofore reported to the department, is considered by Lieut. Commander Flusser as a formidable affair though of light draft. The fortifications at Rainbow Bluff, and the low state of the river, make it impracticable for the navy to destroy her before completion, which is reported near. I have made written application to Major Gen. Peck to send out an expedition to accomplish this desirable object, if practicable. If this is not done, we must have iron-clad defence on the sound, though I do not see how any iron-clads we have now can be got over the bulkhead at Hatteras, where the most water is about nine feet in the best tides." Admiral Lee, September 10th, ordered Lieut. Flusser to co-operate with the land forces of Gen. Foster on an expedition up the Chowan River, having for its destination the destruction of the railroad bridge at Weldon. The object of the expedition not being attained, Lieut. Flusser requested Gen. Foster to detach a small party from the main cavalry force to destroy the boat and battery building at Edward's Ferry, but did not succeed in impressing him with the importance of the move and it was not done.

Secretary Welles, under date of September 17th, 1863, represented to Secretary Stanton the near completion of the ram at Edward's Ferry, and urged a joint expedition of land and naval forces for her destruction. Secretary Stanton merely referred the letter to Gen. Foster for such action as his judgment suggested, by whom it was transmitted to Major Gen. Peck, who advised Admiral Lee, November 13th, 1863, that he had frequently called Gen. Foster's attention to the ram being built at Edward's Ferry, and proposed to him expeditions for burning the same, but "he never attached any importance to it," and Admiral Lee, in a communication to Secretary Welles, November 24th, 1863, says: "The general [Foster] expressed his unconcern about the rebel ram." This "unconcern" cost the Federal army the loss of Plymouth, the destruction of several gunboats, and the death of many brave men, among them Lieut. Flusser.

"In 1863 two citizens, residing near Edward's Ferry,[1] on the Roanoke River, proposed to the Navy Department to construct an iron-clad. Their experience heretofore had been limited to flat-boats, but with the assistance of an intelligent, practical naval officer, coupled with their own natural genius, they felt confident that the desired vessel could be built and rendered formidable for service.

"As Commander Cooke was near at hand, the Secretary of the Navy very judiciously directed him to assume control of the work for the construction of this earnestly desired vessel, whose province was expected to be the rescue of Albemarle and Pamlico Sounds from the possession of the enemy. When aroused to action Cooke was one of the most industrious and indefatigable officers in the navy. With hearty zeal he embarked in the enterprise.

"Iron in all shapes was a necessity. In person Cooke ransacked the country, gathering bolts and bars and the precious metal in any shape that admitted of application to his needs by the manipulation of the blacksmith. His greed for iron became amusingly notorious. At the Tredegar Works in Richmond, and the Clarendon Foundry at Wilmington, he was amusingly known as the 'Ironmonger Captain.' To vamp up from refuse piles serviceable pieces of machinery afforded him excessive delight.

"The building of the iron-clad, under all the disadvantages of place and circumstances, was viewed by the community as a chimerical absurdity. Great was the general astonishment when it became known that the indomitable commander had conquered all obstacles and was about to launch his bantling. On the appointed day 'Cooke & Company' committed their 'nonesuch' to the turbid waters of the Roanoke, christening her, as she glided from the launching-ways, 'the good ship *Albemarle*.'

"Boilers, engines, roofing, and iron shield were to be fitted ere the iron-clad would be ready for service. While this finishing work was in progress Cooke received a communication from Gen. Hoke asking for a careful statement as to the exact time, with increased facilities, that the *Albemarle* could be depended upon for assistance in an important military expedition. The commander's response was quite laconic :

"'In fifteen days, with ten additional mechanics.' The assistance was rendered, Cooke was ordered to prepare the ram, and guns, ammunition, and a few men arrived, with a promise of the remainder of the crew in a few days.

"On the 17th, two young officers with twenty men and the residue of the steamer's outfit arrived. In spite of the herculean exertions of the commander, the *Albemarle* was not entirely completed. The energetic commander had named his day for action, and he was not a man to deal in disappointments.

"At early dawn on the 18th, steam was up; ten portable forges, with numerous sledge-hammers, were placed on board, and thus equipped the never-failing Cooke started on his voyage as a floating workshop. Naval history affords no such remarkable evidence of patriotic zeal and individual perseverance.

<hr>

[1] "Reminiscences of Confederate Navy," by John N. Maffitt. The *United Service,* p. 501.

"On the turtle-back numerous stages were suspended, thronged with sailors wielding huge sledge-hammers. Upon the pilot-house stood Capt. Cooke giving directions. Some of the crew were being exercised at one of the big guns. 'Drive in spike No. 10 !' sang out the commander. 'On nut below and screw up ! In vent and sponge ! Load with cartridge,' was next command. 'Drive in No. 11, port side—so. On nut and screw up hard ! Load with shells—prime ! ' And in this seeming babel of words the floating monster glided by.

"By five in the afternoon the *Albemarle* was secured to the river bank, her forges landed, decks cleared, and the efficiency of the ram ensured, so far as human ingenuity contending against meagre facilities could accomplish.

"The entire construction was one of shreds and patches ; the engine was adapted from incongruous material, ingeniously dove-tailed and put together with a determined will that mastered doubt, but not without some natural anxiety as to derangements that might occur from so heterogenous a combination. The *Albemarle* was built in an open cornfield, of unseasoned timber. A simple blacksmith shop aided the mechanical part of her construction.

"How different the accomplishment of like work at the North. There, convenient docks, elaborate machine shops, material in abundance conveniently at hand, and throngs of machinists accomplish construction with methodical ease and promptness.

"After an active drill at the guns, an aide was dispatched to sound the obstructions placed in the river by the enemy. He returned at midnight and reported favorably, upon which all hands were called, and soon the steamer was under way.

"Soon that dull, leaden concussion which to practiced ears denotes a heavy bombardment, smote upon the ear. Nearer the rapid explosions grew upon the ear, and ere long, by the dawn's early light, the spires of Plymouth greeted the sight. Cooke was up to time, and now for his promise.

"It was 3 A. M. on the 19th of April, 1864, when the *Albemarle* passed in safety over the river obstructions, and received without reply a furious storm of shot from the fort at Warren's Neck. Instantly grasping the situation, amid the cheers of his crew, he made for the Federal gunboats that were chained together in the rear of Fort Williams, guarding its flank, and dashed nine feet of his prow into the *Southfield*, delivering at the same time a broadside into the *Miami*, killing and wounding many of her crew. Among the killed was numbered her commander, the brilliant Flusser. In ten minutes the *Southfield* was at the bottom, the prow of the ram still clinging to her and exciting for a few moments serious apprehensions for the safety of the *Albemarle*. However, she was soon disentangled, and being released from the downward pressure, was fiercely pursuing the enemy, who were finally driven out of the river.

"This brilliant naval success ensured the triumph of Gen. Hoke. The defences of Fort Williams, the citadel of Plymouth, were powerful on the land side, and had already repulsed several Confederate assaults; on the river side the fortification was defective, its open works entirely depending on gunboats. These having been dispersed, Cooke promptly opened with his guns upon the vulnerable part of the fort, soon rendering it untenable, and Gen. Ransom's command entered the town on that flank. This was the prominent part performed by the *Albemarle* in the sanguinary but brilliant capture of Plymouth.

"Major Gen. Peck, the second in command of the Federal forces in the military district, in his official report asserted and demonstrated that, in the absence of the Confederate ram, and with the Federal gunboats intact, Gen. Wessels could have sustained himself for an indefinite length of time.

"After raising the Federal steamer *Bombshell*, which Hoke's artillery had consigned to the bottom, Cooke soon floated and prepared her for service.

"On the 4th of May, Commodore Pinkney, commanding the naval defenses of the Roanoke, ordered Commander Cooke to convoy the steamer *Cotton Planter* (a cotton-clad vessel sent from Halifax with sharp-shooters to aid Gen. Hoke) and the *Bombshell* to Alligator River for military purposes. On the 5th, at noon, the *Albemarle* left the river with her consorts.

"She proceeded about sixteen miles on the east-northeast coast when the Federal fleet, consisting of nine powerfully-armed steamers, hove in sight and gallantly approached in double line of battle. By orders, the *Cotton Planter* instantly returned to Plymouth. Two broadsides received by the *Bombshell* brought down her colors and she surrendered.

"Admiral Lee's instructions to Commander Smith, who commanded the fleet, were imperative: 'At all hazards the rebel ram must be destroyed, by shot, ramming, or torpedoes. Her existence jeopardizes our occupation of this section of North Carolina.'

"These stringent orders were issued to brave and intrepid seamen, who right gallantly (though failing) performed their duty. Their opponent, reared in the same school, was equally brave and as firm as adamant. Though considering his vessel impervious to shot, he was conscious of many defects in her improvised machinery, steering-gear, and fire-draft if, perchance, his smoke-stack should be injured. Combined with these drawbacks was the lack of necessary experience among the very young officers who composed his command. The crew, with but few exceptions, were all landsmen and but slightly practiced in gunnery. All these drawbacks in the aggregate rendered his vessel less formidable than reputation awarded.

"The most serious impediment to a successful issue of a contest against nine fast and well-disciplined men-of-war, using torpedoes, was the lack of *speed*, which, if possessed, would have enabled Cooke to frustrate every critical movement of the enemy, select his own distance for battery effect, and avoid being demolished by their torpedoes.

"At 4 P. M. the Federal fleet fearlessly approached in double columns and delivered their heavy broadsides at less than 100 yards. The *Albemarle* responded effectually, but suffered in return with loss of boats, riddled smoke-stack, broken plates on the shield, and the after-gun cracked some eighteen inches from the muzzle. The fleet grouped around the ram and hurled their 100-pound shot, fired with double charges of powder, aiming particularly at the ports and stern, which they supposed were the vulnerable parts of the vessel. Near sunset, Commander Roe, of the *Sassacus*, selected his opportunity, and with open throttles and a speed of about eight knots, struck the *Albemarle* squarely, just abaft her starboard beam, causing every timber in the vicinity of the impact to crack and complain, but not give way. The pressure from her revolving wheels was so powerful as to force the deck of the iron-clad several feet below the surface of the water and create a momentary impression that she was sinking. The crew became alarmed, and were becoming panic-stricken, when the stern voice of the undismayed Cooke checked incipient disorder and promptly restored discipline as he sang out: 'Stand to your guns! If we must sink, let us perform our duty and go down like brave men.'

"The *Albemarle* soon recovered, and hurled shot after shot through and through her assailer. The last caused howls of agony and shrieks of despair, for one of her boilers was shattered, and the hissing steam embraced with its deadly vapor some twenty of the crew of the *Sassacus*. Notwithstanding the natural consternation under the appalling circumstances, two of her guns' crews continued to energetically fire upon the *Albemarle* until the disabled vessel drifted out of the arena of battle.

"The enemy's fleet were not idle; the incessant roar of their artillery thundered over the placid waters of the sound as their ponderous projectiles thugged upon the shield of the *Albemarle* and ricochetted innocuously beyond. One of the fleet made an ineffectual effort to foul the ram's propeller with a large seine, and the *Miami* failed with her torpedo in consequence of the ram's destructive fire. The contest continued until night shrouded the inland sea, when both parties withdrew from the fierce contest. The Federals suffered severely in their hulls and killed and wounded. His tiller broke when rammed by the *Sassacus*, and it was with great difficulty, from the construction of the vessel, that she could be guided by the relieving tackles.

"One gun was badly cracked in the muzzle by a shot, and the smokestack was so torn and riddled that its draft-power became entirely obliterated, and a small head of steam could only be obtained by burning bacon, lard, and the bulkheads. At last the afflicted *Albemarle* arrived and anchored off Plymouth. Had her speed amounted to ten or eleven knots, the Federal squadron might have been annihilated.

"After being thoroughly repaired the *Albemarle* was detained at Plymouth for harbor defence, awaiting the completion of a sister ironclad, then nearly ready for launching on Tar River.

"The government had decided that two iron-clads acting in concert were necessary for a successful encounter with the formidable force of the enemy then in possession of the Albemarle and Pamlico Sounds.

"The Fates had decided that the career of the *Albemarle* should close.

"On a night of November, 1864, while the Confederate was insufficiently guarded by a section of artillery, the ubiquitous Lieut. Cushing, with hardy daring, entered the harbor with a torpedo-boat, and in spite of the strenuous efforts of Lieut. Warley, then commanding the *Albemarle*, succeeded in blowing her up."

As has been stated by Commander Maffitt, the Confederate authorities, in 1864, had organized and equipped another naval force in the waters of North Carolina.

The co-operating naval expedition was under the command of Commander R. F. Pinkney. Commander J. W. Cooke commanded the iron-clad gunboat *Albemarle*, in Roanoke River, Lieut. B. P. Loyall commanded the iron-clad gunboat *Neuse*, in the Neuse River, and Lieut. R. B. Minor, commanded a flotilla of "cutters" in the Chowan River.

Plymouth is in Washington county, near the mouth of the Roanoke River, and the country around was very rich and full of supplies. The two other places held by the Federal forces on the North Carolina coast were Washington, at the mouth of Tar River, and Newberne, at the mouth of the Neuse. The latter was strongly garrisoned; but it was supposed that the larger part of the forces at Washington had been moved up to Plymouth.

The contest for the capture of Plymouth lasted night and day, from Sunday the 16th to the 20th, and resulted in the capture of the city by Gen. Hoke, including Gen. Wessels and his forces, numbering over 1,500 men, and twenty-five pieces of artillery.

On Monday morning the U. S. gunboat *Bombshell* ran up the Roanoke River to reconnoitre, and observing the ram *Albemarle* approaching turned to steam down to the U. S. fleet, but was struck by a shell from a Confederate battery, and sunk. [1]

[1] The gunboat *Bombshell* was one of the vessels used by the U. S. Marine Artillery corps. She was an ordinary canal boat, mounting one gun and two small light pieces. Her early history may be found among the records of the Erie Canal. She was purchased, with four others, for the

Below the town of Plymouth, in the broad waters of the sounds of North Carolina, were five U. S. gunboats—the *Whitehead*, the *Southfield*, the *Miami*, the *Ceres*, the *Mattabessett*, the *Sassacus*, and the *Wyalusing*.

The approach of the *Albemarle* had been made known to the officers commanding the Federal fleet, and every preparation had been made to meet and overpower her. The *Southfield* and the *Miami* had been chained together for the purpose of running bows on, and possibly in obedience to the instructions of Rear Admiral Lee, that "the great point is to get and hold position on each side of the ram. Have stout lines with small heaving lines thereto, to throw across the ends of the ram, and so secure her between two of our vessels. Her plating will loosen and bolts fly like canister, and the concussion will knock down and demoralize her crew if they keep their ports down."

To encounter that formidable squadron, Commander Cooke[1] steamed slowly down the Roanoke, in the early morning of April 19th. The Federal vessels came on at full speed—the *Miami* and the *Southfield* chained together. The former was struck by the *Albemarle* on the port bow, and later the *Southfield*, pierced by a shot, rapidly sank. The *Miami*, uninjured, surged a little off, passed ahead and delivered her broadside at short range; using her 100-pounder rifle and nine-inch guns, loaded with shells. It was directly after that fire that Flusser, commanding the *Miami*, fell, struck by a piece of shell, which bounded from the side of the ram—and

Burnside expedition. The others were named respectively *Grenade, Rocket, Schrapnel* and *Grapeshot*. They were officered and manned by marine artillerists, under Col. Howard, formerly of the United States revenue service.

[1] Capt. James Wallace Cooke entered the U. S. navy April 1st, 1828, and resigned as lieutenant May 1st, 1861. On May 4th, 1861, he received an appointment in the navy of Virginia, and on June 11th, 1861, entered the service of the C. S. navy. He was engaged in blockading the Potomac at Aquia Creek until after the battle of Manassas, when he was ordered to take command of a small steamer at the Gosport navy-yard for operations in North Carolina waters. He was employed in putting obstructions at the entrance of Albemarle Sound to prevent the entrance of the Federal gunboats to Roanoke Island. These were afterwards removed by order of the commanding general, and the island and Elizabeth City captured. In the battle of Roanoke Island, Lieut. Cooke, while in command of the *Ellis*, was the last to haul off, after he had fired all his ammunition and that taken from the *Curlew*, which was disabled. In his official report of the naval engagement at Elizabeth City he said: "Being surrounded and boarded by two of the enemy's vessels; and having made every possible effort of resistance, and seeing that it was in vain to resist further, I gave the order to blow up the vessel. I ordered the men to save themselves, if possible, as the vessel was near shore. Several had been killed. The order to blow up the boat was betrayed by

a negro coal-heaver to the enemy, who prevented it. Midshipman William C. Jackson was shot and taken on board a Federal vessel where he died in twenty hours. He was a meritorious officer."

Lieut. Commander Cooke in this desperate engagement displayed the greatest gallantry. He fired all the muskets brought to him by Mr Bagley from the armory, and was badly wounded in the right arm, and received a thrust from a bayonet in the leg. He was kindly and courteously treated by his captors, and paroled and allowed to return to his home at Portsmouth, Va., until exchanged. He remained in Portsmouth until March 8th, 1862, when he removed to Warrenton, N. C. He was exchanged in September, and on the 17th of that month was promoted to Commander in the C. S. navy, with orders to proceed to Halifax on the Roanoke River, in North Carolina, to build a gunboat. He selected as his navy-yard the farm of Peter E. Smith at Edward's Ferry. From this land the timber for building the *Albemarle* was cut, and here her keel was laid. The citizens of the neighborhood rendered Commander Cooke every assistance in their power. There were, however, no machine shops, no shipwrights, and no collection of material for ship-building. There was an inexhaustible supply of pine for the frame, but even this was sprouting and blooming in the green tree. Iron, so indispensable in the equipment of an iron-clad, in the neighborhood of Commander Cooke's navy-yard, was scarce to the degree of a famine. His entreaties at the Tredegar Iron Works, in Richmond, for

COMMANDER JAMES W. COOKE, C. S. N.

THE MOUND BATTERY.

several others were wounded at the same time. At that moment the bow-hawser parted and the after-hawser being cut or broken, the *Miami* swung round to starboard and the *Southfield* sank. The *Albemarle* then turned again upon the *Miami*, whose officer reported that "from the fatal effects of her prow upon the *Southfield*, and our sustaining injury, I deemed it useless to sacrifice the *Miami* in the same way" and withdrew from action.

This great triumph of the *Albemarle* was a severe disappointment to the Federal authorities, and the Navy Department called upon Capt. Melancton Smith to destroy the ram; and Admiral Lee said to Capt. Smith, "entrusted by the Department with the performance of this signal service, I leave (with the expression of my views) to you the manner of executing it." To the discharge of that duty Capt. Smith, on May 20th, hoisted his flag on the "double ender" *Mattabessett*, and arranged the following order of fighting:

"The steamers will advance in the third order of steaming, the *Miami* leading the second line of steamers. The *Mattabessett, Sassacus, Wyalusing* and *Whitehead* forming the right column, and the *Miami, Ceres, Commodore Hull* and *Seymour* the left.

"The proposed plan of attack will be for the large vessels to pass as close as possible to the ram without endangering their wheels, delivering their fire and rounding to immediately, for a second discharge.

"The steamer *Miami* will attack the ram and endeavor to explode her torpedo at any moment she may have the advantage, or a favorable opportunity. Ramming may be resorted to, but the peculiar construction of the sterns of 'double enders' will render this a matter of serious consideration with their commanders, who may be at liberty to use their judgment as to the propriety of this course when a chance presents itself."

this necessary article secured for him the name of the "Iron Captain." After the launch of the *Albemarle* she was removed to Halifax, N. C., for cor etion. As it was feared the waters of the riv vould be too low to get her down in the sun..ner, about April 1st she was removed about twe ty miles lower down to Hamilton. Here Commander Cooke and his men suffered from the ffects of bad water and poor food, consisting al st wholly of coarse, unbolted corn-meal and b. n. At this time the indefatigable comma'der worked on board of his ship from sunrise until very often to midnight. About the 16t of April Gen. Hoke, commander of the land for s, visited the *Albemarle*, and notwithstanding he was far from being finished, her heroic cc lander promised that she would be ready to operate with him in the Confederate attack on lymouth. How far Commander Cooke kept hi promise, and the distinguished part the *At marle* took in that gallant affair, has been el where shown. After the successful engagerr ts of the *Albemarle*, Commander Cooke was noted to the rank of Captain in the Pro- .nal Navy of the Confederate States. The er conveying the commission was as follows:

aPT. JAMES W. COOKE, *Plymouth, N. C.:*
SIR—You are hereby informed that the Presi- t has appointed you, with the advice and sent of the Senate, a Captain in the Pro- .onal Navy of the Confederate States *for ant and meritorious conduct* in command of iron-clad steam sloop *Albemarle* on the 19th, and 21st days of April, 1864, in attacking

the enemy's ships and batteries; and in cooperating with the army in the capture of Plymouth, N. C.; and in the action of the 5th of May, 1864, between the sloop *Albemarle*, under your command, and nine of the enemy's gunboats in Albemarle Sound.

"S. R. MALLORY, *Secretary of the Navy."*

He was relieved from the immediate command of the *Albemarle* and placed in command of the naval forces operating in the waters of North Carolina, in the neighborhood of Plymouth. Lieut. Commander John N. Maffitt relieved Capt. Cooke in command of the *Albemarle*, and in a short time he being required for other duty, Lieut. Commander A. F. Warley succeeded him. The *Albemarle* was destroyed by a torpedo while under the command of Lieut. Commander Warley. While the *Albemarle* was being built on the Roanoke River, the Confederate government was engaged in building another iron-clad on the Neuse River. This vessel was never completed, but was destroyed after the loss of the *Albemarle*. Capt. Cooke remained at Halifax until that place was abandoned by the Confederates about the 1st of April, 1865. He performed arduous service during this time in facilitating army movements, and laying torpedoes in the rivers, which were very effective in destroying several of the enemy's gunboats, and preventing marauding expeditions in the interior of North Carolina. Capt. Cooke returned to Portsmouth, Va., after the surrender of Gen. Lee, and spent the remaining four years of his life there, dying in 1869.

In that order of battle, Capt. Smith's squadron on May 5th, when near the buoy at the mouth of the river, saw the *Albemarle* moving down to the sound, accompanied by the little transport *Cotton Plant* and captured gunboat *Bombshell.* Observing the enemy's fleet, Commander Cooke ordered the *Cotton Plant* to seek a place of safety and proceeded on with the *Bombshell.* A Confederate eye-witness gives the following description :

"Three very large gunboats were moving swiftly around Sandy Point and directly for the ram. She meanwhile stood still, her brave little consort slightly in the advance, and as the forward vessel came within range, saluted her with one of her deep-mouthed guns. Very promptly the Federal forces responded with one of theirs, and the fight began.

"The enemy came on in single file and at full speed. The foremost vessel ran straight up to the ram, as if she would run her down, veered off a little, passed ahead and gave her a broadside ; then crossed her bows, returned and delivered another broadside, and passed on out of range. The second and third steamers moved and fired in like manner. The first repeated these evolutions, and was again followed by the other two. This terrific grand waltz continued for some time, the ram receiving the tremendous fire apparently with the most stoical coolness and indifference, and delivering her fatal bolts deliberately and accurately, while the enemy fired rapidly and very wildly.

"Meantime the inglorious squadron of observation, with one additional boat, were coming up from the distant rear, and very cautiously joining, one by one, and at long range, in the melee. The little *Bombshell* had been standing up bravely to the large vessels as they passed, they contemptuously sparing her till her sharp fire provoked them to attack her. The rear boat, avoiding closer quarters with the ram, found a nearer and less formidable antagonist in the *Bombshell*, which, undismayed, maintained a brisk fight with nearly the whole squadron for some minutes, till, surrounded and cut off from her consort and protector, she raised a white flag and dropped out of action—a captive, mute and motionless, and awaiting the orders of captors.

"During this time the guns of the ram had been doing execution. From the hold of the largest steamer issued a thick column of smoke, which increased as the cloud of powder smoke was blown away. She ceased firing, and all hands seemed to engage in subduing the flames. After half an hour's work this was accomplished, and again she mingled in the dreadful fray. The battle now raged more fiercely than ever. The ram, to our surprise, began to move slowly toward Plymouth, firing regularly, but at longer intervals, while the enemy pressed her more hotly. The larger steamers kept up their solemn waltz, varied with occasional digressions; the smaller boats moved a little nearer, and the whole nine vomited forth their shell and solid shot at irregular but frequent intervals. Sometimes the whole number, the ram included, were completely shrouded in thick, white smoke, which lay upon the blue, rippling, glancing waters like a thunder cloud in a clear summer sky, while naught else was seen of the fierce conflict behind it but columns of snowy spray, rising successively in long lines as the balls ricochetted across the water. Then the soft south wind would lift the curtain just in time to disclose the red flashes of new broadsides from the enemy, or the jet of lurid fire which preceded one of the sonorous, metallic voices of the iron monster.

"Now one of the enemy's largest vessels has withdrawn from the fight and steams rather slowly behind Sandy Point, where she still lies at this moment, badly crippled; the ram meanwhile steadily pursuing her course towards Roanoke River, and firing leisurely as she moves. The fire of the enemy somewhat slackens, and only the two remaining large vessels continue the pursuit. Presently they stop and wait for two smaller boats coming up, and while the four are lying in a group, as if in consultation, we distinctly hear the dull crash of a ball from the ram as it buries itself in one of the wooden hulks. As if maddened by the blow, they start more eagerly after the retreating monster, who now nears the river's mouth. Away in the distance the battle once more rages furiously, and long after we ceased to distinguish the vessels, the flashes of flame were visible till the gathering gloom of evening put an end to the fight. The last gun, as well as the first, was fired by the *Albemarle* as she entered the Roanoke."

The Federal accounts, now at hand, show that the *Mattabessett*, leading the right column of attack, received two shells from the ram, which did considerable wounding among the crew—and that the first line of the enemy's vessels continued their advance, when the *Albemarle* put her helm to port, with the purpose of ramming the *Mattabessett*, and that vessel put her helm to starboard to avoid the ram—which action threw the two vessels apart. The *Mattabessett* in passing delivered her broadside of two rifled guns and four nine-inch guns, at a distance of 150 yards; the *Sassacus* about this time, while nearly abeam the ram, delivered her broadside, and passed astern of the *Albemarle*, following the *Mattabessett*, which as she passed the little *Bombshell* fired her rifled gun and howitzer, and compelled her surrender. The *Wyalusing* following the *Sassacus* poured in her broadsides and was followed by the *Whitehead;* while the ram thus surrounded was replying to her many foes, the *Sassacus* ran into the *Albemarle*, striking her nearly at right angles, just abaft the casemate, and at a speed estimated by her commanding officer of not less than ten knots. The ram, though jarred, was able to fire her rifle gun and put a shot through both sides of the *Sassacus*. Just at that moment three solid shots from 100-pounder rifles were fired into the *Albemarle*, and shattered on her armor came in fragments on the deck of the *Sassacus*—but at that moment the ram righting herself sent a shell from her Armstrong gun longitudinally through the *Sassacus*, which filled her with steam and drove her out of the fight. Baffled at every attack Capt. Smith now, at 5:20, signalled the *Miami* "to go ahead and try her torpedo"—signals to "keep in line" "close order" and "cease firing" followed at short intervals until at 6:55 the *Wyalusing* replied that she was "sinking"—when the *Mattabessett* steamed inside and delivered her fire as rapidly as possible when on the quarter and abeam the ram, and endeavored ineffectually to lay a seine to entangle the propeller of the *Albemarle*—then the pounding continued until 7:30 P. M., when the enemy retired. In that fight the *Mattabessett* from her two 100-pounder Parrott rifles expended twenty-seven solid shots, from her four nine-inch Dahlgrens expended twenty-three solid shot; four twenty-four-pounder howitzers expended one shrapnel; two twelve-pounder howitzers expended one shell —casualties; three killed, five wounded.

Sassacus battery, two 100-pounders Parrott guns, four nine-inch Dahlgrens, two twenty-four-pounder howitzers, two twelve-pounder howitzers, expenditure not given—casualties, one killed, nineteen wounded.

Wyalusing battery, two 100-pounder Parrott rifles expended forty-seven solid shot, twenty-eight shell; four nine-inch Dahlgrens expended thirty-seven solid shot, thirty-three shell; two twenty-four-pounder howitzers expended twenty-seven Shrapnel, eighteen shell; two twelve-pounder howitzers (one rifled)—casualties, one killed.

Miami battery, one 100-pounder Parrott rifle expended forty-one solid shot; six nine-inch Dahlgren expended seventy-six solid shot; one twenty-four-pounder howitzer.

Whitehead battery, one 100-pounder Parrott rifle expended seventeen solid shot; three twenty-four-pounder howitzers.

Commodore Hull battery, two thirty-pounder Parrot rifles, expended sixty shell; four twenty-four-pounder howitzers, expended twenty-four shell.

Ceres battery, two twenty-pounder Parrott rifles (pivot).

The *Albemarle* had one of her two guns disabled early in the action, but notwithstanding that, she maintained her ground, drove off the enemy, disabled, discomfited and defeated. The "eye-witness," from whom we have already quoted, continued:

"The shore now bears innumerable evidences of the damage done to the enemy—splinters and large fragments of oak sheathing, copper fastened, portions of window sash, with bits of glass and putty still adhering, pieces of paneling and other ornamental work from cabins or saloons, several fine launches, two of which are badly shot to pieces; oars, gun rammers, window shutters, cabin doors, hatchments, fragments of fine furniture, and even of little articles of toilet and table furniture, with hundreds of other little proofs of the destruction wrought by the gun, rather than the guns, of the ram."

On the 24th of May, 1864, the *Albemarle* again made her appearance, dragging for the torpedoes which the enemy had laid in the mouth of the Roanake—the *Whitehead* observed her and from afar fired a single shell and retired out of the way.

From the 24th of May to the 27th of October the *Albemarle* lay in inglorious inactivity at Plymouth. Cooke, her former gallant commander, had broken down in health and had been superseded by Lieut. A. F. Warley, who fought the *Manassas* so gallantly at New Orleans. This long period of inactivity is unexplained either in contemporaneous accounts or in any extant official records—indeed, the published Confederate Official Records at Washington contain nothing whatever of the ram *Albemarle*.

About eleven o'clock at night on May 25th, an effort was made by five volunteers from the U. S. Steamer *Wyalusing* to destroy the *Albemarle* while she was lying at Plymouth. The party left their vessel at two o'clock P. M. on the 25th of May, (having made a reconnoissance two days before,) and ascended the middle river in the *Mattabessett's* dingey, with two torpedoes (each containing 100 pounds of powder), and their appendages, which they transported on a stretcher across the island swamps. Charles Baldwin, coal-heaver, and John W. Loyd, cockswain, then swam the Roanoke River, with a line, and hauled the torpedoes over to the Plymouth shore, above the town. They were then connected by a bridle, floated down with the current, and guided by Charles Baldwin, who designed to place them across the bow of the ram—one on either side—and Allen Crawford, fireman, who was stationed on the opposite side of the river, in the swamp, was to explode them on a given signal.

Everything had worked favorably for the enemy from the time of starting until the torpedoes were within a few yards of the ram, when Baldwin was discovered, and hailed by a sentry on the wharf. Two shots were then fired, and a volley of musketry, which induced John W. Loyd, who heard the challenge and reports of small arms, to cut the guiding line, throw away the coil, and swim the river again to join John Laverty, fireman, who was left in charge of his clothes and arms. These two men, with the boat-keeper, Benjamin Loyd, coal-heaver, returned to the *Wyalusing* on the morning of the 27th, after an absence of thirty-eight hours in the swamps, encountering the additional discomfort of a rainy day and night.

Two days' unsuccessful search was made by the Confederates for Baldwin and Crawford, both of whom made their appearance in the Federal fleet on Sunday, the 29th of May, much fatigued by travel, and somewhat exhausted from want of food. The attempt to blow up the *Albemarle* was defeated by the party accidentally fouling a schooner anchored in the river. The next attempt, however, by Lieut. Commander Wm. B. Cushing, on October 28th, 1864, was more successful.

On the morning of October 27th, the *Albemarle* was moored near the wharf at Plymouth, a gangway connecting her with the shore. Some distance down the river, in the stream, lay the hull of the *Southfield*, sunk there by Capt. Cooke when Plymouth was captured from the Federals. The *Southfield* was used as a picket station by our infantry forces, to which they passed to and from the shore by a boat, and this boat was usually kept at the *Southfield*. The night was dark and stormy, and the Federal expedition under Lieut. Cushing passed the Confederate pickets on the wreck of the *Southfield* unobserved. About 3 A. M. a fire on shore lighted the way for Lieut. Cushing, and showed him the *Albemarle* surrounded by a raft of logs. The lookout on the *Albemarle* did not discover the approaching enemy until they reached the log barricade, about thirty feet from the ram. Although defence was

THE CONFEDERATE STATES NAVY.

attempted, it was too late to prevent the use of torpedoes on the launch from blowing a hole in the bow of the ram, from which she filled and sank.¹

Thus, by negligence and carelessness on the part of the Confederates, and by the enterprise and gallantry of the Federal detachment, the ram *Albemarle*, which had successfully stood the solid shot and shell from the Federal gunboats, was destroyed by a launch and thirty brave men, and with the weapon the Confederates had perfected and appropriated as peculiarly theirs. With the destruction of the *Albemarle* the control of the waters of the North Carolina sounds was again assured to the Federal gunboats. The companion boat of the *Albemarle* that was building on the Neuse River, was destroyed by a raid of the Federal forces under Gen. Foster; and later, the ram *Neuse*, in Cape Fear River, was destroyed by the Confederates, on the retreat of Gen. Hardee after the battle of Kinston.

Wilmington continued to resist all efforts for her capture, until exhaustion had weakened the grasp which no Federal effort had been able during four years to unwrench. But while the forts resisted successfully assault after assault, and blockade runners eluded all the watchfulness of the squadrons—the same fatality seemed to follow Confederate naval vessels at Wilmington, that had destroyed the vessels wherever they displayed their colors in battle.

At half-past seven o'clock on the night of May 6th, 1864, the iron-clad *Raleigh*, Lieut. Pembroke Jones commanding, bearing the broad pennant of Flag-officer Lynch, with the *Yadkin* and *Equator*, two small river steamers, steamed out of New Inlet, Cape Fear River, convoying several blockade runners and in quest of the enemy. The *Raleigh* steamed directly for the U. S. steamer *Britannia*, with the evident purpose of running her down. The intention was discovered in time, but the *Britannia* narrowly escaped being injured from her shot and shell. When the *Britannia* discovered the *Raleigh* she made signals to the Federal fleet of approaching danger, and fired several shots without effect at the advancing ram. Several blockaders, whose stations were convenient,

---

¹ See particulars in chapter on torpedoes elsewhere.

Of Cooke and Cushing, Capt. W. H. Parker says:

"I had not known Capt. Cooke in the old navy, but I saw enough of him at Roanoke Island and Elizabeth City to know that he was a hard fighter. Few men could have accomplished what he did in taking the *Albemarle* down the river with the carpenters still at work upon her. It was only done by his energy and perseverance. He was deservedly promoted for his services.

"Young Cushing had been a pupil of mine at the Naval Academy in 1861. He was rather a delicate-looking youth, fair, with regular, clearcut features, and a clear, greyish-blue eye. He stood low in his classes. He was first brought to my notice during the war by my happening to get hold of his report of the loss of the U. S. Steamer *Ellis*, under his command, at New River Inlet, Nov. 24th, 1862. I was impressed with this part of his official report (the italics are mine): 'and the only alternatives left were a surrender or a pull of one and a half miles under their fire in a small boat. The first of these was not, *of course*, to be thought of.' Knowing him to be at that time only 19 years old, I comprehended his heroic qualities and was not at all surprised to hear more of him. Immediately after the war I went to San Francisco, and my first visitor was Cushing. He was the hero of the hour and the citizens made much of him. Under the circumstances, I thought he conducted himself with much modesty. He died in 1874."—*Recollections of a Navy Officer*, p 340.

stood for the scene, thinking that it was a blockade-runner trying to escape. When the *Raleigh* got within 600 yards of the *Britannia* she began firing, the first shot putting out the *Britannia's* binnacle light, and the next going over her starboard paddle box. The *Britannia* then burned a blue light when the *Raleigh* fired again. The *Britannia* in her efforts to elude the *Raleigh* changed her course three times, until she passed the buoy and got into shallow water, where she burned several Coston signals for assistance from the Federal fleet. The *Raleigh* then changed her course and steering northeast, about midnight, ran for the U. S. Steamer *Nansemond.* The Federal vessel challenged the *Raleigh* a third time, and then ran off and opened fire with her after-howitzer. The *Raleigh* immediately replied by a shot, which passed over and near the *Nansemond's* walking beam, the *Raleigh* at this time not being over 500 yards distant. Several shots were exchanged on both sides until the *Nansemond* got out of range. Near daylight the *Raleigh* sighted the U. S. steamer *Howquah*, which put to sea with all speed after firing twenty shot and shell. The *Raleigh* returned the fire with her bow gun, one shell going through the *Howquah's* smoke-stack. At daylight the *Nansemond, Mount Vernon, Howquah, Britannia, Kansas, Niphon* and the entire Federal fleet came upon the scene of action, when the *Raleigh* and her consorts returned up the river. The ill-fated luck of the Confederate vessels overtook the *Raleigh* as she crossed the bar. She stuck and " broke her back."[1]

The Federal blockading fleet, believing that the iron-clad which had been destroyed on the bar a little above Fort Fisher was the *North Carolina*, organized an expedition under the command of Lieut. Commander William B. Cushing, U. S. N., to attempt the destruction of the only remaining iron-clad in Cape Fear River, which they supposed was the *Raleigh*. Before proceeding on his perilous journey, Lieut. Cushing deemed it prudent to make a thorough reconnoissance of Wilmington harbor, to determine the position of the *Raleigh*, and to post Acting Rear Admiral S. P. Lee, commanding the North Atlantic blockading squadron, in regard to the city, land and

[1] Commander Jones asked for a Court of Inquiry which examined the circumstances with the following result:

AT WILMINGTON, N C., June 6, 1864.
Report of the Court of Inquiry convened to examine into the circumstances connected with the loss of the iron-clad sloop Raleigh, on the Cape Fear River.
The Court having inquired into all the facts connected with the loss of the C. S. steamer *Raleigh*, in the waters of North Carolina, have the honor to report the same, together with our opinion upon the points in which it is required by the precept.
In the opinion of the court, the loss of the *Raleigh* cannot be attributed to the negligence or inattention on the part of any one on board of her, and every effort was made to save said vessel. We further find that the *Raleigh* could have re- mained outside the bar of Cape Fear River for a few hours with apparent [safety]; but, in the opinion of the court, it would have been improper; and, in view of all the circumstances, her commanding officer was justified in attempting to go back into the harbor when he did.
It is further the opinion of the court, that the draft of water of the *Raleigh* was too great, even lightened as she had been on this occasion, to render her passage of the bar, except under favorable circumstances, a safe operation, particularly as her strength seems to have been insufficient to enable her to sustain the weight of her armor long enough to permit every practicable means of lightening her to be exhausted.

GEORGE N. HOLLINS,
Captain and President.
J. W. B. GREENHOW,
Surgeon and Judge Advocate.

water defences of that port. He left the U. S. steamer *Monticello* off Wilmington, N. C., on the night of the 23d of June, in the first cutter, with two officers (Acting Ensign J. E. Jones and Acting Master's Mate William Howorth) and fifteen men, and started in for the west bar. In his official report to Rear Admiral Lee, dated July 2d, he says:

"We succeeded in passing the forts, and also the town and batteries of Smithville, and pulled swiftly up the river. As we neared the Zeke Island batteries, we narrowly escaped being run down by a steamer, and soon after came near detection from the guard boat; evading them all we continued our course. As we came abreast of the Old Brunswick batteries, some fifteen miles from the starting point, the moon came out brightly and discovered us to the sentinels on the banks, who hailed at once, and soon commenced firing muskets and raising an alarm by noises and signal lights. We pulled at once for the other shore, obliquing so as to give them to understand that we were going down; but as soon as I found that we were out of the moon's rays, we continued our course straight up, thereby baffling the enemy and gaining safety. When within seven miles from Wilmington, a good place was selected on the shore; the boat hauled up, and into a marsh, and the men stowed along the bank. It was now nearly day, and I had determined to watch the river, and if possible to capture some one from whom information could be gained. Steamers soon began to ply up and down, the flag-ship of Commodore Lynch, the *Yadkin,* passing within two hundred yards. She is a wooden propeller steamer of about three hundred tons, no masts, one smokestack, clear deck, English build, with awning spread fore and aft, and mounting only two guns; did not seem to have many men. Nine steamers passed in all, three of them being fine, large blockade-runners. Just after dark, as we were preparing to move, two boats rounded the point; and the men thinking it an attack, behaved in the coolest manner. Both boats were captured, but proved to contain a fishing party returning to Wilmington. From them I obtained all the information that I desired, and made them act as my guides in my further explorations of the river.

"Three miles below the city I found a row of obstructions, consisting of iron-pointed spiles driven in at an angle, and only to be passed by going into the channel left open, about two hundred yards from a heavy battery that is on the left bank.

"A short distance nearer the city is a ten-gun navy battery, and another line of obstructions, consisting of diamond-shaped crates, filled and supported in position by two rows of spiles; the channel in this instance being within fifty yards of the guns. A third row of obstructions and another battery complete the upper defences of the city. The river is also obstructed by spiles at Old Brunswick, and there is a very heavy earthwork there. Discovering a creek in the Cypress swamp, we pulled or rather poled up it for some time, and at length came to a road which, upon being explored, proved to connect with the main road from Fort Fisher and the sounds to Wilmington. Dividing my party, I left half to hold the cross-road and creek, while I marched the remainder some two miles to the main road and stowed away. About 11:30 A. M. a mounted soldier appeared with a mail-bag, and seemed much astonished when he was invited to dismount, but as I assured him that I would be responsible for any delay that might take place, he kindly consented to shorten his journey. About two hundred letters were captured, and I gained such information as I desired of the fortifications and enemy's force. As an expedition was contemplated against Fisher by our army about this time, the information was of much value. There are thirteen hundred men in the fort; and the unprotected rear that our troops were to storm is commanded by four light batteries. I enclose rebel requisition and report of provisions on hand.

" I now waited for the courier from the other direction, in order that we might get the papers that were issued at 1 P. M. in Wilmington; but just as he hove in sight, a blue jacket exposed himself, and the fellow took to instant flight. My pursuit on the captured horse was rendered useless from the lack of speed, and the fellow escaped after a race of some two miles.

"In the meantime we captured more prisoners, and discovered that a store was located about two miles distant, and being sadly in need of some grub, Mr. Howorth, dressed in the courier's coat and hat, and mounted upon his horse, proceeded to market. He returned with milk, chickens, and eggs, having passed every one, in and out of service, without suspicion, though conversing with many. At 6 P. M., after destroying a portion of the telegraph wire, we rejoined the party at the creek, and proceeded down, reaching the river at dark. In trying to land our prisoners upon an island, a steamer passed so close that we had to jump overboard, and hold our heads below the boat to prevent being seen. As we had more prisoners than we could look out for, I determined to put a portion of them in small boats, and set them adrift without oars or sails, so that they could not get ashore in time to injure us. This was done, and we proceeded down the river, keeping a bright look out for vessels in order to burn them, if possible. None were found, but I found the pilot to take me to where the ram *Raleigh* was said to be wrecked. She is indeed destroyed, and nothing now remains of her above water. The iron-clad *North Carolina*, Capt. Muse commanding, is in commission, and at anchor off the city. She is but little relied upon, and would not stand long against a monitor. Both torpedo boats were destroyed in the great cotton fire some time since. One was very near completion. As I neared the forts at the east bar, a boat was detected making its way rapidly to the shore, and captured after a short chase. It contained six persons, four of whom were soldiers. Taking them all into one boat, I cut theirs adrift, but soon found that twenty-six persons were more than a load. By questions I discovered that at least one guard-boat was afloat, containing seventy-five musketeers, and situated in the narrow passage between Federal Point and Zeke Island. As I had to pass them, I determined to engage the enemy at once, and capture the boat if possible.

"The moon was now bright, and as we came nearer the entrance, I saw what we supposed to be one large boat just off the battery; but as we prepared to sail into her, and while about twenty yards distant, three more boats suddenly shot out from that side, and five more from the other, completely blocking up the sole avenue of escape. I immediately put the helm down, but found a large sail-boat filled with soldiers to windward, and keeping us right in the glimmer of the moon's rays. In this trying position both officers and men acted with true coolness and bravery.

" Not the stroke of an oar was out of time; there was no thought of surrender, but we determined to outwit the enemy or fight it out. Suddenly turning the boat's head, we dashed off as if for the west bar, and by throwing the dark side of the boat towards them, were soon lost to view. The bait was eagerly seized, and their whole line dashed off at once to intercept us. Then again turning, by the extraordinary pulling of my sailors I gained the passage of the island, and before the enemy could prevent, put the boat into the breakers on Caroline shoals. The rebels dared not follow, and we were lost to view before the guns of the forts, trained on the channel, could be brought to bear upon our unexpected position. Deeply loaded as we were, the boat carried us through in fine style, and we reached the *Cherokee* just as the day was breaking, and after an absence from the squadron of two days and three nights."

The U. S. Navy Department had endeavored, from the winter of 1862, to induce the War Department to make a joint attack upon the defences of Cape Fear River, but the latter department claimed that no troops could be spared for the expedition. Lieut. Gen. Grant, late in the summer of 1864, gave his attention to the subject and decided that a body of troops could be spared to make the attack about the 1st of October. Upon consultation he was of the opinion that the best results would follow the landing of a large army, under the guns of the U. S. navy, on the open beach north of New Inlet, to take possession and intrench across to Cape Fear River, the navy to occupy the attention of the Confederate works on Federal Point with a heavy fire, in conjunction with the army, and at the same time, such force as could run the batteries was to do so, and thus isolate the Confederates. "The operation," says Secretary Welles, "is an important one, as closing the last port of the rebels, and destroying their credit abroad, by preventing the exportation of cotton, as well as preventing the reception of munitions and supplies from abroad."

Rear Admiral David G. Farragut was assigned to the command of the North Atlantic Squadron on the 5th of September, and the whole subject was committed to his hands. The necessity of rest, however, rendered it important that he should come immediately North, and he declined the command of the operating Federal navy forces. The command was then given to Rear Admiral David D. Porter, and every squadron was depleted and vessels detached from other duty to strengthen the expedition.

It was arranged that an attack should be made on the 1st of October, but it was postponed to the 15th, and in the meantime over 150 vessels of war were concentrated at Hampton Roads and Beaufort, to form the attacking squadron.

This immense fleet of war vessels remained idle, awaiting the movements of the army, until the day before Christmas, when it went into position and attacked the forts at the mouth of the Cape Fear River.

William R. Mayo, who was a midshipman in the Confederate States Navy, but who is now (1887) Collector of the port of Norfolk, Va., and who took a prominent part in the defence of Fort Fisher, has kindly furnished the following interesting narrative of the two attacks on that fort :

"During the summer of 1864, the navy of the Confederacy stationed at Wilmington, or a portion of it, together with officers and men from some other stations, were put ashore at the mouth of New Inlet to garrison a battery built at Confederate or Federal Point, which was commanded by Lieut. Robert T. Chapman, formerly of the U. S. navy, then of the C. S navy. This battery was called by Gen. Whiting, 'Buchanan,' after the admiral. It was built somewhat after the fashion of the Mound Battery of Fort Fisher, though a more complete and formidable work. It mounted two Brooke guns of heavy calibre. The names of most of the officers of this battery have escaped me. It is well known that Fort Fisher was built along the Atlantic coast line, which line was about North and South. Battery Buchanan was located to the west of and about a mile from the mound at Fort Fisher on the extreme south point of the Atlantic beach, the land falling back at this point in a westerly direction for about a mile. The first attack of the Federal fleet that was made during the latter days of December, 1864, was confined entirely to Fort Fisher, they paying no attention to Battery Buchanan—indeed if they knew it were there is doubtful. Having no demand for the garrison at home, therefore, about one-half of the men and officers were sent to relieve the Fort Fisher garrison, and were stationed principally at the guns on what is known as the *land* face of the fort—the chief point of attack. The next day these were relieved and the other half of the Buchanan garrison were sent up. Thus, all of the garrison had a chance at this attack to help reply to the salutations of the Federal fleet, and those of the last day to witness at night Mr. Butler's reconnoisance in force—which resulted in his withdrawal the next morning and the sailing away of the fleet. Some two weeks afterwards the second attack was made, Admiral Porter again in command of the fleet, but Mr. Butler was succeeded by Gen. Terry. This time the attack of the fleet was more systematic and well organized. Instead of, as in the first attack, moving around in a circular direction at too great a distance generally for the most effective work of the long range guns of the fleet, and much too far for a *fair* exchange of courtesies, our guns being of shorter range, each ship fired her battery as she came abreast of us. This was the general tactics of the first attack—the iron-clads and lighter gunboats came at once in close to the beach, and the iron-clads apparently anchored. The next of the fleet taking up a position farther out, and all paying their especial attention to the land face of the fort, the idea being to disable this portion of the fort, which was the only obstacle in the way of the army, which had been landed some eight miles up the beach. There must have been some four or five hundred guns brought to bear upon this earthwork during this attack. During the first day of this second attack no special attention was paid to the southern point of the fort, or mound as it was called, but if my memory is not here again at fault, during the morning of the second day one or more of the enemy's vessels seemed to have been directed to shell this particular spot, which they did, and later in the day a detachment of several double-enders and the lighter gunboats, some six or eight, perhaps, in number, came around the south and east of the mound directly in the inlet, and evidently for the purpose of attacking Battery Buchanan and running in the river, thus taking the fort in the rear, which, had it been accomplished, rendered a surrender at once imperative. I think Admiral Porter saw this, and as the work was the navy's, would have been delighted to have stamped it as such while the army was lying hid away among the sand hills up the beach. During all this day, the first of the second attack, the garrison of Battery Buchanan was in Fort Fisher, manning the land face guns (not all of them, of course), which were one by one disabled by the terrific bombardment, and until the demonstration was made upon our own battery and the inlet. At this time the Confederate navy detachment was withdrawn from Fort Fisher and placed in Battery Buchanan. The vessels sent around in front of us were shy, keeping well off, being evidently uncertain of what we were and of the channel also. In a few minutes they had a fleet of several boats out sounding, and these came in and in, until within range of our guns, when they were opened upon by the gun covering this particular point. There is one circumstance which I remember distinctly in this connection which is worthy of note. Each of these boats was in charge of an officer sitting in the stern. One of them more venturesome than the rest came nearer; a shell fired from our gun cut away the flag from his boat; it fell in the water; he backed his boat up to it, picked it up, waved it over his head and replaced it on the broken staff. Another shot was fired at him, which cut his boat in two and spilled him and his jolly tars in the water, but the other boats instantly came to his rescue, gathered them all in and at once took their departure. The gunboats made no effort to run in. I have heard since, and with much pleasure, that no lives were lost on account of this shot, the only casualty being a broken leg. I have never learned the name of the officer who commanded that boat, but he certainly did not leave his flag.

"The Federal fleet, after battering down or disabling all the guns, or nearly all, on the sea face of Fort Fisher, landed a large force of sailors and marines on the beach in front of the sea face of the fort and made an assault, with great loss. Though proving a great failure in itself, this assault occupied the nearly worn-out and depleted garrison, and had the direct result of admitting the army to the ramparts of the disabled land face of the fort before attention could be given to the assaulting column in that direction.

"Among those of the garrison of Battery Buchanan who were actively engaged in repelling the combined attack of the Federal army and navy, were the Confederate marines under Capt. Van Benthuysen of the C. S. Marine Corps, who had with him about fifty men. How they worked that night with the rest of the little garrison falling back from gun chamber to gun chamber can best be told by Col. Lamb. They were all killed or captured. The writer of this took to the water as the Federals, having captured the fort, pushed their way down the beach, and on that January night, in preference to being caught, ran the risk of freezing and drowning too, but finally succeeded in getting in a boat some several hundred yards out. After the fall of Fort Fisher, the navy at Wilmington garrisoned the batteries on the north side of the Cape Fear. The lowermost of them was commanded by Lieut. Gregory, who also escaped from Fisher, and the upper one by Lieut. Camm. I was at the lower one with Lieut. Gregory, and as Gen. Hoke, C. S. army, fell back before the overwhelming numbers of Gen. Terry, this battery finally became the base of the extreme right wing of his army. I think there was some doubt in the Federal mind as to the exact location and character of these batteries. They really amounted to very little, yet great caution was displayed in coming up the river. One morning early, I remember, as the fog lifted, the sentry reported a monitor in full view from around the point a mile below. Glasses were instantly turned that way, and Gregory after a little observation determined it was a decoy, as it was, an old barge of some sort with a sham turret, and so kept quiet. Not so Camm above us, however; being a half mile farther away he was deceived, and very soon opened in good earnest, but after a few shots the monitor (?) retired, having found out where we were, and also that we 'were alive and able to be about.' Here this portion of the navy remained until Wilmington was evacuated, which was brought about by the advance of a force on the south side of the Cape Fear, Gen. Hoke holding Gen. Terry in check on the north side, when he fell back with the army through North Carolina until it arrived in the lines around Petersburg. The naval force from Wilmington with the army then joined the garrison at Drewry's Bluff on the James River."

The part taken by the navy contingent in the defence of Battery Buchanan near Fort Fisher, is reported by Lieut. Com. Robert T. Chapman to Flag-officer R. T. Pinkney, commanding the naval forces at Wilmington, as follows:

"BATTERY BUCHANAN, Dec. 29th, 1864.
"SIR: I reported to you on the 20th inst. that the fleet of the enemy had arrived off this place. They disappeared on the same day and returned on the 23d, and anchored about six miles off Fort Fisher. A detachment of twenty-nine men, under Lieut. Roby, was sent from this battery to man the Brooke guns at Fort Fisher.

"On the 24th, at 12 M., the fleet of the enemy got under way in line ahead (the *Ironsides* leading), and at one o'clock they opened fire on the fort. There were forty-three vessels engaged, throwing every kind of projectiles from a three-inch bolt to a fifteen-inch shell. A most terrific bombardment continued until 5:30 P. M., when the enemy withdrew. On the 25th, at half-past ten, the fight was renewed by the same number of vessels, and the fire was incessant until 5:30 P. M., when the fleet again went beyond the range of our guns.

"At half-past two o'clock a number of boats were lowered from the ships of the fleet and approached the battery. I think they were dragging for torpedoes. We opened fire on them from one gun, and at the fourth discharge sunk one of their boats ; the others quickly withdrew. At 5:20 P. M. a message was received from Fort Fisher saying that the enemy had landed and were advancing on the fort, and asking for reinforcements. Two-thirds of the men belonging to the battery were immediately sent to the fort, under Lieut. Arledge and officers of the companies. They double-quicked to the fort, and got there in time to assist in repelling the assault. We were at quarters nearly all Sunday night, expecting an attack from the boats of the fleet.

"On the 26th, the men belonging to the battery, except those under Lieut. Roby, returned from Fort Fisher. There was no firing on the fort on the 26th or 27th. On the 26th the forces of the enemy re-embarked, and on the night of the 28th the fleet disappeared, leaving only the regular blockading squadron off this place.

"Both of the guns commanded by Lieut. Roby burst. I send his report.

"Passed Midshipmen Cary and Berrien were with Lieut. Roby, and I understand the conduct of these officers and the men with them is above all praise. Out of the twenty-nine men from this battery serving at Fort Fisher nineteen were killed and wounded, and I regret to state that some have since died. Lieuts. Armstrong and Dornin came down as volunteers. They went to the forts and behaved as gallantly as men could do. Lieut. Dornin was painfully wounded by the explosion of a shell."[1]

Major Gen. W. H. C. Whiting, in his report of the attack on Fort Fisher under date of December 31st, 1864, presents his

"Acknowledgements to Flag-officer Pinkney, C. S. N., who was present during the action, for the welcome and efficient aid sent to Col. Lamb, the detachment under Lieut. Roby, which manned the two Brooke guns, and the company of marines under Capt. Van Benthuysen, which reinforced the garrison. Lieut. Chapman, C. S. N., commanding Battery Buchanan, by his skilful gunnery saved us on our right from a movement of the enemy, which, unless checked, might have resulted in a successful passage.

"The navy detachment at the guns, under very trying circumstances, did good work.

"No commendations of mine can be too much for the coolness, discipline and skill displayed by officers and men.

"Their names have not all been furnished to me, but Lieuts. Roby, Dornin, Armstrong and Berrien attracted special attention throughout.

"To Passed Midshipman Cary I wish to give personal thanks. Though wounded he reported after the bursting of his gun, to repel the threatened assault, and actively assisted Col. Tansil on the land front.

"Above all and before all we should be grateful, and I trust all are, for the favor of Almighty God, under which and by which a signal deliverance has been achieved."

The landing of the Federal forces was effected on January 12th, 1865, and during the 14th the fire of the Confederate

[1] Lieuts. Thomas L. Dornin and R. F. Armstrong, although senior in rank to Lieut. Roby who commanded the naval contingent of two guns' crews at Battery Buchanan (named in honor of Admiral Franklin Buchanan, C. S. N.) volunteered, and served one of the guns as sponger and loader until it burst. They served likewise at the second gun until it burst, caused by depressing the guns to sink Lieut. Wm. B. Cushing's boat, close inshore dragging for torpedoes. Lieut. Dornin was wounded, and Roby ordered to another part of the defences of Fort Fisher. Lieut. Armstrong then volunteered in a battery commanded by a North Carolina officer, who by order of Col. Lamb was detached, and Lieut. Armstrong placed in command of the two guns.

cruiser *Chickamauga*, which had returned to Wilmington, killed and wounded a number of men, so that Lieut. O'Keeffe, with his company of the fifteenth regiment N. Y. V., was directed to build a battery of thirty-two-pounder rifle Parrott guns on the bank of the river to drive her off.[1]

The following account of the part taken by the officers of the *Chickamauga* in the defence of Wilmington, is from the pen of Midshipman Clarence Cary, now a prominent member of the New York bar :

"Arrived at Wilmington, the *Chickamauga* had for the next month but little to do. There had been some intention on the part of the naval authorities to send her out on another raid, but rumors of an impending great naval demonstration against Fort Fisher decided them to keep the ship at hand for such service as events might enable her to render. In December, these rumors began to take shape, and it became apparent that the most formidable fleet yet called into being by the war was gathering at Hampton Roads, for the projected attack. About the 22d of December, 1864, affairs had progressed to such a degree that the scanty garrison at Fort Fisher was hastily, although still insufficiently, reinforced, and preparations for resistance hurried forward. A call was made upon the *Chickamauga* for sufficient men and officers to man two seven-inch Brooke rifled and banded guns which, taken recently from the sunken *Roanoke* in the river, had been mounted in a partially completed battery on the sea-face of the fort ; the navy men being desired in this instance, because the soldiers did not understand the tackling and management of the pieces.

"Accordingly on the morning of the 23d, a picked lot of some twenty-nine blue-jackets from the *Chickamauga*, in charge of Lieut. Roby, and two passed midshipmen, were drafted away for shore service, and soon found themselves tramping over the long sand stretches of Fort Fisher, where, during the next few days, they were destined to meet some novel and adverse experiences. If any anticipation of misfortunes troubled these lads, it was not apparent. They had left the ship in high spirits, envied by those who were forced to remain behind, and the usual sailor-like, devil-may-care hunger for adventure possessed them wholly.

"The advance vessels of the fleet were already hovering on the coast, a little way to the northward, and it was 'in the air' that the attack might begin at any moment. The sailor men were quartered in the fort, but the scanty provision for officers' quarters there forced the lieutenant and midshipmen to find temporary accommodation, pending the outbreak of the expected battle, in a deserted hut, a little way up the beach outside the fort. This circumstance led to their being closer than any others of the garrison to the scene of explosion of the famous powder-ship, brought in by the enemy on the following night, a demonstration which was expected by its promoters to level the walls of the fort and produce general havoc and dismay in the ranks of its defenders.

"This is what the *Chickamauga's* officers heard of it: Towards morning on the night of the 23d, while sleeping on the floor of the hut in that uneasy half-consciousness which men have, even while asleep, on the eve of battle—for the great fleet was then close at hand and might come in for attack at any high tide—a half heard muffled report, such as might come from a distant, heavy gun, was noticed. Rousing at once for attention, for they supposed the sound to be that of an alarm gun, and that it would be followed by the long roll beat of the drums calling the men to the batteries, they waited with an alert interest. But nothing more came of the interruption, and the circumstance was forgotten in renewed slumber. It was not learned till afterwards that the sound they heard and

---

[1] Rep. of Ch. of Engineers of U. S. A., year ending Jan. 30th, 1865, p. 63.

puzzled over was the explosion of the powder ship, and that they chanced
to be in such close proximity to a form of attack which, if only half its
expected success had attended it, would have incidently blown themselves
into space.

"On the following morning, that of Christmas Eve, 1864, when the
sky was clear and the sea blue, with just enough westerly breeze to ripple

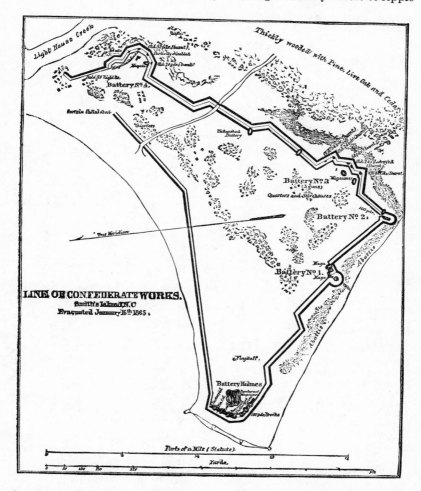

the surface of the ocean and stiffen out the dancing flags overhead, the
splendid fleet steamed slowly in for the attack. In stately line of battle,
three abreast, with the iron-clads in the van and the frigates, sloops of
war and gunboats, all trimmed for action, ranged behind, the fifty-five
vessels of the squadron silently advanced. Inside the fort, from the navy
guns, now manned by the *Chickamauga's* people, all the way up the
quarter mile of sand mounds composing the sea face, and away back

along the more elevated land face which turned off at right angles till it met the marsh and river at the rear, one could see the motionless groups of grey-uniformed gunners standing silently at the barbette guns, no movement showing anywhere, except in the flags which still fluttered gaily in the wind.

"Presently the formidable *Ironsides* took up her desired position, and rounding slightly, jetted out a puff of heavy smoke from one of her bow ports. This, with the screaming, whizzing shell which followed, gave the signal for the heaviest artillery battle of modern times to begin its two days of turmoil.

'At the first shot from the enemy, the fort began its response. The rigid groups unlocked, and a lively, rattling interchange of fire opened between the hundreds of guns of the fleet and the fifty odd pieces perched on the sand mounds of the fortress. What with the continuous roar of the firing, and the scarcely frequent reports of bursting shell, the aggregate noise was not unlike that of a rolling, volleying, long-sustained thunder storm. It continued throughout the day till, with the setting in of the early winter twilight, the fleet hauled off and left the fort to recoup its damages and wonder at the shower of shell fragments and pit-holes so plentifully besprinkling its spacious surface that turbulent Christmas Eve. The *Chickamauga* detachment had found themselves in an unfinished battery, where the incomplete sand mounds, or traverses between the guns, left them somewhat exposed to a raking fire, but they were not without the satisfaction of seeing more than one or two of their chilled bolts and big shells knock a shower of splinters from the wooden ships abreast of the position. An able seaman named Higgins had been the first to figure in the list of casualties. Early in the day he found his left leg spinning away from him across the sand plain before a bursting shell. Later, other mishaps here and there occurred, and in the afternoon a shell burst in the battery of gun No. 1, which sent a five-pound fragment through the shoulder of a sailor, and at the same moment bestowed a crack on the knee to the officer in charge. It had not been deemed expedient to fire the heavy Brooke guns of the navy detachment oftener than at fifteen-minute intervals, by way of saving undue exposure of the guns' crews, and also avoiding heating the pieces; and so, between the discharges, and while crouching in comparative safety under the sand mounds, ample opportunity was found to watch the antics of the hostile missiles showered into the fort. These were of all sorts and sizes, from the big fifteen-inch spherical shot or shell, and the 100-pounder rifled Parrotts, down through the list, and the whiz or whistle of each variety seemed to strike a different and more vicious note. Occasionally a spherical shell, after it had passed safely by, and was nearly spent, exploded with its base turned towards the battery, the result being to toss its bottom-end back among the unprotected gunners, and curiously enough one of these bits delivered a highly-condensed temperance lecture by knocking a bottle of grog just then served out to the sailors, from the hands of the man engaged in taking the first pull. The sympathy of the blue jackets was not addressed to the unfortunate sailor who held the bottle, although he, too, had received a knock from the same fragment.

"In one interval of watching, a young courier was observed running in at top speed across an exposed place to gain cover under the *Chickamauga's* battery. Before the lad reached it, however, an exploding fifteen-inch shell intervened, and almost eliminated him, so much so, that the sailors could find scarcely a recognizable semblance of humanity left to bury in the little hole they hastily scraped out of the sand for that purpose. Some of the missiles striking the sand mounds 'full and by,' sent fountains of dust aloft, while here and there others burrowed in the sand plain, and exploding, left a hole big enough to plant a tree in. Just back of the navy guns, scarcely two hundred yards away, were some framework stables in which a few officers' horses had been left in the emergency of the attack. These buildings, being in the hottest line of concentrated fire, and wholly unsheltered, were speedily breached, and set in flames by the shells, leaving the terrified animals free to escape and gallop madly up and down the plain inside the fort, until one after another they were shotdown. One horse, a handsome grey, came back exhausted after his frantic gallop, with the blood from a wound showing plainly on his neck, and stood patiently as near his stable gate as the flames would permit, until another shell fortunately soon finished his affair.

"Up in the bomb-proof, in the angle formed by the meeting of the land and sea faces of the fort, the surgeons were busily at work over the stream of wounded which trickled in to them during the day, and just outside of their doorway, beyond a little sand-curtain, one found an indication of their whereabouts, in the dozen or so of legs and arms which had been hastily tossed there after amputation. The *Chickamauga* detachment furnished its quota to the hospital, but the worst experience for the sailors was destined to come the following day.

"Then, on Christmas morning, after an harassing night of false alarms spent by the garrison, the fleet came in again, this time earlier, and prepared for a fuller day of it. The same hammering from the ships, and the same sullen and slow response from the fort, characterized the proceedings of the second day's work during the morning hours, but the enemy's fire increased in intensity in the afternoon, as the preliminary of an attack from the land forces of military, which were then disembarking from various transports beyond range up the beach.

"Before this latter demonstration took place, however, the *Chickamauga's* people were treated to a new and highly disagreeable experience.

"While they were engaged in firing gun No. 1, and just as a shell burst over the battery, severely wounding Lieut. Dornin of the navy, who was standing near, the piece itself exploded with terrific force. This heavy gun, weighing about 15,000 pounds, was split by the explosion from the jaws of the cas-cabet horizontally through to the trunnions, and then sliced perpendicularly through the chase. One-half of its breech was blown back over the heads of a group of officers near by, and the other portion smashed through the carriage to the ground, while the heavy bands from around the breech spread apart and miscellaneously damaged the gun's crew. When the officers at the rear struggled to their feet . . . and whether they were knocked down by concussion or astonishment they never knew . . . a strange sight presented itself.

"One man lay dead, with his arms stretched out towards them and his skull blown off, while another appeared twisted in a knot over a piece of iron band lapped across his stomach. Others were more or less hurt, and one man was leaping about the battery like a lunatic, crying out that he was on fire. He could scarcely be comforted, even when on stripping off his shirt he was found only to be tattooed by grains of powder and sand blown into his back and shoulders.

"This finished the work of gun No. 1. Its remaining crew turned to at the other gun, and its midshipmen found duty at headquarters in assisting the staff of Gen. Whiting about the preparations then in course to meet the threatened land attack.

"As it happened curiously enough, Passed Midshipman Berrien's gun, the remaining one of the *Chickamauga's* battery, soon after followed the bad example of its mate, and exploded much in the same manner, with a further but not so disastrous damage to the crew.

"By this time, towards three o'clock in the afternoon, there was a slackening of the shelling on the land face, and a redoubled firing on that fronting the sea, indicating that the land forces were advancing to attack the former portion of the fort. Orders were immediately issued by the general to man the breastworks and parapet on that side, and to this end it became necessary to get from out of the bomb-proofs a battalion of conscripts which had been drafted from home-guard service to eke out the garrison. As these 'Junior Reserves' were the remains of former conscriptions, and composed of decrepit old men and young boys, without experience of service, and wholly unfit for the field, it was somewhat of a task to dislodge them from the 'rat-hole' where they had sheltered in security while the two days' cannonade had thundered overhead. But by dint of scolding and swearing on the part of the officers of the staff, and an occasional use of the flat of the sabre, the unhappy creatures were finally marshalled out on the parapet where they made a show of numbers, and so helped out the gallant soldiers of the regular garrison.

"By this time, a glance over the parapet disclosed an irregular blue line of skirmishers trotting out across the sand plain at the front from a denser body of troops behind them; those in advance alternately putting up their muskets to fire at the men in the fort, and then burrowing like fiddler-crabs, behind hastily tossed-up piles of sand. A lively exchange of musketry fire ensued for a few minutes, but it lacked seriousness on the part of the attack, and presently lulled, showing the blue coats scampering back out of range. This was all that came of the land attack. If it had been pushed with vigor, as was the similar one a few weeks later, it is hardly probable that the fort, weakly garrisoned as it was, could have successfully resisted.

"When it was observed from the fleet that the military were retreating, the ships hauled off, out of action, but not without a long, vindictive spurt of terrific shelling at the land face, by way of parting salute.

"After two days' further waiting, spent in anxiously watching the fleet and the land forces which remained up to the beach, in sight but out of range, the garrison had the agreeable surprise and satisfaction of seeing the troops re-embark, and their transports, accompanied by the host of war-vessels, fade away out of sight to the northward. For the present, at least, the victory was left with Fort Fisher.

"The *Chickamauga's* detachment of thirty-two men and officers, what with the casualties due to their exposed position and to the bursting of their guns, had a 'butcher's bill' of nineteen killed and wounded to show for their share in the two days' affair, and the following morning saw them a shabby, limping squad on foot, with a cart-load of disabled companions trailing on astern; marching back across the sandy plains to where the ship lay anchored in the river.

"They had received a kind congratulation from Gen. Whiting, and a cordial mention in his official report, as also pleasant demonstrations from gallant Col. Lamb and the garrison on leaving the fort; but perhaps the most stirring moments of their lives were still in waiting for them further down the point, at the navy works of Battery Buchanan, where the garrison was composed of some two hundred and fifty of their brother sailors. There, after a brief halt at the shut doors of the sally-port, the *Chickamauga* lads found themselves, cart and all, unexpectedly marched into the centre of a hollow square of tumultuously cheering sailors. After this episode, they were soon again at home and afloat in the *Chickamauga.*

"The second attack on the fort occured on January 15th, a few weeks later, and although the military officers of Fort Fisher kindly applied again for the detachment in the preparation for that affair, the ship was deemed too short-handed to admit of their going back. Thus they escaped a further harsh experience, and, as events proved, a certain capture. Their part in the subsequent operations was limited to such shelling of the attacking troops as the ship was able to accomplish from her position in the river.

"From there they witnessed the second attack and the final capture of the fort. After that the ship was taken back to Wilmington, and subsequently burnt and sunk, higher up the river, where she lay at peace till some enterprising Yankee a few years later raised her hull and converted her into an inglorious West India fruiterer."

The fall of Wilmington was the severest blow to the Confederate cause which it could receive from the loss of any port. It was far more injurious than the capture of Charleston, and but for the moral effect, even more hurtful than the evacuation of Richmond. With Wilmington and the Cape Fear River open, the supplies that reached the Confederate armies would have enabled them to have maintained an unequal contest for years, but with the fall of Fort Fisher the constant stream of supplies was effectually cut off and the blockade made truly effective—not by the navy fleet, but by its captures on land.

CHAPTER XVI.

THE BLOCKADE.

THE diplomacy of Wm. H. Seward, U. S. Secretary of State during the years 1861-5, is a subject of much perplexity, and the more it is examined and analyzed with the light of contemporary and subsequent facts, the greater will be the difficulty in deciding whether it was more harmful to the cause of the United States than to that of the Confederate States. That he accomplished no practical result; that he humiliated the pride of the United States; that he abandoned the historical policy of the government from its beginning without successfully initiating any other in its stead, will be apparent to the most cursory reading of his diplomatic dispatches. And a closer examination will convince the reader that he exhibited an ignorance of geography, of history and of literature, which cannot be traced in the dispatches of any of his official predecessors. [1]

Nor was his temper and discretion suited to the management of diplomatic intercourse. His defects were so well marked and defined that to them may be directly traced several of those rebuffs and discourtesies which were given him

---

[1] A few extracts from his diplomatic correspondence will establish the truth of this assertion. On July 7th, 1862, writing to Mr. Adams of Commodore Farragut's passing the batteries at Vicksburg, he says: "Thus the last obstacle to the navigation of the Mississippi River has been overcome, and it is open to trade once more from the head waters of its tributaries, near the Lakes and *Prince Rupert's Land,* to the Gulf of Mexico."

Prince Rupert's Land lies on the eastern side of Hudson's Bay at least fifteen degrees of latitude, and, as a "bird flies," over a thousand miles from the sources of the Mississippi. So much for geography. His history is not more reliable. After calling the motto of the Order of the Garter, "the motto of the National Arms," he asserts that "Richelieu occupied and fortified a large portion of this continent, extending from the Gulf of Mexico to the Straits of Belle Isle." The cardinal was dead and in his grave in the Sorbonne thirty years before the Missis-

sippi was discovered, either at its source or its mouth. His literature is as defective as his geography and history are incorrect. Commending Mr. Harvey, U. S. Minister at Lisbon, for attending the erection of a monument to Camoens, he says: "The incident seems doubtless the more pleasing to us because it occurs at this conjuncture, when we are engaged in combating, in its full development, a gigantic error which Portugal, *in the age of Camoens,* brought into this continent." Camoens died at Lisbon in 1579, and the Portugese slave trade in this hemisphere began in 1630. Such literary bungling is further clouded with a vulgarity and insensibility to decorum which never before *dirtied* the pages of American diplomacy. The euphemism by which when a household is gladdened by the birth of a babe, the convalescence of the mother is described in technical and courtly phrase: "that the mother is getting on as well as could be expected," was introduced by Mr Seward in a dispatch of July 18th, 1862, to Mr. Adams, by Lord Russell, by M. Drouyn de Lhuys, and by Baron Van Luyden. The moral side of his character involved him in questions of personal veracity with M. Mercier which his most devoted friends have failed to satisfactorily explain. His political fortunes, or some other motive as yet unexplained, induced him to select for diplomatic positions abroad the Pikes and Foggs, and Judds, names which recall the grotesque characters of Dickens' novels, and whose performances and dispatches add to, if they do not embellish, the absurdities and crudities which fill the volumes of diplomatic correspondence for the years 1861-5. Of all the men selected to represent the United States at European courts only Mr. Adams at London, and Mr. Dayton at Paris, and possibly Cassius M. Clay at St. Petersburg, had any reputation for fitness or capacity beyond the narrowest limits of their homes; the rest were obscure and untrained fanatical stump speakers, and newspaper purveyors. To Holland he sent a semi-editor of a New York paper. At religious and bigoted Madrid he placed a German adventurer,—the word is not used in an offensive sense, but as descriptive of the unfitness of Mr. Schurz.

One turns from these mental and moral defects to an absence of political convictions, and a vacillation of political purpose, that is astonishing. It is not surprising to read in a dispatch of March 9th, 1861, that "the President entertains a full confidence in the speedy restoration of the harmony and the unity of the government;" while the powers of Europe were advised by a dispatch to England of April 10th, 1861, that "The President neither looks for nor apprehends any actual and permanent dismemberment of the American Union, especially by a line of latitude. He is not disposed to reject a cardinal dogma of the South, namely, *that the Federal government cannot reduce the seceding States to obedience by conquest*, even although he were disposed to question that proposition. But, in fact, the *President willingly accepts it as true.* Only an imperial or despotic government *could subjugate*

as: "The work of pacification in the region concerned *is going on as successfully as could be expected.* You hear of occasional guerilla raids, but these are the *after-pangs* of revolution in that quarter which has proved *an abortion.*"

He accuses Voltaire of having said, "Dieu est toujours *sur le cote* des gros canons." No educated Frenchman would have said " *sur le cote.*" What Voltaire did say to M. Le Riche was: " Le nombre des sages sera toujours petit. Il est vrai qu'il est augmenté; mais ce n'est rien en comparaison des *sots*, et par malheur on dit que Dieu est toujours *pour* les gros bataillons," and M. Bussy Rabutin wrote : " Dieu est d' ordinaire *pour* les gros escadrons contre les petits," but neither wrote *sur le cote.* And Minister Sandford informs Mr. Seward, July 3d, 1861, that " They would in no case make a treaty which should bind them to perpetual abolition of passports, *vis-a-vis* to my nation." He might have said with equal propriety, *dos-a-dos ! !*

In such tawdry effusions the diplomatic dispatches of Mr. Seward describe the British Colonial Empire as " extending from Gibralter, through the West Indies and Canada, till it begins again on the southern extremity of Africa;" and that "armed insurrections to overturn the government are frequent in Great Britain;" that most of the wars in modern times have been revolutionary wars ;" that "the government of the Netherlands is probably an ally of Japan;" and, lastly, his singular forgetfulness or ignorance of the history of his own country, and of what Silas Deane and Dr. Franklin, and the Lees, and John Adams were sent to do and did, in Europe, when he wrote to Mr. Schurz that "it seems the necessity of faction in every country, that whenever it acquires sufficient boldness to inaugurate revolution, it forgets alike the counsels of prudence, and stifles the instincts of patriotism, and becomes a suitor to foreign courts for aid and assistance." These specimens of literary bungling and ignorance might be multiplied a hundred-fold if space only permitted."

*thoroughly disaffected and insurrectionary members of the
State.* This Federal republican system of ours is, of all forms
of government, the very one which is most unfitted for such a
a labor." The dispatch continues to explain how the Constitu-
tution can be amended by a "National Convention," and concludes that while "the President will not suffer the Federal
authority to fall into abeyance, nor will he, on the other hand,
aggravate existing evils by attempts at *coercion* which must
assume the form of direct war against any of the revolutionary States." Thus Mr. Seward sustained the political doctrine
of the South that the Federal government had no constitutional right to *coerce* a seceded State, and *par consequence*,
no power to declare war, proclaim blockade, or exercise any
other hostile agency to reconstruct the Federal Union. The
British government, thus advised of the principles by
which Mr. Lincoln proposed to conduct his administration,
must have naturally concluded that *secession* had divided the
Federal Union into two confederacies, which were to be reunited only by discussion and agreement. Within ten days
after that pacific declaration, Europe was astonished by the
Proclamation of Blockade, of April 19th, 1861, from the Capes
of Virginia to the mouth of the Rio Grande.

Blockade is a recognized agency of war only between independent nations. European governments had never seen a
nation blockade its *own ports;* and as Mr. Seward had declared
that this government had no constitutional right to coerce a
State back into the Union, and had followed that declaration
with a blockade, the conclusion was irresistible, that the
seceded States were to occupy some intermediate position between independency and restoration to the Federal Union. Is
it surprising that this anomalous and contradicting diplomacy should have determined European governments to assume a neutral position and to declare both the United States
and the Confederate States to be belligerents? What other
course was open to them? Hence, the Queen's Proclamation
of Neutrality of May 13th, and that of the Emperor of the
French of June 10th, 1861, were the consequences of Mr. Seward's diplomacy and of his blockade which constituted the Confederate States belligerents both on land and at sea. England
and France recognized what Mr. Seward had done as the constitutional outcome of the absence of the right to *coerce* the
States back into the Union, and as a declaration of war
against the Confederate States for the purpose of conquering
them, notwithstanding the want of constitutional warrant.

"The only justification that I have heard for this extraordinary concession," said Senator Charles Sumner [1] "which
unleashed upon our country the furies of war to commingle
with the furies of rebellion at home, is that President Lincoln

[1] Speech in the U. S. Senate on the Johnson-Clarendon Treaty.

undertook to proclaim *a blockade* of the rebel ports. By the use of this word ' blockade' the concession (of belligerency) is vindicated. Had President Lincoln proclaimed *a closing* of the rebel ports, there could have been no such concession." And again :

"So far as is now known, the whole case for England is made to stand on the use of the word 'blockade' by President Lincoln. Had he used any other word the concession of belligerency would have been without justification, even such as is now imagined. It was this word which, with magical might, opened the gates to all those bountiful supplies by which hostile expeditions were equipped against the United States. It opened the gates of war. Most appalling is it to think that one little word, unconsciously used by a trusting President, could be caught up by a friendly power and made to play such a part."

It was Mr. Seward that spoke the word "blockade," and whether by ignorance of its import and consequences, or by a design to have that "little blood-letting " which Senator Chandler invoked as the best means of preserving the unity of the Republican party, was immaterial to European powers. They accepted the war agency of Mr. Seward's selection, and made their governments neutrals, in the war between the " belligerents."

Mr. Seward had but two objects before him. One was, to prevent even the indirect recognition of the Confederate States; the other, to effect a complete prohibition of privateering. His diplomacy completely failed in both. His blockade constituted the Confederate States belligerents, and as such they were recognized; and being belligerent, and not having acceded to the Treaty of Paris of 1856, the right of privateering belonged to both the United States and the Confederate States, and was recognized as a rightful war agent to either belligerent. Mr. Seward's blockade, which prevented unrestricted trade between the Confederate States and foreign countries, was not without a multitude of troubles to his department and to his country. While it affected the recognition of the Confederate States as belligerents, it also caused the government of those States to resort to privateering as a counterstroke against the blockade. The Act of the Confederate Congress of May 6th, 1861, by which letters of marque were authorized to be issued, assigned as a reason that the President of the United States " has issued his other proclamation announcing his purpose to set on foot a blockade of the ports of the Confederate States." Thus Mr. Seward's management of the State Department, which had been so bungling and unwise as to cause European powers to invest the Confederate States with a quasi-recognition, had also set loose. "unleashed " as Mr. Sumner put it, a fleet of privateers to prey upon the commerce of the United States. England and France, in accordance with the purpose of the Treaty of Paris to suppress privateering, closed their ports to Confederate and United States privateers, and Mr. Seward's blockade shut up the Confederate ports, so that the condemnation of prizes by admiralty courts was impossible to Confederate captors. The wisdom of a policy which, depriving the merchant owners in the United States of all the advantages of trial of prizes for condemnation by admiralty courts, and compelling the burning on the high seas of many captures, will certainly not be regarded as evincing any very great statesmanship.

The Hon. Charles Sumner, in his speech in the Senate[1] was as unreliable in his statements as the Secretary of State was unwise in his diplomacy. Mr. Sumner averred, years after the war was closed, that at the time when belligerency was conceded to the Confederate States, they were "without prize courts, or other tribunals for the administration of justice on the ocean."[2]   By the Act of March 11th, 1861, the Confederate Congress established "a Court of Admiralty and maritime jurisdiction at Key West, in the State of Florida," and adopted for its guidance the "laws of the United States," until otherwise provided. And the Act of March 16th, 1861, "to establish the Judicial Courts of the Confederate States," gave to all district courts "original cognizance of all civil causes of admiralty and maritime jurisdiction," and gave to "the laws of the United States and the rules of court in refernce to admiralty proceeding in force in the Admiralty Courts of the United States on the 20th day of December, 1860," * * * full force and effect in the courts of the Confederate States." Thus it will be seen that it is not a fact, as Mr. Sumner asserted, that "at the early date when this was done the rebels were, as they remained to the close, without ships on the ocean; without prize courts or other tribunals for the administration of justice on the ocean, without any of those conditions which are the essential prerequisites to such a concession." Adopting, then, Mr. Canning's celebrated declaration made during the Greek Revolution, that ocean belligerency is a "fact," and not a principle—a "fact" to be proved, as any other fact, by

---

[1] On the Johnson-Clarendon Treaty.

[2] If that assertion had been true, there were well-established precedents in American history to sustain the claim of the Confederate States to recognition as a belligerent, and to the use of privateers in the war with the U. S.   Reference need only be made to the Portuguese case and to the correspondence thereon between Chevalier Joseph Corréa de Serra, Portuguese Minister at Washington, with Mr. Monroe, Sec. of State, in 1815-16, with John Quincy Adams, Sec. of State, in 1818, published in Ex. Doc. 1st Sess. 32d Congress, Doc. No. 53, 3d series, No. 1, pp. 161, 163. 166. Also the correspondence on the same case in 1850, between Chevalier de Figauier, Portuguese Minister at Washington, and Mr. Clayton and Mr. Webster, Sec. of State (Ex. Doc. supra pp. 179 and 180). In the latter correspondence Chev. Figauier presents the same state of facts which Mr. Sumner *imagined.*

"Upward of sixty Portuguese vessels, with their cargoes, were captured or plundered, and such ships and cargoes were appropriated to their own use. The fitting out of these privateers at Baltimore was a matter of public notoriety, and many of the leading citizens there, including the sheriff and postmaster, were summoned before the courts as owners or interested in such privateers. It is well known that the noted Banda-Oriental chief, Artigas, held no seaport, had no ships, no sailors; and the privateers. assuming his unrecognized flag, were mostly manned and commanded by citizens of the United States, and in some instances, the officers held commissions in the navy of the United States." The U. S. naval officers were Lieuts. Peleg and Dunham, and Midshipmen Swartout and Grimke. The United States refused positively to entertain the Portuguese claims, to appoint commissions, or in any manner whatever to accept responsibility for the $1,500,000 worth of vessels destroyed by American privateers.

evidence—it is shown that the Confederate States had ships-of-war on the ocean, and possessed admiralty courts, where the laws and proceedings of the United States were recognized and administered; that they were organized in their State autonomies and even confederated by the same kind of league or constitution that bound together the States of the United States; and that Mr. Seward had recognized all these evidences of "fact" by resorting to the blockade of the Confederate ports, the ports of the very States he had declared could not be *coerced* back into the Federal Union.

Events culminated in the assault on Sumter, and on April 19th, 1861, the Proclamation of Blockade was issued. [1]

The administration of Mr. Lincoln was from its beginning greatly embarrassed as to the commercial questions likely to be involved in secession. As early as March 7th, the subject was being discussed in the leading newspapers. The N. Y. *Herald* of that day, voiced the prevailing opinion when it said:

"We may observe in this connection that no government can blockade its own ports. It may lay an embargo on goods leaving its ports, but it cannot legally and constitutionally prevent the ships of other nations entering its ports while it is at peace with those nations. As to laying an embargo on cotton going to England and France, we hardly think Mr. Lincoln will ever try that game with two powerful nations, who so recently cut their way to Pekin to establish the freedom of their commerce." * * * "At present the distinguished rail-splitter is too much engaged in the distribution of the spoils to pay much attention to foreign policies, or to the blockading of the Southern coast, but it is evident from the paragraph in the *Tribune* that that journal feels that the government of Mr. Lincoln will never undertake a blockade." [2]

On March 10th, 1861, the U. S. government had only forty-two vessels in commission and 207 men in all the forts and receiving ships upon the Atlantic coast. Of these vessels, twenty-six were steamers, with eleven knots as the highest

---

[1] "WASHINGTON, April 19.—The President has issued a proclamation as follows :

"An insurrection against the Government of the United States has broken out in the States of South Carolina, Georgia, Alabama, Florida, Mississippi, Louisiana and Texas, and the laws of the United States for the collection of the revenue cannot be effectually executed comfortably to that provision of the Constitution which requires the duties to be uniform throughout the United States.

"And, further, a combination of persons engaged in such insurrection have threatened to grant pretended letters of marque to authorize the bearers thereof to commit assaults on the lives, vessels and property of good citizens of the country, engaged in commerce on the high seas and in the waters of the United States.

"And whereas an Executive proclamation has been already issued, requiring the persons engaged in these disorderly proceedings to desist therefrom, calling out a militia force for the purpose of repressing the same, and convening Congress in extraordinary session to deliberate and determine thereon, the President with a view to the same purposes before mentioned, and to the protection of public peace and the

lives and property of quiet and orderly citizens pursuing their lawful occupations, until Congress shall have assembled and deliberated on the said unlawful proceedings, or until the same shall have ceased, has further deemed it advisable to set on foot a blockade of the ports within the States aforesaid, and in pursuance of the laws of the United States and the law of nations in such case provided.

"For this purpose a competent force will be posted so as to prevent the entrance and exit of vessels from the ports aforesaid.

"If, therefore, with a view to violate such blockade, any vessel shall attempt to leave any of said ports, the vessel will be duly warned by the commander of one of said blockading vessels, who will endorse cn her register the fact and date of such naming, and if the same vessel shall again attempt to enter or leave the blockaded port, she will be captured and sent to the nearest commercial port, for such proceedings against her and her cargo as may be deemed advisable."

[2] In April, 1861, a resolution was adopted by the New York Chamber of Commerce : "That the United States Government be recommended

28

speed. The entire naval force available for defence of the whole
Atlantic coast consisted of the *Brooklyn* (twenty-five guns),
and store-ship *Relief* (two guns), while at that date fifty-six officers had resigned. Orders were hurried abroad for the return of
all war-vessels, the navy-yards were filled with operatives, and
day and night were heard the sounds of earnest preparations
for war, and the Navy Department consulted with some of the
most prominent shipping merchants of New York relative to
the enlargement of the navy by purchase and charter.

The blockade of the Atlantic coast, to be recognized by
foreign powers, "must be effective." The Maritime Law, as
laid down by the Treaty of Paris, would have to be observed
by the United States; and though the blockade law does not
define the effectiveness which it prescribes, yet the accepted
opinion of publicists and naval officers was that from "two to
six" vessels at each port would be necessary. To that end,
ships, barks, schooners, sloops, tugs, ferry-boats, anything
that floated and could carry even a howitzer, were accepted
and put in commission by the U. S. Navy Department, to give
an appearance of effectiveness. In addition to vessels-of-war
at the harbors, a novel mode of blockade was adopted—that
of sinking vessels loaded with stone across the main channel
of entrance to Charleston Harbor and the Savannah River,
and the threat to apply the same mode of closure to every
Southern harbor. The rights to open and close ports of entry, that is, to declare which natural harbors shall be revenue
ports and which shall not be open to trade, was never before
understood to carry the right to destroy the natural roadsteads which offered to vessels a harbor of refuge from the
storms of the coast. Mr. Seward, as the diplomatic chief of
his government, was bound to know that such barbarism
would not be tolerated by enlightened governments, and he
ought to have restrained Secretary Welles, of the navy, from
doing an act so wicked and so uncivilized. Lord John Russell's attention was called to the stone blockade by the Liverpool Ship-owners' Association, and replied that:

"Lord Lyons was told that such a cruel plan would seem to imply
despair of the restoration of the Union, the professed object of the war;
for it never could be the wish of the United States Government to destroy
cities from which their own country was to derive a portion of its riches
and prosperity. Such a plan could only be adopted as a measure of revenge, and of irremediable injury against an enemy.

"Lord Lyons was further told that even as a scheme of embittered
and sanguinary war, such a measure would not be justifiable. It would

and urged to blockade the ports of such States
or any other State that shall join them (in secession), and that this measure is demanded for defence in war, as also for protection to the commerce of the United States *versus* those so-called
privateers invited to enroll under the authority
of such States." As a reply to that resolution, a
public meeting in Marietta, Ga., recommended
the Confederate Congress to throw open all Confederate ports to the shipping and commerce of
neutral nations, granting to those who succeeded
in breaking or running the contemplated blockade, remission of all duties and charges; and
also suggested the propriety of a plan to purchase ocean steamers, by some sort of assurance
from Congress to the owners of those vessels,
suitable for war purposes—that upon their successful entry into our ports they would be purchased for our navy, after examination by a
commission, etc.

be a plot against the commerce of all maritime nations, and against the free intercourse of the Southern States of America with the civilized world. Lord Lyons was desired to speak in this sense to Mr. Seward, who it was hoped would disavow the illegal project.

"Now, however, that the project seems to have been carried into effect at Charleston, Lord Lyons will be instructed to make a further representation to Mr. Seward with a view to prevent similar acts of destruction in other ports."

And in January 1862, Lord Lyons, in response to his call for explanation, was told by Mr. Seward that "the Government of the United States had, last spring, with a navy very little prepared for so extensive an operation, undertaken to blockade upwards of 3,000 miles of coast," and that the Secretary of the Navy had reported that he could "stop up the 'large holes' by means of his ships, but that he could not stop up the 'small ones.' It had been found necessary therefore, to close some of the numerous inlets by sinking vessels in the channel." An ambassador has been said to be a "man sent abroad *to lie* for his State," but the stricture, it appears, can as well be applied to the Federal Secretary of the Navy, for the main channel to Charleston Harbor was not a small inlet. Of that stone blockade, the London *Times* of December 17th, 1861, voiced the universal condemnation and execration in which it was held by all enlightened nations.[1] After ridiculing

1 Of that barbarous act the N. Y. *Herald* said: "There are twenty-five vessels, averaging 335 tons each, and they will be so heavily loaded with stone that, when once sunk, it will be no easy matter to raise them. They will thus become the real blockading fleet, that no storm or fog can interfere with or no small craft pass by. The following are the names of the vessels purchased:

Date.			
1861.	Names.	Port.	Tons.
Oct. 16	Ship Cerea	New London..	356
"	Bark Tenedos	"	245
"	Ship Lewis	"	308
"	Bark Fortune	"	292
"	Ship Robin Hood	Mystic	395
Oct. 17	Ship Archer	New Bedford..	322
"	Bark Cossack	"	254
"	Bark Amazon	Fairhaven	318
"	Bark Frs. Henrietta.	New Bedford..	407
Oct. 18	Bark Garland	"	243
Oct. 21	Bark Harvest	Fairhaven	314
"	Bark America	Edgartown	329
"	Ship Timor	Sag Harbor	289
"	Ship Meteor	Mystic	324
Oct. 22	Ship Rebecca Sims	Fairhaven	400
Oct. 23	Ship L. C. Richmond.	New Bedford.	341
"	Ship Courier	"	381
"	Ship Maria Theresa	"	330
"	Ship Kensington	"	357
"	Ship Herald	"	274
Oct. 28	Ship Potomac	Nantucket	356
"	Bark Peter Demill	New York	300
"	Ship Phoenix	New London..	400
Nov. 1	Bark Leonidas	New Bedford.	231
"	Bark South America.	"	606

25 Vessels ....Total tons...... 8,376
Average tonnage 335

On the day of sailing (the 20th inst.) the captains of the different vessels received sealed orders respecting the destination of the fleet, with injunctions not to open the same until they were out at sea and the pilots had taken their departure. The following is a copy in blank of one of these orders:

SECRET ORDERS.

To Captain ——:—Sir— The ——, now under your command, having been purchased by the Navy Department for service on the Southern coast of the United States, the following are your orders for your proposed voyage:—

You will proceed from this port on —— the —— inst., or with the first fair wind, and when clear of the land make a direct passage to the port of ——, and there deliver your ship to the commanding officer of the blockading fleet off said port, taking his receipt for her to return to me. After the delivery of your vessel, yourself and crew will be provided with passages to the port of New York by the Navy Department, and on arrival there you will call on ——, who will furnish you funds to return to this port.

On the voyage down it would be well, as far as practicable, to keep in company of your consorts, to exhibit lights by night and sound horns or bells in case of fog near the coast.

You will also examine daily the pipe in the quarter of your ship under water, to see that it remains safe.

The only service required of you is the safe delivery of your vessel; and as she is old and heavily laden, you will use special care that she sustains no damage from unskillful seamanship or want of prudence and care.

On a close approach to your port of destination, begin to put between-decks cargo into lower hold, and before anchoring permanently, have your second anchor and chain (if you have one), secured on deck. On leaving your vessel, unless otherwise ordered, you will bring away papers, chronometer, charts, compasses, spyglass and

with pungent severity the naval operations of the United States during 1861, the *Times* said :

" The blockade has been so notoriously a failure that nothing but the extraordinary scrupulousness of the European powers has allowed it to continue. Ships have passed in and out at all times just as they pleased, and, so far as the harbors are concerned, there has never been any difficulty in getting into them or in getting out of them. The Federal government has itself emphatically admitted the failure of their naval blockade by an act of barbarity which is unparalleled in the history of national wars. They have actually endeavored to undo what Columbus had done— to shut up from all mankind forever the ports which the great discoverer opened to the human race, and to destroy by artificial impediments the gates by which men of all nations enter and pass out of some millions of square miles of fertile and productive lands. *This is a crime against all human kind.* If it does not call down universal opposition, it is only because the enterprise is believed to be as impossible as its design is execrable."

The blockade announced by the proclamation of April 19th was extended by that of May 27th to Virginia and North Carolina, and embraced the whole Atlantic coast from the capes of Virginia to the mouth of the Rio Grande.

The terms of the proclamations were that "a competent force will be posted so as to prevent entrance and exit of vessels," and it further provided that "if with a view to violate such blockade, a vessel shall approach or shall attempt to leave any of the said ports, she will be duly warned by the commander of one of the blockading vessels, who will endorse on her register the fact of such warning, and if the same vessel shall again attempt to enter or leave the blockaded port, she will be captured and sent to the nearest convenient port for such proceedings against her, and her cargo as prize, as may be deemed advisable."

The blockade thus proclaimed, was referred to by Mr. Welles as "necessary to interdict commerce at those ports where duties could not be collected"—but that " in performing this *domestic municipal duty,* the property and interests of foreigners" would be guarded by a fifteen days' notice of blockade and a warning before seizure. A blockade carries with it, under the law of nations, the right of visitation and search, which a " domestic municipal duty " did not embrace. If the proclamation of Blockade was merely *domestic municipal duty,* it could not be so exercised as to hinder and embarrass

any other valuable portable articles not required by the commander of the blockading fleet there, and return them safely to me.

In case of disaster to preclude going on, you can call at Fortress Monroe, Hampton Roads, to repair damages, reporting to the flag-officer there.

Wishing you a safe and speedy passage, I am, yours respectfully, —— ——.'

By an examination of the list of vessels comprising the fleet it will be seen that most of them hail from the New England States. In the bottom of each vessel a hole is bored, into which is fitted a piece of lead pipe, five inches in

diameter, with a valve attached, so that the water can be let in with a velocity calculated to sink any of the ships in the space of fifteen or twenty minutes. In case the valves should not work as well as expected each vessel is furnished with large augers, so that there will be no difficulty whatever on the score of sinking.

The crews—which consist of six men to each vessel, will be returned to this city by the men-of-war who assist in the work of sinking. It is intended that the stone vessels shall be anchored broadside in the channel and then sunk, and that the crews shall not leave them until the work has been securely performed."

the commerce of foreign nations. Thus, both Mr. Seward and Mr. Welles blundered in the early days of the war. A blockade may begin by public announcement or proclamation, or by merely stationing a naval force before the port intended to be blockaded. But proclamation without the naval force would not be tolerated — for blockade by mere notification would have been a paper blockade which all nations would have resisted, and a blockade by actual present force could only apply to the particular harbor where the force was stationed. The proclamations, while announcing a blockade *by notification*, also included a *de facto* blockade. By the latter a breach of blockade could only be considered as attempted after notification on the register of the ship and a subsequent attempt to enter. At the date of the two proclamations of intended blockade, there was no naval force at the disposal of Mr. Welles to make a *de facto* blockade, hence it was not until late in the summer of 1861 that the entire coast witnessed the presence of an actual blockading force. Prof. Soley points out the defects of the proclamations :

"In the statement about warning, therefore, the President's proclamation said either to much or too little. If it was intended, as the language might seem to imply, that during the continuance of the blockade—which as it turned out, was the same thing as during the continuance of the war—all neutral vessels might approach the coast and receive individual warning, and that only upon such warning would they be liable to capture, it conceded far more than usage required. If it meant simply that the warning would be given at each point for such time after the force was posted as would enable neutrals generally to become aware of the fact, it conveyed its meaning imperfectly."

And the author might have added that if the proclamation meant both, and was so drawn as to cover any contingency that might arise, it was most likely that Mr. Seward intended this last interpretation. That the proclamation fixed no time for warning to cease, that it permitted such errors as that of Pendegrast, the comprehensiveness of which included ports of North Carolina,[1] where no force was stationed, and that at Charleston, where vessels where warned off the *whole* coast, though no ship of war was at Savannah, were errors which subsequently involved the United States in difficulties which resulted in the payment of "a round sum to their owners in damages for the loss of a market, which was caused by the official warning."

The British consul at Mobile was on May 8th advised by Lord Lyons, that :

"The best advice you can give British ships is to get off as fast as possible, without serious inconvenience. After the effective blockade

---

[1] The following is a copy of the notice of the blockade of Southern ports endorsed on the registers of all vessels, foreign and domestic, bound into the Chesapeake :

"Prussian bark *Edward* from Bremen bound to Baltimore, boarded by United States steam-ship *Quaker City*, of United States blockading squadron, and warned not to enter any port of Virginia, nor any other port of the United States to the south of it.

"S. W. MATHER, *Acting Master U. S. Navy.*
"Off Cape Henry, 18th May, 1861."

has commenced they will be allowed fifteen days to take their departure, but they will not be allowed to carry out any cargo, or part of a cargo, taken on board after the effective blockade was actually begun. Indeed, according to the rules of blockade, I believe they will be liable to confiscation for attempting to go out with a cargo shipped after the commencement of a blockade. But the effective blockade does not begin until the blockading squadron actually appears off the port. The President's proclamation is only the declaration of an intention to blockade."

In the latter part of May, before the arrival off Charleston, S. C., of any blockading vessels, the British schooner *Eliza and Catharine* entered that port, discharged her cargo and loaded immediately, and was proceeding to sea when she was brought to by a shot from the *Minnesota*, and her captain compelled to go on board the man-of-war. After examination the schooner was ordered back to Charleston to discharge her cargo and leave in ballast. Robert Bunch, her Britannic Majesty's consul at Charleston, immediately visited the *Minnesota*, and convinced her commanding officer that, considering the real facts of the blockade at Charleston, it would be best for him to permit the English schooner to depart with her cargo. This permit was immediately given, but the Norwegian bark, *Admiral Zendenskjord*, which entered Charleston under the very same circumstances as the British schooner, was compelled by the blockading officers to leave in ballast. It was impossible for such partiality not to be suspected of proceeding from the very great difference between the English navy and that of Norway and Sweden, and to conclude, at *that early day*, that the favors of the blockading squadron were confined to the ships that could command the protection of the heaviest squadrons.

The general result of inquiries made by Lord Lyons and other foreign ministers, was communicated under date of May 11th by Lord Lyons to Admiral Milne, and may be summarised as follows :

1. "That the date of the commencement of the blockade in each locality will be fixed by the issue of a notice by the commanding officer of the squadron appointed to blockade it. It does not, however, appear to be intended that such notice shall be officially communicated to the governments of neutral nations, or to their representatives in this country.

2. "That fifteen days from the beginning of the effective blockade will be allowed in every case for neutral vessels already in port to put to sea.

3. "That until the fifteen days have expired neutral vessels will be allowed to come out with or without cargoes, and whether their cargoes were shipped before or after the commencement of the blockade.

4. "That except in the last mentioned particular, the ordinary rules of blockade will be strictly enforced.

5. "The armed vessels of neutral States will have the right to enter and depart from the blockaded ports.

"*I continue to be of opinion that, provided the blockade be effective, and be carried on in conformity with the law of nations, we have no other course, in the absence of positive instructions from her Majesty's government, than to recognize it.*"

In October following Lord Lyons addressed to her Majesty's consuls in the Confederate ports the following instructions for their government, and the letter of Mr. Seward as to the commencement of the blockade :

WASHINGTON, Oct. 16th, 1861.

" SIR : On the 11th of May last I made to Her Majesty's consuls in the Southern States the following announcement :

" ' Neutral vessels will be allowed fifteen days to leave port after the actual commencement of the blockade, whether such vessels are with or without cargoes, and whether the cargoes were shipped before or after the commencement of the blockade.'

" I enclose herewith a copy of a note which I have received to-day from the Secretary of State of the United States, and in which he informs me that the law of blockade, which does not permit a vessel in a blockaded port to take on board cargo after the commencement of the blockade, will be.expected to be strictly observed by all vessels in ports blockaded by the naval forces of the United States.

" You will take note of this communication of the Secretary of State for your own guidance and that of the masters of British vessels ; and you will mark carefully, and report to me, the exact date at which the present dispatch and its enclosure reach you.

" You will, without delay, send copies of this dispatch and its enclosure to your vice-consuls, for their information and guidance.

" I am, sir, your most obedient, humble servant,   LYONS.

" *To Her Majesty's Consul at* ———"

" DEPARTMENT OF STATE,)
" WASHINGTON, Oct. 16th, 1861.)

" MY LORD : The Judge of the Court of the United States for the Southern district of New York having recently decided, after elaborate argument of counsel, that the law of blockade does not permit a vessel, in a blockaded port, to take on board cargo after the commencement of the blockade, with a view to avoid any future misunderstanding upon this subject you are informed that the law, as thus interpreted by the judge, will be expected to be strictly observed by all vessels in ports of insurgent States during their blockade by the naval forces of the United States. I avail myself, etc.,   WILLIAM H. SEWARD.

" *The Right Honorable* LORD LYONS."

The great interest taken by foreign nations in the blockade of the ports of the Confederate States will be appreciated from the facts that, in 1860, shipments of tobacco alone amounted to twenty millions of dollars annually, upon which the governments of Europe collected as follows : England, duty on tobacco $21,000,000; Holland, duty on tobacco $20,000,000; revenue in France $18,000,000, revenue in Spain $5,000,000— making a total of $64,000,000 of revenue. When to that sum is added the support derived by thousands of operatives in the manufacture of tobacco, as well as the profits arising from its sale, the hardships of a blockade which could prevent tobacco from reaching Europe would rise into national importance. The cotton exportation of $150,000,000 was the chief support of over five millions of people engaged in its manufacture. The consideration of the effects which a stoppage of exportation of the chief products of the Confederate

States would have upon European nations, created expectations both in the United States and in the Confederate States which were never realized. In the United States the hopes and expectations were stated by the New York *Herald* of May 28th, 1861, that as the blockade bars all outlets in every direction—

"England, France and the other European powers will see the necessity of rendering the war as short as possible; and, therefore, they will not acknowledge the Southern Confederacy, or give it any aid or comfort; but, on the contrary, knowing that it is the only way in which a very speedy termination can be put to the conflict, they will give all the assistance possible to the United States government. Otherwise they cannot get tobacco, or cotton, or turpentine, and they cannot sell their manufactured goods in the markets of the South. *They are completely in our power.* A short war is manifestly the interest of the European nations, and as soon as they understand that any recognition of the Southern Confederacy is likely to prolong the war, they will consult their interest by adopting that course which will put a speedy end to it."

And in the Confederate States the power and resources of "King Cotton" to lift the blockade, admit Confederate cruisers to the Admiralty Courts of foreign nations, and to a speedy recognition of the independence and nationality of the government, was a hope and a belief that never entirely departed from either the government or the people.

Her Majesty's Secretary of State for Foreign Affairs, speaking of the blockade, represented the necessity that existed in England for a supply of cotton, and said : "Thousands are now obliged to resort to the poor-rates for subsistence, owing to this blockade, yet her Majesty's government have not sought to take advantage of the obvious imperfection of this blockade, in order to declare it ineffective. They have, to the loss and detriment of the British nation, scrupulously observed the duties of Great Britain to friendly States." The London *Post* (Lord Palmerston's organ), of July 24th, denying the effectiveness of the blockade, asserted that Charleston had been left for some time without any blockading force, and Admiral Milne, in obedience to orders from home, issued instructions to a frigate under his command that "no port is to be considered efficiently blockaded if any vessel can enter or depart from it unknown to or in spite of the blockading squadron—that an efficient blockade necessitates the complete cutting off of all maritime ingress or egress, and the escape of the *third* vessel from the blockading squadron signifies the invalidity of the blockade."

By that test there was no effective blockade at any Confederate port, and yet England respected a blockade which produced such distresses at home, rather than aid a Confederacy whose-corner stone was to be slavery. The "invalidity of the blockade" by the standard test of Admiral Milne was demonstrated in *one* day at Charleston. A correspondent of the New York *Times*, on board the U. S. steamer *Roanoke,* flag - ship Blockading Squadron off Charleston, Saturday, August 17th, 1861—writes :

" About 8:30 o'clock in the evening of the next day lights were seen crawling along close in shore, in the direction of the harbor, one of which was made out to be quite a large sail, but she passed in *safely*. Since that event other sails have been duly reported. It is but proper to state that the blockading squadron, composed at present of the *Roanoke*, the gunboats *Seminole* and *Iroquois*, and the sloop-of-war *Vandalia*, lay at least twelve miles from the entrance of the harbor.

" But if this should occasion surprise, what will your readers think when they are told that on the 9th inst. a Secession steamer ran the blockade ? She was first seen puffing away toward the coast, on our starboard bow. After spending much valuable time in staring through glasses, hoisting signals, and examining signal books, the *Vandalia* was finally ordered in pursuit, but having only a quarter wind, you may judge the result. After the steamer had made good her retreat, the *Seminole* made chase. Hardly had the excitement of this event subsided, when another steamer, emboldened by the success of the former, accomplished the same exploit."

At Wilmington, Sept. 30th, the steamer *Kate* and two schooners successfully ran the blockade, and though one of the latter grounded on the bar, yet she succeeded in landing her cargo, and was subsequently brought into port. In further evidence of the ineffectiveness of the blockade, and of the strange conduct of England in sustaining its pretended effectiveness, the Evening *Express,* of Halifax, N. C., in August published the following :

" The two principal ports of North Carolina, Wilmington and Beaufort, we learn, have not been and are not now under blockade, and an active trade is carried on in the export of naval stores and the import of provisions. Recent accounts state that six vessels were loading in Beaufort and four in Wilmington, which would shortly sail for Nassau, N. P., and other British ports. The reason the blockade has not been made effective at these two ports is said to be that the government is poorly provided with vessels of draft sufficiently light to enable them to lay off these harbors. Taking advantage of this fact, the rebels are profiting in the exportation of the principal product of the State — naval stores — and weekly receive cargoes of provisions from vessels of light draft, from Nassau, N. P. As a proof of this two vessels have arrived at this port lately from North Carolina, one on Sunday and another yesterday afternoon, both laden with naval stores. It is stated that they had not the slightest difficulty in leaving. Both vessels, we understand, belong to the same person, and we have no doubt that he will make a handsome thing out of the transaction. There have been three arrivals at this port from the same place a few weeks ago."

Nova Scotian vessels continued " to do a good business at the South," and many were " making arrangements to receive a share of the profits to be realized by running the blockade." The sympathies of the people at St. John's, N. B., were largely in favor of the Confederates, and the ship *Alliance,* which sailed from England with a cargo of munitions of war, upon being ordered off from Charleston by the blockading squadron, proceeded to St. John's, N. B., where she added to her contraband list " $1,100 worth of tin plate, $1,200 worth of block tin, $950 worth of quicksilver, etc.. etc., all of which was landed alongside of the *Alliance*; and a correspondent of the Merchants' Exchange states that Mr. Lafitte (the owner) and the captain (both citizens of Charleston) have been pur- chasing, from time to time, such further supplies as would in- dicate a 'forward movement' to Palmettodom. The *Alliance* has kept the 'Confederate flag' flying since her arrival, not- withstanding the protests of the American sea captains and other citizens of St. John."

These, together with many other illustrations and examples of an ineffective blockade, caused the dispatch of the British Admiral Milne with a squadron of "thirty-five men-of-war" to the Gulf of Mexico. The arrival of the British fleet in Southern waters encouraged the hopes of the Confederate peo- ple of an early rupture between England and the United States, the consequence of which would be the recognition of the Con- federate States.

The Mobile *Advertiser and Register* of August 4th thus expressed the hope that was entertained by all classes of peo- ple in the Confederacy :

" Perhaps everybody does not know what a formidable fleet of British ships-of-war are now occupying our Gulf waters, lying right within striking distance of Lincoln's blockaders, whom they are watching with sleepless vigilance and 'evident anxiety to pick a quarrel with on this blockade question.' We have good authority for stating that the British fleet of the Gulf, under Admiral Milne, numbers no less than thirty-five men-of- war, each carrying heavy metal and equipped on a war footing. We know, of course, that this armada is not here to operate against the Con- federacy. We know this, without the avowal of the British government and every other authority, that its object is to oversee and investigate the doings of Lincoln's blockaders.

" Being opposed to the operations of our enemies the British fleet is necessarily in *quasi*, but as yet inactive, alliance with us. It is in our waters as a naval 'corps of observation,' and in force which gives it power at any time to become 'a corps of operation.' Here in our waters will it stay, awaiting a possible, perhaps probable, moment of action, when the British government may deem it necessary to raise the blockade. Should the war not be sooner concluded, we may expect that during the latter part of next fall Great Britain, and perhaps France, will offer to mediate. If the infatuated North rejects propositions we may expect to hear from the British fleet of the Gulf. The way it will run off the Lincolnite ships and open our ports will be a caution to tyrants.

" The tone of Admiral Milne's report to the British government, the substance of which we have published, indicates more fully than any- thing has done heretofore the position of Great Britain with regard to the blockade."

That the possession of the cotton in the Confederate States was as much a motive with the Washington authorities for the blockade, as for the restoration of the Union, will appear very plainly by considering the legislation that followed sharp' upon the proclamation of blockade. By the Act of the United States Congress July 13th, 1861, " to provide for the collection of duties on imports, *and for other purposes*," a forfeiture was

declared of all goods coming from the States of the Confederacy into the United States, with a convenient *proviso,* which
authorized the President "to license and permit commercial
intercourse" with any part of any State in the Confederacy,
"in such articles, and for such time, and by such persons,"
as he may "think conducive to the public interest;" and he
was authorized to establish rules and regulations for the government of such "commercial intercourse," and to do any
other thing that would conduce to the early acquisition of
"all goods and chattels, wares and merchandise" of the people
of the South. While foreign nations were shut out by the
blockade, the President of the United States, having declared
war against the Confederate States by his proclamation of
blockade, was authorized to open up commercial intercourse
with the States, from dealing with whom all other nations were
interdicted. This law authorized the President to proclaim
"an insurrection," whereupon all "commercial intercourse"
was to cease, and all property be confiscated to the United
States. According to the Republican theory the Southern States
were *in the Union,* but in rebellion to its authority ; and if so,
what part of the Constitution authorized Congress to confiscate property and to declare the forfeiture of all goods *in
transitu ?* As between independent nations at war, all commercial intercourse ceases ; but to apply that principle to the
war between the States would have been to recognize their
independence. It was necessary, therefore, to force the Constitution beyond any interpretation yet given to it, and declare
the people to be insurrective, but not at war—to be liable to
blockade, but open to commercial intercourse under the President's permit—to shut out from Europe the cotton and tobacco
of those States, but to open the back door of the United States
to all that could be gotten under license and permit. A book
of "rules and regulations, prescribed by the Secretary of the
Treasury with the approval of the President, concerning commercial intercourse with and in States and parts of States in
insurrection," etc., etc.—was issued to legalize an illegal traffic,
if there existed war between independent States, and unconstitutional if there was merely an insurrection or rebellion to
be suppressed. The law was pronounced unconstitutional,
null and void by Chief Justice Taney in the Carpenter case;
but that made little difference with men and a party which
were running the war on fictions of law and constitution, and
regardless of all the restraints which were declared by the
plainest provisions and principles of American liberty. The
rulings of Chief Justice Taney were of little avail, until supplemented by the orders of General Grant on March 10th, 1865, sus-
pending all these permits; but even he was compelled to revoke
that order on the 11th of April; but on April 29th these regulations ceased by notice of the conquest and subjugation of the
Southern States.

That the administration at Washington forecasted, as early as July, 1861, the effect upon European public sentiment which a stoppage of the cotton supply would create, is hardly to be accepted. These laws and regulations were more likely the results of national and individual cupidity than instrumentalities for securing a supply of cotton to palliate the anger of European public sentiment. But whether these measures proceeded from consummate forecast or from the greed of gain, they preceded by a year the hints of the governments of Great Britain and France, "informally expressed" to Mr. Seward, "for some further relaxation of the blockade in favor of that trade."[1]

The "relaxation," which the laws and regulations above mentioned had given to the scarcity of cotton, was not enough for the English market, and "further" relaxation was suggested. These hints were "not rejected, but are held under consideration, with a view to ascertain more satisfactorily whether they are really necessary, and whether they can be adopted without such serious detriment to our military operations as would render them injurious to the interest of all concerned," and to appease the British sentiment. Mr. Seward added : "We shall speedily open all the channels of commerce and free them from military embarrassments, and cotton, so much desired by all nations, will flow as freely as heretofore. We have ascertained that there are three and a half millions of bales yet remaining in the regions where it was produced, though large quantities of it are yet unginned and otherwise unprepared for market. We have instructed the military authorities to favor, as far as they can consistently with the public safety, its preparation for and dispatch to the markets where it is so much wanted."

From these extracts it is evident that England and France had made some demands on Mr. Seward, with which he was endeavoring to comply, and yet not yield entirely to the pressure from abroad. The contemporaneous expression of New York newspapers are not without light upon those hints which Mr. Seward had received. By the New York *Herald* it was said:

"That the British fleet have not already broken it [the blockade] is owing to an unwillingness to have an open rupture with the United States, and the policy of waiting to see what might turn up — whether our government would defeat the rebels in a decisive battle and thus get cotton for England, or whether the rebels would defeat our government and thus impose on England the necessity of getting cotton for herself. It is now less than two months till the cotton crop will be ready for shipment, and of course it will be necessary for the English government to give previous notice to British merchants and ship-owners that the blockade will not be respected by England, and that they can safely send their vessels for the Southern staple. We may, therefore, at any moment hear of a royal proclamation in Great Britain and Ireland declaring the blockade inefficient, invalid and void."

[1] Mr Seward to Mr. Adams, July 28th, 1862.

The "relaxation" suggested by Lord Lyons to Mr. Seward came in a very limited and unsatisfactory degree from the instruction to collectors of revenue, at the captured ports of Beaufort, Port Royal and New Orleans, issued May 23d, 1862.[1] These "instructions," which were regarded as orders to open certain cotton ports to European trade, were received in England with hope, which was soon disappointed. The London *Times*, of May 17th, before the issue of those instructions, pointed out what might be done from New Orleans:

"Since the beginning of the war both North and South have had a common idea, which has filled the one with anxiety and the other with hope. The Americans have not been able to free themselves from the suspicion that cotton is really king, and that England would go to any extremity to show her allegiance to the sovereign lord of her manufactures. The attitude of the French Emperor and the murmuring of the French operatives have also given the North serious fears. We are almost justified in saying that the expeditions to various points of the Atlantic coast, such as Beaufort, Hatteras, and Newberne, and the occupation of these places, without the hope of producing the smallest effect on the war, have been measures really prompted by the desire to open a cotton port, and thus take away the pretext of European powers for intervening in the affairs of the war.

"The capture of New Orleans makes that easy which before would have hardly been possible. It would have been but a mockery to ask Lancashire to send ships to Beaufort for cotton ; but now that the great emporium of the Mississippi and the access to millions of acres of cotton-growing land are now in the power of the Federals, *it is their obvious policy to declare the trade with New Orleans open, and to let the refusal to supply cotton for the wants of Europe lie on the planters who still assert their allegiance to the Southern Republic.*"

[1] WASHINGTON, May 23d.—The following is a copy of the instructions transmitted to various Collectors of Customs :

"TREASURY DEPARTMENT, May 23d, 1862.

"SIR : In pursuance of the provisions of the Proclamation of the President modifying the blockade of the ports of Beaufort, Port Royal and New Orleans, and of the regulations of the Secretary of the Treasury relating to trade with those ports, no articles contraband of war will be permitted to enter at either of the said ports, and you will accordingly refuse clearance to vessels bound for these ports or either of them with any such articles on board. Until further instructed you will regard as contraband of war the following articles, viz :

"Cannon, mortars, firearms, pistols, bombs, grenades, firelocks, flints, matches, powder, saltpetre, bales, bullets, pikes, swords, sulphur, helmets or boarding caps, sword belts, saddles and bridles (always excepting the quantity of the said articles which may be necessary for the defence of the ship, and of those who compose the crew), cartridge bag material, percussion and other caps, clothing adapted for uniforms, resin, sail cloth of all kinds, hemp and cordage, masts, ship timber, tar and pitch, ardent spirits, military persons in the service of the enemy, dispatches of the enemy, and articles of like character, with these specially enumerated.

"You will also refuse clearances to all vessels which, whatever the ostensible destination, are believed by you on satisfactory grounds to be intended for ports or places in possession or under control of insurgents against the United States, or that there is imminent danger that the goods, wares, or merchandise, of whatever description laden, or such vessels, will fall into the possession or under the control of insurgents; and in all cases where, in your judgment, there is ground for apprehension that any goods, wares, or merchandise shipped to your port will be used in any way for the aid of insurgents or the insurrection, you will require substantial security to be given that such goods, wares or merchandise shall not be transported to any place under insurrectionary control, and shall not in any way be used to give aid or comfort to such insurgents.

"You will be especially careful, upon applications for clearances, to require bonds with sufficient sureties, conditioned for fulfilling faithfully all the conditions imposed by law or departmental regulations, from shippers of the following articles to the ports opened, or to any other ports from which they may easily be, and are probably intended to be, reshipped in aid of the existing insurrection, viz :—Liquors of all kinds, coal, iron, lead, copper, tin, brass, telegraphic instruments, wire, porous cups, platina, sulphuric acid, zinc, and all other telegraphic materials, marine engines, screw propellers, paddle wheels, cylinders, cranks, shafts, boilers, tubes for boilers, fire bars, and every article, or any other component part of an engine or boiler, or any article whatever, which is, can or may become applicable to the manufacture of marine machinery, or for the armor of vessels. I am, very respectfully,

"S. P. CHASE,
"*Secretary of the Treasury.*"

The refusal to supply Europe with cotton through the captured ports followed from the patriotic action of the planters withholding their cotton from markets held by the Federal forces. The press throughout the Confederacy, public sentiment in every State, and the best interest of society and individuals, united in urging the planters not to send their cotton to either the interior towns or ports—that the farmer and planter should keep his cotton at home, avoid the cost of storage and transportation, the certainty of confiscation and seizure at ports held by Federal authority, and lastly that the *torch*[1] was his more patriotic weapon than even the price which his cotton might bring through intermediary agency of his country's enemy. While these considerations did not prevent some cotton from going forward to market, yet the amount was so small that the demand in Europe did not experience much more relief after the fall of Beaufort, Port Royal and New Orleans than before the sailing of the expeditions which were set on foot, with the double purpose of *blockade* and of *opening* cotton ports ; the former to prevent cotton from going forward to Europe, the latter for the purpose of sending cotton forward to Northern markets without the Confederates realizing upon its value.

Another part of this scheme for getting hold of the cotton and other staple products of the States of the Confederacy were the Acts of March 12th, 1863, and July 2d, 1864: " Concerning commercial intercourse between loyal and insurrectionary States, and to provide for the collection of captured and abandoned property, and the *prevention of frauds* in States declared in insurrection ;" and the Act of July 17th, 1862 : " To suppress insurrection, to punish treason and rebellion, to *seize* and *confiscate* the *property* of rebels, and for other purposes." That each and all of these acts had an " eye to business " as well as to patriotism. a purpose to " turn a penny " while restoring the Union, is apparent from even their titles. The scheme overreached the purpose of its inventors, and while it made money for the " baser sort " it impeded military operations to such an extent that Gen. Grant wrote, July 21st, 1863 ·

" My experience in West Tennessee has convinced me that any trade whatever with the rebellious States is weakening to us at least thirty per cent. of our force. No matter what restrictions are thrown around

---

[1] " In 1862, all the planters on the water courses opposed to invasion, had burnt their cotton. This was done in obedience to orders cheerfully obeyed by the people, who were perfectly willing to sacrifice their wealth as well as their lives to attain, or rather to *retain*. as they supposed, their liberties. In 1862 I stood on the balcony of my then pleasant home, and saw the volumes of smoke ascending on every side, for miles and miles, which marked the spots where the planters were burning their crops of cotton, in obedience to Beauregard's orders in the face of the gunboats ascending the Mississippi River. Many of the plantations were nearly submerged by the breaking of the Levee. One gentleman boated his cotton, 550 bales, from his gin-house to an Indian mound, the only spot upon his place that was dry, and burnt it there, on that tumulus of a buried race. This all seems very strange now. but we were desperately in earnest at that time. This cotton - burning was then the policy of the Confederate Government."— *Recollections of Henry Watkins Allen, by Sarah A. Dorsey,* p. 281.

In the winter of 1864 the intention of destroying all the cotton in the State of Louisiana, exposed to Federal capture and invasion, was seriously entertained by Gen. E. Kirby Smith, C. S. A.

trade, if any whatever is allowed, it will be made the means of supplying to the enemy what they want. Restriction, if lived up to, makes trade unprofitable, and hence none but dishonest men go into it. I will venture to say, that no honest man has made money in West Tennessee, in the last year, while many fortunes have been made there during the time. The people in the Mississippi Valley are now nearly subjugated. Keep trade out for a few months, and I doubt not but that the work of subjugation will be so complete that trade can be opened freely with the States of Arkansas, Louisiana and Mississippi."

The *traders* were too strong in influence at Washington for Gen. Grant, and the trade under the license system continued until an end was put to it by a return of peace.

Intimately connected with and growing out of the right to blockade an enemy's port, is the belligerent's right of visitation and search of neutral vessels to prevent a breach of blockade. No nation has more strenuously opposed the exercise of this right than the United States; to enforce "free trade and sailors' rights" the United States went to war with Great Britain in 1812–15, and up to 1861 the United States had championed the rights of neutrals, maintaining the perfect right of a neutral to trade with either belligerent, without restraint as to contraband of war or restrictions of any kind upon the citizens, whether as fillibusters, privateers or sympathizers. No sooner was the war between the States over than the United States Congress returned to its "first love" and asserted the very doctrines of which it complained when practiced by England. The Banks' bill, No. 806, in the Thirty-ninth Congress, first session, enacted in its tenth section "that nothing in this act shall be so construed as to prohibit citizens of the United States from selling vessels, ships or steamers built within the limits thereof, or materials or munitions of war, the growth or product of the same, to inhabitants of other countries, or to governments not at war with the United States."

That England made no objection to the severest exercise of the right of search was because, as expressed by the London *Times:*

"*It is certainly not for our interest as a nation to impeach the belligerent right of search*, and, if the Federals have not actually exceeded their privileges, it *would be impolitic as well as unjust to interfere with their proceedings.* They cannot be allowed to presume, or to encroach; nor can they reasonably complain if we look with more than ordinary suspicion on the movements of an officer so notorious as Commodore Wilkes. Within these limits, however, they are free to exert that power which their maritime ascendancy gives them, and we must say that, with the exception of the case of the *Gladiator,* they do not appear to have materially overstepped their rights. That they have gone to the very verge of illegality is by no means improbable, but neither is it improbable that they have had sound reasons for their eagerness. They assumed, and perhaps with sufficient warrant, that in the Bermuda waters were lying ships consigned to their enemies, which would be lawful prize at sea, but which would be likely enough to elude them if they got clear away. They, therefore, lingered about the harbor and hung about the offing as long as they could justifiably do so, and perhaps a little longer.

They watched the port so closely as almost to blockade it, and they stopped vessels that might have been reasonably allowed to pass without challenge.

"In these proceedings there may have been something extravagant, as well as much that was provoking ; but, on the other side, there was probably the practical provocation of successful smuggling. The population of the islands, we may be pretty sure, is Southern in its sympathies, and many a cargo has doubtless been run through the aid to the venture which these harbors have furnished. The Federals know this, and it is but natural that they should strive, by all the means in their power, to break up the trade. Whether in these proceedings they have transgressed the rules of international law, or whether they have limited their operations *to the sharp practice of a baffled and vindictive belligerent*, is more than we can precisely say at present. In the former case they must be brought to reason ; and they may well indeed be content to observe a law which is operating so decidedly in their own favor. But if, as we should be disposed to surmise, they have done little more than press their privileges as rigorously as possible under the provocation given them by a brisk contraband traffic, *we think we may as well make allowance for their temptations, and put ourselves in their place before we pronounce upon their conduct.*"

The remark that Bermuda was watched so closely "as to almost blockade it" was confirmed in literal truth by the report of the master of the British schooner *Albert,* of Liverpool, that his ship had been stopped and searched by an officer from the *Mercedita* in English waters, and who added:

"Now, in all this there is nothing to complain of if the Bahama Islands and the passages are under blockade by the United States naval force, since all the customary forms prescribed for such a case were complied with ; but up to the time of my sailing from Nassau no notice of such blockade had been made public, and I have been unable to find any such notice in the newspapers since my return to England.

"The United States vessels now on duty off Abaco are the *Mercedita, Quaker City* and *Albatross,* and *their vigilance and attention to the business in hand are such that no vessel bound to or from Nassau can pass either way without being overhauled and searched,* except by a rare and fortunate accident. Such vessels as the commander of the cruiser fancies he seizes ; others he permits to escape. I consider myself fortunate in being among the latter on the present occasion."[1]

The considerations which, apart from the law of nations, induced England to put a construction so lenient upon the practices of Federal cruisers arose from *her own national interests*. The part then being played by the Federal cruisers on the ocean against the commerce of the Confederate States, was exactly that part which England had played very frequently, and which she meant to play again, whenever occasion and opportunity offered. It was as a belligerent and not as a neutral, that she appealed to the doctrines of public law, and it was not to her interest to depreciate or curtail those

---

[1] "I am ignorant, I confess, of the laws of blockade, or indeed if a law there be that allows its enforcement and penalties to be enacted, five hundred miles away from the ports blockaded. But it did seem strange that the men-of-war of a nation at peace with England should be allowed to cruise off her ports, to stop and examine trading vessels of all descriptions, to capture and send to New York, for adjudication, vessels on the mere suspicion of their being intended blockade-runners, and to chase and fire into real blockade-runners so near to the shore that on one occasion the shot and shell fell into a fishing village, and that within sight of an English man-of-war lying at anchor in the harbor at Nassau."—*Sketches from my life, by the late Admiral Hobart Pasha.*

rights which the law of nations placed in her hand, and which her powerful navy could enforce in future against the United States, and plead the precedents of the Federal cruisers against the Confederate commerce.

"It may be our own lot," continued the *Times*, "any day to receive complaints about unjustifiable captures, and to be put upon our defence for acts committed in the course of war. Both interest and equity, therefore, should dispose us to scan the proceedings of the blockading squadron with reasonable indulgence; but, unhappily, there are not wanting considerations on the other side, also. We cannot overlook the appointment of such an officer as Admiral Wilkes[1] to so peculiar a command, nor can we conceal from ourselves that what is now actually charged against the Federals was imputed to them as a deliberate and concerted policy long ago. Already has Mr. Seward been under the necessity of 'instructing' the officers of the Federal navy to observe the dictates of ordinary law, and though the 'instructions' may be quoted to the credit of the Washington government, they are evidence of the previous lawlessness which rendered them necessary. We must wait, however, for the decisions of the American Prize Courts before we can come to any practical conclusion. If the *Adela*, *Peterhoff* and the *Dolphin* are on sufficient evidence fairly condemned, the question is at an end."

The judicial determination in Prize Courts of the United States, of the vessels mentioned by the *Times*, presented occasions where the established doctrines of international law, as applied to blockade, contraband of war and the right of visitation and search, were carried far beyond the extremest rulings of either English or continental prize courts. In the cases of the

---

[1] The conduct of Admiral Wilkes, to which the *Times* takes exception, was not so much that of the "*Trent* affair" as the following behavior in the harbor of Bermuda, which is to be found in the Acadian *Recorder* of Oct., 11th.

"We have been sadly insulted by the three ships of the Union navy, under command of the notorious Wilkes. Three ships arrived here, direct from New York, in four days, on the 25th ult., said to be in want of coal. The Admiral, with one of his fleet, after being presented with a copy of the Queen's proclamation relative to the twenty-four hours' limit, entered the port of St. George for coal, with the understanding that she was to leave at the latest on Monday morning. Monday came—the diver represented that the Admiral's ship required some repairs to her bottom—but no repairs were attempted. On Tuesday, the ships were still in port. Our Governor and the commandant of the troops went on board, to expostulate with Admiral Wilkes, and he promised to leave on Wednesday. Wednesday came—still the obnoxious vessels were in the limited water of the port, and no symptom of their intention to move. On Thursday morning, however, the Admiral and the gunboats he brought in with him left, and the one that was blockading the port was moved in to take coal and undergo repairs.

"The Admiral was induced to leave at length, it seems, by a communication from the Governor, telling him that if he did not he would compel him. The Admiral, after he got to sea, wrote a very offensive letter to the Governor, accusing him of many things—things, indeed, as such men only as Wilkes could and were guilty of in the port of St. George. It would seem that Wilkes had a double object in coming to Bermuda—first, to insult the authorities,

for he must have known in what a defenceless state we were in, and secondly to capture or destroy the vessels in that port—six steamers—that are engaged, either directly or indirectly, with the Confederate ports, and to destroy the powder, of which there is said to be a large quantity stored on one of the small islands in Castle Harbor. The Admiral and one of his steamers have gone out of sight of land, but the other one, having coaled and repaired, is cruising outside of St. George.

"During this rebellion the Americans have taken many liberties with the British, but I do not think any of them equals this.

"The poor Confederates were sadly frightened, for, knowing the character of the Admiral, they knew he would do anything, however illegal, to destroy them; and the inhabitants of St. George were under great apprehension lest some turn might take place which would result in a row, when they would suffer materially.

"*Monday Morning.*—Two of the Admiral's gunboats still close in with the harbor of St. George."

The Halifax *Reporter* of the same date says:

"Considerable excitement was caused this afternoon by a rumor extensively circulated on the authority of several gentlemen who professed to have inquired into the facts of the case, that the Royal mail steamer *Merlin*, on leaving Bermuda, suffered an indignity somewhat similar to that which the *Trent* experienced on a previous occasion, and at the hands of the same valiant individual. The statement is, that Capt. Wilkes, smarting under the affliction of some slights received at Bermuda, stood off the port until the *Merlin* made her appearance, when she was brought to by the firing of a gun across her bows, and detained until she underwent a close examination of her papers, etc."

Peterhoff, the *Bermuda* and the *Springbok*, the Prize Courts of the United States and the Supreme Court, in its final judgment, announced doctrines of prize law against which almost every writer on international law has since vigorously protested.

The facts in the case of the *Peterhoff* were that she was one of a line of steamers owned by Pile, Spence & Co., of London, and trading between England and Matamoras, Mexico; that she was dispatched from London January 7th, 1863, with a general cargo, containing nothing contraband, and having a regular British and Mexican clearance, and conveying her Majesty's mails, as well as dispatches for the Mexican consul; that she was boarded on the 21st of February, when within three miles of St. Thomas, by an officer from the U. S. S. *Alabama*, who, after examining the ship's papers, permitted her to proceed on her voyage; that just after leaving St. Thomas, and when within sight of that port, the U. S. S. *Vanderbilt* hove in sight, and, having communicated with Admiral Wilkes, went in chase of and stopped the *Peterhoff*, and putting an armed crew on board sent her to the United States as a prize.

The facts of seizure were communicated to Earl Russell by the owners of the *Peterhoff* as early as March 26th, 1863, who, after considering all the papers of the vessel and the statements of her owners, replied that:

"The government of the United States has clearly no right to seize British vessels *bona fide* bound from this country or from any other British possession to the ports of Vera Cruz and Matamoras, or either of them, or *vice versa*, unless such vessels attempt to touch at or have an intermediate or contingent destination to some blockaded port or place, or are carriers of contraband of war destined for the Confederate States; and, in any admitted case of such unlawful capture, her Majesty's government would feel it their duty promptly to interfere, with a view to obtain the immediate restitution of the ship and cargo, with full compensation and without the delay of proceedings in a prize court.

"Her Majesty's government, however, cannot, without violating the rules of international law, claim for British vessels, navigating between Great Britain and these places, any general exemption from the belligerent right of visitation by the cruisers of the United States, nor can they proceed upon any general assumption that such vessels may not so act as to render their capture lawful and justifiable.

"Nothing is more common than for those who contemplate a breach of blockade, for the carriage of contraband, to disguise their purpose by a simulated destination and by deceptive papers; and the situation of the ports on the coast of Mexico, with reference to the Confederate States, is such as to make it not only possible, but in many cases probable, that an ostensible Mexican destination would be resorted to as a cover for objects which would really justify capture. It has already happened, in many cases, that British vessels have been seized while engaged in voyages apparently lawful, which vessels have been afterwards proved in the prize courts to have been really guilty of endeavoring to break the blockade, or of carrying contraband to the Confederates.

"It is the right of the belligerent to capture all vessels reasonably suspected of either of these transgressions of international law, and whenever any cause of capture is alleged the case cannot be withdrawn from the consideration of the prize court of the captor.

" After the case has undergone investigation it is the duty of the prize court to restore any such prizes, unlawfully made, with costs and damages ; and the proper time for the interference of her Majesty's government is in general when the prize courts have refused redress for a capture which the evidence shows to have been unjustifiable.

" Her Majesty's government cannot, upon *ex parte* statements, deny the belligerents in this war the exercise of those rights which, in all wars in which Great Britain has been concerned, she has claimed herself to exercise.

" As regards the allusion which has been made to the case of the *Adela*, before her Majesty's government can form any opinion as to the judgment stated to have been given in that case, they must have before them a correct report of that judgment, it being impossible to rely upon the general representation of its effect contained in a newspaper paragraph, founded on printed letters, especially as none of the other judgments of the United States prize courts, which have been reported to her Majesty's government during the present war, evince any disregard of the established principles of international law.

" As regards, however, the particular case of the *Peterhoff*, in which you are more directly interested, her Majesty's government having taken into consideration the papers transmitted by you, and being satisfied that those papers disclose no *prima facie* ground of capture, and that there is every reason to believe the voyage to have been lawful and *bona fide* and the seizure of the vessel wholly unjustifiable, they will instruct Lord Lyons to make an immediate representation of the circumstances of that case to the government at Washington, and if no legal ground of capture should be alleged, then to press for the release of the vessel and her cargo, with compensation and without the delay of proceedings in the prize court. But if any legal grounds of capture should be alleged by the government of the United States, this case, like all others, must unavoidably follow the ordinary course. I am, sir, your most obedient humble servant."

The British Foreign Office was too fully committed to the extremest doctrine of visitation and search to enter any protest against its exercise, in any apparently legal manner, by the United States, which of all the great nations has been the firmest opponent of its exercise. The cargo of the *Peterhoff* was found upon examination by the prize commissioner to be an assorted one, and if not intended for the Confederates to contain just what they stood very much in need of, there being a very large quantity of quinine and other drugs on board, but nothing contraband of war. Nevertheless, the U. S. District Court, Judge Betts, adjudged the *Peterhoff* a legal prize—because :

" First—That the said ship *Peterhoff*, in the premises mentioned, was knowingly, on the voyage aforesaid, laded in whole or in part with articles contraband of war, and had them in the act of transportation at sea. Second—That her voyage with the said cargo was not truly destined to the port of Matamoras, a neutral port, and for purposes of trade and commerce, within the authority and intendment of public law, but, on the contrary, was destined for some other port or place, and in aid and for the use of the enemy, and in violation of the law of nations. Third— That the ship's papers were simulated and false as to her real destination. Wherefore, it is considered by the Court that the said vessel and her cargo are subject to condemnation and forfeiture, and it is ordered that a decree therefor be entered accordingly."

Four years afterwards the Supreme Court overruled the District Court, and the United States compensated the owners.

Upon the *Peterhoff* there were large quantities of mail matter in sealed packages—which were seized upon by Sec. Welles, and their return positively refused. Mr. Seward and Lord Lyons had, previously to the capture of the *Peterhoff*, agreed that mail bags of any captured vessel shall be forwarded unopened to the governments to which they belonged, or whose seals they bore. The refusal of Sec. Welles to deliver up the mails was brought to the attention of the English Parliament, where it was announced that the mails would be forwarded at once. [1]

But it was not known that the delivery of the mails had been made, only after the interchange of notes between Mr. Seward and Mr. Wells and the active interposition of President Lincoln. [2]

The evidence upon which Judge Betts found the cargo of the *Peterhoff* to be contraband of war, throws some light upon the character and description of goods which were being imported into the Confederacy through the *blockade,* as well as illustrates how the U. S. Courts stretched the doctrine of contraband.

The report filed by the Prize Commissioner contains the following language :

" That a very large portion of the said cargo will be found, on examination of the inventory aforesaid, to be particularly adapted to army use; that a large number of cases contain Blucher boots, which are known as army shoes ; a number of cases contain ' cavalry boots,' and are so labelled, samples of said labels being hereto annexed ; that one hundred and ninety-two bales of the said cargo consists of gray blankets, adapted to the use of an army, and are believed to be such as are used in the United States army ; ninety-five cases contain horse-shoes, of a large size ; thirty-six cases, of a large size, contain artillery harness, in sets for four horses, with two riding saddles attached to each set ; there are also on board two hydraulic presses, in pieces, adapted to cotton. That a considerable portion of said cargo consists of drugs, directed to ' Burchard & Co., successors, Matamoras, Mexico, in which, among an assorted cargo of drugs, quinine, calomel, morphine and chloroform form an important portion. The inventory also showed coiled rope, boxes of tin, of sheet zinc, of hoop and of bar iron, anvils and bellows, and ' other articles of a contraband character.' "

As there are but very few articles of commerce which, in a direct or indirect manner, are not "adapted to army use,"

---

[1] In the House of Commons, on the 5th of May, Lord R. Cecil wished to put a question to the Under Secretary for Foreign Affairs. "Some days since the honorable gentleman told the House that Earl Russell had received a letter stating that Mr. Seward had promised that the mails on board the Peterhoff should be forwarded unopened to their destinations. In the newspapers of yesterday, however, it was stated that the captors—that was, Admiral Wilkes—declined to allow the course to be taken. He wished to know whether the Foreign Office had received any information upon that point, and, if so, what course had been determined upon."

"Mr. Layard said that what he had stated to the House on a former day was strictly in accordance with the information then received by the government. It appeared that a difficulty had arisen in the prize court as to what was to be done with the mail bags, which was referred to Mr. Seward, and he informed Lord Lyons that he had sent orders to New York that the mail bags should be forwarded at once to their destinations without being opened. At the same time —as had been stated by Earl Russell in another place—Mr. Seward informed Lord Lyons that a gentleman was coming to this country to settle with the British government the principles upon which the question of mails found on board captured vessels should be treated. No further information had since been received."

[2] History of the United States Navy, by C. B. Boynton, Vol. II., p. 117.

that criterion of contraband, if recognized by all nations, would prohibit all commerce on the part of neutrals in time of war between any two nations. But the court held that a breach of blockade was intended by a voyage from London to Matamoras, Mexico, and that ruling was made in New York, from which port regular clearances to American vessels were given for Matamoras. But, notwithstanding Americans might trade with Mexico, English vessels were liable to seizure going to the same port, because of the known sympathy of that people with the Confederate cause. It was a fact, admitted on the trial, that the Rio Grande "was not blockaded with any declared or actual design to impair the legitimate commerce of any Mexican port."

That the final destination of the trade between England and Matamoras was Texas and the Confederacy, was too plain to deceive ; the abnormal growth of the number of ships that sought the mouth of the Rio Grande, "from two or three to as many hundreds," was a part of the evidence introduced at the trial to prove a "simulated and false destination." But that the trade was legal, that the destination in the ship's papers was the true destination of the ship, was clearly established on the trial. The cargoes for Matamoras were landed and became a part of the goods of the merchants of that port, and were afterwards sold and delivered at Brownsville, Texas, and entered the Confederacy without breach of the blockade, real or technical. The immediate destination of the goods was Matamoras, but their *ulterior* destination was the Confederacy; and though it is a rule of international law that "the *ulterior* destination of the goods determine the character of the trade, no matter how circuitous the route by which they are to reach their destination;" yet, if in that "circuitous route" the goods intermingle with the stock of neutrals, and are sold as part of that stock, the trade of the neutral is legitimate and not liable to interruption by a belligerent.

The aid and comfort derived by the Confederate States from the successful evasion of the blockade, the sympathy and assistance extended by a very large part of the English people, and the derogation from the dignity of the United States which the neutrality of England and France was thought to have effected by recognizing the Confederate States as belligerents, of equal right and consideration with the United States, produced, even among the judges of the highest courts, a condition of mind and temper that unfitted them to administer justice where a subject of Great Britain was a party litigant. [1]

[1] That the minds of the Judges of the Supreme Court were influenced by patriotic feelings has been avowed by one of its most distinguished members—the late Associate Justice Samuel Nelson, who in a letter to the Hon. W. Beach Lawrence, dated 4th August, 1873, and since made public, wrote as follows :—" The truth is that the feeling of the country was deep and strong against England, and the *judges*, as individual citizens, *were no* exception to that feeling. Besides, the court was not familiar with the law of blockade." This avowal was made with reference to the condemnation of the *Circassian*, shortly after Chief Justice Chase had passed from the Department of State to the Chief Justiceship.

The Hon. Wm. M. Evarts seems to have recognized the warp and twist of the judicial mind, in the condemnation by the Supreme Court of the *Springbok*, since he quoted, by way of censure, from the charge of Count Portalis to the prize courts of France, that: "Courts of law deserve the severest censure when, instead of proceeding on the principle of international law, applied with equity, and in a manner favorable to neutrals, they take for their point of departure the interests of belligerents. State policy may have its plans and mysteries, but on the bench reason should ever maintain its empire and its dignity. When arbitrary pretexts, founded on fear or selfishness, direct the judgment seat, all is lost." It was before the Mixed Commission on English and American Claims, in the case of the *Springbok*, to which Mr. Evarts administered that rebuke; and when the extreme limits to which the U. S. Supreme Court carried the law of blockade and contraband, in that and other cases, are considered in connection with the previous ruling of that court and of English prize courts, it will become apparent that unfamiliarity with the law of blockade is not the only reason that will be assigned for rulings which the future interest of the United States will imperatively demand shall be reversed and departed from. To fully comprehend this wide departure from American rulings on international law it is necessary to take a cursory review of the efforts to modify the laws of seizure in the interests of neutral commerce.

The object of the Declaration of the Treaty of Paris, in 1856, was to mitigate the restrictions which the occurrence of war between two or more nations imposes on the commerce of neutrals. The object of the treaty, which the government of the United States urged, was that the treaty did not go far enough in its protection of the commerce of neutrals; and Mr. Marcy proposed, on the part of the United States, to exempt from belligerent capture on the high seas all private property which is not in the nature of contraband. And while objecting to the abolishment of privateering, unless private property at sea was exempt from capture, the United States readily agreed to accept the declarations that the neutral flag covers *enemy's* goods, with the exception of contraband of war; that neutral goods, with the same exception, are not liable to capture under enemy's flag; and that blockades in order to be binding must be effective, that is to say, maintained by a force sufficient really to prevent access to the coast of the enemy. The Confederate States were informally invited by the cabinets of Great Britain and France to accede to the Treaty of Paris, and assented by Resolution of Congress of August 13th, 1861. [1]

[1] Whereas, the Plenipotentiaries of Great Britain, Austria, France, Prussia, Russia, Sardinia, and Turkey, in a conference held at Paris on the 16th of April, 1856, made certain declarations respecting maritime law, to serve as uniform rules for their guidance, in all cases arising under the principles thus proclaimed: *And, whereas*, it being desirable, not only to attain certainty and uniformity, as far as may be practicable in maritime war, but also

The invitation by England and France to the Confederate States to accept the Treaty of Paris, and their formal acceptance of every provision except that against privateering—which had been reserved by the United States—implied a duty on the part of England and France, to enforce the provisions of that treaty in favor of all parties to it. Having invited the Confederate States to guarantee the rights of England, France and all other neutral nations, and the "informal proposals" having been accepted, the faith of treaties was implied that the reciprocal benefits to the Confederate States, as a party to the Treaty of Paris, would be guaranteed by England and France. It was worse than bad faith to make the Confederate States parties, however "informal," to the treaty, and deny to them its benefits. Yet Great Britain, after submitting for one year to an ineffective blockade,[1] went still further and by dispatch on February 11th, 1862, declared that:

"Her Majesty's Government, however, are of the opinion that, assuming that the blockades was duly notified, and also that a number of ships are stationed and remain at the entrance of a port sufficient really to prevent access to it, *or to create an evident danger of entering or leaving it,* and that these ships do not voluntarily permit ingress or egress, the fact that various ships may have successfully escaped through it (as in the particular instance here referred to,) will not of itself prevent the blockade from being an effectual one by international law."

This extract serves well to illustrate how completely Lord Russell and the English Foreign Office overreached Mr. Seward in the diplomacy of blockade; and succeeded in inveigling the United States into acquiesence and compliance with England's ruling in the law of blockade.

From the seventeenth century, and all through the wars of the eighteenth century, the primary and essential condition of a violation of blockade has been held to be the existence of a port "in a state of blockade" in the legal sense. The Fourth Article of the Declaration of Armed Neutrality in 1780, was: " Que pour déterminer ce que charactérise un port bloqué on n'accorde cette dénomination qu'à celui on il y a, par la disposition de la puissance, que l'attaque avec des vaisseaux arrêtés *et* suffisament prôches un danger évident d'entrer." (That in order to determine what characterises a blockaded port, that term shall

to maintain whatever is just and proper in the established usages of nations, the Confederate States of America deem it important to declare the principles by which they will be governed in their intercourse with the rest of mankind. Now therefore—

Be it anacted by the Congress of the Confederate States of America, 1. That we maintain the right of privateering. as it has been long established by the practice and recognized by the law of nations.

2. That the neutral flag covers enemy's goods, with the exception of contraband of war.

3. That neutral goods, with the exception of contraband of war, are not liable to capture, under enemy's flag.

4. That blockades, in order to be binding, must be effectual, that is to say, maintained by a force sufficient really to prevent access to the coast of the enemy.

[1] Lord Russell's dispatch of May 6th, 1862, recites : "This blockade, kept up irregularly, but when enforced, enforced severely, has seriously injured the trade and manufactures of the United Kingdon. * * * Yet, her Majesty's Government have never sought to take advantage of the *obvious* imperfections of this blockade, in order to declare it ineffective," —and May 11th, that the blockade might, no doubt, *be made* effective. considering the small number of harbors on the Southern coasts, even though the extent of three thousand miles were comprehended in the terms of that blockade."

only be applied to a port where, from the arrangement made by the attacking power with vessels stationed off the port, *and* sufficiently near, there is evident danger in entering the port.)

In the Second Armed Neutrality in 1800, the same principle was laid down. " Un port ne peut-être comme bloqué que se non entrée est evidemment dangereux par suite des dispositions prises par une des puissances belligerantes, par le moyen des à vaisseux placés a proximité." (A port shall not be understood as blockaded unless it is evidently hazardous to attempt to enter it, in consequence of the measures adopted by one of the belligerent powers, by vessels of war stationed in its proximity.)

England violated these articles in the grossest manner, and arrogated to herself the right to declare, by Royal Order in Council, ports to be in a state of blockade although there was no blockade stationed off such ports in their proximity. Her cruisers captured neutral vessels bound for such ports, and her courts condemned vessels and cargoes. These "paper blockades," were defended only as "defensive retaliation" justified by necessity. But in the treaty of June 17th, 1801, with Russia, England introduced surreptitiously this novel doctrine, in defining blockade in that treaty, while using the phraseology of the armed neutrality of 1780, a material change was introduced.. The words in the Armed Neutrality of 1780, were : " Avec des vaisseux arrêtés *et* suffisamment prôches;" this language was deftly changed into "avec des vaisseux arrêtés *ou* suffisamment prôches." This same change was made by Lord Russell in sustaining the blockade of Confederate ports; and instead of adhering to the language of the Treaty of Paris—that a blockade is effective only when "maintained by a force sufficient really to prevent access to the coast of the enemy," he added, "*or* to create an evident danger of entering or leaving" the port. This was reviving the blockade " par croisième," (by cruising squadrons) sometimes near and sometimes at a distance from the so-called blockaded port. Mr. Seward did not see the position to which he was committing the United States by accepting Lord Russell's addenda. And the United States now stands committed to a doctrine of blockade similar to that which England maintained against all the principles of international law, and which at some future day will return to plague the commerce of neutral America in the wars of European belligerents.

The solemn protest of the Confederate States against the modification of the provisions of the Treaty of Paris which Lord Russell made in that dispatch, did not avail to correct its great injustice. By the treaty of Paris England engaged to observe blockades only " when maintained by a force sufficient *really to prevent access to the coast* of the enemy." It is difficult to see from what principle of public faith or international law Lord Russell drew the right to interject into that

treaty the important modification, that effectiveness of blockade was complied with where the force at *the entrance of a
port,* not on *" the coast of an enemy,"* was sufficient "to create
an evident danger of entering it or leaving it"! These incon-
sistencies and vacillations were made by the political branches
of the governments of Great Britain and the United States,
and whether excusable or not should have found no sanction
or support from the highest judicial tribunal of the United
States.

International law ought to be more perfect common-sense
than any other law, since there is no supreme power to enforce
it, and its varying problems can never be solved but by an
appeal to the judgments and sentiments of mankind. It is
accordingly one of the first duties of courts of justice, called
upon to administer international law, to repudiate *fictions* of
all kinds, as they are as distasteful to common-sense as a
vacuum is repugnant to nature. The Supreme Court, instead
of rising with the occasion that was presented, to liberalize
and modify the harsher doctrines of international law introduced by British prize courts to protect a colonial trade, embraced the opportunity to enlarge and extend the obsolete
"Rule of the War of 1756," and engrafted on Lord Stowell's old
stock of "continuous voyages," a twig that may yet bear the
most noxious fruit to American commerce. Prior to the war
of 1756, between European States and their transmarine colonies, trade with those colonies was not permitted to other
nations. When, under the stress of war, any one of those States
threw open their interdicted colonial trade to neutrals, the
hostile power refused to recognize this as lawful neutral commerce ; but it was treated as aid to the enemy, in relief of his
trade which the war had strangled, and the adverse belligerent
captured and condemned the ships and cargoes of the neutral
as of an enemy. "As trade, however, in subsequent times,"
said Mr. Evarts, [1] "between the colonies and the neutral State
and the neutral and European States was incontestably open
to the neutral, a trade was attempted of a colorable importation from Cuba, for instance, into Boston and from
Boston to Spain, and so of return voyages, through the interposition of a neutral port. This scheme was denounced and
this commerce was attacked by the belligerent. The question
for the prize court was whether the importation into and the
exportation from the intermediate neutral port were really
transactions of the neutral's own and of course legitimate
commerce, or whether it was really a trade between the colony
and the parent State, and the interposition of the neutral port
was only colorable." It was to meet this novel form of neutral adventure, in aid of an enemy's trade, and to prevent the
produce of an enemy's colony from being imported into the

[1] Brief in the *Springbok* case.

mother country, or *vice versa*, through an apparently legitimate channel, that Lord Stowell took upon himself to invent the doctrine, as it has been termed, of "continuous voyages," and clothed it in language which has enabled the Supreme Court of the United States to apply it with plausibility to a very different class of cases. Lord Stowell's "rule of the war of 1756" was applied only to captures made on the *ulterior voyage*, that is the voyage *from* the neutral port, and it was never applied to captures made on the *immediate* voyage, that is the voyage *to* the neutral port. Under the rule, as laid down by Lord Stowell, condemnation never followed capture made on the voyage *de facto* from one neutral port to another ; but under the application of the rule, or rather its unjustifiable extension by the Supreme Court, captures were condemned by the court on *its presumption* that the first voyage was but a part of the second ; and while, in the cases before Lord Stowell, the *corpus delicti* was incontestable ; in the case of the *Springbok*, before the Supreme Court, the *corpus delicti* was only a matter of argument, presumption and inference.

The *Springbok* was a *sailing* vessel of draft too great to enter any Confederate port, and was upon a voyage from London to Nassau when she was intercepted and seized by a United States cruiser and sent into New York, under a prize crew, and there condemned.[1]

Upon appeal to the Supreme Court the decree of the U. S. District Court, condemning *the vessel*, was reversed ; the Supreme Court holding that the ship was improperly condemned ;[2] but while releasing the ship the Supreme Court *affirmed* the condemnation of the cargo, because the voyage was *one* and the same whether broken or not at Nassau.[3] Upon that ruling Mr. Evarts remarked : "Thus it appears condemnation passed finally upon the cargo, not as taken *in delicto* during a voyage in which the vessel carrying it was to be an agent of transportation with intent to violate the blockade, but simply as set in progress (by and through an innocent

---

[1] "*The United States vs. the Bark Springbok and Cargo.*—This suit having been heard by the Court upon the pleadings, proofs and allegations of the parties, and evidence legally invoked therein from other cases, and the premises being fully considered ; and it being found by the court therefrom that the said vessel, at the time of her capture at sea, was knowingly laden in whole or part with articles contraband of war, with intent to deliver such articles to the aid and use of the enemy ; that the true destination of the said ship and cargo was not to Nassau, a neutral port, and for trade and commerce, but to some port lawfully blockaded by the forces of the United States, and with intent to violate such blockade. And further, that the papers of said vessel were simulated and false. Wherefore, the condemnation and forfeiture of the vessel and cargo is declared. Ordered, that a decree be entered accordingly."

[2] "Her papers were regular and they all showed that the voyage, on which she was cap-

tured, was from London to Nassau, both neutral ports within the definition of neutrality, furnished by international law. The papers too, were all genuine, and there was no concealment of any of them, and no spoliation. Her owners were neutral, and do not appear to have had any interest in the cargo ; and there is insufficient proof that they had any knowledge of its alleged unlawful destination."—5. Wallace p. 21.

[3] "Upon the whole, we cannot doubt that the cargo was originally shipped with intent to violate the blockade ; that the owners of the cargo intended that it should be trans-shipped at Nassau in some vessel more likely to succeed in reaching safely a blockaded port than the *Springbok* ; that the voyage from London to the blockaded port was, both in law and in intent of the parties, one voyage ; and that the liability to condemnation, if captured during any part of that voyage, attached to the cargo from the time of sailing."—5. Wallace, p. 27.

voyage by an innocent vessel to a lawful port) *towards* a purpose of thereafter obtaining transportation by a voyage yet to be commenced, by some unknown and unnamed vessel, to some unknown and unnamed blockaded port." The antiquated and obsolete "rule of the war of 1756" was revived, enlarged and applied by the Supreme Court to the war of 1861, in order to hamper and hinder the Confederate States in obtaining from England the same kind of supplies which the United States obtained by violation of English laws and against the protests of the English Foreign Office.[1]

Surprise is increased that England and France should have continued to respect and observe a blockade which was not only ineffective, according to the rule of the Treaty of Paris, but which was converted into a *paper blockade* by the rulings of the prize courts. European jurists were taken by surprise at the novel doctrine announced in the *Springbok* case ; the learned Dr. Bluntschli, of Heidelberg, observing : " Si cette manière de voir venait à l'emporter dans la pratique, le commerce neutre sera bien plus menacé que par le blocus sur papier."[2]

Whatever effectiveness the blockade had was as much the result of the rulings of the courts, in prize cases, as of the ships that watched the mouths of harbors. The former extended the blockade in reality, if not in avowal, to the English ports in Bermuda, Nassau, St. John, and to the Spanish ports in Cuba. And it was not the stopping of large or " small holes " by ships, but by traps along the paths to the " holes " that the United States cruisers reaped their largest and most profitable prize harvest. Even Lord Russell's interpolation of the law of blockade would not have made that at Wilmington respectable, if he had not permitted the new rulings of the

[1] Lord Russell to Mr. Adams, December 19th, 1862 : " It is right, however, to observe that the party which has profited by far the most by these *unjustifiable practices*, has been the government of the United States, because that government, having a superiority of force by sea, and having blockaded most of the Confederate ports, has been able on the one hand, safely to receive all the warlike supplies *which it has induced* British manufacturers and merchants to send to the United States *in violation of the Queen's proclamation ;* and on the other hand, to intercept and capture a great part of the supplies of the same kind which were destined from this country to the Confederate States. If it be sought to make her Majesty's government responsible to that of the United States because arms and munitions of war have left this country on account of the Confederate government, the Confederate government, as the other belligerent, may very well maintain that it has a just cause of complaint against the British government because the United States arsenals have been replenished from British sources. Nor would it be possible to deny that, in defiance of the Queen's proclamation, many subjects of her Majesty, owing allegiance to her crown, have enlisted in the armies of the United States. Of this fact you cannot be ignorant. Her Majesty's government, therefore, has just ground for complaint against both of the belligerent parties, but most especially against the government of the United States, for having systematically, and in disregard of the comity of nations which it was their duty to observe, induced subjects of her Majesty to violate those orders, which, in conformity with her neutral position, she has enjoined all her subjects to obey."

[2] " Le Droit Internationale Codifie, 2me Editione, Paris, S. 835. Dr. Louis Gessner, Imperial Councillor of the Legation at Berlin, concurred in the same opinion. The United States authority on international law, Wm. Beach Lawrence, wrote to M. Rolin-Jacquemyns, Sept. 30th, 1878, that : " the recent adjudications of our Supreme Court have even gone beyond the cases arising out of " the Rule of Fifty-six. Dr. Heffter, of Berlin; Mr. Carlos Calvo, of Paris; Mr. Westlake, Q. C., of London ; M. G. Rolin-Jacquemyns, of Gaud ; Professor Goldsmidt, of Leyden ; Sir Robert Phillimore, Sir W. Atherton, Sir Roundell Palmer. Lord Selborne, Mr. George Mellish, Sir W. Vernon-Harcourt—all concur in holding that there was a miscarriage of justice in the condemnation of the cargo of the *Springbok.*"

U. S. Supreme Court to extend the blockade back to the English colonial ports.

The *Springbok* case was reviewed before the Mixed Commission on British and American Claims, under the Treaty of Washington, in 1871.   That Mixed Commission held, as to questions arising under the blockade, very nearly the same relation that the Geneva Conference held to those questions which grew up out of the action of Confederate cruisers.   But the Commission that sat at Washington was a very different affair from that at Geneva.   It was composed, on the part of Great Britain, of Mr. Russell Gurney, a mere criminal lawyer, "Recorder" of the city of London, the arbitrator; on the part of the United States was Judge James S. Frazer; and Count Corti, the Italian Minister at Washington, was named as umpire by both governments.   The Commission was provided for in Article XII of the Treaty of Washington, ratified May 8th, 1871, and was limited in duration by Article XIV to two years.   Its session began at Washington on the 26th of September, 1871, and its final award was made at Newport, R. I., on the 25th of September, 1873.   By April 23d, 1872, it had decided eleven cases, and from that date to the 2d of October following it transacted no business whatever, in consequence of the American Commission having refused to adjudicate any British claims while the tribunal at Geneva was at a deadlock.   The Washington Commission refused to hear *oral* argument, gave no reasons for its awards, but curtly announced in stereotyped formula that "this claim is disallowed."   It sat with closed doors, and departed most glaringly from the precedent of the similar Anglo-American Claims Commission, which sat in London in 1853.   The Protocol XXXVI, of April 14th, 1871, provided: "That the Convention of 1853 should be followed as a precedent."   The Convention of 1853 required both commissioners, as well as the umpire or arbitrator, to state *in writing* the grounds of their respective opinions or awards, and a full report of those opinions was published by both governments; the sittings were open, and special counsel were "heard" on behalf of the claimants.   Of these flagrant departures from the precedents of the Commission of 1853, Mr. Beach Lawrence remarked: "Of the Mixed Commission, established by the treaties between the United States and Great Britain of 1794 and 1853, for adjusting the claims of citizens or subjects of the one country or the government of the other, we have *reports more or less complete.*   Moreover, the discussions connected with the arbitrament of the so-called 'Alabama Claims' by the tribunal, created under Article I of the treaty of 1871, whose sittings were held at Geneva, fill many volumes.   But the Mixed Commission, appointed under Article XII of that Treaty, *did not,* save in a few of the early cases, state the reasons on which its adjudications were based.   In the absence of any announcement by the Commissioners of their mode of arriving at their conclusions, we have no means by which to interpret the motives of the decrees. The decisions of arbiters, for the adjustment of international claims, should in every case be furnished in writing to the respective governments."[1]

The number of British claims presented to the Commission was 478, of which 181 were allowed; eight were withdrawn, one was dismissed, and 260 were disallowed. The amount claimed aggregated $96,000,000, exclusive of ten years' interest, and the amount awarded was $1,929,819 in gold, or a trifle over two per cent. on the entire claims. Eighty-seven of the claims were for wrongful seizure of British ships and cargoes; of these four were allowed, but without interest; thirteen were partly allowed, and seventy were disallowed or rejected *in toto*. The aggregate amount of these eighty-seven ship claims was $9,832,680, of which the Commission allowed only $725,630 in gold. Article XVI provided five per cent. on the sums awarded for the expenses of the Commission, and this deduction from the final award amounted to $96,491, which was apportioned to "the two governments in equal moieties." The $45,245 received by the United States the official report of Mr. Hale, the agent and counsel of the United States, shows to have been far short of the amount actually expended, which reached $300,000; which, in contrast with the whole expenses of the Commission of 1853, which sat in London, $12,940, was suggestive of the inquiry: "How the $300,000 had been employed?" Without attempting to solve that riddle it would be interesting and useful to know the grounds upon which the conclusions of the Commission were based. But a far more interesting inquiry is why the British Commissioner concurred in rulings so variant from established international law and so wrongful to British subjects, and which was done in spite of the strong opinion of the law officers of the crown, Dr. Phillimore (Queen's Advocate), Sir William Atherton (Attorney General), and Sir Roundell Palmer (Solicitor General), as well as of Mr. George Mellish (afterwards a Lord Justice of the Court of Chancery), and William Vernon Harcourt, the famous "Historicus" of the *Times*, and Solicitor General under Mr. Gladstone's administration. Were those wrongful awards consented to in the hope and expectation that they would become precedents, profitable to Great Britain against neutrals at some future day, and conclusive against the neutral commerce of the United States when Great Britain should again be at war? If so, the Mixed Commission has sown seeds from which the commerce of the United States may gather fruits more injurious even than those of the war between the States in 1861-65.

[1] Mr. Beach Lawrence's Letter to M. Rolin-Jacquemyns, September 30th, 1873.

The ease with which the blockade at Wilmington was run, and the success with which the blockading fleet was avoided, is explained in that very interesting work of Captain John Wilkinson, C. S. N.,[1] "The Narrative of a Blockade Runner."

"The natural advantages of Wilmington for blockade-running were very great, chiefly owing to the fact that there are two separate and distinct approaches to Cape Fear River, i.e., either by "New Inlet" to the north of Smith's Island, or by the "western bar" to the south of it. This Island is ten or eleven miles in length ; but the Frying Pan Shoals extend ten or twelve miles further south, making the distance by sea between the two bars thirty miles or more, although the direct distance between them is only six or seven miles. From Smithville, a little village nearly equidistant from either bar, both blockading fleets could be distinctly seen, and the outward bound blockade-runners could take their choice through which of them to run the gauntlet. The inward bound blockade-runners, too, were guided by circumstances of wind and weather; selecting that bar over which they would cross after they had passed the Gulf Stream, and shaping their course accordingly. The approaches to both bars were clear of danger, with the single exception of the "Lump" before mentioned ; and so regular are the soundings that the shore can be coasted for miles within a stone's throw of the breakers.

"These facts explain why the United States fleet were unable wholly to stop blockade-running. It was, indeed, impossible to do so ; the result to the very close of the war proves this assertion, for, in spite of the vigilance of the fleet, many blockade-runners were afloat when Fort Fisher was captured. In truth the passage through the fleet was little dreaded ; for although the blockade-runner might receive a shot or two, she was rarely disabled ; and in proportion to the increase of the fleet the greater would be the danger (we knew) of their firing into each other. As the boys before the deluge used to say, they would be very apt "to miss the cow and kill the calf." The chief danger was upon the open sea ; many of the light cruisers having great speed. As soon as one of them discovered

[1] Capt. John Wilkinson was born in Norfolk, Va., in 1821, and was the eldest son of the late Commodore Jesse Wilkinson of the U. S. navy. Capt. John Wilkinson entered the U. S. navy as a midshipman in 1837, served in the Mexican War on board of the *Saratoga ;* and after more than the average amount of sea service, was in command of the steamer *Corwin,* on coast survey when his native State seceded. He then resigned his commission, and offered his services to the State of his birth. Like many of his brother officers, Captain Wilkinson up to that time had meddled so little with politics as never even to have cast a vote ; but having been educated in the belief that his allegiance was due to his State, he did not hesitate to act as honor and patriotism seemed to demand. Speaking of those citizens of Virginia who resigned their commissions, in his interesting *Narrative of a Blockade Runner,* he says : "They were compelled to choose whether they would aid in subjugating their State, or in defending it against invasion ; for it was already evident that coercion would be used by the general government, and that war was inevitable. In reply to the accusation of perjury in breaking their oath of allegiance, since brought against the officers of the army and navy who resigned their commissions to render aid to the South, it need only be stated that, in their belief, the resignation of their commissions absolved them from any special obligation. They then occupied the same position towards the government as other classes of citizens. But this charge was never brought against them till the war was ended. The resignation of their commissions was accepted when their purpose was well known. As to the charge of ingratitude, they reply, their respective States had contributed their full share towards the expenses of the general government, acting as their disbursing agent ; and when these States withdrew from the Union, their citizens belonging to the two branches of the public service did not, and do not, consider themselves amenable to this charge for abandoning their official positions to cast their lot with their kindred and friends. But yielding as they did to necessity, it was nevertheless a painful act to separate themselves from companions with whom they had been long and intimately associated, and from the flag under which they had been proud to serve."

During the brief interval which elapsed between the act of secession and the admission of the State into the Confederacy, the Virginia army and navy were organized ; and all of the naval officers who had tendered their services received commissions in the Virginia navy. Captain Wilkinson's first service was at Fort Powhatan, an earthwork situated on James River, a short distance below City Point, and carrying six or eight guns mounted on ships' carriages. From thence he was transferred to the command of a battery on Acquia Creek. On June 10th, 1861, he entered into the service of

a blockade-runner, during daylight, she would attract other cruisers in the vicinity by sending up a dense column of smoke, visible for many miles in clear weather. A cordon of fast steamers stationed ten or fifteen miles apart, *inside the Gulf Stream*, and in the course from Nassau and Bermuda to Wilmington and Charleston, would have been more effectual in stopping blockade-running than the whole United States navy concentrated off those ports; and it was unaccountable to us why such a plan did not occur to good Mr. Welles; but it was not our place to suggest it. I have no doubt, however, that the fraternity to which I then belonged would have unanimously voted thanks and a service of plate to the Hon. Secretary of the United States Navy for this oversight. I say *inside the Gulf Stream*, because every experienced captain of a blockade-runner made a point to cross "the stream" early enough in the afternoon, if possible, to establish the ship's position by chronometer, so as to escape the influence of that current upon his dead reckoning. The lead always gave indication of our distance from the land, but not, of course, of our position; and the numerous salt works along the coast, where evaporation was produced by fire, and which were at work night and day, were visible long before the low coast could be seen. Occasionally, the whole inward voyage would be made under adverse conditions. Cloudy, thick weather and heavy gales would prevail so as to prevent any solar or lunar observations, and reduce the dead reckoning to mere guess-work. In these cases the nautical knowledge and judgment of the captain would be taxed to the utmost. The current of the Gulf Stream varies in velocity and (within certain limits) in direction; and the stream, itself almost as well defined as a river within its banks under ordinary circumstances, is impelled by a strong gale toward the direction in which the wind is blowing, overflowing its banks as it were. The counter current, too, inside of the Gulf Stream is much influenced by the prevailing winds. Upon one occasion, while in command of the *R. E. Lee*, formerly the Clyde-built iron steamer *Giraffe*, we had experienced very heavy and thick weather, and had crossed the Stream and struck soundings about midday. The weather then clearing, so that we could obtain an altitude near meridian, we found ourselves at least forty miles north of our supposed position, and near the shoals which extend in a southerly direction off Cape Lookout. It would be more perilous to run out to sea than to continue on our

the Confederate States navy, and when the line of the Potomac was abandoned, he was ordered to duty on the Mississippi below New Orleans, first in command of the Confederate States steamer *Jackson*, and afterwards as executive officer of the iron-clad *Louisiana*, carrying the flag of Commodore John K. Mitchell. He succeeded to the command of the *Louisiana* after the mortal wounding of Captain C. F. McIntosh, who fell in the action during the passage of the U. S. fleet under Admiral Farragut. After the destruction of the *Louisiana*, to prevent her from falling into the hands of the enemy, most of the officers (and Lieut. Wilkinson among them) were captured and imprisoned at Fort Warren.

After an exchange he was sent to Europe under orders from the War Department, to purchase a steamer. Besides commanding the *Giraffe*, afterwards named the *R. E. Lee*, he also commanded the secret expedition to attempt the release of the prisoners at Johnson's Island. It is believed the plot was betrayed through the indiscretions of an agent of the C. S. government then residing in Canada. Returning to Bermuda Captain Wilkinson assumed command of the blockade runner *Whisper*, and arrived safely in Wilmington. He was then ordered to the iron-clad *Roanoke*, and after a few weeks to Richmond, where he was given command of the naval portion of the expedition to attempt the release of the Point Lookout prisoners. He was

subsequently relieved, and the naval portion of it was placed under the command of Capt. John Taylor Wood, C. S. N., and one of the President's aides. It is hardly necessary to add, that this expedition also failed, owing to the fact that, secretly as all the preparations had been made, information of it was speedily conveyed to Washington, and prompt measures taken to prevent its success. Captain Wilkinson was then placed in charge of the office of "Orders and Detail," which was charged with lighting the approaches to Wilmington and of detailing pilots and signal officers to the blockade runners. In the later part of September, 1864, he was ordered to the command of the *Chickamauga*, a double screw steamer converted into a man-of-war, and made in her a successful cruise along the Atlantic coast. After his return he was put in command of the *Tallahassee*, which under the name of the *Chameleon* proceeded with all despatch to Bermuda for a cargo of provisions for General Lee's starving army. Procuring her return cargo the *Chameleon* made several attempts to enter a Confederate port but failed. Captain Wilkinson returned to Liverpool, and with the public funds turned her over to Captain Bulloch without appropriating any of the spoils of the perishing ship of state. Capt. Wilkinson with his opportunities could have accumulated a large fortune during the war, but being a gentleman of the purest integrity he returned to his family "dead broke," with a clear conscience.

course, for we had passed through the off-shore line of blockaders, and the sky had become perfectly clear. I determined to personate a transport bound to Beaufort, which was in the possession of the U. S. forces, and the coaling station of the fleet blockading Wilmington. The risk of detection was not very great, for many of the captured blockade-runners were used as transports and dispatch-vessels. Shaping our course for Beaufort, and slowing down, as if we were in no haste to get there, we passed several vessels, showing United States colors to them all. Just as we were crossing through the ripple of shallow water off the 'tail' of the shoals, we dipped our colors to a sloop-of-war which passed three or four miles to the south of us. The courtesy was promptly responded to; but I have no doubt her captain thought me a lubberly and careless seaman to shave the shoals so closely. We stopped the engines when no vessel was in sight, and I was relieved from a heavy burden of anxiety as the sun sank below the horizon, and the course was shaped at full speed for Masonboro' Inlet.

"The staid old town of Wilmington was turned 'topsy turvy during the war. Here resorted the speculators from all parts of the South, to attend the weekly auctions of imported cargoes ; and the town was infested with rogues and desperadoes, who made a livelihood by robbery and murder. It was unsafe to venture into the suburbs at night, and even in daylight there were frequent conflicts in the public streets, between the crews of the steamers in port and the soldiers stationed in the town, in which knives and pistols would be freely used; and not unfrequently a dead body would rise to the surface of the water in one of the docks with marks of violence upon it. The civil authorities were powerless to prevent crime. 'Inter arma silent leges !' The agents and employees of different blockade-running companies lived in magnificent style, paying a king's ransom (in Confederate money) for their household expenses, and nearly monopolizing the supplies in the country market. Towards the end of the war, indeed, fresh provisions were almost beyond the reach of every one. Our family servant, newly arrived from the country in Virginia, would sometimes return from market with an empty basket, having flatly refused to pay what he called 'such nonsense prices' for a bit of fresh beef, or a handful of vegetables. A quarter of lamb, at the time of which I now write, sold for $100, a pound of tea for $500. Confederate money which in September, 1861, was nearly equal to specie in value, had declined in September 1862 to 225 ; in the same month, in 1863, to 400, and before September, 1864, to 2,000 !

"Many of the permanent residents of the town had gone into the country, letting their houses at enormous prices ; those who were compelled to remain kept themselves much secluded ; the ladies rarely being seen upon the more public streets. Many of the fast young officers belonging to the army would get an occasional leave to come to Wilmington ; and would live at free quarters on board the blockade-runners, or at one of the numerous bachelor halls ashore.

"The convalescent soldiers from the Virginia hospitals were sent by the route through Wilmington to their homes in the South. The ladies of the town were organized by Mrs. De R. into a society for the purpose of ministering to the wants of these poor sufferers ; the trains which carried them stopping an hour or two at the depot, that their wounds might be dressed and food and medicine supplied to them. These self-sacrificing, heroic women patiently and faithfully performed the offices of hospital nurses.

"Liberal contributions were made by companies and individuals to this society, and the long tables at the depot were spread with delicacies for the sick, to be found nowhere else in the Confederacy. The remains of the meals were carried by the ladies to a camp of mere boys—home-guards outside of the town. Some of these children were scarcely able to carry a musket, and were altogether unable to endure the exposure and fatigues of field service; and they suffered fearfully from measles, and

LIEUTENANT COMMANDER JOHN WILKINSON, C. S. N.

CAPTURE OF THE "HARRIET LANE," JANUARY 1st, 1863.

typhoid fever. Gen. Grant used a strong figure of speech, when he asserted, that "the cradle and the grave were robbed, to recruit the Confederate armies." The fact of a fearful drain upon the population was scarcely exaggerated, but with this difference in the metaphor, that those who were verging upon both the cradle and the grave, shared the hardships and dangers of war, with equal self-devotion to the cause. It is true that a class of heartless speculators infested the country, who profited by the scarcity of all sorts of supplies, but it makes the self-sacrifice of the mass of the Southern people more conspicuous, and no State made more liberal voluntary contributions to the armies, or furnished better soldiers, than North Carolina.

"On the opposite side of the river from Wilmington, on a low, marshy flat, were erected the steam cotton presses, and there the blockade-runners took in their cargoes. Sentries were posted on the wharves, day and night, to prevent deserters from getting on board, and stowing themselves away; and the additional precaution of fumigating the outward bound steamers at Smithville was adopted; but in spite of this vigilance, many persons succeeded in getting a free passage abroad. These deserters, or 'stowaways,' were in most instances sheltered by one or more of the crew; in which event they kept their places of concealment until the steamer had arrived at her port of destination, when they would profit by the first opportunity to leave the vessel undiscovered. A small bribe would tempt the average blockade-running sailor to connive at this means of escape. The 'impecunious' deserter fared more hardly; and would usually be forced by hunger and thirst to emerge from his hiding place while the steamer was on the outward voyage. A cruel device, employed by one of the captains, effectually put a stop, I believe, certainly a check to the escape of this class of 'stowaways.' He turned three or four of them adrift in the Gulf Stream, in an open boat, with a pair of oars, and a few days' allowance of bread and water."

At the beginning of the war, nearly all the lights along the Southern coast had been discontinued; the apparatus being removed to places of safety. In 1864, it was deemed expedient to re-establish the light on Smith's Island, which had been discontinued ever since the beginning of hostilities, and to erect a structure for a light on the " Mound."[1]

Under special instructions from the Navy Department, Capt. Wilkinson was charged with the duties of relighting the approaches to the Cape Fear River, and of detailing pilots and signal officers to the blockade-runners. To provide the means of light, every blockade-runner was required to bring in a barrel of sperm oil. In addition to these aids to navigation,

[1] The "Mound" was an artificial one, erected by Col. Lamb, who commanded Fort Fisher. Capt. Wilkinson says: "Two heavy guns were mounted upon it, and it eventually became a sight for a light, and very serviceable to blockade runners; but even at this period it was an excellent landmark. Joined by a long, low isthmus of sand with the higher mainland, its regular conical shape enabled the blockade-runners easily to identify it from the offing; and in clear weather, it showed plain and distinct against the sky at night. I believe the military men used to laugh slyly at the colonel for undertaking its erection, predicting that it would not stand; but the result showed the contrary; and whatever difference of opinion may have existed with regard to its value as a military position, there can be but one as to its utility to the blockade-runners, for it was not a landmark, alone, along this monotonous coast, but one of the range lights for crossing New Inlet bar was placed on it. Seamen will appreciate at its full value this advantage; but it may be stated, for the benefit of the unprofessional reader, that while the compass bearing of an object does not enable a pilot to steer a vessel with sufficient accuracy through a narrow channel, range lights answer the purpose completely. These lights were only set after signals had been exchanged between the blockade-runner and the shore station, and were removed immediately after the vessel had entered the river. The range lights were changed as circumstances required; for the New Inlet channel, itself, was and is constantly changing, being materially affected both in depth of water and in its course by a heavy gale of wind or a severe freshet in Cape Fear River."

30

the signal stations were extended farther along the coast, and compulsory service was required of the pilots. Owing to the constantly increasing vigilance of the blockading fleet, and the accession to the United States navy of fast cruisers, many prizes were captured about this time. Their pilots were, of course, held as prisoners of war ; and the demand for those available for service increasing in proportion to their diminished number, there was much competition between the rival companies, to the great detriment of the public service. It was considered necessary, therefore, to establish an office of "Orders and Detail" at Wilmington, in charge of Captain Wilkinson, whence should proceed all orders and assignments in relation to pilots and signal officers. In a short time, the benefit of these arrangements was very perceptible. The blockade-runners were never delayed for want of a pilot, and the casualties were much diminished.

Some of the blockade-runners were constructed regardless of any good quality but speed, consequently their scantling was light and their sea-going qualities very inferior. Many of them came to grief; several were swamped at sea, and others, after being out a few days, struggled back to Queenstown without making a voyage.

The distance from Bermuda to Wilmington is 720 miles, and the in-and-out-voyage, including the time in unloading at the latter port, generally occupied sixteen days. Before making the trip the blockade-runner was prepared for the work by reducing her spars to a light pair of lower masts, without any yards across them; the only break in their sharp outline being a small crow's-nest on the foremast, to be used as a look-out place. The hull, which showed about eight feet above water, was painted a dull, grey color, to render her as nearly as possible invisible in the night. The boats were lowered square with the gunwales. Coal of a smokeless nature (anthracite) was taken on board. The funnel, being what is called "telescope," was lowered close down to the deck. In order that no noise might be made, steam was blown off under water. In fact, every ruse was resorted to, to enable the vessel to evade the vigilance of the Federal cruisers, who were scattered about in great numbers all the way between Bermuda and Wilmington. Among the fowls taken on board as provisions no cocks were allowed, for fear of their proclaiming the whereabouts of the blockade-runner.

The in-shore squadron off Wilmington consisted of about thirty vessels, and lay in the form of a crescent facing the entrance to Cape Fear River, the centre being just out of range of the heavy guns mounted on Fort Fisher, the horns, as it were, gradually approaching the shore on each side; the whole line or curve covered about ten miles.

When the blockade-runner arrived at Wilmington the cargo was landed as quickly as possible and a cargo of cotton immediately shipped. In the first place, the hold was stored by expert stevedores, the cotton bales being so closely packed that a mouse could hardly find room to hide itself among them. The hatches were put on, and a tier of bales put fore and aft in every available spot on the deck, leaving openings for the approaches to the cabins, engine-room, and the men's forecastle; then another somewhat thinner tier on the top of that, after which a few bales for the captain and officers. Loaded in this way, the vessel, with only her foremast up, with her low funnel and grey-painted sides, looked like a huge bale of cotton with a stick placed upright at one end of it.

A'ter the blockade-runner left the quay at Wilmington she steamed down the river, where she was boarded to be searched and smoked; the object of the latter proceeding being to search for runaways, deserters, spies, etc.

On September 1st, 1863, Major-Gen. W. H. C. Whiting issued the following regulations in regard to steamers running the blockade, from and to the port of Wilmington, and they were enforced after that date:

"1. Yankee goods must not be imported, upon penalty of confiscation of the goods, except munitions of war and medicines.

"2. Improper or suspicious persons must not be taken as passengers to this port. They must be properly vouched for, and permission given to embark, *by Major L. Heyliger, at Nassau, or Major Norman Walker, at Bermuda.* Any passenger brought to this port without proper credentials will be sent back by the same steamer.

"3. Steamers will not be permitted to bring in seamen, or other employees of the vessel, to be discharged upon arrival here. In all such cases special permission must be obtained from these headquarters.

"4. Passengers outward bound must obtain permits from headquarters. The officers in charge of boarding vessels will take out such persons as have no permits, and detain the vessel until further orders, if the party is on board by permission of the officers of the vessel.

"5. All vessels, after obtaining proper clearances, must apply to headquarters for permission to sail, and without such permission will be stopped at the forts and sent back.

"6. Letters upon outward and inward bound vessels must be sent to headquarters for inspection and approval. Failure to comply with this rule will involve the offending parties in considerable penalties.

"7. Lists of the officers and crews of all vessels arriving, must be made out for the inspecting officer. As spies can more readily ship as seamen or firemen, care must be taken by captains in selecting their crews.

"8. Copies of manifests of cargoes of vessels arriving will be sent to headquarters.

"9. All vessels from Nassau will remain at quarantine until permission is given to come to the city.

"10. Persons, other than officers of vessels, must be on board by nine o'clock P. M., every night, unless by special permission from headquarters. Such persons violating this order will be arrested and lodged in guardhouse.

"11. Official business at these headquarters in relation to steamers will be attended to by Col. Duncan, A. D. C."

Under Capt. Wilkinson, the *Lee* continued to make her regular trips, either to Nassau or Bermuda, as circumstances required,[1] carrying abroad cotton and naval stores and bringing in "hardware," as munitions of war were then invoiced, until the *Lee* had run the blockade twenty-one times while under his command, and had carried abroad between six and seven thousand bales of cotton, worth at that time about two millions in gold, and had carried into the Confederacy equally valuable cargoes.

The Charleston, S. C., *Mercury*, of November 7th, 1862, in reply to some complaints against the character of the importations through the blockade, explains quite fully the manner in which the Confederate government and cause benefited by blockade-running. It said:

"A single firm in Charleston, John Frasier & Co., have shipped about seven-eighths of the cotton that has gone from the ports of the Con-

THE C. S. BLOCKADE-RUNNER "ROBERT E. LEE."

federate States for some time past. Not one pound of cotton shipped by that house has gone to the United States, either by sale or capture. Every particle of it has gone to Europe. So much for 'the Yankees getting our cotton.'

"It is broadly asserted that 'scarcely a single article applicable to the immediate purposes of the war is brought in by the adventures which 'run the blockade' so constantly.' We affirm, on the contrary, that, in making up the return cargoes, each steamer is first loaded with as much

[1] Lieut. Com. John Wilkinson says that the *Lee*, before she was purchased by the Confederate government for £32,000, plied as a packet between Glasgow and Belfast. She was a very long and narrow side-wheel steamer, of light draft, very strongly built, with a speed of about thirteen and a half knots. She had two short masts on which fore and aft sails could be set and which were only serviceable to keep her steady in a sea abeam. Her beautiful saloon and cabins were dismantled, and bulkheads constructed to separate the quarters for officers and men from the space used for stowage of her cargo. She sailed from Glasgow for Nassau, and arrived there in good time. On December 26th, 1862, she sailed from the latter port, and a little before midnight of the 29th, passed over the Wilmington bar and anchored off Smithville. After having run the blockade twenty-one times, by the culpable mismanagement of the commander who succeeded Lieut. Wilkinson, the *R. E. Lee* fell an easy prey to one of the U. S. cruisers off the coast of North Carolina.

Among those seized on board of the *Lee* was Lieut. Rooks, a British officer.

The following extracts from his diary give an account of the last cruise of the famous blockade-runner:

"THURSDAY, Nov. 5th, 1863.—Start from St. George's in the Confederate steamer *Robert E. Lee*, Capt. Knox, for Wilmington, North Carolina; have fine weather the first three days; third day out (Sunday, 8th) fell in with a Yankee

heavy freight for the government as she can with safety carry, and that then packages of lighter goods are put in to complete the cargo. Most of the latter are also goods of the most importance to the government and the troops, such as shoes, clothes, medicines, etc., etc. The invoices of Messrs. John Frasier & Co. are handed to the agents of the government, and they are allowed to take whatever the government desires, fixing the prices themselves. The balance, which the government does not want, is advertised and sold at auction. Take, for example, the last steamer that run the blockade—the *Minho.* She has brought in of heavy freight for the government, 367 cases of rifles, containing 7,340 ; thirty-five cases of swords, containing 2,100 ; eighty-seven cases ammunition; eighty cases of caps. This was her heavy freight, and as much as she could safely take. Besides this she had aboard salt and cases of shoes, goods, etc., to complete her cargo. It is not customary to tell the public what the government takes. This is but a sample of these adventures. Almost all the goods brought in her are British goods. Some shoes, some cotton cards, some thread, some cases of calicoes, etc., have been bought at Nassau, and brought to Charleston and sold at auction. But they were not paid for in cotton, nor was any cotton sold at Nassau to buy them. The cotton has all gone to Europe. They were paid for by exchange drawn on Liverpool or London. They have generally been articles greatly needed, which we could afford to purchase at Nassau, whether they came from Yankeedom or elsewhere. The Southern people and soldiers need the cloth on which the objectionable ' Herculean Zouave ' is stamped, and

cruiser (the ———), who does not see us; steer away from her: Monday morning at three o'clock, make the land breakers ahead six or seven miles north of Wilmington; the pilot, not knowing where he is, refuses to take the ship in; having run foul of three Yankees, the captain could not put her head out to sea. and had to steer north; when the morning breaks a large Yankee cruiser appears about five miles to the southward, bearing down upon us under sail and steam; the first thing I heard on waking was a passenger coming down the steps, saying: ' By Jove! there's a sail to the south; if she's a cruiser she will be down upon us in five minutes.'

" I dressed and went on deck; saw two vessels—the Yankee and the *Cornubia*—a prize, looming in the distance. We steamed away from her, but could not escape, as we were jammed up in a bay, the light-house on Cape Lookout to the east of us. Seeing she was gaining rapidly, I went down and packed up all my small traps, brought them on deck, and by that time she was less than a mile from us, when bang went the first shot. It fell at least three hundred yards short; the second about fifty, and on the starboard side; the third was better, going straight over, very close to the rigging; the fifth shot, as we afterwards found out, was a shell from a nine-inch Parrott gun. Luckily for us, the fuse was blind, as the line was splendid; it fell about eighty yards astern and *ricochetted* close over us. Bang, bang, bang, went more guns, until they had fired twelve, and they were within eight hundred yards of us when they fired the last. The captain then stopped her, as the firemen, who had been working indifferently the whole time, struck work. As soon as they came alongside, they sent off a boat with a prize crew, and took possession of her.

" As soon as she was captured, it was most amusing to see the snowstorm of paper going overboard—Confederate dispatches, letters, etc. —Webber was seen coming up the stern hold with a bottle of brandy in one hand and a few in his pockets, the rest of the crew following his example. However, on going on board the Yankee (the *James Adger*, as she proved to be),

we were compelled in the most mortifying manner to disgorge our stock. I had one in each great coat pocket. On taking it out I was going to throw it overboard myself; but I told the captain it was excellent brandy, so he put it in his cabin, and I had one drink of it next afternoon. All the officers of the ship were most civil; but we couldn't get over their cold water system. We were only allowed to drink water; it was awful cold, and our stomachs were frozen. Webber and I longed to be on the News' steps at Bermuda calling for drinks.

"Next day I managed to get hold of some smuggled brandy, which was very acceptable. At night six of us were slung up in hammocks in a row in the cockpits, where we had to make shift with the bare hammock as best we could. It was next to impossible to sleep, thanks to the cold and the snoring of the pilot, one of the party. In the morning we had one basin and one towel between us to wash with. At four o'clock in the afternoon the crew were sent on board. The boatswain of the *Lee* (an ex-man-of-war boatswain) tickled my fancy immensely. He came on deck gnawing a huge piece of leather, and when he was asked what he was about, he said he was so hungry. Webber, Mr. Servant and myself went off with the captain, who was very civil throughout; and at thirty-five minutes past five we saw the last of the *James Adger*, and were under way for Fortress Monroe in the United States steamer *Newbern*, 156 in all. She is very uncomfortable, and we were dreadfully crowded.

"The captain very kindly gave us the cabin to sleep in, where I managed to rig up some sort of a bed on the floor with great coats, etc. I slept very little, and in the morning I was aching all over and felt very dirty, as I did not have my clothes off for four days. We arrived at Fortress Monroe at half-past seven, November 11th. Admiral Lee telegraphed to Washington, and we start for New York at three o'clock in the morning. Arrive at New York at five o'clock, November 13th; got to Provost Marshal's office at four o'clock ; were released, and went to the New York Hotel."

can afford to wear it. They are not ashamed to wear Yankee suits and shoes when captured in battle, nor to sleep in Yankee blankets when they can get them. If the Confederate States had twenty mercantile houses with the enterprise and patriotic liberality of John Frasier & Co., we would not want for arms and ordnance, our army would not now be in rags, and our people would not want many of the comforts of life. If other Southern cities had done as much for the purposes of war as Charleston, the South would be in a much better condition. Without Charleston as an emporium of trade the South would be badly off to-day."

An interesting and instructive contemporary account of the blockade auction sales in Charleston, explains the manner in which such portions of the imported cargoes, as the government did not need, made their way into the hands of the people.

"On King and East Bay streets at least four-fifths of the stores are closed, and on Meeting street the only oasis one sees in the great desert of suspension is at the houses where the piles of goods which so constantly run the blockade are auctioneered off. Here, when an auction is to take place, merchants, professional characters and men of leisure, all eager for the accumulation of dollars, congregate in vast numbers, and the store-rooms present a scene of busy life which contrasts strongly with the remaining portions of the city.

"I have, by dint of extraordinary perseverance, worked my way into one of these densely-packed auction rooms, and found the scene presented one of sufficient interest to describe. A burly man, of about 240 pounds avoirdupois, mounts a chair and announces that the sale is about to commence, continuing with the remarks that the conditions are cash, and that no issue of the Hoyer & Ludwig Confederate plate will be taken. The crier, who possesses a strength of lung of which 'Stentor' himself would have been proud, and a rapidity of articulation that has never been surpassed by human tongue, is accompanied by a little, grey-headed man, who wears a woollen cap of richly variegated hues, the crown of which displays the Confederate flag.

"This little man's chief occupation is to exalt the merits of the goods on sale, throw in occasional witticisms, and catch the 'winks and blinks' of bidders which the crier overlooks. A wink is as good as a nod with the little man, and he bawls it out as lustily as if he were giving an alarm of fire, or crying 'stop thief.' The great majority of the crowd who attend these cargo sales are German Jews, and one is as much surprised at their numbers as at their unpronounceable and strangely sounding cognomens, which, at the knock down of every article, grate harshly upon the ear of a stranger. For the amusement of your uninitiated readers, I give a few which it was my privilege to hear, viz.: Litchtenstein, Mittledorfer, Steinlein, Doorflinger, Rosenbaum, Gretzgraw, Zinnlouf, Retscrating, Slinglow, Ungrauphit, etc.

"Many of the merchants here complain that although these immense cargoes are sold at their very doors, yet by means of combinations made among buyers from abroad, they are unable to purchase articles sufficient to justify them in keeping open their stores. For example, three, four, five, or six buyers may combine and purchase a lot of articles amounting in the aggregate to $100,000, or more, and then divide the lot. This is frequently done, as the auctioneers, who have a most extensive catalogue to dispose of, go upon the principle of condensing all they can, the buyer of more limited purse has no means of replenishing his exhausted stock. The magnitude of these sales is really surprising, and the last one made by R. A. Pringle & Co., I understand, footed up over $2,500,000. The parties for whose benefit they are chiefly made, viz.: John Frasier & Co., have already realized $20,000,000. Of the amount $6,000,000 have been invested in Confederate bonds."

Like the *Lee,* the steamer *Kate* became a "regular pack-et"—sailing *on moons*—with a regularity of dispatch which the New York *Times* commended to the officers of the block-ading squadron:

"Can we not extract a similar good from the successes of our Southern rebels in running the national blockade? Here, for instance, we find in the Richmond *Dispatch*, of September 30th, the following item: 'The steamer *Kate*, from Nassau, successfully ran the blockade into Wilmington on Thursday.' This steamer *Kate* ran into Savannah early in July. In the beginning of August she ran out of Savannah and went to Wilming-ton. From Wilmington she started for Nassau about the middle of Au-gust, and now she comes back to Wilmington, of course, with an 'assorted cargo' of arms and ammunition. In other words, the *Kate* is a regular rebel packet, performing her trips with 'regularity and dispatch,' and, no doubt, to the serious advantage of owners, shippers, and consignees. Her successful voyages do not indeed tend to exalt our estimate of the officers of our blockading squadron. Let us console ourselves, therefore, like Mr. Disraeli, by allowing them to 'increase our respect for the energy of human nature.'

The cargoes of the *Kate,* in two trips were:

1,100 kegs of powder.	1 box samples.
400 cases rifles.	1 barrel.
1,405 boxes ammunition.	600 kegs powder.
144 bales of blankets, grey cloth, etc.	780 boxes cartridges.
	21 boxes caps.
218 cases mess-tins, boots, pouches, knapsacks, horse-gear, medi-cines, etc.	124 casks containing mess-tins, boots, horse-gear, medicines, knapsacks. etc.
15 cases medicines.	100 cases rifles.
4 cases instruments.	112 bales blankets.
2 cases lint.	5 packages tarpaulins.
5 packages tarpaulins.	4 cases tarpaulins.
4 cases tarpaulins.	1 case luggage.
1 case.	1 box samples.

Total, 5,048.

The *Kate* made over forty trips.

At Havana, the blockade runners were more frequent call-ers than the regular packets between that city and New York. A correspondent of the *Herald* says:

"Our friends south of Mason and Dixon's line have kept us pretty well posted through the following named vessels, which I give, with the date of arrival.

"April 18—Steamer *W. G. Howes*, 760 tons, New Orleans.
"April 18—Steamer *Arizona*, 670 tons, New Orleans.
"April 20—Steamer *Atlantic*, 660 tons, New Orleans.
"April 21—Steamer *Matagorda*, 650 tons, New Orleans.
"April 22—Schooner *Wide Awake*, 85 tons, New Orleans.
"April 22—Schooner *General Garibaldi*, 85 tons, New Orleans.
"April 23—Steamer *Victoria*, 487 tons, New Orleans.
"April 27—Schooner *Cora*, 63 tons, New Orleans.
"April 27—Schooner *G. Burrows* (Eng.), 57 tons, Mobile.
"April 28—Schooner *Thomas C. Acton*, 130 tons, Mobile.

"All these vessels brought cotton, of which there must be not less than 10,000 bales here at present. Last Monday or Tuesday a few hun-dred bales were sold at twenty-four and a half cents—a pretty good price."

And the arrivals and clearances at Nassau, N. P., for parts of the preceding months were as follows:

"ARRIVED.

"March 16 – Steamer *Granite City*, McEwan, Wilmington, cotton, to H. Adderley & Co.

"March 17—Steamer *Eagle*, Capper, Wilmington, cotton, to H. Adderley & Co.

"March 21—Steamer *Stonewall Jackson*, Black, Havana, ballast, to H. Adderley & Co.

"March 27—Steamer *Gertrude*, Raison, Charleston, cotton, to H. Adderley & Co.

"March 28—Steamer *Charleston*, Robinson, Charleston, cotton to Sawyer & Menendez.

"March 28—Schooner *Convoy*, Roberts, Wilmington, cotton and turpentine, to Saunders & Son.

"March 30—Sloop *Express*, Carey, Charleston, cotton, to H. Adderley & Co.

"April 2—Schooner *James R. Pringle*, Hecklinberg, Charleston, cotton, to H. Adderley & Co.

"April 3—Steamer *Ellie and Annie*, Carlin, Havana, assorted cargo, to H. Adderley & Co.

"April 3—Sloop *Richard*, Mooney, Charleston, cotton, to Saunders & Son.

"April 6—Steamer *Eagle*, Capper, Charleston, cotton, to H. Adderley & Co.

"April 9—Schooner *Victoria*, Wickland, Matamoras, cotton, to T. Darling & Co.

"April 10 – Steamer *Margaret and Jessie*, Wilson, Charleston, cotton, to H. Adderley & Co.

"April 10—Schooner *Julia Gordon*, Wilmington, cotton, to Saunders & Son.

"CLEARED.

"March 16—Sloop *Alfred Haywood*, Wark, Port Royal, S. C., via Abaca, coffee, by Sawyer & Menendez; schooner *Sue*, Erickson, Beaufort, N. C., assorted cargo, H. Adderley & Co.

"March 19—Schooner *Inez*, Edgett, Beaufort, N. C., salt, by the master; steamer *Eagle*, Capper, St. John, N. B., assorted merchandise, by H. Adderley & Co.

"March 20 – Steamer *Granite City*, McEwan, St. John, N. B., assorted merchandise, by H. Adderley & Co.

"March 21—Schooner *William D. S. Hyer*, Marsden, Matamoras, inward cargo, by H. Adderley & Co.; Steamer *Margaret and Jessie*, Wilson, St. John, N. B., assorted merchandise, by H. Adderley & Co.

"April 7—Bark *Nelson*, Irving, England, cotton, by Saunders & Son; brig *San Juan*, Berretiago, Matamoras, assorted cargo, by the R. W. H. Weech.

"April 9—Bark *Earl of Mar*, Still, Liverpool, cotton, by A. Johnson; sloop *Maria Biggs*, Port Royal, S. C., salt, by the master."

As letters from Northern men in Nassau to newspapers at home are not likely to misrepresent affairs unfavorably to the Confederates, the following correspondence of the Buffalo *Commercial Advertiser* may be accepted as giving a fair and truthful account of the effectiveness of the Federal blockade, as well as furnishing some data from which the amount and value of the commerce carried on in blockade-running bottoms:

" The steamers which run to Charleston are all painted a light lead color, which renders them almost undistinguishable from the horizon. They leave here at such a time that a common run will bring them off Charleston about midnight the third day from here, then as they can easily see our fleet, they steer quietly between the blockaders, and being of this dull lead color, and with their single mast, and smoke-pipe lowered, and withal being wonderfully long, low, and swift, they are almost certain of getting in.

" Coming out is still more a certainty, for at sunset they take from Fort Sumter very precise compass observations of our fleet at anchor, and then, as our vessels do not change their positions after dark, it is a perfectly simple matter to steer solely by the compass out into the open sea. Once out there is no danger, for they can show a clean pair of heels to any of our gunboats. Communication is truly more frequent with Charleston than New York, and we have New York dates six and seven days later this way than direct. Since I have been here, now six days, one steamer, the *Calypso*, has arrived from Charleston laden with cotton, and five, the *Ruby*, *Giraffe*, *Antonica*, *Nicholas I.*, and *Leopard*, have sailed for the same place, besides several sail vessels which have cleared for Northern ports, but with cargoes that make it certain they will see Charleston or Wilmington if possible.

" It is a great matter of wonder here to Union men, and Southerners too, that our government has not put forth every exertion to capture Charleston, for it has been by that port and from this place, that their immense supplies of arms have been drawn. Now, if it is captured, it will be shutting the barn door too late, for their supplies are so ample that large quantities of gun-carriages and guns are lying in this place, and not sent across because there is no call for them. These successful affairs, and particularly the naval affair of Charleston (of which we heard before you did), have made the Secessionists very jubilant, of course, and had a contrary effect upon us of the North. We can feel it the more because there was no necessity for it. As long ago as June last, our Consul here, Mr. Whiting (formerly, by the way, a lake captain, running out of Buffalo), officially informed our government that the machinery and iron plates for a ram were here, and being sent to Charleston as fast as opportunity offered. Later, he wrote that, from information he gathered, the ram was about finished, and would be at work very soon.

" Every cargo of cotton is worth from a quarter to a million of dollars, and as the *Antonica* has made six round trips and the *Leopard* the same, they may well put their fingers to their noses, and laugh about their packet and their ferry to Charleston. The authorities here are of course not ignorant of all this. The clearances are taken to Halifax or St. John, but they know perfectly well the real destination. Nearly every white person is in sympathy with the South, and all are more or less engaged in these blockade ventures, which are a perfect game of chance, with chances on the side of the risk. Large quantities of cotton are piled up, waiting shipment to England. Storekeepers put their stocks on shipboard and take their pay in cotton, on the return trip. Cotton sells for sixty cents per pound, specie, and Mr. Storekeeper gets rich."

From July, 1862, to June, 1863, fifty-seven steamers and ninety-one sailing vessels left Nassau for Confederate ports, of which fifty-one of the former and fifty-five of the latter landed their cargoes, and forty-four steamers and forty-five sailing vessels reached Nassau from the Confederacy during the same period; and on the 23d of April there were seventy-three ships, chiefly British, loading with cotton at Matamoras.

As freights were enormous, ranging from $300 to $1,000 per ton, some idea may be formed of the profits of a business in which a party could afford to lose a vessel after two successful trips. [1]

The following letter illustrates, in a measure, the difficulties and embarrassments which, towards the end of the year 1862, began to affect the Confederate government in obtaining certain kinds of supplies:

"RICHMOND, Dec. 15th, 1862.

"*Hon.* J. A. SEDDON, *Secretary of War:*

"SIR—I beg leave to refer to my communication relative to the transfer of the *General Clinch* to us. She is chartered at, I believe, $175 or $200 per day, and valued at $40,000. I would here suggest that, in order to save the charter money, she be purchased by the government, and we will pay for her when she returns with the cargo proposed, if not damaged, her valuation, etc., should the government desire to discontinue the adventure.

"Permit me to say that there is very little prospect of the government receiving on private enterprise certain class of goods, owing to their weight and price, and dangers of capture. These goods are as follows, and are very much needed by all ordnance, engineer, and navy departments, and also by private parties under government contracts, viz.: steel, iron, pig-iron, copper, zinc, ordnance of all kinds, munitions of war, chemicals and acids in particular, boiler iron, engines, etc., etc.

"The freight per ton in Nassau, *payable in advance*, is $500 to a Confederate port. This is equal to $1,500 here; therefore it is self-evident that such classes of goods as above cannot be imported on private account; because many other articles pay much better and take up less room. For instance, we take the article salt, worth $7.50 per ton in Nassau, and will bring $1,700 here; coffee is worth $240 per ton in Nassau and here $5,500, etc., etc.

"By the arrangement we propose the government will get seventy-five tons in weight or measurement of this class of goods for a risk of $40,000— the usual freight being $37,500 in Nassau, equal to at least $100,000 here, and at the same time we will receive facilities which will enable us to import in other ships the necessary goods contracted for.

"We will pay all expenses of the outward and inward trips, except the officers, which the Honorable Secretary of the Navy has promised to detail, *i. e.* an engineer and some other men.

"If we can leave Charleston on the 1st of January, we can return about the 15th. Our other ship will be here about the same time with 'army supplies,' etc., etc.

"I hope that my proposition will meet your approval, and that an order be given accordingly, and that the importance of the subject will be a sufficient apology for so long a letter.

"I have the honor to remain, your obedient servant,

"J. M. VERNON, of Vernon & Co.,
"*Government Contractors*, etc.

"P. S.—I desire to leave for Charleston as soon as possible."

---

[1] New York *Herald*, June 13th, 1863.
The following is a partial list of blockade runners that coaled at and passed through St. Thomas from March, 1862, to March, 1863:

ENGLISH STEAM BLOCKADE RUNNERS.

Arrived	Vessels Name.	Where from.	Cleared	Where bound.
Mch 18.	Adam Kanaris	London	Mch 22.	Berm'da
Ap'l 25.	Circassian	Bordeaux	Ap'l 26.	Havana.
Ap'l 25	Minho	Liverpool	Ap'l 26.	Havana.
May 10.	Patras	London	May 10.	Havana.
May 13.	Pacific	London & Falmouth	May 18.	Nassau.
May 19.	Modern Greece	Falmouth	June 2.	Nassau.
June 14	Ann	London	June 14.	Havana.
Oct. 3.	Bonita	Liverpool	Oct. 4.	Nassau.
Oct. 21.	Kelpie	Limerick	Oct.21.	Nassau.
Dec. 10.	Antona	Liverpool	Dec.16.	Havana.
Dec. 13	Thistle	Liverpool	Dec.27.	Nassau.
Dec. 15.	Nicholas I	Liverpool	Dec.23	Nassau.
Dec. 26.	Havelock	Glasgow	Jan.30.	Nassau.
1863.				
Jan. 1.	Pearl	Glasgow	Jan.13	Nassau.
Jan. 7.	Flora	London	Jan. 7	Nassau.
Jan. 23	Wave Queen	London	Feb. 6.	Nassau.
Jan. 23.	Ruby	Glasgow	Jan.24	V. Cruz.
Jan. 31.	Eagle	Glasgow	Feb. 2	Nassau.
Feb. 5	Granite City	Glasgow	Feb. 5	Nassau.
Feb. 20.	Peterhoff	London	Feb.24.	Mata'ms
Feb. 24.	Aries	Naguabo	Mch13.	Havana.
Mch 3.	Pet	Liverpool	Mch 4	Nassau.
Mch 16.	Neptune	Glasgow	Mch17.	Havana.
Mch 18.	Dolphin	Liverpool	Mch18.	Nassau.

The cause of the Confederacy was beginning to experience the chilling influence of avarice, and men were becoming more disposed to amass wealth than to aid the very cause by which they were able to accumulate immense fortunes. The real blockade capitalists were Englishmen and Northern merchants,[1] rather than Confederates. The companies that owned the vessels were of London, Liverpool and other English cities, and but comparatively few native Southern people were engaged in the business, except as officers and pilots. And notwithstanding the enormous number of captures, aggregating, according to the Report of Assistant Secretary of the Navy, Mr. Fox, up to June, 1863, 855 vessels, the trade and business was at that date as brisk and pushed with as great energy as at any time in the war. The large class of steamers had been abandoned, and a new and different kind had been built expressly for the trade.[2]

During the summer and fall of 1863 the blockade business was at its height, scarcely a dark night passed that one or more did not run into or out of Charleston. Never before, in the annals of blockade, were those low, long and fast Clyde-built steamers so numerous. They came and went in droves. It was said at the time that:

"Every one in London and Liverpool, who has capital enough to purchase a share in a steamer, invests in that way, and looks with composure upon the prospects of running a valuable cargo into some rebel port, and a return trip with the accompanying immense profits. Hence a cloud of steamers mottles the seas, bearing cargoes of valuables to the rebels, and we find them daily, or rather nightly, dashing through our thin shell of blockaders."

An officer from the blockading squadron off Wilmington, writing to the Boston *Traveller* of August 10th, says:

"There ought to be ten blockade-runners caught where we now get one. We have fifteen miles to guard, and to do it we have sometimes four and sometimes only two vessels. Ten vessels is the least number we ought

---

[1] Mr. Charles Cowley, Judge Advocate of the South Atlantic Blockading Squadron, in his very interesting work, entitled "Leaves from a Lawyer's Life Afloat and Ashore," says: "During the whole of Dupont's command, the Charleston newspapers reported the arrival and departure of vessels from that port as regularly and as openly, but, of course, not as numerously, as before the war. Even after Dahlgren established his iron-clad fleet inside the bar, and posted his pickets every night in the throat of the harbor, between Sumter and Moultrie, these arrivals and departures were from time to time announced, but more guardedly, except when the blockade-runner had been run aground, or badly shelled.

"We have been accustomed to berate the commercial classes of Great Britain for exporting goods to the Confederate States, in violation of our blockade. But probably more goods were carried into the Confederate States through the instrumentality of merchants in the United States than by all the merchants of Europe. More secrecy was observed by those residing in New York, who engaged in this business, than

was shown in running the blockade of Mexico, but it is none the less true than it in the Civil War as in the Mexican War, the munitions of war were furnished in very large quantities to the enemies of the United States by citizens of the United States Good old Horace Greeley used to say, not only in his despondent hours, but also in his more hopeful moods, that the ideas and vital aims of the South were 'more generally cherished' in New York than in South Carolina or Louisiana."—*page* 112-113.

[2] On Friday last a handsome looking paddle-wheel steamer of about five hundred tons measurement was launched by Messrs. Stevens, of Kelvinhaugh, a sister to the *Fergus*, built by the same firm, and now about to proceed to Nassau. On Saturday, Messrs. Laird & Co., Greenock, launched a beautiful modelled paddle-wheel steamer of seven hundred and fifty tons, a sister to the *City of Petersburg*, launched by Messrs. Laird and Co. lately. They are each to be supplied with powerful engines of two hundred and fifty horse power. These two vessels were first of all contracted for as steamers for

to have.   The blockade seems to be a farce to me, and I am ashamed and disgusted with the whole thing.   The *Niphon*, the fastest vessel of the fleet, is stationed near Smith's Island, where there is nothing to catch. She was on the North Station a few days, and while there drove the *Hebe* ashore and destroyed her, but for some reason was sent back to Smith's Island.   We have now one steamer less than formerly.

" While we have fifteen miles to guard, we cannot see these blockade runners more than half a mile, and if dark not half that distance, so it is no easy thing to get one.   If one is seen she is soon out of sight, under the guns of the fort.

"The *Niphon* has been trying to destroy a steamer that one of the squadron turned back a few mornings since.   She got on shore, and is there now, but is under the guns of Fort Fisher.   The *Niphon* had a grand shooting match with the fort yesterday, but it was of no use, as she only hit the steamer twice in two hours, firing at two and a half miles. The guns of the fort had a longer range than those of the *Niphon*."

It was that manifest and acknowledged ineffectiveness of the blockade that, in the fall of 1863, revived the discussion by the English press, as to declaring its character and disregarding it altogether.   The London *Times* of September 25th, said :

"With such facility is this accomplished that a question is arising in connection with the blockade *which is likely soon to take a shape seriously affecting ourselves.*   The number of ships that get into the Southern ports is so great and the difficulty of passing the Federal fleet so slight, that the Southern government intends formally to dispute the legality of the blockade under the conditions of the fourth article of the Treaty of Paris.   That article declares that a blockade is not binding unless it is 'efficient,' or maintained with such stringency as 'to prevent access to the coast of the enemy.'   Now, in seven months forty-three steamers have carried cargoes into Charleston and forty-nine into Wilmington.   The difficulty of getting a ship into either harbor *seems to have become only nominal.*   So great is the impunity that the Southern Ordnance Bureau actually imports military stores in vessels of its own, and these ships have made twenty-two voyages from Europe and back in perfect safety.   'No vessel belonging to the Confederate government has yet been captured by the Federals,' and, with rare exceptions, 'the government ships come in and go out without molestation.'   'In fact,' says our correspondent, 'the blockade of the Confederate ports is the veriest farce.'   What has become of the immense Northern navy, how is it distributed or what it is doing, it is difficult to say.   But it appears not to be stopping Southern trade, which seems to be limited only by the Southern power of purchasing.   Of safely receiving all it buys it has not the slightest apprehension.   But on *this very facility the Confederate government founds a demand that the blockade shall be declared illegal and non-existent by the nations of Europe.* President Davis contends that it has lapsed and become void by 'inefficiency.'   This is not the first time the question has arisen, and, like every other, it has two sides.   Against the list of vessels that have made the run in, the Federal government may produce a list of ships captured in the attempt; and if it is shown that there are enough cruisers on the coast, or that the commanders are sufficiently vigilant to 'create an evident danger in entering or leaving' a port, the escape of certain ships, either way, will not invalidate a blockade.   The 'efficiency' implied in the treaty is, we assume, to be decided by the circumstances.   It must admit of a more or less absolute perfection being impossible.   But the conviction is strong in

the Glasgow and Belfast mail service, but were sold while being built.   They are on the same model as the famous *Lord Clyde*, now on her way to Nassau as a blockade-runner, and are expected to be very fast sailors.   The *Nola* was christened by the wife of Captain Rollins, a thorough American sailor, who is nominal owner, and who will take command of this vessel when finished.   [From the *Scotsman*, of Edinburgh, Sept. 15th.]

the South that the terms of the treaty are interpreted too rigidly against it; and if renewed representations of what it considers injustice should fail to obtain a hearing, *there is a prospect of the Floridas and Alabamas enforcing the right of detention and seizure on English ships carrying ' contraband of war ' to Northern ports. This would be a complication of affairs that was scarcely looked for and deserves consideration.* But the very demand proves anything but the increasing weakness of the Confederacy."

The number of vessels that evaded the blockade at Wilmington, between January and July, were forty-three, and forty-nine that succeeded in running out. The number of round trips is not to be ascertained. For the same period of time the following was the statement of the receipts of cotton :

" Total by steamers from Charleston, Wilmington, and Savannah, 28,704
" Received by sailing vessels from Atlantic ports, ... 667
" Received from Matamoras, ... 2,704

" Grand total of bales, ... 32,075

The following is a statement of the exports of cotton from January 1st to June 24th, 1863:

" Exported to European ports, ... 23,817 bales.
" Exported to ports in the United States, ... 2,695 bales.

" Total exports, ... 26,512 bales.

" On hand, ... 5,663 bales.

The cotton from Matamoras was shipped in vessels having regular clearance from New York, and was as much an evasion of the United States blockade as any blockade-running from Nassau. It was the " return cargo " for goods exported from New York to Brownsville, Texas, stopping at Matamoras for lighterage to Brownsville. Notwithstanding the United States authorities regarded that evasion of the blockade as legitimate trade, the United States courts condemned the *Peterhoff* and other vessels, trading between Liverpool and Matamoras, as engaged in *illicit* trade. During the year the loss of the cotton trade of the South began to touch a nerve more sensitive than those of patriotism, and we find the Fayetteville, N. C., *Observer* of July, 1863, noticing the arrival at " Wilmington of a steamer from New York, which merely touched at Nassau, with an unbroken cargo of Yankee goods, on joint account of parties in New York and Wilmington." Between the 11th of May and the 6th of June, 1863, eleven steamers and three sailing vessels arrived at Nassau, and fourteen steamers cleared from that port for the blockaded ports of the Confederacy " loaded with uniforms, blankets, cannon, small arms, percussion caps and other munitions of war to aid and comfort the rebels. If we could capture these vessels we should deprive the rebel armies of their supplies and be paid handsomely for our trouble. Will not our blockading officers be a little more vigilant, active and energetic? Here is a rich game slipping between their fingers every day of their lives."[1]

A Queenstown correspondent of the London *Daily Express* of November 28th, 1863, says that:

" Notwithstanding the season of the year, blockade-running seems to be on the increase. Queenstown is seldom without a vessel of this class among its shipping, and at present there are two anchored there. One of them, which had to put in during the gale of Friday, is of extraordinary length. The other, which came in on Monday night, is very large, and fitted with a double screw of superior workmanship. They can be easily recognized by their long, black, rakish-looking two-funnelled hulls, and by an ostentatious display of the British flag. The larger steamer is bound to Bermuda, the other to Nassau. By all accounts the trade is very profitable, as in case of capture the vessel is insured for far more than its value; and in case of success, the immense profit yielded can well afford the extraordinary premiums charged."

In ten months of 1863, from January to October, ninety vessels ran into Wilmington. During August "one ran in every other day," making fifteen in that month; four on the 11th July and five on the 19th of October.

A dispatch at the Merchant's Exchange room, Boston, reported the following blockade-runners at Bermuda, 4th of August, 1863: British steamers *Gibraltar, Banshee, Harriet Pinckney, Mail, Ella, Gladiator* and *Spalding.* Also the Confederate steamers *Lady Davis, Eugene* and *Advance.* The *Sumter* was also in port.

In the following month, a letter from an officer of the blockading squadron off Wilmington, N. C., stated that:

" Two or three steamers had run into Wilmington each day for five days previous. One large steamer ran in at ten o'clock in the forenoon on the 17th inst. A few mornings since, a steamer of fifteen hundred tons ran in. She was pierced for six guns, in addition to two pivot guns, and probably would receive an armament and be ready to proceed to sea within a week. She is larger than the *Alabama* or *Florida,* and appeared to be very fast. The writer thinks she may be the steamer known as the *Southerner.* The *Niphon* and the *Minnesota* were the only efficient vessels off the port, the *Iroquois* having left a week previous in chase of a blockade-runner."

The clearances from Nassau on the 7th and 9th of May, were: steamers *Britannia, Emma, Norseman, Pet, Antonica, Victory, Calypso,* and *Banshee.* And the N. Y. *Herald's* letter from Nassau, May 20th, called attention to the *Wave Queen, Granite City, Stonewall Jackson, Victory, Flora, Havelock, Emma, Ruby, Hero, St. John's, Margaret and Jesse, Mina, Eagle, Calypso, Nicholas I., Duoro, Antonica, Giraffe, Thistle, Gertrude, Georgiana, Britannia, Pet, Ella, Anne, Charleston, Dolphin* and others—twenty-eight in all.

[1] New York *Herald.*

Of these the following were captured : *Granite City, St. John's, Nicholas I., Gertrude. Thistle, Duoro,* and *Dolphin.*

A month later, June 29th, the same correspondence stated that:

"Charleston or Savannah, in their palmiest days, were never so over-run with cotton as is the city of Nassau at the present time. Every available place large enough to hold half a dozen bales is crammed full and running over. It is piled up six and eight bales deep on all the wharves, vacant lots and even on some of the lawns. It is literally ' laying around loose.' To judge by appearances, bagging must be rather a scarce article in Dixie's land, and it strikes me that some other thing will soon be rather scarce there if Uncle Sam sticks to the bonding business in regard to shipments to Nassau. Already numbers of those who have been coining money by sending western flour and eastern goods and notions to Dixie are beginning to howl. Well, let them; they will howl to a different tune when the time comes for a settlement with England and Englishmen for all the wrong done to us in this war. Of course some innocent people must suffer with the guilty, and there are several firms here who do a legitimate retail business, who are put to considerable trouble and annoyance by this bonding business. The government contractors are among the sufferers. They are for the most part Americans and loyal to the Union. Their contracts were made on the strength of getting supplies from the States, and they have to pay heavy fines for the non-fulfilment of their contracts, and it really looks like a hard case. But it is to be hoped that their Yankee ingenuity will help them out of the scrape.

"The blockade, reported to be so effective two weeks ago that it was impossible for a vessel to leave Charleston, would seem to be relaxed, judging by the arrivals here during the last ten days. The steamers *Charleston, Lizzie, Fanny, Alice, Raccoon, Kate. Ella* and *Annie, Banshee, Antonica, Beauregard* and one or two others, have all arrived during that time from Wilmington and Charleston, with full cargoes of cotton, and some have left again for Dixie."

Nassau became an important point for the arrival and departure of the blockade-runners. All vessels from wherever they came, designed for entering the port of Charleston or engaged in trade with Matamoras, stopped at Nassau either on their way to or returning from these ports. From Nassau, the blockade-runners could watch the opportunities when the cruisers of the U. S. navy were not near to embarrass the movement, and the voyage became an easy one, either to the blockaded port, or to the cotton mart at the mouth of the Rio Grande. As a central point, Nassau became of great importance in changing the character of the cargoes from contraband to British goods. Equally with Nassau, Matamoras became a place of note as soon as the entrance to Charleston harbor became difficult. The cotton that was taken to the Bahamas paid no duty to the government, and the tonnage duty was only one shilling a ton. Notwithstanding this, the arrival of the blockade-runner made trade lively and brisk, and the goods imported from the Confederate States yielded some remuneration to the government. Many of the importations paid 15 per cent. *ad valorem* duty, and others a fixed duty of about the same amount. When these goods were bonded and exported again a drawback of ninety per cent.

was allowed and half the tonnage duty was refunded if the vessel carried away products of the island as a return cargo. Nassau is described as—[1]

" A busy place during the war ; the chief depot of supplies for the Confederacy, and the port to which most of the cotton was shipped. Its proximity to the ports of Charleston and Wilmington gave it superior advantages, while it was easily accessible to the swift, light-draft blockade-runners; all of which carried Bahama bank pilots who knew every channel, while the United States cruisers having no bank pilots and drawing more water were compelled to keep the open sea. Occasionally one of the latter would heave to outside the harbor and send in a boat to communicate with the American consul; but their usual cruising ground was off Abaco Light. Nassau is situated upon the island of New Providence, one of the Bahamas, and is the chief town and capital of the group. All of the islands are surrounded by coral reefs and shoals, through which are channels more or less intricate. That wonderful ' river in the sea'—the Gulf Stream—which flows between the Florida coast and the Bahama banks, is only forty miles broad between the nearest opposite points ; but there is no harbor on that part of the Florida coast. The distance from Charleston to Nassau is about five hundred miles, and from Wilmington about five hundred and fifty. Practically, however, they were equidistant, because blockade-runners bound from either port, in order to evade the cruisers lying in wait off Abaco, were compelled to give that headland a wide berth, by keeping well to the eastward of it. But in avoiding Scylla they ran the risk of striking upon Charybdis; for the dangerous reefs of Eleuthera were fatal to many vessels. The chief industries of the islands before the war were the collection and exportation of sponges, corals, etc., and wrecking, to which was added during the war, the lucrative trade of picking and stealing. The inhabitants may be classed as 'amphibious,' and are known among sailors by the generic name of 'Conchs.' The wharves of Nassau, during the war, were always piled high with cotton, and huge warehouses were stored full of supplies for the Confederacy. The harbor was crowded at times with lead-colored, short masted, rakish-looking steamers; the streets alive with bustle and activity during day-time and swarming with drunken revellers by night. Every nationality on earth, nearly, was represented there; the high wages ashore and afloat tempting adventurers of the baser sort; and the prospect of enormous profits offering equally strong inducements to capitalists of a speculative turn. The monthly wages of a sailor on board a blockade-runner was one hundred dollars in gold, and fifty dollars bounty at the end of a successful trip;[2] and this could be accomplished under favorable circumstances in seven days. The captains and pilots sometimes received as much as five thousand dollars besides perquisites. All of the cotton shipped on account of the Confederate government was landed and transferred to a mercantile firm in Nassau, who received a commission for assuming ownership. It was then shipped under the British or other neutral flag to Europe. The firm is reputed to have made many thousands of dollars by these commissions. But besides the cotton shipped by the Confederate government, many private companies and individuals were engaged in the trade; and it was computed (so large were the gains) that the owner could afford to lose a vessel and cargo after two successful voyages. Three or four steamers were wholly owned by the Confederate government; a few more were owned by it in part, and the balance were

---

[1] Narrative of a Blockade Runner, p. 122.

[2] Capt. John Wilkinson, C. P. N., was offered £2,000 in gold a trip by merchants of Liverpool, but preferred to remain loyal to his government and receive a navy officer's salary. A blockade-runner's crew generally consisted of one cap-
tain, three officers, three engineers and twenty-eight men (ten seamen and eighteen firemen). They were generally all Englishmen. The English men-of-war on the West India station found it a difficult matter to prevent their crews from deserting, so great was th temptation offered by the blockade-runners.

private property; but these last were compelled to carry out, as portion of their cargo, cotton on government account, and to bring in supplies. On board the government steamers, the crew which was shipped abroad, and under the articles regulating the 'merchant marine,' received the same wages as were paid on board the other blockade-runners; but the captains and subordinate officers of the government steamers who belonged to the Confederate States navy, and the pilots, who were detailed from the army for this service, received the pay in gold of their respective grades."[1]

There was one singular fact connected with the blockade-running vessels which speaks well for the C. S. naval officers. Down to August 16th, 1864, and perhaps later, only a single blockade-running vessel was lost while under the command of officers of the navy! Officers in the navy, in the meanwhile, commanded many of them and made many successful trips. The *Coquette*, which was one of the most indifferent of all blockade-vessels, and which was sold in the summer of 1864, made *nine round trips* under the command of Lieut. Robert R. Carter, C. S. N., and saved them every one, clearing for the Confederate government at least six hundred thousand dollars. The *Robert E. Lee*, the *best* ship the Confederates had, was successful in all her numerous trips as long as she was under the able command of Capt. John Wilkinson, C. S. N. As has been stated elsewhere, on the first trip she made after the command had been transferred to a person who was *not* an officer of the navy, she was captured.

---

[1] The following comparison of expenses in running a steamer before the war and those of a blockade-runner will illustrate the profits made in the hazardous trade:

Disbursements of a Steamship before the War.

One captain, per month	$150 00
One clerk, per month.................	100 00
One first Officer......................	75 00
One second officer	60 00
One third officer.....................	45 00
One boatswain........................	40 00
One carpenter	60 00
One steward and three assistants......	110 00
One cook and two assistants	90 00
One engineer and three assistants	250 00
Twelve firemen and coal passers.......	600 00
Twelve deck hands....................	360 00
240 tons of coal at $4.................	960 00
Oil, tallow, packing, etc............ ...	100 00
Stevedores out and home..........,.	2,000· 00
Wharfage and boatage....	400 00
Pilotage, out and in.	256 00
Insurance, 2½ per cent. per month, on $150,000......................	3,750 00
Wear and tear, 2¼ per cent. per month,	4,250 00
Incidental expenses..................	1,000 00
Interest................	875 00
Rations for crew..	405 00
Rations for passengers.......... ..	3,000 00
	$19,136 00

Earnings out and home:

Freight, out and home, four trips.................. $14,800 00	
Passengers 38,000 00	
	52,800 00

Profits made per month previous to war, by a first-class steamer on a specie currency...............$33,664 00

31

Disbursements of a Blockade Steamer.

One captain, per month..............	$5,000 00
First officer, $600, second do., $250 third do, $170...	1,020 00
One boatswain........................	160 00
One carpenter.......................	160 00
One purser...................... ...	1,000 00
One steward, $150; three assistants, $180...................	330 00
One cook, $150; two assistants, $120..	270 00
One engineer and three assistants....	3,500 00
Twelve firemen and coal-heavers......	2,400 00
240 tons of coal at $20...............	4,800 00
Rations for crew....................	2,700 00
Oil, tallow and packing..............	1,000 00
Stevedores	5,000 00
Pilotage, out and in.	3,000 00
Sea Insurance	3,500 00
Wear and tear.......................	4,250 00
Incidental expenses..................	1,000 00
Interest.....	875 00
Risks, 25 per cent....................	37,500 00
Provisions for passengers............	3,000 00
	$80,265 00

Earnings. out and home:

800 bales of cotton for government..............$40,000,00	
800 bales of cotton for owners................ 40,000 00	
Return freight for owners 40,000 00	
Return freight for government 40,000 00	
Passengers, out and home. 12,000 00	
	$172,000 00

Leaving a monthly profit (and if successful in five trips will clear the steamer) of...................... $91,735 00

While the officers of the navy were successful in all their many trips except one, every ship belonging to the Confederate government, not commanded by an officer of the navy, was lost. These officers were skillful seamen, good navigators, gentlemen of standing and character; the cause was their cause, and they were above all the suspicion that could be attached to others less favorably situated.

Several British naval officers of high rank and character were engaged in the same exciting and lucrative occupation of blockade-running; among them the gallant Capt. Burgoyne, who commanded afterwards the unfortunate ship *Captain*, of H. B. M.'s navy, and who perished together with nearly the whole crew when she foundered at sea. The late Hon. August Charles Hobart, Marshal of the Turkish Empire, and Vice-Admiral of the English Navy, was a daring navigator in the blockade-running business, under the name of Capt. Roberts. He made several successful trips.

During the first two years of the war, blockade-running had been a matter of no very great difficulty. Sailing-vessels had time after time eluded the vigilance of the Federal cruisers, and with a steamer of very low pressure success was almost certain. Many that could steam no more than seven or eight knots at their highest speed had run in and out several times without a shot being fired, at a time, too, when cotton could be purchased in the Confederacy at eight cents a pound and sold for six times that sum in Nassau or Bermuda. Most of the captures of that period were made by cruisers falling in with the vessels on their passages from either port, and many that were not legally liable to forfeiture were seized and destroyed by the Federal cruisers in their pursuit of the persevering evaders of their navy. But as the number of blockade-runners increased, the captures became more numerous and the cruisers gained experience. About this time, too, the United States having failed to fulfill their oft-repeated promise of bringing the Confederacy into subjection, Europe began to doubt the power and ability of the United States to accomplish their end, or, at all events, to look upon the fall of the Confederacy as an event far distant; and in the meantime Confederate cruisers were making sad havoc among American merchantmen, and European merchants deemed it no longer safe to trust their goods in American bottoms. Thus hundreds of vessels were thrown out of employment, or were obliged to change their flag; many of their fastest steamers were armed, and employed as cruisers and coastguards. This addition to the U. S. naval power affected the interests and changed the character of the blockade-runner in two ways: first, by placing a larger number of much faster cruisers in the waters between the Confederate States and the British West Indies; and, second, by enabling the U. S. government to add to their blockading squadrons many more of their war steamers, thus rendering the attempts to run in and out a very precarious one indeed. But "the hour has never failed to bring forth the man," and the emergency was promptly met by companies formed for the purpose, with large capitals widely distributed, which immediately ordered vessels from the best English and Scotch builders and spared no expense on their fittings and machinery. These vessels were planned and built expressly for the hazardous trade, and were adapted to carry largely on a light draft of water, and were fitted with steam power to drive them at a rate of speed which even put capture from a fair chase out of the question.

With the advent of these great English blockade-running companies, influenced by no Confederate sentiment or patriotic motive, and inspired only by the greed of gain, the blockade business began to develop influences as hurtful to the Confederate cause as its importations had been helpful to its armies. About the end of 1863, and the beginning of 1864, there began in many quarters of the Confederacy an outcry against a business which was fast degenerating into an illicit and unpatriotic traffic. Its moral effects upon the people were beginning to be most injurious, and to throw out temptation to an extravagance which was ruinous to the finances and demoralizing to society. It was building up a class of influential monied men whose interests lay in a continuation and extension of a business which depleted the country without a corresponding return. It was becoming the agency by which the currency, never founded on any stable or sensible basis, was discredited and brought to an unjust and ruinous discount. The export of cotton, for anything beyond military supplies and for the payment of government indebtedness abroad, began to be regarded as an evil, and many considerate and thoughtful citizens urged upon the government not only a more stringent regulation, but a total control over the business of blockade-running. The Richmond (Va.) *Enquirer* urged that:

"The State governments and the Confederate government *should monopolize the entire blockade business*—controlling all the exportations and all the importations—the former acting for the people and the army, the latter for the army alone. A fleet of fifty steamers owned by the States and by the Confederate States, setting apart each trip a portion of the outgoing cargo as insurance, could be maintained at all times on the ocean, and render the importation and exportation of the country entirely subservient to the cause of national liberty. We would not forbid individual and corporate enterprise, but only regulate it so that it should exist only by making the cause of the country its cause, and subordinating avarice to patriotism. If companies were not willing to run their steamers exclusively for the cause, receiving a liberal compensation, *they should not be permitted to enter the ports, but be treated as public enemies*, which they would be; for, in this war, every citizen that is not with us is against us. The blockade does not require regulating, but controlling—not department rules, but official management.

"By such control of the importations the exports would be made to contribute exclusively to the military defence of the country. By curbing the means of display in dress and on the table the unbecoming vanity of the people would be checked and habits of frugality and economy encouraged. By closing the markets of the country to imported luxuries the disgraceful extravagance that now pervades all classes of the people would be checked, and if the currency was not appreciated it would not be depreciated by a daily comparison with articles of luxury. The blockade regulations of the last Congress were a failure because they impeded individual enterprise, and did not provide that the government should supply the place of the companies that would not run the blockade under those regulations. Fair and liberal compensation should be paid to individual enterprise; but the governments—State and Confederate—should own a fleet of steamers, and run the blockade under a system which, insuring against capture, would supply losses as fast as they occurred. This is a gigantic war, and requires gigantic means and herculean efforts."

The exorbitant prices obtained at the great auction sales of blockade goods, the combination between dealers to purchase all of certain lines of goods, and dividing up the lot prevent all competition, and the positive refusal of the importer to recognize Confederate money as currency, pointed prejudice at both the trade and the auctions. In addition to those evils, the character of much of the goods imported was not in the least contributive to the support of the army or to the necessities of the people. Expensive silks, cloths, brandies, rum, ales, whiskeys, sardines, the use of which cultivated tastes and catered to an extravagance hurtful to that self-denial so necessary to a people struggling for existence against enormous odds. The regulation of the blockade business, rather than its suppression, was demanded both by the sentiment of the people and by the necessities of the army. To have prohibited blockade-running, or to have so hampered it with restrictions as to deprive it of that profit necessary to induce capitalists to incur its risks, and the adventurous to share its dangers, would have been to institute, within Confederate lines, the very system that the United States had attempted on the outside. The aid of the outside world was necessary to the army and people of the Confederate States, but that aid had become encrusted with an evil which it was very difficult to remove.

In response to public sentiment the Confederate Congress enacted laws[1] to regulate foreign commerce, and to prohibit the introduction of "luxuries." The first act prohibited the exportation of cotton, tobacco, military and naval stores, and forbid any vessel, vehicle, slave or animal engaged in loading or transporting such articles, to go beyond the limits of the Confederate States, or to any Confederate port actually within the enemy's lines. And by the law all persons concerned in such exportations were to be deemed guilty of high misdeameanor, unless authorized by special permits to be given under rules to be prescribed by the President.

[1] " An act to prohibit the importation of luxuries, or of articles not necessaries or of common use." Approved February 6th, 1864. " A bill to impose regulations upon the foreign commerce of the Confederate States to provide for the public defence." Approved February 6th, 1864.

The act prohibiting the introduction of " luxuries," after March 1st, 1864, contained a long list of prohibited articles, and limited the liberty of importation into the ports of the Confederate States to articles of prime necessity. It provided that the Secretary of the Treasury should prescribe the maximum prices within which importations of articles partly or wholly of cotton, flax, wool or silk thread should be made, and provided that any article imported contrary to that law should be forfeited, and the owner be required to pay double the value thereof.

The regulations of the Treasury and War Departments, under these laws, required of all vessels going out of Confederate ports that one-half of the tonnage may be employed by the Confederate government for its own use, both on the outward and homeward voyage; and required the owners of vessels to execute a bond conditioned "that the vessel will pursue the voyage designated and that she will return with reasonable dispatch to a Confederate port after her outward cargo shall be discharged, with a cargo consisting of one-half of articles not prohibited by the laws of the Confederate States, and that the other half of such cargo shall be such as the government shall offer for shipment from such port." The regulations fixed the freight to be paid by the Confederate States, on all cotton and tobacco shipped from a Confederate port, at five pence sterling per pound, payable on delivery at the port of destination in coin or sterling exchange ; and the return freight was fixed at the rate of twenty-five pounds per ton in cotton, payable on its delivery at the Confederate port, at ten pence sterling per pound for middling uplands, and a proportionate price for cotton of other qualities. In calculating the ton of freight by weight, 2,240 pounds, and by measure forty cubic feet, were to be allowed. If the outward bound vessels should consent, at the request of the government, to take two-thirds of her cargo on account of the Confederate States, the outward freight was fixed at six pence sterling per pound ; and whenever the government was not prepared to fill up any portion of the tonnage reserved for its use, at the time of sailing, her owners were allowed to fill up the same on their own account; but no vessel was to be allowed to sail on her outward voyage, without the consent of the government, until one-third of her cargo was laden for the use of the government.

The publication of these laws and regulations upon blockade-running created intense interest in Nassau and other ports, where the blockade-runners most congregated. The Nassau *Herald* intimated the probability of a withdrawal of many companies from the business, saying :

" We must conclude that the responsible framers of this measure are fully aware that the agents here will shrink from incurring the responsibility of running the vessels of their principals, without first receiving positive instructions. What then could be the object of the framers of this startling measure, in launching it without even a preliminary announcement, or without specifying a reasonably distant day when it would come into operation? A surprise was clearly intended, and most assuredly has been effected—with what object we forbear to scrutinize too closely; but that less partial pens will probe the motives for so suddenly announcing, and so suddenly carrying into effect, this new and sweeping change, we are quite prepared to expect.

"We have in our former article stated that the sequel may show material advantages to the Confederacy, and those advantages may arise under the measures being adopted by Mr. Slidell, the Confederate Commissioner at Paris. Mr. Slidell has issued instructions to the effect that persons holding cotton-loan bonds for which they wish to obtain cotton must transfer the bonds to his keeping, and on their doing so he will give a certificate or delivery order for the amount of cotton which they represent. If it be the aim of Mr. Slidell, acting of course under instructions, to reissue these bonds at their enhanced value, the Confederate exchequer will be provided with funds, although such a course of procedure will probably meet with censure from the bankholders.

"Large sums have been made and large sums have been lost in these ventures by English sympathizers and speculators, and the authorities at Richmond will find that all such persons will retire as soon as the prospect of gain adequate to the risk incurred ceases. It must not be forgotten that the adventurous spirit of English merchants led the way at the outset in blockade-running, and it is much to be regretted that the Confederates themselves did not take the initiative in the matter, and that even at this date their enterprise (their patriotism is beyond question) has not been more concentrated on so vital an issue as the conveyance of munitions of war and necessary merchandise to the Confederacy.

"We have investigated the merits of the new law with an anxious desire to trace in it marked and decided advantages to Confederate interests, as distinct from all other interests; but we are not of those who consider the cause of the Confederacy will be best served by tacitly assenting to all the measures which may emanate from the executive, and we consider it to be self-evident, that in examining such a measure as the one we are discussing, it is impossible to ignore the interests of the blockade-runner. The Confederates have made great and noble sacrifices, but they cannot surmount the impossibilities, and an impossibility it certainly would prove to be to carry on blockade-running on a comprehensive scale without a large margin of profit being allowed to meet inevitable contingencies."

On the other hand, it was replied to the complaint of the blockade-runner, that the system as it had been conducted had not been beneficial to the Confederate government, nor helpful to the people; that it had depreciated the currency, created an exorbitant rate of prices, and established a widespread and unprincipled extortion; that the English blockade-runners, by refusing to take Confederate money, and demanding gold or cotton, had drained the country of all specie, and greatly increased the price of exchange; that under the then existing system gold flowed out of the country and the supply of cotton was being reduced without a corresponding remuneration; that cotton was not bought with gold, but *swapped* for goods, and sometimes trinkets — not fit for consumption, but adapted only to vanity and display; that silks, satins, laces, broadcloths, liquors, and ladies' goods generally, had made up the bulk of the cargoes of the blockade-runner, and that while they carried a small proportion of army supplies, it was only because they were stowed in that part of the vessel reserved for the government; and that real and substantial aid and help to the army and people had never been the aim or purpose of the English blockade-runner; and, finally, that if the great English blockade-running companies withdrew from the business, the citizens, States, and government of the Confederate States would go back into and conduct it for the purpose of defence only, and not merely for the avarice and greed with which it had been prosecuted.

Though the legislation for the regulation of blockade was adopted in the early part of 1864, there were more vessels, in January, 1865, engaged in blockade-running than when the regulations went into effect.

Notwithstanding the use of swifter blockade vessels, many of them being captured blockade-runners, as well as the largely increased navy of the United States, and the stimulant to increased vigilance which many prizes had given to the officers of the blockading squadron, it was still recognized as impossible for the Federal government to stop blockade-running, except by capturing with the army the ports from which the business was done. This impossibility, so far as the navy was concerned, resulted from physical causes, and not from any neglect, indifference, or absence of stimulating motives. The conformation of the Atlantic coast, and the direction and force of the winds, were the causes that aided blockade-running as well as hindered and embarrassed the blockading squadron. If the wind blew *off* the coast, it drove the squadron to sea, and enlarged the perimiter of the circle through which the blockade-runner could swiftly and safely steam. If the wind blew *landward* the blockading squadron were compelled to haul off to a greater distance to escape the consequences of the heavy seas which dashed with violence upon the coast. The shoals that lined the North Carolina coast extended for miles into the sea, and the whole coast is not surpassed in danger to navigation by any other when a strong easterly wind meets the ebb-tide. And yet it was an easy matter for a pilot experienced in the coast to run a swift-steaming light-draft vessel out to sea or into port, while the heavier and deeper draft vessels of the blockading squadron were buffeting the stormy winds and waves.

The restrictions imposed upon foreign commerce by the above-mentioned Acts of the Confederate Congress had not, in January, 1865, materially reduced the number of vessels engaged in running the blockade. President Davis, in a message to Congress on this subject, said that the number of vessels arriving at only two ports—Charleston and Wilmington—from November 1st to December 6th, had been forty-three, and that only a very small portion of those outward-bound had been captured; that out of 11,796 bales of cotton shipped since July 1st, 1864, but 1,272 bales had been lost. And the special report of the Secretary of the Treasury in relation to the same matter stated, that there had been imported at the ports of Wilmington and Charleston since October 26th, 1864, 8,632,000 pounds of meat, 1,507,000 pounds of lead, 1,933,000 pounds of saltpetre, 546,000 pairs of shoes, 316,000 pairs of blankets, 520,000 pounds of coffee, 69,000 rifles, 97 packages of revolvers, 2,639 packages of medicines, 43 cannon, with a very large quantity of other articles. In addition to these articles, many valuable stores and supplies had been brought in by way of the Northern lines, by way of Florida, and through the port of Galveston, and through Mexico, across the Rio Grande. From March 1st, 1864, to January 1st, 1865, the value of the shipments of cotton on Confederate government account was shown by the Secretary's report to have been $5,296,000 in specie, of which $1,500,000 had been shipped out between July 1st and December 1st, 1864.

A list of vessels which were running the blockade from Nassau and other ports, in the period intervening between November, 1861, and March, 1864, showed that 84 steamers were engaged; of these, 37 were captured by the enemy, 12 were totally lost, 11 were lost and the cargoes partially saved, and 1 foundered at sea. They made 363 trips to Nassau and 65 to other ports. Among the highest number of runs made were those of the *Fanny*, which ran 18 times, and the *Margaret and Jessie*, which performed the same feat, and was captured. Out of 425 runs from Nassau alone (including 100 schooners), only 62—about one in seven—were unsuccessful. A letter from Nassau, on the chances of blockade-running, published in June, 1864, said:

"You will please observe that most of the boats here enumerated were wholly unfit for the purpose to which they had been hastily applied under the inducements of the large profit, and are very different from those which have been more recently built, and expressly for blockade-running. Still, even now it is by no means an uncommon thing for a five or six knot boat to make several successful trips, while the better class pass the blockading squadron almost as carelessly as if none such existed, frequently in open daylight. The average life of a boat, which from the subjoined table would appear to be about five runs, is therefore in reality much higher, and may be safely estimated, with proper management, to be at least four round trips, or eight successful runs. Taking all the craft, good, bad, and indifferent together, you will find that out of eighty-four steamers, eleven only failed on the first run; thirty-seven have been captured, and twenty-five lost from various marine accidents; while twenty-two are still safe, after having paid themselves many times over."

In confirmation of the ineffectiveness of the blockade, as well as of the fact that the restrictive legislation of the Confederate Congress had not materially reduced blockade-running, the New York *Herald*, commenting upon the above exhibit, remarked that:

"Of the vessels which carried this, twenty-five cleared from Matamoras, the quantity brought by them being about 5,000 bales. These figures will serve to give an idea of the immense activity that has prevailed in the traffic between the rebel States and England, despite all the efforts of our cruisers. The shutting up of the port of Wilmington, the principal channel for this trade, will, of course, cut off a large proportion of it. All the means of entry on the rebel line of coast will then be hermetically closed, and their supplies by direct sources cut off. There will remain only the line of supply through Texas; but, as this is circuitous and tedious, it will fail to satisfy the wants of the rebels as fast as needed. The possession by the French of Matamoras will, of course, continue to facilitate the traffic to a certain extent by rendering the articles that pass that way secure from seizure. Had measures been taken by our government to permanently occupy Brownsville and the line of the Rio Grande we should have been enabled to put an estoppal upon all traffic by that route. This, however, will, we presume, be done as soon as a sufficient force can be spared for that purpose; but by that time we should be in a condition to suppress it in another and more effective manner—namely, by clearing the French and their Austrian protegés out of Mexico."

And in its issue of January 21st, 1865, its correspondent from the Bahamas stated that

"The utmost activity prevailed in the Anglo-rebel blockade-running fleet plying between Wilmington, and Charleston and Nassau. Cotton valued at $3,500,000 had been landed at Nassau from the above-named Southern ports within ten days. A large number of British trading vessels had sailed from Liverpool, London, and the Clyde laden with supplies for the rebels. Their names and days of sailing are published in the *Herald*, so that our gallant sailors off Wilmington may have a fair chance of rewarding themselves liberally with the spoils of the common enemy. Two blockade-runners cleared for that port, at Nassau, on the 14th inst. They have probably discovered before now, on arrival in New Inlet, that a change has taken place in the position of affairs there, and that they were just in time to fall into the hands of the national forces."

The military and naval expeditions against Wilmington, in December, 1864, and January, 1865, resulted in the capture of the forts and the closing of the port. Eight vessels left the port of Nassau between the 12th and 16th of January, one of which took four one-hundred-pounder Armstrong guns; and at the time of their sailing there were over two and a half million pounds of bacon stored at Nassau awaiting transportation. The confidence reposed in the defence of Wilmington continued unabated on the part of the blockade-runners, and the *Charlotte*, the *Blenheim*, and the *Stag*, all British steamers, ran in after the fall of Fort Fisher, and were captured by the Federal cruisers in the river. The blockade-runner *Owl*, Capt. John N. Maffitt, C. S. N., in command, succeeded in passing over the bar near Fort Caswell and anchored at Smithville on the night the forts were evacuated, and immediately returned to Bermuda, arriving on the 21st, and carrying the news of the fall of Fort Fisher and the end of blockade-running at Wilmington. Her arrival was timely, stopping the *Maud Campbell, Old Dominion, Florence, Deer* and *Virginia*. Most, if not all, of these steamers now turned their prows toward Charleston, the last harbor remaining accessible; and though the fall of that city was impending, yet a cargo might be safely landed and transported along the interior line to the famishing armies of the Confederate States. To that end Capt. Wilkinson determined to make the effort:

"But it was the part of prudence to ascertain, positively, before sailing, that Charleston was still in our possession. This intelligence was brought by the *Chicora*, which arrived at Nassau on the 30th of January; and on February 1st, the *Owl, Carolina, Dream, Chicora,* and *Chameleon* sailed within a few hours of each other for Charleston."

The effort was a brave and gallant one, but was ineffectual—the U. S. S. *Vanderbilt* intercepted the *Chameleon*, and after an exciting chase was *dodged* by the fast-sailing vessel under the cool seamanship of the gallant Wilkinson. Turning on the *Vanderbilt*, the *Chameleon* again attempted to reach Charleston, but having lost a day in escaping from the *Vanderbilt*, and retarded by unfavorable weather, did not reach the coast near Charleston bar till the fifth night after leaving Nassau. The blockading fleet, reinforced from that off Wilmington, now closed every practical entrance; but it was not until after assurances from the pilot that entrance was impossible that Capt. Wilkinson " turned away from the land, our hearts sank within us, while conviction forced itself upon us that the cause for which so much blood had been shed, so many miseries bravely endured, and so many sacrifices cheerfully made, was about to perish at last." The *Chicora*, more fortunate than the *Chameleon*, ran into Charleston, but finding that city evacuated, ran out, despite the *effectiveness* of the blockade, and reached Nassau on the 28th. The *Fox*, less fortunate, ran into Charleston in ignorance of its capture, and was seized by the Federal cruisers.

Capt. John N. Maffitt, C. S. N., in the *Owl*, left Havana about the middle of March, within "a quarter of an hour" after the U. S. S. *Cherokee* steamed out of the harbor. Passing Morro Castle, the *Owl* hugged the coast towards the west, followed by the *Cherokee*—the chase continued for an hour or more; the *Owl* had the speed, and Maffitt the seamanship, to throw "dust into the eyes" of his pursuer by changing her coal from hard to soft, and clouding the air with dense black smoke, under cover of which the *Owl* turned on the *Cherokee*, and steaming away to the stern of the cruiser, disappeared in the darkness of night and storm.

In the trans-Mississippi, blockade-running continued with some success until the 2d of June, when the terms of surrender in Galveston, by Gens. E. Kirby Smith and J. Bankhead Magruder with Gen. A. J. Smith brought the war to an effectual close. Charleston was evacuated on the 17th of February, and Fort Anderson, the last of the defences at Wilmington, fell on the 19th.

With the termination of blockade-running the commercial importance of Matamoras, Nassau, Bermuda, and other West

India ports, departed. On the 11th of March there were lying in Nassau thirty-five British blockade-runners, which were valued at $15,000,000 in greenbacks, and there were none to do them reverence. Their occupation was gone, their profits at an end, and some other service must be sought to give them employment. There exists no record, if any were kept, from which computation can be made of the amount and value of goods, arms, supplies and stores introduced into the Confederate States during the four years of blockade-running. But the Hon. Zebulon Vance, who was Governor of North Carolina during a large part of the war, has put on record the share, in part, of that State, in blockade-running, from which a general idea of the amount of values introduced may be approximated. In an address before the Association of the Maryland Line, delivered in Baltimore, February 23d, 1885, he said:

" By the general industry and thrift of our people, and by the use of a number of blockade-running steamers carrying out cotton and bringing in supplies from Europe, I had collected and distributed, from time to time, as near as can be gathered from the records of the Quartermaster's Department, the following stores: Large quantities of machinery supplies, 60,000 pairs of handcards, 10,000 grain scythes, 200 barrels blue stone for the wheat growers, leather and shoes for 250,000 pairs, 50,000 blankets, grey-wooled cloth for at least 250,000 suits of uniforms, 12,000 overcoats (ready made), 2,000 best Enfield rifles (with 100 rounds of fixed ammunition), 100,000 pounds of bacon, 500 sacks of coffee for hospital use, $50,000 worth of medicines at gold prices, large quantities of lubricating oils, besides minor supplies of various kinds for the charitable institutions of the State. Not only was the supply of shoes, blankets, and clothing more than sufficient for the supply of the North Carolina troops, but large quantities were turned over to the Confederate government for the troops of other States. In the winter succeeding the battle of Chickamauga, I sent to Gen. Longstreet's corps 14,000 suits of clothing complete. At the surrender of Gen. Johnston, the State had on hand, ready made and in cloth, 92,000 suits of uniform, with great stores of blankets, leather, etc. To make good the warrants on which these purchases had been made abroad, the State purchased and had on hand in trust for the holders 11,000 bales of cotton and 100,000 barrels of rosin. The cotton was partly destroyed before the war closed, the remainder, amounting to several thousand bales, was captured after peace was declared, by certain officers of the Federal army."

The Proclamations of President Andrew Johnson, of the 22d of May and of the 13th, 14th and 23d of June, and that of the 29th of August, 1865, removed all restriction on internal, domestic and coastwise intercourse and trade with the Southern States, as well as all restrictions as to contraband of war; and dispersed the squadrons and put an end to the blockade of the Southern ports. Peace was coming, and, after years of reconstruction almost as hurtful and cruel as war itself, finally settled down to bless a reconstructed Union.

During the whole period of the war, and despite the efforts of the government at Washington, and the vigilance of the generals commanding the armies, there existed a kind of blockade-running across the Potomac and along the whole lines of the armies, between the peoples on both sides, by which large amounts of supplies were introduced into the Confederate States. A kind of legality was thrown around this trade by permits given at Washington, and the whole spirit of the laws relating to trade in "insurrectionary districts," as well as those in regard to "captured and abandoned property," were mere disguises to favor certain persons engaged in illicit traffic. The following letter was captured and published in the New York *Times,* and affords some evidence of how that traffic was conducted and who were engaged in it:

"MY DEAR SIR—Allow me to suggest for your consideration a place for a most profitable adventure, which a little diplomacy can render perfectly safe and practicable.

"To obtain the privilege, either tacit or written, so that it be reliable to run the line of blockade with a cargo of staple articles from a foreign port, and to return with a cargo of Upland or Sea Island cotton.

"Such a vessel coming in at Ossabaw Inlet, under a discreet and reticent master, with vessel and cargo (when within Confederate lines) in my name, would be perfectly safe, and I would furnish her outward cargo—more than sufficient to pay for the inward—and send sterling exchange for your half of the profits.

"The profits would enable you to pay handsomely for the privilege, either by a *pro rata* division or by a direct *bonus*—to whomsoever you negotiate with.

"If you negotiate for such an adventure in any way that is reliable, I will pay my half of all costs and expenses—including that for the pass in and out, and give my personal attention to the sale of the inward and outward purchase of the cargo, and guarantee the latter safely on board. The profits in and out could not fall short of 300 to 500 per cent. on the investment, which would be equally divided after deducting all expenses.

"A reply, addressed to R. W. H. Welch or Alexander Johnson, Esqrs., Nassau, N. P., and to further care of Messrs. John Frazier & Co., Charleston, will reach me.   "I am, etc.,   G. B. LAMAR.

"*To Hon.* FERNANDO WOOD, *New York.*"

The publication of Mr. Lamar's letter in the Confederate States had much influence in shaping the legislation, referred to in the text, for prohibiting commercial intercourse with the enemy. Mr. Lamar's letter, though addressed to the Hon. Fernando Wood, of New York, does not implicate that gentleman, since there exists no evidence that Lamar was authorized by Mr. Wood to make such a proposition, and the mere writing *to* Mr. Wood is only evidence of what Lamar proposed, and not that Mr. Wood assented to or was cognizant in advance of the proposition. The letter, however, is instructive as to the profits arising from that traffic, as well as the shifts and resorts to which men went in making haste to get rich— even in the midst of desolating war. Mr. Lamar acknowledged the genuineness of the letter, defended his scheme for trading with the enemy as "advantageous" and "beneficial" to the Confederate cause, as well as highly profitable to himself. Mr. Lamar—and he was but one example of many people engaged in that trade—failed to comprehend that trading with an enemy in time of war was a crime infamous under every known construction of international law, as well as against the provisions of the statutes of the Confederate States. Such people, realizing enormous profits, disguised from themselves, under the color of helping with their importations the cause of the Confederate States, the crime they were committing as well as the aid they were giving to the enemy.

Before Mr. Lamar's letter was captured, he ventilated his patriotism in the Savannah papers after this fashion:

"I don't own a wharf in the city that I would not sooner sacrifice altogether than the infernal Yankees (now waging the most savage warfare against us, and using the scum of Europe, of all their own large cities, as well as their Billy Wilson regiment of convicts, to kill and destroy our most valuable citizens, as they have done and are doing), should ever be allowed to enjoy any right or privilege within this State."

Such evidence of greed is a melancholy instance of the infirmity which overtook a very large class of people at the South during the war. That class was composed of heavy capitalists, who, rich by accident, were greedy by nature, and while blatant of their patriotism and furious in their advocacy of hostilities, were at all times willing to trade with the enemy and to accumulate fortunes out of the impoverishment of their country.

The interchange of kindnesses and the material aid sent across the Potomac from sympathizing friends in Maryland, and particularly in Baltimore, of which the amount and value was immense, must not be confounded with blockade-running. There was no trading in their kindness, no element of gain, no part of greed or money-making. It was the materializing of sympathy, without the demoralizing influence of trade or traffic.

CHAPTER XVII.

THE TRANS-MISSISSIPPI WATERS.

IN the early days of the war, the operations of the great armies and navies which were then organized, were confined almost exclusively to the territory east of the Mississippi River. In some of the States west of that river, there were a few important military movements before 1863, but the great demonstrations of the Federal government to crush the independence of the Southern States were aimed at those more vital points of the Confederacy from which issued the intelligence and the power that directed and prosecuted the struggle.

The Confederate naval operations west of the Mississippi were confined mainly to the army, or were conducted jointly by both branches of the service—the army and the navy. At the beginning of the war, the few navy officers who were assigned to duty in the trans-Mississippi department were placed under the command of district commanders. They performed meritorious service as engineer officers, building, arming and officering shore batteries and fortifications ; and it can be said of them, that without their co-operation and aid many Confederate successes would not have been obtained. The deeds of enterprise and daring of the navy officers in the trans-Mississippi department, in the early days of the war, are worthy of all praise, and we regret that their labors in the cause of the South are covered up in the operations of the army with which they co-operated.

In 1861 Texas, like all her sister States of the South, was entirely unprepared for war, but her people were ready to answer with alacrity any call from the President of the Confederacy. One of the first accessions to the Confederate States navy was the capture of the U. S. steamship *Star of the West* off Indianola, Texas, by a party of volunteers from Galveston. The *Star of the West* was 1,172 tons burden, and built to run from New York to Aspinwall on the route to California. She was chartered by the U. S. government to take a small force and supplies to Major Anderson at Fort Sumter,

Charleston. She left New York at five o'clock in the afternoon of January 5th, 1861, and proceeded down the bay, hove to and received on board four officers and two hundred and fifty soldiers with their arms and ammunition, and proceeded to sea, crossing the bar at Sandy Hook at nine o'clock the same night. She arrived off Charleston bar at half-past one in the morning of the 9th, and as the lights were all out and no guiding marks to be found, she proceeded slowly until 4 A. M., and then, being in four and a half fathoms of water, lay to until daylight. As the day began to break a small steamer was seen inshore, which, as soon as she discovered the *Star of the West*, burned a blue light and two red lights as signals, and shortly after steamed over the bar into the ship channel. The soldiers were now all put below, and no one allowed on deck except those belonging to the vessel. As soon as there was light enough to see, the *Star of the West* crossed the bar and proceeded up the channel until she was about two miles from Forts Moultrie and Sumter, when a masked battery on Morris Island opened fire on her. The battery floated a red Palmetto flag, and the *Star of the West* the United States flag. The latter continued on under the fire of the battery, which was about five-eights of a mile distant, for over ten minutes. Several of the shots went entirely over her; one shot passed just clear of the pilot-house, another passed between the smokestack and walking-beam of the engine; another struck the ship just abaft of the fore rigging and stove in the planking, while another came near carrying away the rudder. At the same time there was a movement of two steamers from near Fort Moultrie, one of them towing a schooner, which was thought by the officers of the *Star of the West* to be an armed vessel to cut them off. Fearing capture or destruction, Capt. McGowan of the *Star of the West* wore round and steered down the channel, and the battery continued to fire upon him until the shot fell short. He crossed the bar outward at 8.50 A. M. and returned to New York.

A correspondence immediately took place between the commander of Fort Sumter and the Governor of South Carolina, in which the former stated that an unarmed vessel of the United States had been fired on, and wished to know if it had been with the sanction of the Governor. The latter replied, that any attempt to send troops into Charleston harbor by the United States, to re-enforce the forts or to retake and resume possession of the forts within the waters of South Carolina, would be regarded as an act of hostility.

The *Star of the West* was subsequently chartered again by the Federal government, and sent to Texas to receive and convey to New York a part of the regular force withdrawn from that State; but on the 17th of April, 1861, she was boarded off Indianola and captured without resistance.

It appears that in April 1861, Col. Earl Van Dorn, being in Galveston, determined to attempt her capture. He called for volunteers, and in about two hours and a half detachments from the Galveston Artillery, Lieut. Van Buren commanding; the Island City Rifles, Capt. Muller, a German company, and the Wigfall Guards, Capt. McGrath, an Irish company, responded to the call. The entire party amounted to 71 men— 13 artillerists, 29 rifles, and 29 guards. They embarked on the steamer *Matagorda*, which left early on the following morning for Indianola, reaching that point about five in the afternoon. The men were concealed in the state rooms. At Indianola the transport *Fashion* was loading with U. S. troops, numbering about 6,000 men, with baggage, to put on board the *Star of the West*, Capt. Howe, which was lying in deep water outside of the bar. The *Matagorda* put back, and at Siluria, eighteen miles distant, she transferred her armed force to the *General Rusk*. About midnight the *Rusk*, with the soldiers on board, came in hailing distance of the *Star of the West*, and upon being hailed, answered, "The *General Rusk*, with troops on board; can you take our line now?" "Certainly," was the answer from Capt. Howe, he fancying that the troops belonged to the United States. Capt. Howe asked why the *Fashion* did not bring the troops, and was told that she would be along in a few hours, with the *rest* of the troops and their baggage. The sea was rather rough, and after some little trouble the *Rusk* made fast alongside. In a very short time the Galveston soldiers were on board with their guns; and Capt. Howe hardly had time to look at them, when they suddenly presented bayonets, and their officer commanded him to surrender.

"To what flag am I requested to surrender?" asked the astonished captain. Ensign Duggan, of the Wigfall Guards, here displayed the Lone Star flag of Texas, and in his richest brogue exclaimed: "That's it, look at it, me byes; did ye iver see the Texas flag on an Irish jackstaff before?" The captain, having no means of resistance, surrendered without saying a word. He had a crew of forty-two men and 900 barrels of provisions, but nothing else; none of the arms or munitions of the Federal troops had yet arrived on board.

The prisoners were all treated with politeness. The steamer was immediately put about for Galveston; and great must have been the bewilderment of the officers of the *Fashion* and of the Federal troops next morning when they found the *Star of the West* nowhere in sight.

At Galveston, Col. Van Dorn put Mr. Falval, first mate of the *Mexico*, on board the *Star of the West* as captain, and likewise the engineer of the *Mexico;* and ordering the soldiers on board to see her safely into New Orleans, he left, to take charge of some 600 troops who were waiting there for him to go back to Indianola.

The *Star of the West* arrived safely in New Orleans and was moored in the Mississippi River below Algiers. She was turned over to the C. S. navy, and for some time was used as a receiving-ship.

The Texas coast, extending over several hundred miles, was reported, September 27th, 1861, as "in almost a defenceless state," and that the "task of defending successfully any point against an attack of any magnitude amounts to a military impossibility." Earnest efforts were made to put all points of danger in a position of defence. For this purpose, by "Special Orders No. 123," from the Adjutant and Inspector General's office, at Richmond, Va., on August 14th, 1861, Commander W. W. Hunter, C. S. N., was ordered to proceed to Galveston, and "report to Gen. Earl Van Dorn for duty, as superintendent in charge of the works for the defence of the coast of Texas." By the same order, John Withers, Assistant Adjutant General, directed Brig. Gen. Paul O. Hébert to assume command of the Department of Texas in place of Gen. Earl Van Dorn, who was ordered to turn the department over to him and report in Richmond.

On September 27th, upon assuming command, Gen. Hébert reported to the Secretary of War, that "On a coast like this, where in calm weather a landing can be effected at any point, and the bays in the rear and flank of Galveston Island reached in that manner, or by the pass at the west end, the problem of defence, considering the means available to that effect, is certainly one of very difficult, if not impossible, solution." The port of Galveston was partially defended by a few open sand-works, mounted with guns of calibres ranging from eighteen to thirty-two pounders and totally inadequate to resist a bombardment with heavy guns.

Upon his arrival in Texas, Commander Hunter was placed on special duty and assigned to the immediate command of the naval defences of the port of Galveston and the vessels in the employ of the Confederate government. He was subject to the orders of his military superiors in the district and was authorized "to employ such boats propelled by steam or otherwise, as the service, in his judgment, rendered necessary." He was to "take measures to guard against any surprise by the enemy in the harbor and bay of Galveston," and report upon a plan for "establishing a system of alarm signals with the forces on the island and at Virginia Point." His attention was also directed to the railroad bridge.

In obedience to these orders Commander Hunter made a complete inspection of the water approaches and defences of Galveston. On November 17th, 1861, with the chartered steamer *John F. Carr*, drawing two and a half feet of water, he made an examination, and reported on the Rollover, and the practicability of the launches being transported across it, and the necessity of defending that point, and the best means of effecting this. He also examined the water of East Bay; from Bolivar Point to the nearest approachable shore of the Rollover in that direction and examined and recommended the means of defence at Smith's Point. On the 22d of November, by direction of the commanding general, he reported on the practicability of gunboats of the class represented to be in the enemy's fleet being able to reach a position in Galveston Bay to command the bridge from Galveston Island to the mainland; and on December 2d, he reported on "the means of defence of the mouth of Trinity River."

Commander Hunter was exceedingly active, and directed all his energies and talents to fortifying Galveston, Brownsville, Pass Cavallo, and Sabine Pass. There were no vessels under his command, except a few improvised "cotton-clad" river steamers and with these he rendered efficient service to the army in transporting troops and munitions of war, and guarding the coast from the marauding expeditions of the enemy. The "mosquito fleets" of Texas cotton-clad steamers had many severe engagements with the enemy during the war, and their brave actions form a noteworthy series of episodes.

If the Texan authorities found the coast defenceless, and a navy non-existent, in 1861, fortunately the Federal government, in blockading the Atlantic coast, Mobile and New Orleans, exhausted its supply of vessels. We find the following decided opinion expressed of this attempted blockade in the London *Shipping Gazette*, as late in the year 1861, as August:

"There is no doubt that, up to the present time, so far as we have been informed, the blockade of the Southern coast has not been efficient. The more important ports, such as New Orleans, Mobile, Charleston and Pensacola, have been blockaded, but the blockade of these places appears to have nearly exhausted the disposable forces of the national government and the consequence is that other places, such as Wilmington, Beaufort, etc., although declared to be blockaded, have not as yet been legally, that is, efficiently closed against commerce. *It is in vain for the national government to proclaim the blockade of the Southern ports from Baltimore to the Rio Grande.* Neutral States are only bound to respect such a proclamation so far as there is the ability to give effect to it, which on the part of the national government there does not appear to be. All this is, of course, well known to Admiral Milne, who has been placed in the somewhat difficult position of having to witness an inefficient blockade with a force at his disposal adequate to raise it. That he should have applied to his government for precise instructions under the circumstances is more than probable, but with the sincere desire to preserve a strict neutrality between the American belligerents, which animates our government and people, it is equally probable that Admiral Milne has been directed to avoid any collision with the blockading squadron, until at least a fair time has elapsed for establishing the blockade of coast along the line indicated by President Lincoln's proclamation."

To anticipate a little, it was not in fact until 1863 that the blockade of the Texas coast became formidable, and operations began with a purpose to hold the important points.

In July 1861, the *South Carolina*, a vessel previously in the New York and Savannah trade converted into an armed cruiser, Capt. Alden commanding, appeared before Galveston, and captured five small sloops, among them the yacht *Dart*, and the sloops *Shark* and *Falcon*. Great excitement followed the arrival of the *South Carolina*, and the citizens of Galveston immediately dispatched a pilot-boat to Sabine Pass to intercept vessels bound for Galveston. The *Dart* was subsequently armed by the United States; and on August 3rd, the *South Carolina* and *Dart*, against the protest of all the foreign consuls, shelled the shore batteries, and the city of Galveston, but without doing much damage. [1]

Gradually the Federal fleet was re-enforced. The *Rhode Island* and *Santee* were sent to Galveston, the steamer *Montgomery* to cruise off the Brazos; the steamers *Hatteras* and *De Soto* cruised between the passes of the Mississippi and Sabine Pass, and the schooner *Kittatinny* and lighter vessels were on other duties. A letter to the New York *Herald*, however, from the mortar schooner *Henry Janes* off Sabine Pass reported the blockade still "ineffectual." It became necessary to capture Galveston and Sabine Pass. The demand for the surrender of the former was made in the following terms:

"UNITED STATES FRIGATE 'SANTEE,'
"OFF GALVESTON, TEXAS, May 17th, 1862.

" *To the Military Commandant commanding Confederate Forces, Galveston, Texas:*

"SIR: In a few days the naval and land forces of the United States will appear off the town of Galveston to enforce its surrender. To prevent the effusion of blood and destruction of property which would result from the bombardment of your town, I hereby demand the surrender of the place, with all its fortifications and batteries in its vicinity, with all arms and munitions of war. I trust you will comply with this demand.

"I am, respectfully, etc.,
"HENRY EAGLE,

" *Captain Commanding U. S. Naval Force, off Galveston, Texas.*"

The foreign consuls protested, and were curtly answered:

"UNITED STATES FRIGATE 'SANTEE,'
"May 22d, 1862.

"GENTLEMEN: Let me assure you, gentlemen, that no person can deplore more than myself the misery that would result from the bombardment of the town of Galveston and its fortifications, yet it is a duty that

---

[1] The protest of the foreign consuls was as follows:

GALVESTON, August 5th, 1861.

To Captain Jas. Alden, Commanding United States steamer " South Carolina."

SIR: The undersigned, Consuls and Vice-Consuls at Galveston, consider it their duty to enter their solemn protest against your bombardment of this city on the evening of the 3rd inst., without having given any notice so that the women and children might have been removed, and also against your firing a shell into the midst of a large crowd of unarmed citizens, among whom were many women and children, causing thereby the death of an unoffending Portuguese, and wounding boys and peacefully disposed persons, as acts of inhumanity unrecognised in modern warfare, and meriting the condemnation of Christian and civilized nations.

ARTHUR LYNN, British Consul.

JAMES FREDERICK, Hanoverian and Oldenburg Consul; and, in the absence of J. W. Jackorsh, Acting-Consul for Prussia and Hamburg.

J. C. NUHN, Swiss Consul, Vice-Consul for Prussia.

WM. BORKHEIMER, Deputy-Consul for Bremen, Saxony, Belgium, Holland, and Vice-Consul for Austria.

F. JONZALES, Mexican Consul.

T. H ZETIL, Consul for Nassau.

B. THERON, French Agent-Consul, and Consul for Spain.

FREDERICK WAGNER, Consul pro tem for Electoral Hesse.

will become necessary to enforce its surrender. It is not in my power to give you any assurance of security during the bombardment, for it is impossible to tell what direction the shot and shell will take.

"HENRY EAGLE,
" *Captain Commanding U. S. Naval Forces off Galveston.*
"*To the Foreign Consuls, Galveston.*"

As has been previously noticed, the fall of Galveston was, in the opinion of its military commander, Gen. Hébert, inevitable when a strong force should appear before it. The city was therefore evacuated at the approach of the enemy, who took possession. Without proper guns, with no vessels of war of importance, the place was indefensible; but this fact was not known in the interior of the State, where its fall created a profound sensation, and some unjust criticism of the authorities. The Houston *Telegraph* said, editorially:

"To whom censure for this most serious calamity to our State is to be imputed we cannot, nor will we undertake to say—in fact we do not know. It is not now with the past but the future we have to do. We, however, cannot avoid saying that we see with regret, now that Galveston has fallen, and the people do not hesitate to express their deep condemnation of those to whom the country looked as the persons expected to avert this blow. Upon them it is now the fashion not only to charge a supineness criminal in its nature, but a most glaring incompetency and imbecility. Whether these censures be just or not, as we have already stated, it is not within our competency to say. But it appears to us that if founded in truth, many of those who employ these censures are themselves not free from blame. If it be true that the military authorities were either imbecile or neglectful, the fact that it was so has been long apparent, for long has it been believed that Galveston was in peril, and knowing it, it thus became the duty, at least the right, of those whose interests were immediately involved to put in operation measures to avert the apprehended calamity.

"It is true that cannon were removed from the place, but it appears to us that by timely remonstrance this might have been prevented; and there certainly existed no sufficient reason why the people might not themselves have otherwise prepared to meet the foe. But we repeat, that it is not with the past, but the present, we have to do; and as the place has fallen, it now becomes the part of patriotism to so aid the authorities as to confine the enemy to his present limits, and thereby prevent him from using his conquest to the further injury of the State. It is no time for querulous complaint. With the citizens of Galveston exiled by this event we sincerely and deeply sympathize, and so, we have no doubt, does every generous, right-minded person in the State."

All this was unjust. The military authorities made as brave a defence as was in their power. Even after the battle, though the Federal fleet dominated, the army never took possession of the city.

During the floods of the spring of 1862, several steamers were brought away from New Orleans, and with others the *Webb* and the *Cotton*. The former was taken to Alexandria on the Red River, and the latter, a large, fine river steamer, built for the Bayou Sara route, was in the lower Teche, in charge of Capt. E. W. Fuller, a western steamboat man, and one of the bravest of a bold, daring class. The engines of the *Cotton* were compound, high and low pressure. Captain Fuller desired to convert her into a gunboat, and was assisted to the extent of his means by Major J. L. Brent, chief of artillery and ordnance on the staff of Gen. Richard Taylor, who armed her with one thirty-two pounder, smooth-bore, and two twenty four pounders, smooth-bore, in casemate, covered with cotton bales and railroad iron. On her upper or hurricane deck she had one nine-pounder rifled piece, on field carriage. Her casemate extended aft sufficiently to partially protect her boilers and engines.

In October 1862, the Federal General Weitzel brought up a force from New Orleans, with the intention of invading the interior of Louisiana. In connection with gunboats he made several attacks on the small Confederate force below Brisland, on the Teche between Berwick's Bay and Franklin. In these affairs Captain Fuller was always in the advance with the *Cotton*, though her boilers were inadequately protected, and she was too large and unwieldy to be handled in the narrow Teche. We give below the report of Capt. Fuller of one of the most gallant and successful engagements of the war. In the *Cotton* he fairly defeated four Federal gunboats, mounting twenty-seven guns, in a fight which lasted three days. The report was endorsed by Major General Taylor, in command of Western Louisiana, as being "true in every word."

"GUNBOAT 'COTTON,' Nov. 2d, 1862.
" GEN. A. MOUTEN, *Commanding Forces South of Red River:*
"SIR: I embrace the first opportunity of making my report of the recent affair between the *Cotton*, under my command, and the squadron of Federal gunboats that have occupied Berwick's Bay.

"On Saturday evening, November 1st, the smoke from the enemy's boats warned me of their near approach in such force that resistance at the bay was considered by me to be rashness. Acting upon your order, received but a few minutes previously, I immediately gave the necessary orders for leaving the bay. The steamers *Hart* and *Segur* were there at the time, also *Launch No.* 1, under the command of J. M. Rogers, whom I had temporarily appointed to the position of acting master. My order to the officers of those boats was to get immediately under way; the *Hart*, under command of Lieut. E. Montaigue, to proceed up to the Teche with a barge loaded with government sugar in tow. This was safely done according to orders, with one exception. Lieut. Montaigue at one time dropped his barge and returned, like a gallant soldier, to aid the *Cotton* in an unequal conflict. As soon as I could communicate to him my wishes, he resumed his tow, and proceeded safely to his destination.

"*Launch No.* 1 also obeyed the order given to her commander, and conveyed the launch up the lake to a place near Indian Bend, from where he has since safely reported, and is now in position to render valuable service.

" The *Segur*, under the command of Acting Master J. C. Coons, disobeyed the orders I gave of proceeding up the lake, and turned up the Atchafalaya, and was ignobly abandoned to the enemy at a time when the *Cotton* was between the enemy and the *Segur*. The commanding officer has not since reported. I have been informed that he abandoned his men and proceeded as fast as possible to St. Martinsville. Up to the present time the only reliable fact I have about the *Segur* is that it is in the hands of the enemy, prowling about Grand Lake and bayous in the vicinity; of the crew, nothing.

"The enemy came into Berwick's Bay on Saturday evening, just at dark, as the *Cotton* was in range, having had to wait to get the other boats off. They immediately opened fire upon us, and gave chase up the bay with three boats, continuing the fire, which I did not return until rounding into the Atchafalaya, when one of our guns was brought to bear, and we fired one shot, which sped straight to its mark, striking one of the Federal boats in her bows, breaking many timbers, and I have since been informed killing three and wounding five men. The Federals continued to ·ire shot and shell at us from eighteen guns, for about thirty minutes, when they gave up the chase.

"The *Cotton* came up to the Teche turned bows down, and backed · into it, keeping our teeth to the enemy. We backed up to the Fuselier plantation, where we stopped for the night. On Sunday morning, the 2d inst., I received orders to move the *Cotton* above Cornay Bridge, which I did as soon as possible. The bayou had some obstructions thrown across at that point, which I was ordered to defend until it got too hot for me, and then to fall back, turn my boat across the bayou at the second bridge, and, if pursued, sink her.

"On Monday, at 2 o'clock P. M., the four Federal boats, mounting twenty-seven guns, came up and opened fire upon us. They came up in full confidence of overpowering numbers, giving us broadside after broadside, frequently the whole four delivering their fire at once. The shot and shell literally rained on and about our boat, several striking us, but without doing serious damage. We returned their fire, my brave boys cheering frequently, when a well-directed shot struck the Federal boats. One of them retired from the contest in about fifteen minutes, her place being taken by another. One boat, for several minutes, had her colors down. Whether accidentally down or that they hauled them down to indicate a surrender, we had no means of learning. However, they hoisted them again after a delay of about twenty minutes. One, more venturesome than the rest, steadily steamed up the bayou. When in about 200 yards of the obstructions, we gave her a plunging shot from each of our guns, which all struck near the water on the starboard quarter; the boat immediately run her head up on shore, and was listed down so as to throw her guns out of use, and ceased her fire, except occasionally from one gun on the bow. At this time, when but one of the enemy's boats fired with any vigor, when victory seemed to be within our reach, it was announced that we had no more cartridges, having fired the last one. Retreat was all that remained for us; but as we slowly backed up, we had some sacks made, and by cutting off the legs from the pantaloons of some of our men, which we filled up, and returned fire with one as often as we could, in that manner, obtain a cartridge; this we continued until out of range, and the enemy ceased their fire

"We had to mourn the loss of one brave soldier killed by an accidental discharge of his gun, which severely wounded another. Another was accidentally wounded at another gun by recoil of the carriage, and has since died. One man was wounded by a piece of the enemy's shell. These are all the casualties that occurred. The boat sustained no perceptible damage.

"On Tuesday morning we resumed our original position near the obstructions, the enemy having previously retired. We worked hard to improve the condition of our boat, and got up some iron to shield the engines. Nothing occurred worthy of note during the day.

"On Wednesday the 5th inst., the enemy again opened fire upon us with four boats at about half-past ten o'clock. They fired from behind a point out of our range for about twenty minutes; when two of them steamed up into sight. We then immediately returned their fire and with such effect that the enemy retired and abandoned the contest in fifty-five minutes from firing their first shot. The two boats that came into sight were badly damaged and their loss heavy—ours nothing; the only damage being a trifling break in the cabin roof. This day victory was clearly ours; the enemy retired from the action badly discouraged with severe loss. We were unhurt.

"On Thursday the enemy came up and opened fire upon us, but took care not to come into sight. I did not return their fire. They threw shells at us for half an hour and retired without doing us any damage. Since that up to present date they have not assailed us.

"I cannot close this report without returning thanks to officers and men. Where all did their duty gallantly it may seem invidious to mention particular names, yet I must particularly mention the good conduct of O. S. Burdett, Pilot, who for two hours and a half, during the full contest on the 3d inst., manœuvred the boat with the utmost coolness—also the same gallant conduct on the 5th inst. Each of my lieutenants did their duty nobly and ably. Also, F. G. Burbank, gunner, and privates F. D. Wilkinson and Henry Dorning deserve particular mention for their gallant conduct—but all did their duty well, and are again ready to meet the enemy should they come up and try us again.

"Respectfully your obedient servant,
"E. W. FULLER,
"Captain, Commanding Gunboat 'Cotton.'"

In the first days of January, 1863, Weitzel's force was increased to forty-five hundred men, and on the 11th, accompanied by gunboats, he advanced up the Teche and drove in the Confederate pickets at the obstructions "left unprotected by the retreat of the pickets." Gen. Richard Taylor says the *Cotton* was assailed on all sides.[1] Fuller fought manfully, responded to the fire of the enemy's boats with his twenty-fours, and repulsing the riflemen on either bank with his field piece. His pilots were killed and he had an arm broken, but he worked the wheel with his feet, backing up the bayou, as from her great length the boat could not be turned in the narrow channel. Night stopped the enemy's advance, and Mouten, deeming his force too weak to cope with Weitzel, turned the *Cotton* across the bayou, and scuttled and burned her to arrest the further progress of the Federal boats. Weitzel returned to Berwick's, having accomplished his object, the destruction of the *Cotton*, supposed by the Federals to be a formidable iron-clad.[2]

On March 28th, 1863, Gen. Weitzel, who had been quiet at Berwick's Bay for some time, sent the gunboat *Diana*, accompanied by a land force, up the Teche to drive in the Confederate pickets. The capture of the *Queen of the West*, and destruction of the *Indianola*, had impaired the prestige of gunboats, and the troops at Brisland were eager to apply Gen. Taylor's theory of attacking them at close quarters. The *Diana* was armed with one thirty-two pounder Parrott rifle on her open bow and one or two twelve-pounder bronze Dahlgren rifled boat howitzers. As the *Diana* proceeded up the Teche she was engaged by the Valverde battery, Capt. Sayres,

[1] *Destruction and Reconstruction*, p. 121.
[2] The guns removed from the wreck of the *Cotton* were mounted in a work on the west bank of the Teche, to command the bayou and road, and the line of breastworks at Brisland were strengthened.

attached to Sibley's Texas brigade, and a detachment of cavalry. After a great slaughter among her crew she was captured with nearly two hundred infantry on board. The boilers of the *Diana* were protected by two thicknesses of wrought bar-iron, four by one-and-a-quarter inches, laid flat on a wood backing, built at an angle of thirty to forty degrees. The captain and pilot occupied the pilot-house, the former being killed by the side of the pilot, who jumped overboard, and, swimming to the marsh on the left bank of the Teche, made his way to Berwick's Bay and reported the loss of the boat.

The *Diana* was repaired and was posted in the centre of the Confederate line at the battle of Brisland, April 12th and 13th, 1863. Capt. O. J. Semmes, son of Admiral Semmes, C. S. N., an officer of much coolness in action, was detached from his battery and placed in command of the boat. Conical shells from the enemy's Parrott guns had pierced the railway iron, and killed and wounded several of her gunners and crew and cut a steam pipe, and she was lying against the bank disabled. Fortunately Capt. Semmes had kept down his fires, or escaping steam would have driven every one from the boat. It was necessary to take her out of fire for repairs, and she was withdrawn to Franklin, to which point the Confederates retreated. Later, when Gen. Taylor fell back up the bayou, the gallant Semmes, to prevent her from being recaptured by the enemy, after landing his crew applied the torch, and she blew up soon after. Semmes remained too long near the *Diana* to carry out his instructions and was captured.[1]

Following these naval and military movements in western Louisiana came the capture of Galveston, Texas; one of the fiercest and most successful naval captures of the war—one that was most creditable to the Confederates and most mortifying to the Federals—so mortifying that Admiral Farragut, to account for the disaster, did not hesitate to cast a slur upon his officers which was as hasty as it was undeserved. During the month of December, Galveston was blockaded. The *Harriet Lane*, a favorite vessel of the Federal navy, was abreast the city, outside were the steamers *Owasco*, the *Westfield*, the *Clifton* and the *Sachem*—the whole under the command of

---

[1] Capts. Semmes, Fuller, Fusilier, and the prisoners taken from the *Queen of the West* were on the transport *Maple Leaf*, when they were sent from Fortress Monroe to Fort Delaware. Reaching the capes of the Chesapeake at nightfall, the prisoners suddenly attacked and overpowered the guard, ran the transport near to the beach in Princess Anne County, Virginia, landed, and made their way to Richmond, whence they rejoined Gen. Taylor in Louisiana. All the prisoners escaped, excepting Fuller, who from wounds received in his last action was unable to walk. Remaining in charge of the *Maple Leaf* until his friends were ashore, he restored her to the Federals, was taken to Fort Delaware, and died in prison. "A braver man never lived," says Gen. Taylor. Capt. Leclerc Fusilier, who lived in the parish of St. Mary's, twenty miles below New Iberia, was the possessor of great estates and of a hospitable, generous nature. His sons were in the army, and sixty years had not diminished his energy or his enthusiasm. His corn-bins, his flocks and herds, were given to the public service without stint; and no hungry, destitute Confederate was permitted to pass his door. Fusilier was twice captured; after his escape from the *Maple Leaf* he rejoined Gen. Taylor in Louisiana. Again taken, he escaped, while descending the Teche on a steamboat, by springing from the deck and seizing the overhanging branch of a live oak. The guard fired on him, but darkness and the rapid movement of the steamer were in his favor, and he got off unhurt.—*Gen. Taylor's Destruction and Reconstruction.*

Commodore Renshaw.   All December, 1862, the United States naval forces lay at Galveston anticipating an attack.   Letters published in the Northern papers from Commodore Renshaw, and Capt. Wainwright of the *Harriet Lane*, show this apprehension; so that when the attack came in January, 1863, they could not claim to have been unprepared, although the defeat was attempted to be softened by terming it a surprise.

All the winter the Confederate forces under Gen. Magruder had command of all points except the small strip of land upon which Galveston was situated.   The Federals were masters of only the region within the range of their guns. Renewed activity began with the appointment of the fighting Gen. Magruder.   Galveston was to be relieved at all hazards, and the blockade raised.   How well he succeeded the sequel shows.   Throughout December troops were quietly moved to this point.   On Galveston Bay and the Trinity River boats were being cotton-clad and armed.   Major Leon Smith was actively engaged in this work, as in the subsequent fight at Sabine Pass.   The attack was delayed, however, for the co-operation of the land forces, who were to engage first.   The time was spent in completing the fitting out of the boats as speedily as possible.   During Christmas week the expected artillery arrived, and by January 1st, 1863, all was ready.

The *Bayou City*, a packet-boat on the river, had been fitted up as a gunboat under the charge of Capt. Henry Lubbock; she was armed with a thirty-two pound rifled gun on her bow deck; bulwarks of cotton bales were built up on her sides, and a force of 100 men put on board of her.   Capt. Wier was gunner, and the boat was manned by a portion of his regiment. A party of Col. Green's sharp-shooters were among the crew. The *Neptune*, another packet, was also cotton-clad; she was armed with two howitzer guns.   Col. Bayley, of the Seventh Texas cavalry, commanded the sharp-shooters on board.   The men were detailed from the Sibley brigade; all the brigade having stepped forward on a call for volunteers anxious to take part in the affair.   The full number of men was about 150.   The *Lady Gwinn* and the *John F. Carr* accompanied the expedition as tenders.   On the *Carr* were a number of troops and volunteers; and on the *Gwinn* a number of spectators who were prepared to take part in the fight if necessary.   The cutter *Dodge* and the *Royal Yacht* were present, but did not go into action.   The whole naval force was under the command of Major Leon Smith.

The boats moved down about midnight and took position above the town, waiting for the land forces to open the fight. In the meanwhile, the latter, consisting of detachments from some four or five regiments under the command of Brig. Gen. Scurry and Col. X. B. Le Bray, were moved early in the night from their station at Virginia Point.   This point is on the mainland, and from it a bridge, two miles in length, crosses

Galveston Bay to Galveston Island, being about five miles
distant from the city. On crossing this bridge the troops
moved down toward Galveston, but met with unexpected
delays, and did not reach their position until after 4 A. M. The
boats were twelve miles off, at Half Moon Shoals, awaiting
signals.

The town of Galveston was garrisoned by the Federal
naval brigade of Commodore Renshaw, and by Col. Burrill
with the Forty-second Massachusetts regiment, which had
been brought as a reinforcement, and arrived on the preceding
Christmas-day. Lying in the channel were the *Harriet Lane*,
near the town; the *Owasco*, a little distance further, keeping
in deep water, accompanied by the *Westfield*, iron-clad, nine
guns. and the *Clifton* and the *Sachem*, smaller armed vessels.
The *Westfield* was the commodore's flag-ship, and the *Harriet
Lane* was commanded by a brave and capable officer, Commander Wainwright. Three schooners were lying off the bar
at this time—two of them loaded with coal for the fleet.

At about five o'clock on New Year's morning the Confederate troops reached the chosen point for an attack both on
the city and the Federal fleet. Silently the batteries were
placed in position. So quietly was this done that the officer
of the night of the Forty-second Massachusetts on his round
passed within a stone's-throw of where the artillery was
posted without discovering anything wrong. As soon as
everything was in readiness, Gen: Magruder in person fired
the first gun, saying, "Now, boys, I have done my part as
private, I will go and attend to that of general."

Just before this, however, the Confederate gunboats had
been sighted. A letter of January 8th to the Philadelphia
Inquirer states that at this time the *Harriet Lane*, then lying
near the city, signaled an attack on the town. Although it
was night, a beautiful moon plainly revealed everything for
miles, and the course of the gunboats could be distinctly seen.

The artillery duel between the batteries and the Federal
fleet soon became one of the most terrific on record. The Confederates were at one time driven from the batteries by the
appalling rain of iron hail poured upon them from the *Owasco*
and *Harriet Lane*. One of the most gallant exploits of the
contest was the attack on Kuhn's wharf by Col. Cook of the
Confederate forces. The Federal troops there consisted of the
Forty-second Massachusetts militia regiment, over three hundred strong, commanded by Col. Burrill. They were upon the
outer end of the wharf, and had torn up the heavy planks
forming its floor for about fifty feet, making a wall of those
next to the strand, behind which a platform had been erected
for riflemen. The Confederates dashed into the water at the
sides of the wharf, and by the use of planks succeeded in
crossing the gap amidst an enfilading fire of grape and canister from the vessels, which continued with such fury that

Col. Cook withdrew his men to wait for daylight and renew the attack. The *Bayou City* and *Neptune* had now arrived, and their first attack was upon the nearest Federal vessel, the *Harriet Lane*. The *Bayou City* was the first to open fire on the *Lane* with her thirty-two pound rifled gun. Several shots were fired—the second striking her behind the wheel, knocking a large hole in her. As he fired again, Capt. Weir called out, "Well, here goes for a New Year's present!" and the gun exploded, killing him instantly, and wounding Capt. Schneider and one or two others. Deprived of its gun, the pilot, Capt. McCormick, was ordered to use the vessel as a ram, and to hit the *Lane*, so as to allow the men to board her. Going with a strong ebb-tide he ran past her, and damaged the *Bayou City*. Meantime, the *Neptune* came up, striking the *Harriet Lane* on the starboard side, getting her bow stove in, and causing her to leak badly. She then passed round under the stern of the *Lane*, receiving her shots as she passed. One of the shots of the *Lane* struck the *Neptune's* hull, causing her to take water fast. She got on the edge of the channel and soon sank in eight feet water.

By this time the *Bayou City* had rounded-to, with head up stream, and run into the *Harriet Lane*, striking her fairly aft of the larboard wheel-house, and running her bow so far under the gunwale and wheel that she could not be extricated, and the two vessels stuck fast together. The riflemen on the Confederate vessels immediately opened fire upon the deck of the *Harriet Lane* at close quarters from behind the cotton bales and every point of vantage. The fire was terrific for some minutes, and the deck became a scene of flight and slaughter. There were 130 men on the vessel. Commander Wainwright and First Lieutenant Lea fell early in the action. The crew were driven from the deck and took refuge below, first hoisting the white flag; upon which the boarding parties from the *Bayou City* and the *Neptune* sprang on board and took possession. The *Neptune* was so damaged in the encounter that she soon sank, leaving only the *Bayou City* available.

The *Owasco* was the only Federal vessel formidable at this time. About 10 A. M. the *Westfield*, with her splendid battery, had run aground. After removing some personal effects, the commodore determined to burn her. The decks were saturated with turpentine, and the last of the crew, with Commodore Renshaw, were just about to leave the ship. The gig was ready and the commodore was the last to descend. The torch was applied—a bright flash ran along the deck—the commodore turned his face to look at the vessel for the last time. The sailors rested a moment on their oars; all eyes were turned in the direction of the *Westfield*, attracted by the vivid flame. It was a moment of surprise and of perfect silence, and it was only a moment; then there was a flash of blue smoke and a fearful explosion. The shells of the magazine, rising in the air, burst far up.   There was a plunging noise in the water, such as is occasioned by the falling of a heavy body, and then for a radius of four or five hundred feet there was a shower of fragments which sounded like falling rain.   The *Westfield* was seen to part or burst out forward, like a chestnut burr, and when the smoke cleared away there was no sign of life about her.   Forward she was blown into fragments down to the water; but the machinery had not been destroyed, as the singing of the steam was distinctly heard after the explosion.   The commodore's boat and all in it were annihilated in the terrible catastrophe—scattered through the air in fragments.   The smoke-stacks and the after part of

THE "HARRIET LANE," CAPTURED BY THE CONFEDERATES, JANUARY 1ST, 1863.

the ship lay a black mass in the water for ten minutes, when there was another flash, and she was speedily wrapped in flames.

Commodore Renshaw and Commander Wainwright having been killed, the scene in the Federal fleet was one of utter confusion.   The *Westfield* blew up during a truce agreed upon by Capt. Lubbock, commissioned by Major Leon Smith to demand the surrender of the Federal vessels and Capt. Law, of the Federal forces.   The time of the truce was three hours, which Capt. Law of the *Clifton* asked to consult Commodore Renshaw. Instead of respecting this truce, Capt. Law took the opportunity of getting the *Clifton* under way.   Capt. Lubbock charged him with breach of faith, and told him he considered his running away under the circumstances equivalent to stealing so much Confederate property.   Capt. Lubbock and Col. Green had been dispatched by Gen. Magruder, who had come down to the wharf, to close the negotiations for surrender. The *Clifton* and the *Owasco*, in spite of remonstrance, sailed to sea; the latter still having the flag of truce flying at her mainmast. Major Smith, on board the *John F. Carr*, then called for volunteers to follow the *Owasco* and avenge the death of Capt. Weir. He obtained all he wanted and pursued the propeller; but she was too swift for the lumbering cotton-clad and too far on her way out of the harbor, and the pursuit was given up.

The casualties on the Confederate side were 12 killed, including Capt. Weir, and 70 wounded. The Federal loss was estimated by the New York *Herald* correspondent, January 12th, at 150 men killed, besides the wounded and prisoners. The captures were the *Harriet Lane* and her crew, with three 9-inch, one 30-pound rifle, and two 24-pound howitzer guns, with a complete armament, magazine and stores of every description; the 42nd Massachusetts regiment, about 300 strong, with their colonel, arms, and two flags, stores, etc., the barques *Elias Pike* and *Cavallo*, with their crews, guard, 700 tons of coal, 600 bbls. of Irish potatoes, and a complete outfit; a pilot schooner, of fine speed, and the gunboat *Westfield*, partially destroyed, carrying eight heavy guns.[1]

The official report of the battle was as follows:

"*By telegraph from Headquarters, Galveston, to Major Hyllster, via Natchez:*

"This morning, 1st January, at three o'clock, I attacked the enemy's fleet and garrison at this place, and captured the latter and the steamer *Harriet Lane* and two barges, and a schooner of the former. The rest, some four or five, escaped ignominiously under cover of a flag of truce. I

---

[1] Some of the incidents of the memorable battle are interesting enough to preserve. One is quoted from the Jackson *Mississippian* of the 16th of February, and is as follows:

"Dr. Holland was one of the boarding party that cleared the decks of the *Harriet Lane.* Some of the scenes and incidents he describes transcend in strange interest the narratives of Alexander Dumas. Some years ago when the famous steamer *Merrimac*, afterwards changed into a ram by the Confederate government, and forever memorable from her engagement with the *Congress, Cumberland* and *Monitor* in Hampton Roads, made her trial trip across the Atlantic, she entered, as we all remember, Southampton waters, and her officers were received with great hospitality by the authorities of Southampton. Commander Wainwright was then the *Merrimac's* first lieutenant, and on going up to London was entertained by Dr. Holland, who was then living in the great metropolis. The doctor never saw him again alive, and recognized with a feeling of astonishment, in the dead body of the commander of the *Harriet Lane* lying upon her decks, his guest of some years ago in London. The saddest of all the terrible tragedies of this infernal war was enacted upon the same crimsoned and slippery stage when Major Lea, of the Confederate army, encountered in the dying lieutenant of the Federal steamer his own son. Can history or fiction afford any parallel to this? It is a curious fact, too, which

has not been stated, that Capt Leon Smith, to whose skill and gallantry Gen. Magruder attributes the entire success of the attack on the enemy's fleet in Galveston Bay, is the brother of Caleb B. Smith, until very recently the Secretary of the Interior in Lincoln's Cabinet."

The other is from the Houston *Telegraph:*

"Capt. Wm. M. Armstrong went on board the *Lane* after the battle, and found lying in the blood on deck a Bible. He picked it up and remarked, 'Now I am going to open this Bible this New Year's day, and the first passage I read I will take as an omen for the new year.' He opened it carelessly, and the first passage his eye fell on was the 1st verse of the 20th chapter of Deuteronomy: 'When thou goest out to battle against thine enemies, and seest horses and chariots, and a people more than thou, be not afraid of them: for the Lord thy God is with thee, which brought thee up out of the land of Egypt!' It is a good omen, as well as a most startling circumstance."

The United States steamer *Harriet Lane* was well known to most of our citizens She was a side-wheel steamer of 619 tons burden, and was built for, and engaged in, the revenue service as a cutter, under the command of Capt. John Faunce. She was detailed in 1858 from that service, and was engaged in the Paraguay Expedition, under the same commander. During the visit of the Prince of Wales to this country she was used for the purpose of carrying the

have about 600 prisoners, and a large quantity of valuable stores, arms, etc. The *Harriet Lane* is very little injured. She was carried by boarding from two high pressure cotton steamers, manned by Texas cavalry and artillery. The line troops were gallantly commanded by Col. Green, of Sibley's Brigade, and the ships and artillery by Major Leon Smith, to whose indomitable energy and heroic daring the country is indebted for the successful execution of a plan which I had considered for the destruction of the enemy's fleet. Col. Bagby, of Sibley's Brigade, also commanded the volunteers from his regiment for the naval expedition, in which every officer and every man won for himself imperishable renown.

"J. BANKHEAD MAGRUDER, *Major General.*"

Gen. Magruder lost no time in issuing the following also:

"GALVESTON, Jan. 4th, 1863.

"Whereas, the undersigned has succeeded in capturing and destroying a part of the enemy's fleet, and in driving the remainder out of the harbor of Galveston, and beyond the neighboring waters, and the blockade having been thus effectually raised, he therefore proclaims to all concerned that the harbor of Galveston is open for trade to all friendly nations, and their merchants are invited to resume their usual commercial intercourse with this port.

"Done at Galveston, this the 4th day of January, 1863.

"J. B. MAGRUDER, *Major General Commanding.*"

Gen. Magruder's stirring address to the men engaged at Galveston was issued January 14th:

"HEADQUARTERS DISTRICT OF TEXAS, NEW MEXICO AND ARIZONA, ⎰
"GALVESTON, Texas, Jan. 14th, 1863. ⎱

"*Soldiers of the Army of Galveston:*

"The New Year dawned upon an achievement whose glory is unsurpassed. That glory is yours. You have recaptured an island two miles from the mainland. You have repossessed yourselves of your beautiful 'Island City,' and made its hostile garrison, intrenched behind inaccessible barricades, surrender to you at discretion. You have planted your artillery and battalions of infantry within 300 yards of the enemy's formidable fleet, and exposed yourselves to the showers of grape and canister poured into you from his ships.

"You have repossessed yourselves of forts under a concentrated fire of grape, canister and shell, at short ranges, and you have stormed,

royal visitor from Washington to Mount Vernon, and from New York up the Hudson to West Point. When the war broke out she was transferred to the United States navy, and formed, during its early stages, a part of the Potomac flotilla. She was afterwards attached to the West Gulf blockading squadron, from which she was detached for the Galveston expedition, in the capture of which place she figured prominently. The *Harriet Lane* after her capture was transferred by the Secretary of War to the Confederate Navy Department, and Lieut. Joseph N. Barney, C. S. N., was assigned to command her. She was intended as a cruiser, but Lieut. Barney, upon examination, finding her inefficient for that purpose, on March 31st, 1863, the *Lane* was transferred by the Secretary of the Navy back to the War Department, with the request that Captain Smith, who captured her, be placed in command. As will be seen elsewhere, she ran the blockade with a load of cotton, and it is believed never returned to this country.

A Texas paper says: "One of the most affecting incidents of the brilliant and successful recapture of Galveston by the forces under Major General Magruder, was the meeting of Major Lea, of the Confederate army, with his eldest and fondly loved son, who was first lieutenant of the *Harriet Lane.*

"Nearly two years ago, the father then residing in Texas, had written repeatedly to the son, then on the coast of China, suggesting the principles that should determine his course in the then approaching struggle between the North and South, and saying that he could not dictate to one so long accustomed to act on his own judgment ; and that decide as he might, such was his confidence in his high conscientiousness, he would continue to regard him with the respect of a gentleman and the affection of a father ; but that if he should select the side of the enemy, they would probably never meet on earth, unless perchance they should meet in battle.

"The father had served nearly eighteen months eastward of the Mississippi, and, through unsolicited orders, arrived at Houston, en route for San Antonio, late at night on the 30th ult., when hearing of the intended attack on the *Harriet Lane,* aboard of which he had heard was his son, he solicited permission to join the

captured and destroyed a portion of his formidable fleet, and dispersed the rest. With inadequate means, you have conquered the enemy upon that element on which he boasts himself invincible, thus proving yourselves successful rangers of the sea as of the land.

"Your general is proud to command you; your State and country will honor you as long as patriotism and heroism are cherished among men.

"In honor of this victory, you are authorised to inscribe on your banners the words 'Galveston and Galveston Harbor,' to commemorate your success.

"Your commanding general is well assured that wherever you meet the enemy, you will win the right to adorn your standards with the glorious records of your prowess and patriotism.

"The commanding general deems this a fitting occasion to express publicly to the troops his high sense of the indomitable energy and chivalric heroism of the naval commander, and those who so nobly supported him. The country is proud of them. The 'stormers' of the sea and the 'stormers' of the land should greet each other as brothers in battle, and there should be no rivalry, save as to who shall be first permitted to die for his country.

"J. BANKHEAD MAGRUDER,
"General Commanding District of Texas.
"Official:
"ROB'T S. REID, Lieutenant and A. A. A. G."

On the 28th of January, President Davis replied to the official report of Gen. Magruder in complimentary terms:

"RICHMOND, Va., Jan. 28th, 1863.
"Major Gen. J. BANKHEAD MAGRUDER, Galveston, Texas:

"MY DEAR SIR: I am much gratified at the receipt of your letter of January 6th, conveying to me the details of your brilliant exploit in the capture of Galveston and the vessels in the harbor. The boldness of the conception and the daring and skill of its execution were crowned by results substantial as well as splendid. Your success has been a heavy blow to the enemy's hopes, and I trust will be vigorously and effectively followed up.

"It is to be hoped that your prudence and tact will be as successful as your military ability—retaking every position on the Texan coast.

"Your suggestions will receive the favorable consideration due to you.

"The congratulations I tender to you and your brave army are felt by the whole country. I trust your achievement is but the precursor of

expedition, in expectation of nursing or burying his son, whose courage was to expose him fatally to the equal daring of our Texas boys. During the fight Major Lea was ordered by the general to keep a lookout from a housetop for all movements in the bay. As soon as daylight enabled him to see that the *Lane* had been captured, by permission of the general, who knew nothing of the expected meeting, he hastened aboard, where he was not surprised to find his son mortally wounded. Wading through blood, amidst the dying and the dead, he reached the youth, pale and exhausted. 'Edward, 'tis your father.' 'I know you, father, but cannot move,' he said, faintly. 'Are you mortally wounded?' 'Badly, but hope not fatally.' 'Do you suffer pain.' 'Cannot speak,' he whispered. A stimulant was given him. How came you here, father?' When answered, a gleam of surprise and gratification passed over his fine face. He then expended nearly his last words in making arrangements for his wounded comrades. His father knelt and blessed him, and hastened ashore for a litter, and returned just after life had fled.

"When told by the surgeon that he had but a few minutes to live, and asked to express his wishes, he answered confidingly, 'My father is here,' and spoke not again. He was borne in procession to the grave from the headquarters of Gen. Magruder, in company with his captain, and they were buried together, with appropriate military honors, in the presence of many officers of both armies and many generous citizens, all of whom expressed their deep sympathy with the bereaved father, who said the solemn service of the Episcopal Church for the burial of the dead.

"The remains of Captain Wainwright were removed to the North soon after the war closed, but the grave of Lieutenant Lea can be seen in the Episcopal cemetery at Galveston, covered with a plain marble block inscribed:

EDWARD LEA,
Lieut. Commander, U. S. N.
Born 31st January, 1837.
Killed in battle January 1, 1863.
'My father is here.'

"The concluding words were the last ones he uttered. This event made a strange impression and showed the horrible features of the war between the States."

a series of successes, which may redound to the glory and honor of yourself and our country.   " Very respectfully and truly yours,
                                        "JEFFERSON DAVIS."[1]

The blockade was temporarily raised at Galveston and
Sabine Pass by this action, as will be seen by Mr. Benjamin's
declaration issued to foreign nations:

> "DEPARTMENT OF STATE, }
> "RICHMOND, February 7th, 1863. }
>
> "SIR: I have again to inform you of the raising of the blockade of
> two Southern ports by superior forces.
>
> "This government is officially informed of the total dispersion and
> disappearance of the blockading squadron recently stationed off Galves-
> ton harbor by the combined attack of land and naval forces of the Con-
> federacy. In this attack the enemy's steamer *Harriet Lane* was captured,
> and the flag-ship of the squadron, the *Westfield*, was blown up and de-
> stroyed. The blockade of the port of Galveston is therefore at an end.
>
> "The armed river boats which raised the blockade at Galveston then
> proceeded to Sabine Pass, where they again attacked the enemy's block-
> aders, captured thirteen guns, a large quantity of stores, and a number of
> prisoners. No blockading fleet now exists off Sabine Pass, and the steam-
> ers of the Confederacy were, at the last accounts, cruising off the Pass with
> no enemy in sight.
>
> "This information is given for the guidance of such of the merchants
> of your nation as may desire to trade with either of the open ports of Gal-
> veston or Sabine Pass.
>
> "Respectfully, your obedient servant,
>   "J. P. BENJAMIN, *Secretary of State.*"

The Federal disaster at Galveston, followed by that at
Sabine Pass, was the most severe blow the Federal navy had
received. A correspondent of a Texas paper, who was in New
Orleans when the news was received there, states that he was
present when Admiral Farragut raved and "tore his hair"
on hearing of it. However that may be, the Federal admiral
was very much incensed and for the moment lost his head.
There was no reason, no facts, and no fairness, in charging
cowardice upon the officers and crew of the *Harriet Lane.*
Her first and second officers laid down their lives in her defence. Her fire on the shore batteries was so severe as to
drive the gunners once at least from their guns. As to the
conduct of the officer, Capt. Lubbock, who accompanied the
flag of truce, Admiral Farragut traveled out of the record to
cast an unjust imputation upon a brave man, and to cover up
with an unworthy excuse the escape, as charged in Gen.
Magruder's first statement above, of the *Owasco*, the *Clifton,*

---

[1] *Joint Resolution of thanks to Major General J.
Bankhead Magruder, and Officers and Men of
his command, at Galveston, Texas :*
*Resolved by the Congress of the Confederate States
of America,* that the bold, intrepid and gallant
conduct of Major Gen J. Bankhead Magruder,
Col. Thomas Green, Major Leon Smith and
other officers, and of the Texan Rangers and
soldiers engaged in the attack on, and victory
achieved over, the land and naval forces of the
enemy at Galveston, on the first of January,
1863, eminently entitle them to the thanks of
Congress and the country.

2. *Resolved,* That the brilliant achievement, resulting, under the Providence of God, in the
capture of the war steamer *Harriet Lane,* and
the defeat and ignominious flight of the hostile
fleet from the harbor, the recapture of the city
and the raising of the blockade of the port of
Galveston, signally evinces that superior force
may be overcome by skillful conception and
daring courage.

3. *Resolved,* That the foregoing resolutions be
communicated by the Secretary of War to Major
Gen. Magruder, and by him to his command
Approved, February 25th, 1863.

and other vessels "under a flag of truce." Farragut's official report was as follows :

"FLAGSHIP ' HARTFORD,' NEW ORLEANS, Jan. 29th, 1863.

"SIR: I herewith enclose the report of Acting Master J. A. Hannum, of the *Harriet Lane*, by which you will perceive the exaggerations which have been circulated concerning the defence of that vessel; also the pusillanimous conduct of the officer who accompanied the flag of truce and corroborated to Lieut. Commanding Law the enemy's statement, that all the officers and crew of the *Harriet Lane* had perished, save some ten or fifteen persons, whereas there were scarcely that number of killed and wounded. I take it for granted that of the nine slightly wounded the greater part amounted to nothing, so that the testimony of the rebel pilot was very near the truth when he said five killed and six or eight wounded. I cannot think but that for the death of Commodore Wainwright and Lieut. Commanding Lea, the vessel would not have been captured. It is difficult, however, to conceive a more pusillanimous surrender of a vessel to an enemy already in our power, than occurred in the case of the *Harriet Lane*. Very respectfully, your obedient servant,

"D. G. FARRAGUT, *Rear Admiral.*
"HON. GIDEON WELLES, *Secretary of the Navy.*"

The idea that the "pusillanimous surrender" was to an enemy "already in our [the Federal] power" is perfectly absurd, in view of the fact that the Forty-second Massachusetts regiment was captured, the *Westfield* blown up, and the *Harriet Lane* disabled. Discretion was obviously the better part of valor for the remainder of the unfortunate fleet. The "pusillanimity" was not in surrendering or in getting away as fast as possible from an attack so fierce and successful, but in escaping under a flag of truce with vessels which, in the language of Capt. Lubbock, were "already to be regarded as so much Confederate property."

Altogether it was a brilliant victory. Credit is due to the land forces under Gens. Scurry, Green and Le Bray, and especially to Major Gen. Magruder for the foresight with which the affair was planned. The brave men of the land forces on the *Neptune* were under the command of Col. A. P. Bagley, of Green's brigade; and those on the *Bayou City* under the command of Col. Tom Green. Commodore Leon Smith, of the old navy of the Republic of Texas, was in command of the whole naval expedition, which was managed with rare skill. As to the vessels themselves, the *Neptune* was commanded by Capt. William Sangster, with Dave Connor, chief engineer. The *Bayou City* was under command of Capt. Henry Lubbock, with L. C. Hersberger, chief engineer. No mention of this battle can be made without also giving due honor to Capt. Michael McCormack, the brave pilot of the *Neptune*, who was given by Commodore Smith his discretion in steering his vessel for the *Harriet Lane,* and who was the first to begin the attack by water.[1]

[1] Captain McCormack lost his life in 1866, by accidentally falling overboard from a boat commanded by him, running between Galveston and Houston. Twenty-three years after, about one-half of the survivors of the battle of Galveston attended in that city a reunion and encampment, and went over the ground and fought their battles over again.

How thoroughly the harbor was cleared the incident of the attempted capture of the U. S. steamer *Cumbria* shows. The daring attempt of a single pilot-boat to perform such a deed exhibits the confidence of the Confederates in the demoralization of the enemy. Though futile, it was one of the coolest things of the war. It is given from the New Orleans correspondence of the New York *Herald,* and the letter is dated from on board the *Cumbria,* for the vessel put back at once:

"The *Cumbria* left New Orleans on the evening of December 31st, and arrived off Galveston bar, and anchored sixteen miles to the southwest of it, on the evening of Friday, January 2nd. This was the day after our disaster, and the enemy, of course, was in full possession. She lay here during the night. The morning (Saturday) was rainy, and the city of Galveston scarcely visible. At eight o'clock the vessel weighed anchor and approached the bar; but no pilot boat was visible, and she fired a gun as a signal for a pilot. This was not responded to in any manner, which all hands thought extraordinary; yet, while all wondered at the delay, no one really suspected the cause, and during the afternoon a boat was dispatched to the city to report the arrival of the *Cumbria* and secure a pilot. This boat contained Mr. Smith, a Texan refugee, and five of the crew, who, of course, were taken by the rebels the moment they landed.

"Hour after hour passed, and still no return of the boat and no signal or tidings from shore. The officers, by aid of their glasses, were enabled to see flags, notwithstanding the fog; but they were quite unable to make out whether they floated the stars and stripes or the stars and bars. As the entire afternoon passed, however, without any return of the boat which had been dispatched, or any tidings whatever from the shore, all became suspicious that something was wrong, and when night at last settled down upon the water there was a firm determination, strongly felt if not expressed, to exercise the greatest caution before entering the harbor the next morning, even if a pilot should make his appearance.

"On Sunday morning, having already lain off the bar full thirty-six hours, the captain again weighed anchor, and slowly cruised about. At last, about eleven o'clock in the forenoon, a handsome and good-sized sail boat was seen approaching from the direction of the city, with four men in her. She passed the *Cumbria* at some distance, and, making tack, headed for the city, and came alongside, and inquired how much water the vessel drew.

"Capt. Sumner, of the *Cumbria,* replied 'that she drew nine and a half feet,' and the man said 'there were then eleven on the bar.'

"'Are you a pilot?' asked the captain.

"'Yes,' was the answer.

"'Are you the regular pilot?' inquired the captain.

"'No,' was the reply of the spokesman from the boat. 'I am not the regular pilot. The regular pilot is busy. He has to pilot out a bark which is going to sea; but if you will follow me I will pilot you in, and go ahead and take the soundings.'

"Capt. Sumner, whose suspicions were fully aroused by the non-arrival of his boat, was determined not to let the pretended pilot off without bringing him to the point. As he was talking he came to the stern of the boat, bringing himself into full view, and was immediately recognized by a number of the Texans on board the *Cumbria.*

"'How are you, Capt. Payne?' shouted one of the Texans.

"The pretended pilot, finding himself discovered, replied, 'I'm first rate; how are you?'

"'Come aboard, sir,' said Capt. Sumner.

"'No, no,' replied Capt. Payne, 'there are too many damned blue coats aboard there to suit me.'

"'Come aboard, sir!' shouted the captain.

"But Payne had no idea of allowing himself to be caught, and was meantime, making off.

"'I don't want to come aboard,' he shouted. 'Follow me, and I'll guide you over the bar; but I'm not the regular pilot, as I've told you, and I don't want to take the responsibility of your vessel.'

"'Who's in command at Galveston?' inquired the captain.

"'Commodore Wainwright,' was the reply.

"'Come aboard, I say,' cried out the captain.

"'No, no,' said Payne, still making off.

"The captain now ordered the Texans to stand at a 'ready' with their carbines. He also called out, as if giving orders to marines, saying that the portholes must not be opened until the colonel had given the orders to fire. The pilot hearing this, and witnessing the preparations to fire upon him, stopped, and with great reluctance finally came on board. He was then told that he must pilot the vessel in, and that if anything was wrong—if he was leading the vessel into a trap—his brains would be blown out upon the spot.

"'Well, gentlemen,' said the pilot, 'I suppose there is no use of lying to you any more, as I see I am known.' He then told the truth—that Galveston was in possession of the rebels, and that the gunboats had all left. He was made a prisoner; but for some reason not explained the three rebels in the boat were allowed to go back to the city. As they sailed off the pretended pilot shouted out to them:

"'Good bye! Take good care of my clothes, and tell the boys to look out for themselves.'"

The United States made every effort to again blockade Galveston. Admiral Bell was despatched there with a formidable fleet, consisting of the *Brooklyn*, Commander Bell; the *Owasco*, Capt. Wilson; the *Katahdin*, Capt. Johnson; the *Sciota*, Capt. Lowry; and the *Itasca*, Capt. Lewis. The masts of the *Harriet Lane* could be seen from the fleet rising behind the town, and this made the Federals as angry as a hive of bees. A correspondent writing from on board the U. S. steamer *New London*, said: "Galveston is a doomed town. The disgrace attending the capture of the *Harriet Lane* must be wiped out; and the vengeance upon the butchers and captors will be awful."

As soon as the *Brooklyn* arrived, therefore, she began to fire upon the town, at long range and out of danger. Once before all the foreign consuls in the city had protested in the name of humanity and civilization against such an act. This time the action was stopped by a flag of truce and a message from Gen. Magruder that the hospitals containing both Confederate and Federal wounded were within range; further, that there were many women and children in the city; and also, most potent of all, that the Confederate government had proclaimed Galveston a free port, and that the foreign consuls were decidedly of the opinion that the blockade had been successfully broken and could not be recognized until they had communicated with their respective governments. On which Commander Bell deferred further belligerent operations.

At this period the U. S. vessels *Morning Light*, *Rachel Seaman* and *Velocity* were blockading the important outlet of Sabine Pass. Fears were entertained for their safety. Lieut. Read, with the gunboat *Cayuga*, was sent to reinforce the blockading ships. He was too late. He arrived in time to see the *Morning Light* in flames, and the *Velocity* in the hands of the Confederates. The *Rachel Seaman*, he was told, had escaped. The *Morning Light* and *Velocity* had been captured some days before. When Lieut. Read appeared the Confederates were attempting to get the former off the shoals and over the bar, but were compelled to burn her when they saw the *Cayuga*, and knew it was useless to try to save her. The expedition was fitted out against this portion of the Federal fleet soon after the battle of Galveston. It was planned by Gen. Magruder to clear Sabine Pass of the enemy. Two small steamers, the *Josiah Bell* and the *Uncle Ben*, were cotton-clad and placed under the command of Major Watkins, with about three hundred men of Pyron's, Speight's and Cook's regiments. The *Bell* was armed with a 64-pound rifled cannon, and the *Uncle Ben* with two 18-pounders. These vessels reached the pass on Jan. 20th; on the 21st they discovered the *Morning Light* and the *Velocity* twelve miles distant and well out toward the sea. The moment the latter discovered the cotton-clads bearing down upon them they set sail and endeavored to escape. An exciting chase ensued. [1]

The chase continued for fifteen miles, when the *Bell* got within range and fired the first gun at the *Morning Light*. Some ten or twelve shots were fired in all before the vessel came within musket range, when the Texan riflemen on board the *Bell* and the *Uncle Ben* soon cleared her decks. Before the *Bell* could reach her for boarding, the colors of the *Morning Light* were lowered and the Confederates took possession. The *Velocity* was easily captured after this; the Confederates did not lose a man; the loss of the Federals was four killed and fifteen wounded. Major Watkins cruised for several days off the pass waiting for Federal vessels, but found none. The premature absurdity of the following proclamation by Admiral Bell will therefore be readily seen :—

" U. S. STEAM SLOOP 'BROOKLYN,' ⎫
" OFF GALVESTON, Jan. 20th, 1863. ⎭

"*Whereas*, a proclamation dated Galveston, Texas, 4th January, 1863, and signed J. Bankhead Magruder, Major General Commanding, declares the said port of Galveston to be open for trade with all friendly nations, and invites their merchants to resume usual commercial intercourse with the said port of Galveston. Therefore, the undersigned hereby warns all concerned that the port of Galveston, and also Sabine Pass, as well as the

---

[1] It seems almost incredible that these vessels should run away, for the description of the *Morning Light* alone shows her to have been a vessel well able to cope with the two small cotton-clads, to say nothing of the *Velocity* and *Rachel Seaman*, both blockading ships, and armed. The *Morning Light* is thus described in the New York *Herald* after the capture :
" The United States ship *Morning Light* is a purchased vessel, which was put into commission about eighteen months since. She was built in Philadelphia in 1853, has two decks, and is of nine hundred and thirty seven tons burthen. She is constructed of oak, copper and iron fastened, and was metalled in February, 1861. She has a draft of nineteen feet, is one hundred and seventy-two feet long, and thirty-four feet broad and twenty-four feet in depth. She is of sharp model, and was last surveyed in this city in July, 1861. She carries a crew of about one hundred and twenty men, and an armament of eight thirty-two pounders. She was attached to the Gulf blockading squadron under Admiral Farragut."

whole coast of Texas, are under an actual blockade by a sufficient force of United States vessels, and any merchant vessel appearing off the aforesaid ports, or attempting to pass out from the said ports, under any pretext whatever, will be captured, notwithstanding the aforesaid proclamation, and sent into an open port of the United States for adjudication.

"H. H. BELL,
"*Commodore Commanding U. S. Forces*
"*Off Galveston and Coast of Texas.*"

Gen. Magruder's proclamation of the raising of the blockade was true, despite all attempts to hide the fact from foreign countries. Soon after the clearing of the pass Major Watkins bluffed off the *Tennessee*, a boat too swift for his vessels; it was fitted up as a gunboat by the United States. The *Tennessee*, according to a letter to the New York *Tribune*, Jan. 30th, 1863, written on board, arrived on the evening of the 21st of January off Sabine Pass.

"Soon the *Tennessee* sighted a large steamer, strongly resembling the *Morning Light*, though her top spars and the yards on her mizzen-mast had been removed, and her jibboom was rigged English fashion. Behind her lay another vessel, indistinctly made out in the fast gathering darkness. Recognizing the *Morning Light*, in spite of her disguise, and rendered additionally distrustful of what might have happened by the fact that she showed no signal lights in answer to his own, Capt. Child of the *Tennessee* caused her to be hailed and demanded her name. 'The *Morning Light*' was the reply. 'Then send a boat, we have a communication for you.' 'We've neither boat nor crew!' returned the unknown respondent, although the former could be discerned, hanging at the stern, by the officers of the *Tennessee*. 'Where is Capt. Dillingham?' next demanded Capt. Child. The answer came, brief, decisive and exultant! 'Ashore and a prisoner! The Confederates are in possession of the vessel!'

"A short consultation on board the *Tennessee* followed this disastrous intelligence. Some of the officers were disposed to attempt a recapture of the *Morning Light*. It being known, however, that she had no less than eight broadside guns and one thirty-pound Parrott, all of which were in undoubted possession of the rebels, while the *Tennessee* carried but an inconsiderable armament of howitzers, just sufficient for blockade purposes, peaceful counsels prevailed, and Capt. Child steamed for Galveston, forty miles to the southward, there to report the bad news to Commander Bell. From the appearance of the *Morning Light*, it was evident that she had been recently attacked, probably that very day, and no doubt existed that the schooner *Velocity*, her only partner in the blockade of Sabine City, had shared her fate."

Major Watkins at once sent official dispatches of this effective engagement as follows ·

"SABINE PASS, TEXAS,
"ON BOARD C. S. GUNBOAT 'BELL,'
"January 21st, 1863.

"CAPTAIN: We met the enemy this A. M. in the Gulf of Mexico, and whipped them. Brought everything to Sabine Pass. I fought his ten guns to our one. We have captured two vessels—one a full-rigged ship and the other a schooner, and twelve guns, medical stores, ammunition in abundance and 109 prisoners. I am here waiting further orders.

"O. M. WATKINS,
"*Major Commanding Sabine Pass.*
"To Capt. E. P. Turner, A. A. G."

"SABINE PASS, January 21st.

" To Capt. E. P. Turner, A. A. G.:

"I engaged the enemy to-day and captured thirteen guns, about a $1,000,000 worth of property, and 109 prisoners.

"O. M. WATKINS, *Major Commanding.*"[1]

Sabine Pass was an important outlet for the Confederates. The Sabine River is the boundary line between Texas and Louisiana ; and to it, and across it, were sent thousands of bales of cotton to be shipped from Texan ports to Cuba and other points in the West Indies, and to Europe. All the arms and munitions of war from Mexico came to the pass on light-draft blockade-runners, whenever the pass was clear, instead of making the more tedious journey overland.

If Admiral Farragut was correct in his account of these affairs at Galveston and Sabine Pass, the United States navy had more cowards in it than was credited to it at the time. The italics in the lines of his report of the Sabine Pass fight are ours.

Abundant caution seems to have been a characteristic of the Federal vessels in Texan waters, at this time.

FLAGSHIP 'HARTFORD,' NEW ORLEANS, Jan. 29th, 1863.

" SIR: I have received dispatches from Commodore Bell and Lieut. Commander Read, on the coast of Texas, extracts and a copy of which I herewith enclose, by which you will see that our disasters on that coast are not ended. As I had already anticipated, it appears that the enemy came out of Sabine Pass, with two cotton-fortified steamers on a certain morning, and ran out to sea some twelve or fourteen miles where the *Morning Light* was. The latter soon got under weigh; but, by the rebel accounts, and we have no other, they gave chase, soon came up with and captured her without losing a man. *The same course of non-resistance appears to have been pursued by the officers and crew of that vessel as was pursued by those of the Westfield and Harriet Lane.* The schooner *Velocity* was soon made also to surrender and was taken into port. I am very thankful that they did not get the guns of the *Morning Light*, as it would have enabled them to erect a battery of great strength in such a shallow pass.

"You will notice the guns of the *Morning Light* were loaded, and went off when they became heated, by which circumstance I judge the men did not even fire their last charge, but surrendered without a struggle.

"I am pleased to see by Commodore Bell's report that the *Harriet Lane* is still in Galveston harbor, although they have tried to impress us with the idea that she had run out during the last gale, which is now known not to be the case. Your obedient servant,

"D. G. FARRAGUT, *Rear Admiral.*

"To GIDEON WELLES, *Secretary of the Navy.*

" P. S.—I have just learned that the *Morning Light* was captured in a dead calm by a steamer coming up astern of her.

"D. G. FARRAGUT, *Rear Admiral.*"

The obvious purpose is to belittle the Confederate victories. The conquest was easy, says Admiral Farragut in effect,

---

[1] *Joint resolution of thanks to Major Oscar M. Watkins and the officers and men under his command :*

Resolved by the Congress of the Confederate States of America, That the thanks of Congress are due and are hereby tendered, to Major Oscar M. Watkins, and the officers and men under his command, for the signal victory achieved over the naval forces of the United States at Sabine Pass, on the twenty-first of January, 1863, resulting in the dispersion of the blockading squadron of the enemy, and the capture of two of his gunboats.

Approved May 1, 1863.

because the Federal naval officers were cowards. He uses a weapon, however, that wounds the gallant Admiral's own friends more than it does his enemies.

Capt. Wainwright of the *Harriet Lane* at least needs no further defence. He was ably championed by his brother, and it is due to him, and due to the memory of Commodore Smith, who was in an eager and cowardly manner accused by the Federal papers of shooting him after he had surrendered, to give the following card, published in December 1864, in the New York *Herald*, which paper had given currency to the scandalous charge. It is inserted here as pertinent to this part of the history, and as reflecting honor upon the Confederate officers who took part in these engagements. The same respect shown to the body of Capt. Wainwright, it may be said also, was shown to that of the second officer, Lieut. Lea.

"HAVANA, Dec. 8th, 1864.

"To the Editor of the New York Herald:

"My attention has been directed to an article published in your journal of November 30th, headed "Cruise of the United States Steamer *Fort Morgan* - Scenes in the Mexican Port of Bagdad—The Murderer of Commander Wainwright, United States Navy, a Leader of a Lawless Band of Rebels and Mexicans, etc., etc.'—in which the writer, whom I suppose to be an acting officer of the United States Navy, and attached to the *Fort Morgan*, says: 'The state of affairs in Bagdad, a town on the Mexican side of the Rio Grande, is wretched in the extreme. A spirit of lawlessness prevails, and the town is said to be full of rebel desperadoes, who have openly threatened to take the life of any Federal officer they may meet in that town. The notorious Smith, who figured in Galveston Bay in the attack on the *Harriet Lane*, and who shot down Commander Wainwright after he had surrendered, is at this time a leading spirit in Bagdad, and is said to be perfecting his arrangements for the capture of the United States gunboats at anchor off the mouth of the Rio Grande.

"Permit me to say, that justice to myself demands that I should ask space in your columns to contradict at once such portions thereof as refers to me, and which, from beginning to end, are utterly devoid of truth, and could only have emanated in a spirit of wanton desire to defame my character and to pervert well established facts of history.

"During the action of January 1st, 1863, in Galveston Bay, I had the honor to command the Confederate naval forces. I made the attack on the Federal fleet shortly before daylight. The *Harriet Lane* was the first vessel which I engaged by boarding; and it would have been impossible, owing to the darkness then prevailing, to have distinguished her commander from any of her other officers—particularly so, as he wore no uniform or insignia of his rank. After a short struggle the ship was surrendered to me by the senior surviving officer, Acting Master Hamblin, her commander having been killed some twenty minutes previous, gallantly defending himself with his revolver and cutlass.

"A corroboration of my assertion that Commander Wainwright was not killed by me after the surrender of the vessel, as asserted by your correspondent, will be found in the official report of the court of inquiry ordered by Admiral Farragut to investigate the Galveston disaster, a copy of which report I enclose, in which it is stated that 'the *Harriet Lane* was carried by boarding from the *Bayou City*, her commander summoned to surrender, which he refused, gallantly defending himself with his revolver until killed.'

"At the close of the action, I had the dead and wounded taken on shore and cared for. I assisted with my own hands in moving the corpse of Commander Wainwright to the headquarters of Gen. Magruder. While doing so, I was informed that he had been a member of an Order with which I have the honor to be connected. He was dressed in full uniform and laid out in state. I ordered the finest coffin that could be found, and paid for the same out of my own private purse. Although I met and fought him as an enemy, I admired his undaunted courage and bravery, and hence paid every respect to his remains.

"He was buried with military and Masonic honors. I among many other Confederate officers followed him to his grave. I saw to the collection and safe keeping of all of his personal effects, including his two swords, which I placed in charge of the senior surviving officer; but they were subsequently sent out to Commodore Bell, at that time commanding the United States squadron off Galveston, with the request that they should be forwarded to his family in the North, to whom I have every reason to suppose they were safely delivered.

"The statement of my being the leader of a lawless band of Mexicans and rebels at the port of Bagdad is simply ridiculous, and may go for what it is worth.

"If I have done any damage to your government at that point it was done legitimately, from the Confederate side of the Rio Grande, and under the Confederate, not Mexican, flag.

"I have been induced to make this statement of facts in vindication of my character as an officer and a gentleman.

"Very respectfully, etc.,
"LEON SMITH,
"*Confederate States Navy.*"

On March 12th, 1864, Admiral Porter, with nineteen gunboats, followed by ten thousand men of Sherman's army, under the command of Major Gen. N. P. Banks, entered the mouth of Red River. On the 13th, under cover of a part of the fleet, the troops debarked at Semmesport, on the Atchafalaya near the Red River, and on the 14th, under command of Gen. A. J. Smith, captured Fort De Russy. On the 15th of March the advanced boats of Porter's fleet reached Alexandria, where by the mismanagement of a pilot one Confederate steamer was grounded on the falls and had to be burned. On the 26th of April the Federal iron-clad *Eastport* grounded on a bar below Grand Encore, and to prevent her from falling into the hands of the Confederates she was destroyed. While intercepting the Federal gunboats on their way down the Red River at the junction of the Cane, on the 26th, the Confederates crippled one gunboat and exploded the boiler of a transport. The loss of the latter was one hundred dead and seventy-seven severely scalded. On the 1st of May the Confederates captured and sunk the transport *Emma*. On the 3d they captured the transport *City Belle*, on her way up to Alexandria, with the 120th Ohio regiment on board. On the evening of the 4th the Federal gunboats *Covington* and *Signal*, each mounting eight heavy guns, with the transport *Warner*, attempted to pass Davide's Ferry. The *Covington* was blown up by her crew to escape capture, but the *Signal* and *Warner* surrendered.

During these operations the Federals were engaged night and day in the construction of a dam across the Red River, to enable the fleet to escape over the falls. This it finally succeeded in doing, which ended the last Federal campaign undertaken for political objects, or intrusted to political generals.

The Sabine River, between Louisiana and Texas, was a line of great strategic importance to the forces of the United States ; as its possession would give to their forces short lines of operations against the interior of Texas, as well as recover the *morale* that was lost in the harbor of Galveston. For that purpose a fleet of twenty-one vessels was organized and dispatched in September, 1863, accompanied by a force of not less than five thousand men. The Confederate authorities had made no adequate preparations to resist such an army, and at that time it was not possible to promptly organize a force that could repel such an expedition. A few miles above the entrance to Sabine River a small earthwork had been constructed and was at that time garrisoned by a force of forty-two men and two lieutenants, with an armament of six guns. The company constituting the garrison was composed of Irishmen and called the " Davis Guards "; its captain, F. H. Odlum, was temporarily absent and the command devolved on Lieut. R. W. Dowling.

After the first naval battle off Sabine Pass the United States was content for some time to maintain a more or less effective blockade of that estuary, of Galveston and of the mouth of the Rio Grande. Later in the year 1863, however, the Federal authorities saw the necessity, if they would close these ports, of taking possession of them by a formidable land force. Sabine Pass was the first objective point. The expedition against it was organized at New Orleans. The 19th army corps, Major Gen. Franklin in command, constituted the land army, which was embarked on transports on the 4th of December. It was designed to land and hold Sabine Pass as a base of strategic operations against western Louisiana and eastern and central Texas. To cover the landing of the troops there was a navy of four light-draft gunboats—the *Sachem*, the *Clifton*, the *Granite City* and the *Arizona*. The foremost transport was the *Belvedere*, having on board Gen. Adam Weitzel and 500 picked men, who were to occupy the post of honor and make the first landing. The only fortified point at Sabine Pass, as has been stated, was a Confederate earthwork of small proportions with a few light guns, on the Texas side of the pass, known as Fort Griffin, and commanded by Lieut. Dowling, who managed the ensuing fight with a coolness and skill which does him and the men under him infinite credit. The Federals, officered by a general of such eminence as Franklin, and composed in part of picked men recently from the victories on the Mississippi, exulted in the anticipation of an easy conquest.

On the 5th of December the gunboats, accompanied by the transports, started from New Orleans. The rendezvous was Berwick Bay. It was determined that the attack should commence on the 8th of December, should be sudden and secret, and before the Confederates had time to reinforce Fort Griffin, or to erect shore batteries.   On account of the absence of the blockading vessel which they expected to sight, the expedition missed the designated point and was delayed one day.   On the 9th, however, the whole fleet was collected at the Pass and the order of battle arranged.   Capt. Crocker, of the *Clifton*, was to begin the action by feeling and uncovering the Confederate batteries, while Gens. Franklin and Weitzel personally examined the shore of the Pass and ascertained the most eligible point for disembarking the land forces.   Accordingly the *Clifton* was the first to enter the Pass, throwing shells as she did so into Fort Griffin.   She received no response and returned.   Then, the *Clifton* leading, the *Arizona* and the *Sachem* steamed in opposite the fort, and the *Clifton* opened with one of her nine-inch pivot guns.   The shell exploded inside the fort, throwing up a shower of dirt, and was instantly followed by another shell of the same kind.   At once the *Sachem* poured in a broadside from her thirty-two-pounder guns, and the next moment the *Arizona* opened.   Up to this time, and not until thirty or forty shells had exploded apparently in the fort, was a shot fired in return.   The naval commanders began to think the works abandoned.   The only signs of life apparent on water or land were two steamers in the river, one of which ran down to the fort and back just before the action.   The silence did not continue long.   A white cloud of smoke arose from the parapet of the fort and floated away in the still air.   The shot passed directly over the *Arizona*, striking the water beyond, showing that the aim was good and the range effective.   The next shot was at the *Sachem*, and the next at the *Clifton*.   Obviously those in the fort did not intend to allow any of the vessels to complain of neglect.   None of these shots struck the vessel fired at. The engagement now became general.   The *Clifton* and *Arizona* kept moving forward and backward, pouring in broadsides in quick succession, while the *Sachem* was moving steadily forward in order to get in the rear of the fort, where it was open and unprotected.   This move was seen, and the Confederates redoubled their fire at her, answered shot for shot by the three boats, the huge shells every instant bursting in the fort, carrying destruction in their wake and knocking great holes in the parapet, which appeared of sufficient size to admit the passage of a carriage and horses.   The Confederates acted with great bravery, however, and if their fire slackened an instant after one of those terrific explosions, which seemed to shake the very earth around them, it was instantly resumed with increased rather than diminished determination.   Gradually, but surely, the *Sachem* was gaining her desired position. A moment more and she would pass out of range, and the day would be won.   All eyes were bent upon her, when suddenly a shot was seen to strike her amidships, crushing in her sides and tearing her iron plating for the protection of sharp-shooters as a piece of paper, and causing her to career and tremble from stem to stern. An instant more and she was enveloped in the scalding vapor of escaping steam and lay a help-less wreck at the mercy of the fort.[1] The flag was lowered.

The disabling of the *Sachem* enabled the fort to turn its attention to the *Clifton* and the *Arizona*. The latter kept well off; but the former, with a bravery we cannot but admire, fought gallantly, running in toward the batteries and delivering her fire with a quickness and determination which exhibited both courage and good handling by her commander. A large portion of her crew, as well as a majority of that of the *Sachem*, were Irish, and as the troops in the fort were largely of the same nationality, it was Irish pluck against Irish valor. Just as the gunboat, however, ran down to the fort for the last time, her bow was thrown round slightly in the act of turning, and she was driven into the shallow river mud and stuck fast. She offered for a moment a target, of which the Confederate gunners took instant advantage, for she lay broadside on. She still kept firing, and for some time with the hope of keeping down the fire of the fort; but a shot from the battery at length struck the boat in the centre and passed through the boiler. She was now helpless and lay a wreck, exposed to the fort and at its mercy. Her captain had fought her gallantly but uselessly.[2] The white flag was run up and the firing ceased. The *Arizona* was the only boat left, and though the largest of them all, she hesitated to engage the fort alone. She steamed off, and the fleet withdrew, and was next heard of at New Orleans.

This affair at Sabine was highly creditable to all engaged, especially to the Davis Guards, Capt. Dowling, at the fort.[3]

[1] The *Sachem* was built in 1840, in New York, and was formerly owned in Hartford, Conn. She was about 198 tons' burden, and drew about seven feet of water. She had a vertical engine, with a cylinder twenty-four inches in diameter and ten inches stroke. She was rebuilt in 1854, and was sold to the U. S. government early in the war. In the attack upon the forts below New Orleans she was in the Coast Survey service, under the charge of Mr Gerdes, Assistant U. S. Coast Survey. After the taking of New Orleans she was fitted up with heavy armament, and figured prominently at various times and places. Her officers were—Acting Master Commanding, Amos Johnson; Acting Ensign, A. H. Reynolds; Acting Master's Mates, J. C. Dallives, L. C. Granger: Acting Engineers, John Frazier, James R. Wall and George C. M. Woolfe.

[2] The gunboat *Clifton* was built in New York, and was purchased by the Federal Navy Department early in the war. She was a Staten Island ferry boat, and well known in New York. She was attached to the Porter mortar flotilla, and did considerable service in the engagement below the forts at New Orleans. She carried nine guns of heavy calibre. After the mortar flotilla was scattered she served in several expeditions.

After the affair at Galveston she was commanded by Lieut. Frederick Crocker, and was noted on the Texas coast. She served as a Confederate gunboat until the 21st of March, 1864, when, attempting to run the blockade at Sabine Pass with over 700 bales of cotton on board, she ran aground and was burned to prevent her from falling into the hands of the enemy.

[3] A New York *Herald* correspondent noting the action said:—"Considering the number of the forces engaged, it is doubtful if any affair of the whole war can compare with the battle of Sabine Pass in obstinacy of fighting, loss of life and the amount of interest involved. To the enemy it was a matter of life and death, and to the Union forces it was the opening battle of a most brilliant campaign. The enemy retained their prize; but their loss has been undoubtedly without precedent in the annals of the war, and they will, in the midst of their rejoicing, tremble at the thought of a repetition of the attack. There were on board the *Clifton*, besides her crew, a party of seventy-five sharp-shooters and three of the signal corps, and on the *Sachem* a detachment of thirty sharp-shooters. Of the crew of the *Clifton*, five soldiers, one sailor and one signal man escaped down the beach, and were

E. P. Alsbury, a Confederate participant, gives the following interesting account of the fight, and of the part Commodore Leon Smith and his cotton-clads took therein. That it was not a more active one is due to the quick dispatch of the Davis Guards in Fort Griffin, and to the haste of the Federal fleet to get to sea.

The Confederate authorities had notice of the fitting out of the expedition of Gen. Franklin. Its destination was supposed to be Galveston, or Matagorda. The army of Gen. Magruder was distributed in accordance with this view. It was a surprise, therefore, when a dispatch was received by Col. Luckett at Harrisburg, Texas, from Lieut. Dick Dowling at Sabine Pass, stating that a large hostile fleet was in the offing, and that he had at Fort Griffin but forty-two men of the Davis Guards, a Houston company, and five pieces of artillery. Commodore Leon Smith, who was present when the dispatch was received, was at once requested to proceed down the river to the scene of action. At Beaumont, on the river, the steamer *Bell*, fitted up with cotton bales, incased in two-inch plank around her front and boiler, was lying. Commodore Smith took her, and with what men he could muster, steamed down the river. The sound of cannon was heard as the steamer neared Sabine Pass and told that the conflict had already commenced. In the graphic words of Mr. Alsbury—

"The pass was in full view. The white puffs from the advancing gunboats were seen, but the fort was silent. Could it be that it had been deserted? I can better explain the situation by sending the story of the fight, as it was detailed by its chief actor, and by others who supplied the circumstances omitted by the modesty of the young commander. When the fleet first anchored off the bar Lieut. Richard Dowling, a young Irishman, twenty years of age, and the junior officer of his company, was in command of Fort Griffin, with forty-two men present for duty. After transmitting the news to headquarters, he made every preparation necessary for defence, resolving to hold his position until it should become untenable. His men fully entered into the spirit of their young commander, and they calmly awaited the motions of their enemy. Fort Griffin was an unfinished earthwork on the Texas side of the Pass, destitute of any outer defences, presenting three bastioned sides on the east, south and west, the north and rear enclosed by a redoubt about four feet above the level. The work occupied high ground and commanded both the

taken off by a boat from the fleet. The number of killed and wounded must have been large, particularly on the *Clifton*, as she was not only exposed to a cross fire, but was raked from stem to stern by grape. As to the killed and wounded on the *Sachem* nothing is known; but the loss is supposed to be light, and mostly from the escaping steam, as but the one shot was known to have struck her. The loss of the enemy was undoubtedly enormous, as the huge nine-inch shell apparently searched every nook and corner of the earthwork; and when the *Clifton* was aground the same guns poured in a murderous fire of grape, sweeping the parapet from end to end. Their loss, however, will probably never be known."

The correspondent was sadly mistaken, nevertheless, in his assertion that the Davis Guards

would have "trembled at the thought of a repetion of the attack." They were only sorry when the *Arizona* steamed off. The *Granite City* with a broadside of brass guns was not heard of in the action. She was intended to cover the landing of the troops, but none were ever landed. Why, it would be difficult to say; General Franklin had on the transports probably four thousand men, many of them picked troops. He had to cover his landing, the uninjured gunboats *Arizona* and *Granite City*, the latter of light draft and especially chosen for the purpose. It seems an ignominious thing for such a force to sail away and put back to New Orleans, rather than face an earthwork fort of few guns, garisoned by less than three hundred landsmen, and already subjected to a prolonged and severe bombardment.

Texas and Louisiana channels. The former 300 yards; the latter at the distance of three-fourths of a mile.

"The armament consisted of one forty-four-pounder, smooth bore; and four thirty-two-pound Parrotts, and a brass twenty-four-pounder. The latter piece was not used in the action, for the want of suitable ammunition. Sabine village was situated about a mile and a half from the work, up the Pass, and contained only a few families, chiefly women and children of men in the service.

"The morning of the 8th of September, 1863, dawned brightly, and the golden glow from the east was reflected by the white sails of the Federal fleet which were making for a berth as near the shallow bar as possible. Some of the sailing transports were being towed by the steamers and four of the latter, as the sequel proved, were gunboats. Their movements were watched with thrilling interest by the people from the town and fort, and but few of the former anticipated any other result in the coming battle than disaster to the Confederates.

"Finally the cloud of sails on the outer bar, appeared to be arranged to satisfaction, and two steamers headed for the Pass, followed by two others, each with a transport in tow. When they arrived opposite the light-house, about three miles distant, one of the steamers took the Texas channel, while the other turned into that which skirted the Louisiana shore. Lieut. Dowling now understood that the enemy meant business. He had decided on his plan of defence. Ordering the men to enter the bomb-proofs, there to remain until he should fire the first gun, he remained to watch the gunboats, now slowly feeling their way up the two parallel channels. From their long service on the Texan coast, the two vessels were recognized with a glass by the time they had reached the light-house. The gunboat *Clifton*, Capt. Crocker commanding, followed the nearer channel; the other boat was the *Sachem*, under Lieut. Johnson. At a mile distant, the *Clifton* commenced the fight with shell, turning aside occasionally to bring her broadside into play. Several of the missiles fell in the fort and scattered the dirt in all directions. The *Sachem* did not fire, but advanced slowly, throwing the lead. Dowling remained in an angle of a bastion, concealed from view, and watching the approaching foe. This programme obtained until but 400 yards separated the *Clifton* from the Confederate position, when that vessel turned her broadside full to the fort. Until now nothing but silence answered the thunder of the Federal guns, and the commander of the gunboats began to suspect that they were confronted by dummies and a deserted work. But Dowling's opportunity had come. With the cool precision of a target practice, he deliberately sighted the forty-four pounder, and sent a solid shot through the enemy's side. The 'Davies' were not slow to respond to the signal, and soon the fort was wrapped in a curtain of smoke, and shook to the thunders of artillery. Three pieces were turned upon the more distant *Sachem*, now nearly abreast the eastern battery. Her response in quick, successive broadsides added to the din of battle, and hot work was in order for the next few minutes. A shot from the *Clifton* took off a handle of the elevating screw of the forty-four-pounder, hardly a second after Dowling had sighted the piece and moved to one side. The latter vessel fought desperately and in the last attempt to bring her broadside to bear, ran her bow into the mud. While in this position the Confederate shot pierced her steam-chest and boilers, scalding a number of her crew, and her flag was lowered. In a few moments the colors of the *Sachem* were struck, and the cheers from the fort succeeded the roar of cannon. At this moment the *Bell* was noticed coming down the Pass, while far in her rear on the lake the black smoke of another boat was visible. This proved to be an unarmed supply boat from Beaumont, which left shortly after the *Bell*. So soon as hostilities ceased, the other Federal steamers, which were afterwards known to have been the *Arizona* and *Granite City*, steamed back to the fleet, and left their gallant consorts to their fate. Capt.

Crocker came ashore with a boat's crew, and mounting the parapet of the fort, asked for the commanding officer. Dowling, full of the dust of battle, and looking little like a hero, presented himself as the person sought.

"The gallant Federal, in handsome uniform, could scarce believe the dirty boy was his conqueror, or that the handful of men before him comprised the force who had calmly awaited a hostile fleet, and by their unaided effort had subjected it to defeat, with the loss of its two best gunboats.

"As Capt. Crocker and party had come ashore without side-arms, Lieut. Dowling stated that he would accompany him back to the prize and receive his sword. While this formality of receiving the surrender of the *Clifton* was in progress, the steamboat *Bell*, with Leon Smith and party aboard, ran alongside of the *Sachem*, and she was taken possession of and manned by the naval detachment accompanying the commodore. It was discovered that the *Sachem* had also suffered in her boilers, and that fifteen of her men had been scalded. Her brave commander had ordered the canvas spread, and the run completed under sail, but her crew revolted and hauled down her flag. Had the order been obeyed the vessel would doubtless have succeeded in passing out of range, and could have engaged the work from the rear. The officers and men taken on the captured vessels amounted to about 315. In the fort not a single casualty had occurred. The prisoners were landed during the afternoon, and placed under the guard of a militia company of home guards, which hastily assembled on hearing the cannonading, and arrived at the scene of the conflict shortly after it had ceased. This company was composed of men too old to be in active service, and numbered about twenty. Their homespun clothes and rusty old fire locks, some of which still had the flint pans, afforded no little fun for the prisoners, who were neatly uniformed. The majority of the latter were Irish, like their captors, and there was no end to their wit, at the expense of their guard.

"The heroism displayed at Sabine Pass has never been excelled, when the odds are considered and the moral stamina it must have required to brave the presence of little less than an armada bearing a large army with a well-defined object of invasion, and prepared to meet with resistance that must have been believed to be ten or twentyfold its real strength. The young hero, Dick Dowling, has passed away from earth, but his memory will remain green among those who were his fellow soldiers, and still will live in song and story, when Texan valor will be the theme, and heroic deeds recounted."[1]

Sabine Pass was an unlucky spot for the Federal fleet. The Confederates were as active there as hornets. Eight

---

[1] *Joint resolution of thanks to Capt. Odlum, Lieut. Dowling, and the men under their command:*

Resolved, That the thanks of Congress are eminently due, and are hereby cordially given, to Capt. Odlum, Lieut. Richard Dowling, and the forty-one men composing the Davis Guards, under their command, for their daring, gallant and successful defence of Sabine Pass, Texas, against the attack made by the enemy, on the eighth of September last, with a fleet of five gun-boats and twenty-two steam transports, carrying a land force of fifteen thousand men.

Resolved, That this defence, resulting, under the Providence of God, in the defeat of the enemy, the capture of two gun-boats, with more than three hundred prisoners, including the commander of the fleet; the crippling of a third gun-boat, the dispersion of the transports, and preventing the invasion of Texas, constitutes, in the opinion of Congress, one of the most brilliant and heroic achievements in the history of this war, and entitles the Davis Guards to the gratitude and admiration of their country.

Resolved, That the President be requested to

communicate the foregoing resolutions to Capt. Odlum, Lieut. Dowling, and the men under their command.

Approved, February 8th, 1864.

The Federal official dispatch relating to this disastrous event tells its own story. The confident tone of the dispatch of Sept. 4th is in decided contrast with the contents of the subsequent reports.

UNITED STATES STEAM-SLOOP "PENSACOLA,"}
NEW ORLEANS, September 4th, 1863. }

SIR : I have the honor to inform the department that Major General Banks, having organized a force of 4,000 men, under Major Gen. Franklin, to effect a landing at Sabine Pass for military occupation, and requested the co-operation of the navy, which I most gladly acceded to, I assigned the command of the naval force to Acting Vol. Lieut. Frederick Crocker, commanding U. S. steamer *Clifton*, accompanied by the steamer *Sachem*, Acting Vol. Lieut. Amos Johnson; U. S. steamer *Arizona*, Acting Master Howard Tibbetts; and U. S. steamer *Granite City*, Acting Master C. W. Lamson. These being

months after the action just mentioned, the U. S. steamer *Granite City*, which then escaped, together with the steamer *Wave*, were captured at the Pass.

While lying in the river waiting for coal the Confederates threw a pontoon bridge across Mud Bayou, and brought over six pieces of artillery and a force of men. The first intimation the gunboats had of their proximity was the opening of the battery so near that in a few moments the *Granite City* surrendered, and a little while after the *Wave*. The troops on shore were aided by a cotton-clad steamer, probably the *Bell*. The *Granite City* was an iron side-wheel steamer; the crew was made up of the paroled and exchanged men of the unfortunate *Hatteras*. The *Wave*, or *Gunboat* 45, was originally one of Admiral Porter's gunboats and was protected by iron armor. The *Granite* had been on the Texas coast since 1863, and the *Wave* since April 1864. The officers captured with the *Granite City* were Acting Master Commanding, C. W. Lamson; Acting Assistant Surgeon, E. C. Vermulen; Acting Assistant Paymaster, John Reed; Acting Master, A. H. Atkinson; Acting Ensigns, S. R. Tyrrell and A. H. Terry; Acting Master's Mates, T. R. Marshall, J. E. Ashmead and D. Hall; Engineers: Acting Second Assistant, S. Greene; Acting Third Assistants, D. M. Schryver, J. H. Rollins and R. H. Gordon; Paymaster's Clerk, H. H. Faring.

And the officers of the *Wave* were Acting Volunteer Lieutenant, B. W. Loring; Acting Assistant Paymaster, Alfred G. Lathrop; Acting Ensigns, F. J. Latham, Peter Howard, and William Mellen; Acting Master's Mate, Charles Cameron; Engineers: First Assistant, John Thompson; Second Assistant, M. F. Fitzpatrick; Third Assistants, John Rodgers and W. H. Wilson; Paymaster's Clerk, Charles H. Grace.

We have not the official report, but the following letter will be of interest:

"SABINE PASS, Texas, May 8th, 1864.
"MY DEAR ―― I am under the painful necessity of informing you that I was captured at Calcasien Pass on the morning of the 6th. The

the only available vessels of sufficient light draft at my disposal for that service, and as they have good pilots, I have no doubt the force is quite sufficient for the object. The defences afloat and ashore are believed to consist of two thirty-two pounders *en barbette*, and a battery of field pieces, and two bay boats converted into rams.

It was concerted with Gen. Franklin that the squadron of four gun-boats, under the command of Acting Vol. Lieut. Crocker, shall make the attack alone, assisted by about one hundred and eighty sharp-shooters from the army, divided among his vessels; and having driven the enemy from his defences and destroyed or driven off the rams, the transports are then to advance and land their troops.

I regret exceedingly that the officers and crews, who have been on blockade there, cannot participate in the attack, in consequence of the excessive draft of water drawn by their vessels.

The *New London*, drawing 9½ feet, is the lightest draft of all the blockaders, and had

made repeated attempts to go in alone, but without success.

I have the honor to be your obedient servant,
H. H. BELL,
Commodore Commanding W. G. B. Squadron, pro tem.
To the Hon. GIDEON WELLES,
Secretary of the Navy, Washington, D. C.

UNITED STATES STEAMER "ARIZONA,"
SABINE BAR, September 10th, 1883.
SIR :— * * * At 6 A. M. on the 8th, the *Clifton* stood in the bay and opened fire on the fort, to which no reply was made. At 9 A. M. the *Sachem, Arizona,* and *Granite City,* followed by the transports, stood over the bar, and with much difficulty (owing to the shallowness of the water) reached anchorage two miles from the port at 11 A. M., the gunboats covering the transports.

At 3.30 P. M., the *Sachem,* followed by the *Arizona,* advanced up the eastern channel to draw the fire of the forts, while the *Clifton* advanced up the western channel ; the *Granite City* to

Wave was also captured at the same time. We fought for an hour and forty minutes; but the enemy's sharp-shooters picked off our men so that we could not keep our guns manned, and their batteries hulled us every shot.

"The *Granite City* had sixteen shot-holes in her hull, near the water line; two officers were wounded, one severely—so badly that his right arm was obliged to be taken off at the shoulder. Ten men were wounded; two since dead.

"The enemy's sharp-shooters annoyed us most, although we were pretty well cut up by shot and shell.

"I am uninjured and in good health. I have met so far with high-toned polite officers, who have shown me every proper attention.

"We go from here by steamboat and railroad to Houston. Our destination from there is now to me unknown.

"C. W. LAMSON, *Commanding U. S. Steamer 'Granite City.'* "

It will be seen that Commander Lamson pays a tribute to the courtesy and kindness of his captors. In the course of the narrative also it has been observed how generous a tribute was paid to the remains of Commander Wainwright and Lieut. Lea, of the *Harriet Lane*. And further, the letter has been given in which Commodore Smith so indignantly and successfully defended himself against the charge of shooting Commander Wainwright after his surrender. It is the unanimous statement of the officers who were prisoners in Texas from the Federal naval forces that they were well treated, and as well fed, housed and clothed as the circumstances would allow. Of course there were persons who, in Northern papers, tried to influence the feelings of the North by assertions unwarranted by the facts, but time has vindicated the Confederate authorities from all such charges.

cover the landing of a division of troops under General Weitzel; no reply to the fire of the gun-boats being made until we were abreast of the forts, when they opened with eight guns, three of which were rifled. Almost at the same moment the *Clifton* and *Sachem* were struck in their boilers, enveloping the vessels in steam. There not being room to pass the *Sachem*, this vessel was backed down the channel and a boat sent to the *Sachem*, which returned with Engineer Munroe and Fireman Linn badly scalded (since dead). The *Arizona* had now grounded by the stern; the ebb-tide caught her bows and swung her across the channel; she was, with much difficulty, extricated from this position—owing to the engine becoming heated by the collection of mud in the boilers.

The flags of the *Clifton* and *Sachem* were run down and white flags were flying at the fore. As all the transports were now moving out of the bay, this vessel remained covering their movements, until she grounded and remained until midnight, when she was kedged off, as no assistance could be had from any of the tugs of the expedition. There are now on board this vessel, William Low, Peter Benson, George W. Maker, John Howels, Samuel Smith, and George Hurton, of the crew of the *Sachem*.

Very respectfully, your obedient servant,
H. TIBBETTS,
Acting Master Commanding U. S. steamer *Arizona*,
Commodore H. H. BELL,
Commanding W. G. B. Squadron, New Orleans.

UNITED STATES STEAM SLOOP "PENSACOLA,"
NEW ORLEANS, September 13th 1863.

SIR :—My dispatch No. 41 informed you of the repulse of the expedition at Sabine Pass. and the capture of the *Clifton*, Acting-Vol. Lieut. Frederick Crocker, and *Sachem*, Acting-Vol. Lieut. Amos Johnson, by the rebels, and the safe return of the troops and transports to the river without loss.

Lieutenants Crocker and Johnson are reported to have fought their vessels gallantly, and are unhurt. The rebel steamers took the *Clifton* and *Sachem* in tow within twenty minutes after their surrender. The extent of their damage is unknown.

The arrival of the *Owasco* this morning has given me the only reports from the naval officers concerned that I have yet received.

* * * * *

The attack, which was to have been a surprise and made at early dawn on the 7th, was not made until 3 P. M. on the 8th, after the entire expedition had appeared off Sabine for twenty-eight hours, and a reconnoissance had been made on the morning of the 8th, by Generals Franklin and Weitzel and Lieut. Commanding Crocker, when they decided on a form of attack different from that recommended by myself.

* * * * * *

I have the honor to be your obedient servant,
H. H. BELL,
Commodore Com. W. G. B. Squadron, *pro tem.*
Hon. GIDEON WELLES,
Secretary of the Navy, Washington, D. C.

Lieut. Loring of the *Wave* was an officer of distinction. He served the guns that caused the Confederate ram *Atlanta* to surrender, and it is said he fired the first shot at Fort Sumter, and the one that exploded the magazine at Fort Moultrie.

The end was drawing near, however. The United States, with its almost unlimited forces, was proving too strong for the little State of Texas left to itself. Brownsville was occupied by the Banks' expedition; the Matagorda peninsula, commanding Cavallo Pass and Corpus Christi, was firmly held; the blockade of Galveston was strengthened, and only the forts at Sabine Pass were still defiantly held. It was not until May, 1865, that they were evacuated, and then the long war was drawing to a close, and Gens. E. Kirby Smith and Canby were arranging terms of surrender. Acting Volunteer Lieut. Pennington hoisted the United States flag on the memorable Fort Griffin. He found it a small place with five bomb-proofs covered with two feet of solid timber and two layers of railroad iron, and containing five guns, which he spiked.

Acting Rear Admiral Thatcher's report of the capture of the forts at Sabine Pass was as follows:

"NEW ORLEANS, LA., May 31st, 1865.

"SIR : I have the honor to inform the Department that a dispatch, under date of the 25th inst., was this day received from Captain B. F. Sands reporting the evacuation of the defences of Sabine Pass, Forts Mannahassets and Griffin.

"Acting Volunteer Lieut. Commander Pennington hoisted the United States flag on these forts. The guns, five in number, were spiked. Fort Griffin is described as having five bomb-proofs covered with two feet of solid timber, two layers of railroad iron, and four feet of each on top. There were four magazines of like construction. Lieut. Commander Pennington having left force enough to hold the forts, retired to his vessel, leaving the American flag flying.

"Captain Sands, under date of the 27th of May, reports that the rebel army of Texas have generally disbanded and gone home, and the terms of surrender recently executed in New Orleans between the rebel commanders sent by General E. Kirby Smith and General Canby having been complied with on the part of the rebels, it only remains for us to occupy the fortifications. With regard to the rebel naval forces in Texas, I am assured by the Confederate Lieut. Commander Jonathan Carter, who is now here, and declares himself to be the senior naval officer, that there is no naval property nor any officers in Texas on the seaboard, and only one vessel in the Red River—the ram *Missouri*—which will be surrendered to the commander of the Mississippi Squadron.

"Very respectfully, your obedient servant,

"H. B. THATCHER, *Acting Rear Admiral, W. G. B. S.*

"To GIDEON WELLES, *Secretary of the Navy.*

On June 13th the U. S. Navy Department received from Commander W. E. Fitzhugh his report concerning the surrender of the Confederate naval forces on Red River. Commander Fitzhugh, in his dispatch, which was dated on board the *Ouachita*, at Alexandria, Louisiana, June 3d, says that he started up Red River on the 28th of May with the steamers

34

Benton, Ouachita, Fort Hindman and the tug *Fern*, in company with Major Gen. Herron and his steamer *Ida May*, in advance of the troops. He encountered no resistance whatever. All whom he met seemed well disposed. On the morning of June 3d the squadron met Lieut. Commander J. H. Carter, commanding the Confederate naval forces of the trans-Mississippi squadron, and received from him the iron-clad *Missouri* and the paroles of himself, officers and men. Lieut. Commander Carter informed Commander Fitzhugh that the *Missouri* was the only naval vessel on Red River or its tributaries. The *Champion*, one of the pump-boats captured in the expedition, was turned over to the army. The *Missouri* was brought below the Falls, and was to be refitted at the mouth of the river. She was designed to be quite a formidable vessel, made on the plan of the *Tennessee*, captured at Mobile, but was built of timber not thoroughly seasoned, and caulked with cotton, and it was believed that she leaked badly. Her battery was composed of one 11-inch gun, one 9-inch and two heavy thirty-two pounders. Commander Fitzhugh then went up to Shreveport to secure such property as belonged to the navy. The number of Confederate naval prisoners paroled by him at Alexandria was eighteen men and six officers, including Lieut. Commander J. H. Carter.

The end had come, and it only remained for the United States to garrison important points on the Texan coast. Admiral Thatcher reports this fact on June 8th, 1865:

"WEST GULF SQUADRON, U. S. FLAGSHIP ' R. R. CUYLER,')
"OFF GALVESTON, TEXAS, June 8th, 1865. (

"SIR : In my dispatch, No. 136, written at Mobile, I informed the Department that the Rebel Commissioners at Galveston had desired transportation to New Orleans, to meet Gen. Canby, with a view to arrange the terms of surrender, and that I had directed such transportation to be furnished. On the evening of the 28th of May, I arrived at New Orleans, where I remained until the morning of the 5th inst., and, during that period, had several official interviews with Colonel Ashbel Smith, the commander of the defences of Galveston, who assured me that there would be no opposition on the part of the forces under his command or the people to the occupation of Galveston by the navy. On the morning of the 5th I left New Orleans in the U. S. steamer *R. R. Cuyler*, and arrived off Galveston yesterday at 2 P. M. Capt. Sands then informed me that on the 2d inst. Maj. Gen. E. Kirby Smith and Maj. Gen. J. B. Magruder came on board the U. S. steamer *Fort Jackson*, where they were met by Brig. Gen. E. J. Davis, representing E. R. S. Canby, and the terms of surrender heretofore agreed upon between the representatives of Generals Smith and Canby were signed by Gen. E. Kirby Smith. After signing of the articles of surrender, Capt. Sands immediately took the necessary steps to buoy out the channels, and on the 15th inst. proceeded inside the bar in the *Cornelia*, followed by the *Preston*, and landed at Galveston, accompanied by Commander Stevens, Commander Downs, and Lieut. Com. Wilson, and had an interview with the Mayor, C. H. Leonard ; after which the flag of the United States was raised on the Custom House, the citizens conducting themselves in the most orderly manner. The flag is now floating on all the forts in the harbor ; but as we have not sufficient force from the fleet to garrison the latter, I have decided the light-draft gunboats *Cornelia, Preston*, and *New London* to remain inside the bar, where they will be joined by the *Port Royal*. I have also given order to Commander Leroy, of the *Ossipee*, to convey with his vessel the troops which Gen. Canby, it is hoped, will in a few days be ready to dispatch to occupy the different ports on the coast already surrendered to the United States. Gen. Brown, of the U. S. army, on the 1st inst., with a brigade, took possession of the garrison at Brownsville. The other ports on the coast of Texas, which have been heretofore blockaded by our vessels, are now held by the naval forces. Thus blockade running from Galveston and the coast of Texas is at an end. To-day I went on shore and had an interview with the civil and military authorities, by whom I was cordially received, and, in conversation, these gentlemen expressed their anxiety for the restoration of the old order of things, and reiterated their desire that a portion of our naval force should remain in the harbor for their protection. On the visit I was accompanied by Captain Sands and a part of my staff.

"Very respectfully, your obedient servant,
"H. K. THATCHER, *Acting Rear Admiral*,
"*Commanding the Western Gulf Squadron.*
"HON. GIDEON WELLES,
"*Secretary of the Navy, Washington, D. C.*"

The fate of some of the captured vessels, or the river steamers used by the Confederates, remains to be told.

The *Harriet Lane* escaped from Galveston about May 5th, 1864, in company with the blockade-runner *Isabel*, the *Alice* and a schooner. They were loaded with cotton. The *Lane* went by the southwest channel and was discovered by the U. S. steamer *Katahdin*, one of the blockading squadron, which immediately gave chase and got within range. The *Katahdin* fired four shots at the *Lane* without effect. The chase soon became exciting, the vessels being at times so near each other as to distinguish the men on deck. At daylight the *Katahdin* discovered that she was not only chasing the *Lane*, but three other vessels, all keeping together. All the day the chase continued, the *Lane* keeping well out of range, but the *Alice* getting several shots and being compelled to throw her deck load of cotton overboard and break up the timbers of the hurricane deck to burn in the boilers. During the night the *Harriet Lane* and *Isabel* were lost sight of about thirty miles off the west coast of Louisiana, and the next day the two others escaped owing to a head wind springing up, lessening the speed of the *Katahdin* some two points and enabling the steamers to outrun her.

The *Isabel* was captured by the blockading fleet while attempting to enter Galveston Harbor on May 28th, 1864. She was chased by the U. S. steamer *Admiral*, Acting Vol. Lieut. Eaton commanding. The Federal vessel reports that the captain of the *Isabel* handled her "with great skill and desperate courage, not surrendering until he had received two broadsides at short range, every shot hitting his vessel and the fire from the small-arms of the *Admiral* literally driving the men from the wheel." The *Wave* was taken about September 13th, 1863.

The *John F. Carr*, noticed in the recapture of Galveston, while firing upon troops in Matagorda Bay was caught in a gale, driven on shore and wrecked early in 1864.

The Federals captured in Texan waters many blockade-runners, while still more escaped.   Among the unfortunate ones were the Spanish bark *Teriseta*; the *Major Barbour*, of New Orleans; the blockader *Cora*, off Brazos, by the *Quaker City*; the schooners *Loward* and *Julia*, by the U. S. steamer *Chocura*; and the schooner *Hurley*.   The *Anna Dale* was cut out in Matagorda Bay by the boats of the U. S. steamer *Penola*. She struck the bank, however, and was burned.   The blockade running schooners *Pet* and *Annie Sophia* were taken in Galveston Harbor by boats crews from the U. S. steamers *Princess Royal* and *Bienville*.   The noted blockade-runner *Will-o-the-Wisp*, while attempting to get into Galveston on the night of the 3d February, 1865, ran ashore and was wrecked.   The U. S. steamer *Tennessee* captured the British schooner *Friendship* from Havana, and at the same time another schooner, supposed to have been the *Jane*, of Nassau, was blown up. The *Cayuga* captured off the Rio Grande the *J. T. Davis*, which had run out from Galveston.

All these vessels were laden with cotton, stands of arms, or an assorted cargo.

Others were captured of which we have no record, for blockade-running was brisk and often profitable on the Texan coast, and one letter from an officer on board the blockading fleet mentioned ten blockade-runners in sight safe in harbor, or awaiting an opportunity to run out.

Fighting improvised cotton-clads, manned by untrained crews, against regularly armored and equipped steamers manned by experienced sailors; pitting earthworks, with feeble garrisons and insufficient cannon, against blockading vessels, heavily armed and iron-clad—the success which attended the Confederate operations in Texas waters is remarkable and should be as memorable to their descendants as it was honorable to the brave men who planned and executed the capture of Galveston and who fought the battles of Sabine Pass.

COMMANDER RICHARD L. PAGE, C. S. N.

ALSO BRIGADIER GENERAL, C. S. A.

FORT MORGAN,

COMMANDING THE ENTRANCE TO MOBILE BAY.

CHAPTER XVIII.

ALABAMA WATERS.

MONG the earlier of the Southern States to sever connection with the North, alive and vibrant with the impulse for independence, the possessor of a broad water
frontage upon the Gulf of Mexico and its estuaries, and
threaded inland with navigable rivers, every political and geo-
graphical consideration induced Alabama to take an immediate and intimate interest in the maritime operations of
the Confederacy. Her chief city was the second in rank
of the great cotton ports of America; it had maintained
an increasing and lucrative foreign and coastwise commerce, upon which its fortunes had been principally built;
and, whatever might be the fluctuations of war, the contingency that Mobile would become at some time the object of
the enemy's attack by sea could no more be overlooked than
could the value of the harbor for blockade-running purposes,
or the adaptability of the Alabama, Tennessee and Tombigbee
Rivers for the movements of inland flotillas. The alert and
comprehensive genius of the strong men who founded the
Confederate government, and formed its schemes of offence
and defence, was quick to take cognizance of the fact that
Alabama possessed, upon and within her hills, in vast abundance, the raw materials of wood and iron needed for the
creation of ships and their armaments; and that even with the
lack of money, of sufficient dock-yard and machine-shop
facilities and of an adequate number of trained designers,
builders, mechanics and engineers, under which the Confederate States struggled, Alabama would be able to contribute in
a very important degree to their enterprises afloat. Her waters
were destined to become the theatre of naval conflicts of varying magnitude, culminating in that death-grapple of Titans
at the battle of Mobile Bay; of scores of gallant exploits of
seamanlike skill and daring; of marine raids by the adventurous hunters and fishermen of these semi-tropical sounds and
bayous upon the enemy's transports and tenders, and of that

side play of blockade-running which was a constant accompaniment to the main drama of the war.

The primary location of the seat of the new government at Montgomery, and the presence there of such famous officers of the old navy of the United States as Rousseau, Tatnall, Ingraham, Randolph, Semmes, Farrand, Brent and Hartstene, in consultation with the civil heads of the Confederacy upon ways and means of placing the new flag upon the seas, of course were influential in fixing the consideration of the people of Alabama upon the subject.[1]   Quick upon the seizure by their State authorities of the forts in Mobile Bay on January 12th, 1861, they had mooted this question of ships and guns, and in the nature of things it could nowhere have been more a focus of thought than in the seaport town of Mobile. In his "Memoirs of Service Afloat," Admiral Semmes writes that when he reached there on April 19th, 1861, he found it "in a great state of excitement. Always one of the truest of Southern cities, it was boiling over with enthusiasm; the young merchants had dropped their day-books and ledgers and were forming and drilling companies by night and by day, whilst the older ones were discussing questions of finance and anxiously casting about them to see how the Confederate treasury could be supported."

It comes within the domain of those morally well-established facts, the documentary proof of which is missing by reason of the loss of early records, that Alabama, at this opening hour of the struggle, was preparing to do her part for the Southern navy. The first actual evidence we have of the movement in that direction is the signing by the Governor on November 8th, 1861, of a bill which had just passed the Legislature, appropriating $150,000 "for the immediate construction of an iron-clad gunboat and ram in the bay or harbor of Mobile." This bill had been framed by the Select Committee on Harbor Defences, had been reported by Mr. Langdon, and had been passed by both houses, and received the Governor's approval within a week. Messrs. L. J. Fleming, P. J. Pillans, Peter Hamilton, and Duke W. Goodman, of Mobile, and Lieut. Johnson, C. S. N., were appointed commissioners to superintend the work of construction and outfit, and special instructions appear to have been laid upon them by the Legislature to proceed with all practicable speed. They partially completed a fighting machine of the type described, and this is, in all probability, the vessel spoken of in the report of the joint Congressional Committee of Investigation into the Navy Department in the autumn of 1862, as "an unfinished iron-clad ram turned over to the Confederacy by the State of Alabama," as the State had not authorized of itself any other such ship to be built. The only other ship-of-war which was in the possession of Alabama in 1861 was the Federal revenue cutter

---

[1] See chapter III. for details of the organization of the Confederate States navy in Alabama.

Lewis Cass, which on January 31st was surrendered to the State by her commander, Capt. James J. Morrison, of Georgia, and was regularly enrolled in the Confederate navy by a subsequent transfer from the State to the general government. On the 20th of the same month the Mobile Chief of Police seized a small craft, the *Isabella*, which was loading at one of the city wharves with fresh provisions for the Federal fleet off Pensacola. In May, 1861, Col. Bonner, of Alabama, was announced by the New Orleans *Delta* to have invented " an iron-clad steam propelling battery for the defence of Mobile harbor, which is much approved by Cols. Hardee and Chase and by Major Leadbetter of the Confederate States army."

The blockade went into force at Mobile, as at other ports of the Confederacy, on May 28th, 1861, and in anticipation of it the harbor was cleared of all shipping under foreign flags. The first blockader to appear upon this station was the frigate *Powhatan*, under command of Lieut. David D. Porter, who in a communication, of May 28th, to James Magee, the acting British Consul, consented that the Mobile tow-boats should be used in taking out the British merchantmen in port, and added that " it would be better, if it can be done without injury to British interests, to get the ships to sea as soon as practicable." No incident entitled to historical notice marked this cessation of the commerce of Mobile, and from this date until Farragut's attack the port and town passed through three years of closure to marine intercourse, broken only as the low, long, swift ocean racers stole in under the guns of the sentinel fleet, with cargoes of arms, ammunition and stores, and out again with the cotton for which the great mills of Lancashire were waiting. But these were not years of idleness or monotony in these waters. The occasional chase of a blockade-runner by Federal cruisers until the cannon of Fort Morgan stopped the pursuit, the dashes of boat parties upon Federal craft, the strengthening of the fortifications, the work of laying the obstructions in the channel and setting the torpedoes, and the building of the squadron that finally confronted Farragut, made the war a sharp and close reality to the dwellers upon the Mobile shores, the soldiers and the sailors who hereabouts sustained the honor of the Confederate cause.

For some months after the beginning of the war a tolerably regular communication was maintained between Mobile and New Orleans through Mississippi Sound by merchant steamers, but the enemy soon undertook to close this outlet. Early in December 1861, the steamer *Anna*, engaged in this trade, was made a prize by the gunboat *New London*, and as this capture was soon afterward followed by that of the *P. C. Wallace*, another trading steamer, other vessels abandoned a line of travel that it had been found dangerous and unprofitable to pursue.

Actual fighting was opened in the neighborhood on January 29th, 1862, when one of the blockaders chased into Mobile Bay the schooner *Wilder*, which had run the blockade with a cargo of goods from Havana. Seeing the gunboat approach, Capt. Ward, of the *Wilder*, set the British colors and beached his vessel. The Federals came up in launches, into which they began to transfer the cargo of their prize, In the meantime word had been sent to Mobile, and Capt. Cottrill, who commanded a company of rangers, hurried to the shore with his men and opened fire upon the launches, which was returned from their howitzers and small arms, and the Federal steamer sent in several rounds of shot and shell. The launches were driven off, but at night a Federal steamer came in and towed the *Wilder* out. It was claimed by the Confederates that Capt. Cottrill's fire killed twenty-five or thirty of the enemy's party. Nine of their bodies were found upon the beach, and one of their small boats, which was abandoned, was pierced from stem to stern with bullets.

The first occasion of the interchange of the compliments of shot and shell between the beleaguering fleet, the Confederate land defences and the Confederate flotilla, was on the following 3rd of April, when the latter made a reconnoissance down the bay and drew the fire of the Federal gunboats, which they briskly returned but without any injury being accomplished on either side. Having consummated the object of the movement, the Confederate steamers withdrew toward Fort Morgan, and as they were followed by the enemy the batteries of the fort opened on the latter, who were then quick to retire to their stations off the bar. On the night of June 28th the British steamer *Ann* ran the blockade from London *via* St. Thomas and Havana, but being discovered by the Federals the next morning before she could reach the protection of the guns of Fort Morgan, her crew deserted her on the approach of two Federal men-of-war, who easily effected her capture. Her officers had endeavored to scuttle the ship, but her water-tight compartments saved her, and thus the Confederacy lost her valuable cargo of arms and war material.

On August 30th the Federal gunboat *Winona* ran up toward Fort Morgan with a view to dropping shells over Mobile Point upon a Confederate armed vessel lying inside. The latter was in no position for an engagement, but the fort directed so steady a fire upon the *Winona* as to compel her to beat a hasty retreat. The distance, three and a half miles, was too great for any execution to be done, but the little affair served to demonstrate that Fort Morgan's artillerists had an excellent range of the channel, and the enemy's gunboats were thenceforth somewhat more chary of exposing themselves to their fire. This incident preceded by but five days the perilous and splendid rush of the *Florida* under Capt. Maffitt,[1] through

[1] See chapter upon the career of the Florida.

the lines of the blockaders into Mobile, and taught them to keep at a respectful distance from Morgan's batteries during the four months they passed in waiting for Maffitt to repeat his bold exploit on the reverse course by forging out to sea again.

After having refitted for sea at Mobile, the *Florida* celebrated the Christmas Eve of 1862 by a duel at long distance with the Federal ship *New London*, steaming for that purpose down to the westward of Sand Island, while her antagonist took up a position on the gulf side of the bar at that point. It was a lively afternoon spectacle for the garrisons and the blockaders, and it gave Capt. Maffitt the opportunity he desired of exercising his new crew at quarters and putting them through their gun drill with an enemy as a target to practice upon. The contemporary Confederate accounts report that the *Florida* was not struck, but it was believed that three of her shot took effect on the enemy.[1]

Allusion has heretofore been made to the raids of boats' crews of Confederates by way of Mississippi Sound upon Federal vessels. Two that occurred in 1863 are particularly deserving of special description, because of their success and because they illustrate the daring spirit of the Mobile watermen.

On April 6th, 1863, Capt. G. Andrews organized at Mobile a raiding party for the mouth of the Mississippi, where they arrived the next day in a ship's boat, armed with nothing heavier than their revolvers. "So eager were they to take a prize," says the Mobile *Tribune*, of April 10th:

"That they resolved to board the first vessel they saw, but she proved to be the *Illinois*, with six guns and a crew of 400 men. Of course they abandoned the purpose immediately. Shortly afterward they sighted the transport steamer *Fox*, formerly the *Whittemore*, and used as a tow-boat before she was taken from the Confederates. She was lying at a coal-yard in Pass l'Outre. At night, when all was still on board, the brave fifteen boarded her and made all hands (twenty-three) prisoners. She was in command of Capt. Walker, who was formerly captain of one of the Mobile Bay boats. They submitted to the capture peaceably. Steam was immediately raised, and the *Fox*, manned by both crews, (the prisoners as well as the captors worked her) was steered away to Dixie land with the United States flag flying at her masthead. She was not interrupted until she attempted to come in by the Swash Channel at about three o'clock, yesterday morning, when thirty shots were fired at her from the blockading fleet. One struck the top of her smoke-stack and another one of her masts, doing, however, no damage. She came on until she got safely under the guns of Fort Morgan and arrived at the city last evening about six o'clock. Her capture is certainly one of the most daring and well-managed exploits of the war."

[1] "All but these three were seen to strike the water, but the thousands of eyes which watched could not tell where these three went to if they were not stopped by the *New London*. She was evidently hit hard, for after backing out of the fight she signalled the fleet, and one of them ran down and lay alongside of her for several hours, rendering assistance, it is supposed.

"The spectators say that the *Florida's* long and terrible guns were admirably served, the practice being excellent, placing the shot and shell all around the mark, so close, in many instances, as to apparently dash the water upon the Lincolnites' decks. The engagement is said to have been a most animating and exciting scene as witnessed from the forts."—Mobile *Evening News, Dec.* 26th, 1862.

The prize had on board 1,000 barrels of coal. The men who assisted Capt. Andrews were C. W. Austin, M. Riddle, John Brown, Daniel Kernan, R. Hill, Oliver Bowen, D. Mc Mickle, Wm. Brown, Asbell Glenson, J. W. Jones, John Connor, Thomas Nelligan and Charles Stokes.

One of the most daring exploits accomplished at this epoch of the war in the waters of the gulf was consummated by nineteen citizens of Mobile. Cotemporary records have preserved only the name of their leader, Capt. James Duke, although it would have been a solid gratification to have handed down to the future the names of the eighteen volunteers who joined him in the perilous, gallant and successful expedition. Starting from Mobile about the middle of the last week of May, 1863, they pushed through Mississippi Sound in a small boat to the mouth of the Mississippi River. They carried nothing but small arms, and it does not appear that they had any more definite object in view than to reconnoitre the enemy's position and inflict upon him any possible damage the opportunity for which might be presented. After lying three days ambushed in the swamps a few miles above Pass l'Outre light-house, they discovered at dusk of the evening of June 9th the fine steam-propeller *Boston* coming up the river and having in tow the ship *Jenny Lind* from Boston, loaded with ice for New Orleans. Speedily embarking his men on their little boat, Capt. Duke in a few moments laid her alongside of the *Boston*, whose commander had not the most remote suspicion of the presence of a foe in a region patrolled by Federal gunboats. Before he could make any movements toward defence the Mobile men had boarded him with drawn revolvers and compelled his surrender. Capt. Duke cut the hawser connecting the *Boston* with the ship and with his prize stood down the river. The next day he captured the bark *Lenox*, Capt. Cole, from New York for New Orleans, took off the officers, crew and a portion of the passengers, sent the others on shore and burned the vessel and her cargo of general merchandise. Then he stood out to sea, safely passing under the guns of the blockading fleet, and on Sunday, June 14th, came up with the bark *Texana*, Capt. Wulff, also from New York for New Orleans, with a miscellaneous cargo and a quantity of arms. She, too, was boarded and fired; but Capt. Duke was now so encumbered with prisoners that he set all her people on shore except the captain and mate. On the 17th, he brought the *Boston* to the wharf in Mobile, having run the gauntlet of the Federal ships in the bay without injury. He landed eighteen prisoners and turned his prize over to the Confederate government, which subsequently made good use of her. Besides adding this serviceable steamer to the scanty naval strength of the Confederacy, the ships and cargoes destroyed by Capt. Duke's command were valued at $200,000. The merit of his enterprise was properly recognized in Mobile, and the skill and courage of himself and his companions highly applauded. Their daring is attested by the fact that in the Mississippi they were for several hours within speaking distance of the Federal sloop-of-war *Portsmouth*, and half an hour previous to their capture of the *Boston* a gunboat had passed up within gunshot of them. The newspapers of the day speak of the expedition as having been fitted out by Julius Buttner, a citizen of Mobile.

These cool and plucky dashes into the enemy's confines had an inspiriting effect upon the military and naval defenders of Mobile, as affording an indication that notwithstanding the weakness of the Confederacy upon the waters, and the immense resources of the Federals, the latter were not invulnerable against bold hearts and ready hands.

A hitherto unwritten chapter of the war in the Mexican Gulf is that which must record in fitting language the reconnoisance of Pensacola, made by Lieut. James Mc C. Baker,[1] of the *Huntsville*, and his brother Page M. Baker, Master's Mate of the *Tuscaloosa*, and their subsequent project to capture Fort Pickens, which was thwarted by the hesitation of their superior officers. The preliminary scout was an achievement that could only have been carried through by cool men utterly devoid of fear, and the scheme which grew out of it was phenomenal for its shrewdness and possibilities of success even in the days when men who wore the Confederate uniform

[1] James Mc C. Baker entered the Confederate service early in the war as a member of Drew's battalion, and on January 23d, 1862, was transferred to the Washington artillery; but very soon afterward was appointed Acting Master in the Confederate navy and ordered to report to Commodore Whittle, in command at New Orleans, by whom he was assigned to the iron-clad *Louisiana*, then recently launched and still unfinished. As her screw engines were not in position and the recess wheels alone were insufficient to propel her, she was towed down the Mississippi and moored on the bank above Fort St. Philip to aid in the defence of the river against the Federal fleet. Alongside of her was placed the river steamer *W. Burton* as quarters for the officers and crew, and the tug *Landis* was close at hand with a company of artillery detailed to assist in serving her battery. When Farragut's ships advanced to the attack, Lieut. Baker hastened from the *Burton* to his station on the *Louisiana*, making way for Commodore Mitchell to precede him on the ladder that reached the deck, where Mitchell took his stand and passed his orders through Baker to the officers below. The floor not being laid, Baker supported himself astride a scantling in the pilot-house, and when a Federal ship fouled with the *Louisiana* during the battle the shock knocked him from his place and he fell through to the deck. As he rose to his feet, Lieut. John Wilkinson, in charge of the forward division, ordered him to inform Lieut. Ward, who was aft, to look out for the Federal vessel as she swung around on the starboard side of the iron-clad. The commander of the *Louisiana*, Capt. McIntosh, was mortally wounded while in the act of throwing a fire-ball on this vessel, and Baker was detailed to take him ashore, where he placed

him in the temporary hospital established on a flatboat above Fort St. Philip. After the dispersion or destruction of all the Confederate squadron except the *Louisiana* and *McRae*, Lieut. Baker says, engineers and mechanics, by working day and night, put the iron-clad into working and fighting trim; and Baker, learning that Commodore Mitchell contemplated taking her to Mobile, offered himself as pilot. "I am glad to know you are a pilot," responded Mitchell, "as I may need your services." On April 25th he was placed in command of the *Burton*, and on the 26th participated in the council of officers called by Mitchell that decided to destroy the *Louisiana* after hearing of the surrender of the forts. Early on the morning of the 28th Lieut. Baker says he was ordered to report to the commodore, and as he presented himself on board the *Louisiana* Chief Engineer Youngblood stepped up and reported that the auxiliary propeller engines were ready and the whole machinery in running order. Lieut. Wilkinson, who had already received orders to destroy the ship, asked Mitchell, in Baker's presence, "What shall I do?" And the commodore after some hesitation replied: "Go on with the work." Baker was then directed to have the *Burton* ready at a moment's notice to take the crew off the *Louisiana*. All but those engaged in the destruction of the iron-clad were transferred to the tender, and Mitchell, with Wilkinson, Ward and other officers soon followed, leaving the *Louisiana* in flames fore and aft. The *Burton* was headed for the opposite shore, where Baker made her fast, and the *Louisiana* blew up in the position where they had left her. Discovering that the commodore had dispatched Lieut. Whittle to surrender the command, he requested permission to effect his escape, and was the only officer of the

played the most desperate chances if there seemed to be stake on the board of war that might be won.

On March 20th, 1864, Master's Mate Page M. Baker forwarded to Gen. Butler, C. S. A., his draft of a plan for the capture of Fort Pickens by means of a boat expedition to start from Mobile Bay with 150 men, pull along the beach 35 miles to the mouth of Perdido River, where they would lie concealed until the following night, and then row to the head of the Grand Lagoon, whence they would haul the boats over the strip of land, but 30 yards wide, that divides the lagoon from Pensacola Harbor, and would be close upon the fort.   Mr. Baker had given careful attention to the danger of being detected by the sentries, and in the sketch submitted to Gen. Butler he had pointed out that in all probability they could make their landing without attracting the attention of the solitary sentinel outside the fort; and he had ascertained from previous prisoners in Pickens that there was usually but one sentry on the parapet, a second at the gate and a third inside the gate at the guard-room.   He added:

" Having landed we would proceed as cautiously as possible to the east face of the fort, and endeavor to effect our entrance through the embrasures, which are generally left open. Should they be closed, by means of ladders carried with us, in sections, we would mount to the parapet and descend to the centre of the fort by the stairways very fortunately at this point. Once inside, it would be our object to secure the garrison, consisting of from 150 to 200 men. For this purpose we would send a large detachment to the men's quarters on the west side of the fort where they

Louisiana who escaped falling into the hands of the enemy after she was abandoned. Lieut. Murdock, Acting Master Gift and a young volunteer named Wilkinson had permission to leave the ship before she was destroyed and went ashore on the east bank. Lieuts. Arnold and Bowen, and a few others who left the *Burton* with Baker after Lieut. Whittle had started on his errand, were all captured by the Federal pickets on shore. Baker and Mr. Dearing, Chief Engineer of the *Burton*, effected their escape by crawling around the picket. Baker reached New Orleans on May 1st, and on the 3d left for Mobile, from whence he reported to Secretary Mallory, who inquired of him by telegraph whether the *Louisiana* had been destroyed, the wording of the dispatch causing him to infer that up to that time the Secretary had only heard rumors of what had occurred after the battle on the river.

Baker was ordered from Mobile to Georgia, and served some time at Columbus and at the navy-yard in Early County during the building of the iron-clad at Columbus, Ga. He was afterwards transferred to Mobile, and, as a first lieutenant, was included in the surrender of May 10th, 1865, at Nanna Hubba Bluff.

Lieut. Baker's condemnation of the destruction of the *Louisiana* is very emphatic. Three lines of conduct, in his opinion, were open to Commodore Mitchell, the pursuit of either of which, in his opinion, would have immortalized him.   The first was to compel Gen. Duncan to hold the forts when he proposed to surrender; second, to run the gauntlet of the Federal fleet and make his way to Mobile; third, to steam up the river and attack Farragut's wooden ships,

the last course holding out the possibilities of the most brilliant achievement and important results. " I feel no hesitation," Lieut. Baker has written, "in advancing the theory that Mitchell might have fought his ship, for in a conversation with Admiral Buchanan on the subject, the admiral expressed surprise that he had not done so."

Another contribution by Lieut. Baker to the verification of events in connection with this engagement, is his denial of the intimation made by Admiral Porter that after the *Louisiana* was set on fire she was sent adrift in order that she might float down amongst his mortar schooners and communicate the flames to them. In support of this assertion Porter declared that when she blew up she was so near the *Harriet Lane* that the concussion made that vessel heel over, throwing the officers, himself included, from the seats which they were occupying in the cabin. Baker states that at the moment of the explosion the *Burton* was much nearer than the *Harriet Lane* to the *Louisiana*, and no such shaking up was felt on his steamer. The iron-clad, in fact was left by her officers at the spot which she had occupied since the day when she joined the Confederate squadron, and there was no idea in the minds of her officers of setting her adrift as a fire-ship. But Admiral Porter's mortar fleet had proved a good deal of a failure; the Federal honors had been won by Farragut, and to represent himself as in danger from the *Louisiana* was a means of attracting public attention to himself.

Lieut. Baker now resides in New Orleans, and is captain of the steamship *Hutchinson* belonging to the Southern Pacific Company.

sleep with their arms stacked. Another detachment would seize the relief
guard just inside of the gate (also asleep,) and a third the officers in their
quarters on the south side. You will observe there is no boat on the east
or south side of the fort. There are usually from 18 to 20 vessels lying off
the yards, and I have understood by letter recently from Pensacola that
Farragut had removed most of their crews to man his fleet off Mobile; be
that as it may, they would fall an easy prey with the fort once in our possession. At and around the navy-yard there is a force of about 3,500 men,
including one negro regiment. Should Gen. Canby move down with the
force under his command and invest the yard, they being cut off from all
relief must necessarily surrender. As we would need men who could be
relied on in any emergency, I would request permission to select volunteers
and men who have been tried under fire. We would necessarily need a
number of men accustomed to heavy artillery in order to man the guns.
It would be necessary also to take several days' provisions."

If the design of going outside from Fort Morgan to the
mouth of the Perdido was considered too hazardous, Master's
Mate Baker presented the alternative of reaching Perdido
Bay from Bon Secour by hauling the boats over the intervening tongue of land a mile and a half wide. In submitting the
plan to Gen. Butler he hoped that it would be approved, and
asked the general's influence with those who had the power to
aid him in the undertaking. On April 20th, an order was issued
by Admiral Buchanan to Lieut. Jas. McC. Baker, that he
should proceed with all possible dispatch to equip a boat for
an important reconnoissance, and another order on the succeeding day informed him that the object was to reconnoitre
from Mobile to Pensacola by water with the view to ascertain
whether it would be practicable to capture Fort Pickens with
a sufficient force by a boat expedition. "You will, therefore"
the admiral continued, "proceed to Pensacola in one of the
Morgan's cutters, taking with you Acting Master's Mate Page
M. Baker, C. S. N., and a crew of ten men with ten days'
provisions. Confidence is placed in your judgment and discretion to make this reconnoissance and to be careful of your
men."

Lieut. Baker and Master's Mate Baker had the cutter
equipped for the expedition by Monday evening, April 25th,
but took with them only eight seamen. They carried the
boat nearly a mile across the land from Bon Secour Bay to the
gulf and launched her through the breakers—three men remaining in the boat, and the others, entirely nude, shoving
outside until the breakers were passed, when she was bailed
out and all hands taken aboard again. They were then sixteen miles east of Fort Morgan and could plainly see the
blockading fleet as they stepped their mast and set sail for
Fort Pickens. It was Baker's purpose to run direct into the
mouth of Perdido River, but a gale that had been blowing
from the southwest for several days created on Perdido Bar a
sea that nearly swamped the cutter, which with ten men in
her was constantly running her gunwales under water; and as
they could not get into Perdido they kept a course directly for

Pickens and passed the fort in the bright moonlight about three o'clock A. M. of the 26th, going very near to the beach. A few miles to the eastward a large sloop was sighted at anchor and was promptly boarded and captured. She proved to be the fishing-smack *Creole*, of New Orleans, ninety tons burden, commanded by Capt. Benj. Lancashire, and having as crew F. Miller, John McDougal, Bernard Brandon and Edward Stafford, the last named of whom claimed to be a discharged Confederate soldier, captured on the blockade-runner *Alice Vivien, en route* for Havana.[1]

The captain and crew of the *Creole* were completely dazed by being captured, and could not imagine from whence had come the craft that had made prisoners of them in the Federal stronghold in the Western Gulf. They were sent below and the hatch closed upon them, while the venturesome Bakers and their men concealed their cutter, arrayed themselves in the clothes of fishermen, and headed the *Creole* for Fort Pickens, passing so near that in their disguise they spoke to the guards, made a minute examination of the approaches to the fort from the gulf, noted the positions of the sentinels, and were delighted to find that there would be no difficulty in landing a force of men on the beach and effecting an entrance either through ùnguarded sally-ports or by means of scaling-ladders—the moat on the sea-face of the fort having been entirely filled up with sand. Their observations completely confirmed the feasibility of the plan which Page M. Baker had suggested for the capture of the post, and the reconnoissance could not have been more thorough and satisfactory.

After making notes of every point upon which information was desirable, the *Creole* was headed eastward along Santa Rosa Island. A sail was descried, and concluding that it was a vessel from New York or Boston bound for New Orleans with Federal army supplies, Lieut. Baker stood out to sea so as to intercept and capture her. Everything was put in readiness to send to her a boat's crew of the Confederate seamen wearing the fishermen's attire and carrying arms concealed beneath their garments. When they were nearly in position and waiting for the vessel's approach, Lieut. Baker, who had gone to the mast-head, discovered that she was an armed steam-cruiser, having all sails set, burning hard coal and coming along like a racehorse. The *Creole* was quickly

[1] Lieut. Baker prepared on board the *Creole*, while lying off Phillip's Inlet, a dispatch to Admiral Buchanan, conveying valuable information gained from Capt. Lancashire concerning the movements and disposition of the Federal vessels at Pensacola and New Orleans. "Our provisions are running short," he wrote, "but should the wind, which has been blowing constantly from the westward, change in our favor, I will endeavor to make my way back to Mobile Bay, either by running the blockade or hauling our cutter into Little Lagoon, etc., etc., in which case I'll destroy vessel. Should the wind hold as it is, I will be compelled to burn vessel at this point, and make our way overland to Mobile. I trust my course will meet with your approbation, as I have done what under the circumstances seemed best and what necessity forced upon me. Should an opportunity present itself on my return, I will finish the reconnoissance which unfavorable weather has permitted me to only make in part. It is probable I shall see you before this reaches Mobile. In the event of our capture, however, this will give you intelligence of our whereabouts and what we have done up to this time."

put about and headed in shore and measures taken to continue her masquerade as a peaceful fishing craft. The cutter was hauled close under her bow and so fixed as to be cut away and sunk at a moment's notice; dinner, which was just ready, was ordered served on deck; the U. S. flag was conspicuously displayed; and when the gunboat, coming uncomfortably near, stopped her engines and critically surveyed the sloop, the latter was in outward appearance the most innocent and inoffensive fishing-smack ever seen. The cruiser's officers stared at her through marine glasses, while the riflemen in the tops peered over and seemed anxious to try the effect of their fire. A prolonged and careful scrutiny satisfied the Federals that the *Creole* was all right, though she was suspiciously distant from the fishing grounds, and they then went off on their course. The prisoners, who were safely stowed away below, and whose expectations of release had been raised to the highest pitch, were much cast down when they discovered that the cruiser had gone without sending a boat aboard.

Lieut. Baker sailed the *Creole* along the coast for nearly two weeks in the hope of catching favorable winds to enable him to run back to Mobile; but after waiting so long in vain, and the sloop being slow in any wind, he concluded to destroy her and make the best of his way overland to Mobile with his men. She was burned in St. Andrew's Bay, Florida, and the cutter was transported eighty miles across the land to Marianna on ox-wagons furnished by the salt-makers along the coast.[1] From Marianna the party proceeded to Chattahoochee Landing, on the Chattahoochee River, where they took a steamer to Columbus, Ga., going thence by railway to Montgomery, at which point they launched their cutter, which they had carried with them during their circuitous journey, and made their way, by sailing and rowing, to Mobile. Admiral Buchanan was much surprised to see them, and especially proud that they had brought back the cutter, which he had warned them they would lose, but which Lieut. and Master's Mate Baker had determined they would bring back to Mobile at any cost. Four of the prisoners of the *Creole* were permitted to escape when the sloop was burned, but one man insisted on being taken to Mobile, where he said he had friends.

The battle with Farragut's fleet on August 5th blocked the immediate execution of a covert attack on Fort Pickens, but did not cause Lieut. Baker to forget the project. On August 4th he submitted the proposition to Gen. Higgins, reviewing the original plan proposed by Page M. Baker and claiming that the reconnoissance had established its practicability:

[1] Lieut. Baker mentions in his report to Admiral Buchanan: "Mr. Broxton, a citizen of Alabama, whom we accidentally met at this point with his wagon hauling salt, and who has kindly offered to haul a seine of 90 fathoms and a new manilla hawser of 150 fathoms, to a place of safety."

"By the arrival of Mr. Newman [he wrote], who escaped from Fort Pickens on Friday last, I have obtained information concerning sentinels and garrison which leaves no doubt in my mind of the success of an attack on the fort if attempted at the present time. There are in the fort for garrison duty three companies of the Seventh Vermont, numbering in all 100 men, in command of Major Allen. There are but two sentinels, one on the parapet on the east face of the fort and one at the gate opposite Barrancas. In view of this fact, I earnestly desire to obtain permission to attempt the capture of the fort, and should you approve the project, would request your influence with the admiral, in order to have me detached for that purpose. I would require but three or four boats carrying about fifteen men each, with their arms, and five days' provisions. In seven hours after leaving the lagoon we can reach the fort, so that starting about 5 P. M. we would arrive about midnight. The enemy have now withdrawn all their large vessels for an attack on Mobile, and their attention is wholly diverted from Pensacola. In the event of the capture of the fort, with the immense amount of ammunition, stores, etc., there and at the yard, the force of the blow here would be broken, as the enemy obtain all their supplies from that point. Having already reconnoitred the route, I feel confident in asserting its entire feasibility and think it would greatly relieve Mobile. Mr. Newman is an engineer whom I have long known, is intelligent and trustworthy. He is well known by naval men, and very anxious to accompany me on this expedition."

Gen. Higgins indorsed this communication: "I think a diversion might be made in the manner proposed if the necessary officers and men can be obtained"; and Gen. Maury's indorsement was: "I approve of attempting this if the proper outfit can be procured." Both these indorsements were made on August 6th, the day after the battle. The removal, within a few days succeeding, of Admiral Buchanan and other captured Confederate officers to Pensacola, stimulated the ambition of Baker to make a descent on Fort Pickens, for it might include the recapture of the beloved admiral and those who had shared his misfortune. Having secured the favorable judgment of Higgins and Maury, he expected that Commodore Farrand, who had succeeded to the naval command at Mobile, would furnish him with the men and boats for the expedition; but on August 15th he received from Lieut. W. T. Key, secretary of Admiral Buchanan, and who now occupied the same office under Commodore Farrand, a missive that broke rudely upon his lofty aspirations to do a grand deed for the Confederacy. Key wrote him:

Your letter to me, and communication to the commodore enclosed, was received on Saturday evening. On Sunday (yesterday) I handed it to him when he was at leisure, and said and did everything I could to get him to give his consent to the proposed expedition; but all in vain. I am disheartened at the way in which this project, one so perfectly feasible and practicable in all its bearings, has been suffered quietly to be passed over by the authorities that be; and this particularly after it received the full and entire endorsement of both the generals, and Commodore Buchanan especially. 'Tis no further use, I am sorry to say, to push this matter with Commodore Farrand, as he is now decided that we cannot go; if you think it would be right to telegraph the Hon. Secretary of the Navy, do so; but be certain before you do so that you receive not a reprimand for presuming to address him without sending your communication through your commanding officer, and thereby the whole plan fall through. I do not know that it would do so; you know best. I am truly sorry to blight your hopes, but the truth must be told—the expedition will not be allowed to embark by the commodore. I am as sorry as you are; and if you should go by consent of a higher authority, I also will endeavor to go with you."

Baker endeavored to stride over the obstacle interposed by Farrand's supineness by making an appeal to Secretary Mallory.[1] His letter of August 18th to the head of the Navy Department inclosed the proposition submitted to Gens. Maury and Higgins, and pointed out how easily the garrison of 100 men in the fort might be surprised by an inferior force in consequence of the small number of sentinels on duty and the abandonment of Fort McRae. In this communication the daring sailor told Mr. Mallory that the generals had proffered him all the men and arms necessary, and that Farrand "also approved of the project, and indeed ordered me to make the necessary preparations, but afterwards concluded that he could not well spare my services at this juncture."

" Mr. Newman [he continued] says there are immense stores of pro visions, medicines, ordnance, etc., both in the fort and at the yard. In the event of our succeeding, Gen. Maury would send a co-operating force by land against the yard, which being assailed in front and rear, must necessarily surrender. The reinforcements we would receive in the prisoners (numbering some fifty) would enable us to hold the fort without a doubt.

"Believing, sir, that the capture of this place would be of incalculable advantage to us at this time, giving us, as it would, open port, and distracting the attention of the enemy from more vital points, together with the probability of recapturing our noble admiral and the officers confined there, I most respectfully and earnestly request that you will detach myself and brother for the purpose of undertaking this expedition.

"Having already reconnoitred the proposed route, and being perfectly familiar with the coast and the localities in and around the fort, I feel confident in asserting the feasibility of the enterprise."

Their proposal received at Richmond the respectful consideration to which it was entitled, and Commodore Farrand was overruled by the higher authority. It was referred by Secretary Mallory to President Davis, who approved it and directed Gen. Braxton Bragg to co-operate in its execution.

---

[1] While holding the Fort Pickens' expedition in view, Lieut. Baker and his brother also had in contemplation a project to destroy one vessel or more of the blockading fleet with torpedoes. They were to place a spar torpedo in a row-boat and pull out on a dark night to the ship selected for destruction. Lieut. Baker was to keep the boat in position, while Master's Mate Baker was to dive overboard with the torpedo, swim under the side of the ship, and endeavor to explode it below her water-line. The merest statement of such a design is all that need be said to carry conviction of the devotion and heroism of these two young officers. They desired to attempt the task alone, being unwilling that anyone else should venture into the peril which it involved. When it was first proposed to Commodore Farrand he sanctioned it and consented to their detail for the work, but his habitual timidity overcame him afterward, and on August 27th he instructed Lieut. Myers, of the *Huntsville*, to "inform Lieut. Jas. McC. Baker, and request Lieut. Commanding Chas. P. McGary, of the *Tuscaloosa*, to inform also his brother, Master's Mate Page M. Baker, that, upon due deliberation, I am induced to withhold the verbal permission given them a few days since ' to destroy by torpedo, in the manner proposed, any of the enemy's vessels in the bay,' considering the whole scheme from beginning to end impracticable and attended with too great personal risk and danger to the person or persons using the torpedo. They will therefore dismiss all thought of it and return to their respective duties."

35

On September 26th, 1864, Mr. Mallory wrote to Lieut. Baker a letter marked "Confidential," and saying:

"Your plan is approved. Flag-officer Farrand is instructed to take all necessary measures for fitting out the expedition and securing its success, and he will promptly confer with you. * * * My instructions as to secrecy must be rigidly observed. Your success must depend upon a surprise. I earnestly trust, as well for yourself, officers and men as for the country, that there will be no failure."

The Secretary inclosed a communication from Gen. Bragg suggesting that one modification in the plan seemed advisable to him. That was to rely solely on effecting an entrance at the sally-port. "But a small party," he wrote, "would suffice for the ruse, whilst the main force was thrown by scaling-ladders immediately into the fort, over the wall opposite Fort McRae. This point is easily approached, is near the landing-place, and is the lowest part of the wall. It could be scaled by light ladders transported in the boats, which can be carried readily by two stout men. It will afford me pleasure to order the necessary assistance and co-operation from the land forces, and to direct a movement in the diversion whenever the naval expedition shall be in readiness."

In pursuance of Secretary Mallory's authorization, Farrand, on October 6th, issued orders temporarily detaching Lieut. Baker from the *Huntsville* and directing him to report for further instructions. Five days later Baker announced that he was ready to prepare the boats, and requested that they should be turned over to him as soon as possible, and on the 12th he made the following formal requisition upon the flag-officer:

"In accordance with your order, I beg leave respectfully to submit to you the following statement: I will require the following boats, barge and launch at navy-yard, first cutters of *Morgan* and *Huntsville*, launch and first cutter of *Nashville*, with their fixtures, and six wagons with good teams to transport same from Shell Banks to Ross Point; also five officers and 125 men—one-third sailors, the balance heavy artillerists, if possible, armed with revolvers and some short, effective gun; carrying with them seven days' cooked rations, two ladders, forty feet long, in sections of ten feet; six axes, lines for lashing and material for muffling oars will be needed. All to be ready in ten days from date."

On the same day he informed Secretary Mallory that he had reconnoitred and would adopt the route suggested by Gen. Bragg; that the boats, with fixtures, ladders, etc., would be ready by the 19th, the moon serving about that time; but as Commodore Farrand and Gen. Maury had so small a force that they did not like to spare the men, he applied for an order that would enable him to procure them without delay. The necessity thus imposed upon Baker by the commanders at Mobile of communicating with the sources of authority at Richmond at every step of his undertaking had already caused valuable time to be wasted, and this refusal of Farrand and Maury to provide him with the aid that it was most unquestionably intended by President Davis, Secretary Mallory and Gen. Bragg that he should have, without calling for further orders from Richmond, prevented him from starting on the 19th, as he had anticipated doing. However, the Confederate government supported him, and on the 20th Gen. Maury notified Gen. Liddell, commanding the Eastern Division, District of the Gulf, that Lieut. Baker was authorized to receive 100 volunteers from the Fifteenth Confederate cavalry regiment for a special and dangerous service, and he recommended that a portion should, if possible, come from each company. The regiment named was in the brigade commanded by Col. R. McCollock, whose headquarters were at Greenwood, Ala., and on the 21st Baker was informed that McCollock approved of the project of obtaining volunteers. On the 24th, Gen. Maury wrote to Lieut. Baker a letter which to an appreciable extent explains his attitude toward the expedition. In it he said:

"Having discharged my whole duty, and perhaps more, in laying before you my views of your proposed operations, I will now aid you as far as I can in their execution. Confer fully with Gen. Liddell, who will co operate with you as he best can. I regret that my forces are so much reduced as to prevent me from sending to Gen. Liddell any troops from this point. I would not be justified in doing so. I earnestly hope complete success will attend you, and I desire to express my respect for the energy, confidence, tenacity and courage you have evinced. I believe if your future movements be conducted with secrecy, you will capture the fort, and in that case yours shall be all the credit."

Fickle fortune seemed to smile at last upon the expedition. Lieut. Baker and his brother had obtained the steamer *Dick Keys*, and on October 24th he notified Farrand that they would start that night for Blakely, transporting the boats thence in wagons to Ross Point on the Perdido River, from whence it would be easy rowing to Fort Pickens. Once in possession of the fort, he was to signal the land forces that were to co-operate. They did not, however, get away from Mobile until the next evening and had only reached the bay when their ardent hope of making a great *coup* for the Confederacy were blasted by the receipt of an order that they should proceed no further. They returned to Mobile, and on November 1st Lieut. Baker made the annexed report to Secretary Mallory:

"I beg leave respectfully to report that on the evening of the 25th ult. I left this place in the steamer *Dick Keys*, with five launches, fixtures complete, two scaling ladders in sections, wagons, teams, etc.

"We landed at Blakely, at 9 P. M., where I found my men, 100 in number, awaiting me. The better to conceal our movements, started at once under cover of night. At this time I received an order from Brig. Gen. Liddell, commanding me to suspend the expedition temporarily, by order from Maj. Gen. Maury, who had heard of a heavy force of the enemy being landed at the navy-yard. Upon receipt of this I encamped in an obscure spot, off the road, three miles from Blakely. On the 30th ult. news was received by the general of the falsity of the rumor, and I immediately requested permission of Gen. Maury to move forward. He again ordered a temporary suspension of the expedition, as he was not fully prepared to co-operate and feared the enemy had obtained information of the movement. I remonstrated against the delay, stating the impossibility of the enemy having obtained such information, since not even the men in my command were aware of my destination, but the men being under his control I was compelled to acquiesce. He advised that the men be returned to their respective companies, so as to give the impression of the move being abandoned; and on a given day suddenly ordered back, when the expedition might proceed, he thought, with more secrecy and certainty of success. This has been done, and I have left the boats on the wagons concealed, and under cover with a guard in charge of Master's Mate P. M. Baker. Had I been allowed to proceed without delay, I feel confident we should have met with success. It is greatly to be regretted that the men could not be obtained from the navy, as in that case they would have been under my constant control and this delay avoided. I would respectfully suggest that if possible sailors be procured for the enterprise. The generals commanding have recently received intelligence that besides the vast quantities of stores, munitions of war, etc., always at the yard, the enemy have accumulated there immense supplies for Sherman's army. Inclosed you will find a letter to me from Gen. Maury which unfortunately did not reach me until other orders had been issued. As soon as the general is ready to co-operate, I will proceed to carry out the plan without delay."

A week elapsed, and at its end, instead of receiving the renewed instructions to move on to Pensacola that he was pleading for, Baker was peremptorily commanded by Farrand to withdraw from the undertaking. Nothing but his duty to obey a superior officer could have compelled him to abandon a project on which his courageous heart was set and which promised such magnificent results. He did not forego his scheme, however, without making to Secretary Mallory an indignant protest against the vacillating counsels that had embarrassed and ultimately checked him. His last official communication was addressed to Mr. Mallory, from Mobile, on November 9th, and was as follows:

"I beg leave respectfully to report that while acting under orders from the Department, bearing date Richmond, September 26th, 1864, and while awaiting near Blakely, Ala., the co-operation of Maj. Gen. Maury, I received enclosed communication from Flag-officer Farrand, ordering my return with boats, officers, etc., to this point. I obeyed the order, and now respectfully enter my protest, as I conceive myself still under orders from the Department. Furthermore, that upon reporting to Flag-officer Farrand, I was ordered to relinquish the expedition, and return to my ship for duty. Inclosed you will also please find communication from Maj. Gen. Maury ordering a temporary suspension of the expedition."

The Secretary of the Navy responded, under date of November 24th, with a note which closes the narrative: "Maj. Gen. Maury," he wrote to Baker, "having withdrawn his men from the enterprise to the command of which you were assigned, its prosecution became impracticable. It was Capt. Farrand's duty therefore to issue to you the order of which you complain, and against which your protest, for the protection of either your own or the public interests, was unnecessary and irregular. I regret that circumstances beyond the control of the Department or yourself should have thus terminated an enterprise which seemed to promise good results."

It was never questioned at the time or since that the primary cause of the thwarting of the expedition was the opposition of Flag-officer Farrand, who grudgingly consented to it under the positive orders of Secretary Mallory, and even then placed obstacles in its way that delayed it, and in the end brought it to naught. The whole plan of operations had been formulated before Admiral Buchanan was taken prisoner; it had seemed to him practicable and praiseworthy, and we may concur in the belief of Lieut. Baker and Master's Mate Page M. Baker that if he had remained in command of the Confederate naval forces at Mobile, they could have been encouraged to go ahead and furnished with whatever assistance they needed. But Farrand only nominally filled Buchanan's place, and this grand conception of taking a fortified place by a bold dash was more than his spirit could grasp. The youthful officers whom he restrained on the verge of their enterprise have been vindicated as to the judgment which they displayed in formulating and organizing the proposed assault. They felt that they could take Fort Pickens, and since the restoration of peace, Page M. Baker, now the honored editor of the New Orleans *Times-Democrat,* has been informed by the officer in command of the post in the summer and autumn of 1864, that they would, beyond peradventure, have succeeded in capturing it by the movement which they proposed. This confirmation from their former enemy of the foresight and wisdom of their plans renders it all the more regretful that official timorousness balked them. To have taken this important post in the gulf, with its immensely valuable stock of arms and munitions of war, to have released the valiant Buchanan and to have regained Pensacola and the navy-yard would have been of vast benefit to the Southern cause both in the moral and the material aspect, and justified the assent given to the enterprise by the President, the Secretary of the Navy, Gens. Bragg and Maury. That it was created in the mind of Page M. Baker is an instance of the eminent genius for the brilliant surprises of war frequently exhibited by young men of the Confederacy in the face of the excessive strength of the enemy, that partly sufficed to neutralize their superiority.

In anticipation of the assault by the Federal fleet that had been threatened ever since the capture of New Orleans, Admiral Franklin Buchanan had been assigned to the command of the Confederate naval force at Mobile and was gathering a squadron of some respectable power.[1]

---

[1] " We are informed from pretty good authority that Admiral Buchanan, who has just returned from a trip of observation down the bay, determined upon an order which will materially add to the strength of the fleet which has been built and equipped to aid in the defence of Mobile. A crack raft, with a powerful battery and picked crew, ably and gallantly commanded, is the *addendum.* This is the *avant courier* of four other floating engines of war which will

In June 1863, he had ready for operations the iron-clad ram *Baltic*, the steam gunboats *Morgan, Gaines* and *Selma*, and the tender *Crescent*. The history of the *Baltic* is somewhat obscure, and there are no known details of her armament and characteristics. She may have been the former coasting steamer of that name altered for purposes of war, and it is again possible that she was the vessel alluded to in a former paragraph of this chapter as having been partially built by the State of Alabama and then turned over to the Confederate government. The lack of Confederate records renders any precise determination of her identity impossible.

The squadron was officered as follows at this time :

Ram BALTIC, flag-ship of Admiral Franklin Buchanan—Lieutenants, Jas. D. Johnston, Wm. P. A. Campbell, John Grimball; Second Lieutenants, Geo. A. Borchett, E. G. Read, A. G. Hudgins; Surgeons, John T. Mason, Wm. F. Carrington ; Assistant Paymaster, M. M. Leay; Masters, Ivey Foreman, H. W. Perrin; Midshipmen, S. P. Blanc, F. B. Dornin, T. J. H. Hamilton, E. A. Swain ; Engineers, W. M. Fauntleroy, G. Simpson; Gunners, W. H. Haynes, D. G. McComb.

Gunboat MORGAN—Commander, C. H. McBlair ; Lieutenants, C. J. Graves, Thomas L. Harrison ; Assistant Surgeon, Edwin G. Booth ; Assistant Paymaster, R. L. Mackall[1]; Midshipmen H. H. Scott, T. G. Garrot, John A. Wilson, H. H. Tyson, James R. Norris, F. Arthur; Engineer, H. B. Willy.

Gunboat GAINES—Commander, T. T. Hunter; Lieutenants, John W. Bennett, Hilary Cenas ; Assistant Surgeon, T. B. Ford ; Assistant Paymaster, J. E. Armour; Master, E. C. Stockton; Midshipmen, J. A. Merriweather, James M. Gardner, D. D. Colcock, W. D. Goode, W. H. Sterling, James H. Dyke, W. F. Clayton.

Gunboat SELMA—Lieut., P. U. Murphy; Midshipman, J. B. Ratcliffe.

One of the largest naval stations in the Confederacy was located at Selma, on the Alabama River, where in the spring of 1863 five gunboats were in process of construction. The senior officer on duty at this point was Commander Ebenezer Farrand, associated with whom were First Lieut. Van R. Morgan, Assistant Paymaster G. H. O'Neil, Master John Pearson, First Assistant Engineer Wm. Frick and Carpenter John T. Rustic. Besides these the following attachés of the Mobile station did frequent duty at Selma: Lieuts. John R. Eggleston and Alphonso Barbot, Paymaster Thomas R. Ware, Midshipman Wm. S. Hogue and Gunner Benjamin F. Hughes. Surgeons Lewis W. Minor and O. S. Englehart were attached to the Mobile station. The ablest naval designers, engineers and ordnance officers in the Confederate service visited Selma from time to time to assist in the construction and armament of the vessels there fitted out.

The remainder of the year 1863 passed away in naval inactivity around Mobile so far as actual hostilities were

soon take their station in the bay, and oppose their iron sides to the iron shot of the Federal navy. The Federals will find out, after awhile, that 'some things can be done as well as others,' and that Southern men may develop a genius for naval construction and warfare, as they have a splendid aptitude for fighting on *terra firma*. Whether we gain these additions to our navy through cracks in the enemy's blockade, or by other means, we leave him to find out or to infer."—Mobile *Advertiser*, December 27th, 1862.

[1] Died August 11th, 1863.

concerned. Admiral Buchanan was kept on the constant alert by the reports that Farragut was coming at last, and as became so sagacious a commander he busied himself with the various projects of obstructing the channel and placing torpedoes in position that occurred to his keen judgment and fertile invention. He was too wise to underrate the strength of the enemy as compared with the meagre naval equipment of the Confederacy, but his experience in handling the *Virginia* in the battle of Hampton Roads had imparted to him much confidence in that type of fighting machine and he therefore exerted himself in speeding the work upon the iron-clads then building at Selma and Mobile. None but himself and those nearest to him could comprehend the immensity and difficulty of the task of putting afloat even one ship that might cope with the monitors which the ship-yards of the North were turning out with all the rapidity that unlimited money, plant, material and workmen could secure. On that side were all the advantages that invention, science and resources could confer, while from laying the keel of a ship to installing her engines and guns there was not a step at which the Confederate officials were not halted, embarrassed and almost thwarted by their poverty in every appliance that should facilitate their labor. No man can claim to have a truthful understanding of the war who, in studying any of its phases, does not view them by the light of the facts of this vast disparity between the combatants, and it of course follows that the Confederates are to be judged by the obstacles which they overcame rather than by those that proved to be insurmountable.

On February 23d, 1864, the operations of the Federal fleet for the destruction and capture of the seaward defences of Mobile began. Before proceeding with the narrative of the attack it is proper that an accurate description should be given of the approaches to Mobile by water and of the fortifications which guarded the channels.

The city is situated thirty miles from the Gulf of Mexico at the head of the Bay of Mobile, the width of which varies from fifteen miles at the lower end to six at the upper. The principal entrance is by the Swash Channel, which trends at first northeastward from the gulf and closely skirts Mobile Point, a long, low projection from the mainland on the east. On the west side of the bay is Dauphine Island, the easternmost of the chain which bounds Mississippi Sound, the entrance to which is by Grant's Pass, which makes into the bay at the northern side of the island. Because of the deflection of the ship channel to the northeast it is fully three miles distant from Dauphine Island. The most important of the land defences was Fort Morgan, built upon the western extremity of Mobile Point to command the channel, and occupying the site of old Fort Bowyer, which on September 15th, 1814, gallantly repelled the attack of a British fleet. Fort Morgan was a pentagonal bastioned work, built of brick and intended to carry guns both in casemates and barbette, but the Confederates had masked the embrasures of the curtains facing the channel and thrown up an exterior water battery before the northwest curtain.   The main fort mounted seven 10-inch, three 8-inch and twenty-two 32-pounder smooth-bore guns, and two 8-inch, two 6.5-inch and four 5.82-inch rifled cannon.

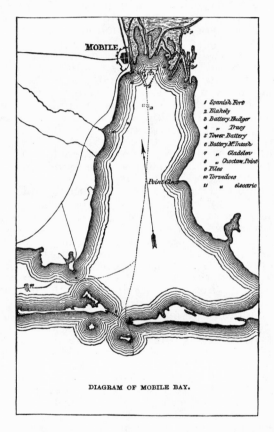

DIAGRAM OF MOBILE BAY.

Twenty-nine more guns were placed in the exterior batteries, the most formidable of which was the water battery, which was armed with four 10-inch Columbiads, one 8-inch rifled gun and two rifled 32-pounders.

On the eastern extremity of Dauphine Island, three nautical miles west-northwest from Fort Morgan, stood Fort Gaines, like Morgan constructed of brick.   It was of secondary importance as a defence of the port, and its armament consisted of but twenty-seven guns, of which three were 10-inch Columbiads, four were rifled 32-pounders, and the remainder smooth-bore 32's, 24's and 18's.   Fort Morgan was commanded by Brig. Gen. R. L. Page,[1] and its garrison numbered 640 officers and men.   The commander of Fort Gaines was Col. Charles D. Anderson, and it was garrisoned by 864 officers and men.

On Tower Island, a diminutive sand hummock at the mouth of Grant's Pass, the Confederates had begun the construction of a battery named Fort Powell, which, although it never reached completion, mounted a 10-inch and an 8-inch Columbiad and four rifled guns.   These three fortifications made up the land defences of Mobile Bay, and we have now to take a look in detail at the squadron under Admiral Buchanan's command.

His flag-ship was the iron-clad steam-ram *Tennessee*, with the exception of the *Arkansas*, destroyed upon the Mississippi River, the most formidable vessel of her class that ever carried the Confederate flag.   The *Tennessee* was 209 feet in

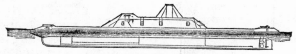

THE C. S. RAM "TENNESSEE."

length, with an extreme beam of 48 feet, and carried her battery in a casemate or shield amidships 79 feet long and 29 feet wide, inside dimensions.   Her frame was composed of yellow pine beams, 13 inches thick, set close together vertically and planked with $5\frac{1}{2}$ inches of yellow pine in horizontal courses, and 4 inches of oak in vertical courses.   Within, the yellow pine frames were sheathed with $2\frac{1}{2}$ inches of oak.   The outer walls of the casemate were inclined at an angle of 45 degrees from the deck, and on this 25 inches of wood backing was laid the plate armor, which was 6 inches thick on the

[1] Gen. Richard L. Page was born in Virginia, and entered the U. S. navy as midshipman on March 12th, 1824, being assigned to the line of battle-ship *North Carolina*, of the Mediterranean squadron. In 1827 he was transferred to the frigate *Constitution*, and in 1828 returned to the United States to complete his studies. Between 1830 and 1834 he served in the sloop *Concord* in the Mediterranean, and the schooner *Fox* at Baltimore. He received his lieutenant's commission March 26th, 1834, and was made executive officer of the schooner *Enterprise*, in which he remained upon the East India station until the autumn of 1837, after which he was granted two years' leave of absence. From 1839 to 1841 he was attached to the frigate *Macedonian* of the West Indian squadron, and the succeeding two years he spent at the Norfolk naval rendezvous, going to sea again in 1844-45 on the sloop *Plymouth*, of the Mediterranean squadron.   In 1845 he was ordered to the line-of-battle-ship *Pennsylvania*, at Norfolk, and the next year was selected as executive officer of the frigate *Independence*, flag-ship of Commodore Shubrick, of the Pacific squadron, in which he remained during the Mexican war. On his return home in 1849, Lieut. Page was again detailed to the Norfolk rendezvous, and in 1851 was selected for special ordnance duty in company with the then Commander Farragut.   In 1852 he was assigned to the command of the brig *Perry*, and was on duty with the African squadron until July, 1854, when he was made executive officer at the Norfolk navy-yard.   On September 14th, 1855, he was promoted to commander and was appointed Assistant Inspector of Ordnance at this navy-yard, where he remained until after the inauguration of President Buchanan in 1857, when he was ordered to the command of the sloop *Germantown*, and attached to the East Indian squadron. He remained with this squadron until April, 1860, when he was recalled to the position of ordnance officer at the

forward wall, and elsewhere 5 inches thick, and was fastened to the wood with bolts 1¼ inch in diameter that went entirely through the wall and were secured by nuts and washers on the inside. The outside deck was plated with two inches of iron. A curious arrangement of the casemate was that its sloping sides were carried down two feet below the water-line and then reversed at the same angle, so that they met the hull seven feet under water. This projection was carried out around the bow, where it was fashioned into a spur or ram. The pilot-house stood on the forward edge of the casemate, and was in fact made by building it up some three feet. There were ten ports, two on each side, three forward and three aft, so arranged that the pivot guns could be fought in broadside, sharp on the bow and quarter and on a direct line with the keel, but the ship never had more than six guns. At each end she carried a Brooke 7⅛-inch rifled gun on pivots, capable of throwing a solid projectile of 110 pounds' weight. There were also four Brooke 6-inch rifles in broadside, each firing a 95-pound solid shot.

So far the *Tennessee* was a credit to her builders, but she had avoidable and unavoidable defects that proved to vastly impair her efficiency in action. One avoidable defect was the manner of constructing the port shutters which revolved upon a pivot and were fatally apt to be jammed in an engagement. Another and greater blunder was that the rudder chains were exposed upon the after-deck, where they were at any moment liable to be shot away. Of the defects that could not be avoided the worst was her lack of speed. Her engines were not built for the ship, but were taken from the high-pressure river steamboat *Alonzo Child;* and though on her trial trip, in March, 1864, her speed was set down at eight nautical miles per hour, she could not make more than six with her battery, ammunition and fuel on board.

Yet, taken in all, the *Tennessee* was a fighting machine of which the Confederacy had a right to feel proud. She was as apt an illustration as the whole war produced of the triumph

Norfolk navy-yard. He resigned from the navy of the United States as soon as his native State had seceded, and was appointed an aide on the staff of Governor Letcher, of Virginia, with special reference to the organization of a State navy. The fortifications at the mouth of James River, the defences of Nansemond River and those of Pagan Creek were constructed under his direction. Upon the formation of the Confederate government, he entered the Confederate States navy, June 10th, 1861, and received the commission of commander in the navy, and acted as ordnance officer at the Norfolk navy-yard until the evacuation of the place by the Confederates. During the battles of the iron-clad *Virginia* in Hampton Roads he volunteered for service at the Sewell's Point battery in working the 11-inch gun against the Federal ships. After the evacuation of Norfolk, Commander Page was promoted to the rank of captain, and with the mechanics and machinery removed from the Norfolk shops established the ordnance and construction depot at Charlotte, N. C., which under his administration became of inestimable value to the Confederacy. For nearly two years he continued in charge of this important post, the only interruption being an assignment to the command of the naval forces at Savannah, during which service he was with Commodore Tatnall in the gunboat *Savannah* at the naval battle of Port Royal; thence returning to the Charlotte station, he was detached from the latter, and ordered to the command of the outer defences of Mobile Bay, making his headquarters at Fort Morgan. This new field of duty necessitated his transfer from the navy to the army, in which he was commissioned brigader-general. After the surrender of Fort Morgan he was held prisoner by the Federals until September, 1865, when he was released. He now resides at Norfolk in the enjoyment of a vigorous old age, after his many years of honorable naval and military service.

of dauntless energy over a host of obstacles, and it can never cease to be a subject of wonder and admiration that Southern builders and seamen, crippled in every department of construction and outfit, could have wrought their little available material to so good a purpose. She was built at the naval station at Selma, in the winter of 1863–64, and so expeditiously was the work done upon her that when her keel was laid, some of the timbers to be used in her were still standing in the forests, and much of what was to be her plating was still ore in the mines. In March 1864, Commander J. D. Johnston was assigned to duty as her captain by Secretary Mallory, and began preparations to take the ship to Mobile. The great problem was to float her over Dog River bar mud flats, on which there were but nine feet of water at high tide. This was accomplished by placing on either side of her keel wooden tanks or caissons, called by sailors camels, which, when pumped free of water, were sufficiently buoyant to lift the *Tennessee* five feet. Thus she was carried over the bar, and on May 18th, all ready for action, she steamed down to the lower

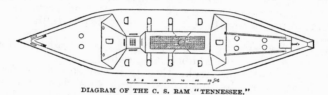

DIAGRAM OF THE C. S. RAM "TENNESSEE."

bay and hoisted her ensign full in the gaze of Farragut's sailors. Admiral Buchanan proposed that night to give the enemy a brush, but after dark the *Tennessee* was found to be hard and fast aground, and he was compelled to abandon his intention. She was officered as follows: Admiral, Franklin Buchanan; Captain, James D. Johnston; Lieutenants, Wm. L. Bradford (also Executive Officer), A. D. Wharton, E. G. McDermott; Masters, J. R. Molry and H. W. Perrin; Engineers, George D. Linning, J. C. O'Connell, John Hayes, Oscar Renson and Wm. B. Patterson; Paymaster's Clerk, J. H. Cohen; Master's Mates, W. A. Forrest, Wm. Beebe and R. M. Carter; Boatswain, John McCredie; Gunner, Herman L. Smith. The crew numbered 110 men.

In addition to the *Tennessee* the Confederate squadron consisted of three small gunboats: *Gaines*, J. W. Bennett, Lieut. Commanding; *Morgan*, George W. Harrison, Commander, and *Selma*, P. U. Murphy, Commander. All were unarmored except for small spaces around the boilers, where a few inches of light iron plating had been put on in order to afford some protection to the boilers and machinery. The *Morgan* and *Gaines* had been hastily constructed by the Confederate government; their frames were of unseasoned wood and their engines were entirely too small for their tonnage. The *Selma* was an open-deck river steamer that had been hurriedly altered into a gunboat. The *Morgan* carried two 7-inch rifles and four 32-pounders; the *Gaines*, one 8-inch rifle and five 32-pounders; the *Selma*, three 8-inch old fashioned Paixhan shell guns and one venerable smooth-bore 33-pounder that had been rather clumsily rifled and was not reliable for close shooting.

The defence of Mobile was not entrusted entirely to the forts and ships. From Fort Gaines a line of closely-planted piles stretched southeasterly along the sand-reef in the direction of Fort Morgan, the heads of the piles being just visible at low water. Where the reef formed the western edge of the channel the piles terminated, their use being to prevent any light-draft vessels from crossing the flats, but from this point a triple row of torpedoes was buoyed across the channel and ended at a red buoy distant less than 800 feet from the water battery of Fort Morgan. Thus there actually existed only an open passage not much more than a hundred yards wide through the channel. This had been left unobstructed as a means of ingress and egress for blockade-runners, who were enabled to navigate it by means of lights displayed from Fort Morgan.[1]

The Confederate torpedo service at Mobile was somewhat elaborate. About 180 torpedoes are said to have been planted in the bay in anticipation of Farragut's advance. One kind was made of tin in the form of a cone. The greater diameter was filled with an air chamber, which floated upward and carried a cap and trigger intended to be fired by a slight blow like that from a passing vessel. The lower compartment contained the charge, which so communicated with the cap that the explosion of the latter would reach it. The other class of torpedo was made of a barrel or beer keg, pitched to make it water tight and with wooden cones secured to the top and bottom to steady it. It was filled with powder and completed by the attachment of half a dozen sensitive primers, which would explode by concussion and transmit their flame to the charge. When prepared with care these torpedoes were much the more reliable as the caps of the can torpedoes got out of working order by long exposure to the action of the water.

In January, 1864, Admiral Farragut began feeling his way toward an attack on Mobile, and on February 23d he opened the bombardment of Fort Powell at Grant's Pass, with his mortar-boats and light-draft vessels that had been able to come up from Mississippi River by way of the sound. For three days the "bummers" and gunboats poured their shot and shell upon the fort without doing it any injury, or so much as wounding one of its garrison, while on the other hand the

---

[1] It was originally contemplated that in case of an attack this entrance should be closed by sinking in it hulks laden with stones; but for some reason this plan was never carried into effect.

fire returned by the Confederates was equally ineffective. During this harmless duel the *Morgan, Gaines* and *Selma* manœvred about in the vicinity of Grant's Pass, but found no opportunity for the exercise of their guns; and the *Tennessee* laid at rest close to Fort Morgan. The attack was indeed intended only to prevent the Confederates from detaching any of the forces around Mobile for service against Sherman, who was at that time making his raid into Mississippi.[1]

We have now pursued the succession of events in and around Mobile up to the consummation of the plans which the Federal government had for two years been maturing for an attack from the sea upon the forts and Admiral Buchanan's squadron. Ever since Admiral Farragut's capture of New Orleans public opinion in the North, no less than the judgment of the Washington authorities, had selected him as the commander under whom should be attempted the reduction of the last stronghold and fleet remaining to the Confederates upon the Gulf of Mexico; and his government was prepared to furnish him with whatever overwhelming force of men and ships he might deem requisite to crush the South at this point. Fully aware of the tremendous odds that were to be brought against them, Admiral Buchanan and Gen. Dabney H. Maury, the military commander at Mobile, threw all their energies into strengthening their squadron and their lines of resistance; but there was literally no single phase of their schemes at which they were not compelled to struggle against their woeful deficiency in everything except the valor of men and the skill of officers that brings to the highest efficiency fleets and armies. For instance, if the resources of the Confederacy had been anywhere near equal to the demand upon them, Buchanan, instead of being compelled to rely so largely upon the *Tennessee* with which to oppose Farragut, would have been able to swing into his line of battle the *Nashville*, and perhaps two or three other iron-clads and gunboats that were lying unfinished at Selma and Mobile because the government was unable to complete them. Speculation upon what might have been the result of the battle of Mobile Bay if Buchanan had been reinforced by these ships may be useless at this late day, but it at least presents an open question when we recall the great preponderance of power that was required to overcome the *Tennessee* alone and oblige Buchanan to strike his flag.[2]

---

[1] Deserters who about this time escaped from the Confederate lines reported that Admiral Buchanan contemplated a dash upon the Mississippi River and New Orleans with his fleet. According to their story he was only waiting for the completion of the iron-clad *Nashville* to attempt this movement. The programme was said to be that the *Tennessee* and *Nashville*, assisted by the iron-clads from the Red River, should proceed up and down the Mississippi, while the troops from Mobile, Gen. Magruder's and Gen. Dick Taylor's commands, were to make a land attack at the same time. If the iron-clads failed in passing Forts St. Philip and Jackson, the *Nashville* and *Tennessee* were to blockade the river at Southwest Pass while the squadron from the Red River attacked the city ; and in case they were repulsed they were to move up the Mississippi and blockade it between New Orleans and Natchez. If such a movement as this was ever proposed it was frustrated by the appearance of Farragut's fleet in the Bay of Mobile and the necessity imposed upon Admiral Buchanan of meeting the enemy there.

[2] Correspondents of the Northern papers added

Farragut's attack was delayed for several weeks because he was waiting for his monitors to arrive. He had no notion of exposing his wooden ships alone to the chances of the combat, and it is, moreover, a very reasonable supposition that in his requisitions upon his government for iron-clads he was, to a certain degree, influenced by the exaggerated reports afloat in the North of the formidable character of the *Tennessee.*[1]

Still another reason for Farragut's delay was the disarrangement of the Federal plans for the co-operation of the army in the movement against Mobile. Grant had assumed in March, 1864, that Banks' expedition up the Red River would be a success, and had consequently ordered that after returning from the Red River, Banks should move against Mobile with 30,000 men, to which he expected to add 5,000 from Missouri. But instead of enjoying the anticipated military promenade in Louisiana and Arkansas, Banks was repulsed in a manner most humiliating to himself, and from his shattered columns had no troops to spare for a diversion that had Mobile as its objective. Consequently, Gen. Canby, the successor of Banks, was so hard pushed by the Confederate army under Gen. Dick Taylor, that he was unable to carry out Grant's instructions, and was compelled to content himself with sending a couple of thousand men under the command of Major Gen. Gordon Granger and Brigadier Gen. McGinnis to invest Fort Gaines; these, on August 3d, were landed on Dauphine Island in the rear of the fort and under the cover of the guns of Lieut. J. C. P. DeKraft's flotilla of light-draft gunboats.

Farragut had formed his plan of battle as far back as July 12th, when he issued a general order regarding the manner in which his fleet should attempt the passage of the forts. In this he provided that the wooden ships should be lashed in couples; that all should open fire as fast as their guns could be brought to bear; that short fuses should be used for the shell and shrapnel; that grape should be fired as soon as a range of 300 or 400 yards was obtained, and that disabled ships must be helped by their consorts. In a subsequent order of July 29th, he instructed his captains to take care to go to the east of the easternmost buoy in order to avoid the triple line of torpedoes, which, as we have previously explained, terminated at the buoy which he mentioned, leaving clear water

to the Confederate squadron "a cigar-shaped torpedo boat," that, according to their letters, " was sunk in the lower bay by the explosion of her boiler."

[1] These reports are amusing reading twenty-two years after the close of the war. In the view of the correspondents of Northern newspapers accompanying Farragut, the *Tennessee* was the most destructive engine of war that had ever floated. Her speed, her armor and her battery were exaggerated to the most remarkable degree, and it was predicted, with all the appearance of confidence on the part of the writers, that if she were ever permitted to escape from Mobile Bay, every port of the North would be at her mercy. They constantly urged upon the Navy Department that if the most deplorable catastrophes were to be averted, Admiral Farragut should have at his disposal every iron-clad that could be spared from imperative duty elsewhere, and Secretary Welles was scorched and slashed with criticism because of his seeming indifferance to the portentous possibilities to the North threatened by this solitary Confederate ship.

between that point and Fort Morgan. No resources of ingenuity were left unexhausted to strengthen the wooden ships. On one of them, the *Richmond*, three thousand bags of sand were used in building a barricade from the port bow around the starboard side to the port quarter, and in various shapes this expedient was adopted on other vessels. Chain cables were hung over the sides to protect the engines and boilers, and the coal in the bunkers was shifted to where it might catch shot coming in a line toward the boilers.

On the evening of August 4th the monitor *Tecumseh*, the last iron-clad for which Farragut had been waiting, steamed into the bay, and the morning of the 5th dawned with the conditions which the Federal admiral desired—a flood-tide to help his ships past the Confederate guns and a westerly wind to blow the smoke of battle away from the fleet and in the direction of Fort Morgan.[1] At 5:30 o'clock his wooden ships were double banked in the prescribed order, and before six the four monitors and the fourteen wooden ships were under way, the golden summer sun of this semi-tropical clime shining from cloudless skies as the prows of this formidable naval array, which could not then have been exceeded by any nation in the world, cut the lapping waves of the bay. They steamed in the following order, the *Hartford* being the flag-ship of Admiral Farragut:

MONITORS—STARBOARD COLUMN.

Tecumseh	1,034 tons—2 guns,	Commander T. A. M. Craven.
Manhattan	" " " "	J. W. A. Nicholson.
Winnebago	970 tons—4 "	" Thomas H. Stephens.
Chickasaw	" " " "	Lieut. Comr. George H. Perkins.

WOODEN SHIPS—PORT COLUMN.

Brooklyn	2,070 tons—24 guns,	Capt. James Alden.
Octorara	829 " 6 "	Lieut. Comr. Chas. A. Greene.
Hartford	1,900 " 21 "	Capt. Percival Drayton.
Metacomet	974 " 6 "	Lieut. Comr. Jas. E. Jouett.
Richmond	1,929 " 20 "	Capt. Thornton A. Jenkins.
Port Royal	805 " 6 "	Lieut. Comr. Bancroft Gherardi.
Lackawanna	1,533 " 8 "	Capt. Jno. B. Marchand.
Seminole	801 " 8 "	Commander Edward Donaldson.
Monongahela	1,378 " 8 "	Commander Jas. H. Strong.
Kennebec	507 " 5 "	Lieut. Comr. W. P. McCann.
Ossipee	1,240 " 11 "	Commander Wm. E. Leroy.
Itasca	507 " 6 "	Lieut. Comr. George Brown.
Oneida	1,032 " 9 "	Commander J. R. M. Mullany.
Galena	738 " 10 "	Lieut. Comr. Clark H. Wells.[2]

At this moment Admiral Buchanan, whose four ships had been riding at anchor to the north of Fort Morgan, gave the

---

[1] As Fort Gaines was more than two miles distant from the channel it did not count for anything in the scheme of engagement.

[2] All these ships carried batteries of the heaviest guns afloat proportionate to their size. Commodore Foxhall A. Parker, of the U. S. navy, states in his paper upon the battle of Mobile Bay, read before the Military Historical Society of Massachusetts, December 10th, 1877, that their total weight of metal was 14,246 pounds, and that they threw at a broadside 9,288 pounds. The total weight of metal that could be thrown from all the *Tennessee's* guns at one discharge was but 600 pounds, while 900 pounds is a large allowance for a single round from the three other Confederate craft. Thus it will be seen that the difference between the concentrated fire of the Federal fleet, and that of Buchanan's squadron, was nearly ten pounds to one in favor

signal to prepare for action, and they stood out across the channel just inside the line of torpedoes, their heads pointed to the westward in order that their port batteries might bring a raking fire to bear upon the advancing enemy. The admiral posted his own ship nearest to the channel and to the Federals [1] in the full expectation of engaging the *Tecumseh*, whose 15-inch guns had been loaded with sixty pounds of powder and cylindrical flat-headed steel bolts that it was supposed would penetrate the armor of the *Tennessee*. By a quarter-past seven o'clock the action had become general, Farragut's ships pouring their broadsides into Fort Morgan, which responded with so much energy that a dense cloud of smoke had already settled down upon the bay, above which loomed the masts and spars of the Federal fleet, while it was incessantly lit up with the flashes of the guns. The spectacle was one of those grand and awful battle-pictures which men who witnessed it confessed their inability to reproduce in words. Still, Admiral Buchanan, stationed in the pilot-house of the *Tennessee*, reserved his fire and kept his gaze fixed upon the *Tecumseh*, whose flat raft of a hull and ominous-looking turret were with every passing second creeping closer to him. There was even a momentary lull in the fury of the fire as all eyes were turned toward these gladiators of the seas, the champions each of its own side of the dreadful combat. [2] Buchanan, determined that the struggle should be at the closest quarters, had transmitted the order through Capt. Johnston to Lieut. Wharton, in charge of the first division of the *Tennessee*, "not to fire until the vessels are in actual contact." "Aye, aye, sir," responded Wharton, [3] tautening

ot the former. Each of Farragut's ships had been built for the naval service, and they constituted the pick of the fighting force of the U. S. government. His monitors were the most powerful iron-clads that had been built. The *Tecumseh* and *Manhattan* were armored with ten inches of iron on their turrets, as against the six inches of the *Tennessee's* casemate, and each carried in her turret two 15-inch guns, the heaviest that in those days had been put on shipboard.

The *Chickasaw* and *Winnebago* were double turret monitors, clad in eight and a half inches of iron, and firing from each turret two eleven inch guns. The *Hartford*, *Brooklyn* and *Richmond* were second-class wooden screw steamers carrying nine-inch Dahlgren guns, and 100-pounder Parrott rifles, and these very effective pieces of ordnance were common throughout the fleet, even the smallest ships mounting at least one nine or eleven-inch gun in addition to the most approved form of rifled cannon and howitzers. There were few such obsolete guns on board of them as the thirty-two pounders of the *Gaines*, *Morgan* and *Selma*. By far the most valuable guns in possession of the Confederates were the Brooke rifles, which were manufactured at Richmond, under the direction of their inventor, Commander John M. Brooke, of the C. S. navy; but the largest of them were but a little over eight inches' calibre, his facilities being too restricted to allow him to turn out pieces like

the eleven and fifteen inch cannon that the Federals placed so great a reliance upon.

[1] Six other Federal ships than those in Farragut's line of battle, the *Sebago*, *Tennessee*, (which must not be confounded with the Confederate iron-clad), *Bienville*, *Pembina*, *Pinola* and *Genesee*, were detailed to attack Fort Morgan on its southward and eastward faces, so as to attract as much as possible of its fire while the fleet was running the gauntlet; but they never steamed close enough to its guns to make an important factor in the action, and the mention of them is only necessary that no feature of the narrative should be left untouched.

[2] Before going into the action Admiral Buchanan addressed his assembled officers and crew upon the *Tennessee's* gun-deck, saying :— "Now men, the enemy is coming, and I want you to do your duty ; and you shall not have it to say when you leave this vessel that you were not near enough to the enemy, for I will meet them, and then you can fight them alongside of their own ships ; and if I fall, lay me on one side and go on with the fight, and never mind me—but whip and sink the Yankees or fight until you sink yourselves, but do not surrender."

[3] Lieut. A. D. Wharton entered the U. S. navy as cadet midshipman September 23d, 1856, and

the lockstring of the bow-gun in his fingers as he spoke the words. Simultaneously the *Tennessee* was moved a very short distance to the westward of the buoy at the end of the torpedo line, and Craven, the commander of the *Tecumseh*, made the fatal mistake of disregarding the order of Farragut to keep to the eastward of this buoy. Ordering his helm put hard-a-starboard, he dashed straight at the *Tennessee*, this course taking him directly across the chain of torpedoes. In a moment, and when the ships were less than a hundred yards apart, a muffled explosion was heard, a column of water like a fountain springing from the sea shot up beside the Federal monitor; she lurched violently, her head settled, her stern went up into the air so that her revolving screw could be plainly seen, and then the waves closed over her, leaving of her officers and crew less than a dozen men swimming about for their lives, while two officers and five men had climbed into a boat that had been washed from her deck. [1]

The suddenness of this catastrophe for an instant called a halt in the action. In Fort Morgan it was imagined that a

graduated at the Annapolis Naval Academy in 1860. He was in the steam-sloop *Seminole* on the Brazil Station when the war began, and his vessel was not ordered home until March 8th, 1861. After returning, he resigned his commission in the U. S. navy, was arrested and imprisoned at Fort Lafayette for two months, and then transferred to Fort Warren, where he was confined for some time, with Capt. Robert Tansell and Lieut. Wilson, who had resigned from the U. S. marine corps. Early in 1862, Lieut. Wharton was exchanged for Lieut. Van Horn, who was surrendered in Texas by Gen. Twiggs. He entered the service of the C. S. navy on February 8th, 1862, and was assigned to duty on board of the C. S. steamer *Arkansas*, then building at Memphis. He was in all the desperate engagements which the *Arkansas* had with the Federal fleets until she left Vicksburg, when he was ordered to Galveston as one of the officers of the captured steamer *Harriet Lane*. This vessel being unfitted for a cruiser, he was ordered to Shreveport, La., where he remained during the year 1863 in charge of the steamer *Webb*, to await the completion of the *Missouri* to which he was to be attached. In the winter of 1863, Lieut. Wharton proposed to the Navy Department to load the *Webb* with cotton and run the blockade at the mouth of the Red River, make an effort to pass New Orleans, and proceed to Havana. Before his proposition reached Richmond, he was ordered to the *Tennessee* at Mobile. Lieut. Read afterwards attempted to run the *Webb* to Havana, and came very near succeeding. Upon one occasion Captain R. H. Meade, of the U. S. navy, said that the attempt of Lieut. Read was one of the most daring feats of the war, and really excited his admiration. Lieut. Wharton bore a distinguished and gallant part in the battle of Mobile Bay, where he was taken prisoner. He was sent to Fort Warren, and, after a short imprisonment, was exchanged and returned to Richmond. He was then ordered as executive officer to the ironclad *Richmond* in the James River squadron. In January, 1865, he conceived the idea of destroying the bridges over the Tennessee River in East Tennessee, to delay what was then supposed to be

the intended advance of Gen. Thomas' army in southwestern Virginia. He thought that by taking a boat with inflammable material and launching it near Abingdon, Va., and passing down the river by night and concealing himself during the day, he could reach the bridges unobserved, and accomplish his mission. The Navy Department assented to the plan and fitted him out with a large flat-bottomed skiff, pulling three oars on a side, with an ample outfit. A dozen men volunteered for the perilous enterprise, among whom we can remember Lieut. Henry Stiles, Lieut. Joseph L. Pearcy, Sergeants William H. Wharton and J. Newton Jones. The boat was conveyed by cars to near Saltville, Va., and launched in the north fork of the Holston River. The journey down the frozen river through cold rains and heavy snows was one of great privation and suffering. Often the party were compelled to wade through ice and carry their boat over shoals and bars, occasionally jumping dams, running afoul of fish traps, and passing camps of the enemy. Upon one occasion the party were wrecked, and finally while they were away from their boat, the river rose so rapidly that it was caught over the overhanging branches of a tree, to which it was fastened, completing destroying all their ammunition and material. It then became necessary for the party to make their escape. They proceeded down the river and passed impotently under the bridge at Strawberry Plains; passing Knoxville and going under a second bridge at London, they were completely used up. Shortly afterwards they were taken prisoners and sent to Camp Chase, Ohio, where they were confined until the close of the war. Lieut. Wharton is at present (1887) in charge of the Hume Grammar and High Schools at Nashville, Tenn. In June, 1886, he was appointed by President Cleveland a member of the Board of Visitors to the Naval Academy.

[1] Twenty-one men in all were saved out of her complement of 141 souls. Commander Craven was among the lost. Of the twenty-one four swam to Fort Morgan and gave themselves up. A week afterwards, when the divers went down

Confederate shot had sunk the *Tecumseh* and a cheer rang out from the garrison. A boat put out from the *Metacomet* to pick up the men struggling with the waves. The roar of battle began again while she was on her errand of mercy, but Gen. Page, with that fine appreciation of an enemy's gallantry characteristic of the chivalrous soldier, ordered his artillerists not to fire upon her.

While these events were occurring, the *Selma*, *Gaines* and *Morgan* were doing their full share toward opposing the passage of the Federal fleet. Their guns were served promptly and efficaciously and from their position across the channel they were enabled to inflict much damage upon the wooden vessels, although their heaviest shot rebounded harmlessly from the impenetrable turrets of the monitors. The latter steered steadily onward, but the *Brooklyn*, leading the wooden ships, was stopped by Capt. Alden because of his fancy that he saw torpedoes in the water ahead. Then she backed down upon the *Hartford* and the Federal line of battle was in peril of becoming involved in inextricable confusion when Farragut dashed to its head in the *Hartford* and so restored order. During this embarrassment the batteries of the Federal men-of-war were almost silent, while Fort Morgan and Buchanan's ships poured into them an incessant and destructive fire. But Farragut took the risk of striking torpedoes and pushed ahead. [1] As he went over the line the keel of the *Hartford* struck several torpedo cases and the primers were heard to snap; but they had been so corroded by the action of the salt water that not one of them exploded and the fleet passed safely through the danger to which the *Tecumseh* had fallen a victim.

With the line of battle restored and the torpedo chain in their rear the Federals pressed on. Fort Morgan hulled each ship repeatedly as it passed, but the chain armor and the sandbag barricades saved every one from being disabled except

to examine the wreck they found nearly all the crew at their posts, as they sank. The chief engineer, who had been married in New York only two weeks before, and who had received from the flag-ship's mail his letters while the line was forming, stood with one hand upon the revolving bar of the turret engine, and in the other an open letter from his bride, which his dead eyes still seemed to be reading.

Lieut. F. S. Barrett, in charge of the torpedo defences at Mobile, on August 13th telegraphed Brig. Gen. G. J. Rains at the office of the Torpedo Bureau, Richmond, that "Monitor *Tecumseh* was sunk by torpedo in thirty seconds," whereupon Gen. Rains made the following communication to the Secretary of War: "I have the honor to enclose the within telegram with the remark that previous to leaving Mobile I had 67 torpedoes planted where this one acted, and had nine submarine mortar batteries under way (three completed) to close the main channel, such as the enemy report kept them out of Charleston, they being unable to remove them. But my instructions and wishes were frustrated after I left; the place left open and the enemy made use of it."

[1] Lieut. A. D. Wharton, who had command of the forward division of the *Tennessee*, writes that when the *Hartford* passed the *Brooklyn* and led the Federal line into the bay, she passed across the *Tennessee's* bow, and not more than 200 yards distant. The seven-inch rifle in the bow of Buchanan's ship was loaded with a percussion shell, and Wharton congratulated himself that he would sink Farragut's flagship under the batteries of Fort Morgan, and that her destruction would lead to the defeat of the others. "I took the lock-string from the captain of the gun myself," he writes, "took a long deliberate aim, and gave the commands: 'Raise,' 'Steady,' 'Raise a little more,' 'Ready,' 'Fire!' I was as confident that our shell would tear a hole in the *Hartford's* side big enough to sink her in a few minutes as I was that I had fired it. It did tear the hole expected, but it was above the water-line. Capt. Drayton refers to this shot in his official report to Farragut. I have often speculated since upon the effect of not having raised the breech of our bow-gun, and thus caused that shell to *ricochet* before striking the *Hartford*. I wish I had let the captain of the gun fire the piece himself."

the *Oneida*, in whose starboard boiler one of Morgan's shells burst, while another exploded in her cabin, and two of her guns were dismounted.   In this condition she was towed past the fort by her consort the *Galena*.

At 8:20 o'clock the hard fighting had lasted a little more than an hour and the Federal fleet was well into Mobile Bay and past the guns of Fort Morgan.   No commander in Gen. Page's place could have done more than he had done to defend the entrance, but it had been proved again, just as it had been demonstrated at New Orleans, Vicksburg and Port Hudson, that forts on shore could not stop the passage of a hostile squadron of steam-vessels handled with skill and determination.   But all hope for the Confederates was not lost with Fort Morgan out of the fight.   Admiral Buchanan and the commanders of his quartette of vessels felt that it now devolved upon them to take up alone the herculean task of turning back the enemy, and they went to their work with steadfast courage against odds that seemed to forbid them to hope for victory.

The *Selma*, *Gaines* and *Morgan* ran close down on the starboard bow of the *Hartford* as she crossed the torpedo line and inflicted upon her the most galling punishment that she suffered during the day.   The rapidity and accuracy of the fire of these gunboats at this stage of the engagement was the perfection of artillery practice.   They were using mainly their stern guns, for they kept a little ahead of the *Hartford*, and the range varied from seven hundred to a thousand yards.   One shot from the *Selma* killed ten and wounded five men at her forward guns, while that division was strewn with the bodies of the dead and wounded, and human limbs and splinters were hurled on to the deck of the consort *Metacomet*. Yet Farragut did not halt,[1] and Buchanan made a dash at him with the *Tennessee*, proposing to give the *Hartford* a taste of the ram, but she easily avoided him by her superior speed, and Buchanan, finding that it was useless to pursue her or to invite her to single combat, stood down the bay again to meet the other Federal wooden ships, which were coming up a mile astern of the *Hartford*, still lashed in couples, the *Brooklyn* and *Octorara* being in the lead.   In a battle where there was so much valor exhibited, it is impossible to specify the most daring deed, but this onslaught of the one ship upon the twelve was not the least brilliant of the undertakings of that memorable 5th of August.

[1] Admiral Farragut told in his own way, after the war, the story of his being "lashed to the mast-head" of the *Hartford* during the battle. "It was a fiction," he said to a reporter who questioned him in San Francisco. "At the commencement of the battle," he continued, "for the purpose of obtaining the best view of the movements of the enemy, and to better govern the fleet under my command, I got into the lower part of the rigging of the *Hartford*, just above what is known as the hammock railing.   As the smoke ascended from the heavy cannonading, my view became more obscured, and I was compelled to ascend the rigging gradually, until finally I got some little distance beneath the maintop.   At this juncture, Capt. Drayton fearing, he said, that I might fall overboard in case of being wounded, called one of the quartermasters, and cutting off a piece of the signal halyard, ordered him to bring it up to me, that I might render my position more secure.   With this rope I attached myself to the rigging, and I was not near the mast-head."

Buchanan had not got well down toward the fleet before he was hampered by the low speed of his vessel and her tardiness in answering her helm. He endeavored in succession to ram the *Brooklyn, Richmond* and *Lackawanna*, but each sheered off and he missed his aim. In passing each, however, he gave her his broadside, "which," says Commodore Parker, "did great injury to the vessels and laid many a brave fellow low, while their fire in reply made not the slightest impression on the iron shield." In fact, for a brief period of time, Buchanan was master of the situation, as nearly every shot that he fired did deadly execution, while he only suffered from the musketry fusillade into his ports as their shutters were swung open to allow of the guns being run out. As the *Tennessee* was invulnerable to the enemy's shot, Capt. Strong, of the sloop-of-war *Monongahela*, which had been fitted with an iron beak below the cutwater, endeavored to dispose of her by ramming, but Buchanan avoided the direct blow and received it on his port quarter. By so doing he rasped along the quarter of the *Kennebec*, the *Monongahela's* consort, and lodged a shell on her berth-deck, which knocked over an officer and four men. Holding his course down the Federal line, he next drove a couple of shots into the *Ossipee* and then swung around under the stern of the *Oneida*, into which ship he discharged two broadsides that disabled two of her guns, carried away much of her lower rigging, and took an arm off Commander Mullany. He had thus pitted the *Tennessee* single-handed against all Farragut's fleet except the *Hartford* and her consort and the three monitors left afloat; he had punished them most severely without being himself crippled in the slightest degree, and he now rested his ship and men for a little while close to the guns of Fort Morgan.

While the *Tennessee* was thus employed with the fleet astern of the *Hartford*, the *Selma, Morgan*, and *Gaines* were continuing their battle with the Federal flag-ship. As soon as Farragut saw that all vessels were clear of Fort Morgan and the torpedoes, he hoisted the signal for his gunboats to cast loose from the larger ships to which they were lashed and to make chase after the Confederate gunboats. They did so, and the latter were forced to retire up the bay, closely followed by the *Metacomet, Itasca, Kennebec, Port Royal* and others of the swift light-draft steamers, which Farragut had kept in hand for this particular duty. Lieut. Murphy, in the *Selma*, Lieut. Harrison, in the *Morgan*, and Lieut. Bennett, in the *Gaines*, were conscious that in speed and weight of metal they were no possible match for their pursuers, but they retreated sullenly and without slackening the fire from their stern guns. This running engagement was in progress when a nine-inch shot hulled the *Gaines* below the water-line and a few moments later a shell struck near the same place and exploded, making a leak that flooded the magazine. The ship was thus placed *hors du combat*, and to save the lives of his ship's company Lieut. Bennett beached her on the sands in front of Fort Morgan and applied the torch to her.

The officers of the gunboat *Gaines* at the battle of Mobile Bay were Lieut. Commander J. W. Bennett; First Lieut. and Executive Officer John Payne; Second Lieut. —— Lambert; Assistant Surgeon O. S. Iglehart; Midshipman Eugene Philips; Master's Mate George Waterman. In addition to her crew of 100 men she had on board a small detachment of marines under command of Lieut. Fendall. Mr. Philips writes in the course of a letter concerning the share that his ship took in the action:

" As the Federal fleet approached we stood out to meet them to keep them as much as possible under the guns of Fort Morgan. Finding that we could not prevent their advance we fell back and opened on the leading vessels at 600 yards. Our fire was very effective, and as we perceived that the Federals wanted to come to closer range, for the purpose of either cutting us off or boarding, we made a running fight. We received an eleven-inch shell under our port counter, which caused us to leak very badly, and the port battery was run over to the starboard side in hopes to list the ship so that the leak might be reached and stopped. This could not be done, and the order was given to stop firing and preparations were made to leave the sinking ship, the men being allowed time to save what few things they had. Marines were stationed at the falls of the ship's boats to prevent confusion, but there was no need for their services, as the men moved quietly and in good order. First putting in the boats our dead and wounded, we rowed away from the *Gaines*, and had gone about 200 yards when she suddenly lurched and went down by the stern, the flag flying from her main topmast ten feet above the water after she had touched bottom. We reached Fort Morgan without any difficulty and offered our services to Gen. Page, but as he did not need us we buried our dead and that night we ran the blockade, taking with us our wounded. We arrived in Mobile the next morning, after rowing all night, reported to Commodore Farrand and were sent to Battery Buchanan."

A heavy rain and wind squall had come in from the gulf, and with a dense mist succeeded the bright sun and unclouded skies of the earlier morning. In the fog the *Morgan* lost her course and went aground, but, getting off as soon as the squall lifted, ran down to a station under the Fort Morgan batteries. The *Selma* was not so fortunate. Lieut. Murphy attempted to steam through the fog, but his vessel was too slow to escape the *Metacomet*, the speediest of all the ships of the Federal force. At nine o'clock, by which time the sky was clear again, the *Metacomet* was across his bow with her nine-inch guns and 100-pounder rifle trained upon him. Still he defiantly kept his colors at the peak and answered the *Metacomet's* fire, which within a few moments killed Executive Officer J. H. Comstock and wounded four men. Lieut. Murphy was himself wounded, and recognizing that there was no means of escape from the swift enemy, and that to prolong the conflict with so much stronger a ship would be but to invite a reckless sacrifice of his men, he struck his flag. The *Morgan* remained near Fort Morgan until nightfall, when, under cover of the darkness, she reached Mobile.

We left the *Tennessee* taking a breathing spell not far distant from Fort Morgan, where she was within medium gunshot of the Federal monitors, which had purposely lingered near the fort to draw its fire until the wooden ships had passed beyond reach of its guns. It is admitted that Farragut supposed that Buchanan had given up the fight and had sought protection from the fort, for he first proposed to attack him as soon as his people had had their breakfasts and then resolved to go in after him as soon as . it became dark with the three monitors.[1]

But Farragut was not put to the necessity of waiting for Buchanan or assuming the offensive against him. When the *Tennessee* hauled off from her first engagement the examination of the ship showed that no essential damage had been done to her, some slight dents in her armor and the carrying away of a portion of her smoke-stack alone revealing that she had been stormed at by the huge ordnance of twelve of the Federal men-of-war. With this discovery made, Buchanan communicated to Capt. Johnston his resolution to once more challenge the enemy. The communication was in this simple language : "Follow them up, Johnston; we can't let them off that way."

Justice cannot be done in any narrative of the battle of Mobile Bay that omits a glance at the situation as it was when Buchanan ventured into this closing scene of that sanguinary day. Commodore Parker compares what he calls Buchanan's quixotic attack upon the three iron-clads and fourteen wooden ships of the Federal fleet to the charge of the light cavalry brigade upon the Russian guns at Balaklava and applies to it the criticism of a French officer upon the onslaught of Cardigan's Six Hundred that "it was magnificent, but it was not war." Yet it would be manifestly absurd to contend that Buchanan should have surrendered the *Tennessee* without making one more effort for the honor and glory of his flag; nobody who understood the iron will and pertinacious courage of the man would have expected him to act differently from

[1] Commander Mahan, of the Federal navy, in his account of the battle contained in his book, "The Gulf and Inland Waters," says that Farragut's resolution to attack the *Tennessee* after breakfast had been served was uttered in response to a remark by Capt. Drayton, of the *Hartford,* and in the hearing of Lieut. Com. Kimberly, Executive Officer of the *Hartford.*

Commodore Parker quotes from a diary, kept by Farragut, that "had Buchanan remained under the fort I should have attacked him as soon as it became dark, with the three monitors." It was probably the ultimate conclusion of the Federal admiral that his advantages would be greater in a day than in a night assault.

what he did.   True, he was absolutely alone; the remainder of his squadron had disappeared and the forts could give him no assistance in the battle into which he was plunging; but it must also be taken into account that he had already proved that his ship was more than a match for a dozen of the enemy's wooden vessels, and although he had not yet engaged their iron-clads it would have evinced a distrust of himself and his men of which he was utterly incapable to have taken it for granted that the monitors would conquer him.   All that is said concerning the desperate character of his effort may be freely conceded, but the exigencies of the situation demanded that he should make it and he acted upon principles that should control any naval warrior in a like emergency.   There were the chances that he might demoralize the Federals by ramming and sinking one or more of their ships; that a lucky shell in a boiler or magazine might have the same effect; or, finally, that he might carry the *Tennessee* up to Mobile and save her for the eventual defence of the city.   These were contingencies that fully warranted him in seeking a second conflict, to say nothing of the battle fervor and devotion to their cause felt by every soul on board the *Tennessee,* from the admiral down to the ammunition-passers.

Shortly after nine o'clock the Federal fleet had come to anchor about four miles inside of Fort Morgan, and most of their crews were at breakfast, when the Confederate flag-ship steamed out from the fort and laid her course directly for the *Hartford*, whereupon Farragut signaled to his monitors and heavy ships to attack with their guns and with bows on at full speed.   The *Monongahela* was the first ship to strike her, which she did on the port beam, and notwithstanding that the blow was delivered at a slightly oblique angle, the shock knocked off their feet many men on both vessels.   Firing was begun on the instant, and while the prow of the *Monongahela* was in actual contact with the *Tennessee's* side the latter planted two shells on the former's berth-deck, wounding an officer and two men. The Federals were less active at the guns, but before the *Tennessee* had passed on ten yards the *Monongahela* rapped her casemate with a broadside that failed to penetrate.   The fleet closed in around her and in ten minutes' time she was the centre of an irregular circle, the periphery of which consisted of the hostile ships, she firing as rapidly as her guns could be handled, while on each side and fore and aft she was pounded with shot and shell.   The second ship to ram her was the *Lackawanna*, whose blow was so forceful that it swung her around and listed her to port, but her recovery was speedily effected, while the *Lackawanna's* stem was stove in for several feet below the water line.   The *Tennessee* did not come unscathed out of the encounter with these two ships.   A shot from the *Lackawanna* smashed one of her gunport shutters, and on sounding the pumps it was found that the two rammings had started a leak which was making water at the rate of six inches an hour; but there was little in these circumstances to discourage Buchanan and he still endeavored to secure a position from which he could ram the *Hartford*, his highest ambition being to come to close quarters with the hostile flag-ship. He was no more to be gratified, however, in this supreme intention than in any other attempts to use his ship as a ram, for every one of the Federal ships not merely exceeded his own in speed, but also in rapidity of manœuvering, and instead of ramming he was rammed.

When the *Lackawanna* drew off he found the *Hartford* close aboard and the two flag-ships struck each other in the bluff of the bow. Nothing more vexing could have happened to Buchanan than what did occur at this conjuncture. He was in as favorable a position as could be desired to pour his shot into the enemy, but one after another, as the order was given to fire, his primers failed to explode except at one gun, whose shell killed and wounded several men on the *Hartford's* berth-deck. It was the most unfortunate moment of the conflict for Buchanan up to that time, for his inability to inflict injury upon the *Hartford* allowed her to get away and she described a circle with the object of again ramming the *Tennessee*, but in so doing she was run into by the *Lackawanna* and cut down nearly to the water's edge.

During the time occupied in the *Tennessee's* combat with the wooden ships, the monitors had come up and she was beset by a foe far more formidable than Farragut's walls of oak. Her shield was impermeable to the latter's shot, but it was yet to undergo the test of a fifteen-inch bolt. Lieut. Wharton has put into a few concise words the effect of the first discharge of one of these monstrous bolts from the *Manhattan*. "The *Monongahela*" he says, " was hardly clear of us when a hideous looking monster came creeping up on our port side, whose slowly revolving turret revealed the cavernous depths of a mammoth gun. 'Stand clear of the port side!' I shouted. A moment after a thunderous report shook us all, while a blast of dense, sulphurous smoke covered our port-holes, and 440 pounds of iron, impelled by sixty pounds[1] of powder, admitted daylight through our side, where, before it struck us, there had been over two feet of solid wood, covered with five inches of solid iron. This was the only 15-inch shot that hit us fair. It did not come through; the inside netting caught the splinters, and there were no casualties from it. I was glad to find myself alive after that shot."

From this moment to the end of the battle the *Tennessee* was vainly contending against the only instrumentalities that could have brought her to disaster. The three monitors, the

[1] This was the maximum charge of powder then used in the fifteen - inch guns. It was afterwards found that they would stand one hundred pounds with a proportionate gain of the velocity and battering power of the projectile.

Manhattan, Winnebago and *Chickasaw*, had her at their mercy.
She could drive shot after shot and shell after shell through
the sides of the wooden ships, but the solid projectiles from
her 8-inch rifles were impotent against the iron-clads, whose
gunners, from their place of safety and advantage in the shot-
proof turrets, could aim and fire with all the coolness and security of participants in an artillery target match. Neither
the *Manhattan* or the *Winnebago* appears to have been handled
with much skill, as the 15-inch shot spoken of by Lieut.
Wharton was the only one that struck the *Tennessee* so as to
do her great harm, and the *Winnebago* planted but a few projectiles upon her; yet the fire of these vessels and especially
the smashing of her shield by the *Manhattan's* bolt were important factors in producing the eventual result. But the most
serious injury was done her by the *Chickasaw*, which took position under her stern and from an average distance of fifty
yards fired over fifty steel-headed cylindrical projectiles, nearly
all of which struck either her hull or her casemate. Simultaneously the wooden ships rammed her in steady succession,
and the unfortunate construction of her port shutters was
evinced by three of them becoming jammed, which reduced
her to fighting with but three guns. Many of her plates
had been started by the 11-inch shot of the *Chickasaw*, and before ten o'clock, according to the statement of Capt. Johnston,
"the smoke-pipe, which had been riddled by shot, was broken
off close to the top of the shield or upper deck by the concussion
produced by the ramming process adopted by the enemy."

The gun-deck was now filled by smoke emitted from the
stump of the pipe and the heat was so great that the men, although many of them had stripped to the waist, were in great
distress. Then the rudder chains, which the enemy knew were
exposed on the deck aft the casemate and had aimed at, were
cut away, probably by a shot from the *Chickasaw*, and although the relieving tackle was promptly manned, that, too,
was shot away in a few moments, and after her heroic fight
the *Tennessee* drifted a helpless hulk upon the waters.

Meanwhile Admiral Buchanan had descended to the gun-
deck and taken personal charge of the battery. He had sent
for a machinist to back out the pivot-pin of a jammed stern
port-shutter in order that the gun might be brought into
action again, when a shot struck the casemate just outside of
where the man was sitting, and the concussion shivered him
into remain that, says Capt. Johnston, "had the appearance
of sausage meat," and that were shoveled into buckets. The
same shot started an iron splinter that struck the admiral
and fractured his leg, and he was carried below to the berth-
deck and placed under the care of Fleet Surgeon D. B.
Conrad.

Just prior to the shooting away of the rudder chains the
admiral had determined to endeavor to seek shelter with the

disabled ship under the batteries of Fort Morgan, and accordingly she had been headed in that direction, it being impossible to carry her away from the enemy and into Mobile, and during the few minutes in which the relieving tackle was available she was still slowly steaming toward Mobile Point; but when that last resource as a steering apparatus had vanished, when the admiral had been struck down, and when the total responsibility of command had fallen upon Capt. Johnston, there was no longer any avenue of escape. The *Tennessee* could revolve her screw, and she could fire three guns at any foe that might place himself in front of their muzzles; but she could not be steered, and without that power everything else was as nothing. Johnston did not want to give her up, but the *Chickasaw* was still banging away at her, the *Manhattan* and *Winnebago* were drawing nigher, and the *Hartford* and *Ossipee* were heading for her at the top of their speed with the desire to do a little more ramming, while she was unable to give them a gun in reply. With poignant regret Capt. Johnston sought the side of Admiral Buchanan, and reported that further resistance was out of the question. From his couch of suffering Buchanan replied: "Do the best you can, Johnston, and when all is done, surrender."

The crisis at which the only alternative of surrender was a vain sacrifice of life had arrived. Johnston returned to the pilot-house and beheld each Federal ship either cannonading the *Tennessee* or preparing to ram her. It had been fifteen minutes since she had discharged a gun and she was encircled by a belt of fire. Within and without she was a picture of the havoc wrought upon a lonely foe by the crushingly preponderating strength of Farragut's fleet. It was imperative that Johnston should make his decision quickly to strike his colors, or let his ship and all hands on board be sent to the bottom of the bay. The staff upon which the Confederate colors were hoisted had been shot away early in the fierce engagement and the flag had been displayed again upon a boat-hook thrust through the grating that covered the casemate. Johnston's decision was that the surrender should be made, and with his own hands he drew in the boat-hook that carried the ensign, but the Federal ships still maintained their fire, and he then mounted to the roof of the casemate and showed a white flag. [1]

This was accepted as the signal of capitulation, the white flag and the figure of Capt. Johnston on the forward edge of

---

[1] Commodore Parker says of Johnston that "hastening to the top of the shield, which was exposed to a perfect shower of solid projectiles, this truly brave man hauled down the Confederate ensign with his own hands ; it had been raised in triumph ; it was lowered without dishonor." Parker meant to render to Johnston the honor which is always the delight of one brave sailor to pay to another, but he failed to exactly comprehend the events that were taking place on board the *Tennessee.* Capt. Johnston had drawn in the boat-hook that bore the ensign before it became necessary for him to throw the white flag to the breeze from the top of the *Tennessee's* shield. In a technical sense Johnston did "haul down the Confederate ensign with his own hands," but he was fired upon after the colors had been lowered, and his extreme feat of daring consisted in his exposure of himself from the top of the shield to the hail of shot and

the roof of the casemate being plainly in view of every vessel in the Federal fleet. The *Ossipee* was approaching to ram the *Tennessee*, but when the sign of surrender made its appearance her helm was shifted and her engines backed. A collision could not be avoided, but it was a gentle one, and the shock was a diminuendo of the stalwart blows that had been administered a half hour previously.[1]

So ended this momentous battle at 10 o'clock in the morning. Com. Johnston made the formal surrender of the *Tennessee* to Commander Le Roy, of the *Ossipee*, and his sword and that of Admiral Buchanan were afterwards delivered to Farragut.[2]

The first Federal officer to board the Confederate flag-ship was Fleet Surgeon Palmer, who had been instructed to assist Dr. Conrad in looking after the wounded, and he thus records his entry into the vessel and his meeting with Admiral Buchanan :

"I scrambled literally through the iron port and threaded my way among the piles of confusion to a ladder, by which I mounted to where Admiral Buchanan was lying in a place like the top of a truncated pyramid. Somebody announced me and he answered (tone polite, but savage), 'I know Dr. Palmer,' but he gave me his hand. I told him I was sorry to see him so badly hurt, but that I should be glad to know his wishes. He answered : 'I only wish to be treated kindly as a prisoner of war.' My reply was : 'Admiral Buchanan, you know perfectly well you will be treated kindly.' Then he said, 'I am a Southern man, an enemy and a rebel.' I felt a little offended at his tone, but rejoined carefully that he was at that moment a wounded person and disabled and that I would engage to have his wishes fulfilled. As to the present disposal of his person, that Admiral Farragut would take him aboard the *Hartford*, or send him to any other ship he might prefer. He said he didn't pretend to be Admiral Farragut's friend and had no right to ask favors of him, but that he would be satisfied with any decision that might be come to. Dr. Conrad, lately an assistant surgeon in our navy, told me he was fleet surgeon and desired to accompany Buchanan wherever he might go. I promised that he should, and returned to the *Hartford* and reported to Admiral Farragut circumstantially. He seemed hurt at Buchanans irritated feeling and said he (Buchanan) had formerly professed friendship for him. I saw there must be some embarrassment in bringing them together and therefore proposed

---

shell while he was again announcing the surrender of the *Tennessee* by the exhibition of the white flag.

[1] As the *Ossipee* drew up beside the *Tennessee* Commander Le Roy came out on his forecastle deck and hailed Johnston. The two men had served in companionship in the old navy, and the warmth of Le Roy's greeting was responded to by the Confederate captain. It was one of those war incidents which excited the wonder of the correspondents of the English newspapers, who could not understand how men who had just been engaged in the bloodiest combat could, when a surrender had taken place, renew their old associations of friendship and amity, take each other by the hand and wish each other well. It is a matter that is plain enough to Americans in the light of the reunion in the North and South, and that even in the war days was illustrated by the fact that Northern and Southern men did not fight as personal enemies or as the machines of monarchial

governments, but as soldiers and sailors who served the flag which they deemed to represent the right. Judged by this truthful standard, the meeting of Johnston and Le Roy is a war episode that it is proper to preserve in history.

[2] Farragut officially reported that Buchanan's sword was delivered to him on board the *Hartford* by Capt. Johnston, which was not the fact. In a note to his report to Secretary Mallory from the Pensacola Hospital on August 26th, Admiral Buchanan says:

"Sept. 17th. Since writing the above, I have seen the report of Admiral Farragut, a portion of which is incorrect. Capt. Johnston did not deliver my sword on board the *Hartford*. After the surrender of the *Tennessee*, Capt. Giraud, the officer who was sent on board to take charge of her, said to me that he was directed by Admiral Farragut to ask for my sword, which was brought from the cabin and delivered to him by one of my aides."

that I should have a steamer to take all the wounded to Pensacola and another one to send all ordinary invalids to New Orleans."[1]

Gen. Page shortly afterward received a communication from Admiral Farragut,[2] under a flag of truce, informing him that Admiral Buchanan had been injured, and requesting that he might be permitted to send all the wounded, also under a flag of truce, on one of his vessels to Pensacola, where they would be properly cared for, the understanding being that the ship should take out nothing but the wounded and bring back nothing that she did not take out. This proposition met the humane impulses of Gen. Page, who at once acceded to it, and the *Metacomet* sailed that night for Pensacola with Admiral Buchanan and a number of the prisoners and wounded, while the Federals proceeded to overhaul the *Tennessee* and *Selma* and fit their prizes out for service.[3]

In making up the lists of killed and wounded, it was found that the Confederates had suffered far less than their vastly out-numbering enemy. Omitting the loss by the sinking of the

[1] Dr. Palmer evidently writes with a strong prejudice against Admiral Buchanan, who may have spoken just as the surgeon reported him without warranting the supposition at which Palmer hints, that he was bent upon saying unpleasant things to Farragut or any other Federal officers with whom he might be brought in contact No man cherished a more punctilious sense of the proprieties than Buchanan, and it is absurd to think of him railing at the enemy to whom fate had given victory like a disappointed beldame. His heartily-expressed gratitude to Palmer for the latter's professional services to him should have convinced Palmer that in defeat as well as in triumph the Confederate commander was incapable of transgressing the code of ceremonial courtesy. We have made use of Dr. Palmer's report of the scene on the *Tennessee* because it is the only record of the incident, but it would be unfair to reprint it without the caution that he seriously misapprehended the character of Buchanan.

[2] FLAG-SHIP "HARTFORD," August 5th, 1864.
SIR : Admiral Buchanan is severely wounded, having lost his leg. There are, in addition, four or five others of the crew of the *Tennessee* who require more comfortable quarters than we can give them in the fleet. Will the commanding officer at Fort Morgan permit a vessel to take them to our hospital at Pensacola, with or without our own wounded ?—the understanding being that the flag of truce vessel takes nothing whatever but the wounded, and brings nothing back that she did not take out, and my honor is given for the above.
Very respectfully,
D. G. FARRAGUT,
Rear Admiral Commanding W. G. B. Squadron.
Brigadier Gen. R. L. PAGE,
Commanding Fort Morgan.

HEADQUARTERS THIRD BRIGADE, D. G., }
FORT MORGAN, ALABAMA, August 5th, 1864. }
SIR : Your communication of this date is received. I am much obliged for the information regarding Admiral Buchanan.
Your request relative to the wounded of the *Tennessee*, and also those of your own command, being taken to Pensacola, will be permit-

ted under a flag of truce, and to return on the conditions you propose.
I would be glad if Admiral Buchanan, having lost a leg, be permitted, under parole, to go to Mobile, where he can receive earlier and more prompt attention.
If the latter request is granted please inform me, and I will have a boat from town to take him up.
Very respectfully,
R. L. PAGE,
Brigadier Gen. Commanding.
Rear Admiral DAVID G. FARRAGUT,
Commanding W. C B. Squadron, Mobile Bay.

FLAG SHIP "HARTFORD," MOBILE BAY, }
August 5th, 1864. }
SIR : In reply to your note of this date, I would say that it is altogether out of the question that I should permit Admiral Buchanan to be sent to Mobile, but I will send him to Pensacola, where he will receive the same comforts as our own wounded, which I apprehend are as good as they could be in Mobile.
It was simply as an act of humanity that I made the proposition I did to-day. I would be glad to bury my dead on shore; but if there is any objection to it, they can have a sailor's grave in the deep, honored by the heartfelt sighs of their shipmates.
Very respectfully,
D G. FARRAGUT,
Rear Admiral Commanding.
Brigadier Gen. R. L. PAGE,
Commanding Fort Morgan.

FORT MORGAN, August 6th, 1864.
SIR : Your note of the fifth received. There is no objection to your burying your dead on shore. When they arrive near the wharf here, a point will be designated for the burial.
Very respectfully, your obedient servant,
R. L PAGE,
Brigadier Gen. C. S. A..
Rear Admiral D. G. FARRAGUT,
Commanding U. S. Naval Forces, Mobile Bay.

[3] Commander Johnston, Lieut P. U. Murphy, and Lieut. W. L. Bradford, were sent north from Pensacola, and arrived at New York on

Tecumseh, the Federals had 52 men killed and 170 wounded, distributed on the various ships as follows:

	Killed.	Wounded.
Hartford	25	28
Brooklyn	11	43
Lackawanna	4	5
Oneida	8	30
Monongahela	0	6
Metacomet	1	2
Ossipee	1	7
Richmond	0	2
Galena	0	1
Octorara	1	10
Kennebec	1	6

The proportion of injury inflicted upon the Federal fleet relatively by Fort Morgan and by Buchanan's squadron cannot be figured out to a certainty, but it is known that the Confederate vessels did much the greater execution, Farragut himself stating in his official report that in the conflict with them " we lost many more men than from the fire of the batteries of Fort Morgan." The Confederate losses were as follows :

Tennessee.—Killed: John Silk, first-class fireman ; Wm. Moore; seaman, mortally wounded and soon afterwards died—2. Wounded : Admiral Franklin Buchanan, leg broken ; Alvah T. Post, pilot, on head ; J. C. O'Connell, second assistant engineer, head and shoulder; James Kelly, boatswain's mate, in knee; Andrew Rossmorson, quartermaster, in head; Wm. Daly, seaman, in head; Robert Barry, marine, in head; James McCann, marine, in shoulder - 8.

Gaines.—Killed : Daniel Ahern, quarter gunner ; Michael Vincent, seaman—2. Wounded: W. W. Smith, first quartermaster, contusions of thighs and legs; Thomas Woods, seaman, contusions of thighs and legs (both these men were wounded by the explosion of a shell while standing at the wheel) ; Newton Williams, landsman, left hand lacerated by a splinter—3.

Selma.—Killed : J. H. Comstock, lieutenant and executive officer; J. R. Murray, acting master's mate ; Wm. Hall,. gunner's mate : James Rooney, seaman ; James Montgomery, seaman; Bernard Riley, ordinary seaman; J. R. Frisley, landsman; Christopher Shepard, landsman—8. Wounded: P. U. Murphy, lieutenant commanding, in wrist; John Villa, seaman, badly in leg and hand; Henry Fratee, landsman, badly in hand; Daniel Linnehan, seaman, slightly in arm; John Shick, seaman, slightly in face; John Davis, fireman, slightly; John Gilliland, seaman, slightly—7.

Morgan.—Killed: None. Wounded: One seaman, slightly—1.

The total Confederate loss was 12 killed and 19 wounded, while the Federals lost 172 killed and 170 wounded, including in the killed the 120 souls who went down with the *Tecumseh*.[1]

September 18th. Admiral Farragut reported the officers of the *Tennessee* captured as follows :— "Admiral F. Buchanan, Commander James D. Johnston, Lieuts. Wm. L. Bradford, A. D. Wharton, E. J. McDermett ; Masters J. R. De Mahy, H. W. Perrin ; Fleet-Surgeon R. C. Bowles ; Engineers G. D. Lining, J. C. O'Connell, John Hayes, O. Benson, W. B. Patterson; Paymaster's Clerk J. H. Conen ; Master's Mates W. S. Forrest, M. J. Beebee, and R. M. Carter; Boatswain John McCredie ; Gunner H. L. Smith."

[1] This is Admiral David D. Porter's estimate of the loss by the sinking of the *Tecumseh*. The earlier Federal accounts of the battle placed the total number of persons on that monitor at but about 100, of whom, as has been said, 21 were rescued. But Porter made up his figures after a thorough scrutiny of all the official documents, and they must be accepted as more reliable than the previous statements, which were compiled without reference to the records to which he had access.

This great disparity in the losses is a fact that bears a volume of evidence to the pluck with which Buchanan's vessels were fought, to the high standard of discipline of his crews, and to the perfection of the aim of his gunners.

Many of the Federal wooden ships were badly cut up. The *Hartford* was struck 20 times by shot and shell, the *Brooklyn* 30 times, the *Octorara* 17 times, the *Metacomet* 11 times, the *Lackawanna* 5 times, the *Ossipee* 4 times, the *Monongahela* 5 times, the *Kennebec* twice, the *Galena* 7 times, and most of the other vessels once or more. Of the monitors, the *Manhattan* was struck 9 times, the *Winnebago* 19 times, and the *Chickasaw* 3 times, but no bolt pierced their invulnerable armor.

How the *Tennessee* came out of the action is best told by the subjoined extract from the report of the Board of Survey ordered by Farragut:

"The injuries to the casemate of the *Tennessee* from shot are very considerable. On its after side nearly all the plating is started ; one bolt

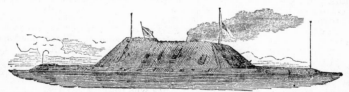

C. S. RAM "TENNESSEE" AS SHE APPEARED AFTER HER SURRENDER TO U. S. SQUADRON, AUGUST 5TH, 1864.

driven in, several nuts knocked off inside, gun-carriage of the after pivot gun damaged, and the steering rod or chain cut near that gun. There are unmistakable marks on the after-part of the casemate of not less than nine 11-inch solid shot having struck within the space of a few square feet in the immediate vicinity of that port. On the port side of the casemate the armor is also badly damaged from shot."

The report then speaks of the effect of the fifteen-inch shot fired by the *Manhattan* and previously alluded to, and continues :

"There are visible between forty and fifty indentations and marks of shot on the hull, deck and casemate, varying from very severe to slight ; nine of the deepest indentations on the after-part of the casemate evidently being eleven-inch shot, and the marks of about thirty of other calibres on different parts of the vessel. There are no external visible marks or evidences of injury inflicted upon the hull of the *Tennessee* by the severe ramming of the *Monongahela*, *Lackawanna* and *Hartford* ; but inasmuch as the decks leaked badly, and when there is a moderate sea running in the bay her reported usual leakage of three inches an hour being now increased to five or six inches an hour, it is fairly to be inferred that the increased leakage is caused by the concussion of the vessels. The *Tennessee* is in a state to do good service now. To restore her to the state of efficiency in which she was when she went into action with this fleet on the 5th inst. it will be necessary to overhaul much of the iron plating on the port and after-sides of the casemate and replace some of it. The iron gun-port slides or shutters, which were damaged, must be either removed or repaired. A new smoke-stack is required, and additional ventilators should be fitted. Blowers are required to produce proper ventilation in the engine-room and on the berth-deck. When these small repairs and additions shall have been made the iron-clad *Tennessee* will be a most formidable vessel for harbor and river service and for operating generally in smooth water, both offensively and defensively."

It is of absorbing interest to turn now to the discussion by the Confederate commanders of this famous battle. Admiral Buchanan's report was not lengthy, it being made from his couch of pain in the United States naval hospital at Pensacola to Secretary Mallory, on August 26th. After relating the order of the Federal vessels as they steamed up the channel, and computing that they carried 199 guns and 2,700 men, he says:

"When they were discovered standing into the channel, signal was made to the Mobile squadron, under my command, consisting of wooden gunboats *Morgan* and *Gaines*, each carrying six guns, and the *Selma* four, to follow my motions, in the ram *Tennessee*, of six guns, in all, twenty-two guns and 470 men. All were soon under way and stood towards the enemy, in a line abreast. As the *Tennessee* approached the fleet, when opposite the fort, we opened our battery, at short range, upon the leading ship, the admiral's flag-ship *Hartford*, and made the attempt to run into her, but, owing to her superior speed, our attempt was frustrated. We then stood towards the next heavy ship, the *Brooklyn*, with the same view; she also avoided us by her superior speed. During this time the gunboats were also closely engaged with the enemy ; all our guns were used to the greatest advantage, and we succeeded in seriously damaging many of the enemy's vessels. The *Selma* and *Gaines*, under Lieut. Commandants P. U. Murphy and J. W. Bennett, fought gallantly, and I was gratified to hear from officers of the enemy's fleet that their fire was very destructive. The *Gaines* was fought until she was found to be in a sinking condition, when she was run on shore near Fort Morgan. Lieut. Commandant Murphy was closely engaged with the *Metacomet* assisted by the *Morgan*, Commander Harrison, who, during the conflict, deserted him, when, upon the approach of another large steamer, the *Selma* surrendered. I refer you to the report of Lieut. Commandant Murphy for the particulars of his action. He lost two promising young officers, Lieut. Comstock and Master's Mate Murray, and a number of his men were killed and wounded; and he was also wounded severely in the wrist. Commander Harrison will no doubt report to the department his reason for leaving the *Selma* in that contest with the enemy, as the *Morgan* was uninjured. His conduct is severely commented on by the officers of the enemy's fleet, much to the injury of that officer and the navy.[1]

"Soon after the gunboats were dispersed by the overwhelming superiority of force, and the enemy's fleet had anchored about four miles above Fort Morgan, we stood for them again in the *Tennessee* and renewed the attack, with the hope of sinking some of them with our prow, and again were foiled by their superior speed in avoiding us. The engagement with the whole fleet soon became general at very close quarters and lasted about an hour, and notwithstanding the serious injury inflicted upon many of their vessels by our guns, we could not sink them. Frequently during the contest we were surrounded by the enemy, and all our guns were in action almost at the same moment. Some of their heaviest vessels ran into us under full steam, with the view of sinking us. One vessel, the *Monongahela*, had been prepared as a ram, and was very formidable. She struck us with great force, injuring us but little. Her prow and stem were knocked off, and the vessel so much injured as to make it necessary to dock her. Several of the other vessels of the fleet were found to require extensive

---

[1] See report of Commander Harrison and accompanying explanations.

repairs. I enclose to you a copy of a drawing of the *Brooklyn*, made by one of her officers after the action; and an officer of the *Hartford* informed me that she was more seriously injured than the *Brooklyn*. I mention these facts to prove that the guns of the *Tennessee* were not idle during this unequal contest. For other details of the action and injuries sustained by the *Tennessee*, I refer you to the report of Commander J. D. Johnston, which has my approval. After I was carried below, unfortunately wounded, I had to be governed by the reports of that valuable officer as to the condition of the ship, and the necessity and time of her surrender; and when he represented to me her utterly hopeless condition to continue the fight with injury to the enemy, and suggested her surrender, I directed him to do the best he could, and when he could no longer damage the enemy, to do so. It affords me much pleasure to state that the officers and men cheerfully fought their guns to the best of their abilities, and gave strong evidence, by their promptness in executing orders, of their willingness to continue the contest as long as they could stand to their guns, notwithstanding the fatigue they had undergone for several hours; and it was only under the circumstances, as presented by Capt. Johnston, that she was surrendered to the fleet, about ten A. M., as painful as it was to do so. I seriously felt the want of experienced officers during the action. All are young and inexperienced, and many had but little familiarity with naval duties, having been appointed from civil life within the year. The reports of Commander Harrison, of the *Morgan*, and Lieut. Commandant Bennett, of the *Gaines*, you have no doubt received from those officers.

"I enclose the report of Fleet Surgeon D. B. Conrad, to whom I am much indebted for his skill, promptness and attention to the wounded. By permission of Admiral Farragut, he accompanied the wounded of the *Tennessee* and *Selma* to this hospital, and is assisted by Assistant Surgeons Booth and Bowles, of the *Selma* and *Tennessee*, all under charge of Fleet Surgeon Palmer, U. S. N., from whom we have received all the attention and consideration we could desire or expect.

"The crews and many officers of the *Tennessee* and *Selma* have been sent to New Orleans. Commander J. D. Johnston, Lieut. Commandant P. U. Murphy, and Lieuts. W. L. Bradford and A. D. Wharton, Second Assistant Engineer J. C. O'Connell and myself, are to be sent North. Master's Mates W. S. Forrest and R. M. Carter, who are with me, acting as my aides, not having any midshipmen, are permitted to accompany me. They are valuable young officers, zealous in the discharge of their duties, and both have served in the army, where they received honorable wounds. Their services are valuable to me.

"I am happy to inform you that my wound is improving, and sincerely hope our exchange will be effected, and that I will soon again be on duty."

Captain Johnston's report to Admiral Buchanan was made from the Pensacola hospital on August 13th. He also recites the advance of the enemy, and thus continues :

"When they had approached sufficiently near to draw the fire from Fort Morgan, signal was made to follow your motions, and the *Tennessee* was moved down to the middle of the channel, just inside the line of torpedoes stretching across it, from whence she immediately opened her battery upon the advancing fleet. Every effort was made, at the same time, to ram each of the leading vessels as they entered the bay, but their superior speed enabled them to avoid this mode of attack ; the first, with the admiral's flag, passing ahead, and all the remainder astern, before the ship could be turned to encounter them. As she followed the fleet into the bay the leading monitor, the *Tecumseh*, was discovered to be sinking, and in a few seconds she disappeared, taking down nearly all on board, consisting, as since learned, of 120 souls. The *Tennessee's* battery was used to the greatest advantage as long as the fleet were within range, and when they reached a point about four miles from Fort Morgan and were in the act of anchoring, she steamed alone up towards them (the other vessels of the squadron having been dispersed), and attacked them as soon as she was near enough to render her fire effective.

"The whole fleet were again put in motion to receive her, and she received four heavy shocks by the heaviest vessels running into her at full speed, soon after which I received an order from you, in person, to steer for Fort Morgan, as it had been reported by the acting chief engineer that the ship was leaking rapidly. At this time it was reported to me that the wheel chains had been carried away; and, ordering the relieving tackles to be used, I made a personal examination of the broken chain to ascertain if it could be repaired. This was found to be impossible, without sending men outside of the shield to expose themselves several minutes to the fire of the enemy's vessels, by which the after-deck (over which the chains lead) was closely watched and constantly swept until the close of the action.

"Returning to the pilot-house for the purpose of more closely observing the movements of the enemy, I soon received a report that you had been wounded, when I went aft to see you, and while there found that the after-port cover had been struck by a shot which instantly killed a man engaged in removing the pivot bolt upon which it revolved, and wounded yourself and one of the gun's crew—the latter mortally. I then learned that the two quarter-ports, out of which the after-gun was intended to be used, had also been so jammed by the fire of the enemy as to render it impracticable to move them, and that the relieving tackles had been shot away and the tiller unshipped from the rudder-head. The smoke-pipe having been completely riddled by shot, was knocked down close to the top of the shield by the concussion of vessels running into the ship. At the same time the monitors were using their eleven and fifteen-inch solid shot against the after-end of the shield, while the largest of the wooden vessels were pouring in repeated broadsides at the distance of only a few feet; and, I regret to say, that many favorable opportunities of sinking these vessels were unavoidably lost by the repeated failure of our gun-primers. The bow-port cover was struck by a heavy shot, as also the cover on the forward port on the port side, and two of the broadside port covers were entirely unshipped by the enemy's shot.

"The enemy was not long in perceiving that our steering gear had been entirely disabled, and his monitors and heaviest vessels at once took position on each quarter and stern, from whence they poured in their fire, without intermission, for a period of nearly half an hour, while we were unable to bring a single gun to bear, as it was impossible to change the position of the vessel, and the steam was rapidly going down, as a natural consequence of the loss of the smoke-pipe.

"Feeling it my duty to inform you of the condition of the vessel, I went to the berth-deck for this purpose, and after making my report, I asked if you did not think we had better surrender, to which you replied : "Do the best you can, sir, and when all is done surrender," or words to that effect. Upon my return to the gun-deck I observed one of the heaviest vessels of the enemy in the act of running into us on the port-quarter, while the shot were fairly raining upon the after-end of the shield, which was now so thoroughly shattered that in a few moments it would have fallen and exposed the gun-deck to a raking fire of shell and grape.

"Realizing our helpless condition at a glance, and conceiving that the ship was now nothing more than a target for the heavy guns of the enemy, I concluded that no good object could be accomplished by sacrificing the lives of the officers and men in such a one-sided contest, and therefore proceeded to the top of the shield and took down the ensign which had been seized on to the handle of a gun-scraper, and stuck up through the grating. While in the act, several shots passed close to me. and when I went below to order the engines to be stopped the firing of the enemy was continued. I then decided, although with an almost bursting heart,

37

to hoist the white flag, and returning again on to the shield, placed it in the same spot where but a few moments before had floated the proud flag for whose honor I would so cheerfully have sacrificed my own life, if I could possibly have become the only victim ; but at the same time it would have been impossible to destroy the ship without the certain loss of many valuable lives, your own among the number.

"It is with the most heartfelt satisfaction that I bear testimony to the undaunted gallantry and cheerful alacrity with which the officers and men under my immediate command discharged all their duties; and to the executive officer, Lieutenant Bradford, it is due that I should commend the regular and rapid manner in which the battery was served in every particular. While a prisoner on board the U. S. steamer *Ossipee*, and since coming into this hospital, I have learned, from personal observation and from other reliable sources of information, that the battery of the *Tennessee* inflicted more damage upon the enemy's vessels than that at Fort Morgan, although she was opposed by 187 guns of the heaviest calibre, in addition to the twelve eleven and fifteen-inch guns on board the three monitors.

"The entire loss of the enemy, most of which is ascribed to the *Tennessee*, amounts to quite three hundred in killed and wounded, exclusive of the one hundred lost in the *Tecumseh*, making a number nearly as large as the entire force under your command in this unequal conflict. Fifty-three shot-marks were found on the *Tennessee's* shield, three of which had penetrated so far as to cause splinters to fly on board, and the washers over the ends of the bolts wounded several men."

Lieut. Commander Murphy, of the *Selma,* made his report to Admiral Buchanan from the Pensacola hospital on August 15th. He wrote:

"The shattered state of my nervous system, produced by the wound I received, has prevented my making my report before this. Between five and six o'clock, on the morning of the 5th inst., it was reported to me that a move was made by the fleet outside. I gave the order at once to get up steam, to weigh anchors, and to lash both securely and then to go to breakfast; and, if we had time, for the crew to clean themselves. The *Selma* was lying to the southward and eastward of the flagship and much nearer the shore. After the anchor was weighed the steamer dropped down with the tide to the northward and eastward. While the crew were at breakfast the engagement commenced, and many shots were fired by both sides before I went to quarters; but as soon as the crew were through with their breakfast and the decks were cleared up, I went to quarters and stood slowly to the northward and westward, under easy steam, and nearly parallel with the vessels coming in, and as soon as I passed the stern of the *Tennessee* I opened on the enemy with all my guns, and continued to fight all of them for some time, when I perceived the *Metacomet* was towing the *Hartford*, the leading ship, when I gave the order to give her all the steam they could that I might get ahead and on the port side of her. My intention was perceived, and before I could get into the position I wanted, the *Metacomet* cast off and gave chase. A constant fire had been kept up all the time, first at one and then at another, as the opportunity offered. Before the *Metacomet* had cast off, my best gunner had been killed by a piece of shell from the *Hartford*, I think; but several vessels were firing at me at the same time, and in a short while my next best gunner met the same fate. The fight was then with the *Metacomet* (carrying eight 9-inch Dahlgren and two 100 pounder Parrott guns), one of the fastest vessels in their squadron. She tried hard to rake me, which was prevented by good steering. The *Metacomet*, being so much faster, soon came quite near, and, firing one of her nine-inch guns, killed six and wounded seven men at the same gun, as well as disabling the gun itself. I had only been able to use two of the four guns which composed the battery of the *Selma* for some time, and the crew of No. 1 gun had just been sent aft to assist in working these two.

"My first lieutenant, Wm. Comstock, and Masters' Mate Murray were both killed by the same shot, and I was wounded in the left arm after firing one or two shots more. I perceived that the *Metacomet* was about to rake me with grape and shrapnel, and that the *Port Royal*, of about the same class, was about to open on me also, and as I did not believe that I was justified in sacrificing more of my men in such an unequal contest, I gave the order, at about half-past nine o'clock, to haul down the colors. My wound was bleeding fast, and I knew if I left the deck for one moment the vessel might be sunk. I had eight killed and seven wounded. My deck was a perfect slaughter-pen when I surrendered. I cannot speak too highly of the officers and crew. Not the least confusion occurred during the action. The wounded were taken below and the men returned instantly to their quarters. The powder division was beautifully attended to; every charge and every shell were sent to the different guns without a single mistake. The enemy acknowledge great loss, in killed and wounded, inflicted on them by the *Selma*."

Lieut. Bennett, having escaped to Mobile after beaching the *Gaines* on Mobile Point and burning her, addressed his report to Secretary Mallory on August 8th, the essential portions of which are the following:

"As soon as the *Tennessee* delivered fire, the *Gaines*, having placed herself next the admiral, commenced at about two thousand yards distance, with her pivot guns, upon the leading wooden ships, supposed to be the *Hartford* and her consort, at about fifty minutes past six, as nearly as I can determine, and continued to deliver a raking fire upon the leading wooden ships until their passage past the fort. She then made circle to prevent too close action, as she was lying nearly in the track of the advancing fleet, and afterwards steered in nearly parallel lines with the enemy at distances gradually diminishing, until she was within at least seven hundred yards, and engaging with her port guns. The enemy now being clear of the fort was enabled to direct attention exclusively to our little squadron.

"Early in the action a shell exploded near the steering wheel, wounding the two men stationed at it, and cutting the wheel-rope. The ship was then steered with the relieving tackles until the after wheel-ropes could be rove. Shortly after this, it was reported that the forward magazine was filled with smoke and thought to be on fire. This, on examination, luckily proved a mistake. An eleven-inch shot had entered the starboard bow, striking the deck above the magazine, had broken it in, and made so much dust that the gunner's mate, serving powder in that magazine, thought it smoke, and believed, from the shock and dust, that a shell had exploded and fired that part of the ship, He reported accordingly. This occasioned a short delay in the serving of powder to the forward division. The firemen of this division, with hose and buckets, went promptly to the spot, under the executive officer, and soon discovered the mistake. About this time the ship was subjected to a very heavy concentrated fire, from the *Hartford*, *Richmond*, and others at short range, as the enemy passed me. Nearly their whole fire seemed, for a time, to be directed at the *Gaines*. The after magazine was now discovered filling with water. I went below to examine it, and found much water had accumulated in it, and was rapidly increasing. Not being aware of any shot having entered, near the water, that part of the ship, and being unable to see any damage, upon inspection from the side, which could have caused such a leak, I directed the executive officer, with the carpenter's mate, to get into a boat and make examination of the counter. He found a shot had broken in the outer planking under the port quarter, about the water-line, and which, from marks, seemed to have glanced below in the direction of the stern-post. This could not be stopped by reason of the impossibility of getting to it, because of the flare of the counter. As this break could not have caused all the water which flowed into the ship, I am of opinion that it was a shell which had caused the break and had probably exploded below the water, under the counter, and had started the timbers near the stern-post. The ship had received a shock during the engagement, which shook her from stem to stern, being much more violent than that of shot passing through. The bilge pumps were immediately worked, but there was no water in the engine-room. Finding the magazine rapidly filling, also the after hold and shell-room, with no water in the engine-room, I caused the after bulk-head of the engine-room to be knocked down so as to allow the flow of water to the bilge pumps. By this time the stern had settled some and the steering became difficult. Under these circumstances I determined to withdraw from action. The enemy's fleet had now passed.

"Finding the ship would sink in a short time, and thinking I might be able to reach the shore, now about two or three miles distant, I withdrew from action, and made the best of my way towards the fort, steering the ship principally with the side wheels, which position I reached without embarrassment from the enemy—thanks to an opportune rain squall which shut me from view—and placed her bow upon the beach within five hundred yards of Fort Morgan, about thirty minutes past nine o'clock.

" I am happy to state there was no confusion or panic under the circumstances of our position, but that every work was done with deliberation and without undue excitement. The ship delivered fire to the enemy at the moment of striking the shore. At the time of beaching, the magazine was nearly filled; I had caused all the powder to be removed to the cabin. The shells were removed as rapidly as possible, but not before many of them might have become submerged. The usefulness of the ship having been destroyed by the enemy, I devoted myself and crew to the preservation of all valuable *materiel*, and landed all the powder, shells, shot, gun equipments, etc., which I gave to the general commanding at Fort Morgan, to whom I thought they might be useful in the expected siege. The crew were then landed, with their bags and blankets, muskets, cutlasses, and small-arm ammunition, and the ship abandoned at twelve o'clock, with her battle-flags flying, and her stern settled as far as it could—about two fathoms. I did not spike the guns because they could be secured by the fort, and could not be taken by the enemy.

"Having thus left my command, it became necessary to devise a retreat for my crew—they were not necessary to the fort, as I was informed when I offered their services. Already I had secured two boats belonging to the *Tennessee*, left by her at anchor, and with four boats of the *Gaines*, one having been destroyed by shot, I left the fort at eight o'clock P. M., and reached Mobile at seven o'clock A. M. on the 6th, with 129 officers and men, small arms, etc., and with six boats passed the enemy's fleet without observation, and reported myself and crew to the senior officer for further service. Not a man was lost by straggling, and I brought up the wounded. The dead were buried on the afternoon of the 5th in the fort's burial-ground. We had only two killed and three wounded.

" Whilst running the gauntlet up the bay, I became apprehensive of capture or of being forced to land and make a march to Mobile. The *Morgan* was being chased by the enemy. As I knew it was her intention to pass near the eastern shore and could see her approach us, I feared she might lead the enemy upon the boats. Under these circumstances I deemed it prudent to drop the signal book into the sea. I did so. The officers and crew of the *Gaines*, for about ten or fifteen minutes, were subjected to a very heavy fire from the enemy at short distance, and, I am proud to say, stood it with great gallantry; there were two exceptional cases only. Without casting censure upon any by my silence, I cannot withhold the expression of my thanks to Lieutenant Payne, Passed Assistant Surgeon Iglehart, Second Assistant Engineer Debois, Gunner Offut, and Paymaster's Clerk Wilson (in charge of the supply of shells to the after division), for their examples of coolness and gallantry under the trying circumstances of this combat against an overwhelming force, and the influence it must have had among the crew, most of whom had never before been in action. Frequent interviews with these officers caused me to regard them with admiration.

"The ship received seventeen shots in her hull and smoke-stack; of these only two can be said to have caused her any distress—that which caused the leak, and the cutting of the wheel-ropes.

"As is usual and proper when a ship is lost, I beg the Department to order a court of inquiry to investigate the causes which led to the abandonment of the *Gaines*."

Under date of August 23d, Secretary Mallory acknowledged the receipt of Lieut. Bennett's report and added :

"Against the overwhelming forces brought to bear upon our little squadron defeat seems to have been inevitable; but the bearing of our officers and men has snatched credit even from defeat; and, mingled with deep regret for the suffering and captivity of the brave old admiral and the loss of our men and ships is the conviction that the triumph of the enemy leaves the honor of our service untarnished.

"The court of inquiry for which you asked is deemed unnecessary. Such a tribunal could but strengthen the public verdict, in which the Department fully concurs, that the loss of your ship resulted from no want of courage, skill or judgment on the part of yourself, your officers or crew."

Commander Harrison was silent concerning his course in running the *Morgan* into Mobile until October 1st, on which date he addressed to Admiral Buchanan a communication which he styles "this letter for the purpose of relating the particular part taken by this vessel in the action with the enemy's fleet." He speaks of engaging the *Hartford* in the earlier moments of the action and of materially injuring her by shells, of which "one in particular, from our forward pivot-gun, must have been considerably destructive (afterwards confirmed by a New Orleans account), as it struck her bulwarks forward and for a time silenced the gun mounted on her forecastle." This fight was continued until the Federal ships had passed Fort Morgan, and of his ensuing movements Commander Harrison wrote :

"The *Gaines* had been disabled and forced out of action and the course we were pursuing was taking us further and further away from the peninsula—which was our only place of refuge in case of being hard pressed—and thus the chances were continually increasing of our being cut off from all retreat by the enemy's gunboats, which I foresaw would soon be thrown off from the fleet in pursuit; so I sheered off to the starboard—the *Selma* doing the same; and, as I anticipated, a double-ender, said to be the *Metacomet*, in a few minutes after, started off from the *Hartford* and soon overhauled and engaged in action with my vessel, whilst the *Selma*, on our bow-port, continued her retreat (unfortunately for her) in a direction to cross the mouth of Bon Secour Bay, and to reach the shore of Mobile Bay. After a short cannonading between us, the *Metacomet* slipped off and steamed rapidly in pursuit of the *Selma*, seeing which, and that my vessel would inevitably be cut off and captured by the two other vessels of the enemy now on the way to join in the pursuit, if I suffered her to engage in a 'stern chase, which is always a long one,' and knowing, furthermore, that with the coal-dust on board, which was my only fuel, I could not possibly make steam enough to overtake two such fast vessels as the *Metacomet* and *Selma*, going off as they were at 'top' speed, I deemed it best to turn the *Morgan's* bow directly into shallow water, and in doing so we grounded on the long stretch of shoals which extends off from the land a little to the eastward of Navy Cove. We backed off, however, in a few minutes, and the *Selma*, having by that time surrendered to the *Metacomet*, and the other chasing gunboats having nearly reached them, I directed my vessel's course toward Fort Morgan, on approaching which we discovered a small Federal gunboat aground on the western side of the seaward channel, about a mile and a half below the fort. I steamed down toward her, and sent a boat, with Lieut. Thomas L. Harrison, to burn her, which was accordingly done. She proved to be the *Phillippi*, disabled by a shot from the fort, and abandoned. Having performed this duty, we returned to the fort and made fast to the wharf.

"A short time before proceeding on this affair of the burning, the *Tennessee*, about four miles distant from us, after a desperate contest with the enemy, had been compelled, by being disabled (as we afterwards learned), to yield to an overwhelming force, and the *Morgan* was now the only vessel left of our little squadron. I felt exceedingly anxious to save her to the Confederacy by 'running the gauntlet' up the bay to Mobile, distant about twenty-five miles, but it seemed so impossible in a noisy, high-pressure steamer, making black smoke, to pass the enemy's fleet unobserved, or to elude the vigilance of his gunboats, which were seen after the action to go up the bay, that I gave up the idea at one time as impracticable, and made preparations to take to the boats, as the *Gaines'* people intended to do when night should come. Upon reconsideration of the matter, however, I determined to make the effort, and having landed three-fourths of my provisions for the use of the garrison, and thrown overboard my coal-dust, for the purpose of picking out all the lumps that could be found, as well as to lighten the vessel, I started at 11 P. M. of a starlight night upon an enterprise which no one on shore or afloat expected to be successful. Not only was this the universal opinion, but all letters and papers from the fort were sent in charge of Lieut. Commanding Bennett in his boats, which were to go up along shore; nor would the two or three town's-people who happened to be down there take passage with us, preferring the longer and safer route by land. But fortune favored us, and although hotly pursued and shelled by the enemy's cruisers for a large portion of the way, we successfully reached the outer obstructions near Mobile at daybreak, having been struck but once slightly. We found the 'gap' through the obstructions, much to our surprise, closed, and it was not until the afternoon that the gate was pulled sufficiently aside to allow us to enter. In the action down the bay we had the good luck to escape with but small damage. We were struck but six times, and only one of that number did any harm, and that entered the port wheel-house and passed out of the starboard, destroying some muskets, boarding-pikes and stanchions in its progress over the deck. Only one person was wounded, and he slightly, by a splinter. I owe this exemption from injury and loss, doubtless, in a great measure, to the excellent position I was enabled to keep generally on the *Hartford's* bow.

"The officers and men, in their conduct, afforded me much satisfaction, particularly as the most of them had never been under fire before; and I am a good deal indebted to my executive officer, Lieut. Thomas L. Harrison, who had especial charge of the after division of guns, owing to an insufficiency of officers, for his hearty co-operation and assistance.

*   *   *   *   *   *   *

"P. S.—Besides the two other double-enders mentioned in the foregoing as having left the fleet shortly after the *Metacomet*, to join in the chase, there was a gunboat also which followed after awhile. It must be understood with regard to the *Selma* that she did not discontinue her retreat to engage the *Metacomet*, but that her fighting was done with her after-gun, fired over her stern, at the approaching vessel, and that she surrendered whilst the *Metacomet* was yet astern or had just got up."

This explanation by Commander Harrison must be contrasted with the criticism made upon him by Admiral Buchanan, who speaks in his official report of Harrison having during the conflict "deserted" the *Selma* while his own vessel was uninjured, and further says that "his (Harrison's) conduct is severely commented upon by the officers of the enemy's fleet, much to the injury of that officer and the navy." The Mobile *Advertiser and Register*, the leading paper of the city, taunted him with having had but one man hurt on his ship. A court of inquiry was, however, subsequently ordered by Secretary Mallory, and its decision exonerated Harrison from blame. [1]

After the surrender and dispersion of Admiral Buchanan's squadron the Federal flotilla commanded by De Kraft, and the monitor *Chickasaw*, bombarded Fort Powell, their fire soon proving so effective that Lieut Col. J. M. Williams, who was in command, telegraphed to Col. Anderson, commandant of Fort Gaines : "Unless I can evacuate, I will be compelled to surrender within forty-eight hours." Anderson replied " Save your garrison when the fort is no longer tenable." Williams had already held out about as long as he thought was possible. He describes in his official report the difficulties under which he labored.

" The front face of the work was nearly completed and in a defensible condition, mounting one 8-inch Columbiad, one 6.4-inch rifle and two 7-inch Brooke guns. The face looking towards Gaines and Little Dauphine Island was half finished. The parapet was nearly complete, but traverses and galleries had only been framed. The rear had only been commenced. Two guns were mounted—one 10-inch Columbiad and one 7-inch Brooke rifled. They were without parapets and exposed from the platform up. During the morning the fort was shelled from five gunboats in the sound at long range. The fort was hit five times, but no particular damage was done. I replied with the four guns bearing on that side, with what effect is not known. About 2:30 P. M. one of the enemy's monitors came up within

[1] CONFEDERATE STATES STEAMER "MORGAN," }
OFF FORT MORGAN, August 4th, 1864. }

MESSRS. CLARK AND FORSYTH, *Editors Advertiser and Register* :

As your recent essays on the navy, and the Mobile squadron in particular, seem to show you to be possessed of a courage quite uncommon as well as an acquaintance with carrying on naval warfare quite marvellous for gentlemen leading peaceable lives like yourselves, I feel particularly anxious to obtain the service of two such valuable recruits, and have therefore, at the suggestion of some of my brother officers, taken the liberty of addressing you this letter for the purpose of requesting the favor of your company on board my vessel when the expected engagement with the enemy's fleet takes place. I promise that you shall have the most conspicuous position on board and the fullest opportunity to display your bravery and naval knowledge. As patriots, you will, I am sure, jump at the opportunity thus offered to serve your country.

Very respectfully,
Your obedient servant,
GEORGE W. HARRISON,
Commander Confederate States Navy.

The Editor of the *Advertiser* replied as follows: A thousand thanks to Capt. George W. Harrison, of the Confederate States steamer *Morgan*, for his polite invitation, and we have to regret that it was only received *yesterday* morning, " the day after the wedding." Had it been in our power to have accepted the invitation, and had we " occupied the most conspicuous position on board," we should still have been in the land of the living to acknowledge his courtesy, for " the most conspicuous position " appears, by the result of the fight, to have been an eminently safe one. Except an engineer, "slightly wounded" by a splinter, "nobody was hurt " on board the *Morgan.*

700 yards of the fort, firing rapidly with shell and grape. I replied from the 7-inch Brooke gun (*razéed*) on the southern angle. It was protected by an unfinished traverse, which, however would not permit it to be depressed sufficiently for *ricochet* firing. The gun was loaded with great difficulty, there being no platform for the gunners in the rear, owing to which, and the delay occasioned by a sponge-head pulling off in the gun, I succeeded in firing but three shots from it while the enemy was in range. One shot struck on the bow, with no apparent effect. The iron-clad's fire made it impossible to man the two guns in the rear and I made no attempt to do so.

"The elevating machine of 10-inch Columbiad was broken by a fragment of shell. A shell entered one of the sally-ports, which are not traversed in the rear, passed entirely through the bomb-proof and buried itself in the opposite wall; fortunately it did not explode. The shells exploding in the face of the work displaced the sand so rapidly that I was convinced that unless the iron-clad was driven off it would explode my magazine and make the bomb-proof chambers untenable in two days at the furthest."

Thus beleaguered, Col. Williams communicated with Col. Anderson, and received the reply advising evacuation. "At the time his dispatch was received," continues Col. Williams, "it was becoming dark. The fleet had not moved up to intercept my communications with Cedar Point; I could not expect to have another opportunity for escape, and I decided promptly that it would be better to save my command and destroy the fort than to allow both to fall into the hands of the enemy, as they certainly would have done in two days."

Soon after dark, on August 5th, he withdrew his garrison of 140 men, left Lieuts. Savage and Jaffers behind long enough for them to spike the guns and blow up the magazine, which they accomplished, crossed to the mainland at low water and marched his troops into Mobile the following morning.

It was an immediate object with Farragut to secure possession of the entrance to Mississippi Sound, in order that troops and supplies might be brought into Mobile Bay from New Orleans, without undertaking to pass the guns of Fort Morgan, and this opening he secured by the Confederate evacuation of Fort Powell. The reduction of Fort Gaines was the next feature on his programme, and on the afternoon of August 6th, he sent in the *Chickasaw* and several gunboats, which opened on it with their heaviest shell at short range. Col. Anderson made no serious reply to this bombardment, and after nightfall he received an invitation by a flag of truce from Farragut to come on board the *Hartford* with his staff. Taking Major Brown with him, he was met on the flag-ship by Farragut and Gen. Gordon Granger, the commander of the Federal land forces. Farragut's intention was at once shown to be to argue him into a surrender, and with this purpose in view he began to expatiate on the hopelessness of attempting to hold the fort. "Gentlemen," he said, "if hard fighting could save that fort, I would advise you to fight to the death; but by all the laws of war, surrounded on three sides by my vessels and on the fourth by the army, you have not even a chance of saving it." Anderson was overcome by this reasoning, without stopping to consider whether his case was as desperate as the Federal admiral made it out to be, and was for capitulation on the spot; but Major Brown was made of sterner fibre, and answered that he, for one, was willing to fight so long as there was a man or gun left. His courage, however, was not shared by Anderson, and becoming convinced that the latter had fully decided to surrender there was nothing left for him to do but agree. They left the ship toward midnight, and on the morning of the 7th, Capt. Drayton and Major Montgomery, representing respectively the Federal navy and army, were admitted to the fort and the surrender took place, the garrison marching out as prisoners of war and being sent to New Orleans. [1]

The loss of Forts Gaines and Powell was, as Gen. Maury reported, a most unfortunate affair for the Confederates, for it enabled Farragut and Granger to concentrate all their efforts upon Fort Morgan, which was speedily invested and besieged by the Federal fleet, now strengthened by the captured *Tennessee* and *Selma*, while Gen. Granger landed 10,000 troops on Mobile Point in its rear, where siege works were thrown up and mounted with shell guns and mortars, to which Farragut contributed four nine-inch guns and their crews from the ships. Farragut's flag-lieutenant, J. Crittenden Watson, and Granger's chief of staff, Major James E. Montgomery, delivered to Gen. Page, on August 8th, a summons to surrender, to which he replied that he would defend his post to the last extremity. He had about 400 effective men to oppose to the 10,000 troops and 2,000 sailors of the enemy, and twenty-six serviceable guns against over 200, but it was his decision that the Federals could not have Fort Morgan without fighting for

[1] The evacuation of Fort Powell and surrender of Gaines gave rise to much amazement and discontent among the Confederates, who had expected Williams and Anderson to defend their positions with the bravery displayed by Buchanan and Page. General Page had instructed Anderson to hold out until the last extremity, and relied upon him to make a strong fight. He had received similar orders from Gen. Dabney H. Maury, commanding the District of the Gulf, who was astounded when the two defences were given up. General Maury touches on the subject in several of his dispatches to Hon. James A. Seddon, Secretary of War. Under date of Aug. 12th, he says : "Lieut. Col. Williams abandoned and blew up his work without having a man injured, nor had any injury been inflicted upon any part of the fort. He had under his bomb-proof fully 30 days' water and two months' provisions. He had hand grenades, revolvers, muskets and howitzers to defend his fort against launches, and eight heavy guns to use against the ships. The fort had just been connected by telegraph with Fort Gaines and Mobile. On the morning of the 5th there were 70 negroes with trenching tools in the fort; the guns on the east face of the work were mounted and in fighting order, but were not yet covered by the parapet, and the men serving them would have

been exposed, as are sailors on an ordinary man-of-war. It is altogether probable that a faithful service of their battery for half an hour would have driven off or sunk the only boat attacking its eastern face, and that it might have been held long enough to compel the fleet to put to sea, or at least to enable Mobile to fully prepare for land attack"

General Maury was still more severe in his strictures upon Anderson's surrender. In the report of August 12th, he writes : "Fort Gaines was garrisoned by six companies, Twenty first Alabama regiment, two companies First Alabama battalion, forty Pelham cadets, 120 reserves and about 40 marines—in all about 600 good troops. The fort was well supplied for six months. The three ten-inch guns were dismounted during the bombardment (by the carelessness of cannoneers, but were subsequently remounted) ; twenty guns remained in good order. The fort was uninjured and could have long withstood attack."

In his report of September 1st Gen. Maury returned to the subject, saying :

"On the evening of August 3rd, the enemy had landed a force on Dauphine Island in order to besiege and reduce Fort Gaines. Gen. Page called for reinforcements to enable him to attack this force, which at time was supposed to be

it, and he gave them a long and stubborn contest. For two weeks preceding the 22d of August they were busy in advancing their lines on the land side, and on the morning of that day they began a bombardment as furious as soldier or sailor ever assisted in. Their heavy guns on Mobile Point were only distant some 250 yards from the fort, and the cannoneers were perfectly sheltered by the high and thick embankments of sand behind which they fought. The ships took their positions at leisure on the north, south and west faces of the fort, the iron-clads lying the closest in and delivering an incessant fire. In twelve hours 3,000 shells were thrown into the fort. Gen. Page replied to this terrific bombardment with all the vigor of which his little force of men and guns was capable, but about nine o'clock at night a shell set fire to the citadel of the fort, and in the renewed impulse of the assault the walls were breached repeatedly and nearly all his best pieces of ordnance disabled. The heroism with which his men kept up the conflict during the weary hours of that fateful night cannot be exaggerated. While some served the few guns still capable of being fired, others labored to extinguish the flames, which were perilously near to the magazines in which an immense quantity of powder was stored; parties were detailed to spike or destroy the dismounted guns, and other squads threw into the cisterns all the powder not required for immediate use. In each sort of work they were under constant exposure to the rain of shot and shell that with the burning citadel lit up the sky, but not a man flinched from his duty.

The flames were extinguished, but soon after dawn of the 23d the citadel was again set on fire and Gen. Page displayed from his scarred and shattered battlements a white flag. He arranged with Capt. Drayton and Gen. Granger the surrender of the fort and garrison, with all the honors of war, at two o'clock P. M., and at that hour the colors which he had fought

---

small. Every available man was sent from Mobile to Fort Gaines. The entrance of the fleet into the bay prevented their return to the city. They were too few to make the proposed attack, but were too many for the proper siege garrison of Fort Gaines, and for the unexplained precipitate surrender made by Col. Anderson of a work which, faithfully defended, could have held the enemy before it at least as long as Fort Morgan. After firing a few shots, Col. Anderson, without authority, entered into negotiations with the enemy, and on the 7th inst., the Confederate flag was lowered and the ensign of the enemy raised and saluted. Gen. Page reports that he visited Fort Gaines and used every proper means to prevent its surrender. He could not with propriety assume command at Fort Gaines, and remain absent from his more important command at Fort Morgan. He ordered Col. Anderson to be relieved from command, and forbade any surrender unless the Federals should return with Col. Anderson to the fort. Nothing more is known of this unfortunate affair."

Col. Anderson wrote from the military prison at New Orleans, on August 18th, a letter to his wife, in which he said that all his officers and men saw that they were cut off and surrounded by an overwhelming force, and expressed themselves decidedly in favor of surrender. He denied that he had acted contrary to the express orders of General Page, and contended that the latter had only instructed him to do the best he could. He gave as a reason for not answering Page's signal that negotiations were then pending under a flag of truce and he had no right to communicate with him. "I expected," he wrote, "to be ostracized, and as I could not maintain the etiquette of the military code without exhibiting too much selfishness, nothing was left me but to consult the great natural and moral law, which prompted me to do exactly as I did. I might have got out of the scrape by demanding to be relieved, but I thought that would only make matters worse; for had any other officer, even General Page himself, attemped to fight that fort another hour, I feel satisfied that there would have been mutiny and a really disgraceful surrender at last."

for until the last chance of beating off the enemy had vanished gave place to the Federal ensign.[1]

Gen. Page made several reports to Gen. Maury upon the participation of Fort Morgan in the events occurring between the 5th and 23d of August. In the report relating to the passage of the fort by the Federal fleet he says :

"The spirit displayed by this garrison was fine, the guns admirably served, and all did their duty nobly; though subjected to a fire which for the time was probably as severe as any known in the annals of this war, our casualties were slight. Four of the enemy's fleet turned from the fire they would have to encounter in passing, and assisted other vessels in an enfilading fire from the gulf side during the action. As to the damage inflicted on those which succeeded in passing I cannot speak definitely; shot after shot was distinctly seen to enter the wooden ships; but, as was evident, their machinery being protected by chains, no vital blow could be given them there. Their loss in men, I am assured, was very great. Four hundred and ninety-one projectiles were delivered from this fort during the passage of the fleet. Our naval forces under Admiral Buchanan fought most gallantly, against odds before unknown to history."

The report of Gen. Page of August 30th sets out in full the defence of Fort Morgan, and is therefore appended:

"After the reduction of Gaines I felt confident that the whole naval and land force of the enemy would be brought against Morgan, and was assiduous in preparing my fort for as good a defence as possible. For the state of the work I beg leave to refer you to Chief Engineer Sheliha's letter to Headquarters' Department, of July 9th, from which time no material changes or addition was made; and further to state, that it had been demonstrated by the fire from the enemy that the *enciente* of the fort (in which was its main strength) protected the scarp of the main wall only about one-half its height from curvated shot; and it was now in the power

---

[1] Official correspondence relating to the capitulation of Fort Morgan:

THE CAPITULATION.

FORT MORGAN, August 23d, 1864.
Rear Admiral D. G. FARRAGUT, *U. S. N., Major General* GORDON GRANGER, *U. S. A., Commanding, etc.*

GENTLEMEN: The further sacrifice of life being unnecessary, my sick and wounded suffering and exposed, humanity demands that I ask for terms of capitulation. Very respectfully,
R. L. PAGE, *Brig. Gen. C. S. A.*

HEADQUARTERS UNITED STATES FORCES, }
MOBILE BAY, August 23d, 1864. }
I have notified Admiral Farragut of your desire to capitulate. Until his arrival hostilities will be suspended, when your proposal will be duly considered.
Respectfully your obedient servant,
G. GRANGER, *Major Gen. U. S. A. Com'dg.*
To Brig. Gen. R. L. PAGE, *Com'dg at Fort Morgan.*

THE TERMS OFFERED.

GENERAL : In reply to your communication of this date, received by Captain Taylor, asking for terms of capitulation, we have to say that the only terms we can make are:
First. The unconditional surrender of yourself and the garrison of Fort Morgan, with all of the public property within its limits, and in the same condition that it is now.
Second. The treatment which is in conformity with the custom of the most civilized nations towards prisoners-of-war.

Third. Private property, with the exception of arms, will be respected.
Very respectfully, your obedient servant,
P. DRAYTON, *Captain U. S. N.,*
On the part of Admiral FARRAGUT, Commanding Naval Forces.
R. ARNOLD, *Brig. Gen. U. S. A.,*
On the part of General GRANGER, Commanding United States Forces.

THE ACCEPTANCE.

FORT MORGAN, August 23d, 1864.
Captain P. DRAYTON, *U. S. N., and Brig. Gen.* R. ARNOLD, *U. S. A., acting on the part, respectively, of Admiral* FARRAGUT *and General* GRANGER.
GENTLEMEN: Your conditions in the communication of to-day are accepted, but I have still to request that the terms asked with regard to my sick be granted and inserted in the capitulation. I will be prepared to surrender at two o'clock, and to embark as soon as possible.
Respectfully, etc.,
R. L. PAGE, *Brig. Gen. C. S. A.*

Official report of Admiral Farragut:
FLAG-SHIP "HARTFORD," }
MOBILE BAY, August 23d, 1864. }
Hon. GIDEON WELLES, *Secretary of the Navy*
SIR : I have the honor to inform the Department that on the evening of the 21st instant General Granger informed me that his batteries would be ready to open on Fort Morgan at daylight the next morning. I accordingly gave

588 THE CONFEDERATE STATES NAVY.

of the enemy to open fire from every point of the compass, and consequently none of the casemates, without heavy traverses in their front, would be safe; that it was manifest, by this concentration of fire, my heavy guns could be dismounted; and my making a protracted resistance depended on my ability to protect my men from the heavy fire and hold the fort from the flank casemates against an assault. With these views, I employed my men day and night, most of the time under fire, in erecting traverses to protect my guns on the main wall as long as possible, to render the casemates selected for the sick and wounded secure, and to provide safe quarters for themselves in their rest from the arduous duties they would have to endure. It was necessary also to put a large traverse at the sally-port, which was entirely exposed.

' Thus, absolutely to prevent the probability of Fort Morgan's being reduced at the first test and onset by the heavy batteries of the enemy it was necessary for my limited garrison (of some 400 effective) to labor to effect a work equal almost in extent to building a new fort.

"On early morning of the 9th the enemy proceeded with monitors and transports, and disembarked troops at Navy Cove, commencing at once their first work of investment by land.

"The 'new redoubt' (2,700 yards from the fort) from which the guns had been withdrawn, and the work formerly known as 'Battery Bragg,' were destroyed as far as possible by burning the wood-work. The buildings around the fort, hospitals, quarters, stables, etc., were also at the same time fired and cleared away as much as possible.

"Two monitors, three sloops-of-war and several gunboats engaged the fort for two or three hours—the wooden vessels at rather long range —with no material damage apparent to either side. Soon thereafter a flag of truce was reported from the fleet, and communicated to this effect:

"*Brigadier Gen.* R. L. PAGE, *Commanding Fort Morgan.*

"SIR : To prevent the unnecessary sacrifice of human life which must follow the opening of our batteries, we demand the unconditional surrender of Fort Morgan and its dependencies.

" We are, very respectfully, your obedient servants,

"D. G. FARRAGUT, *Rear Admiral.*
" GORDON GRANGER, *Major Gen.*"

To which my reply said :

" *Rear Admiral* D. G. FARRAGUT,
" *Major Gen.* GORDON GRANGER,

"SIRS : I am prepared to sacrifice life, and will only surrender when I have no means of defence. I do not understand that while being communicated with under flag of truce, the *Tennessee* should be towed within range of my guns.

" Respectfully, etc.,

"R. L. PAGE, *Brigadier Gen. C. S. A.*"

" From this time to the 15th, day and night, we were engaged by the fleet, sometimes in a brisk fight of several hours' duration, at others in a desultory firing, without any very effective damage being done to our fort,

directions for the monitors and the vessels with suitable guns to move up and be ready to open upon it with the army.

I had previously landed four 9-inch guns and placed them in battery under the command of Lieutenant H. B. Tyson, of the *Hartford*, and manned them with crews taken from the *Hartford*, *Brooklyn*, *Richmond* and *Lackawanna*, in conjunction with the batteries of the army. At daylight, on the 22d, the bombardment began from the shore batteries, the monitors and ships inside the bar and outside, and a more magnificent fire I think has rarely been kept up for twenty-four hours.

At 8:30 P. M. the citadel took fire, and the general ordered the near batteries to redouble

their fire. At 6 this morning an explosion took place in the fort, and at 6:30 the white flag was displayed on the fort. I immediately sent Fleet Captain Drayton to meet General Granger to arrange the terms for the surrender of the fort. These were, that the fort, its garrison, and all public property should be surrendered unconditionally, at 2 o'clock to-day, to the army and navy forces of the United States.

These terms were agreed to by Brigadier General Richard L. Page, formerly a commander in the navy.

I shall send the garrison, officers and men, at once to New Orleans.

Very respectfully, your obedient servant,
D. G. FARRAGUT, *Rear Admiral.*

save a demonstration of the fact that our brick walls were easily pene-
trable to the heavy missiles of the enemy, and that a systematic, concentrated fire would soon breach them. On the 15th, three of the fifteen-
inch shells striking the right flank face of Bastion No. 4 breached the
wall, and disabled the howitzers therein.

"During this time a pretty continuous fire was kept up on the fort
from the Parrott guns in several batteries erected by the enemy; and in
the intervals of serving the guns my men were engaged in the work before mentioned, for their protection, in the anticipation of a vigorous
bombardment. The sharp-shooters in our front had become very numerous and active, and with these encircling us on the land, and the fire delivered from the fleet on the flanks, our guns had to be served with much
care and under great difficulty.

" The land forces of the enemy completed their first approach on the
9th and 10th across the peninsula; the second through the 11th and 12th;
the third, a bayou, near and parallel to gulf shore, 13th and 14th; their
first parallel 500 and 700 yards distant, 15th, 16th, 17th, 18th, 19th; approaches on 20th and 21st to within 200 yards of our glacis.

"Such guns as I could use on this force I annoyed them with, especially at night, and to the extent possible retarded their work; though
nothing very effect've could be accomplished in this way, as their working parties were a concealed in the sand hills, and when our fire was
concentrated on al y one point they would merely, unseen, remove to
some other.

" To the morning of the 22d, our efforts were with the heavy guns
that bore on them to interfere with the investing approaches of the enemy. The topography of our front, however, was to their advantage,
and they made a steady advance, covering it somewhat with an irregular
fire from the batteries already in position, and lining their works already
completed with sharp-shooters to pick off our gunners.

" At daylight the fleet was reported moving up to encircle us, and
shortly its batteries (in conjunction with those on land which numbered
thirty-six guns and mortars) opened a furious fire, which came from
almost every point of the compass, and continued unabated throughout
the day, culminating in increased force at sundown ; after which the
heavy calibres and mortars kept it up during the night. This fire disabled
all the heavy guns save two, which did not bear on the land approach,
partially breached the walls in several places, and cut up the fort to such
an extent as to make the whole work a mere mass of *debris*. Their mortar
practice was accurate.

"Apprehensive, from the great effect already had on the walls, that
my magazines, containing now 80,000 pounds, were in danger in consequence of the continuation of the bombardment in the night, with great
care and under continuous fire I had the powder brought out and flooded.
The guns in the water and lunette batteries, now unserviceable and in
jeopardy from the enemy, I ordered spiked and otherwise effectually
damaged; and all the guns on the main rampart dismounted by the fire
from the enemy were likewise destroyed, as of no further avail in defence.
Early in the night the wood-work of the citadel was fired by the mortar
shells and burned furiously for some hours; the enemy during the conflagration pouring in his missiles with increased vigor. With great efforts
the fire was arrested and prevented from extending around near the magazines, which would have been in immediate danger of explosion. In the
gallant endeavor to prevent this disaster, I would especially mention
privates Murphy, Bembough and Stevens, First Tennessee regiment, for
great courage and daring displayed.

" At daylight on the 23d (all my powder had been destroyed), the
citadel was again set on fire in several places by shells and burned until
it was consumed.

" The report made to me now was that of the casemates which had
been rendered as safe as possible for the men, some had been breached,

others partially (Capts. Johnston, Fisher and Hughes informed me that another shot on them would bring down the walls of their company quarters), so that a resumption of the severe fire from the enemy would in all likelihood inflict great loss of life, there being no bomb-proof in the fort. The enemy's approach was very near the glacis. My guns and powder had all been destroyed; my 'means of defence gone'; the citadel, nearly the entire quartermaster's stores, and a portion of the commissariat burnt by the enemy's shells. It was evident the fort could hold out but a few hours longer under a renewed bombardment. The only question was, hold it for this time, gain in the *eclat*, and sustain the loss of life from the falling of the walls, or save life and capitulate?

"I capitulated to the enemy at two o'clock P. M., and though they refused to insert it in the terms there was a full understanding, and I was assured that my sick and wounded should be sent at once to Mobile by a flag of truce. This was not done. Considering the great exposure to which the men were subjected, and the fact that shells frequently burst among them when in the casemates, the casualties were unusually small. The garrison in this severe test behaved well, and I would make little distinction. Capt. J. Gallimard, engineer in charge, performed his duties to my satisfaction. To the officers of the First Alabama battalion artillery, Major J. T. Gee commanding, and of Capt. Cothran's company, Twenty-first Alabama, I give my thanks for their promptness and alacrity in every duty; and to Col. A. J. Jackson, commanding the First Tennessee, and Capts. Johnston and Fisher and their brave companies of that regiment, for very efficient service. To Capt. C. H. Smith, A. A. G., and Capt. R. T. Thom, A. I. G., for prompt performance of all their duties, I am under obligations; and to my aide-de-camp, Lieut. J. C. Taylor, I owe much for his promptness and energy and for his active and gallant assistance throughout the operations." [1]

Farragut experienced much chagrin when he found that Gen. Page had left him nothing but the battered walls of Fort Morgan, the soaked powder and the disabled guns; and he vented his disappointment in a report, in which he accused the Confederate commander of destroying the armament and ammunition of the fort after displaying the white flag. This charge of a flagrant violation of the laws of civilized warfare was totally unfounded. The report of Gen. Page and the statements of his subordinate officers afford unimpeachable evidence that he destroyed the property of the Confederate government during the night of August 22d and 23d, previous

[1] As soon as Fort Morgan had surrendered Farragut sent out boats to rake the channel for torpedoes. Twenty-one were taken up and one exploded while being handled by the Federal seamen, killing one man and wounding thirteen, of whom four subsequently died from their injuries. There are sound reasons for the belief entertained by Confederate officers that a Federal spy had penetrated within their lines, and informed Federal commanders of their movements and of the location of torpedoes. Lieut. G. A. Arnold, Assistant Enrolling Officer at Mobile in March, 1865, relates that there was frequently seen about Confederate headquarters at that time a soldier known as Sergeant Burke, of the Army of East Tennessee, whose ostensible business was to gather up all the men of that army absent without leave and forward them to their commands. Burke appeared to be very zealous in the Confederate cause, but the day after the surrender Arnold was approached near Canby's headquarters by a man in Federal uniform who called him by name and whom he recognized as Burke. "I looked at him with surprise," Arnold says, "and did not recognize him until he said : 'Lieutenant, don't you know me ?' I then saw that it was Sergeant Burke, and remarked : 'What does this mean, this uniform.' He replied : 'You now know what I have been at the past few weeks.' 'Yes,' I said, 'a spy.' He smiled, and said : 'Lieutenant, if you want protection or aid you will get it by reporting to General Canby. I made a list of deserving citizens for his use, and your name heads the list. Good-bye.' I have not seen Burke since, nor have I any knowledge of what became of him. Burke was a sharp, intelligent American Irishman, and I now have reason to believe that he furnished Farragut with a great deal of valuable information." A Southern correspondent writing from Farragut's fleet at the time, said that the man who laid the torpedoes in Mobile channel had been employed to take them up.

to making any proposition to surrender; and there is not a scintilla of evidence to support the assertion made by Farragut, and reiterated by Admiral Porter in "The Naval History of the Civil War," that any part of the destruction took place after he had opened negotiations for capitulation. It was entirely proper for him to cripple the fort prior to those negotiations, and in so doing he made the last demonstration that was permitted him of his fidelity to his government, for he was thenceforward held a prisoner until the close of the war. But if there were any doubt about the matter, it would be removed by the decision of the Federal Council of War, convened at New Orleans, September 1st, and consisting of Major Gen. S. A. Hurlbut, Brig. Gen. James Totten, and Lieut. Commander S. R. Franklin, U. S. N., which sat for two weeks examining the charges against Gen. Page and reported that no public property was destroyed after the white flag was hoisted on the glacis of Fort Morgan. [1]

With Forts Morgan, Gaines and Powell in their hands the Federals had absolute control of Mobile Bay, but they made no attempt for the time being to move against the city itself, which was defended by an inner line of works, the principal of which was Spanish Fort, on the eastern bank of the Apalachee River. [2] Other defences were Fort Blake and Batteries Huger, Tracy, McIntosh and Gladden, the Tower battery, the Alexis battery on Choctaw Point, and a line of piles and torpedoes across the channel. It was anticipated that after the surrender of Fort Morgan the Federals would push on to the city, and Gen. Maury took command there in person

---

[1] While Gen. Page was a prisoner in Fort Lafayette, in December 1864, he addressed the following to the editor of the New York *Tribune*:

"SIR : In your issue of yesterday was the following paragraph : 'The rebel General Page, captured near Fort Morgan, applied by letter lately to his old classmate, Commodore Rodgers, for assistance in getting exchanged.' The reply was: 'I can do nothing for you. You neither defended your post like a man, nor surrendered like an officer.'

"It does me great injustice; and though a prisoner of war, in the hands of your government, I do not hesitate so far to presume on your sense of right as to solicit a correction of the misstatements involved in the aforesaid paragraph. The facts of the case are just these: Some time ago, while ill and suffering, I sent a private note to Commodore John Rodgers, an old comrade and former friend, requesting him, if he thought proper, to second an application I had addressed to the Union authorities for a parole or a transfer to a warmer climate (which transfer I may add in parenthesis, the surgeon of the post had stated to be essential to my health). To this communication I have never received any reply (written nor verbal), nor has any ever passed through the official channel of correspondence with the inmates of this prison. As to whether the fort, of which I had command, was properly fought and defended, this is a question on which it becomes not me to speak. My own government, and they with whom I shared the perils of the fight, are alone

competent to pronounce on the matter. I am content to abide their opinion. Immediately after the capitulation of Fort Morgan, certain false and injurious reports were circulated, imputing some irregularity and unfairness on my part in the surrender of the work. By a council of war, ordered by Gen. Canby, and composed of officers of the Federal army and navy, I was, after a most searching and protracted investigation, promptly and entirely acquitted of all and every of these imputations.' The opinion and findings of this council were officially published in the New Orleans papers; and it would have been agreeable to my desire to have had the whole 'proceedings' laid before the public, which I yet hope at some future day may be done.

"Your obedient servant,
"R. L. PAGE,
"*Brig. Gen., C. S. army.*
"FORT LAFAYETTE, Dec. 27th, 1864."

[2] The streams entering into the bay of Mobile, near the city, virtually form a delta system. The Mobile River is formed by the confluence of the Alabama and Tombigbee, and has below the city a branch called the Spanish River. The Tensaw River branches off from the Alabama thirty miles above the city, and empties into the bay through two mouths, the Tensaw and the Blakely. The Tensaw and Spanish Rivers come together about a mile from the city, so that there is shoal water navigation between all these streams without entering the bay.

to superintend the defence. He brought together a force of about 6,000 men, only 1,000 of whom had ever been under fire. Brig. Gen. Higgins, who was in command of the harbor defences, issued an order forbidding any officer commanding any fort or battery in and around Mobile to hold any communication, by flag of truce or otherwise, with the land or naval forces of the enemy without authority from headquarters. This prohibition was designed to prevent the examples of Williams and Anderson from being imitated, and Gen. Higgins added that "the forts and batteries of this command must and shall be held to the last extremity."

The city probably had more women and children in it than at any time since the war began, but they and the non-combatants generally were removed in large numbers to the interior towns, and the planters along the Tombigbee and Alabama valleys were asked to send in all the provisions they could spare, and to allow their negro slaves to work upon the fortifications. All the male residents capable of bearing arms were organized into military companies, and the city was placed under martial law. The people were still full of confidence in the future, and when the theatre was opened in the first week of September numerous audiences attended upon the dramatic performances.

Commodore Ebenezer Farrand, who had been in charge of the naval station at Selma, was assigned to the naval command at Mobile in place of Admiral Buchanan, and Major Gen. Frank Gardner was placed in command of the defences, and Major Gen. J. M. Withers in command of all the reserves of Alabama. Col. A. S. Herron was charged with the duty of organizing the Louisianians and the battalion of employes, and Col. T. J. Judge with that of organizing all other troops that might respond to his call.

The squadron left to Farrand was only nominally formidable. It consisted of the *Tuscaloosa, Huntsville, Nashville, Morgan* and *Baltic.* The two first-named were called iron-clads, and were intended to be vessels of the same general plan as the *Tennessee,* although smaller; but they were only partly armored and their engines were still more defective than that of their famous prototype, while neither had a full complement of guns. The obstacles that impeded the Confederate government in the construction and equipment of men-of-war were daily growing in magnitude, and it was sadly acknowledged to be out of the question to complete these two ships. The *Nashville* was a side-wheel steamer, with some little iron-plating upon her, the *Morgan* was Commander Harrison's old ship and the *Baltic* was a small river boat. There were at the Mobile wharves two uncompleted gunboats, on which work never progressed beyond their hulls.

Farragut's lighter vessels and a couple of monitors passed over Dog River Bar within a week after the 5th of August, and on the 15th reconnoitred around the mouth of Mobile River, firing a few shots at the *Tuscaloosa* and *Huntsville*, which were replied to by the *Morgan*. In the second week of September he sent an expedition up Fish River, on the eastern side of Mobile Bay, which destroyed the lumber-mills, salt works, etc., in that vicinity, before it was driven off by Col. Murray at the head of a small force of Confederates with the loss of one officer and two men killed.

These were the last operations around Mobile for six months. The winter was spent in idleness by both Federals and Confederates, but with the opening of spring the former were enabled to spare from other fields of campaign any number of troops and ships for the final assault upon Mobile. Charleston and Fort Fisher had succumbed to the power of the Federal government and over Mobile alone of all the great ports still floated the flag of the Confederacy. Rear Admiral Henry K. Thatcher had succeeded Farragut in the command of the Federal fleet off the city and had had two more monitors and several gunboats added to his strength, while Gen. E. R. S. Canby, in command of the Federal army of the West Mississippi, was given 50,000 troops with which to undertake the investment of Mobile by land.

On March 21st, 1865, the movement against Mobile by land and water was begun, it being first directed against Spanish Fort on the east side of Tensaw River, the siege of which lasted until April 8th, when the garrison was bombarded and starved into evacuating it. Gen. Maury, in an account written within the past few years, says:

"The defence of Spanish Fort was the last death-grapple of the veterans of the Confederate and Federal armies. They brought to it the experience of four years of incessant conflict, and in the attack and defence of that place demonstrated every offensive and defensive art then known to war. It is not too much to say that no position was ever held by Confederate troops with greater hardihood and tenacity, nor evacuated more skilfully after every hope of further defence had gone."

Spanish Fort was garrisoned by 2,100 men and Fort Blakely, five miles above, by 2,600. Nearly 30,000 Federal troops were engaged in the siege of the former, and when it was evacuated they were joined by some 12,000 more, and the whole force went on to the attack on Blakely, which was abandoned on April 11th. Gen. Maury had most ingeniously arranged for the safety of these garrisons, when their positions should become untenable, by constructing bridges across the marshes and streams between them and deep water, so that when the abandonment was made necessary the troops were marched by this route to where steamers were held in readiness to transport them to Mobile.

The Confederate gunboats were able to render but little service in these operations on the eastern side of the Mobile

waters, but they kept along the shore and did some occasional
execution upon the intrenched lines of the enemy. In this
work the *Morgan* was conspicuous. The Federal craft were
very actively employed, and no less than eight of them were
sunk by torpedoes. On March 28th, the monitors *Winnebago*,
Osage, Kickapoo, Chickasaw, and *Milwaukee*, and the gunboat
Octorara steamed toward Spanish Fort to shell a Confederate
transport, and as they were returning to the fleet the *Milwaukee* struck a torpedo, and in three minutes was on the bottom
in ten feet depth of water. All her people escaped to the other
vessels. She was one of the largest and strongest of the Federal iron-clads, having two turrets and two fifteen-inch and
two eleven-inch guns. The next day the deadly effectiveness
of the Confederate torpedo service was proved upon the *Osage*,
a turtle-back iron-clad, which was sunk on the edge of the
channel. Four of her crew were instantly killed, and six
wounded, of whom two subsequently died. The destruction
of these heavy ships caused much exultation among the Confederates, which found expression in salutes from Spanish
Fort and the guns of the *Nashville*. To the Federals the two
disasters, one following the other so closely, were depressing.
As they had swept the channel for torpedoes regularly, and
had taken up 120 within a few days previously, they concluded
that those which had wrecked the *Milwaukee* and *Osage* were
floating instruments of destruction let loose from the rear of
the Confederate obstructions to sweep down with the tide, and
with this fresh peril confronting them they doubled their vigilance, a detail of boats being constantly on duty as torpedo
searchers. Notwithstanding these precautions, however, the
iron-clad *Rodolph* was sunk on April 1st, while towing a scow
with apparatus for raising the *Milwaukee*, and four of her
crew were killed and eleven wounded. Subsequent to the
surrender of Mobile, the gunboats *Ida, Sciota* and *Althea*, a
launch of the monitor *Cincinnati*, and a second launch were
blown up by torpedoes while on search duty, their combined
losses amounting to fourteen killed and wounded. Thus, beginning with the destruction of the *Tecumseh*, the Confederate
torpedo service in the Mobile waters made the remarkable
record of sinking nine vessels, large and small, of the enemy,
and of killing 144 men and wounding twenty-five in addition
to the five killed and eight wounded in handling the torpedoes
dredged from the channel just subsequent to the capture of Fort
Morgan. Nowhere else in the Confederate ports did this service
accomplish such valuable results, and if the officers in charge
of it had possessed the material for manufacturing torpedoes,
primers and fuses that in every instance would have resisted
the action of the water, the calamities to the Federal ships
must necessarily have been much greater than they were.

Batteries Huger and Tracy had been evacuated on the
same day as Blakely (April 11th), and on the 12th Admiral

Thatcher convoyed with his gunboats 8,000 troops under command of Gen. Granger to the front of Mobile, and sent in a demand for the immediate and unconditional surrender of the city. "The city," wrote Mayor R. H. Slough in reply, "has been evacuated by the military authorities, and its municipal authority is now within my control. Your demand has been granted, and I trust, for the sake of humanity, all the safeguards which we can throw around our people will be secured to them."

When the fall of the city was seen to be inevitable, Commodore Farrand sunk the unfinished iron-clads *Huntsville* and *Tuscaloosa* in the main channel of Mobile River, but by moving through the Blakely and Tensaw the Federal gunboats avoided all the obstructions, and anchored with their guns bearing upon the city. With the remainder of his squadron, some river steamers, and several blockade-runners that had been shut up at Mobile after the port was sealed, Farrand started up the Alabama River, hoping to reach Selma, where a further defence might have been made; but that city, and the naval station, had been surrendered already to the Federal land forces, and on April 27th was occupied by a Federal squadron commanded by Lieut. Commander Harmony and an army under command of Major Gen. Steele despatched from Mobile. Commodore Farrand was now closely blockaded in the Tombigbee River, and on the night of May 4th he made to Admiral Thatcher written propositions for surrender, and asked for a conference with the latter at which terms could be settled upon. The two commanders met at Citronelle, a point about twenty-five miles above Mobile, and Farrand's proposals were accepted on the same basis as granted by Gen. Grant to Gen. Lee, Gen. Sherman to Gen. Johnson, and Gen. Canby to Gen. Richard Taylor, which last surrender was made at the same place and time. The memorandum of surrender was as follows:

"Memorandum of the conditions of the surrender of the Confederate naval forces serving under the command of Commodore Ebenezer Farrand in the waters of the State of Alabama, made at Sidney, Alabama, May 4th, 1865.

"*First:* The officers and men to be paroled until duly exchanged, or otherwise released from the obligations of their parole, by the authority of the government of the United States. Duplicate rolls of all officers and men surrendered to be made, one copy to be delivered to the officer appointed by Acting Rear Admiral H. K. Thatcher, and the other retained by the officer appointed by Commodore E. Farrand; officers giving their individual paroles, and commanders of vessels signing a like parole for the men of their respective commands.

"*Second:* All vessels of war, their guns and equipments, all small-arms, and ammunition and stores on board the said vessels, to be delivered over to the officer appointed for that purpose by Acting Rear Admiral Thatcher. Duplicate inventories of the property surrendered to be prepared; one copy to be retained by the officer delivering, and the other by the officer receiving it, for our information.

"*Third:* The officers and men paroled under this agreement will be allowed to return to their homes, with the assurance that they will not be disturbed by the authorities of the United States so long as they continue to observe the condition of their paroles and the laws in force where they reside, except that persons residents of northern States will not be allowed to return without special permission.

"*Fourth:* The surrender of property will not include the side-arms or private baggage of officers.

"*Fifth:* The time and place of surrender will be fixed by us, respectively, and will be carried out by officers appointed by us.

"*Sixth:* After the surrender, transportation and subsistence to be furnished by Acting Rear Admiral H. K. Thatcher for officers and men to the nearest practicable point to their respective homes.

" H. K. THATCHER,
Acting Rear Admiral U. S. N., Commanding West Gulf Squadron.
" E. FARRAND,
Flag Officer, Commanding C. S. Naval Forces in waters of Alabama."

In accordance with these stipulations Lieut. Commanding Julius Myers, the officer designated by Commodore Farrand, on May 10th surrendered to Fleet Capt. Edward Simpson, acting for Admiral Thatcher, at Nanna Hubba Bluff, on the Tombigbee River, the *Nashville*, the *Morgan*, the *Baltic*, the *Black Diamond* and the *Southern Republic*, the last-named being an unarmed steamer on which the stores from the naval station at Mobile had been brought up the river under charge of Lieut. Myers. Capt. Simpson's report states he paroled 112 officers, 285 enlisted men and 24 marines. The paroles and signatures were as follows :

"We, the undersigned, prisoners of war belonging to the Confederate naval forces serving under the command of Commodore Ebenezer Farrand, in the waters of the State of Alabama, this day surrendered by Commodore Ebenezer Farrand to Acting Rear Admiral Henry K. Thatcher, United States navy, commanding the West Gulf squadron, do hereby give our solemn parole of honor that we will not hereafter serve in the navy of the Confederate States, or in any military capacity whatever, against the United States of America, or render aid to the enemies of the latter, until properly exchanged in such manner as shall be mutually approved by the respective authorities.

"Done at Nanna Hubba Bluff, on the Tombigbee River, Alabama, this tenth day of May, eighteen hundred and sixty-five."

L. Rosseau, Captain.
Ebenezer Farrand, Flag-Officer.
Charles W. Hays, Lieutenant.
Julius Myers, Lieutenant.
C. P. McGary, Lieutenant.
Charles E. Yeatman, Lieutenant.
F. Watlington, Lieutenant.
E. G. Booth, Ass't Surgeon.
N. E. Edwards, Ass't Surgeon.
Wm. W. J. Wells, Paymaster.
Robert C. Powell, Ass't Surgeon.
Wm. Fisk, Jr., Chief Engineer.
Albert P. Hulse, Secretary.
P. U. Murphey, Lieutenant.
J. E. Armour, Paymaster.
Lewis W. Munro, Surgeon.
E. Lloyd Winder, Lieutenant.
A. L. Myers, Master.

F. B. Dornin, Passed Midshipman.
J. S. Wooddell, Clerk.
John H. Pippen, Clerk.
John E. O'Connell, 2d Ass't Engineer.
W. B. Patterson, 3d Ass't Engineer.
Edward Cairy, Ass't Surgeon.
Jos. Preble, Acting Master.
G. W. Turner, Acting Master's Mate.
W. A. Gardner, 3d Ass't Engineer.
G. E. Courtin, Paymaster's Clerk.
Edward P. Herssend.
Jos. L. Wilson, Paymaster's Clerk.
Jas. H. Marsh, Navy-Yard Clerk.
Benjamin G. Allen, Gunner
J. R. Shackett, Pilot.
G. H. Lindenberger, Mechanic.
W. D. Crawford.
J.H.Hunt, A.M.M., Com'g St'r *Baltic*.

D. R. Lindsay, Naval Storekeeper.
Thos. G. Lang, 3d Ass't Engineer.
D. B. Conrad, Fleet Surgeon.
Geo. H. Oneal, Ass't Paymaster.
J. M. Pearl, Ass't Paymaster
J. R. Jordan, 1st Ass't Engineer.
S. S. Herrick, Ass't Surgeon.
Howard Quigley, 1st Ass't Engineer.
H. S. Smith, Gunner.
C. H. Mallery, Gunner.
J. M. Smith, Paymaster's Clerk.
George Newton, Sailmaker
Thos. L. Harrison, Lieutenant.
O. S. Iglehart, Passed Ass't Surg.
D. G. Raney, Jr., 1st Lieut. M. C.
W. G. Craig, Master P. N. C. S.
Jos. R. DeMahy, Master P. N. C. S.
M. M. Seay, Ass't Pay'r P. N. C. S.
N. M. Read, Assistant Surgeon.
G. D. Lining, 1st Ass't Engineer.
J. R. Y. Fendall, 1st Lieut. C. S. M.
A. P. Beinre, Passed Midshipman.
R. J. Deas, Passed Midshipman.
E. Debois, 2d Assistant Engineer.
M. M. Rogers, 3d Ass't Engineer.
F. A. Lombard, 3d Ass't Engineer.
Chas. A. Joullian, 3d Ass't Engineer.
J. Fulton, 3d Ass't Engineer.
G. W. Naylor, 3d Ass't Engineer.
Wm. Fink, Paymaster's Clerk.
F. B. Green, Master's Mate.
Avery S. Winston, M. Mate P. N. C. S.
John Curney.
Jos. M. Walker, Pilot.
W. L. Cameron, Paymaster's Clerk.
Lewis Williams, Engineer.
M. L. Shropshire, Act. 1st Ass't Eng'r.
J. V. Harris, Ass't Surgeon.
Benj. Herring, 1st Engineer.

Ira W. Porter, Acting Gunner.
B. H. Weaver, Acting Ass't Engineer.
J. W. Bennett, Lieut. Commanding.
G. A. Joiner,[1] Passed Midshipman.
Wm. Carroll, Passed Midshipman.
G. H. Wellington, 3d Ass't Engineer.
Z. A. Offutt, Gunner.
J. P. Redwood, Clerk.
E. W. Johnston, Master's Mate.
James White, Master's Mate.
Wm. C. Dogger, Engineer.
Wm. P. A. Campbell, 1st Lieutenant.
Julian M. Spencer, 1st Lieutenant.
Jason C. Baker, 1st Lieutenant.
W. F. Robinson, 2d Lieutenant.
Robert F. Freeman, P'ss'd Ass't Sur.
G. W. Claiborne, Ass't Surgeon.
H. E. McDuffie, Ass't Paymaster.
A. N. Bully, Master.
W. Youngblood, Chief Engineer.
John L. Rapier, 2d Lieutenant.
Wm. Fauntleroy, 2d Ass't Engineer.
Geo. J. Weaver, 2d Ass't Engineer.
J. Thomas Maybury, Gunner.
S. H. McMaster, Paymaster's Clerk.
H. L. Manning, Master's Mate.
Joseph Fry, Lieut. Commanding.
Page M. Baker, Master's Mate.
John G. Blackwood, 1st Lieutenant.
Wm. H. Haynes, Gunner.
Hiram G. Goodrich, 3d Ass't Eng'r.
John Applegate, 3d Ass't Engineer.
Edwin Weaver, 3d Ass't Engineer.
Jacob H. Turner, Acting M. Mate.
Thos. A. Wakefield, 3d Ass't Eng'r.
J. D. Johnston, Commander.
W. W. Graves, Ass't Surgeon.
W. T. J. Kunsh, 3d Ass't Engineer.
Henry D. Bassett, Act. Constructor.

Besides the parole signed by the above commissioned and warrant officers of the Confederate navy, there were four other papers of the same character. Acting Fleet-captain Julius

[1] Passed Midshipman George A. Joiner, who was officer of the deck of the *Nashville* when she was surrendered, was appointed in the C. S. navy, January 23d, 1863, and was stationed at the Drewry's Bluff batteries on the James River, until the succeeding summer, when he was ordered to a class on the school-ship *Patrick Henry*. In the spring of 1864, he became aide to Commodore W. H. Parker, in command of the *Richmond*, and was also made signal officer. In the movement to confront Gen. Butler's landing at Bermuda Hundreds, in May, Mr. Joiner commanded a howitzer in the naval contingent, and afterward returned with his class to the school-ship, graduating in July, 1864: as No. 6 of the class. In the detail of midshipmen then ordered to report at Mobile, he and William Carroll, now of Pine Bluff, Ark, were specially designated as aides to Admiral Buchanan, but they did not reach that city until after his capture. Mr. Joiner was assigned to the iron-clad *Huntsville*, Lieut. Commander *Julius Myers*, and was present at the

various engagements of that ship with the Federal batteries during Gen. Canby's investment of Mobile. He was once slightly wounded, and, in company with a sailor named Kelly, distinguished himself by replacing under the enemy's fire the ensign of the ship, which had been shot away in the course of an action in which her smoke-stack was perforated fifty-seven times. When it was decided to sink the *Huntsville* upon the evacuation of Mobile Midshipman Joiner was left in charge of the boat's crew that scuttled her, and was the last person to leave the deck after cutting the feed-pipes of the boiler. He then went to duty on the *Nashville*, and on May 10th, 1865, received at the gangway of the vessel the Federal officer, Lieut. Hamilton, sent to receive her surrender. Her colors had been struck, the officers and crew gathered on deck as they were hauled down and saluted them with raised caps while tears flowed freely. Since the war, Mr. Joiner has resided in his native town of Talladega, Ala., where he is engaged in mercantile pursuits.

Myers gave parole on behalf of the Confederate seamen serving on a portion of the vessels; Lieut. Joseph Fry, commanding the *Morgan*, gave parole on behalf of the 120 men of his ship; Lieut. J. W. Bennett, commanding the *Nashville*, gave parole for his 112 seamen; and Lieut. D. G. Raney, Jr., gave parole for the twenty-four marines under his command.

In addition to the vessels surrendered by Commodore Farrand, the following river steamers in the inland waters of Alabama fell into the hands of the Federals: *St. Nicholas, St. Charles, C. W. Dorrance, Jeff. Davis, Admiral, Reindeer, Cherokee, Marengo, Sumter, Waverly, Magnolia, Robert Watson, Duke, Clipper, Senator, Commodore Farrand,* and *Two Hundred and Ninety.* The blockade-runners *Heroine, Mary, Red Gauntlet* and *Virgin* were also among the prizes.

So fell the curtain upon the defence of Mobile and the adjacent waters. It had been conducted with matchless skill, energy, and gallantry upon meagre resources, against an enemy whose command of men, ships, guns and money was measureless, and it ended without a blemish upon the honor and bravery of the sailors and soldiers who so long held back the enormously superior forces thundering at their gates.

CHAPTER XIX

FLORIDA WATERS.

THE naval operations in Florida waters during the war were not perhaps as brilliant and far-reaching in their character as those in some other parts of the Confederacy, but they are not without a vivid historical interest, and had a solid importance in connection with the whole plan of attack upon the Southern sea-coasts and sea-ports. At the opening of the war, the situation in Florida was not unlike that in other Southern States. The Ordinance of Secession declaring this State "a sovereign and independent nation," was passed by a State Convention which assembled January 10th, 1861. On January 9th, a rumor of the intended seizure of the Pensacola navy-yard, Warrington, by the Confederates, reached the Federal authorities at the Pensacola works. Lieut. Adam J. Slemmer, then in command of the harbor defences, which consisted of Forts Barrancas, McRae and Pickens, determined to concentrate his forces, ammunition, supplies and arms at Fort Pickens, which, besides being the strongest fort, commanded the entrance to the bay and the other forts. The navy-yard, distant about two and a half miles, was beyond the range of the guns at Fort Pickens. On the morning of the 10th, the force under Lieut. Slemmer's command was transferred to Fort Pickens by means of boats from the U. S. steamer *Wyandotte* and the storeship *Supply.* Fort McRae was abandoned, and about 23,000 pounds of powder, together with a quantity of fuses and shot, were destroyed. The guns at Barrancas were spiked, and were in that condition when the Florida troops, under Col. Lomax, took possession of the fort.

Pensacola Bay possesses rare properties as a harbor. It is accessible to large vessels, the bar is near the coast, and the channel across it short and easily passed. The harbor is perfectly land-locked and the roadstead very capacious. There are excellent positions within for repairing, building and launching vessels, and for docks and dock-yards. The supply of good water is abundant. These advantages, in connection with the position of the harbor as regards the coast, induced the U. S. government to select it as a naval station, and a place of rendezvous and repair.

Pensacola Bay, fortified as it was, with all its ordnance in position and properly garrisoned, was deemed impregnable, except by long and hazardous siege by an overwhelming and well appointed land force; and it was said by an enthusiastic writer of the time, "could defy all the navies of the world combined till it filled the harbor's mouth with the carcasses of sunken ships." Fort Pickens is situated on Santa Rosa Island, the west point of which is at the mouth of Pensacola Bay and completely shuts out Pensacola from the sea. The fort was a first-class pentagonal bastioned work, built of stone, brick and bitumen, with covert ways, dry ditch, glacis and outworks complete. Its walls were forty feet in height by twelve feet in thickness, and were embrasured for two tiers of guns in bomb-proof and one tier of guns open or *en barbette*. The guns from this point radiated to every point of the horizon, with flank and enfilading fire in the ditches and at every angle of approach. The work was begun in 1838 and finished in 1853. When on a war footing its garrison consisted of 1,260 soldiers. Its armament in January, 1861, consisted of: in bastion 20 twenty-four-pound howitzers; casemate, 2 forty-two-pounders, 64 thirty-two pounders, 59 twenty-four pounders; in barbette, 24 eight-inch howitzers, 6 eighteen-pounders, 12 twelve-pounders, 1 ten-inch Columbiad mounted, and 4 ten-inch mortars in bad order. The possession of this work by the Confederates was, of course, of the first importance, for unless they could occupy it, it would secure to the U. S. troops a base of operations along the whole gulf coast, and keep open a road into the heart of the South, which could not be obstructed by any fixed fortifications. An enemy holding Fort Pickens could rendezvous a naval force there, and keep up a blockade of all the ports of the gulf, unless it could be met on the sea. The fort was only approachable by land on one side, and, owing to the openness of the country, which was but a barren bed of sand, a party attacking from that quarter would be very much exposed.

Fort McRae,[1] after its abandonment by Slemmer, was in possession of the Florida troops. It was further seaward than Fort Pickens, and was its *vis à vis* across the channel, guarding the west side of the mouth of Pensacola Bay. A vessel entering, then, must needs run the gauntlet of its guns before approaching Fort Pickens, which, however, of itself effectually closed the harbor against the admission of an enemy of even very heavy force. Fort McRae was in poor condition, but was nevertheless a strong water battery. Fort Barrancas, also abandoned by Slemmer, was well built and a powerful defence

---

[1] Correct name believed to be McCrea.

of the entrance of the harbor, but neither its construction nor position was adapted to resist a strong land attack. It stood upon the same shore with Fort McRae, a mile and a quarter farther up the bay. When the Confederate troops took possession of this fort, Capt. O'Hara was put in command. He, by the most untiring efforts. placed it in a proper state of defence. It had a garrison of 300 regularly enlisted men of the army of the Confederate States. The guns were all mounted, and the troops well drilled as cannoneers.[1]

The navy-yard is situated upon the same shore of the bay with Forts McRae and Barrancas, about a mile and a half above the latter. At the outbreak of the war, it was under the command of Commodore James Armstrong; the next officer in rank at the yard being Commander Ebenezer Farrand, who afterwards resigned and entered the C. S. navy. The disposable force at the yard consisted of about seventy sailors or "ordinary men," as they are termed, and forty-eight marines, under the command of Capt. Joseph Watson. There were also at the yard, subject to the commands of Commodore Armstrong, the U. S. storeship *Supply*, with two 30-pounders and thirty-eight men, and the steamer *Wyandotte*, with six 32's and eighty men.

On January 12th, 1861, the navy-yard was surrounded by Florida and Alabama troops, under the command of Major Wm. H. Chase, formerly of the U. S. corps of Engineers, who had been appointed major general by Governor Perry, of Florida, who demanded the surrender of the yard. Opposition was worse than useless, as the navy-yard itself is so situated that no military man would think of defending it against a large attacking force with the means at the commodore's command. The Florida and Alabama troops, numbering seven companies, with nearly five hundred men, rank and file, arrived at the east entrance of the navy-yard about eleven o'clock A. M., and there halted. Col. Lomax, accompanied by Major Marks and Adjutant Burrows of an Alabama regiment, and Col. R. L. Campbell, aide-de-camp to Gen. Ben. Chase, and Capt. Randolph, late of the U. S. army, as also Capt. Farrand of the yard, proceeded immediately to the office of Commodore Armstrong, commanding, for an interview, which was promptly accorded by the venerable chief officer of the yard. After the introduction of the distinguished parties, Col. Lomax read the order from the Governor of Florida, by authority of which he demanded immediate possession of the yard and its stores of every description. Commodore Armstrong responded, his voice trembling with emotion as he announced that he relinquished his authority to the representative of the

[1] The Savannah *Republican* of the 10th of January, 1861, said: "A private letter received yesterday from Bainbridge informs us of the occupation of the Chattahoochee arsenal, situated in Gadsden county, Florida, at the junction of the Flint and Chattahoochee Rivers, by the Quincy Guard. The arsenal contains 500,000 rounds of musket cartridges, 300,000 rifle cartridges and 50,000 pounds of gunpowder. There are no arms except such as is necessary to defend the property against ordinary contingencies."

sovereignty of Florida. The order was immediately given by Lieut. Renshaw to haul down the flag of the Union, which was done; and instead thereof there was run up a flag of thirteen alternate stripes of red and white, and blue field with a large white star, announcing the changed political condition of the State. Everything was conducted in the most orderly and respectful manner, attended with a degree of solemn interest which was manifested upon the countenances of the hundreds of citizens and soldiers present. Capt. Randolph was placed in command of the yard. The magazine, containing a large amount of ammunition, was taken by a detachment of troops as soon as they arrived at the yard. The marines in the barracks, to the number of thirty-six, were made prisoners, together with the laborers and employés in the yard. The wives and children of the command at Fort Pickens had been previously conveyed on board the *Supply*. On the following day the store-ship, under a flag of truce, proceeded to the wharf of the navy-yard, where the laborers and marines were taken on board, Commander Walke having given his parole that they should be landed north of Mason's and Dixon's line. Overtures had been made to the marines to join the State forces, with the alternative of expulsion in case of a refusal. The personal property of the force at Fort Pickens, belonging to the officers' wives, was under flag of truce conveyed on board the *Supply* and taken North, arriving at New York, February 4th, 1861.

In a letter to the New York *Herald*, dated at Pensacola navy-yard, January 29th, 1861, Lieut. B. Renshaw, until a short time before an officer in the U. S. navy, but who resigned and entered the C. S. navy, gave the following account of the circumstances attending the surrender of the navy-yard :

"I have seen in your paper of the 23d inst. a statement, which justice to myself as well as to the naval service of the United States, in which I had the honor of serving for thirty-three years, requires me promptly to request you to correct. The statement referred to recited that the Navy Department had received the resignation of Commander Farrand, who was attached to the Pensacola navy-yard, and who was among those who, in the name of 'Florida,' demanded its surrender, and also that of Lieut. Renshaw who gave the orders to haul down the flag of the Union.

"I submit the following true record of the proceedings which attended and resulted in the surrender of this navy-yard to the authorities of the State of Florida, and I rely upon your sense of right to do me justice by its publication in your columns : On the 12th instant, Flag-officer Armstrong, then commandant at the station, was informed that a commission appointed by the governor of Florida, with a regiment of armed men, were at the navy-yard gate, demanding the surrender of the place. Flag-officer Armstrong directed Commander Farrand, the executive officer at the yard, to conduct the commissioners to his office. The commissioners came accordingly, escorted by Commander Farrand. Colonel Lomax, the commanding officer of the forces on the expedition, with his staff, were then sent for, and conducted to the flag-officer's office by Commander Farrand, to meet the commissioners, who then presented their credentials to

Flag-officer Armstrong, informing him that they had already taken possesion of the magazine, situated about a third of a mile distant from the yard, and demanded the immediate surrender of the navy-yard and the public property within. The veteran commodore declared, with deep emotion, that although he had served under the flag of the United States, in sunshine and in storm, for fifty years, loving and cherishing it as he did his heart's blood, he would strike it now together with the blue pennant, the insignia of his present command, rather than fire a gun or raise his sword against his countrymen, especially in circumstances like the present, when he was without means of defending his position, and when an attempt to do so would result in a useless loss of life and destruction of property. He accordingly ordered the executive officer, Commander Farrand, to cause the flag of the United States, and the blue pennant, to be hauled down; the order was passed, in accordance with usage in the naval service, to the senior lieutenant (myself), under whose directions the time-honored flags were hauled down. The descent was witnessed by none in whose heart the regret and grief at the fate of our longly-beloved Union were more deeply felt than in mine. I now became a prisoner on parole, and remained so for several days, when I resigned my commission in the U. S. navy, which I have held as a lieutenant for twenty years, and tendered my services to the sovereign State of Florida, with whose destiny, whether bright or adverse, I am fully identified."

After the seizure of the navy-yard, Braxton Bragg, formerly an officer of the U. S. army, was ordered to proceed to Pensacola and take command of all the Confederate troops there, and conduct the operations against Fort Pickens. The situation in Florida, January 24th, 1861, was such that there was scarcely a doubt that all the strongholds in the State in the neighborhood of Pensacola would within a week be in the possession of the State troops. There was no one so familiar with the fortifications at Pensacola as Gen. Chase, the commander of the State forces, most of them having been planned and built by him while in the United States service. While investing Fort Pickens he determined to guard against the contingency of a blockade of Pensacola, by providing a six months' supply of provisions for the State troops, and making scaling ladders and other preparations to attempt the capture of Fort Pickens. Lieut. Slemmer, its commander, in reply to the commissioner who waited on him to know if he would surrender the fort, said "that he had orders from his government to defend the fort and that he would do so to the last extremity." Lieut. Berryman, commander of the *Wyandotte*, kept his war steamer at this time, (January 24th, 1861) continually moving opposite the yard and signalizing to the commander at Fort Pickens the movements of the troops.

After the surrender of the navy-yard the Buchanan administration had, as early as January, sent out an artillery force under Capt. Vogdes, on board the steam sloop-of-war *Brooklyn*, to reinforce the garrison in Fort Pickens. The vessel left Hampton Roads January 25th, and stopped at Key West on the 31st. Great excitement existed in Florida, and particularly in Pensacola, relative to the expected reinforcements of the fort. Before the *Brooklyn* reached Fort Pickens the Federal government entered into a truce with certain

Confederate leaders, to the effect that the U. S. government would pursue a policy of inaction, provided the Confederates would make no assault on the fort. Although this agreement was unwritten, it was faithfully kept for a time by the U. S. government, and as faithfully by the Confederates. Capt. Vogdes' command was not permitted to land, but was detained on board until after the expiration of Mr. Buchanan's term. When the *Brooklyn* arrived at Fort Pickens, the provisions were allowed to be delivered at the fort, but she was not allowed to enter the harbor of Pensacola, or to land troops at the fort. Her commander was ordered to act strictly on the defensive, and to give no pretext for hostilities.

When the change of administration took place on the 4th of March, and Mr. Lincoln became President, he found the government without extra means or authority to subdue the Southern States. Commander Jenkins and Capt. Wm. F. Smith, U. S. N., were in the winter of 1861 attached to the Light-house Board, the former as naval secretary, the latter as engineer secretary. Both of these officers were impressed with the danger which threatened Forts Jefferson and Taylor in Florida, and which would, if no steps were taken to prevent it, be likely to pass into the hands of the Confederates. They communicated their apprehensions to Gen. Dix, at that time Secretary of the Treasury, and their purpose to ascertain the condition of things in that quarter. Their suggestions were approved and Capt. Smith visited Tortugas and Key West under the pretext of inspecting the lights. He went to Dry Tortugas and Fort Taylor, saw their danger and satisfied himself as to what was best to be done for their safety. From his communications the U. S. government saw that prompt action was necessary to save the stations off the coast, but more important still was the need that Fort Pickens should be relieved and reinforced. Gen. Scott was much exercised and most anxious that Vogdes' command should be disembarked, and he applied to Secretary Welles for a naval vessel to convey a bearer of dispatches and reinforcements from the war department to Fort Pickens. The *Crusader*, Capt. Craven, and the *Mohawk*, were selected to send to the gulf. After several days of uncertainty caused by receiving no news from Pensacola, an officer, worn-out and exhausted, arrived in Washington, April 5th, with dispatches from Capt. Adams, in command of the squadron off Pensacola. The officer announced himself as Lieut. Gwathmey and unstrapping a belt from beneath his garments delivered a package to the Secretary of the Navy, containing the following letters:

"U. S. FRIGATE ' SABINE,' OFF PENSACOLA, April 1st, 1861.

" SIR : I have the honor to enclose a copy of a letter addressed to me by Capt. Vogdes, U. S. A , who is here in command of some troops sent out in January last to reinforce the garrison of Fort Pickens. I have declined to land the men as Capt. Vogdes requests, as it would be in direct violation of the orders of the Navy Department under which I am acting. The instructions from Gen. Scott to Capt. Vogdes are of old date (March 12th) and may have been given without a full knowledge of the condition of affairs here ; they would be no justification. Such a step is too important to be taken without the clearest orders from proper authority. It would certainly be viewed as a hostile act, and would be resisted to the utmost. No one acquainted with the military assembled under Gen. Bragg can doubt that it would be considered not only a declaration, but an act, of war. It would be a serious thing to bring on, by any precipitation, a collision which may be entirely against the wishes of the administration. At present, both sides are faithfully observing the agreement entered into by the U. S. government, and with Mr. Mallory and Colonel Chase. This agreement binds us not to reinforce Fort Pickens, unless it should be attacked or threatened. It binds them not to attack it unless we should attempt to reinforce it. I saw Gen. Bragg on the 30th ult., who reassured me the conditions on their part should not be violated. While I cannot take upon myself, under such insufficient authority as Gen. Scott's order, the fearful responsibility of an act which seems to render civil war inevitable, I am ready at all times to carry out whatever orders I may receive from the Honorable the Secretary of the Navy.

"In conclusion, I beg you will please to send me instructions as soon as possible that I may be relieved from a painful embarrassment.

"Very respectfully, your obedient servant,

"H. A. ADAMS, *Captain, Senior Officer present.*

" *To the* Hon. GIDEON WELLES,

" *Secretary of the Navy, Washington, D. C.*"

" U. S. FRIGATE ' SABINE,' OFF PENSACOLA, April 1st, 1861.

" *To* Capt. H. A. ADAMS, *Commanding Naval Forces off Pensacola.*

"SIR : Herewith I send you a copy of an order received by me last night. You will see by it that I am directed to land my command at the earliest opportunity. I have therefore to request that you will place at my disposal such boats and other means as will enable me to carry into effect the enclosed order. Yours, etc.,

"J. VOGDES, *Captain First Artillery, Commanding.*"

" HEADQUARTERS OF THE ARMY, WASHINGTON, March 12th, 1861.

"SIR : At the first favorable moment you will land with your company, reinforce Fort Pickens, and hold the same until further notice.

"Report frequently, if opportunities present themselves, on the condition of the fort and the circumstances around you.

"I write by command of Gen. Scott.

"I am, Sir, very respectfully. your obedient servant,

" E. D. TOWNSEND, *Assist. Adjutant Gen.*

"Capt. J. VOGDES, *U. S. A., on board the U. S. Sloop-of-war* ' *Brooklyn,*'

" *Off Fort Pickens, Pensacola, Florida.*"

The course of Capt. Adams caused great disappointment in Washington. It was not understood. Mr. Lincoln, and his Secretary of the Navy, knew of no written truce or orders of the character mentioned in Capt. Adams' letter, and suspicions were entertained of his fidelity to the government. In justice to him, however, it may be stated that he faithfully performed his duty and strictly obeyed the orders sent him. Lieut. Washington Gwathmey, the bearer of Capt. Adams' dispatches, was a Virginian, deeply imbued with the theories prevalent at the South, but, like all the naval officers from the South, his opinions did not prevent him from faithfully discharging the trust confided to him. A few days after his

arrival in Washington he sent in his resignation, which, however, was not accepted. He was dismissed, in accordance
with the petty policy of the new Administration, and soon
after entered the C. S. navy.

The day upon which Lieut. Gwathmey reached Washington was the one upon which the expedition destined for the
relief of Sumter was to sail. It was feared, should the Confederates hear of it, that it would precipitate an attack upon
Fort Pickens before the garrison could be reinforced. It was
determined by the U. S. government that a special messenger
should be sent overland with positive orders to the Federal
forces at Pensacola, directing that the troops should be disembarked without delay. Lieut. John L. Worden, who afterwards commanded the *Monitor* in Hampton Roads, was appointed to perform this duty. The order was made as brief
as possible, as the fact that he was a U. S. naval officer, passing through the South, not in sympathy with the people,
might cause him to be captured. It was as follows:

" [CONFIDENTIAL.]

" NAVY DEPARTMENT, April 6th, 1861.

" *Capt.* HENRY A. ADAMS, *commanding Naval Forces off Pensacola:*

" SIR: Your dispatch of April 1st is received. The Department regrets
that you did not comply with the request of Capt. Vogdes to carry into
effect the orders of Gen. Scott, sent out by the *Crusader*, under the orders
of this Department. You will immediately, on the first favorable opportunity after the receipt of this order, afford every facility to Capt. Vogdes,
by boats and other means, to enable him to land the troops under his
command, it being the wish and intention of the Navy Department to
co-operate with the War Department in that object.

" I am, sir, respectfully, etc.,

" GIDEON WELLES, *Secretary of the Navy.*"

This order was given to Lieut. Worden unsealed; he committed it to memory before he reached Richmond, and then
destroyed it. He hastened on to Pensacola with the greatest
speed, reaching there on the 11th of April. He held an interview with Gen. Bragg, stating that he had a verbal communication from Secretary Welles to Capt. Adams, and received
a pass to visit that officer. He communicated the orders to
Capt. Adams on the 12th of April, and that night the boats of
the squadron, under the command of Lieut. Albert N. Smith,
successfully landed the artillery company of Capt. Vogdes,
consisting of eighty-six men and a detachment of 115 marines.
The garrison in Fort Pickens, previously composed of only
eighty-three men, was reinforced, and for the time made secure.

Gen. Bragg was to have made an attack upon Pickens the
night following that on which the fort was reinforced; but this
additional strength to the garrison defeated this project.
Lieut. Worden, immediately after delivering his message,
began his return journey by land. The Confederates, when
too late, came to the conclusion that this messenger, who had

come and gone so suddenly, was an agent of the government, and that he had been instrumental in the landing of the Federal troops at Fort Pickens. A description of him was telegraphed to the Confederate government, and he was arrested near Montgomery, Alabama, on the 13th of April. The reason assigned for the arrest was that he had violated a pledge given to Gen. Bragg, and that he had been instrumental in reinforcing Fort Pickens, contrary to an agreement with Capt. Adams. The U. S. government held that Worden had given no pledge, and that the agreement alluded to, instead of having been made by Capt. Adams, was an unwritten truce, mentioned in a communication of Secretaries Holt and Toucey, on the 29th of January, addressed to the naval officers of Pensacola, and Lieut. Slemmer in command at Fort Pickens. Indignation was severe against Lieut. Worden, in the South, and he was detained a prisoner for seven months at Montgomery. He was then exchanged for an officer in the Confederate army, and soon after appointed to the command of the *Monitor*.[1]

In regard to the communication of Secretaries Holt and Toucey, referred to above, Gideon Welles, in the *Galaxy* for January, 1871, says:

"The paper or document of Secretaries Holt and Toucey is the only written recognition of the truce or agreement entered into with the rebels

---

[1] W. H. Murdaugh, a distinguished and gallant officer in the C. S. navy, was in the winter and spring of 1861 attached to the frigate *Sabine* off Pensacola, Fla. The latter part of the time he was first lieutenant or executive officer The Confederate flag was flying on Forts McRae and Barrancas and the navy-yard. Fort Pickens was under the U. S. flag and garrisoned by a company of artillery commanded by Lieut. Slemmer, U. S. A. The best of feeling was maintained by the officers of both sides. Boat loads of Confederate officers would come to the ships which were anchored outside the bar, and were entertained, and good fellowship always prevailed, and the U. S. officers had the run of Pensacola and the navy-yard. Capt. Henry A Adams commanded the *Sabine* and was the senior officer afloat. Gen. Bragg and Com. Ingraham, the Confederate commanders, dined with Capt. Adams on board the *Sabine* several times. This pleasant intercourse continued until Fort Sumter fell, when Gen. Bragg cut off communications with the squadron. On board the *Sabine* was a battalion of U. S. artillery commanded by Gen. Vogdes, then a captain of artillery. Soldiers had been sent down to reinforce the garrison of Fort Pickens, but upon their arrival an agreement had been formally entered into by the authorities at Washington and the Confederate Government that the Confederates would not attack Fort Pickens, and that the Federals would not reinforce it. This compact was to be observed by the Federal commanders, so that when their troops arrived, instead of going into Fort Pickens, they were put on board the *Sabine*, where they remained about two months. Some two or three weeks after Mr. Lincoln was inaugurated, a little revenue cutter from Key West came in and anchored under the counter of the *Sabine*. She brought two army officers with dispatches for Capt. Vogdes. Capt. Adams, with whom Capt.

Vogdes messed, gave up the cabin to them, he and Murdaugh coming upon the deck. After a little while, Capt. Vogdes also came on deck with a paper in his hand, saying: "Captain, I have received orders to land my command in Fort Pickens." "From whom?" asked Capt. A. "From General Scott," replied Capt. V. "I do not know Gen. Scott in this matter," said Capt. Adams, "and you cannot land your men until I get proper orders to that effect." "Do you mean to say that your boats cannot land my men?" inquired Capt. Vogdes. "Yes, I do," returned Capt. Adams. "Then I shall charter one or more of these fishing sloops that pass us occasionally, and land my party," said Capt. V. "No," said Capt. Adams, "you do not leave this ship until I get proper orders to that effect."

Mr. Murdaugh writes as follows concerning the events connected with the subsequent reinforcement of Fort Pickens: "Capt. Vogdes asked Capt. Adams if he might send a bearer of dispatches to Washington to tell the condition of things. Capt. Adams readily consented, and one of Capt. Vogdes' lieutenants was landed at the navy-yard that night and took rail to Washington. Not very long after this, Lieut John L. Worden, U. S. N., since the well-known commander of the *Monitor*, came on board the *Sabine*, having permission of Gen. Bragg to do so. After being closeted with Capt. Adams for awhile, I was sent for. On entering the cabin, I found Lieut. Worden writing at the table. Capt. Adams asked me to remain, as he wanted me to be a witness to something. When Lieut. Worden had finished writing, he handed it to Capt. Adams. It was an order for him to send the army forces to Fort Pickens, and as many marines as could be spared from the squadron as soon as possible. At the bottom of the order was a certificate signed by Lieut. Worden, saying that, to the best of his knowledge and belief, the order above was a verbatim copy of a

which I remember to have seen, and of the existence of this document I am not aware that any member of Mr. Lincoln's administration was informed when orders were sent to reinforce Pickens. I never saw it nor knew of it until after the receipt of Capt. Adams' letter of the 1st of April. It has been asserted and denied that the administration of Mr. Buchanan established an armistice, or entered into an arrangement with the rebels by which the functions of the government to suppress insurrection and rebellion were suspended. Capt. Adams states the light in which he and Gen. Bragg viewed the communication of Messrs. Holt and Toucey, which I here insert:

"WASHINGTON, Jan. 29th, 1861.—Received at $\rbrace$
PENSACOLA, Jan. 29th, 1861, at 9 P. M.

"To Capt. JAMES GLYNN, commanding the *Macedonian*; Capt. W. S. WALKER, commanding the *Brooklyn*, or other naval officers in command; and Lieut. ADAM J. SLEMMER, First Reg. Art. U. S. A., commanding Fort Pickens:

"In consequence of the assurances received from Mr. Mallory, in a telegram of yesterday to Messrs. Bigler, Hunter and Slidell, with a request that it should be laid before the President, that Fort Pickens would not be assaulted, and an offer of such an assurance to the same effect from Col. Chase, for the purpose of avoiding a hostile collision upon receiving satisfactory assurances from Mr. Mallory and Col. Chase that Fort Pickens will not be attacked, you are instructed not to land the company on board the *Brooklyn* unless said fort shall be attacked or preparations be made for its attack. The provisions necessary for the supply of the fort you will land. The *Brooklyn* and other vessels-of-war on the station will remain, and you will exercise the utmost vigilance and be prepared at a moment's warning to land the company at Fort Pickens, and you and they will instantly repel any attack on the fort. The President yesterday sent a special message to Congress, commending the Virginia resolutions of compromise. The Commissioners of different States are to meet here on Monday, the 4th of February, and it is important that during their session a collision of arms should be avoided unless an attack should be made, or there should be preparations for such an attack. In either event the *Brooklyn* and other vessels will act promptly. Your right and that of the other officers in command at Pensacola freely to communicate with

dispatch which had been given by the Navy Department at Washington to be delivered to Capt. Adams. That on his way through the Confederate States he had reason to think that his dispatch might be taken from him; he therefore had opened it, committed its contents to memory, and destroyed it. I signed this certificate as a witness. Capt. Adams gave me orders to have everything in readiness to land the men soon after nightfall. These facts are mentioned to show that although I was then what would now be termed 'a rebel,' I was doing my duty in the service from which I could not get away, and by the authority to which I was amenable till my resignation had been accepted. That I was in no way suspected of any desire to neglect duty, nor did I suspect myself of being capable of doing so, never mind how distasteful that duty. I had made all preparations for hoisting out the boats in the afternoon. Capt. Adams thought he had better hoist them out for fear of delays, but I told him it would attract attention on shore; that they could be hoisted out after dark, armed, and the men landed very soon after nightfall. Capt. Adams let me have my way, and all went well. Worden went ashore to return to Washington on that same afternoon. When it was known the next morning that forces had been thrown into Fort Pickens, Gen. Bragg had Worden arrested, and

he was kept a prisoner at Montgomery for some time. The report in the squadron was that when Worden asked leave to communicate with the squadron. Gen. Bragg told him that he could do so if he was not a bearer of dispatches; that he could not if he was. Commodore Ingraham, who was at Pensacola at the time of these occurrences, always maintained that Worden had been treated badly . . . that he had done nothing to justify his imprisonment. On the 25th of April, I heard that Virginia had withdrawn from the Union, and immediately put my resignation of my commission in Capt. Adams' hands. Although a warm friend of mine, and willing to do me any favor, Capt. Adams considered it his duty not to let me leave the squadron until he could hear from Washington. So for six weeks I had to do faithful but most disagreeable duty in the U. S. navy. As a return for an honorable course of duty on my part. the U S. government struck my name from the navy list, and when, after the war, I asked that my political disabilities might be removed, I was required to return to the Treasury one hundred and twenty dollars which I had drawn for services rendered before the receipt of my resignation, my dismissal, of course, being antedated. About four hundred and fifty dollars are yet due me for services honorably discharged. I exchanged from the *Sabine* to the storeship *Supply* in order

the government by special messenger, and its right, in the same manner, to communicate with yourselves and them, will remain intact, as the basis of the present instructions.

"J. HOLT, *Secretary of War.*
"I. TOUCEY, *Secretary of the Navy.*"

"The construction which Capt. Adams put upon what he calls the engagement made by Mr. Mallory and Mr. Chase with the U. S. government, and which restrained him for four weeks from landing troops, will be seen by the following extract from a letter written by him under date of the 18th of March, and sent by Lieut. Gwathmey:

'The officers and men, as I mentioned in my letter of February 19th, are kept in readiness to land at the shortest notice; but I have engaged the assurances of Gen. Bragg, who commands the troops on shore, that he will respect the engagement made by Mr. Mallory and Col. Chase with the U. S. government, and will make no disposition for the attack of Fort Pickens. This engagement, you are aware, binds us not to reinforce Fort Pickens unless it is attacked or threatened. I could easily have thrown any number of men in it almost any time within the last four weeks.'

"This communication, written on the 18th of March, Capt. Adams would not trust to the mails, but withheld for other conveyance; opportunities, however, were rare, and hence the delay in its reception."

Four days after the arrival of Lieut. Worden at Fort Pickens with orders for the reinforcement of that fort, the transport *Atlantic* arrived with Gen. Brown and his force and supplies on board for the reinforcement of that post. Gen. Brown found the place in a miserable condition for hostilities, and in a "complete state of confusion, all requiring the labor of every man in it." The *Powhatan* arrived next day, the 17th of April, but did not attempt to run the batteries and enter the harbor, as had been designed by those who had dispatched the *Powhatan* to Pensacola, the army and navy commanders being opposed to it, as Fort Pickens was not strong enough to resist

to get home, and arrived in New York early in June. I was indebted to the gallant Capt. Foote, U. S. N., to get out of the way of arrest in New York, and so escaped customary imprisonment in Fort Warren. It may seem that much or all that I have written so far is irrelevant to the scheme in hand, but it has a bearing which I consider is very important and one which I confess is very dear, and that is, the standing in the old navy of those who resigned both upon and after they had tendered their resignations. A Yankee pedlar spirit in those who happened to be in power in the times of which I write, brought forth a small and venomous expedient illegal and unjust, that of dismissing from the service instead of accepting these resignations. It was a mean spirit to seek to degrade honorable men, who, without one single exception that I am aware of, did faithful duty in the service in which they were engaged until relieved of that duty by competent authority. Had I been the traitor they would have made me out to be, a single line from me to Gen. Bragg, informing him of the orders from Gen. Scott, to Capt. Vogdes, as narrated above, would have resulted in the immediate capture of Fort Pickens. I am quite sure that it never entered into the minds of any of the 'loyal' officers of the large squadron off Pensacola, that I was less loyal to the U. S. navy while doing duty in it

than themselves. Admiral Porter commanded the *Powhatan* in that squadron. He came there with a plan for the holding of Fort Pickens, of which I was entirely informed, yet he never questioned the propriety of my retaining the position of executive officer of the flag-ship. Political harpies in Washington measured the honor of men by their own possessions in that line. The officers of the U. S. navy, with only the exception of some two or three of the whole body that I ever heard of, were, up to the breaking out of the war, conservative men who believed in the Constitution and the rights of the States, and greatly deplored a condition of things which made it their duty to assist in coercing a portion of their countrymen: nobly they did that duty. At the risk of seeming egotistical, I will mention, in concluding these remarks on the status of Southern officers in the U. S. navy, the fact that only a couple of years ago Admiral Mullaney, the last officer under whom I served in the old navy, spoke to a friend of his with whom he had made acquaintance at a summer resort, of what he was pleased to term my highly honorable conduct under very delicate circumstances, and gave instances of it. After all, he was only speaking of what any Southern officer would have done in like circumstances; by accident I happened to be the man on the occasion."

the fires of the Confederate batteries should the *Powhatan* provoke an attack by entering.[1]

The U. S. transport *Philadelphia*, Capt. Kittridge, sailed for Fort Pickens, April 19th, and arrived there May 2d. She had on board a large cargo of arms and ordnance stores. She approached within three-quarters of a mile of the fort and discharged her cargo. During this time the *Philadelphia* lay within range of the guns of Forts McRae, Barrancas and the land batteries, but no disposition was manifested to attack her. The garrison at the fort were working vigorously at the traverses and all the salient points were well protected with sand-bags. The mortars were planted and protected in like manner. The *Mohawk* also landed heavy guns at Fort Pickens, going up with several small boats and a scow in tow near the fort, but outside the harbor. She lay within the range of guns at Fort McRae, but no demonstration was made against her. The fleet off Pensacola at the time consisted of the U. S. ship *Sabine*, steam sloop-of-war *Brooklyn*, steam sloop *Powhatan*, and steamer *Water Witch;* also the storeship *Supply*, transport *Illinois*, steamer *Wyandotte* and schooner *Oriental*. The *Philadelphia* left Fort Pickens in May, having on board Lieut. Slemmer and his command on their way to Fort Hamilton, New York.

May 4th, the schooner *Oriental*, Lieut. Brown commanding, overhauled two steamers that flew the Southern flag; but as nothing contraband of war was found on them, they were permitted to enter the harbor. On May 7th, two Confederate vessels, bound from Mobile to Pensacola, were captured by the *Powhatan*. They were taken possession of and searched, but neither arms nor ammunition were found. They were laden with provisions for Pensacola, and as they were private property, Capt. Adams did not feel authorized to take them as prizes, but permitted them to return to Mobile.

May 9th, a number of small vessels inside the harbor, passed to and from the forts and Pensacola, taking down large bodies of men and munitions of war. The blockade of the port was proclaimed on the 6th of May, and was rigidly enforced. No vessels, except those in ballast, were permitted to enter the harbor.

At Key West, Commodore Mervine created some anxiety by the publication of the following proclamation :

" *To all whom it may concern:*

"I, William Mervine, Flag-officer, commanding the U. S. naval forces composing the Gulf Squadron, give notice that by virtue of the power

---

[1] On the 12th of March, 1861, at a Naval General Court Martial convened in Washington, Captain James Armstrong of the navy was tried on the charge of neglect of duty and disobedience of orders and conduct unbecoming an officer, at the surrender of the navy-yard at Warrington, Florida. The charges were preferred against him by direction of the Secretary of the Navy, and he was found guilty by the court of both charges. The following sentence was pronounced against him: "That Captain James Armstrong be suspended from duty for the term of five years, with loss of pay for the first half of said term, and be reprimanded by the Honorable Secretary of the Navy in general orders."

and authority in me vested, and in pursuance of the proclamation of his Excellency, the President of the United States, promulgated under date of April 19th and April 27th, respectively, an effective blockade of the port of Key West, Florida, has been established, and will be rigidly enforced and maintained against any and all vessels (public armed vessels of foreign powers alone excepted) which shall attempt to enter or depart from said port of Key West, Florida.

"Given at Key West, June 8th, 1861.

"WILLIAM MERVINE,
" *Flag-officer Mississippi Gulf Blockading Squadron*."

This order took the people of the town by surprise, for if it was rigidly enforced they would be unable to feed themselves. The island was almost a barren, rock-bound desert, and if vessels on their way from New York with supplies for the merchants were ordered off, and the opportunity of leaving the island taken from them, they were fearful of starving. When this state of affairs became known to Commodore Mervine he modified his proclamation as follows:

"The declaration of blockade of this port, made by me the 8th inst., is so far relaxed in its terms as to allow legitimate trading between this port and the ports of the loyal States. Trading between Key West and the Island of Cuba, and any of the West India Islands, so long as it is confined to lawful objects of commerce, may be carried on under such restrictions as may be imposed by the naval commander stationed off this port.

"WM. MERVINE."

A few days after the above publications, the collector of the port of Key West, Charles Howe, issued the following notice:

"By order of Commodore William Mervine, commanding the Gulf Blockading Squadron, the masters and owners of all vessels and boats are required to renew their registers or enrollments and licences on and after this date, as they arrive in port, and take the oath of ownership, according to law.

"And before any vessel or boat will be permitted to leave the harbor of Key West, they must obtain a clearance and permit from the Custom House, setting forth the object of their voyage, excepting pilot boats, on their regular daily cruising grounds, which clearance and permit to be approved by the officer in command of the port. And if any such vessel or boat is found without such clearance, etc., they will be dealt with as violating the blockade. By order as above,

"CHAS. HOWE, *Collector*."

Several small trading vessels were captured, between the 1st and 24th of July, and the U. S. District Judge at Key West was swift to condemn them as prizes.

On the 10th of May, 1861, the Confederate steamer *Spray* captured off Cedar Keys, the U. S. naval schooner *William C. Atwater*, Capt. Henry Allen commander. The *Spray* was armed with small arms, and had a crew of thirty-one men. The *Atwater* was taken to Appalachicola, where her officers and crew of eight men were confined, until sent to Richmond and exchanged. The *Atwater* was confiscated and sold at Appalachicola, and her name changed to the *Lizzie Weston*. She was loaded with 300 bales of cotton, and on the 17th of January, 1862, attempted to run the blockade, but was captured by the U. S. gunboat *Itasca*, Lieut. Caldwell commanding.

The Confederates at this time had a small sand battery at the West Pass entrance to Appalachicola, and eight guns were mounted on the island of St. Vincent, with a garrison of 400 soldiers under the command of Col. Hopkins.

The gunboat *R. R. Cuyler* was blockading the entrance to Tampa Bay. The U. S. steamship *Montgomery* appeared off the West Pass bar on the 11th July, and on the 12th her commander, Capt. Shaw, formally notified the city authorities of the existence of the blockade. The port of St. Marks was not blockaded until about the 1st of August, by the U. S. steamer *Mohawk*. On the the 14th, she scuttled and sunk, across the channel, where it was very narrow, a captured sloop.

In July, the steamer *Massachusetts* captured the schooners *Fanny*, *Bassude* and *Three Brothers*, of New Orleans, and *Olive Branch*, of Mobile, and sent them as prizes to Key West. When off Cedar Keys, they were recaptured by the Florida forces, and Lieut. Sawyer and nineteen seamen taken prisoners and sent to Tallahassee.

In September, Major French, the commanding officer at Key West, issued the following order, which was a great hardship to all those who sympathized with the South. Its promulgation caused a large number of the leading citizens of the town to leave with their families, and take up their residence at Tampa and other towns in Florida:

HEADQUARTERS UNITED STATES TROOPS, }
KEY WEST, FLA., Sept. 6th, 1861. }
ORDER NO. 82.

1. Within ten days from this date all male citizens of the Island of Key West who have taken the oath of allegiance will send their names to these headquarters to be registered.

2. Within thirty days from this date all the citizens of this island are required to take the oath of allegiance to the United States.

3. At the termination of sixty days, all citizens of this island who have failed and refused to take the oath of allegiance to the United States will be removed from Key West. This will also apply to the families of those who have left the island to join the rebel forces.

WM. H. FRENCH, *Commander*.

During the summer of 1861, the Confederate naval officers at Pensacola were busily engaged in constructing batteries and otherwise aiding the army officers in defending the port. The batteries extended over a semi-circle of four and a half miles. They commenced at the navy-yard and terminated at the water battery, beyond McRae. At short intervals, for two miles and a half, there was an uninterrupted line of batteries along this semi-circle. A new battery was constructed one and a half miles from Fort Pickens, named the Quitman, consisting of two thirty-two pounders and one howitzer. It was between Fort Barrancas and Fort McRae, and commanded the eastern entrance to the channel. Besides the two forts, there were nineteen batteries on the Confederate side, between Pensacola and Fort McRae. The batteries were masked, so that they were not visible from the sea or bay, and had strong bomb-proofs. There was a continuous line of batteries between the navy-yard and Barrancas, and between Barrancas and McRae.

The dry-dock, lying at the Warrington navy-yard, was removed by the naval officers into the channel and partly sunk, the object being to intercept the passage of vessels into the bay in case of an engagement. A plan was afterward formed to pump out the water, raise and float it further down to a position opposite Fort McRae, where the channel was very narrow, and where, if it were sunk, it would effectually bar the passage inward of any vessel of size. It was afterwards burned by the enemy.

On the 13th of September a boat expedition, consisting of one launch and two cutters, with a force of about 100 men, officers, sailors and marines, was fitted out by Commodore Mervine of the U. S. flagship *Colorado*, to destroy the schooner *Judah*, which laid off the Pensacola navy-yard, supposed to be fitting out as a privateer, and to spike a gun in battery at the southeast end of the yard. Lieut. John H. Russell had charge of the expedition, and with Lieut. Blake was to attack the schooner, while Lieut. John G. Sproston and Midshipman Steele spiked the gun.

In his exaggerated official report of the affair, Commodore Mervine, U. S. N., says:

"The attack was made on the morning of the 14th inst., at half-past three o'clock. The schooner, named the *Judah*, was found moored to the wharf, under the protection of a battery and field-piece, and to be armed with a pivot and four broadside guns. Her crew were on her, and prepared to receive our forces, pouring in a volley of musketry as the boat neared the vessel. A desperate resistance was made from the decks of the schooner, but her men were driven off on to the wharf by our boarders, where they rallied and were joined by the guard, and kept up a continued fire upon our men.

"In the meantime the vessel was set on fire in several places. That which finally consumed her was lighted in the cabin by Assistant Engineer White and a coal-heaver, Patrick Driscoll, who went as a volunteer. She burned to the water's edge, and has since, while burning, been set free from her moorings and has drifted down opposite Fort Barrancas, where she sunk.

"Of the party assigned to the spiking of the gun, only Lieut. Sproston and Gunner Boreton were able, after considerable search, to find it, the party becoming separated in the darkness. No opposition was made to their landing; Midshipman Steele, with his command, had gone to the aid of those on the schooner, where he performed valuable service. Very fortunately, only one man was found in charge of the gun, and he immediately levelled his piece at Lieut. Sproston, but was shot down by Gunner Horton before he could obtain certain aim. Both pieces exploded simultaneously. The gun, which was found to be a ten-inch Columbiad, was immediately spiked, and, bringing off its tompion, these two officers returned to their boat.

" The work proposed having thus been well and thoroughly done in the short space of fifteen minutes, and the whole force of the enemy in the yard—reported by deserters as over 1,000 strong—being aroused, our boats pulled away, and rallying at a short distance from the shore, fired six charges of canister from their howitzers into the yard, with what result it is impossible to say. Three of the enemy are known to have been killed, and our officers are confident the number is much larger. The boats then returned to the ship, arriving there about daylight.

" But, sir, I am grieved to report that this brilliant affair was not unattended by loss on our side. I have to report as killed by shots from the crosstrees of the schooner, while the boats were approaching, Boatswain's Mate Charles H. Lamphere, and John R. Herring, seaman and captain of the howitzer, two of the best men in our ship, and marine John Smith—the first man to board the schooner, and who behaved most gallantly—who was, by a sad mistake, having lost his distinguishing mark, killed by one of our own men. We have wounded, probably mortally, seaman R. Clark and E. K. Osborn ; severely, nine other seamen. Capt. Reynolds received a severe contusion on his shoulder, and Midshipman Higginson had the end of his thumb shot off. Lieuts. Russell and Blake had narrow escapes, the flesh of each being grazed by one or more musket balls."

The U. S. blockading steamer *Montgomery,* Capt. T. Darragh Shaw, entered the harbor of Appalachicola, with another steamer, on the afternoon of August 27th, and captured the ship *Finland* and schooner *New Plan,* taking the masters and crews of the vessels prisoners. Finding it difficult to secure both vessels, the captors set fire to the *Finland,* but brought the other away.

In October Gen. Yulee commanded at Fernandina, where batteries had been erected and guns brought from St. Augustine mounted. St. John's had a battery of five old guns ; Nassau's battery mounted four old guns, and to bar the entrance to Brunswick there was a battery on St. Simon's Island of three guns. On Jekyl Island there was a battery constructed of railroad iron and palmetto logs. There was a battery on Amelia Island which commanded the channel to Cumberland Islands. Nearly all of these defences at Fernandina, which were afterwards highly commended by Admiral Dupont and some of the best officers of the Union army, were designed and superintended by Lieut. Wm. A. Webb of the C. S. navy. In March 1862, Fernandina was evacuated and most of the Confederate property was removed.

On the 22d of November, the bombardment of Fort McRae by the *Niagara,* and of Fort Barrancas and the navy-yard by Fort Pickens, began. The object of the attack was to destroy the navy-yard and to batter down the fortifications of the Confederates. The action resulted in the Federal forces making terrible breaches in Fort McRae, reducing the village of Warrington to ashes and setting fire three times to the navy-yard. This the Confederates succeeded in extinguishing. The walls of Fort Pickens were badly breached and the *Niagara* was much damaged. The *Richmond* was obliged to haul out early in the action, having received serious damage.

Col. Harvey Brown opened fire from Fort Pickens on January 1st, 1862, upon the Confederate steamer *Times* while loading coal at the Pensacola navy-yard. The fire was gallantly responded to and continued all day from the batteries of Gen. Bragg. The firing was kept up until three in the morning, but as the guns from Fort Pickens did not respond, the fire from the Confederate batteries was suspended.

For some time previous to 1862, the Confederates at Pensacola were busily engaged in removing the commissary stores, munitions of war, guns and everything of value from that place. This having been completed, at midnight on May 9th,

DESTRUCTION OF PENSACOLA NAVY-YARD.

1862, the navy-yard, forts and public buildings were set on fire and the town evacuated. All the public property, excepting the custom house, was destroyed, but all moveable Confederate property was saved. When the enemy discovered what was going on, they opened a furious bombardment, which was kept up during the conflagration, but without doing much damage to anybody at Pensacola. A correspondent of the Mobile *Register*, under date of May 10th, gives a brief but graphic description of the burning of the navy-yard, which we append :

"The scenes of last night closed the long campaign of Pensacola—of its history you are sufficiently familiar. The order for the destruction of the Warrington navy-yard, and all public property at that place and Pensacola that could not be moved, was successfully carried into execution, and thoroughly executed at the yard and Pensacola.

"About 11:30 o'clock the signal being given by Brig. Gen. Thomas Jones, in an instant the torch was applied at every point, and in a few minutes the wood-work, gun-carriages, etc., in Forts Barrancas and McRae and the hospitals, together with all the other buildings in the navy-yard proper, in the villages of Woolsey and Warrington, were in flames. At the same instant the torch was applied to the oil factory and all the government buildings in the city of Pensacola, also to the steamers at the wharf. The scene was grand, thrilling, and sublime. The whole bay was as light as midday, while the murky clouds overhead reflected back an apparently liquid sea of fire. Fort Pickens could be plainly seen, and its garrison seemed to have suddenly aroused, astounded and surprised. In a short while, however, Pickens opened with shot and shell. Our boys, not relishing the compliment, instantly returned it from one or two smooth-bore 44s and 32s, which quickly cleared the ramparts of Pickens of all sight seers. Whether anybody was 'hurt,' is not known. Pickens seemed to be, and must have been, perfectly ignorant of our movements, and from the heaviness of its fire was in a paroxysm of wrath and rage.

"The task of dismantling the forts and batteries, and the removal of everything worth transporting, even to small bits of copper and lead, in the face and very teeth of the enemy, was one of a most difficult and delicate nature. This has been most admirably executed by Gen. Jones. The Federals can now take possession of an unhospitable sand beach."

The greater portion of the population of the city of Pensacola, as well as of the settlements above, on Blackwater Creek and river, and on Escambia Bay, left their homes and sought the interior with their negroes and such of their movable property as they could transport. The *Fulton*, that was on the stocks in the navy-yard, was burned, as was also the iron-clad that was building on the Escambia River.

Early the next morning the *Harriet Lane*, a Federal war steamer (afterwards captured at Galveston, Texas), came up and anchored in front of the city, and the Commodore dispatched a messenger to the mayor of the city with the following communication:

"U. S. Steamer 'Harriet Lane,' off Pensacola, May 8th, 1862.

"Sir: I wish to confer with the authorities of this place, whoever they may be, civil or military, in regard to preserving good order, in case there should be any disposition to commit excesses on unoffending and loyal citizens; and I wish to obtain information relating to late events and the destruction of public property.

"I take this opportunity to say that any abusive or disrespectful conduct from mobs or other parties in this town towards the persons belonging to the naval vessels of the United States, will be treated as an inimical act, and will be resisted as if it was assault and battery.

"No one need fear any interference with their rights or property as long as they conform to good order.

"Very respectfully, your obedient servant,
"D. D. Porter, *Commanding Mortar Fleet.*"

To which the Mayor replied:

"Mayoralty of Pensacola, Pensacola, May 10th, 1862.

"Sir: Your communication of the 8th inst., expressing a desire to confer with the authorities of the city, is to hand.

"In reply, I would state that I am ready to confer with you, either at my office or on board your vessel, in regard to the subject matter of your communication. Very respectfully, your obedient servant,
"Francis B. Bobe, *Mayor.*"

On the same day a large force landed from the Federal fleet and forts and took possession of Pensacola.

On June 13th, 1861, the Confederate vessel *Forest King* was captured at Key West by the U. S. S. *Crusader.* The *Forest King* entered the harbor for supplies, her commander having been told by officers on the U. S. vessels *Sabine, South Carolina* and *Huntsville,* that she could do so; but on entering she was seized and the vessel and cargo were sent to New York. On the 11th of March, 1862, the town of St. Augustine was surrendered to Commander C. R. P. Rodgers, of the U. S. flag-ship *Wabash;* and on the 12th, Jacksonville was peaceably surrendered by the authorities to Lieut. T. H. Stevens, of the gunboat *Ottawa.* This expedition of the South Atlantic squadron resulted in the possession of the whole coast of Georgia from South Carolina to Florida. The harbors were good, and almost any vessel of size could enter and find safe anchorage. This alone made the capture valuable to the United States for the establishment of naval depots.

In May, 1863, the schooner *Fashion*, at anchor in the Chattahoochee River, twenty-five miles above Appalachicola, was loading with cotton, with the intention of running the blockade. She had received sixty bales, and was waiting to complete her cargo, when information was conveyed to the blockading fleet off Appalachicola. The enemy sent nine launches with armed men up the river, captured the schooner with the cotton on board and towed her to the fleet. When the news reached Lieut. Commander John J. Guthrie, of the C. S. gunboat *Chattahoochee*, at Blountstown, Fla., on May 30th, he determined to pass the obstructions in the Chattahoochee, and if possible steam down and relieve the *Fashion.*

The *Chattahoochee* was lying at anchor with only seven pounds of steam on. Lieut. Guthrie ordered steam to be raised, when in a few moments her boilers exploded with the most disastrous results, sixteen persons being killed, many others severely scalded, and the vessel sunk. The disaster happened immediately after cold water had been put into the boilers. A correspondent of the Columbus *Sun* says :

"The magazines of the ship were within three feet of the boiler, and the shell-room as near. As soon as the explosion occurred a panic commenced, the men jumped overboard, fearing the explosion of the magazine and shell-rooms. At this point the gunner, Mr. John A. Lovett, in the absence of the first lieutenant, took charge and displayed great energy and courage in saving life and property and in reassuring the panic-stricken men.

"The ship was found to be filling, when the poor wounded and burned sufferers were landed, together with the personal effects of the crew and officers. It was raining and blowing very hard, and the bank was very muddy upon which the wounded were landed. The poor fellows lay writhing and groaning in the mud for some time before they could be got to a cotton-gin near by.

"The ship was hauled in near the shore and has sunk to her deck, settling firmly on the bottom. The powder and shells are a total loss.

"The guns have been landed, and the nine-inch and rifle are already in position at a strong point, and although the loss of the vessel and the brave men is much to be deplored, yet with the guns ashore, manned by the splendidly-drilled crew of the late *Chattahoochee*, the river is much safer than ever before.

"Midshipman Mallory died at the Ladies' Hospital, in this city, on yesterday evening at five o'clock. He is the same gallant little fellow who pushed his way first aboard the U. S. frigate *Congress*, at Hampton Roads, after she had struck her colors to the *Virginia*."

Those killed by the explosion were: Midshipman Mallory, Assistant Engineers Henry Fagan, Euclid P. Hodges and Frederick W. Arents; Eugene Henderson, Paymaster's Clerk; W. B. Bilbro, Pilot; Charles H. Berry, Quartermaster; four landsmen, two firemen, one coal-heaver and one seaman.

The officers of the *Chattahoochee* were: Lieutenant Commanding, J. J. Guthrie; Lieutenant, G. W. Gift; Surgeon, H. W. W. Washington; Assistant Surgeon, M. R. Ford; Assistant Paymaster, L. E. Brooks; Masters, H. H. Marmaduke, James McC. Baker; Midshipmen, W. J. Craig, W. R. Mayhew, C. K. Mallory; Passed Midshipman, Daniel Trigg; Engineers —First Assistant, John W. Tynan; Second Assistant, Henry Fagan; Third Assistants, John H. Dent, E. P. Hodges; Gunner, John A. Lovett.

The *Chattahoochee* was a strong wooden gunboat of light draft, and carried a battery of four broadside and two pivot guns, one foward and one aft. She had made two efforts previous to her explosion to attack the enemy's vessels off Appalachicola, but each time her machinery became so deranged she was obliged to retire.

When the Federals heard that she was sunk in the river, disabled, they made an attempt to pass the obstructions at the head of the narrows on the Appalachicola River to destroy her. Her guns were mounted in battery on the river bank, and steps were taken by Gen. Cobb to drive the enemy back. A section of Echol's battery and other reinforcements were sent down the river for her defence, and the enemy hearing of the measures adopted did not make an attack, but abandoned the enterprise.

In a short time the *Chattahoochee* was raised, her machinery repaired, and under the command of Lieut. George W. Gift[1] she did efficient service in keeping the Chattahoochee, Flint, and Appalachicola Rivers clear of the enemy.

In the spring of 1864, Lieut. Gift and his officers determined to make a desperate effort to capture one or more vessels blockading Appalachicola. At this time the coast was

[1] Lieut. Commander Gift was born near Nashville, Tenn., on March 1st, 1833. In 1846 he was sent to the Naval Academy at Annapolis, and after two years was assigned as midshipman to the Pacific Squadron. He resigned from the navy in 1852 and went to California, where he established a banking house at Sacramento. At the breaking out of the war, he came overland by way of Texas, with Gen. Albert Sydney John-ston and other distinguished officers from California, and entered the Confederate service, first in the army and afterwards in the navy. He entered the navy on the 18th of March, 1862, and was assigned to the iron-clad *Arkansas*, then building at Memphis, Tenn. He was a brave and daring officer, and took a distinguished part in several gallant exploits of the war. He was one of the boarders that captured and burnt the

blockaded by the U. S. steamers *Somerset* and *Adela*, and the plans of the officers of the *Chattahoochee* were to board in small boats one of these vessels, man her and attempt to capture the other, and if successful, break the blockade, and run the vessels into Mobile or burn them. About seven boats were fitted with muffled oars, grapnels, incendiary materials, signal flags, lanterns, compasses, medical stores, provisions, etc., and manned by the officers and crew of the *Chattahoochee*, numbering about seventy men, and about twenty volunteers from Company F, Bouneau's battalion of Confederate soldiers. The officers and men were armed with rifles, muskets, shot-guns, revolvers and cutlasses, with over 1,000 rounds of ammunition. Everything being made ready, the boats proceeded down the Appalachicola River on their hazardous enterprise. Pilots having been secured, when the boats arrived in St. George's Sound, they proceeded across the bay to East Point, to await a dark night before making the attack. The officers of the party were : Lieut. Commanding, George W. Gift; Passed Midshipmen, Samuel P. Blanc, Henry L. Vaughan, George W. Sparks; Midshipmen, J. Thomas Scharf, Wm. S. Hogue; Assistant Paymaster, Marshal P. Sotheron; Assistant Surgeon, Marcellus Ford; First Assistant Engineer, Loudon Campbell; Third Assistant Engineer, A. De Blanc; Master's Mate, Carman Frazee; Volunteers: Colonel D. P. Holland, aide to the Governor of Florida; Surgeon Cherry, first Georgia regulars; A. G. Sparks, Signal Officer, and Capt. Blunt, in command of the volunteers from Bouneau's battalion.

The expedition landed in the night at East Point, near the east pass of St. George's Sound, which the U. S. steamer *Adela* was blockading. The plan was to remain under cover at this point until a favorable dark or stormy night, when the party was to row to the blockading vessel, and attempt her capture by boarding. Lieut. Gift and his men waited patiently for a favorable opportunity to make the attack, but they were doomed to disappointment. The nights were clear and the sea smooth, and the dipping of the oars in the phosphorescent water emitted a luminous light which shone brightly some distance beyond. In the meantime the provisions of the party gave out, and it was necessary to secure a supply from the town. Intelligence was also received from the Confederate scouts, that information of the contemplated attack had been communicated to the enemy's vessels by Unionists in Appalachicola.

Under these circumstances Lieut. Gift determined to abandon the enterprise and push across the sound and hasten

U. S. steamer *Underwriter*, at Newbern, N. C., and took a prominent part in the defence of the *Arkansas* in her various desperate struggles with the Federal fleets on the Yazoo and Mississippi Rivers. He married Miss Shackleford of Florida while he was stationed on the *Chattahoochee*, and some time after the close of the war he returned to California and settled at Napa. At the time of his death, on February 11th, 1879, he was editor of the Napa City *Reporter*. He left a wife and four children. The writer was his executive officer in the launch he commanded at the time the *Underwriter* was captured at *Newbern*, and was in command of his boat in St. George's Sound during his illness when cast on St. George's Island.

up the Appalachicola River, before the enemy knew of his departure.

The Confederates embarked in their boats with the intention of crossing the sound to Appalachicola, but, as a storm was approaching, only two of the boats—the one containing Lieut. Gift, Midshipman Scharf and the volunteer officers, and the other manned by ten soldiers—attempted to cross the sound, while the others hugged the shore. The latter party, under the command of Passed Midshipman De Blanc, reached the town in safety, while the boat containing the soldiers was swamped; but the men in it were rescued by Lieut. Gift, who was driven fifteen miles across the sound to St. George's Island. The storm raged for several hours, and the heavily ladened boat of Lieut. Gift made vain efforts to reach the town, from which direction the wind was blowing a terrible gale. Lieut. Gift being taken suddenly ill, the command of his boat devolved upon Midshipman Scharf. At this time the boat was half filled with water, with seventeen men inside and ten men from the swamped boat hanging on the outside, and the sea washing over her. The boat was two miles from shore, and all expected every moment would be the last. Finding that it would be impossible to reach the town in the face of the storm, Midshipman Scharf informed Lieut. Gift that their only hope for safety was to turn round and go to sea before the wind. The commander instructed him to do what he thought best, and immediately Midshipman Scharf informed his men of his determination. There was great fear of swamping in the trough of the sea in turning, but having confidence in his judgment the crew were ready to obey his commands. He ordered the boat to be lightened, and all the guns, ammunition, baggage, lanterns, water-casks, etc., thrown overboard. Six of the nearly exhausted men were taken in from the outside and stowed in the bottom of the boat. When everything was ready the order was given and the boat was headed for the Gulf of Mexico as a large wave struck under her quarter, nearly lifting her out of the water. The four men, who were still hanging on the outside, having become nearly exhausted, were taken in the already over-ladened boat, and the storm-driven Confederates proceeded to sea, hoping, if possible, to reach St. George Island off the coast. When the boat approached St. George Island the breakers were heard roaring over the beach, and the pilot gave up all hope of reaching the shore in safety. The men prepared to swim for their lives in the event of the boat being swamped by the breakers, by throwing off all surplus clothing. Fortunately, the boat passed through safely and reached the island, where the party remained for two days in a starving condition, sustaining life only by eating "palmetto cabbage," "alligators," oysters, etc.

In the meantime, the remainder of the boats reached Appalachicola in safety, and took up quarters in the town, to await intelligence from Lieut. Gift. The enemy meanwhile, receiving information of the dispersing of the expedition, landed a force and drove Midshipman DeBlanc and his command to the swamps. In his report, Lieut. Com. Wm. Budd of the U. S. steamer *Somerset,* West Pass, St. George's Sound, May 16th, 1864, said :

"I have the honor to report, that on the night of the 12th inst. I sent the light-draft boats of this vessel and of the U. S. schooner *Chambers* to land a detachment of troops under command of Lieut. Hunter, 110th New York Vols., a few miles below the town of Appalachicola. After landing the troops the officer in charge of the boats (Acting Ensign E. H. Smith) was instructed to proceed slowly along shore, so as to be in communication with them during their march and approach to the town, in the rear of which the whole force was to arrive at daybreak. Taking two launches from this ship, I arrived in front of the place about the same time, and discovered a force of about seventy or eighty of the enemy attempting to embark in boats from the upper end of the wharves. The rapid approach of the first launch caused them to abandon that project and retreat through the town, which movement was hastened by a couple of shells from our howitzer. They passed within a short distance of a portion of our troops under Lieut. Hunter, who unfortunately thought that they were part of his command, and permitted them to gain and escape by the up-river road without molestation. We followed them about two miles, but the density of the undergrowth and number of paths leading through the woods in all directions rendering any further pursuit unwise and futile, we returned to the boats.

"Ascertaining that the commanding officer of the expedition (George W. Gift, Lieutenant C. S. N.), was on the sound with about thirty men, I dispatched my boats and troops after him, but the swiftness of his boat and the approach of night enabled him to escape, having been chased by our first launch, under command of Acting Ensign C. H. Brantingham, who captured one of his small boats and three of his party. * * * We captured six of their boats (all they had except one), four prisoners, a quantity of small arms, (rifles, cutlasses, etc.) 1,000 rounds of ammunition, all their compasses, signal flags, blankets, haversacks, medical stores, etc. They abandoned everything. * * * Had it not been for the unfortunate mistake of the officer in command of our troops, we should have captured or destroyed the entire force."

In a subsequent report dated May 21st, 1864, he said :

"I send down by the U. S. steamer *Honduras,* as prisoners, Thomas McLean, Anthony Murray and James Anderson, citizens of Appalachicola. These men were engaged in active co-operation with the enemy when captured. McLean enacted the role of a scout or spy. Mistaking our troops for those of the enemy, he gave them information respecting my force and position in front of the town on the morning of the 13th inst. Murray and Anderson were acting as scouts for Gift, keeping open his communications and supplying him with provisions when he was absent from the main body of his command. When taken, they were carrying soldiers from the islands back to the main. Heretofore all of them have enjoyed immunity from us as citizens. Their local knowledge makes them dangerous to us and very useful to the enemy ; for the latter they act as scouts, spies and pilots, and in this case they were caught in the act. They pretend to have been forced into Gift's service, but I know them well, and earnestly request that they will not be permitted to return to Appalachicola."

The enemy captured Andrew McCormick, Sergeant of Company F, Bouneau's battalion, Napoleon Terry and Louis

Gay, privates, and Joseph Sire, Captain after-guard of the *Chattahoochee.*

Before Midshipman DeBlanc and his command retreated to the swamps, he sent Thomas McLean, Anthony Murray, and James Anderson, citizens of Appalachicola, with a supply of provisions to search the islands along the coast for Lieut. Gift and his two boats' crews. The relief party found the wrecked crews, and as soon as the storm abated they returned with them to Appalachicola, where they learned for the first time that their comrades had been driven from the town. Lieut. Gift then hastened up the river to avoid the enemy, who were searching the islands for him. He carried his boat some distance up the river, then sank it in a bayou and traveled over-land with his command until he joined the remainder of his party above the obstructions in the Appalachicola River.

Upon the abandonment of the river by the Confederates the *Chattahoochee* was destroyed, together with the iron-clad gunboat *Columbus,* which had been building for a long time at Columbus, Ga., under the direction of Lieut. Andrew McLaughlin. A torpedo boat, nearly completed, was also destroyed at Columbus, together with the navy-yard, machine shops, etc.

CONFEDERATE STEAMER "NASHVILLE" DESTROYING FEDERAL VESSEL

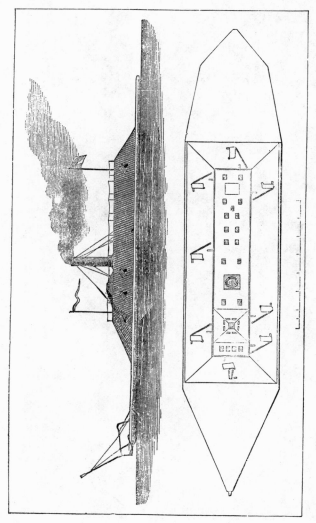

THE C. S. IRON-CLAD "ATLANTA," CAPTURED BY THE FEDERALS JUNE 17TH, 1863.

CHAPTER XX.

GEORGIA WATERS.

FROM the time South Carolina seceded to the secession of Georgia on January 19th, 1861, the relations of the States with one another were peaceful. Neither the Federal government, nor any competent authority, had recognized the existence of a breach between sections of the Republic outside of the competency of Congress and the Executive to heal. But day by day, Mr. Seward was piloting the country with accelerating rapidity towards the "red battle" issue which he declared would be the last act of his "irrepressible conflict."

The first act that paved the way for open hostilities between members of a confederation which, only a few months before, were bound together by ties it was fondly hoped could never be sundered, was the uncalled-for, unwarrantable, and illegal seizure of the property of Savannah merchants in the harbor of New York. This grave and momentous event in the progress toward civil war and military despotism, occurred as early as the 22d of January, 1861. On that day the republican Governor of New York assumed the responsibility of ordering the police of New York City to invade vessels lying in the harbor, and to seize upon such wares as, in their discretion, they might deem to be "contraband of war." Superintendent Kennedy proceeded on board the steamer *Monticello*, at Pier 12, North River, and seized twenty-eight cases of merchandise, which were found to contain 950 muskets. The seizure created the greatest excitement in Savannah, to which port the *Monticello* was bound, and immediately afterwards, ex-Senator Robert Toombs, of Georgia, addressed a telegraphic dispatch to the Mayor of New York, protesting against what had been done, and alluding to the inevitable consequences of such lawlessness. Mayor Wood disavowed participation in it, and declared that it met with his own disapproval, and was reprobated by the vast majority of the people of the city of New York.

In a few days another dispatch was received by telegraph by Governor Morgan of New York, from Governor Brown of Georgia. The latter simply demanded that the property belonging to his citizens should be handed over to G. B. Lamar, the president of the Bank of the Republic. Governor Morgan replied by sending back a telegraphic answer that the subject was too grave a one to reply to cursorily, and that he must wait a more detailed communication from Governor Brown by mail, before giving it his attention. "This was, of course," says the New York *Herald,* of February 10th, 1861, "equivalent to an endorsement of the robbery which the Metropolitan police had committed, with an attempt at evasion, and to gain time, similar to those which have characterized every public leader of the Seward school of Massachusetts politics, since the beginning of the crisis under which the country is laboring."

In retaliation for the illegal seizure by the New York police, under pretence that they were contraband of war, of goods belonging to individuals of that State, the authorities of Georgia, on February 9th, seized, in Savannah, the barks *D. Colden Murray,* the *W. R. Kibby, Golden Lead* and *Adjuster,* and the schooner *Julia A. Hallock.* They were the property of citizens of New York. This was the first act of reprisal at the South, against aggression in the non-slaveholding States, and it was tantamount to a decree of non-intercourse.

"Every sober-minded, intelligent, patriotic American citizen [said the New York *Herald*] will be startled and alarmed by it, and will shrink back with horror from the prospect of blood, carnage and internecine strife which it threatens to inaugurate. Gov. Brown will find an abundant justification of the act he has ordered, in the responsibilities of his position, and in the necessity of indemnifying private citizens, who are his constituents, for an unwarrantable robbery committed by our police, for which they could obtain no other redress. It is the very nearest thing to the beginning of a civil war; but let the blame rest where it belongs, upon the Republican Executive of the State of New York, whose atrocious usurpation of powers that do not belong to him has led to such a sad result."

The seizure of the vessels by the authorities of Georgia also created considerable excitement in Washington among all parties. In the House of Representatives, Hon. John Cochrane offered a resolution calling on the Secretary of the Treasury for information on the subject, but the proposition was objected to and it went over to the following Monday. In the meantime, later in the day, the arms were restored to the agent of the owners, or it was said they were, and the vessels seized in Savannah were released. On the 23d of February Supt. Kennedy refused to give up ten cases of the merchandise referred to, until the legality of the seizure was determined by the "proper tribunals." This unjustifiable act roused the ire of the Georgians, and Gov. Brown showed their spirit of retaliation by holding three vessels belonging to New York, as a surety for the safe return of their property which they contended had been taken from them without any just cause or reason. The vessels seized were the ship *Martha J. Ward*, bark *Adjuster* and bark *Harold*. In consequence of the cargo of the bark *Adjuster* belonging to the subjects of Great Britain, she was released, but the other vessels seized in reprisal by the Georgia authorities were advertised to be sold on the 25th of March. In the meantime, on March 19th, in consideration of the release of the arms by the New York police, the vessels seized in Savannah were released. [1]

At the release of the arms in the keeping of the police of New York, the U. S. revenue officers instituted a strict surveillance over vessels leaving that port to prevent provisions, ammunition and weapons of war from being forwarded to the Southern States, and to stop suspected vessels that it was thought might engage in privateering for the Confederacy. The Secretary of the Treasury, in May, gave orders to the Collector of St. Louis to examine the manifests of all vessels sailing South, and Collector Barney of New York, and the collectors of all ports north of the Potomac, were ordered to make a careful examination of every vessel leaving their respective ports. In this way a complete blockade was maintained in all the collection districts. The revenue cutter *Harriet Lane* was at first used for this purpose at the port of New York, but having been called away, in accordance with the proclamation of Mr. Lincoln, to assist in the blockade of the Southern ports, it became necessary to procure other vessels. Collector Barney therefore impressed into the revenue service three of the vessels engaged in the U. S. coast survey. These were located at three different points to command the several outlets from the harbor of New York. The *Vixen* was placed in Throgg's Neck and guarded the passage from the East River into Long Island Sound. On an average 120 vessels passed this point every day during the flood tide in May, 1861, and each of these had to be boarded and have their papers examined. The *Corwin* was stationed inside the Narrows, where all the large steamers and vessels of extensive tonnage pass out into the ocean. At least fifty vessels a day were boarded at this point. The *Bibb* was

---

[1] The following is a copy of a letter sent by the owners of the *Martha J. Ward* to Mr. Kennedy, which helped to bring about the desired result:

J. A. Kennedy, Esq.:

DEAR SIR: We are the owners of the ship *Martha J. Ward*, now under seizure at Savannah, as stated, in reprisal for the arms seized by you. We have made every effort to save our property, valued at over $40,000, and find that without your friendly aid, we shall be unable to do so, and must submit to such enormous sacrifice. If, in consideration of our unfortunate position, you will deliver the arms to us, we will indemnify you against all damages and costs which may be recovered against you for such seizure.

JAMES E. WARD & Co.

The before-mentioned indemnity read as follows:

In consideration that John A. Kennedy will, at our request, deliver up ten cases of arms seized on board the steamer *Monticello*, and in consideration of one dollar to us paid, we hereby agree to pay all costs and damages and expenses that may be recovered against him for such seizure. Dated this 15th day of March, 1861.

JAMES E. WARD & Co.

The above indemnity was required of the owners of the ship *Martha J. Ward* by Superintendent Kennedy. Upon giving it, the arms were delivered to the owners of the ship, who transmitted them to Savannah to be delivered to Governor Brown.

40

located at the mouth of the Raritan River, in the vicinity of Perth Amboy, and prevented all suspicious looking vessels from passing through Kill von Kull. No vessel was permitted to pass without having a proper clearance, and also undergoing an examination, where it was deemed necessary. The surveyor also detailed officers to visit daily every vessel lying at the wharves, and report the appearance of affairs every twenty-four hours. In addition to this a coast-guard was detailed on both sides of the river to prevent the loading of vessels at night, and no vessel was allowed to leave between sunset and sunrise. The steam tug *Mercury* was employed to ply between New York and the revenue cutters.[1]

These precautions were forced upon the Federal government by the necessity of intercepting the very profitable trade in war material for the South that was being carried on by manufacturers, merchants and shippers in the North, who suffered from an obsession of their "loyalty to the old flag" that was coincident with the offer of Southern agents to pay remunerative prices for anything in the line of guns, ammunition, or army goods that might be useful to the nascent Southern Confederacy.

"We have been accustomed [says Judge Cowley], to berate the commercial classes of Great Britain for exporting goods to the Confederate States in violation of the blockade; but probably more goods were carried into the Confederate States through the instrumentality of merchants in the United States than by all the merchants of Europe. More secrecy was observed by those residing in New York who engaged in the business than was observed in running the blockade of Mexico; but it is none the less true that in the civil war, as in the Mexican war, the munitions of war were furnished in very large quantities by the citizens of the United States to the enemies of the United States."[2]

Mr. Greeley's well-known lament, in "The American Conflict," over the greed of New York commercial men who

---

[1] The following is a complete list of the vessels owned or partly owned by residents of the Southern States which were seized by Surveyor Andrews. of the port of New York, in accordance with the U. S. Confiscation Act of July 13th, 1861:

No. 1, steamer Marion, belonging to New York; owners or consignees, Spofford, Tileston & Co.; 2, steamer Roanoke, New York, N. Y. & Va. S.S. Co.; 3, ship Ohio, N. Bedford, E. Howland ; 4, ship J. W. Fannin, New York, J. H. Brower & Co.; 5, ship W. B. Travis, New York, J. H. Brower & Co.; 6, ship Wm. H. Wharton, New York, J. H. Brower & Co.; 7, ship Crest of the Wave, Thomaston, M. R. Ludwig ; 8, ship St. Charles, New York, W. T. Frost; 9, ship Harriett, Boston, H. L. Richardson & Co.; 10, ship Roger A. Hiern, New York, J. & N. Smith & Co.; 11, ship Trumbull, New York, J. & N. Smith & Co.; 12, ship North Carolina, Norfolk, Hardy Bro.; 13, bark Clara Haxall, Richmond, J. Currie & Co.; 14, bark Virginian, Richmond, D. Currie ; 15, bark Sally Magee, Richmond, D. Currie & Co.; 16, bark Mary Lucretia, New York, J. T. B. Maxwell ; 17, bark Bounding Billow, Boston, A. Pickering & Co.; 18, bark Fame ; 19, bark Parthian, Rich-

mond. D. & W. Currie & Co.; 20, bark Norumbega, New York, J. H. Brower & Co.; 21, bark Winefred, Richmond, J. Currie & Co.; 22, bark General Green, Charles'n, W. G. Armstrong ; 23, bark Pioneer, Richmond, E. D. Voss & Co.; 24, brig Leni, Alexandria, Lambert ; 25, brig Cyrus Starr, 26, brig Champion, Pictou, N. S., J. Ketchune ; 27, brig Fannie Currie, Richmond, J. Currie ; 28, schooner Emily Kieth, New Orleans, J. B Lockwood ; 29, schooner Ned, New York, E. S. Powell; 30, schooner Marshall, Richmond, J. Curry, 31, schooner Crenshaw, Richmond, D. & W. Currie & Co.; 32, schooner Manchester, Richmond, D. & W. Currie & Co ; 33, schooner Lynchburgh, Richmond, D. & W. Currie & Co.; 34, schooner Haxall, Richmond, D & W. Currie & Co.; 35, schooner Forest King, Fairhaven, Fish, Robbins & Co.; 36, schooner Claremont, New York, H. Finch & Co.; 37, schooner Ha'h M. Johnson, Greenport, John Wells. Recapitulation : Steamers, 2; ships, 10; barks, 11 ; Brigs, 3 ; Schooners, 11. Aggregate value, $750,000.

[2] "Leaves from a Lawyer's Life Afloat and Ashore," p. 112.

sacrificed patriotism to pelf, lends additional force to the observations of Judge Cowley in the same line of comment. These dealings by Northern men in war material consigned to Southern ports were so open and flagrant early in 1861 that they were denounced by Judge Smalley, then presiding in the U. S. Circuit Court for New York. On January 14th, in charging the Grand Jury for the term, he delivered an address which has not been preserved in any history of the war written from a Northern standpoint, perhaps because it was too scathing a criticism of the traffic which it became convenient to forget when contractors afterwards found the most lucrative market in their engagements with the War and Navy Departments of the Federal administration. He spoke of their earlier business as embodying " the highest crime known to the law of any civilized country "—that of high treason—in furnishing aid and comfort to an enemy in rebellion against the government; and he extended the charge so far as to include within the offence of misprision of treason all persons who, knowing of the shipments of war material to the States which had seceded, failed to give information thereof to the Federal authorities. It is plain that he meant to throw out a drag-net in which he might catch the money-seekers to whom Georgia and other Southern States were so much indebted, but he failed to intimidate them. They continued to sell the South whatever it wanted until the firing upon Fort Sumter drew the line against their Southern business, and then they plunged, with equal eagerness, their arms elbow-deep into the overflowing treasury at Washington.[1]

Georgia—the " Empire State of the South "—was far removed from the theatre of battle until the war was six months' old. In the meantime she had sent thousands of fighting men to the armies under Beauregard and Johnston in Virginia, but had scarcely given to the establishment of a naval force the consideration that it deserved. Her ordinance of secession was passed on January 19th, 1861; but, by the order of Governor Joseph E. Brown, the State troops took possession of Fort Pulaski, a casemate and barbette fortification at the mouth of the Savannah River, on January 7th, and within the next three weeks all the U. S. military posts in Georgia were surrendered by the officers in charge of them without inviting the compulsion of shot and shell that was used in the argument with Major Anderson at Fort Sumter. The only U. S.

[1] Charles Hallock, in an article on " Bermuda and the Blockade," in the *Galaxy* for April, 1867, speaking of the blockade trade at Bermuda, says : " British goods were always in great demand for the blockade-runners, for they would have no dealings with Yankees. Accordingly, in the shops could be found bushels of Connecticut pins and cases of Massachusetts shoes marked 'London,' elegant felt hats from New York labelled 'Paris,' and good old Irish whiskey from New Jersey; for there were many articles that could be purchased cheaper in the United States than in Europe, and the laws of trade are inflexible—' the longest pole breaks down the most persimmons.' And so quantities of the goods found place in blockade cargoes, to the great profit of shrewd speculators at the North."

vessel in the port of Savannah was the revenue cutter *J. C. Dobbin*, which on the night of January 1st was seized by a party of citizens of Savannah dressed in civic clothes, but armed with muskets and revolvers. They announced to the officer in charge that they had come to take the vessel in the name of the State of Georgia; as they numbered ten times as many as his crew he made no resistance, and they raised the Palmetto flag, saluted it, sent the officers and crew below and closed the hatches on them, and finally ran the vessel ashore. The leader in the seizure was C. A. Greiner, who afterwards went North, and on April 29th was arrested in Philadelphia on a charge of having committed treason in the *Dobbin* affair and in the subsequent capture of Fort Pulaski by the State troops.

Succeeding this incident it was not until the advent of Commodore Josiah Tatnall at Savannah, that public and official attention was seriously turned toward naval affairs. [1] Then the presence of an officer who had attained the highest rank in the U. S. navy, compelled the authorities and the people to think of what Georgia might do toward fighting the battles of the Confederacy on water as well as on land. On February 28th, Governor Brown accepted the tender of the services of Commodore Tatnall to his native State, and appointed him senior flag-officer in the navy of Georgia, which does not appear then to have consisted of a ship or a gun. Tatnall's commission was merely honorary until March, when he was appointed a commander in the provisional navy of the Confederate States, and assigned to the command of whatever navy existed or might be created in the waters of Georgia and South Carolina. He was expected to form a marine force under the Confederate flag, and with the material which he could reach it was a task almost akin to making bricks without straw. He eventually got together a semblance of a naval flotilla by arming a river steamer and a few small tugs that were lying idle at the Savannah wharves with whatever guns he could pick up; and with this "Mosquito Fleet," as it was called, he went into action against the massive frigates and heavy gunboats of the enemy at the battle of Port Royal, only

---

[1] Josiah Tatnall was born at the family estate of Bonaventure, near Savannah, November 9th, 1795, and was appointed midshipman in the U. S. navy, April 1st, 1812, and in August was ordered to the frigate *Constellation*. He participated in the repulse of the British boat expedition by the battery on Craney Island, below Norfolk, which was manned by seamen, June 22d, 1813, and subsequently served on the *Epervier*, *Constellation* and *Ontario*, all attached to the Mediterranean squadron. In April, 1818, he was promoted lieutenant, and assigned to the frigate *Macedonian* on the Pacific Station. In 1823 he was first lieutenant of the schooner *Jackal* in Commodore Porter's squadron, operating against the pirates in the West Indies, and from 1824 to 1826, was on duty on the *Constitution* and *Brandywine* in the Mediterranean. In 1828 he was assigned to the corvette *Erie* of the West India squadron, after which he made the surveys of the site of fortifications on the Tortugas Reef, and in 1831 took command of the schooner *Grampus*. In 1835 he escorted back to Mexico Gen. Santa Anna, who had been captured by the Texans, and turned over to the U. S. government. Three years later he was commissioned commander, and placed in charge of the Boston navy-yard, from which he was detached to command the corvette *Fairfield;* then to the *Saratoga*, and in 1846 to the steam gunboat *Spitfire*, on which he served during the war with Mexico. After being again for two years in command of the Boston navy-yard he was made captain in 1850, and ordered to the steam frigate *Saranac*. Between that year and 1857 he also commanded the *Independence*

to be forced to retire before the swift and strong ships which Commodore Dupont had sent to cut off or destroy his flotilla,[1] but which failed to execute the duty with which they were entrusted. It was the one great drawback to the completeness of the Federal victory at Port Royal that Tatnall did not permit his squadron to be captured, but preserved it intact for future operations. His instructions from the Navy Department at Richmond, were to "distribute" it along the coast from Port Royal to the sounds south of the mouth of the Savannah River, with the special purpose of rendering assistance to vessels expected from England with munitions of war for the Confederacy; but as there were many more sounds than he had vessels, it does not appear on record that he was able to "distribute" his force sufficiently to aid any of the incoming steamers.

Their success at Port Royal enabled the Federals to run their light-draft gunboats into the sounds, rivers, inlets and bays that intervene between the Sea Islands and the mainland of South Carolina and Georgia, on the approaches to which the Confederates had established earthworks without having either the men or guns sufficient to arm them. Expeditions were sent through Ossabaw, Warsaw, St. Helena and Cumberland Sounds all the way down to Fernandina, and as the Confederates had no means of opposing the passage of these squadrons, they retired from their weak fortifications as the enemy drew nigh, and soon the latter were in possession of the whole coast line southward from Port Royal except Savannah and the entrances thereto. Not being then prepared to attack the forts—Pulaski, Jackson and Causton—protecting the Savannah River, they advanced only as far as Tybee Island, at the *embouchure* of the river, which was occupied on November 24th, by Commodore John Rodgers, with a squadron embracing the steamers *Pocahontas*, *Seneca*, *Flag* and *Augusta*, mounting in all about 40 guns, including 11-inch shell guns, and 6-inch rifles. The report of Flag-officer Dupont to Secretary Welles states that Rodgers was sent to make "a preliminary examination of the bars, and for the determination of the most suitable place for sinking the proposed obstructions to the navigation of the

and the naval station on the lakes. In the latter year he was created flag-officer, and assumed command of the naval forces in the East India and China seas. He assisted the English and French allied squadrons in their attack on the Chinese forts at the mouth of the Pei-ho, June 25th, 1859, and the next year brought the Japanese Ambassadors to the United States. He was in command of the naval station at Sackett's Harbor, N. Y., when Georgia seceded, and resigning from the U. S. navy was, on February 28th, 1861, appointed senior flag-officer of the navy of the State of Georgia In March he accepted a commission as captain in the C. S. navy and the command of the naval defence of Georgia and South Carolina. He succeeded Admiral Buchanan as commander of the naval defence of Virginia in March, 1862, but returned to Georgia in July, and in March, 1863, was relieved from the command afloat and limited to shore duty at the Savannah Station, and the work of naval construction. He was paroled as a prisoner of war May 9th, 1865, and from 1866 to 1870 resided in Nova Scotia, near Halifax. He then returned to Savannah in much reduced circumstances, and the city created for him the office of Inspector of the Port, at a salary of $1,200 yearly. His death occurred June 14th, 1871.

[1] See for particulars of Tatnall's fleet the narrative of the battle of Port Royal in chapter upon South Carolina Waters.

river." He was instructed to push his reconnoissance so far as " to form an approximate estimate of the force on Tybee Island, and of the possibility of gaining access to the inner bar." He found the island abandoned, and placed a detachment in the only fortified position, a martello tower, with a battery at its base, but his vessels went no further up the stream; as, to use the language of Dupont, " the rebels themselves have placed sufficient obstructions in the river at Fort Pulaski, and thus by the co-operation of their own fears with our efforts the harbor of Savannah is effectually closed."

The occupation of Tybee Island was not so uneventful as the Federal naval commander represents it. Accounts printed in the Savannah papers state that the enemy first shelled the martello tower and the battery, and obtaining no response, sent several hundred men in a long train of boats on shore. After dark, Captain Read, C. S. A., commanding a company of Irish volunteers in Fort Pulaski, crossed over to Tybee with a squad of his men with the intention of burning the hospital, but found the Federals too numerous around it to warrant him in making the attempt. They were hunting for cotton and rice, with which they expected to pay the expenses of the expedition; as they are said to have done at Port Royal and Beaufort, where they captured a very large quantity of these commodities. Captain Read burned the rice and cotton on several plantations, and withdrew in safety to Cockspur Island, on which Fort Pulaski is situated. Commodore Tatnall's four steamers laid in Cockspur Roads near the fort, and on the 26th he slipped his cables, and running down within range of the enemy's gunboats, opened fire upon them. As they came on he slowly moved backward, hoping to draw them within reach of the guns of Pulaski, but they perceived his purpose and withdrew from the engagement when they were still too far distant from the fort for any of its shot to reach them. The skirmish between Tatnall and the foe continued for an hour, and some forty or fifty shots were exchanged, but the fire was ineffective on either side. For several days afterwards the Federal gunboats pitched shells at long range towards Pulaski, but on December 3d they evacuated Tybee and sailed to the northward, thus relieving the apprehensions which prevailed at Savannah, that an attack upon the city was meditated then. It was so fully expected that the Federal fleet would attempt to fight its way up the river that every preparation was made to receive it. General Robert E. Lee, then an engineer officer in the military department, visited all the works, attended personally to strengthening them and the posting of the garrisons, and made ready for the anticipated combat, but the Federals had accomplished the business upon which they were then bent and which did not include any serious fighting.

On December 26th Tatnall's squadron—consisting of the steamers *Savannah*, flag-ship, Commodore Tatnall ; *Resolute*,

Commander Jones ; *Sampson,* Commander Kennard ; the *Ida,* and *Bartow*—made an excursion down the river which is not recorded except in the biography of the Commodore, prepared by Charles C. Jones, Jr. " With the view," the author says, "to testing the range of some rifle guns lately received on the station, and to afford his men some practice, the Commodore attacked with his flotilla the enemy's blockading vessels then lying in the mouth of the Savannah River. Retiring before his fire, the enemy stood out to sea. After a pursuit of several miles, and having demonstrated the inefficient character of the guns, the Confederate flotilla returned to its anchorage."

The business which had brought the Federals to Tybee, and which is alluded to in Commodore Dupont's report already quoted from, was a part of the scheme of the Federal government to permanently obstruct the entrances to several Southern ports, of which Savannah was one, by sinking in the channels the hulks of whaling ships bought from the thrifty mariners of the decadent Massachusetts ports. One portion of "the stone fleet" was dispatched to Savannah after the reconnoissances by Commander Rodgers' boats had indicated the places at which the hulks should be sunk to obstruct the entrances to the harbor. The plan pursued was the same at Savannah as at Charleston. The blockaders had failed to effectually close these ports, and the notion of sealing them up by sinking ships in the channels was the desperate expedient to which Mr. Lincoln's government resorted. To Savannah were sent some twenty of the hulks, which, after being loaded with stone, were scuttled in the river near Tybee and in the navigable water courses adjacent. This method of compensation for the deficiencies of the legal blockade commanded immense approbation at the North, and was somewhat more sucessful at Savannah than at Charleston.' What effect it produced upon the great maritime powers of Europe has been spoken of elsewhere in this work. The hulks sunk around Savannah barred egress and ingress for a time, but in the end they were washed out or burrowed deep in the sands, and the channels were once more opened.

The campaign afloat and ashore in the Savannah vicinage grew brisk as the old year gave way to the new. After the Federals had closed up the river they were intent upon discovering a route into it above its mouth from Port Royal by way of the inside passages, their primary aim being to take Fort Pulaski in the rear. On Christmas day 1861. an exploring

1 " And if there be any more practical water approaches to Savannah, they can be treated in the same way. This done, there will be no need for vessels of our blockading squadron to be kept on duty there. A gunboat or two, to look in occasionally to see that there is no interference with the barricade, is all that will be necessary. The work then commenced will be continued until the water channels to all the seaboard cities of the South shall have been closed up. The rebels will soon begin to realize that the wiping out of all their seaboard towns, the annihilation of their commerce, and the general distress and ruin which they have brought upon themselves, make their secession whistle altogether too expensive an affair. Fools must be treated according to their folly." —*N. Y. Herald, Nov.* 29*th.*

expedition, under command of Lieut. Wilson, chief of the U.S. corps of Topographical Engineers, started from Hilton Head and pushed through Calibogue Sound and the creeks back of Dawfuskie, Turtle and Jones Islands, until they came out into the Savannah River between Fort Pulaski and the city. On the strength of their report of the practicability of the route a stronger party was sent down to survey it. They found that the entrances of the inlets into the river had been obstructed by barriers of piles which must be removed before the gunboats could get through. This was attempted by putting at the work first a number of men who, obscured from the Confederate sentinels by the tall reeds that grew thick and rank in the marsh, sawed off piles near the edge of the water. Then light draft steamers equipped with derricks and windlasses were brought up, and under cover of the night they fastened chains around the piles and dragged them up. They had nearly cleared the passage before they were detected, but they were finally observed by a sentry on duty at Pulaski. Word was sent to Commodore Tatnall, who came down to the mouth of Wright River with three gunboats and with a few shells drove off their working parties.[1]

Thus foiled on the north side of the Savannah River, the Federals went to the south side and discovered a new passage leading from Warsaw Sound through Wilmington River and St. Augustine Creek to the Savannah just below Fort Jackson; and Dupont and Sherman mutually concluded that this was the avenue that was most accessible for the consummation of their project of reducing Fort Pulaski. Tatnall had foreseen that an attack on the interior lines of communication would be made, and, besides holding his squadron in readiness, he gave his aid to the construction of a battery on a small island opposite Fort Jackson, which, in honor of Dr. Cheves, who superintended its erection, was called Battery Cheves. A part of its armament consisted of some long 32-pounder ship's guns furnished by the Navy Department from the Norfolk navy-yard upon the requisition of the Commodore. This work enfiladed the approach by the river channel above Fort Pulaski and its tenure and defence were confided to the navy. Fire-rafts were also prepared, at Tatnall's suggestion, and placed in the Savannah near Fort Jackson. One of these rafts was completed by Christmas, on which day it, without being ignited, floated down to the Tybee beach, near the Federal position, where its appearance was explained by a deserter from the Confederate lines, who, on coming into the Federal camp, announced that he had cut its moorings and allowed it to go down with the ebb tide.

[1] This is the version of the affair published by the Savannah papers, but according to a statement contributed by Lieut. Thomas Hall, Flag-officer Dupont's chief signal officer, to the "Annals of the War," a publication made in a Northern paper from an incautious letter written by a Federal army officer to a relative exposed the scheme to the Confederates. Official reports that might be useful in clearing away the doubt are lacking.

The attack on Fort Pulaski was not, however, attempted as soon as the Federals opened an inside passage. It had to wait upon the designs of Commodore Dupont to take possession of Fernandina by the route which carried him across the Savannah River to cross into Warsaw Sound. On January 26th, 1862, Fleet Capt. Charles H. Davis and Commander C. P. R. Rodgers, with the gunboats *Ottawa, Seneca, Isaac Smith, Potomska, Ellen* and *Western World* and the armed launches of the frigate *Wabash*, accompanied by transports conveying 2,400 troops under the command of Gen. Horatio G. Wright, passed into the Tybee, and as it was supposed by the Confederates that they meant to attempt a dash upon Fort Pulaski, the garrison and the squadron were put in order to resist them. On the 27th, Davis' gunboats came to anchor in Tybee Roads within sight of the Confederate flotilla, which stood off in contiguity to the fort. Davis had no intention of bringing on an engagement at the time, and the Confederates probably would not have provoked it if they had known that Fort Pulaski was not immediately to be besieged. But under the belief that the fort and the safety of Savannah were threatened, it became of the utmost importance that the garrison in the fort should be provisioned for a long siege. It could not be denied that the possession by the enemy of the interior water courses virtually isolated the fort, and that it must either surrender or be defended against the Federal ships and the batteries which the Federals had established on Tybee Island after their return to it about the middle of January. When Davis' squadron seemed to menace it provisions were running short, and the quantity of ammunition in the magazines was so small that it could not hold out against a siege unless the commissariat was replenished and a new supply of powder, shot, shell, etc., brought in. Commodore Tatnall was requested to convoy a six months' stock of provisions and ammunition to the fort, and undertook to execute the task. He started down the river on January 28th with his flagship the *Savannah*, the steamer *Resolute*, Capt. Jones, and the steamer *Sampson*, Capt. Kennard, escorting the steamer *Ida*, steamer *Bartow* and a scow laden with the desired supplies. They were placed in a very peculiar position as they neared Fort Pulaski. On the northern side of the Savannah River was the Federal squadron commanded by Capt. John Rodgers, and on the south side that commanded by Capt. Davis, both of which had their guns trained upon the channel through which Tatnall must run down to the fort. The distance between the two Federal squadrons was not over three miles, and without any great elevation their guns would carry across the marshy islands which intervened. For Tatnall it was a veritable running of a gauntlet, in which the chances were a hundred to one against his gunboats and their convoy reaching the fort without being cut to pieces or sunk. That they escaped such a fate was due to the blunder of the

Federals in foregoing the advantage which they had in hand, in the hope of destroying the whole Confederate squadron at one blow.   Tatnall's order of movement down the river was with the transports in advance and the armed steamers a short distance in the rear.   He passed within range of the Federal fleet without a shot being fired at him, Davis and Rodgers evidently supposing that after they had let him get below they would run into the Savannah River, cut him off from the city, and easily capture or sink all his vessels by their superior force.   But Tatnall did not propose to be caught that way. After the transports were beyond the range of the Federal guns he left the *Sampson* to accompany them to the wharf of Fort Pulaski and headed the *Savannah* and the *Resolute* back up stream toward the enemy's ships.   It will be understood without further explanation that he was prepared to venture a fight with these two feeble vessels against the thirteen gunboats of the squadrons of Davis and Rodgers in order to protect the *Sampson* and her convoy.   As he proceeded up the river again the enemy attacked him ferociously, Davis on the left and Rodgers on the right, and the singular spectacle was presented of a triangular naval engagement in which the three squadrons concerned were each in a different river, and each, in order to reach the enemy, was obliged to fire across land. Says the Savannah *Republican* of January 29th :

"No sooner had the two steamers turned their bows up stream, than the Federal fleets, seeing they were about to be cheated, opened a terrific fire upon them, which was gallantly returned.   A regular battle ensued, and for forty minutes the shot and shell rained around our little fleet, the latter often exploding directly over them, and the solid shot passing within a few feet of the men on deck.   The fleet kept up a return fire with its rifled cannon and other guns of long range, but with what effect could not be ascertained over the wide space of marsh that intervened on either side. Many of the enemy's shot passed some distance over and beyond our vessels.   Strange as it may appear, not a vessel or man on our side was damaged.   The fleet rode safely through the fire, and the fort is now fully provisioned for six months.   *   *   * The return trip of the *Sampson* and the two unarmed steamers was as perilous as that of their predecessors.   The Yankee fleets poured their iron hail and fire upon the little craft, but with all steam up and hurling defiant shots at the enemy in return, they passed gallantly for two miles or more under the missiles of the enemy.   *   *   * The *Sampson* passed through a terrible ordeal, but without serious damage. She was struck by four English rifled shells, two passing through her, a third lodging on her deck, and a fourth exploding in her store-room, breaking up things around generally, but damaging no one.   Her machinery was unhurt and she plowed gallantly through. In good time they all came up to their wharves and were welcomed by the immense crowds that filled up the dock and balconies, throughout the day."

A small torpedo corps had been organized and had planted some torpedoes in the channels navigated by the Federal gunboats, but they failed to inflict any harm upon the enemy.   Several were discovered on February 13th, by Lieut. Bankhead, in charge of boats surveying the river, who at first supposed them to be empty tin cans. A further examination satisfied him as to their real nature. They were buoyed in the stream and connected by wires. Each can contained thirty pounds of powder, and five cans were set in battery,

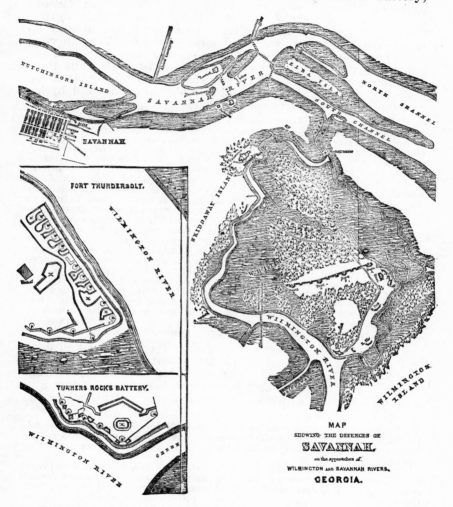

MAP
SHOWING THE DEFENCES OF
SAVANNAH
on the approaches of
WILMINGTON and SAVANNAH RIVERS,
GEORGIA.

the group being connected by wires. The firing apparatus was a friction tube leading from the head of the can into the powder chamber. The arrangement was very defective, for Federal gunboats and launches passed over the torpedo line before it was discovered, without causing an explosion.

The enemy improved the time by constructing on the shore of Tybee, at Venus Point, and on Oakley Island, breaching batteries for an attack on Pulaski, which had become utterly isolated. Towards the end of February, Gen. Lee, commanding the military department, conferred with Tatnall upon the possibility of relieving the fort, and they agreed that it could only be accomplished by a successful assault on the Federal battery at Oakley Island—a forlorn hope in view of the numbers of the Federal men-of-war and troops in the near neighborhood. But while they did not differ in their judgments that the attempt would be entirely too hazardous, Tatnall came very near making it. The story, as told by his biographer, is not devoid of interest:

"Stung [writes Mr. Jones] by some remarks attributed to Gen. Lee, and repeated by some one to the flag-officer, the latter determined to lead his entire force in open boats in an assault upon the battery on Oakley Island. Early on the morning preceding the night upon which this assault was to be made, Gen. Lee, learning the flag-officer's determination, called at Commodore Tatnall's quarters in the city of Savannah, and expressed a desire to see Capt. Tatnall of the marines, one of the flag-officer's aides. To this officer Gen. Lee addressed himself very warmly, and asked how he had best approach Commodore Tatnall in order to attempt to dissuade him from making an attack prompted perhaps by a wounded professional pride, and which if unsuccessful would leave the river approaches to the city practically open to the enemy. The aide responded: he believed the contemplated attack to be very desperate in its character; but, as it would be his duty to accompany the flag-officer, such fact rendered it out of the question for him to take a step toward preventing its execution. Subsequently the General sent a messenger to the flag-officer asking a confidential interview. During that interview Gen. Lee gave distinct utterance to his fears for the fate of Savannah in the event that the attack failed of the desired result. After hearing the General, Commodore Tatnall so far modified his plans as to confess himself willing to be governed by the views of such officers of the navy and army as he should assemble and consult in council."

This council met on the flag-ship *Savannah* on February 28th. It was composed of Lieuts. Commanding John Rutledge, J. S. Kennard, J. Pembroke Jones, O. F. Johnston, Wm. P. A. Campbell and Philip Porcher, of the navy, and Major Edward C. Anderson, of the artillery. They made this report to Tatnall:

"Having been requested by you to express our opinion as to the advisability of an attack by the vessels of your squadron, assisted by 200 men of the army in boats, on the battery at Oakley Island, we report as follows:

"'The boats and vessels would be subjected to a heavy fire of grape and canister at short range from the battery, supported by a cross-fire from the gunboats and battery opposite, and we are of the opinion that the result would in all probability be a failure, attended with great loss of life and vessels. In that event, our *present* preparations for the defence of Savannah would be thrown away, and a fearfully depressing moral effect produced. Should such an expedition prove *successful*, it would result in the spiking of a few of the enemy's guns and a slight retardation in their advance, with such a loss of men and arms on our side as in the result to decrease our means of defending Savannah, which we deem the all-important object, both on shore and afloat.'"

The contemplated attack was consequently relinquished, and Fort Pulaski was perforce left to its fate. On the morning of April 10th, Gen. David Hunter, the Federal commander, summoned Col. Charles H. Olmstead, the commander of the fort, to surrender. "I am here to defend the fort, not to surrender it," was the brief and plucky reply of Olmstead. He withstood a savage bombardment of two days, and capitulation was then decided upon after consultation with all the officers of the garrison.

It need hardly be said that the fall of Fort Pulaski threw Savannah into consternation, but it produced at least the one good effect of stimulating the effort to provide a naval squadron that would not be so feeble as the few steamers with which Tatnall had performed his operations. He was sent on March 25th, 1862, to Norfolk to take command of the *Virginia* after the wounding of Commodore Buchanan in the battle with the *Monitor*, and was succeeded at Savannah by Capt. Richard L. Page. The history of the work done there to create a formidable navy is rather one of effort than of achievement, but whatever were its failures they must be charged to the utter inability of the Confederacy to build the vessels designed by their constructors.

Five Confederate steamers outside of the Mosquito Fleet made matter for history in the waters of Savannah. They were the *Nashville*, the *Atlanta*, the *Georgia*, the *Savannah*,[1] the *Macon*, and the *Milledgeville*. The *Nashville* was the first vessel that was commissioned as a public armed cruiser of the Confederate States. She was a fast side-wheel steamer and had been originally purchased by the Confederate government to convey abroad Messrs. Mason and Slidell, the envoys to Great Britain and France.

In July, 1862, she ran into Savannah with a cargo of arms and was thenceforth blockaded until her destruction, which occurred eight months later during the attack of the Federal iron-clad fleet upon Fort McAllister. This fortification was situated on the Ogechee River, about sixteen miles south of the mouth of the Savannah River, and six miles from Ossabaw Sound. It stood on the mainland directly above the river bank, and commanded the river for a mile and a half on each side. The bluff upon which it was erected was known as Genesis Point. In February, 1863, the Federal monitor *Montauk* was sent into the Ogechee to renew the attack upon the fort, at which time the *Nashville* was in the river waiting an opportunity to run to sea. The report of Capt. George W. Anderson, Jr., commanding Fort McAllister, dated February 28th, and relating the events of the day, says:

"At 7:25 A. M. three gunboats, one mortar-boat and an iron-clad came in sight of our battery. The iron-clad anchored between 800 and 1000

---

[1] This ship was the iron-clad *Savannah*, and must be distinguished from the armed steamer of the same name that served Commodore Tatnall as a flagship in the early days of the war.

yards abreast of our battery, and directed her entire fire at the *Rattlesnake* (*Nashville*),[1] which was aground about three-fourths of a mile from her. * * * At 7:40 o'clock the *Rattlesnake* was set on fire—whether by her commander (Capt. Baker) or by the shells of the enemy, I am unable to say. If by Capt. Baker, I think it was entirely unnecessary, circumstances not demanding her destruction."

Capt. Baker did not deserve the implication of censure contained in Capt. Anderson's report. He had been seeking an opportunity to go to sea past the blockaders, and not thinking it safe to try to evade them on the Savannah River he had resolved to try the Ogechee route, with the result of reaching Fort McAllister just as the Federal fleet were making the attack. He steamed a little to the north and west of the fort, and in so doing ran hard and fast aground in a position affording to the enemy as desirable a target as they could ask for. The reports of Commodore Dupont and of Capt. Worden, the commander of the *Montauk*, are fairly descriptive of her destruction, although, in obedience to the virulent and absurd theory of Secretary Welles, they spoke of her as a "privateer," notwithstanding that they were well informed that she was a ship-of-war of the Confederate States, and entitled to the privileges of a belligerent nation already accorded by the United States, Great Britain and France. Worden wrote :

"By moving up close to the obstructions in the river, I was enabled, although under a heavy fire from the battery, to approach the *Nashville*, still aground, within the distance of 1,200 yards. A few well-directed shells determined the range, and I soon succeeded in striking her with 11-inch and 15-inch shells. * * * I soon had the satisfaction of observing that the *Nashville* had caught fire from the shells exploding in her in several places, and in less than twenty minutes she was in flames forward, aft and amidships. At 9:20 A. M. a large pivot-gun mounted abaft her foremast exploded from the heat, at 9:40 her smoke-chimney went by the board, and at 9:55 her magazine exploded with tremendous violence, shattering her in smoking ruins; nothing remains of her."

Except for the destruction of the *Nashville* the attack on Fort McAllister was sterile of beneficial results for the Federals. In this and in other engagements the fort repulsed them, and her cannoneers shared with those of Fort Sumter the honor of demonstrating that the monitors could be whipped and driven off by heavy ordnance and sharp-shooting gunners on shore.

While the *Nashville* was in quest of an opportunity to escape to sea, the British steamship *Fingal* was being converted into the Confederate iron-clad *Atlanta* in the harbor of Savannah. She was a vessel bought in September, 1861, on the Clyde, in Scotland, by Capt. James D. Bulloch, the European agent of the Confederate States.[2] "She was," says Captain Bulloch, "a new ship; had made but one or two trips to the north of Scotland, was in good order, well-found, and her log gave her speed as thirteen knots in good steaming weather,"

---

[1] The ship was sometimes called the *Rattlesnake*, but the official records of the C. S. Navy Dept. give her no other name than that of the *Nashville*.

[2] "The Secret Service of the Confederate States in Europe."—James D. Bulloch, pp. 109, 151.

Moreover, she was the first ship to attempt to run the blockade inward for the account of the Confederate government, and her cargo was valuable enough to warrant the taking the most perilous risks. It consisted of 10,000 Enfield rifles, 1,000,000 ball cartridges, 2,000,000 percussion caps, 3,000 cavalry sabres, 1,000 short rifles and cutlass bayonets, 1,000 rounds of ammunition per rifle, 500 revolvers and ammunition, a couple of large rifled cannon and their gear, two smaller rifled guns, 400 barrels of cannon powder, and a lot of medical stores and material for clothing. "No single ship," Captain Bulloch states, "ever took into the Confederacy a cargo so entirely composed of military and naval supplies, and the pressing need of them made it necessary to get the *Fingal* off with quick dispatch, and to use every possible effort to get her into a port having railway communication through to Virginia, because the Confederate army, then covering Richmond, was very poorly armed and was distressingly deficient in all field necessaries."

The *Fingal* passed through many adventures in her first voyage under Confederate ownership, of which Captain Bulloch has left an exciting narrative. The passengers beside himself were Col. Edward C. Anderson, of the Confederate army ; Messrs Charles Foster, and — Moffatt, two residents of Charleston, who desired to return to their homes, and Dr. Holland, an ex-surgeon of the U. S. army. For obvious reasons the ship was kept under the British flag, which made it necessary to employ a captain holding a Board of Trade certificate to clear her outward, and to ship the crew in accordance with the Merchant Shipping Law. The second officer was John Low, who made a most honorable record in the Confederate navy. About October 8th or 9th, 1861, the *Fingal* sailed from Greenock, Scotland, with Messrs. Foster and Moffatt on board, and with instructions to call at Holyhead, where Bulloch, Anderson and Holland were waiting to join her. Running into Holyhead on a dark and stormy night she collided and cut down the Austrian brig, *Siccardi*. The character of her mission would not permit delay, and her three passengers going at once on board, she was out of the harbor before the accident was known to any one who would have had authority to stop her, Bulloch first leaving on shore a letter for Fraser, Trenholm & Co., the Confederate financial agents in England, which enabled them to trace the owners of the *Siccardi*, and make proper compensation for the loss of that vessel. On November the 2nd the *Fingal* arrived at St. George, Bermuda, where she found the *Nashville* in port and received from her a pilot, John Makin, for the Southern coast. She had been cleared for Nassau, but was headed from Bermuda for Savannah; and as this necessitated an understanding with the British crew, Bulloch called them aft, explained that his true object was to run the blockade, and offered to put into Nassau if any of them objected to continuing with the ship.' They unanimously consented to go on with the voyage, and he then told them that although the *Fingal* still flew the British flag, he had her bill of sale in his pocket; that he was empowered at any moment to take her from the captain on behalf of the Confederate Navy Department, and that if they would stand by him he would do this and be ready to fight any U. S. blockading ship of equal strength that might intercept him. Not a man backed out and he set them at work to arm the ship. Two 4½-inch rifled guns were hoisted out of the hold and mounted in the forward gangway ports; a couple of boat howitzers were put in position on the quarter-deck; the men were equipped with rifles and revolvers, and a few old man-of-war's men among them were set to drilling their fellows, and the peaceful merchantman was thus metamorphosed into a capable fighting ship. On November 12th she came upon the Georgia shore in a dense fog, and while Bulloch was reasonably sure that he was off Warsaw Inlet, Pilot Makin did not wish to run in on any uncertainty. He bore away for Savannah and made the entrance without catching a glimpse of a blockader. The cargo of arms was sent to the necessitous armies, and it was decided that the *Fingal* should be loaded with cotton on account of the Navy Department and that Captain Bulloch should endeavor to take her back to England. He returned to Savannah on November 23d and found the ship empty and virtually blockaded in the river by the enemy's gunboats and their occupation of Tybee Island. The cotton and coal needed were slow in coming, and he informed Secretary Mallory that if it was desired to send the ship to sea haste should be made to run her out through the Warsaw passage before that was closed by the Federals. He was instructed to take command of the ship, load her with cotton and resin, sail her to a British port and there transfer the command to Lieut. G. T. Sinclair, C. S. N., who would go out from Savannah with him. By December 20th, the cotton was stowed away in her hold and she dropped down to Wilmington Island seeking an opportunity to evade the blockading fleet, being accompanied by Commodore Tatnall's squadron. The Chatham artillery battalion, of Savannah, was sent to Skidaway Island to assist in case there should be a conflict with the Federals. On the 23d, the *Fingal* and the squadron ran down near the enemy's gunboats, which they found in such strong force that they were compelled to retire after an interchange of fire. Tatnall's flagship received a shell in her wheelhouse and was assisted off by the *Resolute*. It was too late now to hope to get the *Fingal* out; every channel was vigilantly patrolled by the enemy's gunboats, and a pilot sent out to see if escape could be effected by way of the Romerly marsh narrowly avoided capture, and reported that five ships-of-war were watching for the *Fingal* in that locality. So close a look-out warranted the suspicion that spies had informed the Federals of her movements, a belief which was strengthened by the desertion of two seamen who accompanied the pilot on his search for an unguarded channel. Just at that time, too, the stone hulks were sunk in the approaches to Savannah, and late in January, 1862, Capt. Bulloch reported to Secretary Mallory that the port was closed and that he could see no prospect of carrying the ship out. By the Secretary's orders he turned her over to Lieut. Sinclair and returned to Europe by way of Wilmington.

Available no longer to the Confederacy as a cruiser or blockade-runner, the *Fingal* was converted into an iron-clad of the familiar type followed in all the Confederate armored ships. Her extreme length was 204 feet, breadth of beam 41 feet, draft of water 15 feet 9 inches. She was cut down to the main-deck, which was widened amidships and overlaid with a foot of wood and iron plating, and upon this foundation was built the casemate, the sides and end inclining at an angle of thirty degrees. The top of the casemate was flat, and the pilot-house rose above the roof about three feet. The sloping sides and ends of the casemate were covered with four inches of iron plates in two layers, secured to a backing of three inches of oak and fifteen inches of pine. A ram was attached to the bow, which was also fitted with a spar to carry a percussion torpedo. Her armament was two 7-inch Brooke guns on bow and stern pivots, and two 6-inch Brooke rifles in broadside. The larger guns were so arranged that they could be worked in broadside as well as for fore-and-aft fire, and the ship could therefore fight two 7-inch and one 6-inch piece on either side. When completed she was renamed the *Atlanta*, and about the same time the iron-clad battery *Georgia* was finished, but proved to be worthless on account of defects in her construction. She was 250 feet in length and sixty feet breadth of beam, with a casemate twelve feet high. Her machinery was of very little use, and whenever she was moved it was by means of tow boats. She carried seven guns and was under the command of Lieut. J. Pembroke Jones, C. S. N. The ladies of Savannah made large contributions to the cost of building her, in the same manner that those of Charleston aided the construction of the iron-clad *Charleston*.

Lieut. Charles H. McBlair, C. S. N., was first placed in command of the *Atlanta*, which, on July 31st, 1862, first showed herself to the Federal fleet. She steamed leisurely down the Savannah toward Fort Pulaski and then returned to the city. It is instructive to learn now of the alarm with which the Federals regarded her. "Unless some monitor comes to our succor," wrote the correspondent of the New York *Herald*, on August 2d, "the fair weather yachts now reposing on the placid bosom of Port Royal Bay have before them an excellent opportunity of learning what it is to be

41

blown out of the water. The rebels have completed their ram. It has been manned and armed and is now ready for sea."

There was no necessity at the time for the extraordinary perturbation evinced by the Federals, as the *Atlanta* was merely on her trial trip, which developed the fact that she steered badly, in consequence of the increased draft caused by her weight of armor and ordnance, and the alteration of form resulting from the projecting overway, which extended several feet below the water line. As a merchant ship, she had made easily twelve knots an hour, but as an iron-clad six to seven was the most that could be got out of her. Believing her, however, to be a miracle of formidableness, the Federals thereafter kept several monitors constantly in the vicinity of Savannah, and on March 3d, 1863, again bombarded Fort McAllister and were again repulsed. In the meantime the *Atlanta* underwent some slight changes that failed to correct her defects. The whole work of constructing her had been entrusted to John A. Tift, and when Commodore Tatnall returned to the naval command at Savannah in July, 1862, he found that he was not permitted to have anything to do with the building of the ship. "Mr. Tift," he wrote to Secretary Mallory," called at my office and showed me his authority from yourself giving him the sole control of her construction, and in reply to a question, he stated that it was intended that the commandant of the station should have nothing to do with her. I, of course, abstained from interfering in any shape whatever."

In January, 1863, Tatnall proposed to attack the blockaders with his fleet, but it was found impossible to get the *Atlanta* through the south channel of the Savannah River, until the obstructions placed there had been removed. The Navy Department was urging him to make a demonstration against the enemy, and his failure to do so was the cause of his removal, in March, from the command afloat; but he was impeded by difficulties that were not fully appreciated at Richmond, or generally in the South, where the people had accepted the Northern opinion of the power of the *Atlanta* as an engine of destruction, and were impatient that she should do something to realize their hopes that she would raise the blockade, and perhaps bombard the Northern seaports. The old commodore's letter of April 24th, 1863, to Secretary Mallory, is a cogent explanation of his intentions in January previous, and his failure to execute them, although he wrote under a sense of indignation at being removed from the command of the squadron. When he resolved on the attack in January, a day was selected when the first high spring tide would enable the *Atlanta*, which drew nearly sixteen feet of water, to pass out of the Savannah; but when she dropped down to the obstructions, it was only to be held back by the inability of the engineer officers to remove them. It was actually a month before the passage could be cleared, and Tatnall then prepared to go through on the next spring tide, which occurred on February 4th. By that date the monitor fleet had gathered in Ossabaw Sound for the assault of Fort McAllister, and Tatnall anchored the *Atlanta* off the Causton's Bluff forts, having been requested by Gen. Mercer to cover that point from an attack by the enemy while a change was being made in the position of the guns of the forts. Continuing his letter to Mr. Mallory, the Commodore wrote that upon the return of the Federal monitors to Port Royal, he took his ship to the head of Warsaw Sound, with a view of running to sea when the enemy made the anticipated attack on Charleston.

"In that event [he said], I had two projects in view—either to attack him at Port Royal, should the force left there justify it, or, sweeping the sounds to the south of the Savannah, push on to Key West in the hope of surprising some of the enemy's vessels in that port. While at this anchorage, however, and when the tides were at the lowest, two of the enemy's iron-clads anchored in the mouth of the Savannah, where none of that class had ever shown themselves before. They could in an hour have attacked the *Georgia*, and, beyond a doubt, destroyed her, for I could not have aided her. Nothing could have prevented this disaster but ignorance of her force and condition. I ordered the return of the ship to the Savannah as soon as possible, which could not be, however, sooner than the 3d of April, and four days before that time I transferred the squadron to Commander Page. It was my purpose not to have left the Savannah River again until the enemy should have fully committed himself in an attack on Charleston, and then to have gone to sea and executed my plan."

Tatnall feared that the *Atlanta* would not be a match for the monitors at close quarters, and his judgment was vindicated by the events, and while he was ready to obey any positive orders given him by the government, he would not rush into a conflict with them upon suggestions from Mr. Mallory that left him a latitude of action. Then Lieut. Wm. A. Webb, C. S. N., was ordered to the command of the ship, the implied condition of his appointment being that he should "do something" with her, and on June 17th, 1863, he got under way before daylight and entered Warsaw Sound. Admiral Dupont had sent the monitors *Weehawken*, Capt. John Rodgers, and *Nahant*, Commander J. Downes, into the sound for the express purpose of meeting the Confederate ram. [1] They were two of the strongest vessels of their class, armored with ten inches of iron on the turret and carrying two 15-inch and two 11-inch guns. Webb was desirous of fighting at close quarters, as he thought that under such circumstances he might pierce the monitor turrets or disable their guns with his rifled shot. He was about 600 yards distant from the *Weehawken* when the *Atlanta* went aground and was backed off with some difficulty, but inside of five minutes she again grounded—this

---

[1] Report of Admiral Dupont to Secretary Welles.

time so hard and fast that the extreme exertions of her engines were powerless to move her.[1] In this position she was at the mercy of the enemy. With the utmost deliberation the *Weehawken* came up to within 300 yards and opened fire. The first shot struck the *Atlanta* upon the side of her casemate, knocking a hole in it and scattering over the gun-deck great quantities of wood and iron splinters, wounding sixteen men and prostrating forty more insensible from the shock. A second shot struck the top of the pilot-house, crushing and driving down the bars on the top and sides, wounding both pilots and one helmsman and stunning the other helmsman. Other shots smashed a port shutter and started the joint of the casemate with the deck. Eight shots were fired from the *Atlanta*, no one of which struck the *Weehawken*, and the *Nahant* did not come into the fight at all. It was impossible for Webb, with his ship fast on the bottom, to bring his guns to bear, and in fifteen minutes it was manifest that the enemy's huge projectiles must soon pierce the casemate and cause fearful slaughter. The *Nahant* was bearing down upon him, and in a few moments would have joined her destructive fire to that of her consort. Webb hoisted the white flag, sent Lieut. J. W. Alexander to inform Capt. Rodgers that he had surrendered, and made the following address to his crew:

"I have surrendered our vessel because circumstances over which I had no control have compelled me to do so. I know that you started upon this expedition with high hopes, and you have been disappointed. I most earnestly wish that it had happened otherwise, but Providence, for some good reason, has interfered with our plans, and we have failed of success. You all know that, if we had not run aground, the result would have been different, and now that a regard for your lives has influenced me in this surrender, I would advise you to submit quietly to the fate which has overtaken us. I hope that we all may soon be returned to our homes, and meet again in a common brotherhood."

The Federals made prisoners of 165 men (officers and crew) of the Atlanta, including 28 marines.[2] With the exception of the wounded, they were sent to prison at Fort Lafayette in New York harbor. The survey ordered by Admiral Dupont reported that the ship could be easily repaired, and she was sent to the navy-yard at Philadelphia, whence she returned in February, 1864, to Fortress Monroe to form one of the Federal North Atlantic squadron.

[1] In a statement made to a Savannah paper, George W. Hardcastle, carpenter of the *Atlanta*, said that upon nearing the *Weehawken* Capt. Webb asked the pilots if there was water enough for the *Atlanta* to make a dash at her. He was informed that there was, and he then ordered all steam up, in order to run into her and blow her up with his torpedo. In a few moments after she had got under full steam she brought to upon a sand-bank and careened over, which rendered her guns useless, and placed the *Atlanta* at the mercy of her two antagonists at short range.

[2] The list of officers was as follows: William A. Webb, Commander; J. W. Alexander, First Lieutenant; Alphonse Barbot, Second Lieutenant; George H. Arledge, Third Lieutenant; Thomas L. Wragg, Master; R. J. Freeman, Passed Assistant Surgeon; E. J. Johnson, First Assistant Engineer; William B. Micou, Paymaster; William J. Morrell, Second Assistant Engineer; Leslie King, Second Assistant Engineer; J. A. G. Williamson, Midshipman; J. A. Peters, Midshipman; William McBlair, Master's Mate; Thomas B. Travers, Gunner; James Thurston, First Lieutenant of Marines; G. W. Carey, Paymaster's Clerk; James M. Fleetwood, Pilot; J. S. West, Second Assistant Engineer.

It was felt throughout the South that the loss of the *Atlanta* was a distressing blow to the Confederacy, and in the thoughtless anger of the moment Lieut. Webb and his officers were harshly spoken of; for the unwarrantable public reports of her fighting capacity had deluded thousands into the opinion that nothing but treachery or incompetency could prevent her from vanquishing the Federal monitors. The newspapers, or some of them, had led the Southern people astray in this matter, and those which had pronounced the vessel the greatest achievement ever accomplished in the way of a battle-ship held to their notion that she could not have been properly defended. "It is painful to hear such a tale," exclaimed the Richmond *Examiner* in commenting on the early reports of the engagement, "nor is the pain alleviated by learning that the unhappy commander, after making a brief address to his crew of Georgians, in which he advised them to be resigned, fainted away upon his quarter-deck." But Lieut. Webb did not faint on his quarter-deck or anywhere else, and his behavior on this occasion was as gallant and sea-manlike as when he carried the cockleshell gunboat *Teaser* into action on the James River. His stranded ship would have become a slaughter-pen under a few more of the *Weehawken's* shots; his men were demoralized, and he had lost the service of his pilots. The crew were in no sense reliable. Out of 140 odd of them only some two-score were indifferent sailors, the remainder having been selected from Georgia infantry, and without experience at sea or any knowledge of naval gunnery, which may be a partial explanation of their failure to inflict any punishment upon the enemy.

After the loss of the *Atlanta* efforts were made to build at Savannah other and superior iron-clads under contract with Mr. Willink, a proficient naval contractor. He built the *Savan-nah*, an armored ship of the casemate type, and had the *Mil-ledgeville*, another vessel of the same class, nearing comple-tion when the city was evacuated; but although the former was armed and manned she never saw any hostile service. The blockade of the port continued uninterrupted. On August 8th, 1863, the Confederate steamer *Robert Habersham*, on duty as a guard-boat, exploded her boilers, killing and wounding many of her crew, and on November 8th the crew of a picket boat in the Savannah River made a prisoner of their com-manding officer, Master's Mate Samuel A. Brockinton, of the *Sampson*, and deserted to the Federals.

The most spirited incident of the last year of the war in Georgia waters was the capture of the U. S. gunboat *Water Witch*, a fine side-wheel steamer, mounting four guns, and having a crew of about eighty men. She was a favorite ship in the navy, having taken part in the Paraguay war of 1855, and fought in Commodore Hollins' attack on the fleet in the Mississippi Passes in October, 1861. As a blockader she was very valuable on account of her speed and handiness. Her station in 1864 was in Ossabaw Sound, south of the Savannah River, and as after the withdrawal of the Federal monitors from attacks upon Fort McAllister she was usually alone in that locality, a plan was arranged to capture her or some other one of the squadron on the coast by a boat expedition operating at night. Capt. W. W. Hunter,[1] commanding the Confederate States' naval forces afloat at Savannah, detailed seven boats, fifteen officers and 117 men from the squadron, and placed the expedition in charge of First Lieut. Thomas P. Pelot, with Lieut. Joseph Price second in command. They left the iron-clad *Georgia* on the afternoon of May 31st, and were towed to the Isle of Hope battery, from where they rowed to Beaulain battery, on Vernon River, where they camped for the night. The next day scouts reported one of the enemy's vessels at anchor in the Little Ogeechee River, close under Racoon Key, and she was selected for attack. The report of Lieut. Price to Flag-officer Hunter says:

"At 8 o'clock P. M., the expedition got under way and formed two columns. Boats Nos. 1, 3, 5 and 7, composing the port column, Nos. 2, 4 and 6 the starboard column; Lieut. Thomas P. Pelot commanding, with Second Assistant Engineer Caldwell, C. S. N., and Moses Dallas (colored) pilot, led in boat 1; Lieut Price, with Master's Mate Gray and Second Assistant Engineer Fabein, in No. 2; Midshipman Minor, with Master's Mate Freeman, in boat No. 3; Midshipman Trimble, in boat No. 4; Boatswain Seymour, with Master's Mate Baccalay, in boat No. 5; Master's Mate H. Golder, with Assistant Surgeon Thomas, in boat No. 6; Master's Mate

---

[1] Commodore William Wallace Hunter was the son of Dr. George Hunter, a distinguished physician of Edinburgh, Scotland. Emigrating to America early in life, he rendered his adopted country eminent service as an officer in the Revolution, and as a member of the society of the Cincinnati. His son, the subject of this sketch, was born in the city of Philadelphia, in 1803. This was about the period of the purchase of Louisiana by the United States, and Dr. Hunter was appointed by President Jefferson to take charge of the new acquisition. The greater part of his youth was spent on the sea, and that, too, contrary to the wishes of his father, who was then a man of wealth and position and who had planned for his son a far different line of pursuit in life. He made many voyages to Europe on commercial vessels, and his first work on board ship was as cabin boy. Dr. Hunter becoming satisfied that young Hunter was determined to adopt a seafaring life, wrote to his friend Hon. James Monroe, then President of the United States, with regard to the boy, and the result was that the future commodore was on May 1st, 1822, given an appointment as midshipman in the U. S. navy. He performed his first service in the squadron of Commodore David Porter, which had been organized for the suppression of piracy in the West Indies. In the course of that service he was captured by the pirates, but succeeded in securing his escape under circumstances which reflected the greatest credit on his courage and ingenuity. It was under Commodore John Rodgers, then commanding the U. S. naval forces in the Mediterranean, and on the flagship *North Carolina*, that young Hunter acquired his chief training as a

naval officer. His subsequent service was for years on the West Indian and Pacific oceans. He was the inventor in 1847 of a mode of propulsion of vessels familiarly known as "Hunter's Horizontal Wheel," which was applied to the first iron ocean steamer of the U. S. This vessel, which was called the *Alleghany*, was constructed at Pittsburgh, Pa., according to plans and designs originated by Hunter and under his personal supervision. The *Alleghany* was commanded by the commodore for over seven years. She passed from Pittsburgh to the ocean, and over the falls of the Ohio, the keel never touching the ground. She was a 1,040 ton vessel, and her battery, which consisted of four 9-inch pivot-guns, each weighing 10,000 pounds, had a range entirely around the compass without changing the position of the vessel.

In 1861, he resigned his commission in the U. S. navy, being then in charge of the Baltimore station, and almost at the head of the list of commanders. Simultaneously with his resignation in the U. S. navy, he tendered his services to the Southern Confederacy at Montgomery, and was immediately given the rank of captain, with a station at New Orleans, embracing the command of the coast of Texas to Mexico. Subsequently he was ordered to the batteries of the Rappahanock, where he served four months; after which he was ordered to Richmond and thence to Savannah to command that station. Nine vessels were under Commodore Hunter's command at Savannah, two of which were iron-clads. After the surrender Commodore Hunter went to Virginia, where his family at the time were residing. He is now (1887) an honored citizen of New Orleans, La

Rostler, with Assistant Surgeon Jones, in boat No. 7; and proceeded with muffled oars to the spot where we supposed the enemy's vessel to be. On arriving, we found that she had either shifted her anchorage or that we had been mistaken as to her position. After searching in vain till nearly day-light, Lieut. Pelot ordered Boatswain Seymour, with one man, to remain on Racoon Keys as scouts, and the expedition to return to camp at Beau-lain battery.

"On the next day (June 3,) at 9 o'clock P. M., we got under way and proceeded to Racoon Keys, where we took on board our scouts, who re-ported that one of the enemy's vessels was lying in Ossabaw Sound, about three miles from where we then were. After waiting there until midnight we were ordered to get under way and pull cautiously. The night being dark and rainy, we got close aboard of her without being dis-covered. On being hailed, Lieut. Pelot answered we were 'rebels,' and gave the order to 'board' her. The vessel having steam up at the time, as soon as the alarm was given, commenced turning her wheels backwards and forwards rapidly, thus thwarting the earnest efforts of Boatswain Seymour and Master's Mate Rostler to get on board with the entire boat's crew.

"The port column, led by Lieut. Pelot, boarded on the port side; star-board column, led by Lieut. Price, boarded on the starboard side. In coming alongside, the enemy's fire with small arms was quite severe; in fact it was during that time, and while the boarding netting, which was triced up, was being cut through, that the most of our loss in killed and wounded was sustained. After a sharp hand-to-hand fight of some ten minutes, the ship was taken. Lieut. Pelot was the first to gain the deck, and while bravely fighting was shot and instantly killed. In his death the country has lost a brave and gallant officer, and society one of her highest ornaments.

"The command then devolved upon me, and I proceeded forthwith to extricate the vessel from the position she was then in to avoid recap-ture by the enemy. Our pilot having been killed before the boats reached the side of the ship, I sought for the enemy's pilot and found that he was too badly wounded to assist me, but finally procured one of the quarter-masters, whom I compelled to pilot me to the upper end of Racoon Key, where, at the top of high water, the ship grounded. I then found it neces-sary to lighten her, which I did by throwing overboard some barrels of beef and pork, a few coils of hemp rigging, the remainder of the chain, which I had slipped as soon as we took the vessel, and lowering two of the guns in the boats. On getting ashore I immediately landed the killed, wounded and prisoners at Beaulain battery. At 4 o'clock P. M., having in the meantime obtained a pilot from the shore, I succeeded in getting off and anchored her at 7 o'clock P. M., under the guns of Beaulain bat-tery above the obstructions, when Lieut. W. W. Carnes, C. S. N., by your order, arrived on board and assumed command.

"In the darkness and confusion on board it was impossible for me to observe each and every man; but I will state, with pride, every one, officers and men, did their duty most gallantly. I would state, however, that I owe my life to E. D. Davis, ordinary seaman of the C. S. steamer *Savannah*, he having cut down every opponent when I was sorely pressed by them.

"Boatswain's Mate J. Perry, of the steamer *Savannah*, and Boat-swain's Mate W. S. Johnston, of the steamer *Sampson*, rendered me most valuable assistance in lightening the vessel and general duties on board. The former, although severely wounded, remained on deck as long as he could."

The Federal reports amplify the modest narrative of Lieut. Price, and confer additional honor upon the officers and men of the Confederate navy engaged in the capture of the *Water Witch*. Acting Master's Mate E. D. Parsons was in charge of the deck when the boats approached in the

midst of the storm, flashes of lightning only casting illumi-
nation upon the scene. Whether Parsons was panic-stricken,
or merely lost his head in the confusion, is uncertain, but he
was charged in the reports of Lieut. Commanding Pendergrast
and Master Charles W. Buck with taking refuge below deck,
without giving the order to slip the cable and start the engine
or calling all hands to repel boarders. Pendergrast and Buck
were in their bunks, and when the fighting began rushed on
deck to find it already partly in possession of the enemy. Such
of the crew and officers as had tumbled up from below were
opposing the Confederates with pistols and cutlasses, the latter
using similar weapons in a hand-to-hand desperate conflict.
Buck endeavored to train a howitzer upon them, but was
struck down before he could apply the primer. Pendergrast,
it is said, came face to face with Lieut. Pelot and their swords
crossed. Pendergrast received a cut which knocked him
senseless upon the deck, but at that moment Billings, the
paymaster of the *Water Witch*, caught a glimpse of the Confederate commander by the glare of the lightning, and shot
him dead. So well organized were the boarders, however,
that the loss of this able and gallant officer did not cause any
confusion or delay, Lieut. Price taking his place and leading
them on to victory. In a very short space of time they had
driven below most of the people of the *Water Witch*, a few of
whom, mostly officers, were continuing the fight in little detached squads about the deck. The crack of pistol-shots and
the clash of sabres alone broke the silence of the night, for it
is the testimony in all the descriptions of the engagement that
after the first hail and answer there was an almost entire absence of the shouts and cheering usually characteristic of close
combat on shipboard. Lieut. Price was badly hurt by a sabre
blow on the head, but continued fighting on the quarter-deck
until he had cleared it, after which it was the task of an instant to send his men below and secure his prisoners. The
condition of things he discovered there was discreditable to
the U. S. navy; he found scores of cowering men who courted
nothing so much as a chance to surrender.

"The men [wrote Lieut. Pendergrast in his report], seemed paralyzed with fear, and remained under the hurricane deck without giving
the officers the least support, though they were ordered out by Paymaster Billings and Ensign Hill. I found it impossible to discover the whereabouts of all the men, owing to the darkness, and there was but little
opportunity for the officers to give many orders, as all were engaged in
combat the moment they reached the deck, and continued to fight until
struck down. I regret to say the watch below evinced no desire to come
on deck and defend the ship. Had the crew but emulated the noble example shown them by their officers, the result would have been different.
* * * I regret to say the engineers acted in the most cowardly manner.
They were the only officers who surrendered, and that to one man. Had
they obeyed my orders to work the engine, the enemy would have been
unable to board us; but, so far from fighting the rebels, they surrendered
at the first summons, and thereby lost the ship."

This condemnation of the engineers is corroborated by Surgeon W. H. Pierson, who reported that when a Confederate officer came into the ward-room, Engineer Genther called out : " I surrender, we surrender, the ship surrenders." The poltroonery of some of the officers and crew is stated to have been in revenge for not having been sent home when they expected. For nearly all the men, their terms of enlistment had expired, and they were dissatisfied because still detained on the ship. But while Lieut. Pendergrast had so many excuses to offer for his defeat, they neither lessened the merit of the Confederate achievement nor satisfied his government. He was tried by court martial for culpable inefficiency in the discharge of duty in not taking proper precautions to secure his ship against surprise and attack, was found guilty and was sentenced to be suspended from duty for two years, on half-pay, and with loss of rank from the date of suspension.

The fighting on the deck of the *Water Witch* was close and deadly while it lasted. Besides Lieut. Pelot, the Confederates lost in killed Pilot Moses Dallas (colored), Quarter-gunner Patrick Lotin, and seamen W. R. Jones, James Stapleton, and —— Crosby; while their wounded were Lieut. Price, Midshipman Minor, Boatswain Seymour, Surgeon's Steward Harley, and seamen J. R. Rice, J. Barnett, A. McDonald, E. J. Murphy, E. Lee, A. Williams, T. King, and —— Champion. Of the Federals, two were killed and twelve wounded. Only one man escaped from the ship. He was a negro named McIntosh, who jumped overboard in the darkness and swam a mile to the south end of Ossabaw Island, where he was next day picked up by the U. S. ship *Fernandina.* The alarm was communicated to other blockaders, and Lieut. Price was thus disappointed in his expectations that by remaining in the sound with the *Water Witch* he might effect the capture of other vessels that should come into those waters in ignorance of her fate. Half a dozen Federal gunboats were sent in pursuit of her, but by placing a pistol at the head of the Federal quartermaster whom he called upon to pilot her, Price brought her safely under the guns of Beaulain. The prisoners captured numbered 77. The wounded were attended by Dr. Pierson, the Federal surgeon, and Dr. C. Wesley Thomas, surgeon, C. S. N., of whom Pierson says in his report, that "should he ever fall into our hands, I bespeak for him the courtesy due to an honorable and gentlemanly adversary."[1] The *Water*

[1] Admiral Porter's "Naval History of the Civil War" accuses the Confederates of "having departed from the usages of war and practiced unnecessary cruelty on their prisoners"—the officers and men of the *Water Witch.* This reckless indictment has no other foundation than the fact that Surgeon Pierson "understood" that there was an arrangement between the Federals and the Confederates that medical officers taken prisoners should, after attending to their own wounded, and their being no necessity for their further services, be allowed to depart. Although such a practice as this existed to some extent during the war, there was no binding agreement between the belligerents concerning it, and when Dr. Pierson's case was referred to Secretary Mallory he replied that the surgeon should be treated as any other prisoner of war when his attention on the Federal sick and wounded in the Savannah hospital ceased. As to the treatment he and his patients met with there, he speaks for himself thus in his report to Admiral Dahlgren: " My patients were placed under my care at a hospital called the Savannah

Witch was enrolled in the Confederate naval force and was destroyed when Savannah fell into the hands of the enemy.

With this incident, so thoroughly demonstrative of the fearlessness and energy of the men of the C. S. navy, ended the hostile activities in which they were permitted to engage in the waters of Georgia. No more surprises of the blockaders were possible ; their vigilance forbade another *Water Witch* affair, and while the naval establishment was maintained at Savannah, and the construction of iron-clads continued, no opportunity again presented itself for attack or defence. The remainder of the war history of the Georgia metropolis is much like that of Charleston and Mobile—it could hold out indefinitely against a foe approaching from the sea, but in its landward rear it was open to the enemy. Unlike Charleston, however, it suffered no Federal bombardment, and the naval officers and men on the station did not enjoy the privilege of their mates of Charleston of serving in the land batteries or in combats around the city. The tedious routine of harbor guard was their lot until December, when the march of Sherman's army threw against the city an irresistible power. Its military defences on the land side consisted merely of some slight earthworks, behind which were a few thousand of Gen. Hardee's troops, and as there were no men to spare to reinforce him, the evacuation of the city was an event not to be long staved off. On December 10th, Secretary Mallory telegraphed to Commodore Tatnall: "should Savannah fall do not permit our vessels under construction or any of the public property in your charge to fall into the hands of the enemy. Destroy everything when necessary to prevent this."

On the 13th, Gen. Sherman captured Fort McAllister by sending against it a division of his army, and on the 18th he demanded from Hardee the surrender of the city, to which the latter replied that be held his two lines of defence, was in communication with his superior authority, and could hold out for an indefinite period. The Confederate general was in fact playing for time in which to save the public property or destroy that which he could not carry away. Sherman resolved

---

Naval Hospital, under the charge of Surgeon Jeffery, C. S. N. This hospital was devoid of some of the luxuries which may be found in Northern hospitals, but was airy and comfortable, and the patients there received every care and comfort which the somewhat limited resources of the country permitted. I myself was treated with gentlemanly consideration by Dr. Jeffery and the assistant surgeons, as well as by the numerous rebel officers who frequently called there." As for the alleged semi-starvation of prisoners at Macon, whither they were removed from Savannah, Dr. Pierson speaks of the food as being meagre in quantity and wretched in quality, but immediately adds: "We were told by the guard, to console us, that this ration was the same as they got themselves, and I think it likely enough that they told the truth. I know that while at Savan-nah, I tabled with the rebel surgeons in the hospital, and that during all my stay there, nearly six weeks, we had coffee never, tea only about five or six times, butter about as often; and to the credit of the surgeons be it said that while they denied themselves the luxuries of tea at $30 to $40 per pound, they had it furnished to our wounded, and generally fed them better than they fed themselves. Afterwards, at Charleston, our rations were somewhat better, the meal being bolted, and wheat flour and fresh beef being issued occasionally. At Macon, as well as at Charleston, we had the opportunity to buy of sutlers within our quarters" This language of Dr. Pierson is a complete exculpation of the Confederate authorities from the accusation brought by Admiral Porter, who made no quotations from the surgeon's report, although he seems to have had it before him as he wrote.

on a siege or assault, as should be necessary, and as Dahlgren had been informed that Commodore Tatnall meditated a dash seaward with his squadron, he placed seven monitors in the Savannah River and thereabouts to intercept him, while his remaining ships cannonaded Battery Beaulain and other works on the Ogeechee, Ossabaw and Vernon waters; which were evacuated by the Confederates on the 21st. Sherman's army had appeared before the earthworks on the land side of Savannah on the 8th of December, and on the 10th some sharp fighting occurred. Several strong assaults were made, in which the Federals were signally repulsed. Attacks were intermittently made and repelled until Hardee had perfected his plans for the abandoment of the city. On the 20th the Confederate iron-clad *Savannah*, Commander W. T. Brent, moved up the river near Hutchinson's Island and vigorously shelled the enemy's left, while the batteries within range joined in with her fire. This was done to cover Hardee's retreat and effected its purpose. Under cover of this fire he crossed his troops to Hutchinson's Island and thence by the Union causeway into South Carolina territory. On the next day Sherman entered Savannah and received the surrender of the city from Mayor Arnold.

Commodore Tatnall had proceeded on the night of the 20th to execute his orders regarding the ships and naval property at the port. The *Georgia* was set on fire and blown up at the moorings where for two years she had laid practically useless for any purpose of warfare. The iron-clad *Milledgeville*, which had recently been launched, was burned to the water's edge and sunk in the middle of the river. A ship partially constructed was burned on the stocks at the yard of Kenston Hawkes. The navy-yard and a large quantity of valuable ship-timber were destroyed by fire, and the captured gunboat *Water Witch*, Acting Master Vaughn, which had been lying at Thunderbolt, was also burned.

While Sherman's army was surrounding Savannah, Commodore William Wallace Hunter, C. S. N., received instructions from Gen. Hardee to proceed up the Savannah River with a sufficient force and destroy the Charleston and Savannah Railroad bridge, to prevent Gen. Sherman from sending a portion of his army across the river into South Carolina to prevent the escape of the retreating Confederates from Savannah. With his flag-ship, the *Sampson*, and the gunboat *Macon*, and a small transport steamer laden with supplies, Commodore Hunter proceeded up the river to the bridge. On the Georgia side of the river the smoking ruins along Sherman's line of march could be seen in every direction. Not a single house was spared, not even a church. Vandalism marked the progress of the Federal army, and along the river banks were only encountered helpless women and children fleeing from the enemy. The arson of the dwelling houses of non-combatants and the robbery of their property, extending even to the trinkets worn by women, made the devastation of Sherman's army as relentless as savage instincts could suggest.

Arriving at his destination during the night, Commodore Hunter sent armed boats with combustible materials on the bridge and soon it was a mass of flames from one end to the other. Remaining alongside to see it completely destroyed, in the morning the gunboats proceeded down the river to take position on the right of Hardee's lines at Savannah. The enemy having received intelligence of the return of the gunboats, lined the river bank with the heaviest of their artillery, and as the vessels approached made every preparation for the attack. They had secured the range at various bends in the narrow stream, and only waited for Commodore Hunter to get in the line of their fire before opening the engagement. Commodore Hunter had received notice from a refugee of the preparations to attempt the capture of his vessels on their passage down the river, and saw the enemy securing the range of the river at various points. The crews were called to quarters and final instructions given when the enemy opened fire at long range with rifle shot. The gunboats withheld their fire until they got nearly opposite, when a terrific fire was opened on both sides. The Federal artillery being stationed on the high bluffs had the advantage of position, and being light-rifled siege guns and field artillery could fire with great rapidity and precision. Commodore Hunter's two small wooden gunboats had their machinery and magazines exposed, and being within a few hundred yards of the enemy, nearly every shot from the latter took effect. As the gunboats approached nearer to the batteries, the fire of the guns of the enemy, which lined the river bank for some distance, was increased. In the hottest of the fight the little transport steamer became disabled in her machinery, and she floated ashore and surrendered. The Sampson and the Macon, although struck several times, continued the running fight for some time. The enemy, believing the gunboats could not pass their batteries, sent several batteries at full speed up the river to prevent their escape in that direction. Commodore Hunter was directing the movements of his vessels from the hurricane deck of the Sampson. Midshipman Scharf, who had charge of the bow gun of the Sampson, observing the attempt of the enemy to prevent the escape of the gunboats up the river, called the attention of the Commodore to the movements of the enemy, and he gave the orders to retreat at full speed before the Federal batteries in his rear could get into position. The Sampson and Macon were turned up stream under a heavy fire, and with the aid of a barrel of bacon in the furnaces, the boats soon steamed from under fire.

At this time there was a flood in the Savannah River, and Com. Hunter concluded to make an attempt to pass the obstructions before Augusta, and reach that city. With his two gunboats he reached Augusta; his vessels being the only ones saved of the Confederate navy at Savannah. At Augusta several of the naval officers received orders to proceed to other points, but the majority of them, including Com. Hunter, were surrendered under Gen. Johnson's capitulation.

When the Federal colors were raised upon the parapet of Fort Jackson, below Savannah, on the afternoon of December 21st, the iron-clad *Savannah* was still in the river, and at once hoisted her flag and opened fire upon the enemy. She continued this for several hours, shelling the troops in Fort Jackson with sufficient vigor to drive them from their guns. Their return fire inflicted no damage upon her, and during the remainder of the day she displayed the Confederate colors in the face of the victorious Federals—the last emblem of the Southern Confederacy to float in hostility over the waters of Georgia. After dark Capt. Brent ran her over to the South Carolina shore, when he was joined by Com. Tatnall. They and the crew started on the march to Hardeeville, where the retreating Confederates were ordered to concentrate, first applying a slow match to the magazine of the *Savannah*. A little after ten o'clock she blew up with a tremendous explosion. A flash of light occurred and then an immense column of flames shot up in the air. The concussion shook the vessels lying in Tybee Roads, and made houses tremble for miles around.

The Federals captured at Savannah 32,000 bales of cotton, a large quantity of rice and some naval stores. They also got an uncompleted torpedo-boat and the small steamers *Beauregard* and *General Lee*, besides 150 pieces of ordnance in the fortifications. It was not until the 23d of January, 1865, that they cleared the river of the obstructions that had held back their ships.

While the naval defence of the port was marked by no such stirring events as were enacted on the South Carolina seaboard, it is a record on the Confederate side of persevering and determined battling against adverse circumstances, sometimes brightened by victories against great odds. The work of naval construction was more energetic and on a larger scale at Savannah than in any other Confederate coast city, but it failed to achieve important results because it was not concentrated. No other port was possessed of so many strong iron-clads as the *Atlanta*, *Georgia* and *Savannah;* but the first and last, which might have done good service for the Confederacy, were not in existence at the same time, and the *Georgia* was a marine abortion. It was the oft-told tale of no money or material to build more than one good ship at a time, and of the eventual bottling up of the squadron by the massive iron-clads of the enemy. The torpedo service, so efficient at Charleston and elsewhere, amounted to nothing at Savannah.

A few explosive machines were placed near or in the obstructions of the river, but they were never heard from until the Federals dug them up after the evacuation. Some were placed in the neighborhood of Fort McAllister, but the only one that did any duty exploded under the monitor *Weehawken* without injuring her.

Yet there is nothing in the Confederate naval records in Georgia waters derogatory to the professional merit, the gallantry, or the fidelity of the officers and men of the service. They deserved well of their country, and they were the peers in every honorable attribute of those who worked and fought where more prominent reputations could be made.

COMMANDER JAMES H. ROCHELLE.

CONFEDERATE STATES NAVY.

CAPTAIN DUNCAN N. INGRAHAM,

CONFEDERATE STATES NAVY.

CHAPTER XXI.

SOUTH CAROLINA WATERS.

FROM the sounding of the first note of the Civil War a sentimental as well as practical interest was focused upon the attack and defence of Charleston. It was the metropolis, the embodiment of the intellectual power and impetus of the commonwealth, whose political giants had thirty years previously enunciated the doctrine of States rights that underlaid the Southern movement of 1861; the State which held that doctrine was the first to point the way of independence; it was virtually in arms almost as soon as the election of Mr. Lincoln became a certainty, and in its harbor the shot that became the signal for armies and navies to rise, and battle-flags to tempt the breeze, was fired. What wonder, then, that there prevailed throughout the North a fierce and passionate hunger that it should be conquered at any sacrifice of life and treasure, while Southern men and women chained their hearts to its fate, and during the two years of the siege the ragged Confederate veterans in field and trench and camp asked first for the news from Charleston! In these sober days of peace the faithful history of the battle fury that within twenty-five years past raged around the spot where less than a century previous Sergeant Jasper had flung out the flag of the new-born American Republic in defiance of British shot and shell, brings back the stirring memories of the long beleaguerment of "the cradle of secession" by ships and forts, the close and murderous conflicts on water and on shore, the diapason of the guns that thundered through more than six hundred nights and days, and the crimsoned pictures of the blood that was shed. No intelligent American can to-day pass the ocean gateways of the city without reverting, as the keel under him cuts the tossing waves of the bay, to the epoch when war held merciless sway over those beautiful waters and men died for the flag under which they served.

The naval records of the war in South Carolina precede the birth of the nation which Mr. Gladstone said that Jefferson

Davis created. When the Ordinance of Secession was passed on December 20th, 1860, there were not wanting in Charleston men whose thoughts had already been drawn toward the subject of naval offence and defence, and who were turning over in their minds sundry projects of putting ships-of-war afloat. After Major Anderson transferred the garrison of U. S. troops from Fort Moultrie to Fort Sumter on the night of Christmas Eve, and the talk at Washington and in the North was devoted to sending a naval expedition to his relief, their ideas of meeting ships with ships could not but become more strongly fixed; and before the provisional government of the Confederacy was formed at Montgomery the palmetto flag had been hoisted over vessels equipped for war purposes by the people of South Carolina, and Governor F. W. Pickens had issued commissions in the naval service of the State. The destruction of the records, when Sherman's army fired Columbia, swept out of existence the official documents upon which a full statement of these commissions, to whom issued and the assignments to vessels, could be based, but newspaper files and communications from the surviving officers supply the deficiency to some extent.

The U. S. government vessels in South Carolina waters were taken possession of by authority of the State toward the close of December 1860, but they were of such small value as scarcely to be worth seizing. They comprised a venerable revenue-cutter known as the *Aiken ;* the schooner *Petrel,* a relic of the Florida war ; the light-house tender *Governor Aiken,* and the coast-survey schooner *Crawford.* They were all sailing-vessels, and carried less than half a dozen light guns among them all. A river steamer called the *General Clinch* was bought in January 1861, and when mounted with a couple of brass cannon was put into service as the first ship of the South Carolina navy.

The report of Major Anderson of December 27th, 1860, states that on that afternoon an armed steamer, two of which had been watching Forts Sumter and Moultrie, between which they had been passing to and fro, or had been anchored for the preceding ten nights, took possession by escalade of Castle Pinckney, Lieut. Meade, the U. S. officer in command, retiring without resistance to Fort Sumter.

On January 10th, 1861, the New York agents of the New York and Charleston steamship line were notified that their steamship, the *Marion,* a side-wheel vessel of 800 tons burden, which had that day arrived at Charleston, had been taken for the service of the State by Governor Pickens' orders. The fact was that the Governor had proposed to buy the ship with the consent of the Charleston stockholders of the company, and workmen were put on board to begin fitting her out for a vessel-of-war; but they had done very little before it was decided that she was not available for that purpose and she was restored to her owners.[1] The anxiety of the South Carolina authorities to establish a naval force was increased by the attempt of the Federal government to reinforce Fort Sumter, the steamer *Star of the West*, with 200 troops on board, having, on January 9th, been only prevented from reaching the fort by the guns of the batteries on Morris Island. Capt. John McGowan, the commander of the steamer, in his report says, after speaking of being fired upon from the island:

"At the same time there was a movement of two steamers from near Fort Moultrie, one of them towing a schooner (I presume an armed schooner) with the intention of cutting us off. Our position now became rather critical, as we had to approach Fort Moultrie within three-quarters of a mile before we could keep away for Fort Sumter. A steamer approaching us with an armed schooner in tow and the battery on the island firing at us all the time, and having no cannon to defend ourselves from the attack of the vessels, we concluded that to avoid certain capture or destruction we would endeavor to get to sea. * * * A steamer from Charleston followed us for about three hours watching our movements."

The report of Lieut. Charles R. Woods, Ninth Infantry. U. S. A., commanding the troops on the *Star of the West*, states that the armed schooner was supposed to be the cutter *Aiken*.

So it seems that three months before the war was begun, South Carolina had provided herself with vessels that could take some part in belligerent operations. It is also quite probable that the idea of iron-plating for forts and ships was first mooted in Charleston. In January, Col. C. H. Stevens, of the 24th S. C. Regt., then a private citizen of Charleston, began the erection of an iron-armored battery of two guns on Morris Island. It was built of heavy yellow pine timber with great solidity; it face was inclined at an angle of forty degrees and was covered with bars of railroad iron.[2] In this battery, which participated in the bombardment of Fort Sumter, and as a first experiment proved successful, we may clearly recognize the germ of such armored ships as the *Virginia* and her congeners; but it does not follow that the designers of the *Virginia* were prompted by the device of Col. Stevens. In Europe and America, speculations upon the possibility of sheathing ships with shot-proof metal were rife in naval circles before the war, and in France and England the topic had been discussed in a desultory way ever since the allied fleets of wooden vessels had demonstrated that they could not endure the fire of the Russian forts at Sevastopol, or so much as venture an attack upon the defences of Cronstadt. Another invention tried at Charleston came much nearer than Col. Stevens' construction to the scheme of iron-clad ships. This was the floating battery that performed an important part in the Sumter

[1] This ship was afterwards bought by the Federal government, as were also the *Columbia*, *James Adger*, *South Carolina* and *Massachusetts*, all of which belonged to the New York and Charleston line, and all were fitted out as armed cruisers for blockading purposes.

[2] " Charleston Year Book for 1883."

bombardment. It was constructed of palmetto logs and armored with boiler iron, over which railroad iron was fastened. The roof was bomb-proof and it mounted four heavy guns. The plating was said to have been subsequently removed to use on one of the iron-clad ships. The battery was designed and constructed by Lieut. J. R. Hamilton, of the C. S. navy.

Shortly after the secession of the State the South Carolina Legislature passed a law, establishing the Coast and Harbor Police, of which Capt. James H. North was placed in command. On January 23d, 1861, Wm. G. Dozier was appointed lieutenant in this force, and on March 13th was ordered to report for duty to Lieut. Thomas B. Huger on the steamer *James Grey.* This vessel was a large steam-tug and was rechristened the *Lady Davis.* She was armed with a small English rifled cannon, of the Whitworth patent, the gift of C. K. Prioleàu, a Charlestonian then residing in Liverpool.

In April Capt. W. J. Hartstein took charge of naval affairs at Charleston with the rank of commander in the C. S. navy, his squadron then consisting of the steamers *Gordon, Lady, Davis* and *General Clinch,* the first named being his flag-ship. On April 5th he issued an order to Lieut. Dozier, commanding the *Lady Davis,* to prepare for sea immediately, taking on board ten days' provisions and as much fuel as possible. What was intended was manifest in the following instruction sent to Dozier the succeeding day:

"The object of the present expedition under my command, consisting of the *Lady Davis, General Clinch* and *Gordon,* is to guard the approaches to this harbor from the sea and prevent a reinforcement of Fort Sumter. You will therefore most rigidly obey all orders by signal or otherwise, using the utmost vigilance and giving immediate notice of any vessel or boat approaching. You will take station in Moffatt's Channel and keep always within signal distance of this vessel (the *Gordon*) in main ship channel. Economize your fuel, and if necessary to replenish it and if you are not able to communicate with me, proceed to Stono and return as soon as possible. If necessary to avoid the enemy, seek shelter under the guns of the nearest battery or run for Stono Inlet or Bull's Bay or Charleston if possible. If compelled to abandon your vessel, set her on fire to prevent her falling into the hands of the enemy. Be particularly cautious at night to guard against the approach or attack from boats, against which you will find it convenient and useful to use your stem by running them down, having small arms ready to repel boarders. Every morning at daylight get under way with me and run as far as Bull's Bay under short steam and cruise to and fro to observe any vessels in the bay or off shore for ten or fifteen miles, being certain to return to your station off the Moultrie house on Sullivan's Island. From dark to daylight you will keep a boat, if the weather is not bad, with two trusty men moving slowly between the *Clinch* in the Swash Channel and your vessel. Allow no lights, except signals, to be shown; be always ready to get under way. Examine all vessels or boats passing in and let none pass with an unusual number or anything suspicious. Allow nothing to pass in except in daylight; if not certain of a vessel's character follow her in past Sumter, keeping her closely observed."

Much interest attaches to the above order, because it is in itself a lucid showing of the part which the naval forces were preparing to take in the opening of the war by the bombardment of Fort Sumter. The Confederate authorities were well apprized of the expedition being fitted out at New York under the command of Capt. G. V. Fox for the relief of Major Anderson, and Capt. Hartstein was charged with the duty of keeping watch for its advent. On April 10th, he wrote to Beauregard that he had had under his charge during the preceding night, in addition to his three steamers, the *Charleston,* while the *Seabrook* and *Catawba* were also out on guard service. A noteworthy feature of this communication is its evidence of his anxiety to begin the bombardment. "It is my opinion," he stated, "that Sumter can be relieved by boats from vessels outside on any night as dark as the last, so if we have to take it you had better be making a beginning. If a vessel-of-war is placed off each bar when Sumter opens, I will lose all my steamers, as there will be no escape for me. Therefore, before firing, these steamers should be called in. If the steamers are to guard the entrances, please send them down before dark that they may be positioned."

On April 11th Gen. Beauregard made his demand upon Major Anderson for the surrender of Sumter, and in anticipation of the attack that would by daylight of the 12th follow a negative reply, certain work was cut out on that day for the naval service to perform. Lieut. Dozier was instructed to take the *Lady Davis* into the harbor, place her in charge of his first officer and obtain from the Quartermaster's Department two rafts, which he was to have towed as near as possible to the southwest side of Fort Sumter and anchored. After dark he was to set them on fire and withdraw, as soon as the Confederate batteries opened on approaching boats or vessels. "The object," Hartstein wrote, "is to place the rafts in such positions as to give the best light on the southwest side of Sumter, that the gunners may see to fire upon a party disembarking from vessels or boats. This service is very important, and much is left to your good discretion. If the rafts burn out before daylight you must replenish and fire up, retreating as before."

Capt. Fox found that the bambardment had begun when he arrived off the bar on the 12th inst. with the gunboats *Pocahontas, Pawnee* and *Harriet Lane,* and the troop-ship *Baltic,* and he refrained from any effort to succor Major Anderson. [1] The presence of his vessels within view of the batteries was, however, disquieting to the Confederates, who expected them to make an attempt to enter. On April 13th Hartstein, writing from Fort Moultrie, informed Gen. Beauregard that he would

[1] Secretary Welles had ordered the steam frigate *Powhatan* to form part of the expedition, but without his knowledge President Lincoln dispatched her out of New York to relieve Fort Pickens under command of Lieut. D. D. Porter. Fox claimed that he had relied upon the boats of the *Powhatan* to attempt to land troops and supplies at Fort Sumter, and that without them he was powerless to execute the plans of relief. Welles and Fox charged that the diversion of the *Powhatan* to another purpose was brought about by the secret machinations of Secretary Seward.

reconnoitre them that night from a small boat, but he thought that with good lookouts on duty and the channel lit up by the fire-hulks there was not any danger of their getting in. The Confederate gunboats did not enter the engagement, and such of the naval officers as could be spared from them did duty on shore. Gen. Beauregard, in his report to Gen. Samuel Cooper, Adj. Gen. C. S. A., spoke warmly of the meritorious services of "the naval department, especially Capt. Hartstein, one of my volunteer aides, who was perfectly indefatigable in guarding the entrance into the harbor; Lieut. T. B. Huger, who was also of much service, first as Inspecting Ordnance Officer of batteries, and then in charge of the batteries on the south end of Morris Island ; Lieut. Warley, who commanded the Dahlgren Channel Battery; also the school-ship, which was kindly offered by the Board of Directors, and was of much service; Lieut. Rutledge, who was Acting Inspector General of Ordnance of all the batteries, in which capacity he was of much service in organizing and distributing the ammunition ; Capts. Childs and Jones, Assistant Commanders of batteries." Lieut. J. R. Hamilton, C. S. N., commanding the Point Battery on Sullivan's Island and also the floating iron-plated battery, was commended in Gen. R. S. Ripley's report for "firing with great precision and skill" to prevent the working of the barbette guns of Sumter and dismount them.[1] As soon as the white flag was displayed from the fort on the 13th, Gen. R. G. M. Dunovant, commanding on Sullivan's Island, sent Capt. Hartstein and Surgeon Arthur Lynch, C. S. N., to ascertain whether Major Anderson had surrendered, but they had been preceded by members of Gen. Beauregard's staff, with whom the terms were negotiated. On the same afternoon Capt. Hartstein returned to the fort, in company with Major D. R. Jones, Capt. Wm. Porcher Miles, and Capt. Roger A. Pryor, to arrange with the Federal commander the means most acceptable to him for his evacuation the following day. In accordance with his desire, the Confederate steamers transferred him and his men to the U. S. transport *Baltic*, one of the ships of Fox's squadron, and they sailed for New York.[2]

Succeeding the surrender of Fort Sumter increased zeal was shown in the formation of a navy. Commissions were issued in May by Governor Pickens, making Thomas P. Pelot

---

[1] On April 15th, Hon. L. P. Walker telegraphed to Gen. Beauregard from Montgomery that if the floating battery worked well he would order one for Pensacola, and asked if Lieut. Hamilton could go there to construct it. Gen. Beauregard answered that it worked well for enfilading, and that he wanted Hamilton for a few days. He decided to place it at Wappoo Cut for defence against boats, and Hamilton suggested that its armament should be changed to 8-inch siege howitzers, and that he could make it further useful if he was authorized to enlist twenty-four seamen, and Lieuts. Grimball and John H. Ingraham could be assigned to him.

[2] Before their departure Lieut. T. B. Huger addressed this communication to Gen. Beauregard : "These vessels of the enemy, which are causing us some anxiety, and at any rate treating us with great disrespect, I would like to have the pleasure of driving off from our port ; and if we cannot succeed in that at least make them keep at a respectable distance. I volunteer for the service. If you will allow me to put the rifled cannon on the *Lady Davis*, under my command, I can go out and at long range try the effect of the shot on them. I think in this way I may be able to annoy them, if not drive them off."

lieutenant, Dr. J. N. Pelot surgeon, and J. J. Darcy second assistant engineer in the navy of South Carolina. Lieut. Stockton was placed in command of the *Lady Davis*, and from the Messrs. Eason's foundry at Charleston a large number of bolts was turned out to fit the Prioleau cannon. Another vessel then added to the navy was the schooner *Helen*, Capt. Coste, which, with the schooner *Petrel*, Capt. Murden, was ordered to stations along the coast. The declaration of the blockade in May, and the speedy appearance before the Southern ports of the fleets which the Federal government was building or buying with an extravagant expenditure of its illimitable treasury resources, spurred the Confederacy to every exertion within its narrow means to repel invasion by water. The authorities were urged to put in requisition every harbor steamer, every sloop, schooner and pilot-boat that could carry a gun, and nowhere was the demand for a naval establishment more urgently made than in South Carolina. Experience with the ironed floating battery in the attack on Fort Sumter had been flattering to its efficacy, and steps were taken to construct others on the same plan at various points liable to attack, while the few steamers in Southern ports were utilized for the hastily-improvised navy.

Blockade-running began quickly upon the establishment of the blockade, and the first prize captured by the Federals on the So. Carolina coast was the ship *General Parkhill*, owned in Charleston, which was taken by the frigate *Niagara*, on May 15th, while endeavoring to make port homeward bound from Liverpool. Upon observing her signals, two small Confederate steamers ran out of the harbor to assist her, but they were too weak to cope with the *Niagara* and were constrained to put back. In the early days of blockade-running some of the craft engaged in the business were armed and commissioned as privateers, or bore letters-of-marque from President Davis, in order that while on their voyages they might strike a blow at the enemy's commerce as occasion offered. Of this class were the schooner *Dixie* and Capt. Hartstein's former flag-ship, the *Gordon*, which when renamed the *Theodora* took out from Charleston Messrs. Mason and Slidell, the Confederate envoys to Great Britain and France.

On October 11th, Messrs. Mason and Slidell left Charleston in the *Theodora* to take the English mail steamer at some point in the West Indies for their posts at London and Paris, but the secret of their movements was so carefully kept that it was not until November 2d that the fact of their departure was published in the city newspapers. Besides the two Confederate envoys the party comprised Mr. Macfarland, secretary to Mr. Mason; Mr. Eustis, secretary to Mr. Slidell; Mrs. Slidell, Miss Mathilde Slidell, Miss Rosine Slidell and Mrs. Eustis. The steamer evaded the blockaders by sailing on a dark and stormy midnight, and reached Nassau on the 13th, where the envoys had anticipated taking passage on the English steamer, but were deterred because they found that she would stop at New York on the way to Liverpool. They continued on the *Theodora* to Cardenas and Havana, reaching the latter port on the 17th with the Confederate colors flying. Their reception there was most cordial, and the ladies of the Cuban city presented Capt. Lockwood of the *Theodora* with a handsome Confederate flag. The ship returned to Charleston and the envoys started for Europe on the steamer *Trent*, which was overhauled by the U. S. frigate *San Jacinto*, Capt. Charles Wilkes, at sea, on November 8th, 1861, and the commissioners taken out of the *Trent*. This outrage created the greatest excitement in England, and to prevent a collision between the two governments the United States gave up the commissioners to the representatives of the British government authorized to receive them. They subsequently arrived safely in England.

A matter which created at the time an uproar that turned out to be ludicrously disproportionate to its importance was the effort of the Federals to close the port of Charleston, as well as other sea-coast cities, with the celebrated "Stone Fleet." Disgusted with the failure of the ships-of-war to stop blockade-running, some of President Lincoln's advisers conceived the brilliant scheme of sealing up the Southern ports by sinking in their channels hulks loaded with stone. The New England whaling men had plenty of worn-out ships for which the government thus provided them a market, and some fifty or sixty of such craft were purchased. Twenty vessels, carrying over six thousand tons of stone, were brought to Charleston on December 20th, 1861, and scuttled in the channels, and the Federals exulted in the supposition that the blockade was effectual at last. But such a barbarous mode of warfare as the attempt to close forever the avenues through which commerce must seek ingress to and egress from a seaport, brought from England and France most emphatic expressions of condemnation. The Ministers of those countries at Washington were instructed by their governments to enter formal protests. Lord Lyons, the British representative, was directed by Lord John Russell to state to Secretary Seward that, in the opinion of her Majesty's government,

" Such a cruel plan would seem to imply despair of the restoration of the Union, the professed object of the war; for it never could be the wish of the U. S. government to destroy cities from which their own country was to derive a portion of its riches and prosperity. Such a plan could only be adopted as a measure of revenge and of irremediable injury against an enemy. Lord Lyons was further told that even as a scheme of embittered and sanguinary war such a measure would not be justifiable. It would be a plot against the commerce of all maritime nations, and against the free intercourse of the Southern States of America with the civilized world."

The protest of France was of the same tenor, and when the French Chambers and the British Parliament met in January and February 1862, the subject was vehemently discussed. While the Washington government might have remained insensible to simple remonstrances from the European powers, it was confronted with their strong disposition to declare illegal a blockade that could not be maintained by ships afloat, and to establish which it was needful to resort to practices not recognized by the Treaty of Paris as legitimate between belligerents. Mr. Seward's tortuous diplomacy was strained to postpone and prevent this dreaded declaration, and the official correspondence was still in progress when the disputation was suddenly terminated by the discovery that the stone fleet scheme at Charleston was one of the blunders of the Federal authorities. The sapient landsmen who invented it had never counted upon the power of the tidal currents of the harbor, by which some of the hulks were broken up and their fragments washed away; others settled below the ever-shifting sands, and such as remained in place helped, by concentrating the currents jetty-fashion, to scour the channels deeper. Mr. Lincoln and his counsellors breathed easier after the forces of nature extricated them from one of the most difficult dilemmas in which they mired themselves by their inordinate craving to disregard the laws of civilized warfare in hostilities against the Confederacy.

The blockade had not been long declared by the government at Washington before it was perceived that it could not be maintained without a coaling, refitting and supply station at some convenient point on the Southern coast, and a joint military and naval expedition was formed under the command of Gen. Thomas W. Sherman and Commodore S. F. Dupont for the purpose of seizing such a location as might be determined upon. After discussion upon the comparative advantages of Fernandina, Bull's Bay and Port Royal, the magnificent land-locked harbor of the latter caused it to be selected, and in the last week of October the fleet of men-of-war and transports rendezvoused at Fortress Monroe, from whence it set sail on the 29th with sealed orders, which were not to be communicated to the commanders of ships until they were at sea.[1] Commodore Dupont hoisted his flag on the frigate *Wabash*, and his other fighting ships were the frigate *Susquehannah*, the sloops-of-war *Mohican, Seminole, Pawnee* and *Vandalia*, and the gunboats *Unadilla, Ottawa, Paulina, Bienville, Seneca, Curlew, Penguin, Augusta, R. B. Forbes* and *Isaac Smith*. This was a much more formidable force than had attacked Hatteras Inlet in the preceding Aug., the vessels mounting in all about 175 guns, many of which were 11-inch pieces. The troops numbered over 12,000, and were convoyed

[1] Secret information of the destination of the enemy had been obtained by the Confederate government On November 1st Acting Secretary of War Benjamin telegraphed from Richmond to Governor Pickens at Columbia, General Ripley at Charleston, and General Drayton at Port Royal: "I have just received information which I consider entirely reliable that the enemy's expedition is intended for Port Royal."

in fifty transports. It was the largest fleet that had ever been under the command of an American officer. A severe gale scattered the ships off Hatteras on Nov. 1st, but only one transport was lost, and the fleet assembled off Port Royal on the 5th, 6th and 7th.

The Confederate defences consisted of Fort Walker on Hilton Head and Fort Beauregard at Bay Point, which form respectively the western and eastern entrances to the harbor, and are distant from each other nearly three miles. They were exceedingly well-built earthworks and were rather heavily armed, Fort Walker mounting 23 guns and Fort Beauregard 18, a total of 41; but 22 of these were only 32-pounders or lighter pieces, so that there were in fact but 19 guns fit to cope with the at least 100 heavy rifles and shell-guns of the Federal ships. Gen. Thomas F. Drayton was in command of both posts, with his head-quarters at Hilton Head, and Col. R. M. Dunovant had immediate command of Fort Beauregard. The defences were garrisoned by about 2,000 men, but this force was very deficient in trained artillerists, and a small supply of shot and shell forbade much practice with the larger guns.

From the time that Port Royal was menaced, Commodore Josiah Tatnall had moved to its vicinity through the sounds the little squadron under his command in the Savannah River. It comprised the river steamer *Savannah* (flag-ship), improvised into a man-of-war, Lieut. J. N. Maffitt commanding, and the armed tugs *Resolute*, Lieut. J. Pembroke Jones; *Sampson*, Lieut. J. Kennard, and *Lady Davis*, Lieut. J. Rutledge. On the morning of Nov. 5th they were lying in the mouth of Skull Creek, a short distance from Fort Walker. The editor of the Savannah *Republican*, who had accompanied Commodore Tatnall as a spectator, describes the subsequent events:

"The Monday after his arrival, he found the enemy, forty-four sail strong, off the mouth of the harbor. Perceiving several of their vessels to be engaged near the bar in taking soundings, he instantly, with his small force, attacked them at a distance of but a mile and a half ; and, after a cannonading of forty minutes, during which he succeeded in entrapping three of the enemy's screw vessels under the fire of our batteries, finding that he had to encounter English rifled guns, he retired inside the harbor.

"The day after (Tuesday), he again engaged the enemy at long shots for upwards of half an hour, apparently with some effect; the flag-ship *Savannah* receiving no further injury from the reception of two shots, than a temporary one to her upper works, and the remaining vessels of the squadron receiving no hurt whatever.

"Early in the evening of this day we were all much gratified by the arrival of Capt. Page, C. S. N., of Virginia, the second in command to Flag-officer Tatnall, of the Georgia and Carolina coast. This accomplished officer, whose reputation in the old service, to which he has long been a bright ornament, is well known, was a most valuable addition to our force, and, as events proved, to the army also, which is somewhat indebted to his personal exertions for the satisfactory retreat made by them, when even their usual bravery, most memorably displayed as it was, failed to quite support them in their hour of need.

"Every one on board the little fleet expected an attack from the ene-my during the night, yet every officer and man of it was cool and collected. Sensible of the fearful odds which, at any moment, they might be called upon to encounter, and fully resolved to meet, as far as lay in their power, any issue forced upon them with the spirit of 'true Southern sailors,' they awaited, with courage in their hearts and resolve stamped upon their every countenance, the approach of a foe to whom, from old association, they took peculiar pride in showing themselves ready to stand by their cause like men '*sans peur et sans reproche*.' But the American fleet did not at-tempt an entrance, and morning dawn showed it to be in the position of the day previous. Another twenty-four hours passed only to reveal the same mysterious inaction on the part of the enemy.

"Thursday morning, however, at about half-past nine, their fleet was seen to 'get under way' and stand into the harbor in the following order: The *Minnesota*, 51, a screw, leading, the flag of Flag-officer Dupont at the mizzen, closely followed by the paddle-wheel steam frigate *Susquehanna*, 15 ; the *San Jacinto*, 14, screw steam corvette, and a number of screw and paddle pelters, mounting rifled guns, one of which towed in a sailing 'Jackass frigate,' not recognized by our officers with certainty, but sup-posed to have been the *Cumberland*, 24. At nine o'clock, having got with-in range, they opened quite a heavy fire upon the batteries, which was re-turned by them with spirit.

"Flag-officer Tatnall ordered the anchor of the *Savannah* hove up when the enemy had advanced to within a mile and a half of him, and steaming up toward Hilton Head battery, took a raking position upon the bow of the largest American frigate, then hotly engaging it, and opened fire with his thirty-two's upon her, to which, however, she did not deign immediately to reply.

"Our distance was too great (being that of a mile), and our guns were of too light a calibre to enable us to do her much, if any, injury. Several excellent shots were made by Midshipman B. Moses, commanding the after gun, but with what effect was, of course, impossible for us to determine. All this time the enemy's frigate was gradually nearing us for the double purpose of enfilading the battery and returning the respects of our little vessel; but the Commodore, disliking to *run* unless under a fire, and that a hot one, only gave the order to retreat when the frigate, rounding to, discharged her first gun at us, and the *Susquehanna* commenced a pursuit.

"We soon found the frigate to be rapidly gaining upon us, and that if we were not in the meantime blown out of the water, Skull Creek was our only haven of refuge from a prison in the great American metropolis. The *Minnesota*, evidently disposed to return our attentions of the last two days once and forever, discharged, at a distance of 800 yards, three broad-sides in quick succession against our miserable cockle-shell, but thanks to her poor gunnery and our luck, we were only hit once by an 11-inch shell that entered our port wheel-house, carrying away bulk-heads and stanch-ions, though hurting no one, from the fact that it did not explode, and lit upon the starboard side of the gun-deck, passing within two feet of Capt. Page, who was superintending the working of the forward gun. At this juncture we were so close to the enemy's ships that their crews could, with the naked eye, be distinctly seen ramming home the guns, and Flag-officer Tatnall, regretting his inability to return the high flown compliments of Flag-officer Dupont in a more satisfactory manner, ordered his blue flag dipped three times to him in token of his acknowledgments of the same.

"We reached Skull Creek in safety at about eleven o'clock and went alongside of Seabrook's Landing, when the flag-officer instantly dispatched our marines, under the command of Capt. G. Holmes, of Savannah, an experienced officer, over the other side of the island to render assistance to the fatigued garrison of the battery—Capt. Page, at the request of the flag-officer, superintending the debarkation.

"They were followed an hour afterwards by Flag-officer Tatnall, Capt. Page and Midshipman Barron Carter, of Augusta - the flag officer's aide --

who preceded all the available seamen of the steam gun-vessels *Savannah* and *Sampson*, with some few marines of the latter vessel under the command of Lieut. Philip Porcher, of South Carolina, ordered to make speed with all our naval ammunition to the battery which, at this time, appeared to be hard pressed.

"I accompanied the command of Lieut. Porcher to within a half mile of the battery. Before reaching that point, however, the firing between the battery and shipping had ceased, and the lieutenant, from the number of straggling soldiers *en route* to the landing ' in search of their companies.' thought things not exactly as they should be, and so remarked, but he nevertheless kept on his course until informed officially by an army officer of the garrison being in the enemy's possession, and advised him to ' make the best of his way back to his vessel.' This advice he partially followed by countermarching his men, in good order, at common time.

"I, however, not being an active participant in the affair, but merely a spectator, pushed further on to learn the fate of the flag-officer and Capt. Holmes' command, and met them at a distance of a quarter of a mile from the battery. Capt. Holmes was missing. He, upon his near approach to the fort, had gone in advance of his company to see how matters stood and had not returned, when the Commodore, finding all to be lost, and conceiving the captain to have been captured, ordered Lieut. Raney, of Florida, the second in command, to follow after him with his men to the steamer; to use his own words, ' feeling no fear for the success of the retreat, or his personal safety, with so reliable an officer in his rear.'

"When we reached Seabrook's Landing the steamer *Savannah* had left for the city to repair damages sustained in the engagement, but the paddle gun-vessel *Sampson*, Lieut. Commanding Kennard, received us all on board; and afterwards, at the request of certain army officers, many of the volunteers who, most unfortunately, had not yet been able to find their companies, and were consequently in much disorder. The embarkation of these last was superintended by Capt. Page, and detained us until late in the evening.

*   *   *   *   *   *

"Flag-officer Tatnall left the island, with the *Resolute* and *Sampson*, at about 2 A. M. for Savannah, which he reached a little after daylight, carrying with him as passengers many of the officers and men from the captured garrison."

The Federal gunboats with which Tatnall was first engaged with his mosquito fleet were the *Ottawa, Pembina, Seneca, Curlew, Penguin, Pawnee* and *Isaac P. Smith.* The skirmish was continued for an hour at too great a distance for much execution to be done, although the *Isaac P. Smith*, the *Ottawa* and the *Pembina* were struck several times and portions of their rigging cut away, while the *Lady Davis* received a solid shot on the quarter. As Dupont's gunboats came under the fire of Fort Beauregard they were shelled so smartly that they retreated, the Confederate flotilla following and firing upon them, the correspondent of the New York *Herald* wrote, "as proudly and defiantly as if Commodore Tatnall had a hundred line-of-battle ships under his command."

At nine o'clock on the morning of the 7th, Dupont had his sixteen ships formed in a main and a flanking column, with the *Wabash* leading, and the battle opened. According to his plan, the vessels steamed in an ellipse between the two forts, delivering their fire upon each as their broadsides were brought to bear—a novel evolution, which, however, was favored by the situation of the contending forces. Tatnall's squadron laid behind an imaginary line connecting the two forts, and the commanders of the four gunboats constituting the Federal flanking division were particularly instructed to attack him if they saw an opportunity.[1] He assisted the forts as far as was within his power, slowly retreating, but keeping within range, as the gunboats advanced upon him. His fire was of some value in the first hours of the engagement in occupying the attention of Federal guns that would otherwise have been devoted to Walker and Beauregard, and when too hard pressed by the overwhelmingly superior power of the gunboats he withdrew to a safe position at the mouth of Skull Creek. To have attempted close fighting with them would have been suicidal, and his toy steamers would have been blown out of the water or sunk by the 11-inch shells if he had ventured it.

There could be but one ending of a contest so unequal as that waged between Dupont and Drayton. During the battle the former was reinforced by the steam frigate *Pocahontas*, Commander Percival Drayton, brother of the Confederate general, which also took part in the assault. The inexperienced artillerists of the forts could rarely plant a shot in the moving steamers, while the latter maintained an unceasing rain of fire upon them. Speaking of Fort Walker, which was the main object of attack, Gen. Drayton's report says:

"Besides this moving battery, the fort was enfiladed by the gunboats anchored to the north off the mouth of Fish Hall Creek, and another on the edge of the shoal to the south. This enfilading fire on so still a sea annoyed and damaged us excessively, particularly as we had no gun on either flank of the bastion to reply with, for the 32-pounder on the right flank was shattered by a round shot, and on the north flank, for want of a carriage, no gun was mounted. After the fourth fire the 10-inch Columbiad bounded over the hurter and became useless. The 24-pounder rifle was choked while ramming down a shell and lay idle during nearly the whole engagement. * * * Two o'clock had now arrived, when I noticed our men coming out of the fort, which they had bravely defended for four and a half hours against fearful odds, and then only retiring when all but three of the guns on the water front had become disabled and only 500 pounds of powder remained in the magazine; commencing the action with 220 men inside the fort, afterwards increased to 255 by the accession of Read's Battery. These heroic men retired slowly and sadly from their well-fought guns, which to have defended longer would have exhibited the energy of despair rather than the manly pluck of the soldier."

At 2:30 P. M. a detachment of sailors hoisted the Federal flag over Fort Walker, and at 3:35 the Confederates evacuated

[1] "In giving these instructions the flag-officer stated that he knew Tatnall well; he was an officer of courage and plan, and that it was not at all unlikely that in the heat of action and smoke of battle he would endeavor to pass out and destroy the transports, and the vital duty of the flanking column was to take care of Tatnall and destroy his vessels if he attempted that experiment. * * * The vessels composing it (Tatnall's squadron) were poorly adapted for successfully opposing those advancing and now within fair range of the earthworks. Tatnall's were what were known as 'river steamers,' extremely vulnerable, boilers and machinery fully exposed, and the guns carried, although rifled, were of inferior calibre."—"The Atlantic Coast." By Rear Admiral Daniel Ammen, U. S. N.

the works on Bay Point, Gen. Drayton retiring with all his troops in safety into the interior, while Commodore Tatnall returned with his flotilla to Savannah. The Federals had eight men killed and twenty-five wounded on board the ships, and the Confederate loss was as follows: killed in Fort Walker 10, wounded 20; killed in Col. De Saussure's regiment 1, wounded 15; wounded in Fort Beauregard 13. Their victory gave the Federals access to the inland waters between Charleston and Savannah and confined Confederate naval operations on this coast to those two ports and their vicinage.

An affair, the importance of which was vastly overrated in the Federal reports, occurred on May 13th, 1862, when Robert Smalls, a slave, stole the steamer *Planter* out of Charleston harbor and delivered her over to the blockading fleet. These reports, and every account of the incident published to this day by Northern writers, speak of Smalls as the pilot of the *Planter*, and as having exhibited extreme daring. Yet he was not the pilot of the vessel, and he took no extraordinary risk, the ease with which he accomplished his undertaking being due to the negligence of her officers, who were Capt. Robert Relyea, Pilot Samuel H. Smith and Engineer Zerich Pitcher. On that day, in disobedience of Gen. Ripley's orders that the officers and crews of all light-draft steamers should remain on board day and night, they had left the boat in charge of the negro hands, of whom Smalls was one. Two white men, a white woman, and the negro crew were privy to his plot, and shortly after three o'clock, on the morning of May 13th, they got up steam and stood down the harbor. As the *Planter* was regularly used in the transportation of ordnance and army stores, there was nothing in her movements to excite the suspicions of the sentinels upon the fortifications, and she was allowed to pass unchallenged.[1] Once outside the line of fire, Smalls hauled down the Confederate ensign and hoisted a white flag, and gave up the *Planter* to a Federal vessel that was just about to fire upon her. The net result was that the Federals acquired a small steamer, the two guns with which she was armed, the four which had been put on her for transportation to the forts, the refugees, and a man (Smalls), who knew all the intricate channels of the vicinity; while Smalls obtained a notoriety which sent him to the South Carolina Legislature, and then to Congress in the reconstruction era. He was eventually convicted of receiving a $5,000 bribe as a legislator and got a term of imprisonment for his offence, none of his Northern admirers, who had so applauded him in 1862, coming forward to help him out of his trouble and disgrace.

In Nov. 1862, it was deemed advisable to take measures toward the establishment of a naval construction and repair

---

[1] The report of Major Alfred Rhett, commandant at Fort Sumter, says that "at 4:15 o'clock this morning the sentinel on the parapet called for the corporal of the guard and reported the guard-boat going out. It was so reported to the officer of the day, and as it is by no means unusual for the guard-boat to run out at that hour no further notice was taken of the occurrence."

depot on the interior waters of South Carolina, where it would not be affected by movements on the seaboard. Lieut. A. Barbot, C. S. N., in compliance with instructions from Flag-officer Ingraham, proceeded to Cheraw, Chesterfield County, on a tour of inspection of feasible sites, and reported that a gunboat could be built at Society Hill Landing on the Pedee River, from whence an average depth of eight feet by water could be carried to the Georgetown entrance. Lieut. Van Rensselaer Morgan[1] was sent into the vicinity to carry out the project, and he soon had the "Pedee navy-yard," as it was termed, under way. His force embraced a naval constructor, a surgeon, a commissary, and about one hundred carpenters, shipwrights and other workmen, most of them detailed from the army. They went into the forests, cut the timber, rafted it down the river, and soon laid the keel of a gunboat. Quite a colony was formed at this point, but great difficulty was encountered in obtaining supplies from the surrounding country, and if the gunboat was ever finished it performed no services that were noticed in official or other reports.

The history of the navy in South Carolina waters for the most part of 1862 presents little beyond reconnoissances of Federal positions. After their victory at Port Royal the enemy's gunboats pushed up into the intricate maze of sounds and inlets between that point and Charleston, and occasional skirmishes took place between them and the Confederate forces on shore, but the list of killed on both sides was not lengthy. The principal point of advantage gained by the Federals was the possession of Stono Inlet, into which they entered on May 29th, and thus secured an important base for the future siege operations against Charleston; but their attempt to then gain a foothold on James Island was frustrated by their defeat at the battle of Secessionville.

On August 14th, the Federal gunboats *Pocahontas* and *Treaty* made a raid up the Black River to Georgetown with a view of capturing the C. S. steamer *Nina*. They took alarm, however, at the reports of a large hostile force being not far distant, and hurried out towards sea again without effecting the object for which the expedition was designed. On their way down the stream they were heavily shelled from batteries on the banks and fired into by riflemen. The raid was entirely a failure.

---

[1] Van Rensselaer Morgan entered the Confederate naval service in 1861, and in the fall of that year commanded the floating battery at the Norfolk navy-yard and the old sloop-of-war *Plymouth*. When the evacuation of the yard was ordered from Richmond, he was directed to have the latter vessel towed up to that city with supplies, but that being impossible on account of the blockade of James River, instructions were given to him to set her on fire in the stream. He reluctantly complied, but not until he had thrown overboard the great quantity of provisions on board, which were gathered up by the people of Norfolk and Portsmouth, who swarmed out in boats. He then established the navy-yard on the Pedee River, and while engaged in building a gunboat there was detached and ordered to report to Commodore Ingraham at Charleston. At the surrender of that city he hurried to the Pedee navy-yard, and obtaining seven men from the commandant, impressed into service enough horses and wagons to transfer the ammunition in the yard to the railroad at Cheraw, from whence it was sent on to Charlotte. He was surrendered and paroled with Flag-officer Forrest's command at Greensboro, N. C., May 1st, 1865.

On Jan. 30th, 1863, the Confederates acquired a notable addition to the navy in Charleston waters by the capture of the Federal gunboat *Isaac P. Smith,* which was cleverly trapped in the Stono River above Legareville. The light-draft steamers were in the habit of patrolling this stream, and Gen. Beauregard, who had assumed command of the Dept. of South Carolina and Georgia on Sept. 24th, 1862, saw that it might be feasible to cut off some of them by masked batteries on shore. Lieut. Col. Joseph A. Yates, First S. C. artillery, was detailed to command an expedition of seven companies of artillery and one of infantry, which on the day mentioned posted their guns at convenient points along the river. The *Smith* was suffered to pass above them, but when she endeavored to return the batteries shelled her repeatedly, until at Legare's Point Place a shot disabled her machinery and she was surrendered, having lost eight men killed and seventeen wounded. She was a very swift steamer of 450 tons, mounting one rifled gun and eight 8-inch Columbiads. The Confederates renamed their prize the *Stono,* adopted her into the fleet and kept her on active duty around Charleston until the city was surrendered. Capt. H. J. Hartstene, C. S. N., was placed in command of this prize.

Every nerve was being strained throughout 1862 to put an iron-clad flotilla afloat, the State and the C. S. governments working along parallel lines with kindred intensity of purposes. Flag-officer Duncan N. Ingraham, who had been appointed to the command of the naval forces in South Carolina, arrived in Charleston early in the year, and one of his duties was to superintend the construction of an armored ram, the keel of which was laid in January. She was named the *Palmetto State,* and was ready for service the succeeding summer. Her iron-plating was four inches thick, and her battery consisted of an 80-pounder rifle gun forward, a 60-pounder rifle aft, and one 8-inch shell gun on each broadside.

Two months after the keel of the *Palmetto State* had been laid by the Confederate government, James M. Eason was intrusted by the State of South Carolina with the building of the second armored ship under the authority of an act of the General Assembly appropriating $300,000 for constructing marine batteries. This keel was laid in the rear of the Charleston post-office in March 1862, the plans calling for a vessel 150 feet long, 35 feet beam and 12 feet depth of hold. The armor consisted of two layers of 2-inch iron plating, which on the casemate was laid upon a wooden backing of twenty-two inches of oak and pine. The plating was continued on the hull for five feet below the water-line and also covered the ram, which was a very strong elongation of the bow. In August the ship was launched, and before September her machinery and battery were on board and she was placed in commission as the *Chicora.* Five hundred tons of iron were used in her armor, and she was propelled by an engine thirty inches diameter of cylinder and twenty-six inches stroke, driving a three-bladed screw eight feet in diameter. Her battery consisted of two 9 inch smooth-bore guns and four of the banded and rifled 32-pounders, each of which thus altered fired a 60-pound projectile.

We find in the Charleston Year Book for 1883 certain correspondence. not elsewhere printed, that illustrates at once the difficulties that stood in the way of the Confederate shipbuilders and the stubborn energy with which they pushed their contracts to completion. Mr. Jno. L. Porter, naval constructor, writing from Charleston, June 20th, 1862, to Mr. Eason, said:

"It affords me pleasure to state that the iron-clad gunboat and ram which you are now building for the State Commission of South Carolina, after drawings and specifications made by myself, is a good job in all respects, and of the very best material. She will compare with the very best of these vessels in all respects, and will afford great protection to the harbor of Charleston when completed. The work has progressed with great rapidity, and is in advance of the two boats of the same class now being built at Wilmington; also the one being built for the C. S. navy at this place. I was much gratified at the appearance of things about the ship and the spirit with which everything seemed to move, and can only hope you will soon finish her."

Yet, despite the speedy work which so gratified Mr. Porter, Mr. Eason was sorely embarrassed by the lack of material, and on June 25th wrote to Secretary Mallory that he could finish his contract in advance if he could obtain the iron-plating, but that he was then without one bar to work upon, and begged to have supplies forwarded him from the mills. When the vessel was finished in November, the State Marine Battery Commission, whose members were Messrs. J. K. Sass, George A. Trenholm, C. M. Furman, W. C. Courtney and W. B. Heriot, passed a resolution complimenting Mr. Eason upon the promptitude and skill that he had displayed, and tendering him $3,000 as compensation. He had built the *Chicora* at the comparatively moderate cost of $263,892.

Mr. Eason, having a complete plant and organization of workmen, and having proved his competency in this new line of ship-building, was commissioned to construct a larger iron-clad, and the keel of the *Charleston* was laid in Dec. 1862. She was 180 feet long, 36 feet beam, and 12½ feet depth of hold, and required 600 tons of iron plate for her four inches of armor and her ram. Her engine was 36 inches in diameter and her propeller wheel 8½ feet. Of her six guns, four were Brooke rifles, carrying shot weighing from 90 to 110 pounds, and two were 9-inch smooth-bores. The boilers and engine, placed in her by Mr. Eason, worked moderately well, and she was in every respect the strongest and swiftest of the Confederate squadron in South Carolina waters, but it was nine months from the time of the laying of her keel before she was ready to be put in commission.[1]

[1] A portion of the amount of money required for the building of the *Charleston* was the contribution of the ladies of Charleston. Judge Charles Cowley, Judge Advocate of the South

The fourth of the iron-clads contracted for at Charleston was named the *Columbia*. F. M. Jones was awarded by the Confederate Navy Department the contract for the hull, and Mr. Eason that for the plating and machinery, but the ship was not completed when Charleston was evacuated.[1]

Like the *Virginia*, the *Mississippi*, the *Arkansas*, the *Tennessee*, and other Confederate iron-clads, all of which were constructed upon the same general plan of an iron-plated wooden hull supporting a more heavily armored battery casemate, the *Palmetto State* and the *Chicora* will always deserve to figure prominently in the history of naval architecture, as reflecting some degree of professional lustre upon the men who designed and built them. Out of the still raging and yet undecided contention as to the piercing power of steel projectiles from 100-ton guns, the resistant quality of chilled steel armor and the most available types of armored ships for offence and defence, there has been developed a very unjust comparison between the Federal turreted monitors and the Confederate casemated ships unfavorable to the latter. According to these critics the Confederate naval constructors were blunderers at their business because their vessels were overcome in battle by the turret craft, and the Federal constructors are exalted to the pinnacle of fame because the monitors won victories over the casemate type. It is self-evident that such comparisons and conclusions are wholly disregardful of the facts that must be the foundation of any just and worthy balancing of the merits of these two opposing classes of marine fighting machines. If the Navy Department of the Confederacy had had behind it an inexhaustible treasury upon which it was privileged to draw at pleasure; if it had been permitted to

Atlantic Blockading Squadron, in his book, " Leaves from a Lawyer's Life Afloat and Ashore,' erroneously states that either the *Palmetto State* or the *Chicora* had been " recently built by the proceeds of a great fair held by the ladies of Charleston," and that " there was a general demand on the part of the ladies who led society in Charleston for a demonstration by the Confederate navy commensurate with their own efforts for that cause." He is referring to the breaking of the blockade by the *Palmetto State* and *Chicora*, but he confounds those ships with the *Charleston*, which was actually the vessel whose existence was so largely due to the efforts of the patriotic women of the beleaguered city, who contributed their money, jewelry, and in some instances their silverware. They held fairs and gave entertainments to increase the fund, and because the ship was so largely the fruit of their work and generosity the *Charleston* was always known in the Southern Confederacy as " The Ladies' Iron-clad Gunboat."

[1] Capt. Jas. Henry Rochelle, who commanded the *Palmetto State* toward the close of the war, when that vessel with the *Charleston* and *Chicora* constituted the squadron, says in a recent letter to the author: " The iron-clads were all slow vessels with imperfect engines, which required frequent repairing. For that day, and considering the paucity of naval resources in the South, they were fairly officered, manned and armed. Their iron armor was four inches thick, and they were all of the type of the *Virginia*. The *Palmetto State's* officers, excepting myself, all belonged to the Provisional navy, but they were competent for the duty required of them, and performed it well at all times and under all circumstances. Her crew consisted of about 120 men: some of them were old sailors, and they were all efficient and reliable men. Each of the iron-clads carried a torpedo fitted to the end of a spar some 15 or 20 feet long, projecting from the bow on a line with the keel, and so arranged that it could be carried either triced up clear of the water or submerged five or six feet below the surface. These vessels were in a good state of discipline, and, so far as their defective engines and bad plan of construction allowed, were efficient vessels of war. Every night one or more of the iron-clads anchored in the channel near Sumter for the purpose of resisting a night attack on Sumter or a dash into the harbor by the Federal vessels. Not long before the evacuation of Charleston, an iron-clad named the *Columbia* was launched there. She had a thickness of six inches of iron on her casemate, and was otherwise superior to the other iron-clads. Unfortunately, the *Columbia* was bilged in consequence of the ignorance, carelessness or treachery of her pilot, and rendered no service whatever."

fling away millions of money upon any experiments with ships and guns that Secretary Mallory desired to make;[1] if it had been possessed of half a dozen navy-yards equipped with the most perfect plants that could be devised; if it had been able to call a dozen private establishments into its service by the temptation of fat contracts; if it had been so provided as to avail itself of the products of unnumbered forges and mills and gun foundries—if it had been endowed with all these advantages, each of which was possessed by the Federal government, it would only have stood upon even ground with its opponent: but with its poverty in ship-yards, in machinery, in mills, in mechanics, and in experience, it relatively accomplished much greater results than did the North. The casemate type of ship grew out of its necessities and limitations, for that was the easiest and cheapest class to build in a country where there were no means of constructing the enormous hulls and engines fitted to support and propel the thousands of tons of 10-inch and 12-inch armor which the Northern builders piled upon their later monitors. It was an ingenious and wise adaptation of means to an end; and it would be a reckless assertion to say that the Confederate ships would still have been inferior to the monitors if they had carried the same thickness of plating, the same engine power and the same weight of ordnance. To sum up this brief diversion into a still pending question, it must be remembered that the most powerful ships of the great European navies partake of both the casemate and the turret plans—perhaps rather more of the former than of the latter; for the so-called citadel iron-clads, upon which England and Italy in particular have spent enormous sums, are the evolution of the casemate design, which is especially prominent in the *Benbow*, the latest of the English vessels. The revolving turret has practically been abandoned everywhere, not even the United States proposing to use it in the new navy now under process of construction, while Congress has refused large appropriations to complete the unfinished vessels of that type. In the essential qualification of rapidity of fire, the broadside batteries of the casemate ships were far superior to the guns of the turreted monitors, as the Federals discovered with the *New Ironsides* at Charleston, which came very much nearer to the designs

[1] Chief Engineer Alban C. Stimers, U. S. N., in the spring of 1863, made designs and detailed drawings for twenty-one light-draft monitors that theoretically were superior to all their predecessors. When the first one, the *Chimo*, was launched at Boston, her hull, without guns or machinery, was but three inches out of water, while according to Stimers' calculations it should have had fifteen inches freeboard. He was just a foot wrong in his specifications for displacement, but his designs had passed through the Navy Department without any discovery by its experts of his blunders. The other twenty monitors of the same type were in various stages of completion, and the whole unique collection was worth about what it would bring for junk. There are no official reports as to what Mr. Stimers' experiment cost the Federal government, but the amount must have been nearly or quite as many millions as the Confederacy spent upon all the iron-clads that it ever got afloat. No Confederate naval constructor made any blunder that may be mentioned in comparison with the wonderful Stimers' monitors, nor did any of the Southern ship-yards turn out iron-clads like the *Galena* and *Keokuk*, on each of which large sums were expended, while the former was shot through and through in engaging the Drewry's Bluff batteries in the James River, and the latter was easily sunk by the guns of Fort Sumter.

of the Confederate constructors than to those of John Ericsson, and was for general fighting uses a much more serviceable ship than any of the monitors. On any fair discrimination the Southern builders may fearlessly rest their claims to professional honors.

There were no maritime operations of importance in Charleston harbor during 1862, but as that year drew to its ending signs were not wanting of preparations to take the offensive against the Federal fleet; whose people, excepting those of the unlucky *Isaac P. Smith,* had had nothing more serious to engage their attention than the pursuit of blockade-runners or an occasional artillery duel with the outer forts. The uniform of the Confederate navy became more conspicuous about the streets, workshops and wharves, drafts were made upon the receiving ship *Indian Chief* to fill up the crews of the *Palmetto State* and *Chicora,* and Commodore Ingraham[1] and Gen. Beauregard were in long and frequent consultation. A list of the officers of the navy then on duty at Charleston is as follows:

"C. S. iron clad *Palmetto State :* Flag-officer, D. N. Ingraham, commanding squadron ; Lieut. Commander, John Rutledge ; Lieuts. W. H. Parker, Philip Porcher, George S. Shyrock, Robt. J. Bowen ; Master, F. T. Chew ; Surgeon, A. M. Lynah ; Paymaster, John S. Banks ; Engineers : Chief M. P. Jordan; Assistants, J. J. Darcy, William Ahern, John

[1] Commodore Duncan N. Ingraham was born at Charleston, Dec. 2d, 1802, and was descended from a line of naval warriors, his father, Nathaniel Ingraham, having fought under Capt. Paul Jones in *Le Bon Homme Richard* in the desperate battle with the British frigate *Serapis* in 1779. By intermarriage he was connected with some of the most distinguished officers of the British navy, among whom were Capt. Marryat the novelist, and Sir Edward Belcher, who commanded an exploring expedition around the world, and the expedition sent in 1853 to the Arctic regions in search of Sir John Franklin. Commodore Ingraham's wife was Miss Harriet H. Laurens, of So. Car., granddaughter on the paternal side of Henry Laurens, President of the Continental Congress and Commissioner with Franklin and Jay to negotiate the treaty of peace with Great Britain, which was signed at Paris. Nov. 30th, 1782. Her maternal grandfather was John Rutledge, Governor of S. C. during the Revolution, member of the Continental Congress, and, by the appointment of President Washington, Chief Justice of the Supreme Court. Commodore Ingraham entered the U. S. navy as midshipman in 1812, and in 1813 was ordered for service in the frigate *Congress,* on the Brazil station. When she returned to the Portsmouth, N. H., navy-yard she was blockaded by British ships, and Midshipman Ingraham was transferred to the sloop-of-war *Madison* on Lake Ontario. After the close of the war with England he served successively on the brig *Boxer,* the sloop-of-war *Hornet,* the schooner *Revenge,* and the frigate *Macedonian,* and was present at the transfer of Florida from the Spanish to the American flag. In 1825 he was promoted to lieutenant and in 1838 to commander, and during the Mexican war commanded the brig *Somers* in the blockade of the Mexican ports. From 1850 to 1852 he was commandant of the Philadelphia navy-yard, after which he was assigned to the sloop-of-war *St. Louis,* and joined Commodore Stringham's

squadron in the Mediterranean. With this ship he performed an exploit the fame of which rang round the world, and which was the boldest deed done to assert the inviolability of American citizenship since the United States went to war with England to protect her marine from the so-called "right of search." This was the historic Kostza affair. Martin Kostza, by birth a Hungarian, and an Austrian subject, took part in the Hungarian revolution against the empire in 1848–49, and when it was suppressed was among those who took refuge in Turkey, where the government refused to surrender them to Austria. Kostza came to New York in company with Louis Kossuth,and on July 31st, 1852,took the initiatory steps to become an American citizen by naturalization. In 1853 he made a trip to Smyrna, Asiatic Turkey, on business, and on June 21st was kidnapped by Greek mercenaries hired by the Austrian consul, and confined in irons on the Austrian man-of-war *Huzzar.* At this critical moment Ingraham came into the harbor with the *St. Louis* and addressed a communication to Mr. Brown, American chargé d'affaires at Constantinople, notifying him of the circumstances and asking advice as to his action. Before an answer could be received the Austrian representative at Smyrna ordered the *Huzzar* to sail with Kostza for an Austrian port on June 29th, but Ingraham halted him by clearing his ship for action, bringing his batteries to bear on the *Huzzar* and the two Austrian mail steamers that had in the meantime arrived, and giving the Austrian captain notice that he would open fire if any attempt was made to remove Kostza before a reply was received from Constantinople. The Austrian hastened to assure him that the prisoner should not be sent away, and thus Ingraham's resolute attitude prevailed, although the Austrian force was strengthened on July 1st, by the arrival of another ship-of-war,which made it far superior to the *St. Louis.* The next day Commander Ingraham received letters from Mr.

C. Johnson; Midshipmen, C. F. Sevier, W. P. Hamilton, C. Cary; Boatswain, Thos. Wilson ; Gunner, George M. Thompson ; Pilots, G. D. Gladdon, Andrew Johnson. C. S. iron-clad *Chicora :* Capt. J. R. Tucker ; Lieuts. George H. Bier, Wm. T. Glassell, Wm. H. Wall ; Master, A. M. Mason ; Acting Master, John A. Payne ; Passed Midshipman, Jos. P. Claybrooke; Midshipmen, R. H. Bacot,[1] Palmer Saunders, Roger Pinckney; Surgeon, Wm. Mason Turner ; Engineers, First Assistant, Hugh Clarke; Second Assistant, J. W. Toombs; Third Assistants, William F. Jones, J. J. Lyell; Gunner, E. R. Johnson; Carpenter, James F. Weaver; Acting Paymaster, Ed. A. West; Pilots, Thomas Payne, Jas. Aldert.

Besides the above the following officers were assigned to the Charleston naval station:

"First Lieut. N. K. Van Zandt ; Surgeon, W. F. Patton; Paymaster, Henry Myers ; Master, W. D. Porter; Midshipman, W. P. Hamilton; Engineer, Virginius Freeman ; First Ass't Engineers, M. P. Jordon, C. H. Levy; Sailmaker, M. P. Beaufort.

On January 31st, 1863, occurred the famous breaking of the blockade by the iron-clads *Palmetto State* and *Chicora*, an event which demonstrated the power of those vessels and the gallantry of the officers and men of the Confederate navy. Col. Alfred Roman, author of "The Military Operations of General Beauregard," assigns to the latter the credit of initiating this bold and successful enterprise. "Gen. Beauregard,"

Brown, stating that Kostza was an American citizen and entitled to the protection of the flag, whereupon Ingraham went on board the *Huzzar* and laid down the ultimatum that the prisoner must be sent on shore by four o'clock that afternoon. He again prepared his ship for battle and to the protest of the Austrian captain returned no answer save a repetition of his demands. As four o'clock approached the populace crowded the shore in expectation of witnessing a fight ; but the Austrians, although they were also standing to their guns, weakened and a compromise was arranged by which Kostza was transferred to the care of the French consul pending the settlement of the question between the Austrian and American governments. Austria made a demand upon the United States for the surrender of the refugee as an Austrian subject ; but President Pierce and Hon. Wm. M. Marcy, Secretary of State, fully justified Commander Ingraham's action, and Mr. Marcy answered the Austrian Minister with a full assertion of Kostza's status as an American citizen, and demanded that the Emperor should take measures to restore Kostza to the same condition he was in when arrested. Austria ate the leek and he was placed on an American bark bound to this country. When Ingraham arrived in the United States in 1855, his name was on every tongue; Congress passed a resolution requesting the President to present him with a gold medal; a gold medal was also presented to him by a great meeting of the citizens of New York; other testimonials were sent him from various American cities ; and the working people of England presented him, by penny subscription, with a superb chronometer and a finely engraved letter. His conduct at Smyrna, and its endorsement by the administration, had formulated a policy for the protection of American citizens that has ever since been maintained.

In 1855 Commodore Ingraham was appointed Chief of the Bureau of Ordnance and Hydrography in the Navy Department, which position he retained until August, 1860, when he was ordered to the command of the frigate *Richmond*, the flagship of the Mediterranean squadron. At the breaking out of the civil war he returned to the United States, in January, 1861, and resigned his commission. He entered the service of the Confederate States on March 26th, 1861, and at Montgomery, Ala., was made a member of the board to consider the water defences of the Confederacy. He was afterwards placed in charge of the Pensacola navy-yard, and continued in command until its evacuation, when he was ordered to command the naval forces on the coast of South Carolina, with headquarters at Charleston.

[1] Lieut. Richard H. Bacot entered the U. S. naval academy by appointment from South Carolina in Sept. 1859, and resigned on Dec. 10th, 1860, the date of the meeting of the convention of his native State, that passed the ordinance of secession. On Jan. 1st, 1861, Gov. Pickens commissioned him instructor of Artillery, to drill the troops in the fortifications of Charleston at the heavy guns, and he also served in the S. C. coast police in the guard steamers off Fort Sumter. He entered the C. S. navy as soon as his class was reached in the order of appointment and was assigned to the steamer *Resolute*, Capt. J. P. Jones, at Savannah. In April 1862, he was ordered to Memphis to duty on the iron-clad *Arkansas*, but before the year was out was transferred to South Carolina waters, where he served in the *Chicora* and *Charleston* until he was detached to command one of the launches in the capture of the Federal gunboat *Underwriter* in North Carolina. During the later months of the war he was on duty on the iron-clad *Neuse* in Eastern North Carolina. At this time (1887) Lieut. Bacot is U. S. Ass't Engineer employed in the improvement of the Missouri River.

says Col. Roman, "advised a night attack by the Confederate rams against the wooden fleet of the enemy, and felt sure that the blockade might be thus raised, or at any rate that considerable damage could thus be effected." Flag-officer Ingraham heartily accorded with the suggestion, and about eleven o'clock on the night of January 30th, he left the harbor on the *Palmetto State*, Lieut. Com. John Rutledge, and in company with the *Chicora*, Com. John R. Tucker, followed by the three steam tenders *General Clinch*, *Etowan* and *Chesterfield*. Before five o'clock the next morning they were over the bar and in the haze of the early dawn; the *Palmetto State* stood for the nearest blockader, which proved to be the *Mercedita*, a large gunboat, carrying seven heavy guns, which had just returned from a chase, and was consequently in trim for action. Lieut. Com. Abbott was in charge of her deck, Capt. H. S. Stellwagen having retired to his cabin. She was taken completely by surprise, no one of her officers anticipating that a Confederate commander would have the temerity to attack the greatly superior force of the blockading squadron. The watch on deck hailed the stranger, and was answered "This is the Confederate States steamer *Palmetto State*." Almost on the moment of giving the reply the *Palmetto State* plunged her ram deep into the quarter of the *Mercedita*, and fired from her bow-gun a shell which went through the enemy's boiler, and exploded on the other side of the ship, tearing a great hole in her planking. Two men were killed by the shell and many more were scalded by the escaping steam. Capt. Stellwagen had not fired a gun during the encounter, and he now appeared on his quarter-deck to announce to Com. Ingraham the surrender of his ship. The latter demanded that a boat be sent aboard, and one came under command of Lieut. Abbott, who gave the name of the ship, stated that she was in a sinking condition, and begged for relief. Several men of his boat's crew were nearly destitute of clothing, and it was learned that the *Mercedita* had been run down so suddenly that all her people, except the watch on duty, had not had time to dress before they found the ship going down under them. The "account of an eye-witness," printed in the Charleston *Courier*, says:

"Lieut. Abbott begged Com. Ingraham to take the men with him on board the *Palmetto State*, as in their haste to come to us they had neglected to put the plug in their small boat, and it was only kept afloat by the strenuous efforts of the men bailing. He also stated that the water in the *Mercedita* had, at the time of his leaving, already risen as high as the engine floors. Com. Ingraham regretted that he could not comply with the request, as he had no room to accommodate them on board his vessel, and no small boats or any other means of affording them relief."

As subsequent events showed, the Federal ship was in no immediate danger of going to the bottom, but all hands had

been panic-stricken, and thought of their personal safety before any other consideration.

On the demand of Com. Ingraham, Lieut. Abbott, as the
representative of Capt. Stellwagen, and speaking for all the
officers and crew of the *Mercedita*, gave his parole of honor
that they would not "take up arms against the Confederate
States during the war, unless legally and regularly exchanged
as prisoners of war," and he was permitted to return to his
ship, on which four men had been killed, and three wounded.
Other vessels of the fleet assisted her to Port Royal for
repairs.

The *Palmetto State* was then headed further to sea, where
the *Chicora* was in vigorous combat with several of the Federal ships, and within an hour the two rams engaged the
Quaker City, the *Ottawa*, the *Keystone State*, the *Unadilla*,
the *Augusta*, the *Stettin*, the *Flag* and the *Memphis*. None of
these gunboats were taken unawares, as the *Mercedita* had
given the alarm by burning signal lights, but not one seemed
desirous of coming to close quarters with the rams, although
all could have done so by their superior speed. Commander
Tucker, of the *Chicora*, thus was not so fortunate in employing his ram upon the foe as his companion had been. The
"account of an eye-witness" says of the movements of the
Chicora, after passing the *Palmetto State*, at work upon the
Mercedita :

"Keeping on our course, we proceeded to within fifty yards of the
vessel on the left, and then gave her a shot from our bow-gun, the blockader at the time being under full headway. We rounded-to and gave her
the full benefit of our broadside guns and after-gun. She immediately
rang her bell for fire, and made signals of distress to the rest of the fleet.
The last seen of her by Signal-officer Saunders, she was stern down, very
low in the water, and disappeared very suddenly. This vessel is supposed
to have gone down. Notwithstanding the *Chicora* immediately steamed
towards her, nothing could be discovered of the vessel.

"The *Chicora*, proceeding farther out to sea, stood northward and
eastward, and met two vessels apparently coming to the relief of the
missing steamer. We engaged them. One of them, after firing a few
guns, withdrew. Standing to the northward, about daybreak, we steamed
up to a small side-wheel two-masted steamer, and endeavored to come to
close quarters. She kept clear of us, driving away as rapidly as possible,
not however without receiving our compliments, and carrying with her
four or five of our shots. Shortly after, the steamship *Quaker City* and
another side-wheel steamer came gallantly bearing down upon the
Chicora and commenced firing at long range.

"Neither would permit our boat to get within a respectable distance.
Two of our shots struck the *Quaker City*, and she left apparently perfectly satisfied, in a critical condition. Another side-wheel two-masted
steamer with walking beams now steamed towards the *Chicora*, coming
down on our stern. Capt. Tucker perceiving it, we rounded-to and proceeded until within about five hundred yards, when the belligerent
steamer also rounded-to and gave us both broadsides and a shot from her
pivot-gun. We fired our forward pivot-gun with an incendiary shell, and
struck her just forward of her wheel-house, setting her on fire, disabling
and stopping her port wheel. This vessel was fired both fore and aft,
and volumes of smoke observed to issue from every aperture. As we

neared her, she hauled down her flag and made a signal of surrender, but still kept under way with her starboard wheel, and changing her direction. This was just after daybreak. We succeeded in catching this vessel, but having surrendered, and the captain supposing her boilers struck and the escaping steam preventing the engineers from going into the engine-room to stop her, ordered us not to fire. She thus made her escape. After this vessel had got out of our reach, to the perfectly safe distance of about three miles, she fired her port rifled gun, again hoisted her flag, and setting all sails, firing her rifled guns repeatedly at us as she left. The *Chicora* now engaged six more of the enemy's vessels at one time-- three side-wheel steamers and three propellers—all at long range. Discovering that the flag-boat *Palmetto State* had ceased firing and was standing in shore, orders were given to follow her. On our return, we again came across a three-masted bark-rigged vessel, which we engaged, firing our guns as we passed, striking her once or twice. We then kept on our course to the bar, having sustained no damage in the action nor a single casualty on board. The last ship mentioned above kept firing at us until we got out of range, and we giving them our return compliments. One of the blockaders was certainly sunk. We engaged her at the distance of only one hundred yards, and she settled down with her stern clear under water.

" The *Chicora* anchored in Beach Channel at 8:30 A. M., and arrived at her wharf in the city about six o'clock, receiving a salute from all the forts and batteries as she passed on her return. The number of shots fired by the *Chicora* during the whole engagement was twenty-seven, mostly incendiary shells. Lieut. Glassell commanded the forward pivot-gun¦ assisted by Midshipman R. H. Pinckney; Lieut. W. H. Wall, the after-pivot ; Master Mason, the starboard broadside; Master Payne, the larboard broadside. The different divisions were commanded by First Lieut. G. H. Bier and Lieut. J. C. Claybrook, assisted by Midshipman R. H. Bacot and Signal-officer Saunders."

The ship which hauled down her colors was the *Keystone State*, Com. LeRoy, who supposed his vessel to be sinking. One of the *Chicora's* shells had set fire to her forward hold and another had destroyed her steam chimneys, filling all the forward part of the vessel with steam. She had twenty men killed, and as many more wounded.

Having accomplished the object of his expedition, Com. Ingraham signalled a return to Charleston, not one ship of the blockading squadron being then in sight from the pilot-house of the *Palmetto State*, all having made off to escape the fate of the *Mercedita* and *Keystone State*. No injury was done to either of the rams, not a man was hurt on them, and when they arrived back in the harbor they were in condition for another battle.

The reports of Com. Ingraham and Com. Tucker, which are appended, will be read with interest:

"OFFICE NAVAL STATION, CHARLESTON, Feb. 2d, 1863.
"SIR: I have the honor to inform you that upon the night of the 30th ultimo, I left the wharf at this place, in company with the steam-ram *Chicora*, Com. John R. Tucker, at 11.15 P. M., and steamed slowly down to the bar, as, from our draft, we could not cross until high water. At 4.30 A. M. we crossed the bar, with about a foot and a half to spare, and soon after made a steamer at an anchor. Stood directly for her, and directed Lieut. Commanding Rutledge to strike her with our prow. When quite near we were hailed: "What steamer is that? Drop your anchor; you

will be into us." He was informed that it was the Confederate steamer *Palmetto State*. At this moment we struck her, and fired the seven-inch gun into her, as he gave an order to fire. I then inquired if he surrendered, and was answered in the affirmative. I then directed him to send a boat on board, which was done. After some delay, Lieut. Commanding Abbott came on board and informed me that the vessel was the U. S. steamer *Mercedita*, Com. Stellwagen, and that she was in a sinking condition, and had a crew of 158 all told, and wished to be relieved; that all his boats were lowered without the plugs being in, and were full of water. At this time the *Chicora* was engaged with the enemy, and the alarm was given.

"I knew our only opportunity was to take the enemy unawares, as the moment he was under way, from his superior speed, we could not close with him. I then directed Lieut. Commanding Rutledge to require from Lieut. Commanding Abbott his word of honor for his commander, officers and crew that they would not serve against the Confederate States until regularly exchanged, when he was directed to return with his boat to his vessel to render what assistance he could. I then stood to the northward and eastward, and soon after made another steamer getting under way. We stood for her and fired several shot at her; but as we had to fight the vessel in a circle to bring the different guns to bear, she was soon out of our range. In this way we engaged several vessels, they keeping at long range and steering to the southward. Just as the day broke we made a large steamer (supposed to be the *Powhatan*),[1] on starboard bow, with another steamer in company, which had just got under way. They stood to the southward under full steam, and opened their batteries upon the *Chicora*, who was some distance astern of us. I then turned and stood to the southward to support the *Chicora* if necessary, but the enemy kept on his course to the southward. I then made signal to Com. Tucker to come to an anchor, and led the way to the entrance of Beach Channel, where we anchored at 8:45 A. M., and had to remain seven hours for the tide, as the vessel cannot cross the bar excepting at high water. * * *

"The sea was perfectly smooth, as much so as in the harbor; everything was most favorable for us, and gave us no opportunity to test the sea qualities of the boats. The engines worked well and we obtained a greater speed than they had ever before sustained.

"I cannot speak in too high terms of the conduct of Com. Tucker and Lieut. Com. Rutledge; the former handled his vessel in a beautiful manner, and did the enemy much damage. I refer you to his official report. Lieut. Com. Rutledge also fought the *Palmetto State* in a manner highly gratifying to me. Every officer and man did his duty nobly, and deserve well of his country.

"We had but little opportunity of trying our vessels, as the enemy did not close, and not a single shot struck either vessel. I am highly indebted to Com. Hartstene, who gallantly volunteered to take charge of three steamers with fifty soldiers on board, who accompanied us in case we should need their services; but they could not get over the bar, but joined us after daylight at the North Channel, and rendered us their assistance in getting through the channel, which is very narrow.

"Of the conduct of Mr. Gladden, the pilot of the *Palmetto State*, I cannot speak in too high terms; he was perfectly cool under the great responsibility he had in taking the vessel over at night with so great a draft, and during the action rendered me great assistance in pointing out the vessels as we approached them in the uncertain light.

"I am, sir, very respectfully,
"Your obedient servant,
"D. N. INGRAHAM,
"*Flag-officer Commanding.*
"*Hon.* S. R. MALLORY, *Secretary of the Navy, Richmond, Va.*"

---

[1] Commodore Ingraham was mistaken in the name of this ship, as the *Powhatan*, according to the Federal official reports, was then coaling at Port Royal.

"CONFEDERATE STATES STEAMER 'CHICORA,' Jan. 31st, 1863.

"SIR: In obedience to your order, I got under way at 11.30 P. M., yes-terday, and stood down the harbor in company with the Confederate States steamer *Palmetto State*, bearing your flag. We crossed the bar at 4:40 A. M., and commenced the action at 5.20 A. M., by firing into a schooner-rigged propeller, which we set on fire, and have every reason to believe sunk, as she was nowhere to be seen at daylight. We then en-gaged a large side-wheel steamer, twice our length from us on the port bow, firing three shots into her with telling effect, when she made a run for it. This vessel was supposed to be the *Quaker City*. We then engaged a schooner-rigged propeller and a large side-wheel steamer, partially crip-pling both, and setting the latter on fire, causing her to strike her flag; at this time the latter vessel, supposed to be the *Keystone State*, was com-pletely at my mercy, I having taken position astern, distant some 200 yards; I at once gave the order to cease firing upon her, and directed Lieut. Bier, First Lieutenant of the *Chicora*, to man a boat and take charge of the prize, if possible to save her; if that was not possible, to rescue her crew. While the boat was in the act of being manned, I dis-covered that she was endeavoring to make her escape, by working her starboard wheel, the other being disabled. Her colors being down, I at once started in pursuit, and renewed the engagement. Owing to her superior steaming qualities, she soon widened the distance to some 200 yards. She then hoisted her flag, and commenced firing her rifled guns; her commander, by this faithless act, placing himself beyond the pale of civilized and honorable warfare. We next engaged two schooners, one brig, and one bark-rigged propeller, but not having the requisite speed were unable to bring them to close quarters. We pursued them six or seven miles seaward. During the latter part of the combat, I was engaged at long range with a large bark-rigged steam sloop-of-war; but in spite of all our efforts, was unable to bring her to close quarters, owing to her superior steaming qualities. At 7:30 A. M., in obedience to your orders, we stood in shore, leaving the partially crippled and fleeing enemy about *seven miles clear of the bar*, standing to the southward and eastward. At 8 A. M., in obedience to signal, we anchored in four fathoms water off the Beach Channel.

"It gives me pleasure to testify to the good conduct and efficiency of the officers and crew of the "*Chicora*." I am particularly indebted to the pilots, Messrs. Payne and Aldert, for the skillful pilotage of the vessel.

"It gives me pleasure to report that I have no injuries or casualties.
"Very respectfully, your obedient servant,
"J. R. TUCKER, *Commander C. S. N.*
"*Flag-officer* D. N. INGRAHAM, *C. S. N., commanding Station, Charles-ton, S. C.*"

This intrepid exploit of the Confederate squadron fell like a thunder-clap on the North and woke the Federal govern-ment from its comfortable indifference as to the prowess of the Southern officers and the efficacy of their ships. While the Northern newspapers heaped invective upon the Washington authorities, and Admiral Dupont and his subordinates, for per-mitting Ingraham and his two small vessels to catch the great Federal armada off its guard and play havoc with it, there arose also a vociferous demand for official contradictions of the reports of the most serious injuries inflicted upon the fleet; and statements meant to minimize the Confederate victory were soon prepared under the supervision of Secretary Welles and his coadjutors. President Lincoln's administration had tremendous stakes at issue. There was the popular fury at the North to be allayed by creating the belief that the Federal disaster was an accident that could not have been provided against, and that the Confederates were favored by circumstances over which they had no control ; there was the reputation of the navy to be upheld, and the European powers were to be convinced of the falsity of the Confederate claim that the blockade had been raised for any period, however brief. It was an hour of anxiety and doubt at Washington, for on shore and at sea, in Jan., 1863, misfortunes had accumulated on the Federal arms, and the elections of the preceding October and November had been strongly adverse to the war policy of the administration. As fast as the reports belittling the Confederate success at Charleston could be written up they were rushed into print for circulation throughout the North. And they differed so irreconcilably from the reports of Ingraham and Tucker, that they merit review before we proceed to the consideration of the diplomatic questions springing out of the dispersion of the blockading fleet.

At the outset of the controversy over the facts of the battle the Federals possessed a fictitious advantage, because they could prove that the Confederate commanders erroneously reported that they had sunk one or more of the enemy's ships. But if it is remembered that the fight took place about dawn of a foggy January morning, that Lieut. Abbott gave Commodore Ingraham to understand that the *Mercedita* was in peril of sinking, and that when the *Keystone State* escaped after striking her colors she was heeled far over, any impartial critic must admit that Ingraham and Tucker, who made their reports on the same day that the action took place, were entirely justified in their opinion that these two vessels had gone down. The strenuous insistence by the Federals that Commodore Ingraham had made or sanctioned reports which he knew to be false in this respect, was convincing evidence that they were exceedingly perplexed to buttress a weak case and resorted to an undignified evasion.

Com. Ingraham, whose conscientiousness no officer who had served with him during his illustrious career in the old navy would call in question, was fully persuaded that he had broken the blockade, and so reported to Gen. Beauregard upon his return to Charleston. The latter, a soldier versed in statecraft, knew that if this claim could be sustained by the consuls of European nations at Charleston, and if their governments would act upon such representations by declaring the blockade raised, Charleston would be an open port for the transaction of commerce, and the reception of war material for the Confederacy, until the United States had established a fresh blockade in accordance with the laws of nations. But before the consuls could be asked to pass their judgment upon the status of affairs, it was proper to make public proclamation of the situation, and on January 31st the following was issued:

"HEADQUARTERS, LAND AND NAVAL FORCES, }
"CHARLESTON, S. C., January 31st, 1863. }
    "At about five o'clock this morning, the Confederate States naval force on this station attacked the U. S. blockading fleet off the harbor of the city of Charleston, and sunk, dispersed, or drove off and out of sight for the time the entire hostile fleet.
    "Therefore we, the undersigned, commanders respectively of the C. S. naval and land forces in this quarter, do hereby *formally declare the blockade by the United States of the said city of Charleston, S. C., to be raised by a superior force of the Confederate States from and after this 31st day of January, A. D.* 1863.
            "G. T. BEAUREGARD, *General Commanding.*
            "D. N. INGRAHAM,
    "*Flag-officer Commanding Naval Forces in South Carolina.*
"*Official.*—THOMAS JORDAN, *Chief of Staff.*"

Hon. Judah P. Benjamin, Confederate Secretary of State, was advised of this proclamation by telegraph, and on the same day he addressed the subjoined communications to the consular representatives of the European powers in the Confederate States :

        "DEPARTMENT OF STATE, RICHMOND, Jan. 31st, 1860.
    "SIR: I am instructed by the President of the Confederate States of America to inform you that this government has received an official dispatch from Flag-officer Ingraham, commanding the naval forces of the Confederacy on the coast of South Carolina, stating that the blockade of the harbor of Charleston has been broken by the complete dispersion and disappearance of the blockading squadron, in consequence of a successful attack made on it by the iron-clad steamers commanded by Flag-officer Ingraham. During this attack one or more of the blockading vessels were sunk or burnt.
    "As you are doubtless aware that, by the law of nations, a blockade when thus broken by superior force ceases to exist, and cannot be subsequently enforced unless established *de novo*, with adequate forces and after due notice to neutral powers, it has been deemed proper to give you the information herein contained for the guidance of such vessels of your nation as may choose to carry on commerce with the now open port of Charleston.
    "Respectfully, your obedient servant,
            "J. P. BENJAMIN, *Secretary of State.*"

Also, on the same day, Gen. Jordan addressed the following communication to Robert Bunce, consular agent of Great Britain; Baron de St. Andre, consul of France, and Senor Francisco Munez Moncada, consul of Spain at Charleston:

    "I am instructed to call your attention officially to the fact that the Confederate States naval forces on this station this morning, about the hour of 5 o'clock, attacked the U. S. blockading squadron off the harbor of Charleston, at their habitual place of anchorage, and after a brief engagement sunk, dispersed or drove off, and out of sight for the time, the whole hostile fleet. And I am further instructed to call your attention to the fact that this summary destruction of the fleet of the United States, constituting the blockading force of this harbor, by the superior force of the Confederate States, operates as an entire defeasance of the blockade of the port of Charleston and of its operation. The rule of public law requiring that there should be a notification of a new blockade before foreign nations can be affected with an obligation of observing it as a blockade still existing, it is deemed necessary to give you now this formal notification of the fact. Should you desire, I shall be pleased to place at your disposal a steamer for the purpose of satisfying yourself of the unobstructed condition of this port."

Baron de St. André and Senor Moncada accepted the invitation, and on the afternoon of January 31st they accompanied Gen. Ripley, on the steamer *General Clinch*, on a visit of inspection, as far as the bar. Mr. Bunce did not accompany them, because earlier in the day he had gone to the same locality in the British corvette *Petrel*, which was in the harbor at that time. The three consuls were back in the city that night, and at a joint conference concurred in the opinion that the blockade had been legally raised.[1] Mr. Bunce strengthened this conclusion with his assertion that on the *Petrel* he had gone five miles beyond the usual anchorage of the blockaders and could see nothing of them with marine glasses, in which positive declaration he was confirmed by the statement of the captain and other officers of the *Petrel*.

The French and Spanish consuls were not quite so emphatic, in their official replies to Gen. Jordan, as they are reported to have been at the conference on the night of January 31st. Senor Moncada wrote the next day to Gen. Jordan :

"I take pleasure in replying to your communication of the 31st of January, respecting the notification of the raising of the blockade at Charleston by the naval forces of the Confederate States. I should inform you that I remitted a copy of the same communication to his Excellency the Minister Plenipotentiary, at Washington. I thank you for your kind offer in placing a steamer at my disposal, so that I might go and satisfy myself as to the condition of the port. Having gone out in company with the French consul, and arrived at the point where the Confederate naval forces were, we discovered three steamers and a pilot-boat returning. I must also mention that the British consul at this port manifested to me verbally, that some time subsequent to this naval combat not a single blockading vessel was in sight."

Diplomatic caution is observable in the statement which Senor Moncada committed to paper for himself and for Baron de St. André, but Mr. Bunce chose to assume a larger responsibility, regardless of what might be the results of his bold avowal of his convictions. The Spanish and French consuls might as well have coincided with him for all the good that their temporizing attitude did them in the judgment of the Federal government and the Northern people. Because they did not certify that the vessels which they saw beyond the bar were blockading ships, and because they did not declare that the blockade was not broken, they were included by the Northern newspapers and the authors of the Federal official reports in the unsparing condemnation thrust upon Beauregard,

[1] The Charleston newspapers of February 1st are the authority for this statement of the conclusions of the meeting. There are no official records concerning it in existence, but it has been accepted by all historians of the war that the consuls united in this declaration.

Ingraham, Jordan, Tucker, Rutledge and Bunce, as the makers of wilfully false reports.

A steamer was at once dispatched from Charleston to Nassau to place in the British mail from the latter point dispatches conveying to Messrs. Mason and Slidell information of the raising of the blockade, in order that they might, if possible, secure acknowledgments from the governments of England and France to that effect. Mr. Mason's correspondence with Earl Russell, British Minister of Foreign Affairs, which related to the dispersion of the blockaders at Galveston as well as at Charleston, epitomizes the history of the refusal of England to accept the Confederate view. In a communication of Feb. 16th, Mr. Mason said:

"I have the honor to submit, therefore, that any alleged pre-existing blockade of the ports aforesaid was terminated at Galveston the 1st day of January last, and at Charleston on the 31st of the same month; a principle clearly stated in a letter I have had the honor to receive from your lordship, dated on the 10th instant, in the following words : ' *The driving off a blockading force by a superior force does break a blockade, which must be renewed de novo, in the usual form, to be binding upon neutrals*'— a principle uniformly admitted by all text writers on public law, and established by decisions of Courts of Admiralty."

Lord Russell's only immediate reply was an acknowledgment of the receipt of the note, and on Feb. 18th Mr. Mason again wrote to him, this second communication having reference also to a note from Lord Russell on Feb. 10th, in which he replied to questions concerning the interpretation placed by her Majesty's government on the declaration of the principles of blockade agreed to in the Convention of Paris. This construction was far from being satisfactory to Mr. Mason or President Davis, Mr. Mason saying in the communication of the 18th that: " It is considered by him [Davis] that the terms used in that convention are too precise to admit of being qualified—or perhaps it may be more appropriate to say revoked—by the super-additions thereto contained in your lordship's exposition of them." The point made by Lord Russell to which Mr. Davis took exception was thus set forth by the former:

" It appears to be sufficiently clear to her Majesty's government that the declaration of Paris could not have been intended to mean that a port must be so blockaded in all winds, and independently of whether the communication might be carried on of a dark night or by means of small, low steamers or coasting craft creeping along the shore."

In other words, the British government stood out inflexibly against the doctrine advanced by Mr. Davis and Mr. Mason, that the habitual evasion of a blockade by the ships of neutrals should be regarded in law as nullifying it; and Lord Russell also refused to admit that the blockade had been raised by the events of Jan. 31st. On Feb. 19th he informed Mr. Mason that "the information which her Majesty's government have derived from your letter and from the public journals on this subject is not sufficiently accurate to admit of their forming an opinion, and they will accordingly, by the first opportunity, instruct Lord Lyons (British Minister at Washington) to report fully on the matter."

On Feb. 27th, Lord Russell went a little deeper into the question by writing to Mr. Mason:

"I have already, in my previous letters, fully explained to you the views of her Majesty's government on this matter; *and I have nothing further to add in reply* to your last letter, except to observe that I have not intended to state that any number of vessels of a certain build or tonnage might be left at liberty freely to enter a blockaded port without vitiating the blockade; but the occasional escape of small vessels on dark nights, or under other particular circumstances, from the vigilance of a competent blockading fleet, *did not evince that laxity in the belligerent which enured, according to international law, to the raising of a block-ade.*"

The people of Charleston publicly celebrated the victory of the *Palmetto State* and *Chicora* by a ceremony, on Feb. 3d, at St. Philip's Church, at which the *Te Deum* was sung, some of the officers and crews of the ships attending and receiving conspicuous attention for the gallant services they had performed. The raid had the effect of hurrying the efforts of the Federal government to place the largest possible number of iron-clads in the waters where the wooden vessels had proved so vulnerable to the attacks of Ingraham's squadron; and Dupont soon had under his command the broadside frigate *New Ironsides*, mounting fourteen 11-inch Dahlgren guns, two 150-pounder rifles and two 50-pounder rifles; the Ericsson monitors *Weehawken*, *Passaic*, *Montauk*, *Patapsco*, *Catskill*, *Nantucket* and *Nahant*, and the Whitney monitor *Keokuk*, which was a turtle-back armored floating battery with two fixed turrets. The monitors carried 15-inch and 11-inch guns and 150-pounder Parrott rifles. It was with this fleet that Dupont determined to attempt the reduction of Fort Sumter and to bombard or run past the other fortifications, and thus capture the city. In order that, if the opportunity served, his wooden ships might take part in the engagement, the *Canandaigua*, *Housatonic*, *Unadilla*, *Wissahickon* and *Huron* were constituted the reserve and were held in readiness outside the bar.

The land defences of Charleston were as perfect as the engineering skill and the resources of the Confederacy could make them. They had been planned and constructed under the direction of Gens. Beauregard and R. S. Ripley, and embraced three lines of fortifications and three lines or circles of fire, each converging or crossing so as to command the channels. Fort Sumter was the centre of the first line, and on the south it was continued to Battery Gregg and Fort Wagner on Morris Island. On the north side a row of defences stretched along the shore of Sullivan's Island, beginning with the new battery at the inner point and comprising successively, in a direction toward the bar, Battery Bee, Battery Marion, Fort Moultrie, Battery Rutledge, Fort Beauregard, four small detached batteries and Fort Marshall, which latter was the outer limit of the line. If an enemy had passed this circle of fire he would have been exposed to the second circle, which consisted of Fort Johnson, Battery Cheves, Battery Wampler, Battery Glover, and some minor earthworks on James Island southeast of the city; Fort Ripley, in the Folly Island channel; Castle Pinckney, on Shute's Folly Island; one battery on Hog Island, and two on Mt. Pleasant, on the northern side of the inner harbor. The third circle embraced the fortifications in the city and on the banks of the Cooper and Ashley Rivers. Within the municipal limits were the King Street Battery, White Point Battery, Vanderhorst Wharf Battery, Frazier's Wharf Battery and the Half-Moon Battery. These and two earthworks at the Calhoun and Laurens Street wharves extended from the southern point of the city around the Cooper River front. On the Ashley River side were Battery Waring and two forts near either end of the Savannah Railroad bridge. Torpedoes were thickly sown in the main channel, as well as in the Swash, the North and Beach channels, and all the way up in Rebellion Roads, the Folly Island channels, and in the entrance to Cooper and Ashley Rivers. A line of rope, pile, log and chain obstructions was stretched across the channel from Cumming's Point to Fort Sumter and Mount Pleasant, and was arranged with openings to allow the passage of blockade-runners and the Confederate squadron.

Dupont's attack was made on April 7th, 1863, with the *New Ironsides* and the eight monitors.

While the battle was being fought, the *Chicora* and *Palmetto State* remained with steam up a little in the rear of a line drawn from Fort Sumter to Cumming's Point. Commodore Ingraham was prepared, in accordance with an understanding with Gen. Beauregard, to take a share in the fighting if the Federal fleet should pass the guns of Sumter and Morris Island, in which case he was to attack; but Dupont's defeat by the forts gave his men no harder work than standing to their guns for three hours.

On the night of their repulse the commanders of the Federal iron-clads were called into consultation with Admiral Dupont on his flag-ship. It was his purpose to renew the attack the next morning; but, after listening to the verbal reports of those officers as to the crippled condition of the monitors, he gave up any such idea.

Before and after the breaking of the blockade, Beauregard and Ingraham had thought it of importance that the rams should be utilized in other localities than Charleston harbor without passing outside the bar. On December 2d, 1862, Major Harris, then chief of engineers, was instructed to cut a channel in Wappoo River, between the Ashley and the Stono, to allow the squadron to operate in that direction; and after the frustration of the attack on Sumter, the presence of the monitors in the outer harbor, without even a timber-guard around them, was like a welcome to an assault by torpedo boats. The torpedo service had been legalized by an act of the Confederate States Congress in October, 1862, and Major F. D. Lee had been placed in charge of it at Charleston. More than two months previous to the attack on Fort Sumter, a plan had been mooted at the Navy Department, by which it was hoped to disable the monitors, or perhaps capture them with all hands on board. It was probably suggested by the plan formed by Admiral Buchanan after the battle of Hampton Roads, when he had determined that if he had another engagement with the original *Monitor*, she should be boarded, and attempts made to block the turret with iron wedges, throw hand grenades down the turret openings and cover her hatchways and ventilators with blankets and tarpaulins in the hope of smothering the crew. Even that looked like a desperate scheme, but it was a crude project in comparison to that which it was proposed to undertake at Charleston. Mr. Mallory did not need to be informed that among the Confederate officers and seamen any number could be had that were required to voluntarily endeavor to carry out his wishes; for there was rather an excess than a lack of impetuous daring in the service which could only find exercise in adventures outside of the routine of warfare.

At a meeting of a board of officers at Richmond, it was decided to equip a special expedition for the work of destroying the monitors in Charleston harbor. Secretary Mallory selected to command it Lieut. William A. Webb, C. S. N., and issued the following order:

" NAVY DEPARTMENT, RICHMOND, February 19th, 1863.
" *Lieutenant Wm. A. Webb, C. S. N.:*

" SIR : Should it be deemed advisable to attack the enemy's fleet by boarding, the following suggestions are recommended for your consideration :

MEANS OF BOARDING THE ENEMY.

" FIRST—Row-boats and barges, of which Charleston can furnish a large number.

" SECOND—Small steamers, two or three to attack each vessel.

" THIRD—The hull of a single-decked vessel without spars, divided into several water-tight compartments by cross bulkheads, and with decks and hatches tight, may have a deck-load of compressed cotton so placed on either side, and forward and aft, as to leave a space fore and aft in the centre. A light scaffold to extend from the upper tier of cotton ten or fifteen feet over the side, and leading to the enemy's turret when alongside the iron-clad, and over which it can be boarded, at the same time that boarding would be done from forward and aft. This could be made permanent or to lower at will.

" The boarding force to be divided into parties of tens and twenties, each under a leader. One of these parties to be prepared with iron wedges, to wedge between the turret and the deck ; a second party to cover the pilot-house with wet blankets ; a third party of twenty to throw powder down the smoke-stack or to cover it ; another party of twenty provided with turpentine or camphine in glass vessels, to smash over the turret, and with an inextinguishable liquid fire to follow it ; another party of twenty to watch every opening in the turret or deck, provided with sulphuretted cartridges, etc., to smoke the enemy out. Light ladders, weighing a few pounds only, could be provided to reach the top of the turret. A rough drawing illustrative of this design is enclosed.

"I am, respectfully, your obedient servant,

"S. R. MALLORY, *Secretary of the Navy.*"

Webb proceeded to Charleston with about thirty officers and men, and with much trouble collected a few cutters and a lot of canoes and skiffs, which were fitted with poles twenty feet long, at their stems, each pole carrying a 60-pound torpedo. "It was not at all uncommon" says Capt. W. H. Parker, "to see a sailor rolling down to his boat, when they were called for exercise, with a quid of tobacco in his cheek and a torpedo slung over his back ; and when it is recollected that each torpedo had seven sensitive fuses which a tap with a stick or blow with a stone was sufficient to explode and blow half the street down, it can readily be believed that we gave him a wide berth."

An organization of the special service was effected quickly after the arrival of its *personnel* at Charleston. A small steamer called the *Sumter* was procured to lead the boats, and Lieut. W. G. Dozier[1] was placed in command of it with officers and crew arranged as follows, for an attempt to smother the monitors:

STACK MEN.

T. S. Wilson, Capt., C. S. N., in charge ; I. A. Mercer, Sergt. *Bottle and Sulphur:* Hugh Aird, Pat'k Hart, Wm. Bell, Stephen Caul. *Blankets and Powder:* Henry Calvin, Jas. Gorgan, Thos. Crilley, Theodore Davis. *Ladder, Bottles and Sulphur:* Richard McGregor, John Barratt. *Axe:* W. A. Bassant, Anthony Cannon. *Plateman:* S. C. Curtis.

[1] Wm. G. Dozier was appointed to the U. S. navy from South Carolina, and in the autumn of 1860 was lieutenant and acting-master of the frigate *Richmond,* of the Mediterranean squadron. The indications of the secession of his native State prompted him to obtain leave of absence to return home and tender his resignation. He reached New York on the day that South Carolina passed the ordinance of secession, and the next day his resignation was accepted by Mr. Toucey, Secretary of the Navy. His services were accepted by his State, and he was appointed to the coast and harbor police, in which he remained until transferred to the C. S. navy. While in the State service he was sent to Baltimore to purchase vessels suitable for gunboats, but succeeded only in procuring the tug *James Gray,* which afterwards became the *Lady Davis.* He was on duty in Charleston Harbor until the fall of Fort Sumter, and accompanied Capt. Hartstene to the fort to take part in the surrender, being assigned to the task of hoisting the Confederate colors after Major Anderson had saluted his flag and hauled it down. On April 19th he was appointed inspector of the first lighthouse district, extending from the northeastern boundary of South Carolina to St. Augustine, from which he was detached on July 13th, and ordered to report to Commander L. Rousseau at New Orleans In August he was engaged in transporting guns from Pensacola to New Orleans for the defence of that city, and on September 2d was appointed to the command of the steamer *Pamlico,* cruising in the lower Mississippi. After making several requests to the Navy Department to be transferred to South Carolina because of the invasion of his native State, and these applications being refused, in March, 1862, he sent in his resignation, which, under date of the 24th, Secretary Mallory declined to accept, but ordered him to report for duty to Flag-officer Ingraham at Charleston. In this letter the Secretary wrote that the Department desired to manifest its appreciation of his services and its desire to retain them. In Charleston Harbor he commanded the steamer *Huntress* and the receiving ship *Indian Chief,* and was afterwards assigned to command of the special expedition designed to operate with torpedo boats against the Federal iron-clads He commanded the naval battalion during the military operations on James Island in August, 1864. Subsequently he was appointed executive officer of the C. S. steamer *Chickamauga,* and participated in her cruises and engagements at the battle of Fort Fisher. After the fall of Wilmington, he took part in the defence of Drewry's Bluff, on the James River, and was paroled at Appomattox Court House. In 1869 he was removed to California, and in August, 1866, was appointed postmaster at Rio Vista, in that State.

TURRETMEN.

S. M. Roof, Capt. C. S. A., Vol., in charge ; A. D. Jean, Sergt. *Bottle and Sulphur :* O. Hackabon, C. Backman, M. B. Buff, C. Blackwell, P. P. Clarke. *Cleavemen, Bottles and Sulphur :* J. J. Chanus, J. J. Dooley, H. H. Bankman, J. K. Dooley. *Wedge and Hammermen :* E. E. Gabell, S. Gregores, J. A. Gregores, E. Human. *Sailmen, Bottles and Sulphur :* Paul Hutts, S. M. Hutts, A. Howard, J. Hook, W. Leach.

HATCH AND VENTILATOR MEN.

J. J. Hook, Lieut. C. S. A., Vol., in charge ; D. S. Griffith, Corporal. *Bottles and Sulphur :* G. D. Lacombs, F. M. Mathios, S. Miller, J. Mack, M. Hutts. *Tarpaulin, Hammer and Nails :* S. B. Parr, H. Pool, J. Pool.

SEAMEN.

John Berry, with grapline; John Cronan, with grapline.

There were on this one steamer 46 men assigned to the work outlined in Secretary Mallory's instructions, and about 50 more. Lieut. Webb having been reinforced by a detachment of sailors from Wilmington, they were distributed among the spar-torpedo boats that were to assist in the undertaking. Although it was under the supervision of Lieut. Webb, Lieut. Dozier was personally charged with the execution of the project. Webb addressed him a letter on March 23d, saying .

" You are selected in this important expedition to carry out the designs of the Navy Department, and you will be careful to preserve order and enforce strict obedience at all hazards. Be careful to select the coolest and best men under your command to discharge the torpedoes; and should the iron-clads pass the batteries, the first and main object is to destroy them by means of torpedoes; failing in which you will immediately board them, and carry into effect the programme herewith enclosed. [1]   You will keep a vigilant watch upon your leader, and follow his motions. If you do not gain a foothold upon the first iron-clad, you will sheer off, and attack the next in order. After the first attack is made, confusion in some degree may follow, when, I trust, your own judgment may be equal to the contest."

In March, Flag-officer Ingraham was relieved by Commodore Tucker, who assumed command of the vessels afloat, with his flag on board the *Chicora,* Com. Ingraham retaining command of the station. On April 9th, Gen. Beauregard, Com. Tucker and Lieut. Webb held a conference, and resolved that the torpedo expedition should be put in motion at once. Executive officer Parker, of the *Palmetto State,* relates that on the next day he was appointed by Tucker to command it, and received an order on Webb for the boats, the attack to be made on the night of the 10th, on the three monitors lying furthest up in the channel. He selected six cutters with their officers and crews, but later in the day changed the plan, because he concluded it would be better to take all the torpedo boats and attack the entire fleet of monitors. " Upon further reflection," he wrote to Webb, " after the discussion with yourself and Captain Tucker, I think it would be preferable to attack each of the enemy's iron-clads now inside the outer bar, with at least two of your spar-torpedo row-boats, instead of the number

[1] The programme contained in Secretary Mallory's letter.

44

already agreed upon. I believe it to be as easy to surprise at the same time all the iron-clads as a part of them."

Beauregard's suggestions were that all the boats should rendezvous on the first calm night at the mouth of the creek in the rear of Cumming's Point, and coast along the beach of Morris Island to a point nearest the enemy's position, where Gen. Ripley would station a picket to show proper lights and guide their return. Having reached the designated point of the beach, they should form line of attack and place torpedoes in position, and should attack by twos the *New Ironsides* or any monitor they should encounter on their way out, answering to the enemy's hail, "Boats on secret expedition," or "Contrabands." After the attack each boat should make for the nearest point on shore, where it could be stranded in case of pursuit, or return to the Cumming's Point rendezvous.

The night of April 12th was fixed for the expedition, and in the evening Capt. Parker had the officers detailed for it in conference with him in the cabin of the *Stono*, where written orders were given that each commander must explode his torpedo against a monitor before returning to Charleston. Fifteen boats were drawn up alongside the *Stono* with torpedoes and the smothering devices, and the intention was to drop down with the tide and reach the hostile fleet by midnight, the moon not rising until 1 A. M. Everything was in readiness for the start when Commodore Tucker came on board to announce that the monitors had left the bar, some going to Port Royal for repairs and others to the North Edisto. It is probable that some of them made a narrow escape from destruction; for, with the favoring conditions that prevailed, the supposition may rationally be entertained that against a portion of them the torpedoes or the apparatus for smothering their crews would have prevailed. The officers and men of the expedition, as a rule, were sanguine of some degree of success, although Capt. Parker has since confessed that he entertained many apprehensions because the boats were frail and leaky and the crews inexperienced. But, granting that these drawbacks existed, they more sharply define the intrepidity and zeal of the men who were ready to go to sea "in half-swamped skiffs and canoes" to fling themselves upon the most powerful squadron afloat.

"The *Ironsides* was still with the blockaders, however," writes the author of the "Military Operations of Gen. Beauregard," "and as Gen. Beauregard looked upon her as our most dangerous antagonist, he determined to strike her a blow—destroy her, if possible—and so raise the blockade on that occasion as to forbid all denial of the fact. Capt. Tucker was again ready to execute Gen. Beauregard's plan, which had assumed much larger proportions than heretofore; when, at the eleventh hour, as it were, a telegram was received from the Navy Department at Richmond ordering back to that city the officers and men of the ' special expedition,' who had been sent to aid in the defence of Charleston, and under whose charge—our own iron-clad boats joining in—was to have been placed that hazardous but very tempting enterprise. Gen. Beauregard did all he could to retain their services, but without success."

The project for the destruction of the *New Ironsides* called for four or five harbor steamers and blockade runners, each to tow four torpedo-boats, and to be followed by the *Palmetto State* and *Chicora*. So soon as the first line of steamers could well distinguish the lights of the blockaders without themselves being seen, the torpedo-boats were to be cast loose—the two first on the left, to attack the first light in that direction; the next two the second light; the third two the third light, and so on towards the right, thus using them as skirmishers in battle. Immediately after their charge the gunboats were to follow, making directly for the position of the *New Ironsides*, and sinking her as soon as practicable. The small boats were to make for the nearest point of shore immediately after their attack, and then retire to the protection of the forts, while the *Palmetto State* and *Chicora* "will," said Beauregard's orders, "remain outside long enough to effectually raise the blockade in such a way that it cannot this time be gainsaid;" but they were not to expose themselves to the monitors if the latter should return to the bar.

Col. Roman's assertion that this effort to break the blockade was defeated by an absolute recall of the special expedition is misleading when so broadly made, and without qualification. On April 18th, five days after the issue of Beauregard's instructions, Lieut. Webb notified Lieut. Dozier that he (Webb) had been "authorized by the Secretary of the Navy to turn the command over to him." Dozier informed Mr. Mallory on the same day that he had assumed the command, and that the expedition then consisted of eleven officers (most of whom were inexperienced) and forty odd men fit for duty. He requested that if the organization was to be kept up an older and more experienced officer than himself should be put in command. The expedition was evidently not dissolved, for on the 21st Flag-officer Tucker ordered him to have the best of his torpedo-boats prepared, and their crews organized for immediate service, as "information just received renders it important that no time be lost." On the 25th, Tucker wrote to Dozier, "the Secretary of the Navy having ordered the men and officers of the special expedition to remain here, you will take charge of it, and organize it as before." On May 8th, Dozier was instructed by him to have four boats thoroughly equipped and manned for torpedo service and supplied with cooked provisions for three days for an expedition in charge of Capt. Parker. On July 2d, eighteen sailors of the special expedition, who had served under Lieut. Dozier since April

24th, addressed him a petition that he would exert his influence to keep the small party together under his command,[1] they being perfectly satisfied as long as they remained under him. "But," they continued, "we do not wish to be placed with the *Stono's* crew. We have understood that we were kept here for the purpose of manning the new torpedo-boat which is now building, and it is our wish to be placed on board of her with you as our commander. We have submitted to the selection that was made when there was every prospect of making money by running the blockade in the C. S. steamer *Stono*. We were then satisfied to serve for the small sum of money which was allowed us by the government, and now that there is some hopes of this new boat being finished pretty shortly, we earnestly solicit your influence as regards keeping us together for that boat."

Indeed, the title and form of the special expedition survived all through the summer of 1863, and although its original aim of destroying the monitors had been abandoned, it was still relied upon as one of the potent safeguards of Charleston. Thus, on Aug. 17th, Lieut. Dozier received orders from Com. Tucker to have everything under his command made ready for action without the least delay; the torpedo steamers to be kept under banked fires and ready to operate should the enemy run past Fort Sumter. A week later he was again directed to have torpedo boats in readiness alongside the *Indian Chief*, the receiving ship, and it was not until Sept. that his men were distributed for general service on the torpedo steamers and the gunboats.

The order of May 8th to Lieut. Dozier to have four torpedo boats equipped for immediate service was the result of a reconnoissance of the monitors in the North Edisto River by Capt. Parker,[2] who, after surveying them in their positions, made up his mind that they were vulnerable to a torpedo attack by way of Bohicket Creek. With Dozier's four boats and one each from the *Palmetto State* and *Chicora* he started from Charleston on the 10th in tow of an army tug for a part of the route, which was to be up the Ashley River to Wappoo Creek, through Wappoo Creek into the Stono, thence to the Wardmelaw and into the North Edisto. Instead of fastening the torpedo poles to the stems they were carried about six feet below the keels of the boats, where they could be let go by keys when it was desired to have them explode. Lieut. W. T. Glassell was second in command. They reached White Point on the North Edisto on the night of the 10th, and the next day Gen. Hagood agreed to co-operate with his troops in the movement. After nightfall the boats were rowed into

---

[1] The signers were William Mothersead, Bartlet A. Grimes, A. S. Speekins, Augustus Eleison, William H. Clapdore, Henry D. Eggens, Peter S. Evans, Noel Sames, Banister Dowdry, Tylor Robinson, Emmerson Walker, Thomas S Buckley, Wm. Smith, John Berry, Garret Hunt, Josiah Noble, Daniel Bummigan and Joseph Gosh.

[2] "Recollections of a Naval Officer," by Capt. Wm. Harwar Parker.

Bohicket Creek, passing the monitors without being detected, and the party hauled the boats under the bank and spent the night in a deserted mansion. Soon after daybreak on the 12th, Glassell's coxswain reported that one of his best men was missing—a man who had accompanied Glassell in the torpedo movements in Charleston harbor and was thoroughly posted on the arrangements.

Scouts were sent out and a picket who had occupied the church steeple at Rockville during the night came in and reported that about dawn he had seen a boat from one of the monitors pull into the marsh and take a *stake* from it. "That ' stake ' was our man," said Capt. Parker. " He had made a straight wake for the fleet, waded through the marsh to the water's edge, and waved his hat for a boat to take him on board."

It was plainly indicated by the movements of the Federal vessels that the deserter had revealed everything concerning the expedition, [1] and as its success depended upon a surprise it could be carried no further. Parker obtained wagons from Gen. Hagood, and mounting his boats upon them, struck across the country to the Stono River, where he launched the boats and returned by Wappoo Creek to Charleston.

Many changes were taking place in the *personnel* of the Charleston naval station, and between April 1863 and Sept. 1864, the following officers were on duty on the ships or ashore : Commanders, T. T. Hunter, I. N. Brown, and James Henry Rochelle; Lieuts. John Rutledge, A. F. Warley, George H. Bier, Philip Porcher, W. G. Dozier, W. T. Glassell, E. C. Stockton, W. H. Wall, Clarence L. Stanton, John Payne, Henry W. Ray, W. H. Ward and C. H. Hasker ; Assist. Surgeons, W. M. Turner, J. P. Lipscomb, A. M. Moffatt, —— Henderson and Daniel E. Ewart ; Chief Engineer, C. S. Tombs ; Engineers, Charles Levy, John Tucker, Charles Tucker, —— Clark and W. F. Jones ; Midshipmen, D. M. Lee, Palmer Saunders, Clarence Cary, John Waller, T. J. Phelps, J. Thomas Scharf, Roger Pinkney, C. F. Sevier, and —— Williams ; Lieut. of Marines, A. S. Berry ; Flag-officer's Secretary, Edward West. In addition to the *Chicora* and *Palmetto State*, the squadron embraced the *Torch*, an unfinished vessel fashioned after the order of the rams, but never iron-plated, and but little used owing to some fault of construction. [2] The *Stono* and the *Juno* were doing guard-boat duty, from which they were relieved in order to run the blockade with cargoes of cotton on account of the Confederate government. The *Stono*, under command of Com. James Henry Rochelle, sailed from Charleston for Nassau on this errand on

---

[1] Capt. (now Rear Admiral) Ammen was the senior officer at the North Edisto. To Capt. Parker, after the war, he stated that the deserter had given him very accurate information of the programme of the torpedo expedition.

[2] This information concerning the *Torch* is contained in a communication from Lieut. Clarence L. Stanton to the author. The name of the vessel does not appear in any official record of operations around Charleston.

the night of June 5th, 1863, but having nothing with which to make steam except soft coal and coke, she was soon discovered by the blockading squadron on account of the sparks which rolled from her smoke-stack. Rochelle endeavored to regain Charleston harbor, but the pilot of the steamer ran her on the breakwater ledge of rocks near Fort Moultrie. It was found impossible to get the vessel off and she went to pieces on the reef, but by Rochelle's promptitude and energy everything on board was saved.

Some time in the autumn of 1863 the *Juno* ran the blockade, also bound for Nassau with cotton, but foundered the day after leaving port, and all hands except Pilot Payne and a fireman were lost. After being adrift in a small boat 48 hours, the two survivors were picked up by an English vessel and taken to Liverpool. Among the officers lost were Lieut. Philip Porcher, who was in command, and Engineer Charles Tucker, son of Flag-officer Tucker. The crew and officers of the *Juno* were volunteers from the fleet.

On July 6th Dahlgren relieved Dupont in command of the Federal naval forces off Charleston; his iron-clads returned to the bar on the 10th, and then began that long and terrible siege of the defences and of the city by the navy and army that was in itself fruitless, and that only terminated when General Sherman entered it by the back door late in February, 1865.

Naturally the thoughts of Beauregard turned toward an attack on the monitors by the Confederate iron-clads and torpedo boats, during the severe attack on Forts Wagner and Gregg. On July 18th he wrote to Com. Tucker:

"I believe it to be my duty to acquaint you with the fact that I consider it of the utmost importance to the defence of the works at the entrance of the harbor that some effort should be made to sink either the *Ironsides* or one of the monitors now attacking the works on Morris Island, not only because of the diminution thus effected in the enemy's means of offence, but because of the great moral effect that would inevitably result from such an occurrence. The stake is manifestly a great one, worthy of so small a risk. For its accomplishment, one vessel such as the *Juno*, provided with the spar-torpedo, with two or three officers and a few men, it is believed would be as effective at night for the end in view as a flotilla of vessels so arranged of the same class."

The *Juno* was not available at the moment for the purpose for which Beauregard had designated her, and Tucker replied that in any event he could be of no assistance, owing to the excessive draft of his iron-clads, their low speed and the short range of their guns, which could not be sufficiently elevated because of the small size of the port-holes. The project rested for a brief space of time, and in the meanwhile a spirited affair took place, on Aug. 7th, in the creek between James and Morris Island, that resulted in the capture of a Federal barge and its crew. For several nights it was known that the enemy had been posting pickets in the marsh for the purpose of observing Confederate movements at Cumming's Point and giving notice to Gillmore's batteries when to open fire on the transports conveying the reliefs to Fort Wagner. An expedition was formed to drive off or capture these pickets, and on the night of Aug. 7th Lieuts. A. F. Warley and John Payne started off with two boats' crews of men from the *Chicora* and *Palmetto State*. They were met below Fort Johnson by Capt. Sellers of the 25th S. C. regiment, with two boats and a detachment of thirty men, and the combined force went into the creek, where it was soon sharply engaged with the Federals. An exhilarating skirmish ensued, the result of which was that one of the Federal boats made off and the other was captured by Payne and Warley. Lieut. Payne found that he had made a prisoner of Master John Haynes, of the U. S. navy, with whom were taken a sergeant and ten men. Two of the enemy were killed and five wounded in this affair.

On the following night, Aug. 8th, Commodore Tucker went on board the *Juno* and ordered Lieut. Porcher to set out on a reconnoitering tour of the harbor. Porcher had ten of his crew armed with rifles, and their instructions were to fire upon any of the Federal picket boats that might be encountered. Steaming cautiously along below Morris Island the *Juno* came upon and took by surprise the first launch of the frigate *Wabash*, which had on board a crew of twenty-three men and a twelve-pounder howitzer, while the steamer was unarmed save for her riflemen, her two guns having been removed when she was put in trim for a blockade-runner. Porcher did not hesitate for that reason, but ran down the launch, and his onslaught was so swift and sudden that the crew attempted no defence. A dozen threw themselves into the sea; five were drowned and seven swam to other picket boats, by which they were rescued. The remainder surrendered and Porcher took possession of the launch and brought eleven prisoners to Charleston. He was highly complimented by Flag-officer Tucker, and the fine launch and her gun came into good use against their former owners. [1]

These naval pastimes soon gave way to more serious business. Most of the boat expeditions and scouting parties had been sent out with a view to discovering the possibilities of a torpedo attack upon the *New Ironsides*, which was more troublesome to Fort Wagner than all the monitors combined, her quick-firing broadsides of 11-inch shell guns being far more annoying than the slow discharges from the turret vessels. As she laid usually about 1,000 or 1,200 yards from the Morris Island beach and well out into the main ship channel, and the

[1] Admiral Dahlgren complained to Gen. Beauregard that the men of the launch were fired upon from the *Juno* while they were struggling in the water. The communication having been referred to Commodore Tucker, he replied to Dahlgren: "I am happy to be able to state, from information received from the C. S. naval officer in command at the time, that the men were not fired at in the water. I highly appreciate your desire to conduct the war upon civilized principles, and it affords me great pleasure to join in so laudable a desire."

Federals had not yet learned the caution of protection against torpedoes by booms and nettings, the provocation to blow her up was irresistible to the experts, who, as Capt. Parker says of Commodore Tucker and himself, "had torpedo on the brain." None of the torpedo steamers which Maj. Lee was constructing had been completed; but by authority of Secretary Mallory he obtained the transfer of an unfinished hull on the stocks at Charleston, which was designed for a gunboat, or rather floating battery, as she was not arranged for any motive power, but was intended to be anchored in position. In a report to Gen. Beauregard, he said that he completed this hull and placed in it a second-hand and much-worn engine that he obtained in Savannah. Despite her tub-like model and the inefficiency of her engine, Capt. Carlin, master of the blockade-runner *Ella and Annie*, took charge of her in an attack against the *New Ironsides* on the night of August 21st. Besides a few seamen, he had with him eight men of the First Regt. S. C. Art'y, who had offered to go along to protect the boat from an assault by the Federal picket launches, which swarmed thick in the lower harbor. The steamer was in such bad order that she could only be kept afloat by bailing as she moved out to the Federal anchorage. She was furnished with a spar designed to carry three torpedoes of 100 pounds each. The lateral spars suggested by Beauregard Capt. Carlin declined to use, as they would interfere very seriously with the movements of the vessel, which, even without them, could with the utmost difficulty stem the current. The boat was almost entirely submerged, and painted gray like the blockade-runners, and, like them, made no smoke by burning anthracite coal. The night selected for the attack was very dark, and the *New Ironsides* was not seen until quite near. Capt. Carlin immediately made for her, but her side being oblique to the direction of his approach, he ordered his steersman, who was below deck, to change the course. This order was misunderstood, and, in place of going "bow on" as was proposed, she ran alongside of the *New Ironsides* and entangled her spar in the anchor chain of that vessel. In attempting to back, the engine hung on the centre, and some delay occurred before it was pried off. During this critical period, Capt. Carlin, in answer to threats and inquiries, declared his boat to be the *Live Yankee*, from Port Royal, with dispatches for the admiral. This deception was not discovered until after Carlin had backed out and his vessel was lost in the darkness. [1]

Little has been said of the part that the squadron took in the defence of Wagner, but to the share of its officers and men fell much labor that was difficult and dangerous while holding

[1] The *New Ironsides* was incapacitated from sharing in future movements against the Confederate defences by an attack made upon her by Lieutenant William T. Glassell, which is related elsewhere in the Chapter on Torpedoes. The blowing up of the *Housatonic* by a torpedo is also described in the same chapter.

out no prospect of decisive battle or glory. As the siege grew hotter the commands on duty in the fort were relieved every three days by fresh troops brought down in boats through Vincent's Creek, on the north side of the island; and this constant changing of the garrison, together with the necessity of conveying provisions, ammunition and even potable water to the post and bringing off the wounded, established what might be almost called a ferriage line on the creek. But it was a ferry operated in the hours of the night and in the presence of imminent peril by the naval force detached from the Confederate vessels. A flotilla of Federal launches scoured the waters as close as they dare go to the batteries, and signals were arranged by which they could direct the fire of their ships upon any indicated point. As early as July 30th, they secured the range of Cumming's Point, on which they threw shells each night. Previously the light-draft Confederate steamers could run in on that edge of the island, but when it was closed to them the only means of communication was by row-boats across the creek, and at this work the sailors and their commanders toiled until Wagner was evacuated. They were equal to the demand upon them, and they never lost a man except on the night of August 4th, when a small boat conveying Major W. F. Warley, a wounded officer of the Second S. C. Art'y, to Charleston, was captured by a Federal launch belonging to a flotilla that was attempting an attack by surprise on Battery Gregg. The prize, however, was not worth what it cost the enemy, for the firing upon the boat aroused the garrison of Gregg and defeated the object of the expedition. Idleness was enforced upon the Confederate iron-clads during the siege, as to pit them against the Federal fleet would have been only to throw them away; but as we have already seen the torpedo service was busy. A loss that occurred was that of the little steamer *Sumter*, which in passing Sullivan's Island was sunk by the batteries there in the belief that she was a hostile vessel. She was then transporting troops for Morris Island to the city, and by the blunder five men were killed, others wounded and twenty drowned, while some 600 were saved by the navy barges.

Heroic endurance was all that remained to the besieged at Battery Wagner. Even a sortie toward the enemy was denied them, for an ingenious system of torpedo mines, to be exploded by the tread of persons walking over them, had been established by the Confederates in the narrow causeway on that side of the fort. Soon after dark, on the night of Sept. 5th, the Federal sappers had pushed around the east and south front so as to completely mask the guns. The long and heavy bombardment had so torn and cut down both scarp and counterscarp as to render the mounting of the parapets by a storming party comparatively easy. Powerful calcium lights, placed on monitors at a safe distance abreast the fort, turned

night into day, blinding the defenders, giving light to the
sappers, and enabling the Federal artillerists and sharp-
shooters to fire with as much precision as in broad sunshine.
That night they again moved to the attack of Battery Gregg
by boats, but were beaten off by its guns. This was the last
of the Confederate triumphs on Morris Island, which had been
held for fifty-seven days under the furious cannonade. On
the 6th. Col. L. M. Keith, then in command at Wagner, informed Beauregard that the garrison would be sacrificed unless boats were sent to take them away that night, and the
latter gave minute instructions for the evacuation of Morris
Island, to effect which the services of the navy were called into
such important requisition that to it is mainly due the proper
execution of the movement. The *Chicora* and *Palmetto State*
took up positions just after dark near Fort Sumter, their guns
bearing on Cumming's Point and to the eastward of it. Transport steamers were stationed as near Cumming's Point as prudence would permit, to receive the men from the small boats
in which they were to leave the island. There were forty of
these boats, manned by oarsmen from the squadron, the whole
commanded by Lieut. Ward, C. S. N., with whom were associated Lieut. Clarence L. Stanton, Lieut. Charles H. Hasker,
Lieut. Odenheimer, Midshipman D. M. Lee, and other officers.
Immediately after dark the movement was begun, and was
made quietly and in admirable order, the majority of the men
being under the impression that they were about to be relieved
as usual, after having served their turn of duty in the fort.
They embraced details of the 25th S. C. regt., 27th Georgia,
28th Georgia, and 1st S. C. As soon as the infantry had left
Cumming's Point, Capt. H. R. Lesesne, commanding Battery
Gregg, spiked his guns and embarked his men. Capt. T. A.
Huguenin, of the 1st S. C., was left to remain in Wagner for
a short time with twenty-five men to keep up a slow fire to
deceive the enemy while the embarkation was going on, and
to lay the train to burst the 10-inch gun and blow up the magazine. Capt. Lesesne was to make the preparations for a similar explosion at Gregg, and finding that his fuse was burning
more rapidly than he calculated, he re-entered the magazine
and cut off the lighted end, so as to give time for the arrival
of Huguenin with the rear-guard from Fort Wagner; and
when they were seen approaching he relit it, as it had been intended that the two explosions should be as nearly simultaneous as they could be. The whole party, except Capt. Huguenin, who had fallen to the rear with a wound in his knee, then
embarked in the boat commanded by Lieut. Odenheimer.
About this time the Federal barges were swarming around
Cumming's Point and commanded the adjacent waters, and
Lieut. Odenheimer put boldly out to sea under the fire of their
boat howitzers. As they skirted the beach they were hailed
by Capt. Huguenin, who waded out to his armpits, and was

drawn into the boat by one of Odenheimer's men. The Federals threw grape and canister hot and quick at the boats and captured two, one of which was commanded by Lieut. Hasker, and made prisoners also of nineteen of the seamen and twenty-seven soldiers. Lieut. Stanton's boat returned in the direction of the enemy under a heavy fire and rescued John Brown, a seaman from the *Chicora*, who had jumped overboard from one of the captured boats.

Under all the circumstances of difficulty and peril which attended the evacuation in the face of an overwhelming numerical force it was wonderfully well done. "The operation," Beauregard had said in his order, "is one of the most delicate ever attempted in war ; coolness, resolute courage, and judgment and inflexibility on the part of officers, obedience to orders and a constant sense of the necessity for silence on the part of the men, are essential for complete success and the credit which must attach to those who deserve it." "To the admirable discipline of the crews of the barges," wrote Maj. Gilchrist, "is mainly due the success of the embarkation. Their boats kept abreast, with the length of an oar from the gunwale to the blade separating them. The oars thus interlocked never touched or interfered with each other. As each detachment left, other boats grounded on the beach to receive their load, and thus silently and without confusion the embarkation was accomplished."

Fort Sumter having been converted into an infantry post, and mounting but a single gun, Major Stephen Elliott was placed in command of it with 200 troops, and Com. Tucker stationed his iron-clads between Sullivan's Island and the fort for the purpose of assisting to protect the latter, and dispute the passage of Dahlgren's fleet into the harbor. On September 7th the Federal admiral summoned Sumter to capitulate and received the reply, "come and take it." He and General Gillmore were then meditating an assault upon it from small boats, laboring under the false impression that there would be little trouble in seizing it since its artillery fire had ceased, and after he was so peremptorily answered by Elliott he communicated with Gillmore by signals, and announced the attack for the night of September 8th. The Confederate signal officers were able to interpret these signals and Elliott was saved a surprise. [1]

About 2 o'clock on the afternoon of the 8th, Lieut. Clarence L. Stanton was officer of the deck of the *Chicora*. A signal officer named Daniels stood near him and was watching some signalling being made from Dahlgren's flag-ship.

[1] This knowledge of the Federal code was obtained by shrewd strategy. A trap was laid for one of their signal pickets in the Florida district, and he was captured and brought to Charleston. In confinement with him was placed Capt. Pliny Bryan, Assist. Adjt. Gen. on Beauregard's staff, disguised in the Federal uniform, and passing himself off as a prisoner. Capt. Bryan had made a study of the signal flags taken from the wreck of the *Keokuk*, and by some adroit questioning he drew all the essential secrets of the code out of his quondam comrade, and soon was as familiar with them as any Federal officer. The Confederate signal service men were taught the system and were able to read any of the messages that passed between the ships or between them and the shore.

Turning suddenly to Stanton, he said: "Fort Sumter will be attacked to-night." "How do you know?" asked Stanton. "I have just read," he replied, "a message from the flag-ship for a boat from each ship, commanded by a lieutenant, to assemble at the flag-ship at 10 o'clock for such an attack." Stanton reported the information to Com. Tucker, who in turn transmitted it to Gen. Beauregard, and effective preparations were made to repel the assault. With the single exception of the fiasco of their second attempt to carry Fort Wagner by storm, it was the most mortifying defeat which the Federals had suffered in Charleston waters. They approached the fort about 10 o'clock on the morning of the 9th in five divisions of boats containing in all about 450 or 500 sailors and marines, whom Admiral Dahlgren says were picked men. Com. T. H. Stevens was in command, and Lieut. Com. E. P. Williams, Lieuts. Remey, Preston and Higginson and Ensign Craven had charge of the respective divisions. Coming on in gallant style, the boats were beached and the assailants sought modes of entrance to the fort on the southern and southeastern faces. Then the hitherto silent sand-heap blazed with the fire of musketry and hand grenades, while the *Chicora* from a few hundred yards' distance poured in canister and shrapnel, and Fort Johnson and the Sullivan's Island batteries swept the narrow beach on which the landing had been made. It was an understanding between the Confederate commanders that they should not spring the trap until the mice had walked into it, and their agreement could not have been more successfully executed. Not even Dahlgren's "picked men" could endure the withering cross-fire that struck at them in front and on both flanks. "The enemy," says the report of Lieut. Com. Williams, "sunk or disabled all my boats by shot or by bricks thrown from the walls. Finding it impossible to get over the walls, I ordered the men to shelter themselves in the holes made by our shells. The enemy kept up a constant fire on us, throwing hand-grenades, bricks, fire-balls, and other missiles amongst us. Hoping something might be done for our relief, I would not surrender, but some of the men from Lieut. Bradford's boat, he having been mortally wounded in landing, surrendered, and were ordered around on the left to come into the fort. I stopped these and ordered them under the walls. Soon finding I was only losing my men without gaining anything, on a consultation with the officers I surrendered, and was shown inside the fort, where we were courteously treated by Maj. Elliott."

By the quickness of the Federals in taking shelter close under the walls of Sumter they lost only three men killed, but Elliott made prisoners of thirteen officers and 102 men and captured four boats and three stands of colors. One of the flags was that which had been hoisted on Sumter in 1861 by Maj. Anderson, and which he had taken to New York with him after the evacuation, where it had excited the utmost enthusiasm and been a powerful stimulus of the war fever. It had been intrusted to the boat expedition in expectation that they would replace it where it had once waved.

On Sept. 10th, Lieut. James H. Rochelle, C. S. N., arrived from Richmond with 130 officers and men, who were ordered to Charleston for harbor service, and reported to Commodore Tucker. Two days later all row-boats, barges, etc., not required for military purposes, were turned over by Gen. Ripley to Lieut. Rochelle to be used for transportation and guard duty in the harbor. On Oct. 30th, orders were issued to Tucker, Ripley and Gen. Hagood to arrange with Maj. Elliott some signal, which, when given by the latter, would notify the iron-clads and the batteries on Sullivan and James Islands to sweep with their fire every point of approach to Fort Sumter, the bombardment of which was steadily kept up. There were apprehensions at the time of a concerted attack upon the defences of Charleston by the Federal fleet and army, and Tucker's squadron took positions that would enable them to command the face of James Island. In case the enemy's iron-clads should endeavor to remove the obstructions between Sumter and Moultrie, the *Chicora* and *Palmetto State* were to assail them from the vicinity of Fort Sumter, and if they attempted to run into the harbor, Tucker was to meet them in the rear of the second line of defence. They did not, however, make the expected movement, and for the remainder of the year one of the few incidents that broke the monotony of the siege was Gen. Gillmore's effort on the night of Nov. 19th to surprise and capture Sumter. He sent in some 300 men in barges, and Dahlgren had an additional force of some 200 sailors in boats upon the scene, but they were discovered when within 300 yards of the fort and made off under a fire which wounded a few of their men. [1]

After nightfall on Feb. 26th, 1864, the first cutter of the Federal steamer *Nipsic*, under command of Acting Master's Mate J. H. Kitching, was on picket about 150 yards from Fort Sumter, where it was discovered by a barge from the *Palmetto State*. The officer in charge of the Confederate boat brought the enemy within his reach, by a series of hails that led the latter to suppose that it was one of his own launches, and then opened a fire which almost instantly compelled him to surrender. Kitching and five men of his crew were taken prisoners. Lieut. G. C. Wiltse, of the monitor *Montauk*, was in the immediate vicinity with another armed Federal boat, but refrained from going to the assistance of Kitching.

Early in 1864, the new iron-clad, *Charleston*, was added to the Confederate squadron, and Com. Tucker transferred his flag to her from the *Chicora*. She was commanded by Com.

[1] Dahlgren wrote in his journal that the garrison of Sumter were aroused, as the boats approached, by the barking of a dog that was in the fort.

Isaac N. Brown ; Com. Thomas T. Hunter was assigned to the *Chicora,* and Com. James H. Rochelle to the *Palmetto State.* [1]

On March 23d, a boat party of Federals that endeavored to cut out the steamer *Little Ada,* in the Suwanee River, near McClellanville, were handsomely repulsed by her own men, aided by a body of troops on shore. The enemy, who were under the command of Acting Master E. H. Sheffield, of the *Winona,* were allowed to come on board the steamer, which they found deserted by her crew; but while they were endeavouring to raise steam in her boilers, with the view of carrying her off, the crew and a small company of artillerists drove them off with a sharp fire from a masked battery of three field-pieces on the adjacent bank.

On July 4th, 1864, the Confederate naval force was engaged in repelling the attack of the Federals upon Fort Johnson and Battery Simkins, on James Island. Early in the morning the 127th N. Y. reg't, the 52d Penn., and a detachment of sixty men from the 3d R. I. artillery, all under the command of Col. William Gurney, embarked in boats from Morris Island with the expectation of taking these Confederate positions by surprise. Misadventure attended the undertaking from the start. Judge Cowley, who has written a clear narrative of the event, says that Col. Gurney, without the knowledge of his command, remained on Morris Island, and in his absence the command devolved upon Col. Hoyt, of the Penn. regiment, who, however, seems not to have been aware of the fact. He was separated from his command and taken prisoner. Lieut. Col. Conyngham, then the senior officer of the Federals, looked about for Hoyt, and became a prisoner himself. "Then," says Judge Cowley, "ensued confusion, baffling description. One

---

[1] James Henry Rochelle was appointed an acting midshipman in the U. S. navy September 9th, 1841, and after six months' service at sea received a warrant as midshipman, bearing the same date as his acting appointment. During the war with Mexico he served on the sloops-of-war *Falmouth* and *Decatur* in the Gulf, and took part in the capture of Tuxpan and Tabasco. He reported to the Naval Academy November 13th, 1847, and graduated on July 10th, 1848, his warrant as passed midshipman assigning him that rank from August 10th, 1847. After duty in the Mediterranean squadron on the frigate *Constitution,* steamer *Alleghany,* steamer *Princeton* and frigate *Independence,* he was ordered to the storeship *Southampton,* which formed part of Comdore Perry's expedition to Japan in 1853. On his return to the United States he was assigned to the coast survey, and on the steamer *Corwin* and schooner *Madison,* the latter of which was for some time in his charge, assisted in the survey of the New York Harbor, Casco Bay and Florida Reef. On September 14th, 1855, he was promoted to master, and on the next day was commissioned lieutenant. He was assigned to the steamer *Southern Star* in the Paraguay expedition, commanded by Flag-officer W. B. Shubrick, and was on the steam-frigate *Fulton* when she was wrecked on the coast of Florida. His final service in the U. S. navy was on the sloop-of-war *Cumberland* in the home squadron, and

he resigned his commission April 17th, 1861, while his ship was at the Norfolk navy-yard. While awaiting the action of the department upon his resignation he was placed in a very painful position by the false alarm of an attack on the navy-yard by the Virginia forces. "I had resolved," Capt. Rochelle writes "that I was bound to obey the command of the Virginia Convention and leave the navy of the United States, and here was the probability of my having to do the very thing I had resigned my commission to escape from doing. I cannot say, however, that the situation caused any hesitation on my part. As long as I was on duty as a lieutenant in the U. S. navy I was fully determined to do that duty, and in case of necessity would have stood to my guns." To be relieved from this embarrassing position, he obtained permission from Flag-officer Pendergrast to leave the *Cumberland,* and on May 2d was appointed lieutenant in the Virginia navy, and on the 29th was ordered to command the gunboat *Teaser.* His commission as lieutenant in the C. S. navy was issued June 6th, and until June 27th he commanded the gunboat *Jackson* at Memphis, when he was ordered to the *Patrick Henry,* then fitting out at Richmond, as executive officer. He participated in the subsequent operations of the James River squadron, including the battle of Hampton Roads and the repulse of the Federal vessels at Drewry's Bluff, shortly after which he

company of the N. Y. regiment, and the R. I. artillerymen landed unobserved within fifty yards of Fort Johnson. They were soon discovered by the garrison, but upon one volley being fired, some officer gave the order to retreat to the boats, and thus this opportunity to capture these important works was lost. The Confederate force then on James Island was small, some reports putting it as low as 150. Our loss in killed, wounded and captured must have exceeded the whole number of men in the two forts assailed; for we lost 137 enlisted men and six officers."

It is well to place stress upon this Federal account of an affair to which they attached so much importance, for the garrison in Fort Johnson principally consisted of men from Com. Tucker's squadron, and it was this little band that poured in the fire that demoralized the Federals. It was one of their very many achievements in the vicinity of Charleston, in connection with which they have heretofore escaped mention, but for which other branches of the service received the honors. The remark becomes wearying that the absence of Confederate records consigns to oblivion the names of the sailors who did one or the other gallant thing, but the repulse of the assault upon Fort Johnson was so brilliant an exploit, that it is a marked misfortune that the men who accomplished it must remain anonymous. On the part of the enemy, the movement was most shrewdly planned by Gen. Schimmelfennig, and if it had succeeded might have decided the fate of Charleston then, as Admiral Dahlgren reported to Secretary Welles. The salvation of Fort Johnson depended that morning on the steadiness of the handful of seamen and their officers in its garrison, and they were worthy of the reliance placed upon them. [1]

was transferred to the command of the gunboat *Nansemond*, and thence to the steamer *Stono*, which was preparing to run the blockade at Charleston. The *Stono* was discovered by the Federals in the bay and in attempting to regain the city was wrecked on the rocks near Fort Moultrie, June 5th, 1863. Resuming command of the *Nansemond*, Capt. Rochelle continued on the James River until September 6th, when he was sent to Charleston to organize the flotilla of guard-boats. On April 2d, 1864, he was ordered to the command of the iron-clad *Palmetto State*, remaining on that duty until the evacuation of Charleston, when he was dispatched to Wilmington in command of a detachment of about 300 officers and men of the Charleston squadron, and co-operated with the army in the defence of that city. From Wilmington he was ordered to report at Richmond as commandant of the midshipmen of the C. S. naval school, and after the evacuation guarded the specie and bullion of the treasury to its transfer to the army at Abbeville. S. C. When paroled after the downfall of the Confederacy he remained at his home in Southampton Co., Va., until June 19th, 1871, when he accepted a position tendered him by the government of Peru as a member of the Peruvian Hydrographical Commission of the Amazon. He joined the Commission at Ignitos, Peru, and was employed in surveying the upper Amazon River and its tributaries. He was senior member and for a time president of the Commission. During his sojourn in Peru they surveyed 3,393 statute miles of the courses of the Amazon and Meayali Rivers and their affluents. They encountered many hardships, and were much annoyed by the Indians, who on two occasions attacked them with considerable spirit. In the autumn of 1874 Captain Rochelle was ordered to New York to assist Commodore John R. Tucker, President of the Commission, in the preparation for publication of charts of the surveys, but the financial troubles of Peru, then nearing her war with Chili, stopped the work, and in April, 1877, the Commission was dissolved. Since then Captain Rochelle has resided in his Virginia home and has held no public position except that of honorary commander of the Southampton Camp of Confederate veterans

[1] Lieut. Wm. G. Dozier on August 26th received the following from Flag-officer Hunter: "I have received a letter from Major Gen. Sam Jones, commanding the Department of South Carolina, Georgia and Florida, in which he expresses his high appreciation of the services rendered by the naval battalion under your command during the recent military operations on James Island, and it affords me great pleasure to inform you of it, and request that you will communicate it to the command."

Other engagements occurred about the same time in which the Confederate navy grasped at the opportunities to distinguish itself. On June 20th Dahlgren was notified that the Confederates were preparing for a simultaneous movement on the blockade inside and outside in order to cover the exit of a large quantity of cotton, and sent two of his cruisers to the vicinity of Port Royal, where his lines were weakest. At the same time he arranged with Gen. Foster for a combined army and navy movement into the Stono, and to cut the Charleston and Savannah railroad, in order to prevent the movement of Confederate troops by that route. Foster, Schimmelfennig and Hatch were to land with 7,000 men, and Gen. Birney, with 3,000 more, was to go up the North Edisto and destroy the railway. Dahlgren accompanied them on July 2d with the monitors *Lehigh* and *Montauk*, and the gunboats *Pawnee*, *McDonough* and *Racer*, while the gunboats *Dai Ching*, *Wamsutta* and *Geranium* were sent into the North Edisto to help Birney. The latter, however, was driven back after some desultory fighting, and on the 4th the whole force of 10,000 men, with the monitors, gunboats and mortar-schooners, was assembled in the Stono, the troops being in position on John's Island. It was determined to make an attack from this direction on the Confederate works on James' Island, but Foster, after reconnoitering them, judged that they were too strong to carry by storm. But Dahlgren could not resist the allurement of an encounter with Battery Pringle, and on July 5th he opened on it from the two monitors, two gunboats and a couple of mortar-vessels.

The guns of Battery Pringle were manned by the men of the Confederate squadron, and before the day was over the Federal vessels retired down the river to cover the retreat of Foster's troops. They had failed to make any impression upon Pringle, and had received very much the worst of the engagement. The *Montauk's* deck was shattered by a shot, and two of her men were badly wounded. As a rule, the fire of the Confederate seamen in the land batteries was quite accurate, and on this day it was especially telling. For the reason that they were not permitted to engage the monitors in their own ships, it was always a source of gratification to them to hammer them from the fortifications.

On Dec. 21st, two boats and their crews from the Federal steamer *Dai Ching* were captured in the Stono by a Confederate force, and on the last day of the year two of the picket launches in Charleston harbor were gathered in by the active Confederate patrols.

In Jan. 1865, the monitors were exceedingly brisk in their movements around the entrance to the harbor, and to render their ingress still more perilous the Confederate engineers planted sixteen large torpedoes just in front of the rope obstructions. Dahlgren had instructed the commanders of the

monitors to examine the channels carefully, as he was meditating an attack on the defences in conjunction with Sherman's army then advancing northward, and on the night of
the 15th the *Patapsco* was the picket iron-clad. She was steaming slowly about between Sumter and Moultrie, covering the
operations of the scout boats that were hunting for the obstructions with grapnel drags, when suddenly there was a
shock, a sound of explosion, a cloud of smoke on the port side,
and in less than half a minute her deck was under the surface
of the water. The torpedo had struck the vessel under the
overhang and had lifted the deck. The first impression of
Lieutenant Sampson, the executive officer, was that she
had been hit by a shot, but the column of water and smoke
which immediately shot up convinced him of the real nature
of the explosion. So quickly did the *Patapsco* go down
that, although a dozen boats were within a few hundred
yards, only forty-seven of her 109 officers and men escaped
drowning.

The concluding months of the war in these waters were
the reverse of fortunate for the U. S. ships. On Jan. 26th, the
gunboat *Dai Ching* was proceeding up the Combahee River to
co-operate with an army movement, and in the neighborhood
of Tar Bluff came upon the Confederate battery. In endeavoring to turn the ship she grounded, and for seven hours a brisk
artillery duel was kept up with the battery. She was struck
thirty times with shot and shell, her guns disabled and her
machinery shot through and through. Her commander, Lieut.
J. C. Chaplin, abandoned and set fire to her and retreated in
his boats, with the loss of a cutter and crew who were made
prisoners, and nine men wounded.

On March 1st, the steamer *Harvest Moon*, flag-ship of Admiral Dahlgren, was sunk by a torpedo while returning from
Georgetown to Charleston. She was then in Georgetown Bay.

It only remains now to follow up the army and navy
operations of the Federals attendant upon the evacuation of
Charleston and the coincident proceedings of the Confederates.
After its pertinacious and lofty resistance from the inauguration of the war to all the forces on sea and land that the enemy
could bring against it, it was nevertheless doomed when Sherman's army started toward it along the sea coast from the
south. It had literally been worn out; the troops that had
held it against superior power had been mostly drawn off to
the armies of Lee or Johnston, and though its batteries still
forbade entrance to the enemy from the water front, it was
vulnerable to them from the rear. Since the latter part of
November, 1864, Dahlgren had been co-operating with Sherman, who by the 24th of Jan., 1865, was at Pocotaligo, on the
Charleston and Savannah railroad, while the Federal admiral
had collected all his vessels near Charleston to keep the rivers
clear of torpedoes and light batteries, so that his transports

could reach certain points and supply the wants of the Federal armies. On Feb. 7th, Sherman was within fifty miles of Charleston; and on the 11th and 17th, monitors and gunboats were sent into Bull's Bay and the South Edisto River to assist him in case of opposition. On the latter date a naval force went into Stono River to assail the Confederate works on that side, and Gen. Schimmelfennig moved on the front of Charleston from Cole's Island. The naval battery on Cumming's Point was ordered to open on Sullivan's Island and fire continually through the night. Contiguous batteries were put in operation, and the monitors would have participated but for their failure to receive orders. During the night a few guns were fired from Fort Moultrie, but the main body of the Confederates had left it at eight P. M. and on the morning of the 18th the Federal scouts found it and all the other defences on Sullivan's Island evacuated. The scouting officer, Acting Master Gifford, with the two tugs on duty, entered the harbor, touching at the various fortified points and at Mount Pleasant, where the intendant and wardens tendered their submission. Castle Pinckney was also first entered by a naval officer, the other defences, including Fort Sumter, Fort Johnson and the lines of works around the city, having been taken possession of by military detachments. Gen. Hardee, C. S. A., who had succeeded Gen. Jones in command of the Department of South Carolina, Georgia and Florida, had moved off all his troops without encountering the enemy. The officers and men of the squadron had been sent off in detachments, the first, which consisted of about 300 men, under command of Capt. Rochelle, having been dispatched several days previously to Wilmington to take part in the defence of that place. Lieut. Bowen, executive officer of the *Palmetto State*, was left behind with a squad, charged with destroying that vessel and the *Charleston* and *Chicora*. He set fire to them, and in a few hours they exploded. Commodore Tucker, Commanders Brown and Hunter and other officers, with the remainder of the seamen, went North, and in the last battle fought by the army of Gen. Lee the gallant officers and crews of the Charleston naval station were reunited at Saylor's Creek in Virginia.

The Federals captured the iron-clad *Columbia*, and the steamers *Mab, Lady Davis* and *Transport*, and three torpedo boats of the David type. The *Columbia* they found on the rocks near Fort Moultrie, where she had run aground on January 12th. They raised and repaired her, and on May 25th she arrived in Hampton Roads, having been towed around by the *Vanderbilt*. She was 216 feet long, 51 feet beam and 15 feet depth of hold, and was plated with six inches of armor on her shield or casemate, which was pierced for eight guns. During her passage north she exhibited excellent sea-going qualities, and probably if she had been completed earlier in the war, and it had been the good fortune of Commodore Tucker to put her into battle with the enemy's iron-clads, she would have proved her first-class fighting qualities.

At last the Federal government had possession of Charleston, and the defences upon which it had concentrated attacks second in magnitude to none endured by any sea-coast city of the Southern Confederacy. In all the history of the war upon the sea-board the operations around Charleston easily take first place. The progress of the siege, the changing tides of victory and defeat, the novel experiments in the opposition of forts to iron-clad fleets, the development of heavy ordnance, the evolution of torpedo warfare in these waters, were studied with the most profound interest by the civilized world; but of more import than all the technicalities of the strife was that unquenchable fire of patriotism and fortitude that never burned brighter in the hearts of the people, and the defenders of the illustrious city, than when they were overcome by numerical force.

CHAPTER XXII.

VIRGINIA WATERS—(Concluded).

ALMOST from the day of the establishment of his position at Yorktown, in March, 1862, Gen. J. Bankhead Magruder, commanding the Confederate Army of the Peninsula, had endeavored to impress upon the Navy Department the wisdom of his views regarding the employment of the squadron in hostile operations in support of his movements; and even after the impossibility of sending the *Virginia* into the York River had been authoritatively pointed out to him, he called for the services of the *Patrick Henry, Jamestown*, and other gunboats to assist in preventing the army of McClellan from crossing Warwick River, which formed a portion of his line of defence. On April 16th, his dispatch to Secretary of War Randolph acknowledged the arrival of the *Teaser*, a small tug carrying one 32-pounder rifle, and commanded by Lieut. Hunter Davidson, in the Warwick; and on the 19th, Commodore Tatnall sent the *Jamestown*, Lieut. Barney, and the *Raleigh*, Lieut. Alexander, up the James River to protect Magruder's flank. These vessels, with the *Patrick Henry*, Capt. John R. Tucker, and the *Beaufort*, had been assembled at the mouth of the James River by April 21st, the squadron being under command of Capt. Tucker, and from that time until the evacuation of Yorktown and Norfolk it had no work to do, except that the *Teaser* was of service to Gen. Magruder on the Warwick River, and that Capt. Thomas Jefferson Page and Capt. Frederick Chatard were employed in the defensive works on shore. Magruder's report of May 3d to Adj. Gen. Cooper has this paragraph:

"That accomplished officer, Capt. T. J. Page, of the navy, successfully applied the resources of his genius and ripe experience to the defence of Gloucester Point. * * * My thanks are due to Capt. F. Chatard,[1] of the navy, for valuable services

---

[1] Frederick Chatard, born in Baltimore, May 17th, 1807, entered the U. S. navy in November, 1824, and made his first cruise on the Mediterranean in the *North Carolina*, 74, bearing the broad pennant of Com. John Rodgers. He also served on the Brazil, West Indies and Pacific stations, and participated in the Seminole war as lieut. of the sloop-of-war *Vandalia*. During the war with Mexico he was attached to the frigate *Independence*, Commodore Shubrick's flag-ship,

as inspector of batteries, and to Lieut. Col. Noland, late of the navy, the efficient commander of the batteries at Mulberry Island Point."

After the abandonment of Yorktown (May 3d), and that of Norfolk, the squadron moved up the James River. Two other gunboats, the *Nansemond* and *Hampton*, which had been built at the Norfolk navy-yard, were sent to Richmond in advance. "These vessels," Capt. W. H. Parker writes, "had saw-mill engines, and when they got under way there was such a wheezing and blowing that one would suppose all hands had been attacked with the asthma or heaves." Two fine gunboats, nearly finished, were burned at the Norfolk yard because there was not time to put their engines into them ; Parker had been assigned to the command of one and Lieut. John Rutledge to that of the other.

McClellan was at this time advancing up the peninsula, between the York and James rivers, and the Federal fleet at Fortress Monroe was made ready to support his "on to Richmond" movement by taking possession of the James, and destroying the Confederate squadron.

Occasional resistance was offered to the progress of Federal ships up the river by the Confederate batteries and squadron. On May 8th, they halted two hours at Fort Boykin, Isle of Wight Co., and shelled the works, which responded until the Confederate commander, Capt. John U. Shivers, was ordered to withdraw after spiking his guns and burning his quarters. They next attacked, on the same day, Fort Huger, at Hardy's Bluff, and after an engagement lasting from 11 A. M. to 2 P. M. passed on out of the range of its guns, having in vain endeavored to drive the defenders, who were commanded by Capt. J. M. Maury, C. S. N., out of the works. At Rock Wharf and Mother Line's Bluff, on May 9th, the *Patrick Henry* and *Jamestown* assisted the shore defences in their fire upon the *Galena*, *Aroostook* and *Port Royal*, and did not retire until the batteries had been silenced by the enemy. At Little Brandon, on the 12th, they were prepared to co-operate with the batteries, but the Federal gunboats ran past the latter and were too powerful for Tucker to think of fighting unaided. Near James' Island he

and in a merchant brig called the *Brighton*, which had been hired by the Commodore and armed, participated in the capture of Mazatlan, and blockaded Manzanilla. He was then variously employed as first lieut. of the frigate *Columbia* on the Pacific station, lieut. commanding of the sloop *Lexington*, and lieut. of the *Columbus*, 74. On receiving his promotion to commander, he was assigned to command the sloop-of-war *Saratoga*, and co-operated with Com. Paulding in the capture of Gen. Walker's fillibustering expedition in Nicaragua. When the civil war began he was in command of the receiving ship *Pennsylvania*. His sympathies turning strongly toward the South, he resigned his commission and tendered his services to the Confederacy.

He was sent to the Manassas fortifications to drill the men in the use of their guns, and next took command of the batteries on the Potomac at Evansport, which blockaded Washington and cut off supplies. Thence he was transferred to service in the Drewry's Bluff batteries, and later on to the command of Gen. J. B. Magruder on the peninsula, where he acted as chief of heavy artillery and constructor of batteries. On page 507 of the "Official Reports of Battles," published by order of the Confederate Congress, appears the following from Gen. Magruder: "My thanks are due to Capt. Chatard of the navy, for valuable services as inspector of batteries." At the close of the war Capt. Chatard removed to St. Louis, where he still resides.

was joined by the remainder of his force. He had in effect decoyed the Federals a long distance up the river in a chase after him, during which they had neglected to pay judicious attention to the danger of leaving Confederate shore batteries in their rear occupied and in fighting shape. This appears confessed in the dispatch of May 14th, from Com. L. M. Goldsborough to Secretary Welles informing the latter that Rodgers had reported to him that " he was unable to resist the five gunboats of the enemy above him because the *Galena* would inevitably be grounded in passing the bar, and thus leave only the *Aroostook* and *Port Royal* to resist them." "Notwithstanding," Goldsborough added, "my orders to Lieut. Com. Jeffers to reduce all the enemy's works on the James River as he went along, spike their guns and blow up their magazines, and thus leave the river entirely open, so that supplies of any sort might be forwarded without difficulty, he has not carried them out; and I now am informed that two of their works on James River—one at Rock Wharf Landing and the other at Harden's or Mother Line's Bluff—both between here [Hampton Roads] and our vessels up the James River, must be taken before the river can be navigated by our supply vessels."

But the Federals did not need to do any more fighting at these points. They had only been held by the Confederates because their temporary retention was in accordance with the military plan of campaign on the peninsula being wrought out by Johnston and Lee, which involved the detention of the Federal fleet in the river for a brief period and an eventual sturdy stand against them at Drewry's Bluff, where was to be fought the most serious engagement that had taken place upon the river. A dispatch from Gen. Lee, March 22d, to Gen. Magruder, announced that obstructions were being placed in the James at that point, and on May 8th, Capt. Tucker was instructed to remove thither the heavy guns that had been placed in battery at Mulberry Point and Jamestown. On the 9th Gen. Lee reported: " In addition to the three guns originally at Drewry's Bluff several navy guns have been mounted, and every exertion is being made to render the obstructions effective and the battery commanding them as formidable as possible." Capt. Ebenezer Farrand, C. S. N., was placed in charge of the battery, and Lieut. T. J. Page, C. S. N., commanded another heavy battery at Chapin's Bluff, a few miles lower down and on the opposite bank of the river. On May 15th, Capt. S. S. Lee was ordered to relieve Capt. Farrand and arrived on the scene while the battle was being fought. [1]

Drewry's Bluff is an elevation of an average height of 200 feet on the right bank of the James River a little more than

[1] Sydney Smith Lee was born in 1805, at Camden, N. J., while his father, a member of Congress from Virginia, was attending the sessions of that body, which were then being held in Philadelphia. His early inclinations showing a strong tendency towards a naval career he was appointed midshipman in the U. S. navy when but a little more than fourteen years of age, in which his services were continuous and distinguished for over forty years. He commanded a

seven miles below Richmond. The rise from the stream is rather precipitous, and the river at that point is less than a mile wide, making it suitable for the placing of obstructions to bar the passage of an enemy. So obvious were the advantages of the locality for defence that the construction of a strong earthwork was determined upon as soon as it became evident that the aim of the Federals was directed toward Richmond, and the building of the fort was entrusted to Capt. A. L. Rives, an engineer officer of the Confederate army. When the naval force was summoned to aid in the defence of the position an additional battery was constructed, or the fort was extended, by counter-sinking the naval guns on the brow of the hill, and cribbing them with logs to prevent caving by the fire of the enemy. Bombproofs were thrown over these pits, and the guns were mounted on navy carriages with all the tackle used upon a man-of-war, and all the trees that might obstruct the range of fire were cut away. Nine guns were mounted in the defences, the heaviest of which was a ten-inch Columbiad, and the others were Brooke rifles, landed from Capt. Tucker's squadron. The steamers *Jamestown*, *Curtis Peck* and *Northampton*, and several sloops and schooners were sunk in the channel to strengthen the obstructions, which were stretched across the river above the fort and consisted of piles driven into the bottom and filled in with logs, stones and iron rubbish, leaving only a narrow and intricate passage close under the guns of Fort Drewry.[1]

Capt. Tucker had superintended the construction of the naval battery, and had mounted upon it the guns landed from the *Patrick Henry* and *Jamestown*. It was manned by the officers and crews of the *Patrick Henry*, *Jamestown* and *Virginia*, included among whom, in addition to Capt. Tucker, were Lieuts. James Henry Rochelle and Francis Lyell Hoge, and Midshipman Carroll, of the *Patrick Henry*; Lieut. Com. Nicholas Barney and Acting Master Samuel Barron, Jr., of the *Jamestown*; Lieuts. Catesby Roger Jones, John Taylor Wood and Walter R. Butt, of the *Virginia*, and Lieut. Hunter Davidson. There were in addition about a score of men who

steam vessel of war in the conflict with Mexico and was prominently engaged at the siege of Vera Cruz, where his brother, the future Gen. Robert E. Lee, also won renown as an engineer and artillery officer. Capt. Lee was commandant of the U. S. naval academy at Annapolis for three years and for the same space of time was in charge of the Philadelphia navy-yard. He commanded the flag-ship *Mississippi* in Com. M. C. Perry's expedition to Japan, and when the Japanese ambassadors came to this country Capt. Lee, Capt D. G. Farragut, and Lieut. D. D. Porter were appointed the Naval Board to receive and entertain them in the United States. The last duty he performed in the U. S. navy was as chief of the Bureau of Coast Survey at Washington. On the withdrawal of Virginia from the Federal Union he resigned his commission, sold all his possessions of every kind and offered his services to the Confederate government. He was

ordered to the Norfolk navy-yard, and after its evacuation was placed in command of the fortifications at Drewry's Bluff, on the James River. His further duty to the Confederacy was discharged mainly as chief of the Bureau of Orders and Detail at Richmond. He died at Richland, Stafford Co., Va., July 22nd, 1869. He was the father of the eminent Confederate General Fitzhugh Lee, now the Governor of Virginia.

[1] The fort took its name from being built upon the property of Capt. A. Drewry, C. S. A. To the Federals it was known as Fort Darling, and in their reports the engagement is styled the battle of Fort Darling. On some of the old maps of James River the location is called Darling's Bluff, but the site of the fort had passed into the possession of the Drewry family many years previous to the war.

had come through from the fleet on the Lower Mississippi after its dispersion by Farragut. These latter had been brought to Norfolk and thence up the James by Lieut. Robert B. Pegram and Master's Mate F. W. Dawson,[1] who had met them while they were themselves approaching New Orleans to go on duty there, and had returned North.

After passing with so little difficulty the defences lower down the river, the Federals felt some confidence that they would make their way to Richmond without encountering any resistance that they could not overcome. The pressure that was being exerted upon Secretary Welles, to have the navy perform some startling exploits, had found voice in a public meeting at Boston on March 29th, in which his removal from office was demanded of President Lincoln, because of his incompetency; and it was a matter of common newspaper report that he had given his commanders of fleets and stations to understand that the news of some creditable achievements in Southern waters would be exceedingly welcome to the Administration and the North. Flag-officer Goldsborough, commanding the North Atlantic squadron, was more than willing to oblige Mr. Welles, and manifested a sublime faith in his ability to reach the Confederate capital while McClellan was wearily struggling in the marshes of the peninsula. On May 12th he wrote to Mr. Welles:

"The *Monitor* and *Stevens* (*Naugatuck*) have both gone up the James River, with orders from me to reduce all the works of the enemy as they go along, spike all their guns, blow up all their magazines, and then get up to Richmond, all with the least possible delay, and shell the city to a surrender. With the above works reduced, I can keep our vessels supplied with coal, ordnance stores, provisions, etc., without difficulty."

On the other hand, there were evidences of a slight trepidation in Richmond, outside of official and military and naval circles, that the powerful Federal iron-clads and gunboats

---

[1] Francis W. Dawson was a native of England, born in London, May 17th, 1840. He felt a deep interest in American politics, and when the news of the fall of Fort Sumter was received in London, he resolved to take passage for America and serve the Southern Confederacy. No opportunity offered until the steamship *Nashville* arrived at Southampton, when he presented to Lieut. Com. Pegram letters of introduction, and asked the privilege of returning to the South on his ship. He was so youthful that Pegram refused to encourage him to leave his own land for war in a distant and alien country ; but Dawson was too much in earnest to accept such a dismissal. Taking advantage of Pegram's absence from the ship a few days before she was to sail on her return voyage, he assumed a seaman's garb and was enlisted by her lieutenant. During the homeward run he earned the favor of Lieut. Pegram and the other officers by his good conduct, and immediately after running the blockade at Beaufort, N. C., he was appointed master's mate in the C. S. navy upon the recommendation of his commander. He was first ordered to duty at Norfolk, and thence to New Orleans, but before he could reach that city it had fallen into the hands of Farragut and Butler. He was then assigned to duty in the James River squadron, but after the battle at Drewry's Bluff resigned his naval commission and enlisted as a private in the Purcell artillery battery. At the battle of Mechanicsville, June 25th 1862, he was badly wounded, and for his bravery on the field was promoted to lieutenant. In August he was commissioned first lieutenant, and for nearly two years was assistant ordnance officer of Longstreet's corps. He was taken prisoner at the battle of South Mountain, in September, 1862, and exchanged in time to take part in the battle of Fredericksburg. In May 1864 he was promoted to be captain of artillery and made ordnance officer of Gen. Fitzhugh Lee's division, in which capacity he served until the end of the war, receiving wounds at the battles of Harrisonburg and Five Forks. He entered journalism as a reporter of the Richmond *Examiner* in the autumn of 1865, and a year later was assistant editor of the Charleston *Mercury*. In 1867, he and B. R. Riordan bought an interest in the Charleston *News*, and in 1873 purchased the Charleston *Courier*, and consolidated the two papers as the *News and Courier*, a journal which has won an enviable place in the newspaper world by its honesty, liberality and enterprise.

CAPTAIN SIDNEY S. LEE,
CONFEDERATE STATES NAVY.

ADMIRAL RAPHAEL SEMMES, C. S. N.,

COMMANDER OF THE "FLORIDA."

could force a passage up to the city. On the morning of May 15th the following communication was published by the Richmond *Dispatch*, under the heading of "Save Richmond":

"I will be one of 100 to join any party, officered by determined and resolute officers, to board the whole fleet of gunboats and take them at all hazards, to save this beautiful city from destruction. I am not a resident of this State, but of the Confederate States, and if such a scheme can be got up, my name can be had by applying at this office."

The suggestion struck the editor so favorably that he endorsed it thus :

"A DASHING ENTERPRISE.

"It will be seen by an advertisement in to-day's *Dispatch* that a proposition is made to organize a party for the purpose of boarding and capturing the Yankee gunboats now endeavoring to make their way up James River to our city. That such a feat may be accomplished by bold and determined men, is not to be doubted ; and surely the invaders will not be allowed to possess themselves of the capital of the Old Dominion without opposition."

There was no necessity for anxiety for the safety of the capital. On the morning that the boarding plan was proposed, Capt. Tucker and his sailors and an artillery battalion under the command of Capt. Drewry, C. S. A., stood behind the guns at Drewry's Bluff, and riflemen were concealed in pits on the left bank of the river, while the Confederate squadron laid ready for action just in the rear of the obstructions. The plan of battle had been arranged in Richmond and the orders delivered at Drewry's Bluff by Lieut. Chas. M. Fauntleroy.

At 7:30 o'clock the three Federal iron-clads, *Monitor*, *Naugatuck* and *Galena*, followed at some distance by the wooden gunboats *Aroostook* and *Port Royal*, steamed up to open the ball. Capt. Rodgers led in the *Galena*, and handled his vessels so perfectly as to draw forth the following tribute from Master Hasker, C. S. N., who commanded a gun on the bluff: "The attack on the part of the *Galena*, I think, was one of the most masterly pieces of seamanship of the whole war. She was brought into action in the coolest manner; indeed, she was brought to and sprung across the channel in a much more masterly way than I have often seen at mere target practice. She steamed up to within 700 or 800 yards of the bluff, let go her starboard anchor, ran out the chains, put her head in shore, backed astern, let go her stream anchor from the starboard quarter, hove ahead, and made ready for action before firing a gun. I could not but admire this manœuvre, although executed to bring death or wounds to so many of my brave comrades."

The skill with which the Federal ships were manœuvred and fought brings into increased prominence the honors which the Confederate sailors and soldiers won in the battle. As the enemy's vessels came up the river they suffered severely from the sharp-shooters in the rifle-pits, under the command of Lieut. John Taylor Wood, C. S. N., who picked off many of their men in spite of the steady fire of grape and shrapnel with which the ships endeavored to silence this annoying and constant fusilade. The *Galena* ran within 600 yards of the batteries before firing a gun and then opened vigorously, the fight lasting from 7:45 to 11:05 A. M. It was conducted with the greatest spirit on both sides, but the Federals were virtually beaten within two hours after it had begun. In accordance with the orders of Capt. Tucker, the *Galena* received most of the attention of the Confederate gunners, and the experienced artillerists whom he had brought from his ships did splendid execution with their rifled ordnance. Almost every shot found its mark. "We fought the enemy for almost four hours," wrote an officer, "and such a perfect tornado of shot and shell, right, left, front, rear, and on top of us, never was seen before. It was an awful sight to see our killed and wounded, some with an arm or leg blown off, some entirely disembowelled."

The action was still young when it was revealed that the *Galena* was not the sort of iron-clad to be proof against a plunging fire directed by the competent cannoneers who were making a target of her. They had her range perfectly, and drove shot after shot from the Brooke rifles through her iron skin and its backing. "Balls came through," said Capt. Rodgers, in his report, "and many men were killed with fragments of her own iron. One fairly penetrated just above the water-line and exploded in the steerage. The greater part of the balls, however, at the water-line, after breaking the iron, stuck in the wood. The port-side is much injured—knees, planks and timbers started. No shot penetrated the spar-deck, but in three places are large holes—one of them about a yard long and eight inches wide, made by a shot which, in glancing, completely broke through the deck, killing several men with fragments of the deck plating."

Thirteen men were killed and eleven wounded on this ship, and yet Capt. Rodgers states that after this heavy loss, and the riddling of the vessel, he only drew out of the action because he had fired 283 shot and shell, and expended all his ammunition except six charges for his Parrott rifles. It seems a foregone conclusion that a much longer exposure to the Confederate fire would have sunk the *Galena*. She did not obtain a great amount of assistance from her consorts. The *Monitor* first passed ahead, but found that from the position she took her guns could not be sufficiently elevated to reach the fort, and she then came into line with the *Galena*, and kept up fire until the baffled squadron retreated. Aware of the uselessness of attempting to penetrate her impervious armor by his guns, Capt. Tucker let her severely alone, and she was struck but three times, no shot causing any more injury than a slight bending of her plates. Nobody was hurt on board of her. The Parrott rifled gun of the *Naugatuck* burst at the seventeenth fire, and she dropped out of the engagement with two men wounded. The wooden gun-boats took no considerable part in the engagement. Once the *Port Royal* steamed into fair range of the fort, but retired on being struck by a shell that slightly wounded her commander, but she and the *Aroostook* were found very useful in towing into a position of safety the two crippled iron-clads.

The badly-battered fleet headed for City Point to repair damages, bury their fourteen dead and provide for their eighteen wounded, the parting salute being given them by Lieut. J. T. Wood, C. S. N., who had been stationed on the bank with a party of sharp-shooters. He was so close to the *Monitor* as she passed down, that he called out to an officer in her pilot-house: "Tell Capt. Jeffers that is not the way to Richmond." The Confederate victory had been won at comparatively small cost. Midshipman Carroll, of the *Patrick Henry*, was killed while acting as signal officer and aide to Com. Farrand. The total loss of the Confederates was seven killed and nine wounded. Michael McMore, one of the *Virginia's* crew, was the only member of the naval force, besides Mr. Carroll, killed, but five of Capt. Drewry's artillerymen were killed. Eight of the latter were wounded, as was also W. Johnson, gunner's mate of the *Virginia's* crew. The casualties among the seamen were caused by a shell from the *Monitor*, which, early in the day, burst in an embrasure of the fort and disabled a gun, that, however, was quickly repaired and became the most efficient piece in the action.

Reports of eye-witnesses of the engagement published in the Southern newspapers were rather brief. The Richmond *Dispatch's* correspondent told the story thus:

"The enemy fired rapidly, many of his shots striking our works, his shells flying and bursting around us, cutting down quite a number of trees near us, but doing our guns no injury, and killing and wounding only some thirteen or fourteen of our men. We struck the *Monitor* and *Galena* again and again, and I think from the manner in which they seemed to recoil at our heavy shot, that something about them must have been put out of place. The *Galena* began to run first, apparently much crippled. We continued to fire upon them as they retreated, amidst loud cheers from our boys. * * * Our men stood to their guns with the greatest bravery and determination. Capts. Tucker and Barney, of the *Patrick Henry* and *Jamestown*, and Capts. Drewry, Jordon and Preston, of Chesterfield, Bedford and Lynchburg, have command of the guns here. They have seen something of the enemy's Chinese gongs before, and, I presume, will not be easily driven from their position by the loud noise the enemy can make with his guns. Let the good citizens of Richmond be quiet. We do not intend the enemy to reach Richmond this way."

In his official report Com. Farrand said:

"The enemy came up the river at half-past six A. M., the *Galena* ahead, the *Monitor* and a small iron steamer, a side-wheel, and a smaller gunboat following in succession.

"When about four hundred yards from our obstructions our batteries opened fire upon the *Monitor* and *Galena*. They did not reply until the *Galena* had placed herself directly athwart the channel. After which she and the *Monitor* opened a brisk fire, the other vessels keeping under way, and at about from a quarter to a mile lower down and so close under the opposite shore that only four of our guns could bear upon them. Our fire was mostly directed upon the *Galena*, only occasionally paying a compliment to the others.

"Several of our shots at long range passed through and through them, and they soon dropped out of range. The small iron-clad and the side-wheel gunboats were badly crippled. We turned our attention to the *Galena*—nearly every one of our shots telling upon her iron surface—at 11 o'clock A. M., one of the *Patrick Henry's* eight-inch solid shot passed into her bow port. Immediately the smoke rushed out of her own ports, showing, evidently, that she was on fire. We gave her three hearty cheers as she slipped her cables and moved down the river. Our pickets heard her captain say to one of the other gunboats, that she was "in a sinking condition.

"Our sharp-shooters did good service, picking off every man who showed himself.

"There is no doubt we struck them a hard blow. The last that was seen of them they were steaming down the river.

"Every officer and man discharged their duties with coolness and determination, and it would be doing injustice to many if I should mention or particularize any. Capt. Drewry and his men fought their guns with great effect."

As stated by Com. Farrand, the service done by the sharp-shooters was a feature of the battle. Lieut. John Taylor Wood, C. S. N., reported as follows to Lieut. Jones concerning that duty performed by his men from the squadron:

"Hearing on the evening of the 14th inst, that the enemy were but a few miles of coming up, I crossed to the north bank with a small party of sharp-shooters armed with Enfield rifles, and proceeded down to Chapin's Bluff. The gunboats were in sight below, lying in a position not easy to assail them, for both banks were low. They were examining the shores very closely with their small boats as well as all drift wood, evidently on the look out for infernal machines. I had several shots at them at long range—they threw as many well-directed shells. Night approaching, I returned to this place, leaving my men at the request of the commanding officer of a battery of the Washington artillery, with him as a covering party.

"Early on the morning of the 15th I returned and soon after met Col. Stewart with a regiment of infantry. I told him where my men were, and that it was the best place for us all; he said that he learned from a number of soldiers that the enemy were landing and was afraid of being cut off. We afterwards followed and met down to the river, about twenty men. The Washington artillery and Dabney artillery were both on the bank, but as the enemy came up left without firing a shot, dreading a landing. I assured them there was no danger of it, and that I would keep below them and give them early intelligence of what was going on. I distributed the men along the high bank with orders to each one to select his position and harass the enemy. For three hours an incessant fire was kept up on their vessels. Two or three times everybody was driven from the guns on board the wooden ships. They replied with their heavy guns, boat guns and small arms. We followed them down the river for a mile or more."

Another party of sharp-shooters was the battalion of marines commanded by Capt. John D. Simms, of the C. S. marine corps, who reported:

"On the 15th inst. the enemy's gunboats having made their appearance near the battery at Drewry's Bluff, I stationed my command on the bluffs some two hundred yards from them, to act as sharp-shooters. We immediately opened a sharp fire upon them, killing three of the crew of the

Galena certainly, and no doubt many more. The fire of the enemy was materially silenced at intervals by the fire of our troops. It gives me much pleasure to call your attention to the coolness of the officers and men under the severe fire of the enemy. The companies composing my battalion were commanded by Capts. A. C. Van Benthuysen and J. E. Meiere."

Secretary Mallory wrote to Com. Farrand that "the thanks of the country are due to yourself, your officers and your gallant men," and added: "The enemy has retired, but to return with a larger force; and the sacred duty of confronting and repelling his advances upon the river is devolved upon the navy. The country expects much from your command, and I feel assured that it will do its duty and nobly sustain the character of the navy."

When Congress met it extended its compliments to the victors by the passage of the following:

"*Resolved by the Congress of the Confederate States of America*, That the thanks of Congress are eminently due, and are hereby most cordially tendered to Commander E. Farrand, senior officer in command of the combined naval and military forces engaged, and Capt. A. Drewry, senior military officer, and the officers and men under their command, for the great and signal victory achieved over the naval forces of the United States in the engagement on the 15th day of May, 1862, at Drewry's Bluff; and the gallantry, courage and endurance in that protracted fight, which achieved a victory over the fleet of iron-clad gunboats of the enemy, entitle all who contributed thereto to the gratitude of the country.

"*Resolved further*, That the President be requested, in appropriate general orders, to communicate the foregoing resolution to the officers and men to whom it is addressed.

"APPROVED September 16th, 1862."

Although the name of Capt. S. S. Lee, who had been, on May 15th, ordered to relieve Com. Farrand, does not appear in the official dispatches, he rendered much service in the defence of the position. Finding that the engagement had commenced when he arrived at Drewry's Bluff, he refrained from taking command, but contented himself with acting in co-operation with the officer whose place he had been sent to fill. As a matter of fact, there was a slight confusion in regard to the forces, and command at the fort. On the 14th, Secretary of War Randolph had ordered Gen. Huger to send from Petersburg to Drewry's Bluff four companies of light troops, and Gen. Mahone's brigade, Mahone to assume command upon his arrival. By some mischance Gen. Mahone did not arrive at the Bluff until the 16th, but he was preceded thither and to Chapin's Bluff by eight companies of heavy artillery belonging to his command. The instructions of Gen. Lee to Gen. Mahone contemplated co-ordinate action between the army and navy, but the latter professed a doubt as to who should exercise the supreme authority at the post. He was informed that the work was placed in immediate charge of the navy and that the President was "unwilling to disturb the arrangement with the Navy Department now existing," further than to insure to Mahone the general control of military operations. Mahone still protested that he "would not be responsible for any co-partnership authority;" and that, although there had been no difficulty between the two arms of the service, "interferences had occurred in the prosecution of the works to the prejudice of the common object." The trouble was settled by Gen. Huger, Mahone's superior officer, taking personal command of the position; and on June 12th, Capt. T. J. Page, C. S. N., was appointed colonel of artillery, and appointed to the command of the batteries at Chapin's and Ball's Bluff. Capt. Lee continued to exercise control at Drewry's Bluff, and under his supervision the obstructions in the river were completed.

There was no year of the war during which Confederate seamen did not find upon the broad expanse of Chesapeake Bay, and its many tributaries between the Potomac and the ocean, opportunities for naval raids and skirmishes that included numerous daring exploits and inflicted much annoyance upon the enemy. The bay being a highway of communication between the North and Fortress Monroe and Washington, and serving also for operations which comprised Baltimore and Annapolis within their scope, it was obvious that any measures which could interrupt or embarrass its navigation by Federal vessels would be of service to the Confederate cause, and the first to suggest itself was the destruction or disabling of the light-houses. In April, 1861, the lights of Cape Henry and Cape Charles and all those on the seaward side of Hampton Roads were extinguished by volunteers from among the population of the seaside counties of Va., except that of the Willoughby Spit Light-ship, which was only kept burning under a guard from the sloop-of-war *Cumberland*. During the same month an expedition—the sole information regarding the *personnel* of which is the statement of a Richmond paper, that it was "a party of gentlemen organized under the Act of Congress for the creation of a volunteer navy"—ran down to Smith's Island, near the mouth of the Potomac, captured the light-ship by boarding and took it into the Great Wicomico River. On May 16th, Gen. Butler sent an armed steamer after the vessel and recaptured it after a sharp fight with a body of Southern troops on shore. In the last week of April, the schooner *George M. Smith* was made a prize off the capes of the Chesapeake, by the *Cumberland*. She had on board a cargo of field-guns and carriages, shipped for a Southern port, by some Northern merchants not too patriotic to sell material of war to the Confederacy when there was no apparent danger of being detected by Federal spies.

Quite a number of privateers, of which no record remains, were sent out of the rivers of Virginia into the bay during the summer, and were at least useful in running the Federal blockade with recruits, small arms and ammunition for the Confederate troops south of the Potomac.

On Nov. 28th, 1862, Lieuts. Wood and Lee', C. S. N., were cruising in the Chesapeake with a boat's crew from the steamer *Patrick Henry.* Below the mouth of the Rappahannock they found the fine ship *Alleghanian,* hailing from New York, and bound from Baltimore to London, which had come to anchor in the prevailing storm. She was quickly boarded by the boat's crew, and Lieut. Wood informed her captain that his ship was a prize and he and his people were prisoners. They made no resistance, and were transferred to their own boats, and the ship set on fire, after the Confederates had selected from her stores such articles as they desired. In the darkness one boat's crew of prisoners managed to escape, but the remainder and the officers were sent to Richmond as prisoners. The ship and her cargo were valued at $200,000, which was a total loss to her owners and consignees. In making this successful dash, Lieuts. Wood and Lee passed close to several gunboats of the enemy, and one of them, the *Crusader,* was only a few miles distant when they captured the *Alleghanian.*

With exploits of this character in these waters in 1863 the name of John Yates Beall is indissolubly associated. Early in the year he suggested to Secretary Mallory a project for privateering on the Chesapeake and Potomac, and receiving the sanction of the government he was commissioned acting master in the C. S. navy. He and an officer of the navy then on the retired list on account of ill-health set about organizing an expedition, and among their first recruits secured Bennett G. Burley, a young Scotchman, who was pressing a submarine torpedo battery upon the attention of the Navy Deparment, and another Scotchman named John Maxwell. They started from Richmond about April 1st with nine or ten men, but for some months accomplished nothing more important than dispersing a camp of negroes in Elizabeth City Co. within ten miles of Fortress Monroe. The young officer alluded to then left the expedition to accept a commission in the army, and Beall was left in sole command. His force was increased to about twenty, provided with open boats, and it was his aim to become the " Mosby " of the Chesapeake, burning light-houses, severing submarine telegraph wires, capturing transports and steamers and otherwise harassing the enemy. Matthews Co. was his rendezvous and base of operations. In July he sent a squad under Roy McDonald to seize a steamer plying between Cherrystone and Fortress Monroe, but they missed her and returned after cutting the U. S. telegraph cable across the Chesapeake. About the 1st of Aug. Beall and all his men crossed to the eastern shore of Va. and made a wreck of the light-house at Cape Charles. On Sept. 18th they started from Matthews Co. on the most enterprising project they had undertaken. The party were divided into two crews, Beall commmanding one in the *Swan* and assigning McDonald to the charge of the second in the *Raven.* Near Cape Charles they made prizes of the Northern sloop *Mary Anne* and two fishing vessels, and ran them into Watchapreague Inlet on the eastern shore, near where, on the night of Sept. 21st, during the heavy equinoctial gale, their boats almost swamped by the high sea, they boarded the schooner *Alliance*, bound from Philadelphia to Port Royal, S. C., with a valuable cargo of sutler's stores. The captain of the schooner showed fight, but was brought under control and his vessel captured. Leaving her at anchor with a prize crew, Beall sallied out in his boats the next night and took the schooners *Horseman, Pearsall* and *Alexander*, which he scuttled, and returned with his prisoners to the *Alliance*, on board of which he placed them and his crews and sailed to Cobb's Island. Here he paroled the prisoners of the *Mary Anne* and the fishing smacks and sent McDonald to Matthews Co. with the others. Because of the value of the cargo of the *Alliance*, he determined to run her up the Piankatank River, from whence he might transport the stores to Richmond; but the pilot grounded the schooner in the mouth of that river, where Beall burned her. He saved some of the stores, however, and got with them into Richmond, where their sale netted a handsome dividend for his party, his agreement with Secretary Mallory being that they should receive no pay, but were entitled to all they could legitimately capture.

They had accomplished so much with so small a force, that an exaggerated notion of their numbers was entertained at the Federal headquarters, and a regiment of infantry, two of cavalry, a battalion of artillery, and three gunboats were sent into Matthews Co. to operate against the squad of twenty. McDonald and two of the men were made prisoners on October 5th; Beall and the remaining sixteen narrowly escaped, and on account of the hot pursuit he disbanded the party and returned to Richmond. He reassembled them in a few weeks, and about November 10th returning to his boats, which he had left concealed, crossed the bay once more to the Accomac shore, where he captured a schooner. Daylight coming on, he sent a squad of his men with one boat to conceal themselves, while he and six others remained on the prize. Accompanying him at that time was Acting Master Edward McGuire, C. S. N. The party sent out endeavored to make a landing, but were ambushed by a large detachment of the Federal coast guard, who extorted from one of their number a betrayal of the whereabouts of Beall. Gen. Lockwood, the Federal commander on the eastern shore, armed a flotilla of boats and captured Beall and his comrades on board their prize. They were taken to Drummondtown, November 15th, and from thence to Fort McHenry. On the passage, Beall tried to induce his men to attempt the seizure of the steamer, but they prudently declined, and it was well they did, for in the hold were concealed a company of Federal troops.

It was the determination of the Federal authorities to place Beall and his command on trial as pirates, although he held a regular commission in the navy of the Confederate States and his men were properly enlisted. It is impossible to discover any charges upon which they could have been convicted by an impartial court and jury. Their captures were lawfully made of vessels owned by citizens of the power with which the Confederate States were at war, and in no instance had they transgressed the rights of a belligerent nation, which had already been recognized by the United States. During their six weeks of imprisonment at Fort McHenry they were ironed and treated to gross indignities. Upon receiving information of their hardships and danger, President Davis promptly ordered Lieut. Com. E. P. Williams, Ensign Benj. H. Porter and fifteen seamen of the U. S. navy made prisoners in Charleston harbor, to be placed in similar close confinement at Richmond and held as hostages for the treatment of Beall and his party as prisoners-of-war. Such summary retaliation instantly brought the government at Washington to terms; the manacles were stricken from the limbs of the Confederate captives, and nothing more was heard of trying them for piracy. Beall was forwarded along with other officers from Fort McHenry to City Point on March 20th, 1864, where he remained until May 5th, when he was duly exchanged and returned to Richmond. The balance of the party, including Beall's brother, William, were not exchanged until the following October.

The capture of the transport steamer *Maple Leaf* was one of the enlivening incidents of 1863. She was chartered by the U. S. government from her owner, who was also her captain, and on July 7th started from Fortress Monroe for Fort Delaware, with 93 Confederate officers who had been taken prisoners on the Mississippi, and sent east for confinement. The ranking officer was Col. A. K. Witt, of the 10th Ark. regt., and he, with Lieut. Semmes, and others of the prisoners, had conceived a scheme to take possession of any vessel upon which they might be placed. They were in charge of a Federal lieutenant and sixteen men. After getting out to sea at night, the lieutenant arranged his guard in three reliefs, the men not on duty stacking their arms, and he retired to rest. Col. Witt and Lieut. Semmes, seeing the opportunity, had arranged that one of their men should be on the upper deck, and at a given signal tap the bell, while the officers generally should cluster around the guard so far as they might do so without exciting suspicion. When the bell struck, the stacked muskets were seized by the men in the secret, the guard was overpowered without a shot being fired, and in five minutes Col. Witt was in command of the *Maple Leaf*, and the Federal soldiers became the prisoners. Col. Witt desired to run the steamer to Nassau, and turn her over to the Confederate agents there;

46

but her captain protested that she would never be able to make the ocean voyage, although he offered to steer for any other point the colonel might designate. It was then decided to make for the coast of North Carolina, which was reached ten miles below Cape Henry, and seventy of the Confederate officers landed, the remaining twenty-three, who were wounded men, being left on board. It was proposed at first to take them off and disable the engine of the boat, but upon the plea of the captain that she represented his fortune, and that he would take the wounded men direct to Fort Delaware, no harm was done her. He repaid this leniency by returning, as quickly as steam could carry him, to Fortress Monroe, and informing Gen. Dix of the affair. Cavalry were sent out after the bold seventy, but they reached the Confederate lines without further adventure.

On March 6th, 1864, another of the Chesapeake Bay surprise parties took place. Lieut. John Taylor Wood, of the Confederate navy, and Capt. Thaddeus Fitzhugh, of the 5th Va. cavalry, who was at his home in Matthews Co. on furlough, gathered together a party of fifteen men, and crossed the bay in open boats to Cherrystone harbor on the eastern shore. Running in at night, and taking the precaution of cutting the telegraph wires, they captured the Federal cavalry pickets, and waited in concealment for larger game. It came in the shape of the U. S. dispatch boat *Iolas*, which arrived during the night from Fortress Monroe, and was promptly seized. Before morning another dispatch steamer, the *Titan*, came in too, and also fell into their hands as a prize. The cavalry guard and the crews of the two steamers outnumbered them three to one, but they acted with such swiftness that their pistols were at the heads of each batch of the enemy before the latter could fire a shot. Warehouses on the wharf containing commissary stores valued at $50,000 were given to the flames. By the orders of Lieut. Wood the torch was also to be applied to the *Iolas*, but the captain offered to bond his vessel for $10,000, and when he executed the document she was spared, and he and his crew were released on parole. The raiders then embarked in the *Titan*, taking with them the cavalrymen whom they had captured, and steamed off for the Piankatank River, which they reached during the day. Several gunboats were sent in pursuit of them, and after running up to Freeport, and removing from their prize everything of value they set her on fire. Both the captured steamers were fine new vessels that cost $40,000 each to build.

These daring expeditions from the western shore of Virginia determined the Federals to strike at their source, and on April 18th, Capt. Foxhall A. Parker entered the Rappahannock River with the Potomac flotilla and destroyed a large amount of navy material which the Confederates had accumulated there, including ship timber and boats. He, however, failed in the principal purpose of his foray, which was to make inmates of Northern prisons of the venturesome raiders; and finding that the river was dangerously sown with torpedoes, he made his way out. About the middle of May, he returned with several vessels equipped with torpedo searchers, and with their aid and by marching seamen along shore to look for pits from which infernal machines might be exploded, he reached Fredericksburg without the loss of a boat. At Powatt's Island he sent into the country a strong party of sailors, who encountered Acting Masters Burley and Maxwell, with nine men. Although the Confederates were so greatly in the minority, they made a gallant fight, which did not end until Maxwell and six of his men had been killed, and Burley and the others made prisoners.

In April, 1865, Capt. Fitzhugh, who was associated with Lieut. Wood in the capture of the *Iolas* and *Titan*, carried to success an equally adventurous undertaking within sixty miles of Baltimore and under the noses of the enemy. Passing into Maryland with his band, he placed all except a dozen in hiding on the Chesapeake shore near the mouth of the Patuxent River, and with the dozen proceeded in disguise, on April 4th, to the steamboat wharf at Fair Haven and took passage on the steamer *Harriet Deford* for Baltimore. When the vessel was well out in the stream they threw off their disguises and revealed themselves in the uniform of the Confederacy. Taking possession of the steamer they headed her down the bay and by signal brought from on shore their comrades, after which they returned to Fair Haven and landed the passengers and most of the crew. They then laid their course again down the Chesapeake with the intention of capturing any government vessel they might be able to overcome or one of the large steamers of the Baltimore and Norfolk line, which were then carrying large numbers of officers and men to and from the army, and were frequently laden with stores of much value and sometimes paymasters' safes. About midnight the steamer *Louisiana* of that line was sighted. All lights on the *Harriet Deford* were extinguished and Capt. Fitzhugh prepared his men for boarding, but a heavy gale was blowing, the seas were running high, and he found it impossible to get the *Deford*, which was of but 150 tons burden, up to the large vessel, which thus escaped capture. The next day the alarm had spread all over the bay, and knowing that the Federal gunboats would be after him he took her into Dimer's Creek and destroyed her.

The last privateering exploit in the Chesapeake was the capture of the schooner *St. Marys* off the mouth of the Patuxent on April 6th, 1865, by Lieut. Commander John C. Brain, who burned the vessel on the Virginia shore. Much obloquy was visited upon the heroes of these adventures by the Federal commanders in their reports, and although the

Washington government did not dare, for fear of retaliation, to renew the Beall experiment of treating as pirates any of them who were captured, the Northern newspapers never spoke of their achievements as anything else than "piracy." But the term was simply employed in vindictiveness and without warrant. The enterprises of Beall, Wood, Brain and Fitzhugh were sanctioned by the rules of civilized warfare, which permitted them, as officers of the Confederate navy or army, to seize the property of citizens of a hostile government or to destroy it. They scrupulously refrained from interference with the personal property of individuals, and in the case of the *Harriet Deford*, for instance, every passenger was set on shore without harm or loss. "Pirates" would have cleaned their pockets out as thoroughly as Sherman swept the homes of Georgia, or Sheridan those of the Shenandoah valley.

In the cotemporaneous chronicles of the advance of the Federals upon Richmond in the spring and summer of 1862, the battle of Drewry's Bluff was made a minor affair in comparison with the clash of the great armies of Lee and McClellan upon the peninsula; but the revelations of later days, the present knowledge of the conditions of invasion and defence as shown in the historical writings of the commanders of opposing fleets and armies, raise it to the rank of an engagement upon which the fate of Richmond depended when it was fought. The dispatch of May 12th, in which Flag-officer Goldsborough promised Secretary Welles the capture of Richmond, was not ridiculous at that date; absurd as it proved to be, it was founded on possibilities that might have been realized if the Federals had been quick enough to seize them. If their fleet of iron-clads and gunboats had started up the James River on the 10th of May, when it was known at Fortress Monroe that they were no longer threatened by the *Virginia*, they might have passed Drewry's Bluff with very little more trouble than they met with at Day's Point or at the other Confederate batteries which, as we have seen, they silenced or passed. They could have easily covered the distance between Newport News and Richmond in 24 hours, and on any day before the 13th of May they would have found at Drewry's Bluff only an uncompleted line of obstructions, a battery mounting but three guns, and the opposition of the Confederate squadron of flimsy gunboats that they could have blown out of the water in a few moments of a close fight. But they lagged behind and passed in inaction their opportune moment, and when they did approach Richmond, Drewry's Bluff was a strong defensive work, whose guns, to employ the language of Lieut. Constable, the commander of the *Naugatuck*, "were manned by the best artillerists in the world— seamen commanded by officers late of the navy of the United States." It was Tucker and his sailors who saved Richmond, and these few hundred men were just then more precious as guardians of the city than the splendid army that warded off the assaults of McClellan.

Richmond was not unconscious of her salvation, nor was she unappreciative of the importance of the creation of a stronger naval force than that which constituted the squadron under the command of Com. Tucker. There was never at any time an indifference in Virginia to the prominence which should be given the navy in the defence of the Confederacy, and the battles in Hampton Roads of the ship which bore the name of the State were an incentive to the prevailing ambition that the bosom of the James should bear iron-clad ships over which the Confederate ensign should float. This pregnant desire gave birth to the *Richmond*, the first fully-armored ship that the South put afloat on the James River. The vessel was consecrated from the laying of her keel with the ardent hopes of a community around which the battle lines were drawn. On March 17th, 1862, Col. Blanton Duncan caused to be published in the Richmond *Dispatch* an appeal for funds with which to build an iron-clad ship, under the supervision of officers designated by the Navy Department, to be presented to the government upon its completion. He instanced the example of the women of South Carolina and Georgia, who were endeavoring to raise a fund for a similar purpose and appealed to the patriotism of the " rich men in our community who can afford to give from $500 to $5,000 each and not miss it," and offered to head a subscription list with his individual gift of $2,000. The first response was made by Charles M. Wallace, who enrolled himself as a contributor in the sum of $1,000, and then Milton P. Jarnagin telegraphed from Athens, Tenn., a subscription of $500. Next the venerable Edmund Ruffin pledged himself to add $500 to the fund, and after him came Edmund Ruffin, Jr., with a subscription of $1,000. Col. Edmund Fontaine requested that his name should be inscribed on the list for $1,500, and then the matter was taken up by the devoted women of Virginia, and eventually it was mainly through their patriotism and self-sacrifice that the project was consummated. Their organization began at Williamsburg, and is set forth in the following letter from that historic Virginia town printed in the Richmond *Dispatch* of March 28th :

" TO THE EDITOR: Please state in your paper that the ladies of Williamsburg, Va., impressed with the importance of every effort to defend our country, have organized a society for the purpose of building an iron-clad gunboat to aid in protecting our coast from depredation and our capital from an attack by water. Their efforts so far have been crowned with signal success, and it is to be hoped that, with like enthusiasm, their countrywomen throughout the State will at once form similar societies for the purpose of obtaining funds for this object, which, if promptly undertaken and actively carried out, may prove of incalculable benefit to our State and country.

" By the energy, industry and patriotism of the women of Virginia, and the influence they can wield over those who are able to contribute to so laudable a design, a fund may soon be collected sufficient to place upon our waters a valuable ally of the mail-clad *Virginia*, the best defence of our harbors and rivers from the attacks of an insolent enemy, whose naval power has already inflicted heavy blows upon our coasts.

"The ladies of Williamsburg, therefore, earnestly invite the co-operation of their sisters throughout the State, and recommend the immediate adoption of such means as may secure the desired result. Contributions from societies or individuals may be forwarded to either of the following ladies: Mrs. Judge B. Tucker, Mrs. W. W. Vest, Mrs. Ro. Saunders, Mrs. Thos. Ambler, Mrs. Jas. Semple, Mrs. C. W. Coleman, Mrs. Dr. Williamson, Mrs. Cornelia Jones, Mrs. Isabella Sully."

The "Ladies Defence Association" was then formed at Richmond, with Mrs. Maria G. Clofton, president; Mrs. General Henningsen, vice-president, and Mrs. R. H. Maury, treasurer. At its meeting on April 9th an address, prepared by Capt. J. S. Maury,[1] was read by Rev. Dr. Doggett. In this address it was eloquently stated that the first efforts of the association would be " directed to the building and putting afloat in the waters of the James River a steam man-of-war, clad in shot-proof armor ; her panoply to be after the manner of that gallant ship, the noble *Virginia*." Committees were appointed to solicit subscriptions, and so much encouragement was received that the managers of the association called upon President Davis for sanction of its purpose, which he gladly gave ; and it was announced that the keel of the vessel would be laid in a few days, that Com. Farrand would be in charge of the work, and that he would be assisted by ship-builder Graves.

Words can but inadequately represent the energy with which the women of Virginia undertook this work, or the sacrifices which they made to complete it. That their jewels and their household plate, heirlooms, in many instances, that had been handed down from generation to generation and were the embodiments of ancestral rank and tradition, were freely given up, is known. "Virginia;" said they in their appeal, "when she sent her sons into this war, gave up her jewels to it. Let not her daughters hold back. Mothers, wives, sisters ! what are your ornaments of silver and gold in decoration, when by dedicating them to a cause like this, you may in times like these strengthen the hand or nerve the arm, or give comfort to the heart that beats and strikes in your defence ! Send them to us."

The organization, moreover, did not confine itself to urging upon the women of the State that this was particularly their contribution to the maintenance of the Confederacy. It solicited materials, tools and metals. "Iron railings," the address

---

[1] John S. Maury held the rank of lieutenant in the U. S. navy previous to the outbreak of the war, and in April, 1861, was stationed on the sloop-of-war *Cumberland*, at Norfolk. He resigned his commission, and entering the C. S. navy, was made lieutenant and assigned to duty at the Norfolk navy-yard after it had been abandoned by the Federals. He was employed there in fitting out the vessels of the Confederate squadron and in transporting guns to Southern ports. After the Confederate evacuation of Norfolk, he was ordered to Drewry's Bluff, and then to the command of the gunboat *Hampton*. He subsequently commanded the iron-clad *Richmond*, from which he was detached to duty in the ordnance bureau in the city of Richmond, where he remained until the evacuation, and was paroled at Danville. Since the war he has resided in Baltimore, where he has been engaged in the insurance business.

continued, "old and new, scrap-iron about the house, broken plough-shares about the farm, and iron in any shape, though given in quantities ever so small, will be thankfully received if delivered at the Tredegar works, where it may be put into the furnace, reduced and wrought into shape or turned into shot and shell." A friendly invasion of the tobacco factories was made by a committee of ladies consisting of Mrs. Brooke Gwathmey, Mrs. B. Smith, and Mrs. George T. Brooker, and the owners cheerfully broke up much of their machinery that was available for the specified purpose. Mrs. R. H. Maury, treasurer of the association, took charge of the contributions in money, plate and jewelry ; the materials and tools were sent to Com. Farrand, and an agent, S. D. Hicks, was appointed to receive the contributions of grain, country produce, etc., that were sent in by Virginia farmers to be converted into cash. By the end of April the construction had reached an advanced stage ; President Davis and Secretary Mallory had congratulated the Ladies' Association upon the assured success of its self-allotted task, and by the sale of articles donated to a public bazaar or fair, almost a sufficient sum to complete the ship was secured. [1]

The *Richmond* was completed in July, 1862, and although detailed descriptions are lacking, all mention made of her is unanimous that she was an excellent ship of her type. Capt. Parker says that "she was a fine vessel, built on the plan of the *Virginia*. She was not so large, and her ends were not submerged. She carried a bow and stern pivot, and two guns in broadside." Federal prisoners coming out of Richmond made many efforts to catch a glimpse of her as she laid at the dock and brought North such exaggerated reports of her size and strength that the Federals christened her " *Merrimac No. 2.*" She gave the Federal commanders an opportunity to see for themselves what she was like on July 30th, when she steamed down to Drewry's Bluff, near where the enemy's squadron was lying. The *Galena* and *Monitor*, according to the letter of a correspondent of the Philadelphia *Inquirer*, hurried off to Harrison's Landing to inform Flag-officer Wilkes[2] that the dreaded "Confederate rams" were coming down the river. Wilkes made no great hurry to provoke an action. On board his flag-ship, the *Wachusett*, he proceeded in the direction of Drewry's Bluff, followed by the *Monitor*, the *Galena* and six gunboats. With this strong squadron he was willing to try the issue of battle with the *Richmond*, but she

---

[1] Just previous to this time there had been received at the Ordnance Office, Richmond, a tender of the church bells of Marietta, Ga., to be cast into cannon, which was accepted. The letter making the offer was signed by Rev. E. Porter Palmer, pastor of the Presbyterian church; Rev. T. B. Cooper, pastor of Baptist church; Rev. Samuel Benedict, rector of St. James Protestant Episcopal church and Rev. Alexander Graham, pastor of the Methodist Episcopal church. The total weight of the bells was 1623 pounds.

[2] Capt. Charles Wilkes, of *San Jacinto* and *Trent* fame, had been appointed to the command of the Federal fleet on the James River. He was chosen for that command because of an expectation on the part of the Federal administration, that he would inaugurate a policy of hard and heavy fighting against the land and naval forces of the Confederacy.

had retired up the river and he refrained from drawing the fire of the batteries on the Bluff.

The Federal knowledge of the fighting capacity of the *Richmond* was by this time tolerably accurate. By their capture of the little gunboat *Teaser* they had come into the possession of papers that fairly described the ship. This capture was effected on the afternoon of July 4th. Balloon reconnoissances were then practiced by both armies ; and the *Teaser,* under command of Lieut. Hunter Davidson, had gone down into Turkey Bend with a balloon on board, which it was proposed to send up in order that an observation might be made of McClellan's positions at City Point and Harrison's Landing. The *Teaser* got aground, and while thus situated was discovered by the Federal gunboat *Maratanza,* a ship carrying several 9-inch Dahlgren guns. Davidson could not retreat, so he opened fire upon the *Maratanza* with his two small guns, a 9-pounder and a 32-pounder rifle. He put a shot into the wheel-house of the *Maratanza,* but by her answering fire a shell was exploded in the boiler of the *Teaser,* and Davidson and his crew abandoned their vessel. They escaped to shore, but left behind them their balloon and papers that the Federals claimed contained valuable information, including particulars concerning the *Richmond* and her armament. Lieut. Davidson, in reporting the loss of his vessel, requested a court of inquiry, which Secretary Mallory did not see fit to grant. "The Department," the Secretary wrote, "does not deem an inquiry as to the loss of the *Teaser,* by a court, necessary, nor does it attach blame to yourself, your officers or crew in consequence thereof. Your conduct under the circumstances was judicious and creditable to the service."

To a Confederate officer, Lieut. James Barry, who had served both afloat and ashore, was due the invention and construction of an iron-clad railway battery. He and some of his men, members of the Norfolk United artillery, had served on the *Virginia* in Hampton Roads ; and when the Confederate army was drawn behind the railroad lines around Richmond he conceived the project of, as the Richmond newspapers styled it, the "Dry Land *Merrimac.*" Upon a double set of car-trucks he built a firm floor, upon which he erected an armor-plated casemate similar to that of the Confederate ironclads, and mounted in it one of the Brooke banded and rifled guns so admirably adapted to firing either shot or shell. It was on several occasions brought into action on the York River railroad in the neighborhood of Fair Oaks and Savage's Station, and did commendable service as long as the enemy were on the line of the road. Railway batteries are now a part of the equipment of all armies, but it is probable that the one built by Lieut. Barry was the first to go into actual service.

Under Wilkes as flag-officer the Federal fleet on the James was considerable strengthened, and when McClellan's shattered army was driven upon Harrison's Landing after the seven days of battle it materially served to protect him from further Confederate assaults ; but no desire was manifested to again try conclusions with the batteries on Drewry's Bluff. The fleet suffered from several minor conflicts in which Confederate army and navy men took part. On May 19th the surgeon, chief engineer, signal officer, and a boat's crew from the gunboat *Wachusett*, went ashore at City Point. Leaving six men in the boat, the others went into the town and were captured by a scouting party of Confederates, who afterwards fired upon the boat and killed or wounded all but one man of the six. At Watkins Bluff, on June 20th, the gunboat *Jacob Bell*, while going up the river to meet the *Monitor*, came within the fire of a masked battery that crippled her. Her pilot-house was carried away, her port wheel and upper works shot off; but the arrival of the *Monitor* saved her from capture.

During the night of July 25th-26th, 1862, the fleet of Federal transports and supply ships near Harrison's Landing were awakened by a bold invasion by a boat's crew embracing Corporal Cocke, Thomas Martin, William Daniel, Alexander Dimitry and William Williams. Martin, an old seaman, was the virtual leader of the party, who stole into the midst of the vessels in a small boat and picked out for attack a large schooner, the *Louisa Rives*, of New York, loaded with army stores. The barking of a dog on the schooner revealed their approach, but they went ahead, although two gunboats were but a few hundred yards distant. Martin jumped upon the deck, followed by his comrades, and to prevent the captain from giving an alarm, they told him they had come to arrest him by orders of Gen. McClellan. Tumbling him into their boat, they set fire to the cabin, and as they pulled for the shore the schooner broke into flames and her crew saved themselves in her boats, while the gunboats slipped their cables and began a search for the party, who were by that time out of reach.

There was no cessation of the apprehensions of the correspondents of Northern papers that the *Merrimac No. 2* was coming out to engage the Federal fleet. On the night of July 29th, Gen. Pendleton, Chief of Artillery, C. S. A., brought several field batteries down to the shore between City Point and Drewry's Bluff, from which he shelled the Federal vessels, and under the supposition that the *Richmond* would make an attack under cover of this fire, the *Monitor*, *Galena* and the gunboats were hastily advanced to confront her. The 15th of Aug. was set as the day by which Flag-officer Wilkes was to reduce Drewry's Bluff and annihilate the Confederate squadron, but it passed without any demonstration on his part, and with the retirement of McClellan's army from Harrison's Landing comparative quiet was restored to the James River. The only addition made to the Confederate squadron meantime was the *Drewry*, Lieut. Com. W. H. Parker, a gunboat mounting one

large rifle gun at the bow, which was protected by an iron shield
in the form of a V. Com. French Forrest was placed in command of the squadron, which toward the close of the year consisted of the *Richmond, Patrick Henry, Nansemond, Hampton,
Beaufort, Raleigh* and *Drewry.* Two gunboats that were
being built on the Pamunkey River had been destroyed by the
Federals in May, and in November they burned another gunboat that was on the stocks in Mobjack Bay, Matthews Co.

The year 1863 was the quietest of the war upon the James
River. In July the Federal iron-clad fleet, which then comprised several monitors, hovered around Fort Drewry, but did
not open fire upon it. On August 4th the most important
event of the year upon the river occurred. Maj. Gen. Foster,
Brig. Gen. Nagle, Brig. Gen. Potter and their staffs started
from Fortress Monroe with a strong squadron for a reconnoissance of Fort Drewry. Their vessels were the monitor *Sangamon* and the gunboats *Commodore Barney* and *Cohasset.* Near
Varina, about five miles below Drewry's Bluff, they reached
a line of torpedoes that had been planted by Lieut. Hunter
Davidson, C. S. N., who had been placed in charge of this
branch of defence and had brought it to a state of remarkable
efficiency by his inventions and supervision. His torpedoes
were connected by wires with electric arrangements on shore
by which they could be exploded, and he, with one or more
of the members of his torpedo corps, would daily visit the
lines in the steam launch that had been set apart for his use
and see that charges, fuses and firing apparatus were in reliable working order. Despite, however, all his carefulness, on
this occasion the torpedoes failed to realize all that had been
expected of them. The *Sangamon* and the gunboats were close
upon the line of the machines when an attempt was made
from the shore to fire them. Only one exploded, and that was
nearly under the keel of the *Commodore Barney,* but a little
too far forward to exert its greatest force upon her. Her bow
was lifted high in the air, planking and timbers were torn
from her side, and she seemed to disappear in the commotion
of the waters, but by her violent careening so much heavy
material went overboard from her spar-deck that thus lightened she righted herself. Twenty of her crew were washed
off the deck, but all except two were rescued by boats from
the consort vessels. "This explosion," said Lieut. Davidson's
report of Aug. 6th, " panic-struck the enemy, as their shrieks
and cries could be heard a long distance, and effectually arrested their progress up the river, not one of their vessels passing our position at any time." There were 500 lbs. of powder in
the torpedoes, which Lieut. Davidson alludes to as being of
the tank pattern; and, perhaps not desiring to make any closer
acquaintance with others like it, Gen. Foster deferred until
a more auspicious hour his reconnoissance of Fort Drewry.
The squadron of observation put back down the river, and at

Deep Bottom, on the following day, steamed unawares within range of a Confederate artillery and infantry force masked behind the thick forest growth of the river bank. The already crippled *Commodore Barney* received a shell in her boiler, the engine of the *Cohasset* was damaged by a solid shot, and only the impenetrable turret-ship came out of the fight unscathed. "The officers don't want to try it over again," wrote a seaman of the *Barney* in a letter that found its way into print, "and I don't blame them."

The lethargy that prevailed on the James in 1863, gave way the next year to extreme military and naval activity, and from May, 1864, to the close of the war, momentous events succeeded each other in swift and stirring procession. In that month the Confederate squadron ready to resume belligerent operations was the most formidable of which the navy was possessed. There had been added to it the iron-clad *Virginia*, a vessel of the same type as her famous name-sake, minus the submerged ends; but plated with six inches of armor on the sides of her casemate, and eight inches on the ends. Her battery consisted of two 6-inch and two 8-inch Brooke rifled guns, so placed that three could be fired in broadside. Another recruit to the squadron was the iron-clad *Fredericksburg*, but she was a much weaker ship, having but four inches of armor. She also carried four guns, all 6-inch rifles. The iron-clad *Richmond* was still on duty, as were the gunboats previously mentioned as constituting the naval force in 1862. Com. John K. Mitchell relieved Capt. French Forrest in the command of the squadron; the *Virginia* was com-manded by Com. R. B. Pegram, the *Richmond* by Lieut. Com. W. H. Parker, and the *Fredericksburg* by Com. T. R. Rootes.[1]

On May 5th, 1864, Gen. B. F. Butler effected the transfer of the Federal army of the James from the York River to Bermuda Hundreds under the protection of four monitors, the iron-clad *Atlanta*, captured near Savannah, and seven gunboats. One duty assigned to the latter was the dragging of the river for torpedoes, but on the 6th the gunboat *Commodore Jones* rested near Four and a Half Mile Creek, directly over one of Lieut. Davidson's tank machines which was connected by a wire with a galvanic battery secreted in a pit on shore and operated by three of the subordinates of his corps. At the proper moment they transmitted the spark, the 400 pounds of powder which the machine contained exploded, and the enemy's ves-sel was literally blown into fragments. More than half her crew were killed or wounded by the concussion or were thrown into the river and drowned. Her total loss was stated to be 75 out of a ship's company of 120. Fifty were killed outright and the mangled portions of their bodies were mingled with the splinters of the vessel that thickly strewed the surface of

---

[1] Lieut. Com. Parker was for much of the time in command of the schoolship *Patrick Henry*, and was several times transferred from that vessel to the *Richmond*, and *vice versa*.

the water. On the next day the gunboat *Shawsheen* was destroyed in the same manner near Turkey Bend, and all of her people not killed were made prisoners.

The Federals obtained some recompense for these losses. When the *Commodore Jones* was destroyed, a boat from another gunboat put for the shore and there captured Acting Master P. W. Smith, C. S. N., and Jeffries Johnson, a private of the submarine battery service, who were in charge of the torpedoes. The captors at once examined them as to the location of other infernal machines, and while Master Smith courageously refused to betray his cause by giving the information which would enable the enemy to avoid them, Private Johnson is said by the report of the Federal fleet captain to have weakened when he was placed in the forward gunboat searching for torpedoes, and to have told all he knew concerning the points where they were laid down by Commander Davidson. From his revelations the Federals were enabled to take up a number of the explosive machines and make more rapid progress up the river. They found that each of the pits, in which a man was stationed to fire torpedoes, contained a simplified form of the Bunsen electric battery, from which insulated wires led under ground and under water to the tank that held the powder, and conducted the spark that fired the charge. Within a month the Federals moved twenty torpedoes from the river, one containing a charge of 1900 lbs. of powder. What destruction they might have caused but for the treachery of one man is beyond the bounds of speculation.

The movement of Butler's army to Bermuda Hundreds was made known at Drewry's Bluff on May 5th by messages from the Confederate signal men. It was seen that the post was in danger of an attack from the land side. Lieut. Col. Terrett of the marine corps was commander of the position, but in his temporary absence he was represented by Maj. Frank Smith. Com. Mitchell and Capt. Pegram were also away, and Capt. W. H. Parker was the senior officer on the river. Very few troops were at the fort, and Capt. Parker took on shore all the men that could be spared from the squadron and assisted Maj. Smith to man the inner line of defences, their force being too weak to hold the outer line. They sent dispatches to Gen. Lee and to Richmond asking for reinforcements, and remained in arms all night expecting an attack that they knew they were too feeble to resist. Gen. Bushrod Johnson arrived with his brigade at daylight, but was compelled to move in obedience to orders, and in the afternoon the alarm was given that the enemy were close at hand. Provisions and ammunition were thrown into the fort, and Capt. Pegram, who had returned to the Bluff, arrayed the squadron so that it might render all possible aid to the defence, but Butler never came. It was his one opportunity to capture Drewry's Bluff, which within the next twenty-four hours was

heavily reinforced. On the 16th Gen. Beauregard drove Butler back to Trent's Reach, and by erecting a strong battery at
the Howlett House held him in that safe position and obtained
an additional command of the river.

Torpedoes were attached to the bows of all the vessels of
the Confederate squadron now, and they were frequently
drilled with them. At the end of May the obstructions were
sufficiently removed to permit the vessels to pass through, and
they went through and anchored off Chapin's Bluff. An
engagement with the Federal fleet was immediately expected,
and on May 30th Admiral Lee, the Federal commander, sent
the following dispatch to Secretary Welles :

" A deserter from the rebel vessel-of-war *Hampton*, reports to-day that
the enemy have now below Drewry's Bluff three iron-clads, six small gunboats, plated with boiler-iron, each mounting two guns of 6-inch and 4-
inch bore, all fitted with torpedoes, and nine fire-ships, fitted with combustible material, with which they propose to attack the fleet in James
River, at as early a moment as practicable, by sending down their fire-
ships first, followed by the iron-clads and other vessels."

So impetuous a desire had been expressed by the Federal
authorities for an engagement between their fleet and the Confederate vessels, that it is impossible to underrate the surprise
felt when it became known that the Federals were obstructing the river at Trent's Reach, by sinking hulks in order to
prevent the Confederate squadron from coming down. The
official correspondence of Gen. Butler, Adm. Lee and Secretary
Welles, contained in the latter's report for 1864, irresistibly
establishes the conclusion that, if the Federal commanders
were anxious to try the gage of battle with Com. Mitchell's
squadron, their confidence in their ability to win a victory was
not shared by their superiors. Adm. Lee was informed early
in June that the passage of the river was to be barred, and on
the 7th he entered his protest to the Navy Department:

"The navy," he said, " is not accustomed to putting down obstructions
before it, and the act might be construed as implying an admission of
superiority of resources on the part of the enemy. The object of the
operation would be to make the river more secure against the attempts of
the enemy upon our vessels by fire and explosive rafts, followed by torpedoes and iron-clad vessels and boats. * * * Of course myself and officers
desire the opportunity of encountering the enemy, and feel reluctant to
discourage his approach. But the point of embarrassment with me is the
consequences that would follow a failure of the campaign should the novel
plan of the enemy succeed in crippling the monitor force."

Adm. Lee's object was to place the responsibility of obstructing the river entirely upon Gen. Butler, and thus acquit the
navy of erecting a barrier against an action with the Confederate squadron, but the wily military lawyer was altogether
too shrewd to permit the burden to be placed upon his
shoulders. On June 2d, he had written to the Admiral:

" I have no difficulty as to the point at which we desire to secure the
river. It is the right of my line near Curtis' house at the ravine, but
whether the river should be secured by obstructions or by vessels, or a

disposition of your obstructions or of the vessels of your navy, neither myself nor my engineers have any right to feel ourselves competent to give
our opinion. The vessels are wholly at your service, but upon your
judgment, not mine, must rest their use."

This clever strategy threw upon the Admiral the onus of
deciding whether he would rely upon the fighting qualities of
his fleet to protect the army lines, or whether he would resort
to obstructions for protection. He appealed the question to
Mr. Welles, but meanwhile gave Butler a non-commital
answer, in which he said :

"The first consideration with me is the necessity of holding this river
beyond a peradventure for the great military purposes of Gen. Grant and
yourself. In consulting my own desires, I would do everything to induce,
and nothing to prevent, the enemy from trying to assert their strength in
a pure naval contest, which in my opinion would give us a naval victory.
The only contingency of such a battle is the unknown effect of the novel
instruments of war—torpedo vessels—which are to be employed by them,
and which, as the attacking party, give them perhaps an advantage which
might possibly balance our certain superiority in all other fighting material."

This diplomatic fencing between the army and the navy
was brought to a termination by Gen. Grant himself. On
June 11th, Secretary Welles replied to Adm. Lee by declining
to decide the question of the obstructions and referring it
back to the discretion of the latter, but before Lee received
this answer Grant had been badly defeated at the battle of
Cold Harbor, and was rushing his army across to the south
side of the James. He did not elect to take the chances of the
Federal ships being driven out of the river by Com. Mitchell,
and he issued his peremptory orders that the hulks already
provided should be scuttled to form the obstructions on Trent's
Reach Bar. This was done, and when booms and cables were
stretched between them the river was closed. The navy was at
any rate saved from the discredit of voluntarily seeking protection from its antagonist, and Mr. Welles was allowed the latitude of boasting in his next annual report of what it might
have done if it had not been overruled.

The Federal fleet available for an engagement embraced
the first-class monitors *Saugus, Tecumseh, Canonicus* and *Onondaga*, mounting 11-inch and 15-inch guns, and 150-pounder
rifles, and some dozen of heavily-armed gunboats, while the
Confederate force that could be depended upon for effective
work was really limited to the three iron-clad rams and Davidson's torpedo-boat; but still Grant was not willing that
there should be a naval action, even with the odds so favorable
to the Federals. Until the obstructions were so far finished
as to make it evident that the enemy would not accept his
challenge to a combat Com. Mitchell remained near Trent's
Reach, and then withdrew to Drewry's Bluff. Loth, however,
to abandon all effort to disturb the enemy, he established a
naval battery on the hill at Howlett's House, from which, by
firing across the neck of land around which the river makes

one of the many great curves that intervene between City Point and Richmond, he might hope to reach the fleet in Trent's Reach. Manning this work with some of his seamen, his iron-clads were instructed to co-operate from a position on the north side of Dutch Gap, and the gunboats to remain close at hand for any assistance feasible for them to render. The *Virginia, Fredericksburg*, and the gunboats got into position on the morning of June 21st, but the *Richmond* was delayed in consequence of a wheel-rope parting, and fouling the propeller; and did not arrive at the scene of action until afternoon. The naval battery opened fire briskly upon the monitors at 10:30 A. M. and the squadron joined in the work, the vessels being concealed from the view of the Federals by the trees. It was an artillery duel at moderately long range that was not of serious effect to either party concerned. The monitor *Saugus* was struck once and the *Canonicus* twice by shot from the battery, but the damage was trifling; 229 projectiles were fired by the monitors, and the sole result was to silence one gun in the naval battery. Mitchell's vessels were not once struck, and the firing was discontinued at sunset.

The squadron was not again engaged until August 13th, when a portion of it participated in harassing the working parties on the canal which Gen. Butler was building at Dutch Gap for the purpose of opening a new route from below Howlett's Battery to the upper reach of the James River. From time to time the pick and shovel brigade on this useless project of the commander of the Federal army of the James had been shelled by the guns of the naval battery at Howlett's so severely that from a dozen to a score was the daily average of casualties among them; but on the 13th they were attacked with a more definite purpose. At 5 A. M. the *Virginia* and *Fredericksburg* opened fire from a position about a mile distant, while the *Richmond* and several of the gunboats dropped down to Cox's Reach, and with the battery on Signal Hill and at Howlett's took part in the cannonade. The Federal monitor *Saugus*, and the gunboats *Mackinaw* and *Delaware*, endeavored to protect the working parties by firing upon the Confederate vessels, but their fire was altogether unproductive of results. As the Confederate squadron was partially hidden from the enemy by a wooded bluff, the guns of the latter could only be aimed by directions from the masthead of the *Mackinaw*, and in fact were so elevated that it was only by chance that they could hit their mark. The *Virginia* was struck twice and the *Fredericksburg* once, but suffered no damage beyond the starting of a few bolts. They paid no attention to the enemy's vessels, but all day long maintained a slow and accurate fire upon the laborers in the canal, with the result, according to the Federal reports, of killing and wounding thirty men.

While a demonstration of this character seemed, standing alone, to be aimless, it was, in truth, an incident of the policy of annoying the Federals that produced beneficent consequences. It compelled the detention of a powerful iron-clad fleet in the James that might otherwise have been detached for operations against Southern ports, and it constantly troubled Gen. Grant concerning the security of his all-important line of communication by water. The authorities at Washington thought that the monitors could be withdrawn from the James for operations against Charleston or Fort Fisher, but when they proposed to strip Adm. Lee of this element of his force, his vigorous remonstrance was so energetically supported by Grant that the administration was obliged to recede from its purpose. "Whilst I believe," wrote Grant on June 9th to Lee, "we will never require the armored vessels to meet those of the enemy, I think it would be imprudent to withdraw them. * * * They stand a constant threat to the enemy, and prevent him taking the offensive. There is no disguising the fact that if the enemy should take the offensive on the water—although we would probably destroy his whole James River navy—such damage would be done our shipping and stores, all accumulated on the water near where the conflict would begin, that our victory would be dearly bought." Lee's reasoning was in accordance with that of Grant. He told Mr. Welles that the application of a few torpedoes would clear a passage through the barricade, and proposed the question: "What, if the draft of the rebel iron-clads allow them to pass the bar in Trent's Reach, would become of the communications of the army if our iron-clads were withdrawn?" They were not withdrawn, and the sleep of the General and the Admiral was not haunted by the spectre of Com. Mitchell's squadron sinking and burning the James River armada.

Making use of another period of inaction on the river, Acting Masters John Maxwell and Hines and three men from the squadron on Sept. 17th went into Warwick River with an open boat and captured the Federal schooner *Jane F. Durfee* and her officers and crew, numbering eight persons. The vessel was bonded and her people paroled. This exploit, successfully performed so far within the enemy's lines, reflected much credit upon those engaged in it.

The most severe test to which the squadron had been subjected was that which they experienced on October 22d, 1864, in an encounter with a new battery at the Boulware House on the left bank of the river, nearly two miles below Chapin's Bluff, and connecting with the fortification on Signal Hill. These works had been erected by the Federals since their capture of Fort Harrison on September 19th, and their armament included several 100-pounder Parrott rifles. They were masked until the morning of the engagement, when the forest growth in front of them was cut away and they were revealed within practicable range of the *Virginia, Richmond, Fredericksburg, Hampton* and *Drewry*, lying near Cox's Landing.

The small gunboats, which were not calculated to withstand the fire of the heavy Federal ordnance, moved out of their reach, not however before Lieut. Alexander's vessel, the *Drewry*, received a shell which struck one of her gun carriages, wounding two men severely and three slightly. Com. Mitchell, with his flag-ship, the *Virginia*, passed down to within 500 yards of the battery, signalling Capts. Maury and Rootes to follow with the *Richmond* and *Fredericksburg;* and for two hours they maintained so steady and well-directed a fire that the replies of the enemy grew slower and then nearly ceased, whereupon the squadron, which had almost exhausted their ammunition, returned toward Drewry's Bluff. It was admitted by the correspondents of Northern papers that the aim of the Confederate gunners was remarkably precise, shell after shell bursting in the earthen face of the battery and driving the men from their pieces. This being the first test of the resisting quality of the casemates of the ships under a close fire of heavy rifled guns, the result was of much practical importance and interest. It was encouraging except in the case of the *Fredericksburg*, the weakest of the three vessels. Capt. Rootes had gallantly exposed her to the sharpest of the enemy's fire, and as the Federal officers had acquired from deserters an acquaintance with the details of the several ships, their thickness of plating and weight of battery, it is rather more than conjecture that they intentionally hammered the *Fredericksburg* harder and more frequently than they did her stronger consorts. Her comparatively vulnerable casemate was struck several times, and although the wooden backing was not penetrated a few plates were started and bolt-heads knocked off ; yet there was no damage done that incapacitated her from continuing the battle, and she emerged from the ordeal in better trim than could have been expected. The only loss in men suffered was on this vessel, a shell that exploded immediately upon the grating of the roof of the casemate wounding seriously two and slightly four of her crew. With the *Virginia* it was demonstrated that her thick armor was proof against the 100-pound conical bolts from the enemy's rifles. She was hit by seven projectiles, no one of which did more than make a slight indentation in the six inches of iron. Not a bolt was started, and she came out of the engagement as tight and sound as when she went into it. Nearly the same thing may be said of the *Richmond*, except that she was more frequently struck and that her smokestack was shot away.

This affair offered the four Federal monitors an enticing opportunity to engage the Confederate squadron if their commanders were spoiling for a fight. As we have seen, Adm. Lee had already indicated that the obstructions on Trent's Reach bar could be removed, with little trouble or loss of time, sufficiently to make a gateway for the passage of vessels, and as the

47

nearest Confederate battery was 2,000 yards distant it could not have materially interfered with their working parties making the opening. Com. Mitchell, whom his associates in the old navy knew as an officer who would not have declined such an engagement, remained in the vicinity of Dutch Gap quite long enough to have permitted the monitors to come up to him, but they did not stir from their moorings. It is no impeachment of the courage of their officers that the vessels were held off; but it is another fragment of evidence that the supreme Federal authorities were cautiously averse to an honest fight with the Confederate ships. All through the autumn of 1864 the latter were most of the time below the obstructions at Drewry's Bluff and in the attitude of challenging the enemy to a combat that was never accepted, notwithstanding the asserted confidence of Gen. Grant and Adm. Lee that the Federals would be victors in a naval battle. The Admiral does, indeed, in his dispatches speak of the channels above Trent's Reach being too shallow for his vessels, but the monitors were of no deeper draft than the Confederate ironclads, and in the negro boatmen who had flocked to him he possessed as capable and skillful pilots as any on the river.

On Dec. 7th the *Richmond* again came down within a mile of Trent's Reach, the *Virginia* and *Fredericksburg* following, and challenged Fort Brady, a Federal work on the right bank of the James, to a shelling match. It was nearly sunset when the firing began, and it ceased with the approach of darkness. The *Richmond* was rapped on her casemate with a big rifle-bolt, but it did no harm, and none of the other ships were hit.

The closing naval event of the year upon the James and contingent waters was the disastrous Federal expedition to Rainbow Bluff, on the Roanoke River, on which occasion Lieut. Davidson's torpedo inventions made a flattering record for him. Five steamers composed the expedition, which on the evening of Dec. 9th came to anchor near Jamesville. The gunboat *Otsego*, fitted with a torpedo catcher, was exploring for infernal machines, but she failed to detect two that exploded directly under her and blew her whole bottom out. On the next day the gunboat *Bazely* was also sunk by a torpedo, and the river was found to be so full of them that the flotilla, now reduced to three vessels, fell back with all the speed that it could make. On the way out of the river the steamers were attacked by sharp-shooters from the shore and almost disabled before they reached the James. Some twenty men were lost by the torpedo explosions and the fire of the sharp-shooters.

We are nearing the *finale* of the James River squadron, but before it shared in the fate which overtook the Confederate States its ships and its men were to do their part in the heroic struggles of the perishing Confederacy. The gloom that overspread the South when the dawn of 1865 introduced the ultimate months of the war was nowhere darker than over the horizon of Richmond, and with the ponderous weight of Grant's armies pressing upon the enfeebled lines of Lee, military resistance was fast giving way. Yet one hope remained —that if the squadron could pass down the James, it might disperse the Federal fleet at City Point and there destroy Grant's base of supplies; Gen. Lee's veterans might pursue this advantage by an attack in mass upon the military lines that were being tightened around Richmond and even break them at any important points—that if all this could be accomplished the throttling grasp of the enemy would be shaken off, the capital would be relieved and new strength gained for the further struggle. It was the mission of the navy to begin the execution of this bold and brilliant programme, which had been planned in conferences between Flag-officer Mitchell and Gen. Lee. To the unflinching spirit of Mitchell, chafing at the forced inaction of his ships, it came as the most welcome incident of his career upon the James.

The circumstances that prevailed in the third week of January seemed to be a harbinger of success. Their suspicions of a naval raid from the direction of Richmond lulled by their confidence in the security of the obstructions, which had been planted with torpedoes, the Federals had sent to the attack on Fort Fisher all their monitors except the *Onondaga*, or Quintard battery, as it was sometimes called, a powerful double-turret vessel, mounting two 15-inch guns, and two very heavy rifles ; but for all her formidable character she could scarcely be forced into a fight, as the sequel showed. A flood in the river was awaited to afford the *Virginia* plenty of water in which to manœuvre, and the outlooks were instructed to report the indications of a freshet, which, it was believed, might wash out the Federal booms stretched across Trent's Reach. The high water came on January 22d, and all day the ice was running out in great fields and hummocks. That night Lieut. C. W. Read, in command of naval Battery Wood, sent Master's Mate Billups and two men down the river in a dug-out to examine the obstructions, and received from Billups the report that, after carefully sounding, he had ascertained that for a width of 80 feet there was a depth of 14 feet through the obstructions, which were only closed by a large spar lying diagonally across the entrance. Read went at once to Gen. Pickett's headquarters and reported the result of the observations. Gen. Pickett directed him to hasten to Petersburg and advise Gen. Lee. Gen Lee asked him if he thought the channel sufficiently wide and deep to admit the passage of the Confederate iron-clads. He replied that he had no doubt of it, and that at any rate it might be tried. Gen. Lee ordered him to go at once to the Secretary of the Navy and ask that the iron-clads be sent down that night. He rode as fast as possible to Richmond, and went to see Mr. Mallory and explain everything to him. Without the least hesitation the latter wrote an order to

Flag-officer Mitchell, directing him to move as soon as possible if he deemed it practicable.

Lieut. Read delivered the orders to Com. Mitchell at 3 P. M. of the 23d, and the commanders of the iron-clads were promptly directed to prepare for the movement. They were Lieut Dunnington, of the flag-ship *Virginia*; Lieut. Kell, of the *Richmond*, and Lieut. Sheppard of the *Fredericksburg*. The remainder of the squadron comprised the gunboat *Drewry*, the torpedo boat *Torpedo*, and the torpedo launches *Scorpion*, *Wasp* and *Hornet*, as it was contemplated that torpedoes should be employed against the Federal vessels. Capt. Read was placed in command of the launches. His narrative of the expedition says :

"Just after dark we got under way and proceeded down the river, the wooden gunboats and the torpedo-boats being placed on the starboard side of the iron-clads. The night was dark and very cold. We passed three or four miles in range of the enemy's batteries and were not discerned, the Federal pickets being all under cover in their rifle-pits around the fires. When we arrived near the obstructions, Capt. Mitchell brought the fleet to anchor. He then went in the *Scorpion*, with Flag Lieut. Graves and myself. We went down and sounded through the obstructions, which verified the report that Billups had made. While we were sounding, the Federal picket boat discerned us and gave the alarm. As the enemy occupied both banks, a heavy fire of big guns, field-pieces and musketry was opened on us, and a perfect rain of missiles swept over our heads. Capt. Mitchell was the coolest man under fire that I ever saw ; he stood by the man at the lead, and was not satisfied until soundings had been made many times across the gap in the obstructions. The spar that was lying diagonally across above the opening of the obstructions, was anchored at each end. A few licks with a cold chisel set it adrift. We then went on board the *Fredericksburg*, which was the lightest draft of the iron-clads. Capt. Mitchell ordered Sheppard to get under weigh, which was soon done, and Capt. Mitchell himself took the ship through the obstructions. He then returned to the *Virginia* in the *Scorpion*. When we went on board the *Virginia*, we found that she had been anchored too close to the north shore and had grounded. The *Richmond* was in the same condition. The tugs were pulling at those two ships, but could not move them. The firing from the southern shore was now tremendous and much more accurate than at first. The Confederate batteries had opened all along the line. About 4 o'clock next morning Capt. Mitchell sent me down in the *Scorpion* with orders to the *Fredericksburg* to return. I found Sheppard about a mile below the obstructions, and piloted the ship up the river and anchored her close by the iron-clads aground near the Confederate battery at the Howlett House."

The grounding of the *Virginia* and *Richmond* was the virtual collapse of the enterprise, the successful consummation of which was balanced upon a quick dash upon the enemy and a surprise. While Mitchell was on his way to the *Fredericksburg* Lieut. Sheppard, puzzled to account for the failure of the other ships to follow him through the obstructions, had sent Master E. T. Eggleston to look for them, but before the latter found them the flag-officer had communicated with the *Fredericksburg* and ordered her return, as stated by Lieut. Read.

The break of day disclosed the Confederate squadron reassembled in Trent's Reach directly under the guns of Fort Parsons, which opened upon them a tremendous fire from rifled guns and mortars. Shortly a shell pierced the *Drewry* and shattered her, but her people had been just previously removed to another vessel. Next the torpedo launch *Wasp* was smashed by a shot, and the other wooden steamers took shelter under a bank where the missiles could not reach them. Several projectiles struck the iron-clads, but did not pierce their armor or at all impair their fighting capacity. But a more dangerous enemy was at hand. The monitor *Onondaga*, which had at first retired down the river upon discovery at daylight of the proximity of Mitchell's squadron, came up again at nine o'clock, and brought her 15-inch guns to bear on the *Virginia* and *Richmond*, which were still helplessly grounded.[1]

They endeavored to reply, but their batteries could not be worked from the embarrassing position in which they were situated, and when the port shutters were opened to allow a gun to be run out the musketry fire from the Federal infantry on the high land of the right bank of the river was so fierce as to prevent any accurate aim. The same cause interfered with the gunners of the *Fredericksburg*, and the small number of shots which they succeeded in discharging passed ineffectively by the *Onondaga*. Her position was on the broadside of the *Virginia*, and she planted a 15-inch solid shot squarely above the after-port of the flag-ship, knocking a clear hole through her armor and wood backing and sending in a whirl along the gun-deck huge iron fragments and wooden splinters that killed six and wounded fourteen of the crew. Luckily she was floated by the rising of the tide and moved out of the range of shot that would pierce any armor then placed on a ship. The *Richmond* got off at the same time. She had been less exposed than the flag-ship and was not injured.

Flag-officer Mitchell summoned a council on board the *Virginia*, of the commanders of vessels, at noon. Lieut. Read states, as he was the junior, his opinion was asked first. He advised an immediate attack on the *Onondaga*, while the squadron had the advantage of daylight for passing through the obstructions, and for striking her with the torpedoes, and trying the effect of steel-pointed shot upon her turrets. The opinions of the other officers were divided, some preferring to wait until after dark; but the decision was to resume hostilities at 9 P. M., at which time the *Virginia* headed down the stream with the *Scorpion* on her port side, followed by the *Richmond* and *Hornet*, and the *Fredericksburg* in the rear. As the squadron arrived opposite the Point of Rocks, a bold bluff half a mile above Trent's Reach Bar, a blazing

[1] Capt. Parker, of the *Onondaga*, was tried by court-martial on the charges of keeping out of this danger, to which he should have exposed himself and failing to do his utmost to overtake and capture or destroy a vessel of the enemy. His defence was that he only retired down the river to obtain room in which to work his ship, but he was found guilty and sentenced to be dismissed from the navy of the United States. Secretary Welles disapproved the sentence on the ground of technical irregularity in the findings of the court, but Capt. Parker was relieved of his command and placed on the retired list.

calcium light that threw a broad glare over the river was turned upon them from a Federal battery, and simultaneously the forts broke the murky night with the flashes of scores of guns trained upon the channel. The pilot who was conning the *Virginia* from the roof of her casemate lost control of himself and rushed for the comparative safety of the pilot-house. Once there, he declared that it was impossible to steer the ship from the small eye-holes in the house, and that he could not have from them a broad enough field of vision to take her through the obstructions. The expedition had reached its end. Com. Mitchell gave the signal for retreat, and in a few hours the squadron was at anchor near Chapin's Bluff.

The Federals strengthened the obstructions in the river after this episode, and added two monitors to the fleet as a safeguard against another such raid. It was the expiring effort of the Confederate squadron that had just been frustrated by untoward influences not to be foreseen or averted, but the withdrawal of the ships was not accepted by some sternly venturesome spirits among their officers as the finality of all projects for assailing the enemy upon the water. Torpedo operations were still possible; and by the use of this favorite weapon, which in the Confederacy had been developed to a state of efficiency previously unknown to the world, the clutch of the enemy might be shaken off where it bore hardest.

On the morning of February 10th, 1865, a party of about 100 officers and men in the uniform of the C. S. navy assembled for inspection at Drewry's Bluff. The weather was bitterly cold, and as the arms and equipments were inspected it was easily seen that serious work and imminent peril were to be encountered by the close attention given to the examination of weapons, and the expression of the men, who, in those stirring times, were familiar with danger and hardships. The detachment was under the command of Lieut. C. W. Read, and the other officers were Lieut. W. H. Ward, Master W. F. Shippey, Passed Mipshipmen Scott and Williamson, all of the navy, and Lieut. of Marines Crenshaw. Lieut. Read had organized the expedition, which embraced ninety seamen and marines, which was to effect in one way what the squadron had failed to do in another—to gain possession of the river and compel Grant to abandon his position at City Point. The details of the plan were to carry torpedo-boats on wheels to a point beyond the Federal left wing, near Petersburg,[1] cross the Blackwater River, launch the boats upon the James, below City Point, capture any passing tugs or river steamers, fix the torpedoes to them, ascend the river and blow up the monitors. These destroyed and the obstructions removed, the Confederate

---

[1] "A Leaf from My Log-Book." Master W. F. Shippey, C. S. N. Southern Historical Society Papers, Volume XII., 1884, pages 416-421.

iron-clads could make short work of the wooden gun-boats, and the James would be open from Richmond to Hampton Roads. Master Shippey, the only chronicler of the expedition, has told how it was conducted, and why it failed. His narrative runs thus:

"The boats were placed in chocks on four wagon-wheels, torpedoes, poles and gear inside, and each drawn by four mules. One Lewis, a volunteer officer of the navy, had been sent ahead to reconnoitre, and was to meet us at the ford of the Blackwater and pilot us to the James. How he fulfilled his engagement will be shown in the sequel. This man Lewis was mate of an American ship lying in Norfolk harbor at the time of the secession of Virginia, and had left his ship to join the Confederates, had served faithfully in the army, been wounded at Bull Run, transferred to the navy and commissioned as acting lieutenant, and was considered worthy of trust and confidence.

"Our first day's march brought us to Gen. Anderson's headquarters, the right of our army, where we encamped that night, and, breaking camp early the following morning, we struck out from our picket line to gain the old Jerusalem plank road. Our march was in three detachments, the advance under Read and Ward, about one hundred yards ahead of the wagon train; Crenshaw, with his marines, about the same distance in rear of them, and Shippey commanding the centre, with the wagon train. Fortunately, we met no stragglers or foraging parties of the enemy, and were not disturbed, and after a good day's march we bivouacked in good spirits and very tired. The following day's march was without incident worthy of mention, an occasional false alarm or seeking the cover of woods to screen us from chance observers. Indeed, we were out of the line of travel; the Federals did all their business at City Point, and there was little more to attract any one to this part of the country than to the Siberian deserts.

"During the night the weather turned very cold, and our poor, tired fellows lay close to the fires. The following morning we took up our march in the face of a storm of sleet, and we had to stop after a few hours, the sleet being so blinding that our mules could not make headway, besides the road being frozen and slippery. We took shelter in an old deserted farmhouse only a few miles from our rendezvous on the Blackwater, once, doubtless, the happy home of some Southern family, now changed into the rude scenes of a soldiers' bivouac.

"While resting and 'thawing' out here by the warmth of bright fires in big fireplaces, impatiently awaiting the breaking up of the storm and anxious to continue our journey, a young man in gray uniform came in and informed us that our plan had been betrayed, and that Lewis was at the ford to meet us, according to promise, but accompanied by a regiment of Federals lying in ambuscade and awaiting our arrival, when they were to give us a warm reception. Had it not been for the storm and our having to take shelter, we would have marched into the net spread for us, and most likely all have been killed, or suffered such other *worse* punishment as a court-martial should inflict.

"This young man had been a prisoner of war at Fortress Monroe, and from his window heard the conversation between Lewis and the Yankee officer, in which the former betrayed us, and the plan to capture the whole party, and having perfected his plans of escape, resolved to put them in execution that night, and, if possible, frustrate his designs by giving us information of his treachery.

"After a hurried council of war, it was decided that we should go back about a mile and find a hiding place in the woods, efface our tracks, and remain concealed, while Lieut. Read should make a reconnoissance to satisfy himself that things were as bad as had been reported, and if, indeed, we would have to return to Richmond without accomplishing our object. Accordingly, we hitched up and filed out into the road and took it back, and when we thought we had gone a safe distance, turned into the woods and camped, Read taking leave of us, disguised, and saying he would rejoin us the next day, when if he did not by sunset we were to conclude he was captured and make our way back to Richmond. The night passed drearily away, the weather being very cold and we afraid to make fires for fear of exposing our situation should they be already on the hunt for us, as we had no doubt they would be as soon as they discovered we were not going into their trap; and the following day, though but a short winter one, seemed endless, so great was our anxiety for our leader, who had thrust his head into the lion's jaws. At length, about 4 P. M., Read made his appearance in camp, cool and collected as ever, and told us that what we had heard was true, and gave orders to hitch up, form line and retreat. The enemy's cavalry was already scouring the country in search of us, and every road of retreat was guarded. We marched by night, avoiding main roads, and during the following day halted and concealed ourselves in the woods.

"Headed off at one turn, we took another and pursued our way, resolved to sell our lives dearly should the enemy fall upon us. Every path now seemed guarded, and our retreat apparently cut off, when an old gentleman in citizen's clothes and a 'stove-pipe' hat on, who had joined us as guide, determined to take us through the water of the Appomattox, and thus 'take soundings' on them. There was a horseshoe bend in the river, which, by fording, we could pass through between their pickets and reach our picket-lines. This was decided upon, and our guide marched us to the ford. It was not a pleasant prospect, that of taking water with the thermometer hanging around freezing point, but it was better than falling in the hands of Yankees, so of the two evils we choose the least. My teeth chatter yet to think of that cold wade through water waist deep, covered with a thin coat of ice, but we passed it successfully, wagons and all, and then double-quicked to keep from freezing ; our clothes freezing stiff on us as we came out of the water.

"We had now the inside track of our pursuers, and leaving them waiting for us to march up one of the many roads they had so well guarded, made our way back towards our lines, which we reached safely, without loss of a man, wagon or mule.

"The results accomplished by this expedition were nothing, but I thought it worthy of a place in history, because of the effort. Our flag waved in the James River two months after the events I have endeavored to describe, but of the hundred and one men who composed this expedition, fully seventy-five were in the naval hospital in Richmond, suffering from the effects of their winter march, on the sad day on which we turned our backs upon that city."

Rear Adm. Semmes was appointed to the command of the James River squadron, and entered upon his duties on the 18th of February, 1865. As reorganized, the vessels and their commanders were the *Virginia*, Capt. Dunnington; *Richmond*, Capt. Johnson; *Fredericksburg*, Capt. Glassel; *Hampton*, Capt. Wilson; *Nansemond*, Capt. Butt; *Roanoke*, Capt. Pollock; *Beaufort*, Capt. Wyatt; *Torpedo*, Capt. Roberts. The squadron was not heavily manned, many of its officers and men having been detached to the naval brigade, which, under command of Com. John Randolph Tucker, was distributed in the fortifications on Drewry's Bluff and in Battery Brooke, Battery Wood and Battery Semmes.

Accustomed to the rigid discipline of the navy which he had enforced on the *Alabama*, Semmes was not prepossessed by the condition in which he found the squadron, although he could not but recognize that it was an unavoidable consequence of the foreshadowed triumph of the Federals. The *personnel* of the crews had lost its distinctive naval character, and with the exception of the principal officers and about half a dozen sailors in each ship, the men were drawn from the army. Demoralization prevailed and desertions were frequent.

"Sometimes [the Admiral wrote], an entire boat's crew would run off, leaving the officer to find his way on board the best he might. The strain upon them had been too great. It was scarcely to be expected of men, of the class of those who usually form the rank and file of ships' companies, that they would rise above their natures, and sacrifice themselves by slow but sure degrees, in any cause, however holy. The visions of home and fireside, and freedom from restraint, were too tempting to be resisted. The general understanding, that the collapse of the Confederacy was at hand, had its influence with some of the more honorable of them. They reasoned that their desertion would be but an anticipation of the event by a few weeks."[1]

The evacuation of Charleston and Wilmington and the destruction of Confederate vessels at those places, released three hundred officers and men of the navy, who were ordered to duty at Richmond and assigned to the batteries near Drewry's Bluff. With this addition the naval brigade became a large and important force, and the familiarity of its men with the handling of great guns was apparent in the bombardments that were the most common occurrences on the lines around Richmond during Feb. and March, 1865.[2] The men were also organized into companies by the commanding officer, Com. Tucker, and drilled as infantry. Among the officers on duty with the brigade at the time were Capt. T. T. Hunter, Lieuts. W. G. Dozier, Clarence L. Stanton, M. M. Benton,[3] W. H. Ward, F. N. Roby, D. M. Trigg, C. R. Mayo, W. L. Bradford, Gwathmey, Marmaduke and Gardner; Lieut. of Marines A. S. Berry, Master's Mate Charles Hunter, and a large contingent of midshipmen. The same causes which had sent these many seamen and their officers from the Southern ports to Richmond had also multiplied the Federal naval force in the

[1] "Memoirs of Service Afloat."

[2] Lieut. W. H. Murdaugh writes: "The last time I saw Gen. Lee was in the Office of Detail in the Navy Department at Richmond. He came in from the Secretary's office, and in replying to a question from Com Forrest and Lieut. Arthur Sinclair, whether they could do anything for him," he replied: "You can do a great deal, I want navy officers, they are the best heavy artillerists we have. I went to see the President last night to ask for them, and I have just come from the Secretary of the Navy to whom I made the same request."

[3] Mortimer Murray Benton was born at Covington, Ky., Feb. 18th, 1841, and entered the U. S. navy as midshipman at the naval academy at Annapolis in Sept. 1858. In April, 1860, he resigned, and in June, 1861, was appointed lieut. of engineers in the Ky. State Guard. Feb. 1862, he received a commission as midshipman in the C. S. navy, and was ordered to the gunboat *Gaines* at Mobile. After passing an examination he was promoted to be master and assigned to service on the captured ship *Harriet Lane* at Galveston; thence to the *Webb* at Shreveport, La., and thence to duty at Richmond in Nov. 1863; but in passing through Mobile he was detained by Adm. Buchanan and placed in charge of equipping the *Tennessee*. He was commissioned as lieutenant in 1863, and in May, 1864, was assigned to command of the gunboat *Raleigh* of the James River squadron. In July he and his crew participated in the Point Lookout expedition. He next served on the *Tallahassee*, and then in torpedo operations at Charleston. On the evacuation of that city he was ordered to Drewry's Bluff, commanded a company of the naval brigade and was made prisoner at the battle of Saylor's Creek. In 1869 he was ordained deacon, and the next year priest, of the Protestant Episcopal Church, and is now (1887) rector of the Parish of the Advent, Louisville.

James, where had been concentrated the most of the vessels that were previously engaged in operations on the coasts of North and South Carolina. The assembling of this imposing and mighty fleet seemed to forbode an attack upon the capital by water, but as Adm. Semmes says, Richmond was secure on that side. No fleet of the enemy could have passed his three iron-clads moored across the stream in the only available channel, with obstructions that would hold it under the fire of the ships and the flanking batteries; and if Adm. Porter, the new commander upon the river, ever thought of such a movement he never attempted it. The remainder of the winter passed slowly and tediously into the spring, and Semmes' visits to the Navy Department for instructions or suggestions from the government resulted merely in permission to him to do about as he pleased. It may be presumed that if the restless and intrepid sailor who carried the *Alabama* into a dozen seas had found any employment for the James River squadron the barnacles would not have gathered upon his hulls, but the opportunities for action were numbered with the past. He has himself told how, as he sat in his cabin, on board the *Virginia*, in March, and studied upon the maps the approach of Sherman, and knew of the reinforcement of Grant by the army of Sheridan, the prospect was to him hopeless enough. Richmond was invested by 160,000 men, and Lee defended it with 33,000 ragged and half-starved troops, with which he was compelled to guard an intrenched line of 40 miles in length, extending from the north side of the James River, below Richmond, to Hatcher's Run, south of Petersburg. In all military history there is recorded no more stubborn and skillful defence of a beleaguered city, but it could not last much longer. The fate of Richmond was decided on the morning of April 2d, when Grant broke through the Confederate lines at Petersburg. Adm. Semmes was at dinner on the *Virginia* that afternoon when he received this message from the Navy Department:

"CONFEDERATE STATES OF AMERICA, }
"EXECUTIVE OFFICE, RICHMOND, VA., April 2d, 1865. }
"REAR ADMIRAL RAPHAEL SEMMES, *Commanding James River Squadron:*
"SIR : Gen. Lee advises the government to withdraw from this city, and the officers will leave this evening, accordingly. I presume that Gen. Lee has advised you of this and of his movements, and made suggestions as to the disposition to be made of your squadron. He withdraws upon his lines toward Danville this night ; and unless otherwise directed by Gen. Lee, upon you is devolved the duty of destroying your ships this night, and with all the forces under your command joining Gen. Lee. Confer with him, if practicable, before destroying them. Let your people be rationed, as far as possible, for the march, and armed and equipped for duty in the field. Very respectfully, your obedient servant,
"S. R. MALLORY, *Secretary of the Navy.*"

The enemy being only a few miles distant it was imperative that the Admiral should conduct his movements with careful secrecy. At nightfall he got the squadron under way and ran up to Drewry's Bluff, intending to blow up the iron-clads there, throw their crews on the wooden gunboats, and proceed in the latter to Manchester, opposite Richmond, on his way to join Gen. Lee. But these plans he was compelled to change when, an hour or two after dark, the flames that lit up the horizon on the north side of the James revealed to him that the army was burning its quarters as it left the intrench-ments. Concealment on his part was no longer practicable. He made his preparations for burning the fleet, first serving out arms, provisions and clothing to the men who were to ex-change the decks for the shore. The various occupations occupied them until a late hour. It was between two and three o'clock on the morning of April 3d before the crews of the iron-clads were all safely embarked on the wooden gun-boats and the iron-clads were well on fire. The little squadron of wooden boats then moved off up the river by the glare of the burning iron-clads. "They had not proceeded far before an explosion like the shock of an earthquake took place, and the air was filled with missiles. It was the blowing up of the *Virginia*, the late flag-ship. The spectacle was grand beyond description. Her shell-rooms had been full of loaded shells. The explosion of the magazine threw all these shells, with their fuses lighted, into the air. The fuses were of different lengths, and as the shells exploded by twos and threes, and by the dozen, the pyrotechnic effect was very fine. The ex-plosion shook the houses in Richmond and waked the echoes of the night for forty miles around."

At one of the bridges across the James the boats were de-tained until after sunrise on account of the draw being down to allow of the passage of troops. Then the Admiral landed his 500 sailors in the midst of the troops and civilians hurrying away from the forsaken city. The wooden gunboats were fired and, wrapped in flames, floated down the stream, while he asked himself what he was to do with his seamen, loaded down with pots and pans, mess-kettles, bags of bread, chunks of salted pork, sugar, tea, tobacco and pipes. His orders were to join Gen. Lee, but he did not know where to find him, he was without transportation, and it was as much as his men could do to stagger under their loads. Fortunately, he found at the railroad depot a small locomotive and some cars, and the steam engineers from the squadron soon had the former in running condition and a train made up ; but while still directly opposite Richmond the engine stuck on an up-grade ; it was not strong enough to pull the train. Another locomo-tive was discovered in the railroad shops, and after it was hitched on the two drew the train off at the rate of six miles an hour. It reached at midnight of April 4th the city of Dan-ville, having passed Burksville Junction an hour and a half before Sheridan's cavalry tore up the rails. Here the Admiral found President Davis and Secretary Mallory, who ordered him to form his command as a brigade of artillery for the occupation of the defences around Danville, his own rank to be that of brigadier general. He arranged with Capt. Sidney Smith Lee and Adjt. Gen. Cooper for the transformation of his sailors into soldiers. Only 400 men were left him, but these he broke in two skeleton regiments, appointing Capts. Dunnington and Johnston their colonels. Midshipman Semmes was assigned to a position on the staff; Mr. Daniel, the Admiral's secretary, became the other aide, and Capt. Rutt was appointed Assistant Adjutant General. Admiral Semmes writes:

" We remained in the trenches before Danville ten days ; and anxious and weary days they were. Raiding parties were careering around us in various directions, robbing and maltreating the inhabitants, but none of the thieves ventured within reach of our guns. Lee abandoned his lines on the 3d of April, and surrendered his army, or the small remnant that was left of it, to Grant, on the 9th, at Appomattox Court-House. The first news we received of his surrender came to us from the stream of fugitives which now came pressing into our lines at Danville. It was heart-rending to look upon these men, some on foot, some on horseback, some nearly famished for want of food, and others barely able to totter along from disease. It was, indeed, a rabble rout. Hopes had been entertained that Lee might escape to Lynchburg, or to Danville, and save his army. The President had entertained this hope, and had issued a proclamation of encouragement to the people before he left Danville. But the fatal tidings came at last, and when they did come we all felt that the fate of the Confederacy was sealed."

These fatal tidings were the melting away of Gen. Johnston's army and its dispersion in accordance with the terms arranged between that commander and Gen. Sherman at Greensboro' on May 1st. This agreement included the admiral's command, which he dispersed on the same day.

While the flag-officer afloat was making his way out of Richmond and to Danville, as just described, with the men of the squadron, Com. Tucker's naval brigade evacuated the positions at Drewry's Bluff on April 2d, and was attached to Gen. Custis Lee's division of Gen. Ewell's corps, which formed the rear-guard of the Confederate army on the retreat from Richmond. It was the post of danger, and never in any of the great emergencies of the war did the sailors win brighter renown than during this perilous march and at the battle of Saylor's Creek. From the 2d to the 6th of April they were allowed no rest and were without food; the spring rains and the passage of troops, wagons and artillery had mired the roads knee-deep; clouds of the enemy's cavalry hovered around them and swooped down upon their flanks; but they tramped on, maintained a compact organization and responded quickly to the orders of commanders. Upon no portion of the dwindling army did the sufferings of the retreat fall heavier than upon this little plucky band, and none bore them with more fortitude. The story of their conduct at Saylor's Creek is an illustrious ending of their history.

That last of the great battles of the war was fought on April 6th. Ewell's depleted ranks were enveloped by the masses of Sheridan's infantry and cavalry, and came to a stand at the creek for their final resistance to the overwhelming thousands of the enemy. The naval brigade held the right of the line, where it repulsed two assaults of cavalry and one of infantry with its firm formation and rapid, steady fire, the Federals splitting on its front and going to the right and left of it. In one of the dashes of the cavalry, Gen Ewell and his staff were captured, and he passed the order of surrender to his troops, whose line, except that held by the sailors, had been pierced by the Federal charges. The naval brigade and 200 marines, under command of Maj. Simmons, were holding precisely the same position then which had been assigned them in the morning. Com. Tucker was informed that Ewell had ordered a surrender, but refused to believe it. The brigades of infantry on either side of him had ceased firing, but with the remark, "I can't surrender," he ordered his men to continue the engagement. Gen. Wright, the commander of the Federal Sixth corps, had directed the fire of a dozen batteries upon him, and a mass of cavalry were making ready to ride him down, when he was informed for the second time, by Lieut. Clarence L. Stanton, C. S. N., who was on staff duty, of the surrender, and he followed the example of the infantry. He had continued the fighting fifteen minutes after they had lowered their arms, and the naval colors were the last to be laid down. The bravery of the sailors was observed along the Federal lines, and when they did surrender the enemy cheered them long and vigorously.[1]

The salutations of the foe to the men who "didn't know when to surrender," brought to a close the history of the navy of the Confederate States upon the waters of Virginia. Unconsciously, Com. Tucker and his three hundred sailors had emphasized with a force beyond the limitations of language to convey, the part which this branch of the service had borne through the years when Virginia was the great fighting ground of the war. They had given the final proof of the strength of the convictions which enrolled them under the Southern colors, and of their unswerving fidelity in the painful hour of irresistible disaster. They had sought every opportunity to fire a shot or strike a blow for the liberties of their States ; they had unflinchingly obeyed orders leading them into combat against outnumbering enemies ; and from they day when the *Virginia* swept Hampton Roads to that upon which they stood in embattled line at Saylor's Creek they made an unsmirched record as hard and honest fighters, obedient subordinates and loyal patriots.

---

[1] Capt. W. H. Parker says in his "Recollections of a Naval Officer," that Com. Tucker told him afterwards that he had never been in a land battle before, and supposed that everything was going on well. Some years after the war Lieut. Mayo, then in command of a Chesapeake Bay steamer, had Gen. Wright as a passenger and recalled to his memory the battle of Saylor's Creek. Wright said he remembered with what obstinacy one portion of the Confederate line had been held, and could not account for it until he found that it had been held by sailors who did not know when they were whipped.

CHAPTER XXIII.

THE TORPEDO SERVICE.

ON July 7th, 1861, occurred the earliest instance of the use of torpedoes in the war between the States, in an attempt to destroy an enemy's vessel. The effort was directed against the Federal squadron in the Potomac River at Aquia Creek, the torpedoes consisting of oil casks which buoyed cylinders of boiler-iron containing the explosive material. Fuses led from the casks into the cylinders, and each pair of casks was connected by a rope in order that, going down stream with the tide, they would bring up against the bows of an enemy's ship, the cylinders would swing against her side and the explosion would take place. The apparatus was sent down by the Confederates on the ebb tide, but being observed from the squadron, a boat's crew extinguished the fuses and it was harmlessly secured. In the latter part of July the Federals found adrift in Hampton Roads a barrel of powder so arranged with a floating line, that if the line fouled the anchor chains or the wheel of a ship it would fire a percussion cap placed upon the powder. This was probably the invention of some Confederate at the Norfolk navy-yard, and had been rendered innocuous by the leakage of the barrel.

Subaqueous and subterranean infernal machines came into use about the same time. During January, 1862, in some experiments on the Mississippi River with a submarine torpedo, the Confederates blew up an immense flat-boat " so high that only a few splinters were heard from; " and on entering Columbus, Ky., in March, the Federals found pear-shaped iron casks three feet long, and half as much in diameter, filled with grape, canister and powder, buried in mines under the river bank, and having an electric firing arrangement communicating with stations in the town. Other torpedoes (called the pronged torpedoes), were picked up in the river. On February 13th, 1862, the U. S. gunboat *Pembina* discovered in the Savannah River, near the mouth of the Wright River, a battery of five tin-can torpedoes anchored by grapnels and

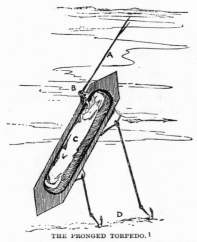

THE PRONGED TORPEDO.[1]

connected with wires, which by the tension exerted upon them by the contact of a passing vessel would fire friction tubes (cannon primers) inserted in the head of each powder chamber. One of these machines was exploded that night when a convoy of artillery was but 200 yards distant, and this induced the Federal commander to suspect that some of them were connected by galvanic wires with Fort Pulaski. Torpedoes of this description were placed in large numbers in the rivers along the Southern coast. Another pattern was the "frame torpedo," which so seriously delayed Burnside's progress up the Neuse River, in March 1862, and was used in narrow channels both for obstruction and destruction. They were thus described:

"Three heavy pieces of timber, placed in the position, at the bottom of which was placed a box filled with old iron, stones and other heavy materials, was sunk in the river, and then inclined forward at an angle of forty-five degrees by means of ropes and weights. This heavy frame was capped by a cylinder of iron, about ten inches in diameter. Into this was fitted a shell, which was heavily loaded, resting on a set of springs, so arranged that the least pressure on the cylinder would instantly discharge the shell by means of a percussion cap ingeniously placed."

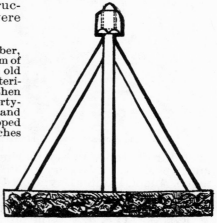

A FRAME TORPEDO.

A FRAME TORPEDO.

[1] A, iron rod armed with prongs to fasten upon bottom of boats going up-stream and act upon B, a lever connecting with trigger to explode a cap and ignite powder. C, canvas bag containing 70 lbs. powder. D, anchors to hold torpedo in place.

This torpedo consisted of a stout sheet-iron cylinder, pointed at both ends, about 5½ feet long and 1 foot diameter. The iron lever was 3½ feet long, and armed with prongs to catch in the bottom of a boat. This lever was constructed to move the iron rod on inside of cylinder, thus acting upon the trigger of the lock to explode the cap and fire the powder. The machine was anchored, presenting the prongs in such a way that boats going down-stream should slide over them, but those coming up should catch.

In the retreat of the Confederates from Williamsburg, Va., in May, 1862, Gen. G. J. Rains, subsequently chief of the torpedo service, arranged some ordinary shells beneath the road and fitted them with sensitive primers. A body of Federal cavalry suffered severely from the explosion of these primitive torpedoes as they rode over them, and Gen. McClellan complained of what he styled this "most murderous and barbarous conduct." Gens. Joseph E. Johnston and Longstreet forbade Rains to use these implements of warfare, and the question was referred to Mr. Randolph, Secretary of War, who decided that torpedoes must only be used in a parapet or on a road to repel assaults or check the enemy, or in a river or harbor to drive off blockading or attacking fleets. After the battle of Seven Pines, Gen. Lee suggested to Rains the employment of torpedoes in the James River. The latter was

U. S. IRON-CLAD "CAIRO" (BLOWN UP BY CONFEDERATE TORPEDO).

placed in charge of the submarine defences, and claims to have put in position, at Drewry's Bluff, the first submarine torpedo made. Lieut. Hunter Davidson, C. S. N., lays claim to not only the first successful application of electrical torpedoes, but also to having established the system upon the James River. Capt. M. F. Maury, C. S. N., was the predecessor of Davidson in charge of the work, but went to Europe before it was far advanced, where he continued his experiments and invented an ingenious method of arranging and testing torpedo mines, which he was about to put into use at Galveston against the blockaders when Gen. Lee surrendered. Still another claimant to early operations with electric torpedoes is Lieut. Beverley Kennon, C. S. N., who writes that he experimented with devices of his own on Lake Ponchartrain in August, 1861. He also states that at Vicksburg, in the autumn of 1862, he gave torpedo instruction to Acting Master Zedekiah McDaniel, C. S. N., who, with Acting Master Francis M. Ewing, subsequently blew up the U. S. iron-clad gunboat Cairo in the Yazoo River. The expedition to which that vessel belonged was under the command of Lieut. Com. Thomas O. Selfridge, U. S. N., and embraced also the *Pittsburg, Marmora, Signal* and ram *Queen of the West.* On December 12th, 1862, the vessels were a little below Haines' Bluff, where McDaniel and Ewing were stationed in charge of the torpedoes. Two were fired without doing any damage, but the third exploded under the *Cairo's* bow and sent her to the bottom in 12 minutes. The torpedo which accomplished this was a large demijohn inclosed in a wooden box and fired with a friction primer by a trigger line leading to torpedo pits on shore. It was the first instance of the destruction of a vessel-of-war engaged in active warfare by a torpedo.

In October, 1862, the "Torpedo Bureau" was established at Richmond, under the charge of Brig. Gen. G. J. Rains, and the "Naval Submarine Battery Service" was organized under command of Capt. M. F. Maury, who relinquished it to Lieut. Hunter Davidson. An act of Congress, April 21st, 1862, provided that the inventor of a device by which a vessel of the enemy should be destroyed should receive 50 per cent. of the value of the vessel and armament, and the general appropriation bill of May 1st, 1863, embraced an item of $20,000 for this branch of the public service, to be expended under the direction of the Navy Department, which was the first appropriation of the kind. By the act of February 17th, 1864, $100,000 was appropriated for the construction of submarine batteries, and by the act of June 13th, 1864, $250,000 was appropriated for the same purpose. Legislation, however, was not as prompt as it should have been.[1]

Torpedo stations were established at Richmond, Wilmington, Charleston, Savannah and Mobile, with sub-stations at other points. The men of the corps were sworn to secrecy and granted extraordinary privileges on account of the perilous and arduous nature of the service. Several boats engaged in laying torpedoes were destroyed with all their crews by accidental explosions.

The spar torpedo was an important invention which played a conspicuous part in this service of the Confederacy. Many such machines were left by the Confederates at Charleston and Richmond when those places were evacuated. Some were cylindrical-shaped copper vessels with convex ends for boats and tugs; others were larger and were shaped like an egg, the butt being carried forward to bring the greater power of the charge nearest to the object to be destroyed. All were intended to be operated at the extremity of a pole or spar projecting from the stem of the torpedo boat or other vessel. This spar was attached to the vessel by a goose-neck, fitted to a socket bolted to the bow, near the water-line.

[1] "For three years the Confederate Congress legislated on this subject, a bill passing each house alternately for an organized torpedo corps, until the third year, when it passed both houses with acclamation, and $6,000,000 appropriated, but too late, and the delay was not shortened by this enormous appropriation." Gen. G. J. Rains, *So. Historical Society Papers, Vol. III., Nos. 5-6, p. 256.*

Guys from the spar to the side of the vessel kept the spar in its position when the torpedo was submerged for an attack, and it was lowered and raised by tricing lines and tackles. Usually seven fuses made to explode by contact were fixed to each torpedo. Gen. Beauregard and Com. Wm. T. Glassell, C. S. N.,[1] state that the spar torpedo was designed by Capt. Francis D. Lee of the engineer corps, on duty at Charleston, and Glassell mentions that after seeing the device successfully tested there, he endeavored to induce Com. Ingraham, flag-officer at Charleston, to equip a flotilla of such

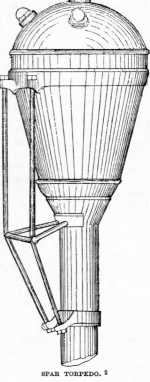

SPAR TORPEDO. [2]

boats for operations against the blockaders. But Ingraham did not believe in what he called "new-fangled notions," and it was only by the aid and at the expense of Geo. A. Trenholm that Glassell at last fitted out some row-boats with the spar-torpedoes. He obtained volunteers for an expedition, but the flag-officer refused to sanction it, on the ground that his rank and age did not entitle him to the command of more than one boat. Finally, Glassell started out with one

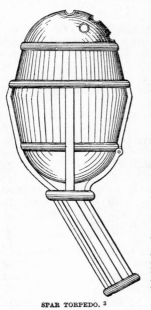

SPAR TORPEDO. [3]

[1] Commander W. T. Glassel was a lieutenant in the U. S. navy, and returned from China in the *Hartford* in the summer of 1862. Immediately upon his arrival in Philadelphia, (August 5th, 1862), he was informed that he must take a new oath of allegiance or be sent to Fort Warren. He refused to take this oath, on the ground that it was inconsistent with one he had already taken to support the Constitution of the United States. He was kept in Fort Warren eight months, and then exchanged as a prisoner of war, on the banks of the James River. Being actually placed in the ranks of the Confederate States, he entered the navy as lieutenant, his commission being dated August 5th, 1862, the same day on which he was sent to Fort Warren. He received orders to report for duty on the iron-clad *Chicora* at Charleston, and participated in the attack upon the Federal blockading fleet. He died at Los Angelos, California, on the 28th of January, 1879.

[2] This class of torpedo was generally used on all the Confederate gunboats. The braces were intended to support the weight of the torpedo, particularly when lifting out of water.

[3] This class of torpedo was among the first used. It was a soda water copper tank supported by iron straps, and had five chemical or sensitive fuses projecting from the upper half of the hemispherical surface.

row-boat and a crew of six men.
and approached the Federal
frigate *Powhatan* at one o'clock
in the morning. He was aiming
to strike her with his torpedoes
when one of his men, from terror or treason, backed his oar;
the others gave up in despair; a
boat put out from the enemy's
ship; and thus thwarted Glassell cut the torpedo loose and
returned to Charleston.

On February 28th, 1863, the
monitor *Montauk* destroyed the
C. S. cruiser *Nashville* in the
Ogechee River, Ga.; and as she
was returning to her anchorage a torpedo exploded under her. By running
her upon a mud-bank and stopping the
hole blown in her hull, she was saved
from sinking, but she was retired from
service for a month
while repairs were
being made. This
disaster and the loss
of the *Cairo* made

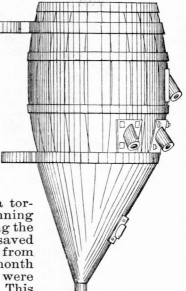

SPAR TORPEDO. [1]

the Federal naval commanders exceedingly cautious about venturing
into waters where the presence of
torpedoes was suspected; and the
government applied to Capt. Ericsson, the constructor of the *Monitor,*
to furnish something to remove or
destroy the submarine batteries.
The next vessel to suffer was the U.S.
iron-clad ram *Baron DeKalb*, which
was completely destroyed on the
Yazoo River, July 22d, 1863. The
torpedo which sunk her was anchored
in the channel, and burst under her
when she struck it in passing over.
On August 8th, as the U. S. steamer
Commodore Barney was descending
the James River an electric torpedo,
fired from the shore, was exploded
just astern of her. She was badly
disabled, and some men were washed
from her deck and drowned; and but

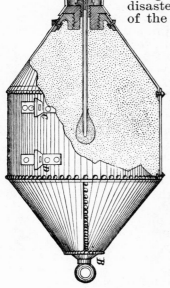

THE ELECTRIC TORPEDO.

[1] This form of "ram torpedo" was taken from the iron-clad *Charleston*, at Charleston, S.C. It was made from a strong wood cask, and had 7 sensi-tive fuses. It contained about 150 lbs. of fine pow-der, and was fixed on the end of an iron spar about 30 ft. long, attached to the bow near the water line.

for the fact that the electric battery had acted slowly, she would have been destroyed.

The electric torpedo represented in the diagram afforded the best protection to the wires, and brought the charge very near the object to be destroyed. It was made of $\frac{3}{4}$-inch boiler iron and filled with fine powder. Two wires connected it with the electric battery on shore, the conductor being covered with gutta percha, the submerged ends being additionally protected by a covering of tarred hemp, and weighted with chain. The torpedo was anchored

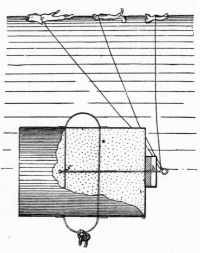

THE DRIFT TORPEDO.

to bolts (C and D), and castings were bolted to the ends (A and B), the former to cover and protect the circuit wires.[1]

The drift torpedo gave the Federals in James River great annoyance. It was a tin case containing about 70 pounds of powder. A number of wires from the friction fuse led from the powder to small pieces of drift-wood on the surface of the water. The torpedo was floated at the proper depth by a line fastened to a floating log. The torpedo was turned adrift at night, with the view of fouling the trigger lines by the propellers of the enemy's vessels. In January, 1863, one of these torpedoes was picked up by the U. S. gunboat *Essex* in the Mississippi River.

On August 17th, 1863, the Federals picked up in Light-house Creek, Charleston harbor, a torpedo made of three metallic cases, on the upper side of which were delicately arranged hammers connected with cords. The cords were to catch on a vessel, when the cases would swing against her, the hammers would fall on percussion caps, and thus the explosion would be caused in the powder chambers under the caps. Another style of torpedo that the

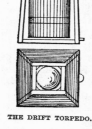

THE DRIFT TORPEDO.

[1] "Barnes Submarine Warfare," p. 77.

Federals discovered around Charleston they christened "devil fish." These were about four feet long, very slender, and shaped like a fish. A number were fastened together by lines of wire which would explode their fuses on becoming entangled with the bows of vessels. On November 14th, Capt. Gansevoort, of the U. S. iron-clad *Roanoke* captured a machine floating down the James River that looked like a big lantern gone adrift. The wick was fixed to communicate with a combustible substance supposed to ignite by friction, and from it a tube ran down to a can containing about 35 lbs. of powder. There were several of these torpedoes similarly constructed and lashed together.

In November, 1863, a number of the keg torpedoes invented by Gen. Rains were taken up off Charleston by the Union fleet. Lager-beer barrels were confiscated everywhere in the Confederacy for making these instruments, and when calked and pitched, loaded with from 35 to 120 pounds of powder, capped with friction fuses and moored in a channel, they

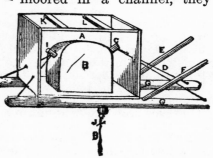

A KEG TORPEDO.   A RAFT TORPEDO.[1]

proved excellent for defence, causing the loss of more vessels than any other kind used by the Confederates. Six vessels and a steam launch were blown up by them in Mobile waters, between March 28th and April 18th, 1865; and they also destroyed the Confederate steamers *Ettiwan* and *Marion* in Charleston harbor, having drifted from their moorings into the navigable channel.

Another design was a raft torpedo, such as was secured by the U. S. gunboat *Gertrude*, westward of the main channel

[1] A—The open top of the box. B—The iron tank. C—Brass tube. D—Iron rods connecting from tube to the end of the raft. E, F—Parts of spars morticed to the runners of raft. G—The runners on which the box lay. H—The mooring. I—Tube with iron rods attached. J—The place where the warp was cut. K, L—Braces across the top.

in Mobile Bay, Jan. 30th, 1864. The moorings were cut by an officer in charge of a boat who found on the raft a box five feet long, four and a half feet wide and four and three-fourths feet high, inclosing a powder-tank two and one-fourth feet square, and three feet high.

The U. S. frigate *New Ironsides* narrowly escaped destruction during the bombardment in Charleston harbor, April 7th, 1863, when she laid for an hour directly over a boiler-iron torpedo containing 2,000 pounds of powder off Fort Wagner. It was designed to be exploded from an electric battery on shore, but every attempt to fire it failed, and the operator was suspected of treachery, until it was ascertained that one of the wires had been cut by an ordnance wagon passing over it. In August the first attempt was made to destroy this ship with a torpedo-boat. It was an improvised affair made from the *razeed* hulk of a gunboat that had been abandoned at Charleston before completion. Capt. Lee, of the engineer corps, obtained it from Secretary Mallory, and fixed a spar torpedo to the bow. Capt. Carlin, of the blockade-runner *Ella and Annie*, offered his services as commander and a volunteer crew was obtained from the squadron. The boat ran close aboard of the *New Ironsides*, but became entangled with her anchor chains, and on being discovered from the deck retreated into the harbor. On October 5th, the second attack was attempted, and although the huge iron-clad was not sunk she was so much injured as to be withdrawn from the coast of South Carolina, and she took no active part in the war afterward until the bombardment of Fort Fisher. The assault of October 5th was made by a *David*, one of the double-ended steam torpedo craft constructed in the Confederacy. They were of wood or iron, forty to sixty feet long, and about seven feet in diameter at the centre. The boiler was forward, the engine aft, and between them was a cuddy-hole for the captain, engineer and whatever crew the boat might carry, and which was entered by a hatchway. The torpedo was carried on a spar that protruded from the bow, and which could be raised or lowered at will by a line passing back into the cuddy-hole. A two-bladed propeller drove the craft along. The torpedo was made of copper, with a mechanical fuse, and carried from fifty to seventy pounds of powder. When ready for action, the boat was so well submerged that nothing was visible except her stunt smoke-stack, the hatch-coaming and the stanchion upon which the torpedo-line was brought aft.

Lieut. W. T. Glassell was placed in command of the first *David* built, which had been constructed at private expense by Theodore Stoney, of Charleston, and had under him C. S. Tombs, engineer of the iron-clad *Chicora*, James Sullivan, fireman of the *Chicora*, and J. W. Cannon, assistant pilot of the iron-clad *Palmetto State*. The night selected for the expedition was slightly hazy, and shortly after nine o'clock the *David* was within 300 yards of the *New Ironsides*, off Morris Island, and making directly for her side, when she was discovered by a sentinel. Without making any reply to his hail, Glassell kept on and fired with a shotgun at the officer of the deck (Acting Master Howard), who fell mortally wounded. The next moment the *David* struck the frigate, the torpedo exploded, the little craft plunged violently, and a deluge of water thrown up by the concussion descended on her smoke-pipe and hatchway. Her fires were extinguished and her machinery jammed. In the midst of a rattling fire of musketry from the *New Ironsides*, Glassell directed his men to save themselves by swimming, as it seemed impossible that the *David* could be made to move. After being in the water

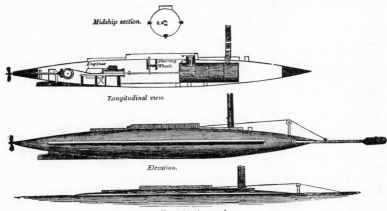

VIEWS OF A CONFEDERATE "DAVID."

himself more than an hour, he was picked up by the boat of a transport schooner and handed over as a prisoner to Adm. Dahlgren, who ordered him into confinement on the guard-ship *Ottawa*. [1]

Engineer Tombs started to swim down the harbor with the intention of catching the chain of the monitor, but changed his mind when he saw that the *David* was afloat and had drifted away from the frigate. Swimming to her he found Pilot Cannon, who could not swim, holding on for life. Tombs got into the boat, pulled Cannon on board, fixed the engine, started up the fire under the boiler and headed for Charleston, where he arrived the next morning. The *David* bore the scars of 13 bullet holes received from the small arms of the *New Ironsides*. Sullivan, the fireman, saved himself by catching the rudder chains of the frigate, from whence he was taken on board as a prisoner.

[1] Lieut. W. T. Glassell, Southern Historical Society Papers. Vol. IV., No. 5, Nov. 1877.

Upon examining the *New Ironsides*, it was found that the torpedo exploded only three feet under water and against 4½ inches of armor, and 27 inches of wood backing. By the explosion the ponderous ship was shaken from stem to stern. It knocked down a bulkhead, started some timbers, and threw two or three rooms into confusion. A marine was dashed against the ceiling and his leg broken, while several other men were slightly injured. The attack upon this ship made such an impression on the Federal naval commanders, that every imaginable precaution was taken to guard against torpedoes, and high steam was carried at night on all the vessels so that they could move at speed upon the instant.

Lieut. Glassell was promoted to commander, and Engineer Tombs to lieutenant for their participation in this affair. Capt. M. M. Gray was in charge of the submarine defences of Charleston at this time, and was exceedingly active in developing this mode of warfare. Sixty officers and men were then on torpedo duty at that point.

The fish torpedo boat that destroyed the Federal gunboat *Housatonic* off Charleston harbor was built at Mobile in 1863, by Hundley & McClintock, and was arranged with a pair of lateral fins by the use of which she could be submerged or brought to the surface. Her motive power was a hand propeller worked by eight men, and it was intended that she should dive under a vessel, dragging a torpedo after her which would explode on contact with the hull or keel of the enemy, the "fish" making off on the other side. She was provided with tanks which could be filled or emptied of water, to increase or decrease her displacement, but there was no provision for a storage of air. During an experiment at Mobile she sank, and before she could be raised the whole crew were suffocated.

Beauregard, in February 1864, accepted this boat for use at Charleston. Lieut. Payne, C. S. N., and a crew of eight men were preparing to take her out for action one night when she was swamped by the wash of a passing steamer and all hands except Payne were drowned. Again she was raised and once more sunk—this time at Fort Sumter wharf, when six men were drowned, Payne and two others escaping. When she was brought to the surface, Hundley took her into the Stono River, where, after making several successful dives, she stuck her nose into the mud and every soul on board perished by suffocation. For the fourth time she was raised and experiments were made with her in Charleston harbor. She worked beautifully until she attempted to dive under the receiving ship *Indian Chief*, when she fouled a cable and once more she proved a coffin for every man within her. Divers brought her up a week later, and Lieut. George E. Dixon, of Capt. Cothran's Co. of the 21st Ala. Inf'y, asked permission of Gen. Beauregard to try her against the *Housatonic*, a splendid new ship-of-war, which lay in the North Channel off Beach

Inlet. Beauregard consented, but only on the condition that she should not be used as a submarine machine, but operating on the surface of the water and with a spar torpedo in the same manner as the *David*. All the thirty or more men who had met death in the "fish" were volunteers, but Dixon had no difficulty in finding another volunteer crew ready to take the same risks. They were Arnold Becker, C. Simpkins, James A. Wicks, F. Collins, and —— Ridgway, all of the Confederate navy, and Capt. J. F. Carlson, of Capt. Wagoner's company of artillery. It was a little before nine o'clock on the evening of Feb. 17th, when Master J. K. Crosby, officer of the deck of the *Housatonic*, detected the torpedo-boat, a scant hundred yards away from the ship. It looked to him, he said, "like a plank moving along the water," and before he decided to give the alarm, he had lost the seconds in which he might have saved his vessel. When he did pass the word, her cable was slipped, her engine backed and all hands called to quarters; but Dixon had closed on her and fired his torpedo on the starboard side, just forward of her mainmast. A hole was knocked in her side extending below her water line and she went down in four minutes. Five of the *Housatonic's* people were killed by the shock or drowned; the remainder took refuge in the rigging, from which they were rescued by other vessels of the fleet. But the victory of the "fish" was fatal to herself and her crew. Whether she was swamped by the column of water thrown up by the explosion, or was carried down by the suction of the sinking *Housatonic* will never be known; but she went under never to rise again, and the lives of all on board were sacrificed. After the war, when the wrecks off Charleston were removed, she was discovered lying on the bottom about 100 feet from the *Housatonic*, with her bow pointing to the latter.

A somewhat similar torpedo boat was dredged up in July, 1878, in the canal, near Spanish Fort, New Orleans. It had undoubtedly been built by the Confederates and sunk when they evacuated the city in 1862.

The next torpedo boat attack was directed against the U. S. steamer *Memphis* in North Edisto River, S. C., March 6th, 1864, and was made by a *David*. It failed because the torpedo boat was seen from the steamer in time to allow her to get under way, and the *David* in running under her counter is supposed to have broken the torpedo pole by coming into contact with her screw. Although a heavy fire was aimed at the *David* she escaped under cover of the night.

General Beauregard was deeply interested in a scheme to construct at Charleston an iron-clad torpedo-ram on designs prepared by Captain F. D. Lee. In 1862, the State of South Carolina appropriated $50,000 to aid in building one or more such craft ; but the Confederate Navy Department was sparing in granting assistance, preferring to expend its resources upon the iron-clad gunboats. Nevertheless, in Feb., 1863, the vessel was ready to receive her iron plating and only $20,000 more was needed for her completion. That amount was never obtained, and the incomplete torpedo-ram fell into the possession of the enemy when they found their way into Charleston.

On April 9th, 1864, Com. Hunter Davidson, in his steam torpedo-boat, *Torpedo*. having made the run of 120 miles down the James River from Drewry's Bluff, exploded a torpedo alongside the U. S. steam frigate *Minnesota*, flag-ship of Rear-Admiral S. P. Lee, at anchor off Newport News. This affair was particularly daring, as the river swarmed with the enemy's vessels, and a guard tug was lying by the *Minnesota*, but her commander had allowed his steam to go down. Davidson hit the great ship full and fair, but his torpedo charge was only 53 pounds of powder and it failed to break in her sides. A frame was shattered, planks started, several gun-carriages broken, and a lot of stores damaged. The daring Confederates got away without harm.

In March, 1864, amongst a lot of correspondence captured from a Confederate mail-carrier on the Red River, was a letter dated at Richmond, January 19th, and addressed by T. E.

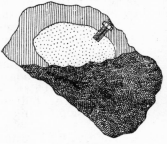

Courtenay to Col. H. E. Clark, of the 7th Mo. Cav., C. S. A., in which the writer spoke of certain torpedo inventions of his own, and alluded to a bill to be presented to the Confederate Congress for the establishment of a secret service corps for the destruction of the property of the enemy. One of these devices was the " coal torpedo," which Lieut. Barnes, U. S. N., in his book on " Submarine Warfare," said "appears to be an innocent lump of coal,

COAL TORPEDO.

but is a block of cast-iron with a core containing about ten pounds of powder." When covered with a mixture of tar and coal-dust, it was impossible to detect their character. They could be placed in coal-piles on barges from which Federal vessels took their supplies, and exploded with terrible effect in their boilers. It was said that to this torpedo was traced a number of mysterious explosions, including the destruction of Gen. Butler's headquarters' boat, the *Greyhound*, on the James River, November 27th, 1864.

The machine which caused the great explosion at City Point, on the James River, Aug. 9th, 1864, was a Confederate clock-work torpedo—a box containing a quantity of powder, and a clock arrangement set to fire a detonating cap at a given hour. John Maxwell and R. K. Dillard, of the torpedo corps, arrived at City Point in disguise, as laborers, and the former, with the machine in charge, handed it to a man on a Federal barge, with the remark that the captain had told him to put it on board. Maxwell retired to watch the effect. The clock-work had been set to run an hour, and at the end of that time the explosion occurred, destroying several vessels loaded with ordnance stores, and the warehouses on the wharf, filled with army supplies, and killing and wounding some fifty men.

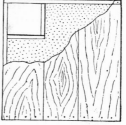

CLOCK-WORK TORPEDO.

The wharf-boat at Mound City, Ill., containing the reserve supplies of ammunition and stores for Adm. Porter's fleet, was blown up by a similar contrivance. On April 1st, 1864, the U. S. army transport *Maple Leaf* was totally destroyed by a floating torpedo, in the St. John's River, Fla.; and exactly abreast of the spot the transport steamer *General Hunter* was blown up on the 5th of April, in the same way. Also, on April 15th, the U. S. iron-clad *Eastport* was sunk in the Red River, by a floating torpedo. On April 18th a bold effort was made by the submarine corps in Charleston to destroy the U. S. steam frigate *Wabash*, one of the blockaders, with a *David*, but they were discovered and fired into, and they retreated.

When Admiral Lee convoyed Gen. Butler's army up the James River to Bermuda Hundreds in May, 1864, he organized a torpedo picket division that in a few days secured eleven of the Confederate "infernal machines;" but despite these precautions, the gunboat *Commodore Jones* was on May 6th knocked into fragments at Deep Bottom by an electric torpedo containing 2,000 pounds of powder, and exploded from pits on shore by men of Com. Hunter Davidson's corps. Forty officers and men of the gunboat were killed. The men who fired the torpedo ran from the pits; one of them (Mr. Britten) was killed by a shot from the Federals, and the other two were made prisoners. Gen. Butler sent one of them to Lieut. Homer C. Blake, commanding the gunboat *Eutaw*, with the instructions: "If you can use him, do so; if not, hang him." Blake handed him over to Lieut. Fyffe, who soon started up the river with the prisoner lashed to the cutwater of his ship. "He only went about 300 yards," Blake said, "when the man called out: 'Stop, captain, for God's sake! There's a torpedo just over there.' This one removed, it was not long before another was pointed out by the terrified man, and so we cleared the channel."

At Dutch Gap, on the James River, the Federals would sometimes pick up floating torpedoes sent against the fleet, at the rate of a hundred a day. These torpedoes were suspended in pairs to wooden buoys, and were connected by trigger-lines which would explode them on contact with a ship; but the Federals guarded against them by putting out booms and nettings in such a way that the torpedo floats were sheered off and passed harmlessly by.

The most dangerous torpedoes were stationary ones, planted across the shallows at frequent intervals. They comprised a spar fastened by a universal joint to a fixed block at the bottom of the river and bearing the torpedo at its summit. Swinging with the current and tide, this torpedo was always kept at a uniform depth below the surface, and was out of sight. The torpedo was studded with sensitive caps, and no matter where a ship touched it it would explode. They could not be grappled for, and it was only by good luck, care and ingenuity that the Federals got them out of the channel.

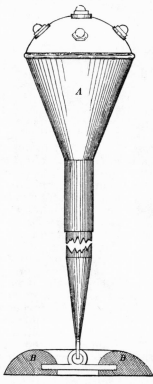

A BOUYANT TORPEDO.

In May, 1864, the U. S. Potomac flotilla cleared the Rappahannock River of torpedoes, taking up four and exploding six. On the 9th of that month, the transport *Harriet A. Weed* was destroyed by a torpedo on the St. John's River, ten miles below Jacksonville. Out of 44 persons on the steamer five were killed, and all the remainder were more or less injured.

This was the third vessel lost in the St. John's within sixty days in the same manner, and on June 19th the transport *Alice Price* was blown up on the same stream by a torpedo. Following the destruction of the *Price* occurred the most fearful work of submarine batteries during the war—the loss of the monitor *Tecumseh*, with over 100 of her officers and men, during Farragut's attack on the defences of Mobile Bay, August 5th, 1864.[1] After the capture of the bay forts the city was protected for nearly ten months from the Federal fleet by the torpedo system in the channels of approach. Besides the *Tecumseh*, eleven U. S. vessels, men-of-war and transports, were sunk by torpedoes in Mobile Bay; some of them after the Confederates had evacuated the city. The Confederates had at Mobile a torpedo-boat named the *St. Patrick*, with which Lieut. Walker, C. S. N., on Jan. 27th, 1865, attacked the Federal flag-ship *Octorara;* but the torpedo did not explode and no damage was done. While the Federals were removing the obstructions in Mobile Bay, on Aug. 25th, 1864, a torpedo exploded, killing five men and wounding nine. On Dec. 7th, the U. S. gunboat *Narcissus* was sunk in the bay by a torpedo;

[1] See Chapter on Alabama Waters.

and in April, 1865, a launch from the U. S. iron-clad *Cincinnati* exploded a torpedo for which she was grappling, and three men were killed.

In 1863 the U. S. government took up the idea of a torpedo service, for which it had previously savagely denounced the Confederates, and invited plans from inventors and mechanics. In that year numerous torpedoes were placed in the Roanoke River to prevent the Confederate ram *Albemarle* from descending to attack the Federal gunboats in Albemarle Sound. Adm. Dahlgren, in February, 1864, wrote to the Navy Department that he "had attached more importance to the use of torpedoes than others had done," and he suggested the offer of $20,000 or $30,000 prize-money for the capture or destruction of a *David*. Adm. Farragut had very little faith in torpedoes at first, but on March 25th, 1864, he wrote to the Department from Mobile Bay, that he would have torpedoes, and added : " Torpedoes are not so agreeable when used on both sides ; therefore I have reluctantly brought myself to it. I have always deemed it unworthy of a chivalrous nation, but it does not do to give your enemy such a decided superiority over you."

A spar torpedo was attached to the monitor *Manhattan* for use during the attack on Mobile, but it was previously carried away by heavy seas washing over the deck.

In the action of May 5th, 1864, between the *Albemarle* and a fleet of U. S. gunboats, the *Miami* was rigged with a spar torpedo, and endeavored to strike the Confederate ram, but was unsuccessful, owing, as her commander stated, to the clumsiness of his vessel. The most important event in the use of the spar torpedo by the Unionists was the destruction of the *Albemarle*, at Plymouth, N. C., Oct. 28th, 1864. Lieut. W. B. Cushing, U. S. N., effected this achievement with a steam launch that had originally been intended for the torpedo picket service in Charleston harbor. He found the *Albemarle* at the wharf, with a pen of logs around her, about 30 feet from her side, and under a sharp fire from the ram and on shore, he made a way through and over the logs, succeeded in lowering his torpedo-pole, which projected twenty-eight feet, against the side of the ram, and exploded the torpedo. A large hole was broken under the water-line of the ram, and she went down in a few minutes. Cushing's own boat was swamped by the rush of water, and of his thirteen officers and men, all but himself and one other were either shot, drowned, or made prisoners. He escaped by swimming. Lieut. A. F. Warley, C. S. N., commanding the *Albemarle*, stated that the pickets gave no notice of the approach of the enemy, and that the artillery stationed by the vessel for protection gave no assistance. She was raised by the Federals in April, 1865, and an Admiralty Court appraised her value at $282,856, of which $79,954 was distributed as prize-money among the men who destroyed her.

A Federal gunboat expedition up the Roanoke River, Dec. 1864, came upon a nest of torpedoes opposite Jamestown. On the 9th the "double-ender" *Otsego*, was destroyed by one of them ; on the next day the *Bazely* was sunk close by, and shortly afterwards Picket-boat No. 5, met the same fate ; and the expedition was abandoned. These calamities were followed on January 15th, 1865, by the destruction of the monitor *Patapsco*, in Charleston harbor, while she was covering the boats engaged in dragging for torpedoes. She struck one herself, and went down like a pig of lead, carrying with her seven officers and about sixty men. She had torpedo-fenders and netting out at the time. Three boats, with drags, had preceded her, searching to some depth the water they had passed over, while steam-tugs and several boats were in different positions on her bow, stern and quarter.

The channels of Cape Fear River, from Forts Fisher and Caswell up to Wilmington, were carefully planted by the Confederates with electric and barrel torpedoes; and the operators for the electric torpedoes were stationed with their firing apparatus in the bomb-proofs of the forts. When Adm. Porter and Gen. Butler, in the winter of 1864–65, were ordered to the command of the Federal naval and military forces for the assault on Fort Fisher, the latter conceived the notion of demolishing the fort and "paralyzing" the garrison by the explosion of the hugest powder-boat ever devised. Porter was an unwilling party to the scheme, as he perceived its absurdity. An old steamer, the *Louisiana*, was procured, and 180 tons of powder placed on board, to be exploded by a time fuse that would burn 90 minutes. She was towed in on the beach, within 400 yards of the fort, and her big display of fireworks went off between one and two o'clock on the morning of Dec. 24th, with the result of hurting nobody and scarcely disturbing the sleeping men in the fort. At the time Midshipman Clarence Cary, C. S. N., with others of the officers and crew of the C. S. steamer *Chickamauga*, occupied a deserted hut a little way up the beach outside the fort, and were nearer than the garrison to the powder-boat, and yet they slept through the explosion and "supposed its report," writes Mr. Cary, "no more than that of a distant gun. Possibly the first ton or so of powder ignited blew the remainder harmlessly into the sea, or it may be the ship got adrift in the hour and half the time fuse allowed her after she was abandoned, and thus wreaked her expected havoc at some remote point, where only the fish and sea-gulls, instead of sleeping men, were within range."

After the capture of Fort Anderson, the Federals were busy in removing the torpedo defences between that point and Wilmington. On Feb. 20th, 1865, Adm. Porter says, "the Confederates sent down 200 floating torpedoes from Wilmington upon the fleet. One damaged the gunboat *Osceola*, and a second blew to pieces a cutter from the *Shawmut*, killing and wounding four men." Porter spread fishing nets across the river to catch the torpedoes as they came down.

On Feb. 17th, 1865, the Confederate flag of truce steamer *Schultz*, Capt. Hill, ran over a torpedo in the James River, a few miles above Cox's Landing, and quickly sank. Several members of the Richmond ambulance committee were on board, but were saved, and the only lives lost were those of two of the guards and two firemen. Adm. Dahlgren's flag-ship, the *Harvest Moon*, was destroyed by a torpedo in Georgetown Bay, S. C., March 1st, with a loss to him of everything on board except the clothes he stood in. He was rescued by a gunboat. On March 4th, the U. S. transport *Thorn* was blown up in Cape Fear River, just below Fort Anderson; and on the 12th, the gunboat *Althea* met destruction on Blakely River, Mobile, losing two men killed and three wounded. Succeeding the evacuation of Charleston by the Confederates, the Federals picked up a hundred torpedoes in the harbor, and in the Cooper and Ashley Rivers. One exploded on March 17th under the U. S. survey steamer *Bibb*, and damaged her engines.

The worst destruction in the concluding months of the war was done around Mobile. On March 28th, 1865, the U. S. monitor *Milwaukee* was destroyed in the Blakely river by a buoyant torpedo, and the next day the monitor *Osage* was sunk on Blakely Bar by a similar machine; she lost two killed and ten wounded. On April 1st the gunboat *Rodolph* was blown up near the scene of the *Milwaukee's* catastrophe, with a loss of four killed and eleven wounded. The U. S. gunboat *Scioto*, on April 14th, was sunk off Mobile by striking a torpedo, and had four men killed and six wounded. On the preceding day, the U. S. steamer *Ida* was destroyed below the obstructions in Mobile Bay. On the 14th the cutter of the iron-clad *Cincinnati* hit a torpedo in the bay with the usual result, and on the same day the gunboat *Itasca* was blown up; five men were killed and six injured by these two disasters. Late the same afternoon the steamer *Rose* was destroyed, and two men were killed and three wounded. A few days later the transport *St. Mary's* was blown up by a torpedo in the Alabama River, and the steamer *Hamilton* from New Orleans, with the Third Mich. cavalry on board, was struck by a torpedo in the Lower Gap channel entrance to Mobile, making a wreck of the boat, and killing and wounding thirteen persons. Thus in less than a month ten vessels of the Federal Government, including two monitors, were destroyed by the Confederate torpedo service, a fact that may be left to stand alone as an evidence of its efficiency.

The last craft to suffer from a torpedo was the U. S. gunboat *Jonquil*, which was much injured on June 6th, 1865, by an explosion in the Ashley River, near Charleston.

Now that torpedo warfare is recognised as legitimate by all the nations of the world, history cannot omit to record that the Confederate States were the first government to bring it into existence as a formidable and practicable weapon. The torpedo and the steam-ram were the valuable contributions to the science of war and its implements which they made during their brief existence.

United States Vessels Destroyed or Injured by Confederate Torpedoes.

Date.	Vessel.	Place.	Tonnage.	Injury.
Dec. 12, '62....	Cairo, iron-clad...............	Yazoo River......	512	Destroyed.
Feb. 28, '63....	Montauk, monitor	Ogeechee River...........	844	Serious.
July 22, "	Baron DeKalb, iron-clad.......	Yazoo River..............	512	Destroyed.
Aug. 8, "	Com. Barney, gunboat........	James River..............	513	Disabled.
Sept. .. "	John Farron, transport........	"	....	Serious.
Oct. 5, "	New Ironsides. iron-clad. .	Off Charleston...........	....	"
Feb. 17, '64....	Housatonic, sloop-of-war. ...	"	1240	Destroyed.
April 1, "	Maple Leaf, transport........	St. John's River..........	508	"
" 9, "	Minnesota, frigate.	Newport News...........	3307	Serious.
" 15, "	General Hunter, transport ...	St. John's River.........	350	Destroyed,
" 15, "	Eastport, iron-clad...........	Red River...............	800	"
May 6, "	Com. Jones, gunboat	James River.............	542	"
" 9, "	H. A. Weed, transport........	St. John's River........	290	"
June 19, "	Alice Price, transport.........	"	320	"
Aug. 5, "	Tecumseh, monitor.	Mobile Bay	1034	"
" 9, "	Several vessels	City Point, James River..	....	"
Nov. 27, "	Greyhound, transport.........	James River.............	900	"
Dec. 7, "	Narcissus, gunboat............	Mobile Bay.......	101	Sunk.
" 9, "	Otsego, gunboat..............	Roanoke River...........	974	Destroyed.
" 10, "	Bazely, gunboat...............	"	....	"
" 10, "	Launch No. 5.....	"	....	"
Jan. 15, "	Patapsco, monitor.	Charleston, S. C..........	844	"
Feb. 20, "	Osceola, gunboat...	Cape Fear River..........	974	Slight.
" 20, "	Launch, Shawmut.............	"	....	Destroyed.
March 1, "	Harvest-Moon.................	Georgetown, S. C........	546	"
" 4, "	Thorn, transport.............	Cape Fear River..	403	"
" 12, "	Althea, gunboat	Blakely River...........	....	"
" 17, "	Bibb, coast survey steamer....	Charleston, S. C.........	....	Slight.
" 20, "	Massachusetts, gunboat.......	"	1155	"
" 28, "	Milwaukee, monitor...........	Blakely River...........	970	Destroyed.
" 29, " ..	Osage, monitor...............	"	523	Sunk.
April 1, "	Rodolph, gunboat.............	"	217	Destroyed.
" 13, "	Ida, tug	"	101	"
" 14, "	Scioto, gunboat...............	Mobile Bay.............	507	"
" 14, " ...	Cincinnati, tug	Blakely River...........	....	"
" 14, "	Itasca, gunboat...............	Mobile Bay..............	....	"
" 14, "	Rose, gunboat...............	"	....	"
" .. "	St. Mary's, transport.........	Alabama River...........	....	"
" .. "	R. B. Hamilton, transport....	Mobile Bay	400	"
June 6, "	Jonquil, gunboat..............	Ashley River.....	....	Serious.

CHAPTER XXIV.

THE CONFEDERATE STATES MARINE CORPS.

B Y act of Congress of the Confederate States, March 16th, 1861, the establishment of a corps of marines was provided for, and subsequent legislation of May 20th enlarged its numbers and elevated the rank of its principal officers. It was, in fact, organized under the second act, whose provisions were that it should consist of: " 1 colonel, 1 lieut. col., 1 major, 1 quartermaster with rank of major, 1 adjutant with rank of major, 1 serg.-major, 1 quartermaster-sergeant, 10 captains, 10 first lieutenants, 20 second lieutenants, 40 sergeants, 40 corporals and 840 privates, 10 drummers, 10 fifers and 2 musicians."

The pay and emoluments were the same as those of the army, except that the paymaster and adjutant received the same as the quartermaster, and seamen's rations were allowed to enlisted men. Enlistments were for three years or the war; recruits to receive a bounty of $50 and re-enlisted men $40. An act of Sept. 24th, 1862, authorized the addition of 20 sergeants, 20 corporals, 20 drummers, 20 fifers and two principal musicians; and by an act of Oct. 2d, 1862, men enrolled for the army were permitted to choose service in the marine corps or the navy.

Previous to the war the U. S. marine corps was an exceptionally fine and well-disciplined body of men, and from it came the nucleus of the corresponding establishment of the Confederate service. Its headquarters were at the Washington navy-yard, and the following officers resigned and tendered their swords to the Confederate Government :

Maj. Henry B. Tyler, of Va., adjutant of the corps; Capt. and Brevet Maj. Geo. H. Terret, of Va.; Capt. Robert Tansill,[1] of Va.; Capt. Algernon S.

---

[1] Capt. Tansill was on duty on the U. S. frigate *Congress*, at Monte Video, when the inaugural address of President Lincoln was received there. On May 17th, 1861, he tendered his resignation; and in his letter, after stating that he had read the address, and that it seemed to him that if the policy therein announced was carried out civil war must ensue, added :

" In entering the public service I took an oath to support the Constitution, which necessarily gives me a right to interpret it. Our institutions, according to my understanding, are founded upon the principles and right of self-govern-

ment. The States forming the Confederacy did not relinquish that right, and I believe each State has a clear and unquestionable right to secede whenever the people thereof think proper, and the Federal government has no legal or moral authority to use physical force to keep them in the Union.

" Entertaining these views, I cannot conscientiously join in a war against any of the States which have already seceded, or may hereafter secede, either North or South, for the purpose of coercing them back into the Union. Such a war, in my opinion, would not only certainly

Taylor,[1] of Va.; Capt. John D. Simms, of Va.; First Lieut. Israel Greene, of Va.; First Lieut. John K. H. Tatnall, of Ga.; First Lieut. Julius E. Meire, of Md.; First Lieut. Geo. P. Turner, of Va.; First Lieut. Thos. S. Wilson, of Mo.; First Lieut. Andrew J. Hays, of Ala.; First Lieut. Adam N. Baker; Second Lieut. George Holmes, of Fla.; Second Lieut. Calvin L. Sayre, of Ala.; Second Lieut. Henry L. Ingraham, of So. Car., and Second Lieut. Baker K. Howell, of Miss.

Most of these officers arrived in Richmond by the time that the seat of the Confederate government was transferred from Montgomery to that city; and, with the exception of Capt. Tansill and Lieut. Turner, they thenceforth served in the C. S. marine corps. They met at Richmond, in May 1861, more than a hundred men of their former command in the Federal service, who fully shared in their enthusiasm for the Confederate cause and had left their comfortable berths under the old flag to risk their lives and fortunes in the yet untested possibilities of the success of the South.

There had been no concert of action by which so many of the former men and officers of the U. S. marine corps were assembled at Richmond, but it was not an unfortunate accident for the Confederacy that they did come together at that time. They formed the skeleton of the organization that it was desired to establish, and brought it into order and being with a celerity that would have been impossible to unskilled hands.

The organization of the corps, which had begun at Montgomery, was completed at Richmond. Col. Lloyd J. Beall,[2] a

and permanently destroy the Confederacy, but, if successful, establish an unlimited despotism on the ruins of our liberty. No personal consideration or advantage, however great, can induce me to aid in a cause which my heart tells me is wrong, and I prefer to endure the most terrible hardships rather than to prosper in the destruction of the freedom of my country. And believing, sir, that it would be disingenuous in me to retain my commission until the government might require my services in such a contest and then decline to serve, I consider it but prudent and just to now tender my resignation as a captain in the United States marine corps."

The action of the Navy Department in the case of Capt. Tansill was one of the many incidents of the war that Northern historians, conscious that they could not be glossed over by apologetic casuistry, chose to pass by without mention. Although his sole offence consisted in his expression, in his letter of resignation, of the reasons that prompted him to the step, upon his arrival in New York, on August the 23d, 1861, he was arrested by the order of Secretary Welles, and placed in imprisonment in Fort Lafayette. No hearing or trial was ever granted him ; but on the day after sending him to prison, Mr. Welles forwarded him, not an acceptance of his resignation, but the information that, by direction of the President, his name had been stricken from the roll of the U. S. marine corps. From Fort Lafayette, Capt. Tansill was transferred to Fort Warren, Boston harbor, and was not released until Jan. 10th, 1862, when he was formally exchanged. The gross injustice done him was recognized in an act of the Confederate Congress of April 11th, 1863, which provided that " officers of the navy and marine corps who resigned from the navy and marine corps of the United States in consequence of secession, and

who were arrested and imprisoned in consequence of such resignation, and who subsequently joined the navy and marine corps of the Confederate States," should receive " leave of absence, pay for and during the term of such imprisonment, and up to the time of their appointment in the navy and marine corps of the Confederate States."

[1] Algernon S. Taylor had been an officer of the U. S. army, and in 1838 was transferred to the marine corps as a second lieutenant. He rose to the rank of captain in that corps, and on April 26th, 1861, he offered his resignation to the Secretary of the Navy. It was not accepted, but he was dismissed from the service. Going to Richmond, Capt. Taylor offered his services to Gen. Lee, and was commissioned a colonel of infantry in the Provisional army of Va. He was ordered by Gen. Lee to establish a school of instruction and mustering-in depot at Culpepper C H., and after the amalgamation of the army of Virginia with the Confederate States forces, he was requested by Secretary Mallory to take charge of the quartermaster's and commissary's departments of the marine corps, with the rank of major. He remained in that position until the evacuation of Richmond, when he was ordered to send all his books and papers by his assistant, Lieut. Venable, to Danville, where they were destroyed. Maj. Taylor joined Lee's retreating army, and surrendered at Appomattox C. H.

[2] Colonel Beall, now approaching fourscore years, is a resident of Richmond. His books and papers were destroyed by fire about the close of the war, and in that disaster were lost many of the most valuable records of the corps. " The corps," he says, in a letter to the author, " was composed of enlisted men, many of whom were old soldiers and commissioned officers, a

former officer of the U. S. army, was appointed commandant with the rank of colonel. A commission as paymaster, with the rank of major, was issued to Richard Taylor Allison, who had held similar rank and office in the U. S. navy. [1]

Other commissions issued at Richmond, made Henry B. Tyler lieut. colonel of the corps; Geo. H. Terret, major; Capt. Greene, who captured John Brown, at Harper's Ferry, when the U. S. marines attacked his fortress in the engine-house at the arsenal, was made adjutant, with the rank of major ; Lieut. Taylor became quartermaster, with the rank of major ; and Simms, Tatnall, Holmes, Meire, Wilson and Hays, were appointed captains. Sayre and Howell were made lieutenants, and the lists of that rank were subsequently filled up by appointments made from time to time. Capts. Thom and Van Benthuysen, and all the lieutenants, except Sayre and Howell, were appointed from civil life, or from the army and navy, while the other officers, with the exception of Col. Beall, came from the U. S. marine service.

The corps remained in and around Richmond, practically unbroken, until the summer of 1862. It was engaged in the battle with the Federal iron-clads *Monitor, Naugatuck* and *Galena*, at Drewry's Bluff, on May 15th, when its service at the guns assisted the artillerists of the army and navy in the repulse of those vessels. Major Terrett commanded the corps on that occasion, and soon after detachments from it were ordered to other stations, and to vessels preparing for sea, or for the coast defence. Because of the great lack of trained seamen in the Confederacy, the veteran marines were of inestimable value on board the ships to which they were attached, and they were made use of in numerous capacities that embraced the duties of sailors. One squad of marines that fought at Drewry's Bluff had previously formed a part of the ship's company of the *Virginia*, and had helped work her guns in the battles in Hampton Roads. They were under the command of Capt. R. Thom, and remained with the ship until she was destroyed. Other detachments served on the *Sumter* and the

number of whom had seen service before in the U. S marine corps and elsewhere. The corps was thoroughly trained and disciplined, and in all encounters with the enemy the officers and men were conspicuous for their courage and good conduct."

[1] Richard Taylor Allison is a native of Jefferson county, Ky., and removed to Baltimore in 1845. In 1849 he was appointed paymaster in the U. S. navy by his uncle, President Taylor. He served first in the Pacific squadron and on the coast of California ; then in the Japan expedition, under Com. Perry, and next in the squadron in the Chinese waters. Returning home in 1856, he was assigned to duty as inspector of provisions at Washington, and afterwards was appointed paymaster at the Washington navy-yard. He occupied that position on April 20th, 1861, when he tendered his resignation to Secretary Welles, being moved to that action by the occurrences of the previous day in Baltimore, and wrote to Gen. Geo. H. Stewart,

commanding the Maryland troops in Baltimore, proffering his services. At the same time he informed President Davis of what he had done. Owing to the interruption of railway travel north of Baltimore, no officer could be immediately obtained to relieve him at the Washington navy-yard ; and, in compliance with the request of Secretary Welles, he remained on duty as paymaster until May 1st. His successor took charge on that date, and he did not discover until the end of the war that the Navy Department had not accepted his resignation, but had dismissed him from the service. As soon as he was relieved he went to Richmond and telegraphed thence to President Davis, who summoned him to Montgomery and appointed him paymaster of the marine corps. He served in that capacity until the close of hostilities and surrendered with Gen. Johnston's army at Greensboro', N. C. Since then he has resided in Baltimore, where he was honored with the position of clerk of the Superior Court.

Alabama during their cruises, and were commanded by Lieut. B. K. Howell, who was highly commended by Capt. Semmes. Lieut. James Thurston commanded the marine guard on the *Atlanta*, during her brief and ill-starred career in the waters around Savannah, and had charge, with his men, of a division of the guns, in the short engagement in the Ogeechee that ended with her surrender. When Adm. Buchanan took the *Tennessee* out to fight Farragut's fleet in Mobile Bay, he had on board a marine guard, under the command of Lieut. David G. Raney, which was assigned to one of the gun divisions, and was largely instrumental in the quick and efficient work with her battery that inflicted such great damage upon the enemy. In the same battle a detachment of marines, under the command of Lieut. J. R. T. Fendall, served on the gunboat *Gaines*, and escaped to Mobile with the crew, after the vessel was beached under the guns of Fort Morgan. At the defence of Fort Fisher, Dec. 24th–25th, 1864, and Jan. 5th, 1865, a body of marines participated. They were commanded by Capt. A. C. Van Benthuysen, and Lieuts. Henry N. Doak and J. Campbell Murdoch. Finally, such companies and detachments of the corps as were not isolated at Mobile, or were not away at sea, or had not been captured, were gathered around Richmond in Feb. and March, 1865, and were then assigned to the former positions of the marines in the fortifications on Drewry's Bluff. Then they made up a part of the naval brigade, under Com. John R. Tucker, and with the sailors held out at the battle of Saylor's Creek, after Gen. Ewell had surrendered.

This mention is to be taken only as a scant index of the services of the marines. Their inadequacy in numbers to the tasks required of them necessitated the breaking up of the corps into small detachments, and hence they participated in many actions their share in which has not been recorded. The report of Col. Beall, dated Oct. 30th, 1864, shows that the aggregate strength of the corps then was but 539 men, of which number two captains, three lieutenants, and sixty-two privates were prisoners in the hands of the enemy, and thirty-two recruits had recently been received at the Charleston naval station from the conscript camp near Raleigh, N. C. The report continues :

"The marine corps is distributed at the following naval stations : Mobile, Savannah, Charleston, Wilmington, and at Drewry's Bluff ; also on board of the three iron-clad steamers in the James River, and as guards at the Richmond navy-yards. Marine guards have been assigned to the armed steamers *Tallahassee* and *Chickamauga*, destined to operate against the enemy's commerce on the sea.

"Since my last report the marines have been under the enemy's fire at Drewry's Bluff and on the James River ; also in the land and naval engagements near Mobile, on the 5th and 6th of August last. A marine guard under the command of Lieut. Crenshaw was attached to the Confederate steamship *Tallahassee* during the late cruise, when much damage was inflicted upon the enemy's shipping at sea.

"Upon all occasions when the marines have been called upon for active service, they have displayed the promptness and efficiency of well disciplined soldiers."

COLONEL LLOYD I. BEALL,

CONFEDERATE STATES MARINE CORPS.

C. S. STEAMER "PATRICK HENRY,"

NAVAL SCHOOL SHIP.

CHAPTER XXV.

THE CONFEDERATE STATES NAVAL ACADEMY.

TO establish a naval school for the proper training of the younger officers of the Confederate navy was a project to which Secretary Mallory had given much thought from the time of his entrance upon the duties of his office; but although such an institution was amply authorized by a section of an act of Congress approved March 16th, 1861, which provided that the naval laws of the United States not inconsistent with the act be applied to the navy of the Confederate States, it was not until 1863 that steps to form the academy were taken. Acting midshipmen had previously been appointed, and by an act of Congress approved April 21st, 1862, their number was limited to 106 and that of passed midshipmen to twenty. On March 23d, 1863, Mr. Mallory laid the foundations of the school by an order for the examination by a board of officers of the acting midshipmen at the several stations in seamanship, gunnery, mathematics, steam engineering, navigation, English studies, French, drawing and drafting. Captains Sidney Smith Lee, Samuel Barron and others were assigned to duty as examiners, and in the meantime Lieut. Wm. Harwar Parker[1] was selected as commandant of the school to be formed, and instructed to formulate regulations for its government. The C. S. steamship *Patrick Henry*, of the James River squadron, was chosen as the schoolship; a mast fully rigged with square yards was stepped in her for

---

[1] Lieut. Parker was a son of Com. Foxhall Parker, U. S. N., and brother of Com. Foxhall A. Parker, U. S. N. While one brother went with the South, the other remained in the Federal navy during the war, and attained distinction. Wm. H. Parker entered the U. S. navy in 1841, when he was 14 years old, and graduated at the head of a class at the Naval Academy that gave to the United States and Confederate States service more distinguished officers than any other single class. Previous to the war between the States, he had attained high reputation as an officer and instructor, and held the position of assistant professor of mathematics at the Annapolis Institution. In the Confederate navy he had taken part in the battles in the North Carolina Sounds; had commanded the gunboat *Beaufort* at the battle of Hampton Roads, and was executive officer of the iron-clad *Palmetto State*, at Charleston, in the breaking of the blockade. His professional writings were used as textbooks at Annapolis and in the Confederate Naval Academy. They were "Elements of Seamanship," "Harbor Routine and Evolutions," "Naval Tactics," "Naval Light Artillery Afloat and Ashore," and "Remarks on the Navigation of the Coasts between San Francisco and Panama." After the war he commanded vessels of the Pacific Mail Steamship Company, was subsequently President of the Maryland Agricultural College, and is now (1887) U. S. consul at Bahia.

the practice of the midshipmen and quarters for them were fitted up. On July 23d, 1863, Com. John M. Brooke, in charge of the office of ordnance and hydrography at Richmond, who had supervision of the establishment of the academy, "approved and recommended for adoption" the regulations prepared by Lieut. Parker, and on their approval by Secretary Mallory the naval school went into operation.

In the fall of 1863, the Navy Department selected the following academic staff :

Lieutenant W. B. Hall,[1] commandant of midshipmen; Lieutenant Oscar F. Johnston, professor of astronomy, navigation and surveying ; Lieut. Thomas W. W. Davies, assistant ; Lieut. C. J. Graves, instructor in seamanship ; Lieut. James W. Billups, assistant ; Lieut. Wm. Van Comstock, instructor in gunnery ; Master George M. Peek, mathematics ; Master George W. Armistead, physics ; Master George A. Pepley, French and German ; — Sanxey, infantry tactics ; ——, sword master ; assistant surgeons, W. J. Addison, James G. Bixley; paymaster, Wm. M. Ladd; second assistant engineer, E. G. Hall; boatswain, Andrew Blakie; gunner, E. R. Johnson (subsequently William F. Brittingham); sail-maker, William Bennett.

The staff remained almost intact until the school perished with the Confederacy. In the summer of 1864, Lieut. O. F. Johnson relieved Lieut. Hall as commandant of midshipmen in order that the latter might devote more attention to the instruction of the classes, and in November, Lieut. B. P. Loyall relieved Lieut. Johnson. The only other change of importance was that later Com. James Henry Rochelle was ordered to the school as commandant of midshipmen and executive officer. As far as the exigencies of war would permit, the organization, studies and discipline of the school were modeled upon the curriculum of the U. S. Naval Academy. Cadets were appointed by members of Congress from their respective districts and by the President from the Confederacy at large, and the school began work with fifty acting midshipmen.

[1] Lieut. Wilburn B. Hall was appointed to the U. S. naval academy from Louisiana in 1855 and graduated at the head of his class. In 1861 he was attached as acting flag-lieutenant to Com. Inman, commanding the squadron on the African coast, and at the outbreak of the war re-turned to the United States in a captured slave-ship with 700 negroes on board. Lieut. Hall was ordered to take them back to Africa and de-liver them to the Liberian government. He then entered the Confederate service, for which he purchased and carried South from New York the steamer *Hunters* He took this vessel into Charleston, March 18th, 1861, with the flag of Georgia flying from her masthead. During the war Lieut. Hall served on and commanded vari-ous vessels and at various stations. He was with Com. Tatnall at the fall of Port Royal, in all the actions around Richmond, Charleston, and dur-ing its siege, as well as in those around Savan-nah and in its adjacent waters. He aided Tat-nall to provision Fort Pulaski when that fort was cut off by the United States ships-of-war and batteries, running in under a terrific fire from Federal guns in broad daylight and through a line of thirteen vessels. He marched the crew of the *Harriet Lane* across the State of Texas to man the iron-clad *Louisiana* on Red River, and subsequently commanded the *Webb, Savannah, Drewry, Resolute* and other vessels. He married the daughter of Com. Ingraham, the great grand-daughter of Henry Laurens, president of the Revolutionary Congress, as well as of John Rut-ledge, Governor, with power of dictator, of South Carolina, in the Revolution, and later Justice of the U. S. Supreme Court. He was detached from the naval academy at his own request Nov. 1864, and ordered to the iron-clad *Chicora*, at Charleston, S. C. Since the war Lieut. Hall has served as major of engineers on the staff of the Khedive of Egypt, being selected for that position by General W. T. Sherman. He is now (1887) a leading instructor in Balti-more.

They were required to be not under fourteen or over eighteen years of age, and on the roll were represented many of the most distinguished families of the South. After passing a physical examination and an examination on such elementary studies as reading, writing, spelling and the four principles of arithmetic, they became acting midshipmen and entered upon their studies, which comprised six departments and twenty-two branches. There were four annual courses and the midshipmen were arranged into four classes, each class pursuing one of these courses. The studies of the fourth class embraced practical seamanship, naval gunnery and artillery and infantry tactics, arithmetic, algebra to equations of the first degree, English grammar and descriptive geography; those of the third class, practical seamanship, gunnery and artillery and infantry tactics, algebra, geometry, plane and spherical trigonometry, physical geography, history and the French language; those of the second class, seamanship and steam, gunnery and field artillery, astronomy, navigation, application of algebra and trigonometry to mensuration of planes and solids, political science and French; those of the first class, seamanship and naval tactics, gunnery, infantry tactics, navigation, surveying, French and Spanish.

The Academic Board held examinations in each June and December, and the December examination was attended by a board of visitors, composed of three captains and two commanders, who ascertained and decided upon the qualifications of the midshipmen for promotion; and as rapidly as the latter were deemed proficient they were ordered to ships, batteries or other duty. But while the cadets of the U. S. Naval Academy were being trained far away from the scene of hostilities, at Newport, R. I., where it had been removed during the war, those of the Confederate school received their professional education in the face of actual warfare, in which they were frequently called from their studies to engage. The *Patrick Henry* was usually stationed near Drewry's Bluff, the scene of desperate fighting, and by the time they were sent to distant service they were versed in the practice as well as the theory of war. If the routine of a day was not broken by a summons to man the guns on shore, or do scouting, or take part in boat expeditions, it was full of hard work on board. The morning gun was fired at seven o'clock, and at eight a breakfast of hard-tack and a decoction of sweet potatoes or beans that masqueraded as coffee was served. Sick call, studies and recitations occupied the hours until two o'clock, and then came a dinner of salt-junk, perhaps a mess of vegetables, and the inevitable corn-meal that became a staple article of diet when wheat-flour climbed toward $1,200 per barrel in Confederate currency. School exercises and dress parade took up the remainder of the afternoon, and the day ended with tattoo at 9:30, and taps at ten o'clock.

Near the close of the war, when it became necessary to have the boys on shore pretty much all the time to stand to the guns, they occupied huts in' the Drewry's Bluff batteries. It was a truly unique education for them—school-boys one hour and fighting men the next, dropping their books to take up their carbines and cutlasses, exchanging in a moment their studies for places in the trenches a few hundred yards distant from those of the enemy—and amidst the stern and awful realities of the final struggle around Richmond they retained the happy, hearty, healthy spirit of brave boys and combined it with the courage and understanding of men. Such a training nourished and strengthened their finest qualities, and it is not remarkable that so many of them have since risen to positions of great honor and trust, and exemplified the virtues and worthy ambitions of civil life.

The school had been in existence scarcely a year before their mettle was tested and approved. This was in May, 1864, when Gen. Butler landed his army at Bermuda Hundreds and there were but 3,000 Confederates between the Appomattox River and Richmond. Com. J. K. Mitchell, commanding the James River squadron, threw his men into the fortifications, while the midshipmen were placed in the iron-clads, Lieut. Parker taking one detachment to the *Fredericksburg*, and Lieuts. Hall and Johnson another to the *Virginia*. The Howlett House battery became the left flank of Lee's army on the James, and was itself defended by the ships. In the succeeding engagements with the enemy's gunboats and monitors around the Howlett House and Drewry's Bluff, the midshipmen were landed under the command of Lieut. W. B. Hall, and took part in several interesting skirmishes with the Federal sharp-shooters. During all the summer of 1864, the young academicians had more fighting than studying to do. Lieut. Billups was left in command of the *Patrick Henry*, and the midshipmen who remained on board were mostly employed in directing scouting parties, leading the boat expeditions, and working in the batteries. A lull in the heavier fighting along the river that occurred in September permitted the resumption of exercises on the schoolship under Lieut. Hall, and a month later Lieut. Parker was relieved of the command of the *Fredericksburg* and returned to the *Patrick Henry;* which, when the midshipmen occasionally took up their quarters on shore, was moored first at Wilton and then at Rockets, on the water front of Richmond.

When the fall of Richmond became imminent, Secretary Mallory determined to transfer the naval school to some point in the interior of the Confederacy. Lieut. Graves was sent into North Carolina, South Carolina and Georgia to examine concerning localities and buildings, but could only report that the movements of the enemy prevented the selection of any site to which the institution could safely be removed.

The protection of the bridge over the James River at Wilton was entrusted to the midshipmen in the *Patrick Henry,* and although then a part of the line of battle the routine of the academy was kept up with some approach to regularity. The sixty young men and their ten officers made up an admirable, well-drilled, disciplined and efficient corps. Lieut. Parker had his orders to prepare the ship for sinking in the obstructions of the river if necessary, and he rented a warehouse at the corner of Franklin and 24th Streets in Richmond for the home of the midshipmen, and the location of stores. This was done in March 1865, but there was so little suspicion afloat that Richmond was so soon to be evacuated, that he spent the night of April 1st in the city, and it was not until the afternoon of April 2d that he received the order to have the corps and its officers at the Danville depot at 6 o'clock P. M., and report to the Quartermaster General of the army. He directed Lieut. Rochelle to execute the order, while he would remain by the ship, expecting the corps to return within a few days. In an hour or two he found out that the abandonment of the capital was intended, and then leaving Lieut. Billups and ten men to burn the ship, he joined the corps at the Danville depot. Billups and his squad performed their duty, but in the subsequent movements never overtook their comrades.

No higher compliment could have been paid the midshipmen, than the final duty entrusted to them. It was the guardianship of the train which contained the archives of the Confederate Government and the specie and bullion funds of the treasury. The corps left Richmond on the evening of April 2d, and proceeded to Danville in charge of the treasure, where Midshipman Raphael Semmes, Jr. was detailed to the staff of his father, the Admiral, and Midshipman Breckenridge was made personal aide to his father, the Secretary of War. From the 3d to the 9th the corps remained at Danville, and then moved southward. Greensboro, N. C., was reached on the 10th, and Charlotte on the 13th. At Charlotte the money was transferred to the mint, but taken out again when the escort started for Chester, S. C. At Chester the railroad was abandoned and a wagon train made up. The gold was packed in small square boxes, and the silver in kegs, and the road was taken for Newberry, S. C. Mrs. Jefferson Davis and her child (now Miss Winnie Davis, the "daughter of the Confederacy") had joined the escort at Chester, and travelled in an ambulance to Newberry, where they arrived on the 15th, and left on the cars the same day for Abbeville, S. C. At Abbeville the treasure was transferred once more to wagons, and on the 17th the midshipmen took up the march for Washington, Ga., which was reached on the 19th, and Augusta on the 20th. In all this toilsome, perilous, and responsible march, Lieut. Parker was looking for President Davis or some responsible officer of the Treasury Department to whom he could hand over his precious trust. Beside his brave midshipmen, he had with him a company of good men under Capt. Tabb, who had joined him at the Charlotte naval station ; but this force was small in comparison with the number of marauders he might at any time chance to meet. The impoverished and ravaged country was swarming with them—bummers, looters and deserters hanging on to the rear of Sherman's army, half-starved Confederates rendered desperate by suffering, roving bands of negroes, and all the rabble that infested that war-swept region. They were to be feared ; and moreover, great numbers of Federal cavalry were riding on Sherman's flanks, and were on several occasions so near to the treasure train that they might have swooped down upon it. Its guards, as Parker knew and said, would have died fighting around it ; but an attack by an overwhelming force upon such a tempting prize as millions of gold and silver was always possible ; and he was strongly urged to divide the treasure among the men following him. But he and the corps of midshipmen were inviolate in their sense of duty, and when he placed the coin and bullion in the vaults of a bank at Augusta, they were intact. He turned the charge of the treasure over to a Treasury officer, whom he found in that city, but the midshipmen continued to guard it. They remained in Augusta during the armistice between Gens. Johnston and Sherman, Parker declining to obey an order to disband the corps so long as they were responsible for the safety of the treasure. On the termination of the armistice they took the gold and silver out of the bank and returned to Washington, Ga., still searching for President Davis. Then they struck off for Abbeville, where they arrived on April 29th. The treasure was stored in a warehouse, and President Davis and his escort came into town the next day. Secretary Mallory accompanied him, and by the Secretary's orders Lieut. Parker turned the treasure over to the Acting Secretary of the Confederate Treasury, who directed it to be delivered to Gen. Basil Duke, who commanded the cavalry detachment escorting Mr. Davis. Neither Lieut. Parker nor any of the midshipmen or officers ever knew how much money there was in the packages, which were not broken while in their charge.

The corps of cadet midshipmen was disbanded at Abbeville on May 2d, 1865, though the orders did not so read, and its members were never surrendered to the enemy or paroled. The order issued to each man simply said :

"ABBEVILLE, S. C., May 2d, 1865.
" SIR : You are hereby detached from the Naval School and leave is granted you to visit your home. You will report by letter to the Hon. Secretary of the Navy as soon as possible. Paymaster Wheliss will issue you ten days' rations, and all quartermasters are requested to furnish you transportation.
" Respectfully your obedient servant,
" WM. H. PARKER, *Commanding*."

To have dismissed them so shabbily as indicated in the above order would have been a shameful reward for their faithful and arduous service, and at the intercession of Capt. Parker and a committee of five cadets, Postmaster General Reagan obtained the sum of $1,500, which gave $40 in gold to each midshipman, upon the receipt of which they started for their respective homes in the distant States of the Confederacy. The high esteem in which President Davis held the corps of cadet midshipmen was manifested by him when informed at Abbeville by Capt. Parker that the corps had been disbanded by the order of Secretary Mallory. "Captain," he said, "I am *very* sorry to hear it," and repeated the regret several times. Upon being told that the corps had been disbanded on the peremptory order of the Secretary, the President replied : "Captain, I have no fault to find with you, but I am *very* sorry Mr. Mallory gave you the order." The very great regret of the President was accounted for when his escort of four skeleton brigades of cavalry were seen. Though there were many in the command ready to follow and defend the President, yet demoralization had entered there too. Arms were being sold or thrown away, and it was apparent that but little reliance could be placed upon that escort. Hence the regret with which he learned that the young men, the sons of the leaders of the cause, organized, educated and trained to the discharge of duty, had been scattered, and could no longer guard and protect him in his proposed journey to the trans-Mississippi.

Though the Confederate Naval Academy produced no record of its usefulness, yet the young men who were taught upon the decks of the *Patrick Henry* learned valuable lessons of self-reliance and duty, which in after life made them, without an exception, earnest, thoughtful, law-abiding men. Among those midshipmen we recall the names of Colonel Morgan, after the war a captain in the Egyptian army and subsequently consul general in Australia ; Windom K. Mayo, commander of steamers and collector of customs at Norfolk, Va. ; Jeff. Davis Howell, [1] who lost his life in the brave

---

[1] Jefferson Davis Howell was born at Natchez, Mississippi, in 1846. His father, William Burr Howell, born in New Jersey, was appointed an ensign and third lieutenant in the 15th Regiment of the U. S. Inf , on August the 19th, 1813. He was promoted to second lieutenant in March, 1814, and served throughout the war of 1812-14. While serving as an officer of marines in McDonough's victory on Lake Champlain, on board the ship *Saratoga*, Lieut. Howell greatly distinguished himself. Captain White Youngs, of the 15th Inf., commanding a detachment of acting marines, in his report to Com. McDonough thus mentions him : "Second Lieut. William H. Howell, 15th Inf., in the U. S. ship *Saratoga*, rendered me every assistance; notwithstanding his having been confined for ten days of a fever, yet, at the commencement of the action, he was found on deck, and continued until the enemy

had struck, when he was borne to his bed. I would also recommend him to your notice."

At the close of the war in May, 1815, Lieut. Howell was retained in the artillery branch of the service, but declined the honor, and soon after resigned. He married Margaret Graham Kemp, native of Virginia. She was the daughter of Col. Kemp, of Natchez, Miss., where Mr. Howell resided for many years; he afterwards removed to New Orleans, where he was appointed deputy surveyor of the port. He had eleven children, Jefferson Davis Howell being the youngest. He was named after Hon. Jefferson Davis, who had married his sister on February 26th, 1845.

Jefferson Davis Howell was educated at Burlington, N. J., Washington, D. C., and Richmond, Va. He was of an active and adventurous temperament, and like most young men in the

discharge of duty when the Pacific mail steamship which he commanded was wrecked; the Hon. C. R. Breckenridge, at present a member of the U. S. House of Representatives; Colonel J. T. Scharf, the author of this work, land commissioner of Maryland, commissioner of the National Exposition

South, shared in the excitement just preceding the outbreak of the war between the States. He was well versed in the political history of the time, and his convictions as well as his sympathies induced him to espouse the cause of the Southern States. Though but sixteen years of age he entered a military organization in New Orleans, and after faithfully serving in the army, on February 24th, 1863, he received an appointment as midshipman in the navy of the Confederate States, and was ordered on board the schoolship *Patrick Henry*, then lying at Drewry's Bluff, James River, to stand an examination. Letters of recommendation being required from his previous commanders, they were obtained. All of these spoke in the highest terms of praise of his gallant and meritorious conduct in the military service, his uniform good behavior and the promptness and faithfulness with which he discharged all the duties required of him in camp and elsewhere. After passing his examination, Midshipman Howell was ordered to Charleston, S. C., where he performed hard service during the winter of 1863-64, in picket-boat duty, between Fort Sumter and Morris Island. While engaged in this arduous and exposed service, he captured an armed picket-boat of the enemy engaged in the same duties; assisted in laying a number of torpedoes in Charleston harbor, and aided in placing a raft of logs around Fort Sumter to prevent another assault. After the evacuation of Charleston in 1865, Midshipman Howell was assigned to the artillery with the rank of lieutenant in the naval brigade of Adm. Semmes, formerly the commander of the C. S. steamer *Alabama*. He was captured, paroled, and joined his sister, Mrs. Jefferson Davis, at Washington, Ga., and was with her at the time of the capture of President Davis. He was imprisoned at Fort McHenry for several months, and upon being released went to Savannah, Ga., where he was again imprisoned. From thence he joined his brother in Canada, and accompanied him to England. Returning to the United States by way of Portland, Me., he was again arrested and sent to Fort Warren, where he was detained for a few weeks and then finally released. He returned to Canada, and from thence went to New York to find himself without means or employment. Scorning to live on his friends, he went to sea before the mast, and made several voyages to Bordeaux, the Cape de Verde Islands, and elsewhere in the Atlantic. His devotion to duty and his thorough competency were soon recognized, and he speedily rose to the rank of mate. While serving in this capacity, in some evolution of the ship he was so injured as to compel him to remain ashore for several months. He then accepted a position upon the staff of the New York *News*. Tiring of an inactive life ashore, he obtained a berth on board the Pacific mail steamer *Ariel* as quartermaster, and sailed from New York in the fall of 1869, for China; thence he returned to San Francisco. During his brief residence in that city, he served as first officer on the steamers *John L. Stephens*, *Ajax* and *Oriflamme*. Speedily rising in rank, his first command was the *Idaho*, and thereafter was given charge successively of the steamers *Moses Taylor*, *Pelican*, *California*, *Nevada*, *Los Angelos*, and lastly the ill-fated *Pacific*.

On February 23d, 1874, Capt. Howell was a passenger on board of the *Los Angelos;* on her voyage from San Francisco to Victoria the steamer broke her propeller shaft, the helm refused to do its duty, and no human agency could be brought to dispel the discouraging forebodings which pressed upon the 150 passengers, and officers and crew who were on board. Tossed about by the waves without a sign of release from their agonizing situation, and drifting towards the dreaded breakers, all hands were in despair. At this critical moment Capt. Howell volunteered to take his chances of life or death in his effort to make the land and reach Astoria, where it was known all would be rendered immediately. With a boat's crew he bravely pushed through the raging sea and landed on the beach above Tillamook, walked to Astoria, obtained a tug which came to the rescue of the disabled vessel and towed her into port. The passengers on the *Los Angelos*, mindful of the great service they owed to Capt. Howell, for the heroism he displayed in saving their lives, tendered him the following complimentary resolutions:

"Whereas, Capt. Jefferson D. Howell, by noble deeds of daring succeeded in reaching Astoria, after we had supposed he had lost his own life in the vain endeavor to save us from a terrible death, therefore:

Resolved—That we return our thanks to the Giver of all good for sparing the life of our noble benefactor, thus enabling him to reach a haven wherein succor to ourselves was speedily rendered.

Resolved—That the action of Capt. Howell in this matter entitles him to our most sincere gratitude, and that we hereby pledge and express to him that thankfulness of human hearts which is more precious than gold, more enduring than diamonds, in the tender regard which we bear for him, and shall ever hold towards him, so long as memory shall dwell within its sacred tabernacle."

Talented, brave and true, and whether serving before the mast or in command of a crowded steamship, always the same courteous and chivalric gentleman, Capt. Howell was beloved by all who came in contact with him. No man was ever more ready to take up the cause of the defenceless than he, and his friends can recall many instances of the liberality with which he disposed of his hard-earned salary in acts of generosity. In the course of conversation on his last voyage from Victoria, he gave an account of how he became a communicant of the Episcopal Church. It seems, as he parted from his mother for a long voyage, he promised to be confirmed the first opportunity. Ere the opportunity occurred she was in her grave, but he was not the man to forget his vow. He was confirmed by Bishop Potter, in New York. While relating the circumstance, he said, with honest pride: "Since my confirmation I have never done anything that conflicted with those solemn vows;" and all who know him will bear testimony that such was the life of this Christian gentleman. His was an Anglo-Saxon face

at New Orleans; William P. Hamilton,[1] of South Carolina, and R. H. Fleming, a Presbyterian clergyman of prominence in Virginia. F. C. Morehead, late commissioner general of the New Orleans Exposition and president of the National Cotton and Planters' Association, was another of the young middies of the *Patrick Henry*, as well as Clarence Cary, a lawyer of high standing in New York and a gentleman of fine literary attainments; the Rev. J. G. Minnegerode, J. De B. Northrop, Preston B. Moore, William A. Lee, nephew of General R. E. Lee; John H. Inglis, a son of the late Judge Inglis, president of the South Carolina Secession Convention of 1860, and many others of equal distinction.

of the highest type, with high brow, fair hair, and laughing blue eyes. He combined the tenderness of a woman with the courage of a man. His little room was hung about with the portraits of his friends, and in the centre was an ivory miniature of his dead mother, whom he adored.

The last act of Capt. Howell was worthy of his life. The steamer *Pacific* was foundered in a gale off Cape Flattery, near Victoria. The survivors of the wreck report that Capt. Howell was drowned from a raft on which some of the unfortunate passengers and crew had taken refuge, and that he was the last man to leave the ship. A writer giving an account of the disaster, says: "When one of the occupants of the raft, a woman, was swept away, what did Howell do, though the sea was running mountain high, and experienced sailor as he was, he knew that once from his support he was lost forever? He acted as every one was sure he would act, and at the cry of a perishing woman, plunged in to her assistance, sacrificing his own life in the same locality where, seven short months before, by another act of heroism he saved the lives of 150 persons aboard the steamer *Los Angelos*, which would have gone ashore among the breakers, had he not volunteered his successful assistance."

[1] Capt. Wm. P. Hamilton, son of Col. Paul Hamilton, and Catherine A. Campbell, was born in Beaufort, S. C., Oct. 11th, 1845, and died May 3, 1875. He was a great-grandson of Hon. Paul Hamilton, who was secretary of the navy under President Madison, and great-nephew of Archibald Hamilton, U. S. N., who served under Decatur. In Aug. 1861, William P. Hamilton received an appointment as midshipman in the C. S. navy, and served on the *Lady Davis*, under Lieut. Com. John Rutledge, at Port Royal. He was subsequently stationed on the steamer *Nashville*, until the summer of 1862,

when he was ordered to Richmond to stand his examination on the *Patrick Henry*. He graduated as passed midshipman, and was ordered to the *Palmetto State*, at Charleston. He participated in the attack on the U. S. steamer *Mercedita*, and the Federal blockading fleet, and served in the navy with distinguished gallantry in the defence of Charleston. In April, 1864, he was ordered to the ram *Albemarle*, at Plymouth, N. C., and took a conspicuous part in the fight with the Federal gunboats at that place. He returned to Charleston, and served there until the close of the war. After the war he worked his passage to England, on the bark *Nutfield*. During the voyage the crew were stricken down with the yellow fever, and his cousin, ex-midshipman P. Hamilton Gibbs, died. There were not sufficient hands on board to man the vessel, and the helm was lashed and the bark allowed to run before the wind, until some of the sick were convalescent. She finally arrived at Liverpool, when W. P. Hamilton shipped as a seaman on the *West Indian*, in the South American trade. Upon his return he passed an examination, and received a certificate as second mate in the British merchant service. He first served on the *John Fraser & Co.*, and subsequently was appointed mate of the *Royal George*. After each trip from Liverpool to the East Indies, he was promoted, until he became master of the ship. In 1872 he returned to Charleston, where he married. Finding that his wife could not endure the long voyages to Bombay and Calcutta, he left the Indian service after a year, and went to the Mediterranean. The following year he commanded the Clyde steamer *Atlas*, running between New York and the West Indies, but the rapid changes of climate impaired his health, and Jan. 1875 he came home to die. Capt. Hamilton was a gallant, amiable, courteous and model officer, and his career proved him to be a model man.

CHAPTER XXVI.

THE CONFEDERATE STATES CRUISERS.

IN many respects the most interesting chapter of the history of the Confederate navy is that of the building and operation of the ships-of-war which drove the merchant flag of the United States from the oceans and almost extirpated their carrying trade. But the limitations of space of this volume forbid more than a brief review of the subject. The function of commerce-destroyers is now so well admitted as an attribute of war between recognized belligerents by all the nations of the world, that no apology is necessary for the manner in which the South conducted hostilities upon the high seas against her enemy, and while the Federal officials and organs styled the cruisers " pirates " and their commanders " buccaneers," such stigmatization has long since been swept away along with other rubbish of the war between the States, and their legal status fully and honorably established. We have not the space for quotations from Prof. Soley, Prof. Bolles and other writers upon this point, but what they have said may be summed up in the statement that the government and agents of the Confederacy transgressed no principle of right in this matter, and that if the United States were at war to-day they would strike at the commerce of an enemy in as nearly the same manner as circumstances would permit. The justification of the Confederate authorities is not in the slightest degree affected by the fact that the Geneva Tribunal directed Great Britain to pay to the Federal government $15,500,000 in satisfaction for ships destroyed by cruisers constructed in British ports.

Eleven Confederate cruisers figured in the " Alabama Claims " settlement between the United States and Great Britain. They were the *Alabama, Shenandoah, Florida, Tallahassee, Georgia, Chickamauga, Nashville, Retribution, Sumter, Sallie* and *Boston.* The actual losses inflicted by the *Alabama* ($6,547,609) were only about $60,000 greater than those charged to the *Shenandoah.* The sum total of the claims filed against the eleven cruisers for ships and cargoes was $17,900,633, all but about $4,000,000 being caused by the *Alabama* and *Shenandoah*. The tribunal decided that Great Britain was in no way responsible for the losses inflicted by any cruisers but the *Alabama, Florida* and *Shenandoah*. It disallowed all the claims of the United States for indirect or consequential losses, which included the approximate extinction of American commerce by the capture of ships or their transfer to foreign flags. What this amounted to is shown in the "Case of the United States" presented to the Tribunal. In this it is stated that while in 1860 two-thirds of the commerce of New York was carried on in American bottoms, in 1863 three-fourths was carried on in foreign bottoms. The transfer of American vessels to the British flag to avoid capture is stated thus: In 1861, vessels 126, tonnage 71,673; in 1862, vessels 135, tonnage 64,578; in 1863, vessels 348, tonnage 252,579; in 1864, vessels 106, tonnage 92,052. Commanders of the Confederate cruisers have avowed that the destruction of private property and diversion of legitimate commerce in the performance of their duty was painful in the extreme to them; but in their wars the United States had always practiced this mode of harassing an enemy and had, indeed, been the most conspicuous exemplars of it that the world ever saw.

The cruisers built or purchased in England for the Confederate navy, were the *Florida, Alabama, Shenandoah* and *Rappahannock*. The latter never made a cruise, and the others were procured for the government by James D. Bulloch,[1] naval agent, in the manner hereinafter stated in the sketches of those vessels. He also had constructed in France the armored ram *Stonewall*, whose history is told in succeeding pages. His instructions from the administration of President Davis were to avoid breaches of the neutrality laws of foreign Powers. He was most careful to adhere to this precept, and the complications which occurred were due, not to his infraction of

[1] Capt. James D. Bulloch was born in Georgia and entered the U. S. navy as midshipman, at an early age, in the year 1839, and was ordered at once to join the frigate *United States*, at Boston, and cruised in that ship on the coast, to New York and to Norfolk, Va., and was there transferred with all the officers and crew to the frigate *Potomac*. He proceeded in the *Potomac* to the Brazil station and served in her and the sloop-of-war *Decatur* until 1842, when at his own request he was ordered to the line of battle ship *Delaware*, a day or two before the *Decatur* sailed for the U. S , on the termination of her cruise. He served during the famous cruise of the *Delaware* in the Mediterranean Sea under the late Com Charles Morris, and returned to the U. S. in her in March, 1844. After a short leave of absence he was ordered to the 120-gun ship *Pennsylvania* at Norfolk, and in Aug., 1844, was sent to the naval school, which was then in Philadelphia. He passed No. 2 of his class in June, 1845, and was ordered direct from the naval school to the supply ship *Erie*, at New York. He proceeded in that ship to the Pacific station and served in the squadron on the coast of California during the whole of the Mexican

war, being transferred to several different ships as the necessities of the service required He was acting master of the schooner *Shark* at the time of her cruise to the Columbia River and was in her when she was wrecked on the shoals off the mouth of that river. He returned to the U. S. in the *Lexington* in June, 1849, and after three months leave was ordered for duty on the coast survey, and was actively employed for more than two years.

When Congress subsidized the Law line of steamers for the mail route to California it was made a condition that the ships should be commanded by naval officers. Under that condition he was ordered as first officer of the U. S. mail steamer *Georgia*, commanded by Lieut. (now Admiral) D. D. Porter, and succeeded Porter in the command of that vessel. Shortly after this a company was formed in New York to run a line of mail steamers to and from Cuba, New York and New Orleans. Bulloch was given a special furlough by the Secretary of the Navy to command a steamer in that service, and commanded in succession the *Black Warrior*, *Cahawba, De Soto* and *Bienville*. He resigned his commission as lieutenant in the U. S. navy

their regulations, but to the shifting policy of the British and French governments. When he began to procure men-of-war in England, he was sustained by the opinion of counsel that he acted within the bounds of the law if they were not sent out armed and equipped, and this position was sustained by the decision of her Majesty's Court of Exchequer in the *Alexandra* case; which, in brief, was, that the subjects of a neutral power had as much right to sell to a belligerent ships as they had to sell any other munitions or implements of warfare. This was the only decision ever made during the war by a British court, upon the subject, and it justified the proceedings of Capt. Bulloch, although it was practically overruled by the detention of Confederate ships by order of the government.

Bulloch, however, was successful in getting all his vessels to sea, except the Laird rams, whose history may be related in advance of that of the cruisers. He contracted in March, 1862, with Messrs. Laird, of Birkenhead, for two iron-clad, double turret rams, each to cost £93,750, exclusive of magazines and battery. They were to be plated with from 4½ to 5½ inches of armor, and carry in each turret two 9-inch rifled guns. With them it was expected to break the blockade of the Southern ports, and lay some of the Northern cities under ransom. In January, 1863, when they were more than half completed, intimation was made by Lord Russell, British Foreign Secretary, that he was aware of their destination, although Bulloch had contracted for them in his own name, and as a private individual, and that they would not be permitted to go to sea unless he was satisfied that they were the property of a government not at war. Bulloch then negotiated with the Messrs. Bravay, bankers, of Paris, to purchase the vessels, under the pretence that they were intended for the Khedive of Egypt, and transfer them at sea to agents of the Confederacy. As the Bravays had about that time received an order from the Khedive to buy iron-clads, the arrangement seemed plausible enough; but Earl Russell—prompted by Mr. Adams, the American Minister—insisted that the transaction was not what it appeared to be. The

while in command of the last named ship, at the breaking out of the war between the States. He offered his services to the Confederate government at Montgomery, and was appointed to special service in Europe, being taken into the C. S. navy with the rank of commander. His duties in Europe are recorded in the work, entitled "The Secret Service of the Confederate States in Europe." During his career in the U. S. navy he performed an unusual amount of active sea service, having been only fourteen months unattached during the first twelve years, and he had the somewhat remarkable fortune to serve in every class of war vessel from a schooner of ten guns to the ship-of-the-line of eighty and over, and while in the mail service superintended the construction of two of the ships commanded by him.

These varied experiences were thought to fit him for the special duties assigned to him by the Secretary of the C. S. navy and were given as the reasons for his selection. His original acceptance of duty in England was made conditional upon being ordered to command one of the first cruisers built, but his services as the agent of the navy there were so important that Secretary Mallory refused to permit him to go to sea, insisting that no other individual could be intrusted with the work which he was performing in Europe. In 1863 Capt. Bulloch urged upon Mr. Mallory his right to command one of the Birkenhead rams, and while the Secretary acceded to his request he again pressed him to consider the confusion which must follow his removal from the special agency of the Department and requested him to sacrifice personal ambition for the good of the country. These considerations prevailed with Capt. Bulloch, who remained in Europe, and is now (1887) still a resident of Liverpool.

THE CONFEDERATE IRON-CLAD "STONEWALL."

TURRET SHIP,

BUILT BY LAIRD BROTHERS FOR THE CONFEDERATE GOVERNMENT

Emperor Napoleon was appealed to by the Messrs. Bravay, to intervene and request the release of the rams as the property of subjects of France, but he refused to take any steps. On Oct. 9th, 1863, the vessels were seized by the British authorities, and suit was instituted for their forfeiture. The case, however, was never pushed, and the rams were sold to the British Admiralty, and enrolled in the navy as the *Scorpion* and the *Wivern.* The Admiralty paid for them £30,000 in excess of the contract price; and while the loss of such formidable ships was a severe disappointment to the Confederate government, the money was much needed at the time, and was beneficially applied to other purposes of the navy.

THE SUMTER.—In April, 1861, at the instance of Com. Raphael Semmes,[1] chief of the C. S. Light-house Bureau, Secretary Mallory directed the Naval Board at New Orleans to purchase the screw steamer *Habana;* the name was changed to the *Sumter*, and on the 18th of the month Com. Semmes was ordered to the command of the vessel, with the following officers: Lieuts. John M. Kell, R. T. Chapman, John M. Stribling and Wm. E. Evans; Paymaster Henry Myers; Surgeon Francis L.

[1] Raphael Semmes, a most famous commander in the Confederate navy, was born in Charles County, Md., Sept. 27th, 1809, and was descended from one of the Catholic families who came from England in the second quarter of the seventeenth century under the auspices of the Lords Baltimore and assisted in the establishment of religious liberty on the shores of the Western Continent. President John Quincy Adams appointed him a midshipman in the U. S. navy in 1826, but he did not enter upon active service until 1832, the intermediate years being spent in naval study at Norfolk, and, during his furloughs, in reading law with his brother, Samuel M. Semmes, at Cumberland, Md., a practicing attorney in that city. His tastes for literature and the law were almost as strong as for the sea and at the outset of his career it seems to have been a question with him whether to continue in the navy or devote himself to the peaceful life of a counsellor and author. He had to make his decision in 1824, when, after returning from his first cruise he was admitted to the bar, and it was to remain a seaman. In 1837 he was promoted to be a lieutenant, and in 1842 removed his home to Alabama. At the beginning of the war with Mexico he was made flag-lieutenant under Com. Conner, commanding the squadron in the Gulf, and in the siege of Vera Cruz he commanded one of the naval batteries on shore. He was in command of the U. S. brig *Somers* on the blockade of the Mexican coast when, in chasing a suspicious vessel, the brig was knocked down by a gale of wind and most of her crew were drowned. Lieut. Semmes was rescued, and after the declaration of peace he served for several years as inspector of light-houses on the Gulf coast. In 1855 he was promoted to the rank of commander, and in 1858 was assigned to duty as secretary of the light-house board at Washington. In his intervals of leisure he wrote "Service Afloat and Ashore during the Mexican War," a spirited and valuable contribution to the history of that conflict. Upon the secession of Alabama, Feb. 15th, 1861, he resigned his commission in the U. S. navy and reported to Mr. Davis at Montgomery, who in-

structed him to return North and endeavor to procure mechanics skilled in the manufacture and use of ordnance and rifle machinery, the preparation of fixed ammunition and of percussion caps. He was also to buy any war material that he might be able to procure. Going North, at Richmond he inspected the Virginia State arsenal and the Tredegar Iron Works with a view to their future use for casting cannon, shot and shell; and was in Washington on March 4th, where he witnessed the preparations for the inauguration of President Lincoln. At Washington he examined the machinery of the arsenal and conferred with mechanics whom he desired to induce to go South. Within the next three weeks he made a tour through the principal work-shops of New York, Conn. and Mass. and found that Northern manufacturers were ready to sell him anything in the line of weapons and ammunition that the South asked for. He purchased large quantities of percussion caps in New York, which were sent to Montgomery without any disguise, and made contracts for batteries of light artillery, powder and other munitions of war, and succeeded in getting thousands of pounds of powder shipped to the South. One of his contracts was for the removal to the Southern States of a complete set of machinery for rifling cannon, with the requisite skilled workmen to put it in operation. Adm. Semmes always refused to betray the names of the thrifty Northern merchants who entered into these bargains and dined him at their residences. "It would be a quasi breach of honor," he wrote, "to disclose their names, as they dealt with me pretty much as conspirators against their government are wont to deal with the enemies of their government—secretly and with an implied confidence that I would keep their secret." It was safe with him even after they took the pay of the Federal government with as much avidity as they had displayed in accepting the money of the South. While in New York he received a letter from Secretary Mallory, dated from Montgomery, March 13th, requesting him to investigate the possibilities of purchasing swift, light-draft steamers for the Confederate naval service,

Galt; Midshipmen William A. Hicks, Richard F. Armstrong, Albert G. Hudgins, John F. Holden,[1] and Joseph D. Wilson. To these before sailing were added the following: First Lieut. of Marines B. K. Howell; Engineers Miles J. Freeman, Wm. P. Brooks, Matthew O'Brien, Simeon W. Cummings; Boatswain Benj. P. Mecaskey; Gunner T. C. Cuddy; Sailmaker W. P. Beaufort; Carpenter Wm. Robinson; Captain's Clerk W. Breedlove.

The *Sumter* was a ship of 437 tons register, 184 feet long, 30 feet beam, 12 feet depth of hold, barkentine rigged; her speed was from nine to ten knots an hour; she could carry coal but for eight days' steaming, and was slow under sail alone on account of her propeller dragging. On April 22d Com. Semmes took charge of the ship, and occupied nearly two months in fitting her out for service and mounting the battery, which consisted of an 8-inch shell gun pivoted amidships and four light 32-pounders in broadside. A crew of competent seamen was enlisted from the many merchant vessels laid up at New Orleans, and on June 3d the ship was put in commission as a vessel-of-war of the Confederate States.

but could discover none suitable for the purpose. His mission in the North completed, he returned to Montgomery on April 4th to find that he had been commissioned commander in the navy of the Confederate States and placed in charge of the light-house bureau, which he relinquished within two weeks to go to New Orleans and fit the *Sumter* out for sea. After the blockade of that ship at Gibralter by two U. S. men-of-war and his sale of her, he went to England and thence to the Azores, where he took command of the *Alabama*, having in the meantime been promoted to the rank of captain. His career in that ship is elsewhere described in this history. Upon her loss in the battle with the *Kearsarge* he returned to England, and in London was presented by officers of the British army and navy with a superb sword to replace that which he had cast into the sea from the deck of his sinking ship. The invitations to subscriptions were issued from the Junior United Service Club, and were addressed to "gentlemen wishing to participate in this testimonial to unflinching patriotism and naval daring." Admiral Anson and Capt. Bedford Pim. of the British navy, were the chief movers in the affair. To keep company with the sword, a noble English lady presented Capt. Semmes with a large Confederate flag, wrought with her own hands from the richest silk. On Oct. 3d, 1864, after a tour upon the continent he sailed from England for Havana, from whence he reached Bagdad, a Mexican port on the Gulf, and passing up through Texas and Louisiana, reached Shreveport on Nov. 27th. Public ovations awaited him along the route and he was everywhere lionized. Crossing the Mississippi in a small skiff, in danger of capture from the Federal gunboats, he arrived on the east bank, and after a short stay at his home in Mobile, was appointed rear-admiral in the Provisional navy and ordered to the command of the James River squadron, with which he guarded the water approaches to Richmond, until the city was evacuated. At Greensboro', N. C., on May 1st, 1865. he participated in the capitulation of Gen Johnston's army, taking the precaution to sign himself in the articles of parole as "rear admiral, C S. N. and brigadier general, C. S. A."—a wise foresight which proved

available when it was afterwards claimed that he had deceived Gen. Hartsuff, who acted for Gen. Sherman, and that Hartsuff was unaware that he was extending parole to the commander of the *Alabama*. Dispersing his men, Adm. Semmes went to his Mobile home and opened an office for the practice of law. There, on Dec. 15th, 1865, he was arrested by a squad of U. S. marines in pursuance of an order of Secretary Welles, and was imprisoned, first in the navy-yard and then in the marine corps barracks at Washington. His seizure was in obedience to the Northern cry for the visitation of the death punishment upon "the pirate," and the pretext was, as stated by Mr. Speed, Attorney General of the United States, his liability to trial as a traitor, which he had evaded by his escape after the destruction of the *Alabama*. From his prison he wrote to President Johnson a letter claiming immunity for all past deeds under the military convention to which he was a party at Greensboro' and the subsequent quarrel between Mr. Johnson and the Republican majority of Congress interrupted any proceedings looking to his trial. He was released under the third of the President's amnesty proclamations, after four months of confinement, and, in May, 1866, was elected judge of the Probate Court of Mobile County, but an order from President Johnson forbade him to exercise the functions of the office. He then became the editor of a daily newspaper in Mobile, which he gave up to accept a professorial chair in the La. Military Institute. For a short time subsequently he was engaged in journalism, but returned to Mobile and the practice of law, in which he was occupied to the date of his death, Aug. 30th, 1877. Besides the narrative of the war with Mexico he published, in 1852, "The Campaign of General Scott in the Valley of Mexico;" in 1864, "The Cruise of the *Alabama* and *Sumter*," and in 1869, "Memoirs of Service Afloat during the War between the States."

[1] Midshipman Holden was drowned in the Mississippi River, May 18th, 1861, by the swamping of a boat in which he was carrying out an anchor from the receiving ship. Three of the seamen of the *Sumter* lost their lives at the same time. Mr. Holden was from Louisburg, Tenn.

Com. Semmes' instructions from Secretary Mallory were "to do the enemy's commerce the greatest injury in the shortest time," and on June 30th he started to go to sea, choosing Pass à l'Outre for his exit from the Mississippi into the Gulf of Mexico, as the sloop-of-war *Brooklyn*, the fastest of the Federal blockading vessels on the station, had gone a few miles off to overhaul a strange sail. The *Sumter* was well through the pass before she was detected by the *Brooklyn*, which immediately gave chase, and on account of the "foaming" of her boilers the *Sumter* was at one time in so much danger of being captured that her commander prepared to throw overboard his military chest and public papers. This trouble was soon obviated, however, and with increased speed she drew away from the enemy, who abandoned the pursuit about four o'clock in the afternoon. On July 3d, while running along the

CONFEDERATE STEAM CRUISER "SUMTER."

Cuban coast, the *Sumter* made her first capture, which proved to be the bark *Golden Rocket*, of Maine. Her crew were taken off and the vessel burned. The next prizes were the brigantines *Cuba* and *Machias*, laden with neutral cargoes; and Semmes headed for Cienfugos, Cuba, with them in tow, his intention being to discover whether Spain would follow the example of Great Britain and France by closing her ports to the prizes of the belligerents. Being compelled to cast off the *Cuba*, he ordered Midshipman Hudgins, who was in command of the prize-crew, to follow him into port. They parted company, and the crew of the *Cuba* overpowered the prize-crew, recaptured the vessel and took her into New York, where the *Sumter's* men were first committed on a charge of piracy, but were subsequently exchanged.

The *Sumter* took into Cienfugos six prizes, but was refused permission to leave them there to await the decision of a Confederate Court of Admiralty, and they were subsequently redelivered to their original owners. Semmes next cruised down the Spanish Main, going as far south as Maranham, Brazil, and then made sail for Martinique. He made a number of prizes going southward, but in fifty-five days, between Maranham and Martinique, he fell in with but two vessels bearing the flag of the United States. The captures and burnings which he had accomplished since leaving New Orleans were fast driving the enemy's commerce from the ocean or forcing the transfer of his bottoms to neutrals. On November 13th, 1861, the *Sumter* proceeded to St. Pierre to coal, but before the work could be completed the U. S. gunboat *Iroquois*, Capt. J. S. Palmer, arrived in the harbor. Several times during the night the *Iroquois* steamed around the *Sumter*, as if desirous of attacking, but fearful of doing so in the French waters of Martinique, and Semmes beat to quarters and ran out his guns. Capt. Palmer addressed to the Governor of Martinique a protest against a vessel " engaged in pirating upon the commerce of the United States " being permitted to coal at the port, and asked that she be directed " to leave the protection of the French flag and the immunities of a French port." The Governor replied that he would not refuse an anchorage to " a vessel belonging to the States of the South " and tendered the same hospitalities to the *Iroquois ;* but required the latter, if she proposed to establish a blockade of the Confederate vessel to go outside of the marine jurisdiction of France. The French man-of-war *Acheron* came around from Port de France, and Capt. Palmer was informed that if he remained in the harbor he would not, under international law, be permitted to leave until twenty-four hours after the departure of the *Sumter.* He arranged with the captain of the American schooner *Windward*, moored in the harbor, to notify him by signals if she sailed, and kept up a constant communication with the shore by boats, in violation of the laws of nations, which required that if he wished to communicate he must bring his ship to anchor, when, of course, the twenty-four hour rule would attach.

After being blockaded nine days, Semmes determined to attempt an escape to sea from the greatly superior enemy, and selected the night of October 23d. At the sound of the eight o'clock gun from the fort, the vessel steamed off. Semmes was quite well aware that he was being watched from the schooner *Windward*, and that she was to notify the *Iroquois* by burning two lights if he went south and one light if he went north. Consequently he steered south until the two lights were shown and then halted under the shadow of the mountains, which run abruptly to the sea. The *Iroquois*, in obedience to the signals, went off southward at a furious pace, while the *Sumter* doubled and stood to the northward.[1] Capt. Palmer had done his utmost to capture her, and because Semmes had outwitted him some of the Northern newspapers bullied the Secretary of the Navy into relieving him of his command.

1 "Memoirs of Service Afloat During the War Between the States."

Com. Semmes' intention now was to cross the Atlantic and cruise in European waters. Off the island of Dominica, on Nov. 25th, he captured the ship *Montmorenci*, and ransomed her on a bond for $20,000, payable to the President of the Confederate States, her cargo being coal shipped on English account. On the way across the ocean three prizes were taken.

On Jan. 4th, 1862, the *Sumter* anchored in the harbor of Cadiz, Spain, and the next day Semmes received a peremptory order from the military governor to proceed to sea within twenty-four hours. To this he replied that it was the duty of Spain to extend to his ship the same hospitality that she would extend to the ships of the opposite belligerent; that his vessel was crippled, and that he had forty-three prisoners on board, whom he desired to hand over to the consul of the United States. In pursuance of orders from Madrid the prisoners were landed, and the *Sumter* was permitted to make at Carracca, eight miles east of Cadiz, barely such repairs as would suffice to keep her afloat. On Jan. 17th, Semmes was served with a peremptory order to depart within six hours, and as he had not been permitted to coal, he had barely sufficient fuel to take the ship to the British port of Gibraltar, whither he decided to proceed.

Between Cadiz and Gibraltar the *Sumter* made two prizes, and reached the latter port January 19th, 1862. On Feb. 3d, Com. Semmes received funds from Mr. Mason, Confederate envoy at London, but when he attempted to purchase coal he found that the merchants had closed the market against him, and an application for supplies from the government yard was denied. Then he sent Paymaster Myers and Thomas J. Tunstall, ex-U. S. consul at Gibraltar, to Cadiz, to buy a supply. The French steamer on which they took passage for Cadiz made a stop at the Moorish town of Tangier, where they were arrested by the local authorities on the requisition of the U. S. consul. By the consul they were turned over to the commander of the Federal naval forces at Algesiras, who sent them to the United States in irons.

The *Sumter* was now blockaded at Gibraltar by the Federal steamers *Tuscarora*, *Kearsarge* and *Chippewa*, and as she could obtain no coal, Semmes decided, after consultation by telegraph with Mr. Mason, to lay her up. All hands were paid off; the officers took passage for London, and the sailors were discharged. Midshipman R. F. Armstrong and acting master's mate J. T. Hester were left in charge of the vessel with ten men; and about April 13th or 14th, Com. Semmes started for London, from whence he sailed for the Confederacy, but was overtaken at Nassau by orders to return to England and take command of the *Alabama*. The *Sumter's* cruise had lasted six months, during which time she had captured eighteen vessels, of which eight were burned, and the remainder were released or bonded, with the exception of one, that was recaptured. She was sold by auction at Gibraltar, in Dec. 1862, and was bought by a Liverpool merchant for $19,500, battery and all, who changed her name to the *Gibraltar*. The commander of the Federal steamer *Chippewa* avowed his purpose to capture her if she ventured out of the harbor, but did not risk attempting such an outrage upon the British flag, which she now carried. In July, 1863, she ran the blockade into Wilmington, N. C., and returned to Liverpool in Dec. with a cargo of cotton. After the war the U. S. government entered suit in the admiralty court, at London, for the recovery of the ship as a prize, but the case was decided in favor of her owners, and she was eventually lost in a gale in the North Sea, not far from where the *Alabama* was sunk.

THE FLORIDA.—The first of the Confederate steam cruisers built in England was constructed by William C. Miller & Sons of Liverpool, under contract with Capt. J. D. Bulloch, naval agent of the Confederate States, and bore the dock-yard name of the *Oreto*. In March, 1862, she was ready to go to sea, and English officers and crew were engaged to take her out as an unarmed ship in order to avoid infringement of the neutrality regulations. She sailed from Liverpool, March 22d, having on board, as a passenger, Master John Lowe, C. S. N., who was instructed to deliver the vessel at Nassau to Capt. J. N. Maffitt. Her guns, equipments and stores were dispatched to the same port in the steamer *Bahama*. The *Oreto* arrived at Nassau April 28th, and between that date and Aug. 1st was twice seized by the British governor on the complaint of the U. S. consul that she was intended for the Confederate service, but the admiralty court could only decide from the evidence submitted that she was properly documented as British property, and ordered her release. At Nassau her armament was placed on a schooner, which the *Oreto* met about Aug. 10th, at Green Cay, sixty miles distant. There it was transferred to the steamer, which was regularly commissioned as a ship of war, and the name changed to *Florida*. Her battery embraced two 7-inch and four 6-inch Blakely rifled guns. Maffitt had but eighteen men in all on board, including Lieut. J. M. Stribling, Acting Master W. L. Bradford and Midshipmen Bryan, Floyd and Sinclair. The yellow fever broke out among them, and in five days the working force was reduced to one fireman and four deck hands. The ship was run into Cardenas, Cuba, in a desperate plight, and there Capt. Maffitt was stricken with the disease. Before he recovered, the *Florida* was summoned to Havana by the captain general. She was still far from being fully equipped or manned, and because of the stringency of the Spanish regulations Maffitt determined to run into Mobile. On Sept. 4th, 1862, she was off the bar, and hoisting the British colors stood toward the three blockading vessels. Deceived by her ensign they allowed her to come up to them before ordering her to stop. The only response was the substitution of the Confederate for the British flag; the *Florida* received the broadside of the Federal sloop-of-war *Oneida* within pistol range, and for two hours the little ship was pelted by the enemy, until she found shelter under the guns of Fort Morgan. Two shells had passed through her, and her rigging was badly cut up, and one man was killed and seven wounded. Maffitt came out of his sick berth to handle the ship, and during the whole war there was no incident in which bravery and energy were more brilliantly displayed.

The *Florida* was fully fitted out and manned at Mobile, and on the night of Jan. 15th, 1863, made her escape to sea, although the blockading fleet had been strengthened with a view to her capture, and she was vainly pursued by one fast gunboat, the *R. R. Cuyler.* Under steam and sail (her screw could be lifted clear of the water, when it was intended that she should go under sail alone) she outran the enemy. She was now officered as follows:

Lieut. Commanding, James Newland Maffitt; Lieutenants, S. W. Averett,[1] J. L. Hoole, C. W. Read, S. G. Stone ; Midshipmen, R. S. Floyd, G. D. Bryan, J. H. Dyke, G. T. Sinclair, and W. B. Sinclair;[2] Chief Engineer, A. M. Spidell; Assistants, Chas. W. Quinn, Thos. A. Jackson, E. H. Brown ; Surgeon, Frederick Garrettson ; Paymaster, —— Lynch.

In a few days the *Florida* made the west end of Cuba, and captured her first prize, a small brig, which was burned. Putting into Havana, she remained 48 hours, taking in coal, and on Jan. 25th arrived at Nassau, having taken two more prizes in the meantime. Capt. Wilkes, commanding the U. S. "flying squadron" in the West Indies, was assiduously hunting

[1] Samuel W. Averett, now one of the principals of Roanoke Female College, Danville, Va., graduated from the U. S. naval academy in 1859 and served on the sloop-of-war *Wyoming* in the Pacific squadron until about April 1st, 1861, when he resigned in consequence of the call of Gov. Letcher, of Virginia, upon her sons in the army and navy to give in their allegiance to their native State. Homeward bound by way of Havana, he, with the late Gen. R. B. Garnett and Engineer Geo. D. Lining, of the *Wyoming*, took passage from that port in July on the schooner *Adelaide*, and after evading a Federal sloop-of-war, entered Fernandina in safety. On reporting to the Navy Department at Richmond, Mr. Averett was commissioned lieutenant, C. S. N., and ordered to duty at New Orleans, where he commanded the *Watson*, and was subsequently executive officer of the steamer *Jackson* and of the steamer *Gen. Polk*. At a later date he was in command of the floating battery *New Orleans* at Island No. 10. He knew the channel of the Mississippi above and around the island tolerably well, and the nature of the defences thoroughly, and when asked by Flag-officer Hollins whether he thought the Confederate position could be passed by Adm. Foote's fleet, he replied confidently that if it attempted the passage by day some of the vessels would go through safely, while others would be destroyed, but a vessel might run through on a dark night without receiving a shot in her hull. When the fortifications on the main-land had been aban-

doned and permission had been given to the men of the floating battery to save themselves in any way they could, or to follow their commander in his efforts to reach Gen. Mackall's camp, sixteen Alabamians asked Lieut. Averett to lead them to their comrades there, the others preferring to attempt escape in small boats, two or three together, down the river and by rafts across Reel Foot Lake, and many of them succeeded. Averett and the Alabamians reached Mackall's camp, and were included in the surrender of April 8th, 1862. He was exchanged at Vicksburg in August, and soon thereafter reported for duty on the C. S. steamer *Florida*, of which he was made executive officer, serving as such until May, 1864, when he was ordered home for rest and recuperation. He expected to return to the ship with other officers and money, but the state of his health forbade him from engaging in active duty afterward.

[2] Midshipman W. B. Sinclair was drowned off the capes of the Delaware, July 10th, 1864, while in command of a boat that swamped in transferring stores from a prize to the *Florida*. He gave up to a seaman the oar upon which he was sustaining himself, and thus sacrificed his own life. The Confederate government issued a general naval order reciting his conduct in terms of the highest praise, and directed that the order be read upon the quarter-deck of all vessels in commission, with the colors at half mast.

for the *Florida*. Reasoning that as the *Florida* had just obtained coal at Nassau, she would not, under the neutrality laws, be allowed to coal at another British port for three months, Wilkes concluded that she must go the French island of Martinique for another supply of fuel, and sent his ships off in that direction, to look for her. She had really gone to Barbadoes, where, upon Capt. Maffitt's statement that his fuel had been exhausted from stress of weather, he procured 90 tons of coal on Feb. 24th. Cruising to the southward, a halt was made at Green Cay, to paint the ship, and on the day after leaving that island the U.S. gunboat *Sonoma* was sighted. All hands were called to quarters, but although the *Florida* was slowed down, the enemy, according to a statement made by Lieut. C. W. Read, kept at a distance, and at the approach of night the *Florida* went on her course. Off the Windward Islands she had a long chase after the clipper ship *Jacob Bell*, from Foo Chow, China, for New York, which she caught and burned. The vessel, and her cargo of tea, silks, etc., was valued at $1,500,000, the most valuable single prize taken by any Confederate cruiser. Pernambuco, Brazil, was reached on May 8th, and the *Florida* cruised along the meeting of the great routes of commerce off that coast, taking many prizes. Near there, Maffitt made a tender of the prize brig *Clarence*, whose career will be subsequently related, and then worked his way back to St. George's, Bermuda, where he arrived July 16th, 1863. He had destroyed 14 prizes, and bonded three.[1]

On July 25th, the *Florida* sailed from Bermuda, and after capturing the ships *F. B. Cutting* (bonded) and *Avon* (burned) arrived at Brest, France, Aug. 23d, where she remained six months in a government dock refitting and recruiting. Capt. Maffitt's health was broken, and he was relieved of command by Com. Joseph N. Barney, who was also seized with illness, and about Jan. 4th, 1864, Lieut. Charles Manigault Morris[2] was ordered to the command of the cruiser. He got to sea from Brest on Feb. 12th, and went to the West Indies, but finding no valuable quarry there made a descent upon the coast of the United States. On July 10th, thirty miles off the capes of the Delaware, he captured the U. S. mail steamer *Electric Spark*, from New York for New Orleans, which was scuttled after transferring her people and passengers to a passing English vessel. Other prizes taken in this dash were the *Harriet Stevens*, *Golconda*, *Margaret Y. Davis* and *Mondamin*. Morris then crossed the ocean to Teneriffe, and cruised

[1] The term bonded or ransomed means that the captain of the captured ship, on condition of the release of the vessel, signed a bond for himself and the owners, to pay a stipulated sum to the President of the Confederate States at a fixed date (usually six months) after the ratification of a treaty of peace between the United States and the Confederate States. A prize was bonded when her cargo was owned by neutral parties, or when it was desired to use her to carry to port the prisoners who accu-mulated on the cruisers, and for whom they could find no accommodation.

[2] Lieut. C. M. Morris resigned from the U. S. navy when Georgia seceded, and being appointed lieut. in the Confederate service was ordered to command of the gunboat *Huntress* at Savannah. After doing ordnance duty and being in charge of the Savannah rendezvous, he was ordered to Europe for duty on the Birkenhead rams, but was detailed to the command of the *Florida*, in which he remained until her capture at Bahia.

C. S. CRUISER "FLORIDA"

C. S. CRUISER "ALABAMA."

back leisurely toward Brazil, capturing the *B. F. Hoxie, Cairaissanne, David Lapsley, Estelle, George Latimer, Southern Rights, Greenland, Windward, William C. Clark* and *Zelinda.*

The *Florida* anchored at Bahia, Brazil, Oct. 4th, and found in port the U. S. steam corvette *Wachusett*, Capt. Napoleon Collins. Relying implicitly upon the protection of a neutral power, Morris drew the loads from his guns and gave his crew liberty on shore by watches. On the night of Oct. 6th he was himself in the town with nearly half the ship's company, leaving her in charge of Lieut. Thomas K. Porter and some eighty officers and men. At three o'clock on the morning of the 7th, the *Wachusett* rammed her on the starboard quarter, fired two shots from her battery, poured in a volley from small arms and demanded her surrender. The *Florida's* people on deck replied with pistols and muskets and some fifteen of the crew jumped overboard, of whom nine were either drowned or were killed by being fired upon from the *Wachusett*, while they were trying to swim to the land. Lieut. Porter surrendered his defenceless ship and the *Wachusett* towed her out to sea without giving him any chance for communication with Capt. Morris. The only Brazilian vessel present was a small sloop-of-war, and although she and the fort fired a few shots at the *Wachusett* the latter paid no attention. The *Florida* was sent to Hampton Roads as a prize.

So gross an outrage upon a neutral government was utterly indefensible and the United States made no attempt to defend it. The demand of Brazil that the *Florida* be returned intact to her protection at Bahia with all the prisoners on board was conceded, and then to avoid this reparation a contemptible and violent fraud was resorted to. While she was lying in Hampton Roads she was "accidentally" struck by an army transport, and then, to avoid any more such "accidental" collisions, she was moored in a secluded locality above Newport News, and an engineer and two assistants placed on board. On the morning of Nov. 28th she sank at her moorings, and the United States escaped the humiliation of returning her to Brazil. We have not the space to introduce reports of this disgraceful business, but no fair man can study them without reaching the conviction that the sinking of the ship was an act deliberately committed by those in charge of her in pursuance of instructions or intimations from very high Federal authority. Admiral Porter, who was then in command at Hampton Roads, goes far to confirm this belief by the manner in which he speaks of the affair in his "Naval History of the Civil War." It is tolerably well apparent that the engineer in charge of the ship opened the water-cocks in her hull and purposely left her to go to the bottom.

The captured officers were sent in succession to prison at Point Lookout, Washington and Fort Warren. They were brutally treated and were not set free until Feb. 1st, 1865.

Then they were compelled to sign an agreement to leave the United States within ten days of their release, and were turned into the streets of Boston without a dollar, but managed to secure passage to Europe.

THE CLARENCE, TACONY AND ARCHER.—On May 6th, 1863, the *Florida* captured, off the Brazilian coast, the brig *Clarence*, of Baltimore, and converted her into a Confederate cruiser. Lieut Charles W. Read was placed in command, and selected as his subordinate officers from the *Florida's* complement, Quartermaster Billups, Boatswain's mate Matthewson, and Quarter-gunner Pride, who were made master's mates. Engineer Brown was also taken on board, and 16 men of the *Florida's* crew. The only armament was a 6-pounder boat howitzer, but with some spare spars Read constructed several Quaker guns that frightened some of the American merchant skippers whom he overhauled. He dipped his colors to the *Florida*, and squared away north and east. Off Cape Hatteras he captured the first prize, the bark *Whistling Wind*, bound to New Orleans with army stores. That, and a few more prizes, the *Kate Stewart, Mary Alvina* and *Mary Schindler*, were burned, and the *Alfred H. Partridge* was bonded off the capes of the Delaware, to land the prisoners. The next prize was the fine bark *Tacony*, and as she was a much swifter vessel than the *Clarence*, the crew and battery were transferred to her, and the *Clarence* was destroyed. Read now proceeded along the coast of New England, capturing and burning with immense vigor. His prizes were the *Ada, Arabella, Byzantium, Elizabeth Ann, Florence, Goodspeed, Isaac Webb, Z. A. Macomber, Marengo, Ripple, Rufus Choate, Shattemuc, Umpire* and *Wanderer*. On June 25th, 1863, the schooner *Archer* was captured and converted into a cruiser in place of the *Tacony*, which was destroyed. Read desired to capture a steamer, make a raid down the coast, and run into Wilmington, N. C.; and learning from captured fishermen that the only armed vessel at Portland, Me., was the revenue cutter *Caleb Cushing*, he decided that she would be of use to him in the execution of his project. On June 27th he sailed into Portland harbor in his peaceful appearing schooner, without molestation, and after dark he took the cutter by boarding, securing her crew below deck. Going out of the harbor at dawn of the 28th, with the *Archer* and the *Cushing*, the wind failed, and the Boston steamer passed in, having on board Capt. Merriman, of the U. S. revenue marine, who had been ordered to Portland to take the cutter in search of the *Tacony*. The first known in Portland of the cutting-out of the *Cushing* was Merriman's report that he had seen her going to sea; and Maj. Andrew, commandant at Fort Preble, organized a recapturing expedition of troops and citizens in two steamers, and three tug-boats. At 11 o'clock in the morning they overtook the *Cushing* and *Archer*. Read opened fire on them from his guns, but by making wide detours, they hemmed him in, and kept out of cannon range. He then took to his boats, after setting a slow match to the magazine of the cutter, which soon blew up. Surrounded by the enemy, he surrendered, and they towed the *Archer* into the harbor. The prisoners were charged with piracy, but were finally exchanged.

THE NASHVILLE.—The C. S. cruiser *Nashville*, a fine, swift side-wheel steamer of about 1,300 tons burden, was built by Northern owners for the trade between New York and Charleston, and was seized by the Confederate authorities at the latter port when she entered it after the capture of Fort Sumter. She laid idle until it was decided that she should take Messrs. Mason and Slidell on the first stage of their journey to Europe, and when this intention was revoked, she was sent out as a Confederate States ship-of-war with the following officers, all of the naval service: Robert B. Pegram, lieut. commanding; Charles M. Fauntleroy, first lieut.; John W. Bennett, second lieut.; Wm. C. Whittle, Jr., third lieut.; John H. Ingraham, master; John L. Auchrim, surgeon; Richard Taylor, paymaster; James Hood, chief engineer, and midshipmen Dalton, Sinclair, Cary, Pegram, Hamilton, Thomas and McClintock. She was armed with but two 12-pounder brass guns, mounted on her forecastle deck, and her crew never numbered more than forty men. On the night of Oct. 21st, 1861, the ship ran the blockade out of Charleston, and after stopping a few days at Bermuda headed across the Atlantic, and on Nov. 19th captured in the entrance of the British channel the ship *Harvey Birch*, of New York, homeward bound from Havre. The passengers and crew were taken off and paroled and the ship burned. On the 21st, the *Nashville* arrived at Southampton, where the prisoners were landed, and enjoyed the distinction of being the first war vessel to fly the flag of the Confederate States in the waters of England.

On Jan. 8th, 1862, the Federal steamer *Tuscarora* arrived in port, and her commander, Capt. Craven, established so close a watch of the *Nashville* that he was warned by the government officers to beware of violating the neutrality laws. This blockade of the *Nashville* continued during the month; but in the last week of January the *Tuscarora* moved off to the Isle of Wight, and Capt. Pegram demanded of the admiralty that in accordance with the law she be detained in British waters until twenty-four hours after his own vessel had sailed. The rule was enforced on Capt. Craven, and the *Nashville* went to sea on Feb. 3d, and reached Bermuda on the 20th, where she picked up a pilot, who agreed to take her into Beaufort, N. C. On the passage the schooner *Robert Gilfillan*, of Philadelphia, was made a prize and burned. The *Nashville* evaded the blockading ships at Beaufort by a daring trick, and ran in on Feb. 28th. Capt. Pegram found that the Confederate government had sold the vessel to private parties in Charleston, and he left her at Moorehead City in charge of Lieut. Whittle; but before the new owners could arrive to take possession it became necessary to run the blockade outward to save her from capture by Burnside's expedition. This feat was gallantly accomplished by Whittle under a heavy fire from the enemy, on March 17th. Finding it impossible to get into Charleston through the blockading fleet, he took the ship to Georgetown, S. C., and turned her over to the purchasers, Fraser, Trenholm & Co. They employed her in running the blockade, and on her first trip to Nassau she was placed under the British flag and her name changed to the *Thomas L. Wragg.* As a blockade-runner the steamer was exceedingly successful, and although several times sighted by Federal ships got away from them by her speed; but in the summer of 1862, she ran into Warsaw Sound, Ga., and before a return cargo could be obtained, the enemy bottled her up with a flotilla of gunboats. She was then fitted out as a cruiser and re-christened the *Rattlesnake.* While watching a chance to run out of the Ogechee River, Feb. 27th, 1863, she grounded in Seven Mile Reach, above Fort McAllister, and the next day was attacked by the Federal monitor *Montauk,* which soon set her on fire with shells, and she burned until the flames reached her magazine and blew her into fragments.

YACHT AMERICA.—At the beginning of the war, the Confederate government bought for $60,000 the famous schooner yacht *America,* which had won the Queen's cup in the Cowes regatta of 1852. The intention was to fit her out as a cruiser, but she was blockaded in the St. John's River, Fla., by Federal ships, and was there scuttled by the Confederates. She was raised by the Federals and remained in the navy until after the war, when the U. S. government sold her to Gen. Benj. F. Butler, who still uses her as a yacht.

THE ALABAMA.—While Capt. Bulloch was concluding the negotiations for the construction of the *Florida,* in June, 1861, he opened communication with the Messrs. Laird, proprietors of extensive ship-yards at Birkenhead, opposite Liverpool, for the building of a small steam sloop-of-war, on a model which he described with some exactness. He paid them £47,500 for the vessel, which was known in the yards as " No. 290," and subsequently became the *Alabama.* On July 29th, 1862, she steamed out of the Mersey, a few hours before the British Foreign Office sent down orders to detain her on the complaint of Minister Adams that she was a Confederate ship-of-war. Seven days later she arrived at Terceira, in the Azores Islands, where she was joined by the bark *Agrippina,* bringing her armament and stores, and the steamship *Bahama,* on which her officers and most of her crew had come out from England. On Aug. 24th she was formally commissioned as the Confederate States cruiser *Alabama,* with the subjoined list of officers :

Captain, Raphael Semmes ; First Lieut. and Executive Officer, J. M. Kell ; Second Lieut., Richard F. Armstrong ; Third Lieut., Joseph D. Wilson ; Fourth Lieut., Arthur Sinclair ; Fifth Lieut., John Lowe ; Surgeon, Francis L. Galt ; Asst. Surg., David H. Llewellyn ; Paymaster, Clarence R. Yonge ; Captain's Clerk, Wm. B. Smith ; Lieut. of Marines, Becker K. Howell ; Chief Engineer, Miles J. Freeman ; Asst. Engineers, Wm. P. Brooks, S. W. Cumings, Mather O'Brien, John W. Pundt ; Midshipmen, Wm. H. Sinclair, Irvine S. Bulloch, Eugene Maffitt, Edwin M. Anderson ; Master's Mates, George T. Fullam, James Evans ; Boatswain, Benj. L. McCaskey ; Gunner, J. O. Cuddy ; Carpenter, Wm. Robinson ; Sailmaker, Henry Alcott.

The *Alabama* was a vessel 220 feet long, 32 feet breadth of beam, 1,040 tons burden. She was barkentine-rigged, and her propeller was so constructed that it could be lifted out of the water, and when this was done she was to all intents and purposes a sailing ship. Under sail alone, with the wind abeam, she occasionally made 10 knots an hour, and her best performance was 11¼ knots under sail and steam combined. Her armament consisted of six 32-pounders in broadside, a 100-pounder Blakely rifle in the forecastle, and a smooth bore 8-inch shell gun abaft the mainmast. She made her *debut* as a warship by plunging in among the American whaling fleet, that between the early spring and October finds employment around the Western Islands. On Sept. 14th, 1862, the *Alabama* was off Fayal, and before the equinoctial gales drove the whalers out of those waters he made prizes of a dozen of them. Capt. Semmes selected for his next cruising ground the Newfoundland Banks, and the track of the American grain ships bound from the Eastern ports to Europe. He reached this station October 3d, 1862, and began burning prizes, or ransoming to carry away his prisoners those containing cargoes documented as the indisputable property of neutrals. The first of the wheat ships taken was the *Brilliant*, and the second the *Emily Farnham ;* and the latter returning to New York under bond, with the information that the *Alabama* was on the coast, a panic was created in shipping circles. Between Oct 3d and 21st, Semmes made sixteen captures, and then fell in with a number of ships whose cargoes were certified to be neutral property. A prize court was convened in the cabin of the *Alabama*, and upon its decision that the certificates were fraudulent, the vessels and their ladings were burned. The *Alabama* ran down to within 200 miles of New York, while the Federal men-of-war were looking for her up on the Grand Banks. About Nov. 18th she put into Port de France, Martinique, when some of the men, who had smuggled liquor on board, created the first and only mutiny on the ship, which the commander promptly suppressed by no severer measures than douching the guilty ones with cold water. The U. S. frigate *San Jacinto* made her appearance off the port while the *Alabama* was there, but the latter's speed enabled her to go to sea past her slow and clumsy enemy. After coaling from a tender at Blanquilla, Venezuela, Semmes laid in wait between San Domingo and Hayti, for one of the California treasure steamers bound from Colon to New York. On Dec. 7th, 1862, he captured the steamship *Ariel*, but she was outward bound from New York, with some 500 women and children among her passengers. As he could not take the prize into any port, he was forced to release her on a ransom bond for $261,000, payable after the recognition of the independence of the Confederate States. He got nothing from the prize, except $9,500 in money that her safe contained, while he might have captured a million if he had taken one of the steamers bound into New York.

The *Alabama* next went into the Gulf of Mexico, with a view of attacking the expedition known to be fitting out in the North under Gen. N. P. Banks for a descent upon the Texas coast, but Banks had gone into New Orleans and Semmes found off Galveston a Federal squadron bombarding that city. By concealing the identity of his ship and steaming slowly off he decoyed a vessel of the enemy twenty miles away, and then halted and cleared ship for action. To a hail he responded first, "This is her Britannic Majesty's steamer *Petrel*," and then "This is the Confederate States steamer *Alabama*." She fired the first broadside at nine o'clock on the night of Jan. 11th, 1863; the other ship replied valiantly, and the engagement lasted just thirteen minutes. Closing in with the foe Semmes found that he had defeated the U. S. gunboat *Hatteras*, Lieut. Com. Homer C. Blake, and that she was in a sinking condition. Blake asked for assistance, which was so promptly rendered, that, although the *Hatteras* went to the bottom within fifteen minutes after surrendering, every man on board, including the five wounded, was transferred in safety to the *Alabama*. Two men were killed on the *Hatteras* and the *Alabama* had but one man wounded. The latter steamed for Jamaica, and on Jan. 20th made the harbor of Port Royal, where Semmes expelled from the service his paymaster, Clarence R. Yonge, for debauchery. On Jan. 25th the *Alabama* left Kingston for a cruise down the Brazil coast and thence to the Cape of Good Hope. At the forks of the marine roads, in the fair-way of commerce, he captured twenty-four vessels, all of which were destroyed except the *Conrad*, which was converted into the C. S. cruiser *Tuscaloosa*. Crossing the Atlantic to the southern point of Africa, two more prizes were taken, and on July 28th, 1863, the *Alabama* put into Saldanha Bay. On this coast he captured only the bark *Sea Bride*, which vessel, with her cargo, Semmes sold to an English merchant, making the transfer at Angra Pequena, in the Hottentot country, to avoid any fracture of the British neutrality laws. For the remainder of the year he cruised in the Straits of Sunda, the China Sea and the Bay of Bengal, with moderate success. Beating up the waters of the Atlantic again, between Cape Town and the equatorial line on the Brazil coast, only two more captures were made. The ship *Tycoon* was taken on April 27th, 1864, and she was the last of the long roll of the victims of the *Alabama*.

On June 11th, the cruiser came to anchor in the port of Cherbourg, France, and three days later the U. S. steam corvette *Kearsarge*, Capt. John A. Winslow, came across from Southampton. The vessels fought their famous battle on Sunday, June 19th. Thousands of people gathered on the southern heights overlooking the British Channel to witness the combat, and the French iron-clad *Couronne*, and the English yacht *Deerhound*, owned and sailed by Mr. John Lancaster, moved to and fro outside the line of fire. A brief narrative of the affair is all that our limits will permit.

From the start the *Kearsarge* had some advantage over her adversary. She was the faster ship and her seven guns threw at a broadside 430 pounds of shot to 360 pounds thrown by the eight guns of the *Alabama*. She obtained this superiority from the two 11-inch pivot guns that she carried, and these pieces decided the action. Moreover, her hull was protected by her heavy chain cables hung up and down the sides. Semmes claims that for this reason she was practically an iron-clad and that Winslow took an unfair advantage of him. It is true, however, that the *Kearsarge* was not hit so frequently during the engagement as to make this a question of great practical importance. She had 163 officers and men, and the *Alabama* had 149. The annexed report of Capt. Semmes to Secretary Mallory was dated from Southampton on June 21st, and embraces most of the needful particulars of the battle.

"SOUTHAMPTON, June 21st, 1864.

" SIR : I have the honor to inform you, that in accordance with my intention as previously announced to you, I steamed out of the harbor of Cherbourg between nine and ten o'clock on the morning of the 19th of June, for the purpose of engaging the enemy's steamer *Kearsarge*, which had been lying off and on the port, for several days previously. After clearing the harbor, we descried the enemy, with his head off shore, at the distance of about seven miles. We were three-quarters of an hour in coming up with him. I had previously pivoted my guns to starboard, and made all preparations for engaging the enemy on that side. When within about a mile and a quarter of the enemy, he suddenly wheeled, and, bringing his head in shore, presented his starboard battery to me. By this time, we were distant about one mile from each other, when I opened on him with solid shot, to which he replied in a few minutes, and the action became active on both sides. The enemy now pressed his ship under a full head of steam, and to prevent our passing each other too speedily, and to keep our respective broadsides bearing, it became necessary to fight in a circle ; the two ships steaming around in a common centre, and preserving a distance from each other of from three-quarters to half a mile. When we got within good shell range, we opened upon him with shell. Some ten or fifteen minutes after the commencement of the action, our spanker-gaff was shot away, and our ensign came down by the run. This was immediately replaced by another at the mizzen-masthead. The firing now became very hot, and the enemy's shot and shell soon began to tell upon our hull, knocking down, killing and disabling a number of men, at the same time, in different parts of the ship. Perceiving that our shell, though apparently exploding against the enemy's sides, were doing him but little damage, I returned to solid-shot firing, and from this time onward alternated with shot and shell.

"After the lapse of about one hour and ten minutes, our ship was ascertained to be in a sinking condition, the enemy's shell having exploded in our side and between decks, opening large apertures through which the water rushed with great rapidity. For some few minutes I had hopes of being able to reach the French coast, for which purpose I gave the ship all steam, and set such of the fore-and-aft sails as were available. The ship filled so rapidly, however, that before we had made much progress, the fires were extinguished in the furnaces, and we were evidently on the point of sinking. I now hauled down my colors, to prevent the further destruction of life, and dispatched a boat to inform the enemy of our condition. Although we were now but 400 yards from each other, the enemy fired upon me five times after my colors had been struck. It is charitable to suppose that a ship of war of a Christian nation could not have done this intentionally. We now directed all our exertions toward saving the wounded, and such of the boys of the ship as were unable to swim. These were dispatched in my quarter-boats, the only boats remaining to me ; the waist-boats having been torn to pieces. Some twenty minutes after my furnace fires had been extinguished, and when the ship was on the point of settling, every man, in obedience to a previous order which had been given the crew, jumped overboard, and endeavored to save himself. There was no appearance of any boat coming to me from the enemy, until after my ship went down. Fortunately, however, the steam yacht *Deerhound*, owned by a gentleman of Lancashire, England—Mr. John Lancaster—who was himself on board, steamed up in the midst of my drowning men, and rescued a number of both officers and men from the water. I was fortunate enough myself thus to escape to the shelter of the neutral flag, together with about forty others, all told. About this time the *Kearsarge* sent one, and then, tardily, another boat. Accompanying, you will find lists of the killed and wounded, and of those who were picked up by the *Deerhound ;* the remainder, there is reason to hope, were picked up by the enemy, and by a couple of French pilot boats, which were also fortunately near the scene of action. At the end of the engagement, it was discovered by those of our officers who went alongside of the enemy's ship, with the wounded, that her midship section, on both sides, was thoroughly iron-coated ; this having been done with chains, constructed for the purpose, placed perpendicularly, from the rail to the water's edge, the whole covered over by a thin outer planking, which gave no indication of the armor beneath. This planking had been ripped off, in every direction, by our shot and shell, the chain broken and indented in many places, and forced partly into the ship's side. She was effectually guarded, however, in this section, from penetration, The enemy was much damaged in other parts, but to what extent it is now impossible to say. It is believed he is badly crippled. My officers and men behaved steadily and gallantly, and though they have lost their ship, they have not lost honor. Where all behaved so well, it would be invidious to particularize, but I cannot deny myself the pleasure of saying that Mr. Kell, my first lieutenant, deserves great credit for the fine condition in which the ship went into action, with regard to her battery, magazine and shell-rooms, and that he rendered me great assistance, by his coolness and judgment, as the fight proceeded. The enemy was heavier than myself, both in ship, battery, and crew ; but I did not know until the action was over, that she was also iron-clad. Our total loss in killed and wounded, is 30, to wit : 9 killed and 21 wounded."

It was subsequently discovered that ten of the *Alabama's* people were drowned, including Surgeon D. H. Llewelyn. She fired 370 shot and shell, of which only fourteen hulled the *Kearsarge*, while twice as many inflicted damage on her spars and rigging. There were two reasons for this comparative ineffectiveness of the Confederate fire. The ammunition had been on board two years and had much deteriorated by cruising in a variety of climates, and shells failed to explode. But for this the *Alabama* might have won the fight, for in the first half hour she drove an 8-inch percussion shell into the enemy's hull near the stern-post, where its explosion would perhaps have sunk her, but the cap was bad and the shell did not burst. In the second place, Semmes had only a few good gunners. The assertions that among the crew of the *Alabama* were a great number of skilled artillerists from the British navy were nonsense. He did have a few such men, but they were a very small fraction to the mass, who had had no practice against an enemy except in the engagement with the *Hatteras*, and whom the little schooling they had in test firing upon some of the hulks at sea did not fit to cope with the excellent crew that Winslow commanded.

THE TUSCALOOSA.—When Capt. Semmes converted the captured bark *Conrad*, of Philadelphia, into the C. S. vessel-of-war *Tuscaloosa*, near the Brazil coast, June 20th, 1863, he placed Lieut. John Low in command, with Midshipman George T. Sinclair as his first officer, and the ships parted company. They met again at the Cape of Good Hope in August, where the U. S. consul demanded from the British governor of the colony the surrender of the *Tuscaloosa*, on the ground that she had not been condemned as a prize by any admiralty court of any recognized nation. The Governor replied that on his understanding she was entitled to be regarded as a vessel-of-war, and on Aug. 14th she went to sea for a ninety days' cruise in the South Atlantic, during which, of 100 vessels spoken, only one was under the American flag, and she having an English cargo on board was bonded and released. On Dec. 26th, the *Tuscaloosa* returned to the Cape of Good Hope and was seized by order of the British Foreign Office, on the charge made by the American consul of violation of the neutrality laws in the sale of a part of her captured cargo of wool, which he alleged took place at the island of Ichaboe within British jurisdiction. When Semmes arrived, shortly afterward, he contended that the transactions in question were conducted at Angra Pequena, outside of British territory, and after the interchange of much correspondence the upshot of the whole business was the following announcement in Parliament by Lord Palmerston:

" The *Tuscaloosa* was seized, in the first instance, in consequence of instructions sent out to the Cape, *founded on a former supposed condition of things.* The *Tuscaloosa* was not in port when those instructions arrived; but when she returned the governor, acting upon those instructions, seized her. Upon further representations, however, and a full consideration of the case, it has been determined that there are no proper grounds internationally for seizing her, and orders have been sent out to set her at liberty."

What it all amounted to was a recognition by Great Britain of the legal right of Semmes to commission as a vessel-of-war a prize captured on the high seas, and the name of the

Tuscaloosa is more remembered for this diplomatic skirmish than for any service as a commerce-destroyer that she performed, as her prizes were but two in number.

THE RAPPAHANNOCK.—This ship was originally the dispatch boat *Victor*, of the British navy, and although a handsomely modelled screw-steamer of some 500 tons burden, proved so defective that in 1863 the Admiralty ordered her to be sold at auction, and she was bought by a representative of Capt. M. F. Maury, C. S. naval agent in England, under the pretence that she was to be engaged in the China trade. The intention was to fit her out as a cruiser at an appointed rendezvous, and Capt. Campbell, C. S. N., was designated to command her. Suspecting that she was destined for the Confederate service, the British Foreign Office ordered her to be detained; but on Nov. 24th, 1863, a young Scotchman named Ramsey succeeded in running her out from Sheerness, expecting to meet the *Georgia* off the French coast, and receive the battery and ammunition of the latter. Passing down the Thames, the brasses of the *Rappahannock* blew out, and she drifted across the Channel, and anchored off Calais. There she was docked for repairs, and Lieut. Chas. M. Fauntleroy, C. S. N., was ordered to take command of her by Com. Barron, the naval agent of the Confederacy at Paris. A board of survey found her utterly unsuited for a cruiser, as she was slow under steam or sail, could only carry eleven days' coal, and but six weeks' provisions. The utmost use she ever was to the Confederacy was to keep one or two Federal vessels off Calais, watching her, to see that she did not go to sea. When the news of the surrender of Gen. Lee was received, Lieut. Fauntleroy was ordered to pay off the officers and crew, and turn the vessel over to Capt. Bulloch. Fauntleroy appropriately called her "The Confederate White Elephant."

THE GEORGIANA.—In 1862–63 Messrs. Laird & Co. built at Birkenhead for the Confederate States a fast and powerful steamer called the *Georgiana*. She escaped from British jurisdiction under the pretence of being destined for the Chinese service, and left Liverpool for Nassau Jan. 22d, 1863; the intention being to run the blockade into Charleston, where the ship was to be armed and fitted out as a cruiser. After being detained some time at Nassau she started for Charleston, but was discovered by the blockaders off the port and her captain ran her ashore, about March 20th, on Long Island beach, on the South Carolina coast, to avoid capture. Strenuous efforts were made by the enemy to get at her cargo, which was partly of military stores and known to be very valuable, but the Confederates kept off their landing parties by bringing field batteries to bear upon them. The *Georgiana*, however, was knocked to pieces by their shells. Apart from her cargo, the loss was a serious one to the Confederacy, as she was a much faster and stronger ship than any one of its cruisers afloat and would have made a superb man-of-war.

THE GEORGIA.—Capt. M. F. Maury, C. S. naval agent, bought at Dumbarton, Scotland, March, 1863, a new iron screw-steamer of 600 tons burden and 200 horse-power, named the *Japan*, built for commercial service. April 1st she cleared from Greenock in ballast for the East Indies, her crew of 50 men, shipped at Liverpool, signing articles for a voyage to Singapore and intermediate ports. Although she left Greenock in the condition of an ordinary ship of commerce, her departure was accelerated by a suspicion that the British authorities had received knowledge of the uses for which she was designed, and orders to detain her reached Greenock the day after she had passed out of the Clyde. On the French coast, off Ushant, she met by appointment the steamer *Alar*, from which she received her guns, ordnance stores and supplies. The Confederate flag was hoisted, the officers took charge, and the ship was formally put in commission as the C. S. man-of-war *Georgia*. Her officers, who had come out in the *Alar*, were Com. W. L. Maury, First Lieut. Chapman, Second Lieut. Evans, Third Lieut. Smith, Fourth Lieut. Ingraham, Passed Midshipman Walker, Midshipman Morgan, Paymaster Curtis, Surgeon Wheedon, Chief. Eng. Pearson. The *Georgia* was a swift and powerful ship of her class, her battery consisting of five Whitworth guns, two 100-pdrs., two 24-pdrs. and one 32-pdr. Of the seamen who had come out from Greenock and signed for a trading voyage, only thirteen consented to ship as man-of-warsmen, and the remainder were sent back to England by the *Alar*, and the crew of the *Georgia* was filled up by men brought out in that vessel. The cruiser's field of operations was the Atlantic Ocean, but it had been already so well reaped of the enemy's commerce by other Confederate ships that only the gleanings were left to her; but in her short career she made prizes aggregating in value $406,000. The first was the ship *Dictator*, taken on April 25th and burned, and the *Georgia* ran across to Bahia, Brazil, where she coaled and continued on to the Cape of Good Hope, capturing on the way the ships *George Griswold* and *Constitution* and the barks *Good Hope* and *J. W. Seaver*. She arrived in St. Simon's Bay on Aug. 16th, and on the 29th set out for a return to Europe. During this run she made prizes of the ships *City of Bath*, *Prince of Wales*, *John Watts* and *Bold Hunter*. She put into Cherbourg, France, on Oct. 28th, where Com. Maury was detached on account of ill-health, and Lieut. Evans was promoted to the command. Because of her insufficient sail power, which necessitated frequent coaling, it was not deemed worth while to continue her as a cruiser, and she was taken to Liverpool, where she arrived on May 2d, 1864. There she was dismantled and offered for sale, Edward Bates, a Liverpool merchant, becoming her purchaser for the sum of £15,000. This was done against the protest of Mr. Adams, the U. S. Minister, who gave notice that his government would not recognize the transfer and requested Com. Craven, then in command of the U. S. frigate *Niagara*, lying in the port of Antwerp, that he must endeavor to intercept and capture the converted Confederate. Mr. Bates removed every vestige of war fittings, effected a charter of the ship to the Portuguese government; and on Aug. 8th, 1864, with a British register and under a British flag, she sailed from Liverpool for Lisbon. Off the mouth of the Tagus River she was captured by the *Niagara* and sent to Boston with a prize-crew, where she was condemned and sold as a lawful prize of the United States. Mr. Bates appealed to the British Foreign Office for redress, but was informed that the case of the *Georgia* must go before the prize court in the United States, and that he must be prepared to defend his interests therein. He was fortunate enough, however, to recover £6,000 insurance money in the British courts.

THE RAM STONEWALL.—In 1862, Mr. Slidell, representative of the Confederate States in France, received an intimation from persons in the confidence of Emperor Napoleon III. that the government would not interfere with the building of cruisers in French ship-yards for the Confederacy; and when, in March 1863, funds were provided by the negotiation of the £3,000,000 loan, Capt. Bulloch, Mr. Slidell and M. Arman, a member of the Corps Legislatif and proprietor of a large ship-yard at Bordeaux, held consultations in Paris, at which M. Arman renewed the assurances that such vessels-of-war could be constructed and sent to sea with the connivance of his government. Contracts were entered into with him for the construction of four steam corvettes, two of which, as his own yard was crowded with work, he turned over to M. J. Voruz, of Nantes.[1] On June 30th, Capt. Bulloch received information of the passage by the Confederate Congress of an appropriation of £2,000,000 for the construction of iron-clad ships-of-war, and in accordance with the instructions of Secretary Mallory entered into a contract with M. Arman to build a ship 172 feet long, 33 feet breadth of beam, to steam 12 knots an hour, to be plated amidships with $4\frac{3}{4}$ inches of iron, tapering to $3\frac{1}{2}$ inches at the extremities, to carry a 300-pdr. Armstrong rifle in a forward turret and two 70-pdr. Armstrongs in an after-turret. The vessel had a ram, and was so designed that she might enter the Mississippi River, and a second ship was ordered on the same general plan. In Nov. the corvettes and the iron-clads were more than half finished, and the attention of the U. S. Minister at Paris, Mr. Dayton, was attracted to them. He laid before the Emperor proof that they were intended for the Confederate government; and Napoleon, induced undoubtedly by considerations relative to the war he was then waging in Mexico, and the probability of the fall of the Confederacy, completely revoked the guarantees that had been given Slidell and Bulloch. The builders were notified that the iron-clads would not be permitted to sail, and that the corvettes must not be armed in France, but might be nominally sold to some foreign merchant, and dispatched as

[2] When the French government changed its policy, and forbade the Confederate ships to go to sea, M. Voruz sold these two corvettes to European powers.

ordinary trading vessels. On July 9th, 1864, M. Arman announced that in obedience to the orders of the government he had sold all six of the vessels.

The only one with which we have anything to do, as the others never came into the possession of the Confederacy, was the iron-clad ram *Sphynx,* one of the two armored ships contracted for. M. Arman sold her to Denmark, then at war with Prussia, but when she arrived at Copenhagen hostilities had ceased, and the Danish government was anxious to part with the ship. Arrangements were made to transfer her to the Confederate flag, and on Jan. 6th, 1865, she sailed from Copenhagen, in charge of Capt. T. J. Page, C. S. N., who had been appointed to the command. On the 24th she met at the appointed rendezvous, off Quiberon, on the French coast, the steamer *City of Richmond,* in command of Lieut. H. Davidson, C. S. N., which had been dispatched from London with the remainder of her officers, crew and supplies. The Confederate flag was hoisted on the ram, and she was christened the *Stonewall.* This is the full list of her officers:

Captain, T. J. Page ; Lieuts., R. R. Carter, Geo. S. Shryock, Geo. A. Borchet, E. G. Read, Sam'l Barron, Jr.; Surgeon, B. W. Green ; Assistant Surg., J. W. Herty ; Paymaster, R. W. Curtiers ; Chief Eng., W. P. Brooks ; Assistant Engs., W. H. Jackson and J. C. Klosh; Master, W. W. Wilkinson ; Boatswain, J. M. Dukehart ; Gunner, J. B. King ; Master's Mate, W. H. Savage ; Paymaster's Clerk, Wm. Boynton ; Sergeant of Marines, J. M. Prior.

The *Stonewall* was found to have sprung a leak immediately after leaving Quiberon, and Capt. Page ran into Corunna. and thence to Ferrol, Spain, where he was at first granted all the dock-yard facilities, but was subsequently hurried off by the Spanish authorities, on account of the protest of the American Minister. In the first week of Feb. the Federal frigate *Niagara* and sloop-of-war *Sacramento,* under command of Com. T. T. Craven,[1] anchored at Corunna, nine miles distant, from whence they could watch the *Stonewall.* The *Niagara* was one of the fastest ships of the U. S. navy, and carried a battery of ten 150-pounder Parrott rifles, while the *Sacramento* mounted two 11-inch guns, two 9-inch guns and one 60-pounder rifle. On March 24th, the *Stonewall* steamed out of Ferrol, and cleared for action, in full sight of the enemy ; but to the surprise of Capt. Page, who fully expected an engagement, they declined his challenge by remaining at anchor. He did everything he could to provoke an encounter, standing on and off all day, and " flaunting her flags in his face," as Craven wrote ; but the latter feared to attack, with his superior force of two ships to one, and fifteen guns to three. Finding that the enemy would not fight, the *Stonewall* bore

[1] Com. Craven was brought to trial by court-martial, on the charge of " failing to do his utmost to overtake and capture or destroy a vessel, which it was his duty to encounter." He was found guilty, and sentenced to two years' suspension; but the Secretary of the Navy annulled the sentence, on the ground that it was not sufficiently severe for the offense. On a revision of the proceedings, the court-martial made the same finding, which the Secretary again set aside, for the same reason and the accused was restored to duty. His defence was, that it would have been imprudent for him to risk his wooden vessels against the iron-clad ram.

away for Lisbon, Capt. Page's intention being to cross the Atlantic, and attempt to strike a blow at Port Royal, which was then supposed to be the base of Gen. Sherman's advance through South Carolina. He reached Nassau on May 6th, and proceeded to Havana, where he learned of the end of the war. The ship was surrendered to the Captain General of Cuba, on the payment of $16,000, about the amount of wages due the crew. That official offered Lieut. Carter, who conducted the negotiations, $100,000, and then $50,000, but the larger amounts were refused. The crew were paid off and discharged, and the Spanish officials took charge of the ship. In July, Spain voluntarily delivered her to the U. S. government, by which she was subsequently sold to Japan.

THE TALLAHASSEE (ATLANTA).—This vessel was a splendid twin-screw, 14-knot blockade-runner, built on the Thames, and after making several trips into and out of Wilmington her name was changed from the *Atlanta* to the *Tallahassee*, and she was commissioned as a C. S. ship-of-war under command of Com. J. T. Wood. [1] The other officers were Lieuts. W. H. Ward, M. M. Benton, J. M. Gardner; Acting Master, Alex. Curtis; Engineers: Chief, J. W. Tyman; Assistants, C. H. Leroy, E. G. Hall, J. F. Green, J. J. Lyell, H. H. Roberts, R. M. Ross; Assist. Paymaster, C. L. Jones; Assist. Surgeon, W. L. Sheppardson; Boatswain, J. Cassidy; Gunner, —— Stewart; Master's Mate, C. Russell; Lieut. of Marines, —— Crenshaw, with a crew of about 110 men. The battery consisted of a 32-pounder rifle, a lighter rifle and a brass howitzer. On Aug. 6th, 1864, the *Tallahassee* went to sea from Wilmington under the fire of the blockaders, whom the speedy ship soon left behind. Her cruising ground was the Atlantic coast, and when within 80 miles of Sandy Hook, on Aug. 11th, she took her first prize, the schooner *Sarah A. Boyce*, of Egg Harbor, N. J., which she scuttled. In two days in these waters,

[1] John Taylor Wood is a son of the late Surgeon Gen. Robert C. Wood, of the U. S. army. His mother was a daughter of President Zachary Taylor, and sister of the first wife of Hon. Jefferson Davis. He was born in Louisiana, and entered the U. S. navy as midshipman in April, 1847, serving during the Mexican war in the *Ohio* and *Brandywine*. In 1861 he was assistant professor of seamanship and gunnery at the U. S. naval academy. Resigning his commission, he entered the service of Virginia, and was at the Evansport batteries during the blockade of the Potomac. He was commissioned lieut. in the C. S. navy Oct. 4th, 1861, and about the beginning of Jan., 1862, was ordered to the *Virginia* at Norfolk, and participated in the Hampton Roads battles. In the engagements at Drewry's Bluff he commanded a company of sharp-shooters that picked off many men on the Federal ships, and after the repulse of the latter he was assigned to duty on the staff of President Davis, with the rank of Col. of cavalry. He organized numerous boat expeditions against the enemy on the Chesapeake Bay and tributary waters, and inspected the water defences of all points held by the Confederacy upon the seaboard, as well as Port Hudson and Vicksburg, on the Mississippi. He commanded the boat expeditions that captured the U. S. gunboats *Satellite* and *Reliance* in the Rappahannock River, and the *Underwriter* at Newberne, N. C. He was promoted to post-captain for gallantry, and in Aug., 1864, took command of the *Tallahassee* for her cruise. He took part in the capture of Plymouth, N. C., and in the winter of 1864–65 was offered the command of the James River squadron, but declined it. On April 2d, 1865, he delivered to President Davis, in St. Paul's church, Richmond, Gen. Lee's dispatch announcing his withdrawal from Petersburg, and the last Confederate cabinet meeting or council was held in a house occupied by Col. Wood's family at Greensboro', N. C. He was with Pres. Davis when the latter was captured at Irwinsville, Ga., May 10th, 1865, and made his own escape by bribing the Federal guard. He joined Gen. Breckenridge the next day, and they, with Col. Wilson, an aide to Mr. Davis, crossed Georgia into Florida, descending St. John's River to Jupiter Inlet in a boat. At the inlet they obtained a second boat from some Federal deserters, with which they crossed to Cuba, making a landing at Cardenas. Since the war, Col. Wood has resided at Halifax.

the pilot-boat *James Funk*, brig *Carrie Estelle*, pilot-boat *Wm. Bell* and schooner *Atlantic* were captured. The *Funk* was converted into a tender under command of Acting Master Davis and captured the bark *Bay State*, brig *A. Richards* and schooner *Carroll*. All but the tender and *Carroll* were burned, and the latter was bonded and sent to N. Y. with the paroled prisoners. Her captain broke his oath by landing on Fire Island and telegraphing information to the Federal authorities that a Confederate cruiser was within 60 miles of New York. Six or seven gunboats were sent in pursuit and New York passed through the throes of alarm and excitement. Com. Wood had formed a project to dash upon the Brooklyn navy-yard and escape to sea by way of Hell Gate after doing all the destruction possible; but this scheme was abandoned and the *Tallahassee* ran to the eastward with the tender in tow. Off the eastern end of Long Island the ship *Adriatic* was taken and burned, on Aug. 12th, and the bark *Suliote* was ransomed to land the prisoners. The tender, being of no further use, was destroyed, and the *Tallahassee* wound up this eventful day by capturing the schooner *Spokane*, the brig *Billow* and the schooner *Robert E. Packer*, which latter was sent off with prisoners. Within the next few days the captures were the *Mercy A. Howes, Glenavon, Lamont Dupont, Howard, Floral Wreath, Restless, Sarah B. Harris, Etta Caroline, P. C. Alexander, Leopard, Pearl, Sarah Louisa* and *Magnolia*. In taking these prizes Wood had made his way well up along the coast of Maine and played the mischief with the N. E. fishing trade, and fully a dozen gunboats were added to the fleet already in pursuit of him. Going toward Halifax for coal he captured the *North America, Neva, Josiah Achorne, Ellis* and *Diadem*. All were destroyed except those by which prisoners were sent to the nearest ports. On Aug. 18th the *Tallahassee* arrived at Halifax and was ordered away, after getting only enough coal to take her back to Wilmington. She left Halifax on the 19th, and between there and the Cape Fear River captured the brig *Rowan* and was fruitlessly chased by Federal cruisers. On the 25th she boldly ran into that river, fighting the blockaders as she pushed through their midst until she dropped anchor under the guns of Fort Fisher. She had burned 16 vessels, scuttled 10, bonded 5 and released 2.

Com. Wood was detached from the ship and was succeeded in command by Lieut. Ward. Her name was changed to the *Olustee*, and on Oct. 29th, 1864, she ran through the blockading fleet to sea, but not without sustaining some damage from their shells. Off the capes of the Delaware she captured and destroyed the bark *Empress Theresa*, schooner *A. J. Bird*, schooner *E. F. Lewis* and schooner *Goodspeed*. Near Sandy Hook the ship *Areole*, brig *T. D. Wagner* and schooner *Vapor* were made prizes and destroyed. Coal being nearly exhausted, the *Olustee* went southward again, but halted on Nov. 6th off Cape Charles in the hope of attacking some of

the U. S. transports hove to in the prevailing gale.   Here she
was detected by the gunboat *Sassacus*, which chased her until
she was lost in the darkness.   On the 6th the *Sassacus* again
saw her and kept up an unsuccessful pursuit all day.   The next
day the *Olustee* was 60 miles off Wilmington bar and steam
was allowed to go down for repairs to the engines.   Three vessels looking like blockade-runners hove in sight.   They were
the captured blockade-runners *Margaret and Jessie*, the *Lil-
lian* and the *Banshee*, converted into Federal cruisers, and
were soon joined by the gunboat *Montgomery*.   Ward first
headed the *Olustee* out to sea and then wore short round and
steered for Wilmington bar.   All the vessels opened fire upon
her, but the *Montgomery* was the only one close enough to be
feared.   She replied with her after gun, distanced her pursuers and got into Wilmington unharmed.   Her battery was
taken out and she was renamed the *Chameleon*.   Under the
command of Capt. John Wilkinson, C. S. N., she ran the blockade of the Cape Fear River, Dec. 24th, while the Federal fleet
was bombarding Fort Fisher, and started for Bermuda to procure a cargo of provisions for Lee's army.   On her arrival at
St. George's on the 30th, she was seized by the British authorities on the demand of the U. S. consul, but she had been so
thoroughly "whitewashed" by an ostensible sale at Wilmington that she was to all intents and purposes a merchant ship.
Laden with provisions, she sailed from St. George's Jan. 19th,
1865, but on arriving off New Inlet Wilkinson found it closed
by the fall of Fort Fisher and put back to Nassau.   On Jan.
30th the *Chameleon* left Nassau for Charleston, but the blockaders were too thick for her off that port, and to Nassau she
returned.   When he learned of the evacuation of Charleston,
Wilkinson resolved to take the ship to England and arrived at
Liverpool, April 9th. She was seized and sold by the British government and was about to enter the merchant service under the
name of the *Amelia* when the United States entered suit for possession.   The court awarded the vessel to that government, and
she was handed over to the consul at Liverpool, April 26th,1866.

THE CHICKAMAUGA.—In the autumn of 1864, the Confederate Navy Department found, at Wilmington, the small
twin-screw blockade-runner *Edith*, which was commissioned
as a cruiser under the name of the *Chickamauga*, and with
Capt. John Wilkinson, C. S. N., in command, was equipped
to follow the example of the *Tallahassee* in a raid upon the
enemy's commerce along the coast.   She carried a light spar-
deck battery of three rifled guns, and started to sea on the
night of Oct. 29th.   She got out safely, and although pursued by a gunboat the next day, outfooted her without trouble.
Twenty-four hours afterwards she opened her record as a
commerce destroyer by capturing the bark *Mark L. Potter*,
and within two days she made prizes within fifty miles of
N. Y., of the bark *Emma L. Hall*, ship *Shooting Star*, and
bark *Albion Lincoln*.   All but the *Lincoln* were burned, and

C. S. CRUISER "SHENANDOAH."

COMMANDER JAMES I. WADDELL, C. S. N.,

COMMANDING THE "SHENANDOAH."

she was bonded to land the paroled prisoners, her captain promising to put into no nearer port than Fortress Monroe, but he steered directly for N. Y. and gave the alarm. The *Chickamauga* ran up to the entrance of L. I. Sound, and off Block Island took and scuttled the schooners *Otter Rock* and *Good Speed.* A gale frustrated Capt. Wilkinson's intention of making an incursion upon the ports of the Sound, and going out to sea he captured the bark *Speedwell.* He put into St. George's, Bermuda, and by having the condenser conveniently disabled obtained permission from the authorities to remain a week for repair. Under the neutrality laws, then being strictly enforced, he was allowed only enough coal to take the ship to the nearest Confederate port; but by offering the British customs officer all the alcoholic load that his hold could contain, he was made oblivious to the fact that the *Chickamauga's* bunkers were being pretty well filled up with coal. The supply was still too short to admit of further cruising, and the ship ran the blockade back into Wilmington, thus closing her history as a belligerent upon the high seas. In the defence of Fort Fisher her officers and crew took a very prominent and distinguished part. After that disaster the *Chickamauga* was taken up the river, and burnt and sunk.

THE SHENANDOAH.—The last of the Confederate cruisers, and the one that, with the exception of the *Alabama*, inflicted the largest total of injury upon the commerce of the United States, was the *Shenandoah*, which was purchased by Capt. Bulloch to supply the place of the vessel sunk by the *Kearsarge.* She was originally the British merchant steamer *Sea King*, equipped with a lifting screw so as to be used under sail alone and was fully rigged as a ship, and was very fast under either sail or steam. The whaling fleets of the United States were the largest portion of its commerce remaining, and this cruiser was especially fitted out to swoop down upon them. Bulloch paid £45,000 for the ship, buying her through the medium of an English merchant captain named Corbett, who was to transfer her upon the high seas. At the same time he purchased the blockade-runner *Laurel* and loaded her at Liverpool with the guns, stores, etc., for the cruiser, and the *Laurel* also carried out to the rendezvous all the officers except Lieut. Whittle, who went in the *Sea King* to make himself acquainted with her. She sailed from London and the *Laurel* from Liverpool on Oct. 8th, 1864. The *Sea King* was cleared for Bombay or any port in the East Indies, and the *Laurel* for Nassau. On the 18th they rendezvoused off Funchal, Madeira, and proceeded to Las Desertas, an uninhabited island near by, and in two days the armament and war material were transferred to the *Sea King;* Capt. James I. Waddell hoisted her new colors and took command of her as the Confederate States man-of-war *Shenandoah.* The battery placed on board consisted of four 8-inch smooth-bore guns, two Whitworth 32-pounder rifles and two 12-pounders. The most serious obstacle that met the ship at the outset of her career was the paucity of her crew. Eighty seamen had shipped for the pretended voyage to the East Indies, and but twenty-three consented to remain under the Confederate flag; so that, including her nineteen commissioned and warrant officers, the ship had but forty-two men on board ; but the crew was soon brought up to the requisite number by enlistments from the prizes she took. The roster of officers was as follows:

"Lieut. Commanding James Iredell Waddell;[1] First Lieuts., Wm. C. Whittle, John Grimball, S. Smith Lee, Jr., Francis T. Chew; Second Lieut., Dabney M. Scales; Acting Master, J. S. Bulloch; Acting Chief Eng., Mat. O'Brien; Passed Assist. Surgeon, C. E. Lining; Acting Assist. Paymaster, W. Breedlove Smith; Passed Midshipmen, O. A. Browne; John T. Mason; Acting Assist. Surgeon, F. J. McNulty; Engineers—First Assist., W. H. Codd; Second Assist., John Hutchinson; Third Assist., Ernest Muggaffeney; Acting Master's Mates, C. E. Hunt, J. T. Minor, Lodge Colton; Acting Boatswain, Geo. Harwood; Acting Carpenter, J. O'Shea; Acting Gunner, J. L. Guy; Sailmaker, Henry Alcott; Second Carpenter, J. Lynch.

Capt. Waddell steered for Australia, and before arriving at Melbourne, Jan. 25th, 1865, made prizes of the barks *Alina, Godfrey, Edward,* and *Delphine ;* schooners *Charter Oak* and *Lizzie M. Stacey,* and brig *Susan,* all of which were burned. The steamer *Kate Prince* was ransomed, to take home the prisoners, and the bark *Adelaide* was bonded. At Melbourne, the *Shenandoah* was permitted to go into a private dock for repairs, and then trouble with the colonial authorities arose, on an allegation that Capt. Waddell had shipped a British subject in the port, in violation of the Foreign Enlistment Act. He refused to allow his ship to be searched, and his assurances that he had committed no breach of neutrality were accepted. The *Shenandoah* left Melbourne Feb. 8th, 1865, in excellent condition, and in three months passed from that far southern latitude to the beginning of her destructive work among the whalers in the Okhotsk Sea, Behring's Sea, and the Arctic Ocean. Between June 22d and the 28th she captured, and either destroyed or ransomed, 24 ships. They were taken in couplets, triplets and quartets, and it was necessary to release and bond four of them, in order to get rid of the numerous prisoners. The earliest prizes were the *Edward*

[1] Capt. Waddell was born in Pittsboro', N. C., in 1824, and was appointed midshipman in the U. S. naval service on Sept. 10th, 1841. He was assigned to duty on the U. S. ship *Pennsylvania,* at Portsmouth, Va. A few months after he entered upon the discharge of his duties he was shot in the hip in a duel with another midshipman, which caused him to limp to the day of his death. After several years of sea service, during which he was promoted to lieutenant, he was, in 1858, made assistant professor of navigation at the naval academy at Annapolis. In 1859 he was ordered to the East India squadron, and in 1861, when the war broke out, mailed his resignation from St. Helena. His reason for resigning was given by him in a letter published by him in Jan. 1862, as owing to his "unwillingness to bear arms against his father's home and relatives in the seceded States." He declared explicitly that he had no property in the seceded States, that he was not hostile to the Constitution of the United States; that he venerated the flag and wished that he might hazard life and limb in its defence against some foreign foe. It has been said that one of the causes of his resignation was that he was engaged to be married to Miss Iglehart, the daughter of James Iglehart, of Annapolis, whose family was strongly inclined to the South. He married this lady in Dec. 1861. His resignation at the breaking out of the war was not accepted, and he stands on the U. S. navy register of 1862 as "dismissed." In Feb., 1862, he ran the blockade to Richmond and entered the Confederate navy. His commission as first lieut. bears date March 27th, 1862. He was assigned to duty at Drewry's Bluff defences. Subsequently he had a command in Charleston harbor, from which he was assigned to "special service," and in 1864 ran the blockade to take command of the C. S. privateer *Shenandoah.*

Casey, Hector, Abigail, Euphrates, Wm. Thompson, Sophia Thornton, Jireh Swift, Susan and Abigail, and *Milo,* the latter being sent to San Francisco, with the prisoners. In the next batch were the *Nassau, Brunswick, Hillman, Waverly, Martha 2d, Congress 2d, Favorite, Covington, James Maury* and *Nile.* The two last-named were converted into cartels, and took the prisoners to San Francisco, and the others were burned. On one occasion eight prizes were taken in a lump, as they had gathered around the disabled ship *Brunswick,* and when the octette was fired, that hyperborean sea was lit up with a wondrous mass of fire. This occurred on June 28th, near the mouth of Behring's Straits, and comprised the last war exploit of the *Shenandoah.* She captured in all 38 ships, 34 of which were destroyed, and four ransomed; their total value was stated by the masters at $1,361,-983. Waddell had faithfully executed the programme of obliterating the American whaling industry in those regions.

It will be seen that many of his captures were effected after the close of the war, and in consequence, Secretary Welles accused him of continuing his belligerent operations when he knew that the armies of the South had surrendered. That malicious charge has been easily and completely refuted. From prizes taken on June 23d, he received papers containing the correspondence of the preceding April, between Grant and Lee, relative to the surrender of the latter; but they also informed him that the seat of the Confederate government had been removed from Richmond to Danville, and that Pres. Davis had issued a proclamation giving assurances of the continuation of the struggle by the Confederacy. With his knowledge of the condition of things in America thus limited, Capt. Waddell had no right to suppose that the war had ended, or to cease his hostile endeavors. The *Shenandoah* came out of the Straits on June 29th, and while running towards the California coast spoke, on Aug. 2d, the British bark *Baracouta,* 14 days out from San Francisco, from whose captain Waddell learned of the capture of Pres. Davis, and the capitulation of the remaining military forces of the Confederacy. The *Shenandoah's* guns were at once dismounted, ports closed, funnels whitewashed, and the ship transformed, so far as external appearance went, into an ordinary merchantman. Waddell decided to give the ship up to the British authorities, and brought her into Liverpool on Nov. 6th, not a vessel having been spoken during the long voyage from the North Pacific. He turned her over to Capt. Paynter, commanding her Majesty's ship *Donegal,* who placed a prize-crew on board, and Waddell communicated with Lord Russell, British Secretary for Foreign Affairs. In this letter he stated his opinion that the vessel should revert, with other property of the Confederacy, to the U. S. government, and that point was quickly settled; but Mr. Adams raised the usual question of "piracy" against the officers and men of the ship, and there was also a liability to proceedings under the Foreign Enlistment Act, if British subjects could be found on board. Mr. Adams wanted the officers and crew held, he said, until he could procure evidence from San Francisco, that Capt. Waddell knew of the downfall of the Confederacy before his latest seizures of American vessels; but the law officers of the crown decided that there was no evidence to justify their detention. On Nov. 8th, Capt. Paynter had the roll of the *Shenandoah* called upon her deck, and as not a member of the ship's company acknowledged to being a subject of Great Britain, they were discharged, and allowed to depart. Mr. Adams, however, continued to urge the arrest of Capt. Waddell, on charges of piracy; and when rebuffed by the British government, he brought forward an affidavit made by one Temple, who purported to have sailed in the *Shenandoah.* He alleged that the crew were chiefly British subjects, and Mr. Adams claimed that they should have been held for violation of the Foreign Enlistment Act, but nothing came of his efforts; and he was, indeed, chiefly prompted by a motive to make up the record that was subsequently presented to the Geneva tribunal. Capt. Waddell and his officers were never molested. The *Shenandoah* was sold by the U. S. to the Sultan of Zanzibar, and in 1879 was lost in the Indian Ocean.

BRAINE'S CAPTURE OF THE CHESAPEAKE AND ROANOKE.— Before daylight on the morning of Dec. 7th, 1863, while the steamship *Chesapeake*, Capt. Willetts, was off Cape Cod on her regular trip between N. Y. and Portland, Me., she was seized by John C. Braine, purporting to be a lieutenant of the C. S. navy, and fifteen men; who had come on board the ship at N. Y. as passengers. In the struggle the second engineer was shot dead, and the first mate wounded. To Capt. Willetts Braine exhibited an order from John Parker, captain of the C. S. steamer *Retribution* (whose true name was V. G. Locke), instructing him to capture the vessel, and naming as his assisting officers First Lieut. H. A. Parr, Second Lieut. D. Collins, and Sailing Master Geo. Rowson. Braine headed the vessel for the island of Grand Menan, off the coast of Maine, where he expected to meet Parker. The latter, however, who had left the *Retribution* at Nassau, some months previously, was encountered on a pilot-boat in the Bay of Fundy, and assumed command of the *Chesapeake*, sending Capt. Willetts and the passengers and crew of the steamer to St. Johns by the pilot-boat. The *Chesapeake* made for Shelburne, N. S., to coal, and from thence went to La Havre River, where Parker sold her cargo of provisions and liquors to the people on shore. A half-dozen Federal cruisers had been sent after the *Chesapeake*, and one of them, the *Ella and Annie*, came up with her in Sambro harbor, near Halifax. Parker and his party escaped to the shore, leaving on the steamer only her former engineer, whom they had impressed into their service, and a couple of her hands. Lying near her was the British schooner *Investigator*, on board of which the commander of the gunboat found and arrested a man named Wade, one of Parker's party. He took the *Chesapeake* into Halifax to turn her over to the British authorities for adjudication, and there Wade was aided to escape by a number of citizens who sympathized with the Southern confederacy. The affair gave rise to intense excitement, and several of Braine's men were arrested on warrants issued by a local magistrate, who committed them for extradition on a charge of piracy. Their names were Collins, McKinnon and Seely. An appeal was taken to the Supreme Court of the province; and on March 10th, 1864, Judge Ritchie ordered their release on the grounds that no proper requisition had been made for their extradition; that piracy was not an extraditable offence; that a magistrate had no jurisdiction over questions of piracy, and that the warrant was bad on its face. In these legal proceedings the Confederate States had been represented by Hon. J. P. Holcomb, who made an inquiry into all the circumstances of the capture of the *Chesapeake*, and reported to Mr. Benjamin, Confederate Secretary of State, who disavowed the responsibility of of his government for the acts of Parker and Braine. His decision was founded on the facts that Parker (Locke) was a British subject who had organized the expedition in a British colony, and had assumed to issue commissions in the Confederate service to British subjects without being himself in that service; that it was doubtful whether either Braine or Parr was a Confederate citizen, and that Braine had, in any event, divested himself of the character of an officer engaged in legitimate warfare by selling portions of the cargo of the *Chesapeake* instead of navigating her to a Confederate port. Mr. Benjamin also distinctly disclaimed "all attempts to organize within neutral jurisdictions expeditions composed of neutral subjects for the purpose of carrying on hostilities against the United States." In his view the captors of the *Chesapeake* were men "who, sympathizing with us in a righteous cause, erroneously believed themselves authorized to act as belligerents against the U. S. by virtue of Parker's possession of the letter-of-marque issued to the privateer *Retribution*." Although the Confederate government would not demand the surrender to it of the men arrested by the provincial authorities, as their actual offence was "disobedience to her majesty's proclamation, and to the foreign enlistment law of Great Britain," Mr. Benjamin stated that Pres. Davis was "much gratified that the superior judicial authorities of New Brunswick have rejected the pretensions of the consul of the United States that the parties engaged in this capture should be surrendered under the Ashburton treaty for trial by the courts of the U. S. on charges of murder and piracy." The temptation to the Confederate government to claim the *Chesapeake* as a prize was avoided by the frank avowal of Mr. Holcomb, that

"It is morally certain that the home government would not, under the circumstances, allow a claim for compensation for the surrender of the vessel by the judicial authorities, and I cannot but think that the presentation of such a claim by our government, and its rejection—the case being one, as all must admit, very doubtful both in law and morals—would impair its public prestige and weaken the moral weight which might attach to its interposition upon future and more important occasions."

As the offence of piracy would have been just as triable in the British provinces as in the U. S., new warrants were issued by the provincial courts for the arrest of the implicated men; but they had been warned, and had placed themselves outside the jurisdiction of those tribunals. In Jan. 1864, proceedings were taken in the admiralty court at Halifax upon the disposition to be made of the *Chesapeake*. Judge Stuart refused to consider the suggestion that the Confederate government might make an application for the vessel, the seizure of which declared to be piracy, and ordered her return to her owners.

After escaping from the British provinces in Dec. 1863, Braine and Parr were next heard of in the capture of the steamship *Roanoke*, of the Havana line. She left Havana on Sept. 29th, 1864, and in passing out of the harbor received on board a party of passengers provided with regular tickets and passports properly viséd. These were disguised Confederates under command of Braine and Parr, and that night, when well out at sea, they made prisoners of the officers, and took possession of the vessel. The ship's carpenter made a resistance and was killed, and the second engineer was wounded. Braine took $21,000 in money contained in the ship's safe and headed for Bermuda, arriving at St. George's on Feb. 4th. Without entering the harbor he obtained coal and provisions from a brig that came out to meet him, and going to sea again encountered the British brig *Mathilde*, to which he transferred the crew and passengers of the *Roanoke*, who were landed at Bermuda. He then set the steamer on fire, and went ashore on Bermuda with his men. They were arrested by the British authorities, but were released after a brief detention.

At the close of the war, Braine came into the United States trusting to be protected by Pres. Johnson's amnesty proclamation. In 1866 he was arrested in N. Y. on the old charges of piracy and murder. He was subsequently released from the custody of the U. S. government.

UNITED STATES VESSELS DESTROYED BY CONFEDERATE CRUISERS.

BY THE NASHVILLE.

When destroyed.	Name of Vessel.	Character.	Property destroyed.	Value.
Nov. 19, 1861..	Harvey Birch........	Ship........	Vessel, etc....	66,000.00
Feb. 26, 1862..	Robert Gilfillan...	Schooner.	Personal property. ...	....

BY THE OLUSTEE.

When destroyed.	Name of Vessel.	Character.	Property destroyed.	Value.
Nov. 3, 1864..	A. J. Bird.............	Schooner......	Vessel, etc......	$24,869.00
Nov. 3, 1864..	Arcole.............	Ship....	Cargo........	18,000.00
Nov. 3, 1864..	E. F. Lewis.............	Schooner.. ...	Vessel, etc	....
Nov. 1, 1864..	Empress Theresa.....	Bark	" "	30,000.00
Nov. 3, 1864..	T. D. Wagner....	Brig.....	" "	....
Nov. 3, 1864..	Vapor.............	Schooner......	Cargo.....	....

BY THE ALABAMA.

When destroyed.	Name of Vessel.	Character.	Property destroyed.	Value.
Sept. 9, 1862..	Alert..............	Ship..........	Vessel and outfits.	$ 52,000.00
Sept. 13, 1862..	Altamaha...........	Brig..........	Brig, outfits, etc.......	6,000.00
Nov. 6, 1863..	Amanda....	Bark..	Vessel and freight.....	104,442.00
June 2, 1863..	Amazonian....	Bark	Bark and charter......	97 655.00
July 2, 1863..	Anna F. Schmidt	Ship	Dif. val. and ins.......	350,000.00
Dec. 7, 1862..	Ariel (bonded)........	Steamer........	U. S. Treasury notes ..	261,000.00
Oct. 29, 1862..	Baron de Castine	Brig	Bonded	6,000.00
Sept. 14, 1862..	Benj. Tucker..........	Ship..... ...	Vessel, Outfit, etc.....	70,200.00
March 1, 1863..	Bethia Thayer.........	Ship	Bonded.....	40,000.00
Oct. 3, 1862..	Brilliant....	Ship	Bonded............	164,000.00
March 25, 1863..	Charles Hill............	Ship	Bonded...............	28,450.00
Jan. 27, 1863..	Chastelaine............	Brig..... ...	Vessel and Cargo	10,000.00
Nov. 21, 1862.	Clara L. Sparks........	Schooner......	" " "	....
June 19, 1863..	Conrad	Bark	" " "	69,000 00
Nov. 11, 1863..	Contest	Ship	" " "	122,815.00
Sept. 16, 1862..	Courser...............	Schooner.....	" " "	7,000.00
Oct. 26, 1862 .	Crenshaw	Schooner.....	" " "	33,869 00
April 26, 1863..	Dorcas Prince........	Ship	" " "	44,108.00
Oct. 7, 1862..	Dunkirk	Brig....	" " "	25,000.00
Sept. 18, 1862..	Elisha Dunbar........	Bark	" " "	27,000.00
Oct. 3, 1862..	Emily Farnum........	Ship.........	Released....	....
Jan. 14, 1864..	Emma Jane............	Ship	Vessel and charter.....	40,000.00
July 6, 1863..	Express......	Ship	Vessel and freight....	121,300.00
Feb. 21, 1863..	Golden Eagle.........	Ship	" " "	61,000.00
Jan. 26, 1863..	Golden Rule.	Bark.........	" " "	112,000.00
Nov. 18, 1863..	Harriet Spalding.....	Bark...	....	....
Jan. 11, 1863..	Hatteras..............	Gunboat	....	160,000.00
Dec. 26, 1863..	Highlander	Ship.........	Vessel and freight.....	75,965.00
May 29, 1863..	Jabez Snow...........	Ship.........	" " "	72,881.00
March 2, 1863..	John A. Parks.........	Ship.........	" " "	70,000.00
May 25, 1863..	Justina................	Bark.........	....	7,000.00
April 15, 1863..	Kate Cory............	Brig	Vessel, etc	28,268.25
March 26, 1863..	Kingfisher........	Schooner.....	" "	24,000.00
Oct. 23, 1862..	Lafayette (1)	Ship..........	" "	110,337.00
	Lafayette (2)...........	Bark	" "	36,025.50
Oct. 15, 1862..	Lamplighter........	Bark.........	" "	117,600.00
Oct. 28, 1862..	Lauretta	Bark	" "	32,800.00
Nov. 2, 1862..	Levi Starbuck........	Ship....	" "	203,962.50
April 4, 1863..	Louisa Hatch.........	Ship..........	" "	82,250.00
Oct. 11, 1862..	Manchester	....	" "	164,000 00
Aug. 9, 1863..	Martha Wenzell......	Bark.........	Released............	....
Dec. 24, 1863..	Martaban.............	Ship..........	Vessel, etc	97,628.00
March 23, 1863..	Morning Star....	Ship.........	Bonded	61,750.00
Dec. 5, 1862..	Nina..................	Schooner.	Bonded..............	....
March 25, 1863	Nora..................	Ship...........	Vessel, etc	80,000.00
April 24, 1862..	Nye..................	Bark	" "	31,127.00
Sept. 8, 1862..	Ocean Rover.........	Bark	" "	98,820.00
Sept. 5, 1862..	Ocmulgee.............	Ship	" "	131,712.00
Feb. 21, 1863..	Olive Jane......	Bark	Merchandise...........	43,208.00
Feb. 3, 1863..	Palmetto............	Schooner......	"	18,434.00
Nov. 30, 1862..	Parker Cook...........	Bark..... ..	Vessel, etc	25,399.86
March 15, 1863..	Punjab	Ship	Bonded	52,000.00
April 23, 1864..	Rockingham....	Ship..........	Vessel, etc	105,000.00
Aug. 5, 1863..	Sea Bride	Bark	" "	100,000.00
May 3, 1863.	Sea Lark	Ship	" "	550,000.00
May 25, 1863..	S. Gildersleeve........	Ship.........	" "	62,783.00
Dec. 26, 1863..	Sonora	Ship.........	" "	46,545.00
Sept. 7, 1862..	Starlight.	Schooner	" "	4,000.00
June 5, 1863..	Talisman..............	Ship..........	" "	139,135.00
Nov. 8, 1862..	Thomas B. Wales.	Ship...	" "	245,625.00
Oct. 9, 1862..	Tonawanda............	Ship	Bonded..............	80,000.00
April 27, 1864..	Tycoon....	Bark	Vessel, etc............	88,559.78
Dec. 5, 1862..	Union	Schooner......	Bonded	1,500.00
May 3, 1863..	Union Jack	Bark.........	Vessel, etc......... ...	77,000.00
Sept. 17, 1862..	Virginia	Ship.........	" "	30,074.00
Feb. 27, 1863	Washington..........	Ship	Bonded............	50,000.00
Oct. 7, 1862..	Wave Crest	Bark.........	Vessel, etc	44,000.00
Sept. 9, 1862..	Weather Gage........	Schooner	....	10,000.00
Nov. 10, 1863	Winged Racer........	Ship	Vessel, etc........ ..	150,000.00

BY THE CALHOUN (A STEAMER FITTED OUT AT NEW ORLEANS).

When destroyed.	Name of Vessel.	Character.	Property destroyed.	Value.
May .. 1861..	John Adams...........	Schooner......	....	....
May .. 1861..	Mermaid..............	Schooner......	....	....
May 29, 1861..	Panama................	Brig............	....	....

BY THE FLORIDA.

When destroyed.	Name of Vessel.	Character.	Property destroyed.	Value.
March 13, 1863..	Aldebaran............	Schooner......	Vessel, etc........	$22,998.00
Aug.　20, 1863..	Anglo Saxon..........	Ship...	"　　"	.. ..
Jan.　12, 1863..	Arabella　...........	Brig............		....
March 29, 1864..	Avon..... ·...........	Ship...	Vessel, etc......	....
....	B. F. Hoxie..........	Ship...... ...	"　　"	70,000.00
May　6, 1863..	Clarence....	Brig............		
April 17, 1863..	Commonwealth.......	Ship..........	Vessel, etc......... ...	352,000.00
Jan.　22, 1863..	Corris Ann...........	Brig............	Cargo........	....
May　13, 1863..	Crown Point...	Ship.........	Personal property, etc.	....
. ...	David Lapsley...	Bark...........		....
July　10, 1864..	Electric Spark........	Steamer......	Cargo, etc........	166,000.00
Jan.　19, 1863..	Estelle......	Brig...........	Vessel, etc.......	12,000.00
Aug.　6, 1863	Francis B. Cutting ...	Ship..........		....
May　18, 1864..	Geo. Latimer..........	Schooner......	Bonded............	....
July 10, 1863..	Gen. Berry............	Bark...........		....
July　8, 1864..	Golconda	Bark..........	Vessel, etc......... ..	
....	Greenland　......	Bark.	Personal property, etc.	....
July　1, 1864..	Harriet Stevens.......	Bark..........	Vessel, etc........	10,500.00
April 23, 1863..	Henrietta.............	Bark...	"　　"	57,049 60
Feb.　12, 1863..	Jacob Bell　........	Ship..........	"　　"	1,500,000.00
June　17, 1863..	Kate Dye.............	Ship..........		....
March 9, 1863..	Lapwing.............	Bark.........	....	....
July　9, 1864	Margaret Y. Davis.....	Schooner......	Vessel and cargo......	77,000.00
March 13, 1863..	M. J. Colcord.........	Bark..........	Vessel and cargo......	
Sept.　26, 1864..	Mondamin............	Bark...... ...	"　　"　　"	....
April 24, 1863..	Oneida	Ship..........	"　　"　　"	760,000.00
....	Red Gauntlet....	Ship...... ...	"　　"　　"	....
July　8, 1863..	Rienzi...............	Schooner......	"　　"　　"	....
June　6, 1863..	Southern Cross........	Ship.........	"　　"　　"	....
Aug.　22, 1863..	Southern Rights........	Ship..........	Bonded....	....
March 6, 1863..	Star of Peace.........	Ship.........	Vessel, etc........	
July　7, 1863..	Sunrise..............	Ship......-.....	Bonded..............	60,000.00
June 26, 1863..	Varnum H. Hill........	Schooner.	Bonded..............	70,000.00
July　8, 1863..	Wm. B. Nash..........	Brig..........	Vessel and cargo......	
Jan.　22, 1863..	Windward..	Brig...........	"　　"　　"	....
June 17, 1864..	Wm. C. Clark..........	Brig...........		....
June 10, 1864..	Zelinda................	Bark............	....	....

BY THE TALLAHASSEE.

When destroyed.	Name of Vessel.	Character.	Property destroyed.	Value.
Aug.　12, 1864..	Adriatic..............	Ship...... ...	Vessel, etc..	....
Aug.　11, 1864..	A. Richards...........	Brig....	....	....
....	Atlantic..............	Schooner.		....
Aug.　11, 1864..	Bay State....	Bark...........	....	. ...
Aug.　10, 1864..	Billow................	Brig...........	....	....
Aug.　11, 1864..	Carrie Estelle...	Brig	....	....
....	Castine...............	Ship	....	....
Aug.　11, 1364..	Coral Wreath..........	Brig...........	....	....
Aug.　10, 1864..	Etta Caroline..........	Steamer......	....	....
Aug.　15, 1864..	Floral Wreath..........	Schooner......	Vessel, etc........	....
....	Glenavon...	Bark　.......	"　　"	....
Aug.　12, 1864..	Goodspeed.........	Schooner......	....	....
Aug.　12, 1864..	Howard........	Bark　......	....	....
Aug.　11, 1864..	James Funk	Pilot-boat.. ...	....	$24,000.00
Aug.　14, 1864..	James Littlefield.......	Ship	....	....
Aug.　14, 1864..	J. H. Howen...........	Schooner.'.....	....	....
Aug.　17, 1864..	Josiah Achorne........	Schooner......	....	8,000.00
Aug.　13, 1864..	Lamont Dupont........	Schooner......	....·.	....
Aug.　15, 1864..	Magnolia..............	Schooner......	....	....
Aug.　15, 1864..	Mercy A. Howes.......	Schooner......	....	....
Aug.　17, 1864..	North America........	Schooner......	Vessel, etc........	....
....	P. C. Alexander.	Bark　.......	....	....
Aug.　16, 1864..	Pearl.................	Schooner......	....	....
Aug.　23, 1864..	Restless..............	Schooner......	....	....
Aug.　20, 1864..	Rowan................	Schooner......	....	....
Aug.　11, 1864..	Sarah A. Boyce.......	Schooner......	....	....
....	Sarah Louisa.........	Schooner......	....	....
Aug.　12, 1864..	Spokane..............	Schooner......	....	....
Aug.　11, 1864..	William Bell..........	Pilot-boat......	....	24,000.00

BY THE YORK.

When destroyed.	Name of Vessel.	Character.	Property destroyed.	Value.
Aug.　9, 1861..	George V. Baker.......	Schooner......	Recaptured.....	....

BY THE SHENANDOAH.

When destroyed.	Name of Vessel.	Character.	Property destroyed.	Value.
May 27, 1865..	Abigail................	Bark..........	Vessel, etc...........	$74,659.00
....	Adelaide............	Bark..........	Bonded................	24,000.00
Dec. 4, 1864..	Alina	Bark..........	Vessel, etc..........	95,000.00
Oct. 30, ...	Brunswick...........	Ship...........	" "	16,272.00
June 26, 1865..	Catharine...........	Bark..........	" "	26,174.00
Nov. 5, 1864..	Charter Oak.........	Schooner......	" "	15,000.00
June 28, 1865..	Congress	Schooner......	" "	90,827.00
June 28, 1865..	Covington	Bark..........	" "	43,764.00
Dec. 29, 1864..	Delphine	Bark..........	" "	76,000.00
Nov. 8, 1864..	D. Godfrey.........	Bark..........	" "	36,000.00
Dec. 4, 1864..	Edward............	Bark..........	" "	20,000.00
April 1, 1865..	Edward Casey........	Ship...........	" "	109,582.70
June 21, 1865..	Euphrates	Ship...........	" "	168,688.50
June 28, 1865..	Favorite	Bark..........	" "	130,000.00
June 26, 1865..	Gen. Pike...........	Bark..........	Ransomed....... ...	....
June 26, 1865..	Gipsey..............	Bark..........	Vessel, etc........	80,000.00
April 1, 1865..	Harvest..............	Bark..........	" "	34,759.00
April 1, 1865..	Hector..............	Ship...........	" "	75,000.00
June 28, 1865..	Fillmore............	Ship...........	" "	71,451.75
June 28, 1865..	Isaac Howland........	Ship...........	" "	115,000.00
June 26, 1865..	Isabella	Bark..........	" "	87,765.00
June 28, 1865..	James Maury....... ..	Bark..........	Ransomed............	....
June 24, 1865..	Jireh Swift	Bark..........	Vessel, etc........	61,960.00
Nov. 12, 1864..	Kate Prince...........	Ship	Bonded...........	....
Nov. 13, 1864..	Lizzie M. Stacey.......	Schooner......	Vessel, etc........	30,000.00
June 28, 1865..	Martha................	Bark..........	" "	65,000.00
June 28, 1865..	Nassau	Ship...........	" "	89,424.50
June 28, 1865..	Nile..................	Bark..........	Bonded...........	25,500.00
June 26, 1865..	Nimrod	Bark..........	Vessel, etc......... ..	29,260.00
April 1, 1865..	Pearl	Bark..........	....	10,000.00
June 24, 1865..	Sophia Thornton......	Ship...........	Vessel, etc....	70,000.00
Nov. 10, 1865..	Susan...............	Bark..........	" "	5,436.00
June 25, 1865..	Susan and Abigail.....	Brig....	" "	225,848.37
June 28, 1865..	Waverly.............	Bark..........	" "	84,655.00
June 22, 1865..	Wm. Thompson.	Ship...........	" "	105,093.75
June 26, 1865..	Wm. C. Nye.	Bark	" "	62,087.50

BY THE SUMTER.

When destroyed.	Name of Vessel.	Character.	Property destroyed.	Value.
July 25, 1861..	Abbie Bradford	Schooner..	Recaptured	....
July 5, 1861..	Albert Adams.........	Brig...........	Released............ ...	....
Nov. 26, 1861..	Arcade................	Schooner	....	....
July 5, 1861..	Ben Danning..........	Brig	Released..............	....
July 4, 1861..	Cuba ...	Brig ...,.....	Released..............	....
Oct. 27, 1861..	Daniel Trowbridge ...	Schooner	....	....
Dec. 8, 1861..	Ebenezer Dodge.......	Bark...........	....	....
July 3, 1861..	Golden Rocket.......	Ship...........	.... "".....	$40,000.00
Jan. 18, 1862..	Investigator	Bark...........	Bonded............	15,000 00
July 27, 1861..	Joseph Maxwell......	Bark.	Released............	....
Sept. 25, 1861..	Joseph Parkes....	Brig	....	....
July 6, 1861..	Louis Kilham..........	Bark	Released	....
July 4, 1861..	Machias.	Brig	Released	....
Nov. 25, 1861..	Montmorency.........	....	Bonded	20,000.00
July 6, 1861..	Naiad	Brig	Released..............	....
Jan. 18, 1862..	Neapolitan............	Bark...........	....	40,000.00
Dec. 3, 1861..	Vigilance.............	Ship	....	....
July 6, 1861..	West Wind............	....	Released............	....

BY THE TACONY (A TENDER OF THE FLORIDA).

When destroyed	Name of Vessel.	Character.	Property destroyed.	Value.
June 23, 1863..	Ada......	Schooner......	....	....
June 12, 1863...	Arabella	Brig ...	Bonded	....
June 24, 1863..	Archer................	Schooner.	Recaptured	....
June 16, 1863..	Byzantium	Ship.	Cargo	....
June 22, 1863..	Elizabeth Ann........	Schooner......	....	....
June 22, 1863..	Florence.............	Schooner......	....	....
June 23, 1863..	Goodspeed	Bark....	Bonded.............	....
June 20, 1863..	Isaac Webb.	Ship...........	Bonded............	....
June 20, 1863..	L. A. Macomber.	Schooner......	....	....
June 22, 1863..	Marengo........... .	Schooner......	....	....
June 22, 1863..	Ripple	Schooner......	....	....
June 22, 1863..	Rufus Choate	Schooner......	....	....
June 24, 1863..	Shattemuc	Ship...........	Bonded	....
June 14, 1863..	Umpire	Brig	....	....
June 22, 1863..	Wanderer	Schooner......	Vessel, etc	....

BY THE GEORGIA.

When destroyed.	Name of Vessel.	Character.	Property destroyed.	Value.
Oct. 9, 1863..	Bold Hunter..........	Ship	Vessel, etc......	....
June 26, 1863..	City of Bath....	Ship....	....	....
June 25, 1863..	Constitution....	Ship	Vessel, etc	....
April 25, 1863..	Dictator .. , ...	Ship........	Vessel, etc	....
June 8, 1863..	Geo. Griswold.........	Ship....	Bonded...........	....
June 13, 1863..	Good Hope............	Bark	Vessel, etc...... ..	....
Oct. —, 1863..	John Watt....	Ship....	Bonded............	....
June 22, 1863..	J. W. Seaver	Bark	"	....
July 16, 1863..	Prince of Wales.......	Ship........ ...	"	....

BY THE CLARENCE (A TENDER OF THE FLORIDA).

When destroyed.	Name of Vessel.	Character.	Property destroyed.	Value.
June 7, 1863..	Alfred H. Partridge....	Schooner......	Bonded...............	....
June 24, 1863..	Caleb Cushing.... ...	Cutter........	... .	....
June 12, 1863 .	Kate Stewart..........	Schooner,.....	....	....
June 9, 1863..	Mary Alvina....	Brig	Vessel, etc...	$11,304.00
June 12, 1863..	Mary Schindler........	Schooner......	....	....
June 12, 1863..	Tacony	Bark........	....	....
June 6, 1863..	Whistling Wind	Bark........	....	....
....	Conrad (s. Tuscaloosa)	....		

BY THE JEFF DAVIS (FITTED OUT AT CHARLESTON, JUNE, 28, 1861).

When destroyed.	Name of Vessel.	Character.	Property destroyed.	Value.
June .. 1861..	D. C. Pierce...........	Bark	....	....
.. 1861..	Ella........	Schooner......	....	....
July 16, 1861..	Enchantress...........	Schooner......	....	....
Aug. .. 1861..	John Crawford........	Ship..	....	....
July 16, 1861..	John Welsh...........	Brig........	....	....
June .. 1861..	Rowena	Bark...	....	....
July. 16, 1861..	S. J Waring..........	Schooner......	Recaptured.............	....
July .. 1861..	W. McGilvery	Brig	....	

BY THE WINSLOW (FITTED OUT AT WILMINGTON IN 1861).

When destroyed.	Name of Vessel.	Character.	Property destroyed.	Value.
July 18, 1861..	Herbert................	Schooner......	....	....
Aug. 4, 1861..	Itasca...	Brig....	....	....
July .. 1861..	Mary Alice............	Schooner......	....	....
July .. 1861..	Priscilla..............	Schooner......	....	....
July 15, 1861..	Transit	Schooner......	....	....

BY THE CHICKAMAUGA.

When destroyed.	Name of Vessel.	Character.	Property destroyed.	Value.
Oct. 29, 1864..	Albion Lincoln........	Bark........	....	....
Oct. 31, 1864..	Emma L. Hall....	Bark..........	Vessel, etc	....
Oct. 30, 1864..	M. L. Potter..........	Bark........	Merchandise	....
....	Shooting Star	Bark	Vessel, etc	

BY THE RETRIBUTION (A SCHOONER FITTED OUT IN CAPE FEAR RIVER).

When destroyed.	Name of Vessel.	Character.	Property destroyed.	Value.
Feb. 19, 1863..	Emily Fisher..........	Brig	Cargo	$9,352.26
Jan. 31, 1863..	Hanover..............	Schooner......	Vessel, etc......	11,630.00
Jan. 10. 1863..	J. P. Ellicott.	Brig	.. ..	

BY THE BOSTON (A STEAMER CAPTURED IN JUNE, 1863).

When destroyed.	Name of Vessel.	Character.	Property destroyed.	Value.
June 12, 1863..	Lennox............. ...	Bark..........	....	....
June 12, 1863..	Texana	Bark...	Cargo	....

BY THE ECHO.

When destroyed.	Name of Vessel.	Character.	Property destroyed.	Value.
July 9, 1862..	Mary E. Thompson....	Brig......	....	....
July 9, 1862..	Mary Goodell.... ...	Schooner......	....	....

BY THE TUSCALOOSA (A TENDER OF THE ALABAMA).

When destroyed.	Name of Vessel.	Character.	Property destroyed.	Value.
Sept. 13, 1863..	Living Age............	Ship...........	. ...	....
July 31, 1863..	Santee......	Ship....	Bonded...............	$150,000.00

APPENDIX.

REGISTER OF THE COMMISSIONED AND WARRANT OFFICERS OF THE PROVISIONAL NAVY OF THE CONFEDERATE STATES TO JUNE 1, 1864, FROM THE NAVY REGISTER.

Secretary, S. R. Mallory ; Chief Clerk, E. M. Tidball; Clerks, Z. P. Moses, T. E. Buchanan. T. J. Rapier, C. E. L. Stuart; Messenger, T. J. J. Murray. Office of Orders and Detail : Chief of Bureau, J. K. Mitchell; Register, etc., J. S. Jones; Chief Clerk, G. Lee Brent. Office of Ordnance and Hydrography : Chief of Bureau, John M. Brooke; Chief Clerk, J. P. McCorkle ; Clerk, A. B. Upshur. Office of Provisions and Clothing : Chief of Bureau, John De Bree ; Chief Clerk, T. C. De Leon. Office of Medicine and Surgery: Chief of Bureau, W. A. W. Spotswood; Chief Clerk, C. N. Fennell.

ADMIRAL : Franklin Buchanan.

CAPTAINS : Samuel Barron, Raphael Semmes, W. W. Hunter, E. Farland, J. K. Mitchell, J. R. Tucker, T. J. Page, R. F. Pinckney, J. W. Cooke.

COMMANDERS: T. R. Rootes, T. T. Hunter, I. N. Browne, R. B. Pegram, W. L. Maury, J. N. Maffitt,' J. N. Barney, W. A. Webb, G. T. Sinclair, G. W. Harrison, J. D. Johnston, John Kell, W. T. Glassell, H. Davidson.

FIRST LIEUTENANTS : Washington Gwathmey, John Rutledge, Joel S. Kennard, Charles M. Morris, John S. Maury, Charles W. Hays, Charles J. Simms, J. Myers, A. F. Warley, John W. Bennett, J. H. Carter. W. H. Parker, J. Pembroke Jones, Wm. H. Murdaugh, James H. Rochelle, Robert D. Minor, James I. Waddell, Joseph Fry, Charles P. McGary, Robert R. Carter, John B. Hamilton, Oscar F. Johnston, John R. Egglesten, R. T. Chapman Wm. P. Campbell, B. P. Loyall, Wm. H. Ward, John W. Dunnington, Francis E. Sheppard, Wm. G. Dozier, Wm. L. Bradford, Hamilton H. Dalton, Wm. E. Evans, George E. Shryock, Thomas K. Porter, Joseph W. Alexander, Charles J. Graves, Thos. B. Mills, Wm. C. Whittle, Jr. ; Wm. A. Kerr, John Grimball, Wm. K. Hall, Samuel W. Averett, H. B. Claiborne, George A. Borchert, Hilery Cenas, Walter A. Butt, Wm. Winder Pollock, A. D. Wharton, Thomas L. Dornin, Thomas L. Harrison, James L. Hoole, Francis L. Hoge, Edmund G. Reed, Charles W. Read, S. G. Stone, Alphonso Barbot, Robert J. Bowen, W. Gift, Thomas W. W. Davies, Patrick McCarrick, Wm. F. Carter, Wm. H. Wall, W. W. Carnes, John H. Ingraham, Wm. Van Comstock, Richard F. Armstrong, Albert G. Hudgins, Charles K. King, James H. Comstock, James D. Wilson, Julian M. Spencer, Sidney S. Lee. Samuel Barron. Jr., E. Canty Stockton, J. McCaleb Baker, John W. Murdaugh, Mortimer M. Benton, Charles L. Harralson, Sidney H. McAdam, Francis T. Chew, Alexander M. Mason, Thomas L. Moore, Ivey Foreman, Walter O'Crain, Joseph Price, Alexander Grant, Charles E. Yeatman, Charles B. Oliver, Charles W. Hasker, Francis Watlington, John L. Phillips, George H. Arledge, M. T. Clarke, John A. Payne, Henry W. Ray, Wm. E. Hudgins, John F. Ramsay. H. B. Littlepage, Lewis R. Hill, Edward J. Means, Henry Roberts, Richard H. Gale, Richard C. Foute, Francis M. Roby, Henry H Marmaduke, John Lowe, Arthur Sinclair, Jr. ; Wm. W. Roberts, Edgar A. Lambert, Otey Bradford, Joseph M. Gardner, Matthew P. Goodwyn, Americus V. Wiatt, Thos. L. Skinner, Charles Borum, J. V. Johnson, C. L. Stanton.

SECOND LIEUTENANTS : J. P. Claybrook, R. S. Floyd, W. P. Mason, W. F. Robinson, J. R. Price, D. A. Telfair, Daniel Trigg, I. C. Holcome, W. R. Dalton, A. S. Worth R. A. Camm, D. M. Scales, J. T. Walker. S. S. Gregory, W. W. Read, R. H. Bacot, E. J. McDermott, R. B. Larmour, T. P. Bell, J. W. Billups.

SURGEONS : J. W. B, Greenhow, W. D. Har-

rison, Wm. F. Carrington, Charles H.Williamson, Arthur M. Lynah, Daniel B. Conrad, F. L. Galt, W. M. Page, H. W. M. Washington, A. G. Garnett.

PASSED ASSISTANT SURGEONS : Frederick Garretson, J. W. Sanford, T. J. Charlton, C. E. Lining. M. P. Christian, R. J. Freeman, B. W. Green, J. W. Herty, J. E. Lindsay, O. S. Iglehart.

ASSISTANT SURGEONS: C. M. Morfitt, T. B. Ford, R. R. Gibbs, E. G. Booth, Thos. Emory, W. M. Turner, John De Bree, Marcellus Ford, W. W. Graves, W. J. Addison, N. C. Edwards, S. S. Herrick, N. M. Read, John Leyburn, R. C. Powell. R. C. Bowles, J. P. Lipscomb, W. C. Jones, W. Sheppardson, C. M. Parker, C. W. Thomas, H. B. Melvin, W. S. Stoakly, W. W. Griggs, J. F. Tipton, G. B. Weston, G. N. Halstead, J. V. Cook, J. O. Grant, Pike Brown, H. G. Land, G. W. Claiborne, J. M. Hicks, J. G. King, D. E. Ewart, Ed. Claire, J. V. Harris, L. R. Dickinson, J. B. Rutherford, G. A. Foote, N. K. Henderson, J. W. Beline, W. L. Warner, Robert Kuykendall, J. G. Thomas, W. E. Bondurant, J. E. Moyler, Fred. Peck, H. S. Paisy, J. E. Duffel, J. G. Bigley, K. Goldborough.

PAYMASTERS: Felix Senac, James O. Moore, Richard Taylor, James E. Armour.

ASSISTANT PAYMASTERS: D. F. Forrest, W. B. Micon, L. E. Brooks, J. S. Banks, J. J. McPherson, M. M. Seay, G. H. O'Neal, W. J. Richardson, P. M. DeLeon, Adam Tredwell, Edw. McKean, D. C. Seymour, L. B. Reardon, W. H. Chase, H. E. McDuffie, W. M. Ladd, S. S. Barksdale, S. S. Nicholas, Chas. W. Keim, W. E. Deacon, T. G. Ridgely, J. M. Pearl, L. M. Tucker, C. L. Jones, W. B. Cobb, J. F. Wheliss, M. L. Southron, Marsden Bellamy, B. M. Herriot, N. K. Adams, W. A. Hearne, C. G. Pearson.

MASTERS IN LINE OF PROMOTION: S. P. Blanc, G. D. Bryan, Wyndam R. Mayo, D. D. Colcock, W. P. Hamilton, J. C. Long. H. L.Vaughan, J. M. Pearson, H. S. Cooke, G. W. Sparks, W. J. Craig.

MASTERS NOT IN LINE OF PROMOTION:—John Pearson, Lewis Parrish, A. Pacetty, Richard Evans, F. M. Harris, John C. Minor, C. W. Johnson, W. B. Whitehead, H. W. Perrin, B. W. Guthrie, Charles A. McEvoy, William D. Porter, James W. McCarrick, Lewis Musgrave, Peter W. Smith, G. Andrews, A. L. Myers, J. Y. Beall,, D. W. Nash, Thomas L.Wragg, George M. Peek, Henry Wilkinson, Julian Fairfax, G. A. Peple, Levi G. White, Edward McGuire, John Maxwell, Bennett G. Burley, S. Milliken, Seth Foster, John L. Ahern, John Webb, B. J. Sage, Charles Beck, Lewis N. Huck, G. W. Armistead, B. J. Sherley, George W. Smith, John A. Curtis, William Collins, C. M. Hite, A. Robinson, C. Linn, John M. Gibbs, Henry Yeatman, C. E. Girardy, W. Frank Shippey, Louis Gonnart, James Cahoon, Charles E. Little, John E. Hogg, Joseph R. DeMahy, H. D. Edinborough, Wm. A. Hines, John C. Braine, W. B. Cox, Lemuel Langley.

MIDSHIPMEN—THIRD CLASS, SENIOR : P. H Gibbs. W. N. Shaw, F. C. Morehead, George A. Joiner, Roger Pinckney, C. Cary, R. J. Deas, B. Carter, C. F. Sevier, W. F. Clayton, W. K. Hale, F. M. Berrien, Thomas C. Pinckney, A. O. Wright, H. H. Scott, H. H. Tyson, F. B. Doonin, P. H. McCarrick, F. M. Thomas, F. S. Hunter, W. T. Carroll, D. M. Lee, J. B. Ratcliffe, C. Meyer, James R. Norris, W. D. Goode, L. M. Rootes, R. J. Crawford, L. D. Hamner, Thomas Wherritt, E. M. Jones, D. B. Talbott, R. E. Pinckney, H. J. Ellett, Raphael Semmes, Jr., A. M. Harrison, O. S. Manson, E. B. Prescott.

MIDSHIPMEN—THIRD CLASS, JUNIOR : D. A. Dixon, John T. Lomax, John A. Lee, George B. Cloud, John H. Inglis, H. T. Minor, W. S. Hogue,

J. D. Howell, John Johnson, Lewis Levy, J. G. Minnegerode, A. S. Doak, G. A. Wilkins, John D. Trimble, J. De B. Northrop, Richard Slaughter, Eugene Phillips, H. J. Warren, John T. Scharf, W. A. Lee, A. T. Hunt, Preston B. Moore.

MIDSHIPMEN—FOURTH CLASS: Wm. M. Snead, W. J. Claiborne, W. S. Davidson, W. D. Haldman, J. C. Wright, M. J. McRae, W. H. Payne, B. S. Johnson, F. S. Kennett, F. L. Place, C. R. Breckenridge, C. G. Dandridge, T. D. Stone.

MIDSHIPMEN : R. S. Floyd, R. J. Moses, W. W. Wilkinson, O. A. Browne, John T. Mason, Wm. B. Sinclair, James W. Pegram, J. H. Hamilton, J. H. Dyke, V. Newton, G. D. Bryan, G. T. Sinclair, W. H. Sinclair, I. D. Bulloch, Eugene Maffitt, E. M. Anderson, J. A. Wilson, J. M. Morgan.

CHIEF ENGINEERS: Michael Quinn, Charles Schroeder, Henry X. Wright, James H. Toombs.

FIRST ASSISTANT ENGINEERS : G. W. City, C. H. Levy, Loudon Campbell, G. D. Lining, W. J. Freeman, H. B. Willy, Hugh Clark, M. P. Jordan, J. H. Loper, W. T. Morrell, G. W. Tennant, Benj. Herring, J. T. Tucker, J. R. Jordan, J. J. Darcy, W. Youngblood, C. W. Jordan, E. A. Jack, W. P. Brooks.

SECOND ASSISTANT ENGINEERS : E. G. Hall, Isaac Bowman, J. F. Green, Junius Hanks, J. M. Freeman, Jr., C. H. Collier, N. O'Brien, W. M. Fauntleroy, Leslie King, J. L. Foster, R. J. Kilpatrick, W. B. Brockett, J. C. Johnson, D. H. Pritchard, J. C. O'Connell, E. H. Brown, J. H. Dent, John Langdon, L. A. McCarthy, J. S. West, J. J. Lyell, John Hayes, Jos. Cardy, G. W. Caldwell, Richard Finn, E. L. Dick, J. H. Baily.

THIRD ASSISTANT ENGINEERS: J. T. Doland, R. J. Caswell, W. F. Harding, J. H. Parker, F. G. Miller, S. B. Jordan, J. K. Langhorne, J. W. Tomlinson, H. H. Roberts, E. F. Gill, R. J. Hackley, J. B. Brown, G. A. Bowe, A. De Blanc, C. S. Leavett, C. S. Peek, A. J. Schwarzman, M. P. Young, M. A. Newberry, B. F. Drago, Oscar Benson, J. C. Phillips, W. A. Luddington, Wm. Rogers, W. R. Doury, Peter Faithful, Donald McDonald, W. B. Patterson, E. P. Weaver, M. J. Cohen, J. T. Reams, R. S. Herring, J. W. McGrath, H. B. Goodrich, G. Wainwright, J. J. Kerrish, John Applegate, J. N. Ramsey, J. B. Weaver, R. E. Edwards, J. J McGrath, Wm. C. Purse, T. O. McClosky, C. B. Thompson, R. J. O'Neal, J. F. Robinett, Achilles Lombard, J. P. Miller, W. C. Tilton, A. P. Wright, C. W. Ridle, W. H. Handy, G. H. Wellington, J. L. McDonald, S. K. Mooers, R. J. Smith, J. J. Lacklison, B. H. Bates, E. J. Dennigan, J. E. Viernelson, E. T. Homan, Holmes Ahern, Henry Discher, James Carlon, J. H. Haly.

BOATSWAINS : Lester Seymour, Thos. Ganley, A. J. Wilson, Andrew Blakie, J. C. Cronin, John Kavanaugh, Jas. Smith, W. J. Smith, H. J. Wilson, J. J. Ingraham, John McCredie, Robt. McCalla, Peter Taff, John Cassidy, John Brown.

GUNNERS : John Owens, John A. Lovett, Wm. Cuddy, J. G. McCluskey, Z. A. Offutt, Wm. H. Haynes, T. B. Travers, W. A. Flemming, G. M. Thompson, E. R. Johnson, S. P. Schisano, E. G. Williams, B. F. Hughes, Wm. Shelly, T. Baker, W. F. Brittingham, C. Gormly, B. A. Barrow, W. J. Ballentyne, John Raabe, J. I. Mayberry, John Waters, Hugh McDonald, C. E. Porter, H. L. Smith, R. J. Webb, Ira W. Porter.

CARPENTERS : R. M. Baine, J. T. Rustic, J. M. Burroughs, G. D. Fentress, Wm. R. Jarvis, R. J. Meads.

SAIL-MAKERS : William Bennett, E. A. Mahoney, S. V. Turner, M. P. Beaufort. Geo. Newton.

ACTING MASTERS' MATES : J. L. Ahern, Wm. McBlair, J. T. Mayberry, J. A. Riley, T. T. Hunter, Jr., J. C. Young, W. G. Porter, T. B. Boville, T. L. Wragg, G. Waterman, W. W. Skinner, J. Y. Benson, J. T. Layton, T. J. Hudgins, W. Smith, R. Benthall, A. E. Alberton, T. E. Gibbs, S. S. Foster, C. Russell, T. M. Hazlehurst, B. M. Fogartie, J. C. Turner, C. B. Bohannon, G. Atchison, S. A. Brockenton, J. A. Rosier, E. M. Skinner, H. C. Barr, E. C. Parsons, J. A. Paschall, R. Battle, E. P. Winder, J H. Turner, J. H. Hart, W. H. Fitzgerald, F. B. Green, C. N. Golder, L. S. Seymour, W. M. Snead, W. D. Oliveira, W. N. Brown, Edward W. Jordan. O. L. Jenkins, C. Hunter, C. M. Selden, C. E. Bragden, P. M. Baker, W. B. Littlepage, S. L. Simpson, L. L. Foster, R. N. Spraggins, E. T. Haynie, J. J. Bronson, E. C. Skinner, W. S. Forrest, W. R. Howle, C. R. McBlair, A. Campbell, E. W. C. Maylin, A. G. Hall, J. R. Murray, W. R. Rowe, H. Gilliland, J. R. Chisman, C. Neil, W. A. Lamkin, R. M. Carter, A. McMillan, J. C. Graves, J. E. Ferral, R. Freeman, P. Power. A. G. Corran, J. C. Hill, W. E. Lester, T. S. Gray, M. J. Beebe, L. Pitts, J. J. Whitehead, W. A. Marschalk, R. Webb, T. Mason, G. C. Lyon, J. M. Hazlehurst, C. F. Curtis, A. W. Johnson, F. Marschalk, C. J. Yonge, P. G. Webb, H. Hermier, L. Bowdoin, E. Smith, W. A. Collier, C. Frazee, C. K. Floyd.

The following names of regular officers in the Navy Register of January 1st, 1864, are not among those of the Provisional Navy in the Register of June 1st, 1864: CAPTAINS—Lawrence Rosseau, French Forrest, Josiah Tatnall, V. M. Randolph, Geo. N. Hollins, D. N. Ingraham, Wm. F. Lynch, Isaac S. Sterrett, S. S. Lee, Wm. C. Whittle. COMMANDERS—Robert D. Thorburn, Robt. G. Robb, Murray Mason, C. H. McBlair, A. B. Fairfax, Richard L. Page, Fred'k Chatard, Arthur Sinclair, C. H. Kennedy, Thos.W. Brent, Matthew F. Maury. Geo. Minor, H. J. Hartstene, J. L. Henderson, W. T. Muse. C. F. M. Spotswood, C. Ap. R. Jones, J. Taylor Wood. COMMANDERS FOR THE WAR: Jas. D. Bulloch, James H. North, John M. Brooke. FIRST LIEUTENANTS—F. B. Renshaw, C. B. Poindexter, H. H. Lewis, P. W. Murphy, John J. Guthrie, Van R. Morgan, Edward L. Winder, John H. Parker, John Wilkinson, C. M Fauntleroy, A. McLaughlin, A. M. De Bree, N. H. Van Zant, D. P. McCorkle, Wm. Sharp, Jos. D. Blake, Thos. P. Pelot, Philip Porcher. LIEUTENANTS FOR THE WAR—Joshua Humphreys, S. W. Corbin. Jas. L. Johnson, Thos. W. Benthall, John G. Blackwood, Wm. H. Odenheimer, Edward E. Stiles. SURGEONS—Jas. Cornick, Wm. F. Patton, W. A. W. Spotswood, Lewis W. Minor, W. F. McClenahan, John T. Mason, William B. Sinclair, Richard Jeffery, Jas. F. Harrison, D. D. Phillips, Chas. F. Fahs, Wm. E. Wysham. PAYMASTERS—John De Bree, Thos. R. Ware, Jas. A. Semple, John Johnston, W. W. J. Kelly, Jas. K. Harwood, Geo. H. Ritchie, Henry Myers, John W. Nixon. MASTERS IN LINE OF PROMOTION—Richard H. Bacot. MASTERS NOT IN LINE OF PROMOTION—Wm. H. Carlon. PASSED MIDSHIPMAN—A. P. Beirne. ENGINEER-IN-CHIEF—Wm. P. Williamson. CHIEF ENGINEERS—Jas. H. Warner, Thos. A. Jackson, Virginius Freeman, E.W. Manning, H. A. Ramsey, Wm. Frick, J. W. Tynan. FIRST ASSISTANT ENGINEERS—W. S. Thompson, W. P. Riddle. NAVAL CONSTRUCTORS—John L. Porter, chief; and J. Pearce, W. A. Graves, acting constructors.

The C. S. Navy Register for January, 1864, gives the following roster of the Marine Corps: COLONEL COMMANDANT—L. J. Beall. COLONEL—H. B. Tyler. MAJOR—G. H. Terrette. PAYMASTER WITH RANK OF MAJOR—R. T. Allison. ADJUTANT WITH RANK OF MAJOR—Israel Greene. QUARTERMASTER WITH RANK OF MAJOR—A. S. Taylor. CAPTAINS—J. D. Simms, J. R. F. Tatnall, A. J. Hayes, G. Holmes, R. T. Thom, A. C. Van Benthuysen, J. E. Meiere and T. S. Wilson. FIRST LIEUTENANTS—C. L. Sayre, B. K. Howell, R. H. Henderson, D. G. Raney. J. R. Y. Fendall, T. P. Gwynn, J. Thurston, F. H. Cameron, F. Mac Ree. SECOND LIEUTENANTS—D Bradford, N. E. Venable, H. L. Graves, H. M. Doak, Albert S. Berry, E. F. Neuville, D. G. Brent, J. C. Murdoch, S. M. Roberts, John L. Rapier.